Adventurers of Purse and Person
1607–1624/5
and Their Families

Adventurers
of Purse and Person
VIRGINIA
1607–1624/5

Fourth Edition

Compiled and Edited by

John Frederick Dorman, C.G., F.A.S.G.

VOLUME ONE (in Two Parts)
Families A-F

PART A
Families A-Ch

GENEALOGICAL PUBLISHING CO., INC.

First edition (1956) compiled and edited by
Annie Lash Jester, F.A.S.G., in collaboration
with Martha Woodroof Hiden, F.A.S.G.

Second edition (1964) compiled and edited by
Annie Lash Jester, F.A.S.G., in collaboration
with Martha Woodroof Hiden, F.A.S.G.

Third edition (1987) compiled and edited by
Virginia M. Meyer (1974-1981) and
John Frederick Dorman, F.A.S.G. (1981-1987)

Fourth edition, Volume One (2004)
Published by Genealogical Publishing Company
3600 Clipper Mill Rd., Suite 260
Baltimore, MD 21211-1953
in collaboration with the Order of First Families of Virginia

Library of Congress Catalogue Card Number 2003114023

Reprinted in Two Parts by Genealogical Publishing Company
Baltimore, Maryland, 2012

ISBN, Part A: 978-0-8063-1819-6

Made in the United States of America

This FOURTH EDITION is published

to commemorate the FOUR HUNDREDTH Anniversary

of the

First Settlement at Jamestown

1607

This volume is dedicated

to the memory of

those intrepid Adventurers of their Person

who suffered hardship and gave their lives

that a civilization might be created in the New World

and to those

Adventurers of Purse who dared to invest

in support of the noble venture

THE SEAL OF THE VIRGINIA COMPANY.

The seal of the Virginia Company of London was granted, April 1606, by King James I to the incorporators of the Company and despite the revocation of the Charter, 1624, the seal continued to be the emblem of State until the surrender of Virginia to the Commonwealth in 1652. The obverse of the seal shows the arms of England with the inscription: "For his Council of Virginia." The reverse of the seal shows King James I in royal robes with the inscription: "Seal of the King of Great Britain, France and Ireland."

FOREWORD

The year 2007 marks the four hundredth anniversary of the founding of Jamestown. The Order of First Families of Virginia, 1607-1624/5 is proud to sponsor this publication as its gift to the celebration of the founding of Virginia and our nation. Since its institution on May 11, 1912, the Order has been steadfast in its purpose "to promote historical, biographical and genealogical researches concerning Virginia history during the period when she was the only one of the thirteen original colonies."[*]

From the earliest years, source material both biographical and genealogical has been collected to be enfolded with the history of Virginia in the period 1607-1624/5. The result was the publication in 1956 of *Adventurers of Purse and Person,* edited by Annie Lash Jester in collaboration with Martha Woodroof Hiden. Subsequently, new historical material has been continually discovered at a great rate. English records were becoming available in Virginia, and the quantity of material was expanding the resources offered to the researcher. New lineages have been discovered, and new information concerning previous lineages has likewise been uncovered.

The new historical research resulted in the publication in 1964 of the second edition under the editorship of Annie Lash Jester and of the third edition in 1987 under the editorship initially of Virginia M. Meyer followed by her successor John Frederick Dorman. We are fortunate in having this fourth edition brought to fruition by the genealogist of the Order, John Frederick Dorman, with thanks being extended to the chairman of the Publications Committee, Kenneth Callaway King.

Too large to be published in a single volume, the fourth edition is published in three volumes, with the first volume covering families from A to F. It is unique in expanding from the four generations of Virginia founders enumerated in the first three editions to six generations–truly a monumental work. By offering this greatly expanded edition, the Order of First Families of Virginia hopes to enlarge the public's knowledge and interest in those earliest settlers of Virginia. It is in this spirit that this fourth edition is published on the eve of the celebration of our nation's birth 400 years ago.

Carter Branham Snow Furr
President

---

[*] Certificate of incorporation granted by the Commonwealth of Virginia July 22, 1913.

CONTENTS

INTRODUCTION
(TO FIRST EDITION)

Within a decade after the discovery of America in 1492 by Columbus, Spain was colonizing in the West Indies. In 1522, Cortez, having overcome the opposition of the natives in Mexico, had been appointed governor of New Spain, a political division of Spain. But England, without sufficient economic resources and with unfavorable political conditions, could make no effort to establish a permanent settlement in America until Sir Walter Raleigh in 1585 sent colonists to Roanoke Island, an effort which ended in utter and tragic failure.

English navigators had not been idle. Voyages for trade and exploration were undertaken in the Atlantic and Pacific throughout the 16th century. With the experience gained from the failure of Raleigh's Colony, and with the geographical knowledge of the world acquired from the accounts of the fearless English sea captains, the projectors of the Virginia Company had something substantial to maintain their enthusiasm, and to base their claim for a charter.

James I, on April 10, 1606, granted a charter to Sir Thomas Gates, Sir George Somers, Richard Hakluyt, Edward-Maria Wingfield, Thomas Hanham, Raleigh Gilbert, William Parker and George Popham "To deduce a colony of sundry of our people into that part of America commonly called Virginia." The first four of this group mentioned were to be the directors of the first colony to be located at some point between 34° and 41° north latitude; the second four to develop what was called the second colony, to be located at some point between 38° and 45° north latitude. Sir Thomas Gates and his associates were designated in the Charter as citizens of London; Popham and his three as coming from Bristol, Exeter and Plymouth. The first colony, settled at Jamestown, became permanent; the second colony landing on the coast of Maine in 1607 was abandoned in 1608.

The first charter, owing to inadequate provision for efficient governing powers in London and Jamestown, was revised and was issued as the second charter on May 23, 1609. This charter is notable for the inclusion of the names of all the adventurers (i.e. stockholders) 659 in number and a list of 56 trade guilds of London as subscribers. The corporate title of the Company was specified "The Treasurer and Company of Adventurers and Planters of the City of London for the First Colony in Virginia." A third charter extending the boundaries of Virginia and enlarging the privileges of the Company was granted on March 12, 1612; in this charter the names of new adventurers (i.e.

stockholders) since the date of the second charter were included. The Company continued to operate with ample power until June 26, 1624, a period of eighteen years from the date of the first charter.

It would be too foreign to the scope of this introductory note to enter into the details of the transactions of the Company. It is fitting to observe here that except for the light shed from Raleigh's sad experience at Roanoke Island, there was little of English colonial experience that could be helpful in establishing a colony in a wilderness like Virginia. In that period of eighteen years there was frequent dissension, with extreme bitterness at times; many seriously deplorable decisions were adopted. The Company was violently condemned both at home and at Jamestown for its mistakes; for instance it had to bear much of the blame for the Indian Massacre of 1622.

With few exceptions, historians have not awarded the just credit to the Company that it deserves. In appraising the efforts of the Company, the reflection is pertinent that amidst many distressing circumstances the Company still held on, never withdrawing its support from the main purpose to found a colony. When the Crown took over on June 25, 1624, the colony was still in Virginia and established. The most difficult work in laying a foundation had been done.

The muster of January, 1624/5 shows a population of 1,232. If the colonization had been directly in the hands of the Crown from the first, it is doubtful if Jamestown had survived after two or three years. The Crown, with its appointed officials, would have been as ignorant and naive as the Company as to the problems involved, and would have been far less generous in expenditures.

The settlement at Jamestown was not an experiment in gold digging, in planting a missionary station, in locating a trading post, in placing a military outpost, nor in exploration for a northwest passage. It was all of these in a certain limited degree, and very much more. It was a determined effort to develop a new colony, a New Britain; indeed it was referred to at times as Nova Britannia. It was to be a colony, in the accepted and broadest meaning of that word. Nor was it an endeavor to serve as an example of socialistic living, as some detractors of Jamestown have implied.

Incomplete records do not permit a statement of the exact number of those who came to Virginia from 1607 to 1624; but it is believed that a fair estimate would place the number at one or two hundred more than 7,000. Of this number about one-seventh survived. At least when the muster or census of January,

1624/5 was taken, the number reported to be living was 1,232. The seven thousand have been subjected to the detraction, sometimes even abuse, of careless and uninformed writers; when all the circumstances are considered, they should be acclaimed for their courage, endurance and industry. After living for two to four months in over-crowded and unsanitary ships, they landed, discouraged and sick, in a wilderness in which savage enemies always lurked. Accustomed to living in a temperate climate, they had to become adapted to a semi-tropical one for four months of each year. A sufficient supply of food was never certain, and a balanced diet impossible. In the early years approximate starvation prevailed. Many lost their minds, and it is not surprising that shocking incidents occurred.

The title "Adventurers of Purse and Person, 1607-1624/5" is most appropriate for this volume. The total number of "Adventurers," that is stockholders, mentioned in the first, second and third charters is approximately 900. A few of the "Adventurers" also became "Planters" by actually settling in Virginia. The foundation for this work is the Muster of January 1624/5, which has never before been printed in full. This census was taken so that the Royal Commission which succeeded the Company on June 26, 1624 might have correct information about all the settlements. The name of each colonist appears, with the location of his house, and the number in his family, together with information about his stock of food, his supply of arms and ammunition, his boats, houses and livestock.

The purpose of this volume has been to develop the documents of the following groups: 1. Adventurers of purse who either came to Virginia in the period 1607-1624/5 and had descendants or who did not come to Virginia within that period but whose grandchildren were residents there. 2. Immigrants to Virginia, i.e. Adventurers of person, 1607-1624/5, who left descendants. There are 109 individuals who have been identified as qualifying in these groups. The descendants of each of the 109 individuals are presented through three generations, bringing the history of the family of that individual through the 17th century.

It is astonishing how the marriages of these three generations lead into the web of social life of Virginia of succeeding centuries, touching nearly all of the well-known families. As an example, Christopher Branch, who is listed as living in Henrico County in 1624/5, had a granddaughter Martha Branch, who married Thomas Jefferson, the great-grandfather of Thomas Jefferson, President of the United States. The student of social life in Colonial Virginia will find much food for profitable reflection in these genealogies if he is serious and fully cognizant of the use and value of genealogical information. He will find evidence here of a mingling of families which grew into a fluctuating stratified society of the 18th century. One of the valuable features of this volume is the scrupulous annotation for each family, references being made not only to printed works, but to manuscripts. Earnest, faithful and patient research is evident on every page. The ideal has been to prepare an indispensable tool for the historian, biographer and genealogist, one that must be used by the student of every subject that pertains to Colonial Virginia.

Earl G. Swem

Williamsburg, Virginia

PREFACE

The loss of the great majority of the records of the Virginia colony and of the county records in many of the earlier counties has presented especially difficult problems for the historian or genealogist attempting to determine family relationships during the first centuries of Virginia settlement. Drawing on the research of such pioneers as William Glover Stanard, Robert Alonzo Brock, Lyon Gardiner Tyler and William Clayton Torrence, and more recently of George Harrison Sanford King, Martha Woodroof Hiden and Annie Lash Jester, produced the remarkable first edition of *Adventurers of Purse and Person, Virginia, 1607-1624/5*, which was published by the Order of First Families of Virginia in 1956. Within just seven years, owing both to public demand for the work and to the number of additional items of information that had been brought to the Order's attention following the initial publication, it was necessary to prepare a second edition in which some corrections were made within the text and others were placed, with additional lineages, in an appendix.

Over the ensuing twenty years many abstracts and indexes of early Virginia records were published, providing ready access to information that previously could be located only by long and tedious reading of difficult handwriting in the original volumes. As a result, further proofs of descent from those families which were resident in Virginia prior to the muster of 1624/5 came to light, and the additional information provided an opportunity for the reevaluation of evidence supporting some claims of descent previously made.

In order to bring together the results of the most recent scholarship on these families, the Order commissioned the preparation of a third edition, published in 1987. That research had been nearly completed by Prentiss Price of Richmond at the time of his death. Virginia (Mrs. Harold I.) Meyer then undertook the assembling of the results of his further studies of four Virginia generations and her own investigations regarding the British origins of a number of families. Subsequently, the materials assembled were placed in the hands of the undersigned so that the entire manuscript could be edited for publication.

On reviewing the work previously done and reexamining some of the sources cited, it became evident that there were additional items of information which should be included in the third edition. In some instances, as well, it appeared from an examination of the sources that a further reevaluation of evidence should be made. The relationships previously accepted in a few of the families were, as a result, altered radically to conform to the evidence newly available.

Following the publication of the third edition in 1987, many interested individuals provided additional information to supplement and further correct the accounts appearing therein, and the Order continued to commission investigations to establish newly identified families whose origins extended to the period of the Virginia Company's administration of the colony's affairs.

In his introduction to the first edition in 1956, Dr. Earl Gregg Swem had pointed out the importance of understanding the interrelationship of family connections in 17th-century Virginia. With the passage of time into a new century, the Order recognized that 18th-century family relationships were increasingly in need of study. The decision to assemble data regarding two more generations of each of the families has resulted in a much expanded collection of information covering the entire colonial period of Virginia's history. The continuing publication of copies and abstracts of source material, together with the generous contribution of data by individuals, enabled the identification of additional family members and further reevaluation of evidence concerning the previously accepted relationships and identifications made in the earlier editions.

The paucity of records concerning the earliest decades of Virginia settlement led earlier researchers to conclude that a number of families later resident in Virginia descended from members of the Virginia Company or from pre-1625 settlers. Although the circumstantial evidence then seemed persuasive, new discoveries have raised questions about some identifications. Readers of this fourth edition will note that descendants of several early Virginia settlers are no longer included herein. Other circumstantial connections between the first and second generations have been retained herein since no contrary evidence has been presented, but no new families have been included on the basis of circumstantial evidence alone. In the fifth and sixth generations in particular, some marriages and filial relationships that have not been established conclusively but that appear from available evidence to be reasonable have been included, with the appended use of the designations probably, possibly and perhaps, in descending order of likelihood

As in previous editions, the existence of published accounts of the several families has been noted in footnotes appended to the title of the individual family genealogy. These previously published accounts have served as the basis for the information presented here, but readers will note that the present accounts, following more thorough examination of available evidence, differ in the placement of some individuals and elimination of others who had been assumed in prior genealogical accounts to be related.

Since this volume contains over ten thousand footnote citations, some data derived from the previously published works cited at the beginning of an account have not been identified more specifically. Every effort has been made, however, to identify the source of birth, marriage and death dates and to refer to wills left by each person mentioned. Reference to land ownership indicated by the 1704 quit rent rolls, military service and civil offices held on the county level, revealed in a wide variety of sources readily available to most researchers, usually have not been cited specifically.

No work of this sort, dealing with so many families in the 17th and 18th centuries of the colony's history, can be considered as representing a final determination of family relationships. The accounts presented here are based, in some instances, on the lifetime work of a single individual. New research on specific points will undoubtedly bring to light further data which may require the revision of the conclusions drawn from the evidence presently available. Every effort, however, has been made to eliminate errors and to locate the results of the most recent scholarship relating to the several families discussed herein. This volume must be considered as the cumulation of the research of many persons, too numerous to acknowledge individually, whose interest in providing the results of their investigations is deeply appreciated by the Order of First Families of Virginia and by the undersigned.

Special thanks are due John Anderson Brayton of Memphis, Lyndon H. Hart of Richmond, and Mrs. Eugene E. Mihalyka of Cheriton, who read portions of the text and made many helpful additions.

John Frederick Dorman

EIGHT ORIGINAL SHIRES (COUNTIES) CREATED 1634

D I V I S I O N S *

JAMES CITY COUNTY————James City
└─Surry (formed by April 1652)

HENRICO COUNTY————Henrico
├─Goochland, 1728
└─Chesterfield, 1749

CHARLES CITY COUNTY————Charles City
(enlarged 1637)
└─Prince George, 1703

ELIZABETH CITY COUNTY————Elizabeth City
└─New Norfolk (formed, 1636, from the portion
of Elizabeth City on the south side of
Hampton Roads)
├─Lower County of New Norfolk, 1637
│   (later termed Lower Norfolk)
└─Upper County of New Norfolk, 1637
    (later termed Upper Norfolk and by
    1642, Nansemond)

WARWICK RIVER COUNTY (designated in several land patents, 1635, as
Denbigh Co. from name of the Parish; name changed to Warwick,
March 1642/43)

WARROSQUYOAKE COUNTY (name changed
to Isle of Wight, 1637
├─Isle of Wight
└─Southampton, 1749

CHARLES RIVER COUNTY (name changed
to York, March 1642/43)
├─York
├─New Kent (formed from
│ upper York, 1654)
│   ├─New Kent
│   └─King and Queen, 1691
│   └─King William, 1702
├─Gloucester, 1651
└─Lancaster (formed from York
   and Northumberland, first
   mentioned, 1 Jan. 1651/52)
    ├─[Old] Rappa-
    │ hannock, 1656
    └─Lancaster

NORTHUMBERLAND COUNTY (formed from
the Indian district *Chickacoan*, first mentioned, 31 Jan. 1644/45 in Maryland
records.†
├─Northumberland
└─Westmoreland, 1653
    └─Stafford, 1664

ACCAWMACK COUNTY (name changed
to Northampton, March 1642/43)
├─Accomack, 1663
└─Northampton

* See Morgan Poitaux Robinson, "Virginia Counties," *Bulletin #9 of the Virginia State Library*.

EXPLANATORY NOTES

ANCIENT PLANTER. A colonist in Virginia by 1616, entitled to 100 acres of land provided he paid his own passage and had dwelt in the Colony for three years when application for land was made. In accordance with a predetermined policy of the Virginia Company, no individual assignments of land were made during the first seven years of the Colony's existence. The policy of granting patents for acreage to settlers was inaugurated during the latter part of the regime of Sir Thomas Dale, Governor, 1611-1616.

CALENDAR. The Julian calendar, according to which 25 March was reckoned as the first day of the New Year, was in use together with the Gregorian calendar until 1752 when it was abandoned and the 11 days difference between the two calendars was dropped out of the year. The occurrence of an event between 1 January, the first day of the New Year according to the Gregorian calendar and 25 March, the New Year's day of the Julian calendar, is indicated by a diagonal: thus 16 February 1624/5, which shows that the event took place on 16 February 1624 by the Julian but 1625 by the Gregorian calendar.

COLLEGE LAND. Under provisions of the Great Charter for Virginia, 1618, 10,000 acres of land were set aside in Henrico and the adjoining area Coxendale "for the endowing of a university and college with convenient possessions." Plans then were put under way to establish this "university" for the education of the Indians. The massacre of 1622, which took a heavy toll of life in Henrico, put to an end all plans for a college in that area.

COMPANY LAND. By act of the Council for Virginia, 18 November 1618, each of the four Corporations, Charles City, Henrico, James City, and Kecoughtan (Elizabeth City) was assigned 3,000 acres of land. Those colonists transported to Virginia at the Company's expense were seated on the Company lands and the Company was entitled to one-half of the profits of their labors during seven-year terms. The other half of the profits was to be used to defray costs of government. (*R, Va. Co.* III, p. 101)

CORPORATIONS. In a first attempt to establish governmental divisions in Virginia, seemingly, prior to 17 June 1617 (Alexander Brown, *First Republic*, p. 254) four

Corporations were established: "James City, Charles City, the citty of Henricus and Kiccowtan (Kecoughtan, renamed Elizabeth City, August 1619)." This system did not long continue as the numerous water courses and cultivation of tobacco brought about development of the colony into plantations. In 1619 seven large plantations in addition to the Corporations elected representatives to the First Assembly.

COUNCIL. An advisory group of leading men dwelling in Virginia, appointed by the King, to assist the Governor in the direction of matters affecting the colony.

COUNCIL FOR VIRGINIA. Thirteen members of the Virginia Company originally appointed by King James, as specified in the First Charter (1606), to handle from England the direction of the Company's business affecting the Colony of Virginia.

COUNCIL. In 1623-33, twenty-one plantations or hundreds were represented in the Assembly, and in 1634 these and others were grouped in units and the Colony divided in eight *shires* or *counties* to be governed as the shires in England. These were: *Accawmack*, "on the Eastern Shore, over the bay" (the present Accomack and Northampton counties. Population, 396; *Charles City*, "extending on both sides of the river,–on the south side from Upper Chippokes Creek to Appomattox River, and on the north side from Sandy Point to Turkey Island Creek." Population, 511; *Charles River* (later York) composed of the plantations on the Charles (York) River. Population, 510; *Elizabeth City*, "extending on both sides of Hampton Roads,–on the south side to Chuckatuck Creek, and on the north side to Newport News, and including a small part thereof." Population, with Warwick River, 1670; *Henrico*, "extending from Charles City County indefinitely westward." Population, 419; *James City*, "extending on both sides of the River,–on the south side from Lawne's Creek to Upper Chippokes, and on the north side from Skiffes Creek to above Sandy Point." Population, 886; *Warrosquyoake* (Isle of Wight, 1637) extending from Chuckatuck Creek to Lawne's Creek. Population, 522; *Warwick River* (Warwick, 1642), "extending on the north side from Elizabeth City County to Skiffes Creek." Population, with Elizabeth City, as above, 1670.

COUSIN. Often meant niece or nephew; exact meaning determined by use in the document.

COMMISSIONERS. Before the Counties were formed, for convenience, Commissioners were appointed to hold court for minor causes in the "upper and lower parts" of the Colony; also see Justice.

DISSOLUTION OF THE VIRGINIA COMPANY. From the beginning King James I had favored the colonial enterprise, but as the colony grew in importance and at the same time began to assume the rudiments of self-government, he and his immediate advisors began to view with alarm the growing independence of the Colony under the Virginia Company guided by the policies of the Earl of Southampton. A Court party headed by the Earl of Warwick supporting the King's views developed within the Company and strong influence was brought to bear for surrender of the Company's Charter. The Indian massacre and ensuing troubles in Virginia gave weight to the King's position. On 17 November 1623 the Royal Commissioners for Virginia ordered the surrender of the locked trunk containing the Company's records. Anticipating this move on the part of the King, Nicholas Farrar, some six months earlier procured an expert clerk to copy *all* of the Company's records.[1]

But, when the Company refused to surrender its Charter for Virginia, the case was placed in the hands of Attorney-General Coventry, who prepared a *quo warranto* against the Company. The court hearing the case (the decision being a foregone conclusion) decreed that "the Patent or Charter of the Company of English merchants trading in Virginia and pretending to exercise a power and authority over his Majesty's good subjects there, should thenceforth be nul and void." However, this judgment was not entered on the record until about 1632 when it was done at the instance of Lord Baltimore; but in the beginning of Parliament of 1640, "the opponents to Baltimore's patent for Maryland took out the Virginia patent again under the Broad Seal of England" and it continued as a basis for rights to land and laws.[2]

---

[1] Farrar presented these copies about midsummer 1624 to the Earl of Southampton "who accepted them as a rich treasure, being evidences that concerned his honor." The fate of the original records is unknown. Some of the copies are missing, but those extant were among the collection in Thomas Jefferson's Library when purchased, 30 January 1815, as a basis for the reestablishment of the Library of Congress. These, transcribed by Susan Myra Kingsbury, are published in four volumes.

[2] See Alexander Brown, *First Republic*, pp. 87, 603, 604.

ENTAILS. In colonial Virginia land was held in *fee tail* or *fee simple*. According to the English law, which the colonists adopted, landed estates were held in *fee tail* and automatically passed from father to son or to the nearest male heir. Debts could not be charged against entailed estates.

Lands not inherited could be held in *fee simple*, in which case they were the sole possession of the owner and could be devised by him; however, unless such bequests of land specifically designated that they were to be held in *fee simple*, the law considered the devisee the owner for term of life only and at his death such holdings reverted to the family estate.

During the middle of the 18th century numerous acts for docking entails and by such legal means permitting sales of inherited lands are recorded. Heirs of landed estates frequently found themselves overloaded with thousands of acres and at the same time with insufficient funds or servants to cultivate their holdings profitably, and, also, often without means to meet individual bequests made in the wills of late owners. Yet, no portion of inherited lands could be sold for any purpose without a specific Act of the Assembly. These Acts provide valuable information as to location of entailed lands, trace the family ownership, usually for four generations, specify the use to which proceeds from the sales are to be put and grant permission for the removal of slaves from the land to be sold to other acreage held by the petitioner.

The obligation upon inherited lands came to an end with the Revolutionary War. By an act of the Assembly operative 1 January 1787, "every estate in lands or slaves, which on 7 October 1776 was an estate in *fee tail*" became from that time an estate in *fee simple* and debts were chargeable against the owners who benefited from the estates.

ESQUIRE. A title of respect applied to the son of a Knight, a member of the Council or to a Naval Collector.

GUARDIANSHIP. The Courts appointed guardians for minors. Those over 14 years of age could choose their own guardians, with Court approval.

HEADRIGHT. This term has no significance other than as evidence of right to land. Every person who, after 1616, came into the Colony from over seas or from a neighboring settlement was entitled to 50 acres of land (100 acres if he came by 1616) in his own name or in the name of the person who paid his passage. This provision was made by the Virginia Company in order to stimulate settlement.

The only limit to the number of such claims by an individual was the number of times he came into Virginia. Such rights were merchantable. They could be used by the recipient, sold or transferred. Often they were accumulated over a period of years and presented by the holder for patents of large acreages. Headrights were issued in the names of persons of all social classes–nobility, gentry, yeomanry, indentured servants (often the younger sons of English social classes) and Negroes. The persons named as headrights in a patent did not necessarily arrive in the colony the year the patent was issued, but oftimes such dates are the only clues to first appearances in Virginia. Before a patent was issued the claimant was required to show receipt as proof that passage money was duly paid.

HERETRIX. An heiress, owner in fee simple of heritable property of a Parish. The term used specifically in *Scots Law* was one of many variants from the English legal terminology and conveyed concisely more detailed information than the counterpart in English law. Though rarely used by colonial attorneys or court clerks, it is found in a deed of gift for land, entered in Surry County records, 1657 (Deeds, Wills &c, 1652-72, p.60).

HUNDREDS. A term used in a more liberal sense than in England where it referred to a county district authorized to hold court. The large early plantations, patents for which were issued in the names of several persons, often were designated *hundreds*, such as Martin's Hundred in James City County, Smith's (Southampton) Hundred on the north side of the Chickahominy River, Flowerdieu Hundred, Governor Yeardley's Plantation, Berkeley Hundred on the James River and Bermuda Hundred at the mouth of the Appomattox.

JUSTICE. The government of a county was vested in a body of justices, often eight, called Commissioners before 1661. They were appointed by the Governor for indefinite terms and were authorized to try cases not involving loss of life or limb and for amounts not to exceed £10.

MONEY. "Hard money" was almost non-existent in the early colony. The accepted media of exchange were: tobacco at the rate of 3 shillings for the best and 18 pence for that of second quality, capons, often mentioned as the accepted fee for land rentals, merchantable Indian corn and beaver skins.

PARTICULAR PLANTATION. In order to relieve the Virginia Company of the heavy responsibility of financing all settlements, the Council for Virginia about 1618 adopted a policy of granting large acreages to groups of adventurers (investors), who in turn agreed to transport large numbers of persons to plant (settle) the domain, and to be responsible for shipping to them needed provisions and supplies. These were known as Particular Plantations and very liberal terms and privileges were accorded to the grantees; in fact, their patents indicated a state of quasi-independence to which the grantees of Martin's Hundred, a domain of 80,000 acres in James City, laid claim. The patent issued for "Berkeley" also designated a Particular Plantation (For patent, Martin's Hundred, see *R, Va. Co.,* III, pp. 592-598).

PROCESSIONER. The most important civil function of the vestry of a Parish was the quadrennial processioning or going over the lands in the Parish to determine ownership and bounds of every tract. Two processioners appointed for each district were accompanied as they worked by the persons interested in the boundary to be established.

SERVANT. A term generally used in the modern sense of *employee.* Younger sons of the gentry in England, having no opportunity to acquire a landed estate, often obligated themselves by articles of indenture to serve required years in order to obtain passage to the promising land of Virginia. They, with others, therefore, are listed as "indentured servants." Adam Thorowgood, a well-to-do early colonist, who married the daughter of Robert Offley, Turkey merchant of London, is listed in the muster as a "servant." Randall Holt, apprenticed to Dr. Pott, was required by the Court to serve his "full time" after which he married the heiress Mary Bayly. A daughter of Christopher Calthrope, of a family connected with royalty, married Thomas Ragg listed in the inventory of her father's estate as an "indentured servant."

SON-IN-LAW, DAUGHTER-IN-LAW, ETC.. Often meant step-son, step-daughter, etc. The exact meaning must be determined by careful perusal of the document, often in relation to other facts in hand.

SPELLING. There was no standardized spelling in the 17th century. The same word may vary in spelling on the same page. Proper names especially were subject to variations. Adherence to 17th-century spelling in documents will account for the variations in spelling in this volume.

WILLS, given thus: 20 June 1678-20 February 1681/82, show the testator's signature was affixed 20 June 1678, and the will was entered on the records 20 February 1681/82.

EXPLANATION OF
ARRANGEMENT

In each of the family accounts that follows, the members of the family are numbered consecutively. In most instances the member of the Virginia Company or settler in Virginia prior to 1624/5 from whom the descent has been traced has been assigned the number one (1), his or her children numbers 2, 3, 4, etc., and the members of the succeeding generations, in order, succeeding numbers. However, in several families, such as Epes, in which a number of brothers came to the colony, these brothers are numbered consecutively according to their ages and the children and succeeding generations are numbered in order thereafter.

Preceding the name of the original ancestor and of some members of the second generation or other persons connected by marriage, a plus sign (+) indicates membership in the Virginia Company and an asterisk (*) indicates settlement in Virginia prior to 1624/5.

A superscript number following a given name indicates the generation to which the individual belongs. For example, *1. William^1 Andrews is the original settler of 1617; 32. Jacob^4 Andrews is his great-grandson, a member of the fourth generation of the Andrews family, and 116. Sarah^6 (Parker) Ker is Jacob's granddaughter, a member of the sixth generation.

Each member of the first five generations who left descendants known to have lived in the American colonies has been assigned a separate section in the family account in which information about his or her life, wives or husbands, and children is given. In listing the issue of such individuals, a child whose life, marriage and descendants are discussed subsequently is shown in capital letters to indicate that further information appears later in the account. If the surname of the children is different from that of the original progenitor, the surname is indicated following the word Issue.

Intermarriages between members of the several families discussed herein occurred frequently. In such instances, the name of the husband or wife (or the parent or grandparent named herein) is shown in italics with the number assigned in the family to which he or she belongs and reference to that family.

Since superscript numbers are used to identify footnotes as well as the generations to which an individual belongs, the reader should note that generation numbers are limited almost entirely to the numbers 1, 2, 3, 4, 5 and 6, although a few references to generations 7 and 8 may appear. These numbers are appended only to given names; if a footnote number of necessity must also follow a given name, it is invariably separated from the given name by some mark of punctuation.

KEY TO ABBREVIATIONS

Br. Gen.: Alexander Brown, *The Genesis of the United States* (New York, 1897), 2 v., paged continuously.

Bruce, *Ec/ Hist.*: Philip Alexander Bruce, *Economic History of Virginia in the Seventeenth Century* (New York and London, 1907), 2 v.

C: *Calendar of Virginia State Papers* (Richmond, 1875-93), 11 v.

Co.: County.

CP: *Cavaliers and Pioneers*, v. 1-3, ed. by Nell Marion Nugent (Richmond, 1934-79), v. 4-7, ed. by Dennis Ray Hudgins (Richmond, 1994-99).

Cra. Rep.: Lyon Gardiner Tyler, *The Cradle of the Republic* (Richmond, 1906).

CVR: William Glover Stanard, *Colonial Virginia Register* (Albany, N.Y., 1902)

ES: Ralph T. Whitelaw, *Virginia's Eastern Shore* (Richmond, 1951), 2 v., ed. by George Carrington Mason.

Esqr.: Esquire.

Gent.: Gentleman.

H: William Waller Hening, *The Statutes at Large; Being a Collection of All the Laws of Virginia* (Richmond, etc., 1809-23), 13 v. [References to v. I-IV are to the second edition used in the facsimile reprint, Charlottesville, 1969].

Hinshaw: William Wade Hinshaw, *Encyclopedia of American Quaker Genealogy*, I, *North Carolina* (Ann Arbor, Mich. 1936); IV, *Ohio* (Ann Arbor, Mich., 1946), VI, *Virginia* (Ann Arbor, Mich., 1950).

Hotten: John Camden Hotten, *The Original Lists of Persons of Quality and Others Who Went from Great Britain to the American Plantations 1600-1700* (New York, 1874).

JHB: *Journals of the House of Burgesses of Virginia, 1619-1776* (Richmond, 1905-15), 13 v., ed. by H. R. McIlwaine.

Leonard: Cynthia Miller Leonard, comp., *The General Assembly of Virginia, July 30, 1619-January 11, 1978, A Bicentennial Register of Members* (Richmond, 1978).

MCGC: *Minutes of the Council and General Court of Colonial Virginia*, 2nd ed. (Richmond, 1979), ed. by H. R. McIlwaine.

MHM: *Maryland Historical Magazine* (Baltimore, 1906-   ), 98 v.

Mrs.: Mistress (often a single woman).

N: *Lower Norfolk County, Virginia, Antiquary* (Baltimore, 1895-1906), 5 v., ed. by Edward Wilson James.

NEHGR: *The New England Historical and Genealogical Register* (Boston, 1847-   ), 157 v.

NGSQ: *National Genealogical Society Quarterly* (Washington, 1912-   ), 91 v.

P.C.C.: Prerogative Court of Canterbury.

P.R.O.: Public Record Office, London.

R: *The Virginia Historical Register, and Literary Advertiser* (Richmond, 1848-53), 6 v., ed. by William Maxwell.

R, Va. Co.: *The Records of the Virginia Company of London* (Washington, 1906-35), 4 v., ed. by Susan Myra Kingsbury.

SCH&GM: *The South Carolina Historical & Genealogical Magazine* (Charleston, 1900-51), 52 v.

Smith, *Tra.*: *Travels and Works of Captain John Smith* (Edinburgh, 1910), 2 v., ed. by Edward Arber and A. G. Bradley.

T: *Tyler's Quarterly Historical and Genealogical Magazine* (Richmond, 1919-52), 33 v.

V: *The Virginia Magazine of History and Biography* (Richmond,, 1893-   ), 110 v.

Val. Papers: *The Edward Pleasants Valentine Papers* (Richmond, 1927), 4 v., ed, by William Clayton Torrence.

Va. Carolorum: Edward Duffield Neill, *Virginia Carolorum: The Colony Under the Rule of Charles the First and Second, A.D. 1625-A.D. 1685, Based upon Manuscripts and Documents of the Period* (Albany, N.Y., 1886).

W(1): *William and Mary College Quarterly Historical Magazine*, 1st ser. (Williamsburg, 1892-1919), 27 v.

W(2): *William and Mary College Quarterly Historical Magazine*, 2nd ser. (Williamsburg, 1921-43), 23 v.

W(3): *The William and Mary Quarterly; A Magazine of Early American History*, 3rd ser. (Williamsburg, 1944-   ), _ v.

Waters, *Gleanings*: Henry F. Waters, *Genealogical Gleanings in England* (Boston, 1901), 2 v., paged continuously.

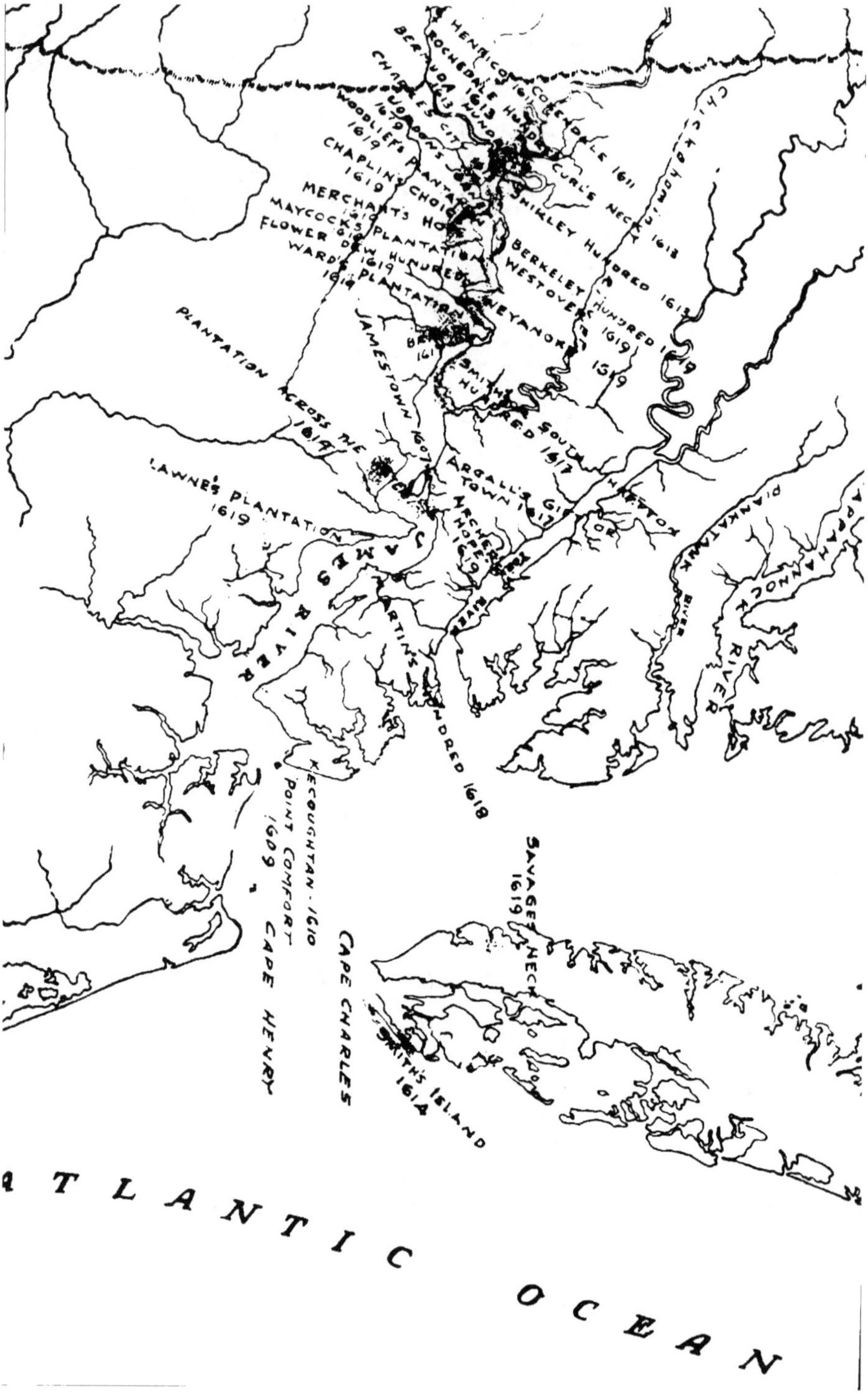
HENRICO 1611
COXENDALE 1611
ROCHEDALE HUNDRED 1613
BERMUDA HUNDRED 1613
CURL'S NECK 1613
SHIRLEY HUNDRED 1613
WOODLIEF'S PLANTATION 1619
CHAPLINS CHOICE 1619
MERCHANT'S HOPE
MAYCOCKS PLANTATION
FLOWER DEW HUNDRED
WARD'S PLANTATION
BERKELEY HUNDRED 1619
WESTOVER 1619
WEYANOKE
SMITH'S HUNDRED 1617
JAMESTOWN 1607
ARGALL'S GIFT TOWN 1617
LAWNE'S PLANTATION 1619
JAMES RIVER
MARTIN'S HUNDRED 1618
KECOUGHTAN 1610
POINT COMFORT 1609
CAPE HENRY
CAPE CHARLES
SAVAGES NECK 1619
SMITH'S ISLAND
CHICKAHOMINY
PIANKATANK RIVER
RAPPAHANNOCK RIVER
ATLANTIC OCEAN

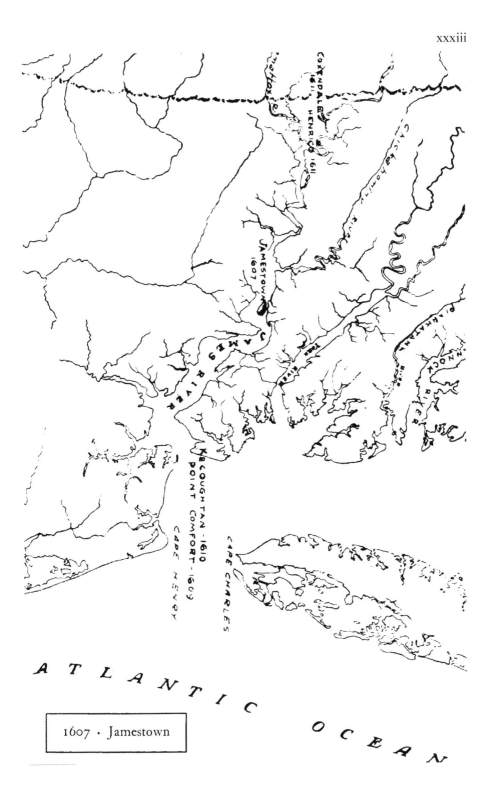

COXNDALE-1611

HENRICO-1611

Appomattox

CHICKAHOMINY

JAMESTOWN 1607

PAMUNKEY

JAMES RIVER

YORK RIVER

NANSEMOND RIVER

RAPPAHANNOCK RIVER

KECOUGHTAN-1610

POINT COMFORT-1609

CAPE HENRY

CAPE CHARLES

A T L A N T I C O C E A N

1607 · Jamestown

THE MUSTER OF THE INHABITANTS OF VIRGINIA
20 JANUARY–7 FEBRUARY
1624/5

[Reproduced from the third edition of 1987.]

IN the late spring of 1622, following the Indian massacre of 22 March 1621/2, George Sandys, Treasurer of the Virginia colony, sent a letter to London by the *Seaflower* informing the authorities that 347 persons had been killed in the tragic uprising of the savages.[1] Immediate action was initiated by John Farrar on behalf of the Virginia Company of London by publishing the list of those slain - "To the end that their lawfull heyres may take speedy order for the inheriting of their lands and estates there: For which the Honourable Company of Virginia are ready to doe them all right and favour."[2]

A letter dated 14 April 1623, from Christopher Davison at James City, Virginia, to John Farrar in London, stated that Davison hoped to send by the next ship "a perfect catalogue" "of the names of all the people, that dyed or were slayne, by the Indyans, & of all that remayne alive."[3]

On 6 Dec. 1623 the Council for Virginia at James City received a letter from the Treasurer and Council for the colony in London, requiring them "to send home by the first oppertunitie of Shipping an exact list as well of all such as have died or ben sleine since the Massacre, as also of all such as are now liveing w[th]in all plantacions."[4] In compliance, the Council directed the commanders of the several plantations to make report, one such order, signed by George Yeardly, George Sandis, Chr: Davison and John Pott, reading

> Theise are to require you Cap[t] W[m] Tucker to send up before the 16th day of this present december a perfect list of the names of all such as have died or ben sleine at Elza: Citty since the Massacre, till the day of the date of yo[r] list as also of all such as are at that day liveing belonging to the said plantacion whether present or absent.[5]

[1] *R, Va. Co.* III, p. 554.
[2] *Ibid.*, pp. 564–71.
[3] *Ibid.*, IV, pp. 115–16.
[4] *Ibid.*, IV, p. 441.
[5] *Ibid.*

In English documents this record is shown under the date 16 Feb. 1623/4 as the List of the Living and the Dead in Virginia. Virginia historians have usually referred to it as a census, and that terminology is used herein for convenience.[6]

When the royal government under King Charles I decided to abrogate the Charter of the Virginia Company and bring affairs of Virginia directly under the control of the Crown, the Privy Council, 24 Oct. 1623, informed John Harvey, John Pory, Abraham Peirsey, Samuel Mathews and John Jefferson:

> His Majesty having taken into his royal care the plantacion in Virginia besides the order hee hath given for the redresse and reformacion of the gouvernment hath bene lykewise pleased for the better advancing of so good a worke to command that informacion be taken of the present state of the plantacion in diverse considerable points: for which cause we have thought fit and doe hereby will and require you in regard you are well acquainted with the coursses and condicions of things there to make diligent enquire of these particulars following, and certify us accordingly what you finde viz., how many severall plantacions there be and which of them be publique and which private and particular, what people, men, women and children be in each plantacion, what fortifications or what place is best to be fortifyed, what howses and how many, what cattle, what armes, ammunicion and ordinance, mounted and serviceable, what corne and other provision of victuals, what boates and barques, what bridges and publique workes, how the colonie standeth in respect of the sauvages, what hopes may be truly and really conceived of that plantacion and lastly the directest means to attaine to those hopes.[7]

On the same day the Governor and Council in Virginia were notified of the appointment of John Harvy, Esquire, and others and directed " . . . to yeald them your best ayde and assistance upon all occasions . . . "[8]

Harvey arrived in Virginia aboard his ship, the *Southampton*, and the commissioners, with the exception of Jefferson who was absent, on 2 March 1623/4 submitted to Governor Sir Francis Wyatt and the General Assembly a request for their opinion in writing regard-

---

[6] Hotten, pp. 169–89, names of the living; 190–95, names of the dead.
[7] *Acts of the Privy Council of England, 1623–1625* (London, 1933), pp. 107–08.
[8] *Ibid.*, p. 108.

ing the four propositions concerning the present state of the colony, to which the Assembly responded the same day.[9] Immediate opposition was encountered, however, to an additional request that the Assembly sign a form testifying thankfulness for the King's care of the colony and consenting to the revocation of old patents and to accept a new charter. To this request Governor Wyatt, the Council and the Assembly quickly replied that they had already given thanks to the King for his tender care over them and that when consent to surrender patents was required would be the proper time to reply to that request. The Assembly further informed the commissioners it desired to see their authority before replying.[10] The Virginia government, which had been appointed by the Company and did not favor the extinction of its authority, and the inhabitants who feared the loss of rights previously held under the liberal policy of the Virginia Company, quite understandably resisted any attempt to relinquish rights without confirmation of the King's specific direction that this be done. Pory, Harvey, Peirsey and Mathews were forced to admit on 3 March that they had no authority to require subscription of that form, but stated they had proposed it "by way of counsel for the good of the plantation." They also informed the Assembly that they "cannot profess that they had no further commission concerning them, for what is unperformed touches their persons, servants, corn, cattle, arms, houses, &c."[11] Despite the opposition, before it was dissolved on 24 May 1624, "to enable the commissioners to take a view of the exact state of the colony, the Assembly ordered that the several plantations should transport them from plantation to plantation, as they should desire."[12]

The Muster of the Inhabitants of Virginia was taken between 20 Jan. and 7 Feb. 1624/5, during the term of office of Governor Sir Francis Wyatt. When Capt. Harvey left Virginia before 16 Feb. 1624/5, he carried with him reports from about 21 plantations, including the Eastern Shore, which give a fairly approximate idea as to the condition of the colony at that time. The muster comprises the answers to the first eight questions propounded in the Privy Council's instructions to the commissioners.[13] Although dated Jan.-

9 W. Noel Sainsbury, ed., *Calendar of State Papers, Colonial Series, 1584–1660* (London, 1860), p. 58.

10 *Ibid.*, p. 59.

11 Ibid.

12 Alexander Brown, *The First Republic in America* (Boston and New York, 1898), pp. 571–72.

13 The text given hereinafter is transcribed from a photocopy of the original (in the Public Record Office, London) in the Virginia State Library.

Feb. 1624/5, it probably was a final compilation of information gathered during the seven or eight months following the dissolution of the Virginia Company. Hence, the Muster is a document pertinent both to the Company's administration in Virginia and to the termination of the authority of this private corporation, originally composed mostly of London merchants who, in 1606, had been given a royal charter to establish a colony in the New World.

MUSTERS
of the Inhabitants in Virginia
1624/1625

THE MUSTER OF THE INHABITANTS
OF THE *COLLEDGE-LAND IN VIRGINIA* TAKEN THE
23TH OF JANUARY 1624.

Liuetennt THOMAS OSBORNE arived in the *Bona Nova* November 1619

SERVANTS

DANIELL SHERLEY aged 30 yeres came in the *Bona Nova* 1619
PETER JORDEN aged 22 in the *London Marchannt* 1620
RICHARD DAVIS aged 16 yeres in the *Jonathan* 1620
   Corne, 12 barrells; Pease, 4 bushells; Fish, 900; Powder, 4 lb; Lead, 40 lb;
*Peeces fixt, 4; Armours, 4; Swords, 4; Swine, 1; Boat, 1; Canow, 1

ROBERT LAPWORTH came in the *Abigaile*
   Corne, 3 barrells; Armour, 1; Peece, 1; House, 1

JOHN WATSON came in the *William & Thomas*
   Corne, 3 barrells; Powder, ½ lb; Lead, 2 lb; Peece, 1; Armour Complett, 1

EDWARD HOBSON came in the *Bona Nova* 1619
   Corne, 3 barrells

CHRISTOPHER BRANCH came in the *London Marchannt*
MARY his wife in the same Shipp
THOMAS his sonne aged 9 Months
   Corne, 2 barrells; Pease, 1 bushell; Fish, 100; Armour Complett, 1; House 1

WILLIAM BROWNINGE came in the *Bona Nova*
   Corne, 1½ barrell; Fish, ½ hundred; Armour Complett, 1; Peece, 1; House, 1

* *Peeces* are guns; however, the term *peeces fixt* was not generally in use in the early
17th century and is not interpreted today (1955) with any certainty. The guns so listed
might be those converted from matchlocks to some faster and surer means of ignition such
as that employed by 1640 in the flintlock. Apparently, between 1611 and 1625 there
was a great deal of activity in remodeling these arms.

MATHEW EDLOW came in the *Neptune* 1618
Corne, 7½ barrells; Fish, 100; Powder, 2 lb; Peece, 1; Armour Complett, 1;
House, 1

WILLIAM WELDON came in the *Bona Nova* 1619
Corne, 5½ barrells; Peece, 1; Armour Complett, 1

FRANCIS WILTON came in the *Jonathan*
Corne, 3 barrells; Pease, 1 bushell; Fish, 100; Powder, 2 lb; Peece, 1; Armour
Complett, 1

EZEKIAH RAUGHTON came in the *Bona Nova*
MARGARET his wife in the *Warwick*
Corne, 3½ barrells; Fish, 100; Peece, 1; Armour Complett, 1

WILLIAM PRICE came in the *Starr*
Corne, 2½ barrells; Fish, ½ hundred; Peece, 1; Armour Complett, 1; House, 1

Colledg Land — ROBERT CAMPION came in the *Bona Nova*
Corne, 2 barrells; Pease, ½ hundred; Fish, 100; Powder, 1 lb; Peece, 1; Armour,
1; House, 1

LEONARD MOORE came in the *Bona Nova*
Corne, 1½ barrell; Fish, 100; Powder, 1 lb; Peece, 1; Armour Complett, 1

THOMAS BAUGH came in the *Supply*
Corne, 2 barrells; Fish, 100; Lead, 10 lb; Peece, 1; Canow, 1; Armour
Complett, 1; House, 1

THOMAS PARKER came in the *Neptune*
Corne, 8 barrells; Powder, 1 lb; Peece, 1; Sword, 1

THEODER MOYSES came in the *London Marchannt*
Corne, 2 barrells; Fish, 100; Peece, 1; Armour, 1; Sword, 1; House, 1

THE MUSTER OF THE INHABITANTS OF THE *NECK-OF-LAND IN THE CORPORATION OF CHARLES CITTIE IN VIRGINIA* TAKEN THE 24TH OF JANUARY 1624.

*[3]

Neck-of-Land Corporation of Charles Citty.

LUKE BOYSE aged 44 yeares arived in the *Edwine* in May 1619
ALLICE his wife arived in the *Bona-Nova* in April 1622

SERVANTS

ROBERT HOLLAM aged 23 yeares in the *Bonaventure* August 1620
JOSEPH ROYALL aged 22 yeares in the *Charitie* July 1622
PROVISIONS: Corne, 60 bushells; Pease and beanes, 3 bushells; Fish, 200. ARMES

* Numbers in brackets on margin show folios of original document.

AND MUNITION: Peeces, 4; Armours, 3; Swords, 2; Powder, 5 lb; Lead and bulletts, 60 lb. CATTELL AND SWINE: Neat Cattell young and old, 11; Swine, 10. HOUSES & BOATS: Dwelling house, 1; Boat, 1.

THE MUSTER OF *JOSUAH CHARD*

JOSUAH CHARD aged 36 yeares in the *Seaventure* May 1607
ANN his wife aged 33 yeares in the *Bony besse* August 1623

PROVISIONS: Corne, 2½ barrells; *Wett fish, 100; ARMES AND MUNITION: Peeces fixt, 3 and one pistoll†; Powder, 1 lb; Lead, 20 lb; Armour, 1; Coat of Male, 1. SWINE AND POULTRIE: Swine, 1 and three piggs; Poultrie, 21. HOUSES: House, 1

THE MUSTER OF *JOHN DODS*

JOHN DODS aged 36 yeares in the *Susan Constant* April 1607
JANE his wife aged 40 yeares

[4]

Neck-of-Land
Charles Cittie

PROVISIONS: Corne, 10 barrells; Pease, ½ bushell; Fish, ½ hundred. ARMES AND MUNITION: Powder, 4 lb; Lead and bulletts, 30 lb; Peeces fixt, 2; Coat of Male, 1 and a head peece; Sword, 1. POULTRIE: Poultrie, 30. HOUSES: House, 1.

THE MUSTER OF *WILLIAM VINCENE*

WILLIAM VINCENE aged 39 yeares in the *Mary & James*
JOANE his wife aged 42 yeares

PROVISIONS: Corne, 6 barrells; Pease, 3½ bushells; Fish, ¼ of a hundred. ARMES & MUNITION: Powder, 6 lb; Lead & shott, 20 lb; Peeces fixt, 2; Coat of Male, 1 and a head peece; Sword, 1. SWINE & POULTRIE: Sow piggs, 2; Poultrie, 25.

THE MUSTER OF *THOMAS HARRIS*

THOMAS HARRIS aged 38 yeares in the *Prosperous* in May
ADRIA his wife aged 23 yeares in the *Marmaduke* in November 1621
ANN WOODLASE theire kinswoman aged 7 yeares

* fish in brine
† This weapon probably derives its name from the word *pistallo* which means pommel, and not from *Pistoja* for it appears not to have been first made at *Pistoja* but at *Perugia* where they made small hand cannons a hand's span in length. (The Roman span is about 7½ inches.)
The *coup de poing*, a small pistol, which the Germans called *Terzerol* was in use in the 16th century. The weapon with a wheel-lock and a barrel only 6½ inches in length was made entirely of iron. This was preceded by the *Monchsbuchse*, a small hand cannon with a rasp.
The revolver pistol, as well as revolver guns, existed in the 17th and 18th centuries and those made later, among which the Colt revolver was the most celebrated, could not be called inventions, but merely improvements of an old invention. See *An Illustrated History of Arms and Armour* by Auguste Demmin trans. by C. C. Black, M.A. (London; George Bell & Sons, 1901).

SERVANTS

ELIZABETH   aged 15 yeares in the *Margaret & John* 1620

PROVISIONS: Corne, 7½ bushells; Pease, 1 bushell. ARMES & MUNITION: Powder, 11 lb; Lead, 2; Peeces fixt, 3; Armour, 1; Coat of Male, 1; Sword, 1. CATTELL & POULTRIE: Cattell young and old, 11; Poultrie, 30. HOUSES AND BOATS: Houses, 2; Boats, 1.

THE MUSTER OF *JOHN PRICE*

JOHN PRICE aged 40 yeares in the *Starr* in May
ANN his wife aged 21 yeares in the *Francis Bonaventure* August 1620
MARY a Child aged 3 Months

PROVISIONS: Corne, 2½ barrells; Pease, 1½ bushell; ARMES AND MUNITION: Powder, 5 lb; Lead, 10 lb; Peeces fixt, 2; Armor, 1; Coat of Steele, 1; Sword & Dager, 2. CATTELL & POULTRIE: Cattell young and old, 5; Poultrie, 15. HOUSES: Houses, 2.

THE MUSTER OF *HUGH HILTON*

HUGH HILTON aged 36 yeares in the *Edwine* in May 1619

PROVISIONS: Corne, 2½ barrells; Pease, 1½ bushell. ARMES AND MUNITION: Powder, 1 lb; Shott, 5 lb; Peeces fixt, 1; Armor, 1; Swords, 2. POULTRIE: Poultrie, 6.

[5]

Neck-of-Land
Charles Cittie

THE MUSTER OF *RICHARD TAYLOR*

RICHARD TAYLOR aged 50 yeares in the *Mary Margrett* September 1608
DOROTHY his wife aged 21 yeares in the *London Marchannt* May 1620
MARY theire Child aged 3 months.

SERVANTS

CHRISTOPHER BROWNE aged 18 yeares in the *Dutie* in May 1620

PROVISIONS: Corne, 9 barrells. ARMES AND MUNITION: Powder, 1½ lb; Lead, 60 lb; Peeces fixt, 2; Coats of Male, 2 and 2 headpeeces. CATTELL SWINE & POULTRIE: Cattell young and old, 3; Sow pigg, 1; Poultrie, 20. HOUSES: House, 1

THE MUSTER OF *THOMAS OAGE*

THOMAS OAGE aged 40 yeares in the *Starr* in May
ANN his wife in the *Neptune* in August 1618
EDWARD theire sonn aged 2 years.

PROVISIONS: Corne, 5½ barrells; Pease & beanes, 2 bushells; Fish, ½ hundred. ARMES AND MUNITION: Powder, 2 lb; Lead, 10 lb; Peeces fixt, 1; Coats of Male, 2 and a head peece; Armour, 1; Sword, 1. POULTRIE: Poultrie, 20. HOUSES: House, 1.

THE MUSTER OF *ROBERT GREENLEAFE*

Robert Greenleafe aged 43 yeres in the *Tryall* August 1610
Susan his wife aged 23 yeres in the *Jonathan* May 1620
Thomas theire sonn aged 3 yeres
Ann a daughter aged 22 weeks

PROVISIONS: Corn, 4½ barrells; Pease and beanes, 1½ bushell. ARMES & MUNITION: Powder, 1 lb; Lead, 3 lb; Peeces fixt, 1. SWINE & POULTRIE: Sow Pigg, 1; Poultrie, 10. HOUSES: House, 1.

THE MUSTER OF *HENERY COLTMAN*

Henery Coltman aged 30 yeres in the *Noah* August 1610
Ann his wife aged 26 yeres in the *London Marchannt* May 1620

PROVISIONS: Corne, 5 barrells; Pease and beanes, 2 bushells. ARMES & MUNITION: Powder, 1 lb; Shott and bulletts, 1 lb; Peece fixt, 1; Armor, 1 and a head [peece]; Coats of Male, 2. POULTRIE: Poultrie, 18. HOUSES: House, 1.

THE MUSTER OF *HUGH PRICE*

[6]

Neck-of-Land
Charles
Cittie

Hugh Price aged 35 yeares in the *William & John* January 1618
Judith his wife aged 24 yeres in the *Marygold* May 1619
John his sonn aged 2 yeres.

PROVISIONS: Corne, 2 barrells. ARMES & MUNITION: Powder, 3 lb; Lead, 1 lb; Peeces fixt, 1; Armour, 1 and a head peece; Coat of Male, 1; Swords, 3. CATTELL SWINE ETC: Cow, 1; Sow pigg, 1; Poultrie, 14. HOUSES: House, 1.

THE MUSTER OF *THOMAS FARMER*

Thomas Farmer aged 30 yeres in the *Tryall* 1616

PROVISIONS: Corne, 2½ barrells. ARMES & MUNITION: Powder, ½ lb; Shott and bulletts, 4 lb; Peeces fixt, 1 and a pistoll; Armour, 1; Steele Coat, 1; Hanger*, 1. POULTRIE: Poultrie, 10.

THE MUSTER OF *THOMAS SHEPPEY*

Thomas Sheppey aged 22 yeres in the *Supply* January 1620

PROVISIONS: Corne, 2 barrells; Pease, 1 bushell. ARMES & MUNITION: Powder, ½ lb; bulletts and Shott, 10 lb; Peeces fixt, 2; Armour, 1 and a headpeece; Coate of Male, 1. POULTRIE: Poultrie, 8. HOUSES: House, 1.

THE MUSTER OF *ALEXANDER BRADWAY*

Alexander Bradway aged 31 yeres in the *Supply* January 1620

* hanger. A seaman's cutlass; a short curved sword.

SISLEY his wife aged 28 yeres in the *Jonathan* May 1620
ADRIA theire daughter aged 9 Months.

PROVISIONS: Corne, 1 barrell; Pease, ½ bushell. ARMES & MUNITION: Powder,
½ lb; Peeces fixt, 1. POULTRIE: Poultrie, 6. HOUSES: House, 1.

THE MUSTER OF *WILLIAM SHARP*

WILLIAM SHARP aged 40 yeres in the *Starr* in May
ELIZABETH his wife aged 25 yeres in the *Bonaventure* August 1620
ISACK his sonn aged 2 yeres
SAMUELL his sonn aged 2 Months

SERVANTS

RICHARD VAUSE aged 20 yeres in the *Jonathan* May 1620

PROVISIONS: Corne, 8 barrells; Pease, 2 bushells; Fish, ¼ of a hundred. ARMES
AND MUNITION: Powder, 3 lb; Lead, 12 lb; Peeces fixt, 2; Coats of Male, 2 and
a headpeece; Swords, 2. CATTELL & POULTRIE: Cattell, 3; Poultrie, 14. HOUSES:
Houses, 2.

[7]

*West &
Sherley
hundred.
Charles
Cittie*

THE MUSTER OF THE INHABITANTS OF WEST AND SHERLEY HUNDRED TAKEN THE 22TH OF JANUARY 1624.

RICHARD BIGGS HIS MUSTER

RICHARD BIGGS aged 41 yeres arived in the *Swann* in August 1610
SARAH his wife aged 35 yeres in the *Marygold* May 1618
RICHARD theire Sonn aged 3 yeres
THOMAS TURNER his Cozen aged 11 yeres in ye *Marygold* 1616
SUSAN OLD his Cozen aged 10 yeres in the *Marygold* 1616

SERVANTS

JAMES GUY aged 20 yeares in the *Marygold* 1622
WILLIAM BROCK aged 26 yeres in the *Margrett* in May 1622
EDWARD TEMPLE aged 20 yeres in the *Margrett* May 1622
MARY PEETERS aged 16 yeres in the *London Marchant* May 1620

PROVISIONS: Corne, 70 bushells; Pease, 9 bushells; Fish, 100. ARMES AND MUNI-
TION: Powder, 30 lb; Lead, 200 wtt; Peeces fixt, 6; Armours compleat, 2. CAT-
TELL SWINE & POULTRY: Neat Cattell young and old, 8; Swine young and old,
21; Poultrie, 30. HOUSES AND BOATS: Houses, 3; Boate, 1.

WILLIAM BAYLEYS MUSTER

WILLIAM BALEY aged 41 yeares in the *Prosperous* in May 1610
MARY his wife aged 24 yeres in the *George* 1617
THOMAS his Sonn aged 4 yeares

PROVISIONS: Corne, 15 bushells; Fish, 1½ hundred. ARMES AND MUNITION: Powder, 1 lb; Lead, 12 lb; Snaphannce*, 1. Poultrie, 7. Houses, 1.

ROBERT PARTINS MUSTER   [8]

ROBERT PARTIN aged 36 yeares in the *Blessinge* in June 1609   *West &*
MARGRETT his wife aged 36 in the *George* 1617   *Sherley*

ROBERT ⎫   ⎧ aged 4 Months.   *hundred*
AVIS   ⎬ theire Children   ⎨ aged 5 yeares.
REBECCA ⎭   ⎩ aged 2 yeares.

SERVANTS

THOMAS HALE aged 20 yeares in the *George* 1623 in Oct.
ELLIN COOKE aged 25 yeares in the *London Marchannt* June 1620

PROVISIONS: Corne, 50 bushells. ARMES AND MUNITION: Powder, 2 lb; Lead, 20 lb; Snaphannce, 1; Armours, 4. CATTELL SWINE ETC: Neat Cattell young and old, 3; Swine, 1; Poultrie, 9. HOUSES: House, 1.

CHRISTOPHER WOODWARDS MUSTER

CHRISTOPHER WOODWARD aged 30 yeares in the *Tryall* in June 1620
JOHN HIGGINS ⎫ his ptn's ⎧ aged 21 yeres in the *George* 1616
RICE HOWE   ⎭   ⎩ aged 26 yeres in the *Gifte* 1618

SERVANTS

MATHEW GLOSTER aged 20 yeres in the *Warwick* 1621
WILLIAM TOTLE aged 18 yeres in the *George* 1623
JOHN CANON aged 20 yeres in the *Abigaile* 1622

PROVISIONS: Corne, 50 bushells; Fish, 1 hundred. ARMES AND MUNITION: Powder, 1 lb; Lead, 4 lb; Peeces fixt, 5; Coate of Male, 1. SWINE & POULTRIE: Swine, 3; Poultrie, 14. HOUSES: House, 1.

THE MUSTER OF *AMIAS BOLTE*   *West &*
                                                      Sherley
AMIAS BOLTE aged 23 yeares in the *Neptune* in August 1618   *hundred*

PROVISIONS: Corne, 8 bushells. ARMES AND MUNITION: Powder, 1 lb; Peece fixt, 1; Coats of Male, 2 and a headpeece. SWINE AND POULTRIE: Swine, 2; Poultrie, 12.

THE MUSTER OF *JOHN COLLINS*

JOHN COLLINS aged 30 yeares in the *Suply* 1620
SUSAN his wife aged 40 yeres in the *Treasurer* 1613
ANN USHER aged 8 yeares born heare

* *Snaphance, Snaphaunce.* The name formerly applied to the spring lock of a firearm. The *snaphaunce* superseded the wheel-lock and fell upon a movable piece of steel, cal' a frizel, which was placed vertically above the pan; hence, a firelock, a musket. The word and object were derived from Continental Europe.

PROVISIONS: Corne, 10 bushells; English wheat, 1 hogshead; Fish, ½ hundred. ARMES AND MUNITION: Powder, 5 lb; Shott, 6 lb; Peeces fixt, 2. CATTELL & POULTRIE: Neat Cattell, 2; Poultrie, 10. HOUSES: House, 1.

THE MUSTER OF *HENERY BENSON*

HENERY BENSON aged 40 yeares in the *Francis Bonaventure* August 1620
NICHOLAS BLACKMAN his ptner aged 40 in the same Shipp

PROVISIONS: Corne, 12 bushells; English Meale, 5 bushells; Fish, 1 hundred. ARMES & MUNITION: Peeces serviceable, 2. POULTRIE: Poultrie, 4.

[9]

West &
Sherley
hundred.
Charles
Cittie

MR *THOMAS PAWLETTS* MUSTER

THOMAS PAWLETT aged 40 yeares in the *Neptune* in August 1618

SERVANTS

JOHN TRUSSELL aged 19 yeres in the *Southampton* 1622

PROVISIONS: Corne, 20 bushells; Fish, 2 hundred. ARMES & MUNITION: Powder, 2 lb; Shott, 6 lb; Coats of Male, 3 and a headpeece; Peeces fixt, 3. POULTRIE: Poultrie, 15. HOUSES: Houses, 2.

THE MUSTER OF *WILLIAM ASKEW*

WILLIAM ASKEW aged 30 yeres in the *Prosperous* in May 1610

PROVISIONS: Corne, 30 bushells. ARMES & MUNITION: Powder, 8 lb; Lead, 50 lb; Peeces fixt, 2 and a pistoll; Armour, 1. POULTRIE: Poultrie, 20. HOUSES: House, 1.

THE MUSTER OF *REBECCA ROSE* Widdow

REBECCA ROSE aged 50 yeares in the *Marygold* in May 1619
MARMADUKE HILL } Children { aged 11 yeres } in the same Shipp
JANE HILL   { aged 14 yeres }

PROVISIONS: Corne, 20 bushells; Pease, 1 bushell. CATTELL SWINE ETC: Neat Cattell, 2; Swine, 6; Poultrie, 20. HOUSES: House, 1.

West &
Sherley
hundred.
Charles
Cittie

THE MUSTER OF M^{RS} *MARY MADISON* Widdow

MARY MADISON aged 30 yeares in the *Treasurer* 1618
KATHERIN LAYDEN a Child aged 7 yeares

SERVANTS

JAMES WATSON aged 20 yeares in the *George* 1623
ROGER LEWES aged 19 yeares in the *Edwin* in May 1617

PROVISIONS: Corne, 100 bushells. ARMES AND MUNITION: Powder, 6 lb; Lead, 100 wtt; Peeces fixt, 3; Coats of Male, 2; Steele coats, 3 and 3 headpeeces. CATTELL SWINE ETC: Neat Cattell, 6; Swine young and old, 20; Poultrie, 30. HOUSES AND BOATS: Houses, 2; boat, 1.

THE MUSTER OF *ROBERT* * *BAGWELL* etc

HENERY BAGWELL aged 35 yeares in the *Deliverance* 1608
SYMON TURGIS aged 30 yeares in the *William & Thomas* 1618

SERVANTS

RANDALL BAWDE aged 30 yeares in the *Due Returne* 1623
CHARLES   aged 19 yeares in the *Jacob* 1624

PROVISIONS: Corne, 80 bushells; Fish, 1 hundred. ARMES AND MUNITION:
Powder, 3 lb; Lead, 50 lb; Peeces fixt, 4; Coats of Male, 2 and 3 headpeeces;
buffe Coat, 1. SWINE & POULTRIE: Sow pigg, 1; Poultrie, 12. HOUSES: House, 1.

THE MUSTER OF *ROBERT MILNER* etc

[10]

*Sherley
hundred.
Charles
Cittie*

ROBERT MILNER aged 24 yeares in the *Francis Bonaventure* Aug 1620
JOHN PASSEMAN aged 29 yeres in the *Jonathan* May 1620
JENKIN OSBORN aged 24 yeres in the *George* 1617
WILLIAM WESTON aged 25 yeres in the *Jonathan* May 1620

PROVISIONS: Corne, 50 bushells; Fish, 3 hundred. ARMES AND MUNITION:
Powder, 3 lb; Lead, 50 lb; Peeces fixt, 6; Coats of Male, 4 and 4 headpeeces.
SWINE AND POULTRIE: Swine, 6; Poultrie, 24. HOUSES: House, 1.

THE MUSTER OF *JOHN THROGMORTON* etc

JOHN THROGMORTON aged 24 yeares in ye *William & Thomas* 1618
CHYNA BOYSE aged 26 yeres in *Georg* in May 1617

SERVANTS

EDWARD SPARSHOTT aged 31 yeares in the *Seafloure* 1621
FRANCIS DOWNING aged 24 yeres in the *Returne* March 1624
ELLIS RIPPING aged 23 yeares in the *Returne* 1624

PROVISIONS: Corne, 20 bushells; Fish, 2 hundred. ARMES AND MUNITION:
Powder, 3 lb; Shott, 7 lb; Peeces fixt, 6; Armour, 1; Coats of Male, 2; Steele
Coat, 1. POULTRIE: Poultrie, 20. HOUSES: House, 1.

THE MUSTER OF *ROGER RATLIFE*

*Sherley
hundred.
Charles
Cittie*

ROGER RATLIFE aged 44 yeares in the *Georg* in May 1619
ANN his wife aged 40 in the *George* in May 1619
ISACK his sonn aged 9 Months

PROVISIONS: Corne, 11 bushells; Fish, ½ hundred. ARMES & MUNITION: Powder,
1 lb; Shott, 2 lb; Peece fixt, 1; Armour, 1. POULTRIE: Poultrie, 13. HOUSES:
House, 1.

* This variation of first name in the heading and first name on the list is in the
original.

THE MUSTER OF *NATHANIELL TATAM*

NATHANIELL TATAM aged 20 yeares in the *George* May 1619

ARMES AND MUNITION: Peece fixt, 1; Armour, 1.

THE MUSTER OF M*RS* *KATHERINE BENETT* Widdow

KATHERINE BENETT aged 24 yeres in the *Abigall* 1622
WILLIAM BENETT her sonn aged 3 weeks

S E R V A N T S

RANDALL CREW aged 20 yeres in the *Charles* 1621

PROVISIONS: Corne, 50 bushells. ARMES AND MUNITION: Peeces serviceable, 2.
SWINE AND POULTRIE: Swine, 1; Poultrie, 23.

[11]   DEAD at West & Sherley and at
              Sherley Hundred 1624

ANDREW DUDLEY, came in the *Truelove* 1622
RALPH FREEMAN, in the *Margrett and John* 1622
Mr WILLIAM BENET Minister in the *Seafloure* 1621
Capt ISACK MADDESON
JAMES CROWDER in the *Returne* 1623
DANIELL VIERO in the *George* 1623
BARNARD JACKSON in the *Margrett & John* 1623
THOMAS WESTON in the *George* 1623
JAMES ROLFE Liuetennt GIBBS Man ⎫
JOHN MICHAELL   ⎬ slaine by the Indians
FRANCIS   Capt MADISONS Man ⎭

THE MUSTER OF THE INHABITANTS

Jordans   OF JORDANS JORNEY AND CHAPLAIN CHOICE
Jorney.   TAKEN THE 21TH OF JANUARY 1624
Charles
Cittie THE MUSTER OF MR *WILLIAM FERRAR* & M^{RS} *JORDAN*

WILLIAM FERRAR aged 31 yeares in the *Neptune* in August 1618
SISLEY JORDAN aged 24 yeres in the *Swan* in August 1610
MARY JORDAN her daughter aged 3 yeares ⎫
MARGRETT JORDAN aged 1 yeare   ⎬ borne heare
TEMPERANCE BALEY aged 7 yeares   ⎭

S E R V A N T S

WILLIAM DAWSON aged 25 yeres in the *Discovery* March 1621
ROBERT TURNER aged 26 yeres in the *Tryall* June 1619

John Hely aged 24 yeares in the *Charles* November 1621
Roger Preston aged 21 yeares in the *Discoverie* March 1621
Robert Manuell aged 25 yeres in the *Charles* November 1621
Thomas Williams aged 24 yeares in the *Dutie* May 1618
Richard Johnson aged 22 yeares in the *Southampton* 1622
William Hatfeild aged in the *Southampton* 1622
John Pead 35 yeares old in the same Shipp
John Freame aged 16 yeares in the same Shipp

provisions: Corne, 200 bushells; Fish, 2 hundred. armes and munition: Powder, 14 lb; Lead, 300 lb; Peeces fixt, 11; Coats of Male, 12. cattle, swine, etc.: Neat cattell young and old, 16; Swine, 4; Poultrie, 20. houses and boats: Houses, 5; Boats, 2.

THE MUSTER OF *THOMAS PALMER*

[12]

Jordans
Jorney.
Charles
Cittie

Thomas Palmer arived in the *Tyger* November 1621
Joane his wife in the same Shipp
Priscilla her daughter aged xi yeares

SERVANTS

Richard English aged xi yeares in the *James* 1622

provisions: Corne, 50 bushells; Fish, 1 hundred. armes & munition: Powder, 1 lb; Shott, 100 lb; Snaphannce Peeces, 3; Armours, 2; Coat of Male, 1. cattle & poultrie: Swine young and old, 6; Poultrie, 19. houses: Houses, 2.

THE MUSTER OF *ROBERT FISHER*

Robert Fisher arived in the *Elsabeth* May 1611
Katherine his wife in the *Marmaduk* October 1621
Sisly theire daughter aged 1 yeare

SERVANTS

Idye Halliers a Maid servant aged 30 yeares in ye *Jonathan* 1619

provisions: Corne, 40 bushells; Fish, ½ hundred. armes and munition: Powder, 3 lb; Lead, 20; Peeces fixt, 3; Coat of Male, 1. swine etc.: Swine, 1; Poultrie, 16. houses: Houses, 2.

THE MUSTER OF *JOHN CLAYE*

John Claye arived in the *Treasuror* February 1613
Ann his wife in the *Ann* August 1623

SERVANTS

William Nicholls aged 26 yeres in the *Dutie* in May 1619

provisions: Corne, 30 bushells; Fish, 1 hundred. armes & munition: Powder,

2 lb; Shott, 20; Peeces, 3; Armour, 1; Steele Coat, 1. CATTELL, SWINE, ETC.:
Neat Cattell, 2; Swine, 1; Poultrie, 10. HOUSES: House, 1.

THE MUSTER OF *CHRISTOPHER SAFFORD*

CHRISTOPHER SAFFORD arived in the *Treasuror* 1613
JOHN GIBBS his ptner in the *Supply* 1619

SERVANTS

HENERY LANE aged 20 yeres in the *Southampton* 1623

PROVISIONS: Corne, 30 bushells; Fish, 2 hundred. ARMES & MUNITION: Powder,
2 lb; Lead, 40 lb; Peeces, 3; Armours, 3; Coats of Male, 3 and 2 headpeeces.
POULTRIE: Poultrie, 20. HOUSES: House, 1.

[13]

*Jordans
Jorney.
Charles
Cittie*

THE MUSTER OF *HENERY WILLIAMS*

HENERY WILLIAMS arived in the *Treasuror* 1613
SUSAN his wife in the *William & Thomas* 1618

PROVISIONS: Corne, 20 bushells. ARMES AND MUNITION: Powder, 2 lb; Lead,
20 lb; Peeces fixt, 2; Coat of Male, 1 and a headpeece. POULTRIE: Poultrie, 10.
HOUSES: House, 1.

THE MUSTER OF *WILLIAM BRANLIN*

WILLIAM BRANLIN arived in the *Margrett & John* 1620
ANN his wife in the *Truelove* 1622

PROVISIONS: Corne, 24 bushells; Fish, 1 hundred. ARMES & MUNITION: Powder,
1 lb; Lead, 6 lb; Peeces, 2; Armour, 1; Coat of Male, 1. POULTRIE: Poultrie, 2.
HOUSES: House, 1.

THE MUSTER OF *JOHN FLUDD*

JOHN FLUDD arived in the *Swan* 1610
MARGRETT his wife in the *Supply* 1620
FRANCES FINCH her daughter in the *Suply* 1620
WILLIAM FLUDD his sonn aged 3 weeks

PROVISIONS: Corne, 30 bushells; Pease and Beanes, 2 bushells. ARMES AND MU-
NITION: Powder, ½ lb; Shott, 10 lb; Peeces fixt, 2 and a Petronell*; Armour, 1;
Coat of Male, 1. SWINE ETC.: Swine, 1; Poultrie, 20. HOUSES: House, 1.

THE MUSTER OF *THOMAS CHAPMAN†*

THOMAS CHAPMAN arived in the *Tryall* 1610
ANN his wife in the *George* 1617

* *petronel.* A portable firearm of the 15th century resembling a carbine of large
caliber.
† In the original CHAPLMAN. The "L" is obviously an error of the recorder.

THOMAS his sonn aged 2 yeare
ANN theire daughter aged 6 weeks

PROVISIONS: Corne, 5 bushells; Fish, ½ hundred. ARMES AND MUNITION: Powder, 1 lb; Lead, 10 lb; Peeces, 1; Armour, 1. CATTELL & POULTRIE: Neat Cattell, 1; Pou̇ltrie, 14. HOUSES: House, 1

THE MUSTER OF *JOSEPH BULL*

JOSEPH BULL arived in the *Abigaile* 1622

PROVISIONS: Corne, 10 bushells. ARMES & MUNITION: Powder, 0; Lead, 12 lb; Peece fixt, 1; Coat of Male, 1 and a headpeece. POULTRIE: Poultrie, 3. HOUSES: House, 1.

THE MUSTER OF *JOHN DAVIS* etc.

JOHN DAVIS arived in the *George* 1617
WILLIAM EMERSON his ptner in the *Sampson* 1618

SERVANTS

WILLIAM POPLETON aged   in the *James* 1622
EUSTICE DOWNES aged 25 yeares in the *Abigall* 1622

PROVISIONS: Corne, 50 bushells; Fish, 4 hundred. ARMES & MUNITION: Powder, 2 lb; Lead, 10; Peeces, 3; Coats of Male, 3 and 2 headpeeces. POULTRIE: Poultrie, 20. HOUSES: House, 1.

THE MUSTER OF *THOMAS CAWSEY*

THOMAS CAWSEY arived in the *Francis Bonaventure* 1620

PROVISIONS: Corne, 12 bushells. ARMES AND MUNITION: Powder, 2 lb; Lead, 6 lb; Peece fixt, 1. POULTRIE: Poultrie, 3. HOUSES: House, 1.

[14]

Jordans Jorney. Charles Cittie

THE MUSTER OF *THOMAS IRON MONGER*

THOMAS IRON MONGER arived in the

PROVISIONS: Corne, 6 bushells. ARMES AND MUNITION: Powder, 1 lb; Peece fixt, 1; Coat of Male, 1.

THE MUSTER OF *RICHARD MILTON*

RICHARD MILTON arived in the *Suply* 1620

PROVISIONS: Corne, 4 bushells. ARMES AND MUNITION: Powder, 2 lb; Lead, 50 lb; Peece fixt, 1; Armour, 1. SWINE & POULTRIE: Swine, 3; Poultrie, 20. HOUSES: Houses, 2.

Jordans
Jorney.
Charles
Cittie

THE MUSTER OF *NATHANIELL CAWSEY*

NATHANIELL CAWSEY arived in the *Phoenix* 1607
THOMASINE his wife in the *Lyon* 1609

SERVANTS

EDWARD DENISON aged 22 yeares ⎫
JAMES BONNER aged 20 yeares   ⎬ arived in the *Truelove* 1623
JAMES DORE aged 19 yeares in the *Bona Nova* 1621
LAURANCE EVANS aged 15 yeares in the *James* 1622
JOANE WINSCOMB aged 20 yeares in the *George* 1618

PROVISIONS: Corne, 50 bushells; Beanes, 1 bushell; Fish, ½ hundred. ARMES & MUNITION: Powder, 4 lb; Lead, 100 lb; Peeces, 3; Armour, 1; Coat of Male, 1. CATTELL, SWINE, ETC.: Neat Cattell, 1; Swine, 8; Poultrie, 50. HOUSES AND BOATS: Houses, 2; Boat, 1.

DEAD at Jordans Jorney 1624

[15]

LIDIA SHERLEY came in the *George* 1623
SUSAN SHERLEY ann Infant.

Chaplains
Choise.
Charles
Cittie

THE MUSTER OF THE INHABITANTS OF CHAPLAINS CHOYSE AND THE TRUELOVES COMPANY TAKEN THE 21TH JANUARY 1624

THE MUSTER OF ENSIGNE *ISACK CHAPLAINE*

ISACK CHAPLAINE arived in the *Starr* 1610
MARY his wife in the *James* 1622
JOHN CHAPLAINE his kinsman aged 15 yeares in the *James* 1622

SERVANTS

ROBERT HUDSON aged 30 yeares ⎫
HENERY THORNE aged 18 yeares ⎪
JOHN DUFFILL aged 14 yeares   ⎬ arived in the *James* 1622
IVIE BANTON a Maid servant   ⎭
ANN MIGHILL a Maid servant arived in the *George* 1619

PROVISIONS: Corne, 100 bushells; Oate-Meale, 2 bushells. ARMES AND MUNITION: Powder, 20 lb; Lead and Shott, 340 wtt; Murderers,* 2; Fauconett†, 1; Peeces

---

* *Murderer, mordrer.* A small piece of ordnance either of brass or of iron. Weapons of this type had chambers in the breeches and were used in ships at the bulkheads of the forecastles in order to clear the decks of boarders. Called also *murdering-piece.*

† fauconett-falconet. A small piece of ordnance, having an outside diameter at the bore of four and a quarter inches, length six feet, weighing four hundred pounds and carrying a shot of about two inches diameter and one and a quarter to two pounds in weight; in use from the 16th to the 18th century.

fixt, 7 and a Pistoll; Coat of Male, 1; Jacketts‡, 2; Armoᵣˢ, 4. SWINE AND POULTRIE: Swine, 3; Poultrie, 20. HOUSES & BOATS: Houses, 2; Boat, 1.

THE MUSTER OF *WALTER PRICE* etc.

WALTER PRICE arived in the *Willm & Thomas* 1618
HENERY TURNER arived in the *John & Francis* 1615

SERVANTS

EDWARD FALLOWES aged 30 yeares in the *Hopewell* 1623

PROVISIONS: Corne, 40 bushells. ARMES & MUNITION: Peeces, 3; Coats of Male, 3. POULTRIE: Poultrie, 9.

THE MUSTER OF THE *THOMAS KEIE* KOMPANY [16]

THOMAS KEIE aged 30 arived in the *Prosperous* June 1619
SARAH his wife in the *Truelove* 1622

Chaplins
Choise.

PROVISIONS: Corne, 23 bushells. ARMES AND MUNITION: Peece fixt, 1 and a Pistoll; Armour, 1. POULTRIE: Poultrie, 6. BOATS: Boat, 1.

Charles
Cittie

THE MUSTER OF *JOHN BROWNE*

JOHN BROWNE aged 28 yeares in the *Bona Nova* Aprill 1621

ARMES AND MUNITION: Peece fixt, 1; Coate of Male, 1. POULTRIE: Poultrie, 6.

THE MUSTER OF *JOHN TREHEARNE*

JOHN TREHEARNE aged 33 yeares in the *Truelove* 1622

ARMES AND MUNITION: Peece fixt, 1; Armour, 1. POULTRIE: Poultrie, 2.

THE MUSTER OF *DAVID JONES*

DAVID JONES aged 22 yeares in the *Truelove* 1622

ARMES AND MUNITION: Peece fixt, 1; Armour, 1. POULTRIE: Poultrie, 3.

THE MUSTER OF *JOHN BOX*

JOHN BOX aged 23 yeares in the *Truelove* 1622

POULTRIE: Poultrie, 2.

PROVISIONS belonging to the *Trueloves* Company: Corne, 90 bushells; Meale, 5 bushells; Pease, 10 bushells; Oatmeale, 1 bushell; Murderers for the forte, 3.

DEAD at Chaplins Choise 1624

HENERY WILSON came in the *Truelove* 1622 slaine by the Indians
NICHOLAS SUTTON in the *James* 1622 slaine by the Indians

‡ Defensive body-armor worn from the 14th to the 17th century inclusive. It consisted of a leathern surcoat worn over the coat of mail and sometimes quilted.

NICHOLAS BALDWIN in the *Truelove* 1622 slaine by the Indians
WILLIAM BARNETT in the *Truelove* 1623.

[17]

*Pierseys
hundred*

THE MUSTER OF THE INHABITANTS OF PEIRSEYS HUNDRED TAKEN THE 20TH OF JANUARY 1624

SAMUELL SHARPE arived in the *Seaventure* 1609
ELIZABETH his wife in the *Margrett and John* 1621

SERVANTS

HENERY CARMAN aged 23 yeares in the *Duty* 1620

Peeces fixt, 2; Armours, 2; Swords, 2; Neat Cattell, 7; Swine, 6; Houses, 2.

THE MUSTER OF MR *GRIVELL POOLEY* MINISTER

GRIVELL POOLEY arived in the *James* 1622

SERVANTS

JOHN CHAMBERS aged 21 yeares in the *Bona Nova* 1622
CHARLES MAGNER aged 16 yeres in the *George* 1623

Corne, 8 barrells; Powder, 4 lb; Lead, 12 lb; Peeces fixt, 3; Armour, 1; Swords, 3; Neat Cattell, 1; Swine, 1.

THE MUSTER OF *HUMFREY KENT*

HUMFREY KENT arived in the *George* 1619
JOANE his wife in the *Tyger* 1621
MARGRETT ARRUNDELL aged 9 yeares in the *Abigaile* 1621

SERVANTS

CHRISTOPHER BEANE aged 40 yeares in the *Neptune* 1618

Corne, 6 barrells; Powder, 2 lb; Lead, 6 lb; Peeces fixt, 2; Swords, 2; Neat Cattell young & old, 3; Swine, 3.

THE MUSTER OF *THOMAS DOUGHTIE*

THOMAS DOUGHTIE arived in the *Marigold* 1619
ANN his wife in the *Marmaduke* 1621

Corne, 3 barrells; Fish, ½ hundred; Powder, 4 lb; Lead, 20 lb; Peece fixt, 1; Coat of Male, 1; Sword, 1; Swine, 1.

THE MUSTER OF *EDWARD AUBORN*

EDWARD AUBORN arived in the *Jonathan* 1620

Corne, 3 barrells; Pease, 1 bushell; Peece fixt, 1; Sword, 1.

THE MUSTER OF *WILLIAM BAKER*

WILLIAM BAKER arived in the *Jonathan* 1609

Corne, 3 barrells; Fish, 50; Powder, 1 lb; Lead, 12 lb; Peece fixt, 1; Coat of Male, 1; Sword, 1.

THE MUSTER OF *JOHN WOODSON*

JOHN WOODSON ⎫
SARAH his wife ⎭ in the *George* 1619

Corne, 4 bushells; Powder, 1 lb; Lead, 3 lb; Peece fixt, 1; Sword, 1.

THE MUSTER OF *EDWARD THRENORDEN*

EDWARD THRENORDEN arived in the *Diana* 1619
ELIZABETH his wife in the *George* 1619

Corne, 3 barrells; Fish, 1 hundred; Peece fixt, 1; Coat of Male, 1; Sword, 1; Swine, 1.

THE MUSTER OF *NICHOLAS BALY*

[18]

*Pierseys
hundred*

NICHOLAS.BALY arived in the *Jonathan* 1620
ANN his wife in the *Marmaduk* 1621

Corne, 4 barrells; Fish, 1 hundreth; Powder, 1 lb; Lead, 12 lb; Peece fixt, 1; Armour, 1; Sword, 1.

THE MUSTER OF *JOHN LIPPS*

JOHN LIPPS arived in the *London Marchannt* 1621

Corne, 10 bushells; Peece, 1; Armour, 1; Sword, 1.

THE MUSTER OF MR *ABRAHAM PEIRSEYS* SERVANTS

THOMAS LEA aged 50 yeres
ANTHONY PAGITT 35 ⎫
SALOMAN JACKMAN 30 ⎪
JOHN DAVIES aged 45 ⎪
CLEMENT ROPER 25 ⎪
JOHN BATES aged 24 ⎪
THOMAS ABBE 20 ⎬ arived in the *Southampton* 1623
THOMAS BROOKS 23 ⎪
WILLIAM JONES 23 ⎪
PEETER JONES 24 ⎪
PIERCE WILLIAMS 23 ⎪
ROBERT GRAVES 30 ⎭

EDWARD HUBBERSTEAD 26
JOHN LATHROP 25
THOMAS CHAMBERS 24
WALTER JACKSON 24   } arived in the *Southampton* 1623
HENERY SANDERS 20
WILLIAM ALLEN 22
GEORG DAWSON 24

JOHN UPTON aged 26 in the *Bona nova* 1622
JOHN BAMFORD aged 23 yeares in the *James* 1622
WILLIAM GARRETT aged 22 in the *George* 1619
THOMAS SAWELL aged 26 in the *George* 1619
HENERY ROWINGE aged 25 yeares in the *Temperance* 1621
NATHANIELL THOMAS aged 23 yeres in the *Temperance* 1621
RICHARD BROADSHAW aged 20 yeares in the same Shipp
ROBERT OKLEY aged 19 yeares in the *William & Thomas* 1618

Negro
Negro
Negro   } 4 Men
Negro

ALLICE THOROWDEN
KATHERINE LOMAN   } maid servants arived in the *Southampton* 1623
NEGRO WOMAN.
NEGRO WOMAN and a young Child of hers.

PROVISIONS, ARMES ETC. of Mr PIERSEY at Peirseys hundred: Corne and Pease, 300 bushells; Fish, 1300; Powder, 1½ barrell; Lead, 200 lb; Peeces of Ordnannce, 6; Peeces fixt, *; Murderes, 2; Armours, 15; Swords, 20; Dwelling houses, 10; Store houses, 3; Tobacco houses, 4; Wind Mill, 1; Boats, 2; Neat Cattell young & old, 25; Swine young & old, 19.

Mr SAMUELL ARGALLS CATTELL: Neat Cattell young and old, 8.

[19]   DEAD at Peirseys hundred Anno Dni 1624

JOHN LINICKER
EDWARD CARLOWE
ROBERT HUSSYE
JACOB LARBEE
JOHN ENGLISH
CHRISTOPHER LEES Wife
ELIZABETH JONES

* Ink blot on original ms. obliterates numeral.

THE MUSTER OF THE INHABITANTS
OF PASBEHAYS' & THE MAINE

TAKEN THE 30TH OF JANUARY 1624 BELONGING
TO THE CORPORATION OF JAMES CITTY

ADAM DIXON arived in the *Margarett & John*
Corne, 10 bushells; Powder, 2 lb; Peece fixt, 1; Sword, 1.

JOSEPH RYALE arived in the *William & Thomas*
Corne, 10 bushells; Peece fixt, 1; Sword, 1.

GEORGE FRIER arived in the *William & Thomas*
URSULA his wife in the *London Marchant*
Corne, 20 bushells; Powder, 2 lb; Armour, 1.

ALLEN KENISTON arived in the *Margarett & John*
Corne, 10 bushells; Armour, 1.

ROBERT PARAMOUR arived in the *Swan*
Corne, 6 bushells; Peece fixt, 1.

WILLIAM KEMP arived in the *George*
MARGRETT his wife in the *George*
ANTHONY his Sonn aged 7 weeks
Corne, 6 bushells; Powder, 1 lb; Peece fixt, 1; Armour, 1.

RICHARD BRIDGWATTER arived in the *London Marchannt*
ISBELL his wife in the same Shipp
Corne, 15 bushells; Peece, 1; Armour, 1.

HUGH HAWARD arived in the *Starr*
SUSAN his wife in the *George*

HENERY TURNER arived in the *London Marchannt*
Corne, 10 bushells; Peece, 1; Armour, 1; Sword, 1.

JOSEPH CREW arived in the *London Marchannt*
Corne, 12½ bushells; Peece, 1; Armour, 1.

THOMAS JONES arived in the *London Marchannt*
MARGRETT his wife in the same Shipp
Corne, 20 bushells; Peece, 1; Armour, 1.

EDWARD BOURBICTH in the *London Marchannt*
Corne, 10 bushells; Coate of Male, 1; Peece, 1.

REVOLL MORCOCK arived in the *Jonathan*
ELIZABETH his wife

THOMAS his Sonne aged 1 yeare.

Corne, 6 bushells; Armour, 1; Peece, 1.

EDWARD FISHER arived in the *Jonathan*
SARAH his wife in the *Warwick*
EDWARD KILDALE her sonn aged 6 yeares
CLARE REN a girle aged 10 yeares.

Corne, 10 bushells; Peece, 1; Armour, 1.

JOHN MOONE arived in the *Returne* 1623

SERVANTS

JULIAN HALLERS aged 19 yeares ⎫
GILES MARTIN aged 23 yeares ⎬ in the *Truelove* 1623
CLINION RUSH aged 13 yeares ⎭

Corne, 40 busheils; Meale, ½ hogshead; Powder, 4 lb; Peeces, 4; Coat of Male, 1; Swords, 3.

RICHARD SMITH arived in the *London Marchannt*

Corne, 7 bushells; Peece, 1; Armour, 1.

Pasbehaighs   THE MUSTER OF THE GOVERNORS MEN
James Citty   AT PASBEHAIGHS

THOMAS JORDEN aged 24 came in the *Diana*.
JOHN MILNHOUSE aged 36 in the *London Marchannt*
RICHARD SANDERS aged 25 in the *Francis Bonaventure*.
GRIFFIN WINNE aged 28 in the *Francis Bonaventure*.
ARTHURE CHANDLER aged 19 in the *Jonathan*.
WILLIAM DORRELL aged 18 in the *Truelove*.
CHRISTOPHER RIPPING 22 in the *Francis Bonaventure*.
THOMAS OSBORN aged 18 in the *Francis Bonaventure*.
GEORGE NELSON aged 19 in the *Francis Bonaventure*.
FRANCIS BUTLER aged 18 in the *Francis Bonaventure*.
THOMAS BLANCKS aged 17 in the *Francis Bonaventure*.
HENERY DOWTIE aged 19 in the *Jonathan*.

Corne, 14 barrells; Fish, 2000; Snaphannce Peeces, 8; Matchcockes,* 2; Armour, 4; Jack-Coat,† 1; Coats of Male, 2; Steele Coat, 1; Corslett, 1 and 2 head peeces; Powder, 10 lb; Shott, 60 lb.

JOHN SWARBECK came in the

Corne, 2 barrells; Peece, 1; Armour, 1; Sword, 1; House, 1.

* Matchcocke. The old form of gun-lock which preceded the wheel-lock and the flint-lock. It had a match which was presented to the priming, whence its name.
† Jack. A coarse medieval coat of defense, especially one of leather.

THOMAS MARLOE came in the *Bona Nova.*

Corne, 15 bushells; Armour, 1; Peece, 1.

THOMAS BUNN
BRIDGITT his wife
THOMAS his sonn aged 1 yeare

SERVANTS

JOHN SMITH aged 30 yeares ⎫
THOMAS SMITH aged 16 yeres ⎭ in the *Abigaile*
THOMAS JONES aged 35 in the *Bona Nova*
JAMES ROBESONN aged 35 in the *Swann.*
ELIZABETH HODGES a Maid servant in the *Abigaile*

Corne, 60 bushells; Pease and Beanes, 6 bushells; Powder, 2 lb; Peeces, 6; Corslett, 1; Swine, 6; House, 1.

THOMAS SWINHOW came in the *Diana.*

SERVANTS

LAWRANCE SMALEPAGE aged 20 yeres in the *Abigaile*

Corne, 20 bushells; Powder, 3 lb; Peeces, 2; House, 1.

JOHN CARTER came in the *Prosperous.*

Corne, 10 bushells; Peece, 1; Armour, 1.

DAVID ELLIS in the *Mary Margrett*
MARGRETT his wife in the *Margrett & John*

Corne, 15 bushells; Powder, 3 lb; Peece, 1; Armour, 1; House, 1.

JAMES TOOKE arived in the

Corne, 6 bushells; Peece, 1; Armour, 1.

WILLIAM BINKS came in the *George*
ANN his wife in the *George*

Corne, 30 bushells; Peece, 1; Armour, 1; Swine, 1; piggs, 11.

MICHAELL BATT came in the *Hercules.*
ELLIN his wife in the *Warwick.*

Corne, 7 bushells; Meale, 1 barrell; Powder, 4 lb; Peece, 1; Armour, 1.

ROBERT LINCE came in the *Treasuror.*

Powder, 2 lb; Peece, 1; Armour, 1.

HUGH BALDWINE came in the *Tryall*
SUSAN his wife in the

Corne, 6 bushells; Peece, 1.

ROBERT SCOTCHMORE came in the *George* 1623
THOMAS KNISTON came in the *George* 1623

SERVANTS

ROGER KIDD aged 24 yeares in the *George* 1623

   Corne, 15 bushells; Pease, 1 hogshead; Peeces, 3; Powder, 10 lb; Armours, 3.

ROBERT CHOLMLE ⎫
JAMES STANDISH ⎬ came in the *Charitie*

   Corne, 3 bushells; Powder, 5 lb.

[22]   THE MUSTER OF DOCTO^R *POTTS* MEN IN THE MAINE

the Maine.   THOMAS LEISTER aged 33 yeares
James Citty   ROGER STANLEY aged 27
   THOMAS PRITCHARD aged 28
   HENERY CROCKER aged 34
   THOMAS CROSSE aged 22   came in the *Abigaile* 1620
   JOHN TRYE aged 20
   WALTER BEARE aged 28
   RANDALL HOLT aged 18 yeares in the *George* 1620

THE REST OF HIS SERVANTS, PROVISIONS, AMUNITION &CT.
AT JAMES CITTY.

DEAD at Pasbehaighs & in the Maine 1624.

JOACHIM ANNDREWS.
HENERY SCOTT.
RICHARD ⎫
RICHARD ⎬ 2 Men of m^r BUNNS.

James Citty   THE MUSTER OF THE INHABITANTS
OF JAMES CITTIE TAKEN THE 24TH
OF JANUARY 1624

THE MUSTER OF S^R *FRANCIS WYATT* K^T &CT.

Sr FRANCIS WYATT K^t Governo^r etc. came in the *George* 1621

SERVANTS

CHRISTOPHER COOKE aged 25 in the *George* 1621
GEORG HALL aged 13 in the *Suply* 1620
JONATHAN GILES 21 in the *Triall* 1619
JOHN MATHEMAN 19 in the *Jonathan* 1619
JANE DAVIS 24 in the *Abigaile* 1622

Corne, 10 barrells; Fish, 4000; Powder, 20 lb; Lead and Shott, 180 lb; Snap-hannce Peeces, 6; Armours, 6; Swords, 6; Cowes, 6; Bull, 1; Yearelings and Calves, 3; Horse, 1; breeding Sowes, 6; young Swine, 14; Dwelling house, 1; Store, 1.

BELONGING TO JAMES CITTY: Church, 1; A Large Court of Guard, 1; Peeces of Ordnannce Mounted, 4; Quilted Coats, 16; Coates of Male, 77; The rest dispersed in the Cunttrie.

THE MUSTER OF S^R *GEORGE YEARLEY* K^T &CT. *James Citty.*

Sr GEORGE YEARLLEY K^t etc. came in the *Deliverance* 1609
TEMPERANCE LADY YEARLLEY came in the *Faulcon* 1608
m^r ARGALL YEARLLEY aged 4 yeares ⎤
m^r FRANCIS YEARLLEY aged 1 yeare ⎬ Children borne heare
m^s ELIZABETH YEARLLEY aged 6 yeres ⎦

SERVANTS AT JAMES CITTY   [23]

RICHARD GREGORY aged 40 ⎤
ANTHONY JONES 26 ⎥
THOMAS DUNN 14 ⎬ came in the *Temperance* 1620
THOMAS PHILDUST 15 ⎦
THOMAS HATCH 17 in the *Duty* 1619
ROBERT PEAKE 22 in the *Margrett & John* 1623
WILLIAM STRANGE 18 in the *George* 1619
ROGER THOMPSON 40 in the *London Marchannt* 1620
ANN his wife
RICHARD ARRUNDELL in the *Abigall* 1620
GEORGE DEVERILL 18 in the *Temperannce* 1620
THOMAS BARNETT 16 in the *Elsabeth* 1620
THEOPHILUS BERISTON 23 in the *Treasuror* 1614
Negro Men. 3
Negro Woemen. 5.
SUSAN HALL in the *William & Thomas* 1618
ANN WILLIS in the *Temperance* 1620
ELIZABETH ARRUNDELL in the *Abigall* 1620.

Corne, 20 barrells; Pease and beanes, 12 bushells; Neat Cattell, 50; Swine, 40; Goats, 8 and 3 kidds; Powder, 20 lb; Lead, 100 lb; Peeces, 30; Armours, 10; Swords, 40; Houses at James Cittie, 3.
A Barque* of 40 Tunn 7 men belonging to her; A Shallop† of 4 Tunn; A Skiffe; The rest of his servants at Hog Island.

* bark, barque. A three-masted vessel, with foremast and mainmast square-rigged, and mizzen-mast fore-and-aft-rigged.
† shallop. A light open boat, used chiefly on rivers, propelled by oars or sails or by both.

*James
Citty*

THE MUSTER OF DOCTO^R *JOHN POTT*

Docto^r John Pott ⎱
m^rs Elizabeth Pott ⎰ arived in the *George* 1620

SERVANTS

Richard Townshend aged 19 yeares in the *Abigaile* 1620
Thomas Wilson aged 27 yeares in the *Abigaile* 1620
Osmond Smith aged 17 yeares in the *Bona Nova* 1620
Susan Blackwood a Maid servant in the *Abigaile* 1622.

Corne, 20 barrells; Meale, ½ hogshead; Fish, 700; Powder, 10 lb; Peeces, 10; Coats of Male, 2; Armours, 3; Swords, 6; Neat Cattell, 1; Goats, 4 and 2 kids; Swine, 2 and 8 piggs; Houses, 2.

THE MUSTER OF CAP^T *ROGER SMITH*

Capt Roger Smith came in the *Abigaile* 1620
m^rs Joane Smith came in the *Blessinge*
Elizabeth Salter aged 7 yeares came in the *Seafloure*
Elizabeth Rolfe aged 4 yeares ⎱
Sarah Macock aged 2 yeares ⎰ borne in Virginia.

SERVANTS

Charles Waller aged 22 came in the *Abigaile* 1620
Christopher Baukus aged 19 yeares in the *Abigaile* 1622
Henery Booth aged 20 in the *Dutie*
Henery Lacton aged 18 yeares in the *Hopewell* 1623

Corne, 20 bushells; Meale, 1 hogshead; Fish, 500; Neat Cattell young and old, 24; Goats, 27; Swine, 2 and 9 piggs.
The rest of his men theire provisions Armes & ct. Over the Watter.

[24]

*James
Citty*

THE MUSTER OF CAP^T *RAPH HAMOR*

Capt Raph Hamor
m^rs Elizabeth Hamor
Jeremy Clement ⎱
Elizabeth Clement ⎰ her children.

SERVANTS

John Lightfoote in the *Seaventure*
Francis Gibbs a boy in the *Seaflower*.
Ann Addams a Maid servant.

Neat Cattell, 8; Swine, 10.
The rest of his servants, Provisions Armes etc. at Hog-Iland.

THE MUSTER OF CAP^T *WILLIAM PIERCE*

Capt WILLIAM PIERCE came in the *Sea-venture.*
m^{rs} JONE PIERCE his wife in the *Blessinge*

SERVANTS

THOMAS SMITH aged 17 yeares in the *Abigaile*
HENERY BRADFORD aged 35 yeres in the *Abigaile*
ESTER EDERIFE a maid servant in the *Jonathan*
ANGELO a Negro Woman in the *Treasuror.*

Neat Cattell, 20; Goats, 20; Swine, 9 and 7 piggs; House, 1.
The rest of his servants; provisions, Armes. Munnition & ct at Mulbery Iland.

THE MUSTER OF MR *ABRAHAM PEIRSEY* Marchannt — James Citty

m^r ABRAHAM PEIRSEY came in the *Susan* 1616
ELIZABETH his daughter aged 15 yeres }
MARY his daughter aged 11 yeres } came in the *Southampton* 1623

SERVANTS

CHRISTOPHER LEE aged 30 yeres }
RICHARD SERIEANT aged 36 yeres }
ALICE CHAMBERS } maid servants. } came in the *Southampton* 1623.
ANNIS SHAW }

Corne, 50 bushells; Fish, 180; Powder, 6; Lead, 200; Peeces fixt, 3; Swords, 2;
Neat Cattell, 2; Goats, 3; Dwelling house, 1; Store houses, 2.
The rest at Peirseys Hundred.

THE MUSTER OF MR *EDWARD BLANEY*

m^r EDWARD BLANEY came in the *Francis Bonaventure*

SERVANTS

ROBERT BEW aged 20 came in the *Dutie.*
JOHN RUSSELL aged 19 in the *Bona Nova.*

Corne, 30 barrells; Meale, ½ hogshead; Oatmeale and Pease, 9 bushells; Fish,
2000; Neat Cattell young and old, 20; Goats, 10 and 5 kidds; Swine, 21 and 8
piggs; Houses, 2; Boats, 2.
The rest of his servants Armes &ct at his plantacon Over ye Watter.

ROBERT POOLE came in the
Corne, 1 bushells; Peeces, 2.

JAMES HICMOTT came in the *Bonaventure*
        his wife in the
Corne, 3 bushells; Peeces, 1 and a Pistoll; Swine, 2 and 7 piggs.

JOHN SOUTHERN came in the *George* 1620

[25]

James
Cittie

THOMAS CRUST aged   came in the *George* 1620

Corne, 2 barrells; Meale, 3 bushells; Fish, 2 hundred; Powder, ½ lb; Peece, 1; Armour, 1; Swine, 4.

RANDALL SMALEWOOD came in the

Corne, 2 barrells; Peeces, 2.

GEORGE GRAVE came in the *Seaventure*
ELNOR his wife in the *Susan*
JOHN GRAVE theire sonne aged 10 yeares
REBECCA SNOW ⎫
SARA SNOW ⎬ her daughters.

Corne, 2 bushells; Fish, 1 hundred; Peece, 1 and a pistoll; Swine, 2; House, 1.

EDWARD CADGE came in the *Marmaduke*
NATHANIELL JEFFREYS came in the *Gift*.

Corne, 2 bushells; Pease, ½ bushell; Fish, 2 hundred; Swine, 1 and 7 piggs; Goats, 2; Peeces, 2 and a pistoll; Swords, 3; House, 1.

James   JOHN JACKSON came in the
Citty   JOHN JACKSON his sonn aged 9 yeares
GERCIAN BUCK aged 10 yeares

Corne, 2 bushells; Peece fixt, 1; Powder, ½ lb; Neat Cattell, 3; Swine, 2 and 2 piggs; Kidds, 3.

THOMAS ALNUTT came in the *Gifte*
         his wife in the *Marygold*

ROGER ROEDS aged 20 yeares in the *Bony bess*.

Corne, 7 barrells; Powder, 2 lb; Lead, 100 lb; Peeces, 5 and a pistoll; Neat Cattell, 3; Kidd, 1; Swine, 7; House, 1; Boat, 1.

PEETER LANGMAN came in the *William & Thomas*.
MARY his wife came in the
PEETER ASCAM her sonn aged 1 yeares
ABIGAILE ASCAM her daughter aged 4 yeres
BENOMY BUCK aged 8 yeres
PELEG BUCK aged 4 yeres

ABRAHAM PORTER aged 36 yeares in the
THOMAS SAWIER aged 23 yeares in the

Corne, 9 barrells; Powder, 1 lb; Peeces, 4; Neat Cattell, 3; Swine, 11 and 3 piggs; House, 1.

m^r JOHN BURROWES came in the
BRIDGETT his wife
MARA BUCK aged 13 yeares

SERVANTS

JOHN COOKE aged 27 yeares
NICHOLAS GOULDFINCH aged 19 yeres
JOHN BRADSTON*
THOMAS THOROWGOOD aged 17 yeres
ELLIAS GAILE aged 14 yeares
ANDREW HOWELL aged 13 yeres
ANN ASHLEY aged 19 yeres

Corne, 12 barrells; Fish, 12 hundred; Peeces, 4; Shott, 150 lb; Armours, 4; Neat Cattell, 4; Swine, 4; Kidds, 2; Houses, 2; Boat, 1.

The Cattell belonging to m^r BUCKS Children: Neat Cattell young & old, 30; Goats, 18; Kidds, 5.

ELIZABETH SOOTHEY came in the *Southampton*
ANN SOOTHEY her daughter

Corne, 2 bushells; Meale, 1 bushell; Fish, 1 hundred; Swine, 1.

JOHN JEFFERSON came in the *Bona Nova*
WALGRAVE MARKS in the *Margrett & John*

Corne, 3 barrells; Powder, 2 lb; Peeces, 3.

WILLIAM MUTCH came in the *Jonathan*
MARGERY his wife in the *George* 1623

Corne, 5 barrells.

RICHARD STEEPHENS came in the *George* 1623

SERVANTS

WASSELL RAYNER aged 28 yeres came in the
THOMAS SPILLMAN aged 28 yeres in the *George* 1623
EDWARD PRISE aged 29 yeres in the *George* 1623
JOANE RAYNER wife of WASSELL RAYNER

Corne, 2 barrells; Meale, ½ hogshead; Powder, 12 lb; Shott, 34 lb; Peeces, 8; Houses, 3; Swine, 5; Boate, 1.

GEORGE MINIFIE arived in the *Samuell* July 1623

SERVANTS

JOHN GRIFFIN aged 26 yeares in the *William & John* 1624
EDWARD WILLIAMS aged 26 yeres in the same Shipp.

* In original "aged 18 yeres" lined out.

Corne, 6 barrells; Pease, 1 hogshead; Fish, 3 hundred; Butter Cheese oyle etc.—
Powder, 6 lb; Shott, 20 lb; Peeces, 3 and a pistoll; Armours, 3; Swords, 3; Swine,
1; Houses, 2; Boats, 1.

JOHN BARNETT aged 26 yeres came in the *Jonathan* 1620

Corne, 2 barrells; Fish, 1 hundred; Powder, 1 lb; Peece fixt, 1; Neat Cattell,
3; Swine, 8 and 6 piggs; Goats, 5 and 3 kidds; House, 1.

[27]

*James
Ileand*

JOHN STOAKS ⎫
ANN his wife ⎭ came in the *Warwick*.

Corne, 1 bushell; Meale, 1 bushell; Fish, 28.

RICHARD TREE came in the *George*
JOHN his Sonne aged 12 yeres

SERVANTS

SILVESTER BULLEN aged 28 yeres came in the

Corne, 7 barrells; Fish, 2 hundred; Peeces, 6; Armours, 2; Swords, 2; Swine,
6 and 7 piggs; Houses, 2.

WILLM LASEY ⎫
SUSAN his wife ⎭ came in the *Southampton* 1624

Corne, 3 barrells; Meale, 1 bushell; Biskett, ½ hundred; Pease, 1 barrell; Fish,
2 hundred; Peeces, 2; Swords, 2; Swine, 2; House, 1.

JOHN WEST came in the *Bony bess*
THOMAS CROMPE came in the

Corne, 5 barrells; Pease and beanes, 3 bushells; Bacon flitches, 2; Peece, 1;
Swords, 2; House, 1.

JOHN GREEVETT came in the
ELLIN his wife in the

Peece, 1; Armour, 1; Sword, 1; Swine, 3.

*James
Iland.*

THOMAS PASSMORE ⎫
JANE his wife ⎭ came in the *George*.

SERVANTS

THOMAS KERFITT aged 24 yeares in the *Hopewell*
ROBERT JULIAN aged 20 yeares in the *Jacob*.
JOHN BUCKMUSTER aged 20 yeres in the *Hopewell*.

Corne, 16 barrells; Meale, 1 hogshead; Pease and beanes, 2½ bushells; Fish,
1 hogshead; drie fish, 4 hundred; Neat cattell, 3; Swine, 6 and 4 piggs; House, 1.

CHRISTOPHER HALL came in the

Powder, 4 lb; Shott, 20; Peeces, 4 and 2 pistolls; Armours, 2.

ROBERT FITT came in the *George*.
ANN his wife in the *Abigaile*

Corne, 1 barrell; Pease, 1½ bushells; Peeces, 3; Sword, 1; Swine, 1 and 5 piggs; House, 1.

GEORGE ONION came in the *Francis bona venture.*
ELIZABETH his wife in the same Shipp.
FRANCIS PALL a boy aged 6 yeares
THOMAS PALL a boy aged 4 yeres
Corne, 1 bushell; Peece, 1; Sword, 1.

JOHN HALL came in the *John & Francis.*
SUSAN his wife in the *London Marchant*
Corne, 1½ barrell; Pease, 1 bushell; Powder, 1 lb; Peece, 1; Armour, 1; Sword, 1; House, 1.

[28]

ROBERT MARSHALL came in the *George*
ANN his wife in the same Shipp
Corne, 4 barrells; Swine, 1.

James Iland

THOMAS GRUBB came in the *George*
Corne, 2 barrells; House, 1.

JOHN OSBORN came in the
MARY his wife in the
Corne, ½ barrell; Powder, ½ lb; Peece, 1; Armour, 1.

WILLIAM SPENCER came in the *Sarah.*
ALLICE his wife in the
ALLICE theire daughter aged 4 yeres.
Corne, 10 barrells; Fish, 2 hundred; Powder, 4 lb; Shott, 8 lb; Peeces, 3; Swine, 12; Goats, 3 and 2 kidds; Houses, 2; Boat, 1.

THOMAS GRAYE came in the
MARGRETT his wife in the
WILLIAM theire Sonn aged 3 yeres
JONE theire daughter aged 6 yeres.
Corne, 11 barrells; Powder, 2 lb; Shott, 10 lb; Peece fixt, 1; Armour, 1; Swine, 5.

GABRIELL HOLLAND came in the *John & Francis.*
REBECCA his wife in the same Shipp
Corne, 7 barrells; Pease & beanes, 2 bushells; Fish, 1 hundred; Peeces, 4; Coate of Male, 1; Swine, 6; House, 1.

JOSIAS TANNER aged 24 yeres came in the
ANDREW RAILEY came in the
WILLIAM COOKSEY
THOMAS BAGLEN
WILLIAM CARTER
JOHN JOHNSON

James Iland

ANN his wife
JOHN his sonn aged 1 yeare
ANN his daughter aged 4 yeres
ALICE KEAN a Maid servant.
JOHN HITCHY
THOMAS DE LA MAIOR.

Provisions in the Marchannts Store to be sould: Fish, 14000; Oyle, 2 hogsheads; wth Butter Cheese and other Necessaries.

DEAD at James Cittie & in the Iland 1624

RICHARD MUMFORD
GEORGE CLARKE
BARTLOMEW BLAKE
WILLIAM WANERTON
SIBILL ROYALL
goodwife JEFFREYS
THOMAS POPKIN
THOMAS SIDES
THOMAS WEST
Wm SPENCER a Child
      a servant of m^r Keths
m^rs PEIRSE
JOHN GEE
      a servant of PEETER LANGMAN
      PHINLOE
m^rs SUSAN KETH.

[29]

Neck of Land
near
James Citty

THE MUSTER OF THE INHABITANTS OF THE NECK-OF-LAND NEAR JAMES CITTY TAKEN FEBR THE 4TH 1624

RICHARD KINGSMELL came in the *Delaware*
JANE his wife in the *Susan*
NATHANIELL his sonne aged 5 yeares.
SUSAN his daughter aged 1 yeare.

SERVANTS

HORTEN WRIGHT aged 20 yeres came in the *Susan*
JOHN JACKSON aged   came in the *Abigall*
EDWARD a Negro
ISBELL PRATT came in the *Jonathan*

Corne, 16 barrells wth other Provisions of flesh and fish; Powder, 11 lb; Shott, 100 lb; Peeces, 6; Murderers, 2; Pistolls, 2; Swords, 2; Houses, 5; Boate, 1; Neat Cattell young & old, 11; Swine young & old, 18.

JOHN SMITH came in the *Bonaventure.*

Corne, 2 barrells; Fish, 1 hundred; Powder, 1 lb; Peeces, 2; Coats of Male, 2; Swine, 8.

THOMAS BAGWELL came in the

Corne, 2½ bushells; Meale, 1 hogshead; Powder, ½ lb; Peece, 1; Sword, 1.

THOMAS BENETT came in the *Bona Nova*
MARGERY his wife in the *Guift*ᵉ
SARAH BROMEDG a Child 2 yeares old.

Neck of Land
neare
James Citty

Corne, 3 barrells; Fish, 1 barrell; Peece, 1; Swine, 1 and 2 piggs.

JOHN REDDISH came in the

Corne, 2 barrells; Fish, 100; Powder, ½ lb; Peece, 1; Sword, 1.

mʳ ALNUTT and his servant here Planted reconed before in the Muster of James Cittie.

DEAD in this Plantacon 1624

a Manservant of mʳ KINGSMELLS.

LIVING

RICHARD PIERCE
ELIZABETH his wife } came in the *Neptune.*

Corne, 3½ barrells; Meale, 2 bushells; Powder, 1 lb; Peeces fixt, 2; Armour, 1; Pigg, 1; House, 1.

THOMAS BRANSBY came in the *Charitie*

[30]

Archers Hope
James Citty

SERVANTS

NICHOLAS GREENHILL aged 24 yeres
CHADWALLADER JONES aged 22 yeres } came in the *Marmaduk* 1623
ROBERT CREW aged 23 yeares

Corne, 30 bushells; Oatmeale and Pease, 6 bushells; Fish, 500; Powder, 12 lb; Lead and Shott, 100 lb; Peeces, 7; Armours, 6; Swords, 6; Piggs, 2; House, 1.

JOHN ELLISON came in the *Prosperous*
ELLIN his wife in the *Charitie*

SERVANTS

JOHN BADELEY aged 24 yeres came in the *Hopwell* 1623

Corne, 22 bushells; Pease and beanes, 1 bushell; Powder, 2 lb; Shott, 12 lb; Peeces, 3; Armour, 1; Sword, 1; House, 1.

THOMAS FARLEY came in the *Ann* 1623
JANE his wife in the same Shipp
ANN a Child

SERVANTS

NICHOLAS SHOTTEN aged 40 yeres in the *Ann* 1623

Corne, 6 bushells; English Meale, 1 hogshead; Pease, 3 bushells; Powder, 2 lb; Lead, 10 lb; Peeces, 2; Armour, 1; Swine, 5 and a pigg; House, 1.

JOSEPH JOHNSON came in the *William & Thomas*
MARGRETT his wife in the *Abigaile*
GEORGE PROUSE came in the *Diana*

Archers Hope   Corne, 15 bushells; Meale, 8 bushells; Pease, 1 bushell; Fish, 1 hundred;
James Citty   Powder, 3 lb; Shott, 12 lb; Peeces, 3 and a pistoll; Armour, 1; House, 1.

DEAD at Archers Hope 1624

GEORGE ELLISON a Child
          a Maid servant of m^r BRANSBYES.
WILLIAM BROWNE.

---

[31]   m^r BURROWES and six of his men wch are planted heare are reconed,
         wth theire Armes Provisions etc, at James Cittie

Burrows Hill
James Citty   JOHN SMITH came in the *Elizabeth* 1611
SUSANNA his wife in the *Bona Nova* 1619
FRANCIS SMITH his sonne aged 1 yeare

SERVANTS

JOHN ELLATT aged 15 yeres in the *Margrett & John* 1621

Corne, 12 barrells; Fish, 14 hundred; Powder, 1 lb; Shott, 30 lb; Snaphannce Peece, 1; Machcocks, 2; Armour, 1; Coate of Steele, 1; Coats of Male, 2; Swine, 1; Houses, 2.

GEORGE PELTON came in the *Furtherance* 1622

Corne, 3 barrells; Peece, 1.

RICHARD RICHARDS came in the *London Marchant* 1620
RICHARD DOLPHINBE came in the *Guift* 1618

Corne, 5 barrells; Fish, 200; Powder, 2 lb; Shott, 12 lb; Peeces, 4; Armour, 1; Buffe Coat, 1; Dwelling house, 1; Tobacco house, 1.

Paces Paines   JOHN PROCTOR came in the *Seaventure* 1607
James Citty   ALLIS his wife in the *George* 1621

SERVANTS

RICHARD GROVE aged 30 yeres in the *George* 1623
EDWARD SMITH aged 20 in the *George* 1621
WILLIAM NAYLE aged 15 in the *Ann* 1623

Corne, 126 bushells; Meale, 2 bushells; Oatmeale, 5 bushells; Fish, ½ hundred; Powder, 22 lb; Peeces, 3 and 2 pistolls & 2 petronells*; Lead, 45 lb; Armours, 5; Neat Cattell, 7 and 5 Calves; Swine, 9; Houses, 2; Boat, 1.

* Petronel. A portable firearm of the 15th century, resembling a carbine of large caliber.

PHETTIPLACE CLOSE came in the *Starr* 1608
DANIELL WATTKINS in the *Charles* 1621

SERVANTS

MARTIN DEMON aged 15 yeres in the *George* 1617
JOHN SKINNER in the *Marmaduk* 1621
  Corne, 46 bushells; Powder, 2 lb; Lead, 10 lb; Peeces, 4; Armours, 1; Sword, 1; Neat Cattell, 2; Swine, 1; House, 1.

THOMAS GATES came in the *Swan* 1609
ELIZABETH his wife in the *Warwick* 1620
WILLIAM BEDFORD in the *James* 1621
  Corne, 40 bushells; Powder, 3 lb; Lead, 60 lb; Peeces, 4; Armours, 3; Swords, 2; Swine, 2; House, 1.

FRANCIS CHAPMAN came in the *Starr* 1608
  Corne, 10 bushells; Peece, 1; Swine, 1; House, 1.

[32]

THE MUSTER OF CAP^T *ROGER SMITHS* MEN
OVER Y^E WATTER

Smiths Plant.
James Citty

FRANCIS FOWLER aged 23 yeres
  Corne, 6 bushells; Peece, 1; Armour, 1.

CHRISTOPHER LAWSON
ALCE his wife
  Corne, 10 bushells; Peece, 1; Armour, 1.

CHRISTOPHER REDHEAD aged 24
  Corne, 10 bushells; Peece, 1; Armour, 1.

STEPHEN WEBB aged 25 yeres
  Corne, 10 bushells; Peece, 1; Armour, 1.

JOHN BUTTERFEILD aged 23 yeres
  Corne, 10 bushells; Peece, 1; Armour, 1.

WILLIAM BAKER aged 24 yeres
  Corne, 10 bushells; Peece, 1; Armour, 1.

RICHARD ALFORD aged 26 yeres
  Corne, 10 bushells; Peece, 1; Armour, 1.

THOMAS HARVIE aged 24 yeres
  Corne, 10 bushells; Peece, 1; Armour, 1.

THOMAS MOLTON aged 25 yeres
  Corne, 10 bushells; Peece, 1; Armour, 1.
  POWDER AMONGST ALL THESE: Powder, 16 lb; Swords, 9.

m^r Blaneys
Plant.
James Citty

THE MUSTER OF MR *EDWARD BLANEYS* MEN
OVER Y^E WATTER

RICE WATKINS aged 30 yeres came in the *Francis bonaventure.*
NATHANIELL FLOID aged 24 in the *Bona Nova.*

GEORGE ROGERS 23
JOHN SHELLEY 23
THOMAS OTTOWELL 40 } in the *Bona Nova.*
THOMAS CROUCH 40

ROBERT SHEPPEARD 20 in the *Hopwell.*
WILLIAM SAWIER 18 in the *Hopwell.*
ROBERT CHAUNTRIE 19 in the *George*
WILLIAM HARTLEY 23 in the *Charles*
LAWLEY DAMPORT 29 in the *Duty*
WILLIAM WARD 20 in the *Jonathan*
JEREMY WHITE 20 in the *Tyger*
JOHN HACKER 17 in the *Hopwell*
ROBERT WHITMORE 22 in the *Duty*

Powder, 7 lb; Lead and Shott, 12 lb; Peeces serviceable, 11 and 3 pistolls; Peeces not fixt, 8; Murderer, 1; Chambers,* 2; Match Cocks, 10; Match,† 6; Armours, 7; Jacks, 6; Coats of Male, 2; Coats quilted, 2; Swords, 12; Dwelling houses, 3; Tobacco houses, 3.

[33]

Capt Mathews
Plant.
James Citty

Capt SAMUELL MATHEWS came in the *Southampton* 1622
m^r DAVID SANDS Minister came in the *Bonaventure* 1620

SERVANTS

ROBERT MATHEWS aged 24 cam.
ROGER WILLIAMS 20
SAMUEL DAVIES 18
HENERY JONES 25
AARON CONAWAY 20 } came in the *Southampton* 1622
JOHN THOMAS 18
MICHAELL LAPWORTH 16
WILLIAM LUSAM 27
WILLIAM FEILD 23 } in the *Charles* 1621
PEETER MONTECUE 21
ROBERT FERNALL 31 in the *London Marchant* 1619

* chamber. That part of the bore of a piece of ordnance which holds the charge.

† match. (Fr. mèche; Sp. & Pg. mecha from the Lat. myxus, a lamp) The match in common use today was not developed until 1827. Prior to that time the match used to fire artillery and firearms was in reality a slow burning fuse. The *slow match* often was a piece of twisted hemp rope soaked in a solution of saltpeter, sugar of lead or the like, or a piece of well twisted cotton rope without preparation.

Walter Cooper 33 in the *Jonathan* 1619
William Walters 27 in the *Bona Nova* 1618
Nicholas Chapman 31 in the *Jonathan* 1619
Gregory Spicer in the *Triall* 1618
Nicholas Peirse 23 in the *Falcon* 1619
Robert Penn 22 in the *Abigaile* 1620
William Dalby 28 in the *Furtherance* 1622
Thomas Hopson 12 in the *Bona Nova* 1618
Abraham Wood 10 in the *Margrett & John* 1620
William Kingsley 24 ⎫
Thomas Bridges 12 ⎭ in the *Marmaduk* 1623
Arthure Goldsmith 26 came in the *Diana* 1618

    Corne, 240 bushells; Powder, 11 lb; Lead, 300 lb; Peeces serviceable, 18; Armours Steele Coats & Coats of Male, 24; Neat Cattell, 5; Calfes, 2; Dwelling House, 1; Stores, 3; Boats, 2.

---

mr Hugh Crowder came in the *Bona Nova* 1619

mr Crowders Plant.
James Citty

SERVANTS

Richard Ball in the *George* 1617
Thomas Hawkins in the *James* 1622
Paule Renalles in the *Tryall* 1619
Nicholas Smith a boy of 18 yeres in the *Bona Nova* 1621
John Verin a boy of 14 yeares in the *George* 1623

    Corne, 16 barrells; Fish, 1000; Powder, 3 lb; Shott and bulletts, 50 lb; Peeces, 12; Armours, 6; Swords, 6; Forte, 1; Houses, 2.

THE MUSTER OF Mr *GEORG SANDS* ESQUIRE

mr Treasurors Plant.

mr Georg Sandis Esquire Treasuror etc came in the *George* 1621

SERVANTS

Martin Turner ⎫
George Bailife
John Sparks
John Dancy
John Edwards ⎬ came in the *George* 1621
Nicholas Tompson
Rosamus Carter
John Stone a boy ⎭
Nicholas Comon ⎫
Nicholas Eyres a boy ⎭ in the *Guifte* 1622
David Mansfeild ⎫
John Claxon ⎭ in the *Bona Nova* 1619 hired servants

THOMAS SWIFTE ⎫ in the *Tyger* freemen. 1622
JOHN BALDWINE ⎭
DANIELL POOLE a french man, hired.
his wife
a yong Child of theires

[34]

m^r Treasurors
Plant.
James Citty

THE MUSTER OF THOSE THAT LIVE IN Y^E TREASURORS PLANT.

ROBERT SHEAPERD came in the *George* 1621
JAMES CHAMBERS in the *Dutie* 1620
JOHN PARSONS ⎫
WILLIAM BENGE ⎪
JOHN EVENS ⎬ in the *Marygold* 1619
ROBERT EDMUNDS ⎪
JOHN COMES ⎭
JOHN TYOS ⎫
WILLIAM PILKINTON ⎪
ELIAS LONGE ⎬ in the *Bona Nova* 1620
THOMAS HALL ⎭
MARGRETT PILKINTON ⎫ woomen
JANE LONG ⎭
m^r VINCENCIO the Italian
m^r BERNARDO
his wife
a Child

Corne, 100 barrells; Powder, 20 lb; Lead & Shott, 300 lb; Peeces, 30; a Peece of Ordnance, 1; Armo^rs Steele Coats & Coats of Male, 30; Swords, 20; Goats, 9 and six kidds; Swine, 2; Dwelling houses, 2; Stores, 2 wth other Cabbens; House framed for silk worms, 1; Garden of an acre & a half, 1; Vnie[Vine]-yard of 2 acres, 1; a Large Forte, 1.

At his other Plantačon: a Large forte Palled in, 1: Peece of Ordnance Mounted, 1; Dwelling house, 1; other houses, 4.

m^r Treasurors
Plant.
James Citty

ZACHARY CRIPPS came in the *Margrett & John* 1621
EDWARD WHITE in the *Bona Nova* 1620
MATHEW HAMON in the *Southampton* 1622
PHILLIP KITHLY in the *Furtherance* 1622
ANTHONY WEST in the *James* 1622

Corne, 12 barrells; Pease, 1 hogshead; Meale, 1 hogshead; Fish, 6 hundred; Powder, 6 lb; Lead, 30 lb; Peeces fixt, 10; Pistolls, 3; Steele Coat, 1; Coats of Male, 2 and 3 headpeeces; Swords, 6; a forte palled in, 1; Dwelling house, 1; Store house, 1.

DEAD at all these Plantations
Over the watter 1624

JOHN PHILMOTT	ELIAS HENTON
WILLIAM PLANT	THO: FITCH
THOMAS ROWLSON	ENECHA FITCH
EDWARD JONES	JOHN SERE
JOHN DIMSDALE	WILLIAM SANDS
JOHN DOCKER	GEORGE GURR
ROBERT ALDRIDGE	WILLIAM COMES } slaine by the Indians
RICHARD GREENE	ROBERT EVARS.
JAMES DAVIS	PEACEABLE SHEREWOOD.
DAVID WILLIAMS	WILLIAM HALL
JOHN FOXEN	

[35]

THE MUSTER OF CAP^T *RAPH HAMORS* SERVANTS

Hog Iland

JEFFEREY HULL came in the *George*
MORDECAY KNIGHT in the *William & John*
THOMAS DOLEMAN in the *Returne*
ELKINTON RATLIFFE in the *Seafloure*
THOMAS POWELL in the *Seafloure*
THOMAS COOPER in the *Returne*
JOHN DAVIES in the *Guifte*.

Corne, 19 barrells; Meale, 1 hogshead; Pease, 1 hogshead; Powder, 20 lb; Shott & Lead, 100 lb; Peeces, 5; Musketts Matchcocks, 6; Corsletts Complett, 4; Swords, 10; Boate, 1; Houses

THE MUSTER OF LIUETENÑT BARKLEY

Liuetenñt EDWARD BARKLEY in the *Unitie*.
m^rs JANE BARKLEY in the *Seafloure*.
JANE BARKLEY his daughter.

SERVANTS

THOMAS PHILLIPS } in the *Bona Nova*
FRANCIS BARRETT }
ROBERT MARTIN in the *George*.
KATHERIN DAVIES in the *Southampton*.

Corne, 9 barrells; Powder, 10 lb; Shott, 40 lb; Peeces, 3; Pistoll, 1; Corslett Complett, 1; Sword, 1; House, 1.

JOHN UTY came in the *Francis Bonaventure*
ANN his wife in the *Seafloure*.
JOHN his Sonn in the *Seafloure*.

Hog Iland

SERVANTS

WILLIAM BURT ⎫
WILLIAM STOCKER ⎬ in the *Bony besse*

RICHARD BICKLEY in the *Returne*.

Corne, 5 barrells; Powder, 6 lb; Shott, 20 lb; Peeces, 3; Swine, 5; House, 1.

JOHN CHEW came in the *Charitie*.
SARAH his wife in the *Seafloure*.

SERVANTS

ROGER DELK in the *Southampton*.
SAMUELL PARSON in the *Hopewell*.
WALTER HASLEWOOD in the *Due Returne*.

Corne, 10 barrells; Powder, 3 lb; Shott, 30 lb; Peeces, 6; Swine, 4; Boate, 1.

HENERY ELWOOD ⎫
WILLIAM RAMSHAW ⎬ in the *Francis Bonaventure*.

JOHN STONE in the *Swann*
SISLY his wife in the *Seafloure*.
HENERY CROCKER in the *Marygold*
JONE his wife in the *Swan*.
HENERY WOODWARD in the *Diana*.
JANE his wife
THOMAS HITCKOCK in the *Marygold*
ALICE his wife
ROGER WEBSTER
JOANE his wife
JOANE DAVIS.

Corne, 41½ bushells.

[36]

*Hog
Iland*

THE MUSTER OF S^R *GEORG YEARLLEYS* MEN

MAXIMILLIAN STONE aged 36 came in the *Temperance* 1620
ELIZABETH his wife in the same Shipp.
MAXIMILLIAN his sonn aged 9 months.
ROBERT GUY 22 in the *Swan* 1619
EDWARD YATES 18 in the *Duty* 1619
CESAR PUGGETT 20 in the *Diana* 1619
ALLEXANDER SANDERS 24 in the *Truelove* 1623
WILLIAM STRACHEY 17 in the *Temperance* 1620
GEORGE WHITEHAND 24 in the *Temperance* 1620
HENERY KING 22 in the *Jonathan* 1620
JOHN DAY 24 in the *London Marchannt* 1620

The wife of JOHN DAY in the same Shipp
JOHN ROOT in the *Guift*
WALTER BLAKE in the *Swan* } Dwellers.
THOMAS WATTS in the *Treasuror.*

DAVID DUTTON } Dead
RICH: BAKER

Houses, 2.
The rest of his servants, Provisions Armes &ct reconed at James Citty.

THE MUSTER OF THE INHABITANTS
OF MARTINS HUNDRED TAKEN THE
4TH OF FEBRUARY 1624.

*Martins
Hundred.*

m^r WILLIAM HARWOOD came in the *Francis Bonaventure*

SERVANTS

HUGH HUGHS came in the *Guifte.*
ANN his wife
THOMAS DOUGHTIE aged 26 } came in the *Abigall.*
JOHN HASLEY aged 22 yeres
SAMUELL WEAVER 20 in the *Bony bess*
ELIZABETH BYGRAVE 12 came in the *Warwick.*

Corne, 10 barrells; Fish, 12 hundred; Powder, 60 lb; Peeces fixt, 10; Machcocks, 25 and 10 lb of Match.; Peece of Ordnance, 1 wth all things thereto belonging; Shott, 300 lb; Armours, 8; Coats of Male, 10; Coats of Steele, 3 and 20 Swords; Neat Cattell, 10 belonging to the Hundred; Houses, 3; Boat, 1.

ELLIS EMERSON
ANN his wife } came in the *George* 1623.
THOMAS his sonn aged 11

*Martins
Hundred*

SERVANTS

THOMAS GOULDING aged 26 yeres came in the *George* 1623.
MARTIN SLATIER aged 20 cam frō Canada in the *Swan* 1624

Corne, 6 barrells; Fish, 3½ hundred; Powder, 12 lb; Shott, 30 lb; Peeces fixt, 1; Matchcock, 1; Armour, 1 and 4 headps; Coats of Male, 2; Coate of Steele, 1; Swords, 2; Swine, 2; House, 1.

ROBERT ADDAMS
AUGUSTINE LEAK } came in the *Bona Nova*
WINIFRED LEAK his wife came in the *George* 1623.

SERVANTS

RICHARD SMITH aged 24 yeres came in the *George* 1623

Corne, 3 barrells; Fish, 11 hundred; Powder, 6 lb; Shott, 5 lb; Peeces fixt, 6; Armour, 1; Coat of plate,* 1; Swords, 2; Piggs, 2; Houses, 2; Boat, 1.

STEPHEN BARKER came in the *James*
HUMPHREY WALDEN in the *Warwick*

Corne, 4 barrells; Fish, 3½ hundred; Powder, 3 lb; Shott, 5 lb; Peeces fixt, 2; Swords, 2.

[37]
───

Martins   JOHN JACKSON   ⎫
Hundred   ANN his wife   ⎬ came in the *Warwick*
               A Child aged 20 weeks

SERVANTS

THOMAS WARD aged 47 yeres ⎫
JOHN STEEPHENS 35 yeres   ⎬ came in the *Warwick*

Corne, 1½ barrell; Fish, 800; Powder, 2 lb; Shott, 6 lb; Peeces fixt, 4; Armours, 3; Coate of Male, 1; Swords, 3; Houses, 1.

───

SAMUEL MARCH came in the *William & Thomas.*
COLLICE his wife in the *Ann* 1623
SAMUELL CULLEY came in the *London Marchamt*

Corne, 5 barrells; Fish, 5 hundred; Powder, 1 lb; Shott, 20 lb; Peeces fixt, 3; Armour, 1; Swords, 2.

ROBERT SCOTCHMORE and his Company now planted heare are reconned before in the Maine†

DEAD at Martins Hundred this yeare

ALLICE EMERSON a girle
ROBERT   a boy of mr EMARSONS
                a girle of JOHN JACKSONS
                a Child of SAMUELL MARCH.

Mulburie   THE MUSTER OF THE INHABITANTS ATT MULBURY
Iland   ILAND TAKEN THE 25TH OF JANUARY 1624.

THE MUSTER OF CAPT *WILLIAM PIERCES* SERVANTS

RICHARD ATTKINS aged 24 came in the *London Marchannt*
ABIGALL his wife   ⎫
                           ⎬ came in the *Abigall*
WILLIAM BAKER aged 20   ⎭
ROBERT ASTON 29 in the *Treasuror*

───

* Coat of plate was constructed of broad metal pieces.
† This plantation in James City County now (1955) bears the same name.

HUGH WING 30 ⎫
ROBERT LATHOM 20 ⎬ came in the *George* 1620
RICHARD ALDON 19 ⎪
THOMAS WOOD 35 ⎭
ROBERT RUCE came in the *Charles*
ALLEXANDER GILL 20 in the *Bony bess*
SAMUEL MORRIS 20 in the *Abigall*
THOMAS ROSE 35 in the *Jonathan*
ROBERT HEDGES aged 40 yeres in the
    Corne, 120 bushells; Powder, 30 lb; Peeces, 14; Armours, 10; Swords, 30.

JOHN VIRGO came in the *Treasuror*
SUSAN his wife in the same Shipp
    Corne, 15 bushells; Powder, 4 lb; Peece, 1; Armour Complett, 1; Sword, 1.

JOHN GATTER came in the *George* 1620
    Corne, 10 bushells; Peece, 1; Armour, 1; Sword, 1.   [38]

WILLIAM RICHARDSON came in the *Edwine*   *Mulbury*
    Corne, 10 bushells; Powder, 2 lb; Peece fixt, 1; Armour, 1; Sword, 1.   *Iland*

RICHARD FINE came in the *Neptune*
    Corne, 10 bushells; Powder, 1 lb; Peece, 1; Armour, 1; Sword, 1.

JOHN NOWELL came in the *Margrett & John*
    Corne, 10 bushells; Powder, 3 lb; Peece, 1; Armour, 1; Sword, 1.

RICHARD DOWNES came in the *Jonathan*
    Corne, 6 bushells; Powder, 2 lb; Peece, 1; Armour, 1; Sword, 1.

JOHN CRANICH came in the *Marygold*
    Corne, 10 bushells; Powder, 1 lb; Peece, 1; Armour, 1; Sword, 1.

PERCEVALL WOOD came in the *George*
ANN his wife in the *George.*
    Corne, 20 bushells; Powder, 2 lb; Peece, 1; Armour, 1; Sword, 1.

WILLIAM RAYMONT came in the *Neptune*   *Mulbury*
    Corne, 12 bushells; Powder, 1 lb; Peece, 1; Armour, 1; Sword, 1.   *Iland*

WILLIAM BULLOCK came in the *Jonathan*
    Corne, 10 bushells; Powder, 2 lb; Peece, 1.

ANTHONY BARAM came in the *Abigall*
ELIZABETH his wife in the *William & Thomas*
    Corne, 15 bushells; Peece, 1; Armour, 1; Sword, 1.

THOMAS HARWOOD came in the *Margrett & John* 1622
GRACE his wife in the *George*

SERVANTS

THOMAS READ aged 65 yeres

Corne, 8 barrells; Powder, 2 lb; Peeces, 2; Armours, 2; Swords, 2.

[39]

Wariscoyack.

THE MUSTER OF THE INHABITANTS AT WARISCOYACK
TAKEN THE 7TH OF FEBR 1624

THE MUSTER OF MR *EDWARD BENNETTS* SERVANTS

HENERY PINKE came in the *London Marchannt* 1619
JOHN BATE in the *Addam* 1621
PEETER COLLINS in the *Addam* 1621

WASSELL WEBLING
ANTONIO a Negro } in the *James* 1621

CHRISTOPHER REYNOLDS
LUKE CHAPPMAN } in the *John & Francis* 1622
EDWARD MAYBANK

JOHN ATTKINS
WILLIAM DENUM } in the *Guifte* 1623
FRANCIS BANKS

MARY a Negro Woman in the *Margrett & John* 1622

Corne, 10 barrells; Powder, 10 lb; Peeces fixt, 13; Armours, 9; Dwelling houses, 2 in serverall Pallisadoes; Store, 1 w^thin one of ye Pallisadoes.

A MUSTER OF THE INHABITANCE
OF BASSES CHOYSE

CAP^T *NATHANIELL BASSE* HIS MUSTER

NATHANIELL BASSE aged 35 in the *Furtherance* 1622
WILLIAM BARNARD aged 21 in the *Furtherance* 1622
EDWARD WIGGE aged 22 in the *Abigall* 1621

Basses Choyse

PROVISION: Corne, 40 bushells; Pease, 6 bushells; Fish, 500 ct.*; Sows, 1; Houses, 2. ARMES: Corsletes, 4; Swords, 6; Coates of Male, 7; peeces, 7; pistoles, 2; petrenell, 1; Murderer, 1; powder, 12 lb; lead, 300 lb.

THE MUSTER OF *THOMAS PHILLIPES*

THOMAS PHILLIPES aged 26 in the *William and Thomas* 1618
ELIZABETH PHILLIPES aged 23 in the *Sea Flower* 1621

* ct. abbreviation for *centum* meaning hundred.

PROVISION: Corne, 12 bushells. ARMES: Corslett, 1; Swords, 2; Coate of Male, 1; peeces, 3; pistole, 1; powder, 5 lb.

THE MUSTER OF *THOMAS BENNETT*

THOMAS BENNETT aged 38 in the *Neptune* 1618
MARY BENNETT aged 18 in the *Southampton* 1622
ROGER HEFORD aged 22 in the *Returne* 1623
BENIAMINE SIMES aged 33 in the
PROVISIŌN Corne, 48 bushells; Fish, 400 ct. ARMES: Corslett, 1; Coate of Male, 1; Sword, 1; peeces, 4; powder, 8 lb.

RICHARD LONGE HIS MUSTER

RICHARD LONGE aged 33 in the
ALICE LONGE aged 23 in the *London Merchant* 1620
ROBERT LONGE a Child borne in Virginia
PROVISION: Corne, 12 bushells; house, 1; ARMES: Corslett, 1; peese, 1; powder, 2 lb.

RICHARD EVANDS HIS MUSTER

[40]
Wariscoyack

RICHARD EVANDS aged 35 in the *Neptune* 1618
PROVISION: Corne, 8 bushells; house, 1. ARMES: Corslett, 1; Sword, 1.

WILLIAM NEWMAN HIS MUSTER

WILLIAM NEWMAN aged 35 in the *Furtherance* 1622
JOHN ARMY aged 35 in the *Furtherance* 1622
PROVISION: Corne, 16 bush; house, 1. ARMES: Corslett, 1; Swords, 2; peeces, 2; powder, 6 lb.

HENRIE WOODWARD HIS MUSTER

HENRIE WOODWARD aged 30 in the
JOHN BROWNINGE aged 22 in the *Abigall* 1621

SERVANTS

AMBROSE   aged 25 in the *Marmiducke* 1621
PEETER   aged 19 in the *Margett and John* 1620
PROVISION: Corne, 40 bushells; houses, 2. ARMES: Corslett, 2; Coates of Male, 2; peeces, 3; pistole, 1.

A list of the DEAD in Wariscoyacke 1624

JOHN SELLEY
NATHANIELL HAUKWURTH

THOMAS SHEWOUD
BENIAMIN HANDCLEARE
MARGRETT SYMES
NATHANIELL ⎫
THOMAS   ⎬ Servants
of Mʳ BENNETS men ⎫
slayne by the Indians ⎬ 5

Newportes   Mᴿ *DANNIELL GOOKINES* MUSTER
newes*   SERVANTES

WILLIAM WADSWORTH aged: 26 ⎫
WILLIAM FOOCKES aged: 24   ⎪
THOMAS CURTIS aged: 24   ⎪
PEETER SHERWOOD aged: 21   ⎬ All wᶜʰ Came in the
GILBERT WHITFILD aged: 23 ⎪ *Flyinge Harte* · 1621
RISE GRIFFIN aged: 24   ⎪
WILLIAM SMITH aged: 23   ⎪
ANTHONIE EBSWORTH aged: 26 ⎭
ISAYE DELYWARR aged 22
HENRIE CARSLEY aged: 23
ROGER WALKER aged: 22
EDMOND MORGAN aged: 22 ⎫
WILLIAM CLARKE aged: 25 ⎬ in the *Providence* 1623
JOSEPH MOSLEY aged: 21 ⎭
JOHN PARRATT aged: 36
ROBART SMITH aged: 22
WILLIAM CRONEY aged: 24
WILLIAM LONGE aged: 19
ANNE EBSWORTH aged: 44
ELLNOR HARRIS aged: 21

PROVISION: Corne, 30 barrells; Fish, 2000; Peese, 3 hodheds; Shott, 200 lb; Peeces, 16; Ordinances Mounted, 3; Armores, 20; Swords, 20; Cattell Neete, 15; Houses, 4; Boate, 1.

DEAD in this Plantatō

one ARMESTRONGE

* *Newportes Newes*, recorded as a settlement, 1619, (*R, Va. Co.* III 227) and later a fishing village, was incorporated as the City of Newport News, 1896. There is no authority for the alliterative name, of which there were several in the Colony, such as: *Pace's Paines, Jordan's Journey, Beggar's Bush.* Thus, tidings brought by Captain Christopher Newport in four voyages to Virginia subsequent to that which founded the settlement at Jamestown, 1607, probably supplied a basis for a euphonious designation of this early outpost at the confluence of the present Hampton Roads and the James River.

CAPT *WILLIAM TUCKER* HIS MUSTER

Capt WILLIAM TUCKER: aged: 36: in the *Mary and James*: [16]10

M^irs^ MARY TUCKER aged: 26: in the *George*: 1623.

ELIZABETH TUCKER borne in Virginia in August:

GEORGE TOMSON aged: 17 ⎫
PAULE TOMSON aged: 14 ⎬ in the *George* 1623:
WILLIAM THOMSON—11 ⎭

PASCOE CHAMPION aged 23 ⎫
STRENGHT SHEERE aged: 23 ⎬ in the *Ellonor* 1621:

THOMAS EVANDS aged: 23 ⎫
STEPHEN COLLOWE aged: 23 ⎬ in the *George*: 1623.
ROBART MUNDAY aged: 18 ⎭

MATHEWE ROBINSONN aged: 24 in the *greate hopewell* 1623

RICHARD APPLETON aged: 19: in the *James* 1622.

JOHN MORRIS aged 24: in the *Bona Nova*: 1619.

MARY MORRIS aged 22: in the *George* 1623

WILLIAM HUTCHINSON aged 21: in the *Diana* 1618

PEETER PORTER aged 20 in the *Tyger* 1621.

WILLIAM CRAWSHAW an Indian Baptised.

ANTONEY Negro: ISABELL Negro: and WILLIAM theire Child Baptised

PROVISION: Corne, 40 barle; Oatmeale, 1 bar; Meale, 1 bar; Fish, 500 ct; Swine, 3; houses, 3; Pallizado, 1; Boate, 1. ARMES: Snaphance peeces, 24; Pistoles, 4; Murderers, 2; Swords, 6; Armors, 10; Powder, 10 lb; Lead, 200 lb.

Elizabeth Cittie

JOHN *DOWNEMAN* HIS MUSTER

JOHN DOWNEMAN aged: 33: in the *John and Francis*: 1611:

ELIZABETH DOWNEMAN aged: 22: in the *Warwicke* 1621.

MOYSES STONES aged: 16: in the *Bone Bes* 1623

PROVISION: Corne, 6 barrels; Goate, 1; Houses, 1; Pallizado, 1. ARMES: Snaphance peeces, 1; Swords, 2; Powder, 1 lb; Lead, 6 lb.

Elzabeth Cittie

JOHN *LAYDON* HIS MUSTER

JOHN LAYDON aged 44: in the *Susan* 1606

ANNE LAYDON aged 30: in the *Mary Margrett* 1608

VIRGINIA LAYDON ⎫
ALICE LAYDON ⎬ borne in Virginia.
KATHERIN LAYDON ⎪
MARGERETT LAYDON ⎭

PROVISION: Corne, 6 barrells; Houses, 2; Pallizado, 1. ARMES: Snaphance peeces, 1; Lead, 40 lb.

WILLIAM COLE HIS MUSTER

WILLIAM COLE aged 26 in the *Neptune* 1618
FRANCIS COLE aged 27 in the *Susan* 1616
ROGER FARBRASE aged 26 in the *Elizabeth* 1621

PROVISION: Corne, 10 barrels; Fish, 50; Houses, 1. ARMES: Snaphance peeces, 3; pistoles, 1; Swords, 1; Armor, 1.

[42]

Elizabeth
Cittie

MILES PRICKETT AND FRANCIS MITCHELL THEIR MUSTERS

MILES PRICKETT aged 36 in the *Starr*: 1610
FRANCIS MITCHELL aged 38 in the *Neptune* 1618
MAUDLIN MITCHELL aged 21 in the *Bona Nova* 1620
JOHN MITCHELL borne in Virginia 1624

PROVISION: Corne, 12 barrels; Fish, 1 ct; Houses, 1; Pallizado, 1. ARMES: Peeces, 4; Armor, 1; Powder, ¼ lb; Lead, 20 lb.

RICHARD YONGE HIS MUSTER

RICHARD YONGE aged 31 in the *George* 1616
JOANE YONGE aged 26 in the *Guifte* 1618
JOANE YONGE aged 2 borne in Virginia
SUSAN   aged 12 in the *Swan* 1624

PROVISION: Corne, 4 barrels; Houses, 1. ARMES: Peeces, 1; Pistole, 1; Swords, 1; Armors, 3; powder, 3 lb; Leade, 40 lb.

LEIUETEN : ALBIANO LUPO HIS MUSTER

ALBIANO LUPO aged 40 in the *Swan* 1610
ELIZABETH LUPO aged 28 in the *George* 1616
TEMPERANCE LUPO aged 4 borne in Virginia

SERVANTS

HENRIE DRAPER aged 14 in the *George* 1621
JOSEPH HAM aged 16 in the *Warwicke* 1621

Elizabeth
Cittie

PROVISION: Corne, 8 barrels; Houses, 1; pallizado, 1; Goates, 4. ARMES: Peeces, 3; powder, 1 lb; Lead, 30 lb; swords, 1.

JOHN POWELL HIS MUSTER

JOHN POWELL aged 29 in the *Swallowe* 1609
KATHREN POWELL aged 22 in the *flyinge Hart* 1622
JOHN POWELL borne in Virginia

SERVANTS

THOMAS PRATER aged 20 in the *Marie Providence* 1622

PROVISION: Corne, 5 barrels; Fish, 700 ct; Houses, 1; pallizado, 1. ARMES: Peeces, 1; Swords, 1; Armor, 1; Powder, 2 lb; Lead, 30 lb.

LARENCE PEALE HIS MUSTER

LARENCE PEALE aged 23 in the *Margett and John* 1620
WILLIAM SMITH aged 30 in the *Jacob* 1624

PROVISION: Corne, 4 barrels; pease, 2 busheles; Fish, 300 ct; houses, 1. ARMES: Peeces, 2; Powder, 6 lb; Lead, 6 lb.

ROBART BRITTIN HIS MUSTER

ROBART BRITTIN aged 30 in the *Edwin* 1618

PROVISION: Corne, 3 barrels; Fish, 200 ct; House, 1. ARMES: Peeces, 1; Lead, 12 lb.

MIHELL WILCOCKES AND *JOHN SLATER* THEIR MUSTER

[43]

Elzabeth Cittie

MIHELL WILCOCKES aged 31 in the *Prosporouse* 1610
ELZABETH WILLCOCKES aged 23 in the *Concord* 1621
JOHN SLATER aged 22 in the *George* 1617
ANNE SLATER aged 17 in the *Guyft* 1622

SERVANTS

JAMES FEILD aged 20 in the *Swan* 1624
JOHN JORNALL aged 20 in the *Ann* 1623
THEODORE JOONES aged 16 in the *Margett and John* 1620

PROVISION: Corne, 9 barrels; Houses, 1. ARMES: Peeces, 3; petronell, 1; Swords, 2; Coates of Male, 2; Lead, 30 lb.

JOSEPH COBB HIS MUSTER

JOSEPH COBB aged 25 in the *Treasoror* 1613
ELZABETH COBB aged 25 in the *Bone Bes* 1623
JOHN SNOWOOD aged 25 in the

PROVISION: Corne, 8 barrels; house, 1. ARMES: Peeces, 1; swords, 2; powder, 3 lb.

CORNELIUS MAY HIS MUSTER

CORNELIUS MAY aged 25 in the *Providence* 1616

PROVISION: Corne, 20 bareis; Fish, 300 ct; Houses, 1. ARMES: Peeces, 1; Lead, 6 lb.

Elzabeth
Cittie

WILLIAM MORGAN als BROOCKES HIS MUSTER

William Morgan aged 30 in the *Starr* 1610
William Morgan aged 2 borne in Virginia

PROVISION: Corne, 4 barrels; Fish, ½ ct; swine, 1; house, 1; goate, 1. ARMES: Peeces, 1; powder, 2 lb; leade, 4 lb.

MR WILLIAM JULIAN HIS MUSTER

William Julian aged: 43: in the *Hercules* 1609
Sara Julian aged 25 in the *Neptune* 1618
William Kemp aged 33 in the *William and Thomas* 1618
Thomas Sully aged 36 in the *Sara* 1611
Maudlyn Sully aged 30 in the *London Marchant* 1620

SERVANTS

Thomas Flower aged 22 in the *George* 1623
Wyatt Masonn aged 16 in the *Ann* 1623

PROVISION: Corne, 19 barrels; swine, 1; house, 1; palizado, 1; goates, 6. ARMES: Peeces, 6; pistole, 1; swords, 4; Armors, 1; Coate of Male, 1; powder, 12 lb; Lead, 600 lb.

[44]

Elzabeth
Cittie

LEIUTEÑ THOMAS PURFRAY HIS MUSTER

Thomas Purfry aged 43 in the *George* 1621
Christopher Colethorpe aged 18: in the *Furtherance* 1622
Danniell Tanner aged 40 in the *Sampson* 1618

SERVANTS

Henrie Feeldes aged 26 in the *Jacob* 1624
William Bauldwin

PROVISION: Corne, 8 barreles; Meale, 1 barrell; fish, 300 ct.; house, 1; pallizado, 1. ARMES: Peeces, 4; petronell, 1; swords, 4; Armor, 1; powder, 1 lb; lead, 100 lb.

JOHN BARNABE HIS MUSTER

John Barnabie aged 21: in the *London Marchant* 1620

PROVISION: Corne, 5 barrels. ARMES: Peeces, 1; Armor, 1; lead, 1 lb.

JOHN HAZARD HIS MUSTER

John Hazard aged 40 in the *William and Thomas* 1618

SERVANTS

Abraham Pelteare aged 14 in the *Swan* 1624

PROVISION: Corne, 14 bushells; house, 1. ARMES: peeces, 1; pistole, 1; sword, 1; lead, 4 lb.

JERIMIAH DICKINSON HIS MUSTER

JERIMIAH DICKINSON aged 26 in the *Margett and John* 1620
ELZABETH DICKINSON aged 38 in the *Margett and John* 1623
PROVISION: Corne, 2 barrels; Fish, 400 ct. ARMES: Peeces, 3; swords, 1; Armor, 1; powder, 1 lb; lead, 20 lb.

PHILLIP LUPO HIS MUSTER

PHILLIP LUPO aged 42 in the *George* 1621
PROVISION: Corne, 2 barreles; Fish, ½ ct. ARMES: Peeces, 1; Swords, 1.

ENSIGNE *THOMAS WILLOBY** HIS MUSTER

THOMAS WILLOBY aged 23 in the *Prosporouse* 1610

SERVANTS

JOHN CHAUNDLER aged 24 in the *Hercules* 1609
THOMAS aged 20 in the *greate hopewell* 1623
ROBERT BENNETT aged 24 In the *Jacob* 1624
NICCOLAS DAVIS aged 13 in the *Mariegould* 1618
PROVISION: Corne, 16 barrels; Fish, 200 ct; houses, 3; pallizado, 1. ARMES: Peeces, 4; pistolle, 1; swords, 3; Armors & Coates, 4; powder, 5 lb; lead, 150 lb.

JOHN HATTON HIS MUSTER

JOHN HATTON aged 26 in the *Tresorer* 1613
OLIVE HATTON aged 32 in the *Abigall* 1620
PROVISION: Corne, 4 barrels; Fish, 200 ct. ARMES: Peeces, 1.

MR *CISSE* MINISTER HIS MUSTER

Mr GEORGE KETH aged 40 ⎫
JAMES WHITINGE aged 16 ⎬ in the *George* 1617
JOHN KETH aged 11 ⎭
PROVISION: Corne, 10 barrels; goates, 4.

SUSAN BUSH HER MUSTER

SUSAN BUSH aged 20 in the *George* 1617
SARA spence aged 4 borne in Virginia

SERVANTS

CLEMENT EVANS aged 30 in the *Edwin* 1616
WILLIAM PARKER aged 20 in the *Charles* 1616
JOHN SEWARD aged 30 in the *Geife* 1622 [Guift]

* elsewhere and usually *Willoughby*.

GILBERT MARBURIE aged 32 in the *Southampton* 1622
THOMAS KILLSON aged 21 in the *Truelove* 1623

PROVISION: Corne, 12 barrels; Shott, 20 lb; Peeces, 7; Rapier, 1; houses, 2.

CAP^T *NICCOLAS MARTUE* HIS MUSTER

NICCOLAS MARTUE aged 33 in the *Francis Bonaventure*
PETER ECCALLOWE aged 30 in the *Southampton*
WILLIAM STAFFORD aged 17 in the *furtherance*

PROVISION: Corne, 10 barrels; Peeces, 12; pistoles, 4; lead, 300 ct; powder, 1 lb;
Fish, 300 ct; houses, 2.

MR *JOHN BANUM* AND *ROBART SWEETE*
THEIRE MUSTER

JOHN BANUM aged 54 in the *Susan* 1616
ELZABETH BANUM aged 43 in the *Bona Nova*, 1620
ROBART SWEETE aged 42 in the *Neptune* 1618

SERVANTS

Elzabeth   NICCOLAS THREDDER aged 30 in the *Katherin* 1623
Cittie   RICHARD ROBISONN aged 22 in the *Bona nova* 1620
JOHN HILL aged 26 in, the *Bona Nova* 1620
WILLIAM MORTON aged 20 in the *Margett and John* 1620
JAMES PASCOLL aged 20 in the *Warwicke* 1621
ROBART DRAPER aged 16 in the *Jacob* 1624
SARA GOULDINGE aged 20 in the *Ann* 1623

PROVISION: Corne, 30 barrels; fish, 1000; Swine, 1; houses, 2; palizado, 1; goates,
6. ARMES: Peeces, 10; pistolles, 2; murderer, 1; swords, 3; Armors, 3; Coats, 1;
powder, 5 lb; lead, 25 lb.

RICHARD MINTRENE HIS MUSTER

RICHARD MINTRENE aged 40 in the *Margett and John* 1620
WILLIAM BEANE aged 25 in the *Diana* 1618
EDWARD MINTRENE aged 12 in the *Margett and John* 1620
JOHN INMAN aged 26 in the *Falcon* 1619
WILLIAM BROWNE aged 14 in the *Southampton* 1622

PROVISION: Corne, 12 barreles; houses, 2. ARMES: Peeces, 8; sword, 1; Armors,
2; lead, 100 lb.

ANTHONEY BURROES HIS MUSTER

ANTHONEY BURROES aged 44 in the *George* 1617

PROVISION: Corne, 3 barreles; house, 1. ARMES: Peeces, 3; sword, 1; Coate, 1;
powder, 1 lb; lead, 40 lb.

JOHN WAINE HIS MUSTER

JOHN WAINE aged 30 in the *Neptune* 1618

*Elzabeth
Cittie*

AMYTE WAINE aged 30 in the *Swan* 1610

GEORGE ACKLAND aged 7 }
MARY ACKLAND aged 4 } borne in Virginia

JOHN HARLOW aged 28 in the *Sampson* 1619

ROBART SABYN aged 30 in the *marget and John* 1622

PHILLIP CHAPMAN aged 23 in the *flyinge hart* 1621

PROVISION: Corne, 12 barreles; fish, 400 ct; houses, 2; pallizado, 1. ARMES: peeces, 4; sword, 1.

MR *ROBART SALFORD* HIS MUSTER
AND *JOHN SALFORD*

Mr ROBART SALFORD aged 56 in the *John and Francis* 1611

JOHN SALFORD aged 24 in the *George* 1616

MARY SALFORD aged 24 in the *Bona Nova* 1620

SERVANTS

WILLIAM ELLISON aged 44 in the *Swan* 1624

THOMAS FAULKNER aged 28 in the *Mary Providense* 1622

PROVISION: Corne, 15 barreles; fish, 300 ct; goates, 23; houses, 4; pallizado, 1. ARMES: Peeces, 4; Pistoles, 2; swords, 3; Armor, 1; Coate of male, 1; powder, 8 lb; lead, 100 lb.

BARTHOLEMEW WETHERSBIE AND
RICHARD BOULTON THEIR MUSTERS

*Elzabeth
Cittie*

BARTHOLEMEW WETHERSBIE aged 30 in the *Providence* 1616

DORYTHIE WETHERSBIE aged 30 in the *London Marchant* 1620

RICHARD BOULTON aged 28 in the *Mary and James* 1610

RICHARD   aged 15 in the *Swan* 1624

PROVISION: Corne, 10 barrels; fish, 400 ct.; goates, 2; house, 1; pallizado, 1. ARMES: peeces, 4; pistole, 1; sword, 1; Coate of male, 1; powder, 14 lb; lead, 30 lb.

JOHN GUNDRIE HIS MUSTER

JOHN GUNDRIE aged 33 in the *Starr* 1610

MARIE GUNDRIE aged 20 in the *George* 1618

JOHN GUNDRIE aged 2 borne in Virginia

PROVISION: Corne, 10 barrels; fish, 100 ct; house, 1. ARMES: Peeces, 4; pistole, 1; sword, 1; powder, 1 lb; lead, 30 lb.

FRANCIS MASON HIS MUSTER

FRANCIS MASON aged 40 in the *John and Francis* 1613
ALICE MASON aged 26 in the *Margett and John* 1622
FRANCIS MASON borne in Virginia

SERVANTS

WILLIAM QUERKE aged 30 in the *Marmaducke* 1621
THOMAS WORTHALL aged 14 in the *Marmaducke* 1621
WILLIAM STAFFORD aged 16 in the *furtherance* 1622
HENRIE GANY aged 21 in the *Dutie* 1619

[47] JOHN ROBINSON aged 21 in the *Margett and John* 1622

> PROVISION: Corne, 10 barreles; houses, 3. ARMES: peeces, 6; pistoles, 2; swords, 2; lead, 6 lb.

FARRAR FLINTON HIS MUSTER

FARRAR FLINTON aged 36 in the *Elzabeth* 1612
JOANE FLINTON aged 38 in the *Elzabeth* 1612
WILLIAM BENTLIE aged 36 in the *Jacob* 1624

SERVANTS

ARTHUR SMYTH aged 25 ⎫
HUGH HALL aged 13   ⎬ in the *Marget and John* 1622
MATHEW HARDCASTELL aged 20 in the *Jacob* 1624
HENRIE NASFEILD aged 19 in the *Swan* 1624

> PROVISION: Corne, 12 barreles; fish, 200 ct; house, 1; boate, 1. ARMES: Peeces, 7; pistole, 1; swords, 4; Armor, 1; Coate, 1; powder, 8 lb; lead, 60 lb.

JAMES SLEIGHT AND *FRANCIS HUFF* THEIRE MUSTER

FRANCIS HUFF aged 20 in the *Swan* 1624
JAMES SLEIGHT aged 42 in the *Tryall* 1610

> PROVISION: Corne, 5 barrels. ARMES: peeces, 2; Sword, 1; powder, 6 lb; lead, 6 lb.

Elzabeth
Cittie

LEIUETEÑ *JOHN CHISMAN* HIS MUSTER

JOHN CHISMAN aged 27 in the *flyinge hart* 1621
EDWARD CHISMAN aged 22 in the *Providence* 1623

> PROVISION: Corne, 2 barreles; house, 1. ARMES: peeces, 6; swords, 2; Armor, 1; powder, 1 lb; lead, 20 lb.

MR *THOMAS SPILMAN* HIS MUSTER

THOMAS SPILMAN aged 24 in the *George* 1616

HANNA SPILMAN aged 23 in the *Bona Nova* 1620
ELIZABETH HILL borne in Virginia

SERVANTS

ROBART BROWNE aged 25 in the *Marygould* 1618
REBECCA BROWNE aged 24 in the *Southampton* 1623
THOMAS PARRISH aged 26 in the *Charity* 1622
JOHN HARRIS aged 21 in the *Jacob* 1624.

PROVISION: Corne, 16 barreles; Swine, 2; houses, 2; pallizado, 1; boate, 1.
ARMES: peeces, 10; swords, 2; Coates of male, 4; powder, 10 lb; lead, 100 ct.

OLIVER JINKINES HIS MUSTER

OLIVER JINKINES aged 30 in the *mary James* 1610
JOANE JINKINES aged 26 in the *George* 1617
ALEXANDER JINKINES borne in Virginia

PROVISION: Corne, 6 busheles. ARMES: peeces, 1; Sword, 1; lead, 10 lb.

[48]

Elzabeth
Cittie

WILLIAM GAYNE AND *ROBART NEWMAN* THEIRE MUSTER

ROBART NEWMAN aged 25 in the *Neptune* 1618
WILLIAM GAYNE aged 36 in the *Bona Nova* 1620
JOHN TAYLOR aged 34 in the *Swan* 1610
REBECCA TAYLOR aged 22 in the *Margett and John* 1623
JOHN COKER aged 20
RICHARD PACKE aged 23 in the *Warwick* 1621
ABRAHAM AVELIN aged 23 ⎫ in the *Elzabeth* 1620
ARTHUR AVELIN aged 26 ⎭

PROVISION: Corne, 10 barreles; Fish, 200 ct; houses, 1. ARMES: peeces, 5; swords,
2; Coate of male, 1; powder, 2 lb; lead, 40 lb.

THOMAS GODBY HIS MUSTER

THOMAS GODBY aged 38 in the *Delivrance* 1608
JOANE GODBY aged 42 in the *Flyinge Hart* 1621
JOHN CURTIS aged 22 in the *Flyinge Hart* 1621
CHRISTOPHER SMITH aged 23 in the *Returne* 1624

PROVISION: Corne, 7 barreles; Fish, 200 ct. ARMES: peeces, 3; Swords, 3; Armor,
1; powder, 1 lb; lead, 20 lb.

MR *EDWARD WATERS* HIS MUSTER

EDWARD WATERS aged 40 in the *Patience* 1608
GRACE WATERS aged 21 in the *Diana* 1618

WILLIAM WATERS ⎫
MARGERETT WATERS ⎭ borne in Virginia

WILLIAM HAMPTON aged 40 in the *Bona Nova* 1620
JOANE HAMPTON aged 25 in the *Abigall* 1621
THOMAS LANE aged 30 in the *Treasorer* 1613
ALICE LANE aged 24 in the *Bona Nova* 1620
THOMAS THORNEBURY aged 20 in the *George* 1616

SERVANTS

ADAM THOROGOOD aged 18 ⎫
NICCOLAS BROWNE aged 18 ⎭ in the *Charles* 1621

PAULE HARWOOD aged 20 in the *Bona Nova* 1622
STEPHEN REEDE aged 17 in the *George* 1618
MATHIAS FRANCISCO aged 18 in the *Jacob* 1624
ROBART PENRISE aged 12 in the *Bona nova* 1620

PROVISION: Corne, 37 barreles; fish, 1500 ct; houses, 4; pallizado, 1; boate, 1. ARMES: Peeces, 11; pistole, 1; swords, 6; Armors & Coates, 4; powder, 10 lb; lead, 100 lb.

CAP^T *THOMAS DAVIS* HIS MUSTER

Capt THOMAS DAVIS aged 40 in the *John and Francis* 1623
THOMAS HEWES aged 40 in the *John and Francis* 1623

PROVISION: Corne, 2 barreles; houses, 1. ARMES: peeces, 1; Murderers, 2; swords, 3; Coates of male, 3; powder, 4 lb; lead, 40 lb.

MR *FRANCIS CHAMBERLIN* HIS MUSTER

FRANCIS CHAMBERLIN aged 45 in the *Marmaducke* 1621
REBECCA CHAMBERLIN aged 37 in the *Bona Nova* 1622
FRANCIS CHAMBERLIN aged 3 borne in Virginia.

[49]

Elizabeth
Cittie

SERVANTS

JOHN FORTH aged 16 ⎫
WILLIAM WORLIDGE aged 18 ⎭ in the *Bona Nova* 1622

sionell* ROWLSTON aged 30 in *Gods Guifte* 1623
RICHARD BURTON aged 28 in the *Swan* 1624

PROVISION: Corne, 15 barreles; fish, 300 ct; house, 1. ARMES: peeces, 5; pistole, 1; swords, 6; Armors, 2; powder, 2 lb; lead, 20 lb.

PERCIVALL IBOTTSON HIS MUSTER

PERCIVALL IBOTTSON aged 24 in the *Neptune* 1618
ELZABETH IBOTTSON aged 23 in the *Flyinge Hart* 1621
JOHN DAVIS aged 24 in the *John and Francis* 1623

* Thus in the original; probably meant for LIONEL.

WILLIAM GREENE aged 28 in the *Hopewell* 1623
ROBART LOCKE aged 18 in the *Warwicke* 1621

PROVISION: Corne, 5 barreles; Meale, 1 hodghead; Fish, 500 ct; houses, 2.
ARMES: Peeces, 4; Swords, 1; powder, 1 lb; lead, 12 lb.

MR *DANNIELL COOKINS** HIS MUSTER

WILLIAM WADSWORTH aged 26
WILLIAM FOULKE aged 24
THOMAS CURTIS aged 24
PEETER SHEREWOOD aged 21

THOMAS BOULDINGE HIS MUSTER

Elizabeth Cittie

THOMAS BOULDINGE aged 40 in the *Swan* 1610
WILLIAM BOULDINGE borne in Virginia
WILLIAM COXE aged 26 in the *Godspeede* 1610
RICHARD EDWARDS aged 23 ⎱
NICCOLAS DALE aged 20 ⎰ in the *Jacob* 1624.

PROVISION: Corne, 10 barreles; Fish, 600 ct; house, 1; pallizado, 1. ARMES: peeces, 3; Armor, 1; Coate of male, 1; swords, 3; powder, 6 lb; lead, 200 lb.

REYNOLD BOOTH HIS MUSTER

REYNOLD BOOTH aged 32 in the *Hercules* 1609
ELIZABETH BOOTH aged 24 in the *Ann* 1623

GEORGE LEVETT aged 29 in the *Bona Nova* 1619
THOMAS SEYWELL aged 20 in the *Tyger* 1623

PROVISION: Corne, 10 barreles; Fish, 100 ct; house, 1. ARMES: peeces, 5; pistole, 1; Coate of male, 1; swords, 3; powd^r, 5 lb; lead, 100 lb.

THOMAS GARNETT HIS MUSTER

THOMAS GARNETT aged 40 in the *Swan* 1610
ELZABETH GARNETT aged 26 in the *Neptune* 1618
SUSAN GARNETT aged 3 borne in Virginia
AMBROSE GYFFITH aged 33 in the *Bona Nova* 1619
JOYSE GYFFITH aged 20 in the *Jacob* 1624

[50]

Elizabeth Cittie

PROVISION: Corne, 5 barreles; fish, 500 ct; house, 1; boate, 1. ARMES: peeces, 3; pistole, 1; Armor, 1; swords, 4; powd^r, 2 lb; lead, 8 lb.

* Thus in the original; usually GOOKIN.

THOMAS DUNTHORNE HIS MUSTER

THOMAS DUNTHORNE aged 27 in the *Margett and John* 1620
ELZABETH DUNTHORNE aged 38 in the *Tryall* 1610

SERVANTS

WILLIAM TOMSON aged 22 ⎫
GEORGE TURNOR aged 27 ⎬ in the *Swan* 1624
GEORGE BANCKES aged 15 ⎭
THOMAS an Indian Boaye
ELZABETH JOONES aged 30 in the *Patience* 1609
SARA JOONES aged 5 borne in Virginia

PROVISION: Corne, 15 barreles; Fish, 400 ct; houses, 2; pallizado, 1; boate, 1.
ARMES: peeces, 5; Coate of Male, 1; Sword, 1; powder, 6 lb; lead, 50 lb.

THOMAS STEPNEY HIS MUSTER

THOMAS STEPNEY aged 35 in the *Swan* 1610

PROVISION: Corne, 4 barreles; Fish, 200 ct; houses, 1. ARMES: peeces, 1; Swords, 1; powder, 4 lb; lead, 12 lb.

Elizabeth Cittie

MR *STOCKTON* HIS MUSTER

JONAS STOCKTON aged 40 in the *Bona Nova* 1620
RICHARD POPELEY aged 26 ⎫
RICHARD DAVIS aged 22 ⎬
WALTER BARRETT aged 26 ⎬ in the *Bona Nova* 1620
TIMOTHEY STOCKTON aged 14 ⎭

SERVANTS

WILLIAM DUGLAS aged 16 in the *Margett and John* 1621
JOHN WATSON aged 24 in the *Swan* 1624

PROVISION: Corne, 16 barreles; Pease, 1 barrell; house, 1. ARMES: peeces, 4; pistole, 1; Swords, 3; Armor, 1; lead, 20 lb.

TOBIAS HURST HIS MUSTER

TOBIAS HURST aged 22 in the *Treasurer* 1618

PROVISION: Corne, 12 busheles; peeces, 4.

MR *WILLIAM GANY* HIS MUSTER

WILLIAM GANY aged 33 in the *George* 1616
ANNA GANY aged 24 in the *Bona Nova* 1620

SERVANTS

ANNA GANY borne in Virginia
THOMASIN EESTER aged 26 in the *Falcon* 1617

Elizabeth Pope aged 8 in the *Abbigall* 1621
John Wright aged 20 ⎫
William Clarke aged 20 ⎪
Hather Tomson aged 18 ⎬ in the *Ambrose* 1623
Thomas Savadge aged 18 ⎭

provision: Corne, 15 barreles; Pease, 1 hoghead; Swine, 11; houses, 3; pallizado, 1. armes: Peeces, 12; pistoles, 2; swords, 6; Armors, 8; Powder, 6 lb;
lead, 100 lb.

*Elizabeth
Cittie*

ALEXANDER MOUNTNEY HIS MUSTER

Alexand.r Mountney aged 33 in the *Mary James* 1610
Lenord Mountney aged 21 in the *Bona Nova* 1620
John Walton aged 28 in the *Elzabeth* 1621
Bryan Rogers aged 18 in the *Elzabeth* 1621
John Washborne aged 25 in the *Jonathan* 1619

provision: Corne, 8 barreles; Houses, 2; Pallizado, 1. armes: peeces, 7; swords,
2; Armores, 2; powder, 5 lb; lead, 10 lb.

A list of the Burialles in Elzabeth Citty 1624.

Weston Browne Aprill. 20.
Richard Wiffe Aprell 26
John Mileman Aprell 28
John Jackson Maye 12
Edward Hill Maye 15
Peeter   Maye 16
James More June 24
M.r Tomson
Phillip Coocke July 8
Thomas Ebes July 12
M.r Chamberlins Man July 17
Sibill Morgon July 18
          Wethersby August 8
James Chamberlin August 11
M.r Fenton Minister Septemb.r 5.
William White Septemb.r 12.
James Chamberlin Septemb.r 22
Mary Downeman a Child Novemb.r 23
John Stamford Septemb.r 30
Thomas Davis
Peeter Dickenson
Richard Easte

THOMAS HUNTER
JOHN SIMNELL
HENRIE MIDDELLTON
SAMMUELL LAMBERT

[52]

JOHN BUSH.

Elzabeth
Cittie

A MUSTER OF THE INHABITENTE
OF ELZABETH CITTIE BEYOND HAMPTON RIVER.

BEINGE THE COMPANYES LAND.

CAP^T *FRANCIS WEST* HIS MUSTER

Capt FRANCIS WEST Counseler aged 36 in the *Mary Ann Margett* 1610
Mrs FRANCIS WEST Widdowe in the *Supply* 1620
NATHANIELL WEST borne in Virginia

SERVANTS

JOANE FAIRCHILD aged 20 in the *George* 1618
BENIAMIN OWIN aged 18 in the *Swan* 1623
WILLIAM PARNELL aged 18 in the *Southampton* 1622
WALTER COUPER aged 22 in the *Neptune* 1618
REINOULD GODWIN aged 30 in the *Abigall* 1620
JOHN PEDRO a Neger aged 30 in the *Swan* 1623.

PROVISION: Corne, 2 barreles; Fish, 300 ct; goates, 14; Kiddes, 18; Houses, 2; Pallizado, 1; boate, 1. ARMES: Armors, 4; peeces, 10; pistoles, 3; Swords, 6; powder 4 lb; lead, 10 lb.

CAP^T *JOHN MARTIN* HIS MUSTER

Capt JOHN MARTIN
SACKFORD WETHERELL aged 21
JOHN SMITH aged 31 } in the *Swan* 1624
JOHN HOWARD aged 24
JOHN ANTHONIE aged 23

PROVISION: Meale, 2 hogheads ½. ARMES: Armor, 1; Targett,* 1; peeces, 5; Machcockes, 11; powder, 20 lb; Lead, 500 lb; Roules of Macht†, 4.

GEORGE MEDCALFE HIS MUSTER

GEORGE MEDCALFE aged 46
SARA MEDCALFE aged 30 in the *Hopewell* 1624
JOANE A Child.

* *target*. [Old French *targette*, later *targuete*, diminutive of *targue*, *targe*.] A kind of small shield or buckler, especially one of circular form.
† *Rouleaus of matches*. Literally, little rolls of matches.

PROVISION: Corne, 3 barrels; Fish, 200 ct; house. ARMES: peeces, 2; powder, 1 lb; lead, 10 lb.

EDWARD JOHNSON HIS MUSTER

EDWARD JOHNSON aged 26 in the *Abigall* 1621
in the *Bona Nova* 1621
A Child borne in Virginia

PROVISION: Corne, 4 barreles. ARMES: peece, 1; powder, 4 lb; lead, 30 lb; house, 1; Stores, 2; Ordnance Mounted, 2.

JOHN LAUCKFILD HIS MUSTER

JOHN LAUCKFILD aged 24 in the *Bona Nova* 1621
ALICE LAUCKFILD aged 24 in the *Abbigall* 1621
SAMMUELL KENNELL aged 30 in the *Abigall* 1621

PROVISION: Corne, 7 barreles; Fish, 200 ct. ARMES: peeces, 4; Swords, 2; powder, 2 lb; lead, 20 lb; house, 1.

WILLIAM FOWLER HIS MUSTER

WILLIAM FOWLER aged 30 in the *Abigall* 1621
MARGRETT FOWLER aged 30 in the *Abigall* 1621

PROVISION: Corne, 3 barreles; Fish, 50; house, 1. ARMES: peeces, 2; powder, 1 lb; lead, 6 lb.

[53]

Elzabeth Cittie

WALTER ELY HIS MUSTER

WALTER ELY
ELZABETH ELY aged 30 in the *Warwicke* 1622
ANN ELY borne in Virginia

PROVISION: Corne, 4 barrels; Fish, 900 ct. ARMES: peeces, 1; lead, 30 lb; house, 1.

WILLIAM TILER HIS MUSTER

WILLIAM TILER in the *Francis Bonaventure* 1620
ELIZABETH TILER in the *Francis Bonaventure* 1620

SERVANTS

ROBART MORE aged 50 in the *Providence* 1622
WILLIAM BROWNE aged 26 in the *Providence* 1622
ROBART TODD aged 20 in the *Hopewell* 1622
ANTHONIE BURT aged 18 in the *Hopewell* 1622
SAMIELL BENNETT aged 40 in the *Providence* 1622
JOANE BENNETT in the *providence* 1622

PROVISION: Corne, 17 barreles; Meale, 1 hoghead; Fish, 300. ARMES: peeces, 9; Coates, 3; swords, 4; powder, 3 lb; lead, 50 lb. CATTELL: Milch Cowes, 4; Bull, 1; Piges, 3; house, 1; Sowes, 2.

THOMAS FLYNT HIS MUSTER

Elzabeth THOMAS FLYNT in the *Diana* 1618
Cittie THOMAS MERRES aged 21 in the *Francis Bonaventure* 1620
HENRIE WHEELER aged 20 in the *Tryall* 1620.
JOHN BROCKE aged 19 in the *Bona Nova* 1619
JAMES BROOKES aged 19 in the *Jonathan* 1619
ROBART SAVADGE aged 18 in the *Elzabeth* 1621.

PROVISION: Corne, 8 barreles. ARMES: peeces, 8; Armors, 2; powder, 10 lb; lead, 20 lb; house, 1; Store, 1.

JOHN WARD HIS MUSTER

JOHN WARD in the *Elzabeth* 1621
ADAM RIMWELL aged 24 in the *Bona Nova* 1619
CHRISTOPHER WYNWILL aged 26 in the *Bona Nova* 1619
OLIVER JENKIN aged 40
JOANE JENKIN & a littell Child
HENRIE POTTER aged 50
ANN POTTER in the *London Marchant*
ROBART GOODMAN aged 24 in the *Bona Nova* 1619

PROVISION: Corne, 20 barreles; Fish, 500 ct. ARMES: peeces, 8; Armors, 2; powder, 8 lb; lead, 20 lb; houses, 2; stores, 2.

[54]

GREGORIE DORIE HIS MUSTER

Elzabeth GREGORIE DORIE aged 36 in the *Bona Nova* 1620.
Cittie his wiffe & a littell Child borne in Virginia

PROVISION: Corne, 5 barreles. ARMES: peeces, 2; powder, 1 lb; lead, 10; Armor, 1; house, 1; pallizado, 1.

JOHN MORE HIS MUSTER

JOHN MORE aged 36 in the *Bona Nova* 1620
ELIZABETH MORE in the *Abigall* 1622.

PROVISION: Corne, 3 barreles; Fish, 400 ct. ARMES: peeces, 3; powder, 2 lb; lead, 16 lb; house, 1; pallizado, 1; Store, 1.

SARGENT *WILLIAM BARRY* HIS MUSTER

WILLIAM BARRY in the *Bona Nova* 1619

SERVANTS

RICHARD FRISBIE aged 34 in the *Jonathan* 1619
WILLIAM ROOKINS aged 26 in the *Bona Nova* 1619
JOSEPH HATTFILD aged 24 in the *Bona Nova* 1619

CUTBERT SEIRSON aged 22 in the *Bona Nova* 1619
JOHN GIBBES aged 24 in the *Abigall* 1621
FRANCIS HILL aged 22 in the *Bona Nova* 1619
JOHN VAGHAN aged 23 in the *Bona Nova* 1619
EDWARD MARSHALL aged 26 in the *Abigall* 1621
WILLIAM JOYCE aged 26 in the *Abigall* 1621
WILLIAM EVANDS aged 23 in the *Bona Nova* 1619
RALPH OSBORNE aged 22 in the *Bona Nova* 1619
MORRIS STANLEY aged 26 in the *hopewell* 1624
NICCOLAS WEASELL aged 28 in the *Abigall* 1621
STEPHEN DICKSON aged 25 in the *Bona Nova* 1619
THOMAS CALDER aged 24 in the *Bona Nova* 1619

PROVISION: Corne, 80 barreles. ARMES: peeces, 10; Armores, 3; powder, 10 lb; lead, 20 lb; houses, 2; Stores, 6.

WILLIAM HAMPTON HIS MUSTER

Elzabeth Cittie

WILLIAM HAMPTON age 34 in the *Bona Nova* 1621
JOANE HAMPTON
JOHN ARNDELL age 22 in the *Abigall* 1621

PROVISION: Corne, 5 barreles; Fish, 200 ct. ARMES: peeces, 8; powder, 1 lb; lead, 20 lb; house, 1.

ANTHONIE BONALL HIS MUSTER

ANTHONIE BONALL age 42 ⎫
ELIAS LEGARDO age 38 ⎬ in the *Abigall* 1621
ROBART WRIGHT age 45 in the *Swan* 1608
JOANE WRIGHT and two Children borne in virginia
WILLIAM BINSLEY age 18 in the *Jacob* 1624
ROBART GODWIN age 19 in the *Swan* 1624

PROVISION: Corne, 5 barreles. ARMES: peeces, 6; swords, 4; powder, 2 lb; lead, 6 lb; house, 1; pallizado, 1; Stores, 3.

VIRBRITT ⎫
OBLE HERO ⎬ two frenchmen in the *Abigall* 1622

PROVISION: Corne, 10 barreles; Fish, 100 ct. ARMES: peeces, 2; Armores, 2; sword, 1; lead, 20 lb; house, 1.

ROBART THRASHER HIS MUSTER

[55]

Elzabeth Cittie

ROBART THRASHER age 22 in the *Bona Nova* 1620
ROLAND WILLIAMES age 20 in the *Jonathan* 1623.

SERVANT

JOHN SACKER age 20 in the *Marget and John* 1623

PROVISION: Corne, 8 barrels. ARMES: peeces, 4; Armor, 1; sword, 1; powder, 2 lb; lead, 10 lb; house, 1.

JOHN HANEY age 27 in the *Margett and John* 1621
ELZABETH HANIE in the *Abigall* 1622
NICHOLAS ROWE in the *Elzabeth* 1621
MARY ROWE in the London *Marchant* 1620

SERVANTS

THOMAS MORELAND ⎫
RALPH HOODE ⎭ age 19 in the *Abigall* 1621

PROVISION: Corne, 9 barreles; Fish, 100 ct. ARMES: Peeces, 3; Armor, 1; Swords, 2; powder, 1 lb; lead, 3 lb; house, 1; pallizado, 1; Stores, 3.

A list of the DEAD beyond Hampton River

of Mr BONALES Servant, 1
Mr DOWSE his men, 2
Mr PEETER ARNDELL

A MUSTER OF THE INHABITANCE OF THE EASTERNE SHORE OVER THE BAYE.

Capt WILLIAM EPES his Muster. (in the *William and Thomas*)
MARGRETT EPES in the *George* 1621

SERVANTS

NICCHOLAS RAYNBERD age 22 in the *Swan* 1624
WILLIAM BURDITT age 25 in the *Susan* 1615
THOMAS CORNISH age 25 in the *Dutie* 1620
PEETER PORTER age 19 in the *Tiger* 1621
JOHN BAKER age 20 in the *Ann* 1623
EDWARD ROGERS age 26 in the *Ann* 1623
THOMAS WARDEN age 24 in the *Ann* 1623
BENIAMINE KNIGHT age 28 in the *Bona Nova* 1620
NICCOLAS GRANGER age 15 in the *George* 1618
WILLIAM MUNNES age 25 in the *Sampson* 1619
HENRIE WILSON age 24 in the *Sampson* 1619
JAMES BLACKBORNE age 20 in the *Sampson* 1619
NICHOLAS SUMERFILD age 15 in the *Sampson* 1619

PROVISION: Corne, 65 barreles; hoges, 2. ARMES: powder, 120 lb; lead, 200 lb; peeces, 5; Armores, 6; Coates of steele, 6; Coates of Male, 4; houses, 2; forte, 1; Stores, 3; shallop*, 1.

* shallop. A light open boat, used chiefly on rivers, propelled by oars or sails or by both.

CAP^T *JOHN WILLCOCKES* HIS MUSTER

Capt JOHN WILLCOCKES in the *Bona Nova* 1620
HENRIE CHARLTON age 19 in the *George* 1623

[*56*]

*Easterne
shore*

   PROVISION: Corne, 28 barreles. ARMES: peeces, 5; Armores, 4; powder, 4 lb; lead, 82 lb; house, 1; Store, 1; boate, 1.

ANCIENT *THOMAS SAVAGE* HIS MUSTER

THOMAS SAVAGE in the *John and Francis* 1607
ANN SAVAGE in the *Sea Flower* 1621

SERVANTS

JOHN WASHBORNE age 30 in the *Jonathan* 1620
THOMAS BELSON age 12

   PROVISION: Corne, 9 barreles. ARMES: powder, 4 lb; Shott, 20 lb; peeces, 2; pistole, 1; Armores, 3; sword, 1; House, 1; Store, 1; boate, 1.

CAP^T THŌ: *GRAVES* HIS MUSTER

Capt THOMAS GRAVES in the *Mary and Margrett* 1607

   PROVISION: Corne, 4 barreles. ARMES: powder, 4 lb; shott, 45 lb; house, 1; Store, 1.

WALTER SCOTT HIS MUSTER

WALTER SCOTT in the *Hercules* 1618
APPHIA SCOTT in the *Gift* 1618
PERCIS SCOTT borne in Virginia

   PROVISION: Corne, 6 barreles. ARMES: peeces, 2; swords, 2; house, 1.

THOMAS POWELL HIS MUSTER

*Easterne
shore*

THOMAS POWELL in the *Samson* 1618

   PROVISION: Corne, 15 barreles. ARMES: peece, 1; powder, ¼ lb; lead, 1 lb; house, 1; Store, 1.

WILLIAM SMITH HIS MUSTER

WILLIAM SMITH age 26 in the *Samson* 1618

   PROVISION: Corne, 8 barreles ½. ARMES: peece, 1; house, 1; store, 1.

EDWARD DREWE HIS MUSTER

EDWARD DREWE age 22 in the *Samson* 1618

   PROVISION: Corne, 8 barreles. ARMES: lead, 2 lb; peeces, 4; house, 1; Store, 1.

CHARLES HARMAN HIS MUSTER

CHARLES HARMAN age 24 in the *Furtherance* 1622
JOHN ASKUME age 22 in the ⎫
ROBERT FENNELL age 20 in the ⎬ *Charles* 1624
JAMES KNOTT age 23 in the *George* 1617

   PROVISION: Corne, 24 barreles. ARMES: peeces, 6; powder, 10 lb; Shott, 200 lb; houses, 2; Store, 1; boate, 1.

[57]

Easterne shore

NICHOLAS HODGSKINS HIS MUSTER

NICHOLAS HODGSKINES age 27 in the *Edwin* 1616
TEMPORANCE HODGSKINES in the *Jonathan* 1620
MARGRETT HODGSKINS borne in Virginia

   PROVISION: Corne, 8 barreles; house, 1; Store, 1.

SOLLOMAN GREENE HIS MUSTER

SOLLOMAN GREENE age 27 in the *Diana* 1618

   PROVISION: house, 1; Store, 1.

THOMAS GASKOYNE HIS MUSTER

THOMAS GASKOYNE age 34 in the *Bona Nova* 1619

   PROVISION: Corne, 3 barreles.

WILLIAM ANDROS at the age of 25 in the *Treasuror* 1617
DANNIELL CUGLEY age 28 in the *London Marchant* 1620

   PROVISION: Corne, 15 barreles. ARMES: powder, 4 lb; shott, 45 lb; house, 1; Store, 1.

JOHN BLORE HIS MUSTER

JOHN BLORE age 27 in the *Star* 1610
FRANCIS BLORE age 25 in the *London Marchant* 1620

SERVANTS

JOHN PARRAMORE age 17 in the *Bona Venture* 1622
JOHN WILKINES

   PROVISION: Corne, 15 barreles. ARMES: powder, 2 lb; lead, 30 lb; peeces, 2; Armor, 1; house, 1; Store, 1; boate, 1.

Easterne shore

ROBART BALL HIS MUSTER

ROBART BALL age 27 in the *London Marchant* 1619

   PROVISION: Corne, 3 barreles. ARMES: peece, 1; powder, 1 lb; shott, 1 lb; Armor, 1; house, 1.

WILLIAM BIBBIE HIS MUSTER

WILLIAM BIBBIE age 22 in the *Swan* 1621*
THOMAS SPARKES age 24 in the *Susan* 1616
   PROVISION: Corne, 15 barreles. ARMES: peece, 1; house, 1; Store, 1.

JOHN HOME HIS MUSTER

JOHN HOME age 25 in the *Margerett and John* 1621
   PROVISION: Corne, 5 barreles. ARMES: peeces, 2; Armores, 2; powder, 5 lb;
shott, 20 lb; house, 1; Store, 1.

JOHN WILKINES HIS MUSTER

JOHN WILKINES age 26 in the *Mary gould* 1618
BRIGGETT WILKINES age 20 in the *Warwicke* 1621
   PROVISION: Corne, 7 barreles. ARMES: peeces, 1; house, 1.

[58]

*Easterne
shore*

PERREGRIM WATKINES HIS MUSTER

PERREGRIM WATKINES age 24 in the *George* 1621
   PROVISION: Corne, 2 barreles. ARMES: Armor, 1.

WILLIAM DAVIS HIS MUSTER

WILLIAM DAVIS age 33 in the *William and Thomas* 1618
   PROVISION: Corne, 8 barreles. ARMES: peece, 1; house, 1; Store, 1.

DEAD in this plantation 1624

THOMAS HELCOTT
JOHN WILKINES

* An o marked over with the numeral 1 makes this date uncertain. It may be either
1620 or 1621.

*Adventurers of Purse and Person
and Their Families*

ANDREWS[1]

*1. WILLIAM[1] ANDREWS sailed for Virginia from Gravesend, England, 21 March 1616/7, aboard the *Treasurer*, with Capt. Samuel Argall, returning to the colony as Lieutenant-Governor, in command. The ship reached Virginia 25 May 1617 and by 1623/4 when he was listed in the census[2] Andrews had settled on the Eastern Shore where he was also listed, as William Andros, in the muster, 1624/5. On 7 March 1623/4 he made a deposition as aged about 25 or 26.[3] He was mentioned in his patent for 100 acres, 14 March 1628/9, as a "Planter of Accomack".[4] A patent, 25 June 1635, for 100 acres on Old Plantation Creek was "due him by order of the Court 9 October 1627" and a patent, same date, for 200 acres recited that 50 of the aforesaid acres were for the "personal adventure of his wife Susanna Andrews"[5] On 30 April 1644 along with Stephen Charlton he was appointed commander of the district from Nassawattocks to Hungars.[6] As Capt. William Andrews he was appointed, 9 Oct. 1651, to command the military district of Hungars Creek[7] and he was later major of militia[8] and lieutenant colonel at the time of his death. He served as one of the commissioners of Northampton County, 1633-54,[9] and was high sheriff, 1655.[10]

William[1] Andrews married (1) Susanna ___ and (2), by Jan. 1653/4, Mary Stringer,[11] sister of Stephen Stringer, who married (2), by 20 June 1657, William Smart[12] and died before 19 Feb. 1659/60.[13] The will of William Andrews "of Hungars in the county of Northampton," 20 Feb. 1654/5-28 Feb. 1655/6, named his wife Mary, four sons, a married daughter, and directed that

---

[1] Martha Woodroof Hiden, "Notes on Andrews and Allied Families," *W*(2) VIII, pp. 36-41; Stratton Nottingham, "Andrews-Corrections and Additions," *W*(2) X, pp. 181-83.

[2] Hotten, p. 188.

[3] *MCGC*, p. 11.

[4] Patent Bk. 1, p. 71; *CP* I, p. 13; *MCGC*, pp. 154, 188.

[5] Patent Bk. 1, pp. 181-82.

[6] Northampton Co. Orders, Deeds, Wills &c 2, 1640-45, p. 194.

[7] Northampton Co. Deeds, Wills &c 4, 1651-54, p. 47.

[8] *H* I, p. 384.

[9] *Ibid.*; Northampton Co. Orders, Deeds, Wills &c 1, 1632-40, transcript, p. 8.

[10] Jean M. Mihalyka, *Loose Papers and Sundry Court Cases, 1628-1731, Northampton County, Virginia*, I (Eastville, Va., 1997), p. 1.

[11] Northampton Co. Deeds, Wills &c 4, 1651-54, p. 190.

[12] Northampton Co. Deeds, Wills &c 7, p. 70.

[13] Northampton Co. Deeds, Wills &c 1657-66, p. 42.

his minor daughters be of age at sixteen or marriage.[14]

Issue: (by 1) 2. WILLIAM[2]; 3. Robert[2], whose undated will, proved 30 March 1657,[15] left to his wife (name not given) for her lifetime, with reversion to his nephews William[3] and Obedience[3] Andrews, 500 acres on Nandua Creek which had been bequeathed to him by his father,[16] and also made bequest to his sister Susanna Stringer (or her child when she had one), married 3. *Rebecca*[2] *Bagwell* (see BAGWELL), who married (2), shortly after 20 April 1657,[17] 3. *Stephen*[2] *Fisher* (see FISHER); 4. SUSANNA[2]; (by 2)[18] 5. Mary[2], placed under the care of Lt. Col. John Stringer after her mother's death; 6. John[2], died before 4 April 1678;[19] 7. ANDREW[2]; 8. Ann[2], placed under the care of Thomas Harmanson after her mother's death.

2. WILLIAM[2] ANDREWS (William[1]) as Lt. William Andrews was appointed sheriff of Northampton County, 3 April 1655.[20] He deposed, as Capt. William Andrews, 30 Dec. 1662, that he was aged 30 and upwards.[21] He was commissioned justice of Northampton County 10 March 1656/7,[22] was major of militia, and a member of the House of Burgesses, 1663-64.[23]

He married (1), 17 Jan. 1651/2, Elizabeth Travellor, daughter of George and Alisha Travellor,[24] and (2), before 24 July 1673,[25] 4. *Dorothea*[2] *(Robins) Evelyn* (see EVELYN and O'NEAL-ROBINS), who was living 2 Nov. 1682 and deceased by 2 March 1682/3.[26] Administration on her estate was granted to William[3] Andrews, 29 March 1683, on behalf of his brothers and sisters.[27]

His will, 24 July 1673-28 Aug. 1673,[28] mentions "the plantation I now dwell on ... bounded ... by Old Plantation Creeke" and named his brothers-in-law

---

[14] Northampton Co. Deeds & Wills 5, 1654-55, p. 85.

[15] Northampton Co. Deeds, Wills &c 7, p. 44.

[16] *ES* I, p. 664.

[17] Northampton Co. Deeds, Wills &c 7, p. 48.

[18] Northampton Co. Deeds, Wills &c 1657-66, p. 42.

[19] Patent Bk. 6, p. 639; *ES* I, p. 414.

[20] Northampton Co. Deeds, Wills &c 5, 1654-55, p. 52; Deeds & Wills 6, p. 18.

[21] Northampton Co. Order Bk. 1657-66, p. 133.

[22] Northampton Co. Deeds, Wills &c 5, 1654-55, p. 137.

[23] *MCGC*, p. 213; Leonard, p. 39.

[24] Northampton Co. Deeds, Wills &c 5, 1654-55, p. 47.

[25] Northampton Co. Prders, Wills &c 10, 1774-79, p. 210.

[26] Northampton Co. Wills & Orders 13, 1678-83, pp. 245, 285.

[27] Northampton Co. Order Bk. 11, 1678-83, p. 293.

[28] Northampton Co. Order Bk. 10, 1664-74, pp. 210-12.

William Waters and John Robins as executors, his son-in-law [step-son] George Evelyn, and

Issue: (by 1) 9. ELISHEBA[3]; 10. Elizabeth[3], born 1 Jan. 1664/5;[29] (by 2) 11. WILLIAM[3]; 12. Obedience[3], who deposed, 28 Jan. 1683/4, he was aged 23,[30] acknowledged, 21 March 1692/3, to John Shepherd the sale of land which he purchased 9 Oct. 1685 from his brother William and which had been given "by my grandfather Lt. Coll. William Andrews Deceased to my Uncle Robert Andrews dec'd:";[31] 13. John[3], who gave receipt, 28 July 1685, to his brother William for his part of his mother's estate,[32] left will 7 April 1688-28 May 1688,[33] and died without issue; 14. ROBERT[3]; 15. GRACE[3]; 16. SUSANNA[3].

4. SUSANNA[2] ANDREWS (William[1]) married (1) Stephen Stringer who died by 29 Jan. 1655/6 without issue,[34] and (2) ___.

Issue: (by 2) 17. (CHILD)[3].

7. ANDREW[2] ANDREWS (William[1]), on whose estate administration was granted 28 May 1688 to his widow,[35] married Elizabeth Johnson, who married (2) Isaac Haggoman.[36] Haggoman deposed 29 March 1682 that he was aged 22[37] and resided in Accomack County, 1702.[38]

Issue: 18 JOHN[3]; 19. ANDREW[3]; 20. William[3], died 28 Jan. 1711/2,[39] left nuncuptive will, 24 Jan. 1711/2-19 Feb. 1711/2, giving his estate to his brother Andrew;[40] 21. Temperance[3]; 22. Mary[3], gave discharge to her "father-in-law" Isaac Haggaman for her part of the estate of her father Andrew Andrews, 9 Oct. 1702.[41]

9. ELISHEBA[3] ANDREWS (William[2], William[1]), to whom her father

---

[29] Northampton Co. Orders, Deeds, Wills &c 5, 1654-55, p. 67, deed of gift of a yearling cow calf by William Hinsley to the "youngest Daught[r] of M[r] W[m] Andrewes Junior."

[30] Northampton Co. Order Bk. 9, p. 56.

[31] Accomack Co. Deeds, Wills &c 1692-1715, p. 8.

[32] Northampton Co. Order Bk. 12, 1683-89, pp. 153-54.

[33] *Ibid.*, pp. 369-70.

[34] Northampton Co. Deeds, Wills &c 5, 1654-55, p. 128. Capt. John Stringer released any claim as heir of his brother.

[35] Northampton Co. Order Bk. 12, p. 357.

[36] Northampton Co. Order Bk. 14, p. 61.

[37] Northampton Co. Order Bk. 11, p. 218.

[38] Northampton Co. Order Bk. 14, p. 109.

[39] Northampton Co. Order Bk. 15, 1710-11, p. 53.

[40] Northampton Co. Wills, Deeds &c 1711-18, p. 19.

[41] Northampton Co. Deeds & Wills 12, 1692-1707, p. 327.

conveyed a heifer, 6 June 1655,[42] married, before 1670,[43] Peter Reverdy, alias Greene, who was engaged in salt making with Col. John Custis, 1668.[44] She and her husband were given land by her grandmother, Alisha (____) Travellor Burdette Walker Custis, 29 Jan. 1676/7, and sold it the same day.[45]

Issue: [REVERDY] 23. Katherine[4], named in the will of her grandfather.

10. WILLIAM[3] ANDREWS (William[2], William[1]), planter of Accomack County, 1692,[46] owned 300 acres there in 1704. He married, probably (1) ___.[47] (2) Comfort Haggoman,[48] daughter of John and Margaret (___) Haggoman,[49] and probably (3), by 3 June 1718,[50] Ann ___, widow of Thomas Ward.

Issue: (probably by 1)[51] 24. MARCUS[4]; 25. WILLIAM[4]; (by 2) 26. Margaret[4], named in the will of her uncle John Haggoman; 27. NATHANIEL[4]; 28. ISAAC[4]; 29. Dorothy[4], named in will of brother Nathaniel[4], married John Hastings on whose estate she relinquished administration 25 Sept. 1739.[52]

14. ROBERT[3] ANDREWS (William[2], William[1]) deposed 2 April 1688 that he was aged 21.[53] He owned 300 acres in Northampton County and 500 acres in Accomack County, 1704, married, by 28 July 1696, Elizabeth Sheppard, daughter of John and Elizabeth (Jordan) Sheppard,[54] and left will 23 June

---

[42] Northampton Co. Orders. Deeds. Wills &c 5, 1654-55, p. 47.

[43] *ES* I, pp. 133, 141.

[44] *Ibid.*, p. 90; Northampton Co. Deeds, Wills &c 1666-68, p. 23.

[45] Northampton Co. Deeds &c 1668-80, pp. 135-38.

[46] Accomack Co. Wills, Orders &c 1682-97, pp. 239-40.

[47] Possibly daughter of Daniel Howard, the "predecessor" of 24. Marcus[4] in ownership of 100 acres which Marcus sold, 1720 (see note 75). Although Comfort (Haggoman) Andrews had a brother Marcus Haggoman, which might suggest that 24. Marcus[4] and 25. William[4] were her children, such a conclusion is precluded by 28. Isaac's inheritance as heir at law of his niece 56. Elizabeth[5] Andrews.

[48] Northampton Co. Orders & Wills 12, 1683-89, pp. 373-75.

[49] Northampton Co. Orders 10, 1664-74, p. 158, will of John Hagamond, 10 Oct. 1672-28 Nov. 1672; Orders & Wills 12, 1683-89, pp. 373-75, will of John Haggaman [Jr.], 3 May 1688-28 May 1688.

[50] Accomack Co. Orders 1717-19, p. 12.

[51] The children of his (1) marriage are identified circumstantially on the basis of onomastics and association.

[52] Accomack Co. Order Bk. 1737-44, p. 192.

[53] Accomack Co. Wills, Orders &c 1682-97, p. 134.

[54] Northampton Co. Deeds & Wills 1692-1707, pp. 91-93; Accomack Co. Wills &c 1692-1715, p. 482.

1718-16 Sept. 1718.[55]

Issue: 30. JOHN[4]; 31. ROBERT[4]; 32. JACOB[4]; 33. Nathaniel[4], left will 31 Dec. 1739-12 Feb. 1739/40;[56] 34. Southey[4], under 14 in 1718; 35. Sarah[4], under 16 in 1718, married (1) 23. *Thomas[4] Gascoigne* (see FISHER) and (2) John Coombe; 36. Rachel[4], under 14 in 1718, living 1739, married ___ Gascoigne.[57]

15. GRACE[3] ANDREWS (William[2], William[1]) married (1) Thomas Harmanson, Jr., who deposed, 5 Nov. 1680, he was aged 21 and, 29 Dec. 1686, he was aged 26,[58] owned 400 acres in Northampton County, 1704, and left will 31 March 1709-28 May 1709.[59]

She married (2), (bond 19) March 1709/10, William Rabyshaw,[60] who left will 26 Feb. 1727/8-10 April 1728.[61]

Issue:[62] (by 1) [HARMANSON] 37. Thomas[4], married 14. *Elizabeth[3] Robins* (see O'NEAL-ROBINS); 38. ELISHE[4].

16. SUSANNA[3] ANDREWS (William[2], William[1]) married (1) 12. *Nathaniel[4] Littleton* (see SOUTHEY-HARMAR-LITTLETON), who died 1703, and (2) Stephen Maxfield, the inventory of whose estate was returned 18 April 1711 by Southey[4] Littleton, administrator.[63] She left will 22 Dec. 1710-20 March 1710/l.[64]

Issue: (by 1) [LITTLETON] 39. Southey[4], left will 31 Dec. 1712-17 Feb. 1712/3,[65] married Mary Eyre, daughter of Daniel and Anne (___) Eyre, who married (2) Edward Mifflin and left will 18 June 1772-28 March 1775;[66] 40. Esther[4], married 19. *Thomas[4] Savage* (see SAVAGE); 41. Sarah Custis[4],

---

[55] Northampton Co. Wills & Deeds 1711-18, pp. 152-54.

[56] Northampton Co. Wills & Inventories 18, pp. 332-33.

[57] Did she marry 44. *Harmanson[4] Gascoigne* (see FISHER)?

[58] Northampton Co. Order Bk. 11, 1678-83, p. 110; Order Bk. 12, 1683-89, p. 261.

[59] Northampton Co. Will Bk. 19, pp. 40-43.

[60] Jean M. Mihalyka, *Marriages, Northampton County, Virginia, 1660/1-1854* (Bowie, Md., 1990), p. 87.

[61] Northampton Co. Wills, Deeds &c 26, p. 113.

[62] Also named in will of grandfather Thomas Harmanson, 26 March 1696-28 Nov. 1702 (Northampton Co. Order Bk. 14, pp. 112-19).

[63] Northampton Co. Order Bk. 15, p. 14.

[64] Northampton Co. Will Bk. 19, pp. 222-23.

[65] Northampton Co. Wills, Deeds &c 1711-18, pp. 40-41.

[66] *ES* I, p. 678; Accomack Co. Wills &c 1772-77, p. 312.

married ___ King;[67] (by 2) [MAXFIELD] 42. JOSEPH[4].

17. ____[3] (Susanna[2] Andrews, William[1]), son or daughter and surname undetermined, married ___.

Issue: [surname undetermined] 43. MARGARET[4].

18. JOHN[3] ANDREWS (Andrew[2], William[1]) chose Col. John Custis as his guardian, 29 May 1700,[68] and was of age by 1 March 1702/3.[69] He sold to his brother Andrew[3], 6 Aug. 1703, 100 acres of the land inherited from his father and disposed of the remaining 500 acres and 50 acres of marsh land to Andrew Hamilton, 29 May 1704.[70] He died before 4 Dec. 1716 when Nathaniel Broad, his administrator, returned the inventory of his estate.[71] He married ___.

Issue: 44. ANDREW[4].

19. ANDREW[3] ANDREWS (Andrew[2], William[1]) owned 100 acres in Northampton County, 1704, which he sold to Joseph Dolby, 1709.[72] He married Eleanor Waterfield, daughter of William Waterfield,[73] and left will 18 July 1728-10 Sept. 1728.[74]

Issue: 45. WILLIAM[4]; 46. ANDREW[4]; 47. JOHN[4].

24 MARCUS[4] ANDREWS (William[3], William[2], William[1]), planter of Accomack County when he sold, 29 Aug. 1720, 100 acres where he lived to 30. John[4] Andrews,[75] purchased 244 acres, "Raccoon Point" in Dorchester Co., Md., 26 Jan. 1722,[76] and left will 24 April 1750-9 May 1750.[77] He married Rebeckah ___, who died after 8 Oct. 1757 when she conveyed to her son Marcus[5] all her goods and chattles at her death.[78]

Issue: 48. Sarah[5]; 49. Daniel[5]; 50. Rebeckah[5]; 51. Nathaniel[5]; 52. Marcus[5];

---

[67] Northampton Co. Deeds, Wills &c 1718-25, p. 81, will of Sarah Custis, 14 April 1720-17 May 1720.

[68] Northampton Co. Orders, Wills &c 14, 1698-1714., p. 40.

[69] *Ibid.*, p. 128.

[70] Northampton Co. Deeds & Wills 12, 1692-1707, pp. 338, 396.

[71] Accomack Co. Orders 1714-17, p. 26.

[72] Northampton Co. Deeds & Wills 19, 1708-17, pp. 117-19.

[73] Northampton Co. Wills &c 23, 1718-25, p. 74, will of William Waterfield, 12 April 1720-17 May 1720.

[74] Northampton Co. Wills, Deeds &c 26, p. 155.

[75] Accomack Co. Deeds, Wills &c 1715-29, p. 119.

[76] Dorchester Co., Md., Old Deed Bk. 2, p. 148. He and Rebecca sold half of this tract 27 Sept. 1732 (Dorchester Co., Md., Old Deed Bk. 9, p. 13).

[77] Maryland Prerogative Court Wills 27, p. 383.

[78] Dorchester Co., Md., Old Deed Bk. 15, p. 520.

53. Isaac[5].

25. WILLIAM[4] ANDREWS (William[3], William[2], William[1]) took oaths as justice of Accomack County, 4 July 1732,[79] and left will 24 Sept. 1763-29 Nov. 1763.[80] He married between 5 April 1720 and 1732 Mary (Selby) Gore, daughter of Daniel and Mary (Parker) Selby and widow of Daniel Gore,[81] who left will 13 March 1764-24 April 1764.[82]

Issue: 54. WILLIAM[5]; 55. LEAH[5].

27. NATHANIEL[4] ANDREWS (William[3], William[2], William[1]), named in the wills of his uncles John[3] Andrews and John Haggoman, left will 16 Feb, 1720/1-2 May 1721.[83] He married Elizabeth, widow of Robert Pitt and daughter of Dennis and Elizabeth Morris.[84]

Issue:[85] 56. Elizabeth[5], under 16 in 1721, died unmarried.

28. ISAAC[4] ANDREWS (William[3], William[2], William[1]) was of Dorchester Co., Md., by 1732, when he sold the land inherited on the death of his brother Nathaniel's daughter[86] and deposed, 1743, that he was aged about 40.[87] He married Mary Stanaway[88] and left will 20 Dec. 1757-6 Jan. 1758.[89]

Issue: 57. Joseph[5]; 58. STEPHEN[5]; 59. Mary[5]; 60. BETTEY[5].

30. JOHN[4] ANDREWS (Robert[3], William[2], William[1]) moved to Somerset Co., Md., and died before 10 Nov. 1741 when administration of his estate was granted to his widow.[90] He married Rebecca Peale, daughter of Thomas Peale of Worcester Co., Md.[91]

---

[79] Accomack Co. Orders 1731-36, p. 32.

[80] Accomack Co. Wills 1761-67, p. 225.

[81] *ES* II, pp. 1196-97; will of Daniel Gore, Accomack Co. Wills, Deeds &c 1715-1729, pt. 1, p. 252; Donna Valley Russell, *Selby Families of Colonial America* (Middletown, Md., 1990), p. 37.

[82] Accomack Co. Wills 1761-67, p. 268.

[83] Accomack Co. Wills, Deeds &c 1715-29, p. 333.

[84] Accomack Co. Wills 1692-1715, pp. 327, 623.

[85] *ES* II, p. 1264.

[86] *Ibid.*

[87] Dorchester Co., Md., Old Deed Bk. 12, p. 167.

[88] Andrews Bible, in Nellie M. Marshall, *Bible Records of Dorchester County, Maryland, 1612-1969* (Cambridge, Md., 1971), pp. 8-9.

[89] Maryland Prerogative Court Wills 30, p. 468.

[90] Northampton Co. Order Bk. 20, 1732-42, p. 461.

[91] Maryland Prerogative Court Wills 23, p. 526, will of Thomas Peale, 13 Feb. 1742-7 June 1744.

Issue: 61. John[5], taxpayer, Pocomoke Hundred, Somerset Co., Md., 1730-40; 62. ROBERTSON[5]; 63. Peale[5], taxpayer, Pocomoke Hundred, 1733-40, died by 8 Feb. 1757 when administration on his estate was granted to widow Tabitha ___,[92] who married (2), by 14 May 1766, Benjamin Kipp.[93]

31. ROBERT[4] ANDREWS (Robert[3], William[2], William[1]) was bequeathed land at Nandua and died intestate before 27 March 1750.[94] He married Elizabeth ___, who died intestate before 30 April 1751.[95]

Issue: 64. Susanna[5], named in the division of her father's estate, returned 30 July 1751;[96] 65. WILLIAM[5].

32. JACOB[4] ANDREWS (Robert[3], William[2], William[1]) was born 8 Nov. 1701, died 21 Feb. 1770,[97] and left will 15 Feb. 1770-24 April 1770.[98] He was bequeathed land at Nandua provided he make over his right to a piece of land given him by his grandfather Sheppard.[99] He married, (bond 19) Aug. 1752,[100] Margaret Joyne, born 11 Nov. 1724, died 29 Sept. 1784,[101] who left will 28 April 1784-1 Dec. 1784.[102]

Issue: 66. SARAH[5].

38. ELISHE[4] HARMANSON (Grace[3] Andrews, William[2], William[1]) left will 15 March 1744/5-9 April 1745.[103] She married (1) Jacob Stringer,

---

[92] Northampton Co. Orders 24, 1753-56, p. 389, with Littleton Andrews as a security. Although evidence is lacking, it appears possible that they were the parents of Littleton Andrews who married Margaret (_____) White, widow of John White (Northampton Co. Wills & Inventories 21, 1754-60, p. 347, will of John White, 31 Jan. 1758-11 April 1758); Wills &c 27, 1783-88, p. 446, will of Caleb White, 20 March 1786-13 Feb. 1787) and of Rachel Andrews who married, (bond 14) Dec. 1756, John Joyne (Mihalyka, *Marriages, Northampton County*, p. 62).

[93] Northampton Co. Minutes 27, 1765-71, p. 43.

[94] Accomack Co. Order Bk. 1744-53, p. 400.

[95] *Ibid.*, p. 479.

[96] Accomack Co. Wills 1749-52, pp. 274-80.

[97] Gravestone, "Sylvan Retreat," Accomack County, in Jean Merritt Mihalyka and Faye Downing Wilson, *Graven Stones of Lower Accomack County, Virginia* (Bowie, Md., 1986), p. 5.

[98] Accomack Co. Wills &c 1767-72, p. 395.

[99] Accomack Co. Wills 1692-1715, p. 482; *ES* I, p. 669.

[100] Mihalyka, *Marriages, Northampton County.*, p. 3.

[101] Gravestone, "Sylvan Retreat," *loc. cit.*

[102] Accomack Co. Wills &c 1784-87, p. 86.

[103] Northampton Co. Wills & Inventories 15, pp. 176-77.

who left will 26 July 1737-14 Dec. 1737,[104] and (2), (bond 16) Nov. 1741, Capt. Robert Nottingham,[105] who left will 27 Jan. 1744/5-9 April 1745.[106]

Issue: (by 1) [STRINGER][107] 67. Elishe[5], born 13 Sept. 1724, died 29 Aug. 1745,[108] married Nathaniel Bell, Jr., who left will 10 Dec. 1796-25 Feb. 1799;[109] 68. Isabell[5], married, (bond 12) March 1744,[110] Levin Denwood of Maryland; 69. ELIZABETH HARMANSON[5]; 70. Mary[5], married (1) 18. *Savage*[4] *Bloxom* (see SAVAGE) and (2), as his (2) wife, John Marshall, who left will 19 Feb. 1744-8 Jan. 1750.[111]

42. JOSEPH[4] MAXFIELD (Susanna[3] Andrews, William[2], William[1]), placed under guardianship of his half-sister-in-law Mary Littleton, widow of Southey[4], 17 March 1712/3,[112] resided at Mulberry Grove, Worcester Co., Md., and left will 7 March 1750-19 May 1750.[113] He married, 14 Nov. 1744, Sarah Warner, born 10 March 1724/5, who married (2), 27 Sept. 1753, Ezekiel Nock[114] and died 1773.

Issue: [MAXFIELD][115] 71. Stephen[5], born 21 Jan. 1748/9, granted a certificate of removal to Philadelphia, Pa., to be apprenticed; 72. Susanna[5], born 15 Oct. 1750, married, 29 March 1768 at Duck Creek Monthly Meeting, Kent Co., Del., James Berry; 73. Esther[5], died Aug. 1751, aged 2 yrs.[116]

43. MARGARET[4] _____ (_____[3], Susanna[2] Andrews, William[1]) married Randolph Hewitt of "Cape May in new West Jersie." She in 1698 was sole heir

---

[104] Northampton Co. Wills & Inventories 18, pp. 231-32.

[105] Mihalyka, *Marriages, Northampton County*, p. 79.

[106] Northampton Co. Wills & Inventories 15, pp. 178-80.

[107] Parents' wills; division of mother's estate, Northampton Co. Wills & Inventories 15, pp. 212-13.

[108] Gravestone, Bell's Neck, in Mihalyka and Wilson, *op. cit.*, p. 19.

[109] Accomack Co. Wills &c 1798-1800, p. 80. This identification is based on *ES* I. p. 580. The children named in the will were probably all by his widow Susannah.

[110] Mihalyka, *Marriages, Northampton County*, p. 26.

[111] Northampton Co. Wills & Inventories 19, 1740-50, p. 545.

[112] Northampton Co. Order Bk. 15, p. 104.

[113] Maryland Prerogative Court Wills 27, pp. 340-41.

[114] Kenneth Carroll, *Quakerism on the Eastern Shore* (Baltimore, 1970), pp. 97, 228, 274, 277.

[115] Named in Joseph Maxwell's will; information provided by Friends Historical Library, Swarthmore, Pa.

[116] Third Haven Monthly Meeting, Talbot Co., Md., records.

of Susanna[2] Andrews.[117]

Issue: [HEWITT][118] 74. Randall[5]; 75. Reuben[5]; 76. Joseph[5]; 77. Jacob[5]; 78. Nathaniel[5]; 79. Ebenezer[5].

44. ANDREW[4] ANDREWS (John[3], Andrew[2], William[1]), on whose estate administration was granted to his widow, 24 Sept. 1745,[119] married Sarah, daughter of Richard Rowley,[120] who married (2) Samuel Tillet.[121]

Issue: 80. Sarah[5], married, by 28 May 1765,[122] John Stinson [Stevenson] of Worcester Co., Md.

45. WILLIAM[4] ANDREWS (Andrew[3], Andrew[2], William[1]) of Northampton County left will 12 Nov. 1760-13 July 1762.[123] He married Ann ___, who married (2), (bond 15) Feb. 1770,[124] Abraham Westerhouse and left nuncupative will 6 Jan. 1797-15 Feb. 1797.[125]

Issue:[126] 81. SOUTHEY[5]; 82. Nelly[5]; 83. RACHEL[5]; 84. Anne[5]; 85. John[5]; 86. Susanna[5], married, (bond 17) Sept. 1778,[127] Spencer Wilson; 87. William[5].

46. ANDREW[4] ANDREWS (Andrew[3], Andrew[2], William[1]). of Northampton County, left will 24 Feb. 1787-10 April 1787.[128] He married, before 22 Feb. 1766,[129] Mary Waterfield, daughter of Jacob Waterfield, Sr.[130]

Issue: 88. Smart[5]; 89. Sarah[5], married, (bond 4) Aug. 1786,[131] Robert Davis.

---

[117] Accomack Co. Wills &c 1697-1715, pp. 334-35.

[118] Based on the assumption he is the Randall Hewett of Cape May Co., N.J., yeoman, who left will naming sons Randall, Reuben, Joseph, Jacob, Nathaniel and Ebenezer and mentioning (but not naming) wife, which was proved when son Randall, 27 June 1733, was granted administration, no executor being named (West Jersey Wills 3, p. 346, in *New Jersey Archives*, 1st ser., XXX, p. 235).

[119] Accomack Co. Order Bk. 1744-53, p. 81.

[120] Accomack Co. Wills &c 1743-49, p. 135.

[121] Accomack Co. Order Bk. 1744-53, p. 255.

[122] Accomack Co. Deeds 3, 1757-70, p. 376, sale of land south of the Maryland border to Skinner Marshall and his wife Leah; *ES* II, p. 1369.

[123] Northampton Co. Wills & Inventories 22, p. 488.

[124] Mihalyka, *Marriages, Northampton County*, p. 123.

[125] Northampton Co. Wills &c 30, 1795-98, p. 188.

[126] Northampton Co. Wills & Inventories 24, 1766-72, p. 284.

[127] Mihalyka, *Marriages, Northampton County*, p. 132.

[128] Northampton Co. Wills &c 27, 1783-88, p. 454.

[129] Northampton Co. Wills & Inventories 24, 1766-72, p. 40.

[130] Northampton Co., Va., Wills & Inventories 24, 1766-72, p. 40, will of Jacob Waterfield, Sr. 2 Feb. 1766-14 Oct. 1766.

[131] Mihalyka, *Marriages, Northampton County*, p. 25.

47. JOHN[4] ANDREWS (Andrew[3], Andrew[2], William[1]) of Northampton County, left will 14 Jan. 1766-12 Aug. 1766.[132] He married, before March 1754, Elizabeth Dunton, daughter of Michael Dunton.[133]

Issue: 90. William[5]; 91. John[5]; 92. Ann[5]; 93. Peggy[5].

54. WILLIAM[5] ANDREWS (William[4], William[3], William[2], William[1]), possibly the William who died before 24 April 1789 when administration on his estate was granted to Thomas Fletcher,[134] married (1) ____ and (2) Susannah Mason, daughter of William Mason, Sr.[135]

Issue: (by 1) 94. Mary[6]; 95. Leah[6], named with Mary as granddaughters in will of Mary (Selby) Gore Andrews, 1764; (by 2) 96. Ishmael[6], born before his parents were married, left will 22 Aug. 1792-28 Jan. 1794,[136] lieutenant of Virginia State Navy on *Accomack* galley, 1777-78,[137] married Mary Ann ___;[138] 97. Rachel[6], married, (bond 4) Feb. 1811,[139] Reuben Rew, who left will 7 Oct. 1806-1 Nov. 1814, naming Rachel Andrews and Southey Rew, son of Rachel Andrews;[140] 98. Jacob[6], named with Rachel in will of brother Ishmael, married, (bond 16) Dec. 1801,[141] Anne Porter; 99. William[6], aged 63 in 1824, seaman in the *Accomack* galley, 1777-80,[142] never married; 100. (probably) Elkanah[6], aged 63 in 1824, born in Accomack County, seaman in the *Accomack* galley, 1777-80,[143] left will 3 Feb. 1844-30 Sept. 1844,[144] married, (bond 11) Jan. 1810,[145]

---

[132] Northampton Co. Wills & Inventories 24, 1766-72, pp. 21-22, which named brother-in-law Elias Dunton.

[133] Northampton Co. Wills & Inventories 20, 1750-54, p. 503, will of Michael Dunton, 5 March 1754-12 March 1754.

[134] Accomack Co. Order Bk. 1798-1800, p. 105.

[135] *ES* II, p. 1218; Accomack Co. Wills &c 1757-61, p. 164, will of William Mason, 12 Feb. 1759-28 Nov. 1759.

[136] Accomack Co. Will Bk. 1788-94, p. 808.

[137] Revolutionary War pension application, Scarborough Bloxom, widow Leah, W.5843, National Archives.

[138] *ES* II, p. 1258.

[139] Nora Miller Turman, *Marriage Records of Accomack County, Virginia, 1776-1854* (Bowie Md., 1994), p. 234.

[140] Accomack Co. Wills &c 1814-16, p. 16.

[141] Turman, *op. cit.*, p. 8.

[142] Revolutionary War pension application, William Andrews, R.—, National Archives.

[143] Revolutionary War pension application, Elkanah Andrews, widow Hetty, S.6505, National Archives.

[144] Accomack Co. Will Bk. 1828-46, p. 526.

[145] Turman, *op. cit.*, p. 8.

Hetty Taylor, aged 40 in 1824.

55. LEAH[5] ANDREWS (William[4], William[3], William[2], William[1]) left will 18 March 1773-27 April 1773.[146] She married James Pettigrew who left will 20 April 1771-26 May 1772.[147]

Issue: [PETTIGREW] 101. John[6], left will 8 Oct. 1811-13 July 1812,[148] married Anne ___, who joined him in selling land in Accomack County, 1777, and moved to Milford, Kent Co., Del.; 102. Gavin[6], under age in 1771; 103. William[6], named in grandmother's will but not in parents' wills.

58. STEPHEN[5] ANDREWS (Isaac[4], William[3], William[2], William[1]) was born 10 May 1741 and died Spring 1772. He married, 24 March 1763, Mary Medford, daughter of William and Ann (Thomas) Medford, born 7 Feb. 1745 and died 7 Feb. 1766.[149]

Issue: 104. Medford[6], born 19 Jan. 1766, died 14 Nov. 1843, married, 26 Jan. 1794, Sarah Parker, daughter of Daniel and Elizabeth Parker, born 29 Oct. 1769.[150]

60. BETTEY[5] ANDREWS (Isaac[4], William[3], William[2], William[1]) married (1) ___ Losin and (2), by 10 April 1757,[151] Samuel League.

Issue: (by 1) [LOSIN] 105. Isaac[6].

62. ROBERTSON[5] ANDREWS (John[4], Robert[3], William[2], William[1]), a taxpayer of Pocomoke Hundred, Somerset Co., Md., 1733-40, was left 200 acres, "Coventree," by his grandfather Peale, and left will 22 Jan. 1750-5 March 1750.[152] He married Sarah ___, who perhaps married (2) ___ Waltham..

Issue: 106. Thomas[6], possibly the Thomas, carpenter, who left will 24 Nov. 1779-11 Dec. 1779;[153] 107. Elizabeth[6], baptized 22 May 1745.[154]

65. WILLIAM[5] ANDREWS (Robert[4], Robert[3], William[2], William[1]) was

---

[146] Accomack Co. Wills &c 1772-77, p. 83.

[147] Accomack Co. Wills &c 1767-72, p. 713.

[148] Accomack Co. Will Bk. 1826-46, p. 75, probated in Kent Co., Del., rerecorded 1 Dec. 1830.

[149] Andrews Bible, *loc. cit.*

[150] *Ibid.*

[151] Dorchester Co., Md., Old Deed Bk. 15, p. 464.

[152] Sussex Co., Del., Will Bk. A, pp. 435-36.

[153] Sussex Co., Del., Will Bk. C, pp. 215-17.

[154] St. George's Parish, Indian River, Sussex Co., Del., Register, in F. Edward Wright, *Vital Records of Kent and Sussex Counties, Delaware, 1686-1800* (2nd ed.; Silver Spring, Md., 1987), pp. 93-94.

born 26 Aug. 1733 and died 4 April 1777,[155] and left will 31 March 1777-30 June 1778.[156] He married Anna Maria (Hall) Parker, born 30 Nov. 1738, died 13 Feb. 1815,[157] left will 10 March 1814-27 Feb. 1815,[158] daughter of Col. Thomas and Elizabeth (Scarburgh) Hall and widow of Caleb Parker.

Issue:[159] 108. Robert[6], born 24 April 1761, died 14 Feb. 1803,[160] left will 20 Oct. 1800-25 Feb. 1803,[161] married, (bond 11) Dec. 1788,[162] 459. *Elizabeth[6] Stratton* (see WILKINS), born 12 April 1767;[163] 109. Susanna[6], married (1) 218. *Edward[6] Revell* (see BAGWELL) and (2) 282. *Revell[6] West* (see WEST, Anthony); 110. Jane[6], born 29 Aug. 1768, died 4 March 1815,[164] left will 16 Jan. 1814-28 March/30 May 1819,[165] married Augustine LeCato, who died before March 1808 when the inventory of his estate was made;[166] 111. Margaret[6], died 5 Sept. 1847, aged 79 yrs. 8 days,[167] married Dr. Augustus Davezac, Sr., of New Orleans, La.; 112. Anna Maria[6], married 620. *Samuel[6] Galt* (see WILKINS); 113. Priscilla Hall[6], died 11 Oct. 1797, aged 27,[168] married Martin A. Davis; 114. Elizabeth[6], married 211. Col. *Thomas[6] Parker* (see BAGWELL); 115. Tabitha[6], born 29 July 1774, died 29 Sept. 1854, married, 22 March 1801, William P. Moore, born 4 Nov. 1780, died 7 Nov. 1872,[169] leaving will 1 Nov. 1872-11 Nov. 1872.[170]

66. SARAH[5] ANDREWS (Jacob[4], Robert[3], William[2]. William[1]), under 18 in 1770 when father made his will, living 1806, married, Jan. 1775,[171] as his (2) wife, 179. *George[6] Parker* (see UTIE-BENNETT), of "Sylvan Retreat,"

[155] Gravestone, in Mihalyka and Wilson, *op. cit.*, p. 5.
[156] Accomack Co. Wills &c 1777-80, p. 110.
[157] Gravestone, in Mihalyka and Wilson, *loc. cit.*
[158] Accomack Co. Wills &c 1814-16, p. 115.
[159] *W*(2) VIII, pp. 36-41.
[160] *Ibid.*
[161] Accomack Co. Wills &c 1800-04, pp. 595-96.
[162] Mihalyka, *Marriages, Northampton County.*, p. 3.
[163] Harriet Russell Stratton, *The Book of Strattons* (New York, 1908), p. 343.
[164] Gravestone, in *ibid.*, p. 149.
[165] Accomack Co. Wills &c 1812-14, p. 423.
[166] *Ibid.*, p. 62.
[167] Gravestone, in Mihalyka and Wilson, *op. cit.*, p. 66.
[168] Gravestone, in Mihalyka and Wilson, *op. cit.*, p. 67.
[169] Gravestones, "Vaux Hall," in Mihalyka and Wilson, *op. cit.*, p. 185.
[170] Northampton Co. Wills & Inventories 39, 1854-97, pp. 148-50.
[171] *V* VI, p. 416.

Accomack County, born 28 Oct. 1735, died 3 Sept. 1784,[172] who left will 13 Aug. 1784-27 Oct. 1784,[173] and married (1) 92. *Adah⁵ Bagwell* (see BAGWELL).

Issue: [PARKER][174] 116. Sarah⁶, born 5 Nov. 1776, died 19 Oct. 1822,[175] married, 6 Jan. 1806,[176] as his (2) wife, George Ker, of Scotland; 117. Maj. John Andrews⁶, born 20 Sept. 1779, died 11 Aug. 1810,[177] member of the House of Delegates from Accomack County, 1801-03,[178] left will 1 Feb. 1806-10 Sept. 1810,[179] married, 2 June 1802,[180] Harriet Burleigh⁸ Darby, born 1 Feb. 1785, died Aug. 1840,[181] daughter of Col. John and Esther⁷ (Christian) Darby and granddaughter of 47. *Michael⁶ Christian* (see YEARDLEY); 118. Jacob Godwin⁶, born 10 Nov. 1782, died 12 May 1829,[182] physician of "Park Hall" at Eastville, Northampton County, married, 5 Feb. 1811,[183] Ann Gertrude⁷ Stratton, born 2 Fen. 1795, died 28 May 1883,[184] daughter of 466. *John⁶ Stratton* and 177. *Lucy⁶ Digges* (see WILKINS and DIGGES).

69. ELIZABETH HARMANSON⁵ STRINGER (Elishe⁴ Harmanson, Grace³ Andrews, William², William¹) married Hezekiah Tilney and resided in Worcester Co., Md., 1747.[185] He left will dated 15 Jan. 1754 and died before 13 July 1754 when his widow petitioned for dower in his estate.[186]

Issue: [TILNEY] 119. Elishe⁶; 120. Jonathan⁶, of Sussex Co., Del., married

[172] Gravestone, "Sylvan Retreat," in Mihalyka and Wilson, *op. cit.*, p. 193.

[173] Accomack Co. Wills &c 1784-87, pp. 77-78.

[174] *V* VI, p. 416.

[175] Gravestone, "Sylvan Retreat," in Mihalyka and Wilson, *op. cit.*, p. 142.

[176] Mihalyka, *Marriages, Northampton County*, p. 66.

[177] Gravestone, Darby's Wharf Farm, in Jean Merritt Mihalyka, *Gravestone Inscriptions in Northampton County, Virginia* (Richmond, 1984), p. 63.

[178] Leonard, pp. 223, 227.

[179] Northampton Co. Wills & Inventories 33, 1808-13, pp. 178-79.

[180] Mihalyka, *Marriages, Northampton County*, p. 82.

[181] Gravestone, Darby's Wharf Farm, *loc. cit.*

[182] Jacob G. Parker Bible (Philadelphia, 1812), in Jean M. Mihalyka, "Bible Records. Accomack and Northampton Counties, Virginia," Virginia State Archives, Miscellaneous Bible Records, XXXVI, p. 81; gravestone, "Park Hall," in Jean Merritt Mihalyka, *Gravestone Inscriptions in Northampton County, Virginia* (Richmond, 1984), p. 68; *Enquirer*, Richmond, 2 June 1829.

[183] Jacob G. Parker Bible, *loc. cit.*

[184] *Ibid.*; gravestone, "Park Hall," *loc. cit.*

[185] *ES* I, p. 522.

[186] Maryland Prerogative Court Wills 29, pp. 252, 209.

Elizabeth ___; 121. Stringer[6], married Elizabeth ___.

81. SOUTHEY[5] ANDREWS (William[4], Andrew[3], Andrew[3], William[1]), died before 8 Feb. 1774 when the inventory of his estate was ordered.[187] He married Sarah ____, who married (2), (bond 12) Feb. 1778,[188] John Tankard and (3), (bond 26) April 1781,[189] Henry Abdeel.

Issue:[190] 122. Esther[6], married, (bond 24) Dec. 1790,[191] Thomas Smith; 123. Rosanna[6], married, (consent 26) Dec. 1786,[192] Edmund Watson, who married (2), (bond 3) Feb. 1801, Peggy Thomas and (3), (bond 2) Aug. 1802,[193] Peggy Westcot and left will 1 May 1834-9 Feb. 1835.[194]

83. RACHEL[5] ANDREWS (William[4], Andrew[3], Andrew[2], William[1]) married, (bond 7) Nov. 1772,[195] Henry Dolby.

Issue: [DOLBY] 124. Nancy[6], named in grandmother's will.

---

[187] Northampton Co. Wills & Inventories 26, 1777-83, pp. 121-23, inventory returned 9 June 1778.

[188] Mihalyka, *Marriages, Northampton County*, p. 109.

[189] *Ibid.*, p. 1.

[190] ES, I, pp. 376-77.

[191] Mihalyka, *Marriages, Northampton County*, p. 102.

[192] *Ibid.*, p. 120.

[193] *Ibid.*

[194] Northampton Co. Wills & Inventories 38, 1829-53, p. 41.

[195] Mihalyka, *Marriages, Northampton County*, p. 27.

BAGWELL

*1. HENRY[1] BAGWELL was probably the Henry, son of David Bagwell of St. Petrock, Exeter, Devonshire, and his wife Joanna Chappelle, who was baptized there 29 Oct. 1589.[1] He was a passenger on the ill-fated *Sea Venture* and finally reached Virginia in the *Deliverance* which landed at Jamestown, May 1610.[2] He settled at West and Shirley Hundred in the Corporation of Charles City by 14 April 1623;[3] he was still there, aged 35 years, when the muster of Robert Bagwell, with whom he was living, was recorded on 22 Jan. 1624/5.[4]

Henry[1] Bagwell's right to 50 acres of land in the Corporation of Charles City was entered on a list sent to England by Sir Francis Wyatt, 25 May 1625, showing all titles and estates of land then held by Virginia settlers.[5] By 1632 he was established on the Eastern Shore where he became first clerk of courts when the County of Accawmack was established.[6] He served in the House of Burgesses from Accawmack, 1630 and 1632.[7] His land on Old Plantation Creek, mentioned 24 June 1636,[8] is of record in a patent for 400 acres issued to him 13 Aug. 1639.[9]

By 1 Jan. 1636/7 Henry[1] Bagwell had married Alice (___) Stratton Chilcott,

---

[1] Patricia Law Hatcher, "Notes on the English Origins of Henry Bagwell of Jamestown," *The Virginia Genealogist*, XLVI, pp. 265-74; Mary Burton Derrickson McCurdy, "The English Origins and History of Henry Bagwell and Thomas Stratton of Early Eastern Shore Virginia," *The Virginia Genealogist*, XXX, p. 3-16. He deposed, 19 Feb. 1633/4, he was aged 43 (Northampton Co. Orders, Deeds, Wills &c 1, 1632-40, transcript, p. 13). The identification of his parentage is tentative because at the time of the census, 1623/4 he and Thomas Bagwell were listed together at West and Shirley Hundred; no record of a Thomas Bagwell has been found in Exeter records.

[2] Hotten, p. 268.

[3] McDonald Papers, Public Record Office, Colonial, III, no. 2, p. 39.

[4] The variation of the first name in the heading and the first name on this census list appears in the photocopy obtained from the Public Record Office, London, C72, Archives Division, Library of Virginia. No other mention of Robert Bagwell has been found.

[5] *R*, Va. Co. IV, p. 553.

[6] Susie M. Ames, *County Court Records of Accomack-Northampton, Virginia, 1632-1640* (*American Legal Records*, VII; Washington, 1954), p. 4.

[7] Leonard, pp. 9, 11.

[8] Patent Bk. 1, p. 367.

[9] *Ibid.*, p. 664.

widow of Benjamin Stratton and ___ Chilcott.[10] On that day she petitioned for and received from the Accawmack County court 200 acres due for her own transportation and for that of her son Thomas Stratton and two servants John Walthum and John Crowder. At the same court she disposed of this land by deeding 100 acres each to Thomas Stratton and to a daughter Mary Chilcott.[11] Henry[1] Bagwell did not leave a will but his eldest son, John[2] Bagwell, fell heir to his land and on 28 April 1663 deeded half of the 400 acre patent to his brother.[12] Thomas Stratton in his will, 13 Oct. 1659-2 Nov. 1659, refers to his brothers (half-brothers) John and Thomas Bagwell.[13]

Issue: 2. JOHN[2]; 3. REBECCA[2]; 4. THOMAS[2].

2. JOHN[2] BAGWELL (Henry[1]), deposed 22 March 1665/6 he was aged 25, 30 Dec. 1680 he was aged 43, 16 May 1681 he was aged 42, and 5 Aug. 1684 he was aged 46.[14] He patented 600 acres at the head of Great Matomkin Creek in Accomack, 25 March 1672, and was charged with this land on the quit rent roll, 1683.[15] He married Ann ___, who deposed 22 March 1665/6 she was aged 19 and 5 Aug. 1684 she was aged 38.[16] The will of John[2] Bagwell, 18 Sept. 1685-30 Nov. 1686,[17] named his wife and children. His widow married (2), by 29 Dec. 1687, Edmund Allen.[18]

Issue: 5. John[3], died before 19 May 1681, being drawn between the cogwheel and trundlehead of the mill belonging to his father;[19] 6. HENRY[3]; 7.

---

[10] McCurdy, *op. cit.*, pp. 5-8. Henry Bagwell was named sole executor in the will of Ann Hawkins, widow of William Hawkins, 8 Nov. 1646-11 Nov. 1646 (Northampton Co. Deeds, Wills &c 1645-51, p. 134a, recorded 6 Jan. 1648/9), which also named (relationship not stated) Alice Bagwell overseer of will and gave bequests to Thomas Stratton and Richard Smyth, who were to share her plantation for four years, Mary Buckland, John Bagwell, Tho. Bagwell, Rebecca Bagwell and others. John Handy and Thomas Stratton were witnesses. William and Ann Hawkins had previously been assumed to be the parents of Alice Bagwell.

[11] Northampton Co. Orders, Deeds, Wills &c 1, 1632-40, p. 80 (transcript, p. 65).

[12] Northampton Co. Deeds &c 1668-80, p. 7.

[13] Northampton Co. Deeds & Wills 1657-66, p. 247. The will was recorded 29 June 1666.

[14] Accomack Co. Deeds, Wills &c 1663-66, p. 119; Northampton Co. Order Bk. 616, 1678-83, p. 129; Accomack Co. Wills, Deeds, Orders 1678-82, p. 229; Accomack Co. Wills, Orders &c 1682-97, p. 46.

[15] Patent Bk. 6, p. 400; *Magazine of Virginia Genealogy*, XXIII, no. 3, p. 70.

[16] Accomack Co. Deeds, Wills &c 1663-66, p. 119; Wills & Orders 1682-97, p. 46.

[17] Accomack Co. Wills & Deeds 1676-90, p. 433.

[18] Northampton Co. Order Bk. 1683-89, p. 324.

[19] *Ibid.*, p. 264.

ALEXANDER[3]; 8. REBECCA[3].

    3. REBECCA[2] BAGWELL (Henry[1]) married (1) *3. Robert[2] Andrews* (see ANDREWS) and (2) *3. Stephen[2] Fisher* (see FISHER). Her will, 3 June 1658-28 June 1658,[20] named as residuary heirs sister Mary Hanby, brothers Thomas Stratton, John Bagwell, Thomas Bagwell and Philip Fisher.[21]

    Issue: see FISHER.

    4. THOMAS[2] BAGWELL (Henry[1]), deposed, 18 May 1678, he was aged about 36 and 17 June 1682 he was aged 40.[22] On 30 Aug. 1669 he conveyed to "my loving brother John Bagwell" 50 acres on Old Plantation Creek, the remainder of 200 acres which his brother John, by deed of gift 28 April 1663, conveyed to him, being one-half of 400 acres granted to "my late deceased father, Henry Bagwell, Gent., by patent dated 13 August 1639."[23] He married Ann Stockley[24] who relinquished her dower right in this land. He held 400 acres in Accomack County, 1683.[25] On 11 Aug. 1682 he received a warrant for the survey of 1000 acres in Sussex Co., Del.[26] His will, 15 April 1690-16 Sept. 1690,[27] named his wife Ann, children and grandchildren. Ann may have moved briefly to Sussex Co., Del., where "Widow Baggwell" was named on the assessment list of 1693,[28] but by 1695 she married (2) William Nicholson and returned to Accomack County.[29]

    Issue: 9. THOMAS[3]; 10. JOHN[3]; 11. COMFORT[3]; 12. ELIZABETH[3]; 13. FRANCIS[3]; 14. WILLIAM[3]; 15. VALLANCE[3]; 16. ANN[3].

    6. HENRY[3] BAGWELL (John[2], Henry[1]) married (1) ___[30] and (2), after 2

---

[20] Northampton Co. Deeds & Wills 1657-66, p. 12.

[21] Mary (Chilcott) Buckland Hanby and Thomas Stratton were her half-sister and half-brother, John and Thomas Bagwell were her full brothers, and Philip Fisher was her husband's brother.

[22] Accomack Co. Order Bk. 1676-78, p. 156; Wills, Deeds, Orders 1678-82, p. 309.

[23] Northampton Co. Deeds & Wills 1668-80, p. 7.

[24] Lucy Ames Edwards, *Ames, Mears and Allied Lines* (n.p., 1967), p. 363.

[25] *Magazine of Virginia Genealogy*, XXIII, no. 3, p. 69.

[26] Sussex Co., Del., Warrants B[1], no. 7, Delaware Hall of Records.

[27] Accomack Co. Wills & Deeds 1676-90, p. 525.

[28] Ronald Vern Jackson and Gary Ronald Teeples, *Early Deleware Census Records, 1665-1697* (Bountiful, Utah, 1977), p. 2.

[29] Accomack Co. Order Bk. 1690-97, p. 154a.

[30] She may have been a sister of Thomas Crippen the Elder whose son Thomas in will, 27 Dec. 1727-5 March 1727/8 (Accomack Co. Wills, Deeds &c 1715-29, pt. 2, p. 303), named uncle Henry Bagwell.

Oct. 1711,[31] Margaret (Drummond) Allen, widow of Edmund Allen and daughter of John Drummond (1635-1713) and his wife Patience Hill of Accomack County.[32] His will, 12 Aug. 1734-1 Oct. 1734,[33] named his wife, grandson Charles Bagwell, and children. He owned 412 acres in Accomack County in 1704.

Issue: (by 1) 17 HENRY[4]; 18. JOHN[4]; 19. Elizabeth[4], married Isaac Rogers; (by 2) 20. William[4], died before his father;[34] 21. THOMAS[4]; 22. TABITHA[4]; 23. Ann[4].

7. ALEXANDER[3] BAGWELL (John[2], Henry[1]) married (1) Elizabeth __, widow of William Sterling,[35] and (2) Neomy Maddux, daughter of Thomas and Rebecca Maddux.[36] He owned 413 acres in Accomack County in 1704. His will, 27 Oct. 1722-8 Jan. 1722/3,[37] named his wife, cozens (nephews) William and Thomas, sons of Henry Bagwell, son-in-law Nathaniel Maddux, and children. His widow married (2) Joseph Stockley.

Issue: 24. Rebecca[4]; 25. Sarah[4]; 26. Anne[4]; 27. MARGARET[4]; 28. Mary[4], under age 1722, gave receipt for her estate to Joseph Stockley, 30 Sept. 1742,[38] sold land she inherited from her father by General Court deed, Oct. 1742,[39] married 135. *William Robinson[5] Smith* (see WEST, Anthony), who married (2) ___ and (3) 161. *Mary Robinson[5] Wise* (see WEST, Anthony) and left will 14 Dec. 1759-30 Jan. 1760.[40]

8. REBECCA[3] BAGWELL (John[2], Henry[1]) married (1) Thomas Mills who deposed 30 Dec. 1680 he was aged 18[41] and left will, 17 Feb. 1708/9-5 April 1709,[42] which named his wife, brother Alexander Bagwell and children. She

---

[31] Accomack Co. Order Bk. 1710-14, p. 27.

[32] Accomack Co. Wills &c 1692-1715, p. 615; *The Colonial Genealogist*, VIII, p. 172. She was his step-father's widow.

[33] Accomack Co. Deeds & Wills 1729-37, pp. 179-80.

[34] Northampton Co. Land Causes 1731-54, pp. 36-41, in Stratton Nottingham, *Virginia Land Causes, Lancaster County 1795-1848, Northampton County 1731-1868* (Onancock, Va., 1931), p. 28.

[35] *Ibid.*

[36] Northampton Co. Order Bk. 1710-15, p. 147.

[37] Northampton Co. Deeds, Wills &c 1718-25, pp. 161-62.

[38] Accomack Co. Deeds &c 1737-46, p.. 244.

[39] Accomack Co. Deeds &c 1737-46, pp. 333-34.

[40] Accomack Co. Wills &c 1757-61, p. 177.

[41] Northampton Co. Order Bk. 11, 1678-83, p. 130.

[42] Accomack Co. Wills &c 1692-1715, p. 479.

married (2) Charles Stockley who left will, 6 May 1718-5 May 1719,[43] which named wife Rebecca, son-in-law (step-son) William Mills and children by his previous marriage.

Issue: (by 1) [MILLS] 29. Edmond[4]; 30. Thomas[4], died without issue; 31. Alexander[4]; 32. Elizabeth[4]; 33. Ann[4]; 34. WILLIAM[4].

9. THOMAS[3] BAGWELL (Thomas[2], Henry[1]) married Elizabeth Eyre, daughter of John and Elizabeth Eyre.[44] He owned 465 acres in Accomack County, 1704. His will, 15 Aug. 1712-6 Jan. 1712/3,[45] mentioned his wife and named his children. His widow married (2) Francis Stockley,[46] who married (3) Tabitha (___) Young and left will 18 Nov. 1740-28 April 1741.[47]

Issue:35. THOMAS[4]; 36. JOHN[4]; 37. Elizabeth[4]; 38. Susanna[4]; 39. Ann[4]; 40. Comfort[4]; 41. SARA[4].

10. Capt. JOHN[3] BAGWELL (Thomas[2], Henry[1]), under 18 in 1690, was left "the plantation where I now live" by his father and owned 465 acres in Accomack County, 1704. He married 14. *Tabitha[3] Scarburgh* (see UTIE-BENNETT), who predeceased him. He left will 1 Nov. 1748-28 Feb. 1749/50.[48]

Issue: 42. JOHN[4]; 43. ELIZABETH[4]; 44. (Daughter)[4], married John Coleburn, who married (2) 77. *Elizabeth[5] Scarburgh* (see UTIE-BENNETT) and (3) Catherine ___ and left will 24 Feb. 1776-26 March 1776.[49]

11. COMFORT[3] BAGWELL (Thomas[2], Henry[1]) married (1) Perry Leatherbury, son of Thomas and Eleanor Leatherbury. He owned 1750 acres in Accomack County, 1704, and left will, 19 Feb. 1708/9-5 April 1709,[50] which named his wife and children. She married (2), as his (2) wife, Robert Burton, who arrived in Accomack County prior to 18 Dec. 1665 and declared, 19 Jan. 1677/8, that he had "formerly gon under the name of Rob[t]: Spencer from my Infancy and now [was] better Informed out of England by Letters from my

---

[43] Accomack Co. Wills, Deeds &c 1715-29, pt. 1, p. 188.

[44] Edwards, op. cit., pp. 270-71; Northampton Co. Deeds, Wills &c 1718-25, p. 24, will of John Eyre, 21 April 1819-21 July 1719.

[45] Accomack Co. Wills &c 1692-1715, p. 592.

[46] Northampton Co. Wills 1718-25, pp. 24-25, will of John Eyre, 1 April 1719-21 July 1719, naming daughter Elizabeth Stockley and grandsons John and Thomas Bagwell. Administration with the will annexed was granted to Francis Stockley and Elizabeth his wife.

[47] Accomack Co. Wills 1737-43, pp. 298-300.

[48] Accomack Co. Wills 1749-52, p. 52.

[49] Accomack Co. Wills &c 1772-77, p. 415.

[50] Accomack Co. Wills &c 1692-1715, p. 481.

relations my true and right name is Robert Burton."[51] He moved, 1692, to Somerset Co., Md., and shortly thereafter to Sussex Co., Del., where he became a member of the Provincial Council of Pennsylvania and, 14 April 1704, petitioned for a separate legislature for the people of New Castle, Kent and Sussex counties.[52] He left will, 16 Sept. 1724-16 Oct. 1725,[53] naming wife Comfort and children and grandchildren.

Issue: (by 1) [LEATHERBURY][54] 45. Patience[4], named in her grandfather Bagwell's will; 46. Perry[4], on whose estate Robert Burton of Sussex County upon Delaware, his "father-in-law", was granted administration 3 Sept. 1717, with consent of his brother Edmund;[55] 47. ANN BAGWELL[4]; 48. Edmund[4], married 12. *Mary[3] (Scarburgh) Baily Bayly* (see UTIE-BENNETT); 49. THOMAS[4]; 50. Charles[4]; 51. COMFORT[4]; 52. (possibly) Elenor[4], born after 19 Feb. 1708/9.

12. ELIZABETH[3] BAGWELL (Thomas[2], Henry[1]) married (1) William Tilney, son of John and Ann Tilney, who was baptized 29 Nov. 1661[56] and died 9 March 1695/6.[57] As a widow Elizabeth Tilney held 200 acres in Accomack County, 1704. She married (2), between 4 Feb. and 6 May 1707,[58] James Davis who left will 9 April 1712-2 June 1713.[59]

---

[51] Accomack Co. Wills & Deeds 1676-90, p. 84.

[52] John Goodwin Herndon, "Notes on the Ancestry of Robert Burton (1730-1785) ...," *The Pennsylvania Genealogical Magazine*, XVIII, pp. 143-52.

[53] Sussex Co., Del., Will Bk. A, pp. 187-90.

[54] Patricia Law Hatcher, "Were the 'Daughters' of Robert Burton of Sussex County, Delaware, Really the Daughters of Comfort (Bagwell) Leatherbury?," *The American Genealogist*, LXXV, pp. 250-66. Herndon, *op. cit.*, pp. 152-53, identified daughter Comfort as wife of (1) Thomas Prettyman, (2) Thomas Walker and (3) Reese Wolfe, daughter Patience as wife of Paul Waples, and daughter Ann as wife of (1) Woolsey Burton and (2) John Plasket, concluding that, although Robert Burton designated them as his daughters in his will, they were his step-daughters. Subsequent deeds disposing of property devised to these daughters (e.g. Sussex Co., Del., Deed Bk. 19, pp. 289-90, and Deed Bk. K10, pp. 22-23, 141, 176) in each instance, however, also refer to them as Robert Burton's daughters rather than step-daughters. It appears, therefore, that Robert Burton and Comfort (Bagwell) Leatherbury both had daughters with these names

[55] Accomack Co. Order Bk. 1717-19, p. 1.

[56] Northampton Co. Deeds, Wills &c 1657-66, p. 134.

[57] Accomack Co. Wills &c 1692-1715, p. 427.

[58] Accomack Co. Deeds, Wills &c 1692-1715, pp. 402-03; Order Bk. 1703-09, pp. 92a, 96; Order Bk. 1719-24, pp. 30, 71.

[59] Accomack Co. Wills 1692-1715, p. 599.

Issue: (by 1) [TILNEY][60] 53. WILLIAM[4]; 54. COMFORT[4]; 55. Ann[4]; 56. PATIENCE[4]; 57. Elizabeth[4], chose Charles Leatherbury as her guardian, 1 June 1708, married John Chambers.

13. FRANCIS[3] BAGWELL (Thomas[2], Henry[1]) was left by his father, jointly with his brother William[3], "all my Land att the Horekill in Sussix County in the teretorys of Penselvania" and released his interest to William 1 Aug. 1710. He married (1) Catherine Burton, daughter of Robert Burton by his (1) wife, and (2) Susannah (_____) Drake, widow of James Drake,[61] and left will 12 March 1720/1-23 March 1720/1.[62]

Issue: (by 1) 58. THOMAS[4].

14. WILLIAM[3] BAGWELL (Thomas[2], Henry[1]) moved to Sussex Co., Del., where he was named in the commission of the peace, 20 April 1704,[63] and served at least until 1712.[64] He represented Sussex County in the Delaware Assembly, 1704.[65] He married, by 3 Oct. 1700, Elizabeth _____, widow of William Parker.[66] On 1 Aug. 1710 his brother Francis[3] released to him his interest in a neck of land called Long Neck in Indian River Hundred in Sussex County.[67] He died before 14 Oct. 1715 when Elizabeth Bagwell, relict of William Bagwell, and Wolsey Burton, both of Sussex County, petitioned for a resurvey of a tract called Long Neck on the south side of Rehoboth Bay, formerly granted to William Burton and Thomas Bagwell and from them descended to the children of William Bagwell and to Wolsey Burton.[68] She married (3), (marriage contract

---

[60] Accomack Co. Deeds, Wills &c 1715-29, p. 116; Order Bk. 1703-09, pp. 92a, 117; Order Bk. 1719-24, pp. 30, 71.

[61] Sussex Co., Del., Orphans Court Docket Bk. 1, 1728-43, p. 4.

[62] Sussex Co., Del., Will Bk. A, pp. 145-46. He bequeathed to Ann Drake items which were her mother's, suggesting Ann was his step-daughter.

[63] C. H. B. Turner, *Some Records of Sussex County, Delaware* (Philadelphia, 1909), p. 45; *Pennsylvania Archives*, Ser. 2, IX (Philadelphia, 1896), p. 683.

[64] Sussex Co., Del., Deed Bk. A, *passim.*

[65] Bruce A. Bendler, *Colonial Delaware Assemblymen, 1682-1776* (Westminster, Md., 1989), p. 3.

[66] Accomack Co. Wills &c 1692-1715, p. 261. Since William Parker in his will, 13 Aug. 1696-2 June 1697 (*ibid.*, p. 162), mentioned brother-in-law John Powell, she may have been Elizabeth, daughter of Nicholas Powell (Northampton Co. Deeds & Wills 1668-80, p. 82).

[67] Sussex Co., Del., Deed Bk. F-6, p. 126.

[68] Sussex Co., Del., Warrants B[1], no. 87.

15) Nov. 1715, John Coe.[69]

Issue:[70] 59. AGNES[4]; 60. William[4], under guardianship of John Adams, 9 May 1729,[71] made a division with William Burton, 6 Sept. 1737, of the land "formerly purchased by our ancestors";[72] 61. Anne[4], died by 1725.

15. VALLANCE[3] BAGWELL (Thomas[2], Henry[1]) was under age 14 in June 1697.[73] She married Charles Leatherbury, a cordwainer, who held 1100 acres in Accomack County, 1704, and left will, 2 March 1721 [1720/1]-4 April 1721,[74] mentioning his wife and leaving land to each of his children.

Issue: [LEATHERBURY] 62. THOMAS[4]; 63. JOHN[4]; 64. Perry[4]; 65. Elizabeth[4]; 66. Ann[4].

16. ANN[3] BAGWELL (Thomas[2], Henry[1]) chose her brother-in-law Perry Leatherbury as her guardian, 8 Jan. 1696/7.[75] She married Griffith Savage who married (2) Patience ____ and left will, 5 Jan. 1738/9-27 June 1739.[76]

Issue: [SAVAGE] 67. BRIDGET[4].

17. HENRY[4] BAGWELL (Henry[3], John[2], Henry[1]) left will 1 March 1734/5-3 June 1735.[77] He married (1) ___ Custis, daughter of Edward Custis,[78] and (2) Sabra Milby, who married (2) John Dix[79] and left will 5 Jan. 1764-28 Feb. 1764.[80]

Issue: (by 1) 68. SPENCER[5]; (by 2) 69. Heli[5], left will 21 March 1761-31 March 1761,[81] never married.

18. JOHN[4] BAGWELL (Henry[3], John[2], Henry[1]) died before 7 Jan. 1729/30

---

[69] Sussex Co., Del., Orphans Court Docket 1728-43, p. 50, petition of William[4] Bagwell, 5 June 1733, for a Negro boy specified in the contract.

[70] Sussex Co., Del., Deed Bk. A-1, p. 293, 5 May 1713; Deed Bk. F-6, pp. 143-44, division of land of William[3] Bagwell, 12 May 1725.

[71] Sussex Co., Del., Orphans Court Docket 1728-43, p. 9.

[72] Sussex Co., Del., Deed Bk. G, pp. 218-20.

[73] Accomack Co. Order Bk. 1690-98, pp. 240-240a.

[74] Accomack Co. Deeds, Wills &c 1715-29, pt. 1, p. 324.

[75] Accomack Co. Order Bk. 1690-97, p. 215a.

[76] Accomack Co. Wills &c 1737-43, pp. 157-59.

[77] *Ibid.*, p. 442.

[78] Accomack Co. Will Bk. 1737-43, p. 175, will of Edward Custis, 3 June 1739-a Aug. 1739.

[79] Accomack Co. Wills 1757-61, p. 314.

[80] Accomack Co. Wills 1761-67, p. 241.

[81] Accomack Co. Wills &c 1757-61, p. 314.

when administration on his estate was granted.[82] He married Kesiah ___, who married (2) John Smith and died after 26 Jan. 1741/2 when she presented John's will for probate.[83]

Issue: 70. CHARLES[5].

21. THOMAS[4] BAGWELL, (Henry[3], Thomas[2], Henry[1]) was devised land in Old Plantation Neck by his father and left undated will proved 28 June 1764.[84] He married Patience Nock, daughter of Benjamin Nock,[85] who married (2) ___ Ackworth [Accor] and left will 27 Nov. 1790-27 Feb. 1797.[86]

Issue: 71. Stephen[5]; 72. John[5], administration of his and Stephen's estate granted to John and Rose Arlington, 26 April 1786;[87] 73. ROSE[5].

22. TABITHA[4] BAGWELL (Henry[3], John[2], Henry[1]) married, between 23 Sept. 1738 and 2 Oct. 1744,[88] William Custis, son of Edward Custis, who left will 10 Nov. 1766-25 Nov. 1766.[89]

Issue: [CUSTIS] 74. Scarburgh[5], daughter, born by 1744, died young; 75. JOHN[5]; 76. Bagwell[5], left will 7 Nov. 1774-31 Sept. 1777;[90] 77. WILLIAM SMITH[5]; 78. BETTY[5].

27. MARGARET[4] BAGWELL (Alexander[3], John[2], Henry[1]) was under 18 in 1722. She married, (bond 3) Nov. 1724, Arthur Roberts,[91] who left will 11 March 1747/8-12 July 1748.[92]

Issue: [ROBERTS] 79. FRANCIS[5]; 80.. JOACHIM[5]; 81. ARTHUR[5]; 82. Margaret[5], married 103. *Major[5] Rogers* (see WEST, Anthony); 83. Mary[5]; 84. Rose Ann[5]; 85. Ann Bagwell[5].

34. WILLIAM[4] MILLS (Rebecca[3] Bagwell, John[2], Henry[1]) left will 3 April

---

[82] Accomack Co. Order Bk. 1724-31, p. 177.

[83] Accomack Co. Will Bk. 1737-43, p. 347.

[84] Accomack Co. Wills 1761-67, p. 320.

[85] *Ibid.*, p. 685, will of Benjamin Nock, 7 July 1765-31 Dec. 1766.

[86] Accomack Co. Wills &c 1796-98, p. 143.

[87] Accomack Co. Order Bk. 1784-86, p. 499.

[88] Accomack Co. Wills 1749-52, p. 171, will of her half-brother Stephen Allen, 23 Sept. 1738-27 Feb. 1750/1; Accomack Co. Wills 1743-49, p. 121, will of her half-sister, Patience (Allen) Custis, 2 Oct. 1744-20 Oct. 1744.

[89] Accomack Co. Will Bk. 1761-67, p. 670.

[90] Accomack Co. Wills &c 1777-80, p. 31.

[91] Jean M. Mihalyka, *Marriages, Northampton County, Virginia, 1660/1-1854* (Bowie, Md.,1990), p. 91.

[92] Northampton Co. Wills & Inventories 19, 1740-50, pp. 336-38.

1750-8 May 1750.[93] He married Ann ___ who joined him in the sale, 2 Aug. 1737, of land he inherited as heir at law of his brother Thomas[4],[94] and died before 12 Feb. 1755 when Moses Cox was named administrator of William Mills, the estate having been unadministered by his executrix.[95]

Issue: [MILLS] 86. Thomas[5], left will 8 Jan. 1760-13 Feb. 1760;[96] 87. EDMUND[5]; 88. Ieaca [Jacker][5], married, (bond 24) March 1749,[97] Moses Cox of Norfolk County who died before 11 June 1765 when Walter Hislop was granted administration on his estate.[98]

35. THOMAS[4] BAGWELL (Thomas[3], Thomas[2], Henry[1]), on whose estate administration was granted 26 Feb. 1739/40,[99] was left 165 acres where his father lived. He married Elizabeth Wharton, who left will 20 Oct. 1748-27 Feb. 1749/50.[100]

Issue: 89. ISAIAH[5]; 90. John[5]; 91. Elizabeth[5]; 92. ADAH[5]; 93. Ann[5]; 94. William[5], left land by his great uncle 15. John[3] Bagwell, died by 27 Nov. 1751 when administration on his estate was granted to Smith Snead.[101]

36. JOHN[4] BAGWELL (Thomas[3], Thomas[2], Henry[1]) moved to Sussex Co., Del., and left will 4 Feb. 1766-12 Feb. 1766.[102] He married Sarah Stockley.

Issue: 95. William[5], died about 1787,[103] married Ann [?Burton],[104] who married (2) William Burton; 96. Thomas[5]; 97. Elizabeth[5]; 98. Sarah[5]; 99. LEAH[5]; 100. RACHEL[5].

41. SARA[4] BAGWELL (Thomas[3], Thomas[2], Henry[1]) married Robert

---

[93] Northampton Co. Wills & Inventories 19, 1740-50, pp. 449-50.

[94] Accomack Co. Deeds & Wills 1729-37, pp. 285-86.

[95] Northampton Co. Minute Bk. 25, 1754-61, p. 24.

[96] Northampton Co. Wills & Inventories 21, 1754-60, p. 533.

[97] Mihalyka, *Marriages, Northampton County*, p. 24.

[98] Northampton Co. Minute Bk. 26, 1761-65, p. 176.

[99] Accomack Co. Order Bk. 1737-44, p. 232.

[100] Accomack Co. Wills 1749-52, pp. 50-51.

[101] Accomack Co. Order Bk. 1744-53, p. 552.

[102] Sussex Co., Del., Will Bk. B, pp. 286-88.

[103] Sussex Co., Del., Estate papers A58, pp. 60, 62.

[104] Named as daughter in will of Elizabeth Prettyman, 4 Feb. 1777-4 April 1777 (*ibid.*, A94, p. 57; Sussex Co., Del., Will Bk. C, pp. 76-78). They joined Elizabeth Prettyman, John Stratton Burton and William Burton in selling, 25 April 1772, 91 acres which William Burton of Worcester Co., Md., devised to his grandson Woolsey Burton, who died intestate (Sussex Co., Del., Deed Bk. L #11, p. 205).

Carruthers who married (2) Tabitha (___) Young[105] and left will 24 Feb. 1750/1-25 Jan. 1754.[106]

Issue: [CARRUTHERS] 101. John[5], left 150 acres in Sussex Co., Del.; 102. Leah Bagwell[5]; 103. ROBERT[5].

42. JOHN[4] BAGWELL (John[3], Thomas[2], Henry[1]) died before 1750. He married ___.

Issue:[107] 104. THOMAS[5].

43. ELIZABETH[4] BAGWELL (John[3], Thomas[2], Henry[1]) married John Wharton who left will 5 Sept. 1742-30 Oct. 1744.[108]

Issue: [WHARTON][109] 105. JOHN[5]; 106. JAMES[5]; 107. Ann[5], left will 26 Oct. 1765-24 June 1766,[110] unmarried.

47. ANN BAGWELL[4] LEATHERBURY (Comfort[3] Bagwell. Thomas[2], Henry[1]) died before 5 Dec. 1786 when administration on her estate was granted to Leatherbury Barker.[111] She married Job Barker of Sussex Co., Del., who left will 26 Feb. 1748/9-20 March 1748/9.[112]

Issue: [BARKER] 108. JOHN[5]; 109. Job[5]; 110. Temperance[5]; 111. Elizabeth[5]; 112. PERRY[5]; 113. WILLIAM[5]; 114. LEATHERBURY[5]; 115. Ann[5].

49. THOMAS[4] LEATHERBURY (Comfort[3] Bagwell, Thomas[2], Henry[1]) left will 27 Jan. 1754-15 Feb. 1754.[113] He married Diana ___, who left will 8 Oct. 1773-16 April 1774.[114]

Issue: [LEATHERBURY] 116. Thomas[5], baptized 30 Nov. 1746,[115] on whose estate administration was granted to John and Elizabeth Hammons, 2 Nov.

---

[105] Accomack Co. Wills &c 1757-61, p. 39, will of Tabitha Carrothers, 11 April 1749-28 Feb. 1758.

[106] Accomack Co. Wills 1752-57, p. 212.

[107] Will of John[3] Bagwell.

[108] Accomack Co. Wills &c 1743-49, p. 123.

[109] Lucy Ames Edwards, *Ames, Mears and Allied Lines* (n.p., 1967), pp.372-73.

[110] Accomack Co. Wills 1761-67, p. 630.

[111] Sussex Co., Del., Estate records A58, p. 191, Delaware State Archives. Since this grant of administration was made after the death of her original administrator, Job Barker, she probably died some years earlier.

[112] Sussex Co., Del., Will Bk. A, pp. 402-03.

[113] Sussex Co., Del., Will Bk. B, p. 67.

[114] Sussex Co., Del., Estate records A84, pp. 18-19, Delaware State Archives.

[115] St. George's Parish, Indian River, Register, in F. Edward Wright, *Vital Records of Kent and Sussex Counties, Delaware, 1686-1800* (2nd ed.; Silver Spring, Md., 1986), p. 92.

1774;[116] 117. William Perry[5], left will 15 March 1770-21 April 1770,[117] married Elizabeth __, who married (2) Woodman Stockley;[118] 118. ELIZABETH[5]; 119. COMFORT[5]; 120. BARSHEBA[5]; 121. SARAH[5].

51. COMFORT[4] LEATHERBURY (Comfort[3] Bagwell, Thomas[2], Henry[1]) married John Prettyman who left will 23 Feb. 1754-12 March 1754.[119]

Issue: [PRETTYMAN] 122. William[5], died between 9 June 1768 and 5 May 1770,[120] married Comfort Kollock, who died before 27 July 1772 when Perry Prettyman was granted administration on William's estate;[121].123. Ann[5]; 124. Sarah[5]; 125. Elenor[5]; 126. John[5], married Comfort __; 127. Perry[5], born after 1733, died before 4 May 1780 when his widow had to issue new deeds correcting an error in a deed he executed straightening out the estates of his brother and sister-in-law,[122] married (1), 28 April 1773,[123] Esther Shaver, who was buried 25 Sept. 1776, [124] and (2), 14 Aug. 1777,[125] Prudence (Hazzard) Wiltbank; 128. Elizabeth[5], married, by 15 Aug. 1770,[126] Prettyman Stockley,

53. WILLIAM[4] TILNEY (Elizabeth[3] Bagwell, Thomas[2], Henry[1]) chose Thomas Bagwell as his guardian 1 June 1708. He was a tailor of Accomack County and given power of attorney, 22 Aug. 1720, by two of his sisters and his brother-in-law. He married Elizabeth __, to whom administration on his estate was granted 24 Feb. 1740/1.[127]

Issue: [TILNEY] 129. William[5], ship carpenter, left will 26 May 1774-2 June 1774,[128] married (1) Rachel Revell, daughter of Edward and Rebecca

---

[116] Sussex Co., Del., Estate papers A84, p. 21, Delaware State Archives.

[117] Sussex Co., Del., Will Bk. B, pp. 383-85.

[118] Sussex Co., Del., Estate records A84, p. 23, Delaware State Archives.

[119] Sussex Co., Del., Will Bk. B, pp. 71-73.

[120] Sussex Co., Del., Deed Bk. M12, p. 84; Deed Bk. L11, p. 184.

[121] Sussex Co., Del., Estate records A94, p. 125, Delaware State Archives; Patricia Law Hatcher, "Shepard Prettyman and Shepard Kollock of Delaware and New Jersey," *The American Genealogist*, LXXVI, p. 45.

[122] Sussex Co., Del., Deed Bk. M12, pp. 350-51.

[123] St. George's Parish, Indian River, Register, in Wright, *op. cit.*, p. 127.

[124] St. George's Parish, Indian River, Register, in Wright, *op. cit.*, p. 116, as Kessy.

[125] St. George's Parish, Indian River, Register, in Wright, *op. cit.*, p. 128.

[126] Sussex Co., Del., Orphans' Court Docket Bk. 3, 1751-70, p. 262.

[127] Accomack Co. Order Bk. 1737-44, p. 309.

[128] Accomack Co. Wills &c 1772-77, p. 211.

(Coleburn) Revell,[129] and (2) Naomi ___.[130]

54. COMFORT[4] TILNEY (Elizabeth[3] Bagwell, Thomas[2], Henry[1]) was of age 1707. She married, William Warrington of Sussex Co., Del.,[131] who married (2) Mary ___ and left will 20 Jan. 1755-27 June 1755.[132]

Issue: [WARRINGTON] 130. TILNEY[5]; 131. WILLIAM[5]; 132. COMFORT[5].

56. PATIENCE[4] TILNEY (Elizabeth[3] Bagwell, Thomas[2], Henry[1]) chose Charles Leatherbury as her guardian, 1 June 1708. She married, by 18 June 1723, Benjamin Stockley of Sussex Co., Del.,[133] who left will 30 Nov. 1762-24 June 1766.[134]

Issue: [STOCKLEY] 133. Benjamin[5]; 134. Jean[5]; 135. Temperance[5], married ___ Little; 136. Ann[5], born 22 Aug. 1728,[135] married Wrixam West; 137. Esther[5], married Lewis West; 138. Elizabeth[5], married Daniel Horsman; 139. Abigail[5], left will 25 Feb. 1775-1 March 1775,[136] married William Waples, who left will 12 Nov. 1773-17 Feb. 1774;[137] 140. (DAUGHTER)[5].

58. THOMAS[4] BAGWELL (Francis[3], Thomas[2], Henry[1]) was devised land by his grandfather Robert Burton, 1724, and left will 30 May 1770-3 Aug. 1770.[138] He married Ann ___.

Issue: 141. Ann[5], married ___ McMain; 142. John[5], divided with his brother William, 8 Feb. 1781, land "formerly purchased by our ancestors from William Burton of Accomack County in Virginia and last owned by our father Thomas Bagwell, deceased,"[139] possibly the John who left will 26 April 1795-11June 1799,[140] married Patience ___; 143. Thomas[5]; 144. Sarah[5], baptized 13 July

---

[129] Accomack Co. Deeds 3, 1757-70, p. 393; Will Bk. 1752-57, p. 200, will of Edward Revell, 22 March 1753-25 Sept. 1753.

[130] Accomack Co, Deeds &c 1770-77, p. 79.

[131] Accomack Co. Deeds, Wills &c 1715-29, transcript, p. 276.

[132] Sussex Co., Del., Will Bk. B, pp. 103-06.

[133] Accomack Co. Deeds, Wills &c 1715-29, transcript, p. 488.

[134] Sussex Co., Del., Will Bk. B, pp. 299-300.

[135] St. George's Parish, Indian River, Sussex Co., Del., Register, in Wright, *op. cit.*, p. 95.

[136] Sussex Co., Del., Will Bk. B, p. 538.

[137] *Ibid.*, p. 500.

[138] *Ibid.*, pp. 396-98.

[139] Sussex Co., Del., Deed M #12, pp. 388-89.

[140] Sussex Co., Del., Will Bk. E, pp. 226-27, naming nephew William Bagwell Burton and mentioning Peter Bagwell McHam.

1746;[141] 145. WILLIAM[5]; 146. Elizabeth[5]; 147. Catherine[5], born 14 Aug. 1753;[142] 148. Lydia[5].

59. AGNES[4] BAGWELL (William[3], Thomas[2], Henry[1]) married John Adams, cordwainer of Lewes, Del., and sold 75 acres in Long Neck 3 May 1726.[143]

Issue: [ADAMS] 149. John[5], as mariner of Sussex Co., Del., sold 150 acres, part of Long Neck, to John Holloway, 7 Nov. 1771,[144] but later repurchased 50 acres of that tract,[145] and as a pilot of Indian River Hundred, with wife Cornelia ___,[146] sold part of Long Neck to William Burton, 6 Feb. 1772.[147]

62. THOMAS[4] LEATHERBURY (Vallance[3] Bagwell, Thomas[2], Henry[1]) left will 27 Dec. 1747-29 March 1748.[148] He married Rachael ____, who married (2) Joshua James, whose will, 23 Jan. 1749-27 Feb. 1749/50, named wife Rachel and son-in-law [step-son] Charles Leatherbury.[149]

Issue: [LEATHERBURY][150] 150. CHARLES[5]; 151. Thomas[5]; 152. John[5]; 153. Elizabeth[5], married ___ Giles.[151]

63. JOHN[4] LEATHERBURY (Vallance[3] Bagwell, Thomas[2], Henry[1]) removed to Somerset Co., Md., and left will 1 May 1756-17 Nov. 1756.[152] He married Sarah, daughter of Charles Ballard.[153]

Issue: [LEATHERBURY][154] 154. ELEANOR[5]; 155. Elizabeth[5], perhaps

---

[141] St. George's Parish, Indian River, Register, in Wright, *op. cit.*, p. 92.

[142] St. George's Parish, Indian River, Register, in Wright, *op. cit.*, p. 95.

[143] Sussex Co., Del., Will Bk. E, pp. 217-18.

[144] Sussex Co., Del., Deed Bk. L #11, p. 174.

[145] *Ibid.*, p. 193.

[146] She apparently was a widow since the will of Mary Hugg, widow of Elias Hugg, 14 May 1773-1 July 1774 (Sussex Co., Del., Will Bk. B, pp. 522-23), named mother Cornelia Adams, wife of John Adams, sisters Cornelia King (wife of James) and Rebeckah Westly (wife of John) and uncle Henry Fisher.

[147] Sussex Co., Del., Deed Bk. L #11, p. 191, naming William Bagwell as grandfather of the grantor.

[148] Accomack Co. Wills &c 1745-49, p. 416; *ES* II, p. 836.

[149] Accomack Co. Wills 1749-52, p. 55.

[150] *ES* II, p. 836.

[151] *Maryland Genealogical Society Bulletin*, XXXI, p. 184.

[152] Somerset Co., Md., Will Bk. ED #4, pp. 42-43.

[153] Maryland Proprietary Wills 18, pp. 363-64, will of Charles Ballard, Sr., of Somerset County, 29 Feb. 1723/4-21 Jan. 1724/5.

[154] Named in father's will.

married ___ King; 156. JOHN[5]; 157. ROBERT[5]; 158. MARY[5]; 159. Charles[5], left land on Wicomico Creek, Somerset Co., Md., married Priscilla ___.

67. BRIDGET[4] SAVAGE (Ann[3] Bagwell, Thomas[2], Henry[1]) , identified as only child of her mother by partition deed, 30 Aug. 1748,[155] married Isaac Dix, Sr., who left will 8 Feb. 1750/1-27 Aug. 1751.[156]

Issue: [DIX][157] 160. RICHARD[5]; 161. ISAAC[5]; 162. SOLOMON[5]; 163. GEORGE[5]; 164. Elizabeth[5].

68. SPENCER[5] BAGWELL (Henry[4], Henry[3], John[2], Henry[1]) left will 23 Sept. 1778-23 Feb. 1779.[158] He married Sophia ___, who left will 4 June 1797-31 Aug. 1797.[159]

Issue: 165. John[6]; 166. Betty[6], married ___ Bonnewell, probably Stephen Bonnewell who married (2) Nancy ____and left will 15 Feb. 1805-25 Feb. 1815;[160] 167. Sarah[6]; 168. Anne[6]; 169. Heli[6], died before 28 Dec. 1795 when administration on his estate was granted to his widow,[161] married Ann [Nancy] ___; 170. William[6].

70. CHARLES[5] BAGWELL (John[4], Henry[3], John[2], Henry[1]) was churchwarden of Accomack Parish[162] and member of the Accomack County Committee of Safety, 1774. He left will 26 Aug. 1792-24 June 1793.[163] He married Ann (Kitson) Evans, daughter of John Kitson[164] and widow of John Evans.[165]

Issue: 171. Col. Charles[6], murdered 24 May 1819 while driving home from Drummond Town,[166] left will 9 April 1818-26 July 1819,[167] married, 25 Jan.

---

[155] Accomack Co. Deeds 1746-57, pp. 168-69.

[156] Accomack Co. Wills 1749-52, p. 293.

[157] Will of Isaac Dix; *ES* II, pp. 1082-85.

[158] Accomack Co. Wills &c 1777-80, p. 291.

[159] Accomack Co. Wills&c 1796-98, p. 204.

[160] Accomack Co. Wills &c 1804-06, p. 245.

[161] Accomack Co. Order Bk. 1793-96, p. 406.

[162] *ES* II, p. 1148.

[163] Accomack Co. Wills 1788-94, p. 751.

[164] Accomack Co. Wills 1780-84, p. 244, will of John Kitson naming son-in-law Charles Bagwell and grandson Charles Bagwell.

[165] Accomack Co. Wills &c 1757-61, p. 300, will of John Evans, 30 Jan. 1760-27 Jan. 1761.

[166] *The Lynchburg Press & Public Advertiser*, 14 June 1819.

[167] Accomack Co. Wills &c 1818-19, pp. 381-82.

1791,[168] Ann [Nancy] Grinalds who left will 12 March 1846-29 Jan./28 May 1849.[169]

73. ROSE[5] BAGWELL (Thomas[4], Henry[3], Thomas[2], Henry[1]) married, (bond 5) April 1786,[170] John Arlington, who married (2) Sophia ___ and left will 24 Sept. 1818-28 Sept. 1818.[171]

Issue: [ARLINGTON] 172. Elizabeth[6], married, (bond 6) Jan. 1806,[172] William Mears; 173. Thomas Bagwell[6]; 174. Rose Ann[6], born 16 March 1791, died 9 July 1861,[173] married, 30 Nov. 1814,[174] William Finney, who married (1), 29 Dec. 1810, Lean Parker; 175. Ann S.[6], born 17 Feb. 1793, died 22 Dec. 1853,[175] married, (bond 22) Feb. 1827,[176] John A. Edwards, who died 18 Feb. 1832,[177] leaving will 28 June 1849-30 Dec. 1853.[178]

75. JOHN[5] CUSTIS (Tabitha[4] Bagwell, Henry[3], John[2], Henry[1]), called John Custis (Sea Side), was a captain in the Revolutionary War. He left will 18 Jan. 1808-29 Feb. 1808.[179] He married (1) Esther Savage, daughter of John and _ (Floyd) Savage, (2) 559. *Esther[6] Savage* (see WILKINS) and (3) Margaret _, possibly Evans.[180]

Issue: [CUSTIS] 176. Leah[6], married Washington Milbourn; 177. Susannah[6], died 1788, married (1), (bond 3) Sept. 1783,[181] Thomas Crippen, Jr., who died before 28 March 1786 when administration on his estate was granted to John Custis,[182] and (2) John Finney; 178. Henry Bagwell[6], left will 29 July

---

[168] Nora Miller Turman, *Marriage Records of Accomack County, Virginia, 1776-1854* (Bowie, Md., 1994), p. 14.

[169] Accomack Co. Will Bk. 1846-82, p. 66.

[170] Turman, *op. cit.*, p. 9.

[171] Accomack Co. Wills &c 1818-19, p. 102.

[172] Turman, *op. cit.*, p. 197.

[173] Gravestone, Arlington cemetery, in Mihalyka and Wilson, *op. cit.*, p. 88.

[174] William Finney Bible (Philadelphia, 1803), in Jean M. Mihalyka, "Bible Records, Accomack and Northampton Counties, Virginia," Virginia State Archives, Miscellaneous Bible Records, XXVII, pp. 152-53.

[175] Gravestone, Edwards cemetery, in Mihalyka and Wilson, *op. cit.*, p. 74.

[176] Turman, *op. cit.*, p. 93.

[177] Gravestone, Edwards cemetery, *loc. cit.*

[178] Accomack Co. Will Bk. 1846-82, p. 97.

[179] Accomack Co. Wills &c 1806-09, p. 475.

[180] Marie Ellen Russell, "Who We Are," Virginia Historical Society Mss 6:1 R9195:1.

[181] Turman, *op. cit.*, p. 71.

[182] Accomack Co. Order Bk. 1784-86, p. 484.

1817-29 Dec. 1817,[183] married ___; 179. Catherine[6], married John Coulborn; 180. Anne[6], married Arthur White, who died by 26 Feb. 1805 when administration on his estate was granted to Charles Stockley;[184] 181. Tabitha[6], died young; 182. Elizabeth[6], married (1) Hancock Copes and (2) John Bundick; 183. William Edmund[6], under age in 1808, left will 24 Nov. 1813-27 Dec. 1813.[185]

77. WILLIAM SMITH[5] CUSTIS (Tabitha[4] Bagwell, Henry[3], John[2], Henry[1]) left will 2 Nov. 1817-29 Jan. 1821.[186] He married (1), (bond 2) Jan. 1787,[187] Bridget Pennock and (2) Margaret (___) Savage, widow of Maj. John Savage.

Issue: [CUSTIS] 184. William Smith[6], of "Sea View," Accomack County, left will 18 Jan. 1834-28 Nov. 1836,[188] married, (bond 2) Nov. 1814,[189] 176. *Elizabeth[6] Stran* (see PARRAMORE), who was born 11 Feb. 1792 and died 16 July 1837;[190] 185. Mary[6], married ___ Selby.

78. BETTY[5] CUSTIS (Tabitha[4] Bagwell, Henry[3], John[2], Henry[1]) married William Garrison, who left will 8 Dec. 1787-25 June 1788.[191]

Isue: [GARRISON] 186. John[6], left will 6 July 1790-27 July/26 Oct. 1795;[192] 187. Tabitha[6]; 188. Joshua[6], married ___ Savage; 189. Betsy[6]; 190. William[6]; 191. Bagwell[6], married, (bond 21) March 1809,[193] Catherine Mathews; 192. Edmund[6], born 16 March 1786, died 14 Oct. 1841,[194] left will 27 April 1841-25 Oct. 1841,[195] married, (bond 25) Dec. 1816,[196] Bridget Ross, born 6 May 1798, died 29 Aug. 1826;[197] 193. Rose[6].

79. FRANCIS[5] ROBERTS (Margaret[4] Bagwell, Alexander[3], John[2], Henry[1])

---

[183] Accomack Co. Wills &c 1817-18, p. 218.

[184] Accomack Co. Order Bk. 1804-05, p. 222.

[185] Accomack Co. Wills &c 1812-14, p. 345.

[186] Accomack Co. Wills &c 1819-21, p. 339.

[187] Turman, *op. cit.*, p. 76.

[188] Accomack Co. Will Bk. 1828-46, p. 283.

[189] Turman, *op. cit.*, p. 76.

[190] Gravestone, Stran Cemetery, in Carey, *op. cit.*, p. 95.

[191] Accomack Co. Will Bk. 1788-94, p. 63.

[192] Accomack Co. Wills &c 1794-96, p. 243.

[193] Mihalyka, *Marriages, Northampton County,* p. 43.

[194] Gravestone, Mount Holly Cemetery, Onancock, Va., in Mihalyka and Wilson, *op. cit.*, p. 95.

[195] Accomack Co. Will Bk. 1828-46, p. 41.

[196] Turman, *op. cit.*, p. 109.

[197] Gravestone, Mount Holly Cemetery, *loc. cit.*

left will 15 May 1768-10 Jan. 1769.[198] He married Agnes _____.

Issue: [ROBERTS] 194. Elizabeth[6]; 195. Sarah[6], married, (bond 6) July 1774,[199] James Sanford, who left will 16 May 1818-codicil 25 Sept. 1819-13 Dec. 1819.[200]

80. JOACHIM[5] ROBERTS (Margaret[4] Bagwell, Alexander[3], John[2], Henry[1]) left will 10 Feb. 1791-28 June 1791.[201] He married Sarah ___.

Issue: [ROBERTS][202] 196. John[6], left will 4 Nov. 1834-27 April 1835,[203] married (1) _____[204] and (2), (bond 16) March 1818,[205] Adah[7] Mears, daughter of 121. *John[6] Mears* and Molly Beach (see GRANGER);[206] 197. Mary Bagwell[6]; 198. Rachel James[6]; 199. Francis[6]; 200. Arthur[6]; 201. Joshua[6].

81. ARTHUR[5] ROBERTS (Margaret[4] Bagwell, Alexander[3], John[2], Henry[1]) left will 22 Nov. 1799-24 Feb. 1800.[207] He married Patience ___, who died by 1817.[208]

Issue: [ROBERTS] 202. Arthur[6], left will 17 Sept. 1797-25 Dec. 1797,[209] married, (bond 2) May 1793,[210] Elizabeth (___) Major, widow of John Major; 203. William Simkins[6], died before 29 Jan. 1816 when administration was granted on his estate,[211] married ___, who married (2), by 8 Dec. 1817, Arthur Powell;[212] 204. Peggy Bagwell[6], married Levin Powell; 205. Nancy[6], died by 1818, married (1), (bond 19) July 1784,[213] Coventon Mears of Accomack County

---

[198] Northampton Co. Wills & Inventories 24, 1766-72, pp. 204-05.

[199] Turman, *op. cit.*, p. 245.

[200] Northampton Co. Wills &c 35, 1817-22, pp. 400-03.

[201] Accomack Co. Wills 1788-94, p. 377.

[202] *ES* I, p. 591.

[203] Accomack Co. Wills &c 1828-46, pp. 177-78.

[204] Perhaps, (bond 27) Oct. 1804, Nancy (___) Read, widow of Severn Read (Turman, *op. cit.*, p. 237).

[205] *Ibid.*

[206] Lucy Ames Edwards, *Ames, Mears and Allied Lines* (n.p., 1967), pp. 196-97.

[207] Accomack Co. Wills &c 1798-1800, p. 366.

[208] Accomack Co. Wills &c 1825-26, pp. 241-43, inventory of estate of Arthur Roberts, made pursuant to order of 1 Sept. 1817, and accounting which includes payment for her coffin.

[209] Accomack Co. Wills &c 1796-98, p. 340.

[210] Mihalyka, *Marriages, Northampton County*, p. 90.

[211] Accomack Co. Order Bk. 1815-17, p. 212.

[212] Accomack Co. Wills &c 1817-18, p. 348.

[213] Turman, *op. cit.*, p. 191.

who died 1796,[214] (2), by 1799, William Groten and (3) James Gumby.[215]

87. EDMUND[5] MILLS (William[4], Rebecca[3] Bagwell, John[2], Henry[1]) died before 13 June 1780 when administration on his estate was granted to Daniel Roalls [Rowles] Hall.[216] He married, (bond 23) Feb. 1761,[217] Susanna Fitchet, daughter of Nehemiah Fitchet.[218]

Issue: [MILLS] Unidentified.

89. ISAIAH[5] BAGWELL (Thomas[4], Thomas[3], Thomas[2], Henry[1]), born 23 Dec. 1736, left nuncupative will 10 March 1764-24 April 1764.[219] He married Sarah ___, born 19 Aug. 1737, who married (2) George Oldham.[220]

Issue:[221] 206. William[6], born 25 Nov. 1755; 207. Thomas[6], born 15 May 1758, died 17 May 1816, left will 5 Nov. 1810-27 May 1816,[222] married Margaret Kellam,[223] who married (2), (bond 18) March 1817,[224] Jesse Elliott and left will 3 June 1824-28 June 1824;[225] 208. Isaiah[6], born 13 Sept. 1760, died 8 Oct. 1839,[226] left will 30 June 1837-28 May 1840,[227] private in 9th Virginia Regiment, 1776-78, seaman on the schooner *Betsey* which was captured by the British 12 April 1780, imprisoned until May 1782,[228] married, 3 Jan. 1790, Christina Newton, daughter of Andrew and Catherine (Goldie) Newton, born 29

---

[214] Stratton Nottingham, *Land Causes, Accomack County, Virginia, 1727-1826* (Baltimore, 1999), p. 54. Administration on his estate granted to Nancy 30 Jan. 1797 (Accomack Co. Order Bk. 1796-98, p. 164).

[215] Accomack Co. Wills &c 1825-26, p. 243.

[216] Northampton Co. Minute Bk. 29, 1777-83, p. 239.

[217] Mihalyka, *Marriages, Northampton County*, p. 74.

[218] Northampton Co. Wills &c 23, 1763-65, p. 355, will of Nehemiah Fitchet, 26 Oct. 1764-13 Nov. 1764.

[219] Accomack Co. Will Bk. 1761-67, p. 273.

[220] The heirs of George Oldham (Louis A. Burgess, *Virginia Soldiers of 1776*, III [Richmond, 1929], p. 1020) included the half-sisters named in the will of Thomas[6] Bagwell.

[221] Isaiah Bagwell Bible (Philadelphia, 1807), in Jean M. Mihalyka, "Bible Records, Accomack and Northampton Counties, Virginia" (Cherryton, Va., 1990), Virginia State Archives, Miscellaneous Bible Records XXXVI, pp. 160-62.

[222] Accomack Co. Wills &c 1814-16, p. 524.

[223] Accomack Co. Wills &c 1806-09, p. 601, will of John Kellam, Sr., 11 July 1806-29 Feb./28 July 1808.

[224] Turman, *op. cit.*, p.. 94.

[225] Accomack Co. Wills &c 1824-25, p. 22.

[226] Gravestone, Bagwell Cemetery, in Mihalyka and Wilson, *op. cit.*, p. 10.

[227] Accomack Co. Wills &c 1828-46, pp. 352-53.

[228] Revolutionary War pension, Isaiah Bagwell, S.6550, National Archives.

Oct. 1758, died 11 July 1839;[229] 209. George[6], born 15 Nov. 1762; 210. George Poulson[6], born 13 Sept. 1764, died Feb. 1826, left will 3 Feb. 1826-27 Feb./27 March 1826,[230] married (1) Caty Chandler[231] and (2), (bond 5) June 1799,[232] Margaret Dix, who left will 8 Aug. 1834-25 July 1836.[233]

92. ADAH[5] BAGWELL (Thomas[4], Thomas[3], Thomas[2], Henry[1]), born 12 Sept. 1734, died 26 Aug. 1766,[234] married, 8 March 1756,[235] as his (1) wife, 179. *George[6] Parker* (see UTIE-BENNETT), of "Sylvan Retreat," Accomack County, who married (2) 66. *Sarah[5] Andrews* (see ANDREWS).

Issue: [PARKER][236] 211. Col. Thomas[6], born 8 Jan. 1757, died Nov. 1819,[237] left will 10 Oct. 1804-codicil 22 Sept. 1815-27 Dec. 1819,[238] of "Poplar Grove," Accomack County, ensign in 2nd Virginia Regiment, 4 Jan. 1777, lieutenant, 13 Oct. 1777, wounded and captured at Savannah, exchanged 22 Dec. 1780, served to close of war,[239] married 114. *Elizabeth[6] Andrews* (see ANDREWS); 212. George[6], born 13 May 1758, died 16 Sept. 1759; 213. Elizabeth[6], born 27 Feb. 1760, married (1) __ Teackle, perhaps Arthur Teackle who left will 12 Jan. 1791-27 April/2 Dec. 1791,[240] and (2) ____Reed; 214. George[6], born 10 May 1761, died 12 July 1826 at Richmond,[241] left will 9 Oct. 1825-14 Aug. 1826,[242] represented Accomack County in the Convention of 1788,[243] elected judge of the General Court, Dec. 1825, married (1), 12 Oct. 1786,[244] Margaret Eyre, (2), 25 May 1802,[245] 536. *Elizabeth[6] (Smith) Stith* (see WEST, Anthony), born 26 Feb. 1760, widow of Griffin Stith, and (3), 19 May

---

[229] Gravestone, Bagwell Cemetery, *loc. cit.*

[230] Accomack Co. Wills &c 1825-26, p. 583.

[231] Accomack Co. Order Bk. 1832-36, p. 122.

[232] Turman, *op. cit.*, p. 14.

[233] Accomack Co. Will Bk. 1828-46, p. 207.

[234] Gravestone, "Poplar Cove," in Mihalyka and Wilson, *op. cit.*, p. 192.

[235] Bible, in *V* VI, p. 414.

[236] *V* VI, p. 414.

[237] *Enquirer*, Richmond, 20 Jan. 1820.

[238] Accomack Co. Wills &c 1819-21, p. 128.

[239] *DAR Magazine*, LXI, no. 1, p. 23.

[240] Accomack Co. Wills 1788-94, p. 448.

[241] *Enquirer*, Richmond, 18 July 1826.

[242] Northampton Co. Wills & Inventories 37, 1825-29, pp. 309-11.

[243] Leonard, p. 172.

[244] Mihalyka, *Marriages, Northampton County*, p. 82.

[245] *Ibid.*

1813,[246] her sister 541. *Susannah*[6] (*Smith*) *Savage*, born 8 Nov. 1770, died Sept. 1848;[247] 215. Ann[6], born 25 Aug. 1763, died 18 June 1820, married Littleton Upshur, born 26 April 1758 at "Warwick," Northampton County, died 27 Aug. 1811,[248] of "Vaucluse," Northampton County.

99. LEAH[5] BAGWELL (John[4], Thomas[3], Thomas[2], Henry[1]) left will 21 June 1796-25 July 1796.[249] She married (1) John Revell, who died before 26 June 1764 when administration on his estate was granted to Leah,[250] and (2) 54. *William*[6] *Seymour* (see YEARDLEY), who left will 9 Nov. 1776-31 Dec. 1776.[251]

Issue: (by 1) [REVELL] 216. John[6], left will 26 Nov. 1806-28 April 1807,[252] married, (bond 28) Feb. 1787,[253] Elizabeth Poulson; 217. Sarah[6], married _____ Poulson; 218. Edward[6], died before 28 Dec. 1791 when administration was granted on his estate,[254] married (1) 263. *Ann*[6] *Ker* (see O'NEIL-ROBINS), who died 10 April 1788,[255] and (2) 109. *Susanna*[6] *Andrews* (see ANDREWS), born 4 July 1766, died 9 July 1806,[256] who married (2) 282. *Revell*[6] *West* (see WEST, Anthony); 219. Elizabeth[6], married 258. *John Shepherd*[6] *Ker* (see O'NEIL-ROBINS); (by 2) [SEYMOUR] 220. George[6], died before 29 Dec. 1806 when administration on his estate was granted to Margaret Seymour,[257] married Margaret ___, who married (2), (bond 16) Dec. 1807,[258] Littleton Hammell; 221. Rev. William[6], born 1 Oct. 1773, died 24 Oct. 1821,[259]

---

[246] *Ibid.*

[247] Isaac Smith Bible, in Jean M. Mihalyka, "Bible Records, Accomack and Northampton Counties, Virginia," Virginia State Archives, Miscellaneous Bible Records, XXX, p. 119.

[248] John Andrews Upshur, *Upshur Family in Virginia* (Richmond, 1955), pp. 52-54; *Enquirer*, Richmond, 6 Sept. 1811.

[249] Accomack Co. Wills &c 1794-96, p. 405.

[250] Accomack Co. Order Bk. 1764-65, p. 146.

[251] Accomack Co. Will Bk. 1772-77, p. 469.

[252] Accomack Co. Wills &c 1806-09, p. 127.

[253] Turman, *op. cit.*, p. 234.

[254] Accomack Co. Order Bk. 1790-93, p. 300; Wills &c 1821-23, p. 173, recorded 25 March 1822.

[255] *Norfolk and Portsmouth Journal*, 23 April 1788.

[256] Gravestone, in Mihalyka and Wilson, *op. cit.*, p. 276.

[257] Accomack Co. Order Bk. 1806-07, p. 233.

[258] Turman, *op. cit.*, p. 120.

[259] Gravestone, Seymour-Snead cemetery, Onancock, in Mihalyka and Wilson, *op. cit.*, p. 231.

left will 21 Oct. 1821-29 Oct. 1821,[260] merchant of Onancock in partnership with John S. Ker, married (1) 266. *Elizabeth*[6] *Ker* (see O'NEIL-ROBINS), born 8 June 1771, died 18 Jan. 1811,[261] and (2) her sister 264. *Isabel*[6] *(Ker) Bowman*; 222. Leah[6], married, (bond 30) Aug. 1802,[262] Richard Ames, born 11 April 1776, died 20 Nov. 1834,[263] who married (2), (bond 23) Nov. 1812,[264] Margaret (__) Ames and left will 26 Sept. 1834-24 Nov. 1834.[265]

100. RACHEL[5] BAGWELL (John[4], Thomas[3], Thomas[2], Henry[1]) married __ Walton.

Issue: [WALTON] 223. Bagwell[6].

103. ROBERT[5] CARRUTHERS (Sara[4] Bagwell, Thomas[3], Thomas[2], Henry[1]) was left 125 acres in Accomack County and left will 3 Sept. 1773-1 Dec. 1773. He married ___.

Issue: [CARRUTHERS] 224. William[6]; 225. John[6]; 226. James[6], married ____, probably the Elizabeth on whose estate Lewis L. Snead was granted administration, 31 Jan. 1853;[266] 227. Sarah[6]; 228. Mary[6]; 229. Elizabeth[6]; 230. Margaret[6].

104. THOMAS[5] BAGWELL (John[4], John[3], Thomas[2], Henry[1]), under guardianship of Charles Stockley, 28 Feb. 1749/50,[267] left will 18 Nov. 1770-28 Aug. 1771.[268] He married Sophia ___.

Issue: 231. John[6], under 21 in 1770, referred to in 1808 as "supposed to be deceased" when land was surveyed for sister Rachel; 232. Thomas[6], died unmarried; 233. Rachel[6], died by 1 May 1821 when administration was granted on her estate,[269] married Jesse Kellam, who died by 27 Dec. 1800 when administration on his estate was granted to John Kellam.[270]

105. JOHN[5] WHARTON (Elizabeth[4] Bagwell, John[3], Thomas[2], Henry[1]) left

---

[260] Accomack Co. Wills &c 1821-23, p. 14.
[261] Gravestone, Seymour-Snead cemetery, *loc. cit.*
[262] Turman, *op. cit.*, p. 6.
[263] Gravestone, Ames plot, Painter, in Mihalyka and Wilson, *op. cit.*, p. 4.
[264] Turman, *op. cit.*, p. 6.
[265] Accomack Co. Will Bk. 1828-46, p. 164.
[266] Accomack Co. Order Bk. 1851-54, p. 345.
[267] Accomack Co. Order Bk. 1744-53, p. 392.
[268] Accomack Co. Wills &c 1767-72, p. 607.
[269] Accomack Co. Order Bk. 1819-21, p. 327.
[270] *ES* II, p. 878; Accomack Co. Order Bk. 1800-04, p. 5.

will 29 May 1772-30 July 1776.[271] He married Elizabeth ___.

Issue: [WHARTON] 234. Tabitha[6], under age 12 in 1765, died before 30 Oct. 1825 when administration on her estate was granted to James H. Dix,[272] married Ephraim Watson, who left will 22 May 1822-31 March 1823;[273] 235. John[6], born 25 Nov. 1762 in Accomack County, died 25 Feb. 1811 at Philadelphia, Pa., of "Wharton Place," Accomack County, engaged in coastwise trade, married, 10 June 1784,[274] Elizabeth Williams, daughter of William and Margaret Williams, who was born 24 May 1764 in Accomack County, died 13 Nov. 1831,[275] left will 29 Oct. 1830-26 Dec. 1831;[276] 236. Nanny[6], died by 1772; 237. Bagwell[6], born 24 Sept. 1770, died 12 Feb. 1821,[277] left will 8 Feb. 1821-27 Feb. 1821,[278] of "Sunderland Hall," Accomack County, married (1), 28 Dec. 1791,[279] Esther Tunnell[280] and (2), (bond 15) June 1811,[281] Catherine[7] Custis, daughter of 444. *John[6] Custis* and Catharine Parker (see WEST, Anthony), born 15 Sept. 1782, died 24 Aug. 1839,[282] left will 6 July 1833-27 May 1839;[283] 238. William[5].

106. JAMES[5] WHARTON (Elizabeth[4] Bagwell, John[3], Thomas[2], Henry[1]) died 1792.[284] He married, after 1767, Susannah James, daughter of William and Amey James, who died Oct. 1813,[285] leaving will 2 Feb. 1813-20 Oct. 1813.[286]

Issue: [WHARTON][287] 239. William[6], left will 10 May 1824-28 Dec.

---

[271] Accomack Co. Wills &c 1772-77, p. 432.

[272] Accomack Co. Order Bk. 1824-27, p. 435.

[273] Accomack Co. Wills &c 1823-24, p. 82.

[274] Turman, *op. cit.*, p. 318, bond 6 June 1784.

[275] Gravestones, Wharton Cemetery near Mappsville, in Mary Frances Carey and others, *Tombstone Inscriptions of Upper Accomack County, Virginia* (Bowie, Md., 1995), p. 291.

[276] Accomack Co. Wills 1828-46, p. 101.

[277] Gravestone, "Sunderland Hall," in Carey, *loc. cit.*

[278] Accomack Co. Wills &c 1819-21, pp. 345-46.

[279] Turman, *op. cit.*, p. 318.

[280] *ES* II, p. 1232.

[281] Turman, *op. cit.*, p. 318.

[282] Gravestone, "Sunderland Hall," *loc. cit.*

[283] Accomack Co. Qill Bk. 1828-46, p. 302.

[284] Accomack Co. Land Causes 1812-21, p. 305. Administration granted 24 Feb. 1795 to Susanna Wharton (Accomack Co. Order Bk. 1793-96, p. 288).

[285] Accomack Co. Land Causes 1812-21, p. 305.

[286] Accomack Co. Wills &c 1814-16, pp. 331-32.

[287] Nottingham, *op. cit.*, p. 115; Edwards, *op. cit.*, pp. 373-74.

1824,[288] unmarried; 240. Ann[6], born 1777, died 21 Aug. 1837,[289] married James Edmunds, born 20 Aug. 1774, died 9 Sept. 1844,[290] left will 25 Nov. 1840-30 Sept. 1844.[291] sergeant in Capt. William C. Scott's company, 28th Regiment, Virginia Militia, in War of 1812;[292] 241. John[6], left will 7 Jan. 1821-29 Jan. 1821;[293] 242. Elizabeth[6]; 243. Charles[6], died before 30 Nov. 1813 when administration was granted on his estate,[294] married, (bond 14) Oct. 1806,[295] Elizabeth Shield, who married (2), (bond 21) Sept. 1814,[296] Isaac Wright; 244. James[6], died Aug. 1812,[297] married Sally Shield, who died Aug. 1806.[298]

108. JOHN[5] BARKER (Ann[4] Leatherbury, Comfort[3] Bagwell, Thomas[2], Henry[1]) married ___.

Issue: [BARKER][299] 245. Job[6], baptized 15 June 1746; 246. Ann[6], baptized 22 May 1748.

112. PERRY[5] BARKER (Ann[4] Leatherbury, Comfort[3] Bagwell, Thomas[2], Henry[1]) died before 5 Dec. 1786 when administration on his estate was granted to Leatherbury Barker.[300] He married (1) Sarah ___ and (2) Catherine Burton, daughter of John and Ann Catherine (___) Burton

Issue: [BARKER] (by 1) 247. Aaron[6], born 15 Feb. 1770,[301] died young; 248. Elen[6], born 1 Sept. 1771,[302] died young; 249. Jehu[6], born 8 Oct. 1773;[303] (by which wife undetermined) 250. Comfort[6]; 251. Sarah[6]; 252. Perry[6]; (probably by 2) 253. John Burton[6], perhaps the John who married, 17 Feb.

[288] Accomack Co. Wills &c 1828-46, pp. 53-54.

[289] Jean M. Mihalyka and Faye Downing Wilson, *Graven Stones of Lower Accomack County, Virginia* (Bowie, Md., 1986), p. 79.

[290] *Ibid.*; James Edmunds Bible, Virginia State Archives, Acc.24469b.

[291] Accomack Co. Will Bk. 1828-46, p. 52.

[292] Edwards, *op. cit.*. pp. 263-64.

[293] Accomack Co. Wills &c 1819-21, p. 338.

[294] Accomack Co. Order Bk. 1812-13, p. 329.

[295] Turman, *op. cit.*, p. 318.

[296] *Ibid.*, p. 330.

[297] Nottingham, *op. cit.*, p. 98.

[298] *Ibid.*, pp. 46, 98.

[299] St. George's Parish, Indian River, Register, in Wright, *op. cit.*, pp. 91, 93.

[300] Sussex Co., Del., Estate records A58, p. 102, Delaware State Archives.

[301] St. George's Parish, Indian River, Register, in Wright, *op. cit.*, p. 100.

[302] *Ibid.*

[303] St. George's Parish, Indian River, Register, in Wright, *op. cit.*, p. 101.

1797,[304] Polly Prettyman; 254. David[6].

113. WILLIAM[5] BARKER (Ann[4] Leatherbury, Comfort[3] Bagwell, Thomas[2], Henry[1]) married Comfort ___.

. Issue: [BARKER][305] 255. Job[6], born 14 Feb. __, baptized 12 March 1770; 256. Nanny Bagwell[6], born 3 Feb. __, baptized 12 March 1770, married, 8 Sept. 1789,[306] Noble Lewis.

114. LEATHERBURY[5] BARKER (Ann[4] Leatherbury, Comfort[3] Bagwell, Thomas[2], Henry[1]) left will 20 Jan. 1789-30 June 1789.[307] He married (1) Abigail ___, who died 26 Oct. 1785,[308] and (2) Sarah ___.

Issue: [BARKER] (by 1) 257. Bagwell[6], born 5 Oct. 176_,[309] married Elen ___; 258. George[6], born 13 Feb. 1772,[310] died young; (by 2) 259. Nancy[6]; 260. Joseph[6].

118. ELIZABETH[5] LEATHERBURY (Thomas[4], Comfort[3] Bagwell, Thomas[2], Henry[1]) married John Hemans [Hammons], who left will 28 July 1788-8 Dec. 1789.[311]

Issue: [HAMMONS] 261. Elizabeth[6], married ___ Jacobs; 262. Thomas[6]; 263. Mary[6]; 264. William Leatherbury[6], born 5 May 1771.[312]

119. COMFORT[5] LEATHERBURY (Thomas[4], Comfort[3] Bagwell, Thomas[2], Henry[1]) married William Salmons.

Issue: [SALMONS] 265. Comfort Leatherbury[6], born 4 June 1770.[313]

120. BARSHEBA[5] LEATHERBURY (Thomas[4], Comfort[3] Bagwell, Thomas[2], Henry[1]) married Paul Waples, who was born in Worcester Co., Md., settled in Sussex Co., Del., and left will 13 June 1800-9 Jan. 1801.[314]

Issue: [WAPLES] 266. Paul[6]; 267. John Smith[6], born 6 Jan. 1776 in Sussex Co., Del., died there 3 April 1818, married, 22 July 1802, Nancy Robinson, born

---

[304] St. George's Parish, Indian River, Register, in Wright, *op. cit.*, p. 135.

[305] St. George's Parish, Indian River, Register, in Wright, *op. cit.*, p. 99.

[306] Lewes and Cool Spring Presbyterian Church Register, in Wright, *op. cit.*, p. 133.

[307] Sussex Co., Del. Will Bk. D, pp. 231-32.

[308] St. George's Parish, Indian River, Register, in Wright, *op. cit.*, p. 111.

[309] St. George's Parish, Indian River, Register, in Wright, *op. cit.*, p. 97.

[310] St. George's Parish, Indian River, Register, in Wright, *op. cit.*, p. 100.

[311] Sussex Co., Del., Will Bk. D, pp. 247-48.

[312] St. George's Parish, Indian River, Register, in Wright, *op. cit.*, p. 140.

[313] St. George's Parish, Indian River, Register, in Wright, *op. cit.*, p. 100.

[314] Sussex Co., Del., Probate 1801-18, Delaware State Archives.

20 March 1784, died 29 Nov. 1831 in Sussex Co., Del.;[315] 268. Peter[6]; 269. Betsey[6]; 270. Barshaba[6]; 271. Catharine[6]; 272. Sally[6], married ___ Long.

121. SARAH[5] LEATHERBURY (Thomas[4], Comfort[3] Bagwell, Thomas[2], Henry[1]) married (1) Isaac Prettyman with whom and her sister Comfort she quit claimed their interest in the land of their father to their brothers William Perry and Thomas, 12 March 1754.[316] His will, 23 March 1767-6 May 1767, named her and their son Joseph.[317] She married (2) George Barnes.

Issue: (by 1) [PRETTYMAN] 273. Leah[6], probably died before 1773; 274. Elizabeth[6]; 275. Ann[6]; 276. Phebe[6]; 277. Comfort[6]; 278. Joseph[6]; 279. Sheppard[6], married, 18 Sept. 1777,[318] Peggy Saunders.

130. TILNEY[5] WARRINGTON (Comfort[4] Tilney, Elizabeth[3] Bagwell, Thomas[2], Henry[1]), born 9 Oct. 1711,[319] died before 1755. She married (1) William Woolf and (2) John Little.

Issue:[320] (by 1) [WOOLF] 280. Warrington[6], born 23 March 1731; 281. Comfort[6], born 15 Aug. 1734; (by 2) [LITTLE] 282. William[6], born 3 Dec. 1740, died 5 Jan. 1772 at Reheboth, Del.; 283. Jean[6], born 2 Feb. 1742; 284. John[6], born 9 Sept. 174[ ].

131. WILLIAM[5] WARRINGTON (Comfort[4] Tilney, Elizabeth[3] Bagwell, Thomas[2], Henry[1]), born 23 Dec. 1714,[321] left will 19 June 1782-20 Aug. 1783.[322] He married Sarah ___.

Issue: [WARRINGTON] 285. Betty[6], born 28 March 1742;[323] 286. Leah[6], baptized 3 March 1747, died before 1 July 1797 when administration on her estate was granted to Levi Warrington;[324] 287. Luke[6], born 5 May 1750,[325] left will 3 Jan. 1813-18 May 1813,[326] married Nancy ___; 288. Levi[6], born 15 Jan. 1753,[327] died before 1 March 1819 when administration on his estate was granted

[315] "Delaware Bible Records," VII (typewritten; n.p., 1958), pp. 201-04.

[316] Sussex Co., Del., Deed Bk. I, p. 32.

[317] Sussex Co., Del., Will Bk. B, pp. 319-21.

[318] St. George's Parish, Indian River, Register, in Wright, *op. cit.*, p. 128.

[319] St. George's Parish, Indian River, Register, in Wright, *op. cit.*, p. 92.

[320] St. George's Parish, Indian River, Register, in Wright, *op. cit.*, pp. 92-93.

[321] St. George's Parish, Indian River, Register, in Wright, *op. cit.*, p. 92.

[322] Sussex Co., Del., Will Bk. C, pp. 310-12.

[323] St. George's Parish, Indian River, Register, in Wright, *op. cit.*, p. 92.

[324] Sussex Co., Del., Probate 1797-1806, Delaware State Archives.

[325] St. George's Parish, Indian River, Register, in Wright, *op. cit.*, p. 95.

[326] Sussex Co., Del., Probate 1813-15, Delaware State Archives.

[327] St. George's Parish, Indian River, Register, in Wright, *op. cit.*, p. 95.

to Mary Warrington,[328] married Mary ___; 289. Sarah[6], born 18 Oct. 1755;[329] 290. William[6], born 19 June 1759,[330] died before Aug. 1796 when administration on his estate was granted to his widow and her (2) husband,[331] married, 19 April 1789,[332] Mary Hargis, who married (2) John Lingo.

132. COMFORT[5] WARRINGTON (Comfort[4] Tilney, Elizabeth[3] Bagwell, Thomas[2], Henry[1]) was born about 1716 and died about 1749. She married Lewis Davidson, of Sussex Co., Del., who was born 1712 in Maryland and died 16 Nov. 1793 in Fayette Co., Pa., aged 81,[333] left will 6 July 1787-4 Feb. 1794.[334]

Issue: [DAVIDSON] 291. Jeremiah[6]; 292. William[6], born 20 Nov. 1747 in Sussex Co., Del., died 16 Nov. 1811 at South Point, Ohio, left will 20 June 1810-8 Sept. 1812,[335] moved from Fayette Co., Pa., to Lawrence Co., Ohio, in 1799, married (1) Rosa Anna Hutchinson, and (2), 1783 in Pennsylvania, Barbara McDole (McDowell), born 8 Jan. 1769, died 18 Oct. 1831 at South Point, Ohio;[336] 293. Lewis[6], left will 31 July 1809-11 June 1817,[337] married Nancy Todd; 294. Thomas[6]; 295. Hannah[6], married ____ McMeekin; 296. Rachael[6], married ___ McKee; 297. Elizabeth[6].

140. (DAUGHTER)[5] STOCKLEY (Patience[4] Tilney, Elizabeth[3] Bagwell, Thomas[2], Henry[1]) married ___ Barker.

Issue: [BARKER] 298. Patience[6].

145. WILLIAM[5] BAGWELL (Thomas[4], Francis[3], Thomas[2], Henry[1]), born 30 Dec. 1748,[338] married Ann ___.

Issue: 299. Elizabeth[6], born April [1776?];[339] 300. Catherin[6], born 17 April 1780, died 1 July 1850;[340] 301. (perhaps) William[6], married, 26 March 1799,[341]

---

[328] Sussex Co., Del., Probate 1819, Delaware State Archives.

[329] St. George's Parish, Indian River, Register, in Wright, *op. cit.*, p. 96.

[330] *Ibid.*

[331] Sussex Co., Del., Estate papers A105, p. 176, Delaware Hall of Records.

[332] St. George's Parish, Indian River, Register, in Wright, *op. cit.*, p. 132.

[333] Family records provided by Henry Clay Russell, Ashland, Ky.

[334] Fayette Co., Pa., Will Bk. 1, p. 86.

[335] Gallia Co., Ohio, Wills1-2, p. 232.

[336] *Hardesty's Hand Atlas of Lawrence County, Ohio* (n.p., 1882), p. 27.

[337] Allegany Co., Md., Will Bk. A, p. 113.

[338] St. George's Parish, Indian River, Register, in Wright, *op. cit.*, p. 94.

[339] St. George's Parish, Indian River, Register, in Wright, *op. cit.*, p. 103.

[340] St. George's Parish, Indian River, Register, in Wright, *op. cit.*, p. 112.

[341] Lewes and Coolspring Presbyterian Church Register, in Wright, *op. cit.*, p. 136.

Nancy McCrea.

150. CHARLES[5] LEATHERBURY (Thomas[4], Vallance[3] Bagwell, Thomas[2], Henry[1]), under age in 1747, died by 26 Oct. 1790 when administration on his estate was granted to widow Sarah and Noah Belote.[342] He married Sarah (___) Belote, widow of Noah Belote.

Issue: [LEATHERBURY][343] 302. Charles[6], probably the Charles who married, (bond 2) Oct. 1807,[344] Elizabeth Kellam; 303. Thomas[6], probably the Thomas who married, (bond 31) March 1806,[345] Nancy Elliott; 304. Nancy[6], died 1802, under age;[346] 305. John[6], married, (bond 11) Feb. 1804,[347] Sarah Window; 306. Susanna[6], married, (bond 8) Dec. 1808,[348] Ephraim Outten; 307. Perry[6].

154. ELEANOR[5] LEATHERBURY (John[4], Vallance[3] Bagwell, Thomas[2], Henry[1]) married John McClester.

Issue: [McCLESTER] 308. Sarah[6], named in grandfather's will.

156 JOHN[5] LEATHERBURY (John[4], Vallance[3] Bagwell, Thomas[2], Henry[1]) was left his father's dwelling plantation on Great Money, Somerset Co., Md. He is probably the John who left will 29 Nov. 1753-23 April 1759,[349] married Eleanor ___ and had

Issue: [LEATHERBURY] 309. Thomas[6], born 19 March 1742,[350] died before 6 Jan. 1791 when the inventory of his estate was made,[351] married, 15 Jan. 1771,[352] Ann Taylor; 310. John[6], aged 11 in 1755; 311. Charles[6], aged 9 in 1755; 312. Betty[6],aged 6 in 1755; 313. Eleanor[6], aged 4 in 1775.

157. ROBERT[5] LEATHERBURY (John[4], Vallance[3] Bagwell, Thomas[2], Henry[1]) was left land on Wicomico River, Somerset Co., Md. He deposed 12

---

[342] Accomack Co. Order Bk. 1790-93, p. 56.

[343] Nottingham, *op. cit.*, pp. 47-49.

[344] Turman, *op. cit.*, p. 162.

[345] *Ibid.*, p. 163,

[346] Nottingham, *op. cit.*, p. 53.

[347] Turman, *op. cit.*, p. 163.

[348] *Ibid.*, p. 215.

[349] Maryland Prerogative Court Wills 29, p. 141; Somerset Co., Md., Original wills, Box 7, folder 63, Maryland State Archives.

[350] Stepney Parish, Worcester Co., Md., Register.

[351] Somerset Co., Md., Inventories EB 19, 1791-97, pp. 1-2.

[352] Stepney Parish Register.

May 1768 he was aged 37, a ship carpenter,[353] and left will 27 April 1784-5 Sept. 1784.[354] He married Eleanor ___.

Issue: [LEATHERBURY] 314. John[6], married Sally ___.

158 MARY[5] LEATHERBURY (John[4], Vallance[3] Bagwell, Thomas[2], Henry[1]) married ___ Bozman.

Issue: [BOZMAN] 315. Sarah[6], named in grandfather's will.

160. RICHARD[5] DIX (Bridget[4] Savage, Ann[3] Bagwell, Thomas[2], Henry[1]) left will 8 Nov. 1760-30 Dec. 1760.[355] He married Mary ___, who died after 22 Jan. 1779.[356]

Issue: [DIX] 316. Griffin[6], died under age; 317. Nancy[6], married, by 22 Jan. 1779, as his (1) wife, John Abbott Bundick, Jr., who left will 11 March 1805-24 June 1805;[357] 318. (Child)[6], unborn 1760.

161. ISAAC[5] DIX (Bridget[4] Savage, Ann[3] Bagwell, Thomas[2], Henry[1]) died before 30 Dec. 1760 when administration on his estate was granted to Southy Simpson.[358] He married Wealthy ___.[359]

Issue: [DIX] 319. Levi[6], left will 1 Dec. 1794-30 Dec. 1794,[360] married Treffey ___, perhaps Trephenia Dix on whose estate administration was granted to John G. Bagwell 27 Jan. 1823.[361]

162. SOLOMON[5] DIX (Bridget[4] Savage, Ann[3] Bagwell, Thomas[2], Henry[1]) left will 7 June 1779-26 Jan. 1780.[362] He married Leah ___.

Issue: [DIX] 320. Preson[6], married, (bond 4) Sept. 1808,[363] Polly Johnson; 321. Caleb[6], left will 23 Oct. 1810-26 Nov. 1810,[364] married (1) Rachel ___ and (2), (bond 30) Dec. 1803,[365] Elizabeth Taylor; 322. Mary[6]; 323. Santer[6],

---

[353] Maryland Chancery Record 12, p. 194, in Debbie Hooper, *Abstracts of Chancery Court Records of Maryland, 1669-1782* (Westminster, Md., 1996), p. 114.

[354] Somerset Co., Md. Will Bk. EB1, p. 251.

[355] Accomack Co. Wills &c 1757-61, p. 280.

[356] Accomack Co. Deeds &c 5, 1777-83, pp. 113-15.

[357] Accomack Co. Wills &c 1804-06, pp. 328-29.

[358] Accomack Co. Order Bk. 1753-63, p. 373.

[359] Perhaps Wealthyanna Dix, daughter named in will of Alexander Harrison, 13 May 1760-28 May 1760 (Accomack Co. Wills &c 1757-61, p. 222).

[360] Accomack Co. Wills &c 1794-96, p. 62.

[361] Accomack Co. Order Bk. 1822-24, p. 126.

[362] Accomack Co. Wills &c 1777-80, p. 492.

[363] Turman, *op. cit.*, p. 84.

[364] Accomack Co. Wills &c 1809-12, pp. 278-79.

[365] Turman, *op. cit.*, p. 83.

daughter.

163. GEORGE[5] DIX (Bridget[4] Savage, Ann[3] Bagwell, Thomas[2], Henry[1]) left will 23 Aug. 1784-29 Nov. 1785.[366] He married 539. *Bridget[6] Powell* (see WILKINS).

Issue: [DIX] 324. Richard[6], left will 3 April 1815-27 Jan. 1818,[367] married ___; 325. Isaac[6]; 326. Elizabeth[6].

---

[366] Accomack Co. Wills &c 1784-87, p. 191.
[367] Accomack Co. Wills &c 1817-18, p. 327.

BALEY-COCKE[1]

*1. TEMPERANCE[1] BALEY (Bailey, Bayley), born in Virginia, 1617, as a child of six years was living at Jourdan's Journey in Charles City, 1623/4,[2] and is listed there in the muster of William Farrar and Mistress Sisley Jordan, 1624/5 (see FARRAR). The 200 acres in the Territory of the Great Weyanoke credited to her in the 1626 list of patents had been placed in her name by 10 Dec. 1620 when Samuel Jordan patented 388 acres in or near upon Sandys his hundred, towards land of Temperance Baley.[3] Since she was a land owner at the age of three, it is evident her father was dead and, as there is no record of a guardian to care for her estate, the probability is that she was the daughter of Sisley Jordan by a first marriage.[4] Her marriage to Richard Cocke is posited from a land patent issued to him, 10 Oct. 1652, which includes 100 acres due by patent to Temperance[1] Baley, 20 Sept. 1620.[5]

It would appear that Temperance[1] Baley married (1) John Browne. On 5 June 1632,[6] the General Court ordered:

> Whereas it appeareth by the account of Richard Cocke that hee hath disbursed 6397[ll] of tobacco for the paym[t] of John Brownes debts haueinge

---

[1] James Cocke Southall, "Genealogy of the Cocke Family of Virginia," *V* III, pp. 405-14, IV, pp. 86-89; "Richard Cocke of 'Bremo' and His Children," *V* XLIV, pp. 136-51; "Links in a Chain," V LI, pp. 389-92; Leonie Doss Cocke and Virginia Webb Cocke, *Cockes and Cousins, Volume 1. Descendants of Richard Cocke (c.1600-1665)* (Ann Arbor, Mich., 1967); Virginia Webb Cocke, *Cockes and Cousins, Volume 2, Descendants of Thomas Cocke (c.1639-1697)* (Ann Arbor, Mich., 1974).

[2] Hotten, p. 171.

[3] *Ibid.*, p. 269; *R*, Va. Co. IV, p. 554; Patent Bk. 8, p. 125.

[4] See *V* LI, p. 390. This assumption is based on circumstantial evidence.

[5] Patent Bk. 3, p. 133.

[6] *MCGC*, p. 201. Although the year is not certain, the fact that John Harvey was Governor and that Capt. Francis West (who died before 28 April 1634) was one of the councillors present apparently requires that the year be no later than 1633. Temperance[1] Baley was only about 15 in 1632 and for her to have had children and been widowed by then requires a very early marriage to Browne, but such early marriages of girls whose fathers were deceased and whose mothers had remarried were fairly common in the period. Although Temperance is not named in this record, Richard Cocke's request in his will to be buried beside his "first wife" seems to suggest that this was not a marriage prior to his marriage to Temperance. It should be noted that the eldest Cocke son, Thomas, was not born until about 1638, but infant mortality was high in the period; furthermore, a later John Brown of Henrico County (see note 15) named a daughter Temperance. While present evidence is not entirely conclusive, the circumstances suggest Temperance was the widow Brown when she married Richard Cocke.

maried the relicte of the sayd Brown, and in regard the sayd Brownes estate was praysed in money it is thought fitt that hee the sayd Richard Cocke shall be allowed after the rate of eight pounds sterlinge for euery Thousand weight of the sayd Tobacco out of the sayd Brownes estate And it is likewise held expedient that Richard Cocke shall kepe two Cowe calves of the next fall & to vndergoe the hazard of them vntill they bee a yeare older at wch tyme they are to be marked and kept by the sayd Cocke for the vse of the Children of the sayd Browne ...

She married (2) Richard Cocke, son of John Cocke and his wife Elizabeth of Wallfurlong in the parish of Stottesdon, Shropshire, who was baptized 5 Sept. 1602 at Stottesdon.[7] He possibly was the Richard Cocke who was mentioned, 24 Dec. 1627, as purser of the ship *Thomas and John*,[8] and as attorney for Patrick Canada at Elizabeth City court, 10 Feb. 1628/9,[9] and the Richard Coxe who was Burgess for Weyanoke in Charles City County, 1632.[10]

Richard Cocke patented 3000 acres, 6 March 1636/7, "easterly upon the land of John Price, now in the tenure of Robert Hallum, Westerly upon the land of Thomas Harris and southerly upon the main river." A repatent of 2000 acres of this tract, issued 10 March 1639/40, names the three plantations identified with the Cocke family, "Bremo," "Malvern Hill," and "Curles."[11] An Act of Assembly, 6 Jan. 1639/40, named him as a tobacco viewer for Curles, Bremo and Turkey Island.[12] He was a member of the House of Burgesses from Henrico, 1644, 1654-55,[13] and commander of the county militia.

Richard Cocke married (2), about 1652, Mary Aston, daughter of Lt. Col. Walter Aston, who married as her (2) husband Lt. Col. Daniel Clarke of Charles City. Richard Cocke's will, dated 4 Oct. 1665, directed that his body should be "interred in the orchard near my first wife," named wife Mary and her children, and carefully segregated to his two eldest sons' portions of his estate which had come from their mother.[14]

---

[7] Parish register, Stottesdon, Shropshire, in Virginia Webb Cocke, "Thomas Cocke of Pickthorn," *The Virginia Genealogist*, XXX, pp. 26-30.

[8] *MCGC*, p. 158.

[9] *Ibid.*, p. 186.

[10] Leonard, p. 11.

[11] Patent Bk. 1, pp. 413, 707.

[12] *W* (2) IV, p. 20.

[13] Leonard, pp. 24, 32.

[14] Henrico Co. Miscellaneous Court Records I, pp. 27-28. No date of probate is given.

Issue: (by 1) [BROWN] children, not identified;[15] (by 2) [COCKE][16] 2. THOMAS[2]; 3. RICHARD[2], the elder; 4. Elizabeth[2], probably by his (1) wife as he directed his sons by that marriage to pay her £100 at age 17 or marriage.

2. THOMAS[2] COCKE (Temperance[1] Baley), who deposed, 1 Aug. 1685, he was aged about 46,[17] referred to himself in a deed, 20 Aug. 1672, as of "Pickthorn Farm in the County of Henrico."[18] He later lived at "Malvern Hill,"[19] one of his father's plantations, operating the flour mill there, tanneries, and looms for weaving both woolens and linen. For a specimin of linen fifteen ells in length and three-fourths of a yard wide, of the first quality of home manufacture, he received an award, 1695, of 800 pounds of tobacco offered by the Assembly, 1693.[20] He served as justice of Henrico, 1678, sheriff, 1680, 1688, coroner, 1680, and Burgess, 1677.[21]

He married (1), about 1661, (Agnes Powell?) and (2) Margaret ___, who left will 12 Aug. 1718-4 May 1719,[22] step-daughter of Gen. Abraham Wood and

---

[15] One possible child was John Brown who died before 1 Oct. 1677 (Henrico Co. Orphans Court Bk. 1677-1739, p. 1) and whose widow Sarah married (2) 2. *John[2] Woodson* (see WOODSON). Their children were Jeremiah, who married 5. *Elizabeth[3] Sheppey* (see SHEPPEY) and left will 29 Nov. 1690-1 Dec. 1690 (Henrico Co. Wills & Deeds 1688-97, p. 179), without issue; Temperance, who married (1) Thomas Batte and (2) 9. *John[3] Farrar* (see FARRAR); and Sarah, left will 16 July 1695-1 Dec. 1696 (*ibid.*, p. 671), who married Samuel Knibb, who left will dated 19 Dec. 1691 (*ibid.*, p. 286). The children of Samuel and Sarah (Brown) Knibb were Samuel, left will 11 Oct. 1716-7 Jan. 1716/7 (Henrico Co. Wills & Deeds 1714-18, p. 129), married Elizabeth ___ who married (2), by 6 Oct. 1718, Benjamin Bullington (Henrico Co. Miscellaneous Court Records, II, p. 383); Solomon, died young; John, left will 31 July 1725-6 March 1726/7 (Henrico Co. Wills & Deeds 1725-37, p. 89), married Sarah ___; Thomas, left will 29 Dec. 1744-May 1747 (Henrico Co. Wills & Deeds 1744-48, p. 265), married Anne ___.

[16] Richard Cocke had issue by his (2) wife: William (1655-1693), married (1) Jane Flower and (2), 1691, 12. *Sarah[3] Dennis* (see ROYALL); John (born about 1658), married, 1686, Mary Davis; Richard the younger (born 1660), married Elizabeth ___; Edward (1665/6-1734), married Mary ___.

[17] Henrico Co. Wills & Deeds 1677-92, p. 327.

[18] Henrico Co. Deeds & Wills 1688-97, p. 245.

[19] "Malvern Hill," located on the James River back of Turkey Island, about 15 miles below Richmond, was the scene of one of the bloodiest battles of the Civil War, 1 July 1862, as part of the Seven Days fighting around Richmond.

[20] Bruce, *Ec. Hist.*, II, p. 459.

[21] Leonard, p. 43.

[22] Henrico Co. Miscellaneous Court Records I, p. 433.

widow of Peter Jones (see WOOD). His will, 10 Dec. 1691-1 April 1697,[23] shows he was the owner of some 5000 acres of land, his dwelling house, mill, tanyards, tobacco houses, orchards, gardens, slaves and horses.

Issue: by (1) 5. THOMAS[3]; 6. STEPHEN[3]; 7. JAMES[3]; 8. WILLIAM[3]; 9. AGNES[3]; 10. TEMPERANCE[3].

3. RICHARD[2] COCKE (Temperance[1] Baley), called "the elder" to distinguish him from his young half-brother of the same name, was born 10 Dec. 1639 and died 20 Nov. 1706.[24] He inherited the 640 acre "Bremo" plantation[25] in Henrico from his father and served as surveyor of the county and justice, 1678. He was associated with his brother Thomas[2] in various enterprises, among them the operation of a ferry across the James River, known as "Cocke's Ferry" as late as 1810, and the operation of an ordinary near the courthouse at Varina. He held 2180 acres in Henrico County, 1704. He married Elizabeth ___. His will, 18 Nov. 1706-2 Dec. 1706,[26] named his children and grandchildren.

Issue: 11. RICHARD[3]; 12. ELIZABETH[3]; 13. MARTHA[3]; 14. JOHN[3].

5. Capt THOMAS[3] COCKE (Thomas[2], Temperance[1] Baley), born about 1662, was a member of the House of Burgesses, 1698, 1699, 1700-01,[27] captain of militia, 1698, and sheriff of Henrico, 1699. He married (1), 1687, Mary Brasseur of Nansemond, daughter of John Brasseur and his wife Mary Pitt, and (2) Frances (Anderson) Herbert, widow of John Herbert, who married (3), (contract 10) Feb. 1710/11,[28] Capt. Joshua Wynne and left will 16 Oct. 1725-14 March 1726.[29]

His will, 16 Jan. 1706/7-codicil 14 Feb. 1706/7-1 April 1707,[30] names

Issue: (by 1) 15. Thomas[4], born about 1687, bequeathed 650 acres by his

---

[23] Henrico Co. Wills & Deeds 1688-97, pp. 684-85.

[24] Tombstone at "Bremo" which says he was son of Richard Cocke.

[25] About 1809 the Cocke descendants sold their entire Tidewater estate to John Hartwell Cocke's two sisters and their husbands, Nicholas and John Faulcon, and removed to Fluvanna County where the plantation was also called "Bremo" and where subsequently the mansion was built. For "Lower Bremo" and "Upper Bremo" in Fluvanna see Fiske Kimball, "The Building of Bremo," *V* LVII, pp. 3-13.

[26] Henrico Co. Wills & Deeds 1706-09, pp. 9-10.

[27] Leonard, pp. 58-60.

[28] Prince George Co. Wills & Deeds 1710-13, p. 77.

[29] Prince George Co. Wills & Deeds 1713-28, p. 973; *The American Genealogist*, XXXVII, pp. 234-40, LXXV, pp. 178-80.

[30] Henrico Co. Wills & Deeds 1706-09, p. 24.

father, left will 29 Aug. 1711-5 Nov. 1711;[31] 16. JAMES POWELL[4]; 17. Henry[4], born about 1696, bequeathed land in Henrico, was lost at sea leaving will 1 Feb. 1714/5-4 April 1715;[32] 18. BRAZURE[4]; 19. MARY[4]; 20. Elizabeth[4].

6. STEPHEN[3] COCKE (Thomas[2], Temperance[1] Baley), born about 1664,[33] was deeded by his father, 1687, 200 acres of the "Malvern Hill" tract, and patented, 29 April 1693, 1040 acres in James City and Charles City counties.[34] He married (1), 1688,[35] Mrs. Sarah Marston, and (2), 26 May 1694,[36] Martha (Batte) Jones Banister, daughter of Thomas Batte, Sr., and widow of Lieut. Abraham Jones and the Rev. John Banister.[37] He died before 14 Aug. 1711.[38]

Issue: (by 2) 21. AGNES[4]; 22. Batte[4], died young; 23. ABRAHAM[4]; 24. Charles[4], died young.

7. JAMES[3] COCKE (Thomas[2], Temperance[1] Baley), deposed, Aug. 1697, he was aged 30.[39] He was a member of the House of Burgesses from Henrico, 1696-97, 1699,[40] and clerk of courts for Henrico, 1692-1707, and held 1506 acres in Henrico County, 1704. He married, 11 Jan. 1691/2,[41] Elizabeth Pleasants, born about 1676, daughter of John Pleasants and his wife Jane (Larcombe) Tucker,[42] who were Quakers, and through this marriage acquired the plantation of "Curles" on James River. His will, now lost, was proved 6 Nov.

---

[31] Henrico Co. Wills & Deeds 1710-14, p. 102. On 15 Aug. 1711, however, William Byrd noted "Tom Cocke was dead" (Louis B. Wright and Marion Tinling, eds., *The Secret Diary of William Byrd of Westover, 1709-1712* [Richmond, 1941], p. 389).

[32] Henrico Co. Wills & Deeds 1714-18, p. 17.

[33] He deposed, 16 May 1692, he was aged 24 (Henrico Co. Deeds & Wills 1688-97, p. 297) but must have been older. He is described as his father's second son (Wills & Deeds 1677-92, p. 442).

[34] Patent Bk. 8, p. 300.

[35] Henrico Co. Deeds & Wills 1688-97, p. 97.

[36] *Ibid.*, p. 552.

[37] *The Virginia Genealogist*, XLIII, pp. 220-24.

[38] Prince George Co. Wills & Deeds 1710-13, pp. 53, 66. On 9 July 1717 his widow Martha presented a supplementary audit of debts due his estate (Prince George Co. Wills & Deeds 1713-28, p. 177).

[39] Henrico Co. Deeds & Wills 1688-97, p. 712.

[40] Leonard, pp. 56-59.

[41] Henrico Co. Deeds & Wills 1688-97, p. 357.

[42] *Val. Papers*, II, pp. 1053-63, 1070, 1074-78; IV, p. 2290.

1721.[43] His widow left will 9 Aug. 1751-July 1752.[44]

Issue: 25. JAMES[4]; 26. ELIZABETH[4].

8. WILLIAM[3] COCKE (Thomas[2], Temperance[1] Baley), born about 1670, married, 2 Dec. 1695,[45] 19. *Sarah[3] Perrin* (see ROYALL). He held 1535 acres in Henrico County, 1704. He left will, 5 Nov. 1717-3 Feb. 1717/8.[46]

Issue:[47] 27. Sarah[4], born about 1696, died about 1750, married (1) 22. *William[4] Cox* (see COX) and (2, before 1 Aug. 1743,[48] Thomas Jordan, born about 1700,[49] who married (2) Martha ___ and died after 2 Sept. 1765;[50] 28. WILLIAM[4]; 29. TEMPERANCE[4]; 30. MARY[4]; 31. CATHERINE[4].

9. AGNES[3] COCKE (Thomas[2], Temperance[1]Baley), born 1672, married Capt. Joseph Harwood, justice of Charles City County and member of the House of Burgesses, 1715.[51] He held 659 acres in Charles City County, 1704.

Issue [HARWOOD] 32. THOMAS[4]; 33. Joseph[4]; 34. Agnes[4]; 35. Joyce[4].

10. TEMPERANCE[3] COCKE (Thomas[2], Temperance[1] Baley), married, 14 June 1694,[52] Maj. Samuel Harwood, justice of Charles City County, member of the House of Burgesses, 1710-12, 1712-14,[53] who held 350 acres in Charles City County, 1704, and died before June 1737.[54]

Issue [HARWOOD]: 36. SAMUEL[4].

11. RICHARD[3] COCKE (Richard[2], Temperance[1] Baley) of "Bremo" deposed, 1 April 1689, he was aged 17 and, 1 Oct. 1694, he was aged 21, and on 23 Nov. 1704 while in London, where he had arrived in Aug. 1704, on the second of two trips he had made to England, deposed he was born in Henrico County and was aged 31.[55] He married (1), about 1695, Anne Bowler, born 23

---

[43] Henrico Co. Minute Bk. 1719-24, p., 141.

[44] Henrico Co. Wills & Deeds 1750-67, p. 158.

[45] Henrico Co. Deeds & Wills 1688-97, p. 631.

[46] Henrico Co. Wills & Deeds 1714-18, pp. 225-26.

[47] Goochland Co. Order Bk. 1750-57, p. 402, May Court 1754.

[48] Henrico Co. Order Bk. 1737-46, p. 228.

[49] Henrico Co. Minute Bk. 1719-24, p. 106. He acknowledged, 5 June 1721, he had received his estate from his guardian, John Whitloe.

[50] Henrico Co. Wills & Deeds 1750-67, p. 897; Order Bk. 1763-67, p. 520.

[51] Leonard, p. 68.

[52] Henrico Co. Deeds & Wills 1688-97, p. 552.

[53] Leonard, pp. 65, 67.

[54] Charles City Co. Order Bk. 1737-51, p. 1.

[55] Henrico Co. Deeds & Wills 1688-97, pp. 43, 522; *NGSQ* LXXIV, p. 67.

Jan. 1674/5, died 24 April 1705,[56] daughter of Col. Thomas Bowler of Old Rappahannock County and his wife Tabitha Underwood (see EDLOE), and (2), 1705, Rebecca ___, who may also have been a daughter of Thomas Bowler. His will, now lost, was proved 3 Oct. 1720.[57]

Issue: (by 1)[58] 37. BOWLER[5]; 38. Martha[4]; 39 TABITHA[4]; 40. John[4]; (by 2) 41. RICHARD[4]; 42. BENJAMIN[4]; 43. ANNE[4].

12. ELIZABETH[3] COCKE (Richard[2], Temperance[1] Baley), born about 1675, married (license 22) Aug. 1695,[59] 11. *Miles[4] Cary. Jr.* (see TAYLOR-CARY), who deposed, 1713, that he was aged 42, of "Potash Creek," Warwick County. He was clerk in the office of the Secretary of State at Jamestown, 1691. In 1693 he became clerk of the legislative committees of Privileges and Elections and of Public Claims, and shortly thereafter Clerk of Warwick County, and held all these posts until 1718. He was colonel of the Warwick militia, 1702, and in 1704 held 600 acres in Warwick. He died 1724.[60]

Issue [CARY]:[61] 44. Richard[4], born about 1696, succeeded his father as clerk of Warwick and clerk of the committees of Privilege and Elections and of Public Claims, 1718, and served until his death, 1721; 45. THOMAS[4]; 46. MILES[4]; 47. Nathaniel[4], born about 1703, died before 1761,[62] married ___, living 1761; 48. Anne[4], born about 1707; 49. Elizabeth[4], born about 1709; 50. Bridget[4], born about 1711; 51. Dorothy[4], born about 1712;[63] 52. Martha[4], born about 1714.

13. MARTHA[3] COCKE (Richard[2], Temperance[1] Baley) married (1), 15

---

[56] Tombstone, "Bremo," in *V* IV, p. 92.

[57] Henrico Co. Minute Bk. 1719-24, pp. 48, 61. Ebenezer Adams, the Hon. Nathaniel Harrison and Capt. Henry Harrison were executors.

[58] Named in grandfather's will.

[59] Henrico Co. Deeds, Wills &c 1688-97, p. 604.

[60] Fairfax Harrison, *The Virginia Carys* (New York, 1919), p. 49.

[61] *Ibid.*, pp. 50-53, 62.

[62] Chesterfield Co. Will Bk. 3, p. 543, will of Dorothy (Phillipson) Cary.

[63] Anderson Demandville Abraham in 1852 stated she married George Dudley (*Whig and Public Advertiser*, Richmond, Va., 10 July 1852; see *The Magazine of Virginia Genealogy*, XXIII, no. 4, pp. 31, 38), who died "many years since" in Mathews County. A Dorothy Dudley was living in Kingston Parish, Gloucester County (which became Mathews County in 1791), with five whites in the family in 1783 and four in 1784 (*Heads of Families at the First Census ... 1790 ... State Enumerations: 1782 to 1785, Virginia* [Washington, 1908], pp. 53, 68), but this marriage is not confirmed by any other records.

May 1699,[64] Joseph Pleasants, who left will 9 Sept. 1725-7 Feb. 1725/6,[65] son of John Pleasants and his wife Jane (Larcombe) Tucker. He served as clerk of Henrico Monthly Meeting of the Society of Friends, 1700-10, 1714-22,[66] and held 1709 acres in Henrico County, 1704. She married (2), 5 March 1726/7 at Curles Meeting House,[67] Edward Bennet of Pennsylvania, with whom she presented the inventory of Pleasants' estate, 4 Nov. 1728.[68] His will, now lost, was presented at Court May 1742.[69]

Issue: (by 1) [PLEASANTS] 53. JOSEPH[4]; 54. Elizabeth[4];[70] 55. Jane[4], unmarried, whose will, 9 Sept. 1726-6 Feb. 1726/7,[71] named her mother, brothers and sisters; 56. MARTHA[4]; 57. JOHN[4]; 58. RICHARD[4]; 59. THOMAS[4]; 60. Robert[4], living 6 Dec. 1742, died unmarried before 22 Nov. 1751.[72]

14. JOHN[3] COCKE (Richard[2], Temperance[1] Baley) married Nov. 1696[73] 41. *Obedience[4] Branch* (see BRANCH), who left will 6 Jan. 1745/6-17 June 1746.[74] Administration was granted on the estate of John[3] Cocke 2 Oct. 1699.[75] Obedience married (2) Alexander Trent and (3) Thomas Turpin.

Issue:[76] 61. John[4], died 15 July 1759, left will 12 June 1753-9 Aug. 1759,[77] married, 22 July 1727, Elizabeth _____, widow of Edward Baxter;[78] 62. MARTHA[4].

---

[64] Henrico Co. Deeds, Wills &c 1697-1704, p. 152. He acknowledged to Henrico Monthly Meeting, 10 Nov. 1699, that he was married by a priest (*Val. Papers* II, p. 1184).

[65] Henrico Co. Wills & Deeds 1725-37, pp. 3-4.

[66] Hinshaw, VI, p. 304.

[67] *Val. Papers*, II. 1192.

[68] Henrico Co. Wills & Deeds 1725-37, p. 216.

[69] Henrico Co. Order Bk. 1737-46, p. 181.

[70] Cocke, *Cockes and Cousins*, II, p. 16, suggests she may have married 39, *Joseph[4] Lewis* (see WOODSON). William Kenneth Rutherford and Anna Clay Zimmerman Rutherford, *Genealogical History of Our Ancestors* (rev. ed.; n.p., 1977), I, p. 505, and *W(2)* VIII, p. 134, state she married John Merryman but provide no documentation.

[71] Henrico Co. Wills & Deeds 1725-27, p. 84.

[72] Henrico Co. Deeds & Wills 1750-1767. On 2 Dec. 1754 his brother Joseph made a deed of gift of land Robert inherited from their father (*Val. Papers* II, pp. 1020, 1031).

[73] Henrico Co. Deeds, Wills &c 1688-97, p . 710.

[74] Goochland Co. Deed Bk. 5, p. 139.

[75] Henrico Co. Order Bk. 1694-1701, p. 237.

[76] Philip Turpin notebook, in *The Virginia Genealogist*, XXXI, p. 5.

[77] Albemarle Co. Will Bk. 2, p. 52.

[78] Henrico Co. Order Bk. 1737-46, p. 387.

16. JAMES POWELL[4] COCKE (Thomas[3], Thomas[2], Temperance[1] Baley), born 1688, was bequeathed the "Malvern Hill" tract, and was vestryman of Henrico Parish, and left will 19 Aug. 1747-Sept. 1747.[79] He married, about 1718, his step-sister Martha Herbert, daughter of John Herbert and his wife Frances Anderson.[80]

Issue:[81] 63. JAMES POWELL[5]; 64. Martha[5].

18. BRAZURE[4] COCKE (Thomas[3], Thomas[2], Temperance[1] Baley) deposed, 14 Aug. 1764, he was aged about 73.[82] He was bequeathed 1650 acres and moved to Brunswick County where he left will 20 Sept. 1766-22 Oct. 1770.[83] He married Frances ___.

Issue:[84] 65. James[5], of Lunenburg County, left will 1 Feb. 1761-1 Dec. 1761;[85] 66. WILLIAM[5]; 67. THOMAS[5]; 68. ELIZABETH[5]; 69. Fanny[5], married John Oliver, of St. Andrew's Parish, Brunswick County, when they sold land 4 Dec. 1759;[86] 70. MARY[5]; 71. SUSANNA[5]; 72. Ann[5], married ___ Chick [Cheek], possibly Robert Chick who as of Nottoway Parish, Amelia County, bought land in Brunswick County, 22 Oct. 1753, and with wife Ann, as of St. Andrew's Parish, Brunswick County, sold 150 acres at the mouth of Rocky Run, 25 Feb. 1762;[87] 73. Martha[5], married, (bond 20) July 1767,[88] William Merritt.

19. MARY[4] COCKE (Thomas[3], Thomas[2], Temperance[1] Baley) married, before April 1715, the Rev. William Finney, M.A. University of Glasgow and minister of Henrico Parish from 1714, who left will 3 Feb. 1726/7-5 June 1727.[89]

Issue: [FINNEY] 74. WILLIAM[5]; 75. Mary[5], married, by 17 May 1743 when they sold the land she inherited from her father,[90] John Williamson, Jr., of

---

[79] Henrico Co. Wills & Deeds 1744-48, p. 296.

[80] *Virginia Gazette*, 7 Aug. 1752, p. 3, advertisement for heirs of John Herbert.

[81] Cocke, *op. cit.*, I, pp. 5, 11, 21-22; II, pp. 4, 10, 23-24; R. A. Brock, ed., *Documents ... Relating to the Huguenot Emigration to Virginia* (Richmond, 1886), pp. 193-204.

[82] Amelia Co. Suit papers, Holt *vs.* Cox, Virginia State Archives.

[83] Brunswick Co. Will Bk. 4, pp. 32-33.

[84] Cocke, *op. cit.*, II, pp. 4, 10, 24-25.

[85] Lunenburg Co. Will Bk. 1, p. 336.

[86] Brunswick Co. Deed Bk. 6, pp. 519-22.

[87] Brunswick Co. Deed Bk. 5, p. 475; Deed Bk. 7, p. 82.

[88] Elizabeth Hicks Hummel, *Hicks History of Granville County, North Carolina*, I (Oxford, N.C., 1965), p. 23.

[89] Henrico Co. Wills & Deeds 1725-37, p. 104; Edward Lewis Goodwin, *The Colonial Church in Virginia* (London, 1927), p. 269.

[90] Goochland Co. Deed Bk. 4, p. 164.

Princess Anne County.

21. AGNES[4] COCKE (Stephen[3], Thomas[2], Temperance[1] Baley), born after Dec. 1696, left will 16 Aug. 1773-24 March 1774.[91] She married Richard Smith, who left will 6 July 1757-5 Feb. 1760.[92]

Issue: [SMITH][93] 76. Richard[5], patented, 15 Oct. 1741, 400 acres[94] which, as a resident of South Carolina, he sold to his father, 17 March 1756,[95] was a trader and interpreter with the Cherokee Indians;[96] 77. AGNES[5]; 78. Sarah[5], born 30 April 1724,[97] died after 1773, married ___ Mayes; 79. ABRAHAM[5]; 80. Peter[5], tithable with his mother in Lunenburg County, 1764, and for himself, 1769, 1772, 1774, 1776;[98] 81. Lucy[5], married, after 1757, ____ Miller;[99] 82. JANE[5]; 83. ANN[5]; 84. TEMPERANCE[5]; 85. Martha[5], married ___ Murrel,[100] probably Jeffrey Murrell who as a resident of Dinwiddie County purchased 187 acres in Lunenburg County, 1 Oct. 1753, which as a resident of Pittsylvania County he sold 13 Dec. 1771,[101] was deeded 400 acres on Muster Branch of Leatherwood Creek in Henry County by Thomas Murrell, 4 March 1779, which Jeffrey Murrell and wife Martha sold, 10 Dec. 1779,[102] and was exempted from paying county levies, 25 Sept. 1783;[103] 86. MARY[5]; 87. Benjamin[5], born 22 June 1741,[104] married Agnes ___, who joined him in selling slaves and 200 acres to

---

[91] Amelia Co. Will Bk. 2, p. 1.

[92] Lunenburg Co. Will Bk. 1, p. 286.

[93] Cocke, *op. cit.*, II, pp. 5, 11, 26-27; Ben H. Coke, *Some Early Landowners in Southern Nottoway and Northern Lunenburg Counties, Virginia, and the Cocke (Coke) Family Who Once Lived There* (n.p., 1997), p. 84.

[94] Patent Bk. 20, p. 23.

[95] Lunenburg Co. Deed Bk. 4, pp. 332-33.

[96] *V* LXIV, p. 151.

[97] Bristol Parish Register.

[98] Landon C. Bell, *Sunlight on the Southside* (Philadelphia, 1931), pp. 245, 276, 299, 343, 386.

[99] Her mother's will refers to her as "commonly called" Lucy Miller. Coke, *Some Early Landowners*, p. 84, identifies her husband as Benjamin Milner.

[100] Her name in her mother's will has been read as both March or Munch. But Geoffery Murrel was one of the legatees of Agnes[4] (Cocke) Smith.

[101] Lunenburg Co. Deed Bk. 3, pp. 378-80; Deed Bk. 12, pp. 139-40. No wife relinquished dower at the sale.

[102] Henry Co. Deed Bk. 1, pp. 264-65; Deed Bk. 2, pp. 53-54.

[103] Henry Co. Order Bk. 3, p. 115.

[104] Bristol Parish Register.

Peter[5] Smith, 9 Feb. 1765.[105]

23. ABRAHAM[4] COCKE (Stephen[3], Thomas[2], Temperance[1] Baley) died 10 May 1760,[106] leaving will 23 Sept. 1759-22 May 1760.[107] He was justice of Amelia County, 1745-60, and sheriff, 1751, and a vestryman of Nottoway Parish. He married about 1729, Charles City County, 28. *Mary[5] Batte* (see SHEPPEY), born 1710, died 4 Nov. 1780.[108]

Issue:[109] 88. ABRAHAM[5]; 89. PETER[5]; 90. MARY[5]; 91. AGNES[5]; 92. STEPHEN[5]; 93. John[5], under age in 1759; 94. MARTHA[5]; 95. ELIZABETH[5]; 96. Thomas[5], left land by his father which he sold 11 Oct. 1765, 27 and 28 Aug. 1766;[110] 97. WILLIAM[5].

25. JAMES[4] COCKE (James[3], Thomas[2], Temperance[1] Baley), born about 1692, was executor of his mother's will and left will 18 Dec. 1772-6 Feb. 1775.[111] He married, about 1715, 40. *Sarah[4] Lewis* (see WOODSON).

Issue:[112] 98. JAMES[5]; 99. PLEASANT[5]; 100. THOMAS[5]; 101. TABITHA[5]; 102. Rebecca[5], married 89. *Benjamin[5] Woodson* (see WOODSON); 103. Ann[5].

26. ELIZABETH[4] COCKE (James[3], Thomas[2], Temperance[1] Baley) married Robert Poythress of Martins Brandon Parish, Prince George County, who was accused of furnishing ammunition to the Indians, 1713,[113] and left will 24 May 1743-13 Sept. 1743.[114]

Issue: [POYTHRESS] 104. Robert[5], died unmarried; 105. ELIZABETH[5]; 106. Mary Ann[5], married ___ Minge; 107. Agnes[5], married (1) 36. Samuel[4] Harwood and (2) 81. *Benjamin[5] Cocke* (see HOLT); 108. PETER[5]; 109. William[5], died unmarried; 110. Tabitha[5], married 130. *Henry[5] Randolph* (see EPES); 111. Susannah[5]; 112. JANE[5].

---

[105] Lunenburg Co. Deed Bk. 10, pp. 117-18, 206-08.

[106] Zelma Wells Price, *Of Whom I Came ...* VI (Greenville, Miss., 1963), p. 108.

[107] Amelia Co. Will Bk. 1, p. 169.

[108] Price, *loc. cit.*; *Virginia Genealogical Society Quarterly*, IV, pp. 70-71.

[109] Cocke, *op. cit.*, II, pp. 5, 12-15, 27-36.

[110] Amelia Co. Deed Bk. 8, p. 682; Deed Bk. 9, pp. 32, 34. He may be the Thomas Cocke who married (1), 23 Feb. 1779 (Kathleen Booth Williams, *Marriages of Amelia County, Virginia, 1758-1815* [n.p., 1961], p. 27), Margaret Jones, born 3 Feb. 1759, (2) ___, (3) ___ and (4) ___ Simpson and died 1839, Mooresburg, Hawkins Co., Tenn. (Cocke, *op. cit.*, II, p. 14).

[111] Henrico Co. Miscellaneous Court Records VII, p. 2249.

[112] Cocke, *op. cit.*, II, pp. 6, 16-17, 36-40; *The Virginia Genealogist*, XVI, pp. 311-12.

[113] *Executive Journals of the Council of Colonial Virginia*, III (Richmond, 1928), p. 366.

[114] *The Southside Virginian*, VIII, pp. 147-48.

28. WILLIAM[4] COCKE (William[3], Thomas[2], Temperance[1] Baley), born about 1698, died before 14 March 1734/5 when his estate was appraised.[115] He married 23. *Judith[5] Anderson* (see SHEPPEY),[116] who married (2), before June 1739,[117] Francis Redford.

Issue:[118] 113. (Child)[5], probably Miss Judith Cocke on whose estate administration was granted, 3 Jan. 1742/3, to Abraham Bailey, John Redford, Jr., Thomas Jordan and John Burton;[119] 114. (Child)[5], died young.

29. TEMPERANCE[4] COCKE (William[3], Thomas[2], Temperance[1] Baley) married, before 1720, Abraham Bailey, born about 1694, died after 1774. They resided in Henrico County.

Issue: [BAILEY][120] 115. Abraham[5], of Chesterfield County where he witnessed several deeds, 1750-55, and later of Henrico County where he purchased 100 acres, 9 July 1761,[121] and succeeded his father as constable, Aug. 1761;[122] 116. JOSEPH[5]; 117. PETER[5]; 118. Henry[5], to whom his father gave 200 acres, 5 Sept. 1757;[123] 119. ROGER COCK[5]; 120. DAVID[5]; 121. TEMPERANCE[5].

30. MARY[4] COCKE (William[3], Thomas[2], Temperance[1] Baley) died before 1754. She married John Redford, Jr., son of John and Martha (Milner) Redford, of Henrico County, who was born 1700 and left will dated 1 April 1778.[124]

Issue: [REDFORD][125] 122. Francis[5]; 123. WILLIAM COCKE[5]; 124. Joseph[5]; 125. Martha[5], married ___ Goode; 126. Ann[5], married ___ Frogmorton

---

[115] Henrico Co. Wills & Deeds 1725-37, p. 601.

[116] Although James P. C. Southall in *V* XLII, p. 215 (followed by Cocke, *op. cit.*, II, p. 7) stated she was Judith Stewart, no supporting evidence has been found.

[117] Henrico Co. Order Bk. 1737-46, p. 84. On 5 Aug. 1747 they sold her dower interest in "World's End" and other land of William[4] Cocke (Henrico Co. Wills & Deeds 1744-48, p. 297).

[118] Cocke, *op. cit.*, II, p. 7.

[119] Henrico Co. Order Bk. 1737-46, p. 201.

[120] Cocke, *op. cit.*, II, pp. 8, 20-21, names several other children but the data are obviously confused and only those established by record or reasonable circumstantial evidence are included here.

[121] Henrico Co. Deed Bk. 1750-74, p. 692.

[122] Henrico Co. Order Bk. 1755-62, p. 512.

[123] Henrico Co. Deed Bk. 1750-67, p. 513.

[124] Henrico Co. Proceedings of the Commissioners Respecting Records 1774-82, p. 105.

[125] Cocke, *op. cit.*, II, pp. 8, 22, 48-49. Also named as possible children are Mary, wife of William Bullington, and Agnes, wife of Joseph Bondurant.

[Throgmorton]; 127. James[5]; 128. SARAH[5]; 129. JOHN[5].

31. CATHERINE[4] COCKE (William[3], Thomas[2], Temperance[1] Baley) died 10 Sept. 1725.[126] She married John Burton.[127]

Issue: [BURTON] 130. John[5], born 7 Sept. 1725.[128]

32. THOMAS[4] HARWOOD Agnes[3] Cocke, Thomas[2], Temperance[1] Baley) died before July 1737.[129] He married ___, who married (2), before Sept. 1739, Isaac Hill.[130]

Issue: [HARWOOD] 131. SAMUEL[5].

36. SAMUEL[4] HARWOOD (Temperance[3] Cocke, Thomas[2], Temperance[1] Baley), justice of Charles City County, 1726, sheriff, 1730, member of the House of Burgesses, 1720-34,[131] captain of militia, 1740, married (1), 16 Sept. 1728,[132] Martha Taylor, daughter of the Rev. Daniel Taylor of Blisland Parish, James City County, and (2) 107. Agnes[5] Poythress, who married (2) 81. *Benjamin[5] Cocke* (see HOLT).

Issue: [HARWOOD] (by 1?) 132. Catherine[5], chose Benjamin Cocke as her guardian, July 1750; 133. SAMUEL[5]; (by 2) 134. Tabitha[5], named in will of her maternal grandfather.

37. BOWLER[4] COCKE (Richard[3], Richard[2], Temperance[1] Baley), of "Bremo" and later of "Shirley," born 1696, died 1771,[133] was justice of Henrico County, 1726, and county clerk, 1728-48, and member of the House of Burgesses, 1752-65.[134] He married (1) Sarah Fleming and (2), about 1745, Elizabeth (Hill) Carter, daughter of Col. Edward Hill of "Shirley," Charles City County, and widow of Col. John Carter of "Corotoman," Lancaster County.

Issue: (by 1)[135] 135. Anne[5], born 18 June 1720, Essex County; 136. Susanna[5], born 6 Nov. 1722, "Bremo," Henrico County, died Oct. 1723; 137.

---

126 Bristol Parish Register.

127 Francis Burton Harrison, *Burton Chronicles of Colonial Virginia* (n.p., 1933), pp. 270-72.

128 Bristol Parish Register.

129 Charles City Co. Order Bk. 1737-51, p. 8.

130 *Ibid.*, p. 107.

131 Leonard, pp. 70, 72, 74.

132 Charles City Co. Deeds, Wills &c 1724/5-1731, p. 224, marriage contract stating Samuel Harwood the younger is the only son of Samuel Harwood, Gent., of the Parish of Westover.

133 *Virginia Gazette* (Purdie & Dixon), 22 Aug. 1771, p. 2.

134 Leonard, pp. 84, 86, 88, 92.

135 *V* XXXV, p. 27, citing fragment of Henrico Parish Register.

Tabitha[5], born 25 Sept. 1724; 138. BOWLER[5]; 139. Sarah[5], born 6 Feb. 1728/9; 140. Elizabeth[5], born 15 May 1731;[136] 141. Richard[5], born 7 March 1732/3, died 31 March 1733; 142. Charles[5], born 9 Sept. 1735, died 4 Aug. 1739.

39. TABITHA[4] COCKE (Richard[3], Richard[2], Temperance[1] Baley), living 1760, married, 1718, Ebenezer Adams, died 13 June 1735,[137] emigrant to Virginia before 1714 who settled in New Kent County.[138]

Issue: [ADAMS][139] 143. Richard[5], died 12 Sept. 1721;[140] 144. Bowler[5], born 19 April 1722, died 26 Nov. 1726;[141] 145. William[5], born 4 July 1724,[142] died before 25 Aug. 1763;[143] 146. RICHARD[5]; 147. Tabitha[5], born 7 July 1728,[144] married, as his (2) wife, 119. *Richard[5] Eppes* (see EPES); 148. Thomas[5], born 1730, died Aug. 1788, left will 12 Oct. 1785-22 Oct. 1788,[145] clerk of Henrico County, vestryman of Henrico Parish, 1757-64, resided in Great Britain to attend to his extensive business interests, 1762-74, chairman of the New Kent Committee, 1774, member of Congress, 1778-80, signer of the Articles of Confederation, moved to Augusta County, 1780, member of the Virginia Senate, 1783-86,[146] married, 1775, Elizabeth[7] (Fauntleroy) Cocke, daughter of 54. *William[6] Fauntleroy* (see PEIRSEY) and widow of 138. Bowler[5] Cocke, who died 1792; 149. ANNE[5]; 150. SARAH[5].

41. RICHARD[4] COCKE Richard[3], Richard[2], Temperance[1] Baley), of

---

[136] Can she have married Capt. John Hylton, baptized 26 May 1719 at South Shields, Durham, England, who settled at Bermuda Hundred, engaged in extensive mercantile activities, was justice of Chesterfield County and Comptroller of the Customs in the Upper District pf James River (Glade Ian Nelson, "Hylton of Virginia: A Baronial Descent," *The Virginia Genealogist*, XIX, pp. 12-13), and died at Bermuda Hundred (*Virginia Gazette*, 18 Nov. 1773) leaving will 7 Nov. 1773-2 Feb. 1774 (Chesterfield Co. Will Bk. 2, p. 281; Order Bk. 5, p. 399) which named children John, Bowler, Ralph, Elizabeth and Sarah Cocke? John Hylton's wife was named Elizabeth (Chesterfield Co. Deed Bk. 7, p. 397).

[137] St. Peter's Parish Register.

[138] *W* (1) V, pp. 160-61; *V* XXII, p. 379.

[139] *V* V, pp. 161-64; Cocke, *op. cit.*, pp. 8, 15, 33; *Richmond Standard*, 11 Dec. 1880.

[140] St. Peter's Parish, New Kent Co., Register.

[141] *Ibid.*

[142] *Ibid.*

[143] *V* V, p. 161, source not identified.

[144] St. Peter's Parish Register.

[145] Augusta Co. Will Bk. 7, p. 99.

[146] *Biographical Directory of the American Congress, 1774-1996* (Alexandria, Va., 1997), p. 558; Leonard, pp. 151, 155, 158.

"Shoal Bay," Surry County, born about 1706, died 5 March 1772[147] leaving will 13 Sept. 1771-21 April 1772.[148] He married (1) Elizabeth Hartwell, daughter of John Hartwell of "Swann's Point," and (2), after 1736,[149] Elizabeth (Ruffin) Kinchin, widow of Matthew Kinchin.

Issue: (by 1)[150] 151. HARTWELL[5]; 152. Benjamin[5], died unmarried; 153. ELIZABETH[5]; 154. REBECCA[5]; (by 2) 155. ANNE[5]; 156. RICHARD[5]; 157. LUCY[5]; 158. NATHANIEL[5]; 159. JOHN[5].

42. BENJAMIN[4] COCKE (Richard[3], Richard[2], Temperance[1] Baley), born about 1710, was vestryman of St. James Northam Parish, Goochland County, 1744-47, and later of Surry County. He left will 13 March 1763-17 May 1763.[151] He married Catherine Allen, daughter of Arthur and Elizabeth Allen of Surry County.

Issue:[152] 160. ALLEN[5]; 161. CATHARINE ALLEN[5]; 162. REBECCA[5].

43. ANNE[4] COCKE (Richard[3], Richard[2], Temperance[1] Baley) died about 1755. She married Capt. William Acrill of Charles City County, member of the House of Burgesses, 1736-38,[153] who died 23 March 1737/8 leaving will 20 March 1738-June 1738, presented at Court by Richard Cocke and Bowler Cocke, executors.[154]

Issue; [ACRILL][155] 163. SUSANNA[5]; 164. REBECCA[5]; 165. Hannah[5], left will 24 Aug. 1768-2 Sept. 1778;[156] 166. William[5], justice of Charles City County, captain of militia, Sept. 1762,[157] member of the House of Burgesses, 1766-76, of the five revolutionary conventions, 1774-76, and of the House of

---

[147] *Virginia Gazette* (Rind), 12 March 1772, p. 2.

[148] Surry Co. Will Bk. 10A, p. 191.

[149] Isle of Wight Co. Will Bk. 4, p. 113.

[150] Cocke, *op. cit.*, I (n.p., 1967), pp. 8, 16, 34-37; *V* V, pp. 73-76.

[151] Surry Co. Will Bk. 10, p. 323.

[152] Cocke, *op. cit.*, I, pp. 8, 17.

[153] Leonard, p. 76.

[154] *Virginia Gazette*, 24 March 1737/8, reporting death on "Thursday last" at his house in Charles City, "a great lawyer"; Charles City Co. Order Bk. 1737-51, p. 44; Surry Co. Deed Bk. 7, p. 339.

[155] Charles City Co. Order Bk. 1754-57, p. 198, naming three daughters.

[156] Henrico Co. County Court Chancery papers, 1792-019, Elizabeth Cocke's Admr. *vs.* Hannah Acrill's Exrs.

[157] Charles City Co. Order Bk. 1758-62, p. 453.

Delegates, 1776-78,[158] died by 2 April 1783 when Acrill[6] Cocke gave bond as his executor.[159]

45. THOMAS[4] CARY (Elizabeth[3] Cocke, Richard[2], Temperance[1] Baley), born about 1698, lived most of his life at "Essex Lodge," York County which he purchased, 1728, and sold to his brother Miles, 1753, and then moved to "Pokashock," Chesterfield County, left will 12 Aug. 1754-Oct. 1755.[160] He married Dorothy Philipson who left will 17 --- 1761-7 Oct. 1768.[161]

Issue: [CARY][162] 167. THOMAS[5]; 168. ROBERT[5].

46. MILES[4] CARY (Elizabeth[3] Cocke, Richard[2], Temperance[1] Baley), born 1701, of "Peartree Hall," Warwick County, succeeded his brother Richard as clerk of Warwick and of the committees of Privileges and Elections and of Public Claims and served 1722-48, merchant, left will 11 Oct. 1763-11 Dec. 1766.[163] He married (1) Hannah Armistead, daughter of William Armistead, on whose estate he was granted administration 14 Sept. 1752,[164] and (2) Anne (____) Howard, who left will 26 Jan. 1768-18 July 1768.[165]

Issue: (by 1) [CARY][166] 169. MILES[5]; 170. Rebecca[5], married 73. Rev. *Miles[5] Selden* (see TAYLOR-CARY); 171. Anne[5], married 35. Capt. *Bennett[5] Tompkins* (see BENNETT, Samuel); 172. JOHN[5]; 173. RICHARD[5]; 174. [?] Hannah[5]; 175. Mary[5], perhaps married James Pride of James City County; 176. ELIZABETH[5]; 177. ROBERT[5].

53. JOSEPH[4] PLEASANTS (Martha[3] Cocke, Richard[2], Temperance[1] Baley), of Pickanockey, Henrico County, left will, now lost, 27 Oct. 1758-4 Dec. 1758.[167] He married, (1), by 2 July 1726,[168] Sarah Goode, daughter of

---

[158] *Dictionary of Virginia Biography*, I (Richmond, 1998), pp. 14-15; Leonard, pp. 94, 97, 99, 102, 105, 109, 112, 114, 117, 119, 122, 125.

[159] *The Virginia Genealogist*, XIV, p. 184.

[160] Chesterfield Co. Will Bk. 1, p. 196; Order Bk. 2, p. 131.

[161] Chesterfield Co. Will Bk. 1, p. 543; Order Bk. 4, p. 239.

[162] Harrison, *The Virginia Carys*, p. 62.

[163] *Ibid.*, pp. 174-75, from Warwick County records.

[164] Warwick Co. Order Bk. 1748-62, p. 190.

[165] York Co. Wills & Inventories 21, 1760-71, p. 420.

[166] Harrison, *The Virginia Carys*, pp. 51-73.

[167] Henrico Co. Deed Bk. 1767-74, p. 484; Order Bk. 1755-62, p. 288.

[168] *Val. Papers*, II, p. 1192. He was disowned by the Quakers for marrying out of unity. On 5 Aug. 1732 he presented a paper to Henrico Monthly Meeting "condemning his evil in taking a wife, not amongst friends," and was readmitted (*ibid.*, p. 1194). The name of his wife is not mentioned.

Joseph Goode,[169] who relinquished dower when he divided with his cousin John Pleasants, 1 April 1728, land and a water grist mill on Four Mile Creek,[170] and (2), 5 Nov. 1732,[171] 28. *Elizabeth*[4] *Woodson* (see WOODSON), who left will, now lost, proved 4 Aug. 1766.[172]

Issue: [PLEASANTS][173] (by 1) 178. WILLIAM[5]; 179. JOSEPH[5]; (by 2) 180. JESSE[5]; 181. JACOB[5]; 182. Josiah[5], named in bond of brother Joseph[5], 6 Nov. 1761,[174] married, by 7 March 1772 when disowned by the Society of Friends,[175] ___; 183. PHILIP[5]; 184. Martha[6].[176]

56. MARTHA[4] PLEASANTS (Martha[3] Cocke, Richard[2], Temperance[1] Baley) married, after 5 Feb. 1734/5,[177] Nathaniel Vandewall, referred to as late of London,[178] of Henrico County who married (2) Ann ___ and left will 8 Dec. 1768-Aug. 1769.[179]

Issue: [VANDEWALL][180] 185. MARTHA[5]; 186. Mary[5], married ____ Lewis.[181]

57. JOHN[4] PLEASANTS (Martha[3] Cocke, Richard[2], Temperance[1] Baley), of Pickanockie, Henrico County, left will dated 29 Dec. 1776.[182] He married 7 Nov. 1731[183] 96. *Susanna*[5] *Woodson* (see WOODSON).

---

[169] Chesterfield Co. Deed Bk. 6, p. 67, deed of William[5] Pleasants, 4 Sept. 1767, to Margaret Akin to fulfill a gift made by his grandfather Joseph Goode.

[170] Henrico Co. Wills & Deeds 1725-37, p. 172.

[171] *Val. Papers* II, p. 1194.

[172] Henrico Co. Order Bk. 1763-67, p. 613.

[173] *Val. Papers* IV, pp. 2295-97. Chesterfield Co. Will Bk. 1, p. 371; Order Bk. 3, p. 598, will of Joseph Goode, 14 Aug. 1761-5 Oct. 1764, establishes children by (1) wife. Quaker records establish Jesse and Jacob as by (2) wife. No proof of the parentage of Philip and Martha has been located.

[174] Henrico Co. Deeds & Wills 1750-67, p. 726. He presumably is the Josiah, son of John [*sic*] Pleasants, who chose Jesse Pleasants as his guardian, 2 Jan. 1769 (Henrico Co. Order Bk. 1767-69, p. 377) but was of age by 6 Sept. 1773 (Henrico Co. Deeds & Wills 1767-74, p. 484).

[175] Hinshaw, VI, p. 206.

[176] *Val. Papers* IV, p. 2295, states she married Joseph Pleasants, not otherwise identified.

[177] *Val. Papers*, II, p. 1196; Hinshaw VI, p. 204.

[178] Hinshaw VI, p. 215.

[179] Henrico Co. Proceedings of the Commissioners Regarding Records Destroyed by the British, 1774-82, pp. 24-26; Order Bk. 1767-69, p. 493.

[180] *V VL*, pp. 283-84.

[181] *Val. Papers* IV, p. 2291, states she married William Lewis.

[182] Henrico Co. Deeds & Wills 1774-82, p. 88.

[183] *Val. Papers*, II, p. 1194.

Issue: [PLEASANTS][184] 187. URSULA[5]; 188. SUSANNAH[5]; 189. MATTHEW[5]; 190. ARCHIBALD[5]; 191. JOSEPH[5]; 192. JAMES[5]; 193. Tarleton[5], not named in father's will, 1776; 194. JOHN[5].

58. RICHARD[4] PLEASANTS (Martha[3] Cocke, Richard[2], Temperance[1] Baley), of Goochland County, left will 15 May 1778-21 Sept. 1778.[185] He married Ann Porter.

Issue: [PLEASANTS][186] 195. RICHARD[5]; 196. JOSEPH[5]; 197. MARTHA[5].

59. THOMAS[4] PLEASANTS (Martha[3] Cocke, Richard[2], Temperance[1] Baley), of Goochland County, left will 8 March 1775-21 Aug. 1775.[187] He married Elizabeth Porter.

Issue: [PLEASANTS][188] 198. Robert[5], married, 4 Dec. 1773,[189] Fanny Clark, possibly the Robert, born 15 March 1742 in Goochland County, died 23 Feb. 1843, who served several tours in the Goochland militia during the Revolutionary War[190] and left will 22 Jan. 1840-20 March 1843;[191] 199. THOMAS[5]; 200. Jesse[5]; 201. Ann[5], married, 4 July 1771,[192] Samuel Martin; 202. Elizabeth[5], married, 20 May 1777,[193] Edward Carter.

62. MARTHA[4] COCKE (John[3], Richard[2], Temperance[1] Baley), born 1697/8, married (1) 68. *Arthur[5] Moseley, Jr.* (see HARRIS, Thomas), who died 4 Oct. 1736 from a fall from his horse[194] leaving will 10 July 1735-Feb. 1736/7,[195] and (2), by 7 Feb. 1742/3,[196] Edward Friend of Henrico and later Chesterfield County, widower of 22. *Anne[5] (Anderson) Ward* (see SHEPPEY),

---

[184] *Val. Papers* IV, pp. 2293-95.
[185] Goochland Co. Deed Bk. 12, pp. 178-79.
[186] *Val. Papers* IV, p. 2293.
[187] Goochland Co. Deeds & Wills 11, p. 38.
[188] *Val. Papers*, IV, p. 2293.
[189] Jones, *op. cit.*, p. 39, gives her name as Ann Clarke.
[190] Revolutionary War pension application, Robert Pleasants, S.8961; Alycon Trubey Pierce, *Selected Final Pension Payment Vouchers, 1818-1864, Virginia: Richmond & Wheeling* (Athens, Ga., 1996), II, p. 445.
[191] Goochland Co. Deed Bk. 33, pp. 226-27.
[192] Jones, *op. cit.*, p. 82.
[193] *Ibid.*
[194] Fragment of Henrico Parish Register, in R. A. Brock, *The Vestry Book of Henrico Parish, Virginia, 1730-1773* (Richmond, 1904; Bowie, Md., 1991), p. 155, as Mosby.
[195] Henrico Co. Wills & Deeds 1725-37, p. 599.
[196] Henrico Co. Order Bk. 1737-46, p. 206.

on whose estate Martha was granted administration 2 Jan. 1761.[197]

Issue: (by 1) [MOSELEY][198] 203. ARTHUR[5]; 204. JOHN[5]; 205. Richard[5]; 206. WILLIAM[5]; 207. EDWARD[5]; 208. Thomas[5]; 209. SARAH[5]; 210. Martha[5], died young; 211. Benjamin[5], with brothers John and Thomas grantees in a deed from their mother, proved March 1738/9,[199] chose his brother William as his guardian, 5 Oct. 1753.[200]

63. JAMES POWELL[5] COCKE (James Powell[4], Thomas[3], Thomas[2], Temperance[1] Baley), born 17 Aug. 1718, died 26 May 1753, left will 30 April 1753-3 July 1753.[201] He lived at "Malvern Hills," Henrico County, and in Lunenburg County. He married, 22 Oct. 1742, Mary Magdalene Chastain, born 23 Aug. 1727,[202] who married (2), 17 Jan. 1754, 37. *Peter[5] Farrar* (see FARRAR).

Issue: 212. Chastain[6], born 14 March 1743, died 1748; 213. Martha[6], born 24 July 1745, died 10 April 1796, married, (bond 24) July 1760,[203] 63. Capt. *Henry[6] Anderson* (see SHEPPEY); 214. James Powell[6], born 20 Jan. 1747/8, died 13 Jan. 1829, of "Malvern Hills," Henrico County, until about 1785, then of Augusta County, moved to Albemarle County about 1793 and resided at "Edgemont," married (1), (bond 24) Nov. 1767,[204] Elizabeth Archer, died 1773, and (2), (bond 2) Oct. 1777,[205] Lucy Smith, born 8 Dec. 1756, died 27 Feb. 1816; 215. Chastain[6], born 11 Nov. 1749, died 19 March 1795, married, (bond 11) April 1769,[206] Martha Field Archer, born 21 Dec. 1752, died 27 Feb. 1817; 216. Stephen[6], born 5 Jan. 1750/1, died 13 Nov. 1794, left will 7 Nov. 1794-22 Jan. 1795,[207] married, 5 March 1772, Jane Segar Eggleston, born 8 June 1756, died 1 April 1835; 217. Elizabeth Chastain[6], born 22 Jan. 1753, married, (bond

---

[197] Chesterfield Co. Order Bk. 3, p. 98.

[198] Philip Turpin notebook, in *The Virginia Genealogist*, XXI, p. 5; John Hale Stutesman, "Sorting Out the Moseleys," *The Virginia Genealogist*, XXXIII, pp. 65-70.

[199] Henrico Co. Order Bk. 1737-44, p. 69.

[200] Chesterfield Co. Order Bk. 1, p. 403.

[201] Lunenburg Co. Will Bk. 1, p. 6.

[202] King William Parish Register, in Brock, *op. cit.*, p. 79.

[203] Kathleen Booth Williams, *Marriages of Amelia County, Virginia, 1735-1815* (n.p., 1961), p. 3.

[204] *Ibid.*, p. 27.

[205] Catherine Lindsay Knorr, *Marriage Bonds and Ministers' Returns of Chesterfield County, Virginia, 1771-1815* (Pine Bluff, Ark., 1958), p. 33.

[206] Williams, *op. cit.*, p. 27.

[207] Amelia Co. Will Bk. 5, p. 145.

24) June 1790,[208] as his (2) wife, 151. Col. *William Cannon* (see WOODSON).

66. WILLIAM[5] COCKE (Brazure[4], Thomas[3], Thomas[2], Temperance[1] Baley) of Granville Co., N.C., left will 12 March 1795-Nov. 1796.[209] He married, (bond 23) July 1754,[210] Rebecca Smith Edwards, who died 16 June 1796 leaving nuncupative will proved Feb. 1797.[211]

Issue: 218. William[6], born 27 April 1757, died 20 June 1812, married, (bond 24) May 1784,[212] Elizabeth Bedford; 219. James[6]; 220. Elizabeth[6]; 221. Sarah[6]; married, (bond 30) Nov. 1772,[213] James Daniels; 222. Mary[6], married ___ Roberts.

67. THOMAS[5] COCKE (Brazure[4], Thomas[3], Thomas[2], Temperance[1] Baley), of Cumberland County, was given 150 acres in Brunswick County by his brother William, 7 Jan. 1754, which he sold 3 May 1759.[214] He married ___.

Issue:[215] 223. (possibly) Anderson[6], born about 1758 in Cumberland County, musician in the 4th Virginia Regiment, 1776-78, later of Prince Edward, Campbell, Charlotte and Halifax counties,[216] married, 12 Sept. 1782,[217] 935. *Elizabeth[6] Michaux* (see WOODSON), born 11 July 1766, died 1784;[218] 224. (Other children)[6].

68. ELIZABETH[5] COCKE (Brazure[4], Thomas[3], Thomas[2], Temperance[1] Baley) married ___ Holt.

Issue: [HOLT] 225. Elizabeth[6].

70. MARY[5] COCKE (Brazure[4], Thomas[3], Thomas[2], Temperance[1] Baley)

---

[208] Williams, *op. cit.*, p. 21.

[209] Granville Co., N.C., Will Bk. 4, pp. 50-52.

[210] Catherine Lindsay Knorr, *Marriage Bonds and Ministers' Returns of Brunswick County, Virginia, 1750-1810* (Pine Bluff, Ark., 1953), p. 18.

[211] Granville Co., N.C., Will Bk. 4, p. 69.

[212] Hummel, *op. cit.*, p. 11.

[213] *Ibid.*, p. 29.

[214] Brunswick Co. Deed Bk. 5, p. 536; Deed Bk. 6, p. 353.

[215] Children are mentioned, but not named, in will of their grandfather.

[216] Revolutionary War pension application, Anderson Cocke, S.9232, National Archives; Alycon Trubey Pierce, *Selected Final Pension Payment Vouchers, 1818-1869, Virginia: Richmond and Wheeling* (Athens, Ga., 1996), I, pp. 114-15.

[217] Catherine Lindsay Knorr, *Marriage Bonds and Ministers' Returns of Prince Edward County, Virginia, 1754-1810* (Pine Bluff, Ark., 1950), p. 17.

[218] *V* XLV, p. 220.

married, (bond 15) Feb. 1758,[219] Parsons Anderson, son of Charles Anderson..
He resided in Prince Edward County where he was a member of Capt. John
Morton's company, 4th Virginia Regiment, in 1776,[220] and died in service during
the Revolutionary War.[221]

Issue: [ANDERSON] 226. Brazure Cocke[6]; 227. Mary[6], married, 12 Feb.
1801,[222] Ransone Dudley.

71. SUSANNA[5] COCKE (Brazure[4], Thomas[3], Thomas[2], Temperance[1]
Baley) married Williamson Coleman.

Issue: [COLEMAN] 228. Susanna[6], born 1755, died 1823, married Isham
Reese, born 1748, Dinwiddie County, died 1816, Methodist minister who moved
to South Carolina and then to Hancock Co., Ga., and Jones Co., Ga.

74. WILLIAM[5] FINNEY (Mary[4] Cocke, Thomas[3], Thomas[2], Temperance[1]
Baley) left an undated will proved 26 April 1759.[223] He married Mary __, who
left will 10 Nov. 1784-23 Oct. 1794.[224]

Issue: [FINNEY][225] 229. Elizabeth[6], married 67. *Thomas Branch[5] Willson*
(see BRANCH); 230. Mary Page, married 64. *Branch[5] Tanner* (see BRANCH);
231. Lucy[6], married 183. *Edward[5] Branch* (see BRANCH); 232. Martha[6],
married, (bond 26) June 1766,[226] Edward Haskins; 233. Sarah[6], married __
Haskins; 234. William[6], died before 25 Oct. 1787 when his widow was granted
administration on his estate,[227] of Amelia County, married 556. Hannah[6]
Watkins, who married (2) John Walke; 235. Judith[6]; 236. Frances[6], married
100. *William[6] Osborne* (see OSBORNE); 237. John[6], left undated will proved

[219] Katherine B. Elliott, *Marriages, 1749-1840, Cumberland County, Virginia* (n.p.,
1969), p. 11.

[220] Herbert Clarence Bradshaw, *History of Prince Edward County, Virginia* (Richmond,
1955), p. 737.

[221] Prince Edward Co. Order Bk. 7, p. 261, naming Brazier Cocke Anderson as eldest son
and heir at law, April 1784.

[222] Catherine Lindsay Knorr, *Marriage Bonds and Ministers' Returns of Prince Edward
County, Virginia, 1754-1810* (Pine Bluff, Ark., 1950, pp. 23, 65.

[223] Amelia Co. Will Bk. 1, p. 145.

[224] Amelia Co. Will Bk. 5, p. 126.

[225] *Ibid.*; Amelia Co. Will Bk. 1, p. 145.

[226] Williams, *op. cit.*, p. 51.

[227] Amelia Co. Order Bk. 18, p. 158.

27 Dec. 1798.[228] married, (1), (bond 17) Dec. 1778,[229] 692. Elizabeth[6] Moseley and (2), (bond 24) Feb. 1785,[230] Sarah (Mann) Chappell, widow of Miles Chappell; 238. Ann[6], married (1) 68. *Daniel[5] Willson* (see BRANCH) and (2) 688. John[6] Moseley.

77. AGNES[5] SMITH (Agnes[4] Cocke, Stephen[3], Thomas[2], Temperance[1] Baley), born 9 April 1722,[231] left will 21 Nov. 1805-8 Sept. 1806.[232] She married John May, of Dinwiddie County, clerk of the vestry of Bristol Parish, who died before 31 March 1760,[233] after which his widow lived in Lunenburg County, where she operated an ordinary, in Botetourt County, in Halifax County, perhaps in Kentucky, and finally in Campbell County.[234]

Issue: [MAY][235] 239. Betty[6], born 16 Nov. 1740,[236] probably died unmarried before 1790; 240. Richard[6], born 20 Dec. 1743,[237] died before Feb. 1782 when his mother was granted administration on his estate,[238] surveyor, justice and captain of militia of Botetourt County and justice of Kentucky County and Jefferson County (Kentucky); 241. John[6], born 20 Dec. 1744,[239] killed by Indians 20 March 1790 on the Ohio River at the mouth of the Scioto River,[240] left will 5 March 1790-10 Feb. 1791,[241] of "Belle Vue," Chesterfield County, clerk of Botetourt County, 1769-78, vestryman of Botetourt Parish, quartermaster of militia, clerk of the General Court of Virginia, 1778-80, clerk pro tempore of Jefferson Co., Ky., 1781, member of the House of Delegates from Jefferson County, 1782, for whom the city of Maysville, Ky., was named, married 282.

---

[228] Amelia Co. Will Bk. 5, p. 537.

[229] Catherine Lindsay Knorr, *Marriage Bonds and Ministers' Returns of Powhatan County, Virginia, 1777-1830* (Pine Bluff, Ark., 1957), p. 23.

[230] Williams, *op. cit.*, p. 41.

[231] Bristol Parish Register.

[232] Campbell Co. Will Bk. 2, pp. 284-85.

[233] Landon C. Bell, *Cumberland Parish, Lunenburg County, Virginia, 1746-1816* (Richmond, 1930), p. 509.

[234] Ben H. Coke, *John May, Jr., of Virginia* (Baltimore, 1975), pp. 236-40.

[235] *Ibid.*, pp. 1-4, 240-68.

[236] Bristol Parish Register.

[237] *Ibid.*

[238] Botetourt Co. Order Bk. 1780-84, p. 140.

[239] Bristol Parish Register.

[240] Charles Johnston, *A Narrative of the Incidents Attending the Capture, Detention, and Ransmoe of Charles Johnston* (New York, 1827), pp. 15-16.

[241] Chesterfield Co. Will Bk. 4, p. 304; Order Bk. 8, p. 543.

Ann[6] *Langley* (see JORDAN, Thomas), who married (2) Thomas Lewis and died Sept. 1811; 242. Stephen[6], born 15 Nov. 1745,[242] died after March 1822, of Lunenburg and Botetourt counties, and later of Nelson Co., Ky., married Martha _____; 243. David[6], born 15 May 1747,[243] died shortly after Oct. 1797, student at the College of William and Mary, 1768-70, clerk of the Botetourt County Committee, 1776, deputy clerk of Botetourt County, 1777, and clerk, 1778-88, captain of militia, 1780, incorporator of Botetourt Seminary, 1785, later of Nelson and Hardin cos., Ky., and clerk of Hardin County, 1795-97, married Mary Meredith, niece of Patrick Henry, who died 28 June 1835 in her 86th year;[244] 244. Agnes[6], born 6 Sept. 1749,[245] died after Jan. 1828, married (1) 88. Abraham[5] Cocke and (2), by March 1789,[246] Thomas Hayes, who moved to Nelson Co., Ky., later lived in Hardin and Barren cos., Ky., and left will 19 May 1841- codicil 18 Sept. 1841-Oct. 1841;[247] 245. William[6], born Oct. 1752,[248] left will 28 April 1825-9 Jan. 1826,[249] justice of Kentucky County, quartermaster and adjutant of militia, clerk of Lincoln Co., Ky., 1781-83, participated in the battle of Blue Licks, 1772, surveyor of Jefferson and Nelson cos., Ky., justice of Nelson County and County Lieutenant, member of the Kentucky legislature, 1792; 246. George[6], born 6 Feb. 1756,[250] died 26 April 1822 at Petersburg,[251] student at the College of William and Mary, surveyor of Kentucky County, 1776-80, of Jefferson Co., Ky., 1780-84, justice of Jefferson County, later resident of Dinwiddie County and of Petersburg, married, 1783, Anna Fitzhugh, born 27 May 1765, died 22 Sept. 1805; 247. Lucy[6], married, (bond 5) April 1786,[252] Joel Bott of Botetourt County.

    79. ABRAHAM[5] SMITH (Agnes[4] Cocke, Stephen[3], Thomas[2], Temperance[1]

---

[242] Philip Slaughter, *A History of Bristol Parish, Virginia* (Richmond, 1879), p. 187.
[243] *Ibid.* Baptized 5 Oct. 1749 (Bristol Parish Register).
[244] Gravestone, Elizabethtown, Ky., Cemetery.
[245] Slaughter, *loc. cit.*
[246] Lunenburg Co. Deed Bk. 15, pp. 415-18.
[247] Barren Co., Ky., Will Bk. 3, p. 183, recorded originally in Warren Co., Ky.
[248] Slaughter, *loc. cit.*
[249] Nelson Co., Ky., Will Bk. F, pp. 55-56.
[250] Slaughter, *op. cit.*, p. 188.
[251] *Richmond Daily Mercantile Advertiser*, 4 May 1822.
[252] Catherine Lindsay Knorr, *Marriage Bonds and Ministers' Returns of Halifax County, Virginia, 1753-1800* (Pine Bluff, Ark., 1957), p. 9.

Baley) left will 5 Jan. 1782-Feb. 1782.[253] He was left land in Dinwiddie County and moved briefly to South Carolina,[254] but returned to Dinwiddie County where he had tracts of 9 acres and 2 acres surveyed in Bath Parish, 26 March 1772,[255] and was justice and sheriff. He married Ann ___.

Issue: [SMITH][256] 248. Nancy[6], married Kennon Jones of Dinwiddie County, who died about 1809; 249. Martha[5], married James French of Dinwiddie County, who left will July 1795-Oct. 1795;[257] 250. Richard[6], died unmarried; 251. Elizabeth[6], married (1) Henry Lochhead, who died about 1794, and (2) James Macfarland, who left will 17 May 1834-codicil 4 Nov. 1836-8 May 1837.[258]

82. JANE[5] SMITH (Agnes[4] Cocke, Stephen[3], Thomas[2], Temperance[1] Baley) married William Cross of Amelia County, who died before 23 Dec. 1782.[259]

Issue: [CROSS][260] 252. John[6], married 95. Elizabeth[5] Cocke; 253. Charles[6], married, (bond 8) Nov. 1770,[261] Phebe Tomlinson; 254. Richard[6], married, (bond 23) July 1770,[262] Anne Maclin; 255. Agnes[6], married, (bond 21) Nov. 1759,[263] Robert Chappell of Dinwiddie County, who moved to Lunenburg County and left will 5 Sept. 1794-11 Dec. 1794.[264]

83. ANN[5] SMITH (Agnes[4] Cocke, Stephen[3], Thomas[2], Temperance[1] Baley) married John Hightower, Jr., who with wife Ann sold land in Amelia County, 27 Sept. 1758 and 22 Oct. 1764,[265] and by 29 Sept. 1769 moved to Lunenburg County.[266]

Issue: [HIGHTOWER] 256. Joseph[6], of Amelia County, 1772, and of

---

[253] Hamilton Trustees *vs.* Smith, U..S. Circuit Court records, Box 127, 1829, Virginia State Archives.

[254] Lunenburg Co. Deed Bk. 3, pp. 176-80, 29 Nov. 1750.

[255] Dinwiddie Co. Surveyors' Plat Bk. 1755-1865, p. 25.

[256] Coke, *Some Early Landowners*, p. 123.

[257] *Ibid.*, without citation of location of a copy.

[258] Lunenburg Co. Will Bk. 11, p. 198.

[259] Amelia Co. Will Bk. 3, p. 164.

[260] *Ibid.*, pp. 168, 169; Coke, *Some Early Landowners*, p. 85.

[261] Matheny and Yates, *op. cit.*, p. 29.

[262] Knorr, *Marriage Bonds ... Brunswick County*, p. 22.

[263] Williams, *op. cit.*, p. 23.

[264] Lunenburg Co. Will Bk. 4, pp. 73-74.

[265] Amelia Co. Deed Bk. 6, pp. 409-10; Deed Bk. 8, pp. 652-54, 654-56.

[266] Gibson Jefferson McConnaughey, *Unrecorded Deeds and Other Documents, Amelia County, Virginia, 1750-1902* (Amelia, Va., 1994), p. 25.

Lunenburg County by 1778,[267] who moved to Georgia in 1782,[268] married Amy
___; 257. Mary[6].

84. TEMPERANCE[5] SMITH (Agnes[4] Cocke, Stephen[3], Thomas[2],
Temperance[1] Baley) married Nathaniel Booth, who left will 8 May 1784-8 Dec.
1785.[269]

Issue: [BOOTH] 258. Joel[6], died before 1814, married Nancy ___;[270] 259.
Nathaniel[6], perhaps married, (bond 4) April 1795,[271] Wineford Morgain; 260.
Martha[6]; 261. Jane[6]; 262. Amy[6], married, 18 Jan. 1794,[272] William Townsend;
263. Mary[6], perhaps married, 26 Sept. 1795,[273] John Norvell of Lunenburg
County.

86. MARY[5] SMITH (Agnes[4] Cocke, Stephen[3], Thomas[2], Temperance[1]
Baley) married John Booth of Amelia and later of Franklin County who left will
26 Aug. 1807-7 Dec. 1807.[274]

Issue: [BOOTH][275] 264. Agnes[6], married, by 1773, Benjamin Clardy, and
moved to Pickens Co., S.C.; 265. Richard[6], died 1832; 266. Peter[6], left will 10
Nov. 1826-1 Jan. 1827,[276] married (1), 28 Dec. 1773,[277] Elizabeth Booth, and
(2), (bond 24) Aug. 1808,[278] Nancy Blades; 267. Stephen[6], moved to Tennessee,
married, (bond 15) Sept. 1786,[279] Penelope Guthrey; 268. Mary[6], married, (bond
13) Sept. 1786,[280] David Guthry; 269. Benjamin[6], born 1762, died 1838,

---

[267] Lunenburg Co. Deed Bk. 12, pp. 156-58; Deed Bk. 13, p. 175.

[268] British mercantile claim, T79/79, p. 76, British Public Record Office, in *The Virginia
Genealogist*, XIX, p. 103, report, about 1800, that he "absconded this state about Jan. 1782 and
left all his creditors unpaid. They considered him as an insolvent, worthless man and never
pursued him to South Carolina or Georgia where he died in disgrace many years ago."

[269] Lunenburg Co. Will Bk. 3, p. 234.

[270] Lunenburg Co. Deed Bk. 23, p. 256.

[271] Emma R. Matheny and Helen K. Yates, *Marriages of Lunenburg County, Virginia,
1746-1853* (Richmond, 1967), p. 12.

[272] *Ibid.*, p. 124.

[273] *Ibid.*, p. 88.

[274] Franklin Co. Will Bk. 1, pp. 332-33.

[275] Marshall Wingfield, *Pioneer Families of Franklin County, Virginia* (Berryville, Va.,
1964), p. 12.

[276] Franklin Co. Will Bk. 3, pp. 218-19.

[277] Hinshaw, VI, p. 881, Bedford County.

[278] Marshall Wingfield, *Marriage Bonds of Franklin County, Virginia, 1786-1838*
(Memphis, 1939), p. 40.

[279] *Ibid.*, p. 41.

[280] *Ibid.*, p. 103.

married, (bond 16) Dec. 1795,[281] Elizabeth Divers; 270. Thomas[6], perhaps predeceased his father or perhaps the Thomas of Booth's Store, Franklin County, private in Capt. Gross Scruggs' company in the Revolutionary War and disabled,[282] married ___; 271. John[6], born 13 May 1773, died 1827, married, 10 Oct. 1795,[283] Ann Ford.

88. ABRAHAM[5] COCKE (Abraham[4], Stephen[3], Thomas[2], Temperance[1] Baley), born 30 Sept. 1730,[284] left will 27 Aug. 1781-14 March 1782.[285] He lived in Lunenburg County and in 1781 was taken prisoner by Col. Banastre Tarleton and contracted smallpox, of which he died.[286] He married 244. Agnes[6] May, born 6 Sept.1749,[287] died after Jan. 1828,[288] who married (2) Thomas Hayes and moved to Kentucky about 1794.

Issue:[289] 272. Martha[6], married, by 1790, Thomas Hardy of Lunenburg County, living in Claiborne Co., Tenn., 1825; 273. John[6], died by 18 April 1834 when his estate was appraised,[290] of Nelson Co., Ky., married, 19 Feb. 1801,[291] Martha[7] May, daughter of 242. Stephen[6] May, who died 1853; 274. Mary[6], married, 17 Aug. 1796,[292] Henry Collier of Lunenburg County; 275. William[6], died about 1839, of Breckinridge Co., Ky., married, (bond 25) March 1803,[293] Elizabeth Gore; 276. James[6], died in infancy; 277. (child)[6], unborn at making of father's will, died in infancy.

89. PETER[5] COCKE (Abraham[4], Stephen[3], Thomas[2], Temperance[1] Baley) of Brunswick County and later of Montgomery Co., Tenn., left will 4 Sept. 1803-Oct. 1803.[294] He married (1) ___, (2), (bond 4) May 1769,[295] Mary

[281] *Ibid.*, p. 40.

[282] Revolutionary War pension application, Thomas Booth, S.10383, National Archives.

[283] Williams, *op. cit.*, p. 14.

[284] Bristol Parish Register.

[285] Lunenburg Co. Will Bk. 3, pp. 101-02.

[286] *The Virginia Genealogist*, XVIII, p. 284,

[287] Slaughter, *op. cit.*, p. 187.

[288] Nelson Co., Ky., Deed Bk. 17, pp. 433-35, 476.

[289] Coke, *op. cit.*, pp. 10-12.

[290] Nelson Co., Ky., Will Bk. G, pp. 393-94.

[291] *Nelson County Pioneer*, III, p. 49; Mary Harrel Stancliff, *Marriage Bonds of Nelson County, Kentucky, 1785-1832* (Houston, Tex., 1962), p. 63.

[292] Matheny and Yates, *op. cit.*, p. 24.

[293] Stancliff, *loc. cit.*

[294] Montgomery Co., Tenn., Will Bk. A, p. 198.

[295] Knorr, *Marriage Bonds ... Brunswick County*, p. 18.

Whitehead, (3) ___.[296]

Issue: (by 1) 278. Ann[6], married, (bond 6) Feb. 1781,[297] Freeman Jordan who sold 178 acres in Brunswick County, 21 Oct. 1790[298] and moved to Nottoway County; 279. Stephen[6], died 1829 in Montgomery Co., Tenn.[299]

280. Abraham[6], left will 17 Oct. 1814-Jan. 1815,[300] married (1), (bond 21) Dec. 1787,[301] Anne Hardy and (2) Elizabeth Hagood Biggers; 281. William Batte[6], died 1814, Clarksville, Tenn., married Nancy ___. who left will dated 1 Jan. 1835;[302] (by 2) 282. Richard[6], married, 25 Feb. 1799, Elizabeth Coffee; 283. John[6]; 284. James Whitehead[6], married, 14 Sept. 1802, Lucy C. Hargrove; 285. Elizabeth[6], married ____ Coffee; (by 3) 286. Susannah[6], married ___ Jordan; 287. Patsy[6]; 288. Benjamin[6]; 289. William Biggars[6]; 290. Hartwell[6], married, 12 Sept. 1808, Elizabeth Sanderson.

90. MARY[5] COCKE (Abraham[4], Stephen[3], Thomas[2], Temperance[1] Baley) died after Oct. 1792 She married, (bond 9) Nov. 1754,[303] Richard Ellis, died White Cliffs, Natchez, Miss., left will 17 Oct. 1792-6 Nov. 1792.[304]

Issue: [ELLIS] 291. Richard[6], died after Oct. 1792; 292. John[6]; 293. Jane[6], died 1823, married George Rapelje and resided at Natchez, Miss.; 294. William Cocke[6], married, (bond 29) March 1789,[305] 305. Mary[6] Cocke; 295. Martha[6], married, 29 July 1797, Don Estevan [Stephen] Minor, adjutant major of Natchez, Miss., 1790;[306] 296. Mary[6], born about 1771, died 1820, married Maj. Benjamin Farrar and lived at Laurel Hill, Miss.; 297. Abram[6], died 22 Dec. 1816, married

---

[296] Cocke, *op. cit.*, p. 12, suggests three wives, but the stated first and third are clearly in error. The division of children by three marriages is unconfirmed. His last wife and widow is probably Mrs. Sarah Cocke, aged 98, who died 14 Oct. 1861 in Montgomery Co., Tenn. (*Clarksville Weekly Chronicle*, 1 Nov. 1861, in Jill L. Garrott, *Obituaries from Tennessee Newspapers* [Easley, S.C., 1980], p. 58).

[297] Williams, *op. cit.*, p. 66.

[298] Brunswick Co. Deed Bk. 15, p. 110.

[299] *National Banner*, Nashville, Tenn., in Silas Emmett Lucas, ed., *Obituaries from Early Tennessee Newspapers, 1794-1851* (Easley, S.C., 1978), p. 74.

[300] Montgomery Co., Tenn., Will Bk. B, p. 75.

[301] Knorr, *Marriage Bonds ... Brunswick County*, p. 18.

[302] Montgomery Co., Tenn., Will Bk. G, 1834-37, pp. 142-43, without probate date. The preceding and next records are dated Jan. and Feb. 1837.

[303] Williams, *op. cit.*, p. 38.

[304] Natchez, Miss., Court Records Bk. C, p. 110.

[305] Williams, *op. cit.*, p. 38.

[306] *Mississippi Genealogical Exchange*, V, p. 42.

Marguerite Gaillard.

91. AGNES[5] COCKE (Abraham[4], Stephen[3], Thomas[2], Temperance[1] Baley), born 1737, died 1800, married, (bond 12) Nov. 1757,[307] Charles: Hamlin, Jr., born 1734, left will 5 March 1786-14 Sept. 1786,[308] of Prince George County, Amelia County and "Flat Rock," Lunenburg County, justice of Lunenburg County, 1766-85.

Issue: [HAMLIN][309] 298. John[6], married, 1809, Mary Williams; 299. Thomas[6], born Sept. 1758, died 1857, aged 99, Rockingham Co., N.C., married (1) 320. Elizabeth[6] Cross, died 1806-07, and (2), 5 May 1807,[310] Mary Ligon Stainback; 300. Tabitha[6], married, between Oct. 1785 and May 1786,[311] James Batte; 301. Lucy[6], married (1) Michael McKie, who left will 2 Dec.1796-8 Jan. 1797,[312] and (2), 1801,Warning Peter Robertson, who left will 19 Oct. 1812-10 March 1814;[313] 302. Mary[6], married, 1798 [or 1807?], William Colgate Boswell; 303. Martha Cocke[6], married, (bond 18) Oct. 1800,[314] Thomas Taylor of Mecklenburg County.

92. STEPHEN[5] COCKE (Abraham[4], Stephen[3], Thomas[2], Temperance[1] Baley), born 31 March 1740, left will 19 Dec. 1792-7 Feb. 1793.[315] She married, (bond 4) Dec. 1764,[316] 40. Amey[6] Jones (see PRICE-LLEWELLIN), born 26 Jan. 1747, moved, 1804, to Washington Co., Ky., lived for a time in Grainger Co., Tenn.,[317] and then returned to Kentucky, left will 30 Jan. 1819-8 Nov. 1824.[318]

Issue: 304. Richard Henry[6], born 8 Feb. 1766, died 17 Feb. 1823, moved

---

[307] Williams, *op. cit.*, p. 49.

[308] Lunenburg Co. Will Bk. 3, p. 362.

[309] Charles Hughes Hamlin, *They Went Thataway*, II (Richmond, 1965), pp. 109-12; John Bennett Boddie, *Southside Virginia Families*, I (Redwood City, Calif., 1955), p. 239.

[310] Matheny and Yates, *op. cit.*, p. 55.

[311] *Ibid.*, p. 7.

[312] Lunenburg Co. Will Bk. 4, p. 178b.

[313] Lunenburg Co. Will Bk. 7, p. 82.

[314] Katherine B. Elliott, *Marriage Records, 1765-1810, Mecklenburg County, Virginia* (South Hill, Va., 1963), p. 120.

[315] Nottoway Co. Will Bk. 1789-1802, p. 71.

[316] Williams, *op. cit.*, p. 27.

[317] Nottoway Co. Deed Bk. 3, p. 424.

[318] Washington Co., Ky., Will Bk. D, p. 75.

from Nottoway County to Washington Co., Ky., married, 6 Dec. 1797,[319] Mary Watkins, born 26 Aug. 1778, died 20 Feb. 1823; 305. Mary[6], born 15 March 1768, married (1) 294. William Cocke[6] Ellis and (2) Richard Jones, born about 1749, died 1828, of Springfield, Ky.; 306. Elizabeth[6], born 25 July 1770, married, by 1 May 1794,[320] William Brown of Petersburg and as a widow moved, 1804, to Washington Co., Ky.; 307. Martha[6] [Mariah], married 319. William Cocke[6] Lacy; 308. Sarah Shelton[6], married 326. John Alexander[6] Cocke; 309. Rebecca[6], born 1776, died 1833, married (1) 321. William Cocke[6] Cross and (2) ____ Harbison and moved to Missouri; 310 Amy Jones[6], born 1778, died 1 June 1824; 311 Thomas Jones[6], born 25 Nov. 1780, died 21 Aug. 1845 near Summerville, Tenn., moved to Washington Co., Ky., 1804, then to Christian Co., Ky., then to Limestone Co., Ala., and in 1823 to Fayette Co., Tenn., married, 20 Jan. 1802 in Nottoway County, Lucy Watkins Nicholson, born 4 Feb. 1783, died 2 Nov. 1836; 312 Stephen Jones[6], born Dec. 1784, died 5 April 1822, married, 10 March 1806, Harriet Nantz [Nance].

94. MARTHA[5] COCKE (Abraham[4], Stephen[3], Thomas[2], Temperance[1] Baley), born about 1742, died 1812 in Rockingham Co., N.C.[321] She married, (bond 28) Nov. 1759,[322] Theophilus Lacy, born 4 Nov. 1736 in New Kent County, son of Henry and Angelica (___) Lacy, sheriff of Pittsylvania County, 1773, who died before 18 Nov. 1777 when the Guilford Co., N.C., court ordered an inventory of his estate be made,[323] after which his widow moved to Guilford Co., N.C.

Issue: [LACY][324] 313 Batte Cocke[6], of Rockingham Co., N.C., and Nelson Co., Ky., married Elizabeth Overton; 314 Betsy[6]; 315 Hopkins[6], died 9 Feb.

---

[319] Catherine Lindsay Knorr, *Marriage Bonds and Ministers' Returns of Prince Edward County, Virginia, 1754-1810* (Pine Bluff, Ark., 1950), p. 17.

[320] Nottoway Co. Order Bk. 1, p. 74.

[321] *Raleigh Register*, 23 Oct. 1812, died "some time since."

[322] Williams, *op. cit.*, p. 67.

[323] Pittsylvania Co. Accounts Current 1, 1770-88, pp. 47-57. The earliest date shown in the account is 20 Sept. 1778. Administration on his estate was granted, 23 Oct. 1778, to Stephen Cocke (Pittsylvania Co. Order Bk. 4, p. 37).

[324] Pittsylvania Co. Accounts Current 1, p. 190; Lucy Porter McCollock, *Theophilus Lacy of Colonial Virginia and His Descendants* (Kensington, Md., 1972), pp. 16, 18-26, 199; Jane Hunter Chapter DAR, *Early Families of the North Carolina Counties of Rockingham and Stokes with Revolutionary Service*, II (Easley, S.C., 1990), pp. 71-72; Rockingham Co., N.C., Deed Bk. B, p. 152. One daughter married ____ McNary.

1831, aged 68,[325] of Jefferson Co., Tenn., 1792,[326] and Hawkins Co., Tenn., by 1795,[327] clerk of the Tennessee House of Representatives, moved to Madison Co., Ala., by 1816, married, 15 July 1817, Margaret Simpson; 316 Theophilus[6], died 31 Aug. 1831, aged about 67,[328] left will 30 Aug. 1831-5 Nov. 1831,[329] attorney, represented Rockingham County in the North Carolina Assembly, 1801, moved to Morgan Co., Ala., 1825; 317 John[6], died 13 Nov. 1826, aged about 60,[330] of Rockingham Co., N.C., moved to Morgan Co., Ala., 1823, married (1) ___[331] and (2), 30 May 1803, Mary Henderson, born 16 Jan. 1785, Rockingham Co., N.C., died 4 July 1850, Morgan Co., Ala.;[332] 318 Polly[6]; 319 William Cocke[6], married (1), 24 June 1802 in Rockingham Co., N.C., Sally B. Overton, who died 1 April 1807, and (2), (bond 11) March 1809,[333] 307. Martha[6] Cocke, born 8 April 1772, died 16 Feb. 1824.

95. ELIZABETH[5] COCKE (Abraham[4], Stephen[3], Thomas[2], Temperance[1] Baley), born about 1741, died 1 Oct. 1815, left will 20 July 1814-2 Nov. 1815.[334] She married (1), (bond 26) Sept. 1765,[335] 252. John[6] Cross who left will 13 Nov. 1790-13 Jan. 1791,[336] and (2), 27 Jan. 1795,[337] as his (2) wife, 247. *William[6] Sydnor* (see GASKINS), born 27 April 1752.

Issue: (by 1) [CROSS] 320. Elizabeth[6], married 299. Thomas[6] Hamlin; 321. William Cocke[6], married, by 1 May 1794,[338] 309. Rebecca[6] Cocke; 322. Mary[6],

---

[325] Gravestone, Bartee Cemetery, Lacy Springs, Ala., in *The Virginia Genealogist*, VI, pp. 170-71.

[326] East Tennessee Historical Society, *Publications*, no. 28, p. 147.

[327] Davidson Co., Tenn., Will Bk. 2, p. 36.

[328] Gravestone, Bartee Cemetery, *loc. cit.*

[329] Morgan Co., Ala., Probate Record 6, pp. 100-02.

[330] Gravestone, Bartee Cemetery, *loc. cit.*

[331] Probably, (bond 13) June 1797 (Rockingham Co.,, N.C., Marriage bond), Jane Rogers. His child by this marriage, however, was according to his gravestone born Jan. 1797.

[332] Gravestone, Bartee Cemetery, *loc. cit.*

[333] Kathleen Booth Williams, *Marriages of Pittsylvania County, Virginia, 1706-1830* (Baltimore, 1980), p. 92.

[334] Nottoway Co. Will Bk. 3, p. 301.

[335] Williams, *Marriages of Amelia County* ..., p. 31.

[336] Lunenburg Co. Will Bk. 3, p. 390.

[337] Matheny and Yates, *op. cit.*, p. 119.

[338] Nottoway Co. Order Bk. 1, p. 74.

married, (1), (bond 17) Dec. 1785,[339] Ashley Davis, who died by 1790,[340] and (2), between 11 May and 9 Aug. 1792,[341] as the second of his five wives, William Batte, born 19 Nov. 1763,[342] left will 20 June 1845-1 Sept. 1845;[343] 323. Jean[6], married Peter Lamkin, Jr., born 13 Nov. 1763,[344] colonel of militia, justice of Lunenburg County, 1789-1806, vestryman of Cumberland Parish, member of the House of Delegates, 1802-04,[345] who died before 5 Dec. 1808 when an inventory of his estate was made;[346] 324. Martha[6], living 1824 when named in the will of her son Robert Chappell,[347] married (1), (bond 4) Aug. 1788,[348] John Chappell of Lunenburg County, died before 13 Aug. 1795,[349] and (2), 28 Jan. 1800,[350] Reuben Rogers; 325. Rebecca[6], married 391. *Peter[6] Epes* (see EPES).

97. Gen. WILLIAM[5] COCKE (Abraham[4], Stephen[3], Thomas[2], Temperance[1] Baley), born 6 Sept. 1747, died 22 Aug. 1828 in Columbus, Miss. He studied law and about 1774 moved to the Holston settlements in East Tennessee, where as captain of militia he helped to guard the frontiers during Dunmore's War and in 1775 followed Daniel Boone to Kentucky where he was a member of the House of Delegates of the Transylvania Colony. During the Revolutionary War he fought Indians and Tories. In 1777-78 he represented Washington County in the Virginia House of Delegates and in 1778 and subsequently was a member of the North Carolina legislature. A leader in the movement to establish the State of Franklin in East Tennessee, 1784-88, he helped form its constitution and was a member of its legislature and Brigadier General of its militia, serving on its Council of State and being sent as its delegate to the United States Congress,

---

[339] Matheny and Yates, *op. cit.*, p. 31.

[340] So stated in will of John Cross, 13 Nov. 1790, *loc. cit.* Administration on his estate was granted to Mary Davis 9 June 1791 (Lunenburg Co. Order Bk. 16, p. 72).

[341] Lunenburg Co. Order Bk. 16, pp. 290, 314.

[342] Bristol Parish Register.

[343] Greensville Co. Will Bk. 6, p. 466.

[344] St. Stephen's Parish, Northumberland County, Register.

[345] Bell, *op. cit.*, p. 260; Landon C. Bell, *The Old Free State* (Richmond, 1927), I, p. 330; II, p. 71; Harold E. Wilkins, *The Descendants of Thomas Lamkin* (Boston, 2001), ed. by Barbara J. Mathews, pp. 146-48..

[346] Lunenburg Co. Will Bk. 7, p. 2.

[347] Lunenburg Co. Will Bk. 8, p. 325.

[348] Matheny and Yates, *op. cit.*, p. 20.

[349] Lunenburg Co. Order Bk. 16, p. 579.

[350] Matheny and Yates, *op. cit.*, p. 104.

although never seated and unsuccessful in presenting the memorial for the state's recognition. When the State of Franklin ceased to exist, he returned to the North Carolina legislature where he sponsored the bill to create Blount College (the present University of Tennessee). He was a member of the Tennessee constitutional convention, 1796, and served as United States Senator, 1796-97, 1799-1809. He was then appointed a judge of the Circuit Court but was temperamentally unsuited for that post and in 1812 was removed from office for showing partiality to his friends. He volunteered for a campaign in East Florida, returned to sit in the Tennessee legislature, and then served in the Creek War, and in 1814 was appointed United States Agent to the Chickasaw Indians but failed to gain their confidence and was soon suspended. About 1817 he moved to Mississippi and served in its legislature in 1822.[351] He married (1) Mary Maclin, born 24 March 1772, Brunswick County, and (2) Kesiah (__) Sims, widow of Parris(h) Sims, born 1768, died 1820.

Issue: (by 1) 326. John Alexander[6], born 7 or 28 Dec. 1772, Brunswick County, died Feb. 1854, Rutledge, Grainger Co., Tenn., lawyer of Rutledge, Tenn., member of the Tennessee House of Representatives, 1796-97, 1807, 1809, 1822, 1837 (Speaker, 1812 and 1847), of the Tennessee Senate, 1799-1801, 1843. and of the United States Congress, 1819-27, major general in the Creek War, 1812, colonel of a regiment of Tennessee riflemen at the battle of New Orleans, 1815,[352] married (1) Louisa King and (2) 308. Sarah Shelton[6] Cocke, who died Aug. 1853 in Hawkins Co., Tenn.; 327. Maria Jane[6], married Nathaniel Buckingham of Sevier Co., Tenn., and moved to Aberdeen, Miss., 1817; 328. Sarah Jane[6], born 1785, died 1850-66, married Joseph M. Anderson of Hawkins Co., Tenn., Clerk of the Tennessee Senate, who died 10 Oct. 1823, Murfreesboro, Tenn.; 329. Thomas[6], born 1785, died 1861, aged about 75,[353] left will 9 Aug. 1849-March 1862,[354] of "Mulberry Grove," Hawkins Co., Tenn., married, 26 Sept. 1847 in Hawkins Co., Tenn., Lucinda (Stubblefield) Creed, who married (3) Wilson Harvey and died 1873, aged about 70; 330. Sterling[5],

---

[351] *Biographical Directory of the American Congress, 1774-1996* (Alexandria, Va., 1997), p. 838; *Dictionary of American Biography*, IV (New York, 1932), pp. 255-56.

[352] *Biographical Directory of the American Congress, 1774-1996*, pp. 837-38.

[353] Tombstone, originally in Cocke Cemetery, Hawkins Co., Tenn., removed to Livingston Cemetery, Grainger Co., Tenn., in Hawkins County Genealogical Society, *Gravestones of Hawkins County, Tennessee*, I (n.p., 1985), p. 215, and Clarence McGinnis and Stella Grace McGinnis, *Grayson County, Tennessee, Cemetery Records* II (Morristown, Tenn., 1958), p. 1.

[354] Hawkins Co., Tenn., Will Bk. 1, 1797-1886, pp. 121-24.

born 15 June 1789, died 12 Aug. 1859,[355] clerk of Grainger Co., Tenn., 1810-18, married (1), 6 Sept. 1814,[356] Elizabeth[7] Massingill, daughter of 50. *Michael[6] Massengill* (see COBB), born 1796, died 1816, and (2) Caroline[7] Jones, daughter of Richard and 305. Mary[6] (Cocke) Jones, who was born 17 Feb. 1792 and died 1 Nov. 1857; 331. Elizabeth[6], born May 1792, died 30 June 1866, married Judge John Finley Jack, clerk and judge of Grainger Co., Tenn., who died 22 June 1829, aged about 63;[357] 332. Rebecca[6], died 1821, married, (bond 11) Dec. 1815,[358] John Brown, native of Ireland, of Rutledge, Tenn.; 333. Stephen[6], born 1800, died about 1860, moved to Mississippi about 1817, Chancellor of that state, married, 9 Dec. 1857 in Copiah Co., Miss.,[359] Emily Willing.

98. JAMES[5] COCKE (James[4], James[3], Thomas[2], Temperance[1] Baley), of Henrico County, left will dated 25 April 1772.[360] He married 150. *Mary[5] Lewis* (see WOODSON).

Issue: 334. James[6], born about 1751, died 1812, married, 25 Nov.1774,[361] Martha Holland Parish, born 26 Dec. 1758;[362] 335. Elizabeth Pleasants[6], married, 3 Jan. 1774,[363] William Robards; 336. John[6], born 9 Nov. 1757;[364] 337. William[6], born 1759, of "Cherry Grove," King William County, on ship lost at sea, 1800,[365] married, 1779, Sara New; 338. Sarah Lewis[6], born 5 Feb. 1760;[366]

---

[355] Gravestone, Etter Cemetery, Mooresburg, Tenn., in Hawkins County Genealogical Society, *op. cit.*, p. 224.

[356] Edythe Rucker Whitley, *Marriages of Grainger County, Tennessee, 1796-1837* (Baltimore, 1982), p. 31, as Coke.

[357] Gravestone, Garrett Cemetery, near Bean Station, Tenn., in McGinnis, *op. cit.*, p. 33.

[358] Whitley, *op. cit.*, p. 32.

[359] *The Prairie News*, Okalona, Miss., 13 Jan. 1858, in Betty Couch Wiltshire, *Marriages and Deaths from Mississippi Newspapers*, I (Bowie, Md., 1987), p. 155,

[360] Henrico Co. Proceedings of the Commissioners Respecting the Records Destroyed by the British, 1774-82, p. 27.

[361] W. Mac. Jones, ed., *The Douglas Register*, (Richmond, 1928), p. 16; Kathleen Booth Williams, *Marriages of Goochland County, Virginia,.1733-1815* (n.p., 1960), p. 17.

[362] Jones, *op. cit.*, p. 265.

[363] *Ibid.*, p. 59, as Roberts.

[364] *Ibid.*., p. 175.

[365] Cocke, *op. cit.*, II, p. 37, which states his wife waited three years to prove his will (not further identified).

[366] Jones, *op. cit.*, p. 175.

339. Ann[6], left will 4 Oct. 1822-March 1823,[367] married (1), (bond 31) Dec. 1779,[368] 522. *David[6] Mosby* (see WOODSON) and (2), (bond 15) June 1809,[369] Thomas McGinnis, from whom she secured legal separation 3 Jan. 1810; 340. Susanna[6], married 97. *William[6] Price* (see PRICE).

99. PLEASANT[5] COCKE (James[4], James[3], Thomas[2], Temperance[1] Baley) left will, not now extant, proved Feb. 1743/4.[370] He married Mary Fleming.

Issue:[371] 341. William Fleming[6], died by April 1767 when administration on his estate was granted to his widow,[372] of Cornwall Parish, Lunenburg [*sic*; Halifax, later Charlotte] County, when he and his wife sold two half acre lots in Richmond, 15 May 1764,[373] married Theodosia Cowley.

100. THOMAS[5] COCKE (James[4], James[3], Thomas[2], Temperance[1] Baley) of Goochland County died intestate between 12 Oct. 1797 when he made provision for his daughters Nancy Cocke and Peggy Merridy and 16 Feb. 1798 when his heirs joined in selling portions of his plantation to sons Pleasant and James.[374] He married Ann Johnson.

Issue:[375] 342. William[6], born about 1743, died at Richmond,[376] married (1) ___ and (2) Sarah Wood; 343. Pleasant[6], married, 1 July 1762,[377] Elizabeth Fowler; 344. Benjamin[6], born 1747, died 20 May 1828, married, 23 June 1768,[378] Mary Johnson, born May 1752, died 13 April 1826; 345. Elizabeth[6], married, 2 June 1774,[379] William Hodges, Jr.; 346. Sarah[6], married, 23 Oct.

---

[367] Mercer Co., Ky., Will Bk. 7, p. 167.

[368] Kathleen Booth Williams, *Marriages of Louisa County, Virginia, 1766-1815* (n.p., 1959), p. 76.

[369] Alma Ray Sanders Ison and Rebecca Wilson Conover, *Marriage Bonds and Consents, 1786-1810, Mercer County, Kentucky* (Harrodsburg, Ky., 1970), p. 81.

[370] Henrico Co. Order Bk. 1737-46, p. 247.

[371] Virginia Webb Cocke, "My Grandson William Fleming Cocke," *The Virginia Genealogist*, XV, p. 221.

[372] Henrico Co. Order Bk. 1763-67, p. 716.

[373] Henrico Co. Deed Bk. 1750-74, p. 860.

[374] Goochland Co. Deed Bk. 17, pp. 250, 131, 247-48.

[375] Goochland Co. Deed Bk. 17, pp. 231-32.

[376] Cocke, *Cockes and Cousins*, II, p. 360, which refers to his will dated 26 March 1801 (not further identified).

[377] Jones, *op. cit.*, p. 16, as Pleasants.

[378] *Ibid.*

[379] *Ibid.*, p. 59.

1773,[380] Charles Clarke; 347. James[6], left will 11 Oct. 1819-15 Nov. 1819,[381] married, 30 Oct. 1773,[382] Jean Johnson; 348. Samuel[6], born 21 Jan. 1754;[383] 349. John[6], born 27 July 1756,[384] possibly married, (bond 21) Oct. 1782,[385] 92. *Mary[5] Branch* (see BRANCH), born 18 Jan. 1761;[386] 350. Mary[6] [Peggy?], born 24 Oct. 1758,[387] married, 27 July 1793,[388] Pleasant Meredith; 351. Nancy[6], born 1 Oct. 1760;[389] 352. Martha[6], married, (bond 18) Dec. 1782,[390] Lewis Powers; 353. Agnes[6], born 29 March 1765.[391] married, 21 July 1787, John Bryan.

101. TABITHA[5] COCKE (James[4], James[3], Thomas[2], Temperance[1] Baley) married (1) (probably) 90. *Booth[5] Woodson* (see WOODSON) and (2) John Winston of Hanover County who died about 1785.[392]

Issue: (by 2) [WINSTON][393] 354. William Bobby[6], born about 1757-58, died 1821,[394] of Richmond, served 1776-79 in 1st Virginia State Regiment,[395] married (1) ____ Head and (2), 24 Sept. 1800,[396] Nancy Meriwether, born 13 July 1763;[397] 355. John Geddes[6], of Botetourt County, married, (bond) 1 June 1809,[398] Sallie Hibden; 356. Sarah[6], born 14 May 1761,[399] married, 4 Dec.

---

[380] *Ibid.*

[381] Goochland Co. Deed Bk. 24, p. 540.

[382] Jones, *op. cit.*, p. 16.

[383] *Ibid.*, p. 175.

[384] *Ibid.*, p. 176.

[385] Knorr, *Marriage Bonds ... Powhatan County*, p. 15.

[386] Jones, *op. cit.*, p. 162.

[387] *Ibid.*, p. 176.

[388] Williams, *Marriages of Goochland County ...*, p. 61.

[389] Jones, *op. cit.*, p. 176.

[390] Williams, *Marriages of Goochland County ...*, p. 79.

[391] Jones, *op. cit.*, p. 176.

[392] William Ronald Cocke, *Hanover County Taxpayers, Saint Paul's Parish, 1782-1815* (Columbia, Va., 1956), p. 148.

[393] *Virginia Genealogical Society Quarterly Bulletin*, VII, p. 16.

[394] *Enquirer*, Richmond, 30 March 1821.

[395] Revolutionary War pension application, William Bobby Winston, S.41357, National Archives.

[396] Williams, *Marriages of Louisa County ...*, p. 114.

[397] Jones, *op. cit.*, p. 249.

[398] Michael E. Pollock, *Marriage Bonds of Henrico County, Virginia, 1782-1853* (Baltimore, 1984), p. 181.

[399] Jones, *op. cit.*, p. 321.

1794,[400] Thomas Falconer; 357. Ann[6], born 12 April 1763,[401] died Sept. 1816, Fredericksburg,[402] married Gerard Banks of Culpeper, Louisa and Goochland counties and Richmond, Fredericksburg and Staunton, planter, member of the House of Delegates from Culpeper County, 1797-98,[403] and later publisher of newspapers in Richmond and Staunton.[404]

105. ELIZABETH[5] POYTHRESS (Elizabeth[4] Cocke, James[3], Thomas[2], Temperance[1] Baley) married John Gilliam, born 1712, died 1772, of "Monte Alto," Prince George County.

Issue: [GILLIAM][405] 358. Robert[6], trustee of Blandford, married, 1760, Lucy Skelton, born 1743,[406] who inherited "Elk Island," Goochland County, and left will 23 Feb. 1784-8 Sept. 1789;[407] 359. William[6], died about 1800,[408] of "White Hill," Prince George County, married, 30 April 1789 in Prince George County,[409] 479. *Christian[6] Eppes* (see EPES), who died after March 1807;[410] 360. John[6], born 1742, died 1801, left will dated 19 Sept. 1791,[411] of "Spring Hill," Prince George County, married Jane Henry, daughter of the Rev. Patrick Henry;[412] 361. Jane[6], married, 1772,[413] Charles Duncan, of "Roslin," Chesterfield County, merchant at Blandford; 362. Anne[6], married 89. *Nathaniel[6] Harrison* (see BURWELL).

108. Col. PETER[5] POYTHRESS (Elizabeth[4] Cocke, James[3], Thomas[2], Temperance[1] Baley), of "Branchester," Prince George County, left will 6 Oct.

---

[400] Catherine Lindsay Knorr, *Marriages of Culpeper County, Virginia, 1781-1815* (Pine Bluff, Ark., 1954), p. 32.

[401] Jones, *op. cit.*, p. 321.

[402] *Virginia Herald*, Fredericksburg, 23 Sept. 1816.

[403] Leonard, p. 207.

[404] *T* XV, pp. 123-25, 236-37.

[405] Philip Slaughter, *A History of Bristol Parish, Virginia* (2nd ed.; Richmond, 1879), pp. 174-75.

[406] *W*(2) IX, p. 213.

[407] *W*(1) XII, pp. 62-64, proved in Prince George County.

[408] Prince George Co. Personal property and land tax books, 1800, estate taxed.

[409] The Rev. John Cameron's Register.

[410] Prince George Co. Surveyor's Record 1794-1824, pp. 133-37.

[411] Virginia State Archives, Acc. 21552.

[412] *V* LVIII, pp. 120-25.

[413] *Virginia Gazette*, 15 Oct. 1772.

1785-10 Jan. 1786.[414] He represented that county in the House of Burgesses, 1768-76, in the five Revolutionary Conventions, and in the House of Delegates, 1776, but resigned on account of sickness.[415] He married 68. *Elizabeth[5] Bland* (see BLAND), born 17 March 1732/3.

Issue: [POYTHRESS][416] 363. Elizabeth[6], born 1759, Prince George County, died 6 Aug. 1806, "Powhatan," Henrico County,[417] married William[7] Mayo, son of John and 50. *Mary[6] (Tabb) Mayo* (see PUREFOY), born 26 Sept. 1757, Gloucester County, died 12 Aug. 1833, Richmond, student at the College of William and Mary, 1774, served in the State Line in the Revolutionary War, of "Powhatan Seat," Powhatan County, and after 1810 of Richmond, who married (2) Lucy Fitzhugh;[418] 364. Ann[6], married 350. *John[6] Randolph* (see EPES); 365. William[6], under 21 in 1785, married (1), 10 Feb. 1787,[419] 145. *Elizabeth Bland[6] Blair* (see BLAND), born 1770, and (2) Mrs. __ Marable; 366. Mary[6], married 78. *John[6] Batte* (see SHEPPEY); 367. Susannah[6], under 21 in 1785, married 142. *Richard[6] Bland* (see BLAND); 368. Sally Bland[6], under 21 in 1785, died 28 May 1828,[420] left will 19 April 1828-codicil 16 May 1828-23 June/23 Aug. 1828,[421] married (1) 59. *Richard[5] Lee* (see BLAND) and (2), 23 May 1798, Capt. Willoughby[7] Newton, son of John[7] Newton and 66. *Elizabeth[6] Vaulx* (see BURWELL) and grandson of 30. *Willoughby[6] Newton* (see BEHEATHLAND); 369. Agnes[6], under 21 in 1785, married 289. *Roger[6] Atkinson* (see JORDAN, Thomas); 370. Jane[6], under 21 in 1785, died 20 March 1837, "Woodstock," Fauquier County,[422] married, 28 July 1792,[423] Maj. Joseph Mayo, born 27 March 1771, died 2 Oct. 1820, Richmond;[424] 371. Lucy Bland[6], under 21 in 1785,

---

[414] William Lindsay Hopkins, *Some Wills From the Burned Counties of Virginia* (Richmond, 1987), pp. 116-17.

[415] Leonard, pp. 96, 98, 100, 104, 106, 110, 113, 115, 118, 120, 123.

[416] Hopkins, *loc. cit.*; *W*(2) XV, p. 72.

[417] Gravestone, "Powhatan," Henrico Co., in J. Staunton Moore, ed., *Annals of Henrico Parish* (Richmond, 1904), pp. 198-99.

[418] Alexander Brown, *The Descendants in Virginia for Six Generations of Major William Mayo ...* (Richmond, 1890), pp. 4, 7.

[419] The Rev. John Cameron's Register.

[420] Lee, *op. cit.*, p. 289.

[421] Westmoreland Co. Deeds & Wills 26, pp. 96-97.

[422] *Enquirer*, Richmond, 25 March 1837.

[423] Brown, *op. cit.*, p. 10.

[424] *Richmond Compiler*, 3 Oct. 1820.

married, 23 Jan. 1806,[425] Capt. John[7] Eppes, son of 200. *John*[6] *Eppes* (see EPES), of "Eppesville," Prince George County, who married (2) Hannah Roane and died 1832.[426]

112. JANE[5] POYTHRESS (Elizabeth[4] Cocke, James[3], Thomas[2], Temperance[1] Baley) married John Baird, formerly of "Moorcroft," near Glasgow, Scotland, who settled near Petersburg where he was a merchant in partnership with William McWhann, Gray Briggs and Peter Poythress trading as John Baird & Company.[427]

Issue: [BAIRD] 372. Elizabeth[6], married, (1), 9 July 1786,[428] Joseph Westmore and (2), 21 April 1803,[429] Thomas Gordon, formerly of Galloway, Scotland, widower of 62. *Margaret*[6] *Murray* (see ROLFE), who settled at Petersburg where he was a merchant with the firm of Westmore, Gordon and Maitland, and was a trustee of the town of Blandford; 373. (perhaps) John[6], [Jr.], of Dinwiddie County; 374. (perhaps) Anna[6], married, 7 March 1788,[430] Joseph Weisiger, captain of Prince George County Light Infantry, who died 2 Nov. 1796 in his 37th year.[431]

116. JOSEPH[5] BAILEY (Temperance[4] Cocke, William[3], Thomas[2], Temperance[1] Baley), of Henrico County, left will 24 Jan. 1783-5 March 1783.[432] He married ___.

Issue: [BAILEY] 375. Richard[6], married, (bond 19) Dec. 1792,[433] Elizabeth Pierce; 376. Elizabeth Branch[6], married, 11 Feb. 1786,[434] Thomas Hood; 377. Joseph[8]; 378. William[6], married, 2 July 1785,[435] Milley (___) Whitlow; 379. Mary[6], married ___ Hughes; 380. Sarah[6], married William Bullington;[436] 381.

---

[425] *The Republican*, Petersburg, 27 Jan. 1806.

[426] Prince George Co. Land tax book, 1833, estate taxed.

[427] Peter Wilson Coldham, *American Migrations, 1765-1799* (Baltimore, 2000), pp. 579-80.

[428] The Rev. John Cameron's Register.

[429] *Ibid.*

[430] *Ibid.*

[431] *Virginia Gazette and Petersburg Intelligencer*, 4 Nov. 1796, in Benjamin Boisseau Weisiger, *The Weisiger Family* (Richmond, 1984), p. 32.

[432] Henrico Co. Will Bk. 1, pp. 65-66, mentioning land he bought from Roger Cock Bailey.

[433] Pollock, *op. cit.*, p. 8.

[434] J. Staunton Moore, ed., *Annals of Henrico Parish* (Richmond, 1904), p. 229; Pollock, *op. cit.*, p. 81, bond 6 Feb.

[435] Moore, *loc. cit.*; Pollock, *op. cit.*, p. 8, bond 22 May.

[436] Cocke, *op. cit.*, II, p. 49.

Ann⁶, married ___ Pearce.

117. PETER⁵ BAILEY (Temperance⁴ Cocke, William³, Thomas², Temperance¹ Baley) was given 200 acres by his father, 5 Sept. 1757,[437] and another 100 acres 10 Nov. 1773,[438] and left will 10 March 1786-5 July 1786.[439] He married, (bond 25) Sept. 1770,[440] Frances Winfree, who married (2), (bond 31) May 1796,[441] Thomas Harwood.

Issue: [BAILEY][442] 382. John W.⁶, died before 23 June 1803 when an inventory of his estate was returned by Nathaniel Childers, his administrator;[443] 383. Peter⁶, married, (bond 9) April 1798,[444] Lucy Harwood; 384. Joseph⁶; 385. Sarah H.⁶, married, (bond 1) Dec. 1790,[445] Nathaniel Childers of Henrico County.

119. ROGER COCK⁵ BAILEY (Temperance⁴ Cocke, William³, Thomas², Temperance¹ Baley) was given by his father the 140 acres on Mirey Branch where Abraham lived, 1 March 1763.[446] He lived in Henrico County until he purchased 65 acres in Charlotte County, 27 Aug. 1777, but sold that land, 15 July 1784, as resident of Mecklenburg County.[447] He served as corporal in Capt. James Green's company of the First Virginia Regiment during the French and Indian War.[448] He married (1) ___, who died in Henrico County, and (2) ___.

Issue: [BAILEY] (by 1)[449] 386. Yancey⁶, born 1751, died 4 Sept. 1804, ensign of Prince Edward County militia during the Revolutionary War, later of Person Co., N.C., married (1) ____ and (2) Sarah Fawlkes, who married (2) Jacob Faulkner; 387. Thomas⁶, left will 24 Nov. 1823-codicil 1 Dec. 1823-12

---

[437] Henrico Co. Deed Bk. 1750-67, p. 512.

[438] Henrico Co. Deed Bk. 1767-74, p. 567.

[439] Henrico Co. Will Bk. 1, 1781-87, p. 313.

[440] Katherine B. Elliott, *Marriage Records, 1749-1840, Cumberland County, Virginia* (South Hill, Va., 1969), p. 15.

[441] Pollock, *op. cit.*, p. 76.

[442] Cocke, *op. cit.*, II, pp. 21, 46, misidentifies the children.

[443] Henrico Co. Will Bk. 3, p. 159.

[444] Pollock, *op. cit.*, p. 8.

[445] *Ibid.*, p. 32.

[446] Henrico Co. Deed Bk. 1750-74, p. 774.

[447] Charlotte Co. Deed Bk. 4, pp. 38-38r; Deed Bk. 5, p. 121.

[448] Charlotte Co. Order Bk. 4, p. 210.

[449] Cocke, *op. cit.*, II, pp. 20, 44-45, identifies several other children without evidence, but states "Bible records and other records definitely connect these 5 as siblings," although without specification of the sources.

Jan. 1824,[450] of Campbell County, married (1), (bond 20) Dec. 1779,[451] Mildred Clark and (2), (bond 21) April 1794, [452] Temperance Bailey; 388. Temperance[6], born 16 Dec. 1761, died 1823, married Samuel Cox, who moved to Hopkins Co., Ky., and left will 24 Dec. 1819-July 1820;[453] 389. Martha Dicy[6], born 5 Aug. 1763, married John Bevill of Mecklenburg County until after 30 Dec. 1795 when they sold 50 acres there;[454] 390. Peter Cock[6], born 9 Oct. 1765, died 1844, for whom his father was appointed guardian, 6 Sept. 1779,[455] and Francis Barnes was appointed guardian, 1 Oct. 1781,[456] served during Revolutionary War in Granville Co., N.C., militia, later of Mecklenburg County and after 1831 of Montgomery Co., Tenn.,[457] married (bond 27) Aug. 1792,[458] Sarah Baker.

120. DAVID[5] BAILEY (Temperance[4] Cocke, William[3], Thomas[2], Temperance[1] Bailey) died about 1800.[459] He settled in Charlotte County where he purchased 100 acres on Dunavant Creek, 7 Dec. 1767.[460] On 28 June 1771 his father conveyed in trust to him and his wife Jean and their son Johnston a slave Will[461] and on 5 Aug. 1771 he conveyed Will to his son Johnson.[462] He

---

[450] Campbell Co. Will Bk. 4, p. 527.

[451] Catherine Lindsay Knorr, *Marriage Bonds and Ministers' Returns of Prince Edward County, Virginia, 1754-1810* (Pine Bluff, Ark.), 1950), p. 5.

[452] Lucy Harrison Miller Baber and Hazel Letts Williamson, *Marriages of Campbell County, Virginia, 1782-1810* (Lynchburg, 1971), p. 9.

[453] Hopkins Co., Ky., Will Bk. 1, p. 351.

[454] Mecklenburg Co. Deed Bk. 9, pp. 124-25.

[455] Charlotte Co. Order Bk. 4, p. 192.

[456] Charlotte Co. Order Bk. 5, p. 21.

[457] Revolutionary War pension application, Peter Bailey, S.21618, National Archives.

[458] Katherine B. Elliott, *Marriage Records, 1765-1810, Mecklenburg County, Virginia* (South Hill, Va., 1963), p. 12.

[459] Charlotte Co. Personal property tax list, 1800, last listing. He was charged with two male tithables, 1795-1800. James Bailey was first taxed in 1801. His 100 acres holding, charged to him, 1782-1801, was charged to David Bailey's estate, 1802 (Charlotte Co. Land tax book, 1802). Assuming his death at this time is complicated, however, by the purchase 25 Jan. 1794, by David Bailey of Charlotte County of 178 acres where he then lived (Charlotte Co. Deed Bk. 7, p. 35), although this land was not charged on the tax books until 1803, and sale of 190 acres on 23 Feb. 1805 (Deed Bk. 11, p. 93). Administration on the estate of a David Bailey was granted to William H. Bailey, 5 May 1823 (Order Bk. 24, p. 22); an accounting of this estate indicated he died before 17 Feb. 1817 (Will Bk. 6, pp. 24-24r).

[460] Charlotte Co. Deed Bk. 1, pp. 393-96.

[461] Henrico Co. Deed Bkk. 1767-74, p. 280. Caleb Johnston and Samuel Johnston, Jr., were named as trustees.

[462] Charlotte Co. Deed Bk. 2, p. 472.

married Jean [Johnston?].

Issue: [BAILEY][463] 391. Mary Cook[6], married, (bond 2) June 1794,[464] John Robertson of Pittsylvania County; 392 Ruth[6], married (1), (bond 8) March 1792,[465] Jesse Wilkes and (2), (bond 13) Feb. 1821,[466] Richard Wilson of Charlotte County; 393. James[6]; 394. David[6], of Madison Co., Ala., married Mildred ____; 395. Jane[6], married, (bond 6) Feb. 1797,[467] Thomas Holt of Rockingham Co., N.C.; 396. Samuel Johnson[6], of Barnwell Co., S.C., married Sarah Wilson; 397. Martha[6], married William Wilkes of Charlotte County; 398. Letitia[6]; 399. Holcomb D.[6], moved to Tennessee and later to Missouri, married, 18 Feb. 18_, Martha Drinkard.

121. TEMPERANCE[5] BAILEY (Temperance[4] Cocke, William[3], Thomas[2], Temperance[1] Baley),[468] married Charles Ballow, born 1722, of Cumberland County, who left will 18 May 1762-23 Nov. 1767.[469]

Issue: [BALLOW] 400. William[6], married Elizabeth Smith Davenport; 401. Ann[6], given by her father a Negro boy then at her grandfather Bailey's, perhaps married, 23 March 1770,[470] William Pollock; 402. Charles[6], captain of Cumberland County militia during the Revolutionary War, died before 19 Nov. 1789 when the inventory of his estate was made,[471] married Rebecca ___; 403. Jesse[6]; 404. John[6]; 405. Thomas[6], born 31 Aug. 1759, died 21 April 1809, married, 19 July 1785, Frances Hobson, born 7 July 1766, died 18 April 1808; 406. Mary[6].

123. WILLIAM COCKE[5] REDFORD (Mary[4] Cocke, William[3], Thomas[2], Temperance[1] Baley) was deeded 80 acres on Roundabout Swamp by his father,

---

[463] Cocke, *op. cit.*, II, pp. 21, 46.

[464] Knorr, *Marriage Bonds ... Charlotte County*, p. 72.

[465] *Ibid.*, p. 90.

[466] Joanne Lovelace Nance, *Charlotte County, Virginia, 1816-1850, Marriage Bonds and Ministers' Returns* (Charlottesville, 1987), p. 116.

[467] Knorr, *Marriage Bonds ... Charlotte County*, p. 42.

[468] Daughters of the American Revolution lineage paper 177132, apparently citing a family Bible, states she was born 18 June 1731 and died 9 Feb. 1779, but misidentifies her husband as a Revolutionary War veteran who died in 1800.

[469] Cumberland Co. Will Bk. 1, pp. 333-35.

[470] Jones, *op. cit.*, p. 54,

[471] Cumberland Co. Will Bk. 2, p. 468.

3 Sept. 1761.[472] He married Mary ___.[473]

Issue: [REDFORD] 407. (probably) Patience[6], married, (bond 22) July 1797, William Pearce;[474] 408. Perrin[6], to whom his father, 7 Aug. 1787, gave the plantation where he lived, reserving use for his and his wife Mary's lives,[475] died after 13 July 1826 when he made deeds to four children,[476] married (1) 201. *Susannah[5] Woodson* (see WOODSON) and (2), (bond 26) Jan. 1808,[477] Judith Warriner, who joined him in deeding a half acre near Varina to the Methodist Society, 17 June 1810.[478]

128. SARAH[5] REDFORD (Mary[4] Cocke, William[3], Thomas[2], Temperance[1] Baley) died before 1778. She married Lusby Turpin, born 1728, who left will 2 Jan. 1791-7 March 1791.[479]

Issue: [TURPIN] 409. Priscilla[6], died before 1791, married ___Vandike; 410. Michael[6], left will 1 May 1796-6 June 1796,[480] married Betty (Farrar?) who died before 1796; 411. John[6], captain in Revolutionary War, left will 10 May 1795-7 Sept. 1795,[481] married Hannah Talman, born 6 April 1760, New Kent County; 412. Lusby[6], died about 1791, married, (bond 8) May 1786,[482] Martha Bullington; 413. Thomas[6], married Martha ___; 414. Mary[6], married Edward Goode, of Mecklenburg County and later of Rutherford Co., N.C.,[483] who left will 16 July 1798-Oct. 1798;[484] 415. Alexander[6], died 1 April 1833, left will 22 Feb. 1833-13 June 1833,[485] married, (bond 10) Feb. 1791,[486] Elizabeth

---

[472] Henrico Co. Deed Bk. 1750-74, p. 695.

[473] Cocke, *op. cit.*, II, p. 22, suggests she was perhaps a Perrin or a Bullington and states she died before 7 Aug. 1786. He is assigned a (2) wife Sally Redford, married (bond 28) March 1793 (Joyce H. Lindsay, *Marriages of Henrico County, Virginia, 1680-1808* [Richmond, 1960], p. 71), which is almost certainly incorrect.

[474] Lindsay, *op. cit.*, p. 65. She is named as daughter of Mary Redford, who consented.

[475] Henrico Co. Deed Bk. 2, p. 367.

[476] Henrico Co. Deed Bk. 28, pp. 467-70.

[477] Pollock, *op. cit.*, p. 135.

[478] Henrico Co. Deed Bk. 9, p. 85.

[479] Henrico Co. Will Bk. 2, pp. 187-89.

[480] Henrico Co. Will Bk. 2, pp. 378-79.

[481] Henrico Co. Will Bk. 2, p. 343.

[482] Lindsay, *op. cit.*, p. 87.

[483] George Brown Goode, *Virginia Cousins* (Richmond, 1887), p. 71.

[484] Rutherford Co., N.C., Will Bk. B, p. 98.

[485] Henrico Co. Will Bk. 8, p. 150.

[486] Lindsay, *op. cit.*, p. 86.

Woodcock; 416. Sarah[6], died before 1791, married, (bond 25) March 1782,[487] John DePriest; 417. Elizabeth[6], married, (bond 4) Dec. 1788,[488] William Royster.

129. JOHN[5] REDFORD (Mary[4] Cocke, William[3], Thomas[2], Temperance[1] Baley) died by Feb. 1767 when his widow was granted administration on his estate.[489] His father deeded him 175 acres on Roundabout Creek, 1755,[490] and he gave bond as a tobacco inspector, 1 Feb. 1762.[491] He married Martha ___.

Issue: [REDFORD][492] 418. William[6];.[493] 419. Sarah[6]; 420. Martha[6]; 421. James[6].

131. SAMUEL[5] HARWOOD (Thomas[4], Agnes[3] Cocke, Thomas[2], Temperance[1] Baley) petitioned, Sept. 1739, for an equal division of his father's land with his step-father Isaac Hill[494] and is probably the Samuel Harwood of Oraham whose will was proved July 1747.[495] He married Amadia ___, who joined him in a sale of land to Warwick Hockaday, April 1748, and relinquished dower, April 1744, in a sale to Isaac Hill, Oct. 1740,[496] and perhaps (2) Elizabeth Rebecca ___, who married (2) John Jacob Coignan Danzie.[497]

Issue: [HARWOOD] 422. Samuel[6], of Westover Parish, Charles City County, sold 450 acres, "Oraham," to John Binns, 3 Oct. 1769,[498] married 183. *Elizabeth[5] Eppes* (see EPES); 423. Travis[6], chose John Jacob Danzie as his guardian, Jan. 1754,[499] married, by 15 April 1769,[500] Elizabeth ____; 424. (perhaps) Temperance[6], left will, proved Dec. 1756, of which John Jacob

---

[487] *Ibid.*, p. 26.

[488] *Ibid.*, p. 74.

[489] Henrico Co. Order Bk. 1763-67, p. 646.

[490] Henrico Co. Deed Bk. 1750-74, p. 426.

[491] *Ibid.*, p. 712.

[492] Henrico Co. Order Bk. 1767-69, p. 366, appointment of John Radford as their guardian, 3 Oct. 1768.

[493] Cocke, *op. cit.*, II, p. 49, identifies him as William Radford, merchant of Richmond, who married 431. *Rebecca[6] Winston* (see JORDAN, Thomas).

[494] Charles City Co. Order Bk. 1737-51, p. 101.

[495] *Ibid.*, p. 445.

[496] *Ibid.*, pp. 38, 144, 154.

[497] They joined in the deed when Travis Harwood sold the land he inherited from his father Samuel Harwood.

[498] Charles City Co. Wills & Deeds 1766-74, p. 200.

[499] Charles City Co. Order Bk. 1754-57, p. 25.

[500] Charles City Co. Deeds & Wills 1766-74, p. 144. On 20 Oct. 1770 they sold the land left to him by the will of Samuel Harwood (*ibid.*, p. 254) in which they were joined by John Jacob Coignan Danzie and his wife Elizabeth Rebecca.

Coignan Danzie and his wife Elizabeth were executors.[501]

133. SAMUEL[5] HARWOOD (Samuel[4], Temperance[3] Cocke, Thomas[2], Temperance[1] Cocke) died shortly before 10 March 1778.[502] He resided at "Weyanoke," Charles City County. He married 163. *Margaret[6] Waddrop* (see HOLT), who married (2) Benjamin Edmundson..

Issue: [HARWOOD][503] 425. Agnes[6], buried at "Oak Hill," Fauquier County,[504] married Fielding[7] Lewis, died 13 June 1834, aged 71,[505] son of 440. Col. *Warner[6] Lewis* (see MARTIAU), of "Weyanoke," Charles City County, student in Scotland and at the College of William and Mary, soldier during the Revolutionary War, first president of the Virginia Agricultural Society; 426. Ann[6], married Maj. Thomas[7] Lewis, born 12 Nov. 1760, brother of Agnes' husband, student in Scotland and at the College of William and Mary, captain of a company which marched to Pittsburgh during the Whiskey Rebellion, 1794; 427. Margaret Waddrop[6], died 19 Sept. 1840, "Violet Bank," Gloucester County,[506] married Robert Munford of "Clifton," Charles City County, lieutenant in the Revolutionary War, clerk of Charles City County, 1797-1800,[507] left will 12 Dec. 1799-24 March 1800.[508]

138. BOWLER[5] COCKE (Bowler[4], Richard[3], Richard[2], Temperance[1] Baley), born 7 March 1726/7, died before 19 Nov. 1772 when his land in Hanover County was advertised for sale.[509] He was vestryman of Henrico Parish, 1749-71, clerk of Henrico County, 1751-62, trustee of Richmond, 1752, and member of the House of Burgesses, 1766-68.[510] He married (1) Elizabeth (Smith) Turner, daughter of Nicholas Smith and widow of Harry Turner of King George County, and (2) Elizabeth[7] Fauntleroy, daughter of 54. *William[6] Fauntleroy* (see PEIRSEY), who married (2) 148. Thomas[5] Adams and died

---

[501] Charles City Co. Order Bk. 1754-57, p. 440; Order Bk. 1758-62, p. 201.

[502] Charles City Co. Will Bk. 1, p. 355.

[503] Merrow Egerton Sorley, *Lewis of Warner Hall* (Columbia, Mo., 1935), pp. 102-03; Ransom Badger True, *Plantation on the James, Weyanoke and Her People, 1607-1938* (n.p., 1986), *passim.*

[504] Nancy Chappelear Baird, *Fauquier County, Virginia, Tombstone Inscriptions* (n.p., 1970), p. 41.

[505] Gravestone, "Weyanoke," Charles City County.

[506] *Whig*, Richmond, 2 Oct. 1840.

[507] *T* III, p. 180.

[508] Charles City Co. Will Bk. 1, pp. 478-79.

[509] *Virginia Gazette* (Purdie & Dixon), 19 Nov. 1772.

[510] Leonard, p. 95.

1792.[511]

Issue: (by 2) 428. Bowler[6], left will 1 March 1812-7 Sept. 1812,[512] of "Bremo" and later of "Turkey Island," Henrico County, vestryman of Henrico Parish, 1785, married (1), 1775, Molly Webb,[513] (2), about 1780, King Fox, (3), Nov. 1802, Nancy[7] Dandridge, daughter of 98. Col. *Francis[6] Dandridge* (see WEST), (4) Maria ___, who died 15 March 1806,[514] and (5) 450. Tabitha[6] Fry; 429. William[6], born 1758, "Bremo," died 14 April 1835, "Oakland," Cumberland County, moved to Cumberland County, about 1789, and resided at "Oakland," married, 2 Nov. 1789,[515] Jane[7] Armistead, daughter of 123. *William[6] Armistead* (see BURWELL); 430. Charles Hartwell[6]; 431. Elizabeth[6]; 432. Sarah[6], born 8 March 1760, "Turkey Island," died 20 April 1838, "Level Green," Nelson County, married, 1778, Maj. Thomas Massie, born 22 Aug. 1747, died 2 Feb. 1834, "Level Green," student at the College of William and Mary, 1759-60, captain and major of 2nd Virginia Regiment, 1775-81, aide to Gen. Nelson at Yorktown, member of the Society of the Cincinnati, moved from New Kent County to Frederick County about 1780 and to Nelson County about 1803, justice of Nelson County from 1808 until his death.[516]

146. Col. RICHARD[5] ADAMS (Tabitha[4] Cocke, Richard[3], Richard[2], Temperance[1] Baley), born 17 May 1726,[517] died 1 Aug. 1800, Richmond,[518] left will 30 Jan. 1800-10 Nov. 1800.[519] He was Burgess for New Kent County, 1752-65, and for Henrico County, 1769-76, and was a member of the five Conventions of 1774-76, of the Henrico County Committee, 1774-75, of the House of Delegates, 1776-78, and of the Virginia Senate, 1779-82,[520] and merchant of Richmond.[521] He married, 10 April 1755, Elizabeth Griffin, born

---

[511] Cocke, *op. cit.*, I, pp. 15, 32.

[512] Henrico Co. Will Bk. 4, pp. 247-50.

[513] *Virginia Gazette* (Dixon & Hunter), 14 Jan. 1775.

[514] *Enquirer*, Richmond, 2 April 1806.

[515] Cocke, *op. cit.*, I, p. 32.

[516] *V* XV, p. 125-26; Alexander Brown, *The Cabells and Their Kin* (Boston and New York, 1895), pp. 410-12.

[517] St. Peter's Parish Register.

[518] *Virginia Argus*, Richmond, 5 Aug. 1800.

[519] Kentucky Court of Appeals Deed Bk. Y, p. 84, recorded originally in the General Court.

[520] Leonard, pp. 84, 87, 89, 92, 97, 100, 103, 106, 110, 112, 115, 118, 120, 122, 126, 131, 136, 139, 143.

[521] *Heads of Families at the First Census ... Virginia* (Washington, 1908), p. 112.

1738, died 23 Dec. 1800.

Issue: [ADAMS][522] 433. Tabitha[6], born 4 July 1756, died 10 Feb. 1828, aged 72;[523] 434. Elizabeth Griffin[6], born 17 Dec. 1757,[524] died 1832, aged 72, at Richmond;[525] 435. Thomas Bowler[6], born 18 Sept. 1759, died 28 Nov. 1794, Richmond,[526] left will 24 Oct. 1794-5 Jan. 1795,[527] married, 30 Jan. 1790,[528] 154. *Sarah[6] Morrison* (see BLAND), who died 13 May 1794, Richmond;[529] 436. Richard[6], born 16 Nov. 1760, died 9 Jan. 1817, Richmond,[530] married (1) Elizabeth (Southall) Randolph, born 1771, died 17 Oct. 1809,[531] and (2) Sarah Travers[7] (Daniel) Hay, born 31 Dec. 1765,[532] died June 1815,[533] daughter of 269. *Frances[6] (Moncure) Daniel* (see THOROWGOOD); 437. Anne[6], born 27 Oct. 1762, died 21 Oct. 1820, Richmond,[534] married, 30 Sept. 1789, Col. Mayo Carrington, born 1 April 1753, died 28 Dec. 1803, of "Boston Hill," Cumberland County, ensign in a minute company, later captain, captured at Charleston, 1780, surveyor, justice, sheriff, member of the House of Delegates, 1786-88, lieutenant colonel commandant of 17th Virginia militia regiment;[535] 438. William[6], born 8 June 1764, died 2 June 1787;[536] 439. Sarah[6], born 14 Jan. 1766, died 1 Oct. 1806,[537] married, 7 Feb. 1793, as his (1) wife, George William Smith, born 1762, "Bathurst," Essex County, died 26 Dec. 1811 in the Richmond theater fire, lawyer, member of the House of Delegates for Essex County, 1791-94, and for

---

[522] *Richmond Standard*, 11 Dec. 1780.

[523] *Enquirer*, Richmond, 19 Feb. 1828.

[524] St. Peter's Parish Register.

[525] *Enquirer*, Richmond, 16 Nov. 1832.

[526] *Virginia Gazette and Richmond and Manchester Advertiser*, 1 Dec. 1794.

[527] Henrico Co. Will Bk. 2, pp. 304-06.

[528] *Virginia Independent Chronicle*, Richmond 3 Feb. 1790; Catherine Lindsay Knorr, *Marriage Bonds and Ministers' Returns of Chesterfield County, Virginia, 1771-1815* (Pine Bluff, Ark., 1958), p. 1.

[529] *Virginia Gazette and Richmond and Manchester Advertiser*, 15 May 1794.

[530] *Virginia Patriot*, Richmond, 10 Jan. 1817.

[531] *Virginia Argus*, Richmond, 24 Oct. 1809.

[532] Hayden, *op. cit.*, p. 304.

[533] *Enquirer*, Richmond, 10 June 1815.

[534] *Enquirer*, Richmond, 24 Oct. 1820; *Compiler*, Richmond, 25 Oct. 1820, which gives death as 22 Oct. 1820.

[535] *NGSQ* LXX, pp. 265-66.

[536] *Virginia Gazette and Weekly Advertiser*, Richmond, 7 June 1787.

[537] *Enquirer*, Richmond, 10 Oct. 1803.

Richmond City, 1802-08, member of the Privy Council, 1809, Lieutenant Governor, 1810, and acting Governor of Virginia, 25 Nov.-26 Dec. 1811;[538] 440. Alice[6], born 20 Feb. 1768, died 17 April 1802,[539] married, 28 June 1788,[540] as his (1) wife, William Marshall, born 31 Jan. 1767, Fauquier County, died 27 May 1816, Richmond,[541] Commonwealth Attorney for Richmond and clerk of the Federal District Court, who married (2), 10 Dec. 1803,[542] Mary[7] Macon, daughter of William Hartwell Macon and 151. *Sarah[6] Ambler* (see TAYLOR-CARY) and (3), (bond 2) July 1814,[543] Maria C. (Winston) Price, widow of John Fleming[7] Price, son of 52. *James[6] Price* (see PRICE); 441. Ebenezer[6], born May 1769, died day after birth; 442. Ebenezer[6], born 4 Aug. 1770, died Aug. 1771; 443. John[6], born 14 July 1773, died 23 June 1825,[544] graduated from the University of Edinburgh, 1796, was a physician of Richmond, member of the House of Delegates, 1803-04, and mayor of Richmond, 1819-25,[545] married 434. *Margaret[6] Winston* (see JORDAN, Thomas); 444. Capt. Samuel Griffin[6], born 5 May 1776, died 14 July 1821,[546] married, (bond 5) May 1797,[547] Catherine Innes.

149. ANNE[5] ADAMS (Tabitha[4] Cocke, Richard[3], Richard[2], Temperance[1] Baley) died before 17 Jan. 1775 when her slaves were divided among her children.[548] She married, as his (2) wife, about 1747-48, Francis Smith, who left

---

[538] *W(1)* XXV, p. 176; Margaret Vowell Smith, *Virginia, 1794-1892 ... A History of the Executives* (Washington, 1893), pp. 318-19; *National Cyclopaedia of American Biography* V (New York, 1907), pp. 445-46.

[539] *Virginia Gazette and General Advertiser*, Richmond, 24 April 1802. *Virginia Argus*, Richmond, 21 April 1802, gives 16 April.

[540] Lindsay, *op. cit.*, p. 57, bond 27 June 1788. *Virginia Gazette and Weekly Advertiser*, Richmond, 10 July 1788, gives date as 20 June.

[541] *Virginia Argus*, Richmond, 29 May 1816; *Richmond Compiler*, 28 May 1816. *Virginia Patriot*, Richmond, 29 May 1816, says died yesterday.

[542] *Virginia Gazette and General Advertiser*, Richmond, 14 Dec. 1803; *Virginia Argus*, Richmond, 21 Dec. 1803.

[543] Anne Waller Reddy and Andrew Lewis Riffe, *Virginia Marriage Bonds, Richmond City* I (Staunton, 1939), p. 18.

[544] *Whig*, Richmond, 24 June 1825; *Enquirer*, Richmond, 28 June 1825.

[545] Leonard, pp. 229, 233; Mary Wingfield Scott, *Houses of Old Richmond* (New York, 1941), p. 68; *Dictionary of Virginia Biography*, I (Richmond, 1998), pp. 28-29.

[546] *Enquirer*, Richmond, 17 July 1821.

[547] Lindsay, *op. cit.*, p. 1.

[548] Essex Co. Will Bk. 12, pp. 609-10.

will 5 March 1760-15 March 1762,[549] of Essex County, justice, vestryman, major and colonel of militia, member of the House of Burgesses, 1752-58.[550]

Issue: [SMITH][551] 445. Francis[6], born about 1749, left will 31 Oct. 1812-4 July 1814,[552] of Bedford County, 1771, "Piscataway," Essex County, and Wilkes Co., Ga., ensign in the 6th Virginia Regiment, 1780, married Lucy Wilkinson, who left will 3 Feb. 1822-9 March 1822;[553] 446. William[6], left will 20 June 1783-codicil 8 March 1784-16 May 1785,[554] vestryman and justice of Essex County, member of the Essex County Committee, 1774, and of the House of Delegates, 1777-78,[555] married Mary Belfield, born 17 Feb. 1753; 447. Anne[6].

150. SARAH[5] ADAMS (Tabitha[4] Cocke, Richard[3], Richard[2], Temperance[1] Baley) as a widow moved to Kentucky. She married, 1764, Col. John Fry, born 7 April [or May] 1737 in Essex County, died 1778, aged 41, of Albemarle County, member of the House of Burgesses, 1761-62, vestryman of St. Ann's Parish.[556]

Issue: [FRY][557] 448. Joshua[6], born 1760, died 1839, student at the College of William and Mary, private and lieutenant in the Revolutionary War,[558] magistrate and member of the House of Delegates from Albemarle County, 1785-86,[559] moved to Kentucky and taught a classical school in Garrard County, married, 4 Sept. 1793,[560] 83. Peachy[6] Walker (see CROSHAW), born 6 Feb. 1767, "Castle Hill," Albemarle County; 449. William Adams[6], born 17 Oct. 1761, Albemarle County, served nine months in Revolutionary War, moved to

---

[549] Essex Co. Will Bk. 11, pp. 413-16.

[550] Leonard, pp. 83, 86.

[551] *W*(1) XXV, pp. 173-74, 177-78.

[552] Wilkes Co., Ga., Will Bk. HH, 1810-16, p. 107, in Grace Gillam Davidson, *Early Records of Georgia ... Wilkes County* (Macon, Ga., 1932), I, p. 89.

[553] Wilkes Co., Ga., Will Bk. HH, 1819-36, p. 84, in *ibid.*, II, pp. 151-52.

[554] Essex Co. Will Bk. 13, pp. 495-97.

[555] Leonard, p. 125.

[556] *NGSQ* LIV, pp. 219-21; George W. Frye, *Col. Joshua Fry of Virginia and Some of His Descendants* (Cincinnati, 1966), pt. 2, p. 1; Leonard, p. 91.

[557] Frye, *op. cit.*, pt. 2, pp. 2, 35-41.

[558] Revolutionary War pension application, Joshua Fry, S.37949, National Archives.

[559] Leonard, p. 156.

[560] John Vogt and T. William Kethley, *Albemarle County Marriages, 1780-1853* (Athens, Ga., 1991), I, p. 120. There is a marriage of Joshua Fry and Kitty Walker by the Rev. Matthew Maury, 24 Nov. 1791, in Albemarle County (*The Virginia Genealogist*, XXX, p. 25).

Jessamine Co., Ky.,[561] left will 16 Aug. 1834-Sept. 1835,[562] unmarried; 450. Tabitha[6], married 428. Bowler[6] Cocke; 451. (probably) John[6], born Albemarle County, aged 18 in Sept. 1780, RevolutionaryWar soldier.

151. Col. HARTWELL[5] COCKE (Richard[4], Richard[3], Richard[2], Temperance[1] Baley) died 1772,[563] left will 29 May 1772-25 Aug. 1772.[564] He was a member of House of Burgesses from Surry County, 1758-72.[565] He married Ann Ruffin, probably the Mrs. Ann Cocke of Swann's Point, Surry County, who died 1795.[566]

Issue: 452. John Hartwell[6], born 26 Nov. 1749, died 9 Feb. 1791, left will 29 Jan. 1791-22 Feb. 1791,[567] leaving land in Surry, Brunswick, Halifax and Buckingham counties and in Kentucky, member of the House of Delegates, 1777-78, and of the Convention of 1788,[568] married, 28 Nov. 1773, Elizabeth Kennon, born 13 July 1755, died [10 July] 1791;[569] 453. Hartwell[6], under age 1772, left will 28 Oct. 1792-10 Jan. 1793,[570] married, (bond 25) Feb. 1783,[571] Sarah Clements who married (2), (bond 12) Oct. 1795,[572] Joseph Wilkins and died by March 1799;[573] 454. Mary[6], died 1790,[574] married, 1772, as his (1) wife, Capt. Edward Archer, born 16 June 1747 at Norfolk, died 27 Feb. 1807;[575] 455. Richard[6], died unmarried; 456. Martha[6], born 5 Sept. 1761, died March 1834 at Athens, Ala., moved as a widow to Harrison Co., Ky.,[576] married, (1), (bond 11)

---

[561] Revolutionary War pension application, William A. Fry, S.30425.

[562] Jessamine Co., Ky., Will Bk. E, p. 168.

[563] *Virginia Gazette*, 23 July 1772.

[564] Surry Co. Will Bk. 10A, p. 235.

[565] Leonard, pp. 90, 93, 96, 98, 101, 104.

[566] *Virginia Gazette*, 30 May 1795.

[567] Surry Co. Will Bk. 12, p. 289.

[568] Leonard, pp. 125, 174.

[569] Prayer Book, in *V V*, p. 78.

[570] Southampton Co. Will Bk. 4, p. 351.

[571] Catherine Lindsay Knorr, *Marriage Bonds and Ministers' Returns of Southampton County, Virginia, 1750-1810* (Pine Bluff, Ark., 1955), p. 28.

[572] Knorr, *Marriage Bonds ... Southampton County*, p. 115.

[573] George Wythe, *Decisions of Cases in Virginia by the High Court of Chancery* (Richmond, 1852), pp. 338-54.

[574] *Norfolk & Portsmouth Chronicle*, 8 May 1790.

[575] Robert Archer, *Archer and Silvester Families, A History Written in 1870* (n.p., 1937), pp. 12, 14.

[576] Fredericksburg District Court, file 60, Carneal *vs.* Coleman.

Sept. 1782,[577] Thomas Clements, Jr., who was born 5 Dec. 1760 and left will 19 July 1784-9 Dec. 1785,[578] and (2), as his (2) wife, Col. Daniel Coleman, born 21 Jan. 1753,[579] of "Pine Hill," Caroline County, ensign and captain of militia, 1777-82, member of the House of Delegates, 1800-02, 1803-08. 1811-15,[580] left will 6 Oct. 1815-12 Aug. 1816;[581] 457. Ann[6], married (1), 24 Dec. 1785,[582] Benjamin[8] Browne, son of William Browne and Sarah[7] Edwards, daughter of 92. *Benjamin[6] Edwards* (see BURWELL), and (2) 137. *Thomas[6] Gray* (see GRAY); 458. Benjamin[6], under age 1772, left will 8 June 1794-codicil 14 June 1794-22 July 1794;[583] 459. Robert[6], died 7 June 1796, Surry County, in his 29th year,[584] married (1) 478. Mary[6] Browne, born 6 Feb. 1771, died 5 Jan. 1790,[585] and (2), 12 May 1791,[586] 185. *Martha Ruffin[6] Newsom* (see HOLT), who relinquished her right of administration on his estate, 22 Oct. 1796,[587] and married (2), (bond 30) June 1797,[588] the Rev. Samuel Butler, rector of Southwark Parish; 460. Elizabeth Hartwell[6], living 13 March 1826,[589] married, (bond 22) Dec. 1788,[590] as his (2) wife, William Taliaferro of "Bath," Caroline County, who died 1814.[591]

153. ELIZABETH[5] COCKE (Richard[5], Richard[4], Richard[3], Richard[2], Temperance[1] Baley) married ___ Thornton.

Issue: [THORNTON][592] 461. Nancy[6], married ___ Branch; 462. Rebecca[6]; 463. Francis[6], died about 1812 at New Orleans, La., in military service; 464.

---

[577] Knorr, *Marriage Bonds ... Southampton County*, p. 27.

[578] Southampton Co. Will Bk. 4, p. 141.

[579] *T* IV, p. 440; Wythe, *op. cit.*, p. 338.

[580] Leonard, pp. 219, 223, 231, 235, 239, 245, 247, 265, 269, 273, 277.

[581] Fredericksburg District Court, file 494, Coghill *vs.* Goodloe.

[582] Catherine Lindsay Knorr, *Marriage Bonds and Ministers' Returns of Surry County, Virginia, 1768-1825* (Pine Bluff, Ark., 1960), p. 13.

[583] Surry Co. Will Bk. 1, p. 68.

[584] *Virginia Gazette and Petersburg Intelligencer*, 14 June 1796.

[585] *W*(1) XVI, p. 230.

[586] Knorr, *Marriage Bonds ... Surry County*, p. 20.

[587] Surry Co. Will Bk. 1, p. 186.

[588] Knorr, *Marriage Bonds ... Surry County*, p. 14.

[589] William Lindsay Hopkins, *Caroline County Court Records ...* (Richmond, 1987), p. 96.

[590] Knorr, *Marriage Bonds ... Surry County*, p. 81.

[591] Hopkins, *op. cit.*, pp. 83, 96.

[592] *V* V, p. 74.

Lucy[6], perhaps married, 10 Dec. 1814,[593] John Hunnicutt, Sr.; 465. Elizabeth[6], married (1) William Wilkinson of James City County and (2) 474. Robert H.[6] Taliaferro.

154. REBECCA[5] COCKE (Richard[4], Richard[3], Richard[2], Temperance[1] Baley) left will 8 Sept. 1810-12 Nov. 1810.[594] She married Col. Richard Taliaferro, son of Richard and Elizabeth (Eggleston) Taliaferro, of "Powhatan," James City County, student at the College of William and Mary, 1753-55, who left will 24 Aug. 1788-14 Dec. 1789.[595]

Issue: [TALIAFERRO][596] 466. Richard[6], died 1791,[597] unmarried; 467. Elizabeth[6], married, as his (1) wife, Daniel Call, born 5 May 1762, died 20 May 1840, aged 75,[598] attorney of Richmond, compiler of *Reports of Cases Argues and Determined in the Court of Appeals* (6 volumes, 1790-1818), who married (2) Lucy Nelson[7] Ambler, daughter of 212. *Jacquelin[6]* and 100. *Rebecca Lewis[6] (Burwell) Ambler* (see TAYLOR-CARY and BURWELL);[599] 468. Mary Hartwell[6], married 200. *William[6] Nelson* (see MARTIAU); 469. Anne[6], married Carter Nicholas; 470. Rebecca[6], died 1792, married William Browne; 471. Sarah[6], married William Wilkinson of James City County; 472. Lucy[6], married, 27 March 1800 at Williamsburg,[600] William P. Harris, merchant of Williamsburg; 473. Benjamin[6], died 1801, married, 1795, Sophia Ann[7] Tazewell, daughter of 113. *Henry[6] Tazewell* (see GRAY), died 1802,[601] who married (2) 555. *Larkin[6] Smith* (see CHEW); 474. Robert H.[6], born 1 Nov. 1783, married 465. Elizabeth[6] (Thornton) Wilkinson; 475. Mary Nelson[6], married, 29 Oct.

---

[593] Knorr, *Marriage Bonds ... Surry County*, p. 47.

[594] Jane Alexander Chapter DAR, "Virginia Genealogical Records: (Virginia DAR Genealogical Records Committee, "Report," Ser. 1, X; typewritten, Alexandria, 1938), p. 97.

[595] Tazewell Papers, Box 26, Virginia State Archives, Acc.24194.

[596] *W*(1) XX, p. 269; *W*(1) XII, p. 125, deed of gift from George Wythe, 8 Oct. 1787, naming Ann, Rebecca, Sarah, Lucy, Benjamin and Robert Taliaferro and Elizabeth Call; *V V*, pp. 74-75.

[597] Claude Lanciano, *"Our Most Skillful Architect,"* *Richard Taliaferro and Associated Colonial Virginia Constructions* (Gloucester, Va., 1981), p. 211.

[598] Gravestone, Shockoe Cemetery, Richmond.

[599] *Dictionary of Virginia Biography*, II (Richmond, 2001), pp. 513-15; Louise Pecquet du Bellet, *Some Prominent Virginia Families* (Lynchburg, 1907), I, p. 30; *The South in the Building of a Nation* (Richmond, 1909), XI, p. 162.

[600] *Enquirer*, Richmond, 8 April 1800; *Raleigh Register*, 15 April 1800.

[601] Littleton Waller Tazewell, "Sketches of his own family written for the use of his children" (1823), Virginia State Archives, Acc.29194 (miscellaneous microfilm reel 331).

1803,[602] William McCandlish, merchant of Williamsburg;.

155. ANNE[5] COCKE (Richard[4], Richard[3], Richard[2], Temperance[1] Baley) married, as his (2) wife, Col. William Browne, born 5 March 1739, left will 19 June 1783-codicil 27 March 1786-27 June 1786,[603] of "Four Mile Tree," Surry County, member of the House of Delegates, 1777-81,[604] who married (1) Sarah[7] Edwards, daughter of 92. *Benjamin[6] Edwards* (see BURWELL) and (3) 398. *Dorothy[6] (Jordan) Hay* (see JORDAN, Thomas).

Issue: [BROWNE][605] 476. Richard[6], born 24 Aug. 1769, died 4 Jan. 1789;[606] 477. John[6], born 6 Jan. 1775, died young; 478. Mary[6], married 459. Robert[6] Cocke.

156. RICHARD[5] COCKE (Richard[4], Richard[3], Richard[2], Temperance[1] Baley) of "Greyland," Surry County, and later of "Shoal Bay," Isle of Wight County, wrote an account of the Cocke family in 1813.[607] He married (1), 19 Nov. 1768,[608] 108. *Anne[5] Claiborne* (see CLAIBORNE), born 30 Dec. 1749, and (2) Theodocia (Cowley) White, who resided as a widow in Princess Anne County and left will 29 March 1824-7 Nov. 1825.[609]

Issue: (by 1)[610] 479. Richard Herbert[6], born 5 Sept. 1769,[611] died 11 July 1833, at "Bacon's Castle," Surry County, aged 64,[612] left will 11 May 1833-27 July 1833,[613] of Isle of Wight County where he kept an ordinary and was collector of accounts for the College of William and Mary, later of Norfolk and Portsmouth, and finally of "Bacon's Castle," where he was postmaster, 1811-15, and later operated a stage coach line between Portsmouth and Petersburg,

---

[602] *Norfolk Herald*, 5 Nov. 1803.

[603] Surry Co. Will Bk. 12, p. 115.

[604] Leonard, pp. 127, 131, 135, 139.

[605] *W*(1) XVI, p. 230.

[606] This date must be incorrect since the 1786 codicil to his father's will says he is deceased.

[607] *V* V, pp. 71-79.

[608] *Virginia Gazette* (Purdie & Dixon), 1 Dec. 1768; Catherine Lindsay Knorr, *Marriage Bonds and Ministers' Returns of Sussex County, Virginia, 1754-1810* (Pine Bluff, Ark., 1952), p. 18.

[609] Princess Anne Co. Will Bk. 4, pp. 38, 172.

[610] *W*(2)II, pp. 14-15, account written by John Herbert Peterson, 1839, which omits son Buller[6].

[611] Albemarle Parish Register.

[612] *Enquirer*, Richmond, 19 July 1833.

[613] Surry Co. Will Bk. 4, p. 496.

married (1), (bond 25) Oct. 1798,[614] Charlotte Mackie and (2), 13 Dec. 1810 at Norfolk,[615] 503. Ann Hunt[6] (Cocke) Bradby Adams, who left will 20 July 1837-codicil 13 July 1837-25 June 1838;[616] 480. Augustine[6], born 20 Nov. 1771,[617] a lawyer, died unmarried; 481. Lucy Ruffin[6], died 11 Sept. 1794 in Halifax County,[618] aged 16; 482. Buller[6], born 1777, died 1838,[619] purser and storekeeper in the United States Navy, 1798-1816,[620] of "Monks Dale," Surry County, postmaster at Bacon's Castle, 1831-38, married, 24 Dec. 1801,[621] Elizabeth Barron; (by 2) 483. Nathaniel[6], perhaps of Portsmouth, died 4 Feb. 1837, aged 50;[622] 484. William Henry[6], born 4 Sept. 1791, lieutenant in United States Navy, killed by discharge of a gun off Moro Castle, 8 March 1823,[623] married, 11 Feb. 1819, Eliza Waddrop[7] Johnston, daughter of 67. *Elizabeth[6] (Smith) Johnston* (see SMITH, Arthur), born 1800, died 26 May 1861; 485. John[6], born 24 Feb. 1798, died 1880, married, (bond 20) Dec. 1820,[624] Ann Bressie Webb; 486. Charles Leonard[6], died 4 Aug. 1854, aged 51, left will 12 Nov. 1853-codicil 10 July 1854-21 Aug. 1854,[625] of Portsmouth, married Ann Roe Cowper, who died 5 Aug. 1855, aged 53;[626] 487. Susan Cowley[6], born 20 Jan. 1801, died 7 Sept. 1836, sole legatee of her mother, married, 25 June 1828,[627] as his (2) wife, Henry[7] Cornick, son of 208. *Endymion[6] Cornick* (see WOODHOUSE), born 28

---

[614] Blanche Adams Chapman, *Isle of Wight County Marriages, 1628-1800* (n.p., 1933), p. 68.

[615] *V* XXXIV, p. 264; Knorr, *Marriage Bonds ... Surry County*, p. 18.

[616] Surry Co. Will Bk. 7, p. 527.

[617] Albemarle Parish Register.

[618] *Virginia Gazette and Richmond and Manchester Advertiser*, 29 Sept. 1794.

[619] Bettie Jo Matthews, *Cedar Grove Cemetery, Portsmouth, Virginia, Plat Book 1 and Book 2* (Bowie, Md., 1992), p. 91.

[620] Edward W. Callahan, *List of Officers of the Navy of the United States and of the Marine Corps from 1775 to 1900* (New York, 1901), p. 120.

[621] *Norfolk Herald*, 31 Dec. 1801; George Herbert Tucker, *Abstracts from Norfolk City Marriage Bonds (1797-1850)* (n.p., 1934), p. 14.

[622] *Enquirer*, Richmond, 18 March 1837.

[623] *National Intelligencer*, 7, 14 April, 4 May 1823.

[624] *W*(2) X, p. 135, Norfolk County.

[625] Norfolk Co. Will Bk. 6, pp. 373-75.

[626] Matthews, *loc. cit.*

[627] Carolyn L. Barkley, *Princess Anne County, Virginia, Marriage Bonds, 1822-1850* (Lovettsville, Va., 1997), p. 42, bond 18 June.

Oct. 1781, died 24 June 1830;[628] 488. Edward[6], of Surry County, left will 22 Feb. 1824-5 April 1824.[629]

157. LUCY[5] COCKE (Richard[4], Richard[3], Richard[2], Temperance[1] Baley) married, 1770, William Ruffin of "Rich Neck," Surry County, who married (1) 86. *Mary[5] Bland* (see BLAND) and left will 1 May 1773-26 April 1774.[630]

Issue: [RUFFIN][631] 489. William[6], married, (bond 25) Nov. 1795,[632] Ann Edwards; 490. Elizabeth[6], born 17 May 1771, died 26 July 1799, married, 22 Sept. 1792,[633] William[8] Browne, son of William Browne and Sarah[7] Edwards, daughter of 92. *Benjamin[6] Edwards* (see BURWELL), born 17 Sept. 1759, died 15 Nov. 1799,[634] left will 14 Nov. 1799-24 Dec. 1799,[635] of "Four Mile Tree," Surry County, step-son of her aunt Ann[5] Cocke.

158. NATHANIEL[5] COCKE (Richard[4], Richard[3], Richard[2], Temperance[1] Baley) was a justice of Halifax County, 1773, was commissioned captain in 7th Virginia Regiment, 7 March 1776, was later lieutenant colonel in Virginia State Line, and moved to Richmond Co., Ga., where he left will 27 Aug. 1796-2 Jan. 1797.[636] He married Rebecca Thompson, who was living in Richmond Co., Ga., 6 May 1830.[637]

Issue:[638] 491. Nathaniel[6], attorney, died 18 Dec. 1807, Sandersville, Ga.;[639] 492. Dr. John[6], died 23 July 1818, Liberty Co., Ga.;[640] 493. Dr. William[6], died 22 Oct. 1809 in Columbia Co., Ga.,[641] of Savannah, Ga., married, 31 March

---

[628] Gravestones, Eastern Shore Chapel, in Laurie Boush Green and Virginia Bonney West, *Old Churches, Their Cemeteries and Family Graveyards of Princess Anne County, Virginia* (n.p., 1985), p. 15.

[629] Princess Anne Co. Will Bk. 4, p. 2.

[630] Surry Co. Will Bk. 10A, p. 351.

[631] *W*(1) XVI, p. 230.

[632] Knorr, *Marriage Bonds ... Surry County*, p. 72.

[633] *Ibid.*, p. 13.

[634] Tombstones, "Four Mile Tree, Surry Co.

[635] Surry Co. Will Bk. 1, p. 361.

[636] Richmond Co., Ga., Will Bk. 1, p. 217.

[637] Revolutionary War pension application, Nathaniel Cocke, widow Rebecca, R.13415, Virginia Half Pay, National Archives.

[638] Margie G. Brown, *Genealogical Abstracts, Revolutionary War Veterans, Scrip Act 1852* (Oakton, Va., 1990), pp. 55-56.

[639] Mary Bondurant Warren, *Marriages and Deaths, 1763 to 1820, Abstracted from Extant Georgia Newspapers* (Danielsville, Ga., 1968), p. 22.

[640] *Ibid.* Brown, *loc. cit.*, says living Portsmouth, Va., 1835.

[641] *Mirror of the Times*, Augusta, Ga., 28 Oct. 1809.

1807, Pamela Rice, who died 29 July 1809, aged 20;[642] 494. Eliza Ruffin[6], born 1782, died 18 Nov. 1844 at Columbus, Ga., married, 16 Feb. 1808 at Augusta, Ga.,[643] John Bacon, merchant of Savannah, Ga., who was born 1766 at Augusta and died 20 Jan. 1812 at Columbus;[644] 495. Mary[6], married, 6 March 1821 in Richmond Co., Ga., John Taylor; 496. Augusta[6], born 1795; 497. Rebecca Thompson[6], died 1828 at Augusta, Ga., aged 43,[645] married, 15 Jan. 1799, Augustus Baldwin of Savannah, Ga.[646]

159. JOHN[5] COCKE (Richard[4], Richard[3], Richard[2], Temperance[1] Baley), student at College of William and Mary, 1770-71, was clerk of Sussex County, 1780-86, and left will 19 Nov. 1785-16 March 1786.[647] He married, (bond 21) Sept. 1776,[648] 114. *Lucy Herbert[5] Claiborne* (see CLAIBORNE), born 22 Aug. 1760,[649] who married (2), (bond 8) Sept. 1788,[650] William Thompson.

Issue:[651] 498. Herbert Claiborne[6], of Halifax County, left undated will, proved 20 Oct. 1814,[652] married, 29 Aug. 1798,[653] Sally Roberts; 499. John Ruffin[6], born 15 July 1783, left will 31 Aug. 1827-17 Oct. 1827,[654] married, 24 Dec. 1803,[655] Mary Coleman Scott, born 1787, died 7 Oct. 1857, left will Feb. 1852-5 Dec. 1857.[656]

160. Col. ALLEN[5] COCKE (Benjamin[4], Richard[3], Richard[2], Temperance[1] Baley) of "Bacon's Castle," Surry County, was a member of the House of Burgesses, 1771-76, of the five conventions of 1774-75, and of the House of

---

[642] Warren, *loc. cit.*

[643] *Ibid.*, p. 4.

[644] Bacon family Bible.

[645] *Telegraph*, Macon, Ga., 9 June 1828.

[646] Warren, *op. cit.*, p. 5.

[647] Sussex Co. Will Bk. D, p. 389.

[648] Knorr, *Marriage Bonds ... Sussex County*, p. 18.

[649] Albemarle Parish Register.

[650] Knorr, *Marriage Bonds ... Sussex County.*, p. 79.

[651] James William Cocke, "Descendants of Richard Cocke who Moved from Virginia to Alabama to Mississippi" (typewritten; Jackson, Miss., 1968), no pagination.

[652] Halifax Co. Will Bk. 10, pp. 81-82.

[653] Catherine Lindsay Knorr, *Marriage Bonds and Ministers' Returns of Halifax County, Virginia, 1753-1800* (Pine Bluff, Ark., 1957), p. 21.

[654] Greene Co., Ala., Will Bk. A, p. 60; Probate file 176.

[655] Wirt Johnson Carrington, *A History of Halifax County* (Richmond, 1924), p. 245.

[656] Greene Co., Ala., Will Bk. C, p. 515; Probate file 1432.

Delegates, 1776, 1779-81.[657] He died 1780,[658] left will 20 Nov. 1780-27 March 1781.[659] He married 335. *Anne*[6] *Kennon* (see EPES), who died 1780, Surry County.[660]

Issue: 500. Benjamin Allen[6], left will 20 July 1799-24 Sept. 1799,[661] married, (bond 17) Aug. 1789,[662] Susannah Crichlow, who married (2), (bond 16) Jan. 1800,[663] Patrick H. Adams; 501. Richard[6], married ___; 502. Allen[6], under 21 in 1780, left will 1 Aug. 1802-23 Nov. 1802,[664] never married; 503. Ann Hunt[6], under age in 1780, married (1) 505. Gen. James Allen[6] Bradby, (2), (bond 3) Jan. 1803,[665] Patrick H. Adams, widower of Susanna (Crichlow) Cocke, who left will 10 April 1805-codicil 28 July 1807-25 Aug. 1807,[666] and (3) 479. Richard Herbert[6] Cocke; 504. Catherine[6], under age in 1780, died before 1813, married (1), (bond 14) April 1789,[667] Wilson Curle Wallace of Elizabeth City County, who left will 3 May 1801-27 Jan. 1803,[668] and (2), 21 April 1802,[669] Thomas M. Hare, who after her death moved to Nansemond County and died about 1824.[670]

161. CATHARINE ALLEN[5] COCKE (Benjamin[4], Richard[3], Richard[2], Temperance[1] Baley) married (1), by 1763, Capt. James Rodwell Bradby, who died by Feb. 1772 when she advertised for sale his personal estate,[671] and (2), (bond 24) Sept. 1776,[672] Thomas Haynes of Halifax Co., N.C., who left will 2 May 1796-May 1796.[673]

---

[657] Leonard, pp. 104, 106, 110, 113, 116, 118, 120, 123, 135, 139.

[658] *Virginia Gazette* (Clarkson & Davis), 9 Dec. 1780.

[659] Surry Co. Will Bk. 11, p. 217.

[660] *Virginia Gazette*, 9 Aug. 1780.

[661] Surry Co. Will Bk. 1, p. 332.

[662] Knorr, *Marriage Bonds ... Surry County*, p. 28.

[663] *Ibid.*, p. 1; Goochland Co. Deed Bk. 18, p. 77.

[664] Surry Co. Will Bk. 1, p. 570.

[665] Knorr, *Marriage Bonds ... Surry County*, p. 1.

[666] Surry Co. Wills &c 2, p. 201.

[667] Knorr, *Marriage Bonds ... Suirry County*, p. 85.

[668] Elizabeth City Co. Deeds & Wills 12, 1796-1806, p. 195.

[669] Knorr, *Marriage Bonds ... Surry County*, p. 39.

[670] Surry Co. Land tax book, 1824.

[671] *Virginia Gazette* (Rind), 27 Feb. 1772; Surry Co. Will Bk. 12, p. 2, account current returned by William Hay, his administrator, 22 July 1783.

[672] Knorr, *Marriage Bonds ... Surry County*, p. 42.

[673] Halifax Co., N.C., Will Bk. 3, p. 267; John Bennett Boddie, *Virginia Historical Genealogies* (Redwood City, Calif., 1954), p. 328.

Issue: (by 1) [BRADBY] 505. Gen. James Allen[6], left will 18 Feb. 1802-codicil 10 March 1802-27 April 1802,[674] represented Surry County in the House of Delegates, 1791-93,[675] married, (bond 18) Feb. 1784,[676] 503. Ann Hunt[6] Cocke.

163. SUSANNA[5] ACRILL (Anne[4] Cocke, Richard,[3] Richard[2], Temperance[1] Baley) left will 6 Dec. 1783-24 Feb. 1784.[677] She married 172. *Thomas[6] Cocke* (see HOLT) of Surry County who left will 28 March 1781-25 Feb. 1783.[678]

Issue: [COCKE][679] 506. Acrill[6], born by 1768, died by 1804, of Charles City County, married ____; 507. Archibald[6], under age in 1781, married, 5 Sept. 1793,[680] Mary[7] Thomas Crafford, born out of wedlock to Micajah Thomas and 21. *Elizabeth[6] Crafford* (see CARTER);[681] 508. William[6], born 1763-65, under age in 1784, died about 1813, married, (bond 4) Dec. 1793,[682] Elizabeth Mackie; 509. Benjamin[6], born after 1772, died without issue by 1803; 510. Lucy[6], chose Richard Cocke as her guardian, 25 May 1784,[683] died after 1809 at Staunton,[684] married, 5 Jan. 1792,[685] John Edmundson; 511. Anne [Nancy][6], under age in 1781, died before 26 June 1815 when the inventory of her estate was made,[686] married Thomas Marriott, who died before 3 Dec. 1794 when the inventory of his estate was made.[687]

164. REBECCA[5] ACRILL (Anne[4] Cocke, Richard[3], Richard[2], Temperance[1] Baley) died before 17 April 1784 when her executors advertised her slaves and

---

[674] Surry Co. Will Bk. 1, p. 545.

[675] Leonard, pp. 185, 189, 193.

[676] Knorr, *Marriage Bonds ... Surry County*, p. 12.

[677] Surry Co. Will Bk. 12, p. 23.

[678] Surry Co. Will Bk. 11, p. 344.

[679] *The Virginia Genealogist*, XLV, pp. 32, 208-10.

[680] Knorr, *Marriage Bonds ... Surry County*, p. 20.

[681] John Anderson Brayton, *The Descendants of Robert Harris ... (Colonial Families of Surry and Isle of Wight Counties, Virginia*, II; Memphis, 1999), pp. 325-30.

[682] Blanche Adams Chapman, *Marriages of Isle of Wight County, Virginia, 1628-1800*, p. 68.

[683] Surry Co. Order Bk. 1775-85, p. 298.

[684] Augusta Co. Deed Bk. 56, pp. 229-30.

[685] Knorr, *Marriage Bonds ... Surry County*, p. 29.

[686] Surry Co. Will Bk. 3, pp. 38-39.

[687] Surry Co. Will Bk. 1, pp. 78-80.

livestock for sale.[688] She married Philip Watson,[689] merchant of Henrico County, who died before Nov. 1766.[690] As a widow she resided in Charles City County.

Issue: [WATSON][691] 512. John Sergeant[6]; 513. Nathaniel[6].

167. THOMAS[5] CARY (Thomas[4], Elizabeth[3] Cocke, Richard[2], Temperance[1] Baley) of Chesterfield County, left will 2 Oct. 1784-3 Dec. 1784,[692] married Sally ___, who died by 31 March 1799 when the inventory of her estate was made.[693]

Issue: [CARY][694] 514. William[6], born 14 April 1756, served seven tours in the Chesterfield County militia, moved in 1808 to Claiborne Co., Tenn., and in 1818 to Cumberland Co., Ky.,[695] married Hannah Burton;[696] 515. Nathaniel[6], left will 27 Jan. 1789-10 June 1790,[697] unmarried; 516. John Philipson[6], married, (bond 1) April 1786,[698] Sally Loafman; 517. Robert Philipson[6], moved to Tennessee, married Martha North; 518. Camp [Kemp][6], chose James Harris as his guardian, 10 Nov. 1785,[699] moved to Tennessee, married, (bond 27) April 1790, Rebecca Butler;[700] 519. Edmond[6], as Edward chose Sally Cary as his guardian, 10 Nov. 1785,[701] died 1829 in Cumberland Co., Ky., married, (consent 10) Dec. 1792, Sally Butler;[702] 520. Rev. Peter Minor[6], born 1774, died 1852, of Chesterfield County, for whom Sally Cary was appointed guardian, 10 Nov. 1785,[703] moved to Jefferon Co., Ky., by 1830, married, 31 Jan. 1795,[704] 413. *Rhoda[6] Cox* (see COX), born 1776, died 1872.

---

[688] *Virginia Gazette, or, The American Advertiser*, Richmond, 17 April 1784.

[689] Surry Co. Deed Bk. 7, p. 339.

[690] Henrico Co. Order Bk. 1763-67, pp. 641, 643. 647.

[691] Henrico Co. Order Bk. 1767-69, p. 6, appointment of guardians of orphans, June 1767.

[692] Chesterfield Co. Will Bk. 3, p. 487; Order Bk. 7, p. 80.

[693] Chesterfield Co. Will Bk. 5, p. 273.

[694] Harrison, *op. cit.*, p. 64.

[695] Revolutionary War pension application, William Cary, S.10424, National Archives.

[696] Chesterfield Co. Will Bk. 5, p. 351, will of John Burton, 10 Jan. 1801.

[697] Chesterfield Co. Will Bk. 4, p. 237; Order Bk. 8, p. 441.

[698] Knorr, *Marriage Bonds ... Chesterfield County*, p. 26.

[699] Chesterfield Co. Order Bk. 7, p. 247.

[700] Knorr, *Marriage Bonds ... Chesterfield County*, p. 26.

[701] Chesterfield Co. Order Bk. 7, p. 246.

[702] Knorr, *Marriage Bonds ... Chesterfield County*, p. 26. Harrison, *op. cit.*, p. 64, says he married, 1793, Nancy Bowman; Knorr (*ibid.*) shows (bond 13) Aug. 1810.

[703] Chesterfield Co. Order Bk. 7, p. 246.

[704] Knorr, *Marriage Bonds ... Chesterfield County*, p. 26.

168. ROBERT⁵ CARY (Thomas⁴, Elizabeth³ Cocke, Richard², Temperance¹ Baley) died by 1 March 1782 when administration on his estate was granted to his widow.⁷⁰⁵ He married Mary [Jennings?] who died 19 March 1836 in Chesterfield County, aged about 92.⁷⁰⁶

Issue: [CARY]⁷⁰⁷ 521. Miles⁶, died before 18 Sept. 1813 when Nelson Cary gave bond as his administrator,⁷⁰⁸ married, by 10 March 1791,⁷⁰⁹ Obedience Brummall; 522. Robert⁶, married, (consent 13) May 1793,⁷¹⁰ 262. *Mary Ann⁶ Branch* (see BRANCH), who left will 18 Jan. 1826-8 May 1826;⁷¹¹ 523. Wilson⁶, moved to Union Co., Ky., married, 1793,⁷¹² Judith Baker; 524. Ann⁶, married, 18 Oct. 1794,⁷¹³ Walthall Robertson, born 31 May 1765,⁷¹⁴ who married (1) Frances Cox; 525. Dorothy⁶; 526. Judith⁶, married, 1 Sept. 1804,⁷¹⁵ Henry Burnett; 527. Elizabeth⁶; 528. Henry⁶, moved to Pocahontas County and then to Kentucky, married Elizabeth Morrisette; 529. Thomas⁶, married Mary Grace Bagnall; 530. Nathaniel⁶.

169. MILES⁵ CARY (Thomas⁴, Elizabeth³ Cocke, Richard², Temperance¹ Baley), born 28 May 1727, died 9 Sept. 1766,⁷¹⁶ left will 3 July 1766-11 Dec. 1766.⁷¹⁷ He was an attorney of Southampton County and succeeded his father as Clerk of the Committee of Public Claims, 1748. He married, 23 May 1752, Elizabeth Taylor, daughter of Etheldred and Patience (Kinchen) Taylor,⁷¹⁸ who died 16 March 1774.

---

⁷⁰⁵ Chesterfield Co. Order Bk. 6, p. 339.

⁷⁰⁶ *Enquirer*, Richmond, 26 March 1836.

⁷⁰⁷ Chesterfield Co. Order Bk. 6, p. 476, appointment of Mary Cary as their guardian, 5 Sept. 1783, naming son William rather than Wilson; Harrison, *op. cit.*, pp. 62-63.

⁷⁰⁸ Chesterfield Co. Will Bk. 8, p. 137.

⁷⁰⁹ Knorr, *Marriage Bonds ... Chesterfield County*, p. 26.

⁷¹⁰ *Ibid.*

⁷¹¹ Chesterfield Co. Will Bk. 11, pp. 175-76. Her will was contested (Order Bk. 25, pp. 436, 483).

⁷¹² Knorr, *Marriage Bonds ... Chesterfield County*, p. 26.

⁷¹³ *Ibid.*, p. 103.

⁷¹⁴ Malcolm Elmore Walthall, "The Walthall Family" (typewritten; Charlotte, N.C., 1963), p. 24.

⁷¹⁵ Knorr, *Marriage Bonds ... Chesterfield County.*, p. 24.

⁷¹⁶ Cary Bible, *W*(1) XV, p. 84.

⁷¹⁷ Southampton Co. Will Bk. 2, p. 179.

⁷¹⁸ *V* XXIII, pp. 104-05.

Issue: [CARY][719] 531. Elizabeth[5] born 18 Dec. 1753, died 9 March 1778, married, 18 Dec. 1774, William Hay, born 10/21 Nov. 1748 at Kilsyth, Sterlingshire, Scotland, died 11 Nov. 1825, educated at University of Glasgow, emigrated to Virginia 1768, lawyer of Surry County and then of Richmond until the courts shut down at the beginning of the Revolutionary War, and in later life of Frederick (Clarke) County,[720] who married (2) 57. *Elizabeth[6] Tompkins* (see BENNETT, Samuel); 532. Hannah[6], born 10 Nov. 1755, left will 2 Dec. 1781-1 March 1782;[721] 533. Col. Miles[6], born 1 Sept. 1757, left will 18 June 1806-21 July 1806,[722] of "Bonny Doon," Southampton County, married (1), 26 Dec. 1782,[723] Frances B. Peterson, (2), (bond 31) Jan. 1785,[724] Griselda Buxton, and (3), (bond 5) Nov. 1795,[725] Elizabeth (Booth) Yates; 534. Mary[6], born 29 Aug. 1760; 535. Nathaniel[6], born 19 Oct. 1763, died 15 Nov. 1767, drowned in Nottoway River.

172. Lt. Col. JOHN[5] CARY (Miles[4], Elizabeth[3] Cocke, Richard[2], Temperance[1] Baley), born 1745, died 1795, of Elizabeth City County, member of the Committee of Safety, 1774, captain, 1775, member of Virginia Senate, 1780-81,[726] left will 28 Oct. 1794-23 July 1795.[727] He married (1), 1765, Sally Sclater, born 26 Nov. 1750,[728] died 1775, and (2) Susannah Armistead, born 1753, died 30 Oct. 1834.[729]

Issue: [CARY][730] (by 1) 536. Anne Elizabeth[6], born 1767, died in infancy; 537. Miles[6], born 1771, died 1850, Campbell County, vestryman of St. John's Church, Hampton, 1810, captain of 68th Virginia Infantry, 1812-14, acquired "Buck Roe," Elizabeth City County, on his (2) marriage, moved to Campbell County, 1816, married (1), 27 Feb. 1796, York County,[731] Martha Sclater, born

---

[719] Cary Bible, in *W*(1) XX, p. 84; Harrison, *op. cit.*, pp. 69-70.
[720] Hay Bible, *W*(1) XV, pp. 85-86; *Virginia Gazette* (Purdie & Dixon), 22 Dec. 1774.
[721] Chesterfield Co. Will Bk. 3, p. 292; Order Bk. 6, p. 342.
[722] Southampton Co. Will Bk. 6, p. 361.
[723] Knorr, *Marriage Bonds ... Southampton County*, p. 26.
[724] *Ibid.*
[725] Knorr, *Marriage Bonds ... Sussex County*, p. 14.
[726] Leonard, p. 140.
[727] Elizabeth City Co. Will Bk. 1787-1800, p. 247.
[728] Charles Parish Register.
[729] *W*(1) VI, p. 231.
[730] Harrison, *op. cit.*, pp. 72-73, 78-79, 82.
[731] *V* XXV, p. 301.

17 Dec. 1775,[732] and (2), 1802, Eliza King (Mallory) Page; (by 2) 538 Hannah Armistead[6], born 1778, died 1821, married, 1799, Horatio Gates Whiting. merchant of Elizabeth City County; 539. Elizabeth Allen[6], born 1779, died 1800; 540. John[6], born 1781, died before Oct. 1822, deputy collector of the port of Hampton, married, 1808, Anne Wythe Sweeny, died 24 Oct. 1822 at Hampton,[733] niece of George Wythe; 541. Col. Gill Armistead[6], born 18 March 1783, died 25 March 1843,[734] of Hampton, married, 18 Nov. 1818, Sarah Elizabeth Smith Baytop, born 18 Sept. 1790, died 15 April 1879;[735] 542. Nathaniel Robert[6], born 1784, died 1790; 543. Polly[6], born 1786, died in infancy; 544. Judith Robinson[6], born 1787, died 1821, married, 1803, Col. Henry Howard of York County; 545. Susannah[6], born 1789, died 1873; 546. Richard[6], born 1791, died in infancy; 547. Nathaniel Robert[6], died 25 Aug. 1832, Elizabeth City County, aged 40,[736] unmarried; 548. William Armistead[6], born 1794, died 1798.

173. RICHARD[5] CARY (Miles[4], Elizabeth[3] Cocke, Richard[2], Temperance[1] Baley) died 13 Nov. 1789,[737] left will 25 April 1785-10 Dec. 1784.[738] He was clerk of Warwick County, 1764, member of Committee of Safety, 1774-76, of the Convention of 1776 and of the House of Delegates, 1776,[739] and judge of the Court of Admiralty, 27 Dec. 1776, and of the General Court, 24 Dec. 1788. He married 20. *Mary[5] Cole* (see COLE).

Issue: [CARY][740] 549. Richard[6], born 1760, left will 5 April 1798-codicil 25 Jan. 1800-2 June 1800,[741] dragoon during Revolutionary War, member of the House of Delegates from Warwick County, 1785-88, 1798-1800, Senator, 1792-96, and member of the Convention of 1788,[742] married Catherine Dudley, who married (2) Thomas Pescud; 550. Miles[6], born 1763, died 1797, married (1)

---

[732] Charles Parish Register.

[733] *National Intelligencer*, 29 Oct. 1822; *Enquirer*, Richmond, 1 Nov. 1822.

[734] Gravestone, "Rich Neck," Warwick County, in *W*(1) XIV, pp. 163-67.

[735] William Carter Stubbs, *A History of Two Virginia Families ... Catlett ... Baytop* (New Orleans, n.d.), p. 146.

[736] *Enquirer*, Richmond, 18 Sept. 1832.

[737] *Virginia Independent Chronicle*, Richmond, 18 Nov. 1789.

[738] Southall Papers, Earl Gregg Swem Library, College of William and Mary, folder 128, extract, recorded in Warwick County.

[739] Leonard, pp. 123, 126.

[740] Harrison, *op. cit.*, p. 55.

[741] Southall Papers, *loc. cit.*, recorded in Warwick County.

[742] Leonard, pp. 158, 162, 166, 174, 190, 194, 198, 202, 206, 213, 217, 221.

Elizabeth Jones and (2), 1 Jan. 1797, Anne[7] Robinson, born 2 March 1775, died 25 Nov. 1842,[743] daughter of 192. *Mary[6] (Phillips) Robinson* (see MARTIAU); 551. Polly[6], died before 1789, married, as his (1) wife, William[7] Cary of "Windmill Point," Warwick County,[744] son of 93. *Thomas[6] Cary* (see TAYLOR-CARY); 552. Hannah[6], married 192. Maj. *William[6] Dudley* (see CHISMAN); 553. Anne[6], died 1809, married, 1796, 33. *William Harwood[6] Wynne* (see HARWOOD) of Warwick County; 554. Elizabeth[6], died 6 Dec. 1805, aged 28, in Warwick County,[745] left will 30 Nov. 1805-12 Dec. 1805;[746] 555. Rebecca[6], died 1799, unmarried.

176. ELIZABETH[5] CARY (Miles[4], Elizabeth[3] Cocke, Richard[2], Temperance[1] Baley) died 24 July [*sic*] 1801,[747] left will June 1801-13 July 1801.[748] She married, 25 Oct. 1755, Benjamin Watkins, who died 12 Feb. 1781, leaving will 9 Feb. 1781-6 April 1781.[749] They resided at "The Hermitage," Chesterfield County. He was the first Clerk of Chesterfield County and was a member of the House of Delegates, 1772-76, and of the conventions of 1774.[750]

Issue: [WATKINS][751] 556. Hannah[6], born 7 Feb. 1757, married (1) 234. William[6] Finney and (2), (bond 4) Nov. 1789,[752] John Walke; 557. Benjamin[6], born 29 Nov. 1758, died 29 July [1759?]; 558. Thomas[6], born 4 Sept. 1760, died 4 Jan. 1812, married, (bond 23) Oct. 1783,[753] 181. *Rebecca[6] Selden* (see TAYLOR-CARY); 559. Elizabeth[6], born 10 Dec. 1762, died 5 Jan. 1802, married (1) 21. the Rev. *William[5] Leigh* (see COLE) and (2) 589. *Benjamin[6] Thweatt* (see BRANCH); 560. Miles Cary[6], born 20 Dec. 1764, died 19 July 1765; 561. Benjamin[6], born 8 June 1766, died 27 Feb. 1786; 562. Richard[6], born 8 Aug. 1768, died 4 Jan. 1803; 563. Rebecca[6], born 7 Aug. 1770, died 4 Jan.

---

[743] Hayden, *op. cit.*, p. 573.

[744] Harrison, *op. cit.*, p. 46.

[745] *Virginia Gazette and General Advertiser*, Richmond, 21 Dec. 1805.

[746] William Armstrong Crozier, *Williamsburg Wills* (*Virginia County Records*, III; New York, 1906), p. 14.

[747] Watkins Bible, in *The Southside Virginian*, III, p. 121.

[748] Chesterfield Co. Will Bk. 5, p. 420; Order Bk. 14, p. 116.

[749] Chesterfield Co. Will Bk. 3, p. 267; Order Bk. 6, p. 317.

[750] Leonard, pp. 102, 105, 109, 112, 114, 117, 119, 122; John Hale Stutesman, *Some Watkins Families of Virginia and their Kin* (Baltimore, 1989), pp. 58-60.

[751] Chesterfield Co. Will Bk. 4, p. 226.

[752] Williams, *Marriages of Amelia County*, p. 111.

[753] Joyce H. Lindsay, *Marriages of Henrico County, Virginia, 1680-1808* (n.p., 1960), p. 90.

1833, married Baldwin Pearce; 564. Mary[6], born 25 May 1772, died 25 Feb. 1832; 565. Susanna[6], born 23 March 1774, died 11 March 1832,[754] married Henry Lockett; 566. Ann[6], born 7 Oct. 1776, died 29 March 1796; 567. Jane[6], born 28 Feb. 1779, died 11 May 1799.

177. ROBERT[5] CARY (Miles[4], Elizabeth[3] Cocke, Richard[2], Temperance[1] Baley) died 1807, Buckingham County. He married Judith Ware, died 1788.[755]

Issue: [CARY] 588. (Daughter)[6], died 1788 in infancy.

178. WILLIAM[5] PLEASANTS (Joseph[4], Martha[3] Cocke, Richard[2], Temperance[1] Baley) of Chesterfield County, died 9 Dec. 1784.[756] He married Elizabeth Folkes who died 13 Sept. 1785.

Issue [PLEASANTS][757] 569. Sarah[6], born 18 May 1761, died 7 Oct. 1780; 570. William[6], born 9 Feb. 1763, perhaps married Elvira ___ and moved to Wake Co., N.C.; 571. Edward[6], born 23 May 1765, moved to Lincoln Co., Ky., and about 1830 to Warren Co., Mo., left will 31 Aug. 1838-18 Feb. 1839,[758] married, 9 Oct. 1790,[759] Lucy Humber; 572. Elizabeth R.[6], born 4 June 1767, died May 1790, married, 13 July 1786, as his (1) wife, Arthur Akin, who left will 7 Jan. 1804-12 June 1809;[760] 573. John[6], born 2 July 1771, died 9 July 1838 in Goochland County, for whom William Pleasants was appointed guardian, 1786,[761] married (1), 3 Aug. 1797, 232. *Polly Price[6] Cox* (see COX), and (2), 1 Oct. 1812, Elizabeth Forsee, born 1 Nov. 1779, died 27 Feb. 1862; 574. Joseph[6], twin, born 9 April 1774, died 28 Nov. 1795 at Oster, French Flanders; 575. Josiah[6], twin, born 9 April 1774; 576. Catherine[6], born 21 Jan. 1777, for whom Edward Pleasants was appointed guardian, 1788;[762] 577. Baxter[6], born 13 June 1779; 578. Robert[6], born 25 Dec. 1782, left will 16 July 1845-codicil 31

---

[754] *Enquirer*, Richmond, 23 March 1832, reported the death on 10 March in Powhatan County of Mrs. Susan Lockett, wife of Dr. Henry W. Lockett, aged 28 [*sic*].

[755] Daniel Call, *Report of Cases Argued and Determined in the Court of Appeals* (2nd ed.; Richmond, 1824), p. 269.

[756] Bible, cited in Norma Carter Miller and George Lane Miller, *Pleasants and Allied Families* (n.p., 1980), p. 102. The inventory of his estate was made 20 June 1785 (Chesterfield Co. Will Bk. 3, p. 537).

[757] Bible, *loc. cit.*; Chesterfield Co. Order Bk. 7, p. 261.

[758] Warren Co., Mo., Will Bk.1833-43, pp. 99-100.

[759] Williams, *Marriages of Goochland County*, (n.p., 1960), p. 76.

[760] Chesterfield Co. Will Bk. 7, pp. 114-16.

[761] Chesterfield Co. Order Bk. 7, p. 287.

[762] Chesterfield Co. Order Bk. 8, p. 114.

July 1845-Sept. 1847,[763] married (1) Nancy Dukle and (2), 10 Feb. 1810,[764] Elizabeth Fletcher.

179. JOSEPH[5] PLEASANTS (Joseph[4], Martha[3] Cocke, Richard[2], Temperance[1] Baley) died by 1 Sept. 1766 when his widow Mary was granted administration on his estate.[765] He married Mary Aikin.[766]

Issue: [PLEASANTS] 579. Sarah[6], married, (bond 12) March 1782,[767] James Aiken; 580. Joseph[6], married, (bond 7) Nov. 1792,[768] Frances Price; 581. William[6], born 30 June 1764, married, 25 Nov. 1785,[769] Mary Frances Flournoy, and probably moved to Georgia and died before 1840 in Washington Parish, La.[770]

180. JESSE[5] PLEASANTS (Joseph[4], Martha[3] Cocke, Richard[2], Temperance[1] Baley) left will 25 Nov. 1803-22 Oct. 1804.[771] He married, 4 May 1769, Elizabeth Smith, daughter of William and Mary (Smith) Smith, born 1 Oct. 1745,[772] died 1810.[773]

Issue: [PLEASANTS][774] 582. Joseph[6]; 583. Ann[6], married 317. *John[6] Woodson* (see WOODSON); 584. Mary[6], married, 8 Aug. 1793,[775] William Keen; 585. Elizabeth Woodson[6], died 1830 at Willington, S.C.,[776] married, 14 March 1800,[777] the Rev. Moses Waddel who founded the Willington church and

---

[763] Franklin Co., N.C., Will Bk. M, p. 221.

[764] Franklin Co., N.C., Marriage bond.

[765] Henrico Co. Order Bk. 1763-67, p. 682.

[766] *Val. Papers* IV, p. 2295. Miller, *op. cit.*, p. 88, states he married, 5 Oct. 1747, Mary, daughter of Stephen Woodson, but she married Joseph Parsons.

[767] Knorr, *Marriage Bonds ... Chesterfield County*, p. 2.

[768] Lindsay, *op. cit.*, p. 67.

[769] Knorr, *Marriage Bonds ... Chesterfield County*, p. 97.

[770] Miller, *op. cit.*, p. 89.

[771] Halifax Co. Will Bk. 7, p. 39.

[772] Smith Bible, in Ben Lacy Rose, *Lacy-Burwell Genealogy* (Richmond, 1981), pp. 158-62; Elliott, *Marriage Records ... Cumberland County*, p. 105, bond 2 May. He was disowned by the Society of Friends, 2 Sept. 1769, for marrying out of unity and allowing himself to be baptized.

[773] *Virginia Genealogical Society Quarterly*, XV, p. 32.

[774] *Val. Papers* IV, p. 2296, lists first four; *Virginia Genealogical Society Quarterly, loc. cit.*, names John Smith[6].

[775] Knorr, *Marriage Bonds ... Halifax County*, p. 54.

[776] Obituary, in *South Carolina Historical Magazine*, XXVIII, p. 250; gravestone, Willington, S.C., cemetery, in Augusta Genealogical Society, *Ancestoring*, VI, p. 33.

[777] Knorr, *Marriage Bonds ... Halifax County*, p. 96.

school in South Carolina; 586. John Smith[5], born 25 Jan. 1785, died 16 June 1856, served in War of 1812, represented Halifax County in the House of Delegates, 1823-24,[778] married, 11 Sept. 1806, Nancy Thweatt, born 5 March 1785, died 25 Sept. [1844], aged 59 yrs. 6 mos.;[779] 587. Martha[6], married, April 1807, Matthew Rowlett of Mecklenburg County; 588. Judith[6], born 1787 in Halifax County, died 1834, married, 16 July 1816 in Halifax County, Matthew[8] Ligon, son of Joseph[7] and Lettice (Simms) Ligon and grandson of 159. *Joseph[6] Ligon* (see HARRIS, Thomas), born 1785, died 1843, of Montgomery Co., Tenn.

181. JACOB[5] PLEASANTS (Joseph[4], Martha[3] Cocke, Richard[2], Temperance[1] Baley) left will dated 8 Feb. 1776.[780] He married, 7 May 1765,[781] 236. *Sarah[4] Pleasants* (see JORDAN, Thomas).

Issue: [PLEASANTS][782] 589. John Scott[6], merchant of Richmond, died 31 Aug. 1813 in Charles City County,[783] married, 29 April 1790 at Alexandria,[784] Sarah Lowndes, who moved to Augusta, Ga.;[785] 590. Elizabeth Tucker[6], married (1) 242. *Thomas Snowden[6] Pleasants* (see JORDAN, Thomas) and (2) 257. *Pleasant[6] Younghusband* (see JORDAN, Thomas); 591. Thomas Exum[6], died before 21 Dec. 1829 when George T. Pleasants gave bond as his administrator,[786] married, (bond 2) May 1801,[787] Jane Chewning of Louisa County; 592. Sarah[6].

183. PHILIP[5] PLEASANTS (Joseph[4], Martha[3] Cocke, Richard[2], Temperance[1] Baley) of Goochland County, who reported, 6 April 1776, he had lately accepted an office in the army and was disowned by the Society of Friends, 7 April 1781,[788] left will 21 Dec. 1830-18 July 1831.[789] He married, 1 July 1782, 250. *Mary[6] Pleasants* (see JORDAN, Thomas).

---

[778] Leonard, p. 319.

[779] Bible, in *Virginia Genealogical Society Quarterly*, VX, pp. 30-31.

[780] Henrico Co. Proceedings of the Commissioners Regarding Records Destroyed by the British, 1774-82, pp. 107-10.

[781] Hinshaw, VI, p. 203.

[782] *Val. Papers* IV, p. 2297.

[783] *Virginia Argue*, Richmond, 2 Sept. 1813.

[784] Hinshaw VI, p. 545; *Virginia Gazette and Alexandria Advertiser*, 6 May 1790.

[785] Richmond Co., Ga., 1830 census, Augusta, 3rd Ward, p. 269.

[786] Amherst Co. Will Bk. 7, p. 296.

[787] Kathleen Booth Williams, *Marriages of Louisa County, Virginia, 1766-1815* (n.p., 1959), p. 82.

[788] Hinshaw, VI, p. 207.

[789] Goochland Co. Deed Bk. 29, p. 131.

Issue: [PLEASANTS][790] 593. Martha A.[6], married, 26 Oct. 1829,[791] John A. Goolsby; 594. Joseph Edwin[6], born about 1803, farmer of Goochland County,[792] married, 12 Nov. 1828,[793] Elizabeth S. Davis; 595. Mary Jane[6]; 596. Henrietta M.[6]; 597. Thomas William[6], died 6 Sept. 1859 in Alleghany County, served in War of 1812,[794] of Rockbridge County, married (1), 4 April 1825, Susan H. Goodman, died 17 Jan. 1840, and (2), 19 May1842, Nancy Matheny, died 1889; 598. Margaret W.[6], married, as his (3) wife, 648.Tarleton Woodson[6] Pleasants; 599. Harris T.[6], married Sally Rowsey; 600. Elizabeth W.[6], married, (bond 16) June 1806,[795] Richard C. Bowles; 601. Philip Sidney[6], of Albemarle County, married, (bond 12) Dec. 1812,[796] 674. Elizabeth[6] Pleasants; 602. Lucius C.[6]; 603. Robert Lee[6], of Albemarle and later Goochland counties, moved about 1837 to Washington Co., Ark., married, (bond 21) Oct. 1806,[797] 673. Demaris[6] Pleasants; 604. Henry F.[6], born about 1795, of Rockbridge County, 1834,[798] later of Alleghany County,[799] married, 18 July 1833,[800] Sarah Ann Rowsey who married (2), 14 July1855,[801] John Smith

185. MARTHA[5] VANDEWALL (Martha[4] Pleasants, Martha[3] Cocke, Richard[2], Temperance[1] Baley) died 3 March 1781. She married, 3 Feb. 1756, Col. Turner Southall, born 25 June 1736, died 1791,[802] left will 14 April 1791-6 June 1791,[803] of Westham, Henrico County, tobacco inspector at Shockoe Warehouse, justice of Henrico County, vestryman of Henrico Parish, member of

---

[790] *Val. Papers*, IV, pp. 2295-96. Only 1, 2, 5, 6, 9, 11 and 12 are named in his will.

[791] Thomas P. Hughes and Jewel B. Standefer, *Goochland County, Virginia, Marriage Bonds and Ministers' Returns, 1816-1854* (Memphis, Tenn., 1972), p. 29.

[792] Goochland Co. 1850 census, p. 245 or 123, family 334-334.

[793] Hughes and Standefer, *op. cit.*, p. 81.

[794] War of 1812 pension, Thomas W. Pleasants, widow Nancy, W.C.1280, National Archives.

[795] Williams, *Marriages of Goochland County*, p. 9.

[796] *Ibid.*, p. 76.

[797] *Ibid.*, p. 77.

[798] Goochland Co. Deed Bk. 30, pp. 102, 129.

[799] Alleghany Co. 1850 census, p. 51 or 26, family 344-345.

[800] Rockbridge Co. Marriage Register 1, p. 290.

[801] *Ibid.*, p. 458.

[802] Southall Bible, in *T* VIII, p. 134, and John K. Martin Papers, *Virginia Genealogical Society Quarterly*, XI, p. 82, with variations.

[803] Henrico Co. Will Bk. 2, pp. 192-96.

the House of Delegates, 1778, 1780-85, and of the Senate 1785-90,[804] manager of the arsenal and foundry at Westham during the Revolutionary War.

Issue: [SOUTHALL] 605. Maj. Stephen[6], born 16 June 1757, died 2 March 1799 at Richmond,[805] Assistant Quartermaster General in Revolutionary War, wounded at Guilford Court House, 15 March 1781, original member of the Society of the Cincinnati, of "Whitehall," Goochland County and later of Richmond,[806] married, 1784, 146. *Martha[6] Wood* (see COX), born 12 March 1768, who married (2) George Frederick Stras; 606. William[6], born 4 Jan. 1759, died 13 Oct. 1759; 607. Ann[6], born 2 Nov. 1760, died 8 June 1830, married (1), (bond 7) Jan. 1784,[807] John Shelton and (2), 15 Dec. 1804,[808] Capt. Peter Foster, marine on the ship *Liberty* of the Virginia Navy, 1776, and later orderly sergeant in the 1st Virginia State Regiment, 1777-81,[809] who died 11 March 1833 in Hanover County, aged 74,[810] leaving will dated 10 March 1833;[811] 608. Philip[6], born 5 May 1763, died 27 Oct. 1790; 609. William[6], born 27 [or 22] April 1765, died 2 March 1796; 610. Pleasants[6], born 27 July 1767, died 6 March 1798, Richmond;[812] 611. Polina[6], born 20 [or 24] May 1769, died 9 Oct. 1819, married ____ Jones; 612. James Barrett[6], born 27 Sept. 1772; 613. Cynthia[6], born 12 April 1777; 614. John[6], born 12[or 21] Dec. 1777; 615. Elizabeth[6], born 19 June 1779, married, 13 May 1802 in Goochland County, Thomas Underwood.[813]

187. URSULA[5] PLEASANTS (John[4], Martha[3] Cocke, Richard[2]. Temperance[1] Baley) died 10 Jan. 1819 near Richmond, aged 77.[814] She married (1), 10 July 1766,[815] George Ellis, who came from "Old England," settled in Henrico County, merchant of Richmond, left will dated 21 Feb. 1771,[816] and died at Norfolk,[817] and (2), by 6 April 1776 when she was disowned by the

[804] Leonard, pp. 130, 138, 142, 146, 150, 154, 158, 162, 166, 170, 177, 181.

[805] *Virginia Argus*, Richmond, 5 March 1799.

[806] *V* XLV, p. 288.

[807] Lindsay, *op. cit.*, p. 76.

[808] *Virginia Argus*, Richmond, 19 Dec. 1804.

[809] Revolutionary War pension application, Peter Foster, S.4644, National Archives.

[810] *Enquirer*, Richmond, 22 March 1833.

[811] Shelton-Hine-Oliver papers, Virginia State Archives, Acc.24677(25).

[812] *Virginia Gazette and General Advertiser*, Richmond, 7 March 1798.

[813] *T* XIII, p. 66, which gives her birth as 1780.

[814] *Compiler*, Richmond, 12 Jan. 1819.

[815] Hinshaw VI, p. 203.

[816] Henrico Co. Miscellaneous Records VII, p. 2153.

[817] *Virginia Gazette*, 3 Oct. 1771.

Society of Friends for marrying out of unity,[818] Col. John Brooke, who died before 15 Dec. 1813 when the inventory of his estate was made.[819]

Issue: (by 1) [ELLIS][820] 616. John Woodson[6], paid by Virginia, 1790, for land appropriated for erecting the public buildings in Richmond,[821] later of Hanover County, married, 1808, Agnes Turner, who died 11 Oct. 1843 in Hanover County, in her 64th year;[822] 617. Catherine[6]; (by 2) [BROOKE] 618. Mary R.[6], died 15 March 1833,[823] married, 2 Nov. 1811,[824] William Young, inspector of Shockoe Warehouse at Richmond, who died 22 Dec. 1832.[825]

188. SUSANNAH[5] PLEASANTS (John[4], Martha[3] Cocke, Richard[2], Temperance[1] Baley) married, 7 March 1762,[826] Joshua Storrs who was a member of Brighouse Monthly Meeting in Yorkshire before coming to Virginia,[827] merchant of Richmond, member of the Henrico County Committee of Safety, 1775, and left will dated 18 10 month [Oct.] 1779.[828]

Issue: [STORRS] 619. Susanna Pleasants[6], married, (bond 3) July 1783,[829] Samuel Coleman; 620. Gervas[6], born 1771, died 1848, represented Henrico County in the House of Delegates, 1800-07, 1808-10,[830] married (1), (bond 18) Oct. 1791,[831] 645. Susanna Randolph[6] Pleasants, who died 12 Dec. 1793 at "Contention," Goochland County,[832] and (2), 18 June 1796,[833] Martha F. Trueheart, born about 1775;[834] 621. Hanna[6], married, by 7 April 1781 when disowned by the Society of Friends for marrying out of unity,[835] Maj. John

---

[818] Hinshaw, VI, p. 172.

[819] Henrico Co. Will Bk. 4, pp. 340-41.

[820] Named in will of grandfather John Pleasants, 1776.

[821] *H* XIII, p. 213.

[822] *Whig*, Richmond, 17 Oct. 1843.

[823] *Enquirer*, Richmond, 22 March 1833.

[824] *Virginia Argus*, Richmond, 7 Nov. 1811; Pollock, *op. cit/,* p. 184.

[825] *Enquirer*, Richmond, 27 Dec. 1832.

[826] Hinshaw, VI, p. 203.

[827] *Ibid.*, p. 214.

[828] Henrico Co. Proceedings of the Commissioners Regarding Records Destroyed by the British, p. 30-32.

[829] Lindsay, *op. cit.*, p. 21.

[830] Leonard, pp. 220, 224, 228, 232, 236, 240, 244, 252, 257.

[831] Williams, *Marriages of Goochland County*, p. 95.

[832] *Virginia Gazette and Richmond and Manchester Advertiser*, 16 Dec. 1793.

[833] *Ibid.*, 22 June 1796.

[834] Henrico Co. 1850 census, Western Dist., p. 1070 or 533R, family 434-455.

[835] Hinshaw, VI, p. 214.

Russell, born 1755 in England, died 31 Dec. 1820[836] at LaGrange, Ky., who served as sergeant and second lieutenant in the 1st Virginia State Regiment, 1777-80, and in 1807 settled at "Anita Springs," Henry Co., Ky.

189. MATTHEW[5] PLEASANTS (John[4], Martha[3] Cocke, Richard[2], Temperance[1] Baley) moved to Woodford Co., Ky., 1800, and died 1816. He married, Feb. 1784, Ann Railey, daughter of John and Elizabeth (Randolph) Railey, born 16 Sept. 1757, died 1826, Woodford County.

Issue: [PLEASANTS][837] 622. Susanna[6], born 2 Dec. 1785, died 1865 in Kentucky; 623. Caroline Fleming[6], born 27 July 1787, died 21 Feb. 1852, married, 1808, Col. William Mayo who was proprietor of a tavern in Versailles, Ky., and later in Shelbyville, Ky., and then moved to Cooper Co., Mo.; 624. George Woodson[6], born 1 July 1789, died 8 April 1812,[838] editor of the Frankfort, Ky., *Palladium*; 625. Peyton Randolph[6], born 19 April 1791, died 9 Nov. 1817 in Woodford Co., Ky.,[839] of Frankfort, Ky., married, 14 Oct. 1817, Ann Catharine Humphries; 626. Pauline[6], born 16 July 1793, died 1816, married Robert Johnston of Fayette Co., Ky.; 627. Benjamin Franklin[6], born 10 Nov. 1795, died 2 June 1879 at Washington, D.C., moved from Harrodsburg, Ky., to Washington, D.C., 1830, and was employed with the Treasury Department, married, Feb. 1817, Isabella McCalla Adair, born 1799, "Whitehall," near Harrodsburg, died 1869, Brooklyn, N.Y., daughter of Governor John Adair of Kentucky; 628. Elizabeth Randolph[6], born 9 Jan. 1796, died Dec. 1881, married, 1835, Douglas Young and resided in Woodford Co., Ky.

190. ARCHIBALD[5] PLEASANTS (John[4], Martha[3] Cocke, Richard[2], Temperance[1] Baley), born 11 Jan. 1746/7 in Henrico County, of Goochland County, served two tours in the militia during the Revolutionary War,[840] and left will 29 March 1836-19 Sept. 1836.[841] He married, 5 Aug. 1775,[842] 395. *Jane[6] Woodson* (see WOODSON), who died 29 Jan. 1821, aged 69.[843]

Issue: [PLEASANTS] 629. Virginia[6], died 28 March 1861 in Goochland

---

[836] Gravestone, no longer standing.

[837] William E. Railey, *History of Woodford County, Kentucky* (Frankfort, Ky., 1938), pp. 255-56.

[838] *Kentucky Gazette*, Lexington, Ky., 21 April 1812.

[839] *Reporter*, Lexington, Ky., 19 Nov. 1817.

[840] Revolutionary War pension application Archibald Pleasants, S.5939, National Archives.

[841] Goochland Co. Deed Bk. 31, p. 51.

[842] Jones, *op. cit.*, p. 39; Williams, *Marriages of Goochland County*, p. 76.

[843] *Richmond Compiler*, 2 Feb. 1821; *Enquirer*, 3 Feb. 1821.

County, aged 60, unmarried;[844] 630. Susanna[6], born about 1775, never married;[845] 631. Charles T.[6], not named in father's will; 632. Jane[6], unmarried in 1836; 633. Frederick[6], died 9 Oct. 1827,[846] of firm of Moncure, Robinson & Pleasants of Richmond, married, 8 Nov. 1812,[847] Sarah Maria[7] Eustace, daughter of 144. *Hancock[6] Eustace* (see WILLOUGHBY), of "Woodford," Stafford County, born 24 April 1793, died 24 April 1825;[848] 634. Archibald[6], born 16 Aug. 1781, died 13 Oct. 1854 at Richmond, merchant of firm of Ralston & Pleasants of Richmond, married, 19 Nov. 1812,[849] Mary Brend, born 1789, died 22 July 1846 at Richmond;[850] 635. John Woodson[6], died 31 March 1836,[851] of Richmond, married, 16 May 1807,[852] Elizabeth W.[7] Coleman, daughter of Samuel and 619. Susanna[6] (Storrs) Coleman; 636. Dorothy[6]; 637. Matilda[6], unmarried in 1836.

191. JOSEPH[5] PLEASANTS (John[4], Martha[3] Cocke, Richard[2], Temperance[1] Baley) left will 8 May 1785-4 July 1785.[853] He married, 10 Nov. 1768 at Curles, Henrico County,[854] 120. *Elizabeth[5] Jordan* (see JORDAN, Thomas).

Issue: [PLEASANTS] 638. Joseph Corbin[6], married, (bond 11) Dec. 1809,[855] Susan Burton, daughter of Daniel Burton; 639. Mahala[6]; 640. Clementina[6], married, (bond 7) Sept. 1795,[856] Thomas Burton, died 29 Nov. 1830; 641. Sophia[6], married, (bond 19) May 1802,[857] Thomas Woodfin; 642. Dorothy[6], married, (bond 28) Dec. 1789,[858] John Burch; 643. Jordan[6], of Caroline County, 1793, and Louisa County by 1811, left will 29 July 1837-9

---

[844] Virginia Dept. of Vital Statistics, Goochland County, Deaths.
[845] Goochland Co. 1870 census, Dover Twp., p. 43 or 1, family 12-12.
[846] *Enquirer*, Richmond, 12 Oct. 1827.
[847] *Enquirer*, Richmond, 5 Dec. 1812.
[848] *Enquirer*, Richmond, 26, 29 April 1825; Hayden, p. 277.
[849] *Enquirer*, Richmond, 5 Dec. 1812.
[850] *Whig*, Richmond, 24 July 1846.
[851] *Enquirer*, Richmond, 1 April 1836.
[852] *Virginia Argus*, Richmond, 20 May 1807; Lindsay, *op. cit.*, p. 67.
[853] Henrico Co. Will Bk. 1, p. 222.
[854] Hinshaw, VI, p. 203.
[855] Pollock, *op. cit.*, p. 129.
[856] Lindsay, *op. cit.*, p. 14. Miller, *op. cit.*, p. 261, gives 18 Sept. 1793.
[857] Lindsay, *op. cit.*, p. 95.
[858] *Ibid.*, p. 13.

Oct. 1837,[859] married Elizabeth Tyler, who was living 12 Nov. 1849.[860]

192. JAMES[5] PLEASANTS (John[4], Martha[3] Cocke, Richard[2], Temperance[1] Baley) of "Contention," Goochland County, died 23 Sept. 1824 in Goochland County, aged 86,[861] left will 27 May 1816-21 March 1825.[862] He married (1), 10 Jan. 1765,[863] 119. *Dorothy[5] Jordan* (see JORDAN, Thomas) and (2) Ann (Randolph) Scott Pleasants, widow of 98. *Daniel[5] Scott* (see COX) and 99. *John[5] Pleasants* (see JORDAN, Thomas).

Issue: [PLEASANTS] (by 2) 644. James[6], born 24 Oct. 1769, "Contention," Goochland County, died 9 Nov. 1836, Goochland County,[864] lawyer, member of House of Delegates, 1797-1802, clerk of the House of Delegates, 1802-11, member of the United States House of Representatives, 1811-19, and of United States Senate, 1819-22, Governor of Virginia, 1822-25, and member of the Constitutional Convention, 1829-30,[865] left will 28 Oct. 1836-20 Feb. 1837,[866] married, 8 May 1790,[867] Susannah Lawson Rose, born 24 Oct. 1771, died 1854;[868] 645. Susanna Randolph[6], married 620. Gervas[6] Storrs; 646. Paulina[6], died 10 April 1846 in Woodford Co., Ky.;[869] 647. Ann Scott[6], married, 26 May 1800,[870] Isaac Webster, possibly the Isaac who died 4 June 1816, aged 42, in Chesterfield County;[871] 648. Tarleton Woodson[6], left will 8 Aug. 1845-codicil 15 Jan. 1850-18 Nov. 1850,[872] married (1), 17 May 1803,[873] 145. *Sarah[6] Pleasants* (see JORDAN, Thomas), who died 11 Feb. 1809 in her 34th year,[874]

---

[859] Louisa Co. Will Bk. 9, p. 505.

[860] Louisa Co. Minute Bk. 1847-51, p. 337.

[861] *Enquirer*, Richmond, 28 Sept. 1824.

[862] Goochland Co. Deed Bk. 26, p. 91.

[863] Hinshaw VI, p. 203.

[864] *Compiler*, Richmond, 16 Nov. 1836.

[865] *Biographical Directory of the American Congress, 1774-1996* (Alexandria, Va., 1997), p. 1670; Leonard, pp. 207. 212, 216, 220, 223, 227, 231, 233, 235, 239, 243, 247, 251, 256, 260, 354; *Dictionary of American Biography*, XV (New York, 1935), pp. 6-7.

[866] Goochland Co. Deed Bk. 31, p. 109.

[867] Knorr, *Marriage Bonds ... Chesterfield County*, p. 97.

[868] Christine Rose, *Ancestors and Descendants of the Brothers Rev. Robert Rose and Rev. Charles Rose ...* (San Jose, Calif., 1985), pp. 98-99.

[869] *Whig*, Richmond, 28 April 1846.

[870] Williams, *Marriages of Goochland County*, p. 105.

[871] *Enquirer*, Richmond, 9 March 1816.

[872] Goochland Co. Deed Bk. 36, p. 134.

[873] Hinshaw, VI, p. 263.

[874] *Ibid.*

(2), 13 June 1812 in Hanover County,[875] Talitha Crew, who was born 18 Feb. 1788, and (3) 598. Margaret W.[6] Pleasants; 649. Martha W.[6], born 2 Dec. 1779, died 10 July 1849, "Canebrake," Woodford Co., Ky., married, as his (2) wife, 1819, Randolph Railey, born 14 May 1770, Chesterfield County, died 28 May 1837, "Canebrake";[876] 650. John L.[6]

194. JOHN[5] PLEASANTS (John[4], Martha[3] Cocke, Richard[2], Temperance[1] Baley), carpenter of Henrico County, died by 2 Oct. 1790.[877] He was condemned by the Society of Friends in 1781 for taking "the Test" and the next year was disowned for being concerned in the sale of a Negro and subscribing "the Test."[878] He married (1) Agnes ___[879] and (2), by 3 March 1764,[880] 42. *Sarah[5] Cox* (see COX).

Issue: [PLEASANTS] (by 1)[881] 651. Mary[6], married, 10 Sept. 1776 at Picquenoque, Henrico County, Jesse Hargrave,[882] born 8 July 1752,[883] of Caroline County, disowned by the Society of Friends with his brothers for holding Negroes in slavery contrary to the intent of their father;[884] 652. Susanna[6], married, 2 Aug. 1783, out of unity,[885] ___; (by 2) 653. Samuel[6], died 4 Oct. 1814,[886] printer of Richmond and editor of the *Virginia Argus*, public printer, 1804-14, married, 18 July 1795,[887] Deborah Lownes, born 19 Feb. 1773; 654. Ursula[6], lived in North Carolina, 1791;[888] 655. John[6], of Richmond, died 3 Aug. 1829, aged 43, in Chesterfield County;[889] 656. Elizabeth[6]; 657. Tarleton[6], of

---

[875] *Ibid.*, p. 238.

[876] Railey, *op. cit.*, p. 259.

[877] Hinshaw VI, p. 297.

[878] *Ibid.*, VI, p. 207.

[879] *Val. Papers* IV, p. 2295, identifies her as Agnes Woodson, but her place in that family has not been established.

[880] Hinshaw VI, p. 206.

[881] Henrico Co. Wills & Deeds 1750-67, p. 1022, deed of gift to his daughters Mary and Susanna, recorded 3 Aug. 1767.

[882] Hinshaw VI, p. 203.

[883] *Ibid.*, VI, p. 244.

[884] *Ibid.*

[885] *Ibid.*, VI, p.207.

[886] *Enquirer*, Richmond, 5 Oct. 1814.

[887] *Richmond Chronicle*, 21 July 1795; Lindsay, *op. cit.*, p. 67.

[888] Hinshaw VI, p. 207.

[889] *Whig*, Richmond, 11 Aug. 1829.

"Mahogany Grove," Hanover County, left will dated 24 Oct. 1835,[890] married, by 5 Dec. 1789 when dismissed for marrying out of unity,[891] ___ Quarles.

195. RICHARD[5] PLEASANTS (Richard[4], Martha[3] Cocke, Richard[2], Temperance[1] Baley), of Goochland County, married, 1 July 1762,[892] Ann Leprade, daughter of John Leprade.[893]

Issue: [PLEASANTS] 658. Jane[6], born 2 Nov. 1763,[894] married, (bond 2) May 1785,[895] Robert Blanks, first sergeant of Buckingham County militia, 1781, and settled in Buckingham County where he died before 1800[896] and she continued to reside;[897] 659. Martha[6], born 26 April 1765,[898] married, (bond 1) April 1786,[899] William Suddearth; 660. John[6], born 10 Jan. 1767,[900] of Goochland County; 661. Ann[6]; 662. Robert[6], of age by 15 June 1798;[901] 663. Temperance[6]; 664. Samuel[6]; 665. Union[6]; 666. Richard[6]; 667. Joanna[6].

196. JOSEPH[5] PLEASANTS (Richard[4], Martha[3] Cocke, Richard[2], Temperance[1] Baley) was probably the Joseph whose estate inventory was dated 24 Sept. 1814.[902] He married, 23 April 1772,[903] Mary Guerrant.

Issue: [PLEASANTS] 668. Reuben[6], named in will of his grandfather, 1778, probably the Reuben whose estate inventory was dated 1 March 1830,[904] married Sarah Gouty; 669. Daniel G.[6], married (1) Ann Ormond and (2), 14 Jan. 1819,[905] Susan L. Puryear; 670. Mary[6]; 671. Simeon[6], taxpayer in Goochland County, 1800; 672. Eudocia[6], married, (bond 30) Nov. 1795,[906] Hezekiah Puryear; 673.

---

[890] Copy, from family papers, in Miller, *op. cit.*, pp. 329-30.

[891] Hinshaw VI, p. 207.

[892] Jones, *op. cit.*, p. 39; Williams, *Marriages of Goochland County*, p. 77, bond 16 June.

[893] Presumably she was a child of a marriage prior to John Leprade's marriage to 64. *Temperance[5] Farrar* (see FARRAR).

[894] Jones, *op. cit.*, p. 274.

[895] Williams, *Marriages of Goochland County*, p. 7.

[896] John H. Wilson, *The Blanks Family*, II (Fort Worth, Texas, 1982), p. 49.

[897] Buckingham Co. 1810 census, p. 811; 1820 census, p. 48.

[898] Jones, *op. cit.*, p. 275.

[899] Williams, *Marriages of Goochland County*, p. 95.

[900] Jones, *op. cit.*, p. 275.

[901] Goochland Co. Deed Bk. 17, p. 235.

[902] Goochland Co. Deed Bk. 21, p. 713.

[903] Jones, *op. cit.*, p. 39. Williams, *Marriages of Goochland County*, p. 76, shows bond as dated 21 April 1771.

[904] Goochland Co. Deed Bk. 29, p. 160.

[905] Hughes and Standifer, *op. cit.*, p. 81.

[906] Williams, *Marriages of Goochland County*, p. 81.

Demaris[6], married 603. Robert Lee[6] Pleasants; 674. Elizabeth, married 601. Philip Sidney[6] Pleasants; 675. Samuel[6], married, (bond 28) Aug. 1817 in Powhatan County,[907] 305. *Elizabeth[6] Holman* (see BRANCH); 676. Joseph[6].

197. MARTHA[5] PLEASANTS (Richard[4], Martha[3] Cocke, Richard[2], Temperance[1] Baley) married, 17 Feb. 1767,[908] William Watson of Hanover County.

Issue: [WATSON] 677. Ann[6], born 21 Dec. 1767.[909]

199. THOMAS[5] PLEASANTS (Thomas[4], Martha[3] Cocke, Richard[2], Temperance[1] Baley) left will 3 July 1775-15 April 1776.[910] He married, 2 Jan. 1772,[911] Ann Parsons.

Issue: [PLEASANTS][912] 678. Sally[6].

203. ARTHUR[5] MOSELEY (Martha[4] Cocke, John[3], Richard[2], Temperance[1] Baley) chose Thomas Moseley as his guardian, Feb. 1738/9,[913] settled in Cumberland County, was captain of militia, and left will 16 Dec. 1769-23 July 1770.[914] He married Mary ___.[915]

Issue: [MOSELEY][916] 679. Arthur[6], merchant near Genito Bridge in Powhatan County, left will 1 July 1797-16 Aug. 1797,[917] married 711. Martha[6] Floyd; 680. Charles[6], died Jan. 1807,[918] captain of Buckingham County militia during the Revolutionary War, married, (bond 23) Nov. 1772,[919] Mary Povall; 681. John[6], died 1796-97 in Buckingham County, captain of Buckingham County militia during the Revolutionary War, married, (bond 21) Dec. 1772,[920] Martha

---

[907] *Val. Papers*, II, p. 1167.

[908] Jones, *op. cit.*, p. 82; Williams, *Marriages of Goochland County*, p. 104.

[909] Jones, *op. cit.*, p. 314.

[910] Goochland Co. Deed Bk. 11, p. 103.

[911] Jones, *op. cit.*, p. 39.

[912] His will names only daughter Sally, under age, but *Val. Papers*, IV, p. 2293, shows his children as Thomas and Ann.

[913] Henrico Co. Order Bk. 1737-46, p. 64.

[914] Cumberland Co. Will Bk. 2, p. 16.

[915] He may have married twice. If so, the children William, Benjamin and Edward were probably by his (2) wife. His widow Mary may have been a Lockett.

[916] John Hale Stutesman, "Sorting Out Some Moseleys," *The Virginia Genealogist*, XXXIII, pp. 65-70.

[917] Powhatan Co. Deed Bk. 2, pp. 365-68.

[918] Moseley Bible, Virginia State Archives, Acc.42042a.

[919] Elliott, *Marriage Bonds ... Cumberland County ...*, p. 95.

[920] *Ibid.*

Povall, who died about 1818 or later; 682. Prudence[6]; 683. Mary[6], died 9 May 1834, Lauderdale Co., Ala., married (1) 160. *John[6] Ligon* (see HARRIS, Thomas) and (2) Giles Fuqua, died 28 Sept. 1827, moved from Prince Edward County to Lauderdale Co., Ala., 1815-20, left will 2 Jan. 1826-3 Dec. 1827;[921] 684. (Daughter)[6], married 80. *Samuel[6] Branch* (see BRANCH); 685. William[6], died Sept. 1808, captain and major in the Continental Line, 1776-81, wounded at battle of Brandywine and taken prisoner at Charleston, S.C.,[922] member of the Society of the Cincinnati, Brigadier General of Powhatan County militia, Treasurer of Virginia, married, (bond 1) Dec. 1784,[923] Ann Irvine, born about 1764, died 18 Feb. 1845; 686. Benjamin[6], left will 2 Feb. 1791-9 May 1791,[924] lieutenant in the Continental Line during the Revolutionary War, married, (bond 29) April 1782,[925] 419. *Amy[6] Giles* (see BRANCH), who left will 7 Sept. 1818-9 May 1818;[926] 687. Edward[6], died July 1832,[927] soldier in the Revolutionary War, justice and major of militia of Powhatan County, married (1), (consent 26) Jan. 1787,[928] Rebecca Lewis and (2), (bond 16) Sept. 1806,[929] 575. *Obedience[6] (Branch) Wilkinson* (see BRANCH).

204. JOHN[5] MOSELEY (Martha[4] Cocke, John[3], Richard[2], Temperance[1] Baley) died 16 May 1800-29 Jan, 1802.[930] He married Elizabeth Williamson, daughter of George and Frances (Davis) Williamson.[931]

Issue: [MOSELEY][932] 688. John[6], of Charlotte County, died after 1819, married, 28 Jan. 1784,[933] 238. Ann[6] (Finney) Willson, born 5 Nov. 1759, died

---

[921] Alya Dean Smith Irwin, *Fuqua--A Fight for Freedom* (Houston, Tex., 1974), p. 11; Lauderdale Co., Ala., Will Bk. 5-6, 1825-32, p. 413.

[922] Revolutionary War pension application, William Moseley, widow Nancy, W.5385, National Archives.

[923] Earle S. Dennis and Jane E. Smith, *Marriage Bonds of Bedford County, Virginia, 1755-1800* (Bedford, 1932), p. 44.

[924] Powhatan Co. Will Bk. 1, pp. 195-96.

[925] Williams, *Marriages of Amelia County*, p. 78.

[926] Powhatan Co. Will Bk. 5, pp. 417-18.

[927] *Enquirer*, Richmond, 20 July 1832.

[928] Knorr, *Marriage Bonds ... Chesterfield County*, p. 88.

[929] Williams, *Marriages of Amelia County*, p. 78.

[930] Powhatan Co. Will Bk. 2, pp. 112-13.

[931] Leila Eldridge D'Aiutolo and others, *The Descendants of William Moseley* (n.p., 2000), I, p. 108.

[932] *Ibid.*, pp. 102, 157-59. Elizabeth, however, is not named in John[5]'s will.

[933] *Ibid.*, p. 157; Williams, *Marriages of Amelia County*, p. 71, bond 20 Jan.

13 Aug. 1826 in Charlotte County; 689. Arthur[6], died 1803, married (1), 24 Nov. 1777,[934] Nancy Trigg and (2), 10 May 1799,[935] Pamelia (Thorpe) Crump; 690. Frances[6], left will 26 Sept. 1820-16 Nov. 1820,[936] married (1) Hillary Moseley of Henrico County, who left will, now lost, dated 30 March 1770,[937] and (2) 539. *Thomas[6] Harris* (see BRANCH);   691. Benjamin[6], married Susannah ___, who died 18 Aug. 1820; 692. Elizabeth[6], married 237. John[6] Finney.

206. WILLIAM[5] MOSELEY (Martha[4] Cocke, Richard[2], Temperance[1] Baley) died before 28 March 1763 when administration on his estate was granted to his widow.[938] He married, (bond 4) Feb. 1755,[939] 220. *Mary[6] Watkins* (see HARRIS, Thomas), born 4 Oct. 1756, who married (2) John Cox, perhaps 88. *John[5] Cox* (see COX), resided in Buckingham County and as a widow with her son William Moseley in Powhatan County, and left will 3 Nov. 1820-20 Feb. 1822, stating she was in her 84th year.[940]

Issue: [MOSELEY][941] 693. Benjamin[6], born 2 Dec. 1755, died 26 July 1799, lieutenant of artillery in Continental Line during Revolutionary War,[942] of Buckingham County, married, 25 Dec. 1783,[943] 260. *Mary[6] Branch* (see BRANCH), born 1764, died 1848;[944] 694. John[5], born 7 Sept. 1757, died after 1820, married Rhoda Watkins and moved to Duck River in Tennessee;[945] 695. William[6], born 18 May 1759, died 29 May 1816, aged 52, left will 14 July 1814-19 June 1816,[946] married, 13 March 1788, Rebecca Clarke Townes, born 18 May 1765;[947] 696. Phebe[6], married 903. *Hezekiah[6] Morton* (see WOODSON);

---

[934] Dennis and Smith, *op. cit.*, p. 45.

[935] *Ibid.*, p. 49.

[936] Powhatan Co. Will Bk. 6, pp. 66-67.

[937] Bedford Co. Deed Bk. 6, p. 197.

[938] Cumberland Co. Order Bk. 1762-64, p. 133.

[939] Elliott, *Marriage Bonds ... Cumberland County*, p. 96.

[940] Powhatan Co. Will Bk. 6, p. 369.

[941] *Ibid.*; John Hale Stutesman, *Some Watkins Families of Virginia and their Kin* (Baltimore, 1989), pp. 172-83.

[942] Revolutionary War pension application, Benjamin Moseley, widow Mary, W.5387.

[943] *Ibid.*; Knorr, *Marriage Bonds ... Chesterfield County*, p. 88, bond 3 Nov.

[944] Gravestone, Eldridge graveyard, Buckingham Co., in *The Southside Virginian*, XIV, pp. 95-96.

[945] Letter of John T. Moseley, Shauqualak, Miss., 21 Nov. 1859, George Brown Goode Papers, Virginia State Archives.

[946] Powhatan Co. Will Bk. 5, pp. 94-96.

[947] Letter of John T. Moseley, 7 Feb. 1860, George Brown Goode Papers, *loc. cit.*

697. Elizabeth[6]; 698. Lydia[6].

207. EDWARD[5] MOSELEY (Martha[4] Cocke, John[3], Richard[2], Temperance[1] Baley), born 4 May 1718, died 3 Sept. 1808,[948] left will 20 May 1808-3 Oct. 1808,[949] was a justice of Charlotte County, vestryman of Cornwall Parish, 1765, and captain of militia, 1778. He married 108. *Amey[5] Green* (see CLAY).

Issue: [MOSELEY][950] 699. Martha[6], died in Henry County, married Thomas Bouldin, born 31 Dec. 1738 in Cecil Co., Md., left will 27 March 1825-11 June 1827,[951] of Charlotte County and later of Henry County, ensign in the Revolutionary War; 700. Mary[6], born 14 Oct. 1753, died 15 Feb. 1815 in Charlotte County, married, 15 Dec. 1770,[952] Mackerness Goode, Jr., born 12 Sept. 1744, died 20 Jan. 1814, who left will 5 Jan. 1814-7 Feb. 1814;[953] 701. Amey[6], married, (bond 15) Dec. 1772,[954] Capt. Joseph Collier, born 24 July 1749 in Hanover County, died 2 Feb. 1819 in Edgefield Co., S.C., left will 26 Dec. 1818-10 March 1819;[955] 702. Edward[6], died 21 March 1831, aged 74,[956] lieutenant of Charlotte County militia, 1781, married (1) ___ and (2), 2 June 1790,[957] Martha Dyson; 703. Hillary[6], born 1759-60, died 16 Oct. 1835,[958] captain in American Revolution,[959] left will 4 April 1835-2 Nov. 1835,[960] married (1), 11 Oct. 1785,[961] 311. *Ann[6] Bedford* (see HARRIS, Thomas), who died Aug. 1826 in Charlotte County,[962] and (2), (bond 24) Jan. 1827,[963] Sarah (Williams) Hutcherson; 704. Elizabeth[6], born 4 June 1759, died before 4 Oct. 1813 when

---

[948] William D. Ligon, *The Ligon Family and Connections* (n.p., 1947), p. 562.

[949] Charlotte Co. Will Bk. 3, pp. 95-96.

[950] Warren L. Forsythe, "Resolving Conflict Between Records: A Spurious Moseley Bible," *NGSQ* LXXXIV, pp. 180-99; Ligon, *op. cit.*, pp. 563-66; D'Aiutolo, *op. cit.*, pp. 171-85.

[951] Henry Co. Will Bk. 3, pp. 178-79.

[952] Knorr, *Marriage Bonds ... Charlotte County*, p. 32, as 15 October.

[953] Charlotte Co. Will Bk. 3, pp. 246r-247r.

[954] Knorr, *Marriage Bonds ... Charlotte County*, p. 16.

[955] Edgefield Co., S.C., Will Bk. C, p. 24.

[956] *Enquirer*, Richmond, 2 April 1831.

[957] Knorr, *Marriage Bonds ... Charlotte County*, p. 58.

[958] *Religious Herald*, 30 Oct. 1835.

[959] Ligon, *op. cit.*, II, p. 97.

[960] Charlotte Co. Will Bk. 7, pp. 200r-201.

[961] Knorr, *Marriage Bonds ... Charlotte County*, p. 59.

[962] *Enquirer*, Richmond, 18 Aug. 1826.

[963] Charlotte Co. Marriage bond.

Thomas T. Bouldin was granted administration on her estate,[964] married, 12 Dec. 1779 on a boat in Chesapeake Bay, Richard Bouldin, born 10 May 1744,[965] left will 4 March 1806-7 Jan. 1811;[966] 705. Rebecca[6], married (1), (bond 22) Dec. 1780,[967] William Johnston, and (2), 30 Oct. 1811,[968] Richard Davenport; 706. Letitia[6], died 14 June 1859 in Campbell County, aged 94,[969] married, 4 Jan. 1785,[970] Edmund Herndon of Campbell County, who died before 11 Oct. 1841 when the inventory of his estate was recorded;[971] 707. Arthur[6], died before 21 Nov. 1804 in Charlotte County,[972] married, 6 Aug. 1788,[973] Nancy Bibb, who married (2), (bond 4) May 1807,[974] John Blanks, who was hanged for murdering her and her daughter Sally; 708. Sally[6], married 13 Nov. 1788,[975] John Patrick; 709. William[6], born 3 June 1776, died 12 Dec. 1830,[976] moved, 1808, to Bedford Co., Tenn., then to Madison Co., Ala., and by 1820 to Morgan Co., Ala., married (1), (bond 17) Aug. 1797,[977] Ann Williams, who died 11 Sept. 1807, and (2) 15 April 1809, Temperance Vaughan, who was born 9 Aug. 1783 and died 11 June 1864 in Morgan Co., Ala.; 710. Tully[6], died young.

209. SARAH[5] MOSELEY (Martha[4] Cocke, John[3], Richard[2], Temperance[1] Baley) married ___ Floyd, perhaps Charles Floyd of Westover Parish, Charles City County, who left will 27 Sept. 1768-5 April 1769,[978] naming

Issue: [FLOYD] 711. Martha[6], married 679. Arthur[6] Moseley; 712. Mary[6], married ___ Miller, probably John Miller who was executor of Charles Floyd, and inherited land in Henrico County.

---

[964] Charlotte Co. Order Bk. 19, p. 144.

[965] Ligon, *op. cit.*, II (n.p., 1957), p. 104.

[966] Charlotte Co. Will Bk. 3, p. 159.

[967] Knorr, *Marriage Bonds ... Charlotte County*, p. 47.

[968] *Ibid.*, p. 21.

[969] *Lynchburg Virginian*, tri-weekly, 4 July 1859.

[970] Knorr, *Marriage Bonds ... Charlotte County*, p. 40.

[971] Campbell Co. Will Bk. 9, p. 37.

[972] Charlotte Co. Will Bk. 3, p. 95.

[973] Knorr, *Marriage Bonds ... Charlotte County*, p. 58.

[974] *Ibid.*, p. 7.

[975] Knorr, *Marriage Bonds ... Charlotte County*, p. 64.

[976] Memory Aldridge Lester, *Old Southern Bible Records* (Chapel Hill, N.C., 1960; Baltimore, 1974), p. 230.

[977] Knorr, *Marriage Bonds ... Halifax County*, p. 66.

[978] Charles City Co. Wills & Deeds 1766-74, p. 119.

BARKHAM-JENINGS

+1. Sir EDWARD[1] BARKHAM, son of Edward Barkham of Norfolk and his (2) wife Elizabeth Rolfe, was a draper of London who served as alderman, sheriff, 1611, and Lord Mayor, 1621-22. He was a member of the Virginia Company, to which he was readmitted 3 July 1622, and also of the East India Company and was knighted 16 June 1622.[1]

He married Jane, daughter of John Crouch of Cornbury, Hertfordshire, and died 5 Jan. 1633/4,[2] leaving will, 14 Jan. 1632/3-17 Jan. 1633/4,[3] which mentioned his house at Tottenham High Cross, Middlesex, but directed his burial in the church of Southacre, Norfolk.

Issue:[4] 2. Sir EDWARD[2]; 3. John[2], buried 16 Nov. 1597 at Tottenham; 4. Sir Robert[2], married, 24 Nov. 1625 at Tottenham, Mary, daughter of Richard Wilcox, who was buried at Tottenham 16 Dec. 1644; 5. Margaret[2], buried 15 June 1603 at Tottenham; 6. (Daughter)[2], married Sir John Gerrard; 7. Jane[2], married Sir Charles Caesar of Bennington, Hertfordshire, Master of the Rolls;[5] 8. Margaret[2], baptized 18 Dec. 1603 at Tottenham, died 1640, married Sir Anthony Irby of Boston, Lincolnshire; 9. Susan[2], died 1622, married Robert Walpole of Haughton, Norfolk;[6] 10. John[2], baptized 7 Dec. 1604; 11. Thomas[2], baptized 2 June 1606, buried 29 Nov. 1606.

2. Sir EDWARD[2] BARKHAM (Sir Edward[1]) was created a baronet 26 June 1623. He served as a member of Parliament for Boston, 1625-26, and was sheriff of Norfolk, 1635-36. He married, 31 July 1622 at Tottenham, Middlesex, Frances, daughter of Sir Thomas Barney of Redham, Norfolk, and his wife Julyan Gawdy,[7] who died 1 July 1667. He died at Tottenham 2 Aug. 1667 and both are buried at Southacre, Norfolk.[8]

Issue:[9] 12. Frances[3], baptized 16 Sept. 1624; 13. Sir Edward[3], 2nd Baronet,

[1] *Br. Gen.*, pp, 825-26; *V* XXII, p. 159.

[2] G. E. Cokayne, *Complete Baronetage*, I (Exeter, 1900), p. 219.

[3] P.C.C. 1 Seager, in *V* XXII, pp. 158-59.

[4] Daniel Lysons, *The Environs of London* ..., III (London, 1975), pp. 535, 541-42.

[5] George W. Marshall, ed., *LeNeve's Pedigrees of the Knights made by King Charles II* ... (Harleian Society, *Publications*, VIII; London, 1873), p. 88.

[6] Walter Rye, ed., *The Visitation of Norfolk, Made and Taken ... Anno 1563 ... 1613* (Harleian Society, *Publications*, XXXII; London, 1891), p. 302.

[7] *Ibid.*, p. 17.

[8] Cokayne, *loc. cit.*

[9] *Ibid.*

aged 6 in 1634, sheriff of Norfolk, 1667-68, died 1688 without issue, married (1) Grace, daughter of Sir George Manners, who was buried 30 March 1685 at Southacre, and (2) Frances, daughter of Sir Robert Napier, 2nd Baronet, who married (2) Henry Richardson, 3rd Baron Cramond, died at Norwich and was buried 10 Nov. 1706 at Didlington, Norfolk; 14. Joan[3], baptized 8 Sept. 1630; 15. MARGARET[3]; 16. ANNE[3]; 17. Mary[3], married, 24 June 1656 at Tottenham, Norton Curtis of Gatton, Surrey, who was aged 1 in 1619;[10] 18. Susannah[3], married Anthony Smithson of Gray's Inn;[11] 19. Sir William[3], 3rd Baronet, of East Walton, Norfolk, and Hatton Garden, London, baptized 28 Feb. 1638/9 at Tottenham, buried 28 Dec. 1695 at Southacre, Norfolk, married Judith, daughter of Sir John Halsey of Gladdesden, Hertfordshire, who married (2), 19 June 1697 at Westminster Abbey, John Holsworthy and was buried 19 March 1723/4 at Woolwich, Kent; 20. Lucy[3], baptized 20 Feb. 1639/40 at Tottenham; 21. Julian[3], baptized 22 Feb. 1641/2.

15. MARGARET[3] BARKHAM (Sir Edward[2], Sir Edward[1]) married Sir Edmund Jenings of Ripon, Yorkshire, who was baptized at Farnham, Yorkshire, 30 Nov. 1626, son of Jonathan Jenings and his wife Elizabeth Parker. He represented Ripon in the Parliaments of 1660, 1661, 1678 and 1680, and was sheriff of the city of York, 1675. He was buried at Ripon 1695.[12]

Issue: [JENINGS] 22. Jonathan[4], aged 10 in 1665, member of Parliament for Ripon, 1695-1701, died unmarried; 23. William[4], aged 7 in 1665, died 1707, unmarried; 24. EDMUND[4]; 25. Peter[4], aged 1 in 1665, died unmarried; 26. Anne[4], died 10 May 1691; 27. ELIZABETH[4]; 28. Mary[4], died in infancy.

16. ANNE[3] BARKHAM (Sir Edward[2], Sir Edward[1]) married Sir Jonathan Jenings, brother of her sister's husband. He was member of Parliament for Ripon, 1658-60 and 1688-95, and high sheriff of York, 1690. He was indicted 11 Jan. 1674/5 at York for killing George Aislabie in a duel, 10 January,

---

[10] Robert Hovenden, ed., *The Visitation of Kent, Taken in the Years 1619-1621* (Harleian Society, *Publications*, XLII; London, 1898), p. 89.

[11] Gerald Brenan, *A History of the House of Percy*, ed. by W. A. Lindsay (London, 1902), II, pp. 433, chart betw. Pp. 430-31. He was a younger brother of Sir Jeremy Smithson, 2nd Baronet, great-great-grandfather of James Smithson whose bequest resulted in the establishment of the Smithsonian Institution.

[12] William Dugdale, *The Visitation of the County of York* (Surtees Society, *Publications*, XXXVI; Durham, 1859), p. 58; J. A. Clay, ed., *Dugdale's Visitation of Yorkshire, With Additions*, II (Exeter, 1907), p. 201; *V* XII, p. 308.

but received the King's pardon.[13]

Issue: [JENINGS] 29. Margaret[4]; 30. Peter[4], admitted to Gray's Inn, Nov. 1687, left will dated 28 May 1707, naming 44. Edmund[6] Jenings as his heir.[14]

24. EDMUND[4] JENINGS (Margaret[3] Barkham, Sir Edward[2], Sir Edward[1]), aged 6 in 1665, died 2 June 1727,[15] was colonel of a troop of horse and commander of the York County militia, 1698, member of the Council, 1691-1726, Attorney General, 1680-91, Secretary of the Colony, 1702-12, 1720-22, and acting Governor of Virginia, Aug. 1706-23 June 1710.[16] He held 850 acres in York County and 200 acres in James City County, 1704. He married (1) Frances Corbin who died 22 Nov. 1713 in London,[17] and (2) Sarah ___, who died 27 March 1728.[18]

Issue: [JENINGS][19] (by 1) 31 ELIZABETH[5]; 32. FRANCES[5].; 33. EDMUND[5]; 34. Anne[5], died 8 Dec. 1691.[20]

27. ELIZABETH[4] JENINGS (Margaret[3] Barkham, Sir Edward[2], Sir Edward[1]) married, 7 April 1681,[21] Sir Roger Beckwith of Aldborough, Yorkshire, who was created a Baronet by Charles II, 15 April 1681, shot himself 6 Dec. 1700, left will 7 May 1690-28 Feb. 1700/1, and was buried at Ripon.[22]

Issue: [BECKWITH] 35. Sir ROGER[5]; 36. Sir MARMADUKE[5].

31. ELIZABETH[5] JENINGS (Edmund[4], Margaret[3] Barkham, Sir Edward[2], Sir Edward[1]), died 20 Jan. 1754, aged 60.[23] She married, as his (2) wife, Robert

---

[13] Clay, *op. cit.*, p. 201.

[14] *V* XII, p. 308.

[15] Bruton Parish Register. Clay, *loc. cit.*, gives 27 Dec. 1727.

[16] *V* XXIX, p. 382; Leonard, p. xx; Maurer Maurer, "Notes on the Honorable Edmund Jenings (1659-1727)," *V* LII, pp. 249-61.

[17] Clay, *loc. cit.*

[18] Bruton Parish Register.

[19] 33. Edmund[5] Jennings in his will made a bequest to his "nephew Edmund Jennings" of the Province of Maryland. No evidence to establish this Edmund's parentage has been discovered. See Arliss S. Monk, "Peter Jenings, Firebrand," *Maryland Genealogical Society Bulletin*, XXX, pp. 226-31.

[20] Bruton Parish Register.

[21] Joseph Foster, *Pedigree of the County Families of Yorkshire*, II, North and East Riding (London, 1874), "Pedigree of Beckwith ...," which incorrectly assigns the children of his two marriages.

[22] Clay, *op. cit.*, p. 111.

[23] Buried at St. Martin's Coney Street, York, England.

Porteus, born 1679, died 8 Aug. 1758,[24] of "New Bottle," Gloucester County, who held 892 acres in Petsworth Parish, 1704, was vestryman, 1706-20, member of the Council, 1714-15,[25] moved to York, England, married (1) 132. *Mildred[5] Smith* (see MARTIAU).

Issue: [PORTEUS] 37. Beilby[6], born 8 May 1731, York, England, died 14 May 1808, Fulham, England, graduated Cambridge University, B.A., 1752, chaplain to the king, 1769, Bishop of Chester, 1776, and after 1787 of London, married, 13 May 1785, Margaret Hodgson;[26] 38. Edmund[6], died 28 March 1752, clerk of Charles Co., Md., 1741-52,[27] left will 24 March 1752-30 July 1752,[28] married Martha Hawkins;[29] 39. Nancy[6]; 40. Dr. Edward[6], died before 1808, of York, England, married ___.

32. FRANCES[5] JENINGS (Edmund[4], Margaret[3] Barkham, Sir Edward[2], Sir Edward[1]) married Charles Grymes, who died before 5 March 1743/4 when Col. Philip Ludwell was granted administration on his estate,[30] of "Morattico," Richmond County, student at the College of William and Mary, 1705, sheriff of Richmond County, 1724-25, member of the House of Burgesses, 1728-34.[31]

Issue: [GRYMES][32] 41. Frances[6], married, 1737 at "Morattico,"[33] Philip Ludwell, born 28 Dec. 1716, died 25 March 1767,[34] of "Green Spring," James City County, member of the House of Burgesses for Jamestown, 1748-49, and of the Council, 1751-60,[35] who went to England and left will 28 Feb. 1767-6 May 1767;[36] 42. Lucy[6], born 26 April 1734, married 60. *Henry[5] Lee* (see BLAND).

33. EDMUND[5] JENINGS (Edmund[4], Margaret[3] Barkham, Sir Edward[2], Sir

---

[24] Tombstone, Ripon Cathedral, England, in *V* XIII, p. 312.

[25] Leonard, p. xxi.

[26] *Dictionary of National Biography*, XVI (London, 1921-22), pp. 195-97; Robert Hodgson, *The Life of the Right Reverend Beilby Porteus* ... (New York, 1811).

[27] Donnell MacClure Owings, *His Lordship's Patronage* (Baltimore, 1953), p. 150.

[28] Maryland Prerogative Court Wills 28, p. 380.

[29] *Ibid.*, p. 73, will of Henry Holland Hawkins, 14 April 1746-22 April 1751; Wills 29, p. 486, will of Joan Hawkins, 8 March 1755-25 Julu 1755.

[30] Richmond Co. Order Bk. 1739-46, p. 375.

[31] Leonard, p. 75.

[32] *V* XXVIII, pp. 90-91.

[33] *Virginia Gazette*, 29 July 1737.

[34] He was buried at Bow, near Stratford, England.

[35] Leonard, p. 81, xx.

[36] P.C.C. 183 Legard, in *V* XIX, pp. 288-89.

Edward[1]) died 3 [*sic*] March 1756, aged 59, at Bath, England.[37] He was educated at London and admitted to the Middle Temple, 23 March 1715. Returning to Annapolis, Md., in 1723, he was a member of the Lower House of the Maryland Assembly, 1728-31, of the Upper House, 1732/3-1752, and of the Council, 1733-53, Deputy Secretary of the Province of Maryland, 20 March 1732/3-1753, and Judge of the Land Office, 1732/3-1738, Collector of Patuxent, 1744-45, and was elected vestryman of St. Ann's Parish, 1728. He settled permanently in England, 1753,[38] and left will 10 March 1756-24 March 1756.[39] He married, 2 July 1728, Ariana (Vanderheyden) Bordley, daughter of Matthias Vanderheyden and widow of Thomas Bordley.

Issue: [JENINGS][40] 43. Ariana[6], born 1729, died 2 Feb. 1801, aged 71,[41] left will 28 Aug. 1800-7 Feb. 1801,[42] married John Randolph, born 1728 at "Tazewell Hall," Williamsburg, died 31 June 1784 at Brompton, Yorkshire, student at the College of William and Mary and at the Middle Temple, London, clerk of the House of Burgesses, 1756, Attorney General, Burgess for the College, 1774-75, judge of the Vice-Admiralty Court, moved from Williamsburg to England at the beginning of the Revolutionary War;[43] 44. Edmund[6], born Aug. 1731 at Annapolis, Md., died 27 July 1819 at Kensington, Middlesex,[44] educated at Eton and Cambridge University, of Lincoln's Inn, "constantly manifested his attachment to the rights of America ... and was obliged to depart the kingdom of Great Britain for such his conduct, and to reside during part of the said war, in other countries,"[45] married Elizabeth ___, died 19 March 1838 [or 1836] in her 80th year;[46] 45. Peter[6], died young; 46. Charles[6], died young.

---

[37] Pedigree filed with the College of Arms, in *V* XII, p. 309.

[38] *A Biographical Dictionary of the Maryland Legislature, 1635-1789*, II (Baltimore and London, 1985), p. 487.

[39] P.C.C. 72 Glazier, in *V* XII, pp. 306-07.

[40] George A. Hanson, *Old Kent: The Eastern Shore of Maryland* (Baltimore, 1876), p. 81.

[41] Inscription, churchyard, Kensington, Midx., notation in Jenings Papers Virginia Historical Society, Mss.1 J4105a.

[42] Copy, Virginia Historical Society, Mss. 2 R1523a.

[43] John McGill, *The Beverley Family of Virginia* (Columbia, S.C., 1955), p. 364; *Dictionary of American Biography*, XV (New York, 1935), pp. 362-63; Peter Wilson Coldham, *American Migrations, 1765-1799* (Baltimore, 2000), p. 590.

[44] Inscription, churchyard, Kensington, Midx., *loc. cit.*

[45] Maryland Laws JG #2, p. 375. Lands confiscated as British property during the Revolutionary War were returned to him.

[46] Inscription, churchyard, Kensington, Midx., *loc. cit.*

35. Sir ROGER[5] BECKWITH, Baronet (Elizabeth[4] Jenings, Margaret[3] Beckwith, Sir Edward[2], Sir Edward[1]), born 13 June 1682, died May 1743, of Aldborough, Yorkshire, sheriff of Yorkshire, 1706-07, left will 26 March 1730-Jan. 1749. He married, 10 Oct. 1705, Jane Waddington, born Dec. 1686 at Leeds, died Dec. 1713.[47]

Issue: [BECKWITH] 47. Joane[6], married Beilby Thompson of Escrick, Yorkshire; 48. (others)[6], who did not survive.

36. Sir MARMADUKE[5] BECKWITH (Elizabeth[4] Jenings, Margaret[3] Barkham, Sir Edward[2], Sir Edward[1]), born Jan. 1687, died 1780, was clerk of Richmond County, 1709-80. He married Elizabeth (Brockenbrough) Dickenson, daughter of William and Mary (Newman) Brockenbrough.[48]

Issue: [BECKWITH][49] 49. Tarpley[6], born 2 Oct. 1718, died 7 Nov. 1748; 50. Sir Jonathan[6], born 14 Nov. 1720, died 6 Dec. 1796, Richmond County,[50] married, 27 May 1753,[51] Rebecca Barnes; 51. Betty[6], born 15 Aug. 1723, died 7 April 1726; 52. Margaret[6], born 29 July 1725, married, as his (2) wife, Joseph Morton, born 1715, died 1759, of James City County, member of the House of Burgesses, 1756-58,[52] left will dated 18 May 1758;[53] 53. Mary[6], born 12 June 1727, died 3 Dec. 1755 in her 27th year,[54] married, as his (1) wife, Lawrence Butler of Westmoreland County, who left will 18 Nov. 1773-29 July 1777;[55] 54. Marmaduke[6], named in will of William Hodgkinson, 20 March 1746/7-5 Dec. 1748,[56] married Sybil Elsie;[57] 55. (probably) Roger[6], married, (bond 6) Jan. 1762, Winifred Miskell;[58] 56. Penelope[6], married Alexander Walker but died shortly after marriage.[59]

---

[47] George E. Cokayne, *Complete Baronetage*, IV (Exeter, 1904), p. 115.

[48] George Harrison Sanford King, *Marriages of Richmond County, Virginia, 1668-1853* (Fredericksburg, 1964), p. 13.

[49] North Farnham Parish, Richmond Co., Register, for nos. 48-52; Daniel Morton, "The Mortons and Their Kin," II (typewritten; St. Joseph, Mo., 1920), p. 463.

[50] *Virginia Herald*, Fredericksburg, 13 Dec. 1796.

[51] King, *loc. cit.*

[52] Leonard, p. 87; Margaret B. Kinsey, *Mountjoy Omnibus* (Baltimore, 2001), p. 57.

[53] King George Co. Order Bk. 3, pp. 1202-04.

[54] Tombstone, "Bleak Hill," Westmoreland Co., in Morton, *loc. cit.*

[55] Westmoreland Co. Deeds & Wills 17, 1773-87, p. 80-81.

[56] Richmond Co. Will Bk. 5, p. 564.

[57] Morton, *loc. cit.*

[58] King, *op. cit.*, p. 14.

[59] *T* XIV, p. 38.

BARNE[1]

+1. Sir WILLIAM[1] BARNE, born about 1568, of Woolwich, Kent, England, the son of Sir George Barne (1525-2 Jan. 1592/3), Lord Mayor of London, 1587, and his wife Anne Garrard (died 1611), daughter of Sir William Garrard, also Lord Mayor of London,[2] was knighted at Whitehall, 23 July 1603, and was a subscriber to the Virginia Company, having paid to the Treasurer £37.10.0 for three shares of stock.[3]

He married, May 1586, Anne Sandys, born 21 June 1570, died after 23 May 1629, daughter of Edwin Sandys (1519-10 July 1588), Archbishop of York, 1577-87, and his (2) wife Cicily Wilsford (died 1610).[4] She was a sister of Sir Samuel Sandys (28 Dec. 1560-18 Aug. 1623), whose daughter Margaret married Sir Francis Wyatt, of Sir Edwin Sandys (9 Dec. 1561-Oct. 1629), who was largely responsible for establishing representative government in Virginia, 1619, of George Sandys (2 March 1577/8-1643), the poet, a resident of Virginia, 1621-31, Treasurer, 1621-25, and member of the Council, 1625,[5] and of three other brothers and a sister.

Sir William[1] Barne died 7 May 1619. His widow married (2) Edward Poulter who died 1626.

Issue:[6] 2. ANNE[2]; 3. Sir William[2], married, Oct. 1618, Dorothy Manwood; 4. Robert[2], of Great Grimsby, Lincolnshire, married Elizabeth Twisden; 5. Thomas[2], of Woolwich, Kent, died before March 1629/30, unmarried; 6. Rev. Miles[2], died 1 Nov. 1670, aged 70, rector of Bishopsbourne, Kent, married, 1632, Jane Travers; 7. John[2], married Mildred ___; 8. George[2], married ___.

2. ANNE[2] BARNE (Sir William[1]) was bequeathed by her grandmother, Cicily (Wilsford) Sandys, £40 "towards her preferment in marriage".[7] She married (1), about 1610, 1. *Sir William[1] Lovelace* (see LOVELACE-

---

[1] Also BORNE, BARNES; *V* XXIX, pp. 110-24; Alfred Suckling, *The History and Antiquities of the County of Suffolk*, I (London, 1846), p. 95.

[2] Joseph Jackson Howard and George J. Armytage, *The Visitation of London ... 1568* (Harleian Society, *Publications*, I; London, 1869), pp. 5, 25.

[3] *R*, Va. Co. III, p. 318.

[4] *V* XXIX, pp. 231-43; Br. *Gen.*, pp. 991-94; Joseph Foster, *Pedigrees of the County Families of England*, I, Lancashire (London, 1873), chart. She is named in both her father's and her mother's wills.

[5] *CVR*, p. 24; Leonard, p. xxi.

[6] V XXIX, p. 123. Only Anne left descendants in Virginia.

[7] *Ibid.*, p. 234.

GORSUCH) and (2), 20 Jan. 1630/1 at Greenwich, Kent, Dr. Jonathan Browne, died Dec. 1643, who matriculated at Gloucester Hall, Oxford, 13 Oct. 1620, aged 19, received B.C.L. degree 3 Feb. 1624/5 and D.C.L. degree 30 June 1630, was rector of Shelley, Essex, 1621, St. Faith's, London, 1628, until sequestered, Hertingfordbury, Herts., 1630, was Dean of Hereford, 1636-43, and Canon of Westminster, 1639.[8] Her uncle Francis Barne of Woolwich in his will dated 23 May 1629 bequeathed to "my neece my Lady Lovelesse" 40 shillings to buy a mourning ring.[9]

Issue: (by 1) see LOVELACE-GORSUCH; (by 2) [BROWNE] 9. Anne[3], married Herbert Croft, born 18 Oct. 1603 at Great Thame, Oxfordshire, died 18 May 1691 at Hereford, studied at the English College at St. Omer, later conformed to the Established Church, matriculated at Christ Church College, Oxford, 25 July 1636, aged 34, rector of Uley, Gloucestershire, 1638, and of Harding, Oxfordshire, 1639, chaplain to the Earl of Northumberland in the Scottish expedition, 1639, canon of Salisbury, 1639, D.D. from Oxford, 1640, became chaplain to King Charles I, prebendary of Winchester, 1640, canon of Windsor, 1641, dean of Hereford, 1644, deprived of all his spiritualities during the Commonwealth, restored 1660, elected Bishop of Hereford, 21 Jan. 1662, published, 1674, *The Naked Truth, or The True State of the Primitive Church*, urging compliance with Protestant practices rather than the enforcement of uniformity through penalties and persecution, which caused much controversy.[10]

---

[8] Joseph Foster, *Alumni Oxonienses ... 1500-1714*, I (Oxford and London, 1891), p. 195.

[9] *V* XXIX, pp. 120, 123.

[10] Foster, *Alumni Oxonienses*, I, p. 351; *Dictionary of National Biography*, V (Oxford, 1973), pp. 105-07.

BATES[1]

*1. JOHN[1] BATES came to Virginia in the *Southampton*, 1623, and was listed in the muster of Abraham Peirsey at Peirsey's Hundred, 1624/5, as aged 24. On 15 Sept. 1655 he patented 50 acres of land lying "at the Middle Plantation butting easterly upon the Old paile [palisado]," which he had purchased from George Lake.[2] An entry in York County court records, 24 May 1660, recites that "John Bates of Middletown Parish in this county, an ancient inhabitant of this colony, being 62 years of age and thereby disabled to work, as formerly, is discharged from the countrey and county leavyes by this court for the future".[3] He married Elizabeth ___, named with his four children in his will, 2 Sept. 1666-24 Jan. 1667/8.[4]

Issue:[5] 2. Anne[2], called "oldest daughter" in her father's will, married ___ Belbie; 3. Alse[2], married ___ Deane, probably William who was a witness to the codicil of John[1] Bates' will; 4. GEORGE[2]; 5. JOHN[2].

4. GEORGE[2] BATES (John[1]) married Mary ___ who married (2) Edmund Brewer.[6] On 4 Dec. 1675 George Bates of York County, carpenter, joined by his wife Mary sold 70 acres upon Skiminoe Creek to John Edmondson of James City County.[7] He died 11 Jan. 1676/7,[8] leaving will 6 Jan. 1676/7-24 April 1677.[9] The nuncupative will of Mary Brewer, now lost, was proved 20 June 1720,[10] and seems to have been contested by her (2) husband's heirs. Edmund Brewer and his wife Mary joined with James and John Bates in a division, 11 Nov. 1697, of the land left by George[2] Bates' will.[11]

---

[1] *W*(1) VI, p. 122; Francis Burton Harrison, *The Harrisons of Skiminoe* (n.p., 1910), pp. 29-31.

[2] Patent Bk. 3, p. 377. This patent was renewed 5 March 1665/6 under the Royal government (Patent Bk. 5, p. 465 [566]). In 1697 Middle Plantation became Williamsburg and the capital of colonial Virginia was moved there from Jamestown, 1699.

[3] York Co. Deeds, Orders, Wills &c 3, 1657-62, p. 79.

[4] York Co. Deeds, Orders, Wills &c 4, 1665-72, p. 165.

[5] John[1] Bates may have been married twice, the married daughters named in his will being by a first wife and the two sons by Elizabeth. Such a case would eliminate problems of chronology which otherwise appear to exist.

[6] York Co. Deeds, Orders, Wills &c 10, 1694-97, pp. 406, 424.

[7] York Co. Deeds, Orders, Wills &c 7, 1684-87, pp. 74, 145-46.

[8] Bruton Parish Register, p. 85.

[9] York Co. Deeds, Orders, Wills &c 6, 1677-84, transcript, pp. 13-14.

[10] York Co. Deeds, Orders, Wills 1716-20, p. 622.

[11] York Co. Deeds & Bonds 1, p. 158.

Issue: 6. JAMES[3]; 7. JOHN[3]; 8. Mary[2]; 9. George[3], posthumous son, who in a deed of gift from his mother, 24 April 1677, is referred to as "being not borne at the death of his father,"[12] and on 24 Nov. 1693 petitioned to have John[3] Bates appointed his guardian.[13]

5. JOHN[2] BATES (John[1]) was given by his father his land by patent as "youngest son" and was buried 20 March 1701/2.[14] He married (1) Elizabeth ___ who joined him, 21 Aug. 1689, in selling 50 acres in Bruton Parish.[15] He married (2) Jane ___ who, as wife of John Bates, was buried 10 Nov. 1692.[16]

Issue: 10. John[3], buried 10 March 1686/7;[17] 11. Elizabeth[3], buried Nov. 1692.[18]

6. JAMES[3] BATES (George[2], John[1]) owned land in both York and New Kent counties and lived at Skimino in York where his mill was located. He became a Quaker under Thomas Story's influence and undertook preaching of the doctrine, visiting Europe and Ireland on a mission, 1717.[19] He left a will Jan. 1723/4-17 Feb. 1723/4.[20] He married Sarah Robinson, step-daughter of Joseph Glaister and widow of 10. *Benjamin[3] Jordan* (see JORDAN, Thomas), who left will 29 June 1750-20 June 1768.[21]

---

[12] York Co. Deeds, Orders, Wills &c 6, 1677-84, transcript, p. 14.

[13] York Co. Deeds, Orders, Wills &c 9, 1691-94, p. 267. He presumably is the George Bates granted liberty to marry Elizabeth Crispe, 15 Nov. 1707, and Grace Fleming, 8 Feb. 1711/2 (Hinshaw, VI, p. 155), and may be the father of John Bates of Charles City County who married, before 1 July 1739 (*ibid.*), Sarah Odan and died before 7 Jan. 1758 when it was reported that his widow was about to marry "a man of ill fame," ___ Evans. Children of John and Sarah include Elizabeth (married ___ by 4 Sept. 1773) and James (left will 11 Nov. 1806-17 Sept. 1807 [Charles City Co. Will Bk. 1, p. 689] naming brother Charles Evans).

[14] Bruton Parish Register, p. 99.

[15] York Co. Deeds, Orders, Wills &c 8, 1687-91, p. 318. This may be the 50 acres patented by John[1] Bates and devised to John[2]. John[2] also, however, assigned his interest in 50 acres near Middle Plantation to his brother George[2], 24 April 1674 (York Co. Deeds, Orders, Wills 5, 1672-76, p. 65), although this appears to be only a quit claim by John and George to any interst they might have had in a sale of 50 acres from John White to John Page of Middle Plantation.

[16] Bruton Parish Register, p. 95.

[17] *Ibid.*, p. 90.

[18] *Ibid.*, p. 95.

[19] Harrison, *op. cit.*, pp. 29-30.

[20] York Co. Deeds, Orders, Wills 1720-29, pp. 258-59.

[21] York Co. Wills & Inventories 21, 1760-71, pp. 418-19. *The Friend*, XXXIV (Philadelphia, 1861), 7 9 mo. 1861, states she died 9 Feb. 1756, aged nearly 70.

Issue: 12. JAMES[4]; 13. Mary[4], died by 1738; 14. Hannah[4], married 36. *Samuel[4] Jordan* (see JORDAN, Thomas).

7. JOHN[3] BATES (George[2], John[1]) of Bruton Parish in York County acquired numerous tracts of land with extensive acreage lying in York, James City and New Kent counties. These are described in his will, 25 Dec. 1719-16 May 1720,[22] which named "my Mother Mary Brewer," two sons, three grandsons, two daughters, 37 slaves, two mills and his "sheriff debts". The inventory of his estate, appraised at £1903.12.1/4, referred to him as a merchant, listed property at Poplar Spring Storehouse in James City County and described the contents of each room in his dwelling in York County.[23]

In 1698 the Quaker preacher Thomas Story recorded: "At Skimino in York County, at the house of John Bates, we had a meeting appointed, where no meeting had been before, and though he was not a Friend by profession, yet very forward to provide seats, saying his house, he feared, would be too small for the meeting, but he had room sufficient in his heart," and at the same meeting "both John Bates and his wife were convinced of the truth and from that time professed the same with us."[24]

John[3] Bates married Hannah ___.[25]

Issue: 15. JOHN[4]; 16. ISAAC[4]; 17. Hannah[4], born after 1698, said to have married Tarleton Fleming; 19. Ann[4], born after 1698, said to have married ___ Daniel.[26]

12. JAMES[4] BATES (James[3], George[2], John[1]) was bequeathed by his father land in York and New Kent counties and the mill at Skimino. He married, 23

---

[22] York Co. Deeds, Orders, Wills 1716-20, p. 605.

[23] *Ibid.*, pp. 628-38.

[24] Harrison, *op. cit.*, p. 30.

[25] York Co. Orders, Wills 1716-20, pp. 623, 656. She made an "affirmation relating to the will of Mary Brewer." She may have survived until Aug. 1748 when a Hannah Bates deeded land to Boble Ladd in Albemarle County (Albemarle Co. Order Bk. 1744-48, p. 415).

[26] Tarleton Fleming married Hannah ___, "said to have been a Miss Bates" (*W*[1] XII, p. 46), lived at Rock Castle, Goochland County, and left will 13 Oct. 1750-18 Dec. 1750 (Goochland Co. Deed Bk. 6, 1748-55, p. 113-14). On 21 March 1732/3 Hannah Daniel chose Tarleton Fleming as her guardian (Goochland Co. Order Bk. 3, 1731-35, p. 39). Hannah Daniel's brother John (*T* XII, pp. 211-13) had a wife Ann (Caroline Co. Order Bk. 1740-46, p. 215, 12 Aug. 1743; Order Bk. 1755-58, p. 323, 12 Jan. 1758). Although there appears to be a connection between the families, the evidence to establish the marriages of Hannah[4] and Ann[4] Bates is presently insufficient.

Nov. 1762, Elizabeth Hunnicutt,[27] who, as a Quaker, entered into bond, 19 June 1769, for administration of his estate,[28] and on 14 Oct. 1772, as guardian of their son James[5], sold Skimino Mill.[29] She married (2) Samuel Winston of Caroline County.[30]

Issue: 20. JAMES[5]; 21. Ann[5], married, before 10 July 1790 when disowned by the Society of Friends for marrying out of unity,[31] ___.

15. JOHN[4] BATES (John[3], George[2], John[1]) was bequeathed by his father land "whereon he now lives ... by name of 'Old Martine'", also "my grist water mill by name of 'O'Kenneck Mill,'" and a portion of a tract called "Poplar Springs" on the Chickahominy River. He left will 30 Nov. 1722-15 July 1723.[32] He married, 8 July 1713,[33] Susannah Fleming, daughter of Charles and Susannah Fleming, who married (2), by 14 Feb. 1735/6, 22. *John[4] Woodson* (see WOODSON) and left will 4 May 1757-15 Nov. 1757.[34]

Issue: 22. Fleming[5], married 50. *Sarah[4] Jordan* (see JORDAN. Thomas); 23. JOHN[5]; 24. Charles[5], married 34. *Elizabeth[4]* (*Branch*) *Woodson* (see BRANCH), widow of 26. *Stephen[4] Woodson* (see WOODSON); 25. JAMES[5]; 26. HANNAH[5]; 27. George[5], named as grandson in the will of Charles Fleming,[35] died young.

16. ISAAC[4] BATES (John[3], George[2], John[1]) was directed by his father's will to have his estate at 16 years and to be kept at school until that age. He was devised the remainder of the tract at "Poplar Springs" together with the furniture at "my house" there, and "my clock, my watch and my screwtore [escritoire]." He resided in Westover Parish, Charles City County, March 1728/9, when he sold a mill on Chickahominy River inherited from his father,[36] but settled in Albemarle County and left will 31 Dec. 1747-14 Dec. 1752.[37] He married Elizabeth ___.

---

[27] Hinshaw, VI, p. 100.
[28] York Co. Order Bk. 1768-70, p. 260.
[29] York Co. Deeds & Bonds 8, 1769-77, pp. 272-73.
[30] Hinshaw, VI, p. 229.
[31] *Ibid.*
[32] York Co. Orders, Wills &c 16, pp. 219-20.
[33] Hinshaw, VI, p. 155.
[34] Goochland Co. Deed Bk. 7, p. 209.
[35] Goochland Co. Deed Bk. 2, pp. 197, 206, deeds of John Fleming, April 1736.
[36] Charles City Co. Wills & Deeds 1725-31, p. 230.
[37] Albemarle Co. Will Bk. 2, p. 4.

Issue:[38] 28. JOHN[5]; 29. Isaac[5], married ___;[39] 30. Ann[5]; 31. Lucy[5]; 32. Elizabeth[5].

20. JAMES[5] BATES (James[4], James[3], George[2], John[1]) died 12 Jan. 1820.[40] He resided at "Lebanon," Charles City County, but was taxed for 173 acres in York County, 1791-1806.[41] He married, 4 May 1790,[42] Ann Ladd who died before 16 Feb. 1821 when the inventory of her estate was returned.[43]

Issue: 33. Joseph Denson[6], born 18 May 1791, died 17 Nov. 1872, of Charles City County, moved to Smithfield Monthly Meeting, Jefferson Co., Ohio, 1824, married, 29 June 1825, Mary P. Wood;[44] 34. James[6], born 24 Feb. 1792, died 15 Jan. 1820; 35. Henrietta Maria[6], born 1 March 1795, married, 10 Nov. 1812,[45] Jonathan Butler and moved to Dinwiddie County;[46] 36. Joshua[6], born 2 Aug. 1797, of Charles City County; 37. Elizabeth[6], born 9 Sept. 1799, of Charles City County.

23. JOHN[5] BATES (John[4], John[3], George[2], John[1]), born about 1716, died before 16 Oct. 1766 when Thomas Watkins and Benjamin Lankford were granted administration on his estate,[47] of Goochland County, moved to Lunenburg County, 1750, was Burgess for Halifax County, 1752-58,[48] captain of militia, 1753, justice, and vestryman of Antrim Parish, 1759, 1763. He married Elizabeth Alford, daughter of John and Grace (___) Alford, who was born 1 July 1719[49] and died 1757, Halifax County.

---

[38] One of the daughters married 154. *Abraham[6] Childers* (see WOODSON) of Cumberland County who, 27 May 1765, in declaring his insolvency listed among his possessions "An interest in right of his wife in one fifth part of 480 Acres of land in York County, late Isaac Bates, dec[d], Father of the s[d] Abraham's wife, which right is disputable" (Cumberland Co. Tax and Fiscal Records, Delinquent schedule, 1765, Virginia State Archives).

[39] She was a sister of the wife of 284. *Jesse[5] Woodson* (see WOODSON) (Cumberland Co. Deed Bk. 6, p. 30, 28 Oct. 1776).

[40] Hinshaw VI, p. 155.

[41] York Co. Land tax books, 1791-1806.

[42] Hinshaw VI, p. 155.

[43] Charles City Co. Will Bk. 2, pp. 482-83.

[44] Hinshaw IV, p. 464.

[45] Hinshaw VI, p. 155.

[46] Charles City Co. Deed Bk. 6, pp. 432-33.

[47] Halifax Co. Order Bk. 5, p. 383.

[48] Leonard, pp. 84, 86.

[49] St. Peter's Parish, New Kent Co., Register.

Issue:[50] 38. John[6], left will 19 April 1777-20 Nov. 1777,[51] of Halifax County, married Chloe ____; 39. Susannah[6], died Apr.-Dec. 1771 in Charlotte County, married John Fuqua, on whose estate she was granted administration 1 April 1771,[52] justice of Charlotte County, 1769-71; 40. Ursula[6], married, (bond 19) Jan. 1763,[53] John Wall, who served in 4th Virginia Regiment in Revolutionary War; 41. Elizabeth[6], married, (bond 16) Dec. 1762,[54] Charles Wall, who served in 2nd Virginia Regiment in Revolutionary War; 42. Ann[6], married, (bond 20) July 1769,[55] John Greenwood, who served in the Revolutionary War; 43. Hannah[6], married, (bond 1) April 1771,[56] Samuel Fuqua of Charlotte County, who left will 21 Aug. 1789-4 Jan. 1790;[57] 44. Joseph[6].

25. JAMES[5] BATES (John[4], John[3], George[2], John[1]), born 7 March 1721, died 9 Nov. 1785. He was left part of Poplar Springs, Charles City County, but later moved to Halifax County where he was a justice, vestryman of Antrim Parish, 1771, and acquired large land holdings. He married, 11 Nov. 1746, Winifred Hix, who was born 18 Jan. 1729 and died 7 Feb. 1790.[58]

Issue:[59] 45. Fleming[6], born 22 Nov. 1747, died 22 Nov. 1804, left will 12 March 1801-2 July 1804,[60] captain of Halifax County militia, 1781,[61] moved to Abbeville Dist., S.C., married, 15 Feb. 1787, Margaret McCarter, died 3 July 1841; 46. William[6], born 23 Nov. 1749, of Halifax County, 13 April 1787, when he sold 100 acres on Birches Creek;[62] 47. Samuel[6], born 29 May 1752, of Pittsylvania County, 11 April 1791, when he sold 200 acres on Catawba and

---

[50] Alya Dean Smith Irwin, *Fuqua–A Fight for Freedom* (n.p., 1974), pp. 99-109.

[51] Halifax Co. Will Bk. 1, p. 205.

[52] Charlotte Co. Order Bk. 2, p. 463.

[53] Catherine Lindsay Knorr, *Marriage Bonds and Ministers' Returns of Halifax County, Virginia, 1753-1800* (Pine Bluff, Ark., 1957), p. 98.

[54] *Ibid.*

[55] *Ibid.*, p. 38.

[56] Catherine Lindsay Knorr, *Marriage Bonds and Ministers' Returns of Charlotte County, Virginia, 1764-1815* (Pine Bluff, Ark., 1951), p. 30.

[57] Charlotte Co. Will Bk. 1, p. 425.

[58] James Bates Bible, in *The Bates Booster*, III, no. 2, March 1974, pp. 4-5.

[59] *Ibid.*; Douglas Register for first five children.

[60] Abbeville Co., S.C., Estate Papers, Box 105, packet 2655, in Willie Pauline Young, *Abstracts of Old Ninety-six and Abbeville District Wills and Bonds* (Abbeville, S.C., 1950), p. 380.

[61] *NGSQ* XXXI, p. 10.

[62] Halifax Co. Deed Bk. 14, pp. 72-73.

Terrible creeks,[63] married, (bond 1) Sept. 1790,[64] Biddy East; 48. Stephen[6], born 24 March 1754, moved to Abbeville Dist., S.C., left will 25 Aug. 1788-8 Oct. 1788;[65] 49. Daniel[6], born 6 July 1756, of Halifax County, 6 Nov. 1787, when Fleming[6] sold to him and Nathaniel[6] 200 acres on branches of Catawba and Terrible creeks but of Pittsylvania County, 1 Nov. 1793, when they sold 254 acres on the north fork of Terrible Creek,[66] married, (bond 25) Feb. 1782,[67] Jane Snelson; 50. Sarah Fleming[6], born 15 March 1759, deeded with Charles[6] 200 acres on the south fork of Catawba Creek by Fleming[6], 2 Nov. 1787,[68] married, (bond 27) Sept. 1790,[69] Philip Vaughan; 51. James[6], born 10 May 1761, of Halifax County; 52. Nathaniel[6], born 30 April 1763, of Halifax County; 53. Matthew[6], born 7 Aug. 1765, died 1800, married, 1 Jan. 1789, Mary Bowles Jones, born 14 Oct. 1769;[70] 54. Charles[6], born 25 May 1768, died 1827, of Halifax County, sold, 25 April 1795, to Philip and Sarah Fleming Vaughan the land deeded to him and Sarah Fleming[6] by Fleming[6],[71] married, (bond 27) July 1789,[72] Mary Martin; 55. Elizabeth[6], born 26 Oct. 1770.

26. HANNAH[5] BATES (John[4], John[3], George[2], John[1]) was left land in New Kent and Charles City counties. She married, (bond 23) Dec. 1745,[73] Robert Easley, son of John Easley.[74] He died before 1 Feb. 1750 when Hannah was granted administration on his estate.[75]

Issue: [EASLEY] 56. Susannah[6], for whom Hannah Easley produced accounts as her guardian, 7 Aug. 1767.[76]

28. JOHN[5] BATES (Isaac[4], John[3], George[2], John[1]) was, 10 May 1759, conveyed by John Cannon 250 acres which Isaac[4] had agreed to purchase before

---

[63] Halifax Co. Deed Bk. 16, pp. 365-66.

[64] Knorr, *Marriage Bonds ... Halifax County*, p. 6.

[65] Abbeville Co., S.C., Estate Papers, Box 5, packet 83, in Young, *op. cit.*, p. 18.

[66] Halifax Co. Deed Bk. 14, pp. 581-82; Deed Bk. 16, pp. 365-66.

[67] Knorr, *Marriage Bonds ... Halifax County*, p. 6.

[68] Halifax Co. Deed Bk. 14, pp. 582-84.

[69] Knorr, *Marriage Bonds ... Halifax County*, p. 96.

[70] Jones Bible, Virginia State Archives, Acc.20868.

[71] Halifax Co. Deed Bk. 16, pp. 466-68.

[72] Knorr, *Marriage Bonds ... Halifax County*, p. 6.

[73] Kathleen Booth Williams, *Marriages of Goochland County, Virginia, 1733-1815* (n.p., 1960), p. 26.

[74] Chesterfield Co. Deed Bk. 1, p. 518.

[75] Chesterfield Co. Order Bk. 1, p.79.

[76] Chesterfield Co. Order Bk. 4, p. 79.

his death, the deed reserving to the widow Elizabeth Bates her dower.[77] As a resident of Buckingham County, 6 Nov. 1776, he sold, as son and heir of Isaac Bates, 481 acres in York County.[78] He was a captain of home guards and served in the Continental Line, 1777-80. About 1780 he moved to White's Mill, Madison Co., Ky.[79] He married, Dec. 1761, Sarah Fearn, who as a widow lived at Richmond, Ky., and died there at a very advanced age.[80]

Issue:[81] 57. Thomas[6], born 2 Dec. 1762, left will 7 Nov. 1844-codicil 8 Nov. 1845-6 Dec. 1847,[82] married Judith Walker;[83] 58. Mary[6], born 17 Nov. 17_; 59. Eliza[6], born 27 Feb. 1770; 60. Frances[6], born 7 July 1772, married, 13 Jan. 1802,[84] Samuel Cochran; 61. Jennie[6], born 4 Jan. 1775, married William Walker; 62. Sarah[6]. born 5 Feb. 1776, married, 24 Nov. 1803,[85] William Donaldson; 63. John[6], born Dec. 1781, left will 29 Sept. 1836-May 1837,[86] married, 18 Jan. 1809,[87] Susannah Keith; 64. Lucy Lee[6], born 27 July 1784, left will 24 Jan. 1848-12 Jan. 1863,[88] married, 1 March 1806,[89] Stephen Watkins Walker, born 1755, left will 17 Nov. 1816-16 Dec. 1816;[90] 65. Daniel[6], born 10 Dec. 1787, died 14 Sept.. 1844, murdered by his brother-in-law, left will 25 June 1844-28 Dec. 1844,[91] and another made on his death bed, married, 21 Aug. 1824

---

[77] Albemarle Co. Deed Bk. 2, pp. 120-21.

[78] York Co. Deeds & Bonds 8, pp. 525-27.

[79] Onward Bates, *Bates, et al of Virginia and Missouri* (Chicago, 1914), p. 106.

[80] Elizabeth Lee Fearn Cabell Ferneyhough and Elizabeth Lee Lusk, *The Fearns of Virginia and Some Allied Families* (Richmond, 1973), p. 27.

[81] Bates Prayer Book, in *The Bates Booster*, IV, no. 5, Sept. 1975, p. 3. *Ibid.*, IX, no. 2, March 1980, p. 3, adds Mary, born 12 Nov. 17__, between Thomas and Eliza, but XII, no. 1, Jan. 1983, shows born 12 Nov. 1779.

[82] Madison Co., Ky., Will Bk. 1, p. 281.

[83] Madison Co., Ky., Will Bk. A, p. 414, in Charles M. Franklin, *Madison Co., Kentucky, Wills and Estates, 1785-1812* (Indianapolis, 1986), p. 49.

[84] Madison Co., Ky., Marriage Register 1, p. 27, in *The Register of the Kentucky Historical Society*, XXXVII, p. 192.

[85] Madison Co., Ky., Marriage Register 1, p. 30, in *ibid.*

[86] Clay Co., Ky., Will Bk. 1, pp. 73-74.

[87] Madison Co., Ky., Marriage Register 1, p. 36, in *The Register of the Kentucky Historical Society*, XXXVII, p. 193.

[88] Madison Co., Ky., Will Bk. O, p. 618.

[89] Madison Co., Ky., Marriage Register 1, p. 41, in *The Register of the Kentucky Historical Society*, XXXVII, p. 193.

[90] Madison Co., Ky., Will Bk. B, pp. 330-31.

[91] Clay Co., Ky., Will Bk. 1, pp. 127-28, nuncupative will and revocation, 19 Sept. 1844.

in Clay Co., Ky., Mary Buford Walker, born 22 March 1805, died 6 Sept. 1879.[92]

---

[92] *The Bates Booster*, XII, no. 1, Jan. 1883, pp. 2-3, 5.

BAYLY[1]

*1. JOHN[1] BAYLY, who transported five servants to Virginia in the *William and Thomas*, 24 Aug. 1618,[2] is listed among the dead at James City, 16 Feb. 1623/4.[3] His daughter Mary[2] survived him and fell heir to his dividend of land according to a patent for 710 acres issued 1 Aug. 1643 to "Randall Holt, Sonn & Lawful heire of Mary Bayley, late of Hogg Island, sole daughter and heire of John Bayly of the s^d Island."[4] Of this acreage, 490 acres had been granted to the said Mary "by the name of Mary Bayly, Orphant," 20 Feb. 1619/20.

On 28 June 1624 "Robert Evers as gardian to Mary Baylie, Claymeth by Pattent ye whole Islande, as having by his Pattent A Clause to purchase ye whole of ye Company wch now at this Courte by the voyce of Mr Thresurer [Treasurer] he offers to doe."[5] The Island, originally estimated to contain 490 acres, was found upon survey to include 700 acres, and according to a provision in the original patent granted Bayly, his heirs were permitted to acquire the additional acreage through claim to the five headrights mentioned.[6]

The young heiress was under age, 23 Oct. 1626, when Edward Grindon, acting as attorney "under the hand and seale of Richard Bailye guardian to Mary Bailye daughter and heire to John Bailye late planter here in Virginia", leased Hog Island to "Sir George Yeardley, Knt., for the terme of three yeares, or longer if soe bee the child doe not then come to age."[7]

Although Hog Island has changed owners numerous times since the Bayly-Holt ownership, there is still standing a holly tree estimated to be 475 years old and once said to be the largest specimen of its species in North America, although now much diminished by age.[8]

---

[1] Also Bailey, Bayley, Baley, Bailye, etc.

[2] Patent Bk. 1, p. 880.

[3] Hotten, p. 191.

[4] Patent Bk. 1, p. 880. Ten of the 710 acres patented were on James Island (Jamestown). See patent to Robert Marshall, 20 Sept. 1628, of land on James Island, adjoining Mary Bayly (*ibid.*, p. 92).

[5] *MCGC*, p. 17. Hog Island under modern survey includes about 4000 acres.

[6] They were Hugh Price, William Done (or Dove), Phillip Roper, Henry Broughton and Robert Reddinge.

[7] *MCGC*, p. 122.

[8] Representatives of the Arnold Arboretum examined the tree, 1930, and from its known growth estimated its age and comparative size.

Issue: 2. MARY[2].

2. MARY[2] BAYLY (John[1]) married 1. *Randall[1] Holt* and died before Aug. 1643.

Issue: see HOLT.

BEHEATHLAND[1]

*1. ROBERT[1] BEHEATHLAND came to Virginia in one of the three ships, *Susan Constant*, *Godspeed* or *Discovery* which sailed from the Thames Dec. 1606 and reached Jamestown 13 May 1607. In an account of the first settlement taken from the writings left by contemporaries, among them Thomas Studly, "Cape-Merchant," the "names of them that were the first planters" are given according to their stations in life. In the list of "Gentlemen" is the name of Robert Beheathland.[2] He was the son of Richard Beheathland of the Parish of St. Endelyon, Cornwall, Gent., who left will at Bodman, 8 Oct. 1631-16 Oct. 1635.[3]

Robert[1] Beheathland was among those who accompanied Capt. John Smith on a visit to Powhatan at his seat "Werowocomoco" on the Pamunkey (York) River, Feb. 1607/8,[4] and was a member of the party setting forth in the *Discovery* barge, 29 Dec. 1608, on a second visit to Powhatan.[5] En route, on account of the weather, the party put in at Kecoughtan (Hampton) and the first Christmas of which there is a record in the new world was spent there in company with the Indians.

> The next day being lodged at Kecoughtan 6 or 7 daies, the extreame wind, rain, frost and snow caused us to keepe Christmas amongst the Salvages: where wee were never more merrie, nor fedde on more plentie of good oysters, fish, wild foule and good bread; nor never had better fires in England then in the drie warme Smokie houses of Kecoughtan.[6]

Beheathland was also of the party which visited the Indian chief Opecancanough on the Pamunkey, 1609, and the settlers, fearful of treachery

---

[1] Violet Noland Gray, *Genealogical History of Robert Beheathland, Gentleman* (Baltimore, 1978); John Bailey Calvert Nicklin, "Descendants of Captain Robert Beheathland," W (2) IX, pp. 60-63, 175-85; Alice Elizabeth Trabue, "More Descendants of Captain Robert Beheathland of Jamestown and of Major Francis Dade," W (2) XII, pp. 26-38.

[2] Smith, *Tra.* I, p. 93

[3] J. A. Whitmore and A. W. Hughes-Clarke, *London Visitation Pedigrees* (Harleian Society, *Publications*, XCII; London, 1940), p. 18. The family arms are given (without tinctures) as a chevron between three escallops. The early registers of the Parish of St. Endelyon are lost.

[4] Smith, *Tra.* II, p. 404.

[5] *Ibid.*, I, pp. 131-32.

[6] *Ibid.*; Conway Whittle Sams, *The Conquest of Virginia, the Second Attempt* (Norfolk, 1929), pp. 529-31. Christmas-tide was celebrated up to 6 January, the feast of the Epiphany.

even then, placed "Master Powell and Master Beheathland" on guard.[7] By 1620 Capt. Robert[1] Beheathland had returned to England, for he is recorded there as one of the signers of a petition presented to the Royal Council requesting that a permanent governor for Virginia be appointed and expressing a willingness to return there if this was done.[8]

Robert[1] Beheathland died by 1627 and his widow *Mary (whose maiden name is not known) had married (2) *Lieut. Thomas Flint of Warwick River,[9] for on 14 March 1628/9 "Mary Flint, ancient planter, now wife of Thomas Flint, Gent. of Warwick river" was granted 100 acres in the corporation of Elizabeth City, "commonly called Fox Hill."[10] Mary Flint's identity is established by an entry in the *Minutes of the Council and General Court,* Nov. 1628, when Dorothy[2] Beheathland is mentioned as Thomas Flint's "daughter-in-law" (step-daughter).[11] Mrs. Mary Flint was living 9 April 1651[12] but was dead by 18 Oct. 1670.[13]

Issue: 2. John[2], of St. Endelyon, Cornwall, whose will, 15 June 1636-22 Oct. 1639,[14] says he is about to go to his mother in Virginia; 3. MARY[2]; 4. DOROTHY[2].

3. MARY[2] BEHEATHLAND (Robert[1]) married Capt. Thomas Bernard who owned land, 1631, in the area which later became Warwick County. His patent for 1050 acres, 16 Dec. 1641, recites that the land was "adjacent to Captain Thomas Flint Whereon stands the dwelling house of said Bernard."[15]

---

[7] Smith, *Tra.,* I, p. 142. Opecancanough was said to have been the originator of the plot which culminated in the massacre of 22 March 1621/2 in which 347 white settlers were slain.

[8] *R,* Va. Co. III, p. 231.

[9] Thomas Flint (Flynt) came in the *Diana,* 1618, was living at "Bucke Row" in Elizabeth City, 1623/4 (Hotten, p. 183), patented 1000 acres "upon the southern shoare of Warwick River, adjoining a patent granted to John Rolfe Esq. dec'd. & Capt. Wm. Pierce," 20 Sept. 1628 (Patent Bk. 1, p. 59), and was a member of the House of Burgesses, representing Warwick River, 1629-30, 1640, 1643, Keith's Creek to Mulberry Island and Saxon's Goal, 1631-32, Stanley Hundred, 1632, Denbigh, 1633, and Warwick, 1647-48 (Leonard, pp. 8-12, 18, 21, 26). Descendants, if any, are not known.

[10] Patent Bk. 1, p. 73.

[11] *MCGC,* p. 177.

[12] Warwick Co. Orders 1648-51, p. 16.

[13] *MCGC,* p. 233.

[14] P.C.C. 157 Harvey; Colonial Records Project Survey Report 3985 (4184). The record says he died abroad, unmarried.

[15] Patent Bk. 1, p. 761.

Thomas Bernard served as a member of the House of Burgesses from Warwick 1644-46[16] and was deceased by 10 Nov. 1651, the date of the will of Robert Nicholson of London, merchant, who made a bequest of gloves to "Mrs. Mary Bernard of Warwick River, widow, and to her daughters" and left a diamond ring and a gold ring with the motto *Idem qui pridem* to "Mrs. Veheath Land Vernald (Mrs. Vernald being the daughter of Mrs. Mary Vernald of Warwick River, widow)."[17]

Issue [BERNARD]: 5. BEHEATHLAND[2]; 6. (Daughter)[2].[18]

4. DOROTHY[2] BEHEATHLAND (Robert[1]) was living at Kecoughtan, 1626, when she appeared as a witness in a trial of a woman "accompted a witch amongst all them at Kicotan"[19] and in 1628 was living at the home of her step-father Thomas Flint of Warwick River. She married, as his (2) wife, *1. Randall[1] *Crew.*

Issue: see CREW.[20]

5. BEHEATHLAND[3] BERNARD (Mary[2] Beheathland, Robert[1]), born about 1635, married (1), 1652, Capt. Francis Dade, alias Maj. John Smith, son of William Dade (died 22 Feb. 1659/60, aged 80) of Tannington, Suffolk, and of Ipswich, and his wife Mary Wingfield (died 3 Feb. 1624/5) of Crofield, Suffolk.[21] As John Smith he served as a member from Warwick County and as

---

[16] Leonard, pp. 22-24.

[17] P.C.C. 228 Bowyer, in Colonial Records Project Survey Report 4106 (4308) and Waters, *Gleanings*, I, p. 100. The will was proved 26 Aug. 1652, the testator having died abroad, and also mentions the Mathews family of Virginia.

[18] Claims that Thomas and Mary[2] (Beheathland) Bernard had a daughter Margaret, identified as either wife of Daniel Gaines of Essex County (who died 1684 with son Bernard and daughters Margaret [probably married Francis Slaughter] and Mary [married John Catlett]) or as wife successively of John Prosser, Simon Miller, Hugh French and John Somerville are unfounded. See Margaret R. Amundson, "Margaret Prosser Miller French Somerville and Elizabeth Catlett: A Correction," *The Virginia Genealogist*, XXXVIII, pp. 22-24, and "Daniel Gaines of Colonial Virginia," *The Virginia Genealogist*, XLVII, pp. 226-36.

[19] *MCGC*, p. 112.

[20] The descendants of 3. Mary[2] Beheathland use Beheathland as a given name for women, while the descendants of 4. Dorothy[2] Beheathland use it as a given name for men.

[21]*Genealogical Data Relating to the Family of Dade of Suffolk* (London, 1888), quoted in Gray, *op. cit.*, pp. 28-29; Joseph Jackson Howard and Robert Hovenden, *Some Pedigrees From the Visitation of Kent, 1663-68* (London, 1887), pp. 95-98. The will of William Dade, 10 Oct. 1655-26 April 1660 (P.C.C. 35 Nabbs, in Howard and Hovenden, *op. cit.*, p. 121), gave £300 to his son Francis.

Speaker of the House of Burgesses, 1658.[22] On 20 Jan. 1659/60 "Major John Smyth of Patomak in Westmoreland County" gave a power of attorney to Maj. Edward Griffith of Mulberry Island, Warwick County, and on 13 Feb. 1660/1 his wife Beethland gave Griffith a similar power.[23] He died on a return voyage from England, 1662/3, leaving, as Francis Dade, a nuncupative will.[24] On 29 Dec. 1663 Edward Griffith and Elizabeth, his wife, of Mulberry Island, assigned to Francis[4] Dade, son of Maj. Francis Dade, deceased, right in a patent of land in Westmoreland County with reversion to Mrs. Beheathland[3] Dade, relict of Maj. Francis Dade.[25]

Beheathland[3] (Bernard) Dade married (2) Maj. Andrew Gilson, a justice of Lancaster County, 1652, sheriff of Old Rappahannock County, 1665, and justice of Stafford County,[26] who deposed 9 Sept. 1686 he was aged 50[27] and left will dated 2 April 1697.[28] Her will, 20 Aug. 1716-3 March 1720/1,[29] left a silver quart tankard to her grandson Dade Massey and all else to her grandson William Storke.

Issue: (by 1) [DADE][30] 7. Francis[4], born 7 Nov. 1659,[31] in 1690 called himself "son and heir of his father John Smith,"[32] died 1698,[33] married 4. *Frances[3] Townshend* (see TOWNSHEND), who married (2) Capt. John Withers

---

[22] Jon Kukla, *Speakers and Clerks of the Virginia House of Burgesses, 1643-1776* (Richmond, 1981), pp. 57-59.

[23] Westmoreland Co. Deeds, Wills &c 1661-62, pp. 27-27a.

[24] Westmoreland Co. Deeds & Wills 1, pp. 201-02. Since Capt. Dade had dropped the Smith alias at the time of his death, it appears probable that he had been involved in one or more of the royal plots before coming to Virginia and resumed his name after the Restoration.

[25] *Ibid.*, pp. 215-17.

[26] Lancaster Co. Record Bk. 1, p. 15; Old Rappahannock Co. Deeds 2, p. 427; *V* XXXVIII, pp. 181-90.

[27] Stafford Co. Record Bk. 1686-94, p. 10. Since he was a justice in 1652 he must have been older.

[28] Photocopy of attested copy from lost Stafford County record book provided by George H. S. King, Fredericksburg, Va.

[29] Westmoreland Co. Deeds & Wills 6, pp. 630-31.

[30] Nicklin, *loc. cit.*, and Gray, *loc. cit.*, list a daughter Elizabeth, wife of Maj. Edward Griffith of Mulberry Island, Warwick County. She, however, had two previous husbands (see HARWOOD) and was born far too early to be a child of Beheathland[3] Bernard. Neither is there evidence that there was a son William Bernard Dade.

[31] Stafford Co. Order Bk. 1689-93, pp. 79-82; *V* VL, pp. 17-18.

[32] *Ibid.*

[33] Stafford Co. Will Bk. Z, 1699-1709, p. 167.

and (3), 1699, 3. Col. *Rice*[3] *Hooe* (see HOOE); 8. MARY[4]; 9. (possibly) Christ.[4], died young;[34] (by 2) [GILSON][35] 10. THOMAS[4]; 11. BEHEATHLAND[4].

8. MARY[4] DADE (Beheathland[3] Bernard, Mary[2] Beheathland, Robert[1]) , born about 1661, died about 1694. She married (1) Capt. Robert Massey of Stafford County who left will dated 22 March 1684/5[36] and died by 12 Dec. 1689,[37] and (2) 3. Col. *Rice*[3] *Hooe* (see HOOE).

Issue: (by 1) [MASSEY][38] 12. DADE[5]; 13. Benjamin[5], died 24 June 1725,[39] of Stafford County, married Elizabeth ____. who married (2) 18. *Henry*[5] *Dade* (see TOWNSEND).[40]

10. THOMAS[4] GILSON (Beheathland[3] Bernard, Mary[2] Beheathland, Robert[1]), born 1665, justice of Stafford County, 1702, and captain of militia, died before 8 May 1707 when the inventory of his estate was made.[41] He married Elizabeth Newton, born about 1685, who left will, 14 June 1762-22 Feb. 1763,[42] and married (2), by Oct. 1710, Capt. Benjamin Berryman.[43]

Issue: [GILSON][44] 14. BEHEATHLAND[5]; 15. DOROTHY[5]; 16. Thomas[5], died without issue.

11. BEHEATHLAND[4] GILSON (Beheathland[3] Bernard, Mary[2] Beheathland, Robert[1]), aged 1 year when a patent was issued, 27 Sept. 1667, for

---

[34] Patent Bk. 6, p. 288, to John James, 20 July 1670, for 500 acres in Stafford County, including Frances [*sic*] Dade, Christ. Dade, Francis Dade, Junr., and Mary Dade as headrights.

[35] The daughter Mrs. Buckner, named in Andrew Gilson's will, and the wife of "my wel Beloved sonn in Law Mr. Wm. Lane" to whom Beheathland Gilson gave a power of attorney, 14 Nov. 1667 (Old Rappahannock Co. Deeds &c 3, 1663-68, p. 312), appear to be his children by a previous marriage.

[36] Stafford Co. Deed Bk. P, 1755-67, pp. 93-95, deed from Lee Massey to John Alexander, 13 April 1756. Mary[4] Dade did not marry Gerrard Lowther as Capt. Massey died before Lowther and she was still Mary Massey when she proved Lowther's will, 11 March 1690/1 (*ibid.*, p. 128; Westmoreland Co. Order Bk. 1690-98, pp. 16, 31, 59).

[37] Stafford Co. Order Bk. 1689-93, p. 5.

[38] Stafford Co. Will Bk. Z, 1699-1709, p. 21; *W*(2) XII, pp. 29-30, 32-34.

[39] *Ibid.*

[40] Although John Bailey Calvert Nicklin in 1935 (*T* XVI, p. 161) identified the wife of Henry Dade as possibly Benjamin Massey's daughter, his identification of her in 1949 (*V* LVII, p. 73) as Benjamin's widow seems much more reasonable.

[41] Stafford Co. Will Bk. Z, p. 367.

[42] Westmoreland Co. Deeds & Wills 14, 1761-68, p. 179.

[43] Westmoreland Co. Order Bk. 1705-21, p. 150.

[44] *W*(2) IX, p. 61; *V* XXXVIII, pp. 186-87.

1050 acres in Rappahannock County in the name of Behethlem Gilson, Junr.,[45] left will dated 2 Oct. 1693.[46] She married Nehemiah Storke, justice of Westmoreland County who was living 31 May 1693,[47] whom she survived, the wills of both being presented for probate 29 Nov. 1693.[48]

Issue: [STORKE][49] 17. ELIZABETH[5]; 18. Catherine[5], born about 1689, died young; 19. WILLIAM[5].

12. Capt. DADE[5] MASSEY (Mary[4] Dade, Beheathland[3] Bernard, Mary[2] Beheathland, Robert[1]) deposed 14 April 1700 he was aged 21,[50] died 6 April 1735,[51] and left will 16 April 1735-13 May 1735.[52] He was sheriff of Stafford County, 1703. He married Elizabeth ___, probably daughter of Capt. Charles Ellis.

Issue: [MASSEY] 20. Mary[6], married 14. Capt. *John[4] Washington* (see TOWNSHEND); 21. Robert[6], born about 1706, married, 20 Dec. 1728,[53] Winifred McCarty; 22. Dade[6], married 98. *Parthenia[5] Alexander* (see THOROWGOOD); 23. Thomas[6], born about 1713, married Heliner Bunberry; 24. Sigismund[6], born about 1717, died 16 June 1746,[54] married, 4 April 1743, Mary Stuart, born 24 Feb. 1725/6;[55] 25. Anne[6], born 19 March 1719/20,[56] married (1), 7 Feb. 1737,[57] Francis Wright, who left will 29 March 1742-27 Sept. 1742,[58] and (2) William Stribling, who signed the accounting of Francis Wright's estate, 26 Sept. 1743;[59] 26. Frances[6], born about 1721; 27.

---

[45] R. T. Barton, *Virginia Colonial Decisions* (Boston, 1909) II, p. 174; Patent Bk. 6, p. 64. This land was deserted and was repatented 20 Oct. 1670 to Thomas Gilson (Patent Bk. 6, p. 335; *MCGC*, p. 230).

[46] Westmoreland Co. Deeds & Wills 8, 1732-38, p. 279, bond of Beheathland Berryman to Capt. Thomas Newton.

[47] Westmoreland Co. Order Bk. 1690-98, p. 96a.

[48] *Ibid.*, p. 111a.

[49] *W*(2) IX, p. 61; *V* XXXVIII, p. 185.

[50] Stafford Co. Will Bk. Z, 1699-1709, p. 57.

[51] St. Paul's Parish, Stafford-King George Co., Register.

[52] Stafford Co. Will Bk. M, 1735-48, p. 172.

[53] St. Paul's Parish Register.

[54] *Ibid.*

[55] *Ibid.*

[56] *Ibid.*

[57] *Ibid.*

[58] Prince William Co. Will Bk. C, pp. 376-77.

[59] *Ibid.*, p. 437.

Beheathland[6], born about 1723, married, 30 Aug. 1752,[60] Thomas Bunberry.

14. BEHEATHLAND[5] GILSON (Thomas[4], Beheathland[3] Bernard, Mary[2] Beheathland, Robert[1]) died 9 Oct. 1728.[61] She married (1) John Berryman, died 1727,[62] and (2), 10 Oct. 1727,[63] Thomas Booth.

Issue: (by 1) [BERRYMAN] 28. Gilson[6], died 4 April 1749,[64] married, 1741, Hannah Berryman.

15. DOROTHY[5] GILSON (Thomas[4], Beheathland[3] Bernard, Mary[2] Beheathland, Robert[1]) left will 20 April 1722-31 Oct. 1722.[65] She married John Spiller.

Issue: [SPILLER] 29. (Son)[6], married ___.

17. ELIZABETH[5] STORKE (Beheathland[4] Gilson, Beheathland[3] Bernard, Mary[2] Beheathland, Robert[1]), born 1687,[66] died April 1759 in her 72nd year.[67] She married (1), 1702,[68] Thomas Newton, born 1678, left will 26 Aug. 1727-31 Jan. 1727/8,[69] and (2), 1730, Col. Samuel Oldham.

Issue: (by 1) [NEWTON] 30. Willoughby[6], aged 33 in Oct. 1735,[70] died 11 Feb. 1767,[71] left will 27 Dec. 1766-codicil 28 Jan. 1767-26 May 1767,[72] ,justice of Westmoreland County, married Sarah Eskridge, daughter of George Eskridge, who died 2 Dec. 1753 in her 46th year;[73] 31. Catherine[6], left will 6 Sept. 1760-20 Feb. 1761,[74] married (1) Thomas Martin, who left will 5 April 1727-14 June

---

[60] St. Paul's Parish Register.

[61] *Ibid.*

[62] *T* XX, p. 182. See also Barton, *op. cit.*, II, p. 42.

[63] St. Paul's Parish Register.

[64] *Ibid.*

[65] Westmoreland Co. Deeds & Wills 7, 1720-23, pp. 131-32.

[66] Barton, *op. cit.*, II, p. 174.

[67] Gravestone, "Wilmington," Westmoreland Co., in William Meade, *Old Churches, Ministers and Families of Virginia* (Philadelphia, 1857), II, p. 152; *W*(1) IX, p. 28.

[68] Barton, *op. cit.*, II, p. 174. The marriage occurred before 28 Jan. 1701/2 when Thomas Newton petitioned for the estate left Elizabeth by her father (Westmoreland Co. Order Bk. 1698-1705, p. 142a.

[69] Westmoreland Co. Deeds & Wills 8, 1723-338, pp. 89-89a.

[70] Barton, *op. cit.*, II, p. 174. He deposed 18 Dec. 1760 he was aged 57 (*V* XXXVII, p. 286).

[71] *Virginia Gazette* (Rind), 19 Feb. 1767.

[72] Westmoreland Co. Deeds & Wills 14, 1761-67, pp. 461-67.

[73] Gravestone, in *W*(1) VII, pp. 97-98.

[74] Lancaster Co. Will Bk. 16, p. 123.

1727,[75] and (2), (bond 26) July 1727,[76] James Brent, who left will 19 April 1750-11 May 1750;[77] 32. Elizabeth[6], left will 22 Aug. 1767-14 May 1770,[78] married (1) William Keene, who left will 25 Oct. 1725-16 Feb. 1725/6,[79] and (2) Maj. John Wauchope [Waughop], who died before 13 Nov. 1749 when administration on his estate was granted to Elizabeth;[80] 33. Beheathland[6], married the Rev. Walter Jones, of Llanelly, County Carnarvon, matriculated at Jesus College, Oxford, 9 April 1717, aged 18, received King's Bounty for North Carolina 17 Dec. 1724, but settled in Westmoreland County.[81]

19. WILLIAM[5] STORKE (Beheathland[4] Gilson, Beheathland[3] Bernard, Mary[2] Beheathland, Robert[1]) petitioned 30 July 1707, aged 17, that his grandmother Beheathland Gilson be his guardian,[82] died before 27 July 1727 when Elizabeth Storke of Stafford County was ordered to return an inventory of her husband's estate in Westmoreland County.[83] He married Elizabeth Hart, who married (2), 29 Aug. 1729,[84] Richard Bernard.

Issue: [STORKE][85] 34. Beheathland[6], born 27 Dec. 1716, died 2 Dec. 1753,[86] married, 25 Aug. 1733,[87] as his (1) wife, Anthony Strother, born 1 Aug. 1710 in Richmond County, died 10 Dec. 1765 in Stafford County,[88] left will 29 Aug. 1765-Oct. 1766,[89] merchant of Fredericksburg; 35. Margaret[6], born 18 Jan. 1720/1, died after 1782, married (1), 23 Nov. 1738, John Washington, who left will 12 Nov. 1751-14 April 1752,[90] (2) ___; 36. Catherine[6], born 17 June 1723,

---

[75] Lancaster Co. Will Bk. 10, pp. 549-50.

[76] Lancaster Co. Marriage bond, in *W*(1) VI, p. 105.

[77] Lancaster Co. Will Bk. 14, p. 280; Chester Horton Brent, *The Descendants of Hugh Brent* (Rutland, Vt., 1936), p. 62.

[78] Northumberland Co. Record Bk. 1766-70, p. 491.

[79] Northumberland Co. Record Bk. 1718-26, p. 386a.

[80] Northumberland Co. Order Bk. 1743-49, p. 522.

[81] Edward L. Goodwin, *The Colonial Church in Virginia* (London, 1927), p.p. 283-84.

[82] Westmoreland Co. Order Bk. 1705-21, p. 62a.

[83] Westmoreland Co. Order Bk. 1721-31, pp. 180a, 184a.

[84] St. Paul's Parish Register.

[85] *Ibid.*.

[86] *T* XI, p. 131.

[87] St. Paul's Parish Register.

[88] *T* XI, p. 131,

[89] Stafford Co. Deed [Will] Bk. O, 1748-67, p. 515.

[90] Stafford Co. Deed [Will] Bk. O, 1748-67, pp. 218-20.

died 1804,[91] married, 12 Jan. 1748/9, Bailey Washington, born 10 Sept. 1731, died 22 June 1807,[92] justice of Stafford County; 37. Elizabeth[6], married (1), 18 May 1743,[93] Henry Washington, who died before 25 Feb. 1745/6,[94] (2), 1749, 33. *Robert[5] Vaulx* (see BURWELL), and (3), 1757, Col. Thomas Jett, who left will 19 Feb. 1785-25 Oct. 1785;[95] 38. John[6], married 29. *Frances[5] Hooe* (see HOOE).

---

[91] John A. Washington, *Rev. Lawrence Washington's Descendants–Five Generations* (Chevy Chase, Md., 1982), chart.

[92] *Ibid.*

[93] St. Paul's Parish Register.

[94] Westmoreland Co. Order Bk. 1743-47, p. 124a.

[95] Westmoreland Co. Deeds & Wills 16, pp. 276-78.

BENNETT (Edward)[1]

*1. EDWARD[1] BENNETT was baptized 2 Feb. 1577/8 at Wivelscombe, Somerset, son of Robert Bennett (died 1603) of Wivelscombe, tanner, and his wife Elizabeth Edney. He was a merchant of London, owner of a fleet of vessels trading with Virginia and established one of the early large plantations in the colony. He was for a time Deputy Governor of the English merchants at Delft, Holland,[2] and became an elder, 25 Dec. 1610, in the ancient church of the Pilgrims at Amsterdam.[3] He was the first to advocate the prohibition of the importation of all tobacco to England except Virginia tobacco. This was aimed specifically at Spanish tobacco from "the territories of Caracoes, Cumanagotta, Trinidado, Oronoco, and ... all Maracabo". His concern in the matter brought him membership in the Virginia Company. At the Virginia court held by the Company on 12 April 1621 Sir Edwin Sandys moved that

> in regard Mr Edward Bennet, a Cittizen had so well deserved of this Company by a treatise[4] wch he made touching the inconvenience that the importation of Tobacco out of Spaine had brought into this land: and by his often attendance upon the Committees of the lower howse of Commons about the same (who were well inclyned to afford their best assistance for prohibiting the bringing in of Spanish Tobacco) that therefore he might have the favor to be admitted a free member of the Company[5]

which was done.

Further recognition was extended Bennett, 4 Oct. 1621, when, by action of the Council of the Virginia Company, he and his associates were granted land in Virginia:

> The first Patent was for a gentleman that had deserved singularly well of the

---

[1] John Bennett Boddie, *Seventeenth Century Isle of Wight County, Virginia* (Chicago, 1938), pp. 34-53, 266-88; Rupert Taylor, "The Parentage of James Day (Died 1700) and Wife Mary of Isle of Wight County, Virginia," *T* XVI, pp. 239-42.

[2] *V* XXV, p. 393.

[3] Edward Arber, ed., *The Story of the Pilgrim Fathers* (London, 1897), pp. 122, 125. He became ruling elder when the church split and was referred to as one of the "two principal pillars of that rotten Separation".

[4] The treatise, "quite long, but very interesting," has been preserved.

[5] *R*, Va. Co. I, p. 446; Alexander Brown, *The First Republic in America* (Boston and New York, 1898), pp. 398-99. By proclamation first issued by King James I and confirmed by King Charles I, March 1625, the importation of Spanish tobacco into England was prohibited; nevertheless, an illegal trade flourished and tobacco from the Spanish West Indies continued to flow into England along with cargos from the Bermudas.

Company before he was a member thereof, And since his admittance hee had been att a verie great charge for transportinge of people to Virginia namely Mr. Bennett who now ioynes himselfe in this buisines wth M^r [Thomas] Wiseman, and M^r [Thomas] Ayres, and divers other their associates.[6]

Bennett and his associates proposed to send over immediately 200 immigrants and were assigned land at Wariscoyak [Isle of Wight]. The first contingent of 120 settlers arrived with Capt. Ralph Hamor and by Feb. 1621/2 began readying the land, but scarcely a month passed when the great Indian massacre, instigated by Opecancanough, occurred, Good Friday, 22 March 1621/2. Completely surprised, fifty of Edward[1] Bennett's company were slain. This was a sizable portion of the 347 persons killed out of the 1240 comprising the entire population of Virginia.

In compliance with the order of the Council that settlers in outlying areas gather at Jamestown and other plantation centers for greater protection against the savages, Wariscoyak was abandoned temporarily. However, Edward[1] Bennett's brother Robert (baptized 27 April 1571) wrote to him at his residence in Bartholomew's Lane, London, from "Bennetes Welcome" in Virginia, 9 June 1623, telling him of conditions of trade, of fishing off the Newfoundland coast, of importing commodities from Spain, and describing the retaliation of the Virginia settlers against the Indians after the massacre.[7] The letter also mentions Robert's desire to see his children in England, but he died in Virginia before the year was out and on 20 Nov. 1623 provision was made for settling his estate.[8] Richard Bennett (baptized 9 Oct. 1573), another brother, also died at Edward's plantation in Virginia, 28 Aug. 1626, and the General Court ordered a settlement of his affairs.[9] Soon, however, two nephews of Edward[1] Bennett, of the same

---

[6] *R*, Va. Co. I, p. 534.

[7] *Ibid.*, IV, pp. 220-22. The retaliation included poisoning some 200 and killing (and apparently scalping) some fifty more.

[8] *Ibid.*, p. 402. Robert Bennett had come to Virginia as manager of his brother's affairs. At his death, John Chew was placed in charge. The names and location of Robert's children in England are not known.

[9] *MCGC*, p. 120. Richard Bennett married Judith (probably Harris) and had five children baptized 1610-18 at St. Mary Woolchurch Haw, London. On 8 June 1627 a commission of administration was granted to Edward Benet of London, brother of Richard Benet, lately deceased in Virginia, the relict Judith Benet renouncing (Virginia Colonial Reords Project, Survey report 4329). The will of Judith Bennett, proved 23 Nov. 1638 (P.C.C. 164 Lee), shows that all their children were then dead.

names as those of his deceased brothers, Robert Bennett, aged 18, and Richard Bennett, aged 20, came to Virginia and appeared in Court at James City, 21 Jan. 1628/9, regarding the interests of their uncle.[10]

Edward[1] Bennett was chosen Auditor of the Virginia Company, 22 May 1622, and, 1623, his name appeared on a list of persons "fit to be Deputy Governor of Virginia and the Somers Islands Companies". In the latter year he allied himself with the powerful Court party headed by the Earl of Warwick, determined to wrest control of colonial affairs from the Virginia Company and place the colony directly under the King.[11]

After the transfer of the Company's authority over Virginia to the Crown, Edward[1] Bennett came to Virginia. He was a Burgess for Wariscoyak, 1628,[12] the first called after the revocation of the charter of the Virginia Company and at the command of the new King, Charles I. The King was anxious to monopolize the lucrative Virginia tobacco trade but believed it would be "more thoroughly effected" if the representatives of the planters in the legislative body enacted the matter into law rather than to bring it about by royal proclamation. The assembly was not inclined to accept the King's terms and commissioned Mr. Bennett and Mr. [Michael] Marshart to go to England, confer with Sir Francis Wyatt and "either to refuse the propositions of this contract or to establish a sure and certain means of out subsistence that wee may noe longer bee alwaies subject to ruine upon the uncertainty of the noyse of any contract."[13]

Edward[1] Bennett married Mary Bourne, daughter of Jasper Bourne (died 1636) of Stanmore Magna, Middlesex, and his wife Joan. Jasper Bourne was a nephew of Gilbert Bourne, Bishop of Bath and Wells, during the reign of Mary I.[14]

Edward[1] Bennett apparently never returned to Virginia but he continued his mercantile connections with the colony. On 24 Aug. 1635 Edward[1] Bennett, aged 55, of St. Olave's, Hart Street, London, deposed concerning freight details

---

[10] *MCGC*, pp. 169, 181. Robert Bennett (baptized 29 Dec. 1611) was the son of William Bennett (baptized 15 June 1572) and his wife Alice Storye. Richard Bennett (see UTIE-BENNETT) was the son of Thomas Bennett.

[11] *R*, Va. Co. II, p. 30; IV, pp. 80-81, 90.

[12] Leonard, p. 7.

[13] *JHB* 1619-1658/9, pp. viii, xxx-xxxi, 50-51. For colonial tobacco trade see Bruce, *Ec. Hist.*, pp. 285-99.

[14] *W*(1) XIII, p. 131; John Bennett Boddie, *Historical Southern Families*, VI (Redwood City, Calif., 1962), pp. 1-7.

of the ship *Ann and Margaret* to Virginia in which he was a partner with John Stoner and George Orme.[15] He was still living in 1638 when his son Jasper was buried but dead before 3 June 1651 when Mary Bennett was granted administration *de bonis non administratis* for the part of her father's estate still undistributed at the death of the executor, her brother-in-law John Bennett.[16] She died before 26 May 1659 when administration on her estate was granted to Mary Bland alias Bennett "the well and lawfull daughter of Mary Bennett late of Stanmore in the County of Middlesex deceased."[17] On 8 April 1663 the Virginia lands of Edward[1] Bennett, 1500 acres in Isle of Wight County, were divided between his two daughters and coheiresses, Silvester Hill and Mary Bland.[18]

Issue: 2. Joan[2], baptized 29 April 1621 at St. Dunstan in the East, London; 3. Edward[2], baptized 6 March 1622/3 at St. Bartholomew by the Exchange, London; 4. MARY[2]; 5. Alice[7], baptized 10 Aug. 1626 at St. Dunstan in the East, London; 6. Elizabeth[2], baptized 31 May 1629 at St. Olave, Hart Street, London, buried 27 June 1632 at Stanmore Magna, Middlesex; 7. SILVESTER[2]; 8. John[7], baptized 17 Feb. 1631/2 at St. Olave, Hart Street, London; 9. Ann[2], baptized 13 March 1633/4 at St. Olave, Hart Street, London, buried there 10 May 1634; 10. Jasper[2], baptized 3 July 1635 at St. Olave, Hart Street, London, buried 6 Dec. 1638 at Stanmore Magna, Middlesex.

4. MARY[2] BENNETT (Edward[1]), baptized 3 April 1624 at St. Bartholomew by the Exchange, London, married (1) John Day of Fulham, Middlesex, Gent., whose will, dated 15 Sept. 1657,[19] named wife Mary, sons John and James, and daughters Ann and Elizabeth. She married (2), 27 May 1658,[20] Thomas Bland of London and they, together with "the heirs of the said Mary," received a patent, 1 June 1664, for 750 acres, her share of 1500 acres granted to Richard Bennett and divided between them and Nicholas Hill and his wife Silvester, 8 April 1663.[21] He died a resident of the parish of St. Peter le Poer, London, leaving a will, 2 Oct. 1666-15 Nov. 1667, which described him

---

[15] P.R.O. Class H.C.A., Colonial Virginia Records Project, Survey report 04004, p. 2.

[16] P.C.C. Administration Act Book 1651, no pagination. Presumably she would not have acted in such a capacity if her husband were living.

[17] P.C.C. Administration Act Book 1659, f. 193.

[18] Patent Bk. 5, p. 153 (27).

[19] *T* XVI, p. 241, from the Court of Hustings, London.

[20] St, Bartholomew the Less, London, Parish register, no pagination.

[21] Patent Bk. 6, p. 140.

as "citizen and scrivener of London."[22]   She married (3), 14 Sept. 1668 at Deptford, Kent,[23] Luke Cropley who died at Stratford le Bow, Middlesex,[24] leaving will 11 Feb. 1690/1-22 Aug. 1694.[25] She was mentioned in Governor Richard Bennett's will, 12 April 1675, as "my cousin Mary, wife of Mr. Luke Cropley of London," and in the will of James[3] Day, 10 Aug. 1700, as "my ever honored mother, Mrs. Mary Cropley."

Issue: (by 1) [DAY] 11. John[3]; 12. JAMES[3]; 13. ANNE[3]; 14. Elizabeth[3], married, Dec. 1670, Charles Molloy.[26]

7. SILVESTER[2] BENNETT (Edward[1]), baptized 25 Oct. 1630 at St. Olave, Hart Street, London, married, as his (2) wife, Nicholas Hill, member of the House of Burgesses from Isle of Wight County, 1661-75.[27] On 30 Sept. 1664 Maj. Nicholas Hill and Silvester[2], his wife, patented 750 acres in the Upper Parish of Isle of Wight, "being the moiety of 1500 acres appeartayning unto the said Silvester and her sister who were daughters and coheirs of Mr. Edward Bennett, deceased."[28] The land lay along the banks of the James to a point called "The Rocks."

The will of Lt. Col. Nicholas Hill, 19 April 1675-20 Oct. 1675, named his wife Silvester[2] and directed that she and her six children were to have the legacy "given by Major General Bennett," and mentioned daughter Agnes Hill and sons Ralph and Nicholas Hill, "my three children by a former wife."[29] The will of Silvester[2] (Bennett) Hill, 7 Oct. 1706-9 Jan. 1706/7, did not mention children but

---

[22] P.C.C. 165 Carr.

[23] St. Nicholas, Deptford, Kent, Parish register, no pagination; *Allegations for Marriage Licenses Issued by the Dean and Chapter of Westminster, 1558 to 1699, also ... by the Vicar-General of the Archbishop of Canterbury, 1660 to 1679* (Harleian Society, *Publications*, XXIII; London, 1886), p. 155, 12 Sept. 1668, Luke Cropley, of St. Peter the Poor, London, Gent., widower, about 35, and Mary Bland, of same, widow, about 36 [*sic*], at Deptford or Charlton, Co. Kent, or Newington, Surrey, or St. James Clerkenwell.

[24] P.C.C. Acts, 1694, f. 148, 22 Aug. 1694, as resident of the parish of St. Bride, London.

[25] P.C.C. 190 Box.

[26] *Allegations for Marriage Licenses Issued from the Faculty Office of the Archbishop of Canterbury, 1543-1869* (Harleian Society, *Publications*, XXIV; London, 1886), p. 116, 13 Dec. 1670, Charles Molloy of Lincoln's Inn, Esq., bachelor, 24, and Elizabeth Day, spinster, 19, her father dead, consent of her mother, now wife of Luke Cropley of St. Peter le Poor, Gent., at Barnet or Hadley, Herts.

[27] Leonard, p. 38.

[28] Patent Bk. 5, p. 153 (27).

[29] Isle of Wight Co. Wills & Deeds 2, p. 133.

named her sister's daughter Ann Chapman and her sister's grandsons.[30]

Issue: [HILL][31] 15. George[3]; 16. Martha[3], married John Best and died without issue, 1695, leaving a nuncupative will;[32] 17. MARY[3]; 18. Anna[3]; 19. Richard[3]; 20. Elizabeth[3].

12. JAMES[3] DAY (Mary[2] Bennett, Edward[1]) married Mary Thompson, daughter of William Thompson of Nansemond County.[33] His will, 10 Aug. 1700-9 Jan. 1700/1, named wife Mary, three sons, brother and sister Chapman, brother and sister Swann, aunt Mrs. Silvester Hill, and mother Mrs. Mary Cropley, and mentioned his property in the Parish of St. Peter the Poor, London.[34] Mary (Thompson) Day married (2) John Johnson (died 1707[35]) and (3) Reuben Gladhill (died 1715). Her will, 30 Nov. 1712-26 Jan. 1712/3 named son James[4] Day, "only surviving executor of my deceased husbands James Day and John Johnson" and also named son[-in-law] Nathaniel Ridley.[36]

Issue: [DAY] 21 JAMES[4]; 22. Thomas[4], died without issue leaving will 19 Jan. 1723/4-24 Feb. 1723/4;[37] 23. William[4]; 24. ELIZABETH[4].

13. ANNE[3] DAY (Mary[2] Bennett, Edward[1]) married Charles Chapman, clerk of Isle of Wight County, 1696-1710, who received certificate, 9 April 1694, for the importation of himself, his wife Anne and sons John and Charles into the colony.[38] His will, 20 Dec. 1710-26 Feb. 1710/1, named sons Joseph and John and a grandson.[39] Administration on her estate was granted in the

---

[30] *Ibid.*, p. 475.

[31] See Lyndon H. Hart, "Are There Descendants of Silvester (Bennett) Hill?," *The Southside Virginian*, VIII, pp. 160-61.

[32] Isle of Wight Co. Will Bk. A, p. 149.

[33] *V* XLV, pp. 197-98.

[34] Isle of Wight Co. Wills & Deeds 2, p. 428. Brother and sister Swann were his wife's sister Eliza Thompson and her husband Thomas Swann (John Bennett Boddie, *Historical Southern Families*, II [Redwood City, Calif., 1956], p. 234).

[35] Isle of Wight Co. Deeds & Wills 2, p. 484, will of John Johnson, 7 Jan. 1703-9 Aug. 1707; David A. Avant, *Some Southern Colonial Families*, II (Tallahassee, Fla., 1982), pp. 147-53; Eddis Johnson and Hugh Buckner Johnston, *The Johnsons and Johnstons of Corrowaugh in Isle of Wight County, Virginia* (Martinsville, Ind., 1979), pp. 47-50.

[36] Isle of Wight Co. Wills & Deeds 2, p. 543.

[37] Isle of Wight Co. Great Book, p. 151. He referred to brother-in-law William Bridger, but the nature of the relationship is undetermined. His inventory (*ibid.*, p. 155) contains clothing suggesting he had been married.

[38] Isle of Wight Co. Order Bk. 1693-95, p. 28.

[39] Isle of Wight Co. Wills & Deeds 2, p. 516.

Prerogative Court of Canterbury, Aug. 1716, to John Weeton, attorney for her son John Chapman in Virginia.[40]

Issue: [CHAPMAN] 25. JOHN[4]; 26. Charles[4], living 7 Oct. 1706 when Silvester[2] (Bennett) Hill mentioned Ann Chapman's three sons in her will, died young; 27. JOSEPH[4].

17. MARY[3] HILL (Silvester[2] Bennett, Edward[1]) married John Jennings, Jr.[41] On 20 Oct. 1694 John Jennings and Mary[3] his wife, confirmed to Dr. Luke Haveild of Chuckatuck certain lands in Nansemond County granted by Martha Best, sister to said Mary Jennings.[42] The will of John Jennings, dated 31 Dec. 1695,[43] mentioned son George, sister Sarah Lucks, brother William Thomas and mother[-in-law] Mrs. Silvester Hill.

Issue: [JENNINGS] 28. George[4], left land on Warrisquack Bay and Lawnes' Creek, died young without issue.

21. Capt. JAMES[4] DAY (James[3], Mary[2] Bennett, Edward[1]) owned 1300 acres in Isle of Wight County, 1714,[44] and left will dated 26 Sept. 1725.[45] He married (1) Juliana Norsworthy, daughter of Col. George Norsworthy of Nansemond County, and (2) Anne Allen, sister of Arthur Allen of Surry County, who left will 2 Dec. 1726-23 Jan. 1726/7.[46]

Issue: [DAY] (by 1) 29. James[5], married 15. *Martha[4] (Smith) Bridger* (see SMITH, Arthur); 30. THOMAS[5].

24. ELIZABETH[4] DAY (James[3], Mary[2] Bennett, Edward[1]) died before 11 May 1749 when the inventory of her estate was returned.[47] She married (1) Nathaniel Ridley of Isle of Wight County, sheriff, 1714, captain of militia, left will 10 March 1718/9-27 July 1719,[48] and (2), as his (2) wife, Matthew Jones of

---

[40] *NGSQ*, LXII, p. 92.

[41] John Anderson Brayton, *The Descendants of Capt. John Jennings of Isle of Wight County, Virginia* (*Colonial Families of Surry and Isle of Wight Counties, Virginia*, IV; Memphis, 2001), pp. 25-29.

[42] Isle of Wight Co. Deed Bk. 1, pp. 148-49.

[43] Isle of Wight Co. Will Bk. A, p. 201, without date of recording, rerecorded 9 June 1696 (Wills & Deeds 2, p. 408). The inventory of his estate was ordered made 10 Jan. 1695/6 and recorded June 1696 (*ibid.*, pp. 365, 372).

[44] *V* LXXXVII, p. 176.

[45] Isle of Wight Co. Great Book, p. 172, without probate date. His estate was ordered appraised 13 April 1726 (Will Bk. 3, p. 2).

[46] Isle of Wight Co. Will Bk. 3, p. 14.

[47] Isle of Wight Co. Will Bk. 5, p. 184.

[48] Isle of Wight Co. Great Book, p. 2.

Warwick County, who left will 28 Jan. 1727/8-25 March 1728.[49]

Issue:[50] (by 1) [RIDLEY] 31. NATHANIEL[5]; 32. James[5], married 16. *Jane*[4] *Smith* (see SMITH, Arthur); 33. MARY[5]; 34. Thomas[5], died by 1744; 35. ELIZABETH[5]; 36. LYDIA[5]; (by 2) [JONES] 37. ALBRIDGTON[5]; 38. Anne[5], married Thomas Holt, possibly 28. *Thomas*[4] *Holt* (see HOLT); 39. MARGARET[5]; 40. Agatha[5], died unmarried before 2 Oct. 1744 when the land devised to her by her father was conveyed by her mother and sisters to Albridgton[5] Jones.[51]

25. JOHN[4] CHAPMAN (Ann[3] Day, Mary[2] Bennett, Edward[1]) owned 100 acres in Isle of Wight County, 1714,[52] and left will 10 Sept. 1736-28 Nov. 1737.[53] He married (1), 15 Feb. 1704/5, Frances Ward who died 22 July 1727 in her 39th year,[54] and (2) Mary (Bevan) Marshall.

Issue: [CHAPMAN] (by 1) 40. PATIENCE[5]; 41. Benjamin[5], born 8 Feb. 1706/7, died 23 Aug. 1723;[55] 42. JOHN[5]; 43. CHARLES[5]; 44. Mary[5]; 45. Rachel Norsworthy[5], born 6 Aug. 1722;[56] 46. JOSEPH[5]; (by 2) 47. William[5], born 28 Dec. 1729,[57] died before 7 Oct. 1773 when Joseph Chapman was granted administration on his estate;[58] 48. Thomas[5], under 14 in 1736; 49. Elizabeth[5].

27. JOSEPH[4] CHAPMAN (Ann[3] Day, Mary[2] Bennett, Edward[1]) left undated will, proved 22 Dec. 1729.[59] He married Alice ___.

Issue: [CHAPMAN] 50. CHARLES[5]; 51. Mary[5]; 52. Martha[5]; 53. Elizabeth[5]; 54. Alice[5].

30. THOMAS[5] DAY (James[4], James[3], Mary[2] Bennett, Edward[1]) left will 24 July 1750-3 Oct. 1752.[60] He married 38. *Mary*[5] *Davis* (see MOONE), who

---

[49] Isle of Wight Co. Will Bk. 3, p. 66.

[50] Lyndon Hobbs Hart and Bromfield Bradford Nichol, *Ridley of Southampton, being The Descendants of Nathaniel and Elizabeth Day Ridley ...* (Pensacola, Fla., 1992), pp. 4-5.

[51] Isle of Wight Co. Deed Bk. 6, pp. 500-02.

[52] *V* LXXXVII, p. 180.

[53] Isle of Wight Co. Will Bk. 4, p. 183.

[54] Chapman Bible, in *V* IX, p. 209; *W*(2) X, p. 256.

[55] *Ibid.*

[56] *Ibid.*

[57] *Ibid.*

[58] Isle of Wight Co. Order Bk. 1772-80, p. 193.

[59] Isle of Wight Co. Will Bk. 3, p. 189, which named son-in-law John Applewhite.

[60] Isle of Wight Co. Will Bk. 5, p. 363, with undated codicil, Will Bk. 6, p. 12.

married (2) John Mallory.[61]

Issue: [DAY] 55. Thomas[6], left will 21 Oct. 1769-1 Oct. 1772,[62] married Elizabeth Tynes;[63] 56. John[6], left will 11 March 1776-1 Aug. 1776,[64] married Betty Wentworth,[65] who married (2) Anthony Degge.[66]

31. NATHANIEL[5] RIDLEY (Elizabeth[4] Day, James[3], Mary[2] Bennett, Edward[1]), justice of Isle of Wight and Southampton counties, left will 20 Oct. 1752-10 May 1753.[67] He married, 1742, Priscilla Applewhaite, daughter of Henry and Ann (Marshall) Applewhaite.[68]

Issue: [RIDLEY][69] 57. Nathaniel[6], left will 7 Jan. 1776-11 July 1776,[70] married 47. *Sarah[5] Ridley* (see SMITH, Arthur); 58. Day[6], moved to Hertford Co., N.C., married Martha Thorpe;[71] 59. Col. Thomas[6], died 15 Feb. 1815,[72] left will 3 Dec. 1809-30 March 1815,[73] justice of Southampton County, member of the House of Delegates, 1785-87, and Virginia Senate, 1790-1800,[74] vestryman of St. Luke's Parish, captain 4th Virginia Regiment, 11 March 1776, major, 10th Virginia Regiment, 1 March 1778, original member of the Society of the Cincinnati, colonel of militia, 9 June 1785, married, (bond 9) April 1778,[75] Amey Scott, who died 5 Feb. 1815; 60. Anne[6], probably married John Holladay; 61. Parmillia[6], died by 1795 when administration on her estate was granted, married (1), (bond 9) Feb. 1769,[76] Riddick Holladay and (2), by 1776, William Coffield,

---

[61] Isle of Wight Co. Deed Bk. 9, p. 272; Deed Bk. 14, p. 143.

[62] Isle of Wight Co. Will Bk. 8, p. 170.

[63] Isle of Wight Co. Chancery papers 1804-028.

[64] Isle of Wight Co. Will Bk. 8, p. 430.

[65] Isle of Wight Co. Will Bk. 7, p. 511, will of Mary Wentworth, 31 May 1768-7 July 1768.

[66] *W*(1) XXI, p. 66.

[67] Southampton Co. Will Bk. 1, pp. 120-22.

[68] Isle of Wight Co. Will Bk. 4, p. 329, will of Henry Applewhaite, proved 27 April 1741; Will Bk. 5, p. 97, will of Ann Applewhaite, 26 July 1746-10 March 1747/8.

[69] Hart and Nichol, *op. cit.*, pp. 9-94.

[70] Southampton Co. Will Bk. 3, p. 152.

[71] *Ibid.*, p. 62, accounting of estate of Thomas Thorpe, returned 10 June 1773.

[72] Ridley family record, in Henry W. Lewis, *Southampton County Ridleys and Their Kin* (Chapel Hill, N.C., 1961), p. 85.

[73] Southampton Co. Will Bk. 7, pp. 434-36.

[74] Leonard, pp. 158, 162, 182, 186, 190, 193, 198, 202, 206, 210, 214, 218.

[75] Catherine Lindsay Knorr, *Marriage Bonds and Ministers' Returns of Southampton County, Virginia, 1750-1810* (Pine Bluff, Ark., 1955), p. 91.

[76] *Ibid.*, p. 57.

of Nansemond County.

33. MARY[5] RIDLEY (Elizabeth[4] Day, James[3], Mary[2] Bennett, Edward[1]) married Francis Jones, nephew of her step-father, of Southampton County and later of Edgecombe Co., N.C., who left will 14 Jan. 1750-Aug. 1755.[77]

Issue: [JONES][78] 62. Nathaniel[6], died 25 Jan. 1810,[79] left will 6 March 1809-Feb. 1810,[80] married Anna Snickers; 63. Tignal[6], died 30 Aug. 1807,[81] left will 26 Aug. 1807-Nov. 1807,[82] justice of Wake Co., N.C., which he represented in the Conventions of 1775-76, the North Carolina House of Commons, 1777, and Senate, 1797, married Penelope Cain; 64. John[6], died before 18 Sept. 1797 when the inventory of his estate was made,[83] married Mary Cain; 65. Matthew[6], ordinary keeper of Johnston Co., N.C., married Elizabeth ____; 66. Albridgton[6], left will dated 25 Nov. 1787,[84] married Mary Hardy; 67. Francis[6], of Halifax Co., N.C., died by Feb. 1794, married Frances Yancey; 68. Judith[6], married (1) George Wilson, who left will 20 Feb. 1758-6 April 1758,[85] and (2) Joseph Cutchins, who left will 14 Dec. 1778-7 Jan. 1779;[86] 69. Mary[6], died before Sept. 1769, married John McCullers, who left will 2 Nov. 1767-May 1768;[87] 70. Lucy[6]; 71. Betty Day[6]; 72. Lydia[6], born 1748 in Edgecombe Co., N.C., died 1821 in Edgefield Co., S.C., married, 1768, Drury Mims, born 1744 in Goochland County, left will 13 May 1817-11 Nov. 1818,[88] who moved to Edgefield Co., S.C., where on 1 Aug. 1787 they sold two lots where the county court house was to be set;[89] 73. Ridley[6], left will 7 June 1817-Nov. 1825,[90] married Henry Restore Jones of Halifax Co., N.C., who left will 19 Oct. 1801-

[77] Edgecombe Co., N.C., Original will, Secretary of State Papers, North Carolina Archives.

[78] Hart and Nichol, *op. cit.*, pp. 331-436.

[79] *Raleigh Minerva*, 1 Feb. 1810, Thursday evening last.

[80] Wake Co., N.C., Will Bk. 9, p. 181.

[81] *Raleigh Register*, 2 Sept. 1807.

[82] Wake Co., N.C., Will Bk. 7, pp. 295-98.

[83] Wake Co., N.C., Will Bk. D, p. 34.

[84] Wake Co., N.C., Will Bk. C, p. 156, recorded between documents recorded 30 Jan. 1788.

[85] Isle of Wight Co. Will Bk. 6, p. 379.

[86] Isle of Wight Co. Will Bk. 8, p. 514.

[87] Johnston Co., N.C., Will Bk. 1, p. 413.

[88] Edgefield Co., S.C., Will Bk. C, p. 9.

[89] Edgefield Co., S.C., Deed Bk. 2, pp. 34-38, 69-72.

[90] Halifax Co., N.C., Will Bk. 4, p. 13.

Nov. 1801;[91] 74. Jemima [6], born 22 April 1788, died 21 May 1814,[92] married Lewis Pope, who moved to Oglethorpe Co., Ga., where he purchased 600 acres on the waters of Golden Grove Creek, 27 Dec. 1793,[93] and left will 13 Sept. 1803-4 Feb. 1805.[94]

35. ELIZABETH[5] RIDLEY (Elizabeth[4] Day, James[3], Mary[2] Bennett, Edward[1]) married Dr. Jesse Browne, born 1709, died 3 Dec. 1770,[95] left will 29 Nov. 1770-13 Dec. 1770,[96] who married (2) Pheriba ___.

Issue: [BROWNE][97] 75. Elizabeth Ridley[6], left will 29 June 1824-21 March 1825,[98] married (1), 1760,[99] Kinchen Taylor, merchant of Southampton County, who died before 19 Jan. 1771 when Henry Taylor was granted administration on his estate,[100] and (2), (bond 23) Aug. 1778,[101] William Kello, who was captured by the British during the Revolutionary War; 76. Martha[6], died Spring 1780, married (1) William Wilkinson of Nansemond County and (2) Thomas Jack, born in Scotland, resident of North Carolina and later of Nansemond County, in both places serving as a justice, who was a Loyalist and fled to Britain in Sept. 1777, later living at Airdrie, near Glasgow, Scotland;[102] 77. Samuel Ridley[6], on whose estate his widow was granted administration, 11 June 1795, of Southampton County where he advertised he would continue his father's hospital and practice of surgery,[103] married Mary ___, who died 27 Sept. 1795; 78. Sarah[6], married, by 1770, John Atkinson of Person Co., N.C., who married (2) Frances ___ and left will 5 April 1792-Sept. 1792;[104] 79. Mary[6], born 1750 at Norfolk, died Dec. 1809 in Granville Co., N.C.,[105] married, 1765, Robert

---

[91] Halifax Co., N.C., Will Bk. 3, p. 367.

[92] S. P. Moore Bible.

[93] Oglethorpe Co., Ga., Deed Bk. A, p. 373.

[94] Oglethorpe Co., Ga. Will Bk. A, p. 46.

[95] *Virginia Gazette*, 3 Jan. 1771.

[96] Southampton Co. Will Bk. 2, p. 357.

[97] Hart and Nichol, *op. cit.*, pp. 443-561.

[98] Southampton Co. Will Bk. 9, p. 255.

[99] *V* XXIII, p. 323, says bond 16 Jan. 1768 in Southampton County.

[100] Southampton Co. Order Bk. 1768-72, p. 342.

[101] Knorr, *Marriage Bonds ... Southampton County*, p. 68.

[102] Peter Wilson Coldham, *American Migrations, 1765-1799* (Baltimore, 2000), pp. 571-72.

[103] *Virginia Gazette*, 21 March 1771.

[104] Person Co., N.C., Wills & Inventories 1, pp. 30-33.

[105] Dickins family Bible, in *The Panola Story*, XI, p. 36.

Dickins, born 1748 in England, left will 16 Aug. 1797-March 1804,[106] merchant of Norfolk, colonel of cavalry in Revolutionary War, later moved to the part of Caswell Co., N.C., which became Person County;[107] 80. Lucretia[6], died by 1813 when her estate was taxed,[108] married (1), 12 May 1768, Benjamin Person, justice and surveyor of Bute Co., N.C., delegate to the Provincial Assembly, 1764-71, who died before 13 Nov. 1771 when Thomas Person gave bond as his administrator,[109] and (2), (bond 27) May 1773,[110] John Faulcon, justice and sheriff of Warren Co., N.C., who died Oct. 1812[111] leaving will 30 May 1812-Nov. 1812;[112] 81. Parthenia[6], born 1753, died 2 March 1835, married, 3 Oct. 1772 at Hampton,[113] Peter Pelham, born 1 May 1747 at Boston, Mass., died 20 Aug. 1822 at Xenia, Ohio, quartermaster of Brunswick County militia, 1777,[114] clerk of Brunswick County and after 1791 of Greensville County, who moved to Xenia, Ohio, where he was the first auditor of Greene Co., Ohio, 1812, was county commissioner for seven terms beginning in 1812, and established the first fulling and carding mill at Oldtown, Ohio.[115]

36. LYDIA[5] RIDLEY (Elizabeth[4] Day, James[3], Mary[2] Bennett, Edward[1]) died by 7 Nov. 1771 when the inventory of her estate was returned.[116] She married (1) Charles Portlock, who left will 15 Feb. 1750-2 July 1752,[117] and (2) Hugh Vance, who left will 2 April 1756-1 July 1756.[118]

Issue: (by 1) [PORTLOCK][119] 82. Frances[6], born 6 Feb. 1744/5,[120] died

---

[106] Person Co., N.C. Will Bk. 3, pp. 248-49.

[107] Mary W. B. Hicks, *A History of the Dickins Family of Panola County, Miss.* (Panola, 1860), pp. 5-6.

[108] Warren Co., N.C., Will Bk. 17, p. 297.

[109] Bute Co., N.C., Will Bk. A, p. 200.

[110] Bute Co., N.C., Marriage bond.

[111] *Raleigh Register*, 16 Oct. 1812.

[112] Warren Co., N.C., Will Bk. 16, p. 344.

[113] *Virginia Gazette*, 22 Oct. 1772; Revolutionary War pension application, Charles Pelham, widow Isabella, W.3034, National Archives.

[114] *V* XII, p. 184.

[115] Meredith B. Colket, "The Pelhams of England and New England," *The American Genealogist*, XX, p. 72; Julie Overton, *Revolutionary War Veterans of Greene County, Ohio* (n.p., 1995), p. 151.

[116] Isle of Wight Co. Will Bk. 8, pp. 99-100.

[117] Isle of Wight Co. Will Bk. 5, p. 439.

[118] Isle of Wight Co. Will Bk. 6, p. 226.

[119] Hart and Nichol, *op. cit.*, p. 563.

[120] Newport Parish Vestry Book.

young; 83. Charles[6], left will 1 Nov. 1797-7 Dec. 1797;[121] 84. Nathaniel[6]; (by 2) [VANCE] 85. James[6].

37. ALBRIDGTON[5] JONES (Elizabeth[4] Day, James[3], Mary[2] Bennett, Edward[1]), born 20 Sept. 1720,[122] left will 22 Sept. 1784-codicil 12 Dec. 1785-18 July 1786.[123] He married (1), 17 June 1744,[124] 120. *Elizabeth[5] Simmons* (see MASON) and (2), (bond 19) Feb. 1770,[125] Mary (Wainwright) Simmons, widow of 116. *Charles[5] Simmons* (see MASON).

Issue: [JONES] (by 1) 86. Mathew[6], left will 26 July 1793-12 Sept. 1793,[126] married ___; 87. Albridgton[6], of Southampton County, lieutenant 4th Virginia Regiment, 11 March 1776 to end of the war,[127] original member of the Society of the Cincinnati, married (1), (bond 22) Dec. 1784,[128] 377. *Frances[6] Calvert* (see MASON) and (2), (bond 27) Feb. 1795,[129] her niece Polly[7] Calvert, born 1779, died Dec. 1856; 88. Mary[6], married, (bond 9) Feb. 1764,[130] Benjamin Jarrell, who died before 13 Sept. 1770 when the inventory of his estate was returned;[131] 89. Agatha[6], married, (bond 24) May 1755,[132] Thomas Harvey of North Carolina; 90. Elizabeth[6], married (1), 9 Jan. 1766, as his (2) wife, Col. Miles Harvey, born 17 Dec. 1728 in Perquimans Co., N.C., died 12 Dec. 1776, who left will 1770-Jan. 1777,[133] and (2), as his (2) wife, Benjamin Baker of "South Quay," Nansemond County, who left will dated 6 April 1785;[134] 91. Ann[6], married, as his (1) wife, Lawrence Baker, of "Cole's Hill," Hertford Co., N.C., colonel in the Revolutionary War, justice and later clerk of Gates Co.,

---

[121] Sussex Co. Will Bk. F, p. 79.

[122] Hart and Nichol, *op. cit.*, p. 567.

[123] Southampton Co. Will Bk. 4, p. 183.

[124] Hart and Nichol, *op. cit.*, p. 567.

[125] Knorr, *op. cit.*, p. 63.

[126] Southampton Co. Will Bk. 4, p. 566.

[127] John H. Gwathmey, *Historical Register of Virginians in the Revolution* (Richmond, 1937), p. 425; Revolutionary War Pension, Albridgton Jones, BLWt.359-200.

[128] Knorr, *op. cit.*, p. 63.

[129] *Ibid.*, p. 64.

[130] *Ibid.*, p. 60.

[131] Southampton Co. Will Bk. 2, p. 338.

[132] Knorr, *op. cit.*, p. 54.

[133] Perquimans Co., N.C., Will Bk. C, p. 211.

[134] *The Virginia Genealogist*, XV, pp. 243-45.

N.C., from 1777 until his death,[135] who died 5 Nov. 1807 in Gates County,[136] left will 5 Sept. 1805-Nov. 1807;[137] 92. Simmons[6], married Mary ___, who married (2), (bond 18) April 1778,[138] Thomas Peete of Sussex County; 93. Sarah[6], died 10 April 1815 in Southampton County,[139] married (1), (bond 18) Aug. 1777,[140] the Rev. Henry John Burges, born 1744, left will 14 Feb. 1797-28 March 1797,[141] rector of Nottoway Parish, Southampton County, 1789-97,[142] (2) Howell Adkins and (3), (contract 18) Jan. 1812,[143] 190. *Randolph[6] Newsum* (see SPENCER); (by 2) 94. William[6], left will 22 July 1793-12 Sept. 1793,[144] without issue.

39. MARGARET[5] JONES (Elizabeth[4] Day, James[3], Mary[2] Bennett, Edward[1]) married Thomas Binns, who married (2) Elizabeth ___ and left will 2 April 1765-18 June 1765.[145]

Issue: [BINNS] 95. Ann[6], married Robert Hunnicutt, who married (2), 24 June 1783,[146] her half-sister Elizabeth Binns; 96. Sarah[6], married Henry Gilbert, who died in 1800; 97. Jean[6], married, (bond 4) Feb. 1783,[147] Richard Ellis, who left will 12 March 1824-26 May 1828.[148]

40. PATIENCE[5] CHAPMAN (John[4], Ann[3] Day, Mary[2] Bennett, Edward[1]) married, 13 Feb. 1723/4,[149] Moses Wills.

Issue: [WILLS][150] 98. Mary[6], born 3 May 1725; 99. Ann[6], born 29 Nov. 1730.

42. JOHN[5] CHAPMAN (John[4], Ann[3] Day, Mary[2] Bennett, Edward[1]) died

---

[135] *North Carolina Genealogy*, XV, pp. 2341-42.
[136] *Raleigh Register*, 19 Nov. 1807.
[137] Gates Co., N.C., Will Bk. 2, p. 1.
[138] Knorr, *op. cit.*, p. 84.
[139] *North Carolina Star*, Raleigh, 21 April 1815.
[140] Knorr, *op. cit.*, p. 23.
[141] Southampton Co. Will Bk. 5, p. 17.
[142] *W*(2)XIX, p. 433.
[143] Southampton Co. Superior Court Deed Bk., p. 2.
[144] Southampton Co. Will Bk. 4, p. 568.
[145] Surry Co. Will Bk. 10, p. 284.
[146] Catherine Lindsay Knorr, *Marriage Bonds and Ministers' Returns of Surry County, Virginia, 1768-1825* (Pine Bluff, Ark., 1960), p. 47,
[147] Surry Co. Marriage Register 1768-1853, p. 11.
[148] Surry Co. Wills &c 5, pp. 316-17.
[149] Chapman Bible, in *V* IX, p. 209; *W*(2) X, p. 256.
[150] *Ibid.*

by 26 April 1761 when administration on his estate was granted to Joseph Chapman,[151] married Jordan Harrison, daughter of William Harrison,[152] who left will 8 Aug. 1764-7 Sept. 1769.[153]

Issue: [CHAPMAN] 100. Charles[6], chose Joseph Chapman as his guardian, 1 Jan. 1761, but ordered, 6 Aug. 1761, to be bound out by the churchwardens of Newport Parish;[154] 101. Chloe[6], married ____ Webb; 102. Jordan[6], married Thomas Smelley; 103. (perhaps) (Daughter)[6], married ___ Casey.

43. CHARLES[5] CHAPMAN (John[4], Ann[3] Day, Mary[2] Bennett, Edward[1]) left will 10 Aug. 1749-1 March 1749/50.[155] He married ___.[156]

Issue: [CHAPMAN][157] 104. Rachel[6], married John Whitfield; 105. Ann[6], married 113. Joseph[6] Chapman; 106. Rhoda [Rodeth][6].

46. JOSEPH[5] CHAPMAN (John[4], Ann[3] Day, Mary[2] Bennett, Edward[1]) born 13 Nov. 1724,[158] married Lydia ___.

Issue: [CHAPMAN][159] 107. Sabra[6], born 22 Sept. 1755; 108. John[6], born 29 [*sic*] Feb. 1763.

50. CHARLES[5] CHAPMAN (Joseph[4], Ann[3] Day, Mary[2] Bennett, Edward[1]) left will 10 Feb. 1777-3 July 1777.[160] He married Mary ___.

Issue: [CHAPMAN] 109. John[6], died before 12 Nov. 1794 when the inventory of his estate was made,[161] married Sarah Wiggs; 110. William[6], left will 21 Dec. 1804-7 Jan. 1805,[162] married Mary Crocker;[163] 111. Henry[6],

---

[151] Isle of Wight Co. Order Bk. 1759-63, p. 215.

[152] Isle of Wight Co. Deed Bk. 8, p. 401.

[153] Isle of Wight Co. Will Bk. 8, p. 3.

[154] Isle of Wight Co. Order Bk. 1759-63, pp. 201, 253.

[155] Isle ofWight Co. Will Bk. 5, p. 235.

[156] Probably Ann, wife of Charles, named in will of Rachel Williams, 4 Aug. 1741-27 Sept. 1742 (Isle of Wight Co. Will Bk. 4, p. 422), which also named Mary, relict of Joseph[4] Chapman. Blanche Adams Chapman, *Isle of Wight County Marriages, 1628-1800* (n.p., 1933), p. 10, says she was Ann Parker, daughter of Thomas Parker, but the cited references do not support this.

[157] Isle of Wight Co. Guardian Accounts 1740-67, pp. 43, 48, 63, 67; Isle of Wight Co. Chancery papers 1796-002.

[158] Chapman Bible, *loc. cit.*

[159] *Ibid.*

[160] Isle of Wight Co. Will Bk. 8, p. 469.

[161] Isle of Wight Co. Will Bk. 11, pp. 11-12.

[162] Isle of Wight Co. Will Bk. 12, pp. 73-74.

[163] Isle of Wight Co. Order Bk. 1772-80, p. 125.

married ___; 112. Benjamin[6], left will 15 Feb. 1804-5 Dec. 1814,[164] married Elizabeth ___; 113. Joseph[6], left will 22 Feb. 1791-5 Dec. 1791,[165] married (1) 105. Ann[6] Chapman and (2) Rhoda ___,[166] who died before 3 Oct. 1796 when Joshua Bunkley was granted administration on her estate;[167] 114. Mary[6], married ___ Milliken; 115 Frances[6], died 4 July 1818 when her estate was appraised,[168] married, by 4 Dec. 1766,[169] Thomas Gale, who died after 5 Oct. 1801 when he deeded his land to his sons Joseph[7] and Alexander[7], reserving his wife's life right;[170] 116 Charles[6].

---

[164] Isle of Wight Co. Will Bk. 13, pp. 429-30.
[165] Isle of Wight Co. Will Bk. 10, p. 220.
[166] Perhaps 106. Rhoda[6] Chapman.
[167] Isle of Wight Co. Order Bk. 1795-97, p. 464.
[168] Isle of Wight Co. Will Bk. 15, pp. 218-19.
[169] Isle of Wight Co. Deed Bk. 12, pp. 111-12.
[170] Isle of Wight Co. Deed Bk. 18, pp. 628-29.

BENNETT (Samuel)[1]

*1. SAMUEL[1] BENNETT and his wife Joane came to Virginia in the *Providence* in 1622. They were named in the census, 16 Feb. 1623/4, as living at Elizabeth City with two children, names and gender unspecified.[2] Both children had died by 7 Feb. 1624/5 when they were listed at Elizabeth City in the muster, he aged 40, and described as servants of William Tiler. By 12 April 1633 he had 50 acres within "the precincts of Elizabeth City".[3] No patent now exists, but he is named as an adjoining property owner in several patents for land at the New Poquoson in Charles River (now York) County.[4] Joane Bennett, "widdow", received a patent 6 May 1636 for 450 acres of land in Charles River County.[5] Hannah[2] Bennett, daughter and heir of Samuel[1] Bennett, deceased, repatented this land 1 Nov. 1639.[6]

His widow married (2) Thomas Chapman (see BENNETT-CHAPMAN).

Issue: 2. (Child)[2], died in infancy; 3. (Child)[2], died in infancy; 4. HANNAH[2].

4. HANNAH[2] BENNETT (Samuel[1]), born about 1625, married (1), 11 Dec. 1644 in York County, Abraham Turner.[7] He died in Nov. 1646 at the house of Augustine Warner leaving one child.[8]

Sometime between 25 Oct. 1647 and 25 May 1648,[9] Hannah (Bennett) Turner married (2) Humphrey Tompkins. He died 23 Sept. 1673[10] and his nuncupative will was proved 24 Nov. 1673.[11] On 14 April 1674 Hannah Tompkins of the New Poquoson in the County of York, widow, made a deed of gift of personalty to her children Samuel (eldest son), William, Humphrey, John

---

[1] Jo White Linn, *Drake-Arrington, White-Turner, Linn-Brown* (Salisbury, N.C., 1984), pp. 171-80.

[2] Hotten, p. 183.

[3] Patent Bk. 1, p. 142.

[4] *Ibid*, pp. 298, 343, 425, 576.

[5] *Ibid.*, p. 346.

[6] *Ibid.*, p. 683.

[7] York Co. Deeds, Orders, Wills &c 3, 1657-62, p. 159, deposition, 22 Dec. 1661, by John Hunt, Armiger Wade, John Nesworth, Anthony Rooksby, Augustine Warner and Francis Willis.

[8] York Co. Deeds, Orders, Wills &c 2, 1646-48, p. 418, deposition of John Sharpe, 26 Sept. 1648.

[9] *Ibid.*, pp. 285, 360.

[10] Charles Parish Register.

[11] York Co. Deeds, Orders, Wills &c 5, 1672-76, p. 54.

and Ann, providing that 200 acres of land in Gloucester County, which she had bought since the death of Humphrey Tompkins, should be held for life by a future husband, should she marry again, and then be divided among her sons.[12] The patent for this escheated land was granted to Hannah Tompkins 4 Oct. 1675.[13] The land had originally been granted to Abraham Turner, 10 Oct. 1642, and was repatented as 217½ acres upon the North River, 25 Sept. 1679, by William, Humphrey and John Tompkins, sons of Humphrey, deceased.[14]

She married (3) William Arnold, who left will 30 Jan. 1682/3-24 April 1683,[15] leaving a gold ring to "sonn in Law" Samuel Tompkins and a silver cup to "sonn in Law" William Tompkins" and the residue of his estate to his wife Hannah. She is probably the Hannah Arnolds who died 6 June 1693.[16]

Issue: (by 1) [TURNER] 5. (Child)[3], died in infancy; (by 2) [TOMPKINS][17] 6. MARY[3]; 7. Edith[3], born 2 Feb. 1651/2, died 1660-74; 8. Hannah[3], to whom Edmund Watts, 23 Nov. 1660, gave the reversion of a cow given to his Godson Samuel Tompkins, son of Humphrey and Hannah, with provision that if Hannah died to go to their daughters Edith and Mary;[18] 9. SAMUEL[3]; 10. William[3], born 30 Dec. 1660, purchased lot in Yorktown, 24 Nov. 1691,[19] with brothers Humphrey and John, sons of Humphrey Tomkins, dec'd., owner of 100 acres in Kingston Parish, Gloucester County, 1704; 11. Humphrey[3], born 4 Dec. 1662, owner of 100 acres in Kingston Parish, 1704, married ___, daughter of Armiger

---

[12] *Ibid.*, pp. 65-66.

[13] Patent Bk. 6, p. 562; *MCGC*, p. 358.

[14] Patent Bk. 7, p. 8.

[15] York Co. Deeds, Orders, Wills &c 6, p. 494. Charles Parish Register shows William Arnold died 24 Feb. 1681/2.

[16] Charles Parish Register.

[17] *Ibid.* The loss of Gloucester County records prevents a determination of descendants of sons William[3], Humphrey[3] and John[3]. One grandson was probably Christopher Tompkins, born 17 Oct. 1705 on North River in Gloucester County, who married 32. *Joyce[4] Reade* (see MARTIAU). Another may be the Samuel Tompkins who presumably married 14. *Ann[4] (Manson) Houghton* (see BENNETT-CHAPMAN) and may be the Samuel who had children (by a previous marriage?) James (who left will dated 17 Jan. 1755 [Elizabeth City Co. Original will]), Mary, Martha, Sarah, Anne and Elizabeth. On 28 Feb. 1682/3 Robert Peyton patented 150 acres adjoining land of Humphrey Tompkins, deceased (Patent Bk. 7, p. 233). On 16 June 1733 Thomas Payton patented land on Black Water Creek adjoining Mary Tomkins, Mr. Robert Peyton's 150 acres, and others (Patent Bk. 17, p. 524), suggesting that descendants still held the land in that year. Several Tompkins families appear in the Kingston Parish Register, 1760-70.

[18] York Co. Deeds, Wills, Orders &c 1657-60, p. 96.

[19] York Co. Deeds, Orders, Wills &c 1, p. 383.

Wade, Sr.;[20] 12. Hannah[3], born 4 Sept. 1664, died 11 Sept. 1665; 13. Elizabeth[3], born 22 Feb. 1666/7, died 5 July 1667; 14. Ann[3], born 12 May 1668; 15. John[3], born 5 June 1670.

6. MARY[3] TOMPKINS (Hannah[2] Bennett, Samuel[1]), born 7 March 1649/50, buried 28 March 1687,[21] married John Nixon of Poquoson Parish, York County, who served as constable of the upper precincts of that parish until Oct. 1687[22] and died 4 Feb. 1693/4.[23] He married (2) Elizabeth ___, who with her "son in law" Richard Nixon, petitioned for administration on his estate, 24 May 1694,[24] and by 25 June 1694 married (2) Samuel Snignall.[25]

Issue: [NIXON][26] 16. Richard[4], born 3 Oct. 1670, given a cow calf by Walter Chapman, 23 Nov. 1672,[27] on 25 April 1706 assigned claim to 50 acres, the Oak Swamp in New Poquoson Parish, which his father had purchased in 1691;[28] 17. Hannah[4], born 19 June 1672, died 9 Dec. 1677; 18. William[4], born 21 June 1674, died 8 Dec. 1677; 19. HUMPHREY[4]; 20. Thomas[4], born 17 March 1679/80, on 24 June 1697, aged 16, was given permission by the court to bind himself out to a trade "to the end hee may thereby be the better abled through his industry to maintain himself,"[29] married Mary ___, who joined him in suing Joseph Thomas, 1724;[30] 21. Hannah[4], born 19 Sept. 1682; 22. Ann[4], born [baptized?]17 April 1687

9. SAMUEL[3] TOMPKINS (Hannah[2] Bennett, Samuel[1]), born 13 March 1658/9, lived in York County and died 31 Oct. 1702. He married (1), about 1681, Mrs. Elizabeth Clarke, who died 21 Dec. 1688, and (2), 1689,

---

[20] The will of Armiger Wade, 12 Aug. 1708-24 Nov. 1708 (York Co. Wills, Orders &c 13, 1706-10, pp. 172-74), named son-in-law Humphrey Tompkins. All of Wade's daughters recorded in the Charles Parish Register are accounted for in his will and her identity is undetermined.

[21] Charles Parish Register.

[22] York Co. Deeds, Orders, Wills &c 8, p. 2.

[23] Charles Parish Register.

[24] York Co. Deeds, Orders, Wills &c 9, p. 335.

[25] York Co. Deeds, Orders, Wills &c 10, p. 9.

[26] Charles Parish Register.

[27] York Co. Deeds, Orders, Wills &c 4, p. 482 [382], with provision that if the boy died his mother Mary Nixon was to have the increase.

[28] York Co. Deeds & Bonds 2, p. 164.

[29] York Co. Deeds, Orders, Wills &c 10, p. 420.

[30] York Co. Deeds, Orders, Wills &c 16, 1720-29, pp. 262, 288.

SarahTrevilian, born 5 Oct. 1670, daughter of Samuel and Mary Trevilian.[31] She joined Samuel in selling, 1 Jan. 1690/1, 200 acres she inherited as only sister and heir of Argoll Trevilian[32] and held 250 acres in York County, 1704.

Issue: [TOMPKINS][33] (by 1) 23. Hannah[4], born 23 Dec. 1681; 24. BENNETT[4]; (by 2) 25. Mary[4], born 29 July 1690; 26. Sarah[4], born 26 July 1692; 27. William[4], born 15 May 1695, died 2 Jan. 1700/1; 28. SAMUEL[4]; 29. Frances[4], born 5 Nov. 1699; 30. Elizabeth[4], born 16 Jan. 1702/3.

19. HUMPHREY[4] NIXON (Mary[3] Tompkins, Hannah[2] Bennett, Samuel[1]), born 9 March 1677/8, died 25 March 1718 [1717/8], left will 20 March 1717/8-15 Dec. 1718,[34] purchased 25 acres in York County, 17 Nov. 1705.[35] He married Susanna ___, who married (2) Giles Taverner.[36]

Issue: [NIXON][37] 31. John[5], left land by his father; 32. Rebecca[5]; 33. Mary[5]; 34. Elizabeth[5].

24. BENNETT[4] TOMPKINS (Samuel[3], Hannah[2] Bennett, Samuel[1]), born 1 March 1683/4, died 21 March 1739/40, married (1), by 1711, Hope Tomer, born 29 March 1693, died 1 July 1718, and (2) Mary ___, who left will 5 Dec. 1741-15 Feb. 1741/2.[38]

Issue: [TOMPKINS][39] (by 1) 35. BENNETT[5]; 36. Elizabeth[5], born 29 Sept. 1713; 37. JOHN[5]; (by 2) 38. Mary[5], born 26 Sept. 1720, died 18 Dec. 1720; 39. Edmund[5], born 11 Dec. 1721; 40. Samuel[5], born 15 Jan. 1723; 41. Martha[5], born 22 Nov. 1725; 42. Mary[5]. born 17 Dec. 1727; 43. Frances[5], born 14 Jan. 1730, died 6 April 1730; 44. WILLIAM[5].

28. SAMUEL[4] TOMPKINS (Samuel[3], Hannah[2] Bennett, Samuel[1]), born 19 June 1697, left will proved 21 March 1763.[40] He married (1) Ann Toomer,

---

[31] Charles Parish Register.

[32] York Co. Deeds, Orders, Wills &c 1, pp. 351-52.

[33] Charles Parish Register.

[34] York Co. Deeds, Orders, Wills &c 15, 1716-20, pp. 367-68.

[35] York Co. Deeds & Bonds 2, p. 152.

[36] York Co. Deeds, Orders, Wills &c 15, 1716-20, pp. 399-400, 589.

[37] Although the will of Humphrey[4] Nixon refers to an unborn child, the accounting of his estate, returned 20 July 1730, speaks of 4 children (York Co. Deeds, Orders, Wills &c 17, 1729-32, p. 84). On 18 May 1730 Rebecca and Mary Nixon, being of lawful age, petitioned for their portions of the estate (*ibid.*, p. 64).

[38] York Co. Wills & Inventories 19, 1740-46, pp. 84-85. She may have been a widow since her will names daughter Ann Gibbons.

[39] Charles Parish Register.

[40] York Co. Wills & Inventories 21, 1760-71, pp. 136-38.

daughter of John Toomer, born 24 July 1698, died 6 March 1717/8, (2) Martha Powers, sister of Daniel Powers,[41] and (3), after 3 Feb. 1761, Apphia (Banister) Sheppard.[42]

Issue: [TOMPKINS][43] (by 1) 45. Samuel[5], born before his parents' marriage,[44] died 5 Sept. 1721; (by 2) 46. MARY[5]; 47. MARTHA[5]; 48. Lazarus[5], born 7 July 1725, died 31 Aug. 1747; 49. Sarah[5], born 1 Feb. 1727/8; 50. Frances[5], born 23 Oct. 1730, died 29 Sept. 1733; 51. JAMES[5]; 52. Anne[5]; 53. Elizabeth[5], born 13 Aug. 1739.

35. BENNETT[5] TOMPKINS (Bennett[4], Samuel[3], Hannah[2] Bennett, Samuel[1]), born 31 March 1711, died 1 Sept. 1780.[45] He resided at Bennett's Creek, York County, and was captain of militia, 1762. He married 171. Ann[5] Cary (see BALEY-COCKE), who was living in 1793 in Richmond.[46]

Issue: [TOMPKINS][47] 54. Rebecca[6], born 6 Oct. 1744; 55. Miles[6], born 6 Aug. 1746; 56 Mary[6], born 2 Sept. 1749, married, 1772,[48] Richard Brown of York County, who left will 15 Aug. 1792-20 April 1795;[49] 57. Elizabeth[6], born 2 Jan. 1753, died 9 Dec. 1796, married, 22 May 1780,[50] William Hay, widower of 531. Elizabeth[6] Cary (see BALEY-COCKE); 58. Ann[6], born 23 July 1756[51] 59. Bennett[6], born 24 Jan. 1759, died Nov. 1759.

37. JOHN[5] TOMPKINS (Bennett[4], Samuel[3], Hannah[2] Bennett, Samuel[1]), born 25 May 1718,[52] is presumably the John who moved to Northampton County and married, 25 Feb. 1747/8, 159. Ann[5] (Kendall) Custis (see MASON), widow of 233. John[5] Custis (see THOROWGOOD),[53] who is probably the Ann, widow

---

[41] York Co. Deeds, Orders, Wills 16, 1720-29, p. 476.

[42] Elizabeth City Co. Will Bk. 1758-64, p. 191; Will Bk. 1763-71, p. 12.

[43] Charles Parish Register.

[44] York Co. Deeds, Orders, Wills &c 16, 1720-29, p. 213.

[45] Charles Parish Register.

[46] Deposition, Brunswick Co. District Court judgments, Clausel vs. Armistead.

[47] Charles Parish Register.

[48] Fairfax Harrison, The Virginia Carys (New York, 1919), p. 52.

[49] York Co. Wills & Inventories 23, pp. 435-36.

[50] William Hay Bible, in W(1) XV, p. 85. Charles Parish Register shows birth as 3 Jan.

[51] Charles Parish Register shows deaths of Ann Tompkins on 3 Nov. 1757 and Oct. 1758.

[52] Charles Parish Register.

[53] Custis Bible, in William Fletcher Boogher, Gleanings of Virginia History (Washington, 1903), p. 328, and V XXXIV, p. 371, with variations; Jean Merritt Mihalyka, Marriages, Northampton County, Virginia, 1660/1-1854 (Bowie, Md., 1991), p. 112, bond 19 Feb. The Bible shows his birth as 4 June 1718, the eleven day difference possibly reflecting conversion

of John Custis, who deposed, 10 Feb. 1747/8, she was aged 35,[54] and left will 20 Aug. 1783-10 Feb. 1789.[55] He died 21 Aug. 1757,[56] leaving will 21 July 1757-13 Sept. 1757 which gave all his land in Gloucester County to his sons John and Bennett.[57]

Issue:[58] 60. John Custis[6], born 27 Nov. 1748, died 16 Dec. 1748; 61. William[6], born 16 Sept. 1750, died 24 Sept. 1750; 62. John[6], born 20 Nov. 1751, died 19 Dec. 1819, aged 68 yrs. 1 mo.,[59] left will 23 Nov. 1811-14 Feb. 1820,[60] of "Wellington," Northampton County, married 325. *Frances[6] Hack* (see WEST, Anthony), born 20 Nov. 1745;[61] 63. Bennett[6], born 22 Jan. 1755, died before 8 Oct. 1798 when administration on his estate was granted to John Tompkins.[62]

44. WILLIAM[5] TOMPKINS (Bennett[4], Samuel[3], Hannah[2] Bennett, Samuel[1]), born 13 April 1731, died by 5 Aug. 1760 when administration on his estate was granted to William Reade.[63] He resided in Elizabeth City County. He married Anne ___.

Issue: [TOMPKINS][64] 64. Martha[6], born 4 March 1754; 65. James[6], born 9 Jan. 1757; 66. Bennet[6], born 22 Dec. 1758.

46. MARY[5] TOMPKINS (Samuel[4], Samuel[3], Hannah[2] Bennett, Samuel[1]), born 12 Feb. 1719/20,[65] married (1) William Sandefer, born 14 Oct. 1707,[66] who as a resident of Elizabeth City County bought land in Isle of Wight County, 14

---

to New Style dating after 1752.

[54] Northampton Co. Suit, Custis *vs.* Custis, pack 33, in William R. M. Houston and Jean M. Mihalyka, *Colonial Residents of Virginia's Eastern Shore* (Baltimore, 1985), p. 25.

[55] Northampton Co. Wills & Inventories 28, 1788-92, p. 88.

[56] Custis Bible, *loc. cit.*

[57] Northampton Co. Wills & Inventories 21, 1754-60, p. 290.

[58] Custis Bible, *loc. cit.*

[59] Gravestone, "Wellington," in Jean Merritt Mihalyka, *Gravestone Inscriptions in Northampton County, Virginia* (Richmond, 1984), p. 85, missing year of death.

[60] Northampton Co. Wills &c 35, 1817-22, pp. 409-11.

[61] Bible, in *The Virginia Genealogist*, XXXIII, p. 164.

[62] Northampton Co. Order Bk. 33, 1796-1800, p. 262.

[63] Elizabeth City Co. Order Bk. 1758-64, p. 224.

[64] Charles Parish Register.

[65] *Ibid.*

[66] Sandefer-Arrington Bible, Mary Jones Arrington Papers, The Southern Historical Collection, University of North Carolina Library, in Jo White Linn, *Drake-Arrington, White-Turner, Linn-Brown ...* (Salisbury, N.C., 1984), pp. 165-68.

Aug. 1746,[67] and left will 27 May 1755-13 Nov. 1755.[68] She married (2) Benjamin Hasty.

Issue:[69] (by 1) [SANDEFER] 67. Martha[6], born 18 Sept. 1738; 68. Mary[6], born 29 Sept. 1741, left will 2 Dec. 1804-Feb. 1805,[70] married Arthur Arrington of Edgecombe Co., N.C., justice and sheriff on the formation of Nash Co., N.C., 1777, quartermaster commissioner during the Revolutionary War, who left will 23 May 1795-Nov. 1795;[71] 69. William[6], born 14 Oct. 1743, moved to the part of Edgecombe County which became Nash Co., N.C.; 70. Patsy[6], born 8 Jan. 1745, possibly married Francis Rose of Nash Co., N.C., who left will 7 May 1795-Nov. 1796;[72] 71. Hill[6], born 25 Aug. 17_, died before 25 Nov. 1772 when his brother William was appointed administrator of his estate;[73] 72. Samuel[6], born 1 Sept. 1750 in Southampton County, died 20 Feb. 1836 in Wake Co., N.C., served four tours in the militia in the Revolutionary War,[74] married, 9 April 1771 in Southampton County, Ann Council, born 30 Nov. 1753; 73. Ann[6], born 1 April 1753; 74. Tompkins[6], born Sept. 1755, left will 2 Dec. 1782-April 1783,[75] married Mary ___; (by 2) [HASTY] 75. Benjamin[6], born 10 Oct. 1758; 76. Mary[6], born 11 Jan. 1762, married Joseph Vick, born 6 Sept. 1762.

47. MARTHA[5] TOMPKINS (Samuel[4], Samuel[3], Hannah[2] Bennett, Samuel[1]), born 1 Oct. 1723, left will 15 Nov. 1788-21 Feb. 1799.[76] She married, as his (2) wife, Edward Armistead, son of Maj. William and Rebecca (Moss) Armistead, of Elizabeth City County, who left will 19 Feb. 1771-1 March 1771.[77]

Issue: [ARMISTEAD][78] 77. Samuel[6], born 9 Sept. 1757, married Frances Minson; 78. Rebecca[6], born 20 Jan. 1761, married Robert Walker.

51. JAMES[5] TOMPKINS (Samuel[4], Samuel[3], Hannah[2] Bennett , Samuel[1]),

---

[67] Isle of Wight Co. Deed Bk. 7, p. 345.

[68] Southampton Co. Will Bk. 1, p. 181.

[69] Sandefer-Arrington Bible, *loc. cit.*

[70] Nash Co., N.C., Original will, in Linn, *op. cit.*, pp. 100-01.

[71] Nash Co., N.C., Original will, in Linn, *op. cit.*, pp. 95-97.

[72] Nash Co., N.C., Will Bk. 1, p. 111.

[73] Edgecombe Co., N.C., Estate Papers, North Carolina Archives.

[74] Revolutionary War pension application, Samuel Sandiford (Sandeford), widow Ann, W.19307, National Archives.

[75] Nash Co., N.C., Will Bk. 1, p. 31.

[76] Elizabeth City Co. Will Bk. 1787-1800, p. 449.

[77] Elizabeth City Co. Will Bk. 1763-71, p. 414.

[78] *W*(1) VII, p. 18; Charles Parish Register.

born 27 May 1733, left will dated 17 Jan. 1755.[79] He married ___.
  Issue: [TOMPKINS] 79. Mary[6], died by 6 May 1760.[80]

---

[79] Elizabeth City Co. Original will.
[80] Elizabeth City Co. Order Bk. 1755-60, p. 286.

BENNETT-CHAPMAN

*1. Joan (___) Bennett, widow of Samuel Bennett, married (2) Thomas Chapman of Poquoson Parish, York County, who entered into a controversy with Abraham Turner concerning the Bennett land and, 11 March 1645/6, surrendered his right to the 450 acres.[1] On 20 Dec. 1645 he proved rights to 1200 acres.[2] Following Joan's death he married (2) Elizabeth ___ who married (2) William Bouth.

Issue: [CHAPMAN] 2. WALTER[2]

2. WALTER[2] CHAPMAN (Joan[1] Bennett), for whom Humphrey Tompkins was guardian, 1660,[3] on 23 Nov. 1672 gave a calf to Richard Nixon, son of John Nixon, with provision that if the boy died his mother Mary Nixon was to have the increase.[4] He was buried 1 Oct. 1685.[5] He married Ann ___, who married (2) Francis Callowhill and left will, proved 18 Feb. 1722, naming children and grandchildren.

Issue: [CHAPMAN][6] 3. JOHN[3]; 4. Walter[3], born 8 March 1676/7, died 7 April 1678; 5. ELIZABETH[3].

3. JOHN[3] CHAPMAN (Walter[2], Joan[1] Bennett), born 24 Feb. 1674/5,[7] owned 70 acres in York County, 1704, left will dated 25 Sept. 1750,[8] not now extant, married Elizabeth ___.

Issue: [CHAPMAN][9] 6. ANN[4]; 7. William[4], born 31 Aug. 1700, died 15 Feb. 1700/1; 8. JOHN[4]; 9. William[4], born 13 Jan. 1704/5; 10. Walter[4], born 19 Oct. 1707; 11. ELIZABETH[4]; 12. Mary[4].

5. ELIZABETH[3] CHAPMAN (Walter[2], Joyce[1] Bennett), born 11 Feb.

---

[1] York Co. Deeds, Orders, Wills &c 2, 1645-49, p. 134, "Joane the wife of sd Thomas Chapman hath likewise ... consented to the sd surrender"; Deeds, Orders, Wills &c 1, p. 347-48, 5 Aug. 1657, agreement with Humphrey Tompkins, "Chapman having died intestate and Wm Bouth having married the relict."

[2] York Co. Deeds, Orders, Wills &c 2, 1645-49, p. 55.

[3] York Co. Deeds, Orders, Wills &c 3, 1657-62, p. 169r. At an Orphans Court, 11 Sept. 1660, Humphrey Tomkins was ordered to give account concerning the orphan of Thomas Chapman.

[4] York Co. Deeds, Orders, Wills &c 4, 1665-72, p. 482 (382). The restriction to Mary Nixon is significant in establishing the family relationship (see p. 244, note 27).

[5] Charles Parish Register.

[6] *Ibid.*

[7] *Ibid.*

[8] York Co. Deeds & Bonds 5, 1741-54, pp. 499-502.

[9] Charles Parish Register.

1678/9,[10] married (1) Peter Manson who held 150 acres in York County, 1704, and died 31 Aug. 1721[11] leaving will 20 March 1720-15 Jan. 1721/2 naming his wife, children and brother-in-law John Chapman.[12] She married (2), by 21 March 1725/6,[13] Thomas Kerby, widower of 7. *Frances*[4] *Lowry* (see PUREFOY).

Issue: [MANSON][14] 13. PETER[4]; 14. ANN[4]; 15. Elizabeth[4], born 3 April 1701; 16. JOHN[4]; 17. JAMES[4]; 18. Frances[4], born 28 Jan. 1706/7, died 25 Dec. 1707; 19. Nathaniel[4], born 10 April 1710, died young; 20. Walter[4], born 8 Dec. 1713.

6. ANN[4] CHAPMAN (John[3], Walter[2], Joan[1] Bennett), born 8 Oct. 1698, married John Trotter who left will 25 March 1745-20 May 1745 mentioning father-in-law John Chapman.[15]

Issue: [TROTTER] 21. Thomas[5], of Cumberland County, left will 9 April 1796-codicil 3 Oct. 1798-26 Nov. 1798;[16] 22. ELIZABETH[5].

8. JOHN[4] CHAPMAN (John[3], Walter[2], Joan[1] Bennett), born 24 Jan. 1701/2, of Warwick County, died by June 1749 when administration on his estate was granted to Ann Chapman.[17] He married Ann Allen, who left will 12 March 1770-17 Dec. 1770.[18]

Issue: [CHAPMAN][19] 23. Walter[5], left will 16 April 1751-15 July 1751;[20] 24. JOHN[5]; 25. ELIZABETH[5]; 26. Ann[5]; 27. MARY ALLEN[5]; 28. Hudson[5], left will proved 16 May 1763;[21] 29. ALLEN[5].

11. ELIZABETH[4] CHAPMAN (John[3], Walter[2], Joan[1] Bennett), born 28 Dec. 1709, left will 2 Aug. 1780-17 June 1782.[22] She married (1) 30. *Edmund*[4] *Chisman* (see CHISMAN) and (2) James Goodwin, widower of 40. *Diana*[4]

---

[10] Charles Parish Register.

[11] *Ibid.*

[12] York Co. Deeds, Orders, Wills &c 16, 1720-29, pp. 99-100.

[13] *Ibid.*, p. 376, petition of Peter Manson against Thomas Kirby and Elizabeth his wife for a division of the estate of Peter Manson.

[14] Charles Parish Register.

[15] York Co. Wills & Inventories 19, 1740-46, p. 369.

[16] Cumberland Co. Will Bk. 3, pp. 132-33.

[17] Warwick Co. Minute Bk. 1748-62, p. 34.

[18] York Co. Wills & Inventories 21, 1760-71, pp. 524-25.

[19] York Co. Inventories & Orders 1752-54, p. 91.

[20] York Co. Wills & Inventories 20, 1745-59, pp. 228-29.

[21] York Co. Wills & Inventories 21, 1766-71, pp. 145-46.

[22] York Co. Wills & Inventories 22, p. 511.

Chisman (see CHISMAN), who died 8 Nov. 1757,[23] leaving will 9 Oct. 1757-19 Dec. 1757.[24]

Issue: (by 1) see CHISMAN; (by 2) [GOODWIN][25] 30. PETER[5]; 31. ROBERT[5]; 32. REBECCA[5]; 33. JAMES[5]; 34. ELIZABETH[5]; 35. DIANA WALLACE[5]; 36. RACHEL[5].

13. PETER[4] MANSON (Elizabeth[3] Chapman, Walter[2], Joan[1] Bennett), born 25 Aug. 1697, died 16 Feb. 1755, of Elizabeth City County, left will dated 12 Dec. 1754.[26] He married, 22 April 1725, Hannah Kerby, born 24 Jan. 1708/9, died 8 Dec. 1754.[27]

Issue: [MANSON][28] 37. Mary[5], married 112. *John[5] Patrick* (see CHISMAN); 38. John[5], born 5 Sept. 1728,[29] died 6 Feb. 1758, left will dated 1 Jan. 1758;[30] 39. Frances[5], born 17 Sept. 1732; 40. Elizabeth[5], married 118. William[5] Patrick; 41. Peter[5], born 4 Dec. 1737, died 8 Dec. 1757; 42. Hannah[5], born 21 Jan. 1741/2; 43. ROBERT[5].

14. ANN[4] MANSON (Elizabeth[3] Chapman, Walter[2], Joan[1] Bennett), born 4 June 1699, married (1) William Houghton, born 12 Feb. 1691/2, of Warwick County, who died before 7 July 1757 when his heirs brought suit to divide his estate,[31] and (2) Samuel Tompkins.[32]

Issue: [HOUGHTON][33] 44. WILLIAM[5]; 45. Nathaniel[5], born 14 Feb. 1722/3, died young; 46. Peter[5], born 10 Sept. 1724; 47. John[5], born 11 Aug. 1726, died young; 48. Elizabeth[5], born 11 March 1728/9, married William

---

[23] *W*(1) VI, supplement, p. 14.

[24] York Co. Will Bk. 20, pp. 454-56.

[25] *W*(1) VI, supplement, pp. 14-15.

[26] Elizabeth City Co. Original wills #87. He died before 3 Aug. 1756 (Elizabeth City Co. Order Bk. 1755-60, p. 64).

[27] *W*(1) X, p. 113.

[28] *Ibid.*

[29] Charles Parish Register.

[30] Elizabeth City Co. Original will, which mentions cousin William Houghton. The inventory of his estate was ordered made 7 Feb. 1758 (Elizabeth City Co. Order Bk. 1755-60, p. 165).

[31] Warwick Co. Minute Bk. 1748-63, p. 488.

[32] This marriage is assumed since Samuel Tompkins and wife Ann were parties to the suit for division of William Houghton's estate but did not share in the division. The identity of Samuel Tompkins is undetermined.

[33] Warwick Co. Minute Bk. 1748-63, pp. 488, 505, 524, 544-47; Charles Parish Register.

Smith;[34] 49. Frances[5], born 26 Feb. 1730/1; 50. SARAH[5]; 51. Mary[5], chose William Houghton as her guardian, 7 July 1757.[35]

16. JOHN[4] MANSON (Elizabeth[3] Chapman, Walter[2], Joan[1] Bennett), born 14 Feb. 1702/3, moved to Prince George County where he patented 200 acres on Horsepen Branch, 20 Aug. 1745, and 346 acres between Sapony Creek and Rockey Run, 25 June 1747.[36] He married, by 1733,[37] Martha ___, widow of Edward Lewis.[38]

Issue: [MANSON] 52. PETER[5]; 53. (possibly) NATHANIEL[5]; 54. JANE[5].

17. JAMES[4] MANSON (Elizabeth[3] Chapman, Walter[2], Joan[1] Bennett), born 13 Jan. 1704/5, of Elizabeth City County, left will dated 12 Dec. 1761.[39] He married Sarah ___, widow of George Latimer.[40]

Issue: [MANSON] 55. Chapman[5], of Dinwiddie County, 1763;[41] 56. Sarah[5]; 57. Peter[5], of Elizabeth City County, sold, 30 Nov. 1802, the plantation devised to him by his father,[42] married Diana ___; 58. James[5].

22. ELIZABETH[5] TROTTER (Ann[4] Chapman, John[3], Walter[2], Joan[1] Bennett) married Maurice Langhorne, son of John and Ann (Wade) Langhorne, who moved from Warwick County to Cumberland County where he was a member of the Committee of Safety, 1775-76. He married (2) Mary Moulson and died before 5 March 1791 when the inventory of his estate was made.[43]

Issue: [LANGHORNE][44] 59. Mary[6], born 30 Nov. 1746, married, as his (1) wife, Col. James Callaway, born 21 Dec. 1736, died 1 Nov. 1804 near New

---

[34] She is perhaps the Elizabeth Smith taxed, 1787, in Warwick County; next on list is William Smith with smaller estate, perhaps a son.

[35] Warwick Co. Minute Bk. 1748-62, p. 488.

[36] Patent Bk. 22, p. 430; Patent Bk. 28, p. 104.

[37] Bristol Parish Register, birth of son Peter, 24 Dec. 1733.

[38] Prince George Co. Minute Bk. 1737-40, p. 356.

[39] Elizabeth City Co. Original wills #124. His estate was divided, 5 Feb. 1765, one-third each to Edward Parish, Peter Manson and James Parish (Elizabeth City Co. Deeds & Wills 1763-71, p. 28). It is unclear whether Parish was husband of his widow or his daughter.

[40] Elizabeth City Co. Deeds, Wills, Bonds &c 1737-56, p. 183.

[41] Dinwiddie Co. Clerk's fee book, in *The Virginia Genealogist* XXXVIII, p. 280.

[42] Elizabeth City Co. Deeds & Wills 12, 1798-1806, pp. 246-48.

[43] Cumberland Co. Will Bk. 2, p. 509.

[44] George Norbury Mackenzie, ed., *Colonial Families of the United States of America*, II (Baltimore, 1911), pp. 414-15; *T* XIII, p. 263, which adds son Beverley who married 1146. *Susan*[6] *Woodson* (see WOODSON) and says Mary[6] married (1) Joseph Calland, (2) Thomas Turpin and (3) James Callaway.

London, served in French and Indian War and was colonel and County
Lieutenant of Bedford County during the Revolutionary War, built the first iron
works above Lynchburg, and was owner and operator of lead mines,[45] who
married (2), 1779, Elizabeth Early; 60. John[6], born 8 Dec. 1751, died 14 May
1784, left will 3 March 1784-26 July 1784,[46] married, 30 April 1774, 124.
Sarah[6] Bell (see TAYLOR-CARY), born 24 Aug. 1754, who married (2) Cary
Harrison; 61. Anne[6], married, Dec. 1775, Thomas Miller, clerk of Powhatan
County; 62. Elizabeth[6], born 9 Dec. 1758, died 5 Aug. 1818, married John
Scarsbrook[7] Langhorne, son of 125. *Elizabeth Cary[6]* (*Scasbrook*) *Langhorne*
(see TAYLOR-CARY), born 10 April 1760, died 1797, of Warwick County,
captain in the Revolutionary War; 63. Maurice Cary[6].

24. JOHN[5] CHAPMAN (John[4], John[3], Walter[2], Joan[1] Bennett), of York
County, left will 23 Jan. 1799-15 July 1799.[47] He married (1) Ann Hansford,
daughter of John and Rebecca Hansford, and (2) Elizabeth Dickinson.[48]

Issue: [CHAPMAN] (by 1) 64. Walter[6], of Warwick County, 1787; (by 2)
65. Mary D.[6], married ___ Moody; 66. William[6], died before 21 Feb. 1807 when
the inventory of his estate was ordered made.[49]

25. ELIZABETH[5] CHAPMAN (John[4], John[3], Walter[2], Joan[1] Bennett)
married ___ Brown.

Issue: [BROWN] 67. John[6].

27. MARY ALLEN[5] CHAPMAN (John[4], John[3], Walter[2], Joan[1] Bennett)
married Capt. John Goodwin, son of Peter and Mary (Robinson) Calthorpe
Goodwin, born 8 Dec. 1739, who died before March 1777.[50]

Issue: [GOODWIN] 68. Ann[6]; 69. Elizabeth[6], born 12 March 1766;[51] 70.
Peter[6], born 6 Aug. 1768.[52]

29. ALLEN[5] CHAPMAN (John[4], John[3], Walter[2], Joan[1] Bennett), of York
County, left will 10 July 1794-20 Oct. 1794.[53] He married ___.

---

[45] Alexander Brown, *The Cabells and Their Kin* (Richmond, 1939), pp. 399-400.

[46] Cumberland Co. Will Bk. 2, pp. 339-40.

[47] York Co. Wills & Inventories 23, 1783-1811, p. 538.

[48] Southall Papers, Earl Gregg Swem Library, College of William and Mary, folder 129.
York Co. Wills & Inventories 23, 1783-1811, pp. 585-87.

[49] York Co. Wills & Inventories 23, pp. 715-16.

[50] *Ibid.*, p. 203, earliest date shown in his estate inventory.

[51] Charles Parish Register.

[52] *Ibid.*

[53] York Co. Wills & Inventories 23, 1783-1811, pp. 424-25.

Issue: [CHAPMAN] 71. John[6], left will 26 Nov. 1803-16 July 1804,[54] married Elizabeth ___; 72. Elizabeth Doswell[6], married ___ Goodwin; 73. Mary[6].

30. PETER[5] GOODWIN (Elizabeth[4] Chapman, John[3], Walter[2], Joan[1] Bennett) of "Oakley," Caroline County, married (1) Sarah Coleman and (2) Sarah Coghill.

Issue: [GOODWIN][55] (by 1) 74. James Coleman[6], born 29 March 1761, died 9 Feb. 1814, farmer of Caroline County and of Fayette Co., Ky., married, 8 Sept. 1782, Nancy[7] Graves, daughter of 251. *Joseph[6] Graves* and Frances Coleman (see GRAVES), born 27 May 1765, died 12 Aug. 1844; 75. (Daughter)[6], married ___ Coleman; 76. (Daughter)[6], married Hawes Coleman, son of John and Eunice (Hawes) Coleman, who was born 1 Jan. 1757 in Spotsylvania County, left will 20 March 1835-codicil 11 June 1838-25 Jan. 1841,[56] served four tours in the Spotsylvania County militia, 1775-81, resided there until 1789 and then moved to the part of Amherst County which became Nelson County,[57] married (2) Ann Harris and (3), 26 Aug. 1814,[58] Ann Overton; (by 2) 77. Thomas[6], born 9 Oct. 1770, merchant of Fredericksburg, married, 2 Oct. 1792[59] at Fredericksburg, Ann Maria Smith; 78. Littleton[6], born about 1778, died, aged 46, before 12 May 1823 when Mrs. Elizabeth Goodwin was mentioned as his administratrix,[60] farmer of "Oakley," Caroline County, married, 19 Jan. 1797, 191. *Elizabeth Doswell[6] Goodwin* (see CHISMAN), born 3 Sept. 1781 in Hanover County, died 27 June 1849; 79. Harwood[6], born 3 Sept. 1775, died Aug. 1859, farmer of "Topping Castle," Caroline County, Louisa County and Orange County, married, 1798, Sarah Minor, born 5 Aug. 1775, died 19 Sept. 1852 in Louisa County; 80. Elizabeth Garland[6], married Henry C. Coleman of "Clifton," Caroline County, who was appointed county surveyor, 13 April 1796,[61] was elected to the House of Delegates in 1808, but that election

---

[54] *Ibid.*, p. 660.

[55] *W*(1) VI, Supplement, pp. 24-36.

[56] Nelson Co. Will Bk. F, p. 138.

[57] Revolutionary War pension application, Hawes Coleman, S.16732, National Archives.

[58] Kathleen Booth Williams, *Marriages of Louisa County, Virginia, 1766-1815* (n.p., 1959), p. 21.

[59] *Virginia Herald*, Fredericksburg, 11 Oct. 1792, which does not specify date.

[60] William Lindsay Hopkins, *Caroline County Court Records and Marriages* (Richmond, 1987), p. 46.

[61] Caroline Co. Order Bk. 1794-96, p. 259.

was set aside for irregularity,[62] and married (2), 1 June 1803,[63] Nancy W. Macon.

31. ROBERT[5] GOODWIN (Elizabeth[4] Chapman, John[3], Walter[2], Joan[1] Bennett), born 1739, died 12 May 1789, left will 9 May 1789-8 June 1789.[64] He was a farmer of Louisa County. He married, 11 Dec. 1766,[65] Jane Tulloch.

Issue: [GOODWIN][66] 81. Elizabeth Garland[6], born 2 May 1768, married, (bond 19) May 1787,[67] Spencer Coleman, farmer of Pine Forest, Spotsylvania County; 82. Hugh[6], born 27 Feb. 1770, died 26 Dec. 1844,[68] farmer of Spotsylvania County, married (1), 22 Dec. 1789 Elizabeth Blaydes, born 25 Jan. 1773, died 27 March 1832, and (2) Mrs. ___ Clayton;[69] 83. Mary[6], born 28 Sept. 1772, died 11 Jan. 1815 at "Red House," Spotsylvania County, married, 26 Oct. 1790,[70] as his (1) wife, Joseph[7] Graves, born 10 July 1776, died 6 June 1826 in Fayette Co., Ky., son of 251. *Joseph[6] Graves* and Frances Coleman (see GRAVES); 84. Barbara[6], born 18 Nov. 1774, died 15 March 1794 married, 27 Sept. 1792,[71] William Coghill, born 1754; 85. Robert[6], born 10 Aug. 1777, farmer of Louisa County, married, 11 Oct. 1804, Judith Tyler; 86. John Chapman[6], born 6 Nov. 1779, died 13 Dec. 1845, left will 13 Aug. 1841-codicil 3 Jan. 1843-12 Jan. 1846,[72] farmer at "Oaksby," Louisa Coounty, married, 27 Dec. 1803,[73] Anna Rhodes Thomson, born 26 Dec. 1783, died 11 Aug. 1865; 87. Mildred[6], born 9 June 1782, died 11 Sept. 1784; 88. Archibald Tulloch[6], born 30 Nov. 1785, died 2 Oct. 1845, of Louisa County, married, 19 Sept. 1805,[74] Candace Sandridge.

32. REBECCA[5] GOODWIN (Elizabeth[4] Chapman, John[3], Walter[2], Joan[1] Bennett) married ___ Mask.

---

[62] Leonard, p. 251.

[63] Caroline Co. Marriage Register 1, p. 3.

[64] Louisa Co. Will Bk. 3, p. 248.

[65] *W*(1) VI, supplement, p. 38; Williams, *op. cit.*, p. 42, bond 9 Dec.

[66] *W*(1) VI, supplement, pp. 38-54.

[67] Williams, *op. cit.*, p. 21.

[68] *Religious Herald*, 23 Jan. 1845.

[69] Mary Douglas Meriwether Blaydes, *More Than Skin Deep* (Lexington, Ky., 1979), pp. 12, 19.

[70] Williams, *op. cit.*, p. 43.

[71] *Ibid.*, p. 20.

[72] Louisa Co. Will Bk. 11, pp. 405-07.

[73] Williams, *op. cit.*, p. 42.

[74] *Ibid.*, bond 13 Sept.

Issue: [MASK] 89. Elizabeth[6]; other children unidentified.

33. JAMES[5] GOODWIN (Elizabeth[4] Chapman, John[3], Walter[2], Joan[1] Bennett) of Charles Parish, York County,[75] and of Elizabeth City County, married Margaret ___.

Issue: [GOODWIN] 90. Rachel[6], born 9 March 1780;[76] 91. James[6], born 29 May 1782.[77]

34. ELIZABETH[5] GOODWIN (Elizabeth[4] Chapman, John[3], Walter[2], Joan[1] Bennett) died 16 Sept. 1828.[78] She married Robert Blackwell who moved to Lunenburg County and left will 29 Feb. 1787-8 Oct. 1789.[79]

Issue: [BLACKWELL][80] 92. Robert[6], born 4 Nov. 1766, died 15 April 1823, of Brunswick and later of Lunenburg County, left will 15 Nov. 1822-12 May 1823,[81] married, 5 April 1792,[82] Jane Jones; 93. James Goodwin[6], born 7 April 1768, died 1 May 1785; 94. John[6], born 28 Dec. 1769, died 14 Dec. 1831, of "Hollydale," Lunenburg County, left will 6 Dec. 1831-Jan. 1832,[83] married, 6 July 1796,[84] Mary Dunn Edmondson, born 16 April 1775, died 13 Aug. 1849; 95. Thomas[6], born 18 Dec. 1771, died 3 May 1820, left will 16 Feb. 1819-10 July 1820,[85] married (1), 31 Jan. 1793, Ann[7] Sydnor, daughter of 247. *William[6] Sydnor* (see GASKINS), born 18 Feb. 1779, died 23 Oct. 1793,[86] and (2), Mariah (Bailey) Bridgeforth, born 13 March 1769, died 3 Feb. 1816; 96. Christiana[6], born 20 Dec. 1773, died 27 Jan. 1826, married Robert Jones; 97. Joel[6], born 16 April 1773, of Lunenburg County, married (1), 24 March 1800,[87] Sally B. Gunn and (2), 18 Jan. 1821,[88] Martha Fletcher Dance; 98. Elizabeth

---

[75] *W*(1) VI, supplement, p. 58.

[76] Charles Parish Register.

[77] *Ibid.*

[78] June Banks Evans, *The Blackwells of Blackwell's Neck* (New Orleans, 1997), p. 31.

[79] Lunenburg Co. Will Bk. 3, p. 349.

[80] Evans, *op. cit.*, pp. 31-55.

[81] Lunenburg Co. Will Bk. 8, p. 284.

[82] Catherine Lindsay Knorr, *Marriage Bonds and Ministers' Returns of Brunswick County, Virginia, 1750-1810* (Pine Bluff, Ark., 1953), p. 8.

[83] Lunenburg Co. Will Bk. 10, pp. 141A-142A.

[84] Emma R. Matheny and Helen K. Yates, *Marriages of Lunenburg County, Virginia, 1746-1853* (Richmond, 1967), p. 10.

[85] Lunenburg Co. Will Bk. 8, p. 106.

[86] *T* III, pp. 283-85.

[87] Matheny and Yates, *loc. cit.*

[88] *Ibid.*

Goodwin[6], born 3 Oct. 1778, died 21 July 1823, married, 17 Aug. 1796,[89] Cannon Jones Green; 99 Anna[6], born 24 Aug. 1781, died 8 Dec. 1821, married, 21 March 1799,[90] Peter M. Hawthorne,who died about 1822; 100. Chapman[6], born 11 Jan. 1785, died 16 Sept. 1851, left will 24 June 1847-Dec. 1851,[91] married (1), 2 April 1806,[92] Polly Hatchett and (2), 25 Jan. 1809,[93] Prudence Russell (Jeffress) Rutledge, born 19 April 1796 [*sic*], died 15 Sept. 1873.

35. DIANA WALLACE[5] GOODWIN (Elizabeth[4] Chapman, John[3], Walter[2]. Joan[1] Bennett) left will 27 Jan. 1792-23 Feb. 1792.[94] She married, as his (3) wife, James Wallace Bayley.[95]

Issue: [BAYLEY] 101. Wilson Wallace[6]; 102. Elizabeth Wallace[6].

36. RACHEL[5] GOODWIN (Elizabeth[4] Chapman, John[3], Walter[2], Joan[1] Bennett) married Edward Mallory, son of Johnson and Diana (__) Mallory, of Elizabeth City County, who left will 10 April 1789-23 Sept. 1789.[96] He was a captain of militia of that county, 1781.

Issue: [MALLORY] 103. Johnson[6]; 104. James Goodwin[6]; 105. William[6]; 106. Elizabeth Wallace[6]; 107. Francis[6].

43. ROBERT[5] MANSON (Peter[4], Elizabeth[3] Chapman, Walter[2], Joan[1] Bennett), born 17 Aug. 1748, left will 1 Oct. 1785-19 Sept. 1796.[97] He was a captain of York County militia, 1777. He married 168. *Mary[6] Pescud* (see CHISMAN).

Issue: [MANSON][98] 113. Anna[6], born 20 Aug. 1771; 114. John[6], born 21 Oct. 1773, left land in Elizabeth City County; 115. Mary[6], born 10 Jan. 1776; 116. Hannah[6], born 16 Jan. 1778, died 24 June 1784; 117. Polly[6], born 12 Jan. 1780; 118. Thomas Pescud[6], born 9 April 1782, left father's dwelling plantation; 119. Robert Pescud[6], born 23 Jan. 1784, left 50 acres in the Lodge in York County; 120. Hannah[6], born 30 Jan. 1786.

---

[89] *Ibid.*, p. 52.

[90] Knorr, *op. cit.*, p. 42.

[91] Henderson Co., Ky., Will Bk. C, p. 116; Order Bk. F, p. 2.

[92] Matheny and Yates, *op. cit.*, p. 10.

[93] *Ibid.*

[94] Elizabeth City Co. Original will.

[95] *T* VI, p. 128.

[96] Elizabeth City Co. Original will.

[97] York Co. Will Bk. 11, pp. 179-80, proved and recorded 20 June 1821.

[98] Charles Parish Register; *W*(1) XIV, p. 115.

44. WILLIAM[5] HOUGHTON (Ann[4] Manson, Elizabeth[3] Chapman, Walter[2], Joan[1] Bennett), born 30 Oct. 1721, mentioned in will of John[5] Manson, is probably the William, Sr., taxed in Warwick County, 1787. He married __.

Issue: [HOUGHTON] 121. (possibly) William[6], Jr., taxpayer in Warwick County, 1787; 122. (possibly) Peter[6], taxpayer in Warwick County, 1787.

50. SARAH[5] HOUGHTON (Ann[4] Manson, Elizabeth[3] Chapman, Walter[2], Joan[1] Bennett), born 14 Feb. 1731/2, married William Cross, probably the William who rented land in Sussex County from the College of William and Mary and left will 4 Nov. 1775-21 Sept. 1780[99] naming wife Sarah and children.

Issue: [CROSS] 122. John[6], married, (bond 15) March 1787,[100] Lucy Tomlinson; 123. William[6], married, (bond 18) Dec. 1780,[101] Rebeckah Wallace; 124. Anne[6], married __ Wilson; 125. Elizabeth[6]; 126. Rebecca[6]; 127. Mary[6], perhaps married, (bond 2) Jan. 1787,[102] Edwin Hines; 128. Susanna[6], perhaps married, 1 Oct. 1796,[103] James Inman.

50. Capt. PETER[5] MANSON (John[4], Elizabeth[3] Chapman, Walter[2], Joan[1] Bennett), born 24 Dec. 1733,[104] died about 1793,[105] resided in Dinwiddie County. He married (1) Susan Hardaway, born 27 Sept. 1740, and (2) Agnes Hardaway, born 30 March 1749, both daughters of Thomas and Agnes (Thweatt) Hardaway.[106]

Issue: [MANSON][107] 129. Capt. Peter[6], died about 1818, of Dinwiddie County; 130. James[6], died about 1804, of Dinwiddie County; 131. Thomas[6], of Brunswick County, left will 19 Oct. 1805-28 April 1806,[108] married Ann ___; 132. John[6], of Dinwiddie County, married ____; 133. Capt. Hardaway[6], died about 1812, of Dinwiddie County; 134. Capt. Nathaniel[6], died about 1815, of Dinwiddie County; 135. Mary[6], married, as his (1) wife, Baker Pegram, born 27

---

[99] Sussex Co. Will Bk. C, p. 379.

[100] Catherine Lindsay Knorr, *Marriage Bonds and Ministers' Returns of Sussex County, Virginia, 1754-1810* (Pine Bluff, Ark., 1952), p. 20.

[101] *Ibid.*

[102] *Ibid.*, p. 36.

[103] *Ibid.*, p. 40.

[104] Bristol Parish Register.

[105] He left a will naming Baker Pegram, Thomas Manson, Peter Manson and Hardiway Manson as executors (Kentucky Court of Appeals Deed Bk. G, p. 31).

[106] *The Southside Virginian*, VII, p. 25.

[107] Thomas, John, Hardaway and Nathaniel presumed from their listing in the household of Capt. Peter Manson, Dinwiddie Co. Personal property tax books, 1784-93.

[108] Brunswick Co. Will Bk. 7, p. 163.

Jan. 1758,[109] died 14 Oct. 1830,[110] sergeant in the Revolutionary War, captain of Dinwiddie County militia, 1784.

51. NATHANIEL[5] MANSON (?John[4], Elizabeth[3] Chapman, Walter[2], Joan[1] Bennett) was a merchant of Charlotte County in partnership with Alexander Shaw as late as 7 Dec. 1774 when he purchased land but moved to Halifax County by 20 June 1776 when John Clayton, Sr., deeded a slave to him.[111] He died by Sept. 1785 when the inventory of his estate was made.[112] He married, (bond 18) Aug. 1775,[113] Lucy Willis[7] Clayton, daughter of 459. *Elizabeth[6] (Willis) Clayton* (see MARTIAU), who married (2) Henry Landon Davies.

Issue: [MANSON][114] 136. Nathaniel[6], of "Pebbleton," Bedford County, married Sarah Alexander.

52. JANE[5] MANSON (John[4], Elizabeth[3] Chapman, Walter[2], Joan[1] Bennett) married Burwell Thweatt, son of Miles and Sarah (Green) Thweatt. They resided in Dinwiddie County.

Issue: [THWEATT][115] 137. Priscilla[6]; 138. Elizabeth[6]; 139. Rebecca[6]; 140. Ann[6]; 141. Susanna[6], married, 1793, Thomas Rives, born about 1770, who moved to Chatham Co., N.C., in 1811 to Jones Co., Ga., in 1817 to Jackson Co., Ga., and shortly afterward to Hall Co., Ga.;[116] 142. Mary[6], perhaps married John T. Sydnor, who died 1847; 143. Burwell Green[6]; 144. John Manson[6], died 17 Jan. 1856, aged 73,[117] left will 10 Oct. 1854-18 Feb. 1856,[118] farmer of Dinwiddie County, married (perhaps Martha) ___.

---

[109] *W*(2) II, p. 63.

[110] Samuel William Simmons, *The Pegrams of Virginia and Descendants, 1688-1984* (Atlanta, 1985), p. 94.

[111] Charlotte Co. Deed Bk. 3, pp.. 485, 625.

[112] Bedford Co. Will Bk. 1, pp. 492-93.

[113] Catherine Lindsay Knorr, *Marriage Bonds and Ministers' Returns of Charlotte County, Virginia, 1764-1815* (Pine Bluff, Ark., 1951), p. 54.

[114] Alexander Brown, *The Cabells and Their Kin* (reprint; Harrisonburg, Va., 1978), p. 401, which says he was son of Peter Manson and Lucy Clayton.

[115] *The Southside Virginian*, VII, pp. 28, 30.

[116] James Rives Childs, *Reliques of the Rives* (Lynchburg, 1929), p. 220.

[117] Virginia Dept. of Vital Statistics, Dinwiddie County, Deaths.

[118] Dinwiddie Co. Will Bk. 6, pp. 166-67.

BERNARD[1]

*1. WILLIAM[1] BERNARD, born about 1603, son of Francis Bernard (died 1630) and his wife Mary Woolhouse of Kingsthorpe, Northamptonshire,[2] came to Virginia, 1622, in the *Furtherance* at the age of 18 and was living at Basse's Choice by 1623/4.[3] He was included in the muster of Capt. Nathaniel Basse at the same place, 7 Feb. 1624/5. He left the colony and returned at least three times before 10 Aug. 1642 when a patent for 1200 acres at the head of Lawnes Creek in Isle of Wight County was issued him as "due for his own personal adventure four times and transportation of twenty persons."[4] He was interested in the culture of silk in the colony, as were others of the period, but though the growth of mulberry trees, on which the silk worm could be nurtured, was prolific, skilled workers were needed to carry on the industry. Silk was produced in the colony, but the cultivation of tobacco, for which there was a ready market, and which required less skill, eventually supplanted silk altogether as a marketable product.

William[1] Bernard served as commissioner of Isle of Wight County, 1646, and served in the Council 1641-65.[5] He patented 800 acres in Lancaster County, adjoining Col. Richard Lee, 8 Oct. 1657,[6] but there is no record of his having lived in the Northern Neck. His death, 31 March 1665, is stated in the will of his brother, Sir Robert Bernard, Bart., of Brampton Hall, Huntingdonshire, 5 Dec. 1665.[7]

He married Lucy (Higginson) Burwell, daughter of Robert and Joanna (Tokesy) Higginson,[8] and widow of 6. *Lewis[2] Burwell* (see BURWELL). She married (3) Philip Ludwell and died 6 Nov. 1675.[9]

Issue: 2. George[2], named in the will of George Ludlowe, 1655, as "son of

---

[1] Also BARNARD; Clayton Torrence, *Winston of Virginia and Allied Families* (Richmond, 1927), pp. 98-99, 115-18; *W*(1) XIX, pp. 177-84.

[2] Sophia Elizabeth Higgins, *The Bernards of Abingdon and Nether Winchendon* (London and New York, 1903-04), I, p. 74; IV, p. 318.

[3] Hotten, p. 184.

[4] Patent Bk. 1, p. 798.

[5] Leonard, p. xix.

[6] Patent Bk. 4, p. 271 (372).

[7] Higgins, *op. cit.*, IV, p. 318.

[8] Torrence, *op. cit.*, pp. 121-22.

[9] Joseph Bryan Branch A.P.V.A, *Epitaphs of Gloucester and Mathews Counties* (Richmond, 1959), p. 19.

Colonel William Bernard"[10] and living in England, 1665, with his uncle, Sir Robert Bernard; 3. LUCY[2]; 4. ELIZABETH[2].

3. LUCY[2] BERNARD (William[1]) married (1) Dr. Edmund Gwyn of Gloucester County, who left will, now lost, dated 10 March 1683/4,[11] and (2) Edward Creffield, Jr., merchant of London, who left will 24 Nov. 1694-9 Dec. 1694.[12]

Issue: (by 1) [GWYN] 5. Lucy[3], married 8. *Thomas[3] Reade* (see MARTIAU).

4. ELIZABETH[2] BERNARD (William[1]) married 46. *Thomas[4] Todd* (see LOVELACE-GORSUCH). In a letter to his son just before he sailed on a last voyage to England, 10 April 1676, Capt. Thomas Todd addressed his son "at his house in the North River," presumably the "Toddsbury" plantation first patented by Capt. Thomas Todd, 27 Oct. 1652.[13] In addition to "Toddsbury" and other Virginia lands, Thomas Todd inherited large tracts in Baltimore Co., Md., from his father. He was a captain of militia and justice of Gloucester County, 1698-1702,[14] owned 775 acres in Kingston Parish and 884 acres in Ware Parish and had a quarter in King and Queen County containing 2300 acres, 1704. He died 16 Jan. 1724/5[15] leaving a will, now lost, dated 4 March 1722/3.[16]

Issue: [TODD][17] 6. THOMAS[3]; 7. ANNE[3]; 8. LUCY[3]; 9. RICHARD[3]; 10. WILLIAM[3]; 11. ELIZABETH[3]; 12. PHILIP[3]; 13. CHRISTOPHER[3]; 14. Frances[3], born 12 April 1692, died 5 Nov. 1703;[18] 15. (DAUGHTER)[3]; 16. FRANCES[3].

6. THOMAS[3] TODD (Elizabeth[2] Bernard, William[1]), born about 1681, married Elizabeth ____, and lived in both Virginia and Maryland. As Thomas Todd of the County of Baltimore he left a will, 11 Jan. 1714/5, which

---

[10] P.C.C. 256 Berkeley, in Waters, *Gleanings*, I, p. 173.

[11] *H* VIII, p. 483.

[12] P.C.C. 244 Box, in *V* XIX, pp. 289-90.

[13] *V* XXIV, pp. 429-30; Patent Bk. 3, p. 182.

[14] Polly Cary Mason, *Records of Colonial Gloucester County, Virginia*, I (n.p., 1946), p. 121.

[15] Joseph Bryan Branch A.P.V.A., *op. cit.*, p. 79.

[16] *H* V, p. 395; VII, p. 488; VIII, p. 632.

[17] *V* XXV, p. 91.

[18] Joseph Bryan Branch A.P.V.A., *op. cit.*, p. 79.

was proved in Maryland 3 June 1715 and in Virginia 20 Sept. 1715.[19] His wife survived him and married (2) the Rev. Hugh Conn and died 1717 in her 27th year.[20]

Issue: [TODD][21] 17 THOMAS[4]; 18. Robert[4], died before 1728, aged 7; 19. Frances[4].

7. ANNE[3] TODD (Elizabeth[2] Bernard, William[1]), born 9 Nov. 1682, died 18 July 1720.[22] She married John Cooke of "Wareham," Gloucester County, who married (2) 36. *Mary[6] Smith* (see STRACHEY).

Issue: [COOKE] 20 MORDECAI[4]; 21. LUCY[4].

8. LUCY[3] TODD (Elizabeth[2] Bernard, William[1]) married (1) ___ O'Brien and (2), 1698, John Baylor, born at Tiverton, Devonshire, died before 27 Sept. 1720,[23] merchant, member of the House of Burgesses from Gloucester County, 1693, and from King and Queen County, 1718,[24] who owned 3000 acres in King and Queen, 1704.

Issue: (by 2) [BAYLOR] 22. JOHN[4]; 23. (Son)[4];[25] 24. Frances[4], died aged 17 on her wedding day, married ___.

9. RICHARD[3] TODD (Elizabeth[2] Bernard, William[1]) married ____. He owned 1050 acres in King and Queen County, 1704.

Issue: [TODD][26] 25. Bernard[4], died without issue; 26. William[4], died without issue.

10. Col. WILLIAM[3] TODD (Elizabeth[2] Bernard, William[1]), of King

---

[19] Maryland Prerogative Court Wills 14, pp. 152-54; Essex Co. Wills & Deeds 14, p. 392-94.

[20] Tombstone, Todd graveyard, North Point, Baltimore Co., Md., cited in Helen W. Ridgely, *Historic Graves of Maryland and the District of Columbia* (New York, 1908), p. 115.

[21] *V* XXV, pp. 217-20.

[22] Joseph Bryan Branch A.P.V.A., *op. cit.*, p. 93.

[23] Letter of Robert Carter to his son John, stating that "Mr. John Baylor, the greatest merchant in our country, is lately dead" (Louis B. Wright, *Letters of Robert Carter, 1720-1727* [San Marino, Calif., 1940], pp. 53, 55). Baylor Bible, Caroline County, 1650-1906, photocopy, Archives Division, Library of Virginia, states he died 11 Sept. 1721 at Norfolk. The handwriting and format show this is a 19th century copy of earlier records and is not contemporaneous with the events entered.

[24] Leonard, pp. 52, 69.

[25] No evidence to establish he was Col. Robert Baylor of King and Queen County is known to exist, although circumstantial evidence (see *V* XXV, pp. 319-23) suggests this may be so.

[26] *V* XXV, pp. 220-21.

and Queen County, left will, now lost, dated 12 Jan. 1736/7.[27] He married, shortly after 16 March 1709/10, Martha Vicaris, daughter of the Rev. Thomas Vicaris of Gloucester County,[28] who was living 1750-51.[29]

Issue: [TODD] 27. THOMAS[4]; 28. RICHARD[4]; 29. DOROTHY[4]; 30. ELIZABETH[4]; 31. (perhaps) Sarah[4], left will 19 May 1781-18 Feb. 1788,[30] married James Barbour as his (2) wife.

11. ELIZABETH[3] TODD (Elizabeth[3] Bernard, William[1]) married (1) Henry Seaton, whose (1) wife was 27. ___[4] *Burwell* (see BURWELL) and who owned 170 acres in Gloucester County, 1704, and later moved to King and Queen County. She married (2), about 1714, as his (2) wife, Augustine Moore, born 1685, died 28 July 1743, left will 20 Jan. 1742/3-18 Aug. 1743,[31] of "Chelsea," King William County, justice.

Issue:[32] (by 1) [SEATON] 32. GEORGE[4]; (by 2) [MOORE] 33. ELIZABETH[4]; 34. Augustine[4], justice of King William, died without issue; 35. LUCY[4]; 36. BERNARD[4]; 37. THOMAS[4].

12. PHILIP[3] TODD (Elizabeth[2] Bernard, William[1]), born about 1688, died before 1740, lived in St. Stephen's Parish, King and Queen County, and was sheriff of Gloucester County, 1730. He married Ann Day, daughter of Edward Day of Somerset Co., Md.

Issue: [TODD][33] 38. MARY[4]; 39. ELIZABETH[4].

13. Capt. CHRISTOPHER[3] TODD (Elizabeth[2] Bernard, William[1]), born 2 April 1690, died 26 March 1743,[34] was justice of Gloucester County, 1727.[35]

---

[27] *H* VIII, p. 57. Orange Co. Deed Bk. 18, p. 273, refers to the date as 12 Feb. 1736.

[28] *H* VIII, p. 632; King George Co. Deed Bk. 3, p. 270.

[29] *Magazine of Virginia Genealogy*, XVIII, p. 144.

[30] Culpeper Co. Will Bk. C, p. 282. She is identified as Sarah Todd on the tombstone at her and James Barbour's graves in Madison County erected in 1804 by their grandson, Governor James Barbour.

[31] Charles Campbell, *Genealogy of the Spotswood Family in Scotland and Virginia* (Albany, 1868), pp. 31-41; Caroline Co. Wills &c 1742-1830, pp. 1-3. The will was probated in King William County.

[32] *V* XXV, pp. 431-36; Malcolm Hart Harris, *Old New Kent County* (West Point, 1977), II, pp. 615-22.

[33] *V* XXIX, pp. 364-72.

[34] Joseph Bryan Branch A.P.V.A., *op. cit.*, p. 79. Todd family record, Virginia State Archives, Ac.25023, apparently from a family Bible, gives these dates but with the years as 1689 and 1742.

[35] *Executive Journals of the Council of Colonial Virginia*, IV (Richmond, 1930), p. 158.

He married 29. *Elizabeth*[4] *Mason* (see MASON), born 25 April 1701, died 10 Nov. 1764.[36]

Issue: [TODD][37] 40. LUCY[4]; 41. ELIZABETH[4]; 42. MARY[4]; 43. Thomas[4], born 26 Dec. 1728, died 22 July 1780,[38] without issue, upon which "Toddsbury" passed to his nephew Philip[5] Tabb.

15. (DAUGHTER)[3] TODD[39] (Elizabeth[2] Bernard, William[1]) married, about 1715, Jonathan Hide, a merchant of Gloucester County and of Christ Church Parish, Middlesex County, who deposed, 1704, he was aged 22 and born at Limehouse, Middlesex, England.[40] His will, 15 Dec. 1718-3 March 1718/9, mentioned his infant daughter, George Seaton and Lucy Moore, son and daughter of Eliza Moore, and the eldest son of William Todd.[41]

Issue: [HIDE] 44. Ann[4], left her father's estate when aged 18.

16. FRANCES[3] TODD[42] (Elizabeth[2] Bernard, William[1]), died 25 July 1745 in her 36th year,[43] married, as his (2) wife, 2 July 1729,[44] Robert North, baptized 29 Oct. 1698,[45] died 21 March 1748/9,[46] captain of militia, justice of Baltimore Co., Md., commissioner to lay out Jones Town (now part of Baltimore), 1732, large landowner, who left will 20 March 1748/9-5 April 1749.[47]

Issue: [NORTH][48] 45. ELIZABETH[4]; 46. Thomas[4], born 16 Feb. 1732/3, died 27 Feb. 1750/1; 47. ELLIN[4]; 48. Frances[4], born 1 Nov. 1743, died 24 Dec. 1743.

---

[36] Todd family record, *loc. cit.*

[37] *Ibid.*

[38] Joseph Bryan Branch A.P.V.A., *op. cit.*, p.79.

[39] *V* XXV, pp. 437-38.

[40] Peter Wilson Coldham, *English Adventurers and Emigrants, 1661-1733* (Baltimore, 1985), p. 100.

[41] Middlesex Co. Will Bk. 1713-40, pp. 110-11.

[42] *V* XXV, pp. 438-45; Dawn F. Thomas and Robert Barnes, *The Green Spring Valley* (Baltimore, 1978), II, pp. 72-73.

[43] Tombstone, St. Thomas' Church, Green Spring Valley, Baltimore Co., Md., in *V* XXV, p. 438.

[44] North family Bible, copy made by George N. Moale, 1890, of 1855 copy of records, Maryland Historical Society.

[45] *The Registers of the Parish Church of Whittington* ... (Lancashire Parish Register Society, III; Rochdale, 1899), p. 57.

[46] North family Bible, *loc. cit.*

[47] Maryland Prerogative Court Wills 25, pp. 561-63.

[48] North family Bible, *loc. cit.*

17. THOMAS[4] TODD (Thomas[3], Elizabeth[2] Bernard, William[1]), captain of foot and justice of Baltimore Co., Md., left will 9 Dec. 1738-2 April 1739.[49] He married (1), 7 June 1728,[50] Lettice Thacker, born 26 Feb. 1704/5, died 10 June 1730, daughter of Henry and Elizabeth Thacker of Middlesex County,[51] and (2) Eleanor Dorsey, daughter of Caleb Dorsey of Baltimore County, who married (2), 6 Sept. 1740, William Lynch, and left will 23 July 1760-16 Oct. 1760.[52]

Issue: [TODD][53] (by 1) 49. Lettice[5], born 26 Feb. 1704/5; (by 2) 50. ELIZABETH[5]; 51. Thomas[5], born 27 Nov. 1738, died 1 Sept. 1798, of North Point, Baltimore Co., Md., married Sarah Wilkinson; 52. ELINER[5]; 53. FRANCES[5]; 54. MARY[5].

20. MORDECAI[4] COOKE (Ann[3] Todd, Elizabeth[2] Bernard, William[1]) died 5 April 1751, aged 43. He married Elizabeth Whiting, daughter of Francis and Mary (Perrin) Whiting, born 17 Dec. 1713, died 8 Dec. 1762.[54]

Issue: [COOKE][55] 55. MORDECAI[5]; 56. FRANCIS WHITING[4]; 57. GILES[5]; 58. JOHN[5].

21. LUCY[4] COOKE (Anne[3] Todd, Elizabeth[2] Bernard, William[1]) married (1) Gregory Smith, born 31 Dec. 1712,[56] died after 16 Nov. 1744,[57] of King and Queen County, and (2), as his (3) wife, Thomas Booth of Gloucester County,[58] who left will 16 Feb. 1753-2 Sept. 1756.[59]

Issue:[60] (by 1) [SMITH] 59. Ann[5], married 53. *Robert[5]* Armistead (see

[49] Maryland Prerogative Court Wills 22, p. 37.

[50] Christ Church Parish, Middlesex Co., Register.

[51] *Ibid.*; St. Paul's Parish, Baltimore, Md., Register.

[52] Maryland Prerogative Court Wills 31, pp. 26-28.

[53] *V* XXV, p. 219.

[54] Joseph Bryan Branch APVA, *op. cit.*, p. 93.

[55] William Carter Stubbs, *Descendants of Mordecai Cooke ... and Thomas Booth* (Richmond, 1923), pp. 81-119.

[56] Christ Church Parish, Middlesex Co., Register.

[57] C. G. Chamberlayne, ed., *The Vestry Book of Stratton Major Parish, King and Queen County, Virginia, 1729-1783* (Richmond, 1931), p. 59.

[58] "Family Account of Mrs. Lucy Ann Page, Late of Gloucester County, Virginia," *W*(1) XI, pp. 132-36.

[59] Stubbs, *op. cit.*, p. 193, citing Tomkies *vs.* Booth, Williamsburg Chancery papers, no longer extant.

[60] Stubbs, *op. cit*, pp. 82-83, 219-25.

BURWELL); 60. Col. Gregory[5], left will 29 May 1789-13 Sept. 1790,[61] student at the College of William and Mary, 1765, member of Committee of Safety of King and Queen County, 1774, captain, 7th Virginia Regiment, 1776, resigned 28 Nov. 1776, colonel, 2nd Virginia State Regiment, June 1777-1781; 61. THOMAS[5]; (by 2) [BOOTH] 62. JOHN COOKE[5]; 63. MARY COOKE[5]; 64. MORDECAI COOKE[5].

22. Col. JOHN[4] BAYLOR (Lucy[3] Todd, Elizabeth[3] Bernard, William[1]) of "New Market," Caroline County, born 12 May 1705, at "New Market," died 3 April 1772,[62] was Burgess from Caroline County, 1742-65,[63] County Lieutenant of Orange, 1752, colonel in the French and Indian War, leading importer and breeder of thoroughbred horses in Virginia, and left will 19 Feb. 1770-16 May 1772.[64] He married, 2 Jan. 1743/4, Frances Walker[65] who died 9 July 1783 at "New Market."[66]

Issue: [BAYLOR][67] 65. John[5], died in infancy; 66. COURTNEY[5]; 67. Frances[5], twin, born 17 Oct. 1746, died 16 Oct. 1815, married, Oct. 1802, John Nicholson;[68] 68. Elizabeth[5], twin, born 27 Oct. 1746, died in infancy; 69. LUCY [LUCINDA][5]; 70. JOHN[5]; 71. GEORGE[5]; 72. ROBERT[5]; 73. WALKER[5]; 74. Elizabeth[5], died 6 Dec. 1784, unmarried.

27. THOMAS[4] TODD (William[3], Elizabeth[2] Bernard, William[1]), of King and Queen County, died before 1761. He married Elizabeth Waring.

Issue: [TODD][69] 75. WILLIAM[5]; 76. HENRY[5]; 77. BERNARD[5]; 78. (perhaps) the Rev. Christopher[5], student at College of William and Mary, 1768-

---

[61] Margie G. Brown, *Genealogical Abstracts, Revolutionary War Veterans, Scrip Act 1852* (Oakton, Va., 1990), pp. 210-11.

[62] Baylor Bible, *loc. cit.*; *Virginia Gazette*, 16 April 1772.

[63] Leonard, pp. 78, 81, 86, 88, 91.

[64] *V* XXIV, pp. 367-73.

[65] Baylor Bible, *loc. cit.*; William Meade, *Old Churches, Ministers and Families of Virginia* (Philadelphia, 1857), II, p. 464. Frances Norton Mason, ed., *John Norton & Sons* (Richmond, 1937), p. 515, gives 10 Dec. 1743.

[66] *The Virginia Gazette, or Public Advertiser*, Richmond, Va., 19 July 1783; Baylor Bible, *loc. cit.*

[67] Mrs. John Bennett Boddie, ed., *Historical Southern Families*, XVII (Baltimore, 1972), pp. 61-80; *V* VI, pp. 198-99, 307-09.

[68] Caroline Co. chancery suit, in William Lindsay Hopkins, *Caroline County Court Records ...* (Richmond, 1987), p. 79.

[69] *V* XXV, pp. 306-07.

70,[70] minister of Brunswick Parish, King George (Stafford) County, died 1777.[71]

28. RICHARD[4] TODD (William[3], Elizabeth[2] Bernard, William[1]) died about 1766. He was a justice of King and Queen County, 1751.[72] He married Elizabeth Richards, who moved to Manchester in Chesterfield County and left will 30 Oct. 1777-7 Nov. 1777.[73]

Issue: [TODD] [74] 79. WILLIAM[5]; 80. RICHARD[5]; 81. Mildred[5], died 24 Oct. 1837 at Frankfort, Ky., in her 84th year,[75] married Thomas Tunstall who represented Pittsylvania County in the House of Delegates, 1791-93, and moved to Lincoln Co., Ky., 1794,[76] and later lived in Frankfort, Ky.; 82. THOMAS[5].

29. DOROTHY[4] TODD (William[3], Elizabeth[2] Bernard, William[1]) married (1) ___ Gordon and (2) Thomas Edmundson of Essex County who left will 26 Dec. 1757-19 Dec. 1759.[77]

Issue: (by 1) [GORDON][78] 83. William[5]; (by 2) [EDMUNDSON][79] 84. John[5], died before 23 July1789 when the inventory of his estate was made,[80] justice of Essex County, 1780, member of the House of Delegates, 1777-81, 1782-83;[81] 85. William[5]; 86. Thomas[5]; 87. James[5], left will 4 July 1791-16 April 1792,[82] of "Charleston Hill," Essex County, member of the House of Burgesses from Essex County, 1769-76, of the Conventions of 1774-76, and the House of Delegates, 1776,[83] married (1) Elizabeth Webb, who died 19 Nov. 1773 in her 37th year, and (2) Elizabeth ___, who married (2) Robert Banks and (3), after 1 May 1802, William Edmundson and died before 20 Feb. 1804;[84] 88. Sarah[5];

---

[70] *W*(2) I, p. 40.

[71] *Virginia Gazette* (Dixon & Hunter), 28 Nov. 1777, sale of estate by executors Bernard Todd and Thomas Lowry.

[72] Lunenburg Co. Deed Bk. 3, p. 312-14.

[73] Chesterfield Co. Will Bk. 3, pp. 128, 227; Order Bk. 6, p. 148.

[74] *V* XXV, pp. 309-10.

[75] *Kentucky Gazette*, Lexington, Ky., 9 Nov. 1837; Hattie Marshall Scott, *Scott's Papers, Kentucky Court and Other Records* (Frankfort, Ky., 1953), p. 188.

[76] Clement, *op. cit.*, p. 173.

[77] Essex Co. Wills 11, 1757-62, p. 228.

[78] *H* VIII, p. 57.

[79] *T* VII, pp. 187-89.

[80] Essex Co. Will Bk. 14, pp. 213-19.

[81] Leonard, pp. 125, 129, 133, 137, 145, 149.

[82] Essex Co. Will Bk. 14, p. 292.

[83] Leonard, pp. 99, 103, 105, 109, 112, 114, 117, 119, 122.

[84] *T* XVI, p. 28.

89. Judith[5], married 83. *Gabriel[5] Throckmorton* (see MARTIAU).

30. ELIZABETH[4] TODD (William[3], Elizabeth[2] Bernard, William[1]) married James Barbour of Culpeper County, justice of Orange County, 1734, vestryman of St. Mark's Parish, 1730-40, who left will 23 Feb. 1770-17 April 1775.[85]

Issue: [BARBOUR][86] 90. Richard[5], presumably of age by 25 April 1753 when the age of a slave belonging to him was adjudged,[87] living 13 April 1775 when he witnessed a deed,[88] never married.

32. GEORGE[4] SEATON (El;izabeth[3] Todd, Elizabeth[2] Bernard, William[1]), born 11 Dec. 1711, died 1750,[89] was called "son-in-law" [step-son] in Augustine Moore's will. He married, 27 Dec. 1734, Elizabeth Hill, daughter of Leonard Hill of Essex County.[90]

Issue: [SEATON][91] 91. Elizabeth[5], born 19 Dec. 1735, died 9 Dec. 1738; 92. AUGUSTINE[5]; 93. George[5], born 8 Feb. 1739, died 1791, perhaps the George of Amherst County who married Elizabeth Watson[92] and the George who was appointed, 1776, to sign Virginia paper currency notes; 94. Elizabeth[5], born 28 March 1741, married 58. *John[6] West* of "West Point" (see WEST).

33. ELIZABETH[4] MOORE (Elizabeth[3] Todd, Elizabeth[2] Bernard, William[1]), born about 1716, left will dated dated 10 Sept. 1779.[93] She married (1) Lyonell Lyde, died 20 Jan. 1737/8, and (2) Col. James Macon, born 28 Oct. 1701,[94] died 1768, who was justice of King George County, 1741, King William County, 1744, and sheriff of King William, 1746.[95]

Issue: (by 2) [MACON] 95. ELIZABETH[5]; 96. MARY[5].

35. LUCY[4] MOORE (Elizabeth[3] Todd, Elizabeth[2] Bernard, William[1]), born about 1720, died about 1759. She married, about 1737, as his (2) wife, the

---

[85] Culpeper Co. Will Bk. B, p. 143.

[86] *H* VIII, p. 57; Raleigh Travers Green, *Genealogical and Historical Notes on Culpeper County, Virginia* (Culpeper, Va., 1900), pt. 2, p. 136.

[87] Orange Co. Order Bk. 5, p. 423.

[88] Spotsylvania Co. Deed Bk. H, pp. 463-54.

[89] Oren Andrew Seaton, *The Seaton Family* (Topeka, Kans., 1906), p. 106.

[90] *Ibid.*

[91] Bible (1638) owned, 1906, by Seaton Schroeder, Washington, D.C., in Oren Andrew Seaton, *The Seaton Family* Topeka, Kans., 1906), pp. 106-14.

[92] Amherst Co. Deed Bk. B, p. 97, 9 Oct. 1765.

[93] *W*(1) XIV, pp. 265-66.

[94] St. Peter's Parish, New Kent Co., Register.

[95] Alethea Jane Macon, *Gideon Macon of Virginia* (n.p., 1956), pp. 9-10.

Hon. John Robinson, born 3 Feb. 1704/5, died 11 May 1766, of King and Queen County, Speaker of the House of Burgesses and Treasurer of Virginia, 1738-65.[96]

Issue: [ROBINSON] 97. John[5], born before 1742/3, died young; 98. Lucy[5], died young; 99. Elizabeth[5], married 58. John[5] Cooke; 100. CATHERINE[5].

36. BERNARD[4] MOORE (Elizabeth[3] Todd, Elizabeth[2] Bernard, William[1]) inherited "Chelsea" from his father and was a justice of King William County, colonel of militia and member of the House of Burgesses, 1742-62, 1769-72, and of the House of Delegates, 1782, 1786-88.[97] He married, about 1741, Anne Catherine Spotswood, born 1725, died March 1802, daughter of Governor Alexander Spotswood (1676-1740).

Issue: [MOORE][98] 101. JOHN SPOTSWOOD[5]; 102. ELIZABETH[5]; 103. THOMAS[5]; 104. ALEXANDER SPOTSWOOD[5]; 105. AUGUSTINE[5]; 106. BERNARD[5]; 107. LUCY[5]; 108. ANN BUTLER[5].

37. THOMAS[4] MOORE (Elizabeth[3] Todd, Elizabeth[2] Bernard. William[1]), of "Moorefield," colonel of militia and justice of King William County, died before 30 May 1787.[99] He married Joanna ___ who died 1801.

Issue: [MOORE][100] 109. Thomas[5]; 110. (Child)[5]; 111. (Child)[5]; 112. (Child)[5]; 113. (Child)[5]; 114. (Child)[5]; 115. (Child)[5].

38. MARY[4] TODD (Philip[3], Elizabeth[2] Bernard, William[1]), born about 1710, married John Bickerton, born about 1700, died 1770,[101] who patented 3500 acres in Hanover County, 1740, and was captain and major of militia and a justice.[102]

Issue: [BICKERTON][103] 116. ANN[5]; 117. ELIZABETH[5]; 118. JOHN

---

[96] Jon Kukla, *Speakers and Clerks of the Virginia House of Burgesses, 1643-1776* (Richmond, 1981), pp. 123-26.

[97] Leonard, pp. 79, 81, 87, 92, 100, 146, 161, 165, 169.

[98] Harris, *op. cit.*, II, pp. 616-18; Louise Pecquet du Bellet, *Some Prominent Virginia Families* (Lynchburg, 1907), II, pp. 704-14.

[99] *Virginia Independent Chronicle*, Richmond, 30 May 1787, advertisement of sale of about 1000 acres in King William County, formerly held by Col. Thomas Moore and "subject to his relict's dower."

[100] Harris, *op. cit.*, II, p. 620, referring to a letter of Col. Thomas[4] Moore, 24 April 1770, to Col. John Baylor which spoke of his wife and seven children.

[101] Churchill G. Chamberlayne, *The Vestry Book of St. Paul's Parish, Hanover County* (Richmond, 1940), p. 473.

[102] Torrence, *op. cit.*, pp. 87-88.

[103] Harris, *op. cit.*, I, p. 477.

TODD⁵; 119. ALICE⁵; 120. Philip⁵, died young.

39. ELIZABETH⁴ TODD (Philip³, Elizabeth² Bernard, William¹) married Benjamin Hubbard, merchant at Dunkirk, justice of Caroline County, 1755-59, vestryman of Drysdale Parish, 1762, and member of the Committee of Safety of Caroline County, 1774-75, who died before 12 April 1781 when James Taylor was granted administration on his estate.¹⁰⁴

Issue: [HUBBARD]¹⁰⁵ 121. ANNE⁵; 122. MARY TODD⁵; 123. (Daughter)⁵, married ____ Harris.

40. LUCY⁴ TODD (Christopher³ , Elizabeth² Bernard, William¹), born 20 Nov. 1721, died 18 Feb. 1791,¹⁰⁶ married, 11 Nov. 1749, 15. *Edward⁵ Tabb* (see PUREFOY), born 3 Feb. 1719/20, died 29 Jan. 1782,¹⁰⁷ of Gloucester County.

Issue: [TABB]¹⁰⁸ 124. PHILIP⁵; 125. LUCY⁵; 126. THOMAS⁵; 127. MARTHA⁵; 128. ELIZABETH⁵; 129. Pauline⁵, died 6 April 1794 in her 29th year,¹⁰⁹ married George Wythe Booth, who married (2) 203. Lucy B.⁶ Jones..

41. ELIZABETH⁴ TODD (Christopher³, Elizabeth² Bernard, William¹), born 28 Jan. 1723/4, died 9 Dec. 1788, married (1) Nathaniel Wythe and (2) Mordecai Booth, merchant of Gloucester County.¹¹⁰

Issue: (by 1) [WYTHE] 130. Mary Mason⁵, married (1) ___ Booth and (2) 124. Philip⁵ Tabb.

42. MARY⁴ TODD (Christopher³, Elizabeth² Bernard, William¹) married, as his (2) wife, 28. Capt. *John⁵ Wyatt* (see WYATT), born 15 May 1732, died 5 Jan. 1805.¹¹¹ He was a vestryman of Petsworth Parish from 1755 until 1768 when he removed from the parish and was called John Wyatt, Jr., when he purchased land from Edward and Lucy Tabb, 7 Nov. 1764.¹¹² He later moved to Prince William County.

Issue: [WYATT] 131. WILLIAM EDWARD⁵.

---

¹⁰⁴ Caroline Co. Order Bk. 1781-85, p. 6; *The Virginia Genealogist*, XXX, p. 52.

¹⁰⁵ *V* XXIX, pp. 371-73.

¹⁰⁶ Joseph Bryan Branch A.P.V.A., *op. cit.*, p. 81. Todd family record, *loc. cit.*, gives death as 10 Feb. 1794.

¹⁰⁷ Joseph Bryan Banch A.P.V.A., *op. cit.*, p. 81.

¹⁰⁸ *W*(1) XIII, pp. 169-74.

¹⁰⁹ Tombstone, Ware Parish Cemetery, in Joseph Bryan Branch A.P.V.A., *op. cit.*, p. 81.

¹¹⁰ William Carter Stubbs, *Descendants of Mordecai Cooke and Thomas Booth* (New Orleans, 1923), pp. 225-26.

¹¹¹ *W*(1) X, p. 60.

¹¹² Cumberland Co. Deed Bk. 3, p. 5.

45. ELIZABETH[4] NORTH (Frances[3] Todd, Elizabeth[2], William[1]), born 7 June 1731, died 31 Dec. 1805,[113] married (1), 13 June 1751, Christopher Carnan, merchant and importer of Baltimore, Md., who died 30 Dec. 1769, aged 39,[114] leaving will 8 Dec. 1769-12 Jan. 1770,[115] and (2) Samuel Johnston, born in Ireland, who came to America, 1753, as agent for the Penn family, resided in Philadelphia and York, Pa., moved to Baltimore, Md., 1784, and died 30 July 1810 in his 84th year.[116]

Issue: (by 1) [CARNAN][117] 132. CHARLES NORTH[5]; 133. ROBERT NORTH[5].

47. ELLIN[4] NORTH (Frances[3] Todd, Elizabeth[2] Bernard, William[1]), born 29 Aug. 1741, died 20 March 1825,[118] married, 25 May 1758 at Baltimore,[119] John Moale, born 1 Jan. 1730/1, died 6 July 1798, of Baltimore Co., Md., justice, member of Assembly, member of Committee of Correspondence, and lieutenant colonel of the Baltimore Town battalion of militia from May 1776 to the end of the Revolution.[120]

Issue: [MOALE][121] 134. ELIZABETH[5]; 135. JOHN[5]; 136. Rebecca[5], born 15 March 1763, died 4 Oct. 1840,[122] married, 19 Oct. 1780, Thomas Russell; 137. RICHARD H.[5]; 138 THOMAS[5]; 139. William North[5], born 1 Nov. 1768, died 2 Feb. 1769; 140. Robert[5], born and died 10 Oct. 1769; 141. ROBERT NORTH[5]; 142. SAMUEL[5]; 143. Rachel[5], born 5 Feb. 1775, died 17 Feb. 1776; 144. Frances[5], born 10 Feb. 1777, died 19 Feb. 1781; 145. William[5], born 14 Jan. 1779, died 15 Jan. 1779; 146. George Washington[5], born 19 Jan. 1780, died 19 March 1799;[123] 147. RANDLE HULSE[5]; 148. Mary North[5], born 5 Sept. 1783, died 2 Aug. 1787.

50. ELIZABETH[5] TODD (Thomas[4], Thomas[3], Elizabeth[2] Bernard,

---

[113] *Federal Gazette*, Baltimore, Md., 3 Jan. 1806.

[114] Thomas and Barnes, *op. cit.*, I, pp. 27-28; II, p. 7; Ethan Allen, *The Garrison Church* (New York, 1898), p. 140.

[115] Maryland Prerogative Court Wills 37, p. 457.

[116] *Federal Gazette*, Baltimore, Md., 1 Aug. 1810.

[117] *V* XXV, p. 442.

[118] *Ibid.*, 24 March 1825; *Baltimore American*, 21 and 24 March 1825.

[119] *Maryland Gazette*, Annapolis, Md., 1 June 1758.

[120] Allen, *loc. cit.*, pp. 144-45.

[121] *V* XXV, pp. 444-45.

[122] *Baltimore Sun*, 7 Oct. 1840, says 2 Oct. 1840.

[123] *Baltimore Federal Gazette*, 21 March 1799.

William¹), born 13 Dec. 1732, married John Cromwell of Anne Arundel Co., Md.

Issue: [CROMWELL] 149. Eleanor⁶, named in grandmother's will, 1760.

52. ELINER⁵ TODD (Thomas⁴, Thomas³, Elizabeth² Bernard, William¹) left will 7 Dec. 1799-13 Aug. 1801.¹²⁴ She married, 6 March 1753,¹²⁵ John Ensor, Jr., born 25 Sept. 1723, died by April 1793,¹²⁶ of Baltimore Co., Md.

Issue: [ENSOR]¹²⁷ 150. Elizabeth⁶, born 28 April 1754, married Nathan Griffin; 151. Eleanor⁶, born 19 Nov. 1755, married John Griffith; 152. Frances⁶, born 14 Dec. 1757, married Elijah Merryman, died 3 July 1799, left will 8 Dec. 1798-17 July 1799,¹²⁸ who married (2), (license 14) Nov. 1785, Elizabeth Cromwell;¹²⁹ 153. Mary⁶, born 20 Nov. 1759, married Micajah Merryman; 154. Deborah⁶, married, (license 5) Feb. 1778, as his (1) wife, Nicholas Merryman, born 1751, died 1832, lieutenant and captain of Baltimore Co., Md., militia, 1777.¹³⁰

53. FRANCES⁵ TODD (Thomas⁴, Thomas³, Elizabeth² Bernard, William¹) married, 7 [17?] Aug. 1759,¹³¹ George Risteau of Baltimore Co., Md., who left will 4 April 1783-14 April 1792.¹³²

Issue: [RISTEAU]¹³³ 155. Katherine⁶, born 17 June 1758, married 133. Robert North⁵ Carnan; 156. Eleanor⁶, born 15 Jan. 1760; 157. Thomas⁶, born 16 Jan. 1763; 158. John⁶, born 14 April 1765; 159. Frances⁶, born 26 July 1767, married, 22 Jan. 1786,¹³⁴ Nicholas Owings; 160. Rebecca⁶, born 5 Dec. 1770, married, 19 May 1793,¹³⁵ Bazaleel Wells.

54. MARY⁵ TODD (Thomas⁴, Thomas³, Elizabeth² Bernard, William¹) left will 18 Nov. 1775-3 Feb. 1776.¹³⁶ She married John Worthington of Baltimore

---

¹²⁴ Baltimore Co., Md., Will Bk. 6, pp. 447-52.
¹²⁵ St. Paul's Parish, Baltimore Co., Md., Register.
¹²⁶ Robert W. Barnes, *Baltimore County Families, 1659-1759* (Baltimore, 1989), p. 207.
¹²⁷ *Ibid.*
¹²⁸ Baltimore Co., Md., Will Bk. 6, p. 192.
¹²⁹ *MHM* X, p. 292.
¹³⁰ *Ibid.*, pp. 291-92.
¹³¹ St. Thomas Parish, Baltimore Co., Md., Register.
¹³² Baltimore Co., Md., Will Bk. 5, pp. 42-43.
¹³³ Barnes, *op. cit.*, p. 546.
¹³⁴ Marriage register of the Rev. Lewis Richards, First Baptist Church, Baltimore, Maryland Historical Society, ms. 640.
¹³⁵ St. Thomas Parish, Baltimore Co., Md., Register.
¹³⁶ Maryland Prerogative Court Wills 40, p. 636.

Co., Md., where she resided as a widow.

Issue: [WORTHINGTON] 161. Elioner[6]; 162. Ann[6]; 163. Elizabeth[6]; 164. Hannah[6]; 165. Margaret[6].

55. MORDECAI[5] COOKE (Moredcai[4], Ann[3] Todd, Elizabeth[2] Bernard, William[1]) died 1783, of Gloucester County, where he was commissioner of revenue, 1782. He married ___ (Dawson?).

Issue: [COOKE] 166. Dawson[6], died 14 Nov. 1829, left will 15 May1829-14 Dec. 1829, of King and Queen County, midshipman in the Virginia Navy aboard the *Liberty* and the *Gloucester* during the Revolutionary War, 1776-79, deputy sheriff, 1783-87, married, Dec. 1785, Mildred (Paschal?), who died 14 Aug. 1836;[137] 167. Hannah[6], married (1) ___ Taylor and (2) Samuel Risher, born Charleston, S.C., died 1824, a Methodist minister who retired to his wife's farm in Gloucester County; 168. Elizabeth[6], married (1) John Beverley Whiting, baptized 18 Oct. 1756,[138] and (2), as his (2) wife, Col. James Baytop, born 1754, died 1822, lieutenant and captain, 7th and 5th Virginia regiments, 1776-79, member of the House of Delegates, 1791-94, 1796,[139] justice of Gloucester County, major, 7th Infantry, 1799-1800, member of the Society of the Cincinnati;[140] 169. Mary[6], married (1) Richard John Gregory and (2) Henry Morris, major in the Revolutionary War; 170. Frances[6], married Capt. Peter Wyatt, died 26 Dec. 1815, aged 47, left will dated 20 Oct. 1815,[141] of Gloucester County.

56. FRANCIS WHITING[5] COOKE (Mordecai[4], Ann[3] Todd, Elizabeth[2] Bernard, William[1]) married, 1766, Elizabeth Baytop.

Issue: [COOKE][142] 171. Mordecai[6], died 1823, married Ann Macon (Pendleton) Harwood, born 24 Jan. 1766;[143] 172. Sarah Smith[6], married, as his (2) wife, Col. Mordecai Cooke; 173. Francis Whiting[6], died 1820, married Sarah ___, died 1823.

---

[137] Revolutionary War pension application, Dawson Cooke, widow Mildred, W.4657, National Archives.

[138] Abingdon Parish, Gloucester Co., Register.

[139] Leonard, pp. 183, 187, 191, 195, 203.

[140] William Carter Stubbs, *A History of Two Virginia Families ... Baytop ... Catlett ...* (New Orleans, n.d.), p. 145; Francis B. Heitman, *Historical Register and Dictionary of the United States Army ...* (Washington, 1902), I, p. 201.

[141] Virginia State Archives, Acc. 20890 and 21105.

[142] Stubbs, *A History of Two Virginia Families*, pp. 113-16.

[143] *V* XLIV, p. 71.

57. GILES[5] COOKE (Mordecai[4], Anne[3] Todd, Elizabeth[2] Bernard, William[1]), born 4 Oct. 1744, died 26 Sept. 1805, left will 31 May 1803-15 Sept. 1806.[144] He married, 5 Nov. 1775, Alicia Payne, daughter of William and Susannah (Clark) Brown Payne, born 12 Dec. 1749 in Fairfax County, died 27 July 1837 at Bowling Green, Ky.[145]

Issue: [COOKE][146] 174. Mordecai[6]; 175. Whiting[6]; 176. Giles[6], born 4 Oct. 1778, died 22 Jan. 1819, of Warren Co., Ky., married, 9 April 1807, Mary Ivy Payne, died 5 July 1818; 177. William[6], born 21 Dec 1779, died 4 Oct. 1823, left will 14 July 1823-21 Oct. 1823,[147] married, 31 May 1808,[148] Maria E. Lacey of Loudoun County; 178. Elizabeth[6], born 7 Oct. 1781, died 24 Sept. 1817, married, 21 May 1801, William Robinson Payne, born 12 Oct. 1781, died 27 Feb. 1847, of Warren Co., Ky., who left will 20 Jan. 1847-April 1847;[149] 179. John W.[6], born 30 July 1783, died 8 Nov. 1821, of Warren Co., Ky., married, 28 April 1805, Anna Payne, born 23 July 1787, died 4 Nov. 1859; 180. Anna[6], born 7 Feb. 1785, died 7 July 1826, Frankfort, Ky., left will 5 July 1826-Jan. 1838,[150] married, June 1824, Jeroboam Orville Beauchamp, died 7 July 1826, Frankfort, Ky.;[151] 181. Littleton[6], born 17 Feb. 1789, died 1834, of Warren Co., Ky., and later of Mason Co., Ky. married, 11 April 1812,[152] Margaret Young, born 1788, died 15 Nov. 1854;[153] 182. Peyton[6], born 27 Jan. 1791, died 1856, of Warren Co., Ky., married (1), 8 June 1818,[154] Mary Armistead Lacey, born 24 Jan. 1800, died 20 Oct. 1827, and (2) Catherine T. Jones, born 20 Dec. 1807;

---

[144] Fairfax Co. Will Bk. I, p. 531.

[145] Brooke Payne, *The Paynes of Virginia* (Richmond, 1937), pp. 232, 244.

[146] Stubbs, *loc.cit.*; Payne, *op. cit.*, pp. 244, 266-67, 269.

[147] Warren Co., Ky., Will Bk. D, pp. 22-23, proved in East Feliciana Parish, La.

[148] Mary Alice Wertz, *Marriages of Loudoun County, Virginia, 1757-1853* (Baltimore, 1985), p. 30.

[149] Warren Co., Ky., Will Bk. D, pp. 233-34.

[150] Warren Co., Ky., Will Bk. D, p. 119.

[151] *The Reporter*, Lexington, Ky., 10 July 1826; *The Filson Club History Quarterly*, XXVIII, p. 165; LXV, pp. 209-30. He was the principal in the notorious Beauchamp-Sharp tragedy in Kentucky and was executed for the murder of Solomon P. Sharp. His wife killed herself in the prison the night before he was executed. Their joint tombstone is in Bloomfield, Ky.

[152] *The Kentucky Genealogist*, X, p. 31.

[153] Gravestones, Old Rice Cemetery, Mason Co., Ky., in Kentucky DAR, *Kentucky Cemetery Records*, I (n.p., 1960), p. 303.

[154] Wertz, *op. cit.*, p. 30.

183. Duvall[6], born 19 Feb. 1793, died 13 July 1794; 184. Thomas[6], born 10 Dec. 1794, died 28 Dec. 1818, married, 1813, Julia Fraily, born 1797.

58. JOHN[5] COOKE (Mordecai[4], Ann[3] Todd, Elizabeth[2] Bernard, William[1]) died 1817 in Woodford Co., Ky. He resided in Berkeley Co., W.Va., until 1794 when he moved to Kentucky. He married (1) 99. Elizabeth[5] Robinson and (2), 30 April 1778, Catherine Burton[8] Nourse, daughter of James[7] and Sarah (Fouace) Nourse and grand-daughter of 20. *Eliza[6] (Gregory) Nourse* (see COPE), who was born 9 May 1759 in London, England, and died June 1833 in Lexington, Ky.[155]

Issue: [COOKE] (by 1) 185. Elizabeth Moore[6], married David Humphries of Fayette Co., Ky.; 186. Frances Whiting[6], married Charles Scott, Jr., of Woodford Co.. Ky.; (by 2)[156] 187. John[6], born 2 Jan. 1779, Berkeley County, died there 5 Jan. 1779; 188. Sarah[6] born 4 March 1781, Berkeley County, died 27 Oct. 1867, Versailles, Ky., married, 1812, Bernard Gaines, born 22 June 1767, died 22 June 1839, Woodford Co., Ky., ensign, lieutenant and captain in 1st United States Infantry, 1791-97; 189. Maria Bull[6], born 4 March 1784, Berkeley County, died 2 Oct. 1853, Hickman Co., Ky., married, 15 Sept. 1811 in Woodford Co., Ky., Thomas Winn, born Hanover County, died 7 July 1862 in Hickman Co., Ky., aged 76; 190. Norbourne Berkeley[6], born 14 April 1786, Berkeley County, died 26 Feb. 1866, sheriff of Woodford Co., Ky., married, 12 July 1810, Judith Virginia[7] Markham, daughter of 549. *Mary[6] (Harris) Markham* (see BRANCH), born 9 July 1785,[157] died 1 Aug. 1871 in Henry Co., Ky.; 191. Susan Nourse[6], born 23 Sept. 1788, Berkeley County, died 27 Oct. 1868, Woodford Co., Ky., unmarried; 192. John Francis Whiting[6], born 20 Dec. 1792, Berkeley County, married Sallie Mosby, who married (2) Buckner Miller and died 20 July 1849 in Mercer Co., Ky., in her 53rd year; 193. Charles Nourse[6], born 2 Dec. 1795, Kentucky, died young.

61. Rev. THOMAS[5] SMITH (Lucy[4] Cooke, Anne[3] Todd, Elizabeth[2] Bernard, William[1]) died 20 May 1789 in his 50th year.[158] He was educated at

---

[155] Maria Catharine Nourse Lyle, *James Nourse and His Descendants* (Lexington, Ky., 1897), p. 94.

[156] *Ibid.*, pp. 45-57.

[157] Catherine Lindsay Knorr, *Marriage Bonds and Ministers' Returns of Chesterfield County, Virginia, 1771-1815* (Pine Bluff, Ark., 1958), p. 35, bond 9 July, with statement she was born 9 July 1787.

[158] Bible, in *W*(1) IV, p. 102.

Trinity College, Cambridge, 1759-63 (Bachelor of Arts), was ordained deacon, 24 July 1763, and priest, 3 March 1765, and was curate of Tivetshall, Norfolk, 1763-65, and of Redenhall with Harleton, 1765, before returning to Virginia, where he was minister of Cople Parish, Westmoreland County, 1765-89, and chairman of the Committee of Safety. He married, 7 Dec. 1765, 218. *Mary[6] Smith* (see TAYLOR-CARY), born 1744, died 14 Dec. 1791.[159]

Issue: [SMITH][160] 194. Lucy Cook[6], born 28 Aug. 1766, died 18 Feb. 1768; 195. Mary Jacquelin[6], born 23 June 1769, married 64. *Philip[6] Lee* (see MATHEWS); 196. Gregory[6], born 1 May 1771, died 25 Dec. 1776; 197. Ann[6], born 31 Jan. 1773, killed by lightning 12 July 1786; 198. Sarah[6], born 27 Feb. 1775,[161] died 21 Dec. 1851, married (1), 11 Oct. 1791,[162] Benjamin Dabney, of "Bellevue," King and Queen County, and "Elmington," Gloucester County, attorney, member of the House of Delegates from King and Queen County, 1790-91, 1794-95, 1800-03,[163] who married (1) 12 9. *Martha Burwell[6] Armistead* (see BURWELL) and died 24 May 1806, aged 49,[164] and (2), 4 Aug. 1814, as his (3) wife, Gen. William Hartwell Macon, born 2 March 1759, died 24 Aug. 1843 in his 85th year;[165] 199. Col. Thomas Gregory[6], born 17 Jan. 1778, died 15 April 1823 in King and Queen County,[166] member of the House of Delegates, 1803-06, 1820-22, and of the Virginia Senate, 1812-16,[167] married Ann[7] Dabney, step-daughter of his sister Sarah[6]; 200. Dr. John Augustine[6], born 29 Aug. 1782, died 9 Feb. 1865,[168] left will 12 June 1857-codicil 13 Nov. 1857-28 July 1865,[169] who graduated from the College of William and Mary, 1800, studied medicine at St. Thomas' Hospital, London, practiced briefly in Gloucester County before moving to New York, N.Y., where he joined the first faculty of the College of Physicians and Surgeon, 1807, was president of the College of William and

---

[159] *Ibid.*, p. 103.

[160] *Ibid.*, pp. 102-03.

[161] Macon family record, in *W*(1) XXI, pp. 33-35.

[162] Christ Church Parish, Middlesex Co., Register, gives 8 Oct. 1791.

[163] Leonard, pp. 180, 184, 196, 200, 220, 224, 228.

[164] *Virginia Argus*, Richmond, 19 July 1806; Family record, in *W*(1) IV, p. 103, gives 25 May 1806.

[165] Macon family record, *loc. cit.*

[166] *Enquirer*, Richmond, 18 April 1823.

[167] Leonard, pp. 232, 236, 240, 272, 276, 280, 284, 304, 309.

[168] *New York Times*, 10 Feb. 1865; New York, N.Y., death certificate.

[169] New York, N.Y., Will Bk. 159, p. 84.

Mary, 1814-25, returned to the faculty of the College of Physicians and Surgeons of New York, 1825, and served as its president, 1831-43,[170] married, 1809, 104. Lettice[6] *Lee* (see BLAND), born 1792, died 1827.

62. JOHN COOKE[5] BOOTH (Lucy[4] Cooke, Anne[3] Todd, Elizabeth[2] Bernard, William[1]), born about1748, died June 1773, left will dated 17 May 1773.[171] He married Ann Brown, who married (2) ____ Drummond[172] and as resident of Williamsburg died 1782.[173]

Issue: [BOOTH] 201. Mary C.[6], born 1773, married, as his (1) wife, June 1793, Morgan Tomkies, died 16 Jan. 1815,[174] member of the House of Delegates, 1803-04, 1805-06,[175] sheriff of Gloucester County, 1809, U.S. military storekeeper.

63. MARY COOKE[5] BOOTH (Lucy[4] Cooke, Anne[3] Todd, Elizabeth[2] Bernard, William[1]) died 18 April 1820 in her 71st year.[176] She married the Rev. Emanuel Jones, died by 1787, student at College of William and Mary, 1772-74, minister of St. Bride's Parish, Norfolk County, 1776, and later of King William County.[177] As a widow she resided at "Hickory Hill," Hanover County and later in Gloucester County.

Issue: [JONES][178] 202. Ann[6], died aged 15; 203. Lucy B.[6], married, as his (2) wife, George Wythe Booth, widower of 129. Paulina[5] Tabb, who died 20 Dec. 1808 in his 36th year,[179] major of cavalry in the militia; 204. Richard[6], sheriff of Gloucester County, 1821, married Martha[8] Throckmorton, daughter of Warner[7] and Sarah (Langbourne) Throckmorton and granddaughter of 434. *Sarah[6] (Smith) Cooke Throckmorton* (see MARTIAU).

64. MORDECAI COOKE[5] BOOTH (Lucy[4] Cooke, Anne[3] Todd, Elizabeth[2]

---

[170] *Dictionary of American Biography*, XVII (New York, 1935), pp. 297-98.

[171] Stubbs, *Descendants of Mordecai Cooke ... and Thomas Booth*, pp. 219-20.

[172] *Virginia Gazette* (Rind), 14 Oct. 1773, advertisement of sale of land of John Cooke Booth on Chickahominy River in James City County, subject to dower of Mrs. Drummond.

[173] *Virginia Gazette and Weekly Advertiser*, Richmond, 26 Jan. 1782.

[174] *Compiler*, Richmond, 18 Jan. 1815.

[175] Leonard, pp. 231, 240.

[176] Tombstone, Ware Church, Gloucester County, in Joseph Bryan Branch, A.P.V.A., *Epitaphs of Gloucester and Mathews Counties in Tidewater Virginia Through 1865* (Richmond, 1959), p. 71.

[177] Edward Lewis Goodwin, *The Colonial Church in Virginia* (London, 1927), pp. 282-83.

[178] Stubbs, *Descendants of Mordecai Cooke ... and Thomas Booth*, pp. 220-21.

[179] Tombstone, Ware Church, *loc. cit.*; *Enquirer*, Richmond, 7 Jan. 1809.

Bernard, William[1]), born 1756, was captain of King William County militia, 1775-81. He married (1), 2 July 1774 in King William County, Sarah Dabney and (2), 19 Dec. 1793 in King George County, Ann Mattocks.

Issue: [BOOTH][180] (by 1) 205. William[6], born 1775; 206. Thomas[6], born 1776, died 1777; 207. Lucy[6], born 1778, died 1779; 208. Mordecai Cooke[6], physician of Middlesex County, justice, 1838, married, 10 May 1821,[181] Elizabeth M. Davis.

66. COURTNEY[5] BAYLOR (Jphnr[4], Lucy[3] Todd, Elizabeth[2] Bernard, William[1]) married Jasper[8] Clayton, son of Jasper[7] Clayton and grandson of 18. *John[6] Clayton* (see SALTER-WELD).

Issue: [CLAYTON] 209. Arthur Baylor[6], born Gloucester County, died 31 March 1844 at "New Market," Caroline County, aged 46,[182] of Gloucester County, married, 19 Dec. 1822,[183] 229. Jane Hatley N.[6] Baylor; 210. Baylor[6]; 211. Caroline[6]; 212. Courtenay[6].

69. LUCY [LUCINDA][5] BAYLOR (John[4], Lucy[3] Todd, Elizabeth[2] Bernard, William[1]), born 12 Oct. 1747, died 26 Nov. 1815, Alexandria, Va., in her 71st year,[184] married, 17 March 1764, 124. *John[6] Armistead* (see BURWELL), of Caroline County, who was a student at the College of William and Mary, 1755, and left will 24 March 1788-21 July 1788.[185]

Issue: [ARMISTEAD][186] 213. John Baylor[6], died after 1844, captain of U.S. Light Dragoons, 1799-1800, married, (settlement 22) June 1796, Ann B. Carter, died 1825;[187] 214. William[6], of Prince William County, married Ann Cary Norton; 215. Addison Bowles[6], died 10 Feb. 1813, lieutenant of 7th United States Infantry, 1799-1800, lieutenant, 1801, and captain, 1806, of artillerists and

---

[180] Stubbs, *Descendants of Mordecai Cooke ... and Thomas Booth*, p. 225.

[181] *Enquirer*, Richmond, 25 May 1821.

[182] *Enquirer*, Richmond, 16 April 1844.

[183] *Enquirer*, Richmond, 21 Jan. 1823; Caroline Co. marriage bond, in *V* XXXIV, p. 154.

[184] *Federal Gazette*, Baltimore, Md., 2 Dec. 1816.

[185] Prince William Co. Land Causes 1754-1811, pp. 478-80; Fauquier Co. Land Causes 1816-53, p. 498, probated in Philadelphia, Pa.

[186] *W*(1) VI, pp. 167-69; Virginia Armistead Garber, *The Armistead Family* (Richmond, 1910), pp. 62-66; Prince William Co. Land Causes 1805-16, p. 406; Heitman, *op. cit.*, I, p. 169.

[187] Peachy R. Grattan, *Report of Cases Decided in the Superior Court of Appeals and in the General Court of Virginia*, I (Richmond, 1860), pp. 484, 487; Florence Tyler Carlton, *A Genealogy of the Known Descendants of Robert Carter of Corotoman* (Irvington, Va., 1982), p. 388.

engineers, married Mary Howe Peyton, born 1 May 1781;[188] 216. George[6], born 10 April 1780, "New Market," Caroline County, died 25 April 1818, Baltimore, Md., second lieutenant, United States Army, 8 Jan. 1799, captain, 1806, major of 3rd Artillery, 3 March 1813, breveted lieutenant colonel for the defense of Fort McHenry, 12 Sept. 1814,[189] married, 26 Nov. 1810,[190] Louise Hughes; 217. Lewis Gustavus Adolphus[6], first lieutenant, 1812, and captain of Riflemen, United States Army, killed 17 Sept. 1814 in a sortie from Fort Erie, Canada; 218. Walker Keith[6], born 1785, died 13 Oct. 1845 at Upperville, graduated from United States Military Academy, 5 March 1803, chief engineer of United States Army in Canada, 1812, lieutenant colonel, 31 July 1812, colonel of 3rd Artillery, June 1821, brevetted brigadier general 12 Nov. 1828, married, 20 Dec. 1814,[191] Elizabeth Stanley, died Sept. 1861; 219. Mary Bowles[6], born 1780, died 1840, married, 1800, as his (2) wife, Landon Carter, born 1757, died 29 Aug. 1820, aged 64,[192] of "Sabine Hall," Richmond County; 220. Frances[6], died 29 July 1818 at "Woodberry Farm," Shenandoah County,[193] married Dr. James Gillies, born 1758 in Scotland, of Fredericksnurg and after 1791 of Alexandria,[194] who died 24 Aug. 1807,[195] administration on his estate being granted to Frances Gillies, 19 Sept. 1807;[196] 221. Eleanor Bowles[6], posthumous, died 7 July 1825 at Richmond,[197] married Col. John Dangerfield of Essex County, collector of the port of Tappahannock.

70. JOHN[5] BAYLOR (John[4], Lucy[3] Todd, Elizabeth[2] Bernard, William[1]),

---

[188] Horace Edwin Hayden, *Virginia Genealogies* (Wilkes-Barre, Pa., 1891), p. 530.

[189] *Dictionary of American Biography*, I (New York, 1928), pp. 346-47.

[190] *Federal Gazette*, Baltimore, Md., 27 Nov. 1810.

[191] *Federal Gazette*, Baltimore, Md., 7 Jan. 1815.

[192] *Virginia Patriot and Richmond Daily Mercantile Advertiser*, 16 Sept. 1820; Carlton, *op. cit.*, p. 372.

[193] *Alexandria Herald*, 25 Sept. 1818.

[194] T. Michael Miller, *Artisans and Merchants of Alexandria, Virginia, 1780-1820* (Bowie, Md., 1991), I, p. 160.

[195] *The Times and Alexandria Advertiser*, 25 Aug. 1807; records of the First Presbyterian Church, Alexandria, in F. Edward Wright and Wesley E. Pippenger, *Early Church Records of Alexandria City and Fairfax County* (Westminster, Md., 1996, p. 128, buried 25 Aug. 1807, aged 49.

[196] Alexandria Will Bk. B, p. 524.

[197] *Enquirer*, Richmond, 25 July 1826.

born 4 Sept. 1750, "New Market," died there 5 Feb. 1808,[198] left will 13 Oct. 1807-14 March 1808,[199] was educated at Putney Grammar School and Caius College, Cambridge, 1770-72,[200] and resided at "New Market," Caroline County. He married, 18 Nov. 1778, St. Olave Hart Street, London, England,[201] Frances Norton, born 5 Dec. 1759, Yorktown, died 18 Feb. 1816.[202]

Issue: [BAYLOR] 222. Frances Courtenay[6], born 18 Oct. 1779, died 3 April 1780; 223. Courtney Orange[6], born 31 May 1781, married, (bond 23) March 1803,[203] Thomas Booth[7] Fox, son of 140. *John[6] Fox* and Ann Macon (see WEST), died 1825, sheriff of Gloucester County;[204] 224. Susanna Frances[6], born 2 March 1783, died 19 Feb. 1837, married, (bond 18) May 1804,[205] James A. Sutton; 225. Lucy Elizabeth Todd[6], married, 25 Nov. 1809,[206] John Horace Upshaw, member of the Virginia Senate, 1809-12, and of the House of Delegates, 1828-30,[207] who left will 3 Nov. 1835- codicil 10 Dec. 1835-18 Jan. 1835;[208] 226. Louisa Henryetta[6], married, (bond 28) March 1811,[209] William Tazewell Upshaw of "Mt. Clement," Essex County, who left will 25 Dec. 1852-16 May 1853;[210] 227. John[6], born 18 May 178_, of "Locust Dale" and "New Market," Caroline County, married, 5 May 1819,[211] Maria Roy who left will dated 24 Aug. 1849;[212] 228. Dr. George Daniel[6], born 29 Jan. 1789, "New Market," died 18 April 1848,[213] of "New Market," Caroline County, married, 24 Sept. 1814, Elizabeth Lewis[8] Fox, born 8 Dec. 1794, "Greenwich," Gloucester County, died 3 April 1837, daughter of John[7] Fox (son of 140. *John[6] Fox* and

---

[198] Baylor Bible (Philadelphia, 1816), in *Virginia Genealogical Society Quarterly*, XIX, p. 23, gives 6 Feb.

[199] Fredericksburg District Court, Record of Cases Decided #1, 1820, p. 132.

[200] *Alumni Cantabrigienses*, pt. 2, I (Cambridge, 1940), p. 195.

[201] Baylor Bible, in *Virginia Genealogical Society Quarterly*, XVIII, p. 120.

[202] Baylor Bible (1816) in *Virginia Genealogical Society Quarterly*, XIX, pp. 22-23.

[203] Caroline Co. Marriage Register 1, p. 3.

[204] *T* XXI, p. 228.

[205] Caroline Co. Marriage Register 1, pp. 8, 88.

[206] *Enquirer*, Richmond, 5 Dec. 1809; Caroline Co. Marriage Register 1, p. 21.

[207] Leonard, pp. 259, 263, 268, 343, 348.

[208] Essex Co. Will Bk. 23, p. 447; *W*(2) XVIII, p. 82.

[209] Caroline Co. Marriage bond, in *V* XXIII, p. 200.

[210] *W*(2) XVIII, p. 75.

[211] *Enquirer*, Richmond, 18 May 1819.

[212] Caroline Co. Wills & Deeds 1794-1863, pp. 59-61.

[213] Baylor Bible (1816), *loc. cit.*, gives 17 April.

Ann Macon [see WEST]) and Eleanor[8] Lewis (daughter of Warner[7] Lewis, Jr., son of 440. Col. *Warner[6] Lewis* and Eleanor Bowles [see MARTIAU]);[214] 229. Jane Hatley N.[6], married 209. Arthur Baylor[6] Clayton.

71. GEORGE[5] BAYLOR (John[4], Lucy[3] Todd, Elizabeth[2] Bernard, William[1]), born 12 Jan. 1752, "New Market," died March 1784, at Bridgetown, Barbados,[215] left will 6 May 1783-codicil 4 May 1784-14 April 1785.[216] He resided at "Pine Forest," Caroline County, was aide to Gen. Washington at the battle of Trenton, lieutenant colonel of 3rd Regiment of Light Dragoons, and brevet Brigadier General, 1783.[217] He married, 30 May 1778 in Spotsylvania County, Lucy Page, born 1757, daughter of Mann Page, who married (2) 107. *Nathaniel[6] Burwell* (see BURWELL).

Issue: [BAYLOR] 230. John Walker[6], born 1779, died 26 Sept. 1824, of Lexington, Ky., 1802, married, 19 Dec. 1799, Ann Digges[7] Fitzhugh, daughter of 157. *Mary[6] (Digges) Fitzhugh* (see DIGGES), born 1 Feb. 1781, died 7 Dec. 1860 at Warrenton;[218] 231. Lucy[6], died in infancy; 232. Elizabeth[6], may have married William Lynn.

72. ROBERT[5] BAYLOR (John[4], Lucy[3] Todd, Elizabeth[2] Bernard, William[1]), born 1754, died 1822, near Monticello, Miss., served in brother George's regiment in Revolutionary War, lived in Essex County, Jefferson Co., W.Va., Logan Co., Ky., and after 1804 in Mississippi. He married (Mrs.?) Frances Gwynne of Gwynne's Island, Mathews County.

Issue: [BAYLOR] 233. John George Wythe[6], died 1822, of Logan Co., Ky., married 257. *Lucy Todd Read[6] Barbour* (see MARTIAU), who died 9 June 1831; 234. Frances Gwynn[6], married, 16 Jan. 1799, John Whiting[8] Washington, son of Warner[7] and Mary (Whiting) Washington and grandson of 411. *Warner[6] Washington* (see MARTIAU), born 4 Oct. 1773, who moved to Kentucky; 235. Walker Gwynn[6], died 5 April 1886, married, 18 Nov. 1817, Jane Ashton Alexander[7] Dade, daughter of 82.*Langhorne[6] Dade* (see TOWNSHEND) and 93. *Sarah[6] Ashton* (see HOOE); 236. Robert Tucker[6], married, 27 July 1809,

---

[214] *T* XXI, p. 228; Merrow Egerton Sorley, *Lewis of Warner Hall* (n.p., 1935), p. 89; Baylor Bible (1816), *loc. cit.*

[215] *Dictionary of American Biography*, II (New York, 1929), pp. 76-77. He was buried in St. Michael's Church.

[216] Caroline Co. Wills, Box 1, Virginia State Archives.

[217] Revolutionary War pension application, George Baylor (Lucy Burwell, former widow), W.5966, National Archives; Heitman, *op. cit.*, I, p. 201.

[218] *Southern Churchman*, 11 Jan. 1861.

Barbara New.

73. WALKER[5] BAYLOR (John[4], Lucy[3] Todd, Elizabeth[2] Bernard, William[1]), born 13 Oct. 1762, died 14 Sept. 1822,[219] left will 23 Feb. 1821-Feb. 1823,[220] was a captain in the Revolutionary War to 10 June 1780, wounded at Germantown and Brandywine, resided in Caroline County and later at Woodlawn, near Paris, Ky.[221] He married, 1782, Jane Bledsoe.

Issue: [BAYLOR] 237. Dr. John Walker[6], born 16 March 1782, Bourbon Co., Ky., died 25 Jan. 1835, assistant surgeon, United States Army, married, 2 April 1804,[222] Sophie Marie Weidner, who died 1862, San Antonio, Tex.; 238. Cyrus Alexander[6], born 13 March 1788, died 28 Feb. 1843, lieutenant in War of 1812, lived in Kentucky, married, 12 Feb. 1811, Martha Barrere [or Baere], born 14 Feb. 1790, died 27 Sept. 1876; 239. Betsey Nelson[6], died 31 Jan. 1797, aged 10;[223] 240. George Wythe[6], born 5 Jan. 1785, left will 24 July 1827-Sept. 1827,[224] served in Kentucky legislature from Bourbon County, 1817-18, married, 3 Dec. 1807, Betsy Davis Timberlake, born 19 Oct. 1789, died 5 March 1838, who married (2) Aquilla Chinn;[225] 241. William Miller[6], born 25 Sept. 1791, died 23 Feb. 1859, lieutenant in War of 1812, lived in Kentucky and Texas, married (1), 20 June 1820, Sarah Coleman and (2) Letitia Coleman; 242. Robert Emmett Bledsoe[6], born 10 May 1793, Lincoln Co., Ky., died 6 Jan. 1874, Gay Hill, Texas, served in War of 1812, Black Hawk War and Seminole War, member of Kentucky legislature from Bourbon County, 1819, but moved to Alabama, 1820, practiced law, was ordained a Baptist minister, served in the Alabama legislature, 1824, and United States Congress from Alabama, 1829-31, moved to Texas in 1830 and was judge of the Supreme Court of the Republic of Texas, 1839-45, and member of the convention which framed the first Texas Constitution, one of the founders of Baylor University, then at Independence, Texas, and of Baylor Female College at Belton, Texas, and professor of law at

---

[219] Bible of George Wythe Baylor, in *V* XXXIII, p. 405; *Reporter*, Lexington, Ky., 14 Oct. 1822.

[220] Bourbon Co., Ky., Will Bk. G, p. 78.

[221] Revolutionary War pension application, Walker Baylor, Disability, National Archives.

[222] *Kentucky Gazette*, Lexington, Ky., 10 April 1804.

[223] *Kentucky Gazette*, Lexington, Ky., 8 Feb. 1797.

[224] Bourbon Co., Ky., Will Bk. G, p. 524.

[225] Bible of George Wythe Baylor, in *V* XXXIII, pp. 404-05.

Baylor University;[226] 243. Walker Keith[7], born 1794, died 1848, served in Alabama Senate, 1838-39, and in Texas Senate; 244. Frances Norton[6], born 30 Sept. 1795, died 1870, married, 21 Sept. 1815, John Metcalfe, born 20 Aug. 1791, Bourbon Co., Ky., died 1870, Benham, Texas, soldier in the War of 1812, manufacturer at "Mill Springs," near Monticello, Ky., later resident of Mississippi and Texas;[227] 245. Joseph Addison[6]; 246. Patrick Henry Nelson[6], under age 1821, moved to Ohio, unmarried; 247. Thomas Jefferson[6], died young; 248. Betty Nelson[6], married M. M. Johnson.

75. WILLIAM[5] TODD (Thomas[4], William[3], Elizabeth[2] Bernard, William[1]) was a member of King and Queen County Committee of Safety, 12 Dec. 1774, and proprietor of Todd's Warehouse. He married ___.

Issue: [TODD][228] 249. Elizabeth Payne[6], died 21 Nov. 1794, aged about 32,[229] married Samuel Griffin[7] Fauntleroy, son of 55. *Moore[6] Fauntleroy* (see PEIRSEY), who died 8 Dec. 1826 in his 67th year, of King and Queen County;[230] 250. Martha[6], married, as his (1) wife, John Macon, born 1 Dec. 1757,[231] died 1793,[232] leaving will 9 Feb. 1791-codicil 1 March 1793-19 Dec. 1793,[233] who later moved to Powhatan County which he represented in the House of Delegates, 1789-90, 1793.[234]

76. Dr. HENRY[5] TODD (Thomas[4], William[3], Elizabeth[2] Bernard, William[1]) died 24 Feb. 1788.[235] He was a member of the King and Queen County Committee of Safety, 12 Dec. 1774, and a member of House of Delegates, 1777-78. 1783,[236] but moved to Burke Co., Ga.[237] He married Apphia

---

[226] *Biographical Directory of the American Congress, 1774-1996* (Alexandria, Va., 1997), p. 634; *Dictionary of American Biography*, II (New York, 1929), pp. 77-78.

[227] *Virginia Genealogical Society Quarterly Bulletin*, II, p. 48.

[228] Harris, *op. cit.*, I, pp. 478-79.

[229] *Virginia Gazette and General Advertiser*, Richmond, 3 Dec. 1794.

[230] Harris, *op. cit*, I, pp. 478-79. *Enquirer*, Richmond, 23 Dec. 1826, has obituary of Samuel G. Fauntleroy, Sr., who died 7 Dec. 1826, aged 70.

[231] Alethea Jane Macon, *Gideon Macon of Virginia ...*, rev. and ed. by Jarvis Wood (Jacksonville, Fla., 1979), p. 25.

[232] *Virginia Gazette and General Advertiser*, Richmond, 27 Nov. 1793.

[233] Powhatan Co. Will Bk. 1, p. 279.

[234] Leonard, pp. 176, 181, 192.

[235] *Georgia State Gazette or Independent Register*, Augusta, Ga., 1 March 1788.

[236] Leonard, pp. 126, 150.

[237] Goerge Harrison Sanford King, *Marriages of Richmond County, Virginia, 1668-1853* (Fredericksburg, Va., 1964), p. 216.

Bushrod[7] Fauntleroy, daughter of 56. *John[6] Fauntleroy* (see PEIRSEY).[238]

Issue: [TODD] 251. Thomas Bernard[6], of Augusta, Ga., died 14 June 1803 at Richardsonville, Hancock Co., Ga., aged 28.[239]

77. BERNARD[5] TODD (Thomas[4], William[3], Elizabeth[2] Bernard, William[1]) moved from King William County to Charlotte County where he had purchased land, 1 March 1783,[240] and was a justice, member of the House of Delegates, 1789-91,[241] and pastor of Cubb Creek Baptist Church.[242] He left will 20 June 1810-7 Nov. 1810.[243] He married Elizabeth Pollard.

Issue: [TODD][244] 252. Thomas[6], died 19 Dec. 1828,[245] justice of King William County, married, 1 Dec. 1808,[246] Eliza (Pendleton) Garnett, widow of Musco Garnett and daughter of James and Elizabeth (Peachey) Pendleton, born 2 Sept. 1786,[247] died 25 March 1831, King and Queen County;[248] 253. Mary[6], married, (bond 15) Aug. 1801,[249] Thomas Sumpter; 254. Rev. William[6], born 13 Oct. 1778, died 29 June 1855, deputy clerk of King and Queen County, clerk of the District Court, ordained, 1804, as a Baptist minister and was pastor of Lower King and Queen Church until his death,[250] married (1) Mary Brown, (2) Maria Pendleton Harwood, (3) Frances S. Gwathmey, died 9 June 1820,[251] and (4), 10 Jan. 1822,[252] Harriett (___) Hill; 255. Christopher[6], died aged over 90, moved to Tennessee, married ____; 256. Bartlett Pollard[6], born 1786 in Charlotte

---

[238] Harris, *op. cit.*, II, p. 857.

[239] *Augusta Chronicle*, Augusta, Ga., 25 June and 2 July 1803.

[240] Charlotte Co. Deed Bk. 5, pp. 36-38.

[241] Leonard, pp. 175, 179, 183.

[242] Robert Baylor Semple, *History of the Baptists in Virginia* (Richmond, 1894), p. 277.

[243] Charlotte Co. Will Bk. 5, p. 6-6r.

[244] Alfred Bagby, *King and Queen County, Virginia* (New York and Washington, 1908), pp. 359-60; W(1) XV, pp. 67-68, which omits Christopher, Philip and Henry and adds Garland who may have died in Cincinnati, Ohio.

[245] *Enquirer*, Richmond, 1 Jan. 1829.

[246] *Ibid.*, 2 Dec. 1808.

[247] Pendleton Bible, in Beverley Fleet, *Virginia Colonial Abstracts*, V (Richmond, 1939), p. 96.

[248] *Religious Herald*, 3 June 1831.

[249] Catherine Lindsay Knorr, *Marriage Bonds and Ministers' Returns of Charlotte County, Virginia, 1764-1815* (Pine Bluff, Ark., 1951), p. 80. She is also said to have married ___ Buster, a delegate in the General Assembly, and moved to Kanawha County (W(1) XV, p. 68)..

[250] Harris, *op. cit.*, I, pp. 507-08; Semple, *op. cit.*, p. 162.

[251] *Enquirer*, Richmond, 20 June 1820.

[252] *Ibid.*, 19 Jan. 1822.

County, died 7 Jan. 1863, of Nottoway County where he was justice, 1816, deputy clerk of court, sergeant major and lieutenant in the War of 1812, and lieutenant colonel of militia, 1829, and later of Petersburg, married Mary Williams[7] Epes, daughter of 388. *John*[6] *Epes* (see EPES); 257. Joseph[6], of Prince Edward County, married ___; 258. Betty Waring[6], married, as his (3) wife, Temple[8] Walker, born 5 Dec. 1790, died 30 Dec. 1868, "Mt. Elba," King and Queen County,[253] son of Humphrey[7] and Frances (_____) Walker and grandson of 70. *Baylor*[6] *Walker* (see CROSHAW), justice of King and Queen County and sheriff, 1844-45; 259. Philip Garland[6], died by 26 Oct. 1831,[254] married Minerva Boone Reynolds, who left will 24 April 1836-8 Aug. 1838;[255] 260. Henry[6], died 10 Nov. 1801, aged 19.[256]

79. WILLIAM[5] TODD (Richard[4], William[3], Elizabeth[2] Bernard, William[1]) left will March 1810-7 Aug. 1815.[257] He moved from Chesterfield County to Halifax County and, about 1770, to Pittsylvania County, where he was a justice, 1776, and sheriff, 1786, and later moved to Woodford Co., Ky., where he was clerk of the Board of Trustees of Transylvania Seminary. He married (1) Phoebe Ferguson, living 7 July 1773,[258] and (2), (bond 7) Feb. 1774,[259] Jane Shelton, daughter of Crispin Shelton.

Issue: [TODD] (by 1) 261. Betty[6], named in the will of her grandfather Todd, married William Smith;[260] 262. Lettice[6], died Sept. 1819,[261] married, 1810, William P. Haslett of Woodford Co., Ky.; 263. William[6], perhaps the William who married, 12 April 1804, Catherine Robinson Winslow, born 1776, died 1851-52, Carlisle, Ky.;[262] 264. Lewis[6]; 265. Martha[6], married __ Brackenridge; (by 2) 266. George[6], born 15 May 1783, died 20 July 1831 at Frankfort, Ky.,

---

[253] Walker Bible, in Beverley Fleet, *Virginia Colonial Abstracts*, VI (Richmond, 1939), p. 52-54; sale of his personal estate, 1869, in King and Queen County Historical Society, *Bulletin*, LXVI, Jan. 1989.

[254] Kanawha Co., W.Va., Will Bk. 1, p. 117.

[255] *Ibid.*, pp. 220-21.

[256] *Virginia Gazette and General Advertiser*, Richmond, 27 Nov. 1801.

[257] Woodford Co., Ky., Will Bk. D, pp. 308-09.

[258] Orange Co., Va., Deed Bk. 16, p. 174.

[259] Catherine Lindsay Knorr, *Marriage Bonds and Ministers' Returns of Pittsylvnia County Virginia, 1767-1805* (Pine Bluff, Ark., 1956), p. 88.

[260] *The Virginia Genealogist*, XXV, p. 47.

[261] *The Reporter*, Lexington, Ky., 22 Sept. 1819.

[262] John McGill, *The Beverley Family of Virginia* (Columbia, S.C., 1956), p. 812, which identified him as son of Richard and Elizabeth (Richards) Todd.

married, 31 Aug. 1806 at Frankfort, Mary Ellis[7] Montague, daughter of 115. *Thomas*[6] *Montague* (see MONTAGUE), who was born 8 Dec. 1788 and died 20 July 1829;[263] 267. Abram[6].

80. RICHARD[5] TODD (Richard[4], William[3], Elizabeth[2] Bernard, William[1]), of Pittsylvania County, died 1795. He married. (bond 19) Sept. 1780,[264] Mary Lankford who as a widow made her home with her brother-in-law Thomas Todd in Kentucky.[265]

Issue: [TODD][266] 268. Thomas[6], possibly of Jefferson Co., Ky.; 269. Benjamin L.[6], married, (bond 12) Dec.1813,[267] Elizabeth Green; 270. Mildred B.[6], married (1), (bond 25) Jan. 1809,[268] John Green, died 1813, and (2), 30 Oct. 1818,[269] John Louderback; 271. Richard[6].

82. THOMAS[5] TODD (Richard[4], William[3], Elizabeth[2] Bernard, William[1]), born 23 Jan. 1765, King and Queen County, died 7 Feb. 1826, Frankfort, Ky., leaving will 22 Dec. 1823-20 Feb. 1826.[270]   He was a substitute in the Revolutionary War for six months and later in service in the cavalry, moved to Danville, Ky., 1786, was clerk of most of the conventions for the purpose of devising plans for Kentucky to become a separate state. He studied law, was clerk of the Federal Court for the District of Kentucky to 1792, clerk of the Court of Appeals, 1792-Dec. 1801, clerk of the Kentucky House of Representatives for several years beginning in 1792, was appointed judge of the Court of Appeals, was Chief Justice, 1806, and was Associate Justice of the Supreme Court of the United States, 1807-26, most of his time being spent in traveling the western circuit.[271] He married (1), 1788, Elizabeth Harris, who died

---

[263] *Argus of Western America*, Frankfort, Ky., 5 Aug. 1829; *The Reporter*, Lexington, Ky., 12 Aug. 1829; George William Montague, *History and Genealogy of Peter Montague* (Amherst, Mass., 1894), p. 157.

[264] Knorr, *Marriage Bonds ... Pittsylvania County*, p. 88.

[265] Maud Carter Clement, *The History of Pittsylvania County, Virginia* (Lynchburg, 1929), p. 194.

[266] Ermina Jett Darnell, *Forks of Elkhorn Church* (Louisville, 1946), p. 286.

[267] Mrs. Carl W. McGhee, *Historical Records of the Kentucky Blue Grass Region, Versailles, (Woodford County) Edition* (Washington, 1951), p. 22.

[268] Woodford Co., Ky., Marriage bond.

[269] Franklin Co., Ky., Marriage Bk. 1, p. 46.

[270] Franklin Co., Ky., Will Bk. 2, pp. 7-8.

[271] *Dictionary of American Biography*, XVIII (New York, 1936), pp. 574-75; *National Cyclopedia of American Biography*, II (New York, 1899), pp. 467-68; *Biographical Cyclopedia of the Commonwealth of Kentucky* (Chicago and Philadelphia, 1896), pp. 428-29; *The*

1811, and (2), 22 March 1812 at the President's House, Washington, D.C.,[272] 664. *Lucy*[6] *(Payne) Washington* (see WOODSON), who died 30 Jan. 1846, "Megeville," Jefferson County.[273]

Issue: [TODD][274] (by 1) 272. Harry Innes[6]; 273. Charles Stewart[6], born 22 Jan. 1791, Lincoln Co., Ky., died 14 May 1871, Baton Rouge, La., attended Transylvania University and, 1809, the College of William and Mary, studied law, was ensign in the army and captain of the 17th Infantry and then Inspector General and colonel in the War of 1812, served as Secretary of State of Kentucky, 1816, was member of the Kentucky legislature for Franklin County, 1817-18, minister to Colombia, 1820-23, then farmer of Shelby Co., Ky., where he raised blooded stock, minister to Russia, 1841-45, commissioner to treat with the Indian tribes on the Mexican border, 1850, and an editor of the Louisville *Industrial and Commercial Gazette*, married, 16 June 1816, Letitia Shelby who died 22 July 1868;[275] 274. John Harris[6], born 1796, Frankfort, Ky., died 30 Aug. 1824, in his 28th year,[276] lawyer of Frankfort, Ky., married Maria K. Innes who married (2), Nov. 1826,[277] as his (2) wife, John Jordan Crittenden, Governor of Kentucky and Attorney General of the United States, widower of 183. *Sarah O.*[6] *Lee* (see WILLOUGHBY); 275. Elizabeth R.[6], died 23 Aug. 1814 at Frankfort, Ky.,[278] married, as his (1) wife, John H. Hanna, who was born in Pennsylvania, died 1881 at Frankfort, Ky., clerk of the United States Circuit and District courts at Frankfort for over thirty years and president of the Farmer's Bank there;[279] 276. Ann Maria[6], born 30 May 1801, died 15 Dec. 1832, married, 2 Oct. 1817 at Frankfort, Ky., Edmund Lyne Starling, born 9 May 1795 in Mecklenburg County, died 30 Aug. 1869, of Frankfort, Ky., and Logan Co., Ky., who about

---

Biographical Encyclopedia of Kentucky (Cincinnati, 1878), p. 195; *The Bulletin of the King & Queen County Historical Society*, VL, July 1978.

[272] *Federal Gazette*, Baltimore, Md., 1 April 1812.

[273] *Enquirer*, Richmond, 6 Feb. 1846; *Observer and Reporter*, Lexington, Ky., 11 Feb. 1846.

[274] William E. Railey, *History of Woodford County, Kentucky* (Frankfort, Ky., 1938), p. 389.

[275] *Dictionary of American Biography*, XVIII, pp. 569-70; *The Biographical Encyclopedia of Kentucky*, pp. 518-19; G. W. Griffin, *Memoir of Col. Chas. S. Todd* (Philadelphia, 1873).

[276] *The Reporter*, Lexington, Ky., 6 Sept. 1824.

[277] *Argus of Western America*, Frankfort, Ky., 26 Nov. 1826, in *The Register of the Kentucky Historical Society*, XLVI, p. 313.

[278] *Kentucky Gazette*, Lexington, Ky., 29 Aug. 1814.

[279] *The Biographical Encyclopedia of Kentucky*, pp. 352-53.

1830 settled in Henderson Co., Ky., and in 1851 in Henderson, Ky., and was a justice of the peace, 1835-50;[280] (by 2) 277. James Madison[6], married, 25 May 1847,[281] Allisonia Rennick; 278. Thomas Johnston[6], of Frankfort, Ky., married, 23 April 1838,[282] Mary Willis Rennick, who married (2), 21 April 1868, as his (2) wife, Richard Kidder[7] Woodson, son of 1077. *Samuel Hughes*[6] and 59. *Anna Randolph*[6] *(Meade) Woodson* (see WOODSON and WATERS); 279. Madisonia[6].

92. AUGUSTINE[5] SEATON (George[4], Elizabeth[3] Todd, Elizabeth[2] Bernard, William[1]), born 17 Oct. 1737, died 10 Oct. 1794, "West Point," King William County, resided at "Chelsea," King William County, and was regimental quartermaster, Grayson's Additional Continental Regiment, 24 May 1777-20 Dec. 1777. He married Mary Winston, daughter of Samuel Winston, who died 1 Aug. 1810 at "Ampthill."[283]

Issue: [SEATON][284] 280. Lucy[6], born 10 Dec. 1778, married Thomas Rose; 281. Augustine Hill[6], born 15 Nov. 1780, died Feb. 1810; 282. Leonard Hill[6], born 13 Oct. 1782, died April 1826; 283. William Winston[6], born 11 Jan. 1785, "Chelsea," died 18 July 1866, Washington, D.C., worked on newspapers in Richmond and, 1806, in Petersburg, and in 1807 became editor of the *North Carolina Journal* of Halifax, N.C., was later with the *Raleigh Register*, and in 1812 joined with his brother-in-law Joseph Gales as editor of the *National Intelligencer* in Washington, D.C., continuing until he retired 31 Dec. 1864, was private in the volunteer company of Capt. John Davidson in War of 1812, was captain of the Washington Guards, 1824, was mayor of Washington for ten years, and vice president of the Washington Monument Association, married, 30 March 1809 at Raleigh,[285] Sarah Weston Gales who died 23 Dec. 1863; 284.

---

[280]Joseph Sullivant, *A Genealogy and Family Memorial* (Columbus, Ohio, 1874), pp. 68-69, chart following p. 71; Edmund L. Starling, *History of Henderson County, Kentucky* (Henderson, 1887), pp. 637-40.

[281] *The Register of the Kentucky Historical Society*, II, p. 72.

[282] *Ibid.*

[283] *Raleigh Register*, 12 Aug. 1810. Whether this was the Cary home in Chesterfield County or Harrison home in Cumberland County is undetermined.

[284] Seaton, *op. cit.*, pp. 109-14. Did Augustine marry (1) ___ and have Jane, daughter of Augustine, who married, (bond 9) Oct. 1790, William Allen (Joyce H. Lindsay, *Marriages of Henrico County, Virginia, 1680-1808* [n.p., 1960], p. 2)?

[285] *Visitor*, Richmond, 8 April 1809.

Elizabeth F.[6], born 9 Oct. 1786, died 5 Sept. 1818, married, 25 Feb. 1813,[286] Samuel Scott of Richmond; 285. John[6], born 18 Aug. 1788, died 18 July 1808.[287]

95. ELIZABETH[5] MACON (Elizabeth[4] Moore, Elizabeth[3] Todd, Elizabeth[2] Bernard, William[1]), born by 1742-43, married, as his (1) wife, Bartholomew Dandridge, born 25 Dec. 1737, died 18 April 1785,[288] left will 16 March 1785-13 May 1785.[289]

Issue: [DANDRIDGE] 286. Anne[6], married, as his (1) wife, 119. *William Dandridge[6] Claiborne* (see CLAIBORNE).

96. MARY[5] MACON (Elizabeth[4] Moore, Elizabeth[3] Todd, Elizabeth[2] Bernard, William[1]), born 20 Jan. 1742, married (1), 19 Sept. 1766, 94. Col. *William[6] Aylett* (see WEST), born 21 Sept. 1743, left will 12 April 1780-15 June 1780,[290] of "Fairfield," King William County. He was proprietor of Aylett's Warehouse in King William County, a member of the House of Burgesses, 1772-76, resigning 22 May 1776 to become Deputy Commissary General of the forces of Virginia, and a member of the five conventions, 1775-76.[291]

She married (2), by 1785,[292] Col. Callohill Minnis.

Issue: (by 1) [AYLETT][293] 287. Philip[6], born 12 May 1767, died Sept. 1831, "Mountville," King William County, married, 1786,[294] Elizabeth Henry, daughter of Patrick Henry, born 23 April 1769, died 24 Sept. 1843, "Fountainbleau," King William County; 288. Elizabeth[6], born 1769, died 11 Oct. 1832, Jefferson Co., Tenn., married (1) 104. Alexander Spotswood[5] Moore, as widow moved to Lexington and in 1808 with brother William to Blount Co., Tenn., married (2), 23 Jan. 1821,[295] Col. Joseph Hamilton, of Jefferson Co.,

---

[286] *Enquirer*, Richmond, 5 March 1813; Michael E. Pollock, *Marriage Bonds of Henrico County, Virginia, 1782-1852* (Baltimore, 1984), p. 145.

[287] *Enquirer*, Richmond, 19 July 1808.

[288] Dandridge family record, in Harris, *op. cit.*, II, pp. 82-83. St. Peter's Parish, New Kent Co., Register, gives birth as 26 Dec. 1737. He was the brother of Martha (Dandridge) Custis Washington.

[289] William Armstrong Crozier, *Williamsburg Wills* (*Virginia County Records*, III; New York, 1907), p. 21.

[290] *The Magazine of Virginia Genealogy*, XXVI, pp. 169-70.

[291] Leonard, pp. 103, 106, 110, 113, 115, 118, 120.

[292] King William Co. Land tax alterations, 1785, in *W*(2) VII, p. 121.

[293] Harris, *op. cit.*, II, pp. 828-30.

[294] *Virginia Independent Chronicle*, Richmond, 18 Oct. 1786.

[295] Roscoe Carlisle d'Armand and Virginia Carlisle d'Armand, *Knox County, Tennessee, Marr8iage Records, 1792-1900* (Knoxville, 1970), p. 436; *Knoxville Register*, 30 Jan. 1821.

Tenn., born 1763, Rockbridge County, died 2 July 1834; 289. Mary[6], married, as his (1) wife, Nov. 1795, 171. *Thomas*[6] *Fairfax*, 9th Lord Fairfax (see TAYLOR-CARY); 290. William[6], born 1776, King William County, died 19 Aug. 1847 in his 72nd year, near Salem, Dallas Co., Ala., moved to Blount Co., Tenn., 1808, and to Alabama in 1819, married Martha A. Posey; 291. Ann[6], born 1778, died 10 July 1818, aged 40, married, (bond 17) May 1803, Rockbridge County,[296] Andrew Alexander, born about 1763, died 1844,[297] lieutenant of cavalry in Rockbridge County militia, 1803; 292. Rebecca[6], married, (bond 27) Sept.1804 in Rockbridge County,[298] the Rev. Joseph B. Lapsley, born 5 Oct. 1779, Rockbridge County, died Sept. 1823,[299] graduate of Washington College, Presbyterian minister in Warren Co., Ky., and Tennessee.

100. CATHERINE[5] ROBINSON (Lucy[4] Moore, Elizabeth[3] Todd, Elizabeth[2] Bernard, William[1]) married, 20 Jan. 1776, Robert[8] Throckmorton, son of John[7] and Rebecca (Richardson) Throckmorton and grandson of 434. *Sarah*[6] *(Smith) Cooke Throckmorton* (see MARTIAU), of "Roxton," Jefferson Co., W.Va., student at the College of William and Mary, 1771-72, justice of Berkeley County, 1786, sheriff of Frederick County, 1789, died 19 Sept. 1796,[300] left will 10 Sept. 1796-24 Oct. 1796.[301]

Issue: [THROCKMORTON][302] 293. John[6], born 22 June 1777, "Roxton," Jefferson Co., W.Va., married, 26 Dec. 1805, Margaret Eleanor Llewellyn; 294. Lucy Moore[6], born 16 July 1779, died 10 Oct. 1851,[303] married James Smalley Bate, died 17 Dec. 1834,[304] left will 29 April 1832-5 Jan. 1835,[305] of Jefferson Co., Ky., a founder of Christ Church, Louisville, Ky.

101. JOHN SPOTSWOOD[5] MOORE (Bernard[4], Elizabeth[3] Todd, Elizabeth[2] Bernard, William[1]) in 1788 succeeded Carter Braxton in the office of

---

[296] *The Virginia Genealogist*, XXI, p. 191.

[297] Wesley E. Pippenger, *John Alexander* (Baltimore, 1990), p. 251.

[298] *The Virginia Genealogist*, XXII, p. 182.

[299] *The Reporter*, Lexington, Ky., 13 Oct. 1823.

[300] *Bowen's Virginia Gazette ...*, Winchester, 23 Sept. 1796.

[301] Berkeley Co., W.Va., Will Bk. 3, pp. 1-2.

[302] John McGill, *The Beverley Family of Virginia* (Columbia, S.C., 1956), p. 981.

[303] Gravestone, Bate family cemetery, Jefferson Co., Ky., in *Register of the Kentucky Historical Society* XXVII, p. 639.

[304] *Ibid.*

[305] Jefferson Co., Ky., Will Bk. 3, pp. 27-33.

searcher, a customs official, at West Point.[306] He later settled in Goochland County.[307] He married 113. *Anna Katherine*[6] *Dandridge* (see WEST), born 27 July 1767.[308]

Issue: [MOORE][309] 295. Anne Catherine[6], married, (bond 6) Aug. 1811,[310] Thomas W. Pulliam; 296. Dorothea Spotswood[6], married, 15 Feb. 1816,[311] William Powers; 297. Eliza[6], married, (bond 16) Jan. 1810,[312] Watson Dandridge; 298. Bernard Carter[6]; 299. Robert[6], married ___ Moseley;[313] 300. Nathaniel[6]; 301. John Spotswood[6], married ___ Murray.

102. ELIZABETH[5] MOORE (Bernard[4], Elizabeth[3] Todd, Elizabeth[2] Bernard, William[1]) married 73. Dr. *John*[6] *Walker* (see CROSHAW), born 13 Feb. 1744 at "Castle Hill," Albemarle County, died 2 Dec. 1809 near Madison Mills, Orange County, planter of "Belvoir," Albemarle County. He was a student at the College of William and Mary, 1764, commissioner with his father to make special terms with the Indians at Fort Pitt, Pa., in order to retain their friendship during the Revolutionary War, aide to Gen. Washington 1777 with rank of colonel, member of the House of Burgesses, 1772-76, and of the first two revolutionary conventions, 1774-75, delegate to the Continental Congress, 1780, United States Senator, 31 March-9 Nov. 1790, and for many years Commonwealth Attorney of Albemarle County.[314]

Issue: [WALKER] 302. Mildred[6], married Francis Kinloch, born 7 March 1765 at Charleston, S.C., died there 8 Feb. 1826, of "Kensington," Georgetown Dist., S.C., graduate of Eton College, 1774, student of law at Lincoln's Inn,

---

[306] *C* IV, pp. 400, 467.

[307] Goochland Co. Deed Bk. 19, pp. 346-47. On 10 April 1803 he conveyed to George Woodson Payne slaves, horses, mules and household and kitchen furniture in trust in consideration of the release by his wife Ann Catherine of her dower in tracts totaling 1236 acres in Hanover County and 500 acres in King William County which he wished to sell.

[308] Bible, in *W*(1) V, p. 139.

[309] Pecquet du Bellet, *op. cit.*, II, p. 709.

[310] Kathleen Booth Williams, *Marriages of Goochland County, Virginia, 1733-1815* (n.p., 1960), p. 81, consent of her mother.

[311] Thomas P. Hughes and Jewel B. Standefer, *Goochland County, Virginia, Marriage Bonds and Ministerss' Returns, 1816-1854* (Memphis, 1972), p. 83.

[312] Williams, *op. cit.*, p. 22.

[313] Perhaps Robert of Mason Co., W.Va., who married, "lately" in Buckingham County, Jane Moseley, daughter of Arthur Moseley (*Virginia Argus*, Richmond, 23 Sept. 1808).

[314] *Biographical Directory of the American Congress, 1774-1996* (Alexandria, Va., 1997), p. 2003; Leonard, pp. 102, 105, 109, 112.

1774, and at Paris and Geneva, volunteer lieutenant and captain in the Revolutionary War, 1778-81, member of the South Carolina House of Representatives, 1779, 1786-88, and of the Continental Congress, 1780, delegate to the South Carolina convention that ratified the Articles of Confederation, 1783, and of the South Carolina constitutional convention, 1790, and warden of the city of Charleston and justice, 1789.[315]

103. THOMAS[5] MOORE (Bernard[4], Elizabeth[3] Todd, Elizabeth[2] Bernard, William[1]) married Martha ___.

Issue: [MOORE] 303. Lucy[6], married Alexander Rose of King William County.[316]

104. ALEXANDER SPOTSWOOD[5] MOORE (Bernard[4], Elizabeth[3] Todd, Elizabeth[2] Bernard, William[1]), born 1763, died 1799, Charles City County, married, 19 July 1787,[317] 288. Elizabeth[6] Aylett, who as a widow moved to Lexington and in 1808 to Blount Co., Tenn., married (2) Col. Joseph Hamilton and died 11 Oct. 1832 in Jefferson Co., Tenn..

Issue: [MOORE][318] 304. Mildred Walker[6], born 16 June 1788, living 1858, of Petersburg, married, 7 June 1806, John Wilson Campbell[319] of Rockbridge County; 305. Alexander Spotswood[6], born 10 Oct. 1790, died 29 Aug. 1850, Tuscombia, Ala., in his 61st year,[320] resident of Tennessee; 306. William Augustine[6], born 30 March 1791, died 22 Aug. 1796; 307. Lavenia[6], born 25 Sept. 1792, died 16 Dec. 1809 in Greensville County,[321] married, 18 March 1809 in Blount Co., Tenn., the Rev. William McPheeters, born 28 Sept. 1778, Augusta County, died 7 Nov. 1842 at Raleigh, N.C., who attended Liberty Hall Academy, studied medicine, was a Presbyterian minister in Kentucky and Virginia, and after 1810 in Raleigh, N.C., where he was also principal of Raleigh Academy, 1810-26;[322] 308. Elizabeth Aylett[6], born 25 July 1794, married, 1 June 1813, Col. James McDonald, an officer in the Revolutionary War, and lived at "Glencoe" in Alabama; 309. Mary Fairfax[6], born 12 Jan. 1796, died 28 Sept.

---

[315] *Biographical Directory of the American Congress, 1774-1996*, pp. 1338-39.

[316] Christine Rose, *The Brothers Rev. Robert Rose and Rev. Charles Rose* (San Jose, Calif., 1985), p. 25.

[317] Moore-Johnston Bible.

[318] *Ibid.*; Harris, *op. cit.*, II, pp. 828-39.

[319] They were the parents of Charles Campbell, the historian.

[320] *The Southern Advocate*, Huntsville, Ala., 11 Sept. 1850.

[321] *Raleigh Register*, 1 Feb. 1810.

[322] *The Register of the Kentucky Historical Society*, XXXIV, pp. 287, 349-53.

1875,[323] resident of Franklin Co., Ala., in 1850, married, 1 Jan. 1813, David Kellar, died 2 May 1837 in his 50th year,[324] who settled at Knoxville, Tenn., 1808, and was a merchant and agent of the Tuscumbia, Courtland and DeCarter Railroad; 310. Ann Evilina[6], born 29 Sept. 1797, married, 28 April 1814, Arthur H. Henley, born 1782, died 1849, farmer of "Chota," Monroe Co., Tenn.; 311. William Augustine[6], born 10 Dec. 1798, married Ann Jane Beck.

105. AUGUSTINE[5] MOORE (Bernard[4], Elizabeth[3] Todd, Elizabeth[2] Bernard, William[1]) left will 20 Jan. 1777-17 March 1777.[325] He represented King William County in the House of Burgesses, 1772-74, and the Convention of 1774,[326] and later resided at "Windsor," Essex County. He married, (1) Sarah Ring and (2) Judith Scandrett who died before 1777.

Issue: [MOORE] (by 1) 312. Booth[6]; 313. Bernard[6]; (by 2) 314. Sarah Scandrett[6], born 1766, died 1818, married (1), 26 Jan. 1792,[327] Carter Braxton, Jr., born 1764, died 8 April 1809 at Williamsburg, aged 43,[328] student at the College of William and Mary and an attorney, and (2) Temple Elliott, died 1822.

106. BERNARD[5] MOORE (Bernard[4], Elizabeth[3] Todd, Elizabeth[2] Bernard, William[1]) of "Chelsea," King William County, student at the College of William and Mary, 1760-63, died about 1806.[329] He married, (bond 2) May 1788,[330] Lucy Ann Heabard Leiper, daughter of Dr. James and Elizabeth (Smallwood) Leiper.

Issue: [MOORE][331] 315. Andrew Leiper[6], died 8 March 1828, "Chelsea,"[332] left will 7 March 1828-20 March 1828,[333] married Ann F. Robinson; 316.

---

[323] Tombstone, Tuscumbia, Ala.; *North Alabamian*, Tuscumbia, Ala., 30 Sept. 1875, in *Alabama Historical Quarterly*, VII, pp. 375-76.

[324] *Knoxville Register*, Knoxville, Tenn., 17 May 1837.

[325] Essex Co. Will Bk. 13, 1775-85, pp. 72-73.

[326] Leonard, pp. 103, 110.

[327] Frederick William Pyne, *Descendants of the Signers of the Declaration of Independence*, VI (Rockport, Me., 2000), p. 820, which gives her death as 1833 at "Mount Pleasant," King and Queen County.

[328] *Virginia Argus*, Richmond, 14 April 1809.

[329] King William Co. Personal property tax list, 1806, estate listed.

[330] Lindsay, *op. cit.*, p. 60.

[331] Land Office Military Certificates 8663-8668, Capt. Heaberd Smallwood, Virginia State Archives.

[332] *Enquirer*, Richmond, 28 March 1828.

[333] Land Office Military Certificates, *loc. cit.*, probated in King William County.

Thomas[6], left will 28 Dec. 1830-28 March 1831,[334] married (1) Robinette[7] Nelson, daughter of 199. *Robert[6] Nelson* (see MARTIAU), and (2), 29 May 1821, Anna Henry[8] Aylett, daughter of Philip[7] and Elizabeth (Henry) Aylett and granddaughter of 94. *William[6] Aylett* (see WEST), who died 2 Jan. 1828, aged 24;[335] 317. Elizabeth[6], born 9 Nov. 1795 at "Chelsea," died 5 Dec. 1863 in Caroline County, married, 15 July 1817, William Penn Taylor, born 25 Oct. 1790 in Caroline County, died there 18 June 1863,[336] of "Hayfields," Caroline County, member of the Convention of 1829-30, of the House of Delegates, 1830-31, and of the United States House of Representatives, 1833-35;[337] 318. Lucy Leiper[6], married Benjamin Robinson and resided at "Chelsea";[338] 319. Bernard[6], died young.

107. LUCY[5] MOORE (Bernard[4], Elizabeth[3] Todd, Elizabeth[2] Bernard, William[1]), born 1747, died 26 Sept. 1819, married, 1774, the Rev. Henry Skyrin, born 1729, Whitehaven, England, died 1795, Hampton,[339] curate of Wimondly, Hertfordshire, who came to Virginia, 1763, was minister of St. John's Parish, King William County, 1764-87, and then of Elizabeth City Parish until his death.[340]

Issue: [SKYRIN][341] 320. Robert[6], never married; 321. Elizabeth[6], born Aug. 1779, died 1862, married, 5 Feb. 1799, Robert Temple, born 1774, died Dec. 1876, of "Ampthill," Chesterfield County;[342] 322. Anne Catherine[6], died 25 June 1830, married (1) Richard Frazier and (2), 3 Oct. 1807, Dr. Zachary Lewis, born 25 Nov. 1787, died 5 June 1859, of King and Queen County; 323. Col. John Spotswood[6], born 1780 at "Chelsea," died 1855; 324. Bernard[6], never married; 325. Maria[6], born 1785, died 14 Oct. 1844, married, 18 Dec. 1802, George Tebbs.

108. ANN BUTLER[5] MOORE (Bernard[4], Elizabeth[3] Todd, Elizabeth[2]

---

[334] *Ibid.*, probated in King William County.

[335] Bible, in Harris, *op. cit.*, II, p. 831.

[336] Frank Willing Leach, "Genealogy of the Signers of the Declaration of Independence" (typewritten; n.p., n.d.), XX, p. 5959.

[337] Leonard, pp. xxvii, 354-55.

[338] *V* XIV, p. 197; Harris, *op. cit.*, II, p. 618.

[339] Tombstone, St. John's Church, Hampton, Va.

[340] Harris, *op. cit.*, II, pp. 781-82.

[341] *V* LIV, pp. 161-63.

[342] William Ludwell Harrison Papers, Virginia Historical Society, folder 4.

Bernard, William[1]) died 15 April 1809.[343] She married, 1780,[344] as his (2) wife, Charles Carter, son of John and Elizabeth (Hill) Carter, who died 28 June 1806 at "Shirley," aged 74.[345] They resided at "Shirley," Charles City County.

Issue: [CARTER][346] 326. Robert Hill[6], born 1771; 327. Ann Hill[6], married, as his (2) wife, 106. Gen. *Henry[6] Lee* (see BLAND); 328. Dr. Robert[6], died 14 Nov. 1805, aged 31, at "Shirley,"[347] married, 1792, Mary[7] Nelson, daughter of 196. Gen. *Thomas[6] Nelson* (see MARTIAU), born 17 Dec. 1774; 329. Bernard[6], born 1776, died 1776; 330. John[6], born 1777, died 1784; 331. Kate Spotswood[6], born 1778, died 1809, married, 1796,[348] as his (1) wife, Dr. Carter[7] Berkeley, son of 114. *Nelson[6] Berkeley* (see BURWELL), died 3 Nov. 1839, aged 72,[349] of "Edgewood," Hanover County; 332. Bernard Moore[6], born 1780, died 1843, married, 1803, Lucy[7] Lee, born 1786, died 1860,[350] daughter of 106. Gen. *Henry[6] Lee* and his (1) wife Matilda Lee (see BLAND); 333. Williams[6], born 1782, died after 1860, of Hanover County, married, 31 March 1810,[351] Charlotte Foushee, who died 27 July 1822, aged 35;[352] 334. Butler[6], born 1784, died 1786; 335. Mildred Walker[6], born 1786, died 1808; 336. Lucy[6], born 25 Feb. 1789, died 10 Nov. 1824, Botetourt County,[353] married, 2 Jan. 1809, Nathaniel[7] Burwell, son of 134. *Nathaniel[6] Burwell* (see BURWELL) and 173. *Martha[6] Digges* (see DIGGES), born 16 June 1785, died 21 July 1866,[354] of "Glenmore," Roanoke County, first president of the Roanoke College Board of Trustees; 337. William Fitzhugh[6], born 1791, died 1852, married Anne Lightfoot; 338. (Daughter)[6], born 1792, died 1792; 339. (Stillborn child)[6], born 1794; 340.

---

[343] *Visitor*, Richmond, 6 May 1809; *Virginia Gazette and General Advertiser*, Richmond, 5 May 1809, which says 16 April.

[344] *Virginia Gazette* (Dixon & Hunter), 29 Nov. 1780.

[345] *Virginia Gazette and General Advertiser*, Richmond, 5 July 1806.

[346] Edmund Jennings Lee, *Lee of Virginia* (Philadelphia, 1895), p. 359; Florence Tyler Carlton, *A Genealogy of the Known Descendants of Robert Carter of Corotoman* (Irvington, Va., 1982), pp. 41, 44, 49, 55, 61, 63.

[347] *Virginia Gazette and General Advertiser*, 4 Dec. 1805.

[348] Carlton, *op. cit.*, p. 399.

[349] *Enquirer*, Richmond, 15 Nov. 1839.

[350] Lee, *op. cit.*, p. 340.

[351] *Enquirer*, Richmond, 3 April 1810.

[352] *Enquirer*, Richmond, 30 July 1822.

[353] *Enquirer*, Richmond, 30 Nov. 1824.

[354] Stuart E. Brown, *Burwell Kith and Kin of the Immigrant Lewis Burwell ...* (Berryville, Va., 1994), p. 58.

Calphemia[6], born 1796, died 1797.

116. ANN[5] BICKERTON (Mary[4] Todd, Philip[3], Elizabeth[2] Bernard, William[1]) married, 4 June 1752, as his (2) wife, George Webb, died by 26 June 1758,[355] merchant and planter of New Kent County, vestryman of St. Peter's Parish, 1746-58, sheriff, 1737, justice,[356] and perhaps (2) ___ Dickenson.[357]

Issue: [WEBB][358] 341. Sarah[6], born 3 Jan. 1754; 342. Mary[6], born 25 Sept. 1756; 343. Bernard[6], born 18 May 1758, resided in Richmond, 1787.

117. ELIZABETH[5] BICKERTON (Mary[4] Todd, Philip[3], Elizabeth[2] Bernard, William[1]) married Lewis Webb, her sister's step-son, son of George and Lucy (Foster) Webb, born 19 April 1731,[359] died about 1786,[360] of "Chemokins," New Kent County, vestryman of St. Peter's Parish after his father's death, member of the House of Burgesses, 1756-61, and House of Delegates, 1777-78.[361]

Issue: [WEBB][362] 344. Lewis[6], born 14 July 1759, died 12 July 1841, New Market, Boyle Co., Ky., of New Kent County, captain of marines, assisted in the capture of seventeen prizes, captain in Col. Parker's Virginia Regiment for five years and six months during Revolutionary War, moved to Mercer Co., Ky., and then to Washington Co., Ky., and to Boyle Co., Ky.,[363] married, 29 Sept. 1787,[364] Lucy R. Cary of King William County, born 5 April 1768; 345. Bickerton[6], died before 11 Feb. 1789,[365] of New Castle; 346. Foster[6], died 12 April 1795 in New Kent County, aged 59,[366] of New Kent County, educated at

---

[355] C. G. Chamberlayne, *The Vestry Book and Register of St. Peter's Parish ... 1684-1786* (Richmond, 1937), p. 336.

[356] Harris, *op. cit.*, I, p. 196.

[357] Bernard Webb stated a tract of land in New Kent County had been devised to him by Mrs. Ann Dickenson (*Virginia Gazette, or the American Advertiser*, Richmond, 20 March 1784).

[358] Chamberlayne, *op. cit.*, p. 556.

[359] *Ibid.*, p. 501.

[360] New Kent Co. Personal property tax list, 1786, estate taxed.

[361] Harris, *op. cit.*, I, p. 197; Leonard, pp. 89, 126.

[362] Harris, *op. cit.*, I, pp. 197-98.

[363] Revolutionary War pension application, Lewis Webb, widow Lucy, W.8990; Margie G. Brown, *Genealogical Abstracts, Revolutionary War Veterans, Scrip Act 1852* (Oakton, Va., 1990), p. 262.

[364] Webb Bible, in *Virginia Genealogical Society Quarterly*, XV, pp. 106-07.

[365] *Virginia Independent Chronicle*, 11 Feb. 1789.

[366] *Virginia Gazette and General Advertiser*, Richmond, 22 April 1795.

College of William and Mary, paymaster general of the State of Virginia, married, 17 June 1775, Sarah Shore, died 20 April 1802;[367] 347. Katherine[6].[368]

118. Maj. JOHN TODD[5] BICKERTON (Mary[4] Todd, Philip[3], Elizabeth[2] Bernard, William[1]), of Hanover County, died between 21 Dec. 1774 and 19 Oct. 1775.[369] He married Martha ___, who married (2) ___ Irwin.[370]

Issue: [BICKERTON] 348. Martha, married, by 21 Sept. 1770,[371] Benjamin Lewis, born 16 June 1744, King and Queen County, of Spotsylvania County,[372] who later lived in Louisa County and then in New Kent County.[373]

119. ALICE[5] BICKERTON (Mary[4] Todd, Philip[3] Elizabeth[2] Bernard, William[1]), born 1730/1, died 16 June 1773, married, 3 Feb. 1746/7, John Winston, born 9 June 1724, died 23 Jan. 1772, of St. Paul's Parish, Hanover County.

Issue: [WINSTON][374] 349. William Overton[6], born 6 [16?] Nov. 1747, died 1815, married (1), 1 Dec. 1770, Joanna Robinson, born 15 April 1755, died 11 Dec. 1794,[375] and (2), about 1800, Ann Kidley (Chamberlayne) Posey, died 1812, widow of John Price Posey; 350. Mary Todd[6], born 16 March 1748/9, died 27 Feb. 1751/2; 351. Barbara[6], born 30 Nov. 1750, died 6 Nov. 1823, married, 15 Aug. 1771, Dr. Robert Barret, who died 9 June 1823;[376] 352. James[6], born 12 March 1752/3, died 17 July 1826, officer in Revolutionary War, married, 25 Dec. 1782,[377] Sarah Marks, died 1829; 353. Molly[6], born 28 March 1755, died 13 Nov. 1761; 354. John[6], born 14 Oct. 1757, died 28 April 1800,

---

[367] Harris, *op. cit.*, I. p. 194.

[368] Her 203 acres in the division of her father's land was charged to William H. Macon.

[369] Maryland Provincial Court Record DD #6, pp. 84, 89, in Torrence, *op. cit.*, p.p. 102-04; *Virginia Gazette* (Purdie), 19 Oct. 1775, advertisement by his executors of land in Albemarle and Louisa counties for sale.

[370] *Virginia Gazette* (Dixon & Hunter), 4 Nov. 1775, 1 June 1776.

[371] Spotsylvania Co. Deed Bk. G, p. 416-17.

[372] Hayden, *op. cit.*, p. 386.

[373] Louisa Co. Deed Bk. E, pp. 286-87, 316-17.

[374] George Harrison Sanford King, "Winston Family of Hanover County," *Virginia Genealogical Society Quarterly*, XIII, pp. 89-95; Malcolm Hart Harris, *History of Louisa County, Virginia* (Richmond, 1936), pp. 431-37; "The Register of the Ancestors of Bickerton Winston," *Louisa County Historical Magazine*, I, pp. 25-26.

[375] *V* XVIII, p. 105, citing Winston Bible.

[376] Barret and Winston family Bible, in *Louisa County Historical Magazine*, II, pp. 24-25.

[377] John Vogt and T. William Kethley, *Albemarle County Marriages, 1780-1853* (Athens, Ga., 1991), I, p. 344.

married, 7 Dec. 1780,[378] Mary Johnson, born 30 Aug. 1763,[379] left will 4 Jan. 1822-10 Nov. 1823;[380] 355. Elizabeth[6], married 633. *Tarleton[6] Payne* (see WOODSON); 356. Joseph[6], born 2 April 1763, left will 10 Nov. 1836-14 June 1841,[381] married, (bond 15) Nov. 1790,[382] Rebecca Johnson, born 2 June 1775;[383] 357. Martha[6], born 20 [21?] June 1765, died 29 April 1788, married, 23 Oct. 1782, as his (1) wife, Col. William Overton Callis, born 23 March 1757 [or 4 March 1756], died 30 March 1814, Louisa County,[384] lieutenant in Continental Line in Revolutionary War, 1777-78, major and aide de camp to Gen. Nelson at Yorktown, 1781,[385] later colonel of Louisa County militia; 358. Bickerton[6], born 28 Jan. 1767 [or 1768], left will 13 April 1830-codicil 213 April 1833-14 July 1834,[386] married (1), 19 Feb. 1795,[387] Ann Lysle Smelt, born 29 April [Aug.?] 1779, died 7 April 1816, and (2), 30 March 1818 in Louisa County, Mary Smith, born 1 July 1793, left will 1 Dec. 1849-13 Oct. 1851;[388] 359. Alice Ann[6], born 8 Aug. 1769, died 8 Jan. 1813, married, (bond 25) Oct. 1785,[389] as his (1) wife, Capt. Henry Pendleton, born 4 Dec. 1762, King and Queen County, died 18 Nov. 1822, of Cuckoo, Louisa County, member of Hanover County militia during Revolutionary War, ensign in that county, 1799, member of the House of Delegates from Louisa County, 1804-06.[390]

121. ANNE[5] HUBBARD (Elizabeth[4] Todd, Philip[3], Elizabeth[2] Bernard, William[1]), born 1738, died 27 May 1789, married, June 1758, as his (1) wife, Col. James Taylor, born 27 Dec. 1732, "Midway," Caroline County, died there

---

[378] W. Mac. Jones, ed., *The Douglas Register* (Richmond, 1928), p. 50; Kathleen Booth Williams, *Marriages of Louisa County, Virginia, 1766-1815* (n.p., 1959), p. 114.

[379] Johnson family register, in *Louisa County Historical Magazine*, II, p. 23.

[380] Louisa Co. Will Bk. 6, p. 410.

[381] Louisa Co. Will Bk. 10, p. 389.

[382] Williams, *Marriages of Louisa County,* p. 114.

[383] Johnson family register, *loc. cit.*

[384] *Enquirer*, Richmond, 8 June 1814; Callis family record, in , *History of Louisa County, Virginia* (2nd ed.; n.p., 1963), p. 303A.

[385] Revolutionary War pension application, William Overton Callis, widow Anne, W.6645; *Louisa County Historical Magazine*, XIII, pp. 3-7.

[386] Louisa Co. Will Bk. 9, pp. 131-32.

[387] Spotsylvania Co. Marriage Register 1, p. 1.

[388] Louisa Co. Will Bk. 13, pp. 182-83.

[389] Williams, *Marriages of Louisa County*, p. 80.

[390] *V* XLI, pp. 265-66.

12 March 1814, left will 12 Nov. 1811-codicil 5 March 1814-April 1815,[391] ensign in the French and Indian War, colonel of Caroline County militia during the Revolutionary War, justice, 1759, sheriff, member of the House of Burgesses, 1774-76, of the Committee of Safety of Caroline County, 1774-76, of the conventions of 1774-75 and 1788, and of the House of Delegates, 1776, and Virginia Senate, 1777-91.[392]

Issue: [TAYLOR][393] 360. Lucy[6], born 1759, married James Eubank of Clark Co., Ky.; 361. Col. Hubbard[6], born 2 Aug. 1760, died 7 Oct. 1840,[394] dragoon under Gen. Nelson in Revolutionary War, moved to "Spring Hill," Clark Co., Ky., 1790, was a member of the Kentucky Constitutional Convention, 1792, and of the Kentucky Senate, 1796-1800, 1815-19, and a presidential elector in the six elections between 1805 and 1825,[395] married, 27 July 1782, Clarissa Minor, born 8 Nov. 1762, died 2 June 1841;[396] 362. Elizabeth[6], born 1763, died 8 Dec. 1836,[397] married, 1781, Capt. Thomas Minor, born 1751, died 21 July 1834,[398] of "Locust Grave," Spotsylvania County, second lieutenant and captain in 5th Virginia Regiment, colonel of militia, justice and sheriff of Spotsylvania County;[399] 363. Martha[6], born 1767; 364. Gen. James[6], born 19 April 1769, Caroline County, died 7 Nov. 1848, Newport, Ky., left will 18 Dec. 1844-codicil 1 July 1848-Jan. 1851,[400] surveyor and deputy sheriff of Caroline County, moved to Newport, Ky., where he was clerk of the Campbell County Court, 1795-1830, was a witness for the prosecution in the trial of Aaron Burr, was Brigadier General and Major General of Kentucky militia and during the War of 1812 was

---

[391] Campbell Co., Ky., Will Bk. A, p. 224, originally recorded in Caroline County.

[392] W(1) IX, pp. 55-56; Leonard, pp. 102, 105, 109, 112, 122, 127, 132, 136, 140, 143, 148, 151, 172, 178, 182, 186.

[393] Jouett Taylor Cannon Papers, The Filson Club, Louisville, Ky.; Caroline Co. Will Bk. 19, 1814-18, pp. 20-21.

[394] Kathryn Owen, *Old Graveyards ... of Clark Country, Kentucky* (New Orleans, 1985), p. 100.

[395] *The Biographical Encyclopedia of Kentucky*, p. 200.

[396] Owen, *loc. cit.*

[397] *Virginia Herald*, Fredericksburg, 21 Dec. 1836.

[398] *Virginia Herald*, Fredericksburg, 23 July 1834.

[399] V XI, p. 335; W(1) IX, pp. 55-5; Revolutionary War pension application, Thomas Minor, widow Elizabeth, W.5374.

[400] Campbell Co., Ky., Will Bk. C , p. 45. This will was rejected at Nov. 1848 Court but was directed by the Circuit Court to be recorded for probate, 28 Jan. 1851.

taken prisoner at Detroit,[401] married, 15 Nov. 1795, Keturah (Moss) Leitch, who was born 11 Sept. 1778 in Goochland County and died Jan. 1866;[402] 365. Alice Thornton[6], married 115. *Washington[6] Berry* (see TOWNSHEND); 366. Ann Hubbard[6], died 14 Sept. 1848, married (1), 6 Nov. 1792, Robert Taliaferro, who died 3 May 1805, aged 41,[403] and (2), 25 Dec. 1823,[404] as his (2) wife, John Todd, who left will 17 Oct. 1831-21 Nov. 1831;[405] 367. Reuben Thornton[6], married Mary T. Thornton; 368. Edmund[6], born 1780, died 2 Oct. 1811, married, 4 Sept. 1803,[406] 374. Mary Todd[6] Hinde; 369. Martha [Polly] Todd[6], born 1783, married Peter Thornton, born 1774, died 29 Sept. 1833, aged 59,[407] of "Rosehill," Caroline County.

122. MARY TODD[5] HUBBARD (Elizabeth[4] Todd, Philip[3], Elizabeth[2] Bernard, William[1]), born about 1745, died after 1830. She married, 24 Sept. 1767, Dr. Thomas Hinde, said to have been born in Oxfordshire, England, 1734, studied medicine in London, and served under Wolfe at Quebec in the French and Indian War, settled in Essex County, was a surgeon in Patrick Henry's regiment during the Revolutionary War, moved to Louisa County and in 1797 went to Clark Co., Ky., and died about 1828.[408]

Issue: [HINDE][409] 370. Elizabeth Clifford[6], born 11 June 1768, married Capt. Robert Richardson; 371. Susannah Brooks[6], born 15 Dec. 1770, married the Rev. Leroy Cole; 372. John Woods[6], born 31 March 1774, died April 1856, married, 16 March 1797,[410] Elizabeth Sydnor Marks, died 10 Feb. 1850; 373. Hannah Hubbard[6], born 6 March 1777, Hanover County, died 11 Jan. 1852, Madison Co., Ky., married (1), 1798, Williams Kavanaugh, born in East

---

[401] *The Biographical Encyclopedia of Kentucky*, p. 309.

[402] W. H. Perrin and others, *Kentucky, A History of the State* (7th ed.; Louisville and Chicago, 1887), pp. 897-98.

[403] Dates presumably from a family Bible, source undetermined.

[404] Stephen W. Worrel, *Campbell County, Kentucky, Marriages, 1795-1850* (Falls Church, Va., 1992), p. 202.

[405] Oldham Co., Ky., Will Bk. 1, p. 222.

[406] Worrel, *op. cit.*, p. 205.

[407] *Enquirer*, Richmond, 14 Oct. 1833.

[408] Revolutionary War Rejected Claims, Box 27, Virginia State Archives; *The Virginia Genealogist*, XXX, p. 53.

[409] Hinde Bible, in Ednah Wilson McAdams, *Kentucky Pioneers and Court Records* (Lexington, Ky., 1929), p. 261.

[410] Kathleen Booth Williams, *Marriages of Louisa County, Virginia, 1766-1815* (n.p., 1959), p. 53.

Tennessee, died about 1806-07, minister of the Methodist Church and later of the Episcopal Church, (2), 1812, William Taylor, and (3) Valentine Martin;[411] 374. Mary Todd[6], born 27 Jan. 1780, married (1) 368. Edmund[6] Taylor and (2), 19 March 1817,[412] John McKinney, native of New Jersey, officer in the Revolutionary War and the regular army, who was stationed at Newport, Ky., in 1816;[413] 375. Anna [Mary?] Winston[6], born 12 Dec. 1783, married Richard Southgate, born 1773, New York City, died 17 July 1851, lawyer and merchant of Newport, Ky., who represented Campbell County in the Kentucky House of Representatives, 1803, and served in the state Senate, 1817-21, 1833-37;[414] 376. Thomas Spotswood[6], born 19 April 1785, of Urbana, Ohio, married (1) Belinda Bradford and (2) Sarah (de Cavalier) O'Neal; 377. Martha Harrison[6], born 21 May 1787.

124. PHILIP[5] TABB (Lucy[4] Todd, Christopher[3], Elizabeth[2], William[1]), born 6 Nov. 1750, died 25 Feb. 1822,[415] of "Toddsbury," Gloucester County, married, 7 Dec. 1780, 130. Mary Mason[5] (Wythe) Booth, born 7 Sept. 1751, died 22 Sept. 1814.[416]

Issue: [TABB] 378. Thomas Todd[6], born 4 Dec. 1782, died 20 June 1835, "Toddsbury,"[417] of "Toddsbury," married (1) 403. Lucy Armistead[6] Smith, died 14 Nov. 1821, "Toddsbury," in her 39th year,[418] and (2) Eliza C. Forman, died 1 July 1851 in her 53rd year;[419] 379. John[6], born 15 Sept. 1784, of "White Marsh," Gloucester County, married, 18 Dec. 1817 at Norfolk,[420] Evelina Matilda Prosser; 380. Philip Edward[6], born 17 Oct. 1786, died 30 Sept. 1851,

---

[411] *The Biographical Encyclopedia of Kentucky*, p. 170.

[412] Worrel, *op. cit.*, p. 137.

[413] *The Biographical Cyclopedia of Kentucky*, p. 362.

[414] *Ibid.*, p. 140.

[415] Tombstone, Ware Parish Cemetery, in Joseph Bryan Branch A.P.V.A., *Epitaphs of Gloucester and Mathews Counties in Tidewater Virginia Through 1865* (Richmond, 1959), p. 83; *Enquirer*, Richmond, 9 April 1822.

[416] Tombstone, Ware Parish Cemetery, *loc. cit.*

[417] Tombstone, Ware Parish Cemetery, *loc. cit.*; *Enquirer*, Richmond, 30 June 1835, which gives death as 22 June.

[418] Tombstone, Ware Parish Cemetery, in Joseph Bryan Branch A.P.V.A., *op. cit.*, p. 84; *Enquirer*, Richmond, 30 Nov. 1821.

[419] Tombstone, Ware Parish Cemetery, in Joseph Bryan Branch A.P.V.A., *op. cit.*, p. 85.

[420] *V* XXXIV, p. 266, license from Gloucester County; George Herbert Tucker, *Abstracts from Norfolk City Marriage Bonds (1797-1850)* (n.p., 1934), p. 74.

aged 65,[421] of "Waverly," Gloucester County, married, 15 Jan. 1824,[422] Emeline M. Allmond; 381. Maria Mason[6], born 13 Aug. 1788, died 24 July 1793; 382. Dr. Henry Wythe[6], born 2 July 1791, died 1 April 1864,[423] of "Auburn," Gloucester County, graduate of Yale College, married (1) Hester Van Bibber, born 1800, died 4 Feb. 1823, "North End," Mathews County,[424] (2) Martha[7] Tompkins, born 21 April 1807, died 17 Sept. 1842,[425] daughter of 332. *Christopher⁶ Tompkins* (see MARTIAU) and 404. Elizabeth[6] Smith, and (3), 13 Oct. 1846 at Brooklyn, N.Y.,[426] Ellen Foster, born 29 Oct. 1828, died 5 Feb. 1858.[427]

125. LUCY[5] TABB (Lucy[4] Todd, Christopher[3], Elizabeth[2] Bernard, William[1]), born 25 March 1753, died 14 Jan. 1824 at Athens, Ga.,[428] left will 15 Aug. 1823-12 April 1824.[429] She married, 11 Nov. 1775,[430] Dudley Cary, who moved to Clarke Co., Ga., and left will 30 Dec. 1802-26 Jan. 1804.[431]

Issue: [CARY] 383. Edward[6], born 10 May 1789 in Gloucester County, died 6 June 1870 in Bullock Co., Ala., of Milledgeville, Ga., married (1), 24 Sept. 1811,[432] Lucinda[7] Clayton, born Nov. 1792,[433] daughter of 226. *Mildred⁶ (Dixon) Clayton*, and (2), 26 April 1826 at Milledgeville, Eliza Jane Howard Rutherford, born 1793, died June 1864 in Bullock Co., Ala.; 384. Peyton[6]; 385. Elizabeth Peyton[6], died 7 March 1816,[434] married, 11 Feb. 1809,[435] as his (1) wife, Stephens Thomas, of Athens, Ga., who left will 11 Nov. 1837-10 May

[421] Tombstone, Ware Parish Cemetery, in Joseph Bryan Branch A.P.V.A., *op. cit.*, p. 74.

[422] Tucker, *op. cit.*, p. 96.

[423] *Ibid.*, p. 82; *Southern Churchman*, 23 Sept. 1864.

[424] Tombstone, Ware Parish Cemetery, in Joseph Bryan Branch A.P.V.A., *op. cit.*, p. 145; *Compiler*, Richmond, 11 Feb. 1823.

[425] Tombstone, Auburn Cemetery, Mathews County, in Joseph Bryan Branch A.P.V.A., *op. cit.*, p. 121.

[426] *Richmond Daily Whig*, 15 Oct. 1846.

[427] Tombstone, Ware Parish Cemetery, in Joseph Bryan Branch A.P.V.A., *op. cit.*, p. 82.

[428] *Georgia Journal*, Milledgeville, Ga., 13 March 1816.

[429] Clarke Co., Ga., Will Bk. B, p. 26.

[430] Kingston Parish Register.

[431] Clarke Co., Ga., Administrator's Bond Bk. A, p. 7.

[432] *Mirror of the Times*, Augusta, Ga., 30 Sept. 1811.

[433] Clayton Bible, copied by William Clayton Torrence, Virginia State Archives.

[434] *Georgia Journal*, Milledgeville, Ga., 13 March 1816.

[435] Clarke Co., Ga., Marriage Register A, in *The Georgia Genealogical Magazine*, no. 18, Oct. 1965, p. 1155.

1838;[436] 386. Frances[6], married Alsa Moore of Clarke Co., Ga.; 387. Lucy[6], married ___ Leeland.

126. THOMAS[5] TABB (Lucy[4] Todd, Christopher[3], Elizabeth[2] Bernard, William[1]), born 20 Aug. 1755, died 20 July 1818, aged 62 yrs., 10 mos.,[437] of "Seaford," Mathews County, married, 20 Dec. 1790, Elizabeth Harmanson[7] Teackle, daughter of 407. *Caleb[6] Teackle* (see MASON), born 29 Nov. 1775, died 3 Dec. 1824.[438]

Issue: [TABB] 388. Thomas Teackle Todd[6], born 7 Dec. 1791, died 18 Aug. 1819 on board the ship *Philip Tabb* from Liverpool to America; 389. Philip Mayo[6], born 25 May 1793, married, 8 Oct. 1814, Martha Tabb Mayo, born 31 July 1799; 390. Marianna[6], born 13 Feb. 1796, married, 11 March 1819, Joseph[7] Mayo, Jr., son of Joseph Mayo and 370. *Jane[6] Poythress* (see BALEY-COCKE), mayor of Richmond, 1859; 391. Sarah Emory[6], married 66. *John Custis[5] Parramore* (see PARRAMORE); 392. Elizabeth Susan[6], born 6 Feb. 1800, died 22 March 1800; 393. Elizabeth Susan[6], born 15 April 1801, perhaps the Elizabeth S. who married, 26 June 1823,[439] John A. Riddle, attorney at law of Mathews County; 394. Henrietta Augusta[6], born 26 March 1803; 395. Malvina Mason[6], born 5 June 1805, died 22 Sept. 1809; 396. Charlotte Amelia[6], born 10 June 1807 died six weeks after her marriage, married Dr. ___ Nicholas; 397. Augusta Patterson[6], born 22 March 1809; 398. Malvina Mason[6], born 9 Nov. 1812, married Judge ____ Jeffries; 399. Sarah Emory[6], born 1817, died 1817.

127. MARTHA[5] TABB (Lucy[4] Todd, Christopher[3], Elizabeth[2] Bernard, William[1]), born 21 Oct. 1757, died 16 Sept. 1821,[440] married the Rev. Armistead Smith, born 1 Dec. 1756,[441] died 12 Sept. 1817 at "Toddsbury," aged 60 yrs. 9 mos. 12 days.[442] He was educated at College of William and Mary, enrolled in the College company of militia, was ordained in 1793 and was rector of Kingston Parish, Mathews County until his death.[443]

Issue: [SMITH] 400. Col. Thomas[6], born 5 March 1785, died 13 April

---

[436] Clarke Co., Ga., Will Bk. B, p. 187.

[437] Family record, in *Virginia Genealogical Society Quarterly Bulletin*, V, p. 94.

[438] *Compiler*, Richmond, 8 Dec. 1824, which gives 4 Dec.

[439] *Enquirer*, Richmond, 8 July 1823.

[440] Tombstone, Ware Parish Cemetery, in Joseph Bryan Branch A.P.V.A., *op. cit.*, p. 81.

[441] Kingston Parish, Mathews County, Register.

[442] Tombstone, Ware Parish Cemetery, in Joseph Bryan Branch A.P.V.A., *op. cit.*, p. 80.

[443] *W*(2) XIX, pp. 416-17.

1841,[444] member of the House of Delegates from Gloucester County, 1826-27, 1828-30, 1832-41;[445] 401. Philip A.[6], died 1 Oct. 1813 in his 25th year;[446] 402. William Patterson[6], born 13 July 1796, died 25 March 1878,[447] of Gloucester County, married, 28 May 1839 at Fredericksburg,[448] Marion A. M. Seddon, born 26 April 1819, died 19 May 1853;[449] 403. Lucy Armistead[6], married 378. Thomas Todd[6] Tabb; 404. Elizabeth[6], married, as his (1) wife, 332. Col. *Christopher[6] Tompkins* (see MARTIAU); 405. Sallie[6], married ___ Todd.

128. ELIZABETH[5] TABB (Lucy[4] Todd, Christopher[3], Elizabeth[2] Bernard, William[1]), born 31 July 1760, married John Patterson, died 1 Aug. 1824, Mathews County, aged almost 83,[450] of "Poplar Grove," Mathews County, who was a midshipman in the Virginia Navy during the Revolutionary War,[451] was clerk of the court, a magistrate and member of the House of Delegates, 1819, 1822-25, and the Virginia Senate, 1819-21.[452]

Issue: [PATTERSON] 406. Maria B.[6], married, as his (2) wife, 332. *Christopher[6] Tompkins* (see MARTIAU); 407. Elizabeth[6], born 20 June 1796, died 19 Oct. 1868,[453] married (1) Thomas Robinson Yeatman, born 5 Jan. 1789, died 18 Aug. 1832, "Isleham," Mathews County,[454] of "Isleham," clerk of Mathews County, and (2) Wade[7] Mosby, Jr., son of 533. *Wade[6] Mosby* (see WOODSON); 408. John B.[6], died without issue.

131. WILLIAM EDWARD[5] WYATT (Mary[4] Todd, Christopher[3], Elizabeth[2] Bernard, William[1]), born 1762, died 26 Sept. 1802, a physician of "Sommerville," Gloucester County, married, 8 Feb. 1781, Mary Graham.

---

[444] Tombstone, Ware Parish Cemetery, in Joseph Bryan Branch A.P.V.A., *op. cit.*, p. 79; *Norfolk Herald*, 19 Sept. 1817.

[445] Leonard, pp. 334, 344, 349, 363, 367, 371, 376, 380, 384, 388, 392, 396.

[446] Tombstone, Ware Parish Cemetery, in Joseph Bryan Branch, A.P.V.A., *op. cit.*, p. 78.

[447] Tombstone, Glen Roy Cemetery, Gloucester County, in *ibid.*, p. 34.

[448] *Enquirer*, Richmond, 31 May 1839; George H. S. King, *Marriages of Fredericksburg, Virginia, 1782-1850*, ed. by Catherine Lindsay Knorr (Pine Bluff, Ark., 1954), p. 89.

[449] Tombstone, Glen Roy Cemetery, *loc. cit.*

[450] *Enquirer*, Richmond, 13 Aug. 1824.

[451] Bounty warrant, John Patterson, Virginia State Archives; Margie G. Brown, *Genealogical Abstracts, Revolutionary War Veterans, Scrip Act 1852* (Oakton, Va., 1990), p. 50.

[452] Leonard, pp. 299, 302, 307, 314, 319, 324.

[453] Tombstone, Yeatman Cemetery, Mathews County, in Joseph Bryan Branch A.P.V.A., *op. cit.*, p. 144.

[454] *Ibid.*, p. 143; *Richmond Constitutional Whig*, 28 Sept. 1832.

Issue: [WYATT][455] 409. John[6], married Cecilia Dabney; 410. Dr. William Graham[6], died 26 June 1854, aged 70 yrs. 4 mos. 26 days,[456] sheriff of Gloucester County, 1851, married, 23 Dec. 1821 in Gloucester County,[457] Louisa Campbell[7] Stubbs, daughter of John Segar[8] and 212. *Hannah[6] (Montague) Stubbs* (see MONTAGUE); 411. Eliza Maria[6], married Walker Jones of Petersburg and later of "Shelter," Gloucester County;[458] 412. Eleanor[6], married, 13 Jan. 1820,[459] Col. Joseph Scott of Petersburg; 413. Col. Thomas[6], never married; 414. Col. Hawte[6], never married.

132. CHARLES NORTH[5] CARNAN (Elizabeth[4] North, Frances[3] North, Elizabeth[2] Bernard, William[1]), born 23 June 1752, died 19 Jan. 1809, Garrison Forest, Baltimore Co., Md.,[460] leaving will 25 Aug. 1808-28 Jan. 1809.[461] He married (1) Mary Boyce, born 1756, died July 1776, and (2) Sarah Johnston, daughter of Samuel Johnston, his step-father, who left will 28 Nov. 1818-9 Dec. 1819.[462]

Issue: [CARNAN][463] 415. Rebecca[6], born 8 June 1775, died young; (by 2) 416. Elizabeth Hulse[6], born about 1790, died 5 Jan. 1823, married, 21 May 1816,[464] Nelson Norris; 417. Sarah[6], born 20 April 1795, died 18 June 1814, married, 15 June 1813,[465] Nelson Norris, merchant of Baltimore.

133. ROBERT NORTH[5] CARNAN (Elizabeth[4] North, Frances[3] Todd, Elizabeth[2] Bernard, William[1]), born 8 Aug. 1756, died 12 May 1837, leaving will 14 June 1832-10 June 1836.[466] He resided at "Risteau's Garrison," Baltimore Co., Md. He married (1) 155. Katherine[6] Risteau, who died 5 March 1803 [or 1805], aged 44, and (2) Sarah (Goldsborough) Ennals, who died 24 April 1828, aged 72 yrs. 6 mos.

---

[455] *W*(1) X, p. 60; L. H. Jones, *Captain Roger Jones of London and Virginia* (Albany, N.Y., 1891), p. 98.

[456] Gravestone, Wyatt Cemetery, in Joseph Bryan Branch A.P.V.A., *op. cit.*, p. 103.

[457] *Enquirer*, Richmond, 5 Jan. 1822. *Richmond Compiler*, 3 Jan. 1822, says 22 Dec.

[458] Jones, *loc. cit.*

[459] Thomas P. Hughes and Jewel B. Standefer, *Petersburg, Virginia, Hustings Court Marriage Bonds ... 1784-1854* (Memphis, Tenn., 1971), p. 120.

[460] *Federal Gazette*, Baltimore, Md. 20 Jan. 1809.

[461] Baltimore Co., Md., Will Bk. 8, pp. 376-78.

[462] Baltimore Co., Md., Will Bk. 10, pp. 538-39.

[463] Thomas and Barnes, *op. cit.*, II, p. 8.

[464] *Federal Gazette*, Baltimore, Md., 24 May 1816.

[465] *Federal Gazette*, Baltimore, Md., 17 June 1813.

[466] Baltimore Co., Md., Will Bk. 16, pp. 57-61

Issue: [CARNAN] (by 1)[467] 418. Frances Todd[6], born 24 Nov. 1777, married,, 10 Dec. 1795, Robert Wilkinson, who died 22 Feb. 1853 in his 85th year; 419. George Risteay[6], died young; 420. Elizabeth Risteau[6], died 1832, unmarried; 421. Christopher[6], born 19 July 1780, died 5 April 1845 at Havre de Grace, Md.,[468] married, 9 March 1809,[469] Christiana Sim Holliday, who died 2 May 1823 in Baltimore Co., Md.; 422. Maria North[6], born 9 Dec. 1792, died 1 May 1822,[470] married, 15 Feb. 1815,[471] Eli Simkins of Baltimore, who died 15 May 1817, aged 22;[472] 423. Rebecca Risteau[6], born 23 May 1794, died 4 Nov. 1825,[473] married, 3 June 1813,[474] Joshua Tevis, who later moved to Philadelphia, Pa.;[475] 424. Frances Wilkins[6], died 20 May 1832, aged 32 yrs. 3 mos. 13 days, married, 1 Feb, 1825, William Fell Johnson.

134. ELIZABETH[5] MOALE (Ellin[4] North, Frances[3] Todd, Elizabeth[2] Bernard, William[1]), born 8 Sept. 1759, died 26 Nov. 1802, married, 14 March 1794, Richard Curson, Jr., who died 14 June 1808, Baltimore, in his 45th year.[476]

Issue: [CURSON] 425. Samuel[6], born 9 Jan. 1795, died 12 Aug. 1800; 426. Elizabeth Rebecca Becker[6], born 5 May 1796, died 15 March 1880, married, 7 May 1824, Samuel Hoffman of Baltimore; 427. Anna Maria[6], born 1 Sept. 1797, died 4 Sept. 1798; 428. Ellin Moale[6], born 26 Oct. 1799, died 5 Dec. 1880, married, 30 Sept. 1828, Samuel Poultney of Baltimore.

135. JOHN[5] MOALE (Ellin[4] North, Frances[3] Todd, Elizabeth[2] Bernard, William[1]), born 17 May 1761, died 3 Nov. 1809,[477] married, 2 Oct. 1790, Lucy Morton who died 15 July 1802, aged 35.[478]

Issue: [MOALE] 429. Ellin[6], married, 3 Aug. 1813,[479] Juan Joseph

---

[467] Thomas and Barnes, *op. cit.*, II, pp. 9-10.

[468] *Baltimore Sun*, 9 April 1845.

[469] *Federal Gazette*, Baltimore, Md., 12 March 1802.

[470] *St. Thomas Parish Deaths and Burials, Owings Mills, Maryland, 1728-1995* (Westminister, Md., 2000), p. 97.

[471] *Federal Gazette*, Baltimore, Md., 15 Feb. 1815.

[472] *St. Thomas Parish Deaths and Burials ...*, p. 97.

[473] *Ibid.*, p. 108.

[474] *Federal Gazette*, Baltimore, Md., 5 June 1813.

[475] Thomas and Barnes, *op. cit.*, II, p. 80.

[476] *Federal Gazette*, Baltimore, Md., 23 June 1808.

[477] *Federal Gazette*, Baltimore, 6 Nov. 1809.

[478] *Federal Gazette*, Baltimore, 22 July 1802.

[479] *Federal Gazette*, Baltimore, 4 Aug. 1813.

Bernabeu.

137. RICHARD HALTON[5] MOALE (Ellin[4] North, Frances[3] Todd, Elizabeth[2] Bernard, William[1]), born 28 Jan. 1765, died 22 June 1802,[480] leaving will 1799-30 Oct. 1802.[481]   He married, 16 April 1797,[482] Judith Carter[7] Armistead, born 29 Dec. 1774, died 13 Jan. 1863, daughter of 123. *William[6]* and *Maria[7] (Carter) Armistead* (see BURWELL), who married (2), 6 Jan. 1807,[483] Robert Riddell, and (3), 21 Aug. 1813,[484] Richard Carroll.

Issue: [MOALE][485] 430. John Carter[6], agent of the Baltimore & Norfolk Packet Company, killed 14 April 1842 when the boilers of the *Medora* exploded, married Juliette Taylor; 431. William Armistead[6], born 2 Jan. 1800 at Baltimore, died there 14 Aug. 1880, married, 4 Feb. 1841 at Baltimore, Mary Winchester, born 10 Aug. 1810, died 11 May 1888;[486] 432. Richard Henry[6], born 2 Nov. 1802, died 25 April 1848.[487]

138. THOMAS[5] MOALE (Ellin[4] North, Frances[3] Todd, Elizabeth[2] Bernard, William[1]), born 22 Sept. 1766, died 25 Nov. 1822 at "Walnut Grove," Baltimore Co., Md. He married, 24 March 1793, Eleanor Owings, daughter of Samuel and Deborah (Lynch) Owings, born 7 Feb. 1772, died 29 Oct. 1853.[488]

Issue: [MOALE][489] 433. Ellin North[6], baptized 29 June 1794, aged 4 mos 21 days, married Benjamin Dorsey and moved to Illinois; 434. John Thomas[6], died after 5 April 1856, married, 22 Oct. 1854, Caroline H. Reister, born 2 Sept. 1811, died 11 Oct. 1856;[490] 435. Samuel O.[6], born about 1797, of Baltimore, Md., married, 8 Jan. 1822, Eliza Owings, who died 17 March 1830, aged 32; 436. Deborah Owings[6], died before 8 April 1854, married, on or about 14 Aug. 1819 at "Walnut Grove," Edward H. Ireland; 437. Eleanor O.[6]; 438. Sophia North[6], born 11 Sept. 1802, died 8 Nov. 1881, married, 5 June 1832, William

[480] *Federal Gazette*, Baltimore, Md., 22 June 1802.
[481] Baltimore Co., Md., Will Bk. 7, pp. 92-97.
[482] *Federal Gazette*, Baltimore, Md., 17 April 1797.
[483] *Federal Gazette*, Baltimore, 7 Jan. 1807.
[484] *Federal Gazette*, Baltimore, 27 Aug. 1813.
[485] Thomas and Barnes, *op. cit.*, II, pp. 64, 68.
[486] *St. Thomas Parish Deaths and Burials ...*, pp. 73-74.
[487] *Baltimore Sun*, 26 April 1848.
[488] *MHM* XXV, p. 393, which gives marriage as 21 March 1793.
[489] Thomas and Barnes, *op. cit.*, II, pp. 64-65, 68, 82.
[490] Lillian Bayly Marks, *Reister's Desire, the Origin of Reisterstown, Maryland ...* (Baltimore, 1975), p. 94.

L. Owings, born 7 Aug. 1799, died 25 Aug. 1851; 439. Maria[6], married George U. Long; 440. Elizabeth A.[6], married George Cromwell; 441. Rebecca[6], married __ Crumpton.

141. ROBERT NORTH[5] MOALE (Ellin[4] North, Frances[3] Todd, Elizabeth[2] Bernard, William[1]), born 22 Jan. 1771, died 31 Oct. 1852 at "Green Spring," Baltimore Co., Md., He married, 2 July 1801, Frances Owings, daughter of Samuel and Deborah (Lynch) Owings, born 30 Sept. 1779,[491] died 18 Sept. 1829 at "Green Spring."

Issue: [MOALE][492] 442. Ellin North[6], born 18 July 1802, died 25 Feb. 1888, married, 11 Dec. 1832, George Howard Elder, died 18 July 1866, aged 64, farmer of "Howard's Square,"Baltimore Co., Md., and later of "Green Spring."

142. SAMUEL[5] MOALE (Ellin[4] North, Frances[3] Todd, Elizabeth[2] Bernard, William[1]), born 4 Jan. 1773, died 21 Feb. 1857, left will 1 Nov. 1852-codicil 20 Jan. 1857-20 March 1857.[493] He was one of the defenders of Baltimore, Md., during the War of 1812 and was a lawyer there. He married (1), 22 Sept. 1796,[494] Ann M. Howard, daughter of Samuel H. Howard, who died 14 Sept. 1827, Baltimore, in her 52nd year,[495] and (2) Anne G. White, daughter of Abraham White, who was born 8 Dec. 1800 and died 13 March 1815..

Issue: [MOALE][496] (by 1) 443. Ellen[6], married, 15 Oct. 1816,[497] Samuel Hollingsworth, Jr., born 22 Feb. 1794, died 20 May 1855,[498] of Baltimore and of Elkton, Md.; 444. Susan Rebecca Hanson[6], died 27 Dec. 1822 at Patterson, N.J., in her 24th year, married, 3 April 1816,[499] as his (1) wife, John Travers, Jr., born 30 Oct. 1790 in Baltimore, died there 25 May 1882, merchant of Lisbon, Howard Co., Md.; 445. Samuel Howard[6], died 30 Oct. 1824 at "Clifton," near Baltimore, Md., in his 22nd year, married, 15 Jan. 1822, Eleanor Gittings, who died 9 Jan. 1834 in her 32nd year; 446. (possibly) Catherine[6], married, Dec.

---

[491] *MHM* XXV, p. 193.

[492] Thomas and Barnes, *op. cit.*, II, pp. 32-33, 65.

[493] Baltimore, Md., Will Bk. NH #27, pp. 306-09.

[494] *Federal Gazette*, Baltimore, Md., 23 Sept. 1796.

[495] *Maryland Gazette*, Annapolis, 20 Sept. 1827.

[496] Thomas and Barnes, *op. cit.*, II, pp. 65-66

[497] *Baltimore American*, 17 Oct. 1816.

[498] J. Adger Stewart, *Descendants of Valentine Hollingsworth, Sr.* (Louisville, Ky., 1925), p. 46.

[499] *Federal Gazette*, Baltimore, Md., 5 April 1816; St. Paul's Parish, Baltimore Co., Md., Register.

1832, John Tilyard; (by 2) 447. Mary Susan[6], born about 1829, married, 21 Jan. 1851, Capt. John C. Foster, U.S.A.; 448. Frances North[6], born about 1831; 449. Ann W.[6], born about 1832; 450. William North[6], born 15 July 1834, died 23 March 1835; 451. Henry[6], born about 1837; 452. Edward[6], born 29 Jan. 1840, died 27 Sept. 1913, married, 24 Aug. 1863 at Baltimore, Md., Jeannie Wilson; 453. Augusta[6].

147. RANDLE HULSE[5] MOALE (Ellin[4] North, Frances[3] Todd, Elizabeth[2] Bernard, William[1]), born 26 Jan. 1782, died 11 July 1864. He married, 16 May 1822, Elizabeth Smith Peck, daughter of Nicholas Peck of Bristol, R.I., born about 1807, buried 6 July 1887, aged 85.[500].

Issue: [MOALE][501] 454. Robert North[6], born 21 Nov. 1824, died 24 Nov. 1831; 455. Sarah Gorham[6], born 6 Feb. 1826, died 28 March 1828; 456. Francis V.[6], born about 1828; 457. Benjamin Bradford[6], died 24 Jan. 1832, aged 1 yr. 11 mos. 26 days; 458. Charles H. H.[6], born about 1832, died 18 Ju\an. 1903; 459. George N.[6], born 6 Oct. 1834, died 9 May 1907, of Owings Mills, Md., secretary of the Baltimore and Randallstown Horse Railway Company organized in 1872, vestryman, senior warden and treasurer of St. Thomas' Parish, married Ellen DeCoursey, born 3 May 1839, died 25 Jan. 1902;[502] 460. Susan P.[6], born about 1836; 461. Frederick[6], born about 1839; 462. Isaac G.[6], born about 1841; 463. Clarence[6], died 2 June 1874, aged 33;[503] 464. Elizabeth[6], born about 1845.

---

[500] *St. Thomas Parish Deaths and Burials* ..., p. 72.

[501] Thomas and Barnes, *op. cit.*, II, p. 66.

[502] *St. Thomas Parish Deaths and Burials* ..., pp. 72-73.

[503] *Ibid.*, p. 72.

BIBBY[1]

*1. WILLIAM[1] BIBBY arrived in the *Swan* in 1621 and in the census of 1623/4[2] was listed as a resident on the Eastern Shore. In the muster, 1624/5, he was shown as aged 22.and in a deposition in a boundary dispute, Oct. 1633, stated he was aged "33 yeeres or thereabouts,"[3] and in another deposition, March 1634/5, relating events while he was engaged in clearing a thicket on his land, he stated he was "age 35 or thereabouts."[4]

His patent for 400 acres on the south side of King's Creek, on the Bay side southwest of the present town of Cheriton, and running toward Old Plantation Creek, was issued 24 June 1636, claimed for the importation of himself, his wife Mary ___, and six other persons.[5]

He died before 25 Sept. 1637 when his will, not extant, was proved by Christopher Calvert,[6] who the same day deposed that "William Cozier desireinge to be free from William Bibby, late deceased, the said William Bibby told him he shold be free if the said Cozier would give him a monthes work or fitt up his house."[7] On 12 Feb. 1637/8 it was stated that he "upon his death bedd made Capt. William Roper & George Traveller his overseers."[8] His widow Mary died in Nov. 1637 according to a statement of William Roper, recorded 20 Feb. 1642/3, concerning cattle in his custody.[9]

Issue: 2. EDMUND[2]; 3. ELIZABETH[2].

2. EDMUND[2] BIBBY (William[1]), orphaned at an early age, was under the care of Capt. William Roper and his widow Katherine during his minority. In Jan. 1650/1 the court ordered that he be set at liberty and directed that his livestock be delivered to him.[10] He left will 12 Dec. 1660-31 Dec. 1660.[11] He

[1] John B. Bell, "More Adventurers: William Bibby (1599/1600-1636/7)," *The Virginia Genealogist*, XXXIV, pp. 20-25.

[2] Hotten, p. 188.

[3] Northampton Co. Orders, Deeds, Wills 1, 1632-37, transcript, p. 7.

[4] *Ibid.*, original, p. 45.

[5] Patent Bk. 1, p. 367.

[6] Northampton Co. Orders, Deeds, Wills 1, 1632-40, p. 113.

[7] *Ibid.*, p. 112.

[8] *Ibid.*, p. 134.

[9] Northampton Co. Orders, Deeds, Wills 2, 1640-45, p. 151.

[10] Northampton Co. Orders, Deeds, Wills 2, 1640-45, p. 151.

[11] Northampton Co. Deeds, Wills &c 7, 1657-66, transcript, p. 80.

married, about 1653,[12] Frances Hunt, daughter of Thomas and Joane (Gawton) Drake Hunt, who married (2) 5. *Nathaniel[2] Wilkins* (see WILKINS).

Issue: 4. Elizabeth[5]; 5. EDMUND[3].

3. ELIZABETH[2] BIBBY (William[1]) was under the care of George Travellor and his widow Alice during her minority. On 14 May 1643 Travellor filed an accounting of the cattle he had received Feb. 1636/7 "with Elizabeth Bibby being about 10 months old."[13]

She married George Freshwater who deposed, 29 Aug. 1684, he was aged 50 or thereabouts[14] and left will 19 March 1687-28 May 1688.[15]

Issue: [FRESHWATER] 6. GEORGE[3]; 7. WILLIAM[3]; 8. Alisha[3]; 9. Elizabeth[3]; 10.MARY[6].

5. EDMUND[3] BIBBY (Edmund[2], William[1]) left will 23 March 1694-28 Jan. 1696/7.[16] He married Esther ___, who married (2), between 9 June and 23 July 1698, Thomas Leonard.[17]

Issue:[18] 11. Nathaniel[4]; 12. John[4], left will 22 April 1720-18 Oct. 1720,[19] giving his estate including his plantation on the bay side, his part of Hog Island and 150 acres in the East Jerseys to Elizabeth Benthall and her children; 13. Edmund[4], married, between 28 Nov. 1709 and May 1711 Mary Clarke, daughter of Robert and Mary (Benthall) Clarke;[20] 14. William[4];[21] 15. Esther[4]; 16. Frances[4].

6. GEORGE[3] FRESHWATER (Elizabeth[2] Bibby, William[1]) left will 26 Oct. 1717-17 March 1717/8.[22] He married (1) Elizabeth Mears, daughter of

---

[12] Northampton Co. Deeds, Wills &c 5, 1654-55, 90, will of Thomas Hunt, 26 May 1655-29 Jan. 1655/6, which named daughter Frances Bibby and her daughter Elizabeth.

[13] Northampton Co. Orders, Deeds, Wills 2, p. 243

[14] Northampton Co. Orders, Wills 12, 1683-89, p. 84.

[15] *Ibid.*, pp. 372-73.

[16] Northampton Co. Orders, Wills &c 13, 1689-98, p. 439.

[17] *Ibid.*, pp. 485, 493-98.

[18] *Ibid.*, pp. 493-98.

[19] Northampton Co. Deeds, Wills &c 1718-23, p. 114.

[20] *ES* I, p. 349; Northampton Co. Deeds, Wills &c 1708-17, p. 104; Deeds, Wills &c 1711-18, pp. 4-6.

[21] *ES* I, pp. 745-46, says the land he inherited was later held by Esther Bebbee (died before 1759) who married John Burroughs. On 18 Jan. 1759 John Burroughs and his son William of Sussex Co., Del., sold 450 acres at the head of Revell's Branch (Accomack Co. Deed Bk. 1757-70, pp. 67-68) which John held by right of curtesy and William in fee simple.

[22] Northampton Co. Wills, Deeds &c 1711-18, pp. 138-39.

Bartholomew Mears,[23] and (2) Elizabeth Griffith, daughter of Jerom and Elizabeth (Benthall) Griffith,[24] who left undated will proved 14 Aug. 1733.[25]

Issue: [FRESHWATER] (by 2) 17. JOHN[4]; 18. GEORGE[4]; 19. THOMAS[4]; 20. MARK[4]; 21. MATTHEW[4]; 22. SARAH[4]; 23. ELIZABETH[4]; 24. Roseander[4], married ___ Loughly [Lofland].

7. WILLIAM[3] FRESHWATER (Elizabeth[2] Bibby, William[1]) deposed, Aug. 1684, he was aged 20[26] and left will 19 March 1722-9 Feb. 1724.[27] He married Esther Griffith, daughter of Jerom and Elizabeth (Benthall) Griffith [28].

Issue: [FRESHWATER] 25. WILLIAM[4]; 26. JEROM[4]; 27. SARAH[4]; 28. Elishe[4], married 99. *Culpepper[4] Pigott* (see WILKINS).

10. MARY[3] FRESHWATER (Elizabeth[2] Bibby, William[1]) married John Hawkins.

Issue: [HAWKINS] 29. Grithing[4].

17. JOHN[4] FRESHWATER (George[3], Elizabeth[2] Bibby, William[1]) died before 28 July 1709 when administration on his estate was granted to his widow Elizabeth ___.[29]

Issue: [FRESHWATER] 30. Comfort[5], married ___ Dunton.

18. GEORGE[4] FRESHWATER (George[3], Elizabeth[2] Bibby, William[1]) left will 2 June 1739-9 Oct. 1739.[30] He married ___.

Issue: [FRESHWATER] 31. JOHN[5]; 32. ELIZABETH[5]; 33. Mark[5], chose Jacob Mills as his guardian, 18 Nov. 1739, and referred to as being of age, 10 Aug. 1742.[31]

19. THOMAS[4] FRESHWATER (George[3], Elizabeth[2] Bibby, William[1]) died before 13 Feb. 1738/9 when administration on his estate was granted to his widow Sarah ___.[32]

---

[23] Accomack Co. Wills & Deeds 1676-90, p. 323, will of Bartholomew Mears, 16 Dec. 1682-28 Dec. 1682. It is possible that rather than being the (1) wife of George Freshwater, Jr., she was the (2) wife of his father.

[24] Northampton Co. Orders, Wills &c 14, 1698-1710, p. 420, will of Jerom Griffith, Sr., 14 March 1707/8-28 May 1708.

[25] Northampton Co. Wills & Inventories 18, 1733-40, p. 7.

[26] Northampton Co. Orders, Wills 12, 1783-89, p. 84.

[27] Northampton Co. Deeds, Wills &c 1718-25, p. 219.

[28] Northampton Co. Wills, Deeds &c 1711-18, p. 138; Deeds, Wills &c 1718-23, p. 65.

[29] Northampton Co. Orders, Wills &c 14, 1698-1710, p. 484.

[30] Northampton Co. Wills & Inventories 18, 1733-40, p. 315.

[31] Northampton Co. Order Bk. 20, p. 374; Order Bk. 21, p. 8.

[32] Northampton Co. Order Bk. 20, 1732-42, p. 346.

Issue: [FRESHWATER] 34. William[5], married, between Oct. 1751 and April 1752,[33] Sisley Mook.

20. MARK[4] FRESHWATER (George[3], Elizabeth[2] Bibby, William[1]) left will 7 Feb. 1761-9 Feb. 1762.[34]   He married (1), before May 1734,[35] Elizabeth ___, widow of 109. *John[4] Waterson* (see WILKINS) and (2) Elishe (___) Smaw Nelson, widow of Andrew Smaw and John Nelson, who left will 15 Feb. 1769-8 May 1770.[36]

Issue: [FRESHWATER] (by 1) 35. JACOB[5]; 36. Benjamin[5], left will 21 Aug. 1764-15 May 1765;[37] 37. Joseph[5], left will 4 April 1786-14 June 1786;[38] 38. SARAH[5].

21. MATTHEW[4] FRESHWATER (George[3], Elizabeth[2] Bibby, William[1]) died before 10 Sept. 1745 when administration on his estate was granted to his widow.[39]   He married Hannah Baker, daughter of John and Margaret (___) Baker,[40] who married (2) [Stephen?] Whitehead and left will 18 June 1774-8 April 1777.[41]

Issue: [FRESHWATER] 39. MATTHEW[5].

22. SARAH[4] FRESHWATER (George[3], Elizabeth[2] Bibby, William[1]) married ___ Costin.

Issue: [COSTIN] 40. Matthew[5].

23. ELIZABETH[4] FRESHWATER (George[3], Elizabeth[2] Bibby, William[1]) died before 14 May 1734 when administration on her estate was granted to her eldest son William.[42]   She married, as his (2 [3?]) wife, Arthur Rascoe, who left will 20 March 1719/20-April 1720.[43]

Issue: [RASCOE] 41. William[5]; 42. Peter[5]; 43. Daniel[5], married Sarah ___, who joined him in the sale of land where he lived, 3 March 1749/50 and 10

---

[33] Northampton Co. Court records, pack 41, July 1752, Pigot's executors *vs.* Elliott *et al.*

[34] Northampton Co. Wills & Inventories 22, 1760-62, p. 390.

[35] Northampton Co. Court records, pack 30, March 1744, Freshwater's petition.

[36] Northampton Co. Wills & Inventories 24, 1766-72, p. 255.

[37] Northampton Co. Wills &c 23, 1763-65, p. 437.

[38] Northampton Co. Wills &c 27, 1783-88, p. 343.

[39] Northampton Co. Order Bk. 21, 1742-48, p. 254.

[40] *ES* I, p. 103; Jean M. Mihalyka, *Loose Papers and Sundry Court Cases, 1628-1731, Northampton County, Virginia* (Eastville, Va., 1997), p. 110.

[41] Northampton Co. Wills & Inventories 25, 1772-77, p. 545.

[42] Northampton Co. Order Bk. 26, 1732-42, p. 10.

[43] Northampton Co. Deeds, Wills &c 1718-25, p. 65.

April 1750.[44]

25. WILLIAM[4] FRESHWATER (William[3], Elizabeth[2] Bibby, William[1]) left will 29 April 1720-June 1720.[45] He married ___.

Issue: [FRESHWATER] 44. Charity[5], married Jerome Griffith.[46]

26. JEROM[4] FRESHWATER (William[3], Elizabeth[2] Bibby, William[1]) left will 3 May 1720-July 1720.[47] He married ___.

Issue: [FRESHWATER] 45. Easter[6], chose John Holebrook as her guardian, 11 Aug. 1733, and Thomas Moor as her guardian, 10 Dec. 1734.[48]

27. SARAH[4] FRESHWATER (William[3], Elizabeth[2] Bibby, William[1]) married Thomas Moor who died before 14 July 1752 when administration on his estate was granted to his widow.[49]

Issue: [MOOR] 46. Matthew[5].

31. JOHN[5] FRESHWATER (George[4], George[3], Elizabeth[2] Bibby, William[1]) died before 10 June 1752 when administration on his estate was granted to William Freshwater.[50] He married ___.

Issue: [FRESHWATER] 47. William[6], possibly the William who moved to Gloucester County.[51]

32. ELIZABETH[5] FRESHWATER (George[4], George[3], Elizabeth[2] Bibby, William[1]) married Jacob Mills.

Issue: [MILLS] 48. John[6].

35. JACOB[5] FRESHWATER (Mark[4], George[3], Elizabeth[2] Bibby, William[1]) married, (bond 24) March 1763,[52] Mary Nelson, daughter of his step-mother, who married (2) Robert Greenaway.

Issue: [FRESHWATER] 49. Betty[6], named in will of her uncle Benjamin, 1764, died before 12 April 1786 when administration on her estate was granted

---

[44] Northampton Co. Deeds 18, 1733-50, pp. 423-25.

[45] Northampton Co. Deeds., Wills &c 1718-25, p. 98.

[46] *ES* I, p. 62.

[47] Northampton Co. Deeds, Wills &c 1718-25, pp. 98, 102.

[48] Northampton Co. Order Bk. 20, pp. 69, 144.

[49] Northampton Co. Order Bk. 23, 1751-53, p. 133.

[50] Northampton Co. Order Bk. 23, 1751-53, p. 124.

[51] *The Virginia Genealogist*, XVII, p. 123.

[52] Jean M. Mihalyka, *Marriages, Northampton County, Virginia, 1660/1-1854* (Bowie, Md., 1990), p. 41.

to Robert Greenaway;[53] 50. Nelson[6]; 51. Elishe[6], married, (bond 8) June 1786,[54] Luke Martin; 52. Nancy[6].

38. SARAH[5] FRESHWATER (Mark[4], George[3], Elizabeth[2] Bibby, William[1]) married, (bond 31) Aug. 1748,[55] Isaac Nottingham, who married (2), (bond 23) Nov. 1763,[56] Mary (Holt) Kendall, widow of 398. *Littleton[6] Kendall* (see MASON), and died before 12 April 1768 when administration on his estate was granted to Addison Nottingham.[57]

Issue: [NOTTINGHAM][58] 54. Sarah[6], died by 1770, married, as his (1) wife, 108. *Moses[5] Johnson* (see PARRAMORE); 55. Robert[6], "Jr.," left will 13 April 1774-9 Aug. 1774;[59] 56. Benjamin[6], died before 1778; 57. Peggy[6], died before 1777; 58. Ann[6], died before 1777.

39. MATTHEW[5] FRESHWATER (Matthew[4], George[3], Elizabeth[2] Bibby, William[1]) deposed, 5 Oct. 1768, he was aged 41[60] and died about 1785.[61] He married Jane (_____) Pike Capell, widow of 36. *Edward[5] Capell* (see GRANGER).[62]

Issue: [FRESHWATER][63] 59. Peggy[6]; 60. Elishe[6], married Levin Smith; 61. William[6], on whose estate administration was granted to Nancy Freshwater and William Wilson, 10 April 1798,[64] married Anne ___.

---

[53] Northampton Co. Order Bk. 30, 1783-87, p. 474.

[54] Mihalyka, *Marriages, Northampton County*, p. 70.

[55] *Ibid.*, p. 77.

[56] *Ibid.*.

[57] Northampton Co. Minute Bk. 27, 1765-71, p. 177.

[58] Stratton Nottingham, *Accomack Land Causes, 1728-1825* (reprint, Bowie, Md., 1990), pp. 64-65.

[59] Northampton Co. Wills & Inventories 25, 1772-77, p. 344.

[60] Northampton Co. Court records, pack 69.

[61] *The Virginia Genealogist*, XVII, p. 46.

[62] Northampton Co. Court records, pack 44, Oct. 1755, Freshwater *vs.* Goffigon.

[63] *ES* I, p. 105.

[64] Northampton Co. Order Bk. 33, 1796-1800, p. 211.

BICKLEY[1]

+1. Sir FRANCIS[1] BICKLEY, son of Francis Bickley of Lolworth, Cambridgeshire, and his wife Amey Mayres, was baptized in Feb. 1582/3 at Lolworth. After apprenticeship in London he entered the trade of a draper, was successful in business and later acquired Attleborough Hall, Norfolk, where he made his residence. He acquired one share in the Virginia Company, 7 March 1622/3, from Thomas Viner,[2] his wife's brother-in-law. In 1646 he was Master of the Worshipful Company of Drapers and on 3 Sept. 1661 was created a Baronet.

He married, 15 May 1615 at St. Lawrence Jewry, London, Mary Parsons, daughter of Richard Parsons,[3] who was buried 7 Dec. 1635 at St. Antholin, Budge Row, London.[4] He died at Attleborough 11 Aug. 1670, aged 87½ years,[5] leaving will 28 June 1670-7 Dec. 1670.[6]

Issue: 2. Ann[2], baptized 3 Aug. 1617at St. Antholin, Budge Row, London, married, 11 June 1633, Richard Edisbury, citizen and merchant tailor of London, who was born 18 Jan. 1610/11; 3. Amyee[2], baptized 14 Feb. 1618/9 at St. Antholin, married (1), 15 Jan. 1638/9, Thomas Newton and (2) William Childers; 4. Mary[2], baptized 17 Dec. 1620 at St. Antholin, married, 15 May 1637, Thomas Hoo, of St. Paul's Walden, Hertfordshire, who was admitted fellow commoner at Sidney College, Cambridge University, 14 July 1628, aged 15,[7] and left will 16 Sept. 1648-12 March 1648/9;[8] 5. Sir FRANCIS[2]; 6. Elizabeth[2], baptized 10 Aug. 1624 at St. Antholin, buried 21 Aug. 1624; 7. Richard[2], buried 2 Sept. 1626; 8. Thomas[2], baptized 2 Feb. 1627/7 at St.

[1] John C. Bell, "English Ancestors of Joseph Bickley of Virginia," *The Virginia Genealogist*, XXXII, pp. 3-15, 100-08, 199-208, 273-81; XXXIII, pp. 49-60, 109-21, 190-203, 271-86; G. E. Cokayne, *The Complete Baronetage* (Exeter, 1903), III, pp. 229-30.

[2] *R, Va. Co. II*, p. 46, 295, 327.

[3] A. W. Hughes-Clarke, *Register of St. Lawrence Jewry 1538-1636* (London, 1940), I, p. 90.

[4] Joseph Lemuel Chester and George J. Armytage, eds., *The Parish Registers of St. Antholin, Budge Row, London ... 1588 to 1754* (Harleian Society, *Registers*, VIII; London, 1883), p. 69.

[5] Tombstone, Attleborough Church; E. W. Sanderson, *Attleborough Parish Registers, 1552-1840*, ed. by Patrick Palgrave-Moore (Norfolk-Norwich Genealogical Society, *Norfolk Genealogy*, XII; Norwich , 1980), p. 243, buried 26 Aug.

[6] Prerogative Court of Canterbury, 170 Penn.

[7] John Venn and J. A. Venn, *Alumni Cantabrigienses*, pt. 1, II (Cambridge, 1922), p. 401.

[8] Prerogative Court of Canterbury 1649, f. 27 (P.R.O. Prob. 11, Pc. 207).

Antholin, buried 14 Nov. 1650; 9. John[2], baptized 10 Oct. 1628 at St. Antholin; 10. Elizabeth[2], baptized 25 Dec. 1630 at St. Antholin, married, 30 Jan. 1648/9 at Hackney, Middlesex, Col. William Beale; 11. Margaret[2], baptized 24 Jan. 1634/5 at St. Antholin, buried 27 Jan. 1634/5.

5. Sir FRANCIS[2] BICKLEY (Sir Francis[1]) was baptized 26 Oct. 1622 at St. Antholin, Budge Row, London,[9] matriculated at University College, Oxford, 24 March 1636/7,[10] was a student at Gray's Inn, 1640, and succeeded his father as 2nd Baronet, 1670. He married, 4 April 1643 at St. Mary Bothaw, London, Mary Mann, daughter of Thomas Mann, who left will 18 July 1694-4 Aug. 1694.[11] He was buried 29 April 1681 at Attleborough, Norfolk,[12] leaving will 5 April 1680-6 May 1681.[13]

Issue: 12. Sir FRANCIS[3]; 13. Mary[3], born 22 Nov. 1645, buried 23 June 1656; 14. Anne[3], born 22 Aug. 1647, buried 28 July 1657; 15. Elizabeth[3], buried 8 June 1658; 16. Thomas[3], born 7 Aug. 1652, mercer of London; 17. John[3], born 4 March 1653/4, buried 19 April 1682 at Attleborough, admitted at Magdalen College, Cambridge, 24 April 1669, M.A. 1676;[14] 18. Richard[3], born 21 Dec. 1655; 19. Nathaniel[3], born 28 Aug. 1657, lieutenant in the Duke of Norfolk's Ulster Regiment, died in Ireland; 20. Elizabeth[3], born 16 Jan. 1660/1, married, 15 June 1684 at Attleborouigh, John Ware of London; 21. Mary[3], baptized 18 Feb. 1662/3, buried 24 March 1707/8, married 29 May 1683 at Attleborough, the Rev. Richard Bickley, who was admitted pensioner at Magdalen College, Cambridge University, 8 July 1655, B.A. 1659-60, M.A. 1663, was vicar of Tooting, Surrey, to 1683, and thereafter rector of Attleborough, Norfolk, until his death 25 Nov. 1708;[15] 22. Anne[3], baptized 26 Jan. 1663/4, buried 4 July 1688 at Attleborough, married Thomas Church of Heatherset, Norfolk; 23. Jane[3], baptized 26 Jan. 1663/4, married (license 23) Nov. 1694, William Bernard of St. Giles in the Fields, Middlesex; 24. Charles[3], baptized 18 April 1666, buried 3 July 1694, lieutenant of foot in Ireland

12. Sir FRANCIS[3] BICKLEY (Sir Francis[2], Sir Francis[1]) was baptized

---

[9] Chester and Armytage, *op. cit.*, p. 56.
[10] Joseph Foster, *Alumni Oxonienses*, 1st ser., I (Oxford and London, 1891), p. 121.
[11] P.C.C. 188 Box.
[12] Sanderson, *op. cit.*, p. 246.
[13] Consistory Court of Norfolk, Original wills, 1681, no. 13.
[14] Venn and Venn, *op. cit.*, pt. 1, I (Cambridge, 1922), p. 148.
[15] *Ibid.*

19 April 1644 at St. John's Hackney, succeeded his father as 3rd Baronet in 1681. He was admitted as a fellow commoner at Clare College, Cambridge University, 4 July 1656 but matriculated at Magdalen College, Oxford University, 14 Dec. 1660, aged 16, and was admitted to the Inner Temple 24 Oct. 1662.[16] He married (1) Deborah Vermuyden, daughter of Sir Cornelius Vermuyden, (2) Mary Winch, daughter of Sir Humphrey Winch, Bart., who was buried 26 Jan. 1685/6 at Attleborough, and (3) Rebecca (Warne) Davy, who married (3) Nicholas Poynter and died in 1694, aged 54. He was buried 19 July 1687.[17]

Issue: (by 1) 25. Ann[4]; 26. Sir Francis[4], 4th Baronet, baptized 29 Jan. 1667/8 at Attleborough, died 4 July 1746,[18] of Langford, Norfolk, commissioned major in the Duke of Norfolk's Irish Regiment, serving until 14 Dec. 1690, married, (license 5) May 1691, Alathea Garrard; 27. Charles[4], baptized 20 Feb. 1669/70 at Attleborough, buried 2 Aug. 1671; (by 2) 28. Capt. John[4], baptized 17 Aug. 1675, ensign in the Prince of Hesse's Darmstadt Regiment of Foot, 16 Feb. 1694/5-1698, losing a leg at the battle of Steinkirk near Brussels, appointed captain in Col. Farrington's Regiment, 10 March 1702/3, and later commander of invalid companies at Windsor, Tynemouth Castle and Tillbury Fort; 29. the Rev. Sir Humphrey[4], 5th Baronet, died 14 Aug. 1752 in his 77th year,[19] left will 4 Dec. 1751-21 Nov. 1752 which devised "any overplus ... to the Eldest Son or Grandson of my Brother Mr. Joseph Bickley late of Virginia, Deceased, I mean the Person who at my death will be the Baronet of my family ...,"[20] matriculated at Magdalen College, Cambridge, 11 June 1692, aged 16, received B.A. 1695-6, was ordained deacon in June 1707 and priest Dec. 1708, and was rector of Attleborough until his death'[21] 30. JOSEPH[4]; 31. Maria[4], buried 13 Sept. 1681 at Attleborough; 32. (perhaps) Elizabeth[4].

30. JOSEPH[4] BICKLEY (Sir Francis[3], Sir Francis[2], Sir Francis[1]) died between 4 Sept. 1735 and 25 Oct. 1740. He emigrated to Virginia and resided in King and Queen County by 7 July 1703. He married, 6 Sept. 1703, Sarah

---

[16] *Ibid.*; Foster, *loc. cit.*

[17] Sanderson, *op. cit.*, p. 248.

[18] P.C.C. Edmunds, 199, in *V* XXX, pp. 40-41.

[19] Gravestone, Attleborough Church, Norfolk, in *The Virginia Genealogist*, XXVII, p. 33. Cokayne, *loc. cit.*, gives 18 Sept. 1754, derived from a death notice in the *The Gentleman's Magazine, and Historical Chronicle*, XXIV (London, 1754), p. 435.

[20] Archdeaconry of Norfolk wills, 1751-53, no. 144.

[21] Venn and Venn, *op. cit.*, pt. 1, I, p. 148.

(Shelton) Gissage, widow of Richard Gissage.[22]

Issue:[23] 33. JOSEPH[5]; 34. JANE[5]; 35. Frances[5], born 31 Jan. 1709/10; 36. JOHN[5]; 37. Charles[5], born 7 Nov. 1715, left will 5 March 1753[1758]-27 March 1758,[24] of Louisa County, unmarried; 38. Elizabeth[6], born 12 Dec. 1719.

33. JOSEPH[5] BICKLEY (Joseph[4], Sir Francis[3], Sir Francis[2], Sir Francis), born 16 Oct. 1704, left will 30 Jan. 1749/50-24 April 1750/[25] He was deputy sheriff of Caroline County, 1732, and sheriff of Louisa County, 1742. He married (1) ____, (2) possibly Margaret Overton and (3) Elizabeth Overton, daughter of Capt. James Overton.

Issue: (by 1) 39. Sir William[6], born about 1732-33, died 9 March 1771 in Louisa County,[26] merchant, captain of militia, 1754, succeeded his great-uncle as 6th Baronet, 1752, married, 1763, Sarah Clough; (by 2) 40. Francis[6], under age in 1755, merchant of Hanover County and later ordinary keeper of Louisa County; 41. John[6], died 1801, lieutenant of Louisa County militia, 1773, and of Fluvanna County militia, 1777, married, 28 July 1766, Henrietta Ragland; 42. Joseph[6], died by 8 Nov. 1763 when administration on his estate was granted;[27] 43. Elizabeth[6], died after 1803 when she had two draws in the Georgia land lottery,[28] married Thomas Darracott of Louisa County who moved to Wilkes Co., Ga., and left will 4 Sept. 1792-19 Dec. 1793;[29] (by 3) 44. James[6], born 1750, left undated will, proved 13 May 1776.[30]

34. JANE[5] BICKLEY (Joseph[4], Sir Francis[3], Sir Francis[2], Sir Francis[1]), born 16 July 1707, married James Hurt.

Issue: [HURT] 45. Rev. John, chaplain of 2nd Virginia Regiment, and in United States Army, 1791-94, original member of the Society of the Cincinnati, left will 25 Sept. 1800-11 Jan. 1806.[31]

----

[22] John C. Bell, "Bickleys of the Pamunkey River Watershed of Virginia in the 18th Century," *The Virginia Genealogist*, XXVII, pp. 32-45.

[23] *Ibid.*, XXVII-XXVIII, *passim.*

[24] Louisa Co. Will Bk. 1, p. 35.

[25] *Ibid.*, p. 15.

[26] *Virginia Gazette*, 21 March 1771.

[27] Louisa Co. Bond Bk., pp. 113-16.

[28] Grace Gillam Davidson, *Early Records of Georgia ... Wilkes County*, I (Macon, Ga., 1933), p. 305.

[29] Wilkes Co., Ga., Will Bk. 1792-1801, p. 71.

[30] Louisa Co. Will Bk. 2, p. 261.

[31] Louisa Co. Will Bk. 5, pp. 63-65.

36. JOHN[5] BICKLEY (Joseph[4], Sir Francis[3], Sir Francis[2], Sir Francis[1]), born 7 Dec. 1713, left will 25 Nov. 1792-16 Sept. 1793,[32] was of King William County and, after 1767, of "Red Hill," Amherst County. He married (1), 14 April 1736, Mary Hurt and (2), (bond 21) Dec. 1767,[33] Susanna (Harding) Ellis, widow of Charles Ellis , who died 1817, aged 95, leaving will 17 June 1796-17 March 1819.[34]

Issue: (by 1) 46. Humphrey[6], born 26 March 1737, died 1792-93, of Louisa County, married Sarah ___, who married (2) ___ Hadlock; 47. Sarah[6], born 26 Oct. 1740, married ___ Blackwell; 48. Joseph[6], born 8 Feb. 1742/3, died by 25 Sept. 1801, of Petersburg; 49. Hannah[6], born 8 Jan. 1744/5, married ___ James; 50. Mary[6], born 3 Feb. 1746/7, died 12 June 1826, married Dale Carter who was killed by Indians at Fort Blackmore, 6 Oct. 1774;[35] 51. John[6], born 25 March 1748, died between Nov. 1784 and Sept. 1755, unmarried; 52. Elizabeth[6], born 29 Jan. 1749/50, married, by 1775, James Coleman;.53. Jane[6], born 18 June 1751, married (William?) Holland; 54. Charles[6], born 27 June 1753, died 1 June 1839, left will 31 May 1839-4 June 1839,[36] served in expeditions against the Cherokee Indians, 1775-80,[37] justice of Russell County, married (1), 22 Sept. 1788, Mary Hatler, who died 8 Aug. 1801, and (2), 19 Feb. 1802, Delilah Winfield, who died Aug. 1837; 55. Frances[6], born 19 Feb. 1756, died 4 Jan. 1838, married, 28 Dec. 1772, the Rev. John Lasley, born 5 May 1744, died 7 Aug. 1827, of Louisa County; 56. William[6], born 27 May 1757, died 6 Sept. 1840, left will 23 March 1833-Sept. 1840,[38] served in expeditions against the Cherokee Indians, with Gen. George Rogers Clark at Kaskaskia and Vincennes, and against the British in Virginia in 1780,[39] married Sarah Lewis, who died by 1833; 57. Carolina Matilda[6], born 1 Jan. 1761, died 4 April 1845, married,

---

[32] Amherst Co. Will Bk. 3, p. 278.

[33] William Montgomery Sweeny, *Marriage Bonds and Other Marriage Records of Amherst County, Virginia, 1763-1800* (Lynchburg, 1937), p. 8.

[34] Amherst Co. Will Bk. 6, p. 59. Administration on her estate was granted 21 Sept. 1818 (*ibid.*, p. 51).

[35] *W*(1) XIX, p. 124.

[36] Louisa Co. Will Bk. 5, p. 70.

[37] Revolutionary War Pension application, Charles Bickley, S.30864, National Archives.

[38] Mason Co., Ky., Will Bk. M, pp. 126-27.

[39] Revolutionary War Pension application, William Bickley, S.10091, National Archives.

(bond 28) Dec. 1801,[40] John Bow of Louisa County; (by 2) 58. Mildred[6], born 1768-69, died young.

---

[40] Kathleen Booth Williams, *Marriages of Louisa County, Virginia, 1766-1815* (n.p., 1959), p. 11.

BLAND[1]

+1. JOHN[1] BLAND was baptized 28 Sept. 1572 at St. Gregory by St. Paul, London, the fifth son and tenth child of Adam Bland of London, skinner, made free of his company, 1549, and sergeant-pelletier to Queen Elizabeth I, 1563 (son of Roger Bland) and his wife Joan or Jane Atkyns, daughter of William Atkyns of St. Gregory, London.[2] He married, about 1606, Susanna or Susan Dublere, who was born in Hamburgh, 1590, and died 1 Feb. 1664/5.[3]

John[1] Bland, of Syth's (Sithe) Lane, near the lower end of Cheapside, London, and of Plaistow, Essex, a member of the Grocer's Company,[4] became the owner of four shares in the Virginia Company, 15 Sept. 1618, by acquisition from David Waterhouse.[5] He did not plan to settle in Virginia with the status of Planter and was classified as an Adventurer (or investor) and as such was entitled to 100 acres in Virginia for each share of stock, with the privilege of doubling this allowance under certain conditions as a second dividend.

In order to liquidate his rights to land in Virginia, John[1] Bland, upon joining the Company, was associated with a group of Adventurers headed by Sir John Wolstenholme who established Martin's Hundred, a particular plantation in the area which became James City County. These Adventurers received a patent, 30 Jan. 1621/2, for 20,000 acres and the promise of an additional 20,000 acres when the settlement was sufficiently peopled. At the same time, 1500 acres were allotted for schools and churches, 100 acres for glebe land and 50 acres were to be assigned for every person remaining in the colony for three years.[6] In Jan.

---

[1]   Joseph Hunter, *Familiae Minorum Gentium*, II (Harleian Society, *Publications*, XXXVIII; London, 1895), pp. 421-27; Br. *Gen.*, pp. 829-30; Nicholas Carlisle, *Collections for a History of the Ancient Family of Bland* (London, 1826).; Charles L. Bland, *A Vision of Unity, The Bland Family in England and America, 1555-1900* (n.p., 1982).

[2] Hunter, *op. cit.*, p. 42l; Carlisle, *op. cit.*, pp. 121, 140.

[3] Hunter, *op. cit.*, p. 422.

[4] Seventy members of the Grocer's Company of London contributed about £2500 to the Virginia project under the Virginia Company of London.

[5] *R*, Va. Co. III, pp. 59, 592-93.

[6] "Particular Plantations" (*ibid.*, pp. 98-108) were sub-colonies, intended originally to be self-independent hundreds, and were inaugurated to enable the Adventurers (or investors) to profit from their investments and still remain in England, and also to relieve the Company of the problems and expense of transporting colonists and supplies to Virginia. Although the original plan was abandoned after Virginia became a Crown colony, 1624, Martin's Hundred, apparently the best organized of all the hundreds, continued to send representatives to the Virginia Assembly until 1633. For patent for Martin's Hundred, see *ibid.*, pp. 592-98.

1618/9 200 colonists in the *Guift of God* arrived in Virginia to settle at Martin's Hundred.

Bland was an early supporter of the Company's affairs, associated himself with the group loyal to Sir Edwin Sandys, and as he resided in London all year, he was at hand to attend to details of the business of a colony across the seas. He served on various committees from time to time, was part owner of at least one vessel plying between England and Virginia, sent supplies to the colonists at his own expense, and on 23 June 1623 was one of four men added to the Company's Council for Virginia.[7]

His will, 24 Sept. 1627-20 April 1632,[8] made no mention of his Virginia interests but named his wife Susan and seven of their seventeen children in numerous bequests. The probate entry appears to be dated in error for John[1] Bland, Grocer, was buried 5 May 1632 at St. Antholin, Budge Row, London.[9]

Issue:[10] 2. Thomas[2], died without issue 26 Sept. 1678, barrister-at-law, appointed with brother John Receiver of the Queen's Rents in Yorkshire, 25 June 1640, but put out of office 1648, Lord of the Manors of Upton, Plaistow, West Ham and Stratford, granted the office of Guardian, Collector and Bailiff of the Manor of West-Ham, 9 Jan. 1672/3, by Queen Henrietta Maria, married (1) Elizabeth Witham and (2), 1 May 1677 at the Charter House, London, Katherine Sandys, baptized 25 Dec. 1638 at Beningboro' Grange, parish of Newton on Ouise, Yorkshire, daughter of Edwin Sandys, Esq., of Northbourne, Kent; 3. MARY[2]; 4. JOHN[2]; 5. Susan[2], named in her father's will, married Thomas Pierson of Wisbeach, Isle of Ely, Cambridgeshire; 6. EDWARD[2]; 7. Robert[2], baptized 22 Feb. 1617/8, admitted to Corpus Christi College, Cambridge, 1637, and received A.M., 1644, rector of Wigborough Magna, Essex, 1647-49,[11] married Mary Hinton and left descendants in England; 8. Anne[2], baptized 26 May 1619, married Stephen Jackson of London, merchant, and of Plaistow, Essex; 9. Elizabeth[2], baptized 20 Aug. 1620, married the Rev. William Beare (Burie, Burye), minister of Cowley, near Colnebrook, Middlesex, briefly residents of Virginia, and left descendants in England; 10. (Child)[2], still born,

---

[7] *Ibid.*, II, pp. 447-48, 456-57.

[8] P.C.C. 44 Audley, in Waters, *Gleanings*, I, pp. 813-14; *NEHGR* XLVIII, pp. 112-13.

[9] Joseph Lemuel Chester and George J. Armytage, ed., *The Parish Register of St. Antholin, Budge Row, London* (Harleian Society, *Registers*, VIII; London, 1883), p. 66.

[10] *Ibid.*, pp. 53-58, 60-62, 64-68; Carlisle, *op. cit.*, pp. 142-52.

[11] John Venn and J. Venn, *Alumni Cantabrigienses*, I (Cambridge, 1922), p. 165.

buried 20 Aug. 1621; 11. Adam[2], died unmarried about 1647 on a voyage to Virginia; 12. William[2], baptized 26 Dec. 1622, a merchant of Seville, Spain, where he died 1649; 13. Heaster[2] (Esther), baptized 18 Jan. 1623/4, buried 5 Jan. 1625/6; 14. Richard[2], baptized 11 Feb. 1624/5, died 20 Nov. 1692, a Spanish merchant, free of the Company of Framework Knitters, resident in London and at Hoxton and Beeston Hall, Leeds, Yorkshire, married, 30 Jan. 1650/1, Jane Lane, who died 19 May 1694 in her 70th year, widow of Edmund Pott of London, and left descendants in England; 15. Rachel[2], baptized 14 Nov. 1626, buried 23 Aug. 1633; 16. Arnal[2] (Arnold), baptized 24 Feb. 1627/8, buried 18 Oct. 1634; 17. THEODORICK[2]; 18. Joneane[2] (Joan-Amy), baptized 10 Jan. 1631/2, buried 5 May 1632 with her father.

3. MARY[2] BLAND (John[1]), baptized 11 Nov. 1607, married (1), 8 June 1626 at St. Antholin's, Emanuel Proby of St. Paul's Churchyard, London, woolen draper, fourth son of Sir Peter Proby, Lord Mayor of London.[12] He left a will proved 28 April 1646. She married (2) Thomas Neville, also a woolen draper of St. Paul's Churchyard, London.[13]

Issue: (by 1) [PROBY][14] 19. Peter[3], baptized 12 June 1628, of Putney, Surrey, and of London, merchant, died without surviving issue leaving will 3 June 1684-21 Nov. 1684, married, 27 April 1656 at St. Olave, Grace, daughter of Sir Richard Ford; 20. George[3], baptized 22 Sept. 1630, came to Virginia but died without issue; 21. Susanna[3], baptized 5 Oct. 1632, married George Torriano of London, merchant tailor, who left will 14 Oct. 1685-2 Dec. 1685;[15] 22. Margaret[3], baptized 1 Oct. 1634; 23. Mary[3], baptized 22 Nov. 1635, died young; 24. CHARLES[3]; 25. Samuel[3], baptized 27 March 1640, merchant of London; 26. Mary[3], baptized 25 Feb. 1641/2; 27. Nathaniel[3], baptized 7 July 1643; 28. Elizabeth[3], baptized April 1645, married, April 1675, John Rogerson of Warbus, Dublin, merchant,[16] Alderman of Dublin.

4. JOHN[2] BLAND (John[1]), a Spanish merchant of Old Navy Office, Mark Lane, London, traded in the West Indies and Virginia, had estates in both

[12] Carlisle, *op. cit.*, p. 149.

[13] *Ibid.*

[14] L. G. Pine, *The New Extinct Peerage, 1884-1971* (London, 1972), p. 60.

[15] P.C.C. 157 Can, in Noel Currer-Briggs, *Virginia Settlers and English Adventurers* (Baltimore, 1970), p. 381.

[16] George J. Armytage, ed., *Allegations for Marriage Licenses Issued By the Vicar-General of the Archbishop of Canterbury* (Harleian Society, *Publications*, XXXIV; London, 1892), p. 138.

England and Virginia, and resided for a time in Seville in the early 1640s and in Tangier in the 1660s, serving as its mayor 1668-76.[17] He came to Virginia about 1635 to see to the Bland interests. His two brothers later handled the family affairs in the colony but following the deaths of both, his nephew 29. Edward[3] Bland deeded to him, 20 March 1674/5, the 8000 acre plantation known as "Kimages", in Westover Parish, Charles City County, which was originally Berkeley Hundred and settled in 1619 under terms similar to those granted the patentees of Martin's Hundred.[18]

John[2] Bland married Sarah Green, died 4 March 1712/3, daughter of Giles Green, Esq., of Aflington in the Isle of Purbeck. She was an able and courageous woman who, following the tragic death of her son Giles[3] in Virginia, crossed the ocean alone, 1679, armed with a power of attorney to handle and settle her husband's affairs in Virginia.[19] When these affairs were further complicated by the death of John[2] Bland, his executor in England, Thomas Povey, also gave her a power of attorney.

The will of John[2] Bland of London, merchant, 3 May 1680-23 June 1680,[20] referred to his many adversities and infirmities concerning his unhappy affairs and estates, but praised his wife Sarah who was in Virginia. Due to the uncertainty of the times and her great distance from England he named with her consent a co-executor, Thomas Povey, a good friend. He mentioned that many years before he had greatly improved a house at Tangier which, during his absence, was taken by the Governor "to the services of his Majesty"; Thomas Povey was entrusted to obtain the satisfaction which he had not been able to obtain. The two executors were directed to raise money from all other lands and tenements to pay his debts. He directed that a "competent provision" be made for his daughter-in-law, Frances Bland, and for his grandson John[4] Bland, her son,

---

[17] V LXXII, pp. 19-20. He is mentioned a number of times in *The Diary of Samuel Pepys*, ed. by Robert Latham and William Matthews (10 v.; Berkeley and Los Angeles, 1970).

[18] *H* VI, pp. 303-04. For settlement of Berkeley Hundred, see *R*, Va. Co. III, pp. 201-07. His widow and his executor, Thomas Povey, conveyed this 8000 acres to Benjamin Harrison, 19 Dec. 1692, and Harrison conveyed the land to his son Benjamin, 2 Nov. 1693 (Charles City Co. Wills & Deeds 1692-94, p. 180).

[19] Isle of Wight Co. Wills & Deeds 1, pp. 409-11; Surry Co. Deeds, Wills &c 2, 1671-84, p. 229. This power names the Bland plantations as Bartlett, Rimocky, Herring Creek Mill, Jerdone, Jordans, Westoffer, Upper Chippokes, Sunken Marsh Plantation, Basse's Choice, Jamestown Lott, and Lawne's Creek.

[20] P.C.C. 76 Bath, in Waters, *Gleanings*, I, p. 814.

the child "being in infancy". He died 8 June 1680.[21]

Issue:[22] 29. John[3], died 11 Jan. 1659/60, aged 13; 30. GILES[3]; 31. Thomas[3], buried at St. Antholin's 21 Nov. 1654, aged 5.

6. EDWARD[2] BLAND (John[1]), baptized 5 Feb. 1614,[23] was a merchant of London and in Spain. While still resident in London he purchased from Capt. William Peirce 2000 acres on Lawne's Creek in the area which became Surry County, which he repatented 7 July 1646.[24] By 10 March 1646/7 he evidently was living in Virginia for he patented 1300 acres "on the southside of the James River near Upper Chippokes" and named as headrights Edward Bland, Ja. Bland, Wm. Beare, Eliza. Beare and Geo. Proby.[25] On 27 Aug. 1650 he set out with Abraham Wood, Sackford Brewster and Elias Pennant from Fort Henry at the head of the Appomattox River and explored the territory south into North Carolina. A published account of this journey, 1651, was dedicated to Sir John Danvers.[26] Administration on his estate was granted to his brother John[2], 12 July 1652.[27]

Edward[2] Bland married in England Jane Bland, daughter of his uncle Gregory Bland (born 1567) of Ireland. On 9 May 1652 as "late the wife of Edward Bland," she was granted a patent for his total holdings, being 4300 acres in James City (now Surry) near the head of Chippokes Creek.[28] She married (2), possibly by 1 Feb. 1652/3, John Holmwood and died about 1664, being buried at Westover.[29]

Issue: 32. EDWARD[3].

17. THEODORICK[2] BLAND (John[1]), baptized 6 Jan. 1629/30 at St.

---

[21] Hunter, *op. cit.*, p. 423; W. Bruce Bannerman, ed., *The Registers of St. Olave, Hart Street, London, 1563-1700* (Harleian Society, *Registers*, XLVI; London, 1916), p. 221, burial 12 June.

[22] Carlisle, *op. cit.*, p. 145.

[23] St. Stephen, Coleman Street, London, register, in *Dictionary of Virginia Biography*, II (Richmond, 2001), p. 5.

[24] Patent Bk. 2, p. 50.

[25] *Ibid.*, p. 108.

[26] *V* LXXXVII, pp. 131-57; Edward Bland, *The Discovery of New Brittaine, 1650* (London, 1651).

[27] P.C.C. Admon. Act Bk. 1652, fo. 134, in Waters, *Gleanings*, I, p. 815.

[28] Patent Bk. 3, p. 200.

[29] Carlisle, op. cit., p. 299; Surry Co. Deeds, Wills &c 1, 1652-72, p. 18. Holmwood contracted with Thomas Felton for the erection of a house at "Berkeley" for 1400 pounds of tobacco less what was due from Felton to the estate of Edward Bland, merchant.

Antholin, Budge Row, London, was a merchant with his brother Edward[2] at Santa Lucar, Spain, and in the Canary Islands. He came to Virginia, 1653, following the death of his brother in order to manage the family's large mercantile interests, control of which was vested in his brother John[2] Bland. While attending to these duties, he served as justice of Charles City, 1663-65, Burgess from that county and speaker of the House, 1660, Burgess from Henrico County, 1661-62, and member of the Council, 1663-71,[30] and was "overseer of the horse ferry boate" operating from Westover to the south side of James River, 1664.[31] On 17-18 April 1665 Theodorick[2] Bland purchased "Westover" from Sir John Pawlett whose brother Thomas Pawlett owned the plantation, 1636.[32]

He died 23 April 1672 and his tombstone in the old churchyard now adjoining the garden at "Westover" is covered by a stone erected by his "most disconsolate widow, a daughter of Richard Bennett, Esq."[33]

He married, 1660,[34] 4. *Anne[2] Bennett* (see UTIE-BENNETT), who married (2) 32. *St. Leger[3] Codd* (see ST. LEGER) and died Nov. 1688 at Wharton Creek, Kent Co., Md.[35]

Issue: 33. THEODORICK[3]; 34. RICHARD[3]; 35. JOHN[3].

24. CHARLES[3] PROBY (Mary[2] Bland, John[1]) married Dorothy, sister of George Torriano, who married (2) Thomas Lucas of Fort St. George, Madras.[36]

Issue: [PROBY][37] 36. William[4], of Rans, Buckinghamshire, and Elton, co. Huntingdon, Governor of Fort St. George, Madras, died Jan. 1739, married (1),

---

[30] Charles City Co. Order Bk. 1655-65, pp. 352, 609; Leonard, pp. 36, 38, xix; *H* II, p. 99; Jon Kukla, *Speakers and Clerks of the Virginia House of Burgesses, 1643-1776* (Richmond, 1981), pp. 59-61; Charles Campbell, *The Bland Papers* (Petersburg, 1846), p. 148; *Dictionary of Virginia Biography*, II, p. 14.

[31] Charles City Co. Order Bk. 1655-65, p. 513.

[32] *V* XLVII, pp. 196-206.

[33] *W*(1) IV, p. 143, inscription in Latin, which gives the year as 1671 and age as 41, which is in agreement with the date of his baptism. He was present, however, at a meeting of the General Court, 24 Nov. 1671, and his estate was first mentioned 16 May 1672 (*MCGC*, pp. 286, 306).

[34] *MCGC*, p. 503.

[35] Carlisle, *op. cit.*, p. 301; *Dictionary of Virginia Biography*, II, p. 1, says probably Nov. 1687.

[36] Pine, *loc. cit.*

[37] *The Genealogist*, new ser., XIX, pp. 184, 186, 189; Venn, *op. cit.*, III (Cambridge, 1924), p. 401.

26 Jan. 1692/3 at Fort St. George, Frances Gray and (2) Henrietta Cornwall; 37. Charles[4], born in the East Indies, died 16 Jan. 1727/8, aged 61, graduate of Jesus College, Cambridge, rector of Tewin, Hertfordshire, 1702-27, and of Bramfield [Braintfield], Hertfordshire, 1715-18; 38. Elizabeth[4], married, 25 Aug. 1687 at Fort St. George, Gabriel Roberts.

30. GILES[3] BLAND (John[2], John[1]), baptized 26 Oct. 1647,[38] came to Virginia to act as agent for his father following the death of his uncle Theodorick[2] Bland, 1672. As a young "hot head", he arrived on the turbulent scene preceding Bacon's Rebellion and briefly was a colorful figure, defying Governor Berkeley and members of the Council to the point that he was placed under arrest and suspended from the important office of Collector of Customs, to which he had been appointed. When Bacon organized his forces, Giles[3] Bland allied himself with the leaders of the Rebellion and following the collapse of that brief defiance, he suffered the same ignominious fate to which the others were condemned. Tried at a court martial at "Green Spring" on 8 March 1676/7, he was convicted of treason and summarily hanged, 27 March 1676/7, aged 29.[39] At this point his mother, Sarah Bland, took hold of the family interests and came to Virginia to unravel affairs, greatly complicated by her son's precipitate acts.

Giles[3] Bland married Frances Povey, natural daughter of Thomas Povey of Whitehall. She married (2) Samuel Starkey, barrister-at-law of New Windsor, Berkshire.[40]

Issue: 39. Thomas Posthumous[4], born 5 Nov. 1677, ensign of foot in Queen Anne's service, 1712, married Mary Brown, daughter of John Brown, merchant, citizen and vintner of London.[41]

32. EDWARD[3] BLAND (Edward[2], John[1]) in 1674/5 deeded to his uncle John[2] Bland the 8000 acres included in "Kimages" and in return received from Sarah Bland, his uncle's relict and executrix, 2000 acres of the "Kimages" trace, the deed stating that the land should descend to the heirs of Edward[2] Bland and

---

[38] W. Bruce Bannerman, ed., *The Registers of St. Olave, Hart Street, London, 1563-1700*, (Harleian Society, *Register Series*, XLVI; London, 1916), p. 56.

[39] *V* LXXII, pp. 27-28; Campbell, *op. cit.*, pp. 146-47; *The Virginia Gazette* (Purdie & Dixon)), 23 Feb. 1769, p. 1; *MCGC*, pp. 423, 435, 457, 529; *H* II, pp. 370, 461; John Davenport Neville, *Bacon's Rebellion* (n.p., 1976), pp. 43, 47-48, 51, 53, 61 *et seq.*; *Dictionary of Virginia Biography*, II, pp. 7-8.

[40] Hunter, *op. cit.*, p. 423.

[41] *Ibid.*, which states his legitimacy is doubtful.

his wife.[42] He married Margaret ___ and died about 1690.[43] His widow married (2) Thomas Tanner and, 6 Aug. 1723, sold her one-third part of "Kimages" to Benjamin Harrison.[44]

Issue: 40. John[4], of "Kimages," living 1714, died intestate; 41. SARAH[4].

33. THEODORICK[3] BLAND (Theodorick[2], John[1]), born Feb. 1662/3, heir to the "Westover" plantation, shared his inheritance with his brother Richard[3] and together they sold 1200 acres of the estate, 4 Feb. 1688/9, to William Byrd.[45] He was surveyor of Charles City County, 1680, and of Stafford County, 1691, and laid out the town of Williamsburg, 1699.[46] He married Margaret (___) Man and died Nov. 1700.[47]

Issue: 42. John[4], born 8 Dec. 1698, educated at Leeds, lived at Scarborough, Yorkshire, but went to Virginia where he was described as a merchant of Prince George County when he sold, 1 March 1749/50, land his father had bought from William Byrd, 1 Oct. 1690,[48] and died at "Jordan's," Prince George County, married Ann West, who died 24 Nov. 1758 at Mustens, Yorkshire;[49] 43. Theodorick[4], died soon after his father.

34. RICHARD[3] BLAND (Theodorick[2], John[1]), born 11 Aug. 1665, lived at Williamsburg and at "Jordan's Point" on the James River in Prince George County, was justice of Prince George and a member of the House of Burgesses for Charles City County, 1693, 1700-04, and for Prince George County, 1705-06.[50] He died 6 April 1720,[51] leaving will 4 Feb. 1719/20-12 April 1720.[52]

He married (1), 6 Sept. 1692, Mary Swann, born 5 Oct. 1669,[53] died at "Jordan's" Sept. 1700, daughter of Col. Thomas Swann of "Swann's Point," Surry County, and his (5) wife Mary Mansfield, and (2), 11 Feb. 1701/2,[54]

---

[42] *H* VI, p. 305.

[43] Carlisle, *op. cit.*, p. 299. Hunter, *op. cit.*, p. 423, names his wife as Jane Gilly.

[44] *H* VI, pp. 303-08; Isle of Wight Co. Deeds, Wills &c 7, p. 475, 6 Feb. 1722/3.

[45] *V* XLVII, pp. 211-17.

[46] *Executive Journals of the Council of Colonial Virginia*, I (Richmond, 1925), pp. 440, 460; Stafford Co. Record Bk. 1686-1693/4, p. 212.

[47] Hunter, *op. cit.*, p. 425; Carlisle, *op. cit.*, p. 302.

[48] Chesterfield Co. Deed Bk. 1, p. 67.

[49] Hunter, *op. cit.*, p. 425.

[50] Leonard, pp. 53, 60, 52, 64.

[51] Hunter, *op. cit.*, p. 425.

[52] Prince George Co. Wills & Deeds 1713-28, p. 394.

[53] Swann family record, *V* XXVIII, pp. 30-32.

[54] Hunter, *op. cit.*, p. 425; Henrico Co. Deeds, Wills &c 1697-1704, p. 279.

Elizabeth Randolph, born 1680, died 22 Jan. 1719/20, daughter of Col. William Randolph of "Turkey Island," Henrico County, and his wife Mary Isham.[55]

Issue: (by 1) Several children who died in infancy;[56] (by 2)[57] 44. MARY[4]; 45. ELIZABETH[4]; 46. RICHARD[4]; 47. ANNA[4]; 48. THEODORICK[4].

35. JOHN[3] BLAND (Theodorick[2], John[1]), born 8 Feb. 1681/2, resided at Scarborough, Yorkshire, where he was free of the Committee for Merchant Adventurers of York, and died 1746. He married (1) Mary Breckon, daughter of Francis Breckon, and (2), 9 Nov. 1709, Elizabeth Dale, died 1746, daughter of Thomas Dale of Marsham and Crossbill Hall, Yorkshire.[58]

Issue: (by 2) 49. Richard[4], born 22 Aug. 1710, never married; 50. JOHN[4]; 51. Anne[4], born 4 May 1714, died 1730.

41. SARAH[4] BLAND (Edward[3], Edward[2], John[1]), heir-at-law to her brother, inherited his two-thirds part of "Kimages." She married (1) Edward New of Charles City County and (2) Alexander Horton of Charles City County, who joined her in a deed, 6 Feb. 1722/3, conveying 1530 acres of "Kimages" to Benjamin Harrison[59] and, 16 March 1725, 25 July 1725 and 17 March 1728, once described as of Lawnes Creek Parish, Surry County, sold the land received from Harrison in exchange.[60] In Aug. 1744 Sarah Horton and her son Alexander Horton were committed to jail on suspicion of being privy or accessory to the breaking open of the store of Hugh Miller, merchant, in Prince George County, and robbing goods of the value of £8.14.0, but the court found that Richard Gibbs, a boarder at her house, took the goods there and that she was innocent.[61]

Issue:[62] (by 1) [NEW] 52. JOHN[5]; (by 2) [HORTON][63] 53. Bland[5]; 54. Alexander[5]; 55. [?] Susanna[5]; 56. [?] Lucy[5]; 57. (Other daughters?)[5].

44. MARY[4] BLAND (Richard[3], Theodorick[2], John[1]), born 21 Aug. 1703,[64] left will 19 Oct. 1762-29 May 1764.[65] She married Col. Henry Lee of "Lee

[55] Wassell Randolph, *William Randolph I of Turkey Island* ... (Memphis, 1949), p. 92.
[56] Carlisle, *op. cit.*, p. 302.
[57] Hunter, *op. cit.*, p. 425; Campbell, *op. cit.*, p. xiii.
[58] Hunter, *op. cit.*, p. 426.
[59] *H* VI, pp. 303-08; Isle of Wight Co. Deeds, Wills &c 7, p. 675.
[60] Surry Co. Deeds, Wills &c 7, 1715-30, pp. 589, 528, 899.
[61] Charles City Co. Order Bk. 1737-51, p. 245.
[62] Charles Campbell, ed., *The Bland Papers* (Petersburg, 1846), I, p. 147.
[63] Charles City Co. Order Bk. 1737-51, p. 145.
[64] Hunter, *op. cit.*, p. 425. Campbell, *op. cit.*, p. xiii, gives 1704.
[65] Westmoreland Co. Wills & Deeds 14, 1761-68, pp. 265-67.

Hall," Westmoreland County, lieutenant colonel of militia, who left will 30 July 1746-last codicil 13 June 1747-25 Aug. 1747.[66]

Issue: [LEE][67] 58. John[5], born about 1724, left will 23 Sept. 1765-24 Feb. 1767,[68] without issue, of "Cabin Point," on the Potomac River, clerk of the court of Essex County, 1745-61, member of the House of Burgesses, 1761-65,[69] married, 20 Dec. 1749, 20. *Mary[5] (Smith) Ball* (see MATHEWS), died 1802, who married (3), 30 Aug. 1768, John Smith; 59. RICHARD[5]; 60. HENRY[5]; 61. LAETITIA[5].

45. ELIZABETH[4] BLAND (Richard[3], Theodorick[2], John[1]), born 29 May 1705,[70] married 70. Col. *William[6] Beverley* (see ST. LEGER), born about 1698, died 28 Feb. 1756, of "Blandfield," Essex County, clerk of Essex County, 1714-45, member of the House of Burgesses from Orange, 1736-40, and Essex, 1742-49, County Lieutenant of Orange and Augusta counties, 1741, member of the Council, 1752-55, patentee of "Beverley Manor," Augusta County,[71] left will 3 Dec. 1755-3 May 1756.[72]

Issue: [BEVERLEY][73] 62. ROBERT[5]; 63. URSULA[5]; 64. John[5], died 1743; 65. ELIZABETH[5]; 66. Anna[5], married 79. Col. Robert[5] Munford.

46. RICHARD[4] BLAND (Richard[3], Theodorick[2], John[1]), born 6 May 1710,[74] died 26 Oct. 1776 at Williamsburg.[75] He inherited "Jordan's Point" and was a student at the College of William and Mary and member of the House of Burgesses for Prince George County, 1742-75, of the Virginia Committee of Correspondence, 1773, of the First Continental Congress, 1774-75, of the five

---

[66] Westmoreland Co. Wills & Deeds 10, 1744-48, pp. 364-68; Edmund Jennings Lee, *Lee of Virginia* (Philadelphia, 1895), pp. 131-36.

[67] Lee, *op. cit.*, p. 136.

[68] Westmoreland Co. Deeds & Wills 14, pp. 412-16.

[69] Leonard, p. 91.

[70] Hunter, *op. cit.*, p. 425. Campbell, *op. cit.*, p. xiii, gives 1706.

[71] *Dictionary of Virginia Biography*, I (Richmond, 1998), pp. 477-78; John McGill, *The Beverley Family of Virginia* (Columbia, S.C., 1956), pp. 534-35; *V* III, p. 269; Leonard, pp. 77-78, 81, xix.

[72] *V* XXII, pp. 297-301, proved in the General Court.

[73] John McGill, *The Beverley Family of Virginia* (Columbia, S.C., 1956), pp. 535-36, 549, 571, 581, 590, 593-94, 603, 608, 612; Beverley-Randolph Bible (Oxford, 1747), in *The Virginia Genealogist*, XVI, pp. 130-31, and *V* XXXIV, pp. 161-63, with variations.

[74] Hunter, *op. cit.*, p. 425.

[75] *Virginia Gazette* (Purdie), 1 Nov. 1776.

Virginia conventions, 1774-75, and of the House of Delegates, 1776.[76] He married (1), 21 March 1729/30, Ann Poythress, born 13 Dec. 1712, died 9 April 1758, only daughter and heiress of Peter Poythress,[77] (2), 1 Jan. 1759, Martha (Macon) Massie, born 12 Aug. 1722,[78] died 8 Aug. 1759, daughter of William Macon and widow of William Massie,[79] and (3) Elizabeth (Blair) Bolling, born 4 April 1712, died 22 April 1775, daughter of Dr. Archibald Blair and widow of 8. *John⁵ Bolling* (see ROLFE).[80]

Issue: (by 1) 67. RICHARD⁵; 68. Elizabeth⁵, married 108. *Peter⁵ Poythress* (see BALEY-COCKE); 69. ANNE⁵; 70. PETER RANDOLPH⁵; 71. JOHN⁵; 72. Mary⁵, born 15 Feb. 1740/1, died in infancy; 73. WILLIAM⁵; 74. Theodorick⁵, born 28 Sept. 1744, died 1754; 75. EDWARD⁵; 76. SARAH⁵; 77. Susan⁵, born 20 Feb. 1752, died young; 78. Lucy⁵, born 22 Sept. 1754, married, 31 May 1780, Jacob Rubsamen of Manchester,[81] a native of Germany and physician, trustee of Manchester on whose land the Manchester tobacco inspection was established, who died before 2 May 1792 at Philadelphia, Pa.,[82] leaving will 22 March 1792-14 May 1792.[83]

47. ANNA⁴ BLAND (Richard³, Theodorick², John¹), born 25 Feb. 1711/2,[84] died 1770,[85] married (1) Capt. Robert Munford of Appomattox River, vestryman of Bristol Parish, 1735, member of the House of Burgesses from Prince George

---

[76] *Dictionary of American Biography*, II (New York, 1929), pp. 354-55; *Dictionary of Virginia Biography*, II, pp. 10-13; *Biographical Directory of the American Congress, 1774-1996* (Alexandria, Va., 1997), p. 672; Leonard, pp. 79, 82, 85, 87, 89, 93, 96, 98, 100, 104, 106, 110, 113, 115, 118, 120, 123; Clinton L. Rossiter, "Richard Bland: The Whig in America," *William and Mary Quarterly*, 3rd ser., X, pp. 33-79.

[77] Campbell, *op. cit.*, pp. xiii-xiv. She was niece of Edward Baxter of Charles City County (Henrico Co. Order Bk. 1737-46, p. 387).

[78] Massie Bible, in *V* XLI, p. 349.

[79] Tombstone, New Kent Co., *T* I, pp. 58-59.

[80] Stuart E. Brown and others, *Pocahontas' Descendants* (n.p., 1985), p. 7; *Virginia Gazette* (Purdie), 28 April 1775.

[81] Knorr, *Marriage Bonds ... Chesterfield County*, p. 105, bond 21 May; *Virginia Gazette*, 31 May 1780, in *V* XII, p. 27.

[82] *Virginia Gazette and General Advertiser*, Richmond, 2 May 1792.

[83] Chesterfield Co. Will Bk. 4, p. 479, which named his brothers and sister in Germany; Order Bk. 9, p. 338.

[84] Hunter, *op. cit.*, p. 425.

[85] Bushrod Washington, *Reports of Cases Argued and Determined in the Court of Appeals of Virginia*, I (Richmond, 1798), p. 97.

County, 1736-40,[86] who died Dec. 1744,[87] leaving will 8 Sept. 1743-10 Sept. 1745,[88] and (2) George Currie, jailor, 1753,[89] and clerk of Halifax County, 1752-57, elected to the House of Burgesses, 1753, but unseated,[90] who later was a resident of Prince George County[91] and left will, now lost, recorded 11 Feb. 1772.[92]

Issue: (by 1) [MUNFORD][93] 79. ROBERT[5]; 80. THEODORICK[5]; 81. ELIZABETH[5]; (by 2) [CURRIE][94] 82. Anna[5], left will dated 21 Jan. 1773, now lost, probated in Prince George County; 83. MARGARET[5].

48. THEODORICK[4] BLAND (Richard[3], Theodorick[2], John[1]), born 2 Dec. 1718,[95] of "Kippax" and "Cawson's", Prince George County, and of Amelia County, left will 16 July 1783-28 Oct. 1784.[96] He married (1), 1738, Frances Bolling, born 1724, died 1774, only daughter and heiress of Drury Bolling, and (2) Elizabeth (Randolph) Yates, daughter of Edward Randolph and widow of the Rev. William Yates, who left will dated 17 Dec. 1783.[97]

Issue: (by 1)[98] 84. ELIZABETH[5]; 85. THEODORICK[5]; 86. MARY[5]; 87. ANNA[5]; 88. Jane[5], born 30 Sept. 1749, married Herbert Harris; 89. FRANCES[5].

50. JOHN[4] BLAND (John[3], Theodorick[2], John[1]), born 5 Aug. 1712, died 14 Nov. 1787 at Ilford, Essex, was a Virginia merchant of Lime Street, London. He married 1 July 1739, Ann Buck, born 18 Aug. 1718, died 10 Nov. 1770 at

---

[86] Leonard, p. 77.

[87] Campbell, *op. cit.*, p. xiii.

[88] *T* XII, pp. 88-90; Prince Edward Co. District Court Will Bk. 1, p. 106.

[89] Halifax Co. Pleas No. 1, 1752-55, p. 318, in *Magazine of Virginia Genealogy*, XXV, no. 2, p. 24.

[90] Leonard, p. 84; Wirt Johnson Carrington, *A History of Halifax County* (Richmond, 1924), pp. 45, 49.

[91] Churchill G. Chamberlayne, *The Vestry Book and Register of Bristol Parish* (Richmond, 1898), *passim*.

[92] Halifax Co. Deed Bk. 19, p. 330.

[93] *T* III, pp. 177-79.

[94] Halifax Co. Deed Bk. 19, p. 330.

[95] Hunter, *op. cit.*, p. 425. *V* XLIX, p. 255, gives 19 Dec. 1719.

[96] Amelia Co. Will Bk. 3, pp. 289-91.

[97] *Ibid.*, p. 302, admitted to probate about Dec. 1784. The inventory of her estate was returned 28 Dec. 1786 (Amelia Co. Order Bk. 17, p. 98).

[98] Bristol Parish Register; Philip Slaughter, *A History of Bristol Parish* (2nd ed.; Richmond, 1879), pp. 158-60.

London.

Issue:[99] 90. JOHN[5]; 91. THOMAS[5]; 92. Edward[5], born 30 April 1744 at Scarborough, died 1771 at sea, in British Navy, unmarried; 93. Joseph[5], born 1 Sept. 1745 at Scarborough, died 10 Oct. 1810 at Bush-Hill, Herts., merchant there, married Jane Cockshutt; 94. THEODORICK[5]; 95. William[5], born 16 Jan. 1747/8 at Scarborough, died there Jan. 1748/9; 96. Anna[6], born 26 May 1749 at Scarborough, died 6 Jan. 1838 at Sion Hill, Bath, unmarried; 97. Sarah[6], born 18 March 1750/1 at Scarborough, married Thomas Miller of Iford, Sussex; 98. Elizabeth[6], born 1 Nov. 1752 at Scarborough, died 1770, married Richard Butler, merchant of London; 99. Robert[6], born 16 April 1775 at Scarborough, died 1781, in British Navy, unmarried; 100. Susannah[6], born 1760 at Scarborough, died 5 Nov. 1817 at Sion Hill, unmarried.

52. JOHN[5] NEW (Sarah[4] Bland, Edward[3], Edward[2], John[1]) made deed to Col. Benjamin Harrison proved in June 1745.[100] He engaged in an extended law suit over the title to "Kimages", contending that the 1681 deed entailed the land to the heirs of Edward[3] forever and that the land could not lawfully be sold. The suit was settled by agreement, 1752, which gave John New other land in exchange and left the Harrisons in possession of "Kimages", better known as "Berkeley". As John New of Henrico County, wheelwright, he, 17 March 1760, conveyed 350 acres and four slaves to his son William.[101] He married ___.

Issue: [NEW] 101. William[6], resident of Henrico County, 1782, died before 7 Feb. 1785 when his widow was granted administration on his estate,[102] married Editha ____, who died before 12 Jan. 1795 when the sale of her estate was made.[103]

59. RICHARD[5] LEE (Mary[4] Bland, Richard[3], Theodorick[2], John[1]), born about 1726, left will 16 Feb. 1790-23 March 1795.[104] He resided at "Lee Hall," Westmoreland County, and was justice, vestryman of Cople Parish, member of the House of Burgesses, 1757-74, of the Conventions of 1775-76, and of the House of Delegates, 1777-93, and Naval Officer for the port of South Potomac.

---

[99] Charles L. Bland, *A View of Unity: The Bland Family in England and America, 1550-1900* (n.p., 1982), pp. 35-40.

[100] Charles City Co. Order Bk. 1737-51, p. 260. This was probably for the 2000 acres of "Kimages" which was confirmed by Act of Assembly in 1752 (*H* VI, p. 306).

[101] Henrico Co. Deed Bk. 1750-67, pp. 620-21.

[102] Henrico Co. Order Bk. 2, pp. 25. 474.

[103] Greensville Co. Will Bk. 1, pp. 298-99.

[104] Westmoreland Co. Deeds & Wills 19, pp. 79-80.

He married, when about 60 years old, 368. *Sally Bland⁶ Poythress* (see BALEY-COCKE), who was aged 16 at her marriage, married (2), (bond) 23 May 1798,[105] Capt. Willoughby⁷ Newton , son of 66. *Elizabeth⁶ (Vaulx) Newton* (see BURWELL) and died 28 May 1828, leaving will 19 April 1828-codicil 16 May 1828-23 June 23 Aug. 1828.[106]

Issue: [LEE][107] 102. Richard⁶, died young; 103. Mary⁶, born 12 Feb. 1790, died 18 Sept. 1848, "Belle Vue," Chesterfield County, married, 11 Dec. 1804, Thomas⁷ Jones, born 18 Aug. 1781, died 9 Nov. 1860, "Belle Vue," of Chesterfield County, student at the College of William and Mary, 1799, son of 99. Gen. *Joseph⁵ Jones* (see SHEPPEY) and 288. *Jane⁶ Atkinson* (see JORDAN, Thomas);[108] 104. Lettice⁶, married 200. Dr. *John Augustine⁶ Smith* (see BERNARD); 105. Sally Richardia⁶, married (1) 229. *Presley⁶ Cox* (see FLEET) and (2), (bond 7) Sept. 1824,[109] William D. Robinson.

60. HENRY⁵ LEE (Mary⁴ Bland, Richard³, Theodorick², John¹), died 15 Aug. 1787 in Loudoun County in his 58th year,[110] left will 10 Aug. 1787-1 Oct. 1787.[111] He resided at "Leesylvania," Prince William County, and was a justice, member of the House of Burgesses, 1758-76, of the Conventions of 1774-76, and of the State Senate, 1776-87,[112] and County Lieutenant of Prince William during the Revolutionary War. He married, 1 Dec. 1753 in James City County, 42. *Lucy⁶ Grymes* (see BARKHAM-JENINGS), born 26 April 1734.

Issue: [LEE][113] 106. Henry⁶, born 29 Jan. 1756, "Leesylvania," died 25March 1818, Cumberland Island, Ga., graduate of Princeton College, 1773, officer of dragoons in the Revolutionary War, Governor of Virginia, commander of the United States army in the Whiskey Rebellion, major general 19 July 1798,

---

[105] Stratton Nottingham, *The Marriage License Bonds of Westmoreland County, Virginia, From 1786 to 1850* (Onancock, Va., 1928), p. 50.

[106] Westmoreland Co. Deeds & Wills 26, pp. 95-96.

[107] Lee, *op. cit.*, pp. 285-91.

[108] Augusta B. Fothergill, *Peter Jones and Richard Jones Genealogies* (Richmond, 1924), pp. 42-46.

[109] Nottingham, *op. cit.*, p. 59.

[110] *Virginia Journal and Alexandria Advertiser*, 30 Aug. 1787.

[111] Prince William Co. Will Bk. G, pp. 372-77.

[112] Leonard, pp. 87, 89, 93, 96, 98, 100, 104, 106, 110, 113m 115m 118, 120, 124, 128, 132, 136, 140, 144, 148, 151. 155, 159, 163.

[113] Lee, *op. cit.*, pp. 292-99, 329-82.

discharged 15 June 1800, member of Congress, 1799-1801,[114] married (1), 1782, Matilda Lee, who died 1790,[115] and (2), 18 June 1793, 327. *Anne Hill*[6] *Carter* (see BERNARD), born 1773, died 25 July 1829. "Ravensworth," Fairfax County;[116] 107. Charles[6], born 1758, died 24 June 1815, Fauquier County, educated at Princeton College, 1770, B.A. 1775, M.A. 1777, Naval Officer of South Potomac, 1777, Attorney General, 1795-1801, married (1), 11 Feb. 1789 at "Chantilly," Westmoreland County, Ann Lee, born 1 Dec. 1770, died 9 Sept. 1804,[117] and (2), 19 July 1809, Margaret Christian[7] (Scott) Peyton, born 20 Jan. 1783, Dumfries, died 11 Oct. 1843, daughter of 278. the Rev. *John*[6] *Scott* (see THOROWGOOD) and widow of Yelverton Peyton, who married (3), 27 June 1821, John Glassell;[118] 108. Richard Bland[6], born 20 Jan. 1761, "Leesylvania," died 12 March 1827, Washington, D.C.,[119] of Loudoun County, member of the House of Delegates, 1785-87, 1788, 1796, and for Fairfax County, 1799, member of Congress 1789-95, 1825-27, judge of the Orphans Court of the District of Columbia,[120] married, 19 June 1794, Elizabeth Collins who died 24 June 1858 in her 91st year; 109. Mary[6], born 9 July 1764, "Leesylvania," Prince William County, died 10 Nov. 1827, Washington, D.C.,[121] married, Nov. 1791,[122] as his (3) wife, Philip Richard Fendall, born 1734, left will 5 Nov. 1799-3 May 1805,[123] clery of Charles Co., Md., 1756, merchant and attorney, who moved to Alexandria, 1784, was elected first president of the Bank of Alexandria, 1793, and served on the Board of Aldermen, and was a director of

---

[114] *Biographical Directory of the American Congress, 1774-1996* (Alexandria, Va., 1997), p. 1374.

[115] *Maryland Jounral*, Baltimore, 7 Sept. 1790.

[116] *Alexandria Gazette*, 28 July 1829. They were the parents of Gen. Robert E. Lee, Commander-in-Chief of the Armies of the Confederate States of America.

[117] *Alexandria Gazette*, 13 Sept. 1804.

[118] Horace E. Hayden, *Virginia Genealogies* (Wilkes Barre, Pa., 1891), pp. 540, 615, which shows her birth as 30 January.

[119] *National Intelligencer*, Washington, D.C., 13 March 1827; *Alexandria Gazette*, 14 March 1837, which says died 13 March.

[120] *Biographical Directory of the American Congress, 1774-1996* , p. 1376; Leonard, pp. 154, 157, 161, 169, 204, 215.

[121] *National Intelligencer*, 13 Nov. 1827; *Alexandria Gazette*, 13 Nov. 1827.

[122] *The Virginia Gazette and Alexandria Advertiser*, 17 Nov. 1791.

[123] Alexandria Will Bk. B, p. 344.

the Potomac Company;[124] 110. Theodoric[6], born 3 Sept. 1766, died 10 April 1849, "Eckington," near Washington, D.C., married Catherine Hite; 111. Edmund Jennings[6], born 20 May 1772, "Leesylvania," died 30 May 1843, Alexandria,[125] left will 5 April 1843-5 June 1843,[126] married, 23 May 1796,[127] Sarah Lee, born 27 Nov. 1775, "Chantilly," Westmoreland County, died 8 May 1837, Alexandria;[128] 112. Lucy[6], born 1774, died unmarried;[129] 113. Anne[6], born 1776, died Aug. 1857, married, 10 Aug. 1797,[130] William Byrd Page of "Fairfield," Clarke County.

61. LAETITIA[5] LEE (Mary[4] Bland, Richard[3], Theodorick[2], John[1]) died by 5 Nov. 1788,[131] leaving will 16 Oct. 1788-15 Dec. 1788.[132] She married, 1746-47, as his (2) wife, Col. William Ball, of "Millenbeck," Lancaster County, member of the House of Burgesses from Lancaster, 1756-58,[133] who died by 18 Feb. 1765 when his widow was appointed guardian of their daughter Mary.[134]

Issue: [BALL][135] 114. William[6], M.D., of "Millenbeck," left will 17 June 1785-22 July 1785,[136] married Catherine __; 115. Henry Lee[6]; 116. Mary[6], died 1836 in Kentucky,[137] married (1), (bond 12) March 1765,[138] John Ball of Fauquier County who died by 24 May 1773 when the inventory of his estate was

---

[124] T. Michael Miller, "Philip Richard Fendall, Banker, Lawyer, Entrepreneur, 1734-1805," *Alexandria History*, VIII, pp. 16-27.

[125] *Alexandria Gazette*, 1 June 1843.

[126] Alexandria Will Bk. 4, p. 320.

[127] *The Columbian Mirror and Alexandria Gazette*, 26 May 1796.

[128] *Alexandria Gazette*, 10 May 1837.

[129] Perhaps the Lucy who died 29 May 1837 (*Alexandria Gazette*, 25 May 1837).

[130] *The Columbian Mirror and Alexandria Gazette*, 12 Aug. 1797.

[131] *Virginia Independent Chronicle*, Richmond, 5 Nov. 1788.

[132] Lancaster Co. Will Bk. 22, p. 193.

[133] Leonard, pp. 87, 89. On 9 Nov. 1788, having been "by the Grand Jury of Inquests, for the Body of this Colony, in October General Court last, presented for uttering forged and counterfeit Treasury Notes, knowing them to be so," he was judged forever incapable of sitting and voting in the House (*Journals of the House of Burgesses of Virginia, 1758-1761* [Richmond, 1908], p. 50).

[134] Lancaster Co. Will Bk. 17, p. 98.

[135] Hayden, *op. cit.*, pp. 103-05.

[136] Lancaster Co. Will Bk. 22, pp. 86-87.

[137] George Mason Graham Stafford, *General George Mason Graham of Tryone Plantation* ... (Baton Rouge, La., 1947), p. 35.

[138] Stratton Nottingham, *The Marriage License Bonds of Lancaster County, Virginia, From 1701 to 1848* (Onancock, Va., 1927), p. 2.

returned,[139] and (2), (bond 3) April 1774,[140] Reginald Graham, merchant of Dumfries, who died before 3 June 1782 when the inventory of his estate was ordered made,[141] and as a widow moved to Kentucky.

62. ROBERT[5] BEVERLEY (Elizabeth[4] Bland, Richard[3], Theodorick[2], John[1]), born 21 Aug. 1740 at "Blandfield," Essex County, died there 12 April 1800,[142] leaving will 9 March 1793-9th codicil 24 Jan. 1800-21 April 1800.[143] He was educated at Trinity College, Cambridge. He was a justice of Essex County and a Loyalist during the Revolutionary War. Elected to the Virginia Assembly, 1780, he did not serve. Afterward he settled for a time at "Wakefield," Culpeper County, but returned to "Blandfield."[144] He married, 3 Feb. 1763, Maria[7] Carter, daughter of Landon Carter and 64. *Maria[6] Byrd* (see ST. LEGER), born 22 Nov. 1745, "Sabine Hall," Richmond County, died 20 Aug. 1817, Williamsburg.[145]

Issue: [BEVERLEY][146] 117. William[6], born 27 Oct. 1763, "Blandfield," died Sept. 1823, Paris, France, educated at Cambridge University, resided at Beverley, Yorkshire, where he was a merchant, alderman and mayor, married, about 1795, Mary Midgeley; 118. Maria[6], born 15 Dec. 1764, "Blandfield," died 2 Oct. 1824, Williamsburg, married (1), 1 Dec. 1785, Richard Randolph III, died 18 March 1799, Williamsburg, in his 42nd year,[147] who served in the cavalry during the Revolutionary War, and (2), 12 April 1800,[148] Gawin Lane Corbin, born 1778-79, died 3 Nov. 1821, of "King's Creek," York County, member of the House of Delegates, 1808-13,[149] major of Virginia militia in War of 1812 and wounded at Hampton 25 June 1813; 119. Robert[6], born 30 July 1766, "Blandfield," died there 14 Jan. 1767; 120. Robert[6], born 12 March 1769, died

---

[139] Fauquier Co. Will Bk. 1, pp. 211-13, 215-16, 367-68.

[140] Nottingham, *The Marriage License Bonds of Lancaster County*, p. 34.

[141] Prince William Co. Will Bk. G, 1778-91, pp. 299-302.

[142] Beverley-Randolph Bible, *loc. cit.*; *Virginia Gazette and General Advertiser*, Richmond, 18 April 1800.

[143] Essex Co. Will Bk. 15, pp. 343-53.

[144] *Dictionary of Virginia Biography*, I, pp. 73-74.

[145] *Virginia Patriot*, Richmond, 26 Aug. 1817. Beverley-Randolph Bible, *loc. cit.*, gives death as 21 Aug.

[146] Beverley-Randolph Bible, *loc. cit.*

[147] *Virginia Gazette and General Advertiser*, Richmond, 26 March 1799.

[148] Bible, in *V* XXII, p. 98.

[149] Leonard, pp. 254, 263, 268.

May 1823, of "Blandfield," Essex County, justice of Middlesex County, 1795, married, 27 May 1791 at "Mount Airy,"[150] Jane Tayloe, born 25 March 1774, "Mt. Airy," Richmond County, died 10 May 1816 in Essex County;[151] 121. Lucy[6], born 24 Feb. 1771, "Blandfield," died 1854, "Oakleigh," near Greensboro, Ala., married, 21 Nov. 1789, Brett Randolph, born 20 July 1766, "Curles Neck," Henrico County, died 23 Jan. 1828, "Goshen," Lowndes Co., Miss.;[152] 122. Burton[6], born 24 Nov. 1772, "Blandfield," died there 16 July 1781; 123. Carter[6], born 15 April 1774, "Blandfield," died 10 Feb. 1844, married, 24 Jan. 1795, Jane Wormeley, born 29 Feb. 1776, "Rosegill," Middlesex County, died 23 Feb. 1814;[153] 124. Byrd[6], born 17 Aug. 1775, "Blandfield," died at sea, unmarried; 125. James Mills[6], born 22 Dec. 1776, "Blandfield," died there 8 April 1779; 126. Anna Munford[6], born 6 Jan. 1778, "Blandfield," died 7 Oct. 1830, "The Reeds," Caroline County, married, 3 Dec. 1795,[154] Francis Corbin, born 1759, died 28 May 1821 at "The Reeds," aged 62,[155] admitted to the Inner Temple, 23 Jan. 1777, member of the House of Delegates, 1784-95, and of the Virginia Convention of 1788;[156] 127. Munford[6], born 8 March 1779, "Blandfield," lost at sea Feb. 1820; 128. Peter Randolph[6], born 17 Oct. 1780, "Blandfield," lived in Bordeaux, France, and in Yorkshire but returned to Virginia, married Lovely St. Martin, born Santo Domingo, died 4 Feb. 1849 in her 64th year, left will 5 Jan. 1849-23 April 1849;[157] 129. Evelyn Byrd[6], born 6 June 1782, "Blandfield," died 10 Sept. 1836, married (1) George Lee of "Farmwell," Loudoun County, born 1768, died 1805, left will 28 Oct. 1802-11 Feb. 1805,[158] and (2), 26 Dec. 1806, Dr. Patrick Hume Douglas, born about 1760, died 1820, of "Montrossor" and later of "Farmwell," Loudoun County; 130. McKenzie[6], born 3 June 1783, "Blandfield," of Spotsylvania County, married Isabella Gray; 131. Jane

---

[150] *Virginia Gazette and General Advertiser*, Richmond, 1 June 1791.

[151] *Virginia Argus*, Richmond, 22 May 1816.

[152] *Enquirer*, Richmond, 26 Feb. 1828, which gives death as 26 Jan. 1828.

[153] Beverley Bible in *V* XXXVII, pp. 69-70, gives his birth as 17 April 1774, marriage as 25 June 1795, and death as 11 Jan. 1842.

[154] Christ Church Parish, Middlesex County, Register.

[155] *Enquirer*, Richmond, 5 June 1821. *Richmond Daily Mercantile Advertiser*, 25 May 1821, says died 22 May.

[156] Leonard, pp. 154, 157, 161, 165, 169, 173, 176, 170, 184, 188, 192, 196.

[157] Tombstone, Greenwood Cemetery, Tuscaloosa, Ala.; Tuscaloosa Co., Ala., Will Bk. 1, p. 246, in *The Virginia Genealogist*, XXI, p. 19.

[158] Lee, *op. cit.*, p. 318; Loudoun Co. Will Bk. G, p. 301.

Bradshaw[6], born 27 Aug. 1784, "Blandfield," died 23 Feb. 1814, married Thomas Robertson, hardware merchant of Georgetown, D.C.; 132. Harriet[6], born 12 April 1786, "Blandfield," died May 1829, Philadelphia, Pa., married John Bull Rittenhouse, born 1783, left will 2 May 1814-14 June 1814,[159] of Philadelphia and of Washington, D.C., United States consul in the Netherlands.

63. URSULA[5] BEVERLEY (Elizabeth[4] Bland, Richard[3], Theodorick[2], John[1]), born at "Blandfield," married, about 1752-53, as his (1) wife, Col. William Fitzhugh, born 13 April 1725,[160] died 1790, "Marmion," Stafford County,[161] left will 3 March 1789-2 June 1791,[162] son of Maj. John and Anna Barbara (McCarty) Fitzhugh.

Issue: [FITZHUGH][163] 133. William Beverley[6], born 27 March 1756; 134. Daniel[6], born 15 March 1758, of Caroline County, perhaps the Daniel of King George County, aged about 75 in 1832, who was a volunteer aide de camp under Gen. Muhlenburg for six months, 1781, and died 16 Oct. 1836;[164] 135. Theodorick[6], born 20 July 1760.

65. ELIZABETH[5] BEVERLEY (Elizabeth[4] Bland, Richard[3], Theodorick[2], John[1]), born 15 Jan. 1725/6, "Blandfield," married, 21 Aug. 1743, James Mills, born 4 April 1718, left will 3 May 1781-codicil 24 Sept. 1781-28 Jan. 1782,[165] merchant of Urbana, who married (2), Sept. 1771,[166] Elizabeth (Poythress) Boyd.[167]

Issue: [MILLS] 136. John[6], born 31 Aug. 1744, died 13 Sept. 1744; 137. Elizabeth[6], died aged a few hours; 138. Elizabeth[6]; 139. Anna Beverley[6], died in infancy; 140. William[6], died in infancy; 141. James[6], born 10 June 1757, died 31 Aug. 1757.

67. Col. RICHARD[5] BLAND (Richard[4], Richard[3], Theodorick[2], John[1]),

---

[159] Washington, D.C., Will Bk. 1, pp. 416-18.

[160] St. Paul's Parish, King George Co., Register.

[161] *Virginia Gazette and General Advertiser*, Richmond, 8 Sept. 1790.

[162] King George Co. Will Bk. 2, pp. 133-41.

[163] St. Paul's Parish Register. Some of the children of William Fitzhugh (McGill, *op. cit.*, p. 612) cannot be identified as to which wife was their mother.

[164] Revolutionary War pension application, Daniel Fitzhugh, S.8474, National Archives.

[165] Middlesex Co. Will Bk. F, 1772-87, pp. 215-18.

[166] *Virginia Gazette* (Purdie & Dixon), 14 Nov. 1771.

[167] John Frederick Dorman, *Ancestors and Descendants of Francis Epes I of Virginia*, I (n.p., 1992), pp. 208-09.

born 20 Feb. 1730/1, died 25 Jan. 1786,[168] resided at "Jordan's," Prince George County. He married, 8 Oct. 1761, 31. *Mary*[6] *Bolling* (see ROLFE), born 16 July 1744, died after 18 Jan. 1791.[169]

Issue: 142. Richard[6], born 23 July 1762, died 26 March 1806, qualified as sheriff of Prince George County two months before his death,[170] married, 24 Dec. 1787,[171] 367. *Susannah*[6] *Poythress* (see BALEY-COCKE); 143. Anne Poythress[6], born 1765, married (1) 146. John[6] Morrison and (2), by 14 March 1793[172] 25. *Peter*[6] *Woodlief* (see WOODLIFFE); 144. John[6], born 1767, died 1777; 145. Elizabeth Blair[6], born 1770, married 365. *William*[6] *Poythress* (see BALEY-COCKE).

69. ANNE[5] BLAND (Richard[4], Richard[3], Theodorick[2], John[1]), born 15 Aug. 1735, died before 19 Feb. 1782 when the inventory of her estate was made.[173] She married Alexander Morrison of Ward's Creek, Prince George County.

Issue: [MORRISON][174] 146. John[6], died March 1790,[175] left will 19 April 1785-10 Aug. 1790,[176] clerk of Prince George County, married 143. Anne Poythress[6] Bland; 147. Alexander[6], left will 6 Feb. 1839-6 Jan.1840,[177] of Jackson Co., Ga., married Mary Ann __, who survived him; 148. Theodorick[6], married ____; 149. David[6]; 150. William[6], married Anne ____; 151. Jane[6], married, 27 June 1789,[178] John Green; 152. Elizabeth[6], married 157. Peter Bland; 153. Patience[6], married, 9 Dec. 1786,[179] William Epes; 154. Sarah[6], married 435. *Thomas Bowler*[6] *Adams* (see BALEY-COCKE); 155. Anne[6], married, 6 Dec.

---

[168] *Virginia Gazette and General Advertiser*, Richmond, 28 Jan. 1786.

[169] Prince George Co. Deed Bk. 1787-92, p. 512.

[170] *Virginia Genealogical Society Quarterly*, XIV, p. 120.

[171] *Virginia Gazette and Independent Chronicle*, Richmond, 29 Dec. 1787; The Rev. John Cameron, Register.

[172] Chesterfield Co. Order Bk. 10, p. 53.

[173] Prince George Co. Deed Bk. 1787-92, p. 255.

[174] Prince George Co. Execution Bk. 1801-03, pp. 4, 34, Feb.-March 1801 The listing of defendants entered here names the wives of both John Green and Peter Bland as Anne, amd the wife of William Epes as Palmer. *Ibid.*, p. 100, Feb. 1803, states the (1) wife of. William Epes, by then deceased, was named Patience rather than Palmer

[175] *Virginia Gazette and Petersburg Intelligencer*, 18 March 1790, died "last week."

[176] Prince George Co. Deed Bk. 1787-92, p. 403.

[177] Jackson Co., Ga., Will Bk. A, p. 239.

[178] The Rev. John Cameron's Register.

[179] *Ibid.*

1788,[180] William Harrison..

70. PETER RANDOLPH[5] BLAND (Richard[4], Richard[3], Theodorick[2], John[1]), born 2 Feb. 1736/7, died 16 Feb. 1781, leaving will dated 14 Sept. 1779.[181] He resided in Amelia County and as vestryman of Nottoway Parish took the oath to the government, 27 June 1780.[182] He married, (bond 26) Nov. 1761,[183] Judith Booker, probably daughter of Edward and Judith (Archer) Booker, and died before 3 Dec. 1807 when Peter Bland qualified as her administrator.[184]

Issue:[185] 156. Richard[5], left will 4 April 1807-6 June 1807,[186] married Elizabeth Ridley[7] Dickins, daughter of 79. *Mary*[6] (*Browne*) *Dickins* (see BENNETT, Edward); 157. Peter[6], attorney of Nottoway County, married 152. Elizabeth[6] Morrison; 158. Edward[6], born 8 Aug. 1767, died 10 Nov. 1831,[187] left will 30 Oct. 1831-1 Dec. 1831,[188] married (1), (bond 7) March 1786,[189] 134. *Lettice*[6] (*Greenhill*) *Jones* (see CLAIBORNE), who died by 1795,[190] and (2), 29 June 1808,[191] Rebecca[7] Jones, daughter of 52. *Batte*[6] *Jones* (see PRICE-LLEWELLYN), born 30 Oct. 1791, died 26 Sept. 1841,[192] left will 8 Aug. 1840-7 Oct. 1841;[193] 159. Ann[6], left will 4 Sept. 1806-June 1807.[194]

71. JOHN[5] BLAND (Richard[4], Richard[3], Theodorick[2], John[1]), born 19 Oct. 1739, died before 27 March 1777 when his widow was granted administration on his estate.[195] He married Clara Yates, who died Aug. 1832 in Brunswick

---

[180] *Ibid.*
[181] Amelia Co. Will Bk. 3, p. 181, without probate date.
[182] Amelia Co. Order Bk. 15, 1780-82, p. 4.
[183] Kathleen Booth Williams, *Marriages of Amelia County, Virginia, 1735-1815* (n.p., 1961), p. 12.
[184] Nottoway Co. Order Bk. 5, p. 277.
[185] Amelia Co. Will Bk. 4, pp. 38-40, division of estate of Peter Randolph Bland.
[186] Nottoway Co. Will Bk. 2, pp. 350-51.
[187] Edward Bland Bible, in Evelyn Pierson Georgens, "Bible Records" (John Alexander Chapter DAR; n.p., 1977), pp. 71-72.
[188] Nottoway Co. Will Bk. 6, p. 257.
[189] Williams, *loc. cit.*
[190] Amelia Co. Order Bk. 20, p. 459.
[191] The Rev. John Cameron, Register.
[192] Edward Bland Bible, *loc. cit.*
[193] Nottoway Co. Will Bk. 8, p. 40.
[194] Nottoway Co. Will Bk. 8, pp. 351-52,
[195] Amelia Co. Order Bk. 14, 1776-80, p. 24.

County,[196] daughter of the Rev. William Yates and [his step-mother] Elizabeth Randolph, who married (2), (bond 16) Dec. 1779,[197] Robert Bolling

Issue: 160. Richard Yates[6], born about 1770,[198] died after 2 Aug. 1851,[199] sheriff of Nottoway County, 1827, married Ann Booth, daughter of Gilliam and Martha (____) Booth, born about 1772, who survived him and died 23 May 1853, aged 83;[200] 161. Thomas[6].

73. WILLIAM[5] BLAND (Richard[4], Richard[3], Theodorick[2], John[1]), born 26 Dec. 1742, left will 6 July 1794-24 Oct. 1803.[201] He was a student at the College of William and Mary, 1758-63, ordained priest of Church of England and licensed for Virginia, 24 June 1767, minister of James City Parish to about 1777, and chaplain of the First Virginia Regiment, 1776. He represented Warwick Parish in the church convention of 1785 and Elizabeth City Parish in 1786. His claim to be rector of St. Paul's Parish, Norfolk, was not sustained by the convention, 1789-90, but he continued to preach there until deposed from the ministry by Bishop James Madison, 1794,[202] and made Norfolk his home until his death. He married (1) Elizabeth Yates, died 1772,[203] and (2), 21 June 1773,[204] 20. Ann[5] (*Harwood*) *Wills* (see HARWOOD) of Warwick County, who left will 18 Feb. 1817-26 June 1818.[205]

Issue: (by 1) 162. Anne[6], married 287. *Richard[6] Pryor* (see ROYALL); (by 2) 163. William H.[6], who, aged 19, son of William Bland of Norfolk, absconded from the service of Hillary Butt, 20 Nov. 1794,[206] mentioned as living, 17 Nov. 1801, when his father gave security for money due him;[207] 164. Edward[6]; 165. Theodorick[6], died before 1817, married (1), (bond 4) Nov. 1803,[208] Sarah

---

[196] Revolutionary War pension application, Robert Bolling, widow Clara, R.19363, Virginia Half Pay, National Archives.

[197] Williams, *loc. cit.*

[198] Dinwiddie Co. 1850 census, Southern Dist., p. 985 or 493, family 374-376.

[199] Deposition, Revolutionary War pension application, Robert Bolling, *loc. cit.*

[200] Virginia Dept. of Vital Statistics, Dinwiddie County, Deaths.

[201] Norfolk City Will Bk. 2, pp. 178-79.

[202] *V* XLI, pp. 124-25.

[203] *Virginia Gazette* (Rind), 17 Dec. 1772.

[204] *Ibid.*, 24 June 1773.

[205] Norfolk City Will Bk. 3, pp. 282-84.

[206] *Virginia Chronicle and General Advertiser*, Norfolk, 27 Nov. 1794.

[207] Norfolk City Deed Bk. 7, pp. 449-51.

[208] George Herbert Tucker, *Abstracts from Norfolk City Marriage Bonds (1797-1850)* (n.p., 1934), p. 20.

Lawson and (2) Ann ___.

75. EDWARD⁵ BLAND (Richard⁴, Richard³, Theodorick², John¹), born 16 Dec. 1746, died about 1797.²⁰⁹ He resided in Prince George County and was captain of militia, 1775.²¹⁰ He married Elizabeth Cooke.

Issue:²¹¹ 166. (perhaps) Edward⁶.

76. SARAH⁵ BLAND (Richard⁴, Richard³, Theodorick², John¹), born 19 [or 30] Sept. 1750, died 13 May 1807.²¹² She married, 18 June 1767, 208. Col. *Robert⁶ Goode* (see BRANCH), born 8 Feb. 1743[/4?],²¹³ died 20 April 1809.²¹⁴ He resided at "Whitby," Chesterfield County, and was major and colonel of Chesterfield County militia during the Revolutionary War and a member of the Virginia Council, 1790-97.

Issue: [GOODE]²¹⁵ 167. Robert⁶, born 9 March 1769, died 22 Nov. 1788; 168. Richard Bland⁶, born 7 Dec. 1770, died 28 July 1812, graduated from the College of William and Mary, 1794, married, 10 Dec. 1796, 1084. *Sally Hughes⁶ Woodson* (see WOODSON); 169. Francis⁶, born 5 May 1773, "Whitby," Chesterfield County, died 13 Jan. 1815, of "Post Oak," Powhatan County, married, 28 Oct. 1795,²¹⁶ Martha Hartwell⁷ Hughes, died 5 July 1825, Powhatan County,²¹⁷ daughter of Robert Hughes and 530. *Mary⁶ Mosby* (see WOODSON); 170. Theodorick Bland⁶, born 12 Dec. 1774, died 3 May 1810;²¹⁸ 171. Mary⁶, born 25 July 1776, died 21 July 1847, married, 28 Oct. 1805,²¹⁹

---

²⁰⁹ Prince George Co. Land tax list, 1797, estate taxed. In Dec. 1802 Edward Bland was referred to as his administrator (Prince George Co. Execution Bk. 1801-03, pt. 2, p. 93).

²¹⁰ Revolutionary War pension application, Abram Alley, S.11955, National Archives.

²¹¹ Bland, *op. cit.*, 165, lists his children as Louisa (married Robert Harrison) and John (married [1], 18 Sept. 1814, Mary B. Perkinson and [2] ___ Jones) but chronology suggests they were children of a younger Edward..

²¹² *Virginia Gazette and General Advertiser*, Richmond, 27 May 1807.

²¹³ George Brown Goode, *Virginia Cousins* (Richmond, 1887), pp. 42, 55. His father's will,, written 8 Sept. 1765, however, indicates he was then under age.

²¹⁴ *Virginia Gazette and General Advertiser*, Richmond, 25 April 1809; *The Visitor*, Richmond, 6 May 1809.

²¹⁵ Goode, *op. cit.*, pp. 55, 115, 118-19.

²¹⁶ Catherine Lindsay Knorr, *Marriage Bonds and Ministers' Returns of Powhatan County, Virginia, 1777-1830* (Pine Bluff, Ark., 1957), p. 26, bond 26 October.

²¹⁷ *Enquirer*, Richmond, 19 July 1825.

²¹⁸ *The Visitor*, Richmond, 13 May 1810.

²¹⁹ Catherine Lindsay Knorr, *Marriage Bonds and Ministers' Returns of Chesterfield County, Virginia, 1771-1815* (Pine Bluff, Ark., 1958), p. 112, consent dated 5 Oct. 1795 [*sic*].

John[7] Spotswood, son of 102. *John[6] Spotswood* (see WEST), of "Orange Grove," Orange County; 172. Sally Bland[6], born 5 Aug. 1779, died 30 Jan. 1816,[220] married (1), 18 June 1796,[221] James Lyle, Jr., merchant of Manchester who died 29 July 1806,[222] and (2), 24 Dec. 1807,[223] Tarleton Saunders of Richmond and of "Whitby"; 173. Martha Currie[6], born 22 Feb. 1787, died 1 May 1814,[224] married, 26 July 1804,[225] James Scott, born Roxboroughshire, Scotland, about 1775, who settled at Manchester, 1798, as agent for the firm of Irwin and Sons of Glasgow and engaged in the export of tobacco; 174. Thomas[6], born 4 Jan. 1789, died young.

79. ROBERT[5] MUNFORD (Anna[4] Bland, Richard[3], Theodorick[2], John[1]), aged about 8 at his father's death, 1743,[226] left will 16 Dec. 1783-8 Feb. 1784.[227] He was educated at the Academy in Leeds, England, was captain in the French and Indian War, 1758, County Lieutenant of Mecklenburg County, 1765-84, and member of the House of Burgesses, 1765-75, of the first Convention, 1774, and of the House of Delegates, 1779-81.[228] He married 66. Anna[5] Beverley.

Issue: [MUNFORD][229] 175. Elizabeth Beverley[6], born 28 March 1762, married, (bond 16) May 1780,[230] Richard Kennon, died 1805, aged 44, left will 4 Feb. 1805-8 April 1805,[231] of "Firewood," Mecklenburg County, lieutenant of 5th Virginia Regiment in the Revolutionary War, County Lieutenant of Mecklenburg County, 1789, brigadier general of Virginia militia, member of the Convention 1788, the House of Delegates, 1788-90, 1792, and of the Virginia Senate, 1798-1801 (Speaker 1801),[232] appointed Governor of Louisiana;[233] 176.

---

[220] *Virginia Patriot*, Richmond, 31 Jan. 1816.

[221] Knorr, *Marriage Bonds ... Chesterfield County*, p. 79, consent 10 June; *Virginia Gazette and Richmond and Manchester Advertiser*, 22 June 1796.

[222] *Virginia Gazette and General Advertiser*, Richmond, 2 Aug. 1806.

[223] Knorr, *Marriage Bonds ... Chesterfield County*, p. 107, bond 14 December.

[224] *Enquirer*, Richmond, 7 May 1814.

[225] Knorr, *Marriage Bonds ... Chesterfield County*, p. 107, bond 9 July.

[226] Washington, *loc. cit.*

[227] Mecklenburg Co. Will Bk.E, p. 45.

[228] Leonard, pp. 92, 95, 98, 100, 103, 106, 110, 134, 138.

[229] McGill, *op. cit.*, p. 616.

[230] Katherine B. Elliott, *Marriage Records, 1765-1810, Mecklenburg County, Virginia* (South Hill, Va., 1963), p. 77.

[231] Mecklenburg Co. Will Bk.5 , p. 227-30.

[232] Leonard, pp. 169, 173, 176, 180, 188, 213, 217, 222, 225.

[233] *W*(1) XIV, p. 125.

Ursula Anne⁶, died 21 Aug. 1844, aged 78, as widow resided in Campbell County, married, 6 April 1781 in Mecklenburg County, Francis Otway⁷ Byrd, born 8 May 1756, died 2 Sept. 1800, son of 65. *William⁶ Byrd* III (see ST. LEGER), midshipman in the British navy until he resigned, 1775, lieutenant colonel of 3rd Virginia Light Dragoons in Revolutionary War, sheriff of Charles City County, 1786-87, clerk of that county, 1790-97, collector of the port of Norfolk, 1804;[234] 177. William⁶, born 15 Aug. 1775, Mecklenburg County, died 21 June 1825, Richmond,[235] studied law at College of William and Mary, 1790-94, member of the House of Delegates from Mecklenburg County, 1797-98, 1800-02, and of the Senate, 1802-06,[236] moved to Richmond where he was a member of the Privy Council until 1811, then clerk of the House of Delegates, 1811-25,[237] and reporter for the Virginia Court of Appeals, married, 27 Feb. 1802,[238] Sarah⁷ Radford, born 1785, died 1864, daughter of William Radford and 431. *Rebecca⁶ Winston* (see JORDAN, Thomas).

80. Capt. THEODORICK⁵ MUNFORD (Anna⁴ Bland, Richard³, Theodorick², John¹), born 21 Feb. 1741/2,[239] died Oct. 1772 at Col. John Banister's in Dinwiddie County.[240] He was a student at the grammar school of the College of William and Mary, 1753-54. He married ___.

Issue: [MUNFORD][241] 178. Frances Moseley⁶, married (1), as his (2) wife, 356. *John⁶ Boush* (see MASON) and (2), 17 April 1793,[242] Conway Whittle, merchant of Norfolk.

81. ELIZABETH⁵ MUNFORD (Anna⁴ Bland, Richard³, Theodorick², John¹), born 22 Sept. 1734,[243] married the Rev. Archibald McRobert, born 20 Sept. 1736, died 8 Oct. 1807, Providence, Prince Edward County,[244] left undated

---

[234] Revolutionary War pension application, Francis Otway Byrd, widow Anna, W.6219, National Archives.

[235] *Enquirer*, Richmond, 24 June 1825.

[236] Leonard, pp. 208, 220, 224, 230, 233, 237, 242.

[237] *Ibid.*, pp. 265, 269, 273, 277, 281, 285, 289, 293, 298, 303, 308, 318, 323.

[238] *Virginia Argus*, Richmond, 2 March 1802.

[239] Bristol Parish Register.

[240] *Virginia Gazette*, 19 Nov. 1772.

[241] U.S. District Court, Richmond, Record Bk. 7G, p. 115.

[242] *Virginia Chronicle and Norfolk and Portsmouth Advertiser*, 20 April 1798.

[243] Bristol Parish Register.

[244] *Virginia Argus*, Richmond, 16 Oct. 1807. *Dixon's Observatory* Richmond, 11 Oct. 1798, reported his death.

will proved 21 Dec. 1807.[245] He was licensed for Virginia, 25 Feb. 1761, and was minister of Dale Parish, Chesterfield County, 1773-75, chairman of the Committee of Safety of Chesterfield County, minister of St. Patrick's Parish, Prince Edward County, 1776-79, and later organized a dissenting body and then joined the Presbyterian Church and was trustee of Hampden-Sydney College, 1783.[246]

Issue: [McROBERT] 179. Elizabeth[6], married, 11 Jan. 1798,[247] Samuel Carter; 180. Theodorick B.[6], attorney of Prince Edward County and later of Pittsylvania County, commonwealth attorney, 1795-99, member of House of Delegates, 1799-1800,[248] married, 18 Oct. 1792,[249] 1002. *Agnes Woodson[6] Morton* (see WOODSON), born 13 Sept. 1776;[250] 181. Ebenezer M.[6], died before 22 Feb. 1817 when the inventory of his estate was made,[251] graduate of Hampden-Sydney College, A.B., 1786, of Prince Edward County, married (1), (bond 1) Jan. 1794,[252] Mary Foster and (2), (bond 26) March 1804,[253] Henrietta Maria[7] (Anderson) Feild, daughter of 469. *Sarah[6] (Clarke) Anderson* (see EPES) and widow of James Feild.

83. MARGARET[5] CURRIE (Anna[4] Bland, Richard[3], Theodorick[2], John[1]) left will 19 Aug. 1777-10 Jan. 1792.[254] She married (1) ____ Fawn and (2), (articles 26) Aug. 1775 in Prince George County, Thomas Armistead of Petersburg, who married (2) Juliana ____.

Issue: (by 1) [FAWN] 182. Capt. John Harrison[6], mariner, member of the firm of Theodorick Armistead & Co. and at one time U.S. naval agent at

---

[245] Prince Edward Co. Will Bk. 1, p. 91.

[246] Edward Lewis Goodwin, *The Colonial Church in Virginia* (London, 1928), p. 280; Herbert Clarence Bradshaw, *History of Prince Edward County, Virginia* (Richmond, 1955), pp. 239, 739 *et passim*.

[247] Catherine Lindsay Knorr, *Marriage Bonds and Ministers' Returns of Prince Edward County, Virginia, 1754-1810* (Pine Bluff, Ark., 1950), p. 14.

[248] Leonard, p. 216.

[249] Knorr, *op. cit.*, p. 51.

[250] Henry Morton Woodson, *Historical Genealogy of the Woodsons and Their Connections* (Memphis, 1915), p. 97.

[251] Prince Edward Co. Will Bk. 5, pp. 157-58.

[252] Knorr, *Marriage Bonds ... Prince Edward County*, p. 51.

[253] Augusta B. Fothergill, *Marriage Records of Brunswick County, Virginia, 1730-1852* (n.p., 1953), p. 72.

[254] Prince George Co. Deed Bk. 1787-92, p. 629.

Norfolk, died 17 Jan. 1818 at Jerusalem;[255] (by 2) [ARMISTEAD] 183. Ann Currie[6], died 7 July 1798 near Petersburg in a carriage accident,[256] unmarried; 184. Theodorick[6], born 1777 at Petersburg, died 20 Nov. 1812,[257] left will 10 Nov. 1812-28 Dec. 1812[258] navy agent of the United States at Norfolk, 1812, married, (bond 18) June 1801,[259] Martha T.[7] Newton, daughter of 328. *Thomas[6] Newton* (see MASON), who died in Aug. 1810;[260] 185. Robert Munford[6], of Norfolk, married, 28 April 1804,[261] Ann Lee; 186. Thomas[6], died 20 May 1813 at Norfolk,[262] merchant of Norfolk, married (1) Maria Allison, died Nov. 1805,[263] and (2), 20 March 1810 at Norfolk,[264] Priscilla M. Armistead, died July 1814.[265]

84. ELIZABETH[5] BLAND (Theodorick[4], Richard[3], Theodorick[2], John[1]), born 4 Jan. 1739/40, died 1777,[266] married, as his (2) wife, John Banister, of "Battersea," Dinwiddie County, colonel in Revolutionary War, member of Congress, who was born 26 Dec. 1734, died 30 Sept. 1788 near Petersburg[267] and left will 9 Jan. 1788-20 Oct. 1788.[268]

Issue: [BANISTER] 187. Robert[6]; 188. Wilamatha[6]; 189. (Child)[6].

85. THEODORICK[5] BLAND (Theodorick[4], Richard[3], Theodorick[2], John[1]),

---

[255] *Norfolk Herald*, 28 Jan. 1818. *Raleigh Minerva*, 20 Feb. 1818, gives place of death as near Edenton, N.C.

[256] *Norfolk Herald*, 14 July 1798.

[257] *W*(1) VII, p. 183; *Norfolk Gazette and Public Ledger*, 23 Nov. 1812; *Baltimore Federal Gazette*, 30 Nov. 1812.

[258] Norfolk, Va., Will Bk. 3, pp. 82-83.

[259] Tucker, *op. cit.*, p. 12.

[260] *Norfolk Gazette and Public Ledger*, 15 Aug. 1810.

[261] Tucker, *op. cit.*, p. 21.

[262] *Norfolk Gazette and Public Ledger.*, 22 May 1813; *Raleigh Register*, 28 May 1813.

[263] *Ibid.*, 8 Nov. 1805.

[264] *V* XXXIV, p. 263.

[265] *Norfolk Gazette and Public Ledger*, 27 July 1814.

[266] *Virginia Gazette* (Purdie), 11 July 1777.

[267] *Dictionary of Virginia Biography*, I (Richmond,. 1998), pp. 315-16; *Virginia Gazette and Weekly Advertiser*, Richmond, 16 Oct. 1788.

[268] Land Office Survey Bk. 30, pp. 131-35, in Willie Graham and Mark R. Wenger, "Battersea: A Historical and Architectural Study" (typewritten; n.p., 1988), Appendix IV. William Armstrong Crozier, *Williamsburg Wills* (*Virginia County Records*, III; New York, 1906), p. 6, gives dates.only.

born 21 March 1741/2, died 2 June 1790 at New York,[269] leaving will 5 Nov. 1789-12 Aug. 1790.[270] He was educated in England and graduated M.D. at Edinburgh. Returning to Virginia, 1759, he resided at "Cawsons," Prince George County, was vestryman of Bristol Parish, colonel of cavalry in Revolutionary War, and commander of the Convention troops at Charlottesville. He was a member of the Continental Congress, 1780-83, of the House of Delegates, 1786-88, in the Virginia Convention of 1788 opposed ratification of the federal constitution, and served as a member of Congress, 1789 until his death.[271]

He married Martha Daingerfield, died 1804 in France,[272] who married (2), (marriage agreement 4) Oct. 1791,[273] Nathan Blodget of Dinwiddie County and (3) ___ Corran, a sea captain with whom she went to France.

Issue: 190. (Child)[6], died young.

86. MARY[5] BLAND (Theodorick[4], Richard[3], Theodorick[2], John[1]), born 22 Aug. 1745, married, as his (1) wife, William Ruffin of "Rich Neck," Surry County, who married (2) 157. *Lucy[5] Cocke* (see BALEY-COCKE) and left will 1 May 1773-26 April 1774.[274]

Issue: [RUFFIN] 191. Theodorick Bland[6], married, (bond 14) Jan. 1788,[275] Susan Murray, named in the will of William Browne, 14 Nov. 1799-24 Aug. 1799.[276]

87. ANNA[5] BLAND (Theodorick[4], Richard[3], Theodorick[2], John[1]) married, about 1761, as his (1) wife, Gen. Thomas Eaton, son of William and Mary (Rives) Eaton, who was born about 1739, died June 1809, and left will 30 April 1807-Aug. 1809.[277] He represented Bute Co., N.C., in the North Carolina

---

[269] *Maryland Journal*, Baltimore, 8 June 1790; *Virginia Gazette and Alexandria Advertiser*, 10 June 1790; *Virginia Independent Chronicle*, Richmond, 16 June 1790; *Virginia Gazette and Weekly Advertiser*, Richmond, 19 June 1790. Buried Trinity Church, New York City.

[270] Prince George Co. Deed Bk. 1787-92, p. 404.

[271] *Dictionary of Virginia Biography*, II, pp. 14-16; Leonard, pp. 162, 166, 170, 174.

[272] Slaughter, *op. cit.*, p. 158; *Biographical Directory of the American Congress, 1774-1996* (Alexandria, Va., 1997), p. 672; *Dictionary of American Biography*, II (New York, 1929), pp. 356-57.

[273] Prince George Co. Deed Bk. 1787-92, p. 632; Legislative petition, 25 Oct. 1793, in *Virginia Genealogical Society Quarterly*, XIV, p. 19.

[274] Surry Co. Will Bk. 10A, p. 351.

[275] Elliott, *op. cit.*, p. 108.

[276] Surry Co. Will Bk. 1, p. 361.

[277] Warren Co., N.C., Will Bk. 10, p. 85.

Assembly, 1769-71, was appointed colonel of the Bute County militia, 1771, and brigadier general, 1781, was a member of the Provincial Council, 1775-76, of the provincial congresses, 1775-76, and of the Council of Safety, 1776, and resided in Warren Co., N.C., at Eaton's Ferry on Roanoke River.[278]

Issue: [EATON] 192. Anna Bland[6], born 21 Nov. 1763 in Prince George County, married, 23 May 1784 at Halifax, N.C., Guilford Dudley, born 17 April 1756 in Caroline County, died 3 Feb. 1833, who organized the first volunteer company at Halifax, N.C., 1774, served under Gen. Greene at Guilford, N.C., 1781, as major, was later lieutenant colonel, moved to Franklin, Williamson Co., Tenn.[279]

89. FRANCES[5] BLAND (Theodorick[4], Richard[3], Theodorick[2], John[1]), born 24 Sept. 1752, "Kippax," Prince George County, died 18 Jan. 1788, "Matoax," Chesterfield County,[280] left will proved 13 March 1788.[281] She married (1), 9 March 1769, 20. *John[6] Randolph* (see ROLFE), born 26 [29?] June 1742, "Curles," Henrico County, died 28 Oct. 1775, "Mattoax," Chesterfield County,[282] left will 25 July 1775-codicil 23 Oct. 1775-3 Nov. 1775,[283] and (2), 23 [22?] Sept. 1778, as his (1) wife, St. George Tucker, born 10 July 1752, Port Royal, Bermuda, died 10 Nov. 1827, "Edgewood," Nelson County, who came to Virginia, 1771. As a student at the College of William and Mary, he studied law under George Wythe, then returned to Bermuda, 1775, and again came to Virginia, 1776, with a cargo of salt for the government, having previously been concerned in the seizure of powder in Fort St. George, Bermuda. He was employed by Virginia to ship indigo from Charleston, S.C., to the West Indies for the purchase of arms and ammunition, was aide-de-camp to Gen. Nelson, 1779, major of militia, Feb. 1781, was wounded at Guilford Court House, N.C., March 1781, lieutenant colonel, Sept. 1781, was present at Yorktown, and was a member of the Council of State, 1781, and of the Annapolis Convention, 1786-87, judge of the General Court of Virginia, 1788-1804, professor of law

---

[278] *Dictionary of North Carolina Biography*, II (Chapel Hill and London, 1986), p. 131.

[279] Revolutionary War pension application, Guilford Dudley, widow Anna Bland, W.8681, National Archives; "A Sketch of the Military Services performed by Guilford Dudley, then of the Town of Halifax, North Carolina, during the Revolutionary War," *The Southern Literary Messenger*, XI (1845), pp. 144-48, 231-35, 281-87, 370-75.

[280] Tombstone, "Matoax," in *W*(1) VIII, p. 180.

[281] Chesterfield Co. Order Bk. 8, p. 44. The will is not of record.

[282] Tombstone, "Matoax," *loc. cit.*

[283] Chesterfield Co. Will Bk. 2, p. 328; Order Bk. 6, p. 90.

at the College of William and Mary, 1790-1804, president and judge of the High Court of Appeals, 1804-13, and judge of the United States District Court for Virginia, 1813-14.[284]

Issue: (by 1) [RANDOLPH][285] 193. Richard[6], born 9 March 1770, died 14 June 1796, left will 18 Feb. [1796]-8 April 1797,[286] married, 31 Dec. 1789, Judith Randolph; 194. Theodorick Bland[6], born 22 Jan. 1771, died 14 Feb. 1792; 195. John[6], of "Roanoke," Charlotte County, born 3 [2?] June 1773, died 24 May 1833, Philadelphia, Pa., student at the College of New Jersey and Columbia College, New York, member of Congress, 1799-1813, 1819-25, 1827-29, 1833, United States Senator, 1825-27, and minister to Russia, 1830;[287] (by 2) [TUCKER] 196. Ann Frances Bland[6], born 26 Sept. 1779, "Mattoax," died 12 Sept. 1813, Red Sulphur Springs, W.Va., married, 5 June 1802, as his (3) wife, John Coalter, born 20 Aug. 1769, Rockbridge County, died 2 Feb. 1838, "Chatham," Stafford County, of Augusta County, Richmond, and "Chatham," judge of the Virginia Court of Appeals;[288] 197. Henry St. George[6], born 29 Dec. 1780 at "Mattoax," died 28 Aug. 1848, Winchester, graduate of the College of William and Mary, 1798, captain of cavalry in the War of 1812, member of the House of Delegates, 1807-08, of Congress, 1815-19, and of the Virginia Senate, 1819-23, Chancellor of the Fourth Judicial Circuit, 1824-31, president of the

---

[284] *Dictionary of American Biography*, XIX (New York, 1936), pp. 38=39; *V* XLII, pp. 211-21, letter of St. George Tucker, 27 Oct. 1813. Her obituary in *Virginia Independent Chronicle*, Richmond, 30 Jan. 1788; his obituary in *Enquirer*, Richmond, 20 Nov. 1827, says he died at Warminster.

[285] Wyndham Robertson, *Pocahontas, Alias Matoaka, and her Descendants* (Richmond, 1887), p. 37; Stuart E. Brown and others, *Pocahontas' Descendants* (n.p., 1985), p. 126, which also lists another child Jane[6].

[286] Prince Edward Co. District Court Will Bk. 1, p. 4; *V* XXXIV, pp. 73-76.

[287] *Biographical Directory of the American Congress, 1774-1996* (Alexandria, Va., 1997), pp. 1705-06; *Dictionary of American Biography*, V (New York, 1935), pp. 363-67; William Cabell Bruce, *John Randolph of Roanoke, 1773-1833* (2 v.; New York and London, 1922). For discussion of his several wills, including that dated 1 Jan. 1832 which was admitted to probate by the General Court but on appeal was declared invalid, see Peachy R. Grattan, *Report of Cases Decided in the Superior Court of Appeals and in the General Court of Virginia*, I (Richmond, 1860), pp. 29-38.

[288] Coalter Bible, in Hayden, *op. cit.*, p. 214; his tombstone, in Catherine Lindsay Knorr, *Marriage Bonds and Ministers' Returns of Fredericksburg, Virginia, 1782-1850, Also Tombstone Inscriptions from St. George Cemetery, 1782-1920* (Pine Bluff, Ark., 1954), pp. 69-70.

Court of Appeals, 1831-41, professor of law at the University of Virginia, 1841-45, and author of the 1842 honor system for students there, and president of the Virginia Historical Society, and author of *Commentaries on the Laws of Virginia* (2 v.; 1836-37)[289] married, 23 Sept. 1806, Ann Evalina Hunter; 198. Theodorick Tudor[6], born 17 Sept. 1782, died 3 April 1795; 199. Nathaniel Beverley[6], born 6 Sept. 1784 at "Mattoax," died 26 Aug. 1851 at Winchester, lieutenant in the War of 1812, moved to Missouri, was instrumental in the formation of Jefferson Co., Mo., and later resident of Saline Co., Mo., and judge of the circuit court, returned to Virginia, 1833-34, professor at the College of William and Mary where he was a proponent of the doctrine of state sovereignty, novelist and author of works on political economy,[290] married (1) Mary Coalter who died in Missouri, (2) Eliza Taylor and (3), 13 April 1830, Lucy Ann Smith, born 1812, died 1867; 200. Henrietta Eliza[6], born 16 Dec. 1787, died July 1796.

90. JOHN[5] BLAND (John[4], John[3], Theodorick[2], John[1]), born 8 Dec. 1741 at Scarborough, Yorkshire, died Dec. 1794.[291] He was a merchant of Prince George County.[292] He married, 23 April 1791,[293] Mary Long.

Issue:[294] 201. Anna Buck[6], born 12 March 1792,[295] died 26 March 1832,[296] named in the will of Elizabeth (Randolph) Yates Bland, married, 9 Feb. 1809,[297] Henry J. Harrison of Sussex County; 202. Harriet[6], married Jonas Wood, Jr.

91. THOMAS[5] BLAND (John[4], John[3], Theodorick[2], John[1]), born 6 Dec. 1742 at Scarborough, died 1 June 1807 at Sheffield, Yorks., was a merchant at Sheffield. He married Ann Broadbent.

Issue: 203. Thomas Broadbent[6], in 1805 resident in Baltimore, Md.[298]

94. THEODORICK[5] BLAND (John[4], John[3], Theodorick[2], John[1]), born 21 Sept. 1746 at Scarborough, resided at Williamsburg and on the surrender of the

---

[289] *Dictionary of American Biography*, XIX, pp. 32-33; *Biographical Directory of the American Congress*, 1774-1996 (Alexandria, Va., 1997), p. 1966.

[290] *Dictionary of American Biography*, XIX, pp. 36-37.

[291] Bristol Parish Register.

[292] Bland's heirs *vs.* Woodlief, Brunswick Co. judgments, 1822, in *The Southside Virginian*, VI, p. 3.

[293] The Rev. John Cameron's Register.

[294] Bland's heirs *vs.* Woodlief, *The Southside Virginian*, VI, p. 13.

[295] Bristol Parish Register.

[296] *Enquirer*, Richmond, 6 April 1832.

[297] *Visitor*, Richmond, 11 Feb. 1809.

[298] Bland Papers, Maryland Historical Society.

British at Yorktown escaped to New York.[299] He died in King George County many years before 1800.[300] He married, 5 Dec. 1772,[301] Sarah Fitzhugh, born 12 Aug. 1748, died 1793.

Issue: 204. John[6], born 1 April 1774;[302] 205. Theodorick[6], died 16 Nov. 1846,[303] attorney of Baltimore, Md., commissioned judge of the 6th Judicial District of Maryland, 28 July 1811, and of the United States District Court for Maryland, 23 Nov. 1819,[304] and at his death Chancellor of the State of Maryland, married Elizabeth ___; 206. Sophia[6], died 9 Sept. 1842,[305] made her home at "Bedford," King George County, and later at Baltimore, Md..

---

[299] Peter Wilson Coldham, *American Migrations*, 1765-1799 (Baltimore, 2000), p. 535.
[300] *The Virginia Genealogist*. XI, p. 181.
[301] St. Paul's Parish, King George County, Register.
[302] St. Paul's Parish Register.
[303] *Whig*, Richmond, 19 Nov. 1846.
[304] Bland Papers, Maryland Historical Society.
[305] *The Sun*, Baltimore, Md., 14 Sept. 1842.

BOYCE[1]

*1. Cheney[1] Boyce was listed in the muster of John Throgmorton at West and Sherley Hundred, 1624/5, as aged 26 and having arrived in the *George* in 1617, but eleven years later received a land patent which included 100 acres "as being an Ancient Planter,"[2] which suggests that he had been in Virginia prior to 1616 and the voyage on the *George* was a return trip.. He represented Shirley Hundred Island in the assemblies of 1629, 1630 and 1632.[3]

His grant of 1550 acres on Lime Hill Swamp and Merchants Hope Creek in Charles City County, which included the 100 acres due him as an Ancient Planter, was issued the last of May 1636 and reissued 24 Aug. 1637.[4] He apparently was still alive 23 Aug. and 1 Sept. 1643 when named as an adjoining landowner in patents issued to Thomas Wheeler and John Freeme.[5]

His death and the remarriage of his widow Joyce ___ to Richard Tye are set forth in a subsequent record:

> In anno 1637 Chainey Boyce deceased did pattent in his owne name 1550 Acres of Land lyeing in the wood at a place called the old Towne. In Anno 1643 which was 15 [*sic*] years after Chainey Boyce dyed without seating the sd Land his title being thereby utterly lost, But the Rights reverted into the hands & estate of Joyce his late wife & Executrix as onely a personall Estate, Att which time the Cort in care of the estate of Tho. Boyce the onely sonne of Chainey Boyce did order the sd executrix to pay him an Annuall maintenance & to delivr him a very considerable estate at the age of 21 years to pay all the deacedents debts & then to bee totally discharged all wch shee punctually performed. In Anno 1644 The executrix Intermarried with Capt. Rich: Tye who six years after finding the sd rights wch were then a Chattell and parcell of his estate by his wife did repattent the said Land in his owne Rights & in his owne name seated it & inioyed it seaven yeares & left it by will to his owne children and dyed.[6]

The repatenting by Richard Tye of 1450 acres, "known by the name of the old Towne above Merchants Hope," which had been granted Chene Boys, 25 Aug. 1638 for 1500 acres and surrendered by Tye "who married the relict of sd.

---

[1] John Anderson Brayton, *The Descendants of Cheney Boyce, "Ancient Planter," and of Richard Craven, for Seven Generations* (Winston-Salem, N.C., 1996).

[2] Patent Bk. 1, p. 352.

[3] Leonard, pp. 8-9, 11.

[4] Patent Bk. 1, p. 352, 468.

[5] *Ibid.*, pp. 893, 896.

[6] Charles City Co. Order Bk. 1655-65, p. 355.

Chene Boys," occurred 26 Oct. 1649.[7]   Probate of the will of Capt. Richard Tye was granted, 3 Oct. 1658, to his widow and executrix Mrs. Joyce Tye.[8]

By 3 June 1659 Joyce had married her (3) husband, Dr. John Cogan, "of the Citty of Bristol ... but now resident in Virginia ... chirurgeon,"[9] who was frequently involved in the Charles City County records as managing the estates of Richard Tye's children and possibly thereafter moved to Isle of Wight County.

The last mention of Joyce (___) Boyce Tye Cogan was on 3 Feb. 1661 in a matter concerning a debt.[10]

Issue: 2. THOMAS[2].

2 THOMAS[2] BOYCE (Cheney[1]) was born no earlier than about 1638/9, By 20 Nov. 1663 he and his wife Emelia, as of Westover Parish, Charles City County, sold to John Cogan, Chirurgeon, a tract of 650 acres on the back side of Merchants Hope, which "was granted unto Richd Craven decd & derived to the sd Tho. Boyce by right of marriage wth Emelia the Grandchild of the sd Richd Craven decd."[11] No further records of Thomas and Emelia Boyce are known.[12]

---

[7] Patent Bk. 2, p. 199.

[8] Charles City Co. Order Bk. 1655-65, p. 164.

[9] *Ibid.*, p. 170.

[10] *Ibid.*, p. 320..

[11] *Ibid.*, p. 425. The sparse records, which, however, indicate that *Richard Craven was a resident of Virginia before 1625, are discussed in Brayton, *op. cit.*, pp. 309-12.

[12] Although record evidence is lacking, James Rives Childs, *Reliques of the Rives* (Lynchburg, 1929), p. 430, John Bennett Boddie,*Southside Virginia Families*, I (Redwood City, Calif., 1955), pp. 100-03, David A. Avant, *Florida Pioneers (Some Southern Colonial Families*, I; Tallahassee, Fla., 1974), pp. 383-407, and Brayton, *op. cit.*, p. 13, point out that the names Thomas, Emelia, Boyce and Cheney which appear in the families descended from John Scott of Prince George County and his wife Bethia are strongly suggestive that Bethia may have been a daughter of Thomas and Emelia Boyce. The will of John Scott, 1 June 1724-9 June 1724 (Prince George Co. Wills & Deeds 1713-28, p. 713), named his wife Bethyer, daughters Bridget Tatum [married 7. *Christopher*[3] *Tatum* (see TATUM)], Amelia Tatum [married 17. *Nathaniel*[4] *Tatum* (see TATUM)], Bethyer Burrow [married Philip Burrows, Jr.], and Elizabeth Chappell [married Samuel Chappell], son-in-law James Gee [married Boyce Scott], and grandsons Thomas and John Scott and their mother Amy Scott [widow of John Scott, Jr.].

BOYLE-MOUNTNEY[1]

*1. Hannah Boyle, daughter of Richard Boyle of Blackfriars, London, was born about 1602 and came to Virginia in the *Bona Nova* in 1620. She married (1) *Edward Hill whose tract of 100 acres at Elizabeth City was shown as planted on the list of titles and estates of land sent home by Sir Francis Wyatt, May 1625.[2] In a letter to his brother John Hill, mercer in Lunbarstreet, London, 14 April 1623, he wrote of the recent massacre and added

> So the truth is we lyue in the fearefullest age that ever christians lyued in: And to speake the truth I stay to gett what I have lost and then god willing I will leaue the Contrey: for this is the worst yeare here that euer I saw like to bee. ... The last yeare I had a very hard yeare of it by reason of th' Indians and I feare this wilbe as bad: I lost the last yeare as many Cattle as were worth a 100[lb]: yet if we saue but o[r] liues god willing the next yeare I will see yo[u][3]

His intention to return to England was cut short for his burial, 15 May 1624 at Elizabeth City, was noted in the muster, 1624/5.

Very shortly she married (2) *Thomas Spilman, listed in the muster as aged 24 and as coming in the *George*, 1616,[4] with whom she was listed in the muster at Elizabeth City with her daughter *Elizabeth Hill, born in Virginia. On 1 Dec. 1624 a patent for 50 acres at Kiccoughtan adjoining land of Edward Hill, deceased, was issued to Thomas Spilman, Gent., for his personal adventure, having come in the *George*, 1617.[5] He returned to England where he died in March 1627 at Truro leaving a nuncupative will which described him as lately of Truro, Cornwall, and gave his estate in England to his daughter *Mary, then in Virginia, and that in Virginia to Hannah. In her absence, administration on his estate was granted, 24 April 1627, to his brother Francis Spelman.[6]

Hannah's last (3) marriage, before Dec. 1628, was to *Alexander Mountney who was listed in the muster, 1624/5, as residing at Elizabeth City, aged 33, and

---

[1] Marie Victoria Bobo, "Descendants of Hannah Boyle" (typewritten; Stockbridge, Ga., 2002).

[2] *R, Va. Co.* IV, p. 558.

[3] *Ibid.*, p. 234. On the same day he wrote his father-in-law, Richard Boyle.

[4] Avery E. Kolb, "Early Passengers to Virginia, When Did They Really Arrive," *V* LXXXVIII, p. 409, indicates the earliest arrival of the *George* was May 1617.

[5] Patent Bk. 1, p. 35.

[6] P.C.C. 40 Skinner, in Waters, I, p. 72; P.C.C. 113 Barrington, in Virginia Colonial Records Project, Survey Report 3285.

as having come in the *Mary James*, 1610.[7] As an Ancient Planter he received 100 acres at Kiccoughtan, adjoining land of Edward Hill, 20 Sept. 1624.[8] By 1633 he disposed of his holdings in Elizabeth City[9] and moved across the Bay to Accomack where in Feb. 1633/4 a suit between him and George Seowell regarding a wager whether William Burdett would marry the Widow Saunders was heard.[10] On 14 Sept. 1635 he was appointed as one of the first vestrymen of the parish on the Eastern Shore.[11] On 13 Nov. 1635 he leased for 21 years 84 acres and 13 poles and somewhat later 190 acres 147 poles from Secretary Richard Kemp.[12] On 20 Sept. 1641 he was appointed keeper of the Common Store at King's Creek.[13] He served on a jury, 15 May 1643,[14] but died before 10 Feb. 1643/4 when Hannah was mentioned as his widow.[15]

Over the next decade Hannah conducted her affairs in Northampton County, being mentioned frequently in the court records. She was last mentioned in the records of the Eastern Shore on 9 Nov. 1655 when she made a deposition, giving her age as about 53 years.[16] On 5 Feb. 1657/8 a patent for 1650 acres in Lancaster County near the head of Corotoman River was issued to Mr. Edwin Connaway and Mrs. Hannah Mountney.[17] On 30 Nov. 1659 administration on the estate of Hannah Mountney was granted to William Crompe, "her son in law."[18]

Issue: (by 1) [HILL] *2. ELIZABETH[2]; (by 2) [SPILMAN] *3. Mary[2],

---

[7] Kolb, *op. cit.*, p. 411, suggests a possible arrival date of Aug. 1611 for the *Mary and James*.

[8] Patent Bk. 1, p. 37.

[9] By petition to the Governor and Council, recorded 10 Nov. 1642, he stated he had sold the land belonging to the orphans of Thomas Spilman and Edward Hill to Daniel Tanner and had converted the payment into cattle for use of the orphans (Northampton Co. Deeds, Wills, Orders 2, 1640-45, pp. 110-11).

[10] Northampton Co. Orders, Wills, Deeds 1, 1632-40, transcript, p. 12.

[11] Northampton Co. Orders, Wills, Deeds 1, 1632-40, p. 58.

[12] Northampton Co. Orders, Deeds, Wills &c 2, 1640-45, p. 10.

[13] *Ibid.*, p. 58.

[14] *Ibid.*, p. 147.

[15] *Ibid.*, p. 177, She was referred to as his administratrix, 28 July 1644 (*ibid.*, p. 202).

[16] Northampton Co. Deeds, Wills &c 5, 1654-55, p. 88.

[17] Patent Bk. 4, p. 148 (216).

[18] Lancaster Co. Order Bk. 1655-66, p. 98.

living July 1643;[19] (by 3) [MOUNTNEY][20] 4. ALEXANDER[2]; 5. FRANCES[2].

2. ELIZABETH[2] HILL (Hannah[1] Boyle) was probably the daughter who married William Pindley, referred to as son of Hannah Mountney.[21] He deposed, 15 Dec. 1647, he was aged about 28,[22] and was living 26 Dec. 1649 when he wrote and witnessed the will of Edward Drew,[23] but died before 28 Aug. 1650 when administration on his estate was granted to Mrs. Hanna Mountney on behalf of the orphans.[24]

Issue: [PINDLEY] 6. Dorothy[3], formerly under the guardianship of William Crump, on 14 May 1662, aged about 15, chose Nicholas Porquoy as her guardian,[25] moved with William Crump to Talbot Co., Md., and 14 July 1670 gave a power of attorney to Michael Miller to arrest and prosecute William Crump; [26] 7. William[3], placed under the guardianship of Nicholas Porquoy, 14 May 1662;[27] 8. Thomas[3], on 9 Sept. 1663, aged 14, having been abused by Nich. Porquoy, his former guardian, chose William Crompe as his guardian,[28] moved with William Crump to Talbot Co., Md..

4. ALEXANDER[2] MOUNTNEY (Hannah[1] Boyle) was mentioned in the will of John Holloway, 25 Aug. 1643,[29] and moved to Maryland by 1661.[30] In March 1662 100 acres on the north side of Patapsco River called Mountenay's

---

[19] Northampton Co. Orders, Deeds, Wills &c 2, 1640-45, pp. 157-58.

[20] On 29 May 1655 a certificate for 1750 acres was granted to Mrs. Hanna Mountney naming Alexander, Thomas, John, Leonard and Roger Mountney among the headrights (Northampton Co. Deeds, Wills &c 5, 1654-55, p. 144). Since a Leonard Mountney was listed in the muster, 1624/5, with Alexander Mountney, the last four may be brothers of her husband rather than sons. They were included in her 1657 patent for land in Lancaster County and were also claimed in a patent issued in Northampton County to William Jordan (Patent Bk. 4, p. 140 [206]). Depositions regarding the will of John Holloway (Northampton Co. Deeds & Wills 3, p. 46, 15 Sept. 1646) establish that he told Alexander Mountney he gave a calf to "yor daughter Betty," but she may be his step-daughter Elizabeth Hill.

[21] Northampton Co. Deeds, Wills &c 3, 1645-51, p. 240.

[22] *Ibid.*, p. 140.

[23] *Ibid.*, p. 240.

[24] *Ibid.*, p. 225.

[25] Lancaster Co. Order Bk. 1655-66, pp. 176-77.

[26] Talbot Co., Md., Deed Bk. 1, p. 113.

[27] Lancaster Co. Order Bk. 1655-66, p. 277.

[28] Lancaster Co. Order Bk. 1655-66, p. 227.

[29] Northampton Co. Orders, Deeds, Wills &c 3, 1640-45, p. 164.

[30] Maryland Patent Bk. 17, p. 67, proof, 25 June 1672, of one right for importing himself into the province to inhabit "about eleven years time."

Neck in Baltimore Co., Md., was surveyed for him.[31] He may have been living as late as 2 March 1685/6 when Edward Mumford sold land on the northwest branch on the north side of Patapsco River adjoining land of Alexander Mountney.[32] He presumably married ___ and had

Issue: [MOUNTNEY][33] 9. (possibly) HANNAH[3].

5. FRANCES[2] MOUNTNEY (Hannah[1] Boyle) married William Crump who appears in the records of Lancaster County in an unfavorable light, being sued, 14 May 1662, by Walter Hyrd for defamation, which he "acknowledged ... with sorrow," and charged, 9 July 1662, with breaking into the house of Richard George and taking bags of Indian corn, and, 18 March 1662/3, with threatening Ralph Horton so that "hee goeth in danger of his life."[34]

Very shortly afterward he moved to Talbot Co., Md., where on 20 March 1671 he attested he imported himself, his wife Frances, sons William and John, daughter Elizabeth, and Thomas and Dorothy Pinley in Feb. 1665.[35] On 20 Nov. 1671 he purchased 200 acres, "Costin's Choice," and on 13 Sept. 1679, 150 acres called "Leavington."[36] On 16 Oct. 1683 he and Frances sold 200 acres, "Plain Dealing," on the south side of Chester River and west side of Broadrib's Branch, to James Barber.[37] He was appointed constable of Chester Hundred, 18 March 1672/3[38] and was living as late as 1689 when continued as captain of a foot company in the Talbot County militia[39] but died before 11 Sept. 1695 when John Loyd gave receipt to Frances Crump, widow and executrix of the last will of William Crump, for the legacy of his wife Hannah and John Meriday gave receipt for that of his wife Mary.[40] No copy of the will survives.

---

[31] Baltimore Co., Md., Rent Roll, in *MHM* XXI, p. 340, shown as later in possession of James Todd.

[32] Baltimore Co., Md., Deed Bk. RM #HS, pp. 166-68..

[33] This identification is based solely on the sale by John Hurst of land formerly belonging to Alexander Mountney and his having a wife Hannah and son Alexander.

[34] Lancaster Co. Order Bk. 1655-66, pp. 180, 217.

[35] Maryland Patents 16, p. 463.   See also Patents 6, p. 136, undated but among other records dated 1663; Patent Bk. 7, pp. 551-53, dated 1664.

[36] Talbot Co., Md.., Deed Bk. 1, p. 183; Deed Bk. 3, p. 313.

[37] Talbot Co., Md., Deed Bk. 4, p. 260.

[38] Talbot Co. Court Proceedings BB no. 2, no pagination, in *Archives of Maryland*, LIV (Baltimore, 1937), p. 563.

[39] William Hand Browne, ed., *Proceedings and Acts of the General Assembly of Maryland, April, 1684-June, 1692* (*Archives of Maryland*, XIII; Baltimore, 1894), p. 243.

[40] Kent Co., Md., Bonds & Inventories GL #1, pp. 2c-3.

She died after 2 April 1715 when she gave a deposition.[41]

Issue: [CRUMP] 10. William[3], died unmarried; 11. John[3], died unmarried; 12. Elizabeth[3]; 13. HANNAH[3]; 14. ROBERT[3]; 15. Mary[3], married, by 11 Sept. 1695, John Merriday (Meredith).[42]

9. HANNAH[3] MOUNTNEY (Alexander[2], Hannah[1] Boyle) married John Hurst who, as of Anne Arundel Co., Md., purchased 100 acres in Baltimore Co., Md., 15 April 1695.[43] Described as an innholder in Baltimore, he sold, 13 Oct. 1702, 135½ acres, "Cold Harbor," which he had purchased from James Todd, and 164½ acres which had formerly belonged to Alexander Mountney.[44]

Issue: [HURST][45] 16. John[4]; 17. Alexander[4].

13. HANNAH[3] CRUMP (Frances[2] Mountney, Hannah[1] Boyle) died in 1756.[46] She married (1), Edward Richardson, (2), by 11 Sept. 1695, John Loyd of Talbot Co., Md., who died before 23 Nov. 1713 when Hannah gave bond as his administratrix,[47] and (3) ___ Winn.

Issue: (by 1) [RICHARDSON] 18. ELIZABETH[4]; (by 2) [LOYD] 19. John[4]; 20. William[4], joined, 28 Nov. 1723, his mother Hannah Winn in selling

---

[41] Queen Anne's Co., Md., Deed Bk. IK #A, p. 64.

[42] Henry C. Peden and F. Edward Wright, *Colonial Families of the Eastern Shore of Maryland*, XI (Lewes, Del., 2000), p. 167, states John Meredith by Mary Crump had one son John who married Elizabeth Green and left will 28 May 1748-29 Jan. 1750/1 (Maryland Prerogative Court Wills 27, p. 496), naming children John, Thomas, Benjamin, Catherine, Mary and Rebecca, and that John, the father, married (2), by 23 Nov. 1713 (Maryland Prerogative Court Wills 14, p. 113, will of Thomas Bailey, 23 Nov. 1715-19 March 1715/6), Sophia Bailey, who filed the inventory of his estate 31 May 1729 (Maryland Prerogative Court Inventories 14, p. 261). On 2 April 1750, however, one John Meradith of Queen Anne's Co., Md., deposed he was aged 72 (Maryland Provincial Court Ejectments, Queen Anne's County, folder 050082-2, suit of William Bishop *vs.* Austin), an age consistent with the approximate birth of Mary Crump and with that of the 1748 testator. Evidence presently available is insufficient to resolve the inconsistencies in the Peden and Wright account, including the placement of the Thomas Meredith who deposed 15 March 1760 he was aged about 48 (Maryland Provincial Court Ejectments, Queen Anne's County, folder 050082-28, Richard Tilghman Earle) and whether John (died 1729) or John (died 1751) was Mary Crump's husband.

[43] Baltimore Co., Md., Deed Bk. RM #HS, pp. 456-59.

[44] Baltimore Co., Md., Deed Bk. HW #2, pp. 196-98.

[45] Robert W. Barnes, *Baltimore County Families, 1659-1759* (Baltimore, 1989), p. 349.

[46] Robert W. Barnes and F. Edward Wright, *Colonial Families of the Eastern Shore of Maryland*, II (Westminster, Md., 1996), pp. 111-12, without citation of source.

[47] Maryland Testamentary Proceedings 22, p. 328.

150 acres, the upper part of "Crump's Forest."[48].

14. ROBERT[3] CRUMP (Frances[2] Mountney, Hannah[1] Boyle) died before 2 Feb. 1748/9 when administration was granted on his estate.[49] He married, Elizabeth Tydings, daughter of Richard Tydings.[50] On 10 Jan. 1700 he and Elizabeth sold a tract on Coursegall Creek in Chester Hundred,[51] on 13 Aug. 1702 they sold to James Heath their moiety of 300 acres, "Crump's Forest," which had been patented by his father, but bought it back, 16 Nov. 1708,[52] and on 28 June 1715 they sold 200 acres of "Crump's Forest" to James Williams, Jr.[53] He and Elizabeth also sold "Crumpton" to Darby Mahar, 28 June 1718.[54]

Issue: [CRUMP] 21. ROBERT[4]; 22. MARY[4]; 23. PRECIOSIA[4].

18 ELIZABETH[4] RICHARDSON (Hannah[3] Crump, Frances[2] Mountney, Hannah[1] Boyle) married William Tarbotin (Tarbutton), tailor of Queen Anne's Co., Md., whom she joined, 10 March 1719/20, when they with 14. Robert[3] Crump sold 50 acres, "Crumpton," to James Heath.[55]

Issue: [TARBUTTON] 24. Joseph[5], mentioned as "friend" in the will of Joseph Harris, 1746,[56] granted, 29 Sept. 1756, 100 acres, "Locust Ridge," which he sold, 5 Oct. 1772, along with 55 acres, "Hog Pen Neck," which he had purchased 2 May 1772;[57] 25. WILLIAM[5]; 26. Edward[5], married, 8 Nov. 1744,[58] Rachel Ratcliffe.

21. ROBERT[4] CRUMP (Robert[3], Frances[2] Mountney, Hannah[1] Boyle)

---

[48] Queen Anne's Co., Md., Deed Bk. IK #B, pp, 221-22.

[49] Maryland Prerogative Court Inventories 41, pp. 209-10.

[50] Richard Tydings of Anne Arundel Co., Md., left will dated 2 Feb. 1687.(Maryland Prerogative Court Wills 6, p. 40, without probate entry) which gave 300 acres in Baltimore County to his daughters Charity and Elizabeth. On 25 June 1719 Robert Crump and wife Elizabeth of Queen Anne's Co., Md., sold 375 acres, half of "Nanjemie," of which Robert was seized in right of his wife (Baltimore Co., Md., Deed Bk. TR #DS, pp. 47-51). In Dec. 1750 Charity Sellman, daughter of Richard Tydings [and widow of 77. *William*[4] *Sellman* (see WEST, Anthony)], sold 375 acres, part of "Nanjemoy" (Baltimore Co., Md., Deed Bk. TR #D, p. 197).

[51] Kent Co., Md., Deed Bk. M, p. 110.

[52] Kent Co., Md., Deed Bk. JD #1, pp. 34-35; Queen Anne's Co., Md., Deed Bk. ET #A, p. 34.

[53] Queen Anne's Co., Md., Deed Bk. IK #A, p. 38.

[54] *Ibid.*, p. 188.

[55] Queen Anne's Co., Md., Deed Bk. IK #B, pp. 9-11.

[56] Maryland Prerogative Court Wills 29, p. 365, dated 5 June 1746, proved 17 April 1755.

[57] Queen Anne's Co., Md., Deed Bk. RTK, p. 110; Deed Bk. RTH, p. 407.

[58] St. Luke's Parish, Queen Anne's Co., Md., Register.

married, 28 May 1731,[59] Jane (Lowder) Lazenby, daughter of Charles and Joane (___) Lowder and widow of John Lazenby. By 1752 they moved with relatives to the part of Halifax County[60] which became Pittsylvania County, where he was listed as tithable, 1767.[61] On 30 May 1767 he took up 400 acres on Green Creek.[62]

Issue: [CRUMP] 27. William[5], entered 400 acres on Crooked Creek in Pittsylvania County, 26 Aug. 1768,[63] was granted 340 acres on Beaver Island Creek in Guilford Co., N.C., 14 Oct. 1783,[64] and purchased, 27 Nov.1793,[65] an adjoining 300 acres, which fell into Stokes Co., N.C.; 28. ROBERT[5].

22. MARY[4] CRUMP (Robert[3], Frances[2] Mountney, Hannah[1] Boyle) married (1), 10 June 1719,[66] Abraham Montague and (2) ___ Godfree.[67]

Issue: (by 1) [MONTAGUE] 29. William[5], as son of Abraham, sold a mare to Thomas Baggs, 18 Aug. 1753.[68]

22. PRECIOSIA[4] CRUMP (Robert[3], Frances[2] Mountney, Hannah[1] Boyle) married, 14 Jan. 1730/1,[69] Samuel Bostick of Queen Anne's Co., Md., who deposed, 13 Aug. 1757, he was aged 55 or thereabouts.[70].

Issue: [BOSTICK][71] 30. Elizabeth[5], born 24 Jan. 1735/6; 31. Samuel[5], born 17 Jan. 1738/9; 32. Lucy[5], born 17 March 1751/2.

24. WILLIAM[5] TARBUTTON (Elizabeth[4] Richardson, Mary[3] Crump,

---

[59] St. Luke's Parish, Queen Anne's Co., Md., Register.

[60] Halifax Co. Pleas [Orders] 1, p. 62, order, 20 Dec. 1752, directing that Robert Crump (two tithables), Charles Lowder, Charles Lessenby and Daniel Lessonby, among others, be added to the general list of tithables. On 18 Sept. 1753 Robert Crump, William Crump, David Lessenby, Edward Lowder and Charles Lessenby were added to the list of Joseph Terry (*ibid.*, p. 185).

[61] Maud Carter Clement, *The History of Pittsylvania County, Virginia* (Lynchburg, 1929), p. 282.

[62] Pittsylvania Co. Entry Bk. 1737-70, p. 408.

[63] *Ibid.*, p. 433.

[64] Guilford Co., N.C., Deed Bk. 2, p. 386.

[65] Rockingham Co., N.C., Deed Bk. C, p. 337.

[66] St. Luke's Parish, Queen Anne's Co., Md., Register.

[67] Based on the assumption she is the Mary Godfree who with Precosia Bostick signed as next of kin the inventory of 21. Robert[4] Crump, 11 March 1748/9 (Maryland Prerogative Court Inventories 41, p.. 209).

[68] Queen Anne's Co., Md., Deed Bk. RT #D, p. 194.

[69] St. Luke's Parish Register.

[70] Queen Anne's Co., Md., Land Commission Bk. 1756-68, p. 24.

[71] St. Luke's Parish Register.

Frances[2] Mountney, Hannah[1] Boyle), of Queen Anne's Co., Md., died before 5 April 1770 when the inventory of his estate was made.[72] He purchased 100 acres, part of "Cod Head Manor," 10 March 1740 but sold that land 28 Jan. 1755.[73] He married Rebecca (Satterfield?).[74]

Issue: [TARBUTTON][75] 33. Rebeccah[6]; 34. Dinah[6]; 35. James[6], married, before 18 Aug. 1774, Elizabeth ___, widow of William Burk;[76] 36. William[6]; 37. Solomon[6]; 38. Elizabeth[6]; 39. Mary[6].

26. ROBERT[5] CRUMP (Robert[4], Robert[3], Frances[2] Mountney, Hannah[1] Boyle) died 1823 in Franklin Co., Ga.[77] He married Mary Parr, daughter of John and Miriam (___) Parr,[78] who died about 1830 in Franklin Co., Ga.[79] He was tithable in Pittsylvania County in 1767[80] and later moved to Surry Co., N.C., where he was granted 300 acres on Beaver Island Creek, 3 Nov. 1784, and purchased 213 acres, 1 May 1787.[81] He was head of a household in Stokes Co., N.C., 1790,[82] and by 1808 moved to Franklin Co., Ga., where he then owned 200 acres on Bear Creek.[83] On 1 Aug. 1809 he sold 25 acres, part of the tract where

---

[72] Maryland Prerogative Court Inventories 104, p. 211.

[73] Dorchester Co., Md., Old Deed Bk. 11, p. 154; Queen Anne's Co., Md., Deed Bk. RTD, p. 283.

[74] She signed the inventory of the estate of William Satterfield, 26 March 1770, as one of the next of kin (Maryland Prerogative Court Inventories 103, p. 319).

[75] Maryland Balance of Final Distributions Bk. 6, p. 31.

[76] Maryland Prerogative Court Accounts 71, p. 319.

[77] Bobo, *loc. cit.* He was last named in the Franklin Co., Ga., tax digests in 1825 when Richard Crump was listed for Rob't. Crump, Sr., no poll (Martha Walters Ackor, *Franklin County, Georgia, Tax Digests*, IV, 1825-1839 [Birmingham, Ala., 1981], p. 12).

[78] Patrick Co. Will Bk. 1, p. 103, will of John Parr, 20 Jan. 1808-March 1808.

[79] Bobo, *loc. cit.* She was living 10 Feb. 1826, when Mary Crump, Robert Crump, Richard Crump of Franklin Co., Ga., and James York of St. Clair Co., Ala., as legatees of Robert Crump, deceased, sold 75 acres on the north side of Leatherwood Fork (Franklin Co., Ga., Deed Bk. BBB, 1829-32, pp. 52-53, recorded 13 April 1830) and is probably the female, aged 70-80, in the household of her son Richard Crump in 1830 (Franklin Co., Ga., 1830 census, p. 234).

[80] Clement, *loc. cit.*

[81] Surry Co., N.C., Deed Bk. C, p. 227; Deed Bk. D, p. 116.

[82] *Heads of Families at the First Census ... 1790, North Carolina* (Washington, 1908), p. 178.

[83] Acker, *op. cit.*, II, 1808-1818 (Birmingham, Ala., 1981), p. 24. Mary Crump, wife of Robert Crump, was charged with 100 acres the same year (*ibid.*).

he lived.[84]

Issue: [CRUMP][85] 40. John D.[6], born 1770 in Pittsylvania County, died 4 Dec. 1848 in St. Clair Co., Ala., married, about 1790 in South Carolina, Sarah Cornelius; 41. William Mt. Scar[6], born 1772 in Pittsylvania County, died 31 Octr. 1844 in Tuscaloosa Co., Ala., married, about 1793 in Stokes Co., N.C., Sarah Vawter, who was born 1776 in Madison County and died about 1856 in Tuscaloosa Co., Ala.; 42. Silas[6], born about 1775, died about 17 Nov. 1834 in St. Clair Co., Ala., married , 1795 in Stokes Co., N.C., Sarah Hannah Riggs, who was born about 1780 in Maryland and died about 1856 in St. Clair Co., Ala.; 43. Charles[6], born about 1777, left will 26 Oct. 1820-1 Jan. 1821,[86] moved to Elbert Co., Ga., married about 1796 in Stokes Co., N.C., Agnes Vernon, who was born about 1776 in Surry Co., N.C., and died Dec. 1869 in Hart Co., Ga.; 44. Malissa[6], born 1779, died in Franklin Co., Ga., married, 25 Feb. 1805;[87] Enoch Andrews, who was born 1784 in Fairfield Co., S.C., and died after 1850 in Franklin Co., Ga.; 45. Robert Green[6], born 1781, died 10 June 1856 in Franklin Co., Ga., justice of the Franklin County Inferior Court, 1837-41, married (1), about 1805, Agnes Tyner,[88] who was born about 1785, and (2), 16 Jan. 1846 in Elbert Co., Ga., Nancy Tyner, who died about 1870 in Franklin Co., Ga.; 46. Dinsolendy[6], married, 14 April 1816,[89] Jonathan Bush; 47. Jane[6], born 1783 in Patrick County, married, 3 Oct. 1819,[90] Brazel Anderson; 48. Richard Lee[6], born 1787 in Stokes Co., N.C., died 5 Aug. 1853 in Franklin Co., Ga., married (1), 8 Oct. 1812,[91] Elizabeth Wheeler, who died before 1830, and (2) Elizabeth Kesler, who was born 8 Oct. 1801 in South Carolina and died 23 Sept. 1881 in Franklin Co., Ga.; 49. Ruth[6], born 1 Jan. 1787 in Stokes Co., N.C., died 24 March 1857 in DeKalb Co., Ala., married, 10 April 1803 in South Carolina, George Washington Reeve, who was born 14 April 1782 and died 10 May 1850 in DeKalb Co., Ala.

---

[84] Franklin Co., Ga., Deed Bk. T, 1809-10, pp. 65-66.

[85] Bobo, *loc. cit.*; Franklin County Historical Society, *History of Franklin County, Georgia* (Carnesville, Ga., 1992), p. 441.

[86] Elbert Co., Ga., Will Bk. L, p. 413.

[87] Franklin Co., Ga., Marriage Register 1, p. 11, as Anders.

[88] Elbert Co., Ga., Will Bk. M, p. 339, will of Richard Tyner, 13 Sept. 1824-10 Nov. 1821; Old Will Bk. N, p. 33.

[89] Franklin Co., Ga., Marriage Register 1, p. 115.

[90] Franklin Co., Ga., Marriage Register 1, p. 134, as Adison.

[91] Franklin Co., Ga., Marriage Register 1, p. 92.

BRANCH[1]

*1. CHRISTOPHER[1] BRANCH, the earliest American ancestor of record of Thomas[6] Jefferson, was born probably about 1598 in England, the only son of Lionel Branch (1566-1605) and his wife Valentia Sparke who were married 8 July 1596 at St. Martin, Ludgate, in the city of London. He married at St. Peter's, Westcheap, London, by virtue of a marriage license from the Bishop of London, 2 Sept. 1619, Mary Addy, daughter of Francis Addy of Darton, Yorkshire, and in March 1619/20 embarked in the *London Merchant* for Virginia. Christopher[1] Branch is recorded among the "living" at "The Colledg Land" in present Henrico County, 1623/4,[2] and in the muster, 1624/5, he, his wife and 9 months old son Thomas[2] are listed there. In 1632 he returned briefly to England and unsuccessfully brought suit to recover the Bull Inn at Abingdon which had been owned by his uncle Thomas Branch (1557-1603).

As "Christopher Branch, Planter, of Arrowhattocks in Henrico County," he was granted a lease, 20 Oct. 1634, for 21 years on 100 acres lying "east upon the maine River."[3] The following year, 8 Dec. 1635, he patented 250 acres "at Kingsland over against Arrowhattocks, east upon the maine River ... adjacent to the land of John Griffin, now in the tenure of said Branch ... 50 acres for his own personal adventure and 200 acres for transportation of 4 persons."[4] By 28 Feb. 1638/9 Branch's plantation numbered 450 acres after he had acquired an additional 100 acres through an exchange with James Place and the remaining acreage through additional headrights.[5]

He was named in an Act of Assembly, 6 Jan. 1639/40, as a tobacco viewer

---

[1] James Branch Cabell, *Branch of Abingdon* (Richmond, 1911); James Branch Cabell, *Branchiana* (Richmond, 1907); William Clayton Torrence, "Thomas and William Branch of Henrico and Some of their Descendants," *W*(1) XXV, pp. 59-70, 107-16; James Branch Cabell, "Thomas and William Branch and Some of their Descendants," *W*(1) XXVI, pp. 111-21; Peter Walne, "Branch of Abingdon: A Revision," *V* LXVII, pp. 82-105; John Anderson Brayton, "Notes on the Ancestry of Valentia[A] (Sparke) Branch, Mother of Christopher[1] Branch," *The Virginia Genealogist*, XLVI, pp. 293-98; John Anderson Brayton, "Notes on the Ancestry of Mary (Addy) Branch, Wife of Christopher[1] Branch," *The Virginia Genealogist*, XLVI, pp. 299-305.

[2] Hotten, p. 169.

[3] Patent Bk. 1, p. 155.

[4] *Ibid.*, p. 326.

[5] *Ibid.*, pp. 381, 527, 634.

from the World's End to Henrico,[6] and was Burgess for the county the following year,[7] and justice, 1656. His will, 20 June 1678-20 Feb. 1681/2, described him as "of Kingsland."[8]

Issue: 2. THOMAS[2]; 3. WILLIAM[2]; 4. CHRISTOPHER[2].

2. THOMAS[2] BRANCH (Christopher[1]), born May 1624, aged 9 months in the muster, 1624/5, married Elizabeth (Gough?). They lived on a part of the Kingsland tract on the south side of James River in the area of Henrico which later became Chesterfield County. He left a will, 25 Oct. 1688-1 Feb. 1694/5,[9] which named his wife and children, and his widow left a will, 2 Aug. 1697-20 Aug. 1697.[10]

Issue: 5. THOMAS[3]; 6. MATTHEW[3]; 7. JAMES[3]; 8. Elizabeth[3], married Melchizedek Richardson, who deposed, 1 Dec. 1686, he was aged 38 and, 1 Dec. 1691, he was aged 41,[11] of whose will, now lost, she was granted probate 1 April 1701;[12] 9. Martha[3], married, as his (1) wife, Richard Ward, who deposed, 1 Dec. 1692, he was aged 33,[13] owned 300 acres in Henrico County, 1704, and left will, now lost, proved 6 July 1724.[14]

3. WILLIAM[2] BRANCH (Christopher[1]), born about 1626, resided in Henrico County where he was a planter and died probably about 1670.[15] He married Jane ___,[16] who deposed, 1 Dec. 1688, she was aged 48,[17] married (2) William Baugh, Jr., and (3) Abell Gower, and left will, 7 Dec. 1710-Jan.

---

[6] *W*(2) IV, p. 20.

[7] Leonard, p. 18.

[8] Henrico Co. Wills & Deeds 1677-92, pp. 209-10.

[9] Henrico Co. Deeds & Wills 1688-97, p. 543.

[10] Henrico Co. Wills & Deeds 1697-1704, p. 10.

[11] Henrico Co. Wills & Deeds 1677-91, p. 401; Deeds & Wills 1688-97, p. 263.

[12] Henrico Co. Wills & Deeds 1697-1704, p. 223.

[13] Henrico Co. Deeds & Wills 1688-97, p. 375.

[14] Henrico Co. Minute Bk. 1719-24, p. 349.

[15] Henrico Co. Orphans Court Bk. 1677-1739, p. 2, "Account of cattle & horses belonging to the orphans of Mr. William Branch dec'd., & Mr. Baugh dec'd. presented by Mr. Abell Gower," which names William and John Branch, Mary and Priscilla Baugh. Mary married 7. *John*[3] *Cox* (see COX); Priscilla married 5. *William*[3] *Farrar* (see FARRAR).

[16] Neil D. Thompson, *The Family of Bartholomew Stovall*, I (Fort Worth, Tex., 1993), p. 204, identifies her as probably a daughter of William Hatcher. In her will she left a damask gown and petticoat to "sister Hatcher," presumably the wife of one of William Hatcher's sons.

[17] Henrico Co. Deeds & Wills 1688-97, p. 25.

1710/11.[18]

Issue: 10. William[3], died after 20 Aug. 1678, without issue;[19] 11. JOHN[3].

4. CHRISTOPHER[2] BRANCH (Christopher[1]), born about 1628, removed from Henrico to Charles City County where, in 1657 at the age of 29, he was appointed justice. The inventory of his estate was made 24 Nov. 1665 by William Farrar.[20] The name of his wife is unknown.

Issue:[21] 12. CHRISTOPHER[3]; 13. SAMUEL[3]; 14. MARY[3]; 15. Sarah[3]; 16. BENJAMIN[3].

5. THOMAS[3] BRANCH (Thomas[2], Christopher[1]) deposed 3 March 1710/11 he was aged about 54.[22] He married, by Oct. 1688, Elizabeth Archer, daughter of George Archer.[23] He owned 540 acres in Henrico County, 1704, and left a will, 4 Dec. 1727-Dec. 1728.[24]

Issue: 17. Thomas[4], lived in the part of Henrico which became Chesterfield County, owned 950 acres, 1736,[25] died unmarried leaving will 30 Oct 1765-6 June 1766;[26] 18. William[4], unmarried, owned 400 acres in Henrico County, 1736,[27] left will 4 Oct. 1741-5 March 1762;[28] 19. James[4], unmarried, left will

---

[18] Henrico Co. Wills & Deeds 1710-14, p. 35.

[19] Henrico Co. Orphans Court Bk. 1677-1739, p. 3.

[20] Henrico Co. Miscellaneous Court Records I, p. 31.

[21] Henrico Co. Wills & Deeds 1677-92, pp. 218-19, inventory of estate of Christopher[1] Branch.

[22] Henrico Co. Wills & Deeds 1710-14, p. 48.

[23] Henrico Co. Orphans Court Bk. 1677-1739, p. 23, 12 Oct. 1688, "Mr. Joseph Royall guardian of the orphans of Geo: Archer dec'd. doth give account that he hath taken up two mares belonging to the said orphans, one of which he hath delivered to Thos: Branch who marryed Elizabeth Archer (one of the said orphans)."

[24] Henrico Co. Deeds & Wills 1725-37, p. 221.

[25] Beverley Fleet, *Henrico County-Southside* (*Virginia Colonial Abstracts*, XXI; Richmond, 1944), p. 8.

[26] Chesterfield Co. Will Bk. 1, pp. 535-36; Order Bk. 3, pp. 735, 744. He left his estate to Henry Mitchell, Edward Osborne, Robert Goode (son of Robert Goode late dec'd.), Josiah Tatum, Branch Tanner, Christopher Branch, Thomas Branch Willson and John Goode, equally, and named all of them his executors. These were the oldest sons of his eight sisters.

[27] Fleet, *loc. cit.*

[28] Chesterfield Co. Will Bk. 1, p. 335; Order Bk. 3, p. 209. He left his estate to Henry Mitchell, Edward Osborne, Robert Goode (son of Robert Goode late dec'd.), Josiah Tatum, Branch Tanner, Christopher Branch, Thomas Branch Willson and John Goode, equally, and named all of them his executors. These were the oldest sons of his eight sisters.

5 Aug. 1736-Oct. 1737;[29] 20. TABITHA[4]; 21. AGNES[4]; 22. ELIZABETH[4]; 23. FRANCES[4]; 24. Mary[4], married ___ Tatum, probably 10. *Henry*[3] *Tatum* (see TATUM); 25. Amey[4], married her cousin 43. Henry[4] Branch; 26. MARTHA[4]; 27. MARGERY[4].

6. MATTHEW[3] BRANCH (Thomas[2], Christopher[1]), born about 1661, resided in Henrico County where he owned 947 acres, 1704. He married ___.[30] He left a will, 15 Dec. 1722-4 July 1726.[31]

Issue: 28. MATTHEW[4]; 29. JOHN[4]; 30. OLIVE[4]; 31. DANIEL[4]; 32. THOMAS[4]; 33. Phoebe[4]; 34. ELIZABETH[4].

7. JAMES[3] BRANCH (Thomas[2], Christopher[1]), born about 1666, lived in that part of Henrico which became Chesterfield County in 1749. He owned 555 acres in Henrico, 1704, and 586 acres, 1736.[32] On 2 April 1716 he purchased 100 acres of "Kingsland" from Thomas Turpin and his wife 41. Obedience[4] Branch and on 2 Nov. 1726 he sold this tract to Henry Vanderhood.[33] He left a will 19 Aug. 1726-4 Aug. 1749.[34] He married Mary ___ who left will 28 Nov. 1750-1 April 1757.[35]

Issue: 35. Frances[4]; 36. ELIZABETH[4]; 37. Verlinche[4], married 30. Olive[4] Branch; 38. Mary[4]; 39. JOHN[4]; 40. PHOEBE[4].

11. JOHN[3] BRANCH (William[2], Christopher[1]) married Martha ___ who was granted probate of her husband's will, now lost, 2 April 1688.[36] She married (2) 3. *Thomas*[3] *Osborne* (see OSBORNE) and (3), 26 Oct. 1692, Thomas Edwards.[37]

Issue: 41. OBEDIENCE[4]; 42. PRISCILLA[4].

12. CHRISTOPHER[3] BRANCH (Christopher[2], Christopher[1]) deposed, 1 Oct. 1683, he was aged 24 and, 1 Oct. 1687, that he was aged 29.[38] He married

---

[29] Henrico Co. Deeds & Wills 1725-37, p. 662. He left everything to his brothers Thomas and William.

[30] James Branch Cabell, "Branch of Henrico," *W*(1) XXVI, p. 275, suggests she was probably Frances Ware, a sister of Caleb Ware.

[31] Henrico Co. Wills & Deeds 1725-37, pp. 31-32.

[32] Fleet, *op. cit.*, p. 10.

[33] Henrico Co. Wills & Deeds 1714-18, p. 75; Wills & Deeds 1725-37, pp. 61-62.

[34] Chesterfield Co. Will Bk. 1, p. 55; Order Bk. 1, p. 8.

[35] Chesterfield Co. Will Bk. 1, pp. 235-36; Order Bk. 2, p. 287.

[36] Henrico Co. Order Bk. 1678-93, p. 266.

[37] Henrico Co. Deeds & Wills 1688-97, p. 435.

[38] Henrico Co. Wills & Deeds 1677-92, pp. 254, 466.

Anne (Sherman) Crowley, daughter of Henry Sherman (died 1695) and his wife Cicely (died 1703/4) and childless widow of 7. *John³ Crowley* (see SHARP-BAUGH) who died 1687.[39] He owned 646 acres in Henrico County, 1704, and left will 11 Aug. 1727-1 Jan. 1727/8.[40]

Issue: 43. HENRY⁴; 44. Mary⁴, married ___ Walters;[41] 45. Anne⁴, left a cow by her grandmother Sherman, 1703, probably died young; 46. CICELY⁴; 47. OBEDIENCE⁴.

13. SAMUEL³ BRANCH (Christopher², Christopher¹) deposed, 8 June 1691, he was aged 28.[42] He married Ursula Goode,[43] who married (2), by 1707, Walter Scott of Henrico.[44] Samuel³ left will 3 May 1700-1 Aug. 1700.[45] Ursula was still alive when Walter Scott made his will, 29 March 1743.[46]

Issue: 48. Samuel⁴, died after 10 July 1714 when he gave a power of attorney to his "Trusty & well beloved father Walter Scott,"[47] without issue; 49. Ursula⁴, died without issue; 50. Martha⁴, died without issue.[48]

14. MARY³ BRANCH (Christopher², Christopher¹) married (1), 1678/9, Thomas Jefferson of Henrico County. She petitioned for probate of his will,

---

[39] Henrico Co. Deeds & Wills 1688-97, p. 595; Wills & Deeds 1697-1704, p. 364; Wills & Deeds 1677-92, p. 425; Order Bk. 1710-14, pp. 51 *et seq.* See also FARRAR, note 16.

[40] Henrico Co. Deeds & Wills 1725-37, p. 163.

[41] She may have been the (2) wife of John Walters, who left will 30 Sept. 1734-5 May 1735 (Henrico Co. Wills & Deeds 1725-37, p. 483), by whom she had a son John Walters, and have left will, now lost, proved Sept. 1767 (Henrico Co. Order Bk. 1767-69, p. 137). Malcolm Elmore Walthall, "The Walthall Family" (typewritten; Charlotte, N.C., 1958), p. 13, however, suggests this surname was incorrectly written or transcribed in the will of Christopher³ Branch and her husband was Richard Walthall, who left will 19 June 1744-Oct. 1744 (Henrico Co. Miscellaneous Court Records 1650-1800, IV, p. 1271) naming wife Mary. No evidence is known to establish either identification.

[42] Henrico Co. Deeds & Wills 1688-97, p. 223.

[43] Her surname is based on the naming of Ursula Goode Scott (born 7 June 1785), daughter of William and Elizabeth (Wade) Scott and granddaughter of Walter, Jr., and Agnes (Martin) Scott (*W*[2] VIII, p. 131; Bible of David Street, Virginia Historical Society, Mss.6:4ST833)

[44] Henrico Co. Orphans Court Bk. 1677-1739, p. 50.

[45] Henrico Co. Wills & Deeds 1697-1704, p. 191.

[46] Henrico Co. Wills & Deeds 1744-48, p. 235.

[47] Henrico Co. Order Bk. 1710-14, p. 281.

[48] Bill in chancery, Branch *vs.* Branch, Chesterfield County suit, in *The Southside Virginian*, V, pp. 51-53, showing 129. Christopher⁵ Branch, son of 43. Henry⁴ Branch, as heir at law of 13. Samuel³ Branch.

now lost, 7 Dec. 1697, and his estate accounts, mentioning children Thomas and Martha, were returned 1 Oct. 1698.[49] She married (2), 17 Feb. 1700/01, Joseph Maddox.[50]

Issue: (by 1) [JEFFERSON][51] 51. THOMAS[4]; 52. MARY[4]; 53. MARTHA[4].

16. BENJAMIN[3] BRANCH (Christopher[2], Christopher[1]) was raised by his grandfather, both parents apparently having died during his infancy. In Feb. 1686/7 "Benjamin Branch, an Orph[an] in the tuition of Christopher Branch" [his brother], petitioned that he was of lawful age to receive his estate.[52] On 2 Dec. 1689 he deposed he was aged 24 or thereabouts and on 8 June 1691 that he was aged 25.[53] The family lived at "Kingsland" and Benjamin[3] presumably cleared the western portion of the plantation where his brothers were directed by the will of Christopher[1] Branch to build him a "house of four lengths of board every length of board to be five foot long" and clear him a corn field.[54] He owned 550 acres in Henrico County, 1704.

He married, about 1695, 7. *Tabitha[4] Osborne* (see OSBORNE), who was granted administration on his estate, Dec. 1706.[55] She married (2), 2 Feb. 1706/7, Thomas Cheatham, Jr.[56]

Issue: 54. BENJAMIN[4].

20. TABITHA[4] BRANCH (Thomas[3], Thomas[2], Christopher[1]) died 14 Jan. 1752.[57] She married, before 1727, Henry Mitchell, who moved to that part of Surry County which became Sussex County, married (2) Sarah ___ and died 27 March 1754,[58] leaving will 2 March 1754-8 April 1754.[59]

Issue: [MITCHELL] 55. HENRY[5]; 56. THOMAS[5]; 57. NATHANIEL[5].

---

[49] Henrico Co. Wills & Deeds 1697-1704, p. 114. He is the first certain Jefferson ancestor of Thomas[6] Jefferson. The John Jefferson who came in the *Bona Nova* and was in Elizabeth City, 1623/4, and at James City, 1624/5, went to the West Indies by 1628 (*MCGC*, p. 172) and left no descendants in Virginia.

[50] Henrico Co. Wills & Deeds 1697-1704, p. 243.

[51] Philip Turpin notebook, in *The Virginia Genealogist*, XXXI, pp. 9-10.

[52] Henrico Co. Orders & Wills 1678-93, p. 229.

[53] Henrico Co. Deeds & Wills 1688-97, pp. 107, 223.

[54] Henrico Co. Wills & Deeds 1677-92, pp. 209-10.

[55] Henrico Co. Wills & Deeds 1706-09, p. 33.

[56] *Ibid.*, p. 67.

[57] Albemarle Parish Register.

[58] *Ibid.*

[59] Sussex Co. Will Bk. A, pp. 4-5.

21. AGNES[4] BRANCH (Thomas[3], Thomas[2], Christopher[1]) married (1) 9. *Edward[4] Osborne*, on whose estate she was granted administration, Sept. 1724,[60] and (2), by 11 Oct. 1726,[61] John Worsham, Jr., who left will 11 Oct 1744-Nov. 1745.[62]

Issue: (by 1) see OSBORNE; (by 2) [WORSHAM] 58. EDWARD[5]; 59. Mary[5], married 86. *Richard[5] Wilkinson* (see COX); 60. Capt. John[5], of Bermuda Hundred, left land at Bermuda Hundred by his grandfather John Worsham, Sr.,[63] chose Joshua Worsham as his guardian, 4 Jan. 1754,[64] left will 25 Nov. 1768-7 April 1769,[65] married 147. *Mary[5] Epes* (see EPES) who married (2) 132. Christopher[5] Branch and (3), by July 1773,[66] 181. Benjamin[5] Branch, without issue.

22. ELIZABETH[4] BRANCH (Thomas[3], Thomas[1], Christopher[1]) died 30 Nov. 1766 at "Whitby," Chesterfield County.[67] She married (1), 1710, Robert Goode of "Whitby," who left will 25 May 1718-17 July 1718,[68] (2), by Oct. 1725,[69] Page Punch, born 13 Dec. 1692,[70] who left will 31 Aug. 1726-6 Nov. 1727,[71] and (3), as his (2) wife, Edward Curd, who left will 4 Feb. 1739/40-Dec. 1742.[72]

Issue: (by 1) [GOODE] 61. ROBERT[5]; 62. Francis[5]; (by 2) [PUNCH] 63. Mary[5].

23. FRANCES[4] BRANCH (Thomas[3], Thomas[2], Christopher[1]) married Lodowick Tanner, born 1692, who owned 125 acres in Henrico County, 1736,[73]

---

[60] Henrico Co. Minute Bk. 1719-24, p. 359.

[61] Henrico Co. Wills & Deeds 1725-37, p. 62.

[62] Henrico Co. Wills & Deeds 1744-48, p. 97.

[63] Chesterfield Co. Will Bk. 1, p. 137; Order Bk. 1, p. 402, will of John Worsham, 8 Dec. 1751-5 Oct. 1753.

[64] Chesterfield Co. Order Bk. 1, p. 430.

[65] Chesterfield Co. Will Bk. 3, p. 5; Order Bk. 4, p. 279.

[66] Chesterfield Co. Order Bk. 5, p. 304.

[67] George Brown Goode, *Virginia Cousins* (Richmond, 1887), p. 37.

[68] Henrico Co. Wills & Deeds 1716-18, p. 260.

[69] Henrico Co. Orphans Court Bk. 1677-1739, p. 54.

[70] Prince George's Co., Md., Court Record B, 1699-1705, p. 232. Page Punch, 10 years old on 13 December last, was in March 1702/3 bound by his mother Mary Punch to Mr. Clement Brooke until age 21.

[71] Henrico Co. Wills & Deeds 1725-37, p. 152.

[72] Henrico County Miscellaneous Court Records, IV, p. 1177.

[73] Fleet, *op. cit.*, p. 29.

moved to Amelia County, married (2), (bond 5) May 1764,[74] Ann (___ Johnson, and left will 10 Aug. 1773-23 Dec. 1773.[75]

Issue: [TANNER] 64. BRANCH[5]; 65. Sarah[5], married 17. *Peter[5] Jones* (see PRICE-LLEWELLIN); 66. Elizabeth[5], married 28. *William[5] Osborne* (see OSBORNE).

26. MARTHA[4] BRANCH (Thomas[3], Thomas[2], Christopher[1]) married, after Aug. 1736, Daniel Willson who left will 8 Oct. 1785-23 March 1786.[76]

Issue: [WILLSON] 67. THOMAS BRANCH[5]; 68. DANIEL[5]; 69. ELIZABETH[5].

27. MARGERY[4] BRANCH (Thomas[3], Thomas[2], Christopher[1]) married (1), after Aug. 1736, 516. John[6] Goode, nephew of her sister Elizabeth's (1) husband, who left will, now lost, proved Sept. 1743.[77] He was described as a carpenter of Henrico County in the deed, 12 Nov. 1736, whereby Francis James [his step-father] conveyed to him 173 acres on Stoney Creek in what is now Chesterfield County, adjoining other land belonging to him.[78]

She married (2) Jacob Bugg, born 16 Feb. 1722/3,[79] of Chesterfield County and later a justice of Mecklenburg County, who left will 27 Nov. 1773-13 Dec. 1773.[80]

Issue: (by 1) [GOODE] 70. JOHN[5]; 71. BENNETT[5]; 72. THOMAS[5]; (by 2) [BUGG] 73. Jacob[5], left will 17 May 1787-11 Feb. 1788,[81] unmarried; 74. LUCY[5]; 75. ELIZABETH BRANCH[5].

28. MATTHEW[4] BRANCH (Matthew[3], Thomas[2], Christopher[1]), of "Hanna Spring," Chesterfield County, owned 297 acres, 1736,[82] and left will 7 July 1766-5 June 1767.[83] He married ___.

Issue: 76. MATTHEW[5]; 77. Samuel[5], left "Barbados" on the back of

---

[74] Williams, *Marriages of Amelia County*, p. 104.
[75] Amelia Co. Will Bk. 2, pp. 106-07; Order Bk. 13, p. 233.
[76] Amelia Co. Will Bk. 3, pp. 427-30.
[77] Henrico Co. Order Bk. 1737-46, p. 230.
[78] Henrico Co. Deeds & Wills 1725-37, pp. 596-97.
[79] St. Peter's Parish, New Kent County, Register.
[80] Mecklenburg Co. Will Bk. 1, p. 175; June Banks Evans, *Journals of William Emmanuel Bugg, 1848-1935* (New Orleans, 1986), p. 299.
[81] Mecklenburg Co. Will Bk. 2, p. 246.
[82] Fleet, *op. cit.*, p. 9.
[83] Chesterfield Co. Will Bk. 1, pp. 527-28; Order Bk. 4, p. 45.

"Kingsland," 280 acres, which he sold to Branch Tanner, 3 May 1771;[84] 78. EDWARD[5]; 79. THOMAS[5].

29. JOHN[4] BRANCH (Matthew[3], Thomas[2], Christopher[1]), on whose estate administration was granted 1 Feb. 1750/1,[85] owned 300 acres in Henrico County, 1736.[86] He married 87. *Johannah[5] Hancock* (see HARRIS, Thomas), who left will 11 Jan. 1769-5 July 1771.[87]

Issue: 80. John[5], left will 27 Nov. 1768-6 Jan. 1769,[88] unmarried; 81. SAMUEL[5]; 82. HANNAH [Johannah][5]; 83. MATTHEW[5]; 84. Frances[5], chose Samuel Branch as her guardian, 2 Aug. 1754,[89] died young; 85. Betty[5], for whom Samuel Branch was appointed guardian, 2 Aug. 1754,[90] left will 5 Oct. 1765-1 Aug. 1766.[91]

30. OLIVE[4] BRANCH (Matthew[3], Thomas[2], Christopher[1]) owned 225 acres in Henrico County, 1736,[92] took oaths as tobacco inspector at Rocky Run Warehouse, 3 Jan. 1752,[93] and left will 16 Oct. 1779-5 April 1782.[94] He married his cousin 37. Verlinche[4] Branch.

Issue: 86. James[5], second lieutenant of Capt. David Patterson's company, Chesterfield County militia, Oct. 1778, of Chesterfield County, 1790; 87. OLIVE[5]; 88. Judith[5], married, (bond 7) Sept. 1772,[95] Matthew Anderson.

31. DANIEL[4] BRANCH (Matthew[3], Thomas[2], Christopher[1]) subscribed oath of allegiance in Powhatan County, 1777,[96] and left will 13 April 1782-15 Aug. 1782.[97] He married, before Nov. 1750, Elizabeth Porter of Cumberland

---

[84] Chesterfield Co. Deed Bk. 6, pp. 330-31. This land had been deeded to Matthew[3] by James Branch, 27 Sept. 1684.

[85] Chesterfield Co. Order Bk. 1, p. 80.

[86] Fleet, *op. cit.,* p. 8.

[87] Chesterfield Co. Will Bk. 2, p. 44; Order Bk. 5, p. 12.

[88] Chesterfield Co. Will Bk. 1, p. 528; Order Bk. 4, p. 250.

[89] *Ibid.*

[90] *Ibid.*

[91] Chesterfield Co. Will Bk. 1, p. 535; Order Bk. 3, p. 744.

[92] Fleet, *op. cit.,* p. 10.

[93] Chesterfield Co. Order Bk. 1, p. 166.

[94] Chesterfield Co. Will Bk. 3, p. 299; Order Bk. 6, p. 345.

[95] Knorr, *Marriage Bonds ... Chesterfield County,* p. 3.

[96] *The Virginia Genealogist,* XXVII, p. 195.

[97] Powhatan Co. Will Bk. 1, pp. 76-77.

County, daughter of Thomas Porter.[98]

Issue: 89. DANIEL[5]; 90. THOMAS[5]; 91. Dutoy[5], subscribed oath of allegiance in Powhatan County, 1777;[99] 92. Mary[5], born 18 Nov. 1761,[100] married, (bond 21) Oct. 1782,[101] John Cocke of Goochland County, possibly 349. *John[6] Cocke* (see BALEY-COCKE), born 17 July 1756; 93. Matthew[5], born 30 March 1764,[102] died Oct. 1823 in Powhatan County, aged 58,[103] left will 13 Oct. 1823-20 Nov. 1823,[104] unmarried; 94. ELIZABETH BARBARA[5]; 95. Frances[5], married 45. *John[5] Price* (see PRICE); 96. Samuel[5], devised the land where his father lived.

32. THOMAS[4] BRANCH (Matthew[3], Thomas[2], Christopher[1]), of Shampoke, owned 150 acres, 1736,[105] and left will 29 Aug. 1769-5 Nov. 1773.[106] He married Mary ___, who was born 6 Oct. 1719.[107]

Issue:[108] 97. THOMAS[5]; 98. James[5], born 24 Feb. 174[1/?]2; 99. GARNER[5]; 100. Phoebe[5], born 10 Nov. 1744, married __ Lockett; 101. Patsy[5], born 12 April 1749; 102. EDWARD[5]; 103. Mary[5], born 19 Nov. 1755; 104. Elizabeth[5], born 7 Dec. 1759.

34. ELIZABETH[4] BRANCH (Matthew[3], Thomas[2], Christopher[1]) died 7 Nov. 1789. She married (1), 2 Nov. 1730, 26. *Stephen[4] Woodson* (see WOODSON), who died 18 Jan. 1735/6,[109] and (2) 24. *Charles[5] Bates* (see BATES), who was left a part of "Poplar Springs," Charles City County, was vestryman of St. James Northam Parish, Goochland County, and died 16 May 1790 in his 72nd year.[110]

---

[98] Cumberland Co. Will Bk. 1, p. 51, will of Isaac Dutoy, 26 Nov. 1750-March 1750; Will Bk. 1, p. 321, will of Thomas Porter, 15 April 1765-27 April 1767.

[99] *The Virginia Genealogist*, XXVII, p. 195.

[100] W. Mac. Jones, ed., *The Douglas Register* (Richmond, 1928), p. 162.

[101] Catherine Lindsay Knorr, *Marriage Bonds and Ministers' Returns of Powhatan County, Virginia, 1777-1830* (Pine Bluff, Ark., 1957), p. 15. Note, however, the will of her brother Matthew shows her name as Cox.

[102] Jones, *loc. cit.*.

[103] *The Family Visitor*, Richmond, 1 Nov. 1823.

[104] Powhatan Co. Will Bk. 6, p. 477-79.

[105] Fleet, *op. cit.*, p. 10.

[106] Chesterfield Co. Will Bk. 2, p. 2; Order Bk. 5, p. 349.

[107] John K. Martin Papers, in *Virginia Genealogical Society Quarterly*, XIII, p. 38.

[108] *Ibid.*

[109] Stephen Woodson Bible, *W* (2) VIII, p. 310.

[110] *Ibid.*

Issue: (by 1) see WOODSON; (by 2) [BATES][111] 106. Daniel[5], born 4 March 1744/5, died 19 Sept. 1800;[112] 106. Molley[5], born 27 Feb. 1747/8; 107. Charles Fleming[5], born 26 May 1749.

36. ELIZABETH[4] BRANCH (James[3], Thomas[2], Christopher[1]) married John Wooldridge, son of John and Martha (___) Wooldridge,[113] who in 1748 was licensed to keep an ordinary at his house in Goochland, later Powhatan, County and later was a planter of Chesterfield County,[114] married (2) Margaret ___, died after 20 May 1783,[115] and left will 16 Nov. 1780-4 July 1783.[116]

Issue: [WOOLDRIDGE] 108. RICHARD[5]; 109. JOHN[5]; 110. MARY[5]; 111. WILLIAM[5]; 112. ELIZABETH[5]; 113. EDMOND[5]; 114. VIRLINCHE[5]; 115. PHEBE[5]; 116. (probably) ROBERT[5]; 117. (probably) THOMAS[5].

39. JOHN[4] BRANCH (James[3], Thomas[2], Christopher[1]) was deeded by his mother tracts of 200 and 31 acres, 29 Nov. 1749,[117] but apparently lived for a few years in Lunenburg County, possibly as a merchant.[118] He returned to Chesterfield County where his mother and he sold 20 acres on Bear Creek, 4 Dec. 1755,[119] and he was executor of his mother's will. On 7 June 1766 Thomas Branch deeded to him 100 acres including the plantation where John lived but on 1 April 1772 with wife Susannah he sold this land.[120] He then moved to Bedford County where he died before 24 April 1787 when the inventory of his estate was returned.[121] He married Susannah ___, who died after 10 Sept. 1814 when she joined her son James in a deed.[122]

---

[111] Woodson Bible, in *W*(2) VIII, pp. 310-11.

[112] His will, not recorded, was proved 14 June 1802, the executors refusing to qualify (Chesterfield Co. Order Bk. 14, p. 281).

[113] She may have been 8. *Martha*[4] *Osborne* (see OSBORNE).

[114] William C. Wooldridge, *The Wooldridge Family* (Richmond, 2002), pp. 11-14. Although the 1750 will of Mary (___) Branch establishes that John Wooldridge married her daughter, her identification as Elizabeth rests upon Elizabeth Wooldridge's witnessing the 1755 deed of Mary and her son John[4] Branch (see note 119).

[115] Chesterfield Co. Deed Bk. 10, p. 201.

[116] Chesterfield Co. Will Bk. 3, p. 395; Order Bk. 6, p. 452.

[117] Chesterfield Co. Deed Bk. 1, p. 45.

[118] Lunenburg Co. Order Bks. 2-4, 1751-57, *passim*.

[119] Chesterfield Co. Deed Bk. 2, p. 355.

[120] Chesterfield Co. Deed Bk. Deed Bk. 5, p. 315; Deed Bk. 6, pp. 436-37.

[121] Bedford Co. Will Bk. 1, pp. 521-22.

[122] Bedford Co. Deed Bk. 14, p. 204.

Issue: 118. SARAH[5]; 119. James[5], married (1), 11 Oct. 1789,[123] Frances Terry and (2), 28 April 1792,[124] Martha Minor.

40. PHOEBE[4] BRANCH (James[3], Thomas[2], Christopher[1]) married Edward Hill,[125] son of Edward and Anne (Fowler) Hill, of Chesterfield County, who left will 2 June 1799-13 July 1803.[126]

Issue: [HILL] 120. JAMES[5]; 121. OLIVE[5]; 122. Frances[5], married (1) 99. Garner[5] Branch and (2), (consent 14) Feb. 1792,[127] Thomas Brooks, on whose estate she was granted administration 14 Oct. 1793.[128]

41. OBEDIENCE[4] BRANCH (John[3], William[2], Christopher[1]) left will 26 Jan. 1745/6-17 June 1746.[129] She married (1), Nov. 1696, 14. *John[3] Cocke* (see BALEY-COCKE), (2) Alexander Trent, who left will 27 June 1703-2 Aug. 1703,[130] and (3) Thomas Turpin, on whose estate Obedience gave bond as executrix, 4 May 1724.[131]

Issue: (by 1) see BALEY-COCKE; (by 2) [TRENT] 123. ALEXANDER[5]; (by 3) [TURPIN] 124. THOMAS[5]; 125. Obedience[5], married, as his (2) wife, 54. Benjamin[4] Branch; 126. William[5], died young; 127. Mary[5], married 61. Robert[5] Goode.

42. PRISCILLA[4] BRANCH (John[3], William[2], Christopher[1]) died after 7 Nov. 1760.[132] She married (1), 16 July 1699, Edward Skerme, who left will 21 March 1699/1700-1 Aug. 1700,[133] and (2), by 7 Feb. 1700/1,[134] Joseph Wilkinson of Henrico County,[135] probably son of John Wilkinson and 4. *Sarah[2] Royall* (see ROYALL), who left will 19 Oct. 1750-2 Dec. 1752.[136]

Issue: (by 2) [WILKINSON] 128. JOSEPH[5]; 129. Martha[5], born by 1710,

---

[123] Bedford Co. marriage return, in Hinshaw, VI, p. 881.

[124] *Ibid.*

[125] Lloyd DeWitt Bockstruck, "James Hill," unpublished ms.

[126] Chesterfield Co. Will Bk. 5, p. 421; Order Bk. 14, p. 116.

[127] Knorr, *Marriage Bonds ... Chesterfield Ciunty*, p. 22.

[128] Chesterfield Co. Order Bk. 10, p. 241.

[129] Goochland Co. Deed Bk. 5, p. 139.

[130] Henrico Co. Wills & Deeds 1697-1704, p. 342.

[131] Henrico Co. Miscellaneous Court Records I, p. 601; Minute Bk. 1719-24, p. 337.

[132] Chesterfield Co. Deed Bk. 5, p. 230.

[133] Henrico Co. Wills & Deeds 1697-1704, p. 192.

[134] *Ibid.*, p. 243.

[135] Lloyd DeWitt Bockstruck, "The Wilkinson Family of Southside Virginia," *The Virginia Genealogist*, XXXVI, pp. 133-38.

[136] Chesterfield Co. Will Bk. 1, p. 467; Order Bk. 1, p. 295.

married 18. *Thomas*[4] *Howlett* (see SHARP-BAUGH); 130. EDWARD[5]; 131. Mary[5], born by 1710, named in will of Jane (___) Branch Baugh Gower.

43. HENRY[4] BRANCH (Christopher[3], Christopher[2], Christopher[1]) resided in the part of Henrico County which became Chesterfield County, owned 700 acres, 1736,[137] and died before 28 July 1748 when the inventory of his estate was made.[138] He married 25. Amey[4] Branch.

Issue: 132. CHRISTOPHER[5]; 133. Martha[5], left will 31 Oct. 1773-1 April 1774;[139] 134. ANN[5]; 135. WILLIAM[5]; 136. HENRY[5]; 137. Elizabeth[5], chose Thomas Branch as her guardian, 7 Feb. 1752.[140]

46. CICELY[4] BRANCH (Christopher[3], Christopher[2], Christopher[1]), born 27 Feb. 1695/6, left will 17 Nov. 1769-6 July 1770.[141] She married, 9 Oct. 1718,[142] as his (2) wife, William Bass who left will 27 Feb. 1746/7-2 Feb. 1753.[143]

Issue: [BASS][144] 138. CHRISTOPHER[5]; 139. MARY[5]; 140. Thomas[5], born 4 Feb. 1723/4, died young; 141. Archard[5], born 31 Jan. 1725/6; 142. Thomas[5], born 23 March 1727/8; 143. Edward[5], born 31 July 1730; 144. Peter[5], born 23 Dec. 1732; 145. JOSEPH[5]; 146. Ann[5], chose William Walthall as her guardian, Jan. 1755,[145] married 181. Benjamin[5] Branch; 147. ELIZABETH[5]; 148. Sarah[5], married 91. *Thomas*[5] *Friend* (see COX).

47. OBEDIENCE[4] BRANCH (Christopher[3], Christopher[2], Christopher[1]) left will 12 Feb. 1771-5 Aug. 1774.[146] She married William Cheatham who left will 27 April 1751-6 Oct. 1752.[147]

Issue: [CHEATHAM][148] 149. WILLIAM[5]; 150. Obedience[5], married 23. *Charles*[5] *Cheatham* (see OSBORNE); 151. ANN[5]; 152. THOMAS[5]; 153.

---

[137] Fleet, *op. cit.*, p. 7.

[138] Henrico Co. Deed Bk. 1748-55, pp. 23-24.

[139] Chesterfield Co. Will Bk. 2, p. 232; Order Bk. 6, p. 3.

[140] Chesterfield Co. Order Bk. 1, p. 170.

[141] Chesterfield Co. Will Bk. 2, pp. 38-39; Order Bk. 4, p. 429.

[142] Bass Bible, *The Virginia Genealogist*, IX, p. 81.

[143] Chesterfield Co. Will Bk. 1, pp. 115-19; Order Bk. 1, p. 305.

[144] Bass Bible, in *The Virginia Genealogist*, IX, pp. 81-82. His son William by his (1) wife married 24. *Martha*[4] *Clay* (see CLAY).

[145] Chesterfield Co. Order Bk. 2, p. 30.

[146] Chesterfield Co. Will Bk. 2, pp. 250-51; Order Bk. 6, p. 50.

[147] Chesterfield Co. Will Bk. 1, pp. 90-92; Order Bk. 1, p. 256.

[148] Alberta Marjorie Dennstedt, "The Cheatham Family of Colonial Virginia," *The Virginia Genealogist*, XXX, pp. 17-23,

Mary[5]; 154. CHRISTOPHER[5].

51. THOMAS[4] JEFFERSON (Mary[3] Branch, Christopher[2], Christopher[1]), born 1679, died 15 Feb. 1730/1,[149] owned 492 and 15 acres in Henrico County, 1704, was a justice of Henrico, and left will 15 March 1725/6-6 April 1731.[150] He married (1), 20 Nov. 1697,[151] Mary Field, born 3 Feb. 1679/80, died 13 Aug. 1715, daughter of Maj. Peter Field and his wife Judith (Soane) Randolph, widow of Henry Randolph and daughter of Henry Soane,[152] and (2) Alice [Ailsey] Ward.[153]

Issue: [JEFFERSON] (by 1)[154] 155. Judith[5], married 13. *George[4] Farrar* (see FARRAR); 156. Thomas[5], born 24 Sept. 1700, went to sea and died 14 Feb. 1723/4 aboard the *Williamsburg*, Capt. Isham Randolph, commander, on a return trip to Virginia; 157. FIELD[5]; 158. Martha[5], died young; 159. PETER[5]; 160. Mary[5], married 124. Thomas[5] Turpin; (by 2) 161. MARTHA[5].

52. MARY[4] JEFFERSON (Mary[3] Branch, Christopher[2], Christopher[1]) left will 29 Oct. 1744-Sept. 1745.[155] She married Thomas Harris, who left will 5 Oct. 1729-6 July 1730.[156]

Issue: [HARRIS][157] 162. JOHN[5]; 163. Thomas[5], left will 18 May 1741-Aug. 1741,[158] never married; 164. MARY[5].; 165. EDITH[5]; 166. Sarah[5], left will 12 April 1753-24 Sept. 1753,[159] never married; 167. MARTHA[5]; 168. Phebe[5], died young; 169. ANN[5]; 170. Francis[5], left will 12 May 1743-July 1743,[160] never married; 171. JAMES[5]; 172. BENJAMIN[5]; 173. WILLIAM[5].

53. MARTHA[4] JEFFERSON (Mary[3] Branch, Christopher[2], Christopher[1]) married, as his (1) wife, Robert Wynne [Winn] of Surry County, whom she joined in selling two tracts of land in Prince George County, 8 May 1718,[161] and

---

[149] Jefferson Bible (1668), *T* VII, p. 122.

[150] Henrico Co. Deeds & Wills 1725-37, p. 293.

[151] Henrico Co. Deeds &c 1697-99,p. 96.

[152] Randolph family record, *W*(1) IV, p. 126; Jefferson Bible, *loc. cit.*

[153] Philip Turpin notebook, *loc. cit.*; Henrico Co. Order Bk. 1719-24, pp. 116, 276.

[154] Jefferson Bible, in *T* VII, pp. 121-22.

[155] Henrico Co. Wills & Deeds 1744-48, p. 78.

[156] Henrico Co. Wills & Deeds 1725-37, p. 272.

[157] Philip Turpin notebook, in *The Virginia Genealogist*, XXXI, p. 9, which fails to mention son John and assigns his marriage and children to son Thomas.

[158] Henrico Co. Miscellaneous Records IV, p. 1139.

[159] Cumberland Co. Will Bk. 1, p. 72.

[160] Henrico Co. Miscellaneous Records IV, p. 1231.

[161] Prince George Co. Wills & Deeds 1713-28, pp. 222, 224.

who married (2), (bond 9) Aug. 1753,[162] Mary Philipson and left will 1754-12 Aug. 1754.[163]

Issue: [WYNNE][164] 174. LUCRETIA[5]; 175. MARTHA[5]; 176. ANGELICA[5]; 177. (Son)[5]; 178. ANNE[5].

54. BENJAMIN[4] BRANCH (Benjamin[3], Christopher[2], Christopher[1]), born about 1700, owned 300 acres in Henrico County, 1736,[165] and left will 31 Dec. 1760-5 Nov. 1762.[166] He married (1), before 1727, his cousin 11. *Mary[5] Osborne* (see OSBORNE), and (2) his cousin 125. Obedience[5] Turpin.

Issue:[167] (by 1) 179. Mary[5], died unmarried before 1760; 180. Martha[5], died unmarried before 1760; (by 2) 181. BENJAMIN[5]; 182. Thomas[5], tithable in 1762,[168] left will 22 April 1778-5 June 1778,[169] unmarried; 183. EDWARD[5]; 184. Obedience[5], married (Edward?) Bass; 185. PRUDENCE[5]; 186. Mary[5], chose Robert Goode as her guardian, 5 Nov. 1762.[170]

55. HENRY[5] MITCHELL (Tabitha[4] Branch, Thomas[3], Thomas[2], Christopher[1]) died before 20 Dec. 1770 when his widow was granted administration on his estate.[171] He married Priscilla __, who married (2), (bond 3) Dec. 1774,[172] Samuel Northington..

---

[162] Catherine Lindsay Knorr, *Marriage Bonds and Ministers' Returns of Brunswick County, Virginia, 1750-1810* (Pine Bluff, Ark., 1953), p. 110.

[163] Sussex Co. Will Bk. A, p. 14.

[164] Philip Turpin notebook, in *The Virginia Genealogist*, XXX, p. 9, states they had a son and two daughters. The number of daughters may be incorrect. Angelica[5] had a son named Jefferson; Martha[5] presumably was named for her mother; Lucretia[5] had a granddaughter Martha Jefferson Bell.

[165] Fleet, *op. cit.*, p. 8.

[166] Chesterfield Co. Will Bk. 1, pp. 335-36; Order Bk. 3, pp. 271-72.

[167] James Branch Cabell, *Branchiana* (Richmond, 1907), pp. 43-44. The two eldest daughters are named in the will of their grandfather, Thomas Osborne, 17 Feb. 1730-Hybe 1733 (Henrico Co. Wills & Deeds 1725-37, p. 394). Which wife was the mother of the three sons is not clearly established, but since Edward named a daughter Obedience Turpin and Benjamin a daughter Obedience it appears more likely that Obedience Turpin was the mother of all the younger children.

[168] *The Southside Virginian*, V, p. 82.

[169] Chesterfield Co. Will Bk. 3, p. 150; Order Bk. 6, p. 173.

[170] Chesterfield Co. Order Bk. 3, p. 272.

[171] Sussex Co. Order Bk. 1770-76, p. 16.

[172] Catherine Lindsay Knorr, *Marriage Bonds and Ministers' Returns of Sussex County, Virginia, 1754-1810* (Pine Bluff, Ark., 1952), p. 59.

Issue: [MITCHELL][173] 187. Ann[6], born 9 Aug. 1742; 188. Mary[6], born 3 Dec. 1743;[174] 189. Henry[6], born 31 Aug. 1745,[175] of Prince George County, married Jane (Ambrose?),[176] who joined him, 17 June 1773, in deeding to his mother 327 acres on the south side of Jones' Hole Swamp where she lived;[177] 190. Branch[6], born 14 __ 174_, of Prince George County,[178] and later of Sussex County, married Elizabeth ___; 191. Priscilla[6], born 11 Jan. 1750; 192. Jones[6], born June 1752;[179] 193. Rubin[6], born 14 July 1755;[180] 194. Reaps[6], born 13 Feb. 1758,[181] died 12 March 1803, left will 28 Feb. 1803-4 Aug. 1803,[182] of Prince George and later of Sussex County, married, 30 Dec. 1783, Susannah Rives, born 10 June 1755, died 28 Aug. 1815; 195. Frances[6], born 19 Oct. 1760,[183] married, (bond 7) April 1783,[184] Richard Bonner of Prince George County; 196. Thomas[6], born 25 Feb. 1763, given 327 acres on Jones Hole Swamp by his mother Priscilla Northington, 5 Aug. 1789;[185] 197. Tabitha[6], born 22 Jan. 1767, perhaps the Tabitha who married, 13 Sept. 1785, Frederick Batts.[186]

56. THOMAS[5] MITCHELL (Tabitha[4] Branch, Thomas[3], Thomas[2], Christopher[1]), of Albemarle Parish, Sussex County, left will 20 Oct. 1761-18 [8?] March 1762.[187] He married Amy Goodwyn, born 31 Aug. 1732,[188] who married (2), (bond 5) Oct. 1762, John Raines.[189]

---

[173] Mitchell Bible, in *NGSQ* LX, p. 46.

[174] Albemarle Parish Register shows baptism 20 Dec. 1742.

[175] Albemarle Parish Register.

[176] On 19 Sept. 1771 Henry Mitchell deeded to brother-in-law Thomas Ambrose for love and affection 50 acres on the south side of Jones' Hole Swamp (Sussex Co. Deed Bk. D, p. 397). Since Thomas had a wife Amy (Albemarle Parish Register) he, presumably, did not marry Henry's sister.

[177] Sussex Co. Deed Bk. E, p. 81.

[178] Sussex Co. Deed Bk. D, p. 450.

[179] Albemarle Parish Register.

[180] *Ibid.*

[181] *Ibid.*

[182] Sussex Co. Will Bk. F, p. 339.

[183] Albemarle Parish Register, which shows 14 Dec. 1760.

[184] Knorr, *Marriage Bonds ... Sussex County*, p. 10.

[185] Sussex Co. Deed Bk. G, p. 323.

[186] Knorr, *Marriage Bonds ... Sussex County*, p. 6.

[187] Sussex Co. Will Bk. A, p. 232.

[188] *W*(1) XV, p. 107.

[189] Knorr, *Marriage Bonds ... Sussex County*, p. 68.

Issue: [MITCHELL][190] 198. Thomas[6], died 27 July 1826,[191] of Thomas Co., Ga., married Ann Raines; 199. John[6]; 200. Gen. Henry[6], of Hancock Co., Ga., married Frances Hobbs; 201. Tabitha[6]; 202. Winnefret[6].

57. NATHANIEL[5] MITCHELL (Tabitha[4] Branch, Thomas[3], Thomas[2], Christopher[1]) died by 16 May 1771 when an accounting of his estate was returned.[192] He married Elizabeth ___, who married (2) William Bishop.

Issue: [MITCHELL][193] 203. John[6], twin, born 31 Jan. 1756, left will 6 June 1782-19 Sept. 1782,[194] married, (bond 5) June 1779,[195] Scota Stewart, who married (2) Peter Cain, Jr.; 204. Tabitha[6], born 31 Jan. 1756, married David Golightly and moved to South Carolina, probably Spartanburg County; 205. Lewis[6], born 18 July 1763, named as a reversionary heir of brother John "if he comes back," but living 1786; 206. Ann[6], married Nicholas Ogburn.

58. EDWARD[5] WORSHAM (Agnes[4] Branch, Thomas[3], Thomas[2], Christopher[1]) died before 3 Nov. 1775 when administration on his estate was granted to his widow Elizabeth ___.[196]

Issue: [WORSHAM][197] 207. Edward[6], left will 30 May 1792-10 June 1793,[198] unmarried; 208. Michel[6], daughter; 209. Sarah[6], married, 5 Dec. 1793,[199] Archibald Baugh; 210. John[6].

61. ROBERT[5] GOODE (Elizabeth[4] Branch, Thomas[3], Thomas[2], Christopher[1]), born 19 July 1711, left will 8 Sept. 1765-6 June 1766.[200] He held 360 acres in Henrico County, 1736.[201] He married, 1737, 127. Mary[5] Turpin,

---

[190] *W*(1) XXVI, pp. 126-27.

[191] *Ibid.*, p. 127.

[192] Sussex Co. Will Bk. 3, p. 304.

[193] Albemarle Parish Register; Sussex Co. Deed Bk. D, pp. 40-43, deed of slaves to each of his children, 14 June 1768; Sussex Co. Deed Bk. F, p. 523, sale by devisees under the will of John[6] Mitchell, 15 June 1786.

[194] Sussex Co. Will Bk. D, p. 89.

[195] Knorr, *Marriage Bonds ... Sussex County*, p. 54.

[196] Chesterfield Co. Order Bk. 6, p. 91.

[197] *Ibid.*

[198] Chesterfield Co. Will Bk. 4, p. 354; Order Bk. 10, p. 130. He named uncle John Royall.

[199] Knorr, *Marriage Bonds ... Chesterfield County*, p. 10; Chesterfield Co. Order Bk. 11, p. 42.

[200] Chesterfield Co. Will Bk. 2, p. 108; Order Bk. 3, p. 734. Goode, *op. cit.*, pp. 37, 42, gives 6 March 1765 and 29 Oct. 1760 as dates of his death, both incorrect.

[201] Fleet, *op. cit.*, p. 17.

born 6 Sept. 1720, died 6 March 1765.

Issue: [GOODE][202] 211. Elizabeth[6], born 2 March 1738[/9?], "idiot"; 212. Mary[6], born 6 April 1741, married Seth Ward of Powhatan County; 213. Col. Robert[6], married 76. *Sarah[5] Bland* (see BLAND); 214. Col. Francis[6], of "Seven Oaks," Chesterfield County, born 20 Dec. 1744, died 23 April 1795 on board the sloop *Fanny* on his way home from Philadelphia,[203] left will 22 Nov. 1794-8 June 1795,[204] captain of Chesterfield County militia, 1777, married, (bond 28) Nov. 1774,[205] 551. Alice[6] Harris; 215. Obedience[6], born 12 April 1747, died 1800, unmarried, "idiot"; 216. Martha[6], born 10 Aug. 1749, died 30 Sept. 1751; 217. Martha[6], born 24 Oct. 1751, died 15 Dec. 1752; 218. Thomas[6], born 31 Dec. 1753, died 6 April 1813 at Manchester, married, 1777, Elizabeth Prosser who died 26 March 1838 in Chesterfield County, aged 80;[206] 219. Col. Samuel[6], born 21 March 1756 at "Whitby,", died 14 Nov. 1822 at "Invermay," Mecklenburg County,[207] lieutenant of the Chesterfield County troop of horse during the Revolutionary War, later colonel of militia, lawyer, represented Mecklenburg County in the House of Delegates, 1778-84, member of Congress, 1799-1801,[208] married, 5 Oct. 1786,[209] Mary Armistead[7] Burwell, daughter of 138. *Lewis[6] Burwell* (see BURWELL), who died 20 March 1829; 220. Martha[6], born 13 June 1760, died 29 March 1774.

64. BRANCH[5] TANNER (Frances[4] Branch, Thomas[3], Thomas[2], Christopher[1]), of Amelia County, left will 10 June 1787-25 April 1793.[210] He married, (bond 2) Jan. 1764,[211] 230. *Mary Page[6] Finney* (see BALEY- COCKE).

---

[202] Goode, *op. cit.*, pp. 42, 54-63. These birth dates are not in agreement with the will of Robert[5] Goode, which indicates Mary and Robert were still under age in 1765.

[203] *Virginia Gazette and Richmond and Manchester Advertiser*, 7 May 1795.

[204] Chesterfield Co. Will Bk. 4, p. 476; Order Bk. 11, p. 132.

[205] Katherine B. Elliott, *Marriage Records, 1749-1840, Cumberland County, Virginia* (South Hill, Va., 1959), p. 59.

[206] *Whig*, Richmond, 27 March 1828.

[207] *Enquirer*, Richmond, 3 Dec. 1822.

[208] *Biographical Directory of the American Congress, 1774-1996* (Alexandria, Va., 1997), p. 1102; Leonard, pp. 130, 134, 138, 142, 150, 154.

[209] Katherine B. Elliott, *Marriage Records, 1765-1810, Mecklenburg County, Virginia* (South Hill, Va., 1963), p. 52, bond 28 Sept. 1786.

[210] Amelia Co. Will Bk. 5, p. 13.

[211] Kathleen Booth Williams, *Marriages of Amelia County, Virginia, 1735-1815* (n.p., 1961), p. 104.

Issue: [TANNER] 221. Frances[6], died 1797,[212] married, (bond 22) Oct. 1782,[213] as his (1) wife, Maj. Peter Field Archer, born 1756, died 25 April 1814, aged 58, near Scottsville, Powhatan County,[214] of Henrico and Powhatan counties, lieutenant in Revolutionary War,[215] who married (2), (bond 22) Jan. 1799,[216] Judith Eggleston[7] Cocke, daughter of 216. *Stephen[6] Cocke* (see BALEY-COCKE); 222. Branch[6], left will 9 Jan. 1784-25 Sept. 1794.[217]

67. THOMAS BRANCH[5] WILLSON (Martha[4] Branch, Thomas[3], Thomas[2], Christopher[1]), born 21 Oct. 1739,[218] died Dec. 1850.[219] He was appointed major of Amelia County militia, 23 Oct. 1777, and lieutenant colonel, 23 April 1778. He married (1), (bond 28) Feb. 1760,[220] 229. *Elizabeth[6] Finney* (see BALEY-COCKE), born 12 Nov. 1742, died 15 May 1773, (2), (bond 2) Dec. 1774,[221] 95. *Judith[5] Friend* (see COX), (3), (bond 27) Nov. 1777,[222] Penefee [Puripu] Barrat, and (4), (bond 1) April 1782,[223] Sarah Walthall.

Issue: [WILLSON][224] (by 1) 223. Lucy[6], born 28 Aug. 1762, married, (bond 18) Oct. 1781,[225] William Gray; 224. Rebecca[6], born 14 Nov. 1764, died 7 April 1829, married, 6 Sept. 1782, Gabriel Gray, born 29 Nov. 1762, died 1 June 1844; 225. Martha[6], born 21 April 1767; 226 Daniel[6], born 26 March 1771, died 1841 in Amelia County, married, (bond 27) Aug. 1789,[226] Elizabeth[7] Anderson, daughter of 66. *Francis[6] Anderson* (see SHEPPEY), born 22 Dec. 1777, died 1825.[227]; (by 2) 227. Thomas Friend[6], born 25 May 1776, died 1841

---

[212] Walter A. Watson, *Notes on Southside Virginia* (Richmond, 1925), p. 154.

[213] Williams, *op. cit.*, p. 5.

[214] *Enquirer*, Richmond, 25 May 1814.

[215] Revolutionary War pension application, Peter Field Archer, BLWt.300-300, National Archives.

[216] Williams, *op. cit.*, p. 5.

[217] Amelia Co. Will Bk. 5, p. 112.

[218] Gray Bible, in *W*(2) XIII, p. 193.

[219] Sons of the Revolution, Virginia, *Genealogy of Members* (Richmond, 1939), p. 270.

[220] Williams, *op. cit.*, p. 120.

[221] Knorr, *Marriage Bonds ... Chesterfield County*, p. 130.

[222] Williams, *op. cit.*, p. 120.

[223] *Ibid.*, p. 121.

[224] Gray Bible, *loc. cit.*

[225] Williams, *op. cit.*, p. 48.

[226] *Ibid.*, p. 120.

[227] Carter Watkins Friend, *The Descendants of Captain Thomas Friend ...* (Alexandria, Va., 1961), p. 137.

in Amelia County, married, (bond 15) Aug. 1796,[228] Ann[7] Anderson, daughter of 66. *Francis[6] Anderson* (see SHEPPEY), born 22 Dec. 1777, died 1825;[229] (by 3) 228. Purpu Barrett Booker[6], born 24 Aug. 1778, married, (bond 25), Aug. 1796,[230] Charles Broadfoot.

68. DANIEL[5] WILLSON (Martha[4] Branch, Thomas[3], Thomas[2], Christopher[1]) died before 11 Oct. 1783 when the inventory of his estate was made.[231] He married, (bond 28) Feb. 1776,[232] 238. *Ann[6] Finney* (see BALEY-COCKE), who married (2) 688. *John[6] Moseley* (see BALEY-COCKE).

Issue: [WILLSON][233] 229. Archer[6]; 230. Daniel[6].

69. ELIZABETH[5] WILLSON (Martha[4] Branch, Thomas[3], Thomas[2], Christopher[1]) married, (bond 26) July 1758,[234] Nathaniel Wilkinson of Amelia County and later of "Solitare," Henrico County.

Issue: [WILKINSON][235] 231. Margaret[6], married, (bond 27) July 1784,[236] William Chamberlayne; 232. Elizabeth[6], married 68. *Richard[6] Gregory* (see WEST).

70. JOHN[5] GOODE (Margery[4] Branch, Thomas[3], Thomas[2], Christopher[1]) died before 10 Jan. 1803 when his widow relinquished her right to administer his estate.[237] On 8 July 1749 Francis James [his step-grandfather] conveyed to him, as "son of John Goode, deceased," 100 acres on Stoney Creek in Chesterfield County, adjoining his land and that of Bennett and Robert Goode.[238] He sold, 4 March 1762, to his uncle Robert Goode the "Whitby" estate, 473 acres near the falls of James River, which had been devised to him by his father,[239] and moved to Cox's Creek, Mecklenburg County where he purchased 225 acres, 25 Dec.

---

[228] Williams, *op. cit.*, p. 120.

[229] Friend, *loc. cit.*

[230] Williams, *op. cit.*, p. 17.

[231] Amelia Co. Will Bk. 3, p. 206.

[232] Williams, *op. cit.*, p. 120.

[233] Amelia Co. Order Bk. 21, p. 7, appointment of Tom B. Willson as their guardian, 25 Sept. 1795.

[234] Williams, *op. cit.*, p. 118.

[235] *The Virginia Genealogist*, XXXVI, p. 6.

[236] Joyce H. Lindsay, *Marriages of Henrico County, Virginia, 1680-1808* (n.p., 1960), p. 16.

[237] Mecklenburg Co. Order Bk. 11, p. 294.

[238] Chesterfield Co. Deed Bk. 1, pp. 33-34.

[239] Chesterfield Co. Deed Bk. 5, p. 8. This deed was also acknowledged by Mary [*sic*, Margery] Bugg [his mother].

1764, and 370 acres, 14 Feb. 1767.[240]   He, however, shortly returned to Chesterfield County where on 1 Sept. 1769 he purchased from John Brush Forsie and his wife Jane [his mother-in-law] her dower interest in the land where he then was living.[241]   On 3 April 1792 he gave a power of attorney to his brother Thomas Goode and to Samuel Hopkins authorizing them to sell his real and personal estate to pay his debts.[242]   He married (1) Jane Gordon, daughter of Alexander Gordon, who, as of Chesterfield County, joined him, 3 Jan. 1777, in the sale of her one-fourth interest in land where they then lived, inherited from her father,[243] and 8 June 1778 relinquished dower in 595 acres in Mecklenburg County sold to Sir Peyton Skipwith,[244] (2), (bond 19) April 1790,[245] Martha Moore, and (3), (bond 18) July 1796,[246] Rebecca J. Pulley, who married (2), (bond 28) Jan. 1807,[247] John Short.

Issue: [GOODE] (by 1) 233. John[6] "Twigg," born 1783, died 26 Aug. 1874, unmarried, student at the University of North Carolina, 1797, and an attorney; (by 2) 234. Jane [Jinny][6], born about 1792, died about 1853, married John Bolling of Dinwiddie County; 235. Dr. Alexander[6], born 1794, living in Petersburg, 1814, and Brunswick County, 1816, married (1), (bond 25) April 1816,[248] Sarah Worthington and (2), (bond 14) Jan. 1828,[249] Minerva Jackson (Rawlings) Harrison.; 236. Lucy[6], born about 1794, married Abner Adams, born about 1781, of Dinwiddie County;[250] (by 3) 237. Bennett[6], died 1879, married, 14 Jan. 1818,[251] Sarah L. Rolfe; 238. Elizabeth B.[6], born 4 Aug. 1802, died 14 Feb. 1827, married, 25 March 1819, Jackson Yancey of North Carolina.

71. BENNETT[5] GOODE (Margery[4] Branch, Thomas[3], Thomas[2], Christopher[1]) died before 7 March 1785 when the inventory of his estate was

[240] Mecklenburg Co. Deed Bk. 1, pp. 53, 466.

[241] Chesterfield Co. Deed Bk. 6, p. 211.

[242] Mecklenburg Co. Deed Bk, 8, p. 300.

[243] Chesterfield Co. Deed Bk. 8, p. 109.

[244] Mecklenburg Co. Deed Bk. 5, pp. 478-79.

[245] Elliott, *Marriage Records ... Mecklenburg County*, p. 51.

[246] *Ibid.*, p. 52.

[247] *Ibid.*, p. 111.

[248] Augusta B. Fothergill, *Marriage Records of Brunswick County, Virginia, 1730-1852* (n.p., 1953), p. 39.

[249] *Ibid.*

[250] Dinwiddie Co. 1850 census, Northern Dist., p. 913 or 457, family 352-352.

[251] Prestwould Chapter DAR, *Marriage Records - 1811-1853, Mecklenburg County, Virginia* (South Hill, Va., 1962), p. 69.

made.[252] He was a member of the Mecklenburg County Committee of Safety, 8 May 1775, justice, 11 Aug. 1776, colonel of militia, 8 Dec. 1777,[253] and was a member of the Conventions of 1775-76 and of the House of Delegates, 1776, 1778-81, 1783-85.[254] He married Isabella[7] Lewis, daughter of 452. *Howell[6] Lewis* (see MARTIAU), who married (2), (bond 8) Feb. 1789,[255] Swepson Jeffries, Sr.

Issue: [GOODE][256] 239. John Bennett[6], for whom Samuel Hopkins, Jr., was guardian, 12 Oct. 1789, member of the House of Delegates, 1804-10,[257] married, 4 July 1804, Pamelia B. Hendrick; 240. Ann Branch[6], for whom Swepson Jeffries was guardian, 12 Oct. 1789, and Mark Alexander was guardian, 9 Oct. 1797, died before 28 Dec. 1799 when her estate was divided;[258] 241. Elizabeth Willis[6], died 27 Aug. 1835, for whom Swepson Jeffries was guardian, 12 Oct. 1789, married, 1 March 1796,[259] Joseph[8] Taylor, son of Joseph and Frances[7] (Anderson) Taylor and grandson of 469. *Sarah[6] (Clarke) Anderson* (see EPES), born 14 Aug. 1772, died 12 Aug. 1838,[260] of Granville Co., N.C., who moved to Hardeman Co., Tenn., and left will 20 April 1833-codicil 24 May 1838-6 Sept. 1838.[261]

72. THOMAS[5] GOODE (Margery[4] Branch, Thomas[3], Thomas[2], Christopher[1]) left will 10 Sept. 1812-18 July 1813.[262] He resided for some years in Mecklenburg County where in 1782 he received a certificate for fodder and bacon impressed for the troops and pasturage of horses during the Revolutionary War. He later returned to Chesterfield County where he was a planter. There and at "Inglewood" in Mecklenburg County he bred thoroughbred horses, owning

---

[252] Mecklenburg Co. Will Bk. 2, p. 94.

[253] Katherine B. Elliott, *Revolutionary War Records, Mecklenburg County, Virginia* (South Hill, Va., 1964), p. 67.

[254] Leonard, pp. 110, 113, 115, 118, 120, 123.

[255] Elliott, *Marriage Records, 1765-1810, Mecklenburg County*, p. 72.

[256] Katherine B. Elliott, *Early Settlers, Mecklenburg County, Virginia*, II (South Hill, Va., 1965), pp. 163-64.

[257] Leonard, pp. 236, 240.

[258] Mecklenburg Co. Will Bk. 4, pp. 153-54.

[259] Elliott, *Marriage Records, 1765-1810, Mecklenburg County*, p. 119.

[260] Bible of Mary McCraw, photocopy provided to the Society of the Descendants of Francis Epes by Mrs. Eugene McCraw, Woodland, Calif.

[261] Hardeman Co., Tenn., Will Bk. 2, p. 28-30.

[262] Chesterfield Co. Will Bk. 8, pp. 84-85.

some of the most noted of the time.[263]　He married, 2 Feb. 1769,[264] 97. *Agnes*[6]
Osborne (see OSBORNE), who left will 5 Aug. 1813-13 Sept. 1813.[265]

　　Issue: [GOODE] 242. Elizabeth Eppes[6], born 12 Jan. 1770, died 16 Sept.
1771; 243 Thomas[6], born 21 Aug. 1774, died 4 Sept. 1794, unmarried; 244.
John Chesterfield[6], born 26 May 1775, died 2 Sept. 1832, left will 25 Aug. 1837-
12 Oct. 1837,[266] of "Inglewood," Mecklenburg County, lieutenant in the Virginia
militia, 1814, member of the House of Delegates, 1810-13, 1814-15,[267] married
(1), 11 Nov. 1797 at "Grammarton," Dinwiddie County,[268] 316. *Lucy Herbert*[6]
Claiborne (see CLAIBORNE), who died about 1800, and (2), (bond 22) Feb.
1819,[269] Mary (Smith) Nuttall; 242. Martha[6], born 15 April 1777, died 1801,
married, 1 Sept. 1796,[270] as his (2) wife, William Brown Hamlin of Amelia
County, who died about 1840;[271] 246. Elizabeth Osborne[6], born 21 June 1779,
died 14 Jan. 1850, unmarried; 247. Agnes Eppes[6], born 15 May 1781, died 25
Dec. 1814, married, 18 May 1803, John Tucker of Brunswick County which he
represented in the House of Delegates, 1809-14, and Virginia Senate, 1816-22;[272]
248. Edward[6], born 2 Feb. 1785, died 6 Feb. 1785.

　　74. LUCY[5] BUGG (Margery[4] Branch, Thomas[3], Thomas[2], Christopher[1])
married, (bond 20) May 1789,[273] as his (1) wife, Col. Mark Alexander of
"Salem," Mecklenburg County, justice, member of the House of Delegates,
1783-94, 1796, 1798-99,[274] who died 27 July 1824 in Mecklenburg County.[275]

　　Issue: [ALEXANDER] 249. Mark[6], born 7 Feb. 1792 at "Salem," died 5
or 6 July 1883, student at the University of North Carolina, attorney of "Park

---

　　[263] *V*L, pp. 55-62; Alexander Mackey-Smith, *The Colonial Quarter Racehorse* (Richmond, 1983), pp. 165, 167; John Hervey, *Racing in America, 1665-1865* (New York, 1944), pp. 40, 175.

　　[264] Bible, in Rose Chambers Goode McCullough, *Yesterday When It Is Past* (Richmond, 1957), pp. 56, 174.

　　[265] Chesterfield Co. Will Bk. 8, pp. 109-10.

　　[266] Mecklenburg Co. Circuit Court Will Bk. 1, p. 12.

　　[267] Leonard, pp. 261, 266, 270, 278.

　　[268] *Virginia Gazette and Petersburg Intelligencer*, 17 Nov. 1797.

　　[269] Warren Co., N.C., Marriage bond.

　　[270] Knorr, *Marriage Bonds ... Chesterfield County*, p. 62.

　　[271] Amelia Co. Land tax books, 1840-41.

　　[272] Leonard, pp. 256, 260, 265, 269, 273, 296, 301, 306, 311.

　　[273] Elliott, *Marriage Records, 1765-1810, Mecklenburg County*, p. 7.

　　[274] Leonard, pp. 192, 196, 204, 212.

　　[275] *Enquirer*, Richmond, 10 Aug. 1824.

Forest," Mecklenburg County, lieutenant of militia, member of the House of Delegates, 1815-19, 1845-46, of the United States House of Representatives, 1819-33, and of the Virginia Constitutional Convention, 1829-30,[276] married, 1 June 1831 in Warren Co., N.C.,[277] Sarah Park Turner.

75. ELIZABETH BRANCH[5] BUGG (Margery[4] Branch, Thomas[3], Thomas[2], Christopher[1]), born 1756, died 1831, married, (bond 18) Jan. 1783,[278] Samuel Hopkins, son of Samuel and Isabella (Taylor) Hopkins, born 19 April 1753, Albemarle County, died 16 Sept. 1819, Henderson Co., Ky. He was captain, major and lieutenant colonel of the 14th (later 10th) Virginia Regiment, 1776-80, was taken prisoner at Charleston, later colonel of 1st Virginia Regiment, 1781, and was an original member of the Society of the Cincinnati. A justice of Mecklenburg County, 1785-87, he moved to Kentucky where he was agent for the Henderson Land Grant Company, justice of Henderson County, 1799-1801, member of the Kentucky Legislature, 1800-06, and Senate, 1809-13, Commander in chief of the Western Frontier (Illinois and Indiana) with rank of Major General, 1812, and led 2000 mounted volunteers against the Kickapoo Indians. He served in the United States House of Representatives, 1812-14. He resided at "Spring Garden," Henderson County.[279]

Issue: [HOPKINS][280] 250. Samuel Goode[6], born 1784, died 1833, New Madrid, Mo., unmarried, served in War of 1812 under his father; 251. Lucy Bugg[6], born 1786, died 1873, married (1) Dr. James Coulter Wardlaw and (2) Dr. Levi Jones of Texas; 252. Elizabeth Branch[6], born 28 May 1788, died 13 Sept. 1853, married 253. *Philip[6] Barbour* (see MARTIAU); 253. Jacob Bugg[6], born 11 Feb. 1790, died 1848, of Henderson Co., Ky., married, 26 March 1812, Caroline Imlay Brent, born 15 Feb. 1794, died 30 Aug. 1829; 254. Ann [Nancy] Taylor[6], born 1792, married, 24 June 1809,[281] as his (1) wife, Judge Thomas[7] Towles, son of 556. *Mary Beverley[6] (Smith) Towles* (see CHEW), born 1 June

---

[276] Susan L. Bracey, *Life By the Roaring Roanoke* (n.p., 1977), pp. 158-59; Leonard, pp. 282, 286, 290, 294, 353, 417; *Dictionary of Virginia Biography*, I (Richmond, 1998), pp. 61-62..

[277] *Enquirer*, Richmond, 14 June 1831.

[278] Williams, *op. cit.*, p. 66.

[279] Walter Lee Hopkins, *Hopkins of Virginia and Related Families* (Richmond, 1931), pp. 14-15; *Biographical Directory of the American Congress, 1774-1996* (Alexandria, Va., 1997), pp. 1235-36; *Dictionary of American Biography*, IX (New York, 1932), pp. 218-19.

[280] Hopkins, *op. cit.*, pp. 16-18.

[281] Henderson Co., Ky., Marriage Register A, p. 2.

1784 in Spotsylvania County, died 12 Dec. 1850 in Henderson Co., Ky., where he settled in 1805;[282] 255. Sarah Pettus[6], born 1794, died 7 April 1869, married (1) Nicholas Horseley and (2), 24 Aug. 1831,[283] John B. Bibb, born 27 Oct. 1789, died 13 April 1884 at Frankfort, Ky.,[284] who was a major in War of 1812 and represented Logan County in the Kentucky House of Representatives, 1823-28, and Senate, 1830-34; 256. Martha Isabella[6], born 1796, died 1822, married, 1819, George Lyne; 257. Mary Boush[6], born 1798, died 1874, unmarried.

76. MATTHEW[5] BRANCH (Matthew[4], Matthew[3], Thomas[2], Christopher[1]) of age by 1746, was left land at Warwick, and left will 1 June 1772-11 Sept. 1772.[285] He married, Feb. 1749,[286] 102. Ridley[6] *Jones* (see SHEPPEY), born 9 Aug. 1730,[287] died 21 May 1799 in Buckingham County, aged 69.[288]

Issue: 258. Matthew[6], of Prince Edward County, married (1) ___ and (2). (bond 7) Sept. 1791,[289] Elizabeth (___) Hamblen, widow of John Hamblen; 259. Peter[6], of Chesterfield County, married (1), (bond 24) March 1785,[290] Judith Jones and (2) Martha ___; 260. Mary[6], married 693. *Benjamin[6] Moseley* (see BALEY-COCKE); 261. Elizabeth[6].

78. EDWARD[5] BRANCH (Matthew[4], Matthew[3], Thomas[2], Christopher[1]) was left part of "Hanna Spring" by his father, and left will 14 July 1804-Aug. 1804.[291] He married (1) Margaret ___ and (2) Mary Ann ___.

Issue:[292] 262. Mary Ann[6], married, (consent 13) May 1793,[293] 522. *Robert[6] Cary* (see BALEY-COCKE); 263. Elizabeth[6], married, 16 Feb. 1801,[294] Charles Burton; 264. Stephen[6]; 265. Edward[6]; 266. Matthew[6]; 267. Judith[6], probably

---

[282] Edmund L. Starling, *History of Henderson County, Kentucky* (Henderson, Ky., 1887), p. 781.

[283] Henderson Co., Ky., Marriage Register A, p. 36.

[284]*Ibid.*, p. 2. Bibb Bible, in *The Register of the Kentucky Historical Society*, XXVI, p. 159, gives 22 August.

[285] Chesterfield Co. Will Bk. 2, p. 32; Order Bk. 5, p. 150.

[286] Williams, *Marriages of Amelia County*, p. 16. The bond is defaced and the bride's name is obliterated.

[287] Bristol Parish Register.

[288] *Virginia Argus*, Richmond, 28 June 1799.

[289] Prince Edward Co. Marriage Bonds 1754-1850, no pagination.

[290] Williams, *op. cit.*, p. 16.

[291] Chesterfield Co. Will Bk. 6, pp. 206-07.

[292] Chesterfield Co. Deed Bk. 12, pp. 196-97. Three children were under age in 1804.

[293] Knorr, *Marriage Bonds ... Chesterfield County*, p. 26.

[294] *Ibid.*, p. 24.

married, (bond 28) Feb. 1805,[295] Joseph Warren Robertson.

79. THOMAS[5] BRANCH (Matthew[4], Matthew[3], Thomas[2], Christopher[1]), born 1735, died 4 July 1815.[296] He was left "Hanna Spring" by his father and lived there until 4 May 1808 when, joined by Thomas Cheatham, trustee, he sold 302 acres to Edward Friend.[297] He married, 1760, 56. *Mary[6] Eldridge* (see ROLFE), born 11 March 1742/3,[298] living Nov. 1792.

Issue:[299] 268. Maj. Bolling[6], died 2 Nov. 1829 at Richmond,[300] of Buckingham County, married, (1), 20 Feb. 1800,[301] Rebecca[7] Graves, daughter of 268. *Arthur[6] Graves* (see COX), who died 7 Aug. 1815, and (2), 3 June 1817, Mary H.[7] Bell, born 22 Sept. 1781, died 15 Aug. 1822,[302] daughter of 120. *Henry[6] Bell* (see TAYLOR-CARY); 269. Matthew[6], born about 1776, died 1828,[303] of "Tower Hill," Buckingham County, married (1), about 1795, Martha Cox, daughter of John Cox, perhaps 88. *John[5] Cox* (see COX), and (2) Rebecca[7] Bell, born 18 Jan. 1777, "Cold Comfort," Buckingham County, died 31 Dec. 1858, Buckingham County, sister of his brother's wife;[304] 270. (Son)[6], probably died young.

80. SAMUEL[5] BRANCH (John[4], Matthew[3], Thomas[2], Christopher[1]) left will 11 Dec. 1789-8 July 1790.[305] He married ___.[306]

Issue:[307] 271. Arthur[6], died before 20 Jan. 1801 when his widow gave bond

---

[295] *Ibid.*, p. 102.

[296] Benjamin H. Branch, *The Branch, Harris, Jarvis, and Chinn Book* (n.p., 1963), p. 8.

[297] Chesterfield Co. Deed Bk. 18, pp. 452-54.

[298] Wyndham Robertson, *Pocahontas, Alias Matoaka, and her Descendants* (Richmond, 1887), p. 34.

[299] *Ibid.*, stating they had three sons, no daughters, but p. 39 listing only Bolling and Matthew. Stuart E. Brown and others, *Pocahontas' Descendants*, I (n.p., 1985), p. 278, adds William, Mary and possibly Sarah, who were children of 97. Thomas[5] Branch.

[300] *Religious Herald*, 6 Nov. 1829; *Compiler*, Richmond, 3 Nov. 1829.

[301] *Virginia Argus*, Richmond, 25 March 1800; Knorr, *op. cit.*, p. 19.

[302] Family Bible, in Branch, *op. cit.*, p. 8.

[303] John Hale Stutesman, *Some Watkins Families* (Baltimore, 1989), pp. 180, 189.

[304] Branch, *op. cit.*., p. 9.

[305] Chesterfield Co. Will Bk. 4, p. 329; Order Bk. 8, p. 449.

[306] She may have been a daughter of 203. *Arthur[5] Moseley* (see BALEY-COCKE) since the estate of Samuel Branch was concerned in the division of Arthur Moseley's estate in 1793 (*The Virginia Genealogist*, XXXIII, p. 69).

[307] William Daniel Ligon, *The Ligon Family and Connections* (n.p., 1947), p. 554.

as his administratrix,[308] married, (bond 16) Sept. 1779,[309] Catherine Moseley; 272. Samuel[6], died before his father,[310] married, (bond 19) Sept. 1782,[311] Jane Martin, born 9 Sept. 1764,[312] who married (2), (consent 19) Feb. 1791,[313] Thomas Whitworth; 273. William[6], left will 22 Dec. 1807-14 April 1817,[314] married, (bond 18) Sept. 1790,[315] Sarah Martin, born 6 Dec. 1766;[316] 274. Charles[6], died 11 Sept. 1835 in Powhatan County,[317] left will 5 Jan. 1813-5 Oct. 1835,[318] married, (bond 1) May 1801, Elizabeth (Porter) Porter, widow of Thomas Porter,[319] who died 24 Jan. 1841 in Powhatan County, in her 64th year[320] and left will 1 Dec. 18440-1 March 1841;[321] 275. Thomas[6], chose Archer Branch as his guardian, 9 Dec. 1793;[322] 276. Elizabeth[6], married, (bond 16) Feb. 1779,[323] John Harris; 277. Hannah [Johannah][6], died about 1825,[324] married, (consent 3) Dec. 1784,[325] William Hopkins; 278. Mary[6], married, (bond 27) June 1788,[326] Samuel Marshall.

82. HANNAH [Johannah][5] BRANCH (John[4], Matthew[3], Thomas[2], Christopher[1]) was left a Negro in will of Caleb Ware, 23 June 1740.[327] She married Abraham Sandefur of Cumberland County, who left will 7 July 1784-22

---

[308] Powhatan Co. Will Bk. 2, pp. 117-18.

[309] Knorr, *Marriage Bonds ... Powhatan County*, p. 10, with Thomas Moseley, security.

[310] Administration on his estate was granted to Anthony Martin, 8 April 1790 (Chesterfield Co. Order Bk. 8, p. 394).

[311] Catherine Lindsay Knorr, *Marriage Bonds and Ministers' Returns of Powhatan County, Virginia, 1777-1830* (Pine Bluff, Ark., 1957), p. 10.

[312] Jones, *op. cit.*, p. 243.

[313] Knorr, *Marriage Bonds ... Chesterfield County*, p. 128.

[314] Chesterfield Co. Will Bk. 8, p. 609.

[315] Knorr, *Marriage Bonds ... Powhatan County*, p. 10.

[316] Jones, *op. cit.*, p. 243.

[317] *Enquirer*, Richmond, 20 Oct. 1835.

[318] Powhatan Co. Will Bk. 9, p. 593.

[319] Knorr, *Marriage Bonds ... Powhatan County*, pp. 10, 51.

[320] *Religious Herald*, 22 April 1841.

[321] Powhatan Co. Will Bk. 11, pp. 296-98.

[322] Chesterfield Co. Order Bk. 10, p. 294.

[323] Knorr, *Marriage Bonds ... Chesterfield County*, p. 64.

[324] Hopkins, *op. cit.*, p. 222.

[325] Knorr, *Marriage Bonds ... Chesterfield County*, p. 69, as Hamey Branch.

[326] Knorr, *Marriage Bonds ... Powhatan County*, p. 40.

[327] Chesterfield Co. Will Bk. 1, p. 19.

Nov. 1784.[328]

Issue: [SANDEFUR] 279. Frances[6], born 29 July 1757 in Cumberland County, died 29 Jan. 1831 in Jessamine Co., Ky., married, (bond 26) July 1773,[329] George Stokes Stovall Smith, born 11 April 1850, died 18 Feb. 1810 in Jessamine Co., Ky., a Baptist minister in Virginia and Kentucky,[330] took the oath of allegiance in Powhatan County, 1777;[331] 280. Elizabeth Ridley, married, (bond 18) June 1778,[332] John Deane, who took the oath of allegiance in Powhatan County, 1777;[333] 281. Susannah[6], born 5 Aug. 1764;[334] 282. Diana[6], born 30 Nov. 1766.[335]

83. MATTHEW[5] BRANCH (John[4], Matthew[3], Thomas[2], Christopher[1]) chose Samuel Branch as his guardian, 2 Aug. 1754,[336] and left will 15 Feb. 1786-April 1786.[337] He married, by 28 Dec. 1766,[338] Ann Walthall.

Issue: 283. John[6]; 284. Archibald[6], of Buckingham County, married ___; 285. Thomas Spencer[6]; 286. Mary[6]; 287. Elizabeth[6]; 288. Nancy Spencer[6]; 289. Matthew[6].

87. OLIVE[5] BRANCH (Olive[4], Matthew[3], Thomas[2], Christopher[1]) moved from Chesterfield to Bedford County about 1774 and as a resident of Campbell County with his son Anderson was found guilty of murder by the General Court but was acquitted by the Dec. 1786 court.[339] He married ___.

Issue: 290. Samuel[5] [Jr.], deeded 182 acres by his father, 20 Sept. 1776 [1777];[340] 291. Pleasant[6], deeded 183 acres by his father, 21 Sept. 1777,[341] moved to Bourbon Co., Ky., where he purchased a tract on the waters of Hinkston Creek, 11 Aug. 1809,[342] died before 24 Sept. 1839 when the inventory

---

[328] Cumberland Co. Will Bk. 2, p. 346-48.

[329] Elliott, *Marriage Records, 1749-1840, Cumberland County*, p. 118.

[330] Thompson, *The Family of Bartholomew Stovall*, I, p. 53.

[331] *The Virginia Genealogist*, XXVII, p. 195.

[332] Knorr, *Marriage Bonds ... Powhatan County*, p. 19.

[333] *The Virginia Genealogist*, XXVII, p. 195.

[334] Jones, *op. cit.*, p. 291.

[335] *Ibid.*

[336] Chesterfield Co. Order Bk. 1, p. 524.

[337] Chesterfield Co. Will Bk. 4, p. 6; Order Bk. 7, p. 311.

[338] Chesterfield Co. Will Bk. 2, p. 352, will of Henry Walthall.

[339] *Virginia Journal and Alexandria Advertiser*, 19 Oct. 1786, 4 Jan. 1787.

[340] Bedford Co. Deed Bk. 5, pp. 417-19.

[341] *Ibid.*, pp. 415-17.

[342] Nicholas Co., Ky., Deed Bk. I, pp. 294-95, recorded 30 June 1831.

of his estate was made,[343] married, (bond 14) Feb. 1781,[344] Jenny Mastin; 292. Olive[6], born 1760 in Chesterfield County, died 21 Jan. 1846 in Buckingham County, aged 86,[345] served four tours as private and sergeant in the Bedford County militia during the Revolutionary War, afterward settled in Buckingham County,[346] married ___; 293. Anderson[6].

88. DANIEL[5] BRANCH (Daniel[4], Matthew[3], Thomas[2], Christopher[1]) of Chesterfield County, left undated will, proved 8 Oct 1792.[347] He married Jemima Britton, daughter of William Britton.[348]

Issue: 294. James[6]; 295. Olive[6], married, (bond 6) July 1799,[349] Sally Ash; 296. Daniel[6], left will 5 May 1811-16 Dec. 1824,[350] married (1) Mary Britton and (2), (bond 20) Feb. 1783,[351] Salley Clarke; 297. Sally[6]; 298. Verlinshe[6]; 299. Washington[6], chose James Branch as his guardian, 11 Jan. 1802,[352] married, (bond 15) Sept. 1807,[353] Polly Brachan; 300. Lucy[6]

89. THOMAS[5] BRANCH (Daniel[4], Matthew[3], Thomas[2], Christopher[1]), born 20 July 1757 near Manakintown, Powhatan County, died 22 Sept. 1850. He served at least six tours in the Powhatan County militia during the Revolutionary War and in 1797 moved to Prince Edward County.[354] He married, 31 Dec. 1789,[355] Nancy Clements, who was living, aged 87, 26 June 1856, when she applied for bounty land.

Issue: 301. William[6], born 1 June 1791, died 30 Nov. 1825,[356] left will 10

---

[343] Nicholas Co., Ky., Will Bk. C, 1830-39, p. 549.

[344] Earle S. Dennis and Jane E. Smith, *Marriage Bonds of Bedford County, Virginia, 1755-1800* (n.p., 1932), p. 8.

[345] *Whig*, Richmond, 3 Feb. 1846.

[346] Revolutionary War pension application, Olive Branch, S.8101, National Archives.

[347] Chesterfield Co. Will Bk. 4, p. 494; Order Bk. 9, p. 509.

[348] Branch, *op. cit.*, p. 61; Chesterfield Co. Will Bk. 2, p. 48, will of William Brittain, 22 July 1764-2 March 1770.

[349] Knorr, *Marriage Bonds ... Chesterfield County*, p. 20.

[350] Powhatan Co. Will Bk. 7, p. 131.

[351] Knorr, *Marriage Bonds ... Powhatan County*, p. 10.

[352] Chesterfield Co. Order Bk. 14, p. 196.

[353] Knorr, *Marriage Bonds ... Chesterfield County*, p. 20.

[354] Revolutionary War pension application, Thomas Branch, widow Nancy or Ann, R.1154, BLWt.50806-160-55, National Archives; *Enquirer*, Richmond, 22 Oct. 1850.

[355] *Ibid.*; Williams, *Marriages of Amelia County*, p. 16, bond 26 Dec.

[356] *Enquirer*, Richmond, 30 Dec. 1825.

Dec. 1823-19 Dec. 1825,[357] operated a school at his home, "Golgotha," Prince Edward County, later practiced law,[358] married, 26 Nov. 1812,[359] Jane Davis Booker.

94. ELIZABETH BARBARA[5] BRANCH (Daniel[4], Matthew[3], Thomas[2], Christopher[1]), born 27 March 1766,[360] married, (bond 3) Feb. 1786,[361] Henry Holman of Powhatan County, who left will 1830-4 March 1841.[362]

Issue: [HOLMAN] 302. Jane[6], married, 15 Feb. 1810,[363] Joshua P. Hunnicutt; 303. William[6]; 304. Mary[6], married, 15 Feb. 1810,[364] Philip Deane; 305. Elizabeth[6], married 675. *Samuel[6] Pleasants* (see BALEY-COCKE); 306. James[6]; 307. Sarah[6], married ___ Puryear; 308. Frances[6]; 309. Daniel B.[6], left will 26 March 1832-16 May 1832;[365] 310. Edwin[6]; 311. Matilda[6]; 312. John Henry[6].

97. THOMAS[5] BRANCH (Thomas[4], Matthew[3], Thomas[2], Christopher[1]), born 31 Oct. 1735, resided in Chesterfield County. He married ____ Hays, daughter of Richard Hays.[366]

Issue:[367] 313. Mary[6], married ___ Drew and resided in Buckingham County when deeded two slaves by her father, 28 April 1795;[368] 314. (probably) Sarah[6], married, (consent 3) Sept. 1798,[369] as his (1) wife, Daniel Weisiger, born 15 April 1776 at Manchester, died 26 June 1848, of "The Grove," Chesterfield County, captain of militia, justice, sheriff, proprietor of the Farmer's Tavern in

---

[357] Prince Edward Co. Will Bk. 6, pp. 256-57.

[358] Herbert Clarence Bradshaw, *History of Prince Edward County, Virginia* (Richmond, 1955), p. 838, which shows marriage as 16 Dec.

[359] Williams, *Marriages of Amelia County*, p. 17.

[360] Jones, *op. cit.*, p. 162.

[361] Knorr, *Marriage Bonds ... Powhatan County*, p. 31.

[362] Powhatan Co. Deed & Will Bk. O, pp. 109-11.

[363] Knorr, *Marriage Bonds ... Powhatan County*, p. 32.

[364] *Ibid.*

[365] Powhatan Co. Will Bk. 9, p. 76.

[366] Goode, *op. cit.*, pp. 84-85.

[367] Chesterfield Co. Deed Bk. 16, pp. 306-09, individual deeds of gift, 12 Sept. 1803, of slaves and personalty to last seven children.

[368] Chesterfield Co. Deed Bk. 13, pp. 206-07.

[369] Knorr, *Marriage Bonds ... Chesterfield County*, p. 126.

Manchester,[370] who married (2), (bond 15) Feb. 1815,[371] Seigniora Tabb Smith; 315. Elizabeth[6]; 316 Thomas[6]; 317. Richard Hays[6]; 318. Catharine G.[6]; 319. Ann[6], married, (bond 3) Jan. 1806,[372] David Weisiger, Jr., born 16 Dec. 1777 at Manchester, died 26 May 1825 in Chesterfield County, who married (2), 16 Feb. 1819, Sally S. Gordon;[373] 320. Rebecca H.[6], born about 1775,[374] married, 27 April 1826,[375] Charles Forsee, born 4 March 1754 in Powhatan County, died 14 June 1836 in Chesterfield County, widower of 50. *Judith[6] Bass* (see SHARP-BAUGH), who served many short tours in the Powhatan County militia, 1777-81, and was pastor of Skinquarter Baptist Church, Chesterfield County; 321 William Hays[6].

99. GARNER[5] BRANCH (Thomas[4], Matthew[3], Thomas[2], Christopher[1]) born 28 Jan. 173[8/?]9, died before May 1782 when administration on his estate was granted to Fanny Branch and Edward Hill.[376] He married (1) Elizabeth Branch and (2) 122. Frances[5] Hill.

Issue: (by 1) 322. Edward[6], of Powhatan County, on 9 June 1793 joined by his uncle Edward sold the land they had inherited jointly from 32. Thomas[4] Branch,[377] married, (bond 25) April 1791,[378] Julia Langdon; 323. Jonathan[6], born 2 May 1762.[379]

102. EDWARD[5] BRANCH (Thomas[4], Matthew[3], Thomas[2], Christopher[1]), born 5 June 1752, left will 24 May 1814-8 Aug. 1814.[380] He married, about Nov. 1786,[381] Tabitha Horner, born 15 May 1768.

Issue: 324. Nelson[6], born 22 Feb. 1788; 325. Thomas[6], born 12 Sept. 1790,

---

[370] Benjamin Boisseau Weisiger, *The Weisiger Family* (n.p., 1983), p. 38; *Whig*, Richmond, 30 June 1848.

[371] Knorr, *Marriage Bonds ... Chesterfield County*, p. 126.

[372] *Ibid.*

[373] Weisiger, *op. cit.*, p. 59.

[374] Chesterfield Co. 1850 census, Upper Dist., p. 191 or 96, family 588-622. She deposed, however, she was aged 75, 24 June 1853, and aged 82, 21 March 1855 (Revolutionary War pension application, Charles Forsie [Forsee], widow Rebecca H., W. 11001, National Archives).

[375] Weisiger, *Marriage Bonds ... Chesterfield County*, p. 59.

[376] Chesterfield Co. Order Bk. 6, p. 352.

[377] Chesterfield Co. Deed Bk. 12, pp. 305-07.

[378] Knorr, *Marriage Bonds ... Powhatan County*, p. 10.

[379] Jones, *op. cit.*, p. 162. The Rev. William Douglas, who customarily entered the maiden name of the mother, shows his parents as Gernat Branch and Elizabeth Branch.

[380] Chesterfield Co. Will Bk. 8, p. 205.

[381] Knorr, *Marriage Bonds ... Chesterfield County*, p. 19, shows June 1786-June 1787.

of Chesterfield County, private in Capt. William Fitzgerald's company at Norfolk in War of 1812; 326. Polly[6], born 15 Nov. 1793; 327. Arthur[6], born 22 Oct. 1800; 328. Patsy[6], born 16 April 1803; 329. Garner[6], born 15 March 1807; 330. Edward[6], born 4 June 1810, living Dec. 1852, carpenter of Chesterfield County, married Harriet ___, born about 1815.[382]

108. RICHARD[5] WOOLDRIDGE (Elizabeth[4] Branch, James[3], Thomas[2], Christopher[1]) died before 2 May 1782 when his widow was granted administration on his estate.[383] He was taxable in Bedford County, 1755, and Chesterfield County, about 1757, but settled in Prince Edward County.[384] He married Elizabeth ___, who died about 1806.[385]

Issue: [WOOLDRIDGE][386] 331. John[6], born 1761, died 3 Jan. 1846, served in the Revolutionary War for six months,[387] married, 23 Sept. 1783,[388] Caroline Fleming Creasy, who was born about 1757[389] and died 7 April 1851;[390] 332. Elizabeth[6], died after 1810; 333. Richard[6], of Appomattox County, died 1845-46, married Sarah ___, possibly 341. Sarah[6] Wooldridge, born about 1760;[391] 334. Mary[6], died after 1812; 335. William[6], born about 1772, died 22 Oct. 1857, married, (bond 10) Feb. 1812,[392] Catherine Kelly, born 17 Dec. 1788, died 10 Jan. 1878; 336. Jenny[6], died before 1810; 337. Phoebe[6], died before 1810; 335. Sarah[6], married, 27 Oct. 1802,[393] Pledge Carter.

109. JOHN[5] WOOLDRIDGE (Elizabeth[4] Branch, James[3], Thomas[2], Christopher[1]) died about 1782 in Bedford County.[394] He married (1) ___ Farley,

---

[382] Chesterfield Co. 1850 census, Lower Dist., p. 313 or 157, family 694-694.

[383] Campbell Co. Order Bk. 1, p. 337; Will Bk. 1, p. 10, inventory, 4 July 1782.

[384] Wooldridge, *op. cit.*, I, pp. 43-45.

[385] Campbell Co. Personal property tax list, 1806, estate taxed.

[386] Campbell Co. Order Bk. 10, p. 132; Wooldridge, *op. cit.*, I, pp. 46, 69, 81, 107.

[387] Revolutionary War pension application, John Wooldridge, widow Fleming, W.6582, National Archives.

[388] Lucy Harrison Miller Baber and Hazel Letts Williamson, *Marriages of Campbell County, Virginia, 1782-1810* (Lynchburg, 1971), p. 104.

[389] Appomattox Co. 1850 census, p. 352 or 176R, family 319-319, as Caroline Fleming.

[390] Alycon Trubey Pierce, *Rejected Final Payment Vouchers, 1818-1854, Virginia: Richmond & Wheeling* (Albany, Ga., 1995), II, p. 633.

[391] Appomattox Co. 1850 census, p. 311 or 156, family 5-5.

[392] Prince Edward Co. Marriage Bonds 1754-1850, no pagination.

[393] Baber and Williamson, *op. cit.*, p. 19.

[394] Campbell Co. Personal property tax list, 1782, widow taxed.

daughter of James Farley,[395] and (2) Mary ___.

Issue: [WOOLDRIDGE][396] 339. Elizabeth Branch[6], married, (bond 7) July 1781,[397] Moses Morris; 340. James[6], born 26 Nov. 1760, Chesterfield County, died 1839-40, Revolutionary War soldier,[398] married (1) ___, (2) Ann Coleman, and (3) ___ Staples; 341. Sarah[6], possibly married 333. Richard[6] Wooldridge; 342. John[6], born about 1766, died 1811 in Williamson Co., Tenn., married Nancy ___; 343. (possibly) (Daughter)[6], married Edmund Franklin..

110. MARY[5] WOOLDRIDGE (Elizabeth[4] Branch, James[3], Thomas[2], Christopher[1]) died before 1780. She married John Martin.

Issue: [MARTIN] 344. Elizabeth[6], married ___ Viers.

111. WILLIAM[5] WOOLDRIDGE (Elizabeth[4] Branch, James[3], Thomas[2], Christopher[1]) died before March 1817 when the inventory of his estate was made.[399] He resided in Chesterfield, Powhatan and Bedford counties before moving in 1788-89 to Kentucky where he resided in Bourbon and Montgomery counties. He married Mary Harrison, daughter of Edward and Sarah (Butler) Slaughter Harrison.[400]

Issue: [WOOLDRIDGE][401] 345. Fleming[6], died after 1824, was left 100 acres in Chesterfield County by his grandmother, moved to Bourbon Co., Ky., where he served as captain in the 5th United States Infantry, 1799-1800, married, 23 Oct. 1814,[402] Judith Branch; 346. Harrison[6], died by 1787, unmarried, left 187 acres in Powhatan County by his grandmother; 347. Edmund[6], probably died before 1824, of Bourbon Co., Ky., and later of Green Co., Ky., married Margaret ___, who petitioned for divorce, claiming he "went off with another woman" and abandoned her, and married (2), 1 Aug. 1825,[403] George

---

[395] Chesterfield Co. Will Bk. 3, p. 216; Order Bk. 6, p. 228, will of James Farley, 19 Feb. 1779-4 June 1779.

[396] Wooldridge, *op. cit.*, I, pp. 116-23, 184-86.

[397] Kathleen Booth Williams, *Marriages of Amelia County, Virginia, 1735-1815* (n.p., 1961), p. 77.

[398] Revolutionary War pension applications, James Wooldridge, S.11884, National Archives.

[399] Bourbon Co., Ky., Will Bk. F, p. 28.

[400] Chesterfield Co. Will Bk. 3, p. 358; Order Bk. 6, p. 389, will of Sarah Harrison, 2 Jan. 1781-3 Jan. 1783.

[401] Wooldridge, *op. cit.*, I, pp. 203-07, 221-24, 226.

[402] Bourbon Co., Ky., Marriage bond, dated 19 Oct. 1814.

[403] Green County Historical Society, *Green County, Kentucky, Marriage Records, 1795-1836* (n.p., n.d.), p. 46, bond dated 28 April 1825.

Quisenberry; 348. William Harrison[6], left will 18 April 1810-20 May 1814,[404] lieutenant in the United States army, 1801-04, later settled in Claiborne Co., Miss., where he was colonel of militia and aide to the Governor of Mississippi Territory, married Nancy E. (Bryan) Sugg, who died 31 Aug. 1834; 349. Mary[6], born 12 March 1779, married, (bond 18) Jan. 1797,[405] Mordecai Boulware, born 14 Oct. 1774, left will 18 Oct. 1840-codicil 21 Nov. 1844-24 March 1845,[406] who was minister of North Fork of Elkhorn Baptist Church, Franklin Co., Ky., 1816-25,[407] and later moved to Marion Co., Mo.; 350. (probably) Elizabeth[6], married Richard Brown.

112. ELIZABETH[5] WOOLDRIDGE (Elizabeth[4] Branch, James[3], Thomas[2], Christopher[1]) married (1) John Wooldridge, son of Thomas Wooldridge, who died 1771 in Cumberland County and (2) William Langsdon, son of William and Esther (Jouany) Langsdon,[408] who left will 21 Jan. 1814-18 Jan. 1817.[409]

Issue: (by 1) [WOOLDRIDGE][410] 351. Thomas[6]; 352. Seth[6], died 30 June 1818 in Powhatan County, married, (bond 7) May 1793,[411] 371. Peggy Wooldridge[6] Elam; 353. Frances[6], probably died 1788-89; 354. John[6], born 1771, died 18 April 1859 in Powhatan County,[412] Baptist minister in Powhatan County for about fifty years, married (1), (bond 29) Aug. 1795,[413] Martha Winfree Magruder, who died 28 Sept. 1831, aged 53,[414] (2), 29 Feb. 1832,[415] Karen Hughes, who died 2 Nov. 1841, in her 61st year,[416] and (3), 23 June 1841,[417] Elizabeth Sublett; 355. Phoebe[6], died after 1788-89; (by 2)

---

[404] Claiborne Co., Miss., Will Bk. A, p. 53.

[405] George F. Doyle, "Marriage Bonds of Clark County, Kentucky ... 1793 to 1850 ..." (typewritten; Winchester, Ky., 1931), p. 407.

[406] Marion Co., Mo., Will Bk. B, pp. 292-96.

[407] Ermina Jett Darnell, *Forks of Elkhorn Church* (Louisville, Ky., 1946), p. 84.

[408] Cameron Allen, "Jean Jounay, As American as John Jones," *The Virginia Genealogist*, VII, p. 156.

[409] Powhatan Co. Will Bk. 5, p. 183.

[410] Wooldridge, *op. cit.*, I, pp. 293-95, 304-05, 319-23.

[411] Knorr, *Marriage Bonds ... Chesterfield County*, p. 132.

[412] *The Religious Herald*, 12 May 1859.

[413] Knorr, *Marriage Bonds ... Powhatan County*, p. 75.

[414] *The Religious Herald*, 28 Oct. 1831.

[415] John Vogt and T. William Kethley, *Powhatan County Marriages, 1777-1850* (Athens, Ga., 1985), p. 75.

[416] *The Religious Herald*, 8 April 1841.

[417] Vogt and Kathley, *loc. cit.*

[LANGSDON] 356. (perhaps) Benjamin⁶, married, (bond 4) June 1798,⁴¹⁸ Anna Magruder; 357. (perhaps) Martha⁶; 358. Nancy⁶, married, (bond 21) July 1795,⁴¹⁹ John Maxey; 359. Hanna⁶, married, (bond 2) Nov. 1819,⁴²⁰ Elias G. Bowler; 360. Rebecca⁶, married, (bond 1) Jan. 1816,⁴²¹ Walker Bowler.

113. The Rev. EDMOND⁵ WOOLDRIDGE (Elizabeth⁴ Branch, James³, Thomas², Christopher¹) first went to Kentrucky in 1776 with Daniel Boone and later settled in Woodford Co., Ky., and left will 28 April 1791-Sept. 1791.⁴²² He married, (bond 22) Aug. 1774,⁴²³ 227. *Elizabeth⁶ Watkins* (see HARRIS, Thomas), born 1 Dec. 1755, who married (2), June 1792,⁴²⁴ John Moss and died 11 Feb. 1841.

Issue: [WOOLDRIDGE]⁴²⁵ 361. Edmund⁶, born 17 March 1776 in Cumberland County, died 18 June 1807 in Adams Co., Miss., moved to Mississippi, married, about 1805, Isabella Charlotte (Hutchins) Vousden, who married (3) 272. *Thomas Augustine⁶ Claiborne* (see CLAIBORNE); 362. Samuel C.⁶, born 3 Dec. 1779, died 31 March 1829 at Jackson, Miss., was first Treasurer of Mississippi, 1821, married, (bond 4) Dec. 1819,⁴²⁶ Elizabeth Ann McDaniel; 363. Phoebe⁶, born 15 May 1781, died 13 Oct. 1834, married, (bond 20) Jan.. 1798,⁴²⁷ Philip Watkins, who was deputy sheriff and ensign of militia, 1794, in Chesterfield County, moved to Woodford Co., Ky., and then to Nashville, Tenn.;⁴²⁸ 364. Nancy⁶, born 24 June 1783, died 5 Sept. 1817 at New Orleans, La., married, (bond 17) Sept. 1798,⁴²⁹ Steward Wilkins; 365. John Watkins⁶, born 28 March 1786, died 1836, of Woodford Co., Ky., and after

---

⁴¹⁸ Knorr, *Marriage Bonds ... Powhatan County*, p. 35.

⁴¹⁹ *Ibid.*, p. 41.

⁴²⁰ *Ibid.*, p. 9.

⁴²¹ *Ibid.*

⁴²² Woodford Co., Ky., Will Bk. A, pp. 34-35.

⁴²³ Elliott, *Marriage Records, 1749-1840,Cumberland County*, p. 144.

⁴²⁴ Woodford Co., Ky., Marriage return, in *The Register of the Kentucky Historical Society*, XIX, p. 63.

⁴²⁵ Wooldridge, *op. cit.*, I, pp. 233-36, 243-47, 253-54.

⁴²⁶ Wilena Roberts Bejach and Lillian Johnson Gardiner, *Williamson County, Tennessee, Marriage Records, 1809-1850* (Memphis, Tenn., 1957), p. 292.

⁴²⁷ Donna Adams Wilson, *Woodford County, Kentucky, Marriage Bonds and Consents* (n.p., 1998), p. 175.

⁴²⁸ John Hale Stutesman, *Some Watkins Families of Virginia and Their Kin* (Baltimore, 1989), p. 227.

⁴²⁹ Wilson, *op. cit.*, p. 179.

1822 of Christian Co., Ky., married (1) Elizabeth M. Jeffries and (2), (bond 23) Aug. 1830,[430] Jane (Torbitt) Gilmore; 366. Powhatan[6], born 7 Nov. 1790 in Woodford Co., Ky., died 20 March 1862 in Pettit Co., Mo., worked for a time in a commission house in New Orleans, La., before returning to Woodford County, served in the War of 1812, moved to Christian Co., Ky., where he was sheriff, 1838-40, and later to Pettit Co., Mo., married, 14 March 1815,[431] Mildred Taylor Major, died 1879 in Pettis Co., Mo., aged 90.[432]

114. VIRLINCHE[5] WOOLDRIDGE (Elizabeth[4] Branch, James[3], Thomas[2], Christopher[1]), born about 1751, married Daniel Elam.

Issue: [ELAM][433] 367. Daniel[6], left will 29 Dec. 1792-10 June 1793,[434] married, (consent 10) Feb. 1790,[435] Mary Flournoy; 368. William[6], left will 7 Aug. 1821-14 March 1823,[436] married ___; 369. Robert[6]; 370. Thomas[6]; 371. Peggy Wooldridge[6], married 352. Seth[6] Wooldridge; 372. Virlinche[6], died before 1834, married ___ Saunders.

115. PHEBE[5] WOOLDRIDGE (Elizabeth[4] Branch, James[3], Thomas[2], Christopher[1]) married Richard Elam of Chesterfield County, who left will 9 July 1791-2 Jan. 1792.[437]

Issue: [ELAM][438] 373. Mary[6], married, 27 Dec. 1792,[439] John Porter; 374. Elizabeth[6]; 375. Edward Wooldridge[6], ordered, 10 July 1797, to be bound by the Overseers of the Poor;[440] 376. William Green[6], ordered 10 July 1797, to be bound by the Overseers of the Poor,[441] left will 26 Nov. 1844-9 Dec. 1844,[442] married (1), (consent 26) July 1803,[443] Sallie Cox, daughter of Henry Cox, and

---

[430] *Ibid.*, p. 184.

[431] Franklin Co., Ky., Marriage Bk. 1, p. 42.

[432] Robert Peter, *History of Fayette County, Kentucky*, ed. by William Henry Perrin (Chicago, 1882), p. 739.

[433] Wooldridge, *op. cit.*, I, p. 16.

[434] Chesterfield Co. Will Bk. 4, p. 433; Order Bk. 10, p. 138.

[435] Knorr, *Marriage Bonds ... Chesterfield County*, p. 43.

[436] Chesterfield Co. Will Bk. 10, pp. 486-87.

[437] Chesterfield Co. Will Bk. 4, p. 425; Order Bk. 9, p. 263.

[438] Wooldridge, *op. cit.*, I, pp. 16-17.

[439] Knorr, *Marriage Bonds ... Chesterfield County*, p. 93, as Parter; *ibid.*, p. 09, consent, 18 Dec., as Porter.

[440] Chesterfield Co. Order Bk. 12, p. 238.

[441] *Ibid.*

[442] Chesterfield Co. Will Bk. 16, pp. 309-10.

[443] Knorr, *Marriage Bonds ... Chesterfield County*, p. 44.

(2), 14 June 1830,[444] Jane A. Wooldridge; 377. Pleasant[6], probably died in Jefferson Co., Miss., by 17 Dec. 1841, married __; 378, Nancy[6]; 379. Martha[6]; 380. Richard[6], ordered, 8 Feb. 1802, to be bound by the Overseers of the Poor;[445] 381. John[6], for whom William G. Elam was appointed guardian, 14 June 1802;[446] 382. Joseph[6], for whom William G. Elam was appointed guardian, 14 June 1802,[447] married, (bond 13) Jan. 1812,[448] Caroline Wooldridge.

116. ROBERT[5] WOOLDRIDGE (Elizabeth[4] Branch, James[3], Thomas[2], Christopher[1]) died 1801 in Franklin Co., Ky. He married Susanna Major, who married (2), (bond 5) Feb. 1802,[449] Ritchie Boulware and moved to Christian Co., Ky.

Issue: [WOOLDRIDGE][450] 383. Merritt[6]; 384. John[6], probably died young; 385. Elizabeth Redd[6], married, 29 June 1816,[451] Matthew Jeffries; 386. Thomas Major[6], born about 1800, died 20 Feb. 1872 at Hopkinsville, Ky., married, 9 May 1824,[452] Eliza B. Cates.

117. THOMAS[5] WOOLDRIDGE (Elizabeth[4] Branch, James[3], Thomas[2], Christopher[1]), born 1756 [453] in Chesterfield County, left will 22 Oct. 1840-Jan. 1841.[454] He served a tour in the Chesterfield County militia, 1777, and two tours in the Buckingham County militia, 1779 and 1781, moved to Franklin Co., Ky., in 1793, and four years later settled in Henry Co., Ky.[455] He married (1), (bond

---

[444] Benjamin B. Weisiger, *Marriage Bonds and Ministers' Returns of Chesterfield County, Virginia, 1816-1853* (Richmond, 1981), p. 52.

[445] Chesterfield Co. Order Bk. 14, p. 207.

[446] *Ibid.*, p. 280.

[447] *Ibid.*

[448] Knorr, *Marriage Bonds ... Chesterfield County*, p. 44.

[449] Franklin Co., Ky., Marriage bond, in *The Register of the Kentucky Historical Society*. XII, p. 72.

[450] Wooldridge, *op. cit.*, I, pp. 273-76.

[451] Franklin Co., Ky., Marriage Bk. 1, p. 35, in Hattie M. Scott, "Index to Franklin County, Kentucky, Marriage Bonds, 1810-1830" (typewritten; n.p., n.d.), p. 14.

[452] Christian Co., Ky., Marriage bond, 8 May 1824, in *The Register of the Kentucky Historical Society*, XXV, p. 172.

[453] *A Census of Pensioners for Revolutionary and Military Services* (Washington, 1841), p. 163, as aged 89.

[454] Henry Co., Ky., Will Bk. 7, p. 284.

[455] Revolutionary War pension application, Thomas Wooldridge, S.31494, National Archives.

10) Aug. 1781,[456] Sarah Ann Barnes and (2), 5 July 1826,[457] Agnes (Kelly) Mallory.

IssueL [WOOLDRIDGE][458] (by 1) 387. John Barnes[6], born about 1785, died 5 Aug. 1822 in Franklin Co., Ky.; 388. Mary P.[6], married (1), (bond 24) Dec. 1805,[459] Jeremiah Hall, who died 1825 in Franklin Co., Ky., and (2), 29 June 1830,[460] George W. Oliver; 389. Elizabeth[6], married, (bond 27) Sept. 1805,[461] Thomas S. Wingate and lived in Owen Co., Ky.; 390. Edward Porter[6], born Nov. 1796, died Nov. 1873, married, 20 Feb. 1826,[462] Katherine Atchison, born Nov. 1810, died May 1894.

118 SARAH[5] BRANCH (John[4], James[3], Thomas[2], Christopher[1]), born about 1764, died 30 Dec. 1851.[463] She married, 25 Nov. 1791 in Bedford County, Edmund Goode, who died 15 Oct. 1812. He was a private during the Revolutionary War and was at the battles of Eutaw Springs, Camden and Guilford.[464] They resided in Bedford County and she continued to live there as a widow.

Issue: [GOODE][465] 391. John[6], born Oct. 1796, died Jan. 1876, soldier in the War of 1812, farmer of Bedford County, married, (bond 24) Feb. 1824,[466] Ann M. Leftwich, born March 1804, died Oct. 1868; 392. Susan[6], married, 9 Nov. 1813,[467] Samuel Hobson.

120. JAMES[5] HILL (Phoebe[4] Branch, James[3], Thomas[2], Christopher[1]), betwen age 16-21 in 1786, married ___.

IssueL [HILL] 393. Edward[6].

121 OLIVE[5] HILL (Phoebe[4] Branch, James[3], Thomas[2], Christopher[1]), tithable in 1777, married ___.

---

[456] Knorr, *Marriage Bonds ... Powhatan County*, p. 75.

[457] *Henry County, Kentucky, Marriages, 1798-1850* (Indianapolis, n.d.), p. 55.

[458] Wooldridge, *op. cit.*, I, pp. 284-86.

[459] Franklin Co., Ky., Marriage bond, in *The Register of the Kentucky Historical Society*, XIII, p. 82.

[460] Franklin Co., Ky., Marriage Bk. 1, p. 54.

[461] Franklin Co., Ky., Marriage bond, in *ibid.*, XII, p. 85.

[462] *Henry County, Kentucky, Marriages, 1798-1850, loc. cit.*

[463] Pierce, *op. cit.*, I, p. 221.

[464] Revolutionary War pension application, Edmund Goode, widow Sarah, W.3801, National Archives.

[465] Goode, *Virginia Cousins*, pp. 50-F, 95.

[466] Bedford Co. Marriage bond, in Hinshaw, VI, p. 923.

[467] Bedford Co. Marriage return, in Hinshaw, VI, p. 932.

Issue: [HILL] 394. Edward[6], married, (bond 13) May 1799,[468] Judith Chalkley.

123 ALEXANDER[5] TRENT (Obedience[4] Branch, John[3], Thomas[2], Christopher[1]) of Cumberland County, left will 9 Dec. 1750-22 July 1751.[469] He married Frances Archer, daughter of John Archer.[470]

Issue: [TRENT] 395. Alexander[6], born 3 March 1728/9, died 27 Feb. 1793,[471] left will 5 Feb. 1793-21 March 1793,[472] of "Barter Hill," Cumberland County, justice, member of the House of Burgesses, 1766-72,[473] vestryman of Southam Parish, later merchant of Manchester, married (1), (bond 27) Sept. 1750,[474] Frances Scott, possibly daughter of Edward and 28. *Ann*[4] (*Cox*) *Scott* (see COX) of Goochland County,[475] and (2), (bond 1) Jan. 1753,[476] 104. *Elizabeth*[5] *Woodson* (see WOODSON), born 19 [18?] March 1733/4,[477] died 7 Jan. 1787; 396. Peter Field[6], died 19 Nov. 1794 at an advanced age,[478] merchant of Richmond, married (1) _____ and (2), 3 March 1771,[479] 411. Angelica[6] Wilkinson, who died 8 Feb. 1793 in her 46th year;[480] 397. Elizabeth[6], married 345. *John*[6] *Archer* (see EPES).

124 THOMAS[5] TURPIN (Obedience[4] Branch, John[3], William[2], Christopher[1]), born 17 May 1708, died 20 June 1790,[481] left will 11 March 1789-16 Sept. 1790.[482] He married, 4 May 1732, 160. Mary[5] Jefferson, born

---

[468] Knorr, *Marriage Bonds ... Chesterfield County*, p. 67.

[469] Cumberland Co. Will Bk. 1, p. 44.

[470] Dr. Philip Turpin notebook, in *The Virginia Genealogist*, XXXI, pp. 5-6.

[471] Trent Bible, in David A. Avant, *Some Southern Colonial Families*, IV (Tallahassee, Fla., 1991), p. 749.

[472] Powhatan Co. Will Bk. 1, pp. 251-52.

[473] Leonard, pp. 94, 97, 99, 102.

[474] Katherine B. Elliott, *Marriage Records, 1749-1840, Cumberland County, Virginia* (South Hill, Va., 1969), p. 129.

[475] Goochland Co. Deed Bk. 3, 1737-42, p. 107, will of Edward Scott, 20 Feb. 1737-18 April 1738.

[476] Kathleen Booth Williams, *Marriages of Goochland County, Virginia, 1733-1815* (n.p., 1960), p. 99.

[477] Woodson Bible, in *W*(2) VIII, p. 310.

[478] *Virginia Gazette and Richmond and Manchester Advertiser*, 20 Nov. 1794.

[479] *Virginia Gazette* (Rind), 21 March 1771; marriage contract, 2 March 1770 [*sic*?], Chesterfield Co. Deed Bk. 6, p. 360.

[480] *Virginia Gazette and Public Advertiser*, Richmond, 9 Feb. 1793.

[481] Philip Turpin Notebook, in *The Virginia Genealogist*, XXXI, pp. 7-8.

[482] Powhatan Co. Will Bk. 1, p. 180.

Aug. 1708, died 8 Feb. 1784.[483]

Issue: [TURPIN][484] 398. Thomas[6], born 9 May 1733, died a few months later; 399. Obedience[6], born 17 Sept. 1734, married 513. John[6] Harris; 400. Thomas[6], died 9 March 1797 in Powhatan County,[485] left will 30 May 1796-17 May 1797,[486] member of the House of Delegates, 1786-88, and of the Convention of 1788,[487] married, 9 April 1767,[488] Martha Ward Gaines; 401. Mary[6], married 521. Richard[5] James; 402. William[6], born 6 April 1741, married, (bond 28) June 1773, 552. Sarah[6] Harris, born 17 Jan. 1754;[489] 403. Philip[6], died young; 404. Lucy[6], died young; 405. Dr. Philip[6], died 8 May 1828 at "Salisbury," Chesterfield County,[490] left will 11 April 1828-19 Aug. 1828,[491] married (1), 8 Oct. 1787, Caroline M. Rose, who died 20 Nov. 1793 at "Salisbury,"[492] and (2), 10 Dec. 1796,[493] 40. *Martha[6] (Osborne) McCallum* (see OSBORNE);[494] 406. Peter Field[6], left will 2 Feb. 1789-16 Sept. 1790,[495] unmarried; 407. Horatio[6], of Powhatan County, married, 30 March 1803, Mary Anne Bancroft.[496]

128 JOSEPH[5] WILKINSON (Priscilla[4] Branch, John[3], William[2], Christopher[1]) left will 21 Oct. 1732-Sept. 1733.[497] He married Mary [Green?].

Issue: [WILKINSON] 408. Priscilla[6], married (1) Henry Embry, Jr., member of the House of Burgesses from Brunswick County, 1736-40, and Lunenburg County, 1748-49,[498] justice 1749-50, died before 27 March 1753

---

[483] Philip Turpin Notebook, in *The Virginia Genealogist*, XXXI, p. 8.

[484] *Ibid.*, pp. 6-7; George Wythe, *Decisions of Cases in Virginia By the High Court of Chancery* (Richmond , 1852), pp. 137-43.

[485] *Virginia Argus*, Richmond, 31 March 1797.

[486] Powhatan Co. Deed Bk. 2, pp. 350-54.

[487] Leonard, pp. 161, 166, 173.

[488] Jones, *op. cit.*, p. 47.

[489] Elliott, *op. cit.*, p. 130.

[490] *Enquirer*, Richmond, 16 May 1828.

[491] Chesterfield Co. Will Bk. 11, pp. 320-21.

[492] *Virginia Gazette and Richmond and Manchester Advertiser*, 25 Nov. 1793.

[493] *Virginia Argus*, Richmond, 12 Dec. 1796.

[494] Christine Rose, *Ancestors and Descendants of the Brothers Rev. Robert Rose and Rev. Charles Rose* (San Jose, Calif., 1985), p. 92.

[495] Powhatan Co. Will Bk. 1, p. 137.

[496] Branch, *op. cit.*, p. 69.

[497] Henrico Co. Wills & Deeds 1725-37, p. 406.

[498] Leonard, pp. 76, 82.

when Priscilla was granted administration on his estate,[499] and (2), (bond 24) Oct. 1758,[500] William Hill, who moved to Carteret Co., N.C.;[501] 409. Mary[6].

130. EDWARD[5] WILKINSON (Priscilla[4], John[3], William[2], Christopher[1]), of Chesterfield Parish, left will 29 March 1771-7 June 1771.[502] He married (1) 160. *Ann[4] Epes* (see EPES) and (2), (contract 30) Jan. 1759,[503] Mary (____) Oglesby (Ogilby), widow of Richard Oglesby, who died before 14 May 1793 when her sons John and Richard Ogilby were granted administration on her estate.[504]

Issue: [WILKINSON] (by 1) 410. Joseph[6], married 147. Elizabeth[5] Bass; 411. Angelica[6], named in will of grandfather Epes, married 396. Peter Field[6] Trent.

132 CHRISTOPHER[5] BRANCH (Henry[4], Christopher[3], Christopher[2], Christopher[1]) of "The Grove," Chesterfield County, chose his mother as his guardian, 6 May 1751,[505] and left will 17 March 1772-7 Aug. 1772.[506] He married (1) ____ Archer, whose father, John Archer, named his grandsons Christopher and Archer Branch in his will, 5 Sept. 1773-3 Dec. 1773,[507] and (2) 147. *Mary[5] (Epes) Worsham* (see EPES), widow of 60. John[5] Worsham, who married (3) 181. Benjamin[5] Branch.

Issue: (by 1) 412. Christopher[6], died before 8 June 1798 when William Ball was granted administration on his estate,[508] of Chesterfield County, married Ann __, who joined him in selling land, 21 Nov. 1795;[509] 413. Archer[6], executed 28 Oct. 1796 for horse stealing,[510] his widow being granted administration on his

---

[499] Brunswick Co. Order Bk. 4, p.442; Will Bk. 3, p. 180.

[500] Catherine Lindsay Knorr, *Marriage Bonds and Ministers' Returns of Brunswick County, Virginia, 1750-1810* (Pine Bluff, Ark., 19532), p. 44.

[501] Lunenburg Co. Deed Bk. 10, pp. 18-19, 150-51, sale of land by William Hill to Harwood Jones, 16 July 1764, and Priscilla's relinquishment of dower, 23 March 1764[5?].

[502] Chesterfield Co. Will Bk. 2, p. 359; Order Bk. 5, p. 5.

[503] Chesterfield Co. Deed Bk. 11, pp. 262-63, recorded 23 May 1771; Williams, *Marriages of Amelia County*, p. 117, bond 29 Jan., as Wilkerson.

[504] Chesterfield Co. Order Bk. 10, pp. 91-93.

[505] Chesterfield Co. Order Bk. 1, p. 110.

[506] Chesterfield Co. Will Bk. 2, p. 31; Order Bk. 5, p. 132.

[507] Chesterfield Co. Will Bk. 2, p. 28; Order Bk. 5, p. 378.

[508] Chesterfield Co. Order Bk. 12, p. 373.

[509] Chesterfield Co. Deed Bk. 13, pp. 234-35.

[510] *Norfolk Herald*, 14 Nov. 1796.

estate, 11 June 1798,[511] married, 28 June 1786,[512] Mary Fleming Bernard, who died 30 Jan. 1817 at "Summerville," Chesterfield County, aged 56;[513] 414. Elizabeth[6], chose Henry Anderson as her guardian, 6 June 1782.[514].

134 ANN[5] BRANCH (Henry[4], Christopher[3], Christopher[2], Christopher[1]) chose Thomas Branch as her guardian, 7 Feb. 1752.[515] She married 191. *William[6] Giles* (see HARRIS, Thomas), of Amelia County, who left will 28 Feb. 1793-25 Sept. 1794.[516]

Issue: [GILES][517] 415. William Branch[6], born 12 Aug. 1762 in Amelia County, died 4 Dec. 1830,[518] student at the College of William and Mary and graduate of the College of New Jersey (Princeton), 1781, attorney of Petersburg, member of Congress, 1790-98, 1801-03, and of the United States Senate, 1803-15, member of the House of Delegates, 1798-1800, 1816-17, 1826-27, and of the Convention of 1829-30, Governor of Virginia, 1827-30,[519] married (1) , (bond 6) March 1797,[520] Martha Peyton[7] Tabb, daughter of 48. *John[6] Tabb* (see PUREFOY), who died 30 July 1808,[521] and (2), 22 Feb, 1810 at Georgetown, D.C.,[522] Frances Anne Gwynn, who died 28 Dec. 1821 at "The Wigwam," Amelia County;[523] 416. Elizabeth[6], married 103. *John[6] Booker* (see PUREFOY); 417. Patty[6], married, 13 March 1800,[524] Joshua Chaffin; 418. Mary[6], married 181. *Samuel[6] Jones* (see CLAIBORNE); 419. Amy[6], named in will of her aunt Martha Branch, died about 17 Oct. 1818 in Powhatan County, married, (bond

---

[511] Chesterfield Co. Order Bk. 12, p. 482.

[512] Knorr, *Marriage Bonds ... Chesterfield County*, p. 19.

[513] *Enquirer*, Richmond, 13 Feb. 1817.

[514] Chesterfield Co. Order Bk. 12, p. 482.

[515] Chesterfield Co. Order Bk. 1, p. 170.

[516] Amelia Co. Will Bk. 5, p. 107.

[517] Leila Eldridge d'Aiutolo, *The Descendants of William Moseley* (n.p., 2000), I, pp. 112, 158, 191.

[518] *Compiler*, Richmond, 8 Dec. 1830.

[519] Leonard, pp. 211, 215, 285, 333, 353; *Biographical Directory of the American Congress, 1774-1996*, p. 1090; *Dictionary of American Biography*, VII (New York, 1931), pp. 283-84.

[520] Williams, *Marriages of Amelia County*, p. 46.

[521] *Enquirer*, Richmond, 23 Aug. 1808.

[522] *Enquirer*, Richmond, 9 March 1810.

[523] *Enquirer*, Richmond, 3 Jan. 1822.

[524] Williams, *Marriages of Amelia County*, p. 22.

29) April 1782,[525] 686. *Benjamin*[6] *Moseley* (see BALEY-COCKE), who died 26 Feb. 1791 in Powhatan County.

135. WLLIAM[5] BRANCH (Henry[4], Christopher[3], Christopher[2], Christopher[1]) was bound by the churchwardens to learn a trade, 2 June 1758,[526] and left will 14 Nov. 1796-10 April 1797.[527] He married, (bond 20) Sept. 1764,[528] Judith Scott who died 4 Sept. 1820, aged 79.[529]

Issue:[530] 420. William[6], left 344 acres where he lived; 421. Joseph[6], left will 15 Oct. 1801-14 Dec. 1801,[531] married, 13 Jan. 1798,[532] 427. Susanna[6] Branch; 422. Henry[6], of Chesterfield County, sold 700 acres in Wilkes Co., Ga., 15 Sept. 1799,[533] married Catherine ___; 423. Col. Thomas[6], of Chesterfield County, left land in Georgia; 424. Francis[6], died young; 425. Judith[6], left land in Botetourt County, married, by 3 Jan. 1799, Thomas Ligon; 426. Martha[6], left land in Botetourt County.

138. HENRY[5] BRANCH (Henry[4], Christopher[3], Christopher[2], Christopher[1]) was named in will of brother Christopher and died before 8 Jan. 1798 when his widow was granted administration on his estate.[534] He married Tabitha ____.

Issue:[535] 427. Susanna[6], married 421. Joseph[6] Branch; 428. William[6], left will 9 Nov. 1802-13 Dec. 1802,[536] married Elizabeth ___; 429. Judith[6]; 430. John[6]; 431. Palina Fowler[6], married, (bond 5) Sept. 1805,[537] Thomas Fore; 432. Henry[6]; 433. Matthew Hobson[6]; 434. Robert F.[6], born about 1787, died 9 Nov. 1858 in Dinwiddie County, of Manchester and later of Dinwiddie County, served

---

[525] *Ibid.*, p. 78.

[526] Chesterfield Co. Order Bk. 2, p. 422.

[527] Chesterfield Co. Will Bk. 5, p. 132; Order Bk. 12, p. 1153.

[528] Williams, *Marriages of Amelia County*, p. 17.

[529] *Virginia Patriot and Richmond Daily Mercantile Advertiser*, 20 Sept. 1820.

[530] Chesterfield Co. Will Bk. 7, pp. 130-31, division of estate of William Branch, 3 Jan. 1799.

[531] Chesterfield Co. Will Bk. 5, p. 461; Order Bk. 14, p. 185.

[532] Knorr, *Marriage Bonds ... Chesterfield County*, p. 19.

[533] Wilkes Co., Ga., Deed Bk. RR, pp. 262-63. William Branch had purchased this land, 24 March 1787 (Wilkes Co., Ga., Deed Bk. CC, p. 24).

[534] Chesterfield Co. Order Bk. 12, p. 368.

[535] *Ibid.*, p. 652, division of estate; all children except Susanna under 21 in 1799.

[536] Chesterfield Co. Will Bk. 5, p. 461; Order Bk. 14, p. 185.

[537] *Ibid.*, p. 50.

two brief tours in the Virginia militia during the War of 1812,[538] married (1), (bond 19) Dec. 1811,[539] 227. *Mary*[6] *Tatum* (see TATUM), (2), 12 March 1857, Harriet (Coalman) Johnson, born about 1801; 435. Lucy[6].

138. CHRISTOPHER[5] BASS (Cicely[4] Branch, Christopher[3], Christopher[2], Christopher[1]), born 5 March 1719/20, left will 8 Nov.1772-4 Nov. 1774.[540] He married Frances ___.

Issue: [BASS] 436. William[6]; 437. Christopher[6], chose William Bass as his guardian, 4 Nov. 1774;[541] 438. Mary[6], chose Joseph Bass as her guardian, 4 Nov. 1774.[542]

139. MARY[5] BASS (Cicely[4] Branch, Christopher[3], Christopher[2], Christopher[1]), born 9 Jan. 1721/2, died 19 Nov. 1788. She married, 6 Dec. 1739, William Walthall of Chesterfield County, son of Henry and Mary (___) Walthall, born 16 Aug. 1714, died 12 May 1789,[543] left will 8 Dec. 1788-11 June 1789.[544]

Issue: [WALTHALL][545] 439. William[6], born 7 March 1740/1, died before 6 July 1781 when administration on his estate was granted to Edward Archer and Archibald Walthall,[546] of "Troxdale," Chesterfield County, married Martha Field Archer, who died 1805; 440. Mary[6], born 17 Dec. 1742, left will 27 July 1790-14 Oct. 1790,[547] married Edward Archer who left will 30 Dec. 1789-11 Feb. 1799;[548] 441. John[6], born 7 Oct. 1744, died young; 442. Sally[6], married 92. *Nathaniel*[5] *Friend* (see COX); 443. Archard[6], born 9 Jan. 1750/1, left will 16 Nov. 1805-9 Dec. 1805,[549] of "Valley Farm," Chesterfield County, married Frances Netherland, born 21 Oct. 1765, died before 12 Sept. 1821 when John

---

[538] War of 1812 pension, Robert F. Branch, widow Harriet, W.O.27301, W.C.17123, National Archives.

[539] Knorr, *Marriage Bonds ... Chesterfield County*, p. 20.

[540] Chesterfield Co. Will Bk. 2, p. 229; Order Bk. 6, p. 64.

[541] Chesterfield Co. Order Bk. 6, p. 65.

[542] *Ibid.*, p. 64.

[543] Walthall Bible, 1714-89, Virginia State Archives, Acc.22827.

[544] Chesterfield Co. Will Bk. 4, p. 196; Order Bk. 8, p. 261.

[545] Walthall Bible, *loc. cit.*; Malcolm Elmore Walthall, "The Walthall Family" (typewritten; Charlotte, N.C., 1963), pp. 20, 37-38.

[546] Chesterfield Co. Order Bk. 6, p. 321.

[547] Chesterfield Co. Will Bk. 4, p. 255; Order Bk. 8, p. 495,

[548] Chesterfield Co. Will Bk. 4, p. 244; Order Bk. 8, p. 373.

[549] Chesterfield Co. Will Bk. 6, p. 283.

Walthall, her administrator, sold property.[550]

145. Col. JOSEPH[5] BASS (Cicely[4] Branch, Christopher[3], Christopher[2], Christopher[1]) chose William Walthall as his guardian, 2 March 1753,[551] took the oath as lieutenant colonel of Chesterfield County militia, 4 Jan. 1777, and left will 23 Aug. 1777-2 Oct. 1778.[552] He married Elizabeth ___.[553]

Issue: [BASS][554] 444. Joseph[6], born 30 Nov. 1759 in Chesterfield County, died 30 March 1844 in Dinwiddie County, served two tours as quartermaster sergeant of Chesterfield County militia, 1780, was appointed ensign 6 April 1781 and served two more tours, moved from Chesterfield to Dinwiddie County, 1807,[555] married, 5 Dec. 1790,[556] Jenny Manlove, born about 1773;[557] 445. William[6]; 446. Peter[6]; 447. Elizabeth[6]; 448. Ann[6], died before 7 Feb. 1783 when administration on her estate was granted to her husband,[558] married, (bond 4) Aug. 1780,[559] as his (1) wife, 40. Henry[6] Stratton (see SHEPPEY); 449. Rebecca[6], married, (consent 9) Dec. 1792,[560] James Fountain; 450. Polly[6].

147. ELIZABETH[5] BASS (Cicely[4] Branch, Christopher[3], Christopher[2], Christopher[1]) married 410. Joseph[6] Wilkinson, who was given by his father the 300 acres in Amelia County where he lived, 11 March 1763,[561] and died before 23 July 1767.[562]

Issue: [WILKINSON][563] 451. Edward[6], died after Feb. 1794 in Amelia

---

[550] Chesterfield Co. Will Bk. 9, p. 162.

[551] Chesterfield Co. Order Bk. 1, p. 313.

[552] Chesterfield Co. Will Bk. 3, p. 205; Order Bk. 6, p. 190.

[553] It has been assumed she was Elizabeth Trent since Joseph[5] Bass referred to his brother-in-law 390. Peterfield[6] Trent in his will. This Peter Field Trent's sister 391. Elizabeth[6] Trent, however, married 345. John[6] Archer (see EPES). Perhaps Elizabeth was the sister of 390. Peter Field[6] Trent's unidentified (1) wife.

[554] Chesterfield Co. Chancery papers, 1783-018, Stratton admr. vs. Bass's exrs. & al.

[555] Revolutionary War pension application, Joseph Bass, widow Jenney, W.5765, National Archives; John H. Gwathmey, *Historical Register of Virginians in the Revolution* (Richmond, 1938), p. 46.

[556] Knorr, *Marriage Bonds ... Chesterfield County*, p. 9.

[557] Dinwiddie Co. 1850 census, Southern Dist., p. 951 or 476, family 91-92.

[558] Chesterfield Co. Order Bk. 6, p. 397.

[559] Knorr, *Marriage Bonds ... Chesterfield County*, p. 114.

[560] *Ibid.*, p. 51.

[561] Gibson Jefferson McConnaughey, *Unrecorded Deeds and Other Documents, Amelia County, Virginia, 1750-1902* (Amelia, Va., 1994), p. 73.

[562] Amelia Co. Order Bk. 9, p. 229.

[563] Chesterfield Co. Deed Bk. 13, p. 408.

County; 452. Joseph[6], born after March 1751,[564] left will 5 Jan. 1804-27 June 1805,[565] married, (bond 28) Feb. 1788,[566] 575. Obedience[6] Branch, who married (2), (bond 16) Sept. 1806,[567] 687. *Edward[6] Moseley* (see BALEY-COCKE) and died 29 Dec. 1847, aged 78 yrs. 4 mos.[568]

149. WILLIAM[5] CHEATHAM (Obedience[4] Branch, Christopher[3], Christopher[2], Christopher[1]), of Chesterfield County, left will 12 Dec. 1795-11 July 1796.[569] He married (1) Tabitha Beasley and (2) Frances Pryor.

Issue: [CHEATHAM] (by 1) 453. Sarah[6]; 454. Ann[6]; (by which wife unknown) 455. Elizabeth[6], married Pleasant Bowman who moved to Cumberland Co., Ky.; 456. Rhoda[6], married ____ Walthall; 457. William[6], born 28 Aug. 1762, Chesterfield County,[570] died 1840, Washington, Ark., served five tours in Revolutionary War, moved in 1808 to Cumberland Co., Ky., and about 1838 to Hempstead Co., Ark., married Sarah ___, died 1845; 458. Edmund[6], moved to Cumberland Co., Ky., married, (bond 3) March 1792,[571] Milly Norment; 459. Frances[6]; 460. Rebecca Berry[6], married 483. Christopher[6] Cheatham; 461. Christopher[6], of Chesterfield Conunty, married Nancy ___; 462. Major[6], born 30 May 1787, died about 1843, moved to Woodford Co., Ky., and later to Todd Co., Ky., and St. Clair, Ill., married, 17 March 1808, Martha Wooldridge, who was born 20 March 1789 and died 1844 at Alton, Ill.[572]

151. ANN[5] CHEATHAM (Obedience[4] Branch, Christopher[3], Christopher[2], Christopher[1]) married, before 1751, as his (1) wife, James Hill, born 17 July 1726,[573] son of John and Elizabeth (Pride) Hill, of Chesterfield and later of Amelia County, who married (2), (bond 27) June 1763,[574] Ann Booker and left will 25 Feb. 1765-28 March 1765.[575]

---

[564] Chesterfield Co. Will Bk. 2, p. 38, will of grandfather Wilkinson.

[565] Amelia Co. Will Bk. 7, pp. 182-83.

[566] Williams, *op. cit.*, p. 118.

[567] *Ibid.*, p. 78.

[568] Blandford Cemetery, Petersburg, Register of Interments, 1843-71, pp. 19-20.

[569] Chesterfield Co. Will Bk. 4, pp. 593-94; Order Bk. 11, p. 513.

[570] Revolutionary War pension application, William Cheatham, S.31607, National Archives.

[571] Lindsay, *op. cit.*, p. 17.

[572] Wooldridge, *op. cit.*, p. 920.

[573] Bristol Parish Register.

[574] Williams, *Marriages of Amelia County*, p. 53.

[575] Amelia Co. Will Bk. 2X, p. 91.

Issue: [HILL] 463. James[6], married, (bond 28) June 1781,[576] Frances Booker; 464. John[6]; 465. Elizabeth[6], married Richard Craddock; 466. Ann[6], married James Vaughan; 467. Obedience[6], married William Cross Craddock of Amelia County who left will 27 March 1795-23 July 1796;[577] 468. Sarah[6], married, (bond 18) June 1784,[578] Abraham Lockett; 469. Rebeckah[6].

152. THOMAS[5] CHEATHAM (Obedience[4] Branch, Christopher[3], Christopher[2], Christopher[1]), of Chesterfield County, left will 18 April 1794-April 1795.[579] He married (1) ___ Hobson and (2) Prudence ___, who died after 29 Dec. 1821.[580]

Issue: [CHEATHAM][581] (by 1) 470. Matthew[6], left will 18 Oct. 1815-13 Nov. 1815,[582] married, 12 May 1793,[583] Martha[7] Sherwin, daughter of 357. *Elizabeth[6] (Randolph) Sherwin* (see EPES); 471. Sarah[6], married ___ Graves; 472. William[6], died before his father; 473. Thomas[6], born 26 June 1770, died 15 Sept. 1827, served in War of 1812, married Elizabeth Bruce, who married (2), (bond 14) Feb. 1835,[584] Matthew Winfree; 474. Elizabeth[6], left will 28 Aug. 1820-11 Dec. 1820,[585] married Capt. William Ball, who was born about 1757 in Henrico County[586] and died before 13 Oct. 1817 when Thomas Ball gave bond as his administrator,[587] of "Broad Rock," Chesterfield County; 475. Pollina[6], died before her father; 476. Martha[6], died before 13 Dec. 1802 when administration on her estate was granted to Branch Cheatham,[588] married (1), (consent 20) Sept. 1791,[589] Stephen Beasley, who left will 10 Nov. 1791-9 April 1792,[590] and (2) 40. *Henry[6] Stratton* (see SHEPPEY); (by 2) 477. Branch[6], died by 13 July

---

[576] Williams, *Marriages of Amelia County*, p. 53.
[577] Amelia Co. Will Bk. 5, p. 177.
[578] Williams, *Marriages of Amelia County*, p. 69.
[579] Chesterfield Co. Will Bk. 4, pp. 474-76.
[580] Chesterfield Co. Deed Bk. 24, p. 320.
[581] Dennstedt, *op. cit.*, pp. 100-01.
[582] Chesterfield Co. Will Bk. 8, pp. 383-85.
[583] Knorr, *Marriage Bonds ... Chesterfield County*, p. 29.
[584] Weisiger, *Marriage Bonds ... Chesterfield County*, p. 166.
[585] Chesterfield Co. Will Bk. 9, p. 305.
[586] Donna Rachal Mills, *Some Southern Balls* (Orlando, Fla., and Tuscaloosa, Ala., 1993), p. 45.
[587] Chesterfield Co. Will Bk. 8, pp. 707-08.
[588] Chesterfield Co. Order Bk. 14, p. 395.
[589] Knorr, *Marriage Bonds ... Chesterfield County*, p. 11.
[590] Chesterfield Co. Will Bk. 4, p. 397; Order Bk. 9, p. 329.

1840,[591] married Mary __; 478. Ann[6], died before her mother;[592] 479. Susanna[6], married Peterfield Edwards, who died before Sept. 1841.[593]

154. CHRISTOPHER[5] CHEATHAM (Obedience[4] Branch, Christopher[3], Christopher[2], Christopher[1]), of Chesterfield County, left will 30 Sept. 1770-7 Dec. 1770.[594] He married Elizabeth Akin.[595]

Issue: [CHEATHAM] 480. William[6]; 481. Lucy[6], born 26 March 1764, died 19 March 1836, married, 3 Jan. 1783,[596] Valentine[7] Winfree, son of 277. *Martha[6] (Graves) Winfree* (see COX), born 15 June 1762, died 8 April 1824,[597] left will 22 Feb. 1824-12 April 1824;[598] 482. Polly[6]; 483. Christopher[6], of Cumberland Co., Ky., married, (bond 3) March 1796,[599] 460. Rebecca Berry[6] Cheatham; 484. Thomas[6].

157. FIELD[5] JEFFERSON (Thomas[4], Mary[3] Branch, Christopher[2], Christopher[1]), born 16 March 1702/3, died 10 Feb. 1765,[600] left will 8 June 1762-10 June 1765.[601] He was sheriff of Lunenburg County, 1753. He married (1) Mary Frances Robertson, daughter of the Rev. George Robertson, who died 26 Feb. 1750/1 in her 44th year, and (2), (bond 31) Oct. 1753,[602] Mary (Hunt) Minge Allen, widow of Robert Minge and William Allen.[603]

Issue: [JEFFERSON] (by 1)[604] 485. Thomas[6], died 5 Dec. 1783; 486. Peter Field[6], born 14 March 1735/6, died by Aug. 1798 when his widow and children

---

[591] Chesterfield Co. Deed Bk. 32, p. 397. He left a will, probably in Alabama.

[592] Chesterfield Co. Will Bk. 13, p. 30, division of slaves of Prudence Cheatham, 14 July 1834.

[593] Chesterfield Co. Deed Bk. 33, p. 153.

[594] Chesterfield Co. Will Bk. 2, pp. 65-67; Order Bk. 4, p. 473.

[595] Chesterfield Co. Will Bk. 2, p. 20, will of Elizabeth Akin, 31 July 1771-4 Oct. 1771. His will names wife Elizabeth but 3 Jan. 1783 Lucy Cheatham, widow of Christopher Cheatham, moved that Thomas Cheatham be appointed her guardian (Chesterfield Co. Order Bk. 6, p. 391).

[596] Winfree Bible, Virginia State Archives.

[597] Ellery Farmer, *Descendants of Thomas Farmer ...* (Hendersonville, N.C., 1956), p. 55.

[598] Chesterfield Co. Will Bk. 10, p. 148.

[599] Knorr, *Marriage Bonds ... Chesterfield County*, p. 28.

[600] Jefferson Bible, *loc. cit.*

[601] Mecklenburg Co. Will Bk. 1, p. 4.

[602] Emma R. Matheny and Helen K. Yates, *Marriages of Lunenburg County, Virginia, 1746-1853* (Richmond, 1967), p. 68; prenuptual agreement, 1 Nov. 1753, Lunenburg Co. Deed Bk. 3, pp. 412-13.

[603] *T* XIII, pp. 15-23.

[604] Jefferson Bible, *loc. cit.*

were sued in chancery in Pittsylvania County,[605] married, (bond 29) May 1762,[606] Elizabeth Allen, born 7 Dec. 1739,[607] died 7 May 1828, left will 11 March 1828-16 June 1828;[608] 487. John[6], married, 28 March 1763, Elizabeth Broome; 488. George[6], of Lunenburg County and moved about 1776[609] to Richmond Co., N.C., left will 1780,[610] married, July 1764,[611] Elizabeth Garland; 489. Mary[6], married __ Nicholls; 490. Phoebe[6], died 1823-30, married Alexander Clark, died 1782, of Edgecombe and Chatham cos., N.C., justice and treasurer of Chatham County, member of the North Carolina House of Commons;[612] 491. Judith[6], married, (bond 7) Sept. 1762,[613] Arthur Hopkins of Albemarle, Mecklenburg and Pittsylvania counties,[614] captain of militia, Aug. 1771, member of the Committee of Safety, 26 Jan. 1775, who left will 18 Oct. 1775-26 Sept. 1776;[615] 492. Frances[6], living 7 April 1752,[616] married Henry Delony,[617] who married (2), 11 May 1753,[618] Rebecca B. Walker, was justice of Mecklenburg County, 1765, member of the House of Delegates, 1777-78,[619] kept an ordinary, and left will 29 April 1785-13 June 1785.[620]

159. PETER[5] JEFFERSON (Thomas[4], Mary[3] Branch, Christopher[2], Christopher[1]), born 29 Feb. 1707/8,[621] left will 13 July 1757-13 Oct. 1757.[622] He was vestryman of St. James Northam Parish, 1748, colonel of militia, 1745, County Lieutenant, 1755, member of the House of Burgesses from Albemarle

---

[605] *Lynchburg Weekly Gazette.* 13 Oct. 1798.

[606] Elliott, *Marriage Records ... Cumberland County*, p. 74., bond 29 May.

[607] Allen Bible, in *W*(1) XXII, p. 195, gives 17 Dec.

[608] Pittsylvania Co. Will Bk. 1, p.p. 149-50.

[609] *Virginia Gazette* (Purdie), 13 Sept. 1776.

[610] Richmond Co., N.C., Will Bk. 1, pp. 4-5.

[611] *T* VII, p. 51, letter of consent of her father David Garland, 2 July 1764 (not mentioned in Matheny and Yates, *op. cit.*).

[612] Elizabeth Shown Mills, "A Husband for Phoebe Jefferson," *The Virginia Genealogist*, XXIX, pp. 83-104.

[613] Matheny and Yates, *op. cit.*, p. 63.

[614] Walter Lee Hopkins, *Hopkins of Virginia* (Richmond, 1931), p. 33.

[615] Pittsylvania Co. Will Bk. 5, p. 420.

[616] Lunenburg Co. Deed Bk. 2, pp. 468-70.

[617] *The Southside Virginian*, VII, p. 165.

[618] Knorr, *Marriage Bonds ... Brunswick County*, p. 24.

[619] Leonard, pp. 126, 130.

[620] Mecklenburg Co. Will Bk. 2, p. 103.

[621] Jefferson Bible, *loc. cit.*

[622] Albemarle Co. Will Bk.B, pp. 32-35.

County, 1754-55, ran the boundary line between Virginia and North Carolina with Col. Joshua Fry, 1749, and made a map of Virginia, 1751. He married, (bond 3) Oct. 1739,[623] Jane Randolph, daughter of Isham Randolph of "Dungness," Goochland County, who left will undated will proved Oct. 1778.[624]

Issue: [JEFFERSON][625] 493. Jane[6], born 27 June 1740, died 1 Oct. 1765; 494. Mary[6], born 1 Oct. 1741, married, 24 June 1760, 29. *John[6] Bolling* (see ROLFE); 495. Thomas[6], born 2 April 1743, "Shadwell," Albemarle County, died 4 July 1826, "Monticello," Albemarle County, student at the College of William and Mary, lawyer of "Poplar Forest" and later of "Monticello," Albemarle County, member of the House of Burgesses, 1769-76, the five Virginia conventions, 1774-76, the Continental Congress and author of the Declaration of Independence, the House of Delegates, 1776-79, 1784, Governor of Virginia, 1779-80, member of Congress, 1781-84, minister to France, 1784-89, Secretary of State, 1790-94, Vice President, 1797-1801, and President of the United States, 1801-09, and founder of the University of Virginia, 1825,[626] married, 1 Jan. 1772, 321. *Martha[6] (Wayles) Skelton* (see EPES), born 21 Oct. 1748, died 6 Sept. 1782;[627] 496. Elizabeth[6], born 4 Nov. 1744, died 1 Jan. 1773; 497. Martha[6], born 29 May __, died 3 Sept. 1811 at "Dunlora," Albemarle County, in her 63rd year,[628] married, 20 Jan. 1765, Dabney Carr, born 26 Oct. 1743, "Bear Castle," Louisa County,[629] died 16 May 1773 at Charlottesville,[630] left will 7 Sept. 1772-published 20 April 1773-19 July 1773,[631] attorney, Burgess from Louisa County, 1772-73;[632] 498. Peter Field[6], born 16 Oct. 1748, died 29 Nov. 1748; 499. (son)[6], born and died 9 March 1750; 500. Lucy[6], born 10 Oct. 1752, died between 19 Dec. 1807 and Dec. 1810, married, 12 Sept. 1769, Charles

[623] Williams, *Marriages of Goochland County*, p. 46.

[624] Albemarle Co. Will Bk. B, p. 367.

[625] *T* VI, p. 265.

[626] *Dictionary of American Biography*, X (New York, 1933), pp. 17-35; Leonard, pp. 97, 99, 102, 105, 109, 112, 114, 117, 122, 125, 129, 133, 141, 145.

[627] Jefferson Prayer Book (Oxford, 1752), photocopy, Virginia Historical Society.

[628] *Alexandria Herald*, 19 Sept. 1811.

[629] Malcolm Hart Harris, *History of Louisa County, Virginia* (Richmond, 1936), p. 297.

[630] *Virginia Gazette* (Rind), 27 May 1773.

[631] Goochland Co. Deed Bk. 10, pp. 379-80.

[632] Leonard, p. 103.

Lilburn[7] Lewis, born 1747, died 5 April 1831,[633] son of 448. *Charles*[6] *Lewis* and Mary Randolph (see MARTIAU), of "Buck Island" and "Monteagle," Albemarle County, County Lieutenant of Albemarle, 1782, founder of the town of Milton, moved to Livingston Co., Ky., about 1808-09;[634] 501. Anna Scott[6], born 1 Oct. 1755, twin, married, Oct. 1788, Hastings Marks, who served under Lt. George Gilmer at Williamsburg, July 1775,[635] and later moved to Clark Co., Ky.;[636] 502. Randolph[6], born 1 Oct. 1755, twin, died 7 Aug. 1815, of "Snowden," Fluvanna County, served in Light Dragoons in Revolutionary War, married (1), (bond 30) July 1780,[637] Ann Jefferson[7] Lewis, daughter of 448. *Charles*[6] *Lewis* (see MARTIAU), and (2) Mitchie B. Pryor.[638]

161. MARTHA[5] JEFFERSON[639] (Thomas[4], Mary[3] Branch, Christopher[2], Christopher[1]) married 515. Bennett[6] Goode, who settled in Cumberland, later Powhatan, County and left will 1 Oct. 1771-23 Sept. 1771.[640]

Issue: [GOODE][641] 503. John[6], of "Fine Creek," Powhatan County, born 1743, died 1838, served in the Revolutionary War, married, (bond 31) March 1785,[642] Martha (Embry) Simmons, widow of 310. *Benjamin*[6] *Simmons* (see MASON), who died 1 June 1831 in Powhatan County, aged 76;[643] 504. Bennett[6], died 11 March 1821 in Powhatan County, aged 74,[644] married Susannah ___; 505. Thomas[6], died before 20 Nov. 1777 when administration on his estate was

---

[633] Mrs. John Bennett Boddie, *Historical Southern Families*, XVII (Baltimore, 1972), p. 113.

[634] Merrow Egerton Sorley, *Lewis of Warner Hall* (n.p., 1935), p. 350; Otto A. Rothert, "The Tragedy of the Lewis Brothers," *The Filson Club History Quarterly*, X, pp. 231-53.

[635] Edgar Woods, *Albemarle County in Virginia* (Charlottesville, 1901), p. 365.

[636] Marion Dewoody Pettigrew, *Marks-Barnett Families and Their Kin* (Macon, Ga., 1939), p. 18.

[637] John Vogt and T. William Kethley, *Albemarle County Marriages, 1780-1853* (Athens, Ga., 1991), II, p. 175.

[638] *V* VII, p. 326.

[639] Philip Turpin Notebook (*The Virginia Genealogist,*, XXXI, p. 10) gives her name as Alice.

[640] Cumberland Co. Will Bk. 2, pp. 43-45.

[641] Goode, *op. cit.*, pp. 44, 67-68, 469.

[642] Catherine Lindsay Knorr, *Marriage Bonds and Ministers' Returns of Brunswick County, Virginia, 1750-1810* (Pine Bluff, Ark., 1953), p. 34.

[643] *Enquirer*, Richmond, 14 June 1831.

[644] *Enquirer*, Richmond, 23 March 1821.

granted to his brother John;[645] 506. William[6], born 1765, died 1837, of Elbert Co., Ga., and later of Clarke Co., Ala., married, 17 Sept. 1789,[646] Sarah James, who died 1817 in Elbert Co., Ga.; 507. Lucy[6], born 1760, died 1826 in Henderson Co., Ky.,[647] married, (bond 21) March 1782,[648] Col. William Marshall of Mecklenburg County, who moved to Henderson Co., Ky., 1810,[649] and died before 4 Feb. 1811 when his estate was appraised;[650] 508. Mary[6], married John Hyde Saunders of Lynchburg; 509. Martha[6], married, (bond 9) Oct. 1770,[651] Richard Baskerville of Cumberland County; 510. Ailsey[6], married, (bond 31) May 1785,[652] George Royster and moved to Dinwiddie County; 511. Sally[6], married, Oct. 1783,[653] Charles Povall, born 1763, died 1830, of Powhatan County; 512. Elizabeth[6], married 225. *Samuel[6] Watkins* (see HARRIS, Thomas).

163. JOHN[5] HARRIS (Mary[4] Jefferson, Mary[3] Branch, Christopher[2], Christopher[1]) left will 23 March 1749-May 1751.[654] He married Ursula Jordan.

Issue: [HARRIS][655] 513. John[6], of "Norwood,", Powhatan County, left will 11 March 1797-19 Nov. 1800,[656] married, (bond 27) Aug. 1754,[657] 399. Obedience[6] Turpin; 514. Elizabeth[6], left will 15 May 1789-19 May 1791,[658] married, 9 April 1748,[659] Samuel Flournoy, born 4 Oct. 1727, left will 5 Sept. 1780-21 Dec. 1780;[660] 515. William[6], of Powhatan County, left will 16 Dec. 1791-18 Dec. 1794,[661] married, 15 June 1770,[662] Elizabeth Evans.

164. MARY[5] HARRIS (Mary[4] Jefferson, Mary[3] Branch, Christopher[2],

---

[645] Powhatan Co. Order Bk. 1, p. 17.

[646] Goode, *op. cit.*, p. 473.

[647] *T* X, pp. 66-67.

[648] Knorr, *Marriage Bonds ... Powhatan County*,, p. 40.

[649] Starling, *op. cit.*, p. 632.

[650] Henderson Co., Ky., Will Bk. A, pp. 87-88.

[651] Elliott, *Marriage Records ... Cumberland County*, p. 16.

[652] Knorr, *Marriage Bonds ... Powhatan County*, p. 54.

[653] *Ibid.*, p. 51.

[654] Cumberland Co. Will Bk. 1, p. 37.

[655] Harris, *op. cit.*, p. 333.

[656] Powhatan Co. Will Bk. 2, p. 1.

[657] Elliott, *Marriage Records ... Cumberland County*, p. 63.

[658] Powhatan Co. Will Bk. 1, p. 200.

[659] *V* II, p. 89; Williams, *Marriages of Goochland County*, p. 29.

[660] Powhatan Co. Will Bk. 1, p. 66.

[661] *Ibid.*, p. 301.

[662] Jones, *op. cit.*, p. 24.

Christopher[1]) left will 17 Dec. 1759-25 Aug. 1760.[663] She married (1) John
Goode, of Henrico County, and (2), by 5 Oct. 1725,[664] Francis James of
Cumberland County, who left will 27 July 1756-26 May 1760.[665]

Issue: (by 1) [GOODE] 516. John[6], married 27. Margery[4] Branch; 517.
Bennett[6], married 161. Martha[5] Jefferson; 518. Thomas[6], of Henrico County,
married ___; 519. Mary[6], married, (bond 22) May 1740,[666] William Megginson
of "Clover Plains," Buckingham County, justice of Goochland County, 1741,
and afterward of Albemarle County, captain, 1743, and later County Lieutenant,
who died about 1752;[667] (by 2) [JAMES] 520. Francis[6], left will 24 Sept. 1746-
19 Nov. 1746,[668] married Maudlin Bedford who married (2), (bond 10) June
1747,[669] 136. Micajah[5] Mosby (see WOODSON) and (3), (bond 22) Nov.
1773,[670] 108. John Booker[6] Hoy (see PUREFOY); 521. Col. Richard[6], died 26
Jan. 1802 in his 66th year, married, (bond 10) March 1761,[671] 401. Mary[6]
Turpin, who.died 11 Dec. 1806; 522. Martha[6], married (1) James Meredith of
Cumberland County, who left will 27 Feb. 1750-March 1751,[672] and (2), (bond
27) July 1754,[673] William Clarke; 523. Phebe[6], married, (bond 17) Jan. 1752,[674]
Thomas Merryman, who was licensed to keep an ordinary at his house in
Cumberland County which was continued by his widow,[675] and died before23
Feb.1762 when Phebe was summoned to say whether she would take
administration of his estate;[676] 524. (Son)[6], died young; 525. (Daughter)[6], died
young,

165. EDITH[5] HARRIS (Mary[4] Jefferson, Mary[3] Branch, Christopher[2],
Christopher[1]) married (1) Henry Trent, who left will 8 Jan. 1725-5 Sept. 1726,[677]

---

[663] Cumberland Co. Will Bk. 1, p. 203.
[664] Henrico Co. Orphans Court Bk. 1677-1739, p. 54.
[665] Cumberland Co. Will Bk. 1, p. 196.
[666] Williams, op. cit., p. 61.
[667] George Brown Goode Papers, Virginia State Archives.
[668] Goochland Co. Deed Bk. 5, p. 194.
[669] Williams, Marriages of Goochland County, p. 65.
[670] Elliott, Marriage Records ... Cumberland County, p. 70.
[671] Ibid., p. 74.
[672] Cumberland Co. Will Bk. 1, p. 31.
[673] Elliott, Marriage Records ... Cumberland County, p. 33.
[674] Ibid., p. 90.
[675] Cumberland Co. Order Bk. 1758-62, pp. 9, 233, 461.
[676] Ibid., pp. 449, 462.
[677] Henrico Co. Wills & Deeds 1725-37, p. 40.

(2) 6. *John*[4] *Osborne* (see OSBORNE), and (3), by 3 Nov. 1746,[678] Peter Fitzpatrick.

Issue: (by 1) [TRENT] 526. Henry[6], of Goochland, later Cumberland, County, perhaps married (1) Esther _____, on whose estate he was granted administration, March 1739/40,[679] and (2) ____ Hooper[680] and later lived in Amherst County, left will 27 Dec. 1793-17 Oct. 1796;[681] 527. Edith[6]; 528. Mary[6]; (by 2) see OSBORNE.

167. MARTHA[5] HARRIS (Mary[4] Jefferson, Mary[3] Branch , Christopher[2], Christopher[1]) left will 21 March 1743-19 May 1746.[682] She married, as his (2) wife, Jean Pasteur, native of Genevois, Switzerland, barber and peruke maker who practiced his profession of surgeon in Williamsburg and left will 15 Aug. 1741-16 Nov. 1741.[683]

Issue: [PASTEUR][684] 529. William[6], died 18 June 1791 at Williamsburg,[685] apothecary and practitioner of physic and surgery of Williamsburg, alderman and mayor of Williamsburg, member of the Committee of Safety, surgeon during the Revolutionary War, married Elizabeth Stith, daughter of the Rev. William Stith, who died 1792;[686] 530. Martha[6]; 531. Ann[6], married Thomas Craig;

169. ANN[5] HARRIS (Mary[4] Jefferson, Mary[3] Branch, Christopher[2], Christopher[1]) married (1) ____ Booth and (2), (marriage agreement 10) June 1753,[687] as his (1) wife, Samuel Yeargain, who left will 24 Dec. 1784-Jan. 1785.[688]

Issue: (by 2) [YEARGAIN] 532. Ann[6], left plantation on Roanoke River by her father, married William Alston.

171. JAMES[5] HARRIS (Mary[4] Jefferson, Mary[3] Branch, Christopher[2]

---

[678] Henrico Co. Deeds 1744-48, p. 222, release of their interest in two tracts sold by Henry[6] Trent to Richard Randolph, 7 June 1739.

[679] Henrico Co. Order Bk. 1737-46, p. 98.

[680] Cumberland Co. Will Bk. 1, p. 35, will of Joseph Hooper, 25 Dec. 1750-May 1751, leaving 200 acres where he lived to son-in-law Henry Trent.

[681] Amherst Co. Will Bk. 3, p. 397.

[682] York Co. Deeds, Orders, Wills &c 20, p. 28.

[683] York Co. Deeds, Orders, Wills &c 19, pp. 59, 65.

[684] *Val. Papers* IV, pp. 2285-86.

[685] *Virginia Gazette and General Advertiser*, Richmond, 22 June 1791.

[686] Benjamin Watkins Leigh, *Reports on Cases Argued and Determined in the General Court of Virginia* (2nd ed.; Richmond, 1857), III, p. 378.

[687] Chesterfield Co. Deed Bk. 1, p. 400.

[688] Warren Co., N.C., Will Bk. 4, p. 66.

Christopher[1]) was of Goochland County when he sold land inherited from his father[689] and later of Cumberland County, and left will 27 May 1767-27 July 1767.[690] He married, by Dec. 1744,[691] Sarah Bailey.

Issue: [HARRIS] [692] 533. James[6], of Chesterfield County, married, 26 May 1769,[693] Ursula[7] Flournoy, daughter of Samuel Flournoy and 514. Elizabeth[6] Harris; 534. John[6], of Buckingham County, married ___; 535. William[6], born 1757, died about 1816, of Bedford County, married Mary Pollard, died 1830; 536. Francis[6], of Buckingham County, left will 16 Aug. 1826-13 Aug. 1827,[694] married, (bond 7) June 1773,[695] Ann Diuguid, who as a widow moved to Wilcox Co., Ala., and died 10 July 1836, aged 82 yrs. 6 mos. 17 days;[696] 537. Phoebe[6], married 51. *Joseph Royall[5] Farrar* (see FARRAR); 538. Mary[6]; 539. Col. Thomas[6], of Powhatan County, died 1810,[697] married, 19 Nov. 1778, 690. *Frances[6] (Moseley) Moseley* (see BALEY-COCKE), who died 20 Oct. 1820 in Powhatan County,[698] left will 26 Sept. 1820-15 Nov. 1820.[699]

172. BENJAMIN[5] HARRIS (Mary[4] Jefferson, Mary[3] Branch, Christopher[2], Christopher[1]), of Manakin Town, left will April 1776-Sept. 1776.[700] He married (1) Frances Platt and (2), 1750-53,[701] Priscilla Wager, who died before 15 Jan. 1778 when Edward Moseley was granted administration on her estate.[702]

Issue: (by 2) [HARRIS] 540. Edith[6], left will 5 Oct. 1779-18 Nov. 1779;[703] 541. Sarah[6], became aged 18 in Aug. 1777, married William Yates; 542.

---

[689] Henrico Co. Wills & Deeds 1744-48, p. 225.

[690] Cumberland Co. Will Bk. 1, p. 328.

[691] Henrico Co. Order Bk. 1737-44, p. 287.

[692] Harris, *op. cit.*, pp. 332, 335.

[693] Jones, *op. cit.*, p. 11.

[694] Wilcox Co., Ala., Will Bk. 2, pp. 25-27, in *The Virginia Genealogist*, XXVII, pp. 209-11.

[695] Elliott, *Marriage Records ... Cumberland County*, p. 63.

[696] Gravestone, Harris Cemetery, Wilcox Co., Ala., in Eleanor Harris MacRae, *William Diuguid of Buckingham County, Virginia* (Virginia Beach, Va., 1989), p. 178.

[697] It has been stated he left a will, not extant, proved 22 Nov. 1810 in the General Court.

[698] D'Aiutolo, *op. cit.*, I, p. 102.

[699] Powhatan Co. Will Bk. 6, pp. 66-67.

[700] George Wythe, *Decisions of Cases in Virginia By the High Court of Chancery* (Richmond, 1852), pp. 163-64.

[701] Jones, *op. cit.*, p. 24.

[702] Powhatan Co. Will Bk. 1, p. 5.

[703] *Ibid.*, p. 40.

Benjamin[6]; 543. William Wager[6]; 544. Priscilla[6], baptized 1761,[704] died young; 545. Ann Hinson[6], born 19 Nov. 1764;[705] 546. Phoebe[6], died about 1808, married Nathaniel Carrington, born 28 Feb. 1743/4, died 23 Nov. 1813,[706] left will 10 Feb. 1803-28 Nov. 1803, lieutenant of a Cumberland County minute man company, justice, sheriff and captain of militia;[707] 547. Hinson Wager[6], married, (bond 24) Sept. 1770,[708] 200. *Edward[6] Moseley* (see HARRIS, Thomas); 548. Mary[6], married ___ Spencer.

173. WILLIAM[5] HARRIS (Mary[4] Jefferson, Mary[3] Branch, Christopher[2], Christopher[1]), of "Norwood," Powhatan County, died 30 Oct. 1794 in Powhatan County in his 82nd year[709] and left will 16 June 1791-18 Dec. 1794,[710] He was a Baptist minister.[711] He married (1), by 6 Dec. 1746,[712] 32. *Martha[6] Osborne* (see OSBORNE) and (2) Elizabeth (Ward) Gaines, widow of Bernard Gaines.

Issue: [HARRIS] (by 1) 549. Mary[6], died 3 April 1825 in Henry Co., Ky.,[713] married, 14 May 1767,[714] Bernard Markham, who died 13 July 1802 in Chesterfield County, leaving will 12 July 1801-13 Sept. 1802;[715] 550. Elizabeth[6], married Vincent Markham, brother of Bernard, who was named as justice of Powhatan County in the first commission, 1777;[716] (by 2) 551. Alice[6], married 214. Francis[6] Goode; 552. Sarah[6], married 402. William[6] Turpin; 553. Thomas[6].

174. LUCRETIA[5] WYNNE (Martha[4] Jefferson, Mary[3] Branch, Christopher[2], Christopher[1]) married Joseph Tucker of Prince George and Dinwiddie counties.[717]

---

[704] Jones, *op. cit.*, p. 207.

[705] *Ibid.*

[706] Garland Evans Hopkins, *Colonel Carrington of Cumberland* (Winchester, Va., 1942), p. 87.

[707] *NGSQ* LXX, p. 265; Cumberland Co. Will Bk. 3, p. 238.

[708] Elliott, *Marriage Records ... Cumberland County*, p. 95.

[709] *Virginia Gazette and Richmond and Manchester Advertiser*, 3 Nov. 1794.

[710] Powhatan Co. Will Bk. 1, pp. 301-02.

[711] Harris, *op. cit.*, p. 334.

[712] Henrico Co. Wills & Deeds 1744-48, p. 252.

[713] *V* V, p. 334.

[714] Jones, *op. cit.*, p. 33.

[715] Chesterfield Co. Will Bk. 5, p. 562; Order Bk. 14, p. 351.

[716] *V* V, p. 334.

[717] John Bennett Boddie, *Historical Southern Families*, V (Redwood City, Calif., 1960), p. 296-97.

Issue: [TUCKER] 554. Lucretia[6], born 15 Aug. 1731;[718] 555. Martha[6], married 70. *Benjamin[6] Bell* (see PIERCE-BENNETT); 556. Robert[6], born 8 Sept. 1739,[719] of Dinwiddie County, married Mary Green, born 24 April 1741;[720] 557. Joel[6], died before 20 Aug. 1772 when the inventory of his estate was made,[721] married Judith ___ who married (2), 21 Feb. 1774,[722] Peter Cain; 558. Mary[6], born 3 April 1745.[723]

175. MARTHA[5] WYNNE (Martha[4] Jefferson, Mary[3] Branch, Christopher[2], Christopher[1]) married, as his (2) wife, Mathew Parham, of Sussex County, who left will 2 Sept. 1770-21 May 1772.[724]

Issue: [PARHAM][725] 559. Robert[6], born 17 Jan. 1747/8, left will 27 Oct. 1767-17 Dec. 1767,[726] married 42. *Lucretia[5] Sturdivant* (see HALLOM); 560. Matthew[6], born 27 Feb. 1750/1; 561. Elizabeth[6].

176. ANGELICA[5] WYNNE (Martha[4] Jefferson, Mary[3] Branch, Christopher[2], Christopher[1]) married William Raines and moved to Granville Co., S.C. [*sic?*].

Issue: [RAINES][727] 562. Jean[6], born 26 Aug. 1736; 563. Robert Wynne[6], born 25 June 1739, to whom his parents deeded 400 acres where they resided, 14 Feb. 1763,[728] following their removal to South Carolina, moved briefly to Brunswick County, but then returned to Sussex County,[729] and died before 16 Sept. 1778 when the inventory of his estate in Brunswick County was made,[730] married Jane ___, who joined him, 20 June 1765 and 17 May 1767, in selling two tracts of 400 acres each;[731] 564. Richard[6], born 2 March 1740/1; 565. Jefferson[6], born 20 Nov. 1744; 566. Anne[6], born 22 July 1746; 567. Nathaniel[6],

---

[718] Bristol Parish Register.

[719] Albemarle Parish Register.

[720] *Ibid.*

[721] Sussex Co. Will Bk. C, p. 6.

[722] Catherine Lindsay Knorr, *Marriage Bonds and Ministers' Returns of Sussex County, Virginia, 1754-1810* (Pine Bluff, Ark., 1952), p. 13.

[723] Bristol Parish Register.

[724] Sussex Co. Will Bk. 8, p. 347.

[725] Named in will of grandfather Robert Wynne, *loc. cit.*; Albemarle Parish Register.

[726] Sussex Co. Will Bk. B, p. 45.

[727] Albemarle Parish Register.

[728] Sussex Co. Deed Bk. C, p. 10.

[729] *Ibid.*, pp. 153, 167.

[730] Sussex Co. Will Bk. C, p. 66.

[731] Sussex Co. Deed Bk. C, pp. 163, 266.

born 21 March 1748; 568. Theodosia[6], born 10 Dec. 1749.

178. ANNE[5] WYNNE (?Martha[4] Jefferson, Mary[3] Branch, Christopher[2]. Christopher[1]) married Thomas Butler, who married (2 [3?]) Mary ___and left will 26 June 1784-18 March 1784.[732]

Issue: [BUTLER]:[733] 569. Martha[6], born 8 Nov. 1741, died 10 Oct. 1742; 570. Mary[6], born 21 March 1742/3, died before 29 April 1790 when John Viers sold land where she lately lived,[734] married Thomas Viers, Jr.

181. BENJAMIN[5] BRANCH (Benjamin[4], Benjamin[3], Christopher[2], Christopher[1]) died 29 April 1786 from fall from a horse[735] leaving will 19 April 1782-13 July 1786.[736] He resided at "Willow Hill," Chesterfield County, and was a member of the Committee of Safety, 1774, justice, captain of militia, sheriff, 1780 and 1786. He married (1) 146. Ann [Nancy][5] Bass and (2), (bond 25) Aug. 1773,[737] 147. *Mary[5] (Epes) Worsham Branch* (see EPES).

Issue: (by 1)[738] 571. Benjamin[6], died about 1824, of Chesterfield and later of Dinwiddie County, married, (bond 1) Dec. 1780,[739] 98. *Elizabeth Eppes[6] Osborne* (see OSBORNE); 572. Edward[6], of Chesterfield County, lieutenant and captain of militia, 1787, 1789, married, (bond 15) Dec. 1783,[740] 401. *Anne[6] Eppes* (see EPES); 573. Anne[6], married ___ Jones; 574. Thomas[6], born 4 April 1767, died 10 Sept. 1818, of "Willow Hill," Chesterfield County, married, 1787, Mary Patteson, born 28 Sept. 1770, died 20 Aug. 1825; 575. Obedience[6], died 29 Dec. 1847, aged 78 yrs. 4 mos.,[741] married (1) 452. Joseph[6] Wilkinson and (2), (bond 16) Sept. 1806,[742] 687. *Edward[6] Moseley* (see BALEY-COCKE).

183. EDWARD[5] BRANCH (Benjamin[4], Benjamin[3], Christopher[2],

---

[732] Sussex Co. Will Bk. D, p. 219.

[733] Albemarle Parish Register. Mary Butler is named as a granddaughter by Robert Wynne. Thomas and Amy Butler are listed as the parents of Elizabeth, born 1743, and Lucy, born 25 Nov. 1745. Martha's death was reported by Maj. Wynne but without indication of relationship; her sponsors were William Raines, Angelica Raines and Phoebe Wynne.

[734] Sussex Co. Deed Bk. G, p., 584.

[735] *Virginia Gazette and American Advertiser*, Richmond, 10 May 1785.

[736] Chesterfield Co. Will Bk. 4, p. 119; Order Bk. 7, p. 344.

[737] Knorr, *Marriage Bonds ... Chesterfield County.*, p. 19, as Mazy.

[738] Cabell, *op. cit.*, pp. 46, 48, 151.

[739] Knorr, *Marriage Bonds ... Chesterfield County*, p. 19.

[740] *Ibid.*

[741] Blandford Cemetery, Petersburg, Register of Interments 1843-71, pp. 19-20.

[742] Williams, *Marriages of Amelia County*, p. 78.

Christopher[1]), of Chesterfield County, tithable in 1762,[743] left will 5 Jan. 1781-8 June 1786.[744] He married, (bond 6) July 1764,[745] 231. *Lucy[6] Finney* (see BALEY-COCKE).

Issue:[746] 576. Edward[6], married, 5 Nov. 1787,[747] Martha Bott; 577. Mary[6], married, (bond 18) Oct. 1781,[748] William Parham; 578. Lucy[6], married James Bott; 579. Benjamin[6], married, (bond 5) June 1801,[749] Sarah Bott; 580. Thomas[6], perhaps married, (bond 19) Dec. 1792,[750] Mary Walker; 581. William[6], born 1770, died 1812, married _____, perhaps, (license 28) Oct. 1791,[751] Dicey Callicott; 582. Obedience Turpin[6], married, (bond 28) April 1789,[752] William Williamson Hall; 583. Judith Finney[6], married, (consent 14) Dec. 1793,[753] George Walker; 584. Elizabeth[6], married, (bond 3) June 1794,[754] William Mann; 585. Prudence[6]; 586. Page[6]; 587. Sally[6].

185. PRUDENCE[5] BRANCH (Benjamin[4], Benjamin[3], Christopher[2], Christopher[1]) married William Thweatt of Chesterfield County, who left will 4 Jan. 1804-10 Dec. 1804.[755]

Issue: [THWEATT][756] 588. William[6], died about 1813,[757] of Prince George County, married (1) Judy Foise and (2) Lucretia ___, who left will 12 March 1845-9 Nov. 1848;[758] 589. Benjamin[6], died before 12 July 1802 when Benjamin W. Leigh was granted administration on his estate,[759] married, (contract 10) Feb.

---

[743] *The Southside Virginian*, V, p. 82.

[744] Chesterfield Co. Will Bk. 4, p. 104; Order Bk. 7, p. 335.

[745] Williams, *Marriages of Amelia County*, p. 16.

[746] Chesterfield Co. Order Bk. 7, p. 577, Francis Goode was chosen as guardian by Thomas and William and appointed guardian of Judy, Elizabeth, Prudence, Obedience, Page and Sally, 11 Oct. 1787; Order Bk. 11, p. 466, 16 May 1796.

[747] Williams, *Marriages of Amelia County*, p. 16.

[748] Knorr., *Marriage Bonds ... Chesterfield County*, p. 93.

[749] Williams, *Marriages of Amelia County*, p. 16.

[750] *Ibid.*, p. 17.

[751] *Ibid.*

[752] *Ibid.*, p. 124.

[753] *Ibid.*, p. 124.

[754] *Ibid.*, p. 83.

[755] Chesterfield Co. Will Bk. 6, pp. 220-21; Order Bk. 15, p. 324.

[756] *The Southside Virginian*, VII, p. 31.

[757] Prince George Co. Land tax book, 1813, estate taxed.

[758] Anne Bradbury Peebles, "Prince George County, Virginia, Wills and Marriage Records Before 1865" (typewritten; n.p., 1955), p. 12, Virginia State Archives Acc.27997.

[759] Chesterfield Co. Order Bk. 14, p. 300.

1797,[760] 559. *Elizabeth*[6] (*Watkins*) *Leigh* (see BALEY-COCKE), born 10 Dec. 1763, died 5 Jan. 1802;[761] 590. Thomas Branch[6], born about 1775,[762] moved to Memphis, Tenn., married, 16 Dec. 1812,[763] Nancy Jones[7] Wooldridge, daughter of Daniel and 107. *Agnes*[6] (*Osborne*) *Osborne* (see OSBORNE), who died 9 Sept. 1840.[764]

---

[760] Chesterfield Co. Deed Bk. 14, pp. 82-84.

[761] Watkins Bible, in *The Southside Virginian*, III, p. 121.

[762] Shelby Co., Tenn., 1850 census, 12th Civil Dist., p. 404 or 202R, family 1747.

[763] Knorr, *Marriage Bonds ... Chesterfield County*, p. 117.

[764] Wooldridge, *op. cit.*, I, p. 373.

BUCK[1]

*1. The Rev. RICHARD[1] BUCK, son of Edmund Bucke of Wymongham, County Norfolk, was admitted sizar at Caius College, Cambridge, 26 April 1600, aged 18 years.[2] As chaplain of the expedition headed by Sir Thomas Gates and bound for Virginia in a fleet of seven ships and two pinnaces under the command of Sir George Somers, he sailed from England aboard the *Seaventure*, June 1609, with his wife and family.

The expedition ran into a "vehement storm," the ships were dispersed and the *Seaventure*, driven off her course, encountered a hurricane and was wrecked on the reefs of the Somers Islands [Bermuda]. One hundred and fifty "gentlemen adventurers," sailors, women and children were landed safely on the sandy shores, 600 miles off the Virginia coast. They were assembled by their chaplain who "led them in thanks to God for their safe deliverance."[3] Marooned for nine months, the party finally embarked for Virginia, 10 May 1610, in two pinnaces, *Patience* and *Deliverance*, built on the islands. To the ministry of Mr. Buck during the period, Old St. Peter's of Bermuda dates the origin of that church's parish.[4]

By the time Richard[1] Buck arrived at Jamestown, 21 May 1610, the Rev. Robert Hunt, who had come as minister to the first expedition, 1607, was dead. The colony was found to be barely existing and in desperate straits. Decision to relinquish the settlement was concurred in by Gates and Somers and the colonists, abandoning Jamestown, embarked for the return trip and had dropped down the James River when they were met by a "long boat" with news of the arrival of Lord De La Warr with relief. As soon as his Lordship "came up with his fleet, he went on shore and heard a sermon" and thereafter, as a means of restoring morale and courage to the disheartened, services were ordered held twice daily at Jamestown, at 10 o'clock in the morning and at 4 in the afternoon.[5]

---

[1] Br. *Gen.*, p. 835; William Curry Harllee, *Kinfolks*, II (New Orleans, 1934), pp. 1209-22; *Dictionary of Virginia Biography*, II. (Richmond, 2001), pp. 377-78; William Robert Gann, "Land Patents, a Lost Will, and Legal Battles Prove Family Relationships," *The Magazine of Virginia Genealogy*, XL, pp. 257-78.

[2] John Venn and J. A. Venn, comp., *Alumni Cantabrigienses*, pt. 1, I (Cambridge, 1922), p. 245.

[3] Smith, *Tra.* I, pp. xcv, 171.

[4] *Ibid.*; Margaret K. Murphy, "Old St. Peter's of Bermuda," *The Cathedral Age*, XXXVIII, no. 1, pp. 7-9.

[5] Smith, *Tra.* II, pp. 500-02.

The Rev. Richard[1] Buck opened with prayer the initial meeting of the first representative legislative Assembly held in the new world, 30 July 1619, at Jamestown.[6] He was assigned 750 acres at Archer's Hope in James City with the provision that 100 acres should be laid aside for "gleab land."[7] In a later patent the date is given as 20 Jan. 1619/20.[8] On 18 Dec. 1620 William Fairfax sold to Richard[1] Buck, Minister, of James City "my dwelling howse and my other little howse thereto adjoining with twelve acres of land lying in James Cittie in the Island being my owne howse and land."[9]

In two letters addressed to Sir Edwin Sandys, May and June 1622, Mr. Buck stated that he was sorely in need of funds which had not been forthcoming from the Virginia Company according to their agreement with him and urged payment as he had "a charg of children to provide for & but one boy to be an helper to me in my busines ..." and in the second and more urgent letter he stressed his need for servants and for "mony wch I have allredy payd & left in the hands of the Company ... w^{ch} ... would be a good estate for me & the releife of my wife & Children ..."[10]

Neither Richard[1] Buck nor his wife[11] was recorded in the census, 1623/4, or in the muster, 1624/5, though the four Buck children born in Virginia were listed in both.[12] Richard[1] Buck was dead by 21 June 1624 as a case in the General Court then referred to "the overseers of Mr. Ric. Buck his last will."[13] His children were living with guardians by Jan. 1623/4. His will was produced in court, 10 Oct. 1626, by Mr. Richard Kingsmill, who then was appointed guardian to Peleg[2] Buck in place of Thomas Allnut, deceased.[14] His estate

---

[6] "Reporte of the manner of proceeding in the General Assembly convented at James City, July 30, 31, August 2, 3, 4, 1619," *R*, Va. Co. III, pp. 154-55. "The most convenient place we could find to sitt in was the Quire of the Churche Where Sir George Yeardley, the Governor, being sett downe in his accustomed place, those of the Counsel of Estate sate nexte him ... But forasmuche as men's affaires doe little prosper where God's service is neglected, all the Burgesses tooke their places in the Quire till a prayer was said by Mr. Bucke, the Minister, that it would please God to guide and sanctifie all our proceedings ..."

[7] *R*, Va. Co. IV, p. 555.

[8] Patent Bk. 3, p. 306, to John[3] Crump, 29 Nov. 1654.

[9] Patent Bk. 1, p. 650.

[10] *R*, Va. Co. III, pp. 443, 461.

[11] Stated to have been a Miss Langley.

[12] Hotten, p. 175.

[13] *MCGC*, p. 16.

[14] *Ibid.*, p. 117. The will has not survived.

included land at Archer's Hope, land and houses at Jamestown, cattle and payments due him in tobacco.[15]

Issue:[16] 2. ELIZABETH[2]; 3. Mara[2], born in Virginia, 1611, ward of John Burrowes after the death of her father and upon rumor, 1624, that she was "to be stolen away by a greate one" (the Rev. David Sandys), the case came into the General Court where Mara[2] was described as "very dull to take her learninge" and Burrowes was required to put up "the some of 100 pound that neyther hee nor his wiefe shall ... permit any motione of marriadge to be made of Mara Buck ...";[17] 4. Gercian[2], born in Virginia, 1614, living 1624/5, with the family of John Jackson, purchased, 1 Sept. 1636, 500 acres "within the precincts of Neck of Land" from Thomas Crump,[18] died by 29 May 1638 when Peleg[2] Buck repatented land which had been "bequeathed unto him by his brother Gersham Buck;[19] 5. Benoni[2], born in Virginia, 1616, and called "the first idiot born in that plantation,"[20] living with the family of Peter Langman, 1624/5; 6. Peleg[2], born in Virginia, 1620, ward first of Thomas Allnut and then of Richard Kingsmill, repatented land, 1638, inherited from his brother Gercian[2], died without issue by 29 Nov. 1654 when this tract was again repatented by John[3] Crump and described as "500 acres granted to Peleg Buck, 29 May 1638, and descended unto said Crump by inheritnce."[21]

---

[15] Patent Bk. 1, p. 650; *MCGC*, pp. 17, 36, 47, 86.

[16] The Biblical names of the four youngest children seem to reflect the tribulations through which the family passed: Mara, "bitter," Gercian, "stranger," Benoni, "son of my sorrow," Peleg, "flowing water." The inclusion in previous editions of a son Bermudas, born and died while his parents were marooned in the Somers Islands, 1609-10, is unconfirmed by the source there cited (Samuel Purchas, *Purchas His Pilgrims*, XIX [Glasgow, 1906], pp. 1-41), which (p. 38) refers to only two births there (Bermuda, daughter of John Rolfe, christened 11 Feb. 1609/10, and Bermudas, son of the wife of Edward Eason, born 20 March 1609/10). The naming of a daughter Bridget, wife of John Burrows, resulted from a misinterpretation of the evidence concerning John Burrows' being the guardian of Mara[2] Buck.

[17] *MCGC*, pp. 15-16. According to the late Dr. Lyon Gardiner Tyler, Mara[2] Buck became the (2) wife of Richard Adkins.

[18] Patent Bk. 1, p. 533, land joining the original Buck patent.

[19] *Ibid.*, p. 532.

[20] *V* XII, pp. 390-91, letter of Governor Sir John Harvey, 20 May 1639, concerning Benoni[2] Buck, "newly come to age of 21"; W. Noel Sainsbury, ed., *Calendar of State Papers, Colonial Series, 1574-1660* (London, 1860), pp. 251, 294, petition of Ambrose Harmer, 6 May 1637, stating he had had the tuition of Benoni and his brothers for thirteen years.

[21] Patent Bk. 3, p. 306.

2. ELIZABETH[2] BUCK (Richard[1]) perhaps remained in England when her father came to Virginia as she was mentioned neither in the census, 1623/4, nor the muster, 1624/5. She married, about 1625, 1. Sergeant *Thomas*[1] *Crump*.[22]

Issue: see CRUMP.

---

[22] *JHB* 1619-1658/9, p. 96, Bromfield *vs.* Crump; *H* I, p. 405.

BURWELL[1]

+1. EDWARD[1] BURWELL of Houghton Park, Harlington, Bedfordshire, England, member of the Virginia Company and subscriber to the Second Charter,[2] married Dorothy Bedell, daughter of William Bedell (died 1612[3]) of Catsworth, Huntingdonshire. He made a nuncupative will 18 Oct. 1626 "on his sick bed" and administration on his estate was granted to Dorothea Burwell 9 Nov. 1626.[4] After her husband's death, she married (2) Roger Wingate[5] (died 1641), member of the Council and Treasurer of Virginia, 1639-41,[6] and distinguished for his interest in colonial affairs.

Issue:[7] 2. William[2], of Northampton County where, 11 Jan. 1640/1, he received a certificate for 200 acres for his personal adventure and the transportation of Lewis, George and Elizabeth Burwell,[8] and left will, 17 June 1647-6 Sept. 1647,[9] mentioning his "aged mother," and wife ___, who married (2) William Denham[10] and was perhaps the Elizabeth, wife of Robert Merriott [Marriott],[11] and still later of William Smith;[12] 3. Edward[2], born 14 April 1616, died 4 March 1619/20; 4. DOROTHY[2]; 5. ELIZABETH[2]; 6. LEWIS[2]; 7. George[2], baptized 17 May 1624, died before 1648; 8. Edward[2], baptized 19 Feb. 1625/6, died

---

[1] Clayton Torrence, *Winston and Allied Families* (Richmond, 1927), pp. 361-70; John L. Blair, "The Rise of the Burwells," *V* LXXII, pp. 304-29; Stuart E. Brown, *Burwell Kith and Kin of the Immigrant Lewis Burwell* ... (Berryville, Va., 1994).

[2] Br. *Gen.*, p. 220.

[3] P.C.C. 64 Fenner, in *V* XXIV, pp. 262-64.

[4] P.C.C. 126 Hele, in *V* XXIII, pp. 156-57.

[5] Frederic Augustus Blaydes, ed., *The Visitations of Bedfordshire, Annis Domini 1566, 1582, and 1634* (Harleian Society, *Publications*, XIX; London, 1884), pp. 151, 201. They had a daughter Lucy, aged 1 1/2 in Jan. 1637/8.

[6] *CVR*, p. 24; Leonard, p. xxi.

[7] Parish register, Ampthill, Bedfordshire, in F. G. Emmison, *Bedfordshire Parish Registers*, XVII (Bedford, 1938), pp. A2-A4, A78. Brown, *op. cit.*, pp. 1, 88, also names as children Francis(?), baptized 1623, and John (1627-1629) but without cited evidence. Francis Burwell was named as a headright in a patent granted Lewis Burwell 12 June 1648 (Patent Bk. 2, p. 181).

[8] Susie M. Ames, ed., *County Court Records of Accomack-Northampton, Virginia, 1640-1645* (Virginia Historical Society, *Documents*, X; Charlottesville, 1973), pp. 53-54.

[9] Northampton Co. Deeds, Wills &c 3, 1645-51, p. 115.

[10] *Ibid.*, p. 122.

[11] Northampton Co. Deeds, Wills &c 7, 1657-66, p. 233 (239), will of Robert Merriott, 9 Nov. 1665-Dec. 1665.

[12] Northampton Co. Deeds, Wills &c 8, 1666-68, p. 3.

before 1648.

4. DOROTHY[2] BURWELL (Edward[1]), baptized 24 June 1618, married John Woodington.[13]

Issue: [WOODINGTON][14] 9. John[3], deposed, 28 May 1656, he was aged 19,[15] of Warrany in New Kent County,[16] civil officer [justice] of that county, 1680,[17] died after May 1691;[18] 10. Charles[6], of James City and New Kent counties.[19]

5. ELIZABETH[2] BURWELL (Edward[1]), baptized 25 Feb. 1620/1, married (1) George Hull who patented 200 acres near the head of Old Poquoson River, 12 Oct. 1635,[20] which he included in a patent for 540 acres in Charles River [York] County.[21] He died before 21 Oct. 1643 when Mrs. Elizabeth Hull, widow, patented 850 acres on the south side of Potomac River, for the personal adventure of George Hull, that of his wife Elizabeth and sons Edward and David and others.[22]

She married (2) Robert Vaulx, merchant of London and of York and Westmoreland counties, who, 3 Jan. 1647/8, gave a power of attorney to his

---

[13] Chart prepared by Commander Anthony Bateman, Muscat House, Wroxham, Norfolk, England.

[14] York Co. Deeds & Wills 3, p. 4. On 6 Oct. 1657 Elizabeth Vaulx, wife of Robert Vaulx, by virtue of a commission "given unto mee by my said husband ... dated in England 7 Sept. 1656," gave to "my wel beloved kinsmen John Woodington and Charles Woodington" 400 acres at Potomack (200 acres to each). A deposition of John Mems, Sr., taken 30 Jan. 1707/8 refers to a deposition taken about 20 years past relating to land of William [*sic*; Robert?] Vaulx A parcel of ground called Woodington's field was seated by John Woodington on the road leading down to Nominy (Westmoreland Co. Deeds & Wills 4, 1707-08, pp. 72-73).

[15] Northampton Co. Orders, Deeds, Wills &c 5, p. 148.

[16] Lancaster Co. Record Bk. 2, 1637-40, pp. 390-92, power of attorney and assignment to William Wroughton, 22 May 1660, of a patent for 27 acres granted 15 Jan. 1658/9 (Patent Bk. 4, p. 244 [343]).

[17] *V* I, p. 248.

[18] York Co. Deeds, Orders, Wills &c 8, pp. 195, 247, suit brought, Jan. and May 1691, against Thomas Jefferson.

[19] Patent Bk. 4, pp. 87 (126), (477), 106 (602); Patent Bk. 6, p. 230.

[20] Patent Bk. 1, p. 292.

[21] *Ibid.*, p. 515.

[22] *Ibid.*, p. 925. This land was assigned by her to Thomas Broughton who on 19 Aug. 1648 repatented 1050 acres naming the same headrights and adding four headrights;, Wm. Burwell, Lewis Burwell, Geo. Burwell and Elizabeth Burwell, assigned to him by her (Patent Bk. 2, p. 120).

brother Lewis Burwell[23] and died after 25 Feb. 1672/3.[24]

Issue: (by 1) [HULL] 11. Edward[3]; 12. David[3]; (by 2) [VAULX] 13. ROBERT[3].

6. LEWIS[2] BURWELL[25] (Edward[1]), baptized 5 March 1621/2, came to Virginia when a mere boy with his mother and step-father Roger Wingate.[26] On 12 June 1648 he patented 2350 acres "lying on the north side of York River upon Rosewell Creek," adjacent to George Menifie.[27] This land lay in the area which by 1652 had became Gloucester County and Burwell's plantation was called "Fairfield," later "Carter's Creek."[28]

By deed, 28 July 1648, Dorothy Wingate, widow of Roger Wingate, conveyed to "my only and welbeloved sonn Lewis Burwell" all rents due at Roger's decease and confirmed to Dorothy by the King.[29]

Lewis[2] Burwell died 18 Nov. 1653 and the inscription on his tombstone recites that he was a major of Gloucester County and "descended from the Ancient family of the Burwells of the Counties of Bedford and Northampton in England."[30] He married Lucy Higginson, daughter of Capt. Robert Higginson and his wife Joanna Tokesey. She married (2) 1. *William[1] Bernard* (see BERNARD) and (3) Philip Ludwell (see ST. LEGER)[31] and died 6 Nov. 1675.[32]

Issue: 14. LEWIS[3].

13. ROBERT[3] VAULX (Elizabeth[2] Burwell, Edward[1]) deposed, 10 May 1676, he was aged 25 or thereabouts.[33] He was a merchant, was a justice of

---

[23] York Co. Orders, Wills &c 2, 1645-49, p. 332. The interpretation of "brother" as wife's brother is confirmed by a deposition of John Quisenberry, 31 Jan. 1707/8 (Westmoreland Co. Deeds & Wills 4, 1707-09, pp. 75-76), which speaks of "Mrs. Wingate a nigh relation to old Mrs. Vaulx her husband [i.e. 11. Robert[3] Vaulx]."

[24] Westmoreland Co. Deeds, Patents &c 1665-77, pp. 136a-137.

[25] *Dictionary of Virginia Biography*, II (Richmond, 2000), pp. 431-32.

[26] *V* XV, pp. 297-98.

[27] Patent Bk. 2, p. 181.

[28] R. A. Lancaster, *Historic Virginia Homes and Churches* (Philadelphia and London, 1915), p. 82.

[29] York Co. Deeds, Orders, Wills 2, p. 394.

[30] Joseph Bryan Branch A.P.V.A., *Epitaphs of Gloucester and Mathews Counties* (Richmond, 1959), p. 19. The remains of the members of the Burwell family were removed from the "Fairfield" burying ground and reinterred at Abingdon Church, Gloucester County.

[31] *V* XXV, p. 88.

[32] Joseph Bryan Branch A.P.V.A., *loc. cit.*

[33] Westmoreland Co. Deeds, Patents &c 1665-77, p. 264.

Westmoreland County, 19 March 1672/3,[34] and left will, now lost, 20 March 1684/5-27 May 1685.[35]

He married Mary Foxhall, daughter of John and Martha Foxhall,[36] who deposed, 31 Jan. 1707/8, she was aged 49[37] and left will 2 Feb. 1712/3-26 Aug. 1713.[38] She married (2), by 24 Nov. 1686,[39] Alexander Gorgas, who left will proved 31 Oct. 1688,[40] (3), by 25 July 1688,[41] Edward Duddleston, (4), by 28 Jan. 1690/1,[42] Caleb Butler, who left will 16 Feb. 1708/9-25 May 1709,[43] and (5), (marriage settlement 19) Dec. 1711,[44] the Rev. John Bagge.

Issue: [VAULX] 15. ROBERT[4]; 16. James[4], unmarried, left will 16 Oct. 1710-21 Aug. 1711;[45] 17. ELIZABETH[4].

14. LEWIS[3] BURWELL (Lewis[2], Edward[1]) deposed, 16 Sept. 1693, that he was aged 41.[46] He inherited not only his father's holdings but through his first marriage came into possession of an estate which included "King's Creek" in York County. In 1704 he held 26,650 acres in Gloucester, King William, Charles City, New Kent, James City, York and Isle of Wight counties. He was appointed a member of the Council, 1702, and served until his death. He was also a governor of the College of William and Mary, 1702.[47]

He married (1) Abigail Smith, born 11 March 1656/7, died 12 Nov. 1692,[48] daughter of Anthony Smith of Colchester, England, and his wife Martha Bacon,

---

[34] *Ibid.*, p. 149.

[35] Westmoreland Co. Order Bk. 1675/6-1688/9, p. 408; Deeds & Wills 10, 1744-48, pp. 67-71, deed of Elizabeth Eskridge to Robert Vaulx.

[36] *W*(2) XIII, p. 235.

[37] Westmoreland Co. Deeds & Wills 4, 1707-09, pp. 76-77.

[38] Westmoreland Co. Deeds & Wills 5, 1712-16, pp. 221-23.

[39] Westmoreland Co. Order Bk. 1675/6-1688/9, p. 524.

[40] *Ibid.*, p. 680. He probably was dead by 31 May 1688 when Mary Gorgas was sued in her own right (*ibid.*, p. 651).

[41] *Ibid.*, p. 663.

[42] Westmoreland Co. Order Bk. 1690-98, p. 4.

[43] Westmoreland Co. Deeds & Wills 4, 1707-09, pp. 192-94. Their daughter Jane was the (1) wife of 122. *Augustine*[5] *Washington* (see MARTIAU).

[44] Referred to in her will, *loc. cit.*

[45] Westmoreland Co. Deeds & Wills 7, pp. 239-40; Order Bk. 1705-21, p. 168.

[46] *NGSQ* LXX, p. 41.

[47] *Dictionary of Virginia Biography*, II, pp. 432-33; Leonard, p. xix.

[48] Joseph Bryan Branch A.P.V.A., *op. cit.*, p. 20.

sister of Nathaniel Bacon (1620-1692/3) the Elder.[49] He married (2) Martha (Lear) Cole, died 4 Aug. 1704,[50] daughter of Col. John Lear (died 1695[51]) and widow of 2. *William*[2] *Cole* (see COLE).

Lewis[3] Burwell died 19 Dec. 1710 and the inscription on his tombstone recites that he was "Son of Maj. Lewis Burwell & Lucy his wife," gives the names of his two wives, the number of sons and daughters by each and the number of sons and daughters surviving.[52] He left a will, 11 Oct. 1710-10 Feb. 1710/1.[53]

Issue:[54] (by 1) 18. Joanna[4], died 7 Oct. 1727, in her 53rd year, married 22. *William*[4] *Bassett* (see TAYLOR-CARY); 19. ELIZABETH[4]; 20. NATHANIEL[4]; 21. Lewis[4], born 9 Ot. 1682, died 17 Sept. 1696; 22. LUCY[4]; 23. MARTHA[4]; 24. Bacon[4], born 22 Feb. 1686/7, died before 15 March 1691/2; 25. Jane[4], baptized 16 Nov. 1688, died before 15 March 1691/2; 26. JAMES[4]; 27.(Daughter)[4], born after March 1691/2, married Henry Seaton, who married (2) 11. *Elizabeth*[3] *Todd* (see BERNARD); (by 2) 28.(Son)[4], born about 1695, died young; 29. Mary[4], born 1697, died 20 July 1701; 30. LEWIS[4]; 31. Jane[4], born about 1701, died young; 32. MARTHA[4].

15. Capt. ROBERT[4] VAULX (Robert[3], Elizabeth[2] Burwell, Edward[1]) left will 30 Nov. 1721[*sic*]-29 Nov. 1721.[55] He married, by 19 July 1711,[56] Elizabeth (Kenner) Bushrod, died shortly before 18 July 1754 in St. Mary's Co., Md., widow of Richard Bushrod, who married (3) the Rev. Lawrence DeButts and (4) Arthur St. Clair.[57]

Issue: [VAULX] 33. ROBERT[5]; 34. James[5]; 35. (Child)[5].

17. ELIZABETH[4] VAULX (Robert[3], Elizabeth[2] Burwell, Edward[1]) left

---

[49] *V* II, pp. 125-26; P.C.C. 70 Carr, will of Anthony Smith, in Torrence, *op. cit.*, pp. 384-85.

[50] Joseph Bryan Branch A.P.V.A., *op. cit.*, p. 20.

[51] *V* XVII, pp. 229-31, will of Col. John Lear of Nansemond County, 21 Nov. 1695-12 Dec. 1695.

[52] Joseph Bryan Branch A.P.V.A., *op. cit.*, p. 20.

[53] York Co. Orders, Wills &c 14, pp. 55, 60-64.

[54] Everard Kidder Meade, "The Children of Major Lewis Burwell II ...," Clarke County Historical Association, *Proceedings*, IV (1944), pp. 6-26; Abingdon Parish Register.

[55] Westmoreland Co. Deeds & Wills 7, 1720-26, pp. 252-54, recorded 5 Dec. 1721.

[56] Northumberland Co. Order Bk. 5, pp. 635-36, 739, 750-53.

[57] George Ely Russell, "DeButts Family of Maryland and Virginia," *The Genealogist*, XII (1998), p. 133.

will 20 Oct. 1744-27 Nov. 1744.[58] She married (1) Capt. Richard Craddock, who left will, now lost, 28 Oct. 1710-26 Sept. 1711,[59] (2), by 26 March 1713,[60] 44. *Daniel[4] Porten* (see MASON), and (3), as his (2) wife, George Eskridge of "Sandy Point," Westmoreland County, attorney, member of the House of Burgesses, 1705-14, 1718-34,[61] who left will 27 Oct. 1735-25 Nov. 1735.[62]

Issue: (by 2) [PORTEN] see MASON; (by 3) [ESKRIDGE][63] 36. ELIZABETH[5].

19. ELIZABETH[4] BURWELL (Lewis[3], Lewis[2], Edward[1]), baptized June 1677, died 30 Dec. 1734,[64] married Benjamin Harrison, died 10 April 1710, aged 37,[65] of "Berkeley," Charles City County, where he owned 6350 acres, 1704, clerk of Charles City County, Attorney General, 1697-1702, member of the House of Burgesses from James City County, 1703-05, and from Charles City County and its Speaker, 1705-06, and Treasurer of Virginia, 1705-10,[66] owner of over 20,000 acres in Charles City, James City, Prince George and Surry counties at his death.[67]

Issue: [HARRISON]: 37. BENJAMIN[5]; 38. ELIZABETH[5].

20. NATHANIEL[4] BURWELL (Lewis[3], Lewis[2], Edward[1]), of "Carter's Creek," baptized 14 Oct. 1680, left will dated 20 Aug. 1721-25 Oct. 1721,[68] was a member of the House of Burgesses for Jamestown, 1710-12, and for Gloucester County, 1720-21,[69] justice of Gloucester County, 1714-19. He married, about 1708, Elizabeth Carter, died 1734, daughter of Robert Carter of "Corotoman," Lancaster County, who married (2) Dr. George Nicholas.

Issue: 39. LEWIS[5]; 40 Lucy[5], born 21 April 1715;[70] 41. CARTER[5]; 42.

---

[58] Westmoreland Co. Deeds & Wills 10, 1744-48, pp. 72-74.

[59] Westmoreland Co. Deeds & Wills 5, pp. 311-14; Order Bk. 1705-21, p. 174.

[60] Westmoreland Co. Order Bk. 1705-21, p. 208a.

[61] Leonard, pp. 64, 66-67, 69, 71, 73, 75.

[62] Westmoreland Co. Deeds & Wills 8, 1722-38, pp. 273-273a.

[63] *W*(1) VIII, p. 212.

[64] Tombstone, "Westover," Charles City County, *W*(1) IV, p. 146.

[65] *Ibid.*

[66] *V* XXXI, pp. 180-82; Leonard, pp. 62, 64; Jon Kukla, *Speakers and Clerks of the Virginia House of Burgesses, 1643-1776* (Richmond, 1981), pp. 106-10.

[67] *H* III, pp. 538-40.

[68] Clarke County Historical Assn., *Proceedings*, IV, pp. 6-21. R. T. Barton, *Virginia Colonial Decisions* (Boston, 1909), I, p. R102, gives date as 24 Aug. 1721.

[69] Leonard, pp. 65, 70.

[70] Abingdon Parish Register.

Elizabeth[5], baptized 22 Jan. 1718, married 67. *William[5] Nelson* (see MARTIAU); 43. ROBERT[5]; 44. (Daughter)[5], posthumous, died aged 2 months.[71]

22. LUCY[4] BURWELL (Lewis[3], Lewis[2], Edward[1]), born 21 Nov. 1683, died 16 Dec. 1716,[72] married, 1 Dec. 1704, Edmund Berkeley, who deposed, 18 Nov. 1697, he was aged 25,[73] son of Edmund and Mary (Kempe) Berkeley, of Gloucester County to 1712 and then of "Barn Elms," Middlesex County, member of the Council, 1713-19,[74] and left will 14 Dec. 1718-3 March 1718/9.[75]

Issue: [BERKELEY][76] 45. EDMUND[5]; 46. Lewis[5], born 18 Jan. 1706/7, died before 5 March 1744/5 when Edmund Berkeley gave bond as administrator of his estate;[77] 47. LUCY[5]; 48. MARY[5]; 49. SARAH[5].

23. MARTHA[4] BURWELL (Lewis[3], Lewis[2], Edward[1]), baptized 16 Nov. 1685, died after Dec. 1710. She aroused such passion in Governor Francis Nicholson that his behavior resulted in his recall. She married Henry Armistead, justice of Gloucester County, 1714-26, member of the House of Burgesses from Gloucester, 1728-34,[78] County Lieutenant of Caroline County, 9 Aug. 1733, who died after 13 June 1746.[79]

Issue: [ARMISTEAD][80] 50. WILLIAM[5]; 51. Lucy[5], married 69. *Thomas[5] Nelson* (see MARTIAU); 52. Martha[5], married, as his (1) wife, 71. *Dudley[5] Digges* (see DIGGES); 53. ROBERT[5].

---

[71] Barton, *op. cit.*, I, p. R102.

[72] Gravestone, "Barn Elms," Middlesex Co., in *W*(1) XII, p. 244, which states she died.aged 33 after being married 12 years and 15 days; *Dictionary of Virginia Biography*, II, pp. 436-37.

[73] *NGSQ* LXVII, p. 291. He was then in London but mentioned being in Virginia in April 1697.

[74] *Dictionary of Virginia Biography*, I (Richmond, 1998), pp. 448-49.

[75] Middlesex Co. Will Bk. B, 1713-34, pp. 112-15. The inventory of his estate listed property at Boot Swamp Quarter, King and Queen Quarter, Purton Quarter and the home plantation, and his books by title (*ibid.*, pp. 138-48).

[76] Berkeley Bible, 1703-1888, Virginia State Archives, in *Virginia Genealogical Society Quarterly*, XX, p. 86.

[77] Middlesex Co. Will Bk. C, 1740-48, pp. 197-99.

[78] Leonard, p. 74.

[79] *W*(1) VI, p. 165; Leonard, p. 74; Caroline Co. Order Bk. 1740-46, p. 589. Administration on his estate was granted 10 Dec. 1748 (P.C.C. Admon. Act Bk. 1748, in *V* XI, p. 68).

[80] *W*(1) VI, pp. 165-67, 169-70.

26. JAMES[4] BURWELL (Lewis[3], Lewis[2], Edward[1]) , of "King's Creek," York County, born 4 Feb. 1689/90, died 6 Oct. 1718,[81] member of the House of Burgesses, 1715, 1718,[82] left will 6 Sept. 1718-15 Sept. 1718.[83] He married Mary Armistead, daughter of William Armistead and his wife Anna Lee, who married (2) Philip Lightfoot of Yorktown and died June 1775 at Yorktown in her 79th year[84] leaving will 9 Nov. 1771-codicil 12 May 1775-21 Aug. 1775.[85]

Issue: 54. NATHANIEL BACON[5]; 55. Lucy[5], died before 21 March 1719/20 when Philip and Mary Lightfoot gave bond as administrators of her estate.[86]

30. LEWIS[4] BURWELL (Lewis[3], Lewis[2], Edward[1]), of "Kingsmill," James City County, born 1699, died 19 Nov. 1743, was a justice of James City County, 1726 and 1729, Naval Officer for the upper James River, 1729, and member of the House of Burgesses, 1742-43.[87] He married Elizabeth ___, who died I Oct. 1745, aged 46.[88]

Issue:[89] 56. LEWIS[5]; 57. ARMISTEAD[5]; 58. (probably) Col. Nathaniel[5], born about 1724/5,[90] died before 1779, of King William County, married Margaret ___, who died at her house in King William County, 1779.[91]

---

[81] Tombstone, cited in J. L. Hall, "Ancient Epitaphs and Inscriptions in York and James City Counties, Virginia," Virginia Historical Society, *Collections*, new ser., XI, p. 105. Note discrepancy with dates of will.

[82] Leonard, pp. 68-69.

[83] York Co. Deed, Orders, Wills 15, 1716-20, pp. 331-36.

[84] *Virginia Gazette*, 30 June 1775.

[85] York Co. Wills &c 1771-83, p. 299.

[86] York Co. Deeds, Orders, Wills 15, 1716-20, pp. 581-82.

[87] *Dictionary of Virginia Biography*, II, pp. 433-34; Leonard, p. 79.

[88] *Virginia Gazette*, 10 Oct. 1745. Family tradition suggests she was a Miss Armistead. She may be the daughter of William and Anna (Lee) Armistead.

[89] Although previously published Burwell genealogies identify only Lewis[5] and Armistead[5] as children, and do not mention the existence of Col. Nathaniel Burwell of King William County, it seems likely that he was another brother and that 134. Nathaniel[6] inherited "Vermont" as his nephew and namesake. If there were other children in this family, another may be Anne, wife of Samuel Sheppard of Norfolk County, who wrote (*W*(2) VII, pp. 174-75), 3 Feb. 1792, "I was born on the 3rd of February, 1730 ... I married Anne Burwell in Gloucester ..." and, 15 Nov. 1782, "... my letter, which I send by cousin Burwell ... I have only returned a few days ago from his house of Gloucester, where I also saw much of our other relations..."

[90] Caroline Co. Order Bk. 1759-63, p. 48., undated deposition as aged 34 or thereabouts, made pursuant to order of Feb. 1758 and recorded 15 June 1759.

[91] *Virginia Gazette* (Dixon & Hunter), 3 July 1779.

32. MARTHA[4] BURWELL (Lewis[3], Lewis[2], Edward[1]), born 1703, died 27 May 1738,[92] married Col. John Martin of "Clifton," Caroline County, member of the House of Burgesses from Caroline, 1738-40,[93] later merchant of Bristol and of Dublin, where he left will dated 30 April 1760 with codicil 15 Oct. 1760.[94]

Issue: [MARTIN][95] 59. George[5], merchant of Bristol, England, in partnership with his father, left will proved in Prerogative Court of Dublin, 1811, married Alicia Campbell; 60. Samuel[5], merchant in Virginia and Maryland, and of Dublin, Ireland, who, 17 Sept. 1756, gave a power of attorney concerning his guardianship of his nephew George Barclay,[96] and whose estates in Albemarle and Goochland counties and 107 slaves were confiscated and ten vessels lost by capture and otherwise during the Revolutionary War;[97] 61. Lewis Burwell[5], who owned 1166 acres on Great Bird Creek in Fluvanna County and 2350 acres in Goochland County and 118 slaves confiscated in 1779, became Assistant Judge and member of the Assembly of Jamaica;[98] 62. LUCY[5]; 63. Agnes[5], unmarried in 1760; 64. Patty[5], died 1757, married, 11 June 1756, as his (1) wife, Edmond Sexton Pery, born 1719, died 1806, Speaker of the Irish House of Commons, 1771-85, created Viscount Pery of Newtown Pery, county Limerick, 30 March 1785;[99] 65. ELIZABETH[5].

33. ROBERT[5] VAULX (Robert[4], Robert[3], Elizabeth[2] Burwell, Edward[1]) left will 5 Aug. 1754-codicil 8 Aug. 1754-26 March 1755.[100] He married (1) Sarah Elliott and (2), (contract 1) Aug. 1749,[101] 37. *Elizabeth[6] (Storke) Washington*, widow of Henry Washington (see BEHEATHLAND), who married (3) Col. Thomas Jett.

---

[92] Tombstone, "Clifton," Caroline County, *W*(1) XI, p. 146.

[93] Leonard, pp. 74, 76.

[94] Prerogative Court of Ireland Will Bk. 1761, p. 215, in *V* XXI, p. 372. He was living 20 March 1761 when he gave a power of attorney to recover money in Virginia (Henrico Co. Deed Bk. 1750-74, p. 692).

[95] *V* XIII, p. 198; Malcolm Hart Harris, *Old New Kent County* (West Point, Va., 1977), II, pp. 776-77.

[96] Henrico Co. Deed Bk. 1750-74, p. 485.

[97] Peter Wilson Coldham, *American Migrations, 1765-1799* (Baltimore, 2000), p. 581.

[98] *Ibid.*, p. 580.

[99] Bernard Burke, *A Genealogical History of the Dormant, Abeyant, Forfeited, and Extinct Peerages of the British Empire* (London, 1883), p. 426.

[100] Westmoreland Co. Deeds & Wills 13, pp. 114-20.

[101] Westmoreland Co. Deeds & Wills 11, pp. 174-81.

Issue: [VAULX] (by 1)[102] 66. Elizabeth[6], married John[7] Newton, son of 30. *Willoughby*[6] *Newton* (see BEHEATHLAND), who left will 8 Jan. 1767-24 Feb. 1767;[103] 67. Sarah[6], married, 29 April 1761, as his (1) wife, the Rev. James Marye, Jr., born 8 Sept. 1731 at Manakin Town, died 4 Oct. 1780 at Fredericksburg,[104] left will 21 June 1774-codicil 3 Oct. 1780-21 Dec. 1780,[105] student at College of William and Mary, 1754, minister of St. Thomas' Parish, Orange County, 1761-68. succeeded his father as minister of St. George's Parish, Spotsylvania 1768, and continued until his death,[106] who married (2) 194. *Mary*[6] *Kenner* (see CLAIBORNE); 68. Milly[6]; 69. Mary Higgins[6], married, (license 28) May 1766,[107] James Ball, who left will 21 Dec. 1785-9 Oct. 1786;[108] 70. Catherine[6]; 71. Margaret Kenner[6]; (by 2)[109] 72. Elizabeth[6]; 73. Peggy[6], died 1778, married, April 1772, Col. John Skinker.

36. ELIZABETH[5] ESKRIDGE (Elizabeth[4] Vaulx, Robert[3], Elizabeth[2] Burwell, Edward[1]) died 27 Aug. 1770, Westmoreland County.[110] She married (1), as his (2) wife, Capt. William Aylett, who left will 29 March 1744-28 Aug. 1744,[111] and (2), as his (2) wife, Col. James Steptoe, born about 1709, left will 10 May 1755-28 June 1757,[112] of "Hominy Hall," Westmoreland County, physician and vestryman of Cople Parish.

Issue: (by 1) [AYLETT] 74. Mary[6], married Thomas Ludwell Lee, born 13 Dec. 1730, died 13 April 1778 at "Bellevue," Prince William County;[113] 75. Anne[6], died 12 Dec. 1768, aged 30,[114] married, 3 Dec. 1757, as his (1) wife, Richard Henry Lee, born 20 Jan. 1732 at "Stratford," Westmoreland County,

---

[102] Westmoreland Co. Order Bk. 1758-51, p. 52.

[103] Westmoreland Co. Deeds & Wills 14, pp. 415-17.

[104] James Marye Bible, the Fredericksburg Area Cultural Center and Museum.

[105] Spotsylvania Co. Will Bk. E, pp. 376-79.

[106] St. George's Parish, Vestry Book, 1746-1817, pp. 77 (80); Edward Lewis Goodwin, *The Colonial Church in Virginia* (London, 1924), p. 292; Edith Whitcraft Eberhart and Adaline Marye Robertson, *The Maryes of Virginia, 1730-1985* (Baltimore, 1985), pp. 49-54.

[107] Northumberland Co. marriage license, in *V* XLII, p. 44.

[108] Northumberland Co. Record Bk. 13, 1785-87, p. 163.

[109] Jeter Lee Jett, *The Jett and Allied Families* (Baltimore, 1977), p. 123.

[110] *Virginia Gazette* (Rind), 6, 20 Sept. 1770.

[111] Westmoreland Co. Deeds & Wills 18, pp. 51-54.

[112] Westmoreland Co. Deeds & Wills 14, pp. 97-98.

[113] Edmund Jennings Lee, *Lee of Virginia* (Philadelphia, 1895), p. 168.

[114] Monument, Nomimi Church, in *ibid.*, p. 206.

died 19 June 1794 at "Chantilly," Westmoreland County,[115] who married (2) 215. Anne[6] Gaskins (see GASKINS); (by 2) [STEPTOE] 76. George[6], left will 22 Jan. 1783-27 May 1784,[116] student at University of Edinburgh, 1770, physician of "Windsor," Westmoreland County, member of Westmoreland County Committee of Safety, 1775, married Elizabeth (Ransdell) Davenport;[117] 77. James[6], born 1750, died 9 Feb. 1826, aged 75,[118] of "Federal Hill," Bedford County, student at College of William and Mary, 1777, clerk of the District Court at New London, clerk of Bedford County, 1778-1826, married, 18 Feb. 1781, Fanny Calloway, who died 12 Jan. 1805;[119] 78. Thomas[6], born 1752, died unmarried; 79. William[6], born 1753, of "Hewick," Middlesex County, married, 19 May 1782,[120] Elizabeth Robinson, daughter of Christopher and Sarah (Wormeley) Robinson.

37. BENJAMIN[5] HARRISON (Elizabeth[4] Burwell, Lewis[3], Lewis[2], Edward[1]) of "Berkeley," Charles City County, member of the House of Burgesses, 1736-44, died 12 July 1745,[121] left will 17 Oct. 1743-Aug. 1745.[122] He married Anne Carter, daughter of Robert Carter of "Corotoman," Lancaster County, born 1702, died after 1743.[123]

Issue: [HARRISON] 80. Anne[6], married, about 1735, William Randolph of "Wilton," Henrico County, born about 1719, "Turkey Island," Henrico County, member of the House of Burgesses from Goochland County, 1745-46, and from Henrico County, 1758-61, died at "Wilton" 1761;[124] 81. Elizabeth[6], left

---

[115] Virginia Herald, Fredericksburg, 17 July 1794.

[116] Westmoreland Co. Deeds & Wills 17, p. 11.

[117] W(2) XVII, p. 107.

[118] Enquirer, Richmond, 25 Feb. 1826; gravestone, Steptoe-Callaway Cemetery, Bedford Co., in The Southside Virginian, X, p. 76, aged 76.

[119] Bible of James Steptoe, in Juliet Fauntleroy, "Bible Records From Campbell, Bedford, Pittsylvania Counties, Virginia" (typewritten; n.p., 1938), p. 28. Gravestone, Steptoe-Callaway Cemetery, loc. cit., gives death Dec. 1807, aged 45.

[120] Christ Church Parish, Middlesex County, Register; Virginia Genealogical Society, Marriages of Middlesex County, Virginia, 1740-1852 (Special Publication no. 3; Richmond, 1965), p. 79.

[121] Maryland Gazette, 16 Aug. 1745, killed by lightning with two of his daughters.

[122] V III, pp. 124-31, recorded in Charles City County.

[123] Florence Tyler Carlton, A Genealogy of the Known Descendants of Robert Carter of Corotoman (Irvington, Va., 1982), p. 254.

[124] V VL, p. 69.

will 1 June 1780/23 Oct. 1780-codicil 20 July 1782-17 Feb. 1783,[125] married Peyton Randolph who was admitted to the Middle Temple, 13 Oct. 1739, was called to the Bar 11 Feb. 1743/4, was Attorney General of Virginia, 1748-66, member of the House of Burgesses for Williamsburg, 1749, the College, 1752-58, and Williamsburg, 1758-75, its Speaker 1766-75, President of the Convention of 1775, and elected President of the Continental Congress, March 1774,[126] died at Philadelphia, Pa., 22 Oct. 1775, in his 54th year,[127] left will 18 Aug. 1774-20 Nov. 1775;[128] 82. Benjamin[6], born 15 Aug. 1726 at "Berkeley," died 24 April 1791 at "Berkeley," left will 3 Jan. 1780-17 June 1791,[129] member of the House of Burgesses for Charles City County, 1749-75, of the Revolutionary Conventions, 1775-76, of the Continental Congress, 1774-78, and Signer of the Declaration of Independence, and member of the Virginia House of Delegates, 1776-81, being its Speaker, 1778-81, Governor of Virginia, 30 Nov. 1781-30 Nov. 1784, again member of the House of Delegates from Surry County, 1785-90, and Speaker, 1787-90, and member of the Constitutional Convention of 1788,[130] married 136. *Elizabeth[6] Bassett* (see TAYLOR- CARY), born 13 Dec. 1730 at "Eltham," New Kent County, died 1792;[131] 83. Robert[6], of Charles City County, died before 28 Oct. 1775 when his estate was offered for sale,[132] married, by 17 Dec. 1763,[133] Elizabeth Collier; 84. Henry[6], died young; 85. Lucy[6], born about 1732, married (1) Capt Edward Randolph, with whom she went to England, and (2) Robert Neck;[134] 86. Henry[6], born 1734, died 28 Jan. 1772,[135] of "Hunting Quarter," Sussex County, captain in Virginia Regiment, 1755-57, married (1) Elizabeth Avery and (2) Mary __, who married (2), (bond 2) June 1773,[136] Michael Wall; 87. Carter Henry[6], of "Clifton," Cumberland

---

[125] York Co. Wills & Inventories 23, 1783-1811, pp. 4-6.

[126] *Dictionary of American Biography*, XV (New York, 1935), pp. 367-68.

[127] *Virginia Gazette* (Purdie), 3 Nov. 1775.

[128] York Co. Wills & Inventories 22, 1771-83, pp. 308-11.

[129] Charles City Co. Will Bk. 1, pp. 56-59.

[130] *Dictionary of American Biography*, VIII (New York, 1932), pp. 330-31.

[131] Frederick William Pyne, *Descendants of the Signers of the Declaration of Independence*, VI (Rockport, Me., 2000), p. 380.

[132] *Virginia Gazette* (Dixon & Hunter), 28 Oct. 1775.

[133] Sussex Co. Deed Bk. Deed Bk. C, 1763-68, p. 39.

[134] *V* LXXXIX, pp. 294-307.

[135] Albemarle Parish Register.

[136] Catherine Lindsay Knorr, *Marriage Bonds and Ministers' Returns of Sussex County, Virginia, 1754-1810* (Pine Bluff, Ark., 1952), p. 82.

County, chose his brother Benjamin as his guardian, June 1750,[137] captain in the Virginia Regiment, 1755, member of the Cumberland County Committee of Safety, 1774-76, and of the House of Delegates, 1782-87,[138] left will 8 Oct. 1793-27 Jan. 1794,[139] married, 9 Nov. 1760,[140] Susanna Randolph, daughter of Isham Randolph of "Dungness," Goochland County; 88. Hannah[6], killed by lightning 12 July 1745; 89. Nathaniel[6], of Prince George County, born 30 Sept. 1742, died 24 Dec. 1782, married (1), 11 Oct. 1760, Mary Ruffin, born 5 June 1739, died 10 Sept. 1767, and (2), 12 March 1768,[141] 362. *Anne*[6] *Gilliam* (see BALEY-COCKE); 90. Charles[6], married 105. *Mary*[5] *Claiborne* (see CLAIBORNE); 91. (Daughter)[6], killed by lightning 12 July 1745.

38. ELIZABETH[5] HARRISON (Elizabeth[4] Burwell, Lewis[3], Lewis[2], Edward[1]) married, as his (1) wife, William Edwards, of Surry County, who left will 9 Jan. 1721/2-21 Feb. 1724[/5?].[142] He represented Surry County in the House of Burgesses, 1703-06.[143]

Issue: [EDWARDS] 92. Col. Benjamin[6], died before 20 March 1749/50 when the inventory of his estate was ordered,[144] one of the trustees appointed by Act of Assembly, Aug. 1734, to sell the Nottoway Indians' land in Isle of Wight County,[145] married ___.

39. LEWIS[5] BURWELL (Nathaniel[4], Lewis[3], Lewis[2], Edward[1] was educated at Eton, 1722-29, and at Caius College, Cambridge University, where he was admitted a fellow-commoner, 18 June 1729, aged 17.[146] He was a member of the House of Burgesses for Jamestown, 1736-40, and James City County, 1743-44, Councillor, 1743-51, President of the Council and acting Governor, 14 Nov. 1750-21 Nov. 1751,[147] and died 6 May 1756 at his house in

---

[137] Charles City Co. Order Bk. 1737-51, p. 551.

[138] Leonard, pp. 145, 149, 153, 156, 160.

[139] Cumberland Co. Will Bk. 3, pp. 20-21.

[140] W. Mac. Jones, *The Douglas Register* (Richmond, 1928), p. 25.

[141] *V* XXXIV, p. 187.

[142] Surry Co. Deeds & Wills 7, 1715-30, p. 389.

[143] Leonard, pp. 63-64.

[144] Surry Co. Deeds & Wills 1738-54, p. 660.

[145] *H* IV, pp. 459-61.

[146] John Venn and J. A. Venn, *Alumni Cantabrigienses*, pt. 2, I (Cambridge, 1922), p. 269.

[147] Leonard, pp. 76, 79, xix; John W. Raimo, *Biographical Directory of American Colonial and Revolutionary Governors, 1607-1789* (Westport, Conn., 1980), p. 493.

Gloucester County.[148] He married (1) Anne Holden[149] and (2), Oct. 1736,[150] Mary Willis, who died 22 May 1746 in her 28th year.[151]

Issue:[152] 93. Lewis[6], died 1779,[153] of "White Marsh," Gloucester County, student at the College of William and Mary 1759-60, 1763-64, sheriff of Gloucester County, 1767, Burgess, 1769-76, and member of the five Virginia Revolutionary conventions, 1775, and of the House of Delegates, 1776-78,[154] married Judith Page, daughter of Mann and Alice (Grymes) Page, who died 1777;[155] 94. Elizabeth[6], born 1739-40, "White Marsh," Gloucester County, died 6 Dec. 1803 at "Elmington," married Peter Beverley Whiting, born about 1736 at "Elmington," Gloucester County, killed in a riding accident 28 Nov. 1782,[156] probably the Peter who was a student at the College of William and Mary, about 1754,[157] and was a vestryman of Ware Parish and represented Gloucester and Middlesex counties in the Virginia Senate, 1779;[158] 95. Lucy[6]; 96. Anne[6], born 19 July 1741,[159] married (1), Sept. 1759,[160] Armistead Lightfoot, who died Sept. 1771 at Yorktown,[161] and (2), (contract 15) Nov. 1773, Charles Grymes of Gloucester County;[162] 97. Nathaniel[6]; 98. Judith[6]; 99. Mary[6], died 18 Sept. 1809, married, 1768, Lewis Hale, born 1742, died 12 March 1802, and settled in Grayson County, justice 1792-1802; 100. Rebecca Lewis[6], born 20 May 1746,[163] died 1 Aug. 1806 at Richmond, aged 61,[164] married 212. Col. *Jacquelin[6] Ambler*

---

[148] *Maryland Gazette*, 20 May 1756.

[149] Carlton, *op. cit.*, p. 114.

[150] *Virginia Gazette*, 29 Oct. 1736.

[151] *Ibid.*, 29 May 1746.

[152] Brown, *op. cit.*, pp. 25-27.

[153] *Virginia Gazette* (Dixon & Hunter), 19 March 1779.

[154] Leonard, pp. 97, 99, 103, 105, 109, 112, 115, 117, 119, 122, 125, 129.

[155] *Virginia Gazette* (Purdie), 12 Sept. 1777.

[156] *Virginia Gazette and American Advertiser*, Richmond, 21 Dec. 1782.

[157] *W*(2) I, p. 41.

[158] Leonard, p. 136.

[159] *V* XIV, p. 259.

[160] *V* XVI, p. 208, citing *Virginia Gazette*, 28 Sept. 1759, notes of John Randolph in an interleaved almanac now at Virginia Historical Society.

[161] *Virginia Gazette* (Purdie & Dixon), 19 Sept. 1771. He was son of Philip Lightfoot and Mary (Armistead) Burwell, widow of 24. James[4] Burwell.

[162] York Co. Deed Bk. 8, p. 376.

[163] Abingdon Parish Register; *V* XIV, p. 259.

[164] *Virginia Gazette and General Advertiser*, Richmond, 6 Aug. 1806.

(see TAYLOR-CARY).

41. CARTER[5] BURWELL (Nathaniel[4], Lewis[3], Lewis[2], Edward[1]), born 25 Oct. 1716 at "Fairfield," Gloucester County,[165] of "Carter's Ferry," James City County, was a member of the House of Burgesses, 1742-53,[166] and left will 6 May 1756-codicil 14 May 1756-26 Oct. 1756.[167] He married, 5 Jan. 1737/8,[168] Lucy Grymes, born 18 April 1720.

Issue:[169] 101. Lucy[6], born 23 Oct. 1740, "Brandon," Middlesex County, married Capt. Thomas Lilly of the Virginia Navy, 1776-81, of Yorktown, who died intestate 1 April 1798;[170] 102. Elizabeth[6], born 21 Feb. 1741/2, "Carter's Grove," James City County; 103. Judith[6], born 11 April 1744, "Brandon," died 20 Nov. 1769, married, 8 Nov. 1766, Thomas Bertrand Griffin of Lancaster County who left will 3 Feb. 1778-21 May 1778;[171] 104. Alice[6], born 4 May 1745, "Brandon," married, Dec. 1771,[172] the Rev. James Maury Fontaine, student at the College of William and Mary, 1753-55, minister of of Petsworth Parish, 1762-65, and of Ware Parish, Gloucester County, 1764-95,[173] who died before 12 Oct. 1796 when his estate was mentioned;[174] 105. Sarah[6], born 30 Nov. 1746, Williamsburg, married, Sept. 1776,[175] the Rev. John Bracken, minister of Bruton Parish, James City County, 1773-1818, master of the Grammar School, 1775-79, and professor of moral philosophy and president of the College of William and Mary, 1812-14, who was elected Bishop of Virginia, 1812, but declined,[176] and died 15-16 July 1818;[177] 106. Mary[6], born 6 April

---

[165] Abingdon Parish Register; *V* XIV, p. 259.

[166] *Dictionary of Virginia Biography*, II, pp. 229-31; Leonard, pp. 79, 81, 84.

[167] Cunningham Chapel Parish, Clarke Co., records, pp. 63-64,Virginia State Archives acc.24801, recorded in the General Court.

[168] Burwell Prayer Book, in *W*(1) VI, pp. 145-46; *Virginia Gazette*, 6 Jan. 1737/8; Christ Church Parish, Middlesex County, Register.

[169] Burwell Bible, in *V* XXXI, pp. 357-58, which gives parents' marriage as 16 January.

[170] William Lindsay Hopkins, *Virginia Revolutionary War Land Grant Claims, 1783-1850 (Rejected)* (Richmond, 1988), p. 138.

[171] Lancaster Co. Will Bk. 20, p. 129.

[172] *Virginia Gazette* (Purdie & Dixon), 26 Dec. 1771.

[173] *V* XLI, pp. 138-39.

[174] *Virginia Gazette and General Advertiser*, Richmond, 12 Oct. 1796.

[175] *Virginia Gazette* (Dixon & Hunter), 21 Sept. 1776.

[176] *V* XLI, p. 125; *Dictionary of Virginia Biography*, II, pp. 179-80.

[177] *Enquirer*, Richmond, 24 July 1818, as 15 July; *American Beacon*, Norfolk, 22 July 1818, as 16 July.

1749, "Carter's Grove," married 113. Edmund[6] Berkeley; 107. Nathaniel[6], born 15 April 1750, "Carter's Grove," died 29 March 1814, "Carter Hall," Clarke County,[178] student at the College of William and Mary and in 1772 won the Botetourt medal for proficiency in mathematics, was County Lieutenant of James City County, 1776-81, member of the House of Delegates, 1778-79, 1782, and of the Convention of 1778, lived at "Carter's Grove" and later moved to "Carter Hall,"[179] married (1), 28 Nov. 1772 at "Brandon", Middlesex County,[180] Susanna Grymes, born 4 March 1752,[181] died 24 July 1788 at "Carter's Grove,"[182] and (2), 24 Jan. 1789 at "Mannsfield," near Fredericksburg,[183] Lucy (Page) Baylor, born 1759, died 11 Nov. 1843 in Clarke County,[184] widow of 71. Col. *George[5] Baylor* of "Newmarket," Caroline County (see BERNARD), and daughter of Mann Page; 108. Carter[6], born 25 Jan. 1754, "Carter's Grove," died 1775, buried at St. Martin Orgar, London; 109. Lewis[6], born 5 June 1755, "Carter's Grove," died young.

45. ROBERT[5] BURWELL (Nathaniel[4], Lewis[3], Lewis[2], Edward[1]), born 3 June 1720,[185] died 30 Jan. 1777 at "Newington," King and Queen County,[186] leaving will 16 Aug. 1772-codicil 10 Jan. 1777-13 Oct. 1777.[187] He was a resident of Isle of Wight County, County Lieutenant, 1749-72, vestryman of Newport Parish, and trustee of Smithfield, 1752, member of the House of Burgesses, 1752-58, and of the Council, 1762-74, but moved to "Newington" after 1772. He married (1), before 6 Aug. 1745,[188] Sarah Nelson, daughter of Thomas and Frances (Housden) Tucker Nelson, (2) Elizabeth (Lightfoot)

---

[178] Burwell Bible, in *V* XXXI, p. 359.

[179] *Dictionary of Virginia Biography*, II, pp. 437-38; Leonard, pp. 130, 134, 146, 173.

[180] *Virginia Gazette* (Hunter & Dixon), 3 Dec. 1772; Virginia Genealogical Society, *Marriages of Middlesex County, Virginia, 1740-1852* (*Special Publication*, no. 3; Richmond, 1965), p. 15; Burwell Bible, *V* XXXI, p. 359; Christ Church Parish Register.

[181] *V* XXVIII, p. 96.

[182] *Virginia Gazette and Weekly Advertiser*, Richmond, 31 July 1788; gravestone, "Carter's Grove," in Cunningham Chapel Parish, *op. cit.*, p. 84.

[183] *Virginia Gazette and Weekly Advertiser*, Richmond, 26 Feb. 1789.

[184] Alycon Trubey Pierce, *Virginia Revolutionary Records, Selected Final Pension Payment Vouchers, 1818-1864* (Athens, Ga., 1996), I, p. 80.

[185] Abingdon Parish Register.

[186] *Virginia Gazette* (Purdie), 14 Feb. 1777.

[187] *W*(1) VII, p. 311-13, recorded in King and Queen County.

[188] *W*(1) VI, p. 144, will of Thomas Nelson, her father.

Randolph, widow of Beverley Randolph, who died 6 March 1770, Yorktown,[189] and (3), 31 Dec. 1774,[190] Mary (Blair) Braxton, born 27 Sept. 1734, daughter of John and Mary (Monro) Blair and widow of Col. George Braxton, who married (3), 8 April 1792,[191] Robert Prescott.

Issue: (by 1) 110. Frances[6], died 1784, aged 37, married John Page, born 17 April 1744, died 11 Oct. 1808 at Richmond, of "Rosewell," Gloucester County, graduate of the College of William and Mary, 1763, served under George Washington on an expedition against the French and Indians and was colonel of Gloucester County militia during the Revolutionary War, was delegate to the Virginia constitutional convention, 1776, Lieutenant Governor of Virginia, 1776-79, member of the House of Delegates, 1781-83, 1785-88, 1797-1801, and of Congress, 1789-97, Governor of Virginia, 1802-05, and federal Commissioner of Loans;[192] 111. Nathaniel[6], justice, 1766-72, and clerk of Isle of Wight County, 1772-87, County Lieutenant, 1772, member of the Committee of Safety, 1775, later moved to Lancaster County where he left will 13 May 1784-15 Feb. 1813,[193] but died before 20 Oct. 1789 when his estate was sold by the sheriff, [194] married (1) Mary Wormeley and (2), 20 April 1786,[195] Frances (__) Wormeley, widow of John Wormeley, who married (3), (bond 16) March 1791,[196] Griffin Garland and left will 21 March 1832-17 Oct. 1836.[197]

45. EDMUND[5] BERKELEY (Lucy[4] Burwell, Lewis[3], Lewis[2], Edward[1]), born 26 Nov. 1704, of "Barn Elms," Middlesex County, justice, 1725, member of House of Burgesses, 1736-40,[198] left will 30 March 1761-codicils 14 May 1764/15 March 1765-4 Aug./6 Oct. 1767.[199] He married, 18 May 1728,[200] 68.

---

[189] *Virginia Gazette*, 8 March 1770. She was buried at Sandy Point, Charles City County.

[190] *V* XXXII, p. 386; *Virginia Gazette* (Purdie), 5 Jan. 1775.

[191] *V* XXXII, p. 386.

[192] Richard Channing Moore Page, *Genealogy of the Page Family of Virginia* (2nd ed.; Bridgewater, Va., 1965), p. 71; *Biographical Directory of the American Congress, 1774-1996*, p. 1622; *Dictionary of American Biography*, XIV (New York, 1934), pp. 137-38.

[193] Lancaster Co. Will Bk. 28, p. 139.

[194] Lancaster Co. Will Bk. 20, p. 253.

[195] Stratton Nottingham, *The Marriage License Bonds of Lancaster County, Virginia, From 1701 to 1848* (Onancock, Va., 1927), p. 10.

[196] *Ibid.*, p. 29.

[197] Lancaster Co. Will Bk. 28k, p. 325.

[198] Leonard, p. 77.

[199] Middlesex Co. Will Bk. E, pp. 305-08.

[200] Berkeley Bible, *loc. cit.*

Mary⁵ Nelson (see MARTIAU).

Issue: [BERKELEY][201] 112. Lucy⁶, born 15 June 1729,[202] died young; 113. Edmund⁶, born 5 Dec. 1730,[203] died 8 July 1802,[204] of "Barn Elms," Middlesex County, member of House of Burgesses, 1771-76, the House of Delegates, 1776, and the Conventions of 1775-76,[205] married (1), 5 Nov. 1757, Judith Randolph, who died 28 April 1763[206] and (2), 23 Jan. 1768, 106. Mary⁶ Burwell; 114. Nelson⁶, of "Airwell," Hanover County, born 16 May 1733, died before 9 April 1794 when his executors advertised his estate,[207] member of Hanover County Committee of Safety, married, 11 March 1756, Elizabeth Wormeley Carter, died 1778;[208] 115. Mary⁶, born 15 Jan. 1737/8,[209] married, 20 April 1771,[210] Dr. Corbin Griffin of Yorktown, who died 20 Sept. 1813, aged 74;[211] 116. Sarah⁶, born 27 Jan. 1741/2;[212] 117. Lucy⁶, born 9 June 1744.

47. LUCY⁵ BERKELEY (Lucy⁴ Burwell, Lewis³, Lewis², Edward¹), born 10 May 1709,[213] died 18 Jan. 1731/2,[214] She married Alexander Lister, who died 11 Nov. 1733.[215]

Issue: [LISTER] 118. Sarah⁶, born 9 Jan. 1721/2,[216] married, (bond 9) Aug. 1750,[217] Peter Robinson, who matriculated at Oriel College, Oxford University, 2 April 1737, aged 18, was a member of the House of Burgesses for King William County, 1758-61,[218] and left will dated 8 June 1765.[219]

---

[201] *Ibid.*

[202] Christ Church Parish, Middlesex Co., Register, which shows 20 June.

[203] *Ibid.*

[204] *Ibid.*

[205] Leonard, pp. 100, 103, 106, 110, 113, 115, 118, 120, 123.

[206] Frances Berkeley Young, *The Berkeleys of Barn Elms* (Hamden, Conn., 1964), p. 40.

[207] *Virginia Gazette and General Advertiser*, Richmond, 9 April 1794.

[208] Carlton, *op. cit.*, p. 398.

[209] Christ Church Parish, Middlesex Co., Register.

[210] *Ibid.*

[211] *Virginia Patriot*, Richmond, 5 Oct. 1813.

[212] Christ Church Parish, Middlesex Co., Register. Did she die 16 Aug. 1795?

[213] Louise Pecquet du Bellet, *Some Prominent Virginia Families* (Lynchburg, 1907), II, p. 384; Abingdon Parish Register, baptized 17 May.

[214] Christ Church Parish, Middlesex County, Register.

[215] *Ibid.*

[216] *Ibid.*

[217] Virginia Genealogical Society, *op. cit.*, p. 70.

[218] *V* XVII, p. 208; Leonard, p. 89.

[219] *T* IV, pp. 42-43.

48. MARY[5] BERKELEY (Lucy[4] Burwell, Lewis[3], Lewis[2], Edward[1]), born 24 May 1711,[220] married, as his (1) wife, Christopher Robinson, of "Hewick," Middlesex County, member of the House of Burgesses, 1752-58,[221] left will 17 July 1768-6 Dec. 1768,[222] who married (2), (bond 6) May 1750,[223] Sarah Wormeley.

Issue: [ROBINSON][224] 119. Lucy[6], died 7 March 1734/5; 120. Judith[6], born 2 June 1736, died Dec. 1757, married, (bond 16) June 1755,[225] as his (1) wife, Carter Braxton, born 16 Sept. 1736 at "Newington," King and Queen County, died 10 Oct. 1797 at Richmond, of King William County, graduated of the College of William and Mary, 1755, student at Cambridge University, member of the House of Burgesses, 1761-71, 1775-76, of the first, second and fourth Virginia conventions, 1774-75, of the Continental Congress where he was a Signer of the Declaration of Independence, of the House of Delegates, 1779-81, 1783, 1785-86, 1791-94, and of the Virginia Council of State, 1789 until his death;[226] 121. Christopher[6], born 9 March 1737/8, died young.

49. SARAH[5] BERKELEY (Lucy[4] Burwell, Lewis[3], Lewis[2], Edward[1]), born 9 Feb. 1713/4,[227] married, as his (1) wife, 4 Nov. 1736,[228] Ralph Wormeley of "Rosegill," Middlesex County, member of the House of Burgesses, 1742-64, who died 19 Aug. 1790 at "Rosegill,"[229] left will 7 April 1787-codicil 26 May 1789-1 March 1791.[230]

Issue: 122. Elizabeth[6], born 3 Sept. 1737, married, July 1760, as his (2) wife, 71. *Dudley[5] Digges* (see DIGGES).

50. WILLIAM[5] ARMISTEAD (Martha[4] Burwell, Lewis[3], Lewis[2], Edward[1]), of "Hesse," Gloucester County, left will 23 Dec. 1755-20 April

---

[220] Abingdon Parish Register, which shows 25 May.

[221] Leonard, pp. 84, 87.

[222] Middlesex Co. Will Bk. E, 1760-72, pp. 350-52.

[223] Virginia Genealogical Society, *op. cit.*, p. 70.

[224] Christ Church Parish, Middlesex Co., Register.

[225] Virginia Genealogical Society, *op. cit.*, p. 10.

[226] *Dictionary of American Biography*, II (New York, 1929), pp. 609-10; *Biographical Directory of the American Congress, 1774-1996* (Alexandria, Va., 1997), p. 701; Leonard, pp. 92, 95, 98, 100, 106, 110, 113, 115, 118, 120, 123, 126, 134, 138, 142, 159, 157, 189, 184, 188, 192, 196.

[227] Christ Church Parish, Middlesex Co., Register.

[228] *Virginia Gazette*, 19 Nov. 1736.

[229] *Virginia Gazette & General Advertiser*, Richmond, 25 Aug. 1790.

[230] Middlesex Co. Will Bk. G, 1787-93, pp. 191-95.

1756.[231] He married Mary Bowles who married (2) the Rev. Thomas Price.

Issue: [ARMISTEAD] 123. William[6], of "Hesse," student at William and Mary College, 1755, left will 5 Oct. 1784-8 April 1785,[232] married, 1765, Maria[7] Carter, daughter of Charles Carter of "Cleve" and 63. *Anne[6] Byrd* (see ST. LEGER); 124. John[6], married 69. *Lucy[5] Baylor* (see BERNARD); 125. Bowles[6], of Eley's Ford, Culpeper County, student at William and Mary College, 1763-66, left undated will proved 21 June/15 May[*sic*] 1785,[233] married Mary Anne Fontaine; 126. Henry[6], died by 1773.

53. ROBERT[5] ARMISTEAD (Martha[4] Burwell, Lewis[3], Lewis[2], Lewis[1]) was clerk of King George County, 1752-57. He married (1), about 1750, Elizabeth (Burgess) Ball, widow of Jeduthan Ball who died 5 March 1749/50,[234] and (2) 59. *Ann[5] Smith* (see BERNARD).

Issue: [ARMISTEAD] (by 1) 127. Henry[6], first clerk of the Hustings Court of Fredericksburg, 1782-87, died 20 July 1787 at Fredericksburg,[235] left will 13 July 1787-3 Sept. 1787,[236] married, (bond 14) Oct. 1774,[237] Winifred Peachey, born 8 Jan. 1752;[238] (by 2) 128. Thomas[6], lieutenant and captain of 1st Virginia State Regiment, Aug. 1776-21 May 1782, of Richmond and later a grocer at Brandywine, King William County, died 1 Sept. 1809, leaving will 19 June 1809-6 March 1810,[239] married (1) ___ Marchant of North Carolina and (2) Jane Peachey, living 31 Jan. 1826; 129. Martha Burwell[6], married Benjamin Dabney, of "Bellevue," King and Queen County, and of "Elmington," Gloucester County, attorney at law, who married (2) 198. *Sarah[6] Smith* (see BERNARD) and died 24 May 1806, aged 49;[240] 130. Robert[6], of Portsmouth, left will 16 Jan. 1794-7 Feb. 1794,[241] married ___.

54. Capt. NATHANIEL BACON[5] BURWELL (James[4], Lewis[3], Lewis[2],

[231] Prince William Co. Land Causes 1805-16, pp. 413-15, recorded in Gloucester County.

[232] *T* XXIV, pp. 45-50.

[233] Culpeper Co., Will Bk. C, pp. 114-15.

[234] Horace E. Hayden, *Virginia Genealogies* (Wilkes Barre, Pa., 1891), p. 100.

[235] *Virginia Independent Chronicle*, Richmond, 8 and 22 Aug. 1787.

[236] Fredericksburg Hustings Court Will Bk. A, p. 48; Order Bk. 1784-1800, p. 15.

[237] George Harrison Sanford King, *Marriages of Richmond County, Virginia, 1668-1853* (Fredericksburg, 1964), p. 4.

[238] North Farnham Parish, Richmond Co., Register.

[239] Revolutionary War pension application, Thomas Armistead, R.12157, and Virginia Half Pay file, National Archives.

[240] *Virginia Argus*, Richmond, 19 July 1806.

[241] Norfolk Co. Will Bk. 3, pp. 114a-115.

Edward[1]) of York County, landowner in Isle of Wight County, died before 10 April 1746 when his estate was mentioned.[242] He married Jemima Cocke.[243]

Issue:[244] 131. James[6], of King's Creek, near Williamsburg, died April 1775,[245] married Anne Jones, born 15 Feb. 1739,[246] died Oct. 1779;[247] 132. Elizabeth[6], married (1) the Rev. Richard Hewitt who was a student at William and Mary College, 1753-55, went to England for ordination and was licensed for Virginia 30 Sept. 1760, and was minister of Hungars Parish, Northampton County,[248] and died before 12 April 1774, when William Hewitt was granted administration on his estate, the executors having resigned,[249] and (2) 24. Col. *Edward⁵ Harwood* (see HARWOOD).

56. LEWIS[5] BURWELL (Lewis[4], Lewis[3], Lewis[2], Edward[1]) of "Kingsmill," James City County, Naval officer of the District of Upper James River, 1752, died Oct. 1784, Mecklenburg County,[250] leaving will 1 Aug. 1784-13 Dec. 1784.[251] He was a Loyalist during the Revolutionary War.[252] He married, (bond 21) Jan. 1745/6,[253] Frances (Thacker) Bray, daughter of Edwin Thacker[254] and widow of James Bray, born 2 Oct. 1722,[255] died 1784.

Issue: 133. Lewis[6], of "Kingsmill," married Lucy[7] Randolph, born 1744,[256] died before April 1787 when he was granted administration on her estate,[257] daughter of 78. Anne[6] (Harrison) Randolph;[258] 134. Nathaniel[6], of "Vermont,"

---

[242] *Virginia Gazette*, 10 April 1746.

[243] Brown, *op. cit.*, p. 47.

[244] *W*(1) II, p. 232; III, pp. 107-08; will of half-brother John Lightfoot, 20 April 1751-31 Dec. 1751 (Brunswick Co. Will Bk. 3, p. 42).

[245] *Virginia Gazette* (Purdie), 28 April 1775.

[246] L. H. Jones, *Captain Roger Jones of London and Virginia* (Albany, N.Y., 1891), p. 45.

[247] *Virginia Gazette* (Dixon & Hunter), 30 Oct. 1779.

[248] Edward L. Goodwin, *The Colonial Church in Virginia* (London, 1927), p. 278.

[249] Northampton Co. Minute Bk. 28, 1771-77, p. 238. His will is not of record.

[250] *Virginia Gazette and Weekly Advertiser*, Richmond, 30 Oct. 1784, died "lately."

[251] Mecklenburg Co. Will Bk. 2, p. 80.

[252] Coldham, *op. cit.*, p. 540.

[253] Virginia Genealogical Society, *op. cit.*, p. 15.

[254] *H* VI, p. 214.

[255] Family papers of Judge Francis Wyatt Smith, in Beverley Fleet, *Virginia Colonial Abstracts*, V (Richmond, 1959), p. 59.

[256] *V* XLV, p. 69.

[257] Chesterfield Co. Order Bk. 7, p. 478.

[258] *Virginia Gazette* (Purdie), 12 May 1775.

King William County, born 1750, died 30 March 1802,[259] ensign 1775, captain of artillery, 1776, and major and aide-de-camp to Gen. Howe, 1779, in the Revolutionary War to 1783, member of the Society of the Cincinnati, member of the House of Delegates, 1799-1801,[260] left will 30 March 1802-26 April 1802,[261] married, 5 Nov. 1780,[262] 173. *Martha*[6] *Digges* (see DIGGES), who deposed 16 Nov. 1837 she was aged 80 years, 3 months, and died 3 Feb. 1848 at "Rustic Lodge," near Fincastle, Va.;[263] 135. Thacker[6], born 1752, lieutenant colonel of Mecklenburg County militia, 1777-78, left will 21 Sept. 1780-11 Dec. 1780,[264] married Mary Armistead;[265] 136. Armistead[6], died Jan. 1775;[266] 137. Elizabeth[6], died 26 Dec. 1811, Richmond,[267] married, 1771,[268] John[7] Page, Jr., son of 66. *Jane*[6] (*Byrd*) *Page* (see ST. LEGER). born about 1743, "North End," Mathews County, died 20 April 1789,[269] of Caroline County, original member of Phi Beta Kappa, 1776, at College of William and Mary.[270]

57. ARMISTEAD[5] BURWELL (Lewis[4], Lewis[3], Lewis[2], Edward[1]), vestryman of Bruton Parish and merchant of Williamsburg, and of "Stoneland," Mecklenburg County, died 1754.[271] He married Christian Blair, daughter of John and Mary (Monro) Blair, who was born 1727 and died 2 Jan. 1784.[272]

Issue: 138. Lewis[6], born 26 Sept. 1745[273] at Williamsburg, died 2 July

---

[259] Revolutionary War pension application, Nathaniel Burwell, widow Martha, W.18681, National Archives.

[260] Leonard, pp. 216, 220.

[261] Franklin Co., Ky., Deed Bk. F, p. 238, in *The Register of the Kentucky Historical Society*, XLII, pp. 352-53.

[262] Revolutionary War pension application, *loc. cit.*; *Virginia Gazette*, 11 March 1780.

[263] Gravestone, Fincastle, Va., in Elizabeth Hawes Ryland, *King William County, Virginia, From Old Newspapers & Files* (Richmond, 1955), p. 70; *Enquirer*, Richmond, 21 Nov. 1848.

[264] Mecklenburg Co. Will Bk. 1, p. 342.

[265] *Virginia Gazette* (Purdie & Dixon), 24 Nov. 1774.

[266] *Virginia Gazette* (Dixon & Hunter), 28 Jan. 1775.

[267] *Enquirer*, Richmond, 28 Dec. 1811. She died in the Richmond theater fire.

[268] *Virginia Gazette* (Purdie & Dixon), 11 July 1771.

[269] *Virginia Independent Chronicle*, Richmond, 6 May 1789.

[270] Page, *op. cit.*, p. 101.

[271] Brown, *op. cit.*, p. 63. His executors, Lewis and Nathaniel Burwell, advertised 1600 acres in King William County for sale (*Virginia Gazette*, 6 June 1755).

[272] *V LV*, p. 174.

[273] Bruton Parish Register

1800,[274] of "Stoneland," Mecklenburg County, colonel during Revolutionary War, County Lieutenant of Mecklenburg, member of House of Delegates, 1781-82, 1785-88, 1790,[275] married (1), 24 March 1768, 104. Anne[6] Spotswood (see WEST), who died 14 Feb. 1789 in her 43rd year,[276] and (2), 13 Nov. 1789, Elizabeth[7] Harrison, daughter of 86. Henry[6] Harrison and Elizabeth Avery, who died 19 Nov. 1824; 139. John[6], of Dinwiddie County, born 30 Nov. 1746,[277] died 26 Feb. 1788,[278] married, 1771,[279] Anne Powell, who died 14 Nov. 1788, aged 42.

62. LUCY[5] MARTIN (Martha[4] Burwell, Lewis[3], Lewis[2], Edward[1]) died 26 July 1802 at Twickenham, Middlesex, leaving will as Lucia, Viscountess Clifden, in Prerogative Court of Dublin.   She married (1) Henry Boyle-Walsingham, son of Henry Boyle, first Earl of Shannon, and (2), 20 March 1760, James Agar of County Kilkenny, Ireland, who was born 25 March 1734, was Member of the Irish Parliament for Gowran, 1753-60, for County Kilkenny, 1761-76, and for Gowran again, 1776, Commissioner of Revenue, 1771-85, Commissioner of Excise, 1776-85, joint Postmaster General, 1784-89, created Lord Clifden, Baron of Gowran, County Kilkenny, 27 July 1776 and Viscount Clifden of Gowran, 12 Jan. 1781, and died 1 Jan. 1789 in Ireland, leaving will proved 1789.[280]

Issue: (by 2) [AGAR][281] 140. Henry Welbore[6], born 22 Jan. 1761, clerk of the Privy Council from 1785 until the abolition of that office in 1817, Member of Parliament for County Kilkenny, 1783-89, and for Heytesbury, 1793-1802, Fellow of the Society of Antiquaries, 8 Dec. 1803, by the death of his great-uncle, Welbore, Baron Mendip of Mendip, inherited that peerage and took

---

[274] Monument, St. John's Church, Chase City, Va., in Munsey Adams Moore, *Cemetery and Tombstone Records of Mecklenburg County, Virginia*, I (Chase City, Va., 1982), p. 177, apparently a modern monument.

[275] Susan L. Bracy, *Life By the Roaring Roanoke* (n.p., 1977), pp. 78, 401; Leonard, pp. 142, 157, 161, 165, 169, 180.

[276] *Virginia Independent Chronicle*, Richmond, 4 March 1789.

[277] Bruton Parish Register.

[278] Brown, *op. cit.*, p. 81.

[279] *Virginia Gazette* (Purdie & Dixon), 5 Dec. 1771.

[280] G. E. Cokayne, *The Complete Peerage*, ed. by Vicary Gibbs, III (London, 1913), pp. 287-88.

[281] *Ibid.*; *Burke's Genealogical and Heraldic History of the Peerage ...* (105th ed.; London, 1970), p. 574.

the surname Ellis, died 13 July 1836 at Hanover Square, London, leaving will proved Sept. 1836, married, 10 March 1792 at Sion House, Isleworth, Middlesex, Caroline, born 27 Oct. 1763 and died at Blenheim 23 Nov. 1813, daughter of George (Spencer), Duke of Marlborough;[282] 141. the Rev. John Ellis[6], born 31 Dec. 1764, died 3 Jan. 1797, married, 11 March 1792, Harriet, daughter of William, 2nd Viscount Ashbrook, who married (2), 28 July 1798, Pryse Loveden-Pryse and died 14 Jan. 1813; 142. Charles Bagenal[6], born 13 Aug. 1769, died 16 June 1811, barrister at law, married, 15 Nov. 1804, Anna Maria, daughter of Thomas Hunt of Millington Hall, Cheshire, who was sole heir of her great-uncle the 3rd Earl of Radnor and died 3 March 1861; 143. (Daughter)[6].

65. ELIZABETH[5] MARTIN (Martha[4] Burwell, Lewis[3], Lewis[2], Edward[1]) married, (contract 12) Aug.1742,[283] Patrick Barclay, merchant of King and Queen and Essex counties, who left will 16 May 1746 dated at London-19 July 1749.[284]

Issue: [BARCLAY] 144. George[6], married 27. *Mary[5] Cole* (see COLE).

---

[282] She was the great-granddaughter of John Churchill, 1st Duke of Marlborough, and the great-great-great-aunt of Sir Winston Spencer Churchill, British Prime Minister.

[283] Louisa Co. Deed Bk. A, pp. 23-26.

[284] Essex Co. Will Bk. 8, 1747-50, pp. 296-97.

BUSH

*1. JOHN[1] BUSH came to Virginia in the *Neptune*, 1618. This was the ship in which Lord Delaware was returning to Virginia to resume his office as Governor of the colony. The Governor died on the way, in Nova Scotia, and Sir George Yeardley, appointed in Lord De La Warr's place, sailed for Virginia, 19 Jan. 1618/9. In the fleet of ships bearing the Yeardley party was the *Guifte* with John[1] Bush's wife Elizabeth and two daughters as passengers. After a "sore voyage" the *Guifte* arrived at Jamestown, 19 April 1619.[1]

John[1] Bush and family were located at "Kikatan, now called Elizabeth City," where he had two houses, one occupied by his brother and the latter's wife.

> John Bush haveinge two howses paid for before the said Governor [Yeardley] came in was in like manner turned out and Capt: Nuce put in possession of the same by S[r] George Yeardley, contrary to all right and equity whereby he lost all his goods and his wife in that extreamity, miscarried with child.
>
> The brother of the said John Bush, beinge then dead in the howse and his wife great with Child was likewise turned out.[2]

The charges cited above were presented at a Virginia court held in London, 19 June 1622, by William Kemp, Gent., who made his home with William Julian, a near neighbor of John[1] Bush. Kemp's complaint was registered in behalf of those living at Kecoughtan and against Governor Yeardley for his taking over lands settled by the early colonists, which lands lay within the tract designated as the "Company lands" and which Yeardley placed under Capt. William Nuce, who came in 1620, having been appointed the first Marshal of Virginia.[3]

John[1] Bush and family escaped the massacre of 1622 and he is listed at Elizabeth City in the census of 1623/4.[4] His wife and two children were named in a patent for 300 acres within the parish of Kiccoughtan in Elizabeth City Corporation, adjoining Lieut. Albino Lupo, William Julian and William Prickett, issued, 1 Dec. 1624, to John Bush of Kiccoughtan, Gent., who came to this country in the *Neptune*, in 1618, being for the transportation out of England of his wife Elizabeth, his two children, Elizabeth and Mary, who all came in the *Guifte* in 1619, and 100 acres for the transportation of two servants, Thomas Hand and William Parker, in the *Charles* in 1621.[5]

---

[1] *R*, Va. Co. I, p. 229.
[2] *Ibid.*, II, p. 44.
[3] *Ibid.*, I, pp. 447, 453.
[4] Hotten, p. 188.
[5] Patent Bk. 1, p. 31.

Shortly after John[1] Bush was granted a "letter of administration" by the General Court, Nov. 1624,[6] he died, and his burial was the last in Elizabeth City given in the muster, 1624/5. For some unknown reason his will was not probated until 13 Jan. 1626/7 when

> Captain William Tucker sworn and examined sayeth that the will produced in Court was the will of John Bush, deceased, and that the said John Bush was, at the time of the making of the same, in perfect sence and memory, the will bearing date the 9th of December 1624.[7]

By the 1630s Maj. Thomas Ceeley had acquired the Bush tract and adjoining land where he resided in 1639.[8]

Issue:[9] 2. Elizabeth[2], born in England; 3. Mary[2], born in England.

---

[6] *MCGC*, p. 34.

[7] *Ibid.*, p. 137.

[8] W. T. Stauffer, "Old Farms Out of Which the City of Newport News Was Erected," *W*(2) XV, pp. 251-52.

[9] Abraham Bush of Lancaster County, who is first mentioned in extant records the last of Sept. 1657 when a certificate was issued to Thomas Powell for the "transportation of Abraham Bush, George Spencer, Peter Elinor and Sarah Bannister" (Lancaster Co. Order Bk. 1656-66, p. 34), was living in Lancaster, 25 July 1663, when Richard Merryman conveyed to him a life interest in 200 acres (Lancaster Co. Record Bk. 2, 1654-66, p. 347) and is recorded as 61 years of age in 1683 (Old Rappahannock Co. Deed Bk. 6, reverse, fo. 17), was formerly identified as a son. Since the importation certificate suggests that Abraham Bush was a recent immigrant, further evidence to establish his parentage and a connection with the family of John[1] Bush is needed.

CALTHORPE[1]

*1. CHRISTOPHER[1] CALTHORPE, baptized 22 April 1605 at Ditchingham, Norfolk, was second son of Christopher Calthrope, Esq. (baptized 29 May 1581 at Cockthorp, died 14 March 1624/5 at London) of Blakeney and Cockthorp, Norfolk, England, and his wife Maud Thurton (buried 27 March 1624) of Broome, Norfolk, who were married 8 Sept. 1602 at Broome.[2] As a youth he came to Virginia in 1622 in the *Furtherance*, in company with Lt. Thomas Purefoy, and was listed in the muster, 1624/5, as aged 18. His grandfather, Sir James Calthrope (born 31 Aug. 1558, died 15 June 1615), having married Barbara Bacon (died 3 Nov. 1639), he was probably a relative of President Nathaniel Bacon of the Virginia Council.

On 28 March 1623 George Sandys, at James City, in a letter to Samuel Wrote in London, stated:

> I used Mr. Calthorpe at his landing with all the curtesie I could and brought him acquainted with the Governour. I proferd him the Entertainment of my house and my own Chamber to lodge in wch he refused in that I was to bee but seldome there myselfe in regard of my almost dailie attendance at the Councel ... I have given him from time to time the best Councell I am able, at the first he kept companie too much with his Inferiours who hung upon him while his good liquor lasted. After, he consorted with Captain Whitacres (a man of no good example) with whom he is gone into Kicotan [Hampton], yet wheresoever he bee, hee shall not bee without the reach of my care nor want for anie thing that I or my credit can procure him.[3]

He owned land, 1628, adjoining Lt. Purefoy and William Coxe near Fort Henry in Elizabeth City.[4] When land along the York River opened for settlement, 1630, Capt. Christopher Calthorpe obtained 500 acres on the river and Calthorpe's Creek at "New Poquoson, Elizabeth City County," by order of court, 26 April

---

[1] Lyon Gardiner Tyler, "The Calthorpes," *W*(1) II, pp. 106-12, 160-68. The name is variously spelled Calthrop, Calthrope, Calthorp, Calthorpe. Exact dates of birth and death in the second and later generations are from the Charles Parish Register.

[2] G. H. Holley, "Pedigrees Compiled from the Parish Registers, Wills, Monumental Inscriptions, Court Records, Etc., of Norfolk County, England," (MS, Genealogical Society, Salt Lake City, Utah), II, p. 6; Walter Rye, ed., *The Visitation of Norfolk ... 1563 ... 1613* (Harleian Society, *Publications*, XXXII; London, 1891), p. 66; George W. Marshall, ed., *LeNeve's Pedigrees of the Knights ...* (Harleian Society,*Publications*, VIII; London, 1873), pp. 9-10; John Anderson Brayton, "A Royal Descent for Christopher Calthorpe of York Co., Va.," *The Virginia Genealogist*, XL, pp. 67-70.

[3] Edward Duffield Neill, *Virginia Vetusta* (Albany, N.Y., 1885), pp. 126-27. George Sandys was Treasurer of the Colony, 1621-25.

[4] Patent Bk. 1, pp. 88-89.

1631, for which a patent was issued 13 July 1635.[5] This land, by then described as in Charles River [York] County, was repatented 6 May 1636 with an additional 500 acres and on 5 July 1636 he added another 100 acres adjoining as well as repatenting 100 acres which he had purchased on Waters Creek in Warwick County.[6]

Christopher[1] Calthorpe called his plantation "Thropland"[7] after the family estate in England. The church building of New Poquoson Parish, later Charles Parish, dating back to 1635,[8] stood on the Calthorpe tract and the foundation of an early church on the site is preserved.

In 1646 Capt. Christopher[1] Calthorpe was among eight men fined by the court "for not rendering their accounts as guardians," suggesting that Calthorpe may have married a widow.[9] He served as commissioner of York County but was replaced by order of the Governor, 24 April 1661, as he had gone Southward.[10]

On 13 Aug. 1661 Christopher[1] Calthorpe, "late of the New Poquoson and now of Carolina to the South of Virginia," gave power of attorney to Armiger

---

[5] *Ibid.*, p. 227. The boundary line between the present York County and Elizabeth City County (Hampton since 1952) is the Northwest Branch of Back River (formerly the Old Poquoson) and Bethel Reservoir (formerly the headwaters of the Old Poquoson). The Poquoson River (formerly New Poquoson), flowing into Chesapeake Bay, lies in York County.

[6] *Ibid.*, pp. 347, 368. Waters' Creek has been dammed to form Lake Maury, now enclosed within the part of the Mariners Museum, Newport News.

[7] "Thropland," in 1956 a farm of 100 acres, the property of the Sinclair and Smith families, adjoins Calthorpe Neck Road which traverses land originally part of the plantation.

[8] Anthony Yonge, citizen and grocer of London, in his will, 23 Feb. 1635/6-1 Dec. 1636 (P.C.C. 118 Pile, in *V* XV, p. 177), bequeathed 500 pounds of tobacco to "the church of the newe Poquoson" in Virginia. New Poquoson Parish embraced the region between Back Creek and the [New] Poquoson River and included in its bay frontage section in York now known as *Crab Neck* and *Fish Neck*. Westward the parish probably extended to the Warwick County line. The Parish Register is the earliest extant church record in Virginia, beginning 1644/5, when a minister for the parish was inducted (*MCGC*, p. 502). In 1692 New Poquoson became Charles Parish by Act of the Assembly (see George Carrington Mason, *Colonial Churches of Tidewater Virginia* [Richmond, 1945], pp. 216, 229-33).

[9] York Co. Deeds, Orders, Wills &c 2, 1645-49, p. 184.

[10] York Co. Deeds, Orders, Wills &c 3, 1657-62, p. 117. Southward was the territory with ill-defined boundaries which lay in the region now included in the southeastern part of Virginia and the northeastern part of North Carolina. The location presumably is Perquimans Co., N.C., where in a deposition, 5 Dec. 1687, Richard Watredy, "being designed to go into the Southward about the year 1662," mentioned the "then seated Land of Collo. Caltropp" (Perquimans Co., N.C., Deed Bk. A, #380).

Wade and William Harman of York County to execute a deed, confirmed by Ann Calthorpe.[11] He was a member of the House of Burgesses from York County, 1644-46, 1652-53, 1660, and from Elizabeth City County, 1645,[12] and was captain, major and colonel of militia.

He died before 24 April 1662 when Anne Calthorpe petitioned the court for probate of "the nuncupative will of my deceased husband Coll. Xopher Calthorpe" and gave "bond with very good security."[13] Six months later she submitted an inventory which estimated the estate at 30,380 pounds of tobacco and cask. Omitted from the account was "the land here and at Southward" and she noted that she would given an account of the latter when it came to "her hand."[14] Anne Calthorpe died 9 Dec. 1667 before her husband's estate was divided among the heirs. On 21 Jan. 1667/8 the three daughters, Elinor[2] and Barbara[2] Calthorpe, aged 21 years and upwards, and Ann[2] Calthorpe, aged 16 years and upwards, by their "loving friend Mr. William Harman," petitioned the court for a division and on 24 Jan. 1667/8, upon petition of "James Calthorpe & his sisters Mrs. Ellinor, Barbary & Anne Calthorpe," the court ordered that the "Estate of their Deced Father & Mother be equally divided between them."[15]

Issue: 2. JAMES[2]; 3. Elinor[2], born in the 1630s and named as "Sister Elliner Ragge" in the 1688 will of James[2] Calthorpe, married, by 7 Sept. 1674,[16] Thomas Wragg who was listed in her father's inventory as an indentured servant with seven years to serve[17] and held 500 acres in James City County, 1704; 4. Barbara[2], buried 28 July 1680; 5. Ann[2], buried 7 April 1685.

2. JAMES[2] CALTHORPE (Christopher[1]) served as a justice of York County. He died 3 Aug. 1689 leaving a will, 10 Oct. 1688-26 May 1690, which gave a plantation to his sister Elliner Ragge for her life, another to his wife, unnamed, for life, land under ninety-nine year leases to his sons James and

---

[11] York Co. Deeds, Orders, Wills &c 3, 1657-62, p. 157.

[12] *Dictionary of Virginia Biography*, II (Richmond, 2001), pp. 524-25; Leonard, pp. 22-24, 30-31, 36, spelled Callthrop, Calthrope, Calthropp, Caulthropp and Coltrop.

[13] York Co. Deeds, Orders, Wills &c 3, p. 161.

[14] *Ibid.*, p. 189.

[15] York Co. Deeds, Orders, Wills &c 4, pp. 162, 166.

[16] York Co. Deeds, Orders, Wills &c 5, 1672-76, p. 80, deed of Ellenor Ragg of New Poquoson, with consent of Thomas Ragg, of a cow to Goddaughter Mary Dunning

[17] See note 14. The modern interpretation of the term servant is employee. With opportunities for schooling meager, the system of training was through indenture by which young men bound themselves to serve a number of years under experienced elders.

Elestrange and another tract not yet patented to his son Charles, mentioned his daughters Elizabeth and Barbary and his son Christopher (who by primogeniture would inherit the balance of his real estate), and provided that if his sons died without issue the land should go to "the first Calthorpe that shall personally appear out of England ... of the race of Sir Christopher Calthorpe or of Edward or of John Calthorpe, the two sons of my unckle Edward Calthorpe," and if none appeared to make claim, to the use of a school and the church of New Poquoson Parish.[18]

He married (1) Elizabeth ___ and (2) Mary ___, who died 24 Aug. 1698.

Issue: (by 1) 6. Ann[3], born 15 Feb. 1671/2, died 7 Dec. 1673; 7. Christopher[3], born 20 Feb. 1672/3, died 27 June 1694, unmarried, whose will, 22 June 1694-24 Aug. 1694, named his brothers James and Charles and sister Barbary Calthorpe;[19] 8. JAMES[3]; 9. Elizabeth[3], born 26 Nov. 1677, died 21 Aug. 1698; 10. ELESTRANGE[3]; 11. BARBARA[3]; 12. CHARLES[3].

8. JAMES[3] CALTHORPE (James[2], Christopher[1]), born 5 March 1674/5, married Elizabeth ___. He held 900 acres in York County, 1704, and was master and owner of the *James of Virginia*, built in North Carolina in 1688, which traded in York River, 1699.[20] He died 21 Dec. 1711 leaving will 19 Dec. 1711-21 Jan. 1711/2.[21]

Issue: 13. ELIMELECH[4]; 14. Ruth[4], twin, born 6 Jan. 1710/11.

10. ELESTRANGE[3] CALTHORPE (James[2], Christopher[1]), born 4 Sept. 1680, married (1) Mary Butts, born 4 Sept. 1684, died 24 Oct. 1718, daughter of Anthony and Mary Butts, and (2) Anne ___ who died 31 March 1734. He died 4 Oct. 1726 and the inventory of his estate was recorded 19 June 1727.[22]

Issue: (by 1) 15. James[4], born 27 March 1707, died 2 Nov. 1744, "singleman," who left will, 20 Oct. 1744-17 Dec. 1744, which mentioned his brothers Charles and John;[23] 16. CHARLES[4]; 17. Anthony[4], born 4 Aug. 1712,

---

[18] York Co. Deeds, Orders, Wills &c 8, 1687-91, pp. 427-29. Sir Christopher Calthorpe was the only child of his father's eldest brother, James Calthorpe, and was then unmarried; Edward Calthorpe was his father's next younger brother.

[19] York Co. Deeds, Orders, Wills &c 9, 1691-94, p. 38.

[20] Louis des Cognets, *English Duplicates of Lost Virginia Records* (Princeton, N.J., 1958), p. 284.

[21] York Co. Orders, Wills &c 14, pp. 127-28.

[22] York Co. Deeds, Orders, Wills &c 16, pp. 459, 462.

[23] York Co. Orders, Wills & Inventories 19, pp. 335-36.

died 2 Oct. 1712; 18. JOHN[4]; (by 2) 19. Elizabeth[4], born 21 Dec. 1722, died 7 Aug. 1726.

    11. BARBARA[3] CALTHORPE (James[2], Christopher[1]), born 23 May 1683, died 22 Dec. 1711. She married Henry Freeman of Charles Parish, born 20 Nov. 1675, died 4 April 1720, son of Henry and Martha Freeman, who left will 29 Dec. 1720 [1719]-16 May 1720, which named his (2) wife Elinor, sons Calthorp and John, daughter Ann Freeman and "all my children."[24]

    Issue: [FREEMAN] 20. Elizabeth[4], born 26 May 1702, died 4 Sept. 1702; 21. ANNAMARIA[4]; 22. Calthorpe[4], born 4 Sept. 1706; 23. John[4], born 18 March 1708/9; 24. Charles[4], twin, born 24 Nov. 1711, died 29 Jan. 1711/2; 25. Henry[4], born 24 Nov. 1711.

    12. CHARLES[3] CALTHORPE (James[2], Christopher[1]), born 17 Feb. 1687/8, married Amy ___. A patent for 165 acres in New Poquoson Parish was issued to him 20 Oct. 1691,[25] pursuant to his father's will. He died 16 Dec. 1718 leaving a will, 14 Dec. 1718-19 Jan. 1718/9, which named his wife Amy, brother-in-law Henry Freeman, and "Cousin Charles Calthorp, son of Elestrange Calthorpe, my brother."[26]

    Issue: 26. Elestrange[4], born 21 July 1718, died 22 July 1718.

    13. ELIMELECH[4] CALTHORPE (James[3], James[2], Christopher[1]), twin, born 6 Jan. 1710/11, died 14 Jan. 1733/4, married, by 1729, Mary Robinson, daughter of John and Frances (Wade) Robinson, who married (2) Peter Goodwin.[27]

    Issue:[28] 27. FRANCES[5]; 28. James[5], born 2 June 1731, died 14 Oct. 1732; 29. John[5], born 19 Feb. 1732/3, died 26 Feb. 1732/3; 30. Mary[5], married 77. *Robert[5] Smith* (see MARTIAU).

    16. CHARLES[4] CALTHORPE (Elestrange[3], James[2], Christopher[1]), born 8 Oct. 1709, moved to Nottoway Parish, then Isle of Wight, later Southampton, County, where he purchased 400 acres from the Nottoway Indians, 4 April

---

[24] York Co. Orders, Wills &c 15, p. 597.

[25] Patent Bk. 8, p. 202.

[26] York Co. Orders, Wills &c 15, pp. 379-80.

[27] York Co. Deeds, Orders, Wills &c 18, p. 413; Orders, Wills & Inventories 19, p. 471.

[28] Charles Parish Register.

1742,[29] and left will 8 Nov. 1756-14 April 1763.[30] He married Elinor Clifton, born 13 March 1713/4, left will 7 April 1772-12 Jan. 1775.[31]

Issue:[32] 31. Butts[5], born Dec. 1731, died 17 Oct. 1739; 32. Mary[5], baptized 10 Feb. 1733/4, married John Bayley; 33. SARAH[5]; 34. FRANCES[5]; 35. JAMES[5]; 36. Edward[5], of Southampton County, inherited his father's York County land, which he sold, 29 March 1768,[33] living 1772; 37. Anthony[5], sold 425 acres where he lived, 16 March 1784,[34] and died by 13 Dec. 1794 when his widow Mary ___ relinquished dower in that land;[35] 38. JAMES BUTTS[5]; 39. Elizabeth[5], baptized 19 Aug. 1739; 40. MARTHA[5]; 41. ANNE[5]; 42. ELENER CLIFTON[5]; 43. Diana[5], under 21 in 1764, married, (bond 12) Jan. 1775,[36] Silas Kirby of Southampton County.

18. JOHN[4] CALTHORPE (Elestrange[3], James[2], Christopher[1]) moved to Isle of Wight, later Southampton, County where he purchased 250 acres on the west side of Flatt Swamp, 17 Feb. 1745,[37] and with wife Sarah ___ sold 5 acres to William Blunt, 10 Jan. 1772.[38] He left will 14 April 1785-15 Oct. 1791.[39]

Issue: 44. John[6], probably the John who moved to Mecklenburg County and married, (bond 10) Feb. 1784,[40] Mary Crowder; 45. James[6], sold 17 Jan. 1792, one acre, a part of the land of John Calthorp, deceased,[41] left will 31 Jan. 1799-

---

[29] Southampton Co. Deed Bk. 4, p. 227, sale by his son Anthony to whom he devised the land.

[30] Southampton Co. Will Bk. 2, pp. 30-31, which in probate entry erroneously names his wife as Sarah (see Southampton Co. Chancery papers, Tyler *vs.* Calthorpe, 1764).

[31] Southampton Co. Will Bk. 3, p. 118.

[32] Charles Parish Register; wills of parents; Southampton Co. Guardians' bonds, in *The Virginia Genealogist*, XXV, p. 133; Tyler *vs.* Calthorpe, *loc. cit.*

[33] York Co. July 24, 2002eeds & Bonds 7, pp. 419-21.

[34] Southampton Co. Deed Bk. 6, p. 295.

[35] Southampton Co. Deed Bk. 8, pp. 192-93.

[36] Catherine Lindsay Knorr, *Marriage Bonds and Ministers' Returns of Southampton County, Virginia, 1750-1810* (Pine Bluff, Ark., 1955), p. 69.

[37] Isle of Wight Co. Deed Bk. 7, p. 275.

[38] Southampton Co. Deed Bk. 5, p. 333.

[39] Southampton Co. Will Bk. 4, p. 451.

[40] Katherine B. Elliott, *Marriage Records, 1765-1816, Mecklenburg County, Virginia* (South Hill, Va., 1963), p. 25. John Calthorp was named as son-in-law in the will of James Hamner, 14 Dec. 1792-14 Jan. 1793 (Mecklenburg Co. Will Bk. 3, p. 144).

[41] Southampton Co. Unrecorded deed, in *The Southside Virginian*, II, p. 168.

12 Dec. 1793;[42] 46. Henry[6], married, 8 Aug. 1780,[43] Edy Harris; 47. Nowell[6].

21. ANNAMARIA[4] FREEMAN (Barbara[3] Calthorpe, James[2], Christopher[1]), born 22 Oct. 1703, died after 1783.[44] She married John Wellons, who left will 18 Dec. 1773-6 Oct. 1778.[45] On 13 April 1749 he purchased 850 acres in Nottoway Parish[46] and moved to Southampton County where, 12 April 1753, they sold 200 acres out of this tract.[47].

Issue: [WELLONS][48] 48. JOHN[5]; 49. HENRY[5]; 50. CHARLES[5]; 51. Barbara[5], born 13 April 1735, married, (bond 17) May 1756,[49] Benjamin Oney; 52. William[5], born 10 Feb. 1737/8, died young; 53. ELIZABETH[5]; 54. Anna Maria[5], born 30 May 1743, died young; 55. Mary[5], born 18 March 1745, died young.

27. FRANCES[5] CALTHORPE (Elimelech[4], James[3], James[2], Christopher[1]), born 19 Sept. 1729, married Henry Howard of York County, who married (2), (bond 12) May 1777,[50] Martha ___, widow of Richard Sclater, and left will 10 Nov. 1781-17 June 1782.[51]

Issue: [HOWARD] 56. Mary[6], born 1746, died 2 Oct. 1747; 57. Francis[6], born 7 Jan. 1748/9, died young; 58. John[6], born 19 Dec. 1750, died 22 Aug. 1752; 59. Elizabeth[4], born 15 Aug. 1752, died after 1817; 60. Henry[6], born 1 July 1755, died 2 March 1756; 61. Edward Calthorpe[6], born 1757, died 1810, married Sarah Russell, born 8 May 1753, died 24 Jan. 1816;[52] 62. William[6], born 23 Feb. 1759, left will 23 March 1811-18 Oct. 1813,[53] married, (bond 24) Nov. 1777,[54] 148. Anne[6] Chisman (see CHISMAN), born 28 Aug. 1755,

---

[42] Southampton Co. Will Bk. 4, p. 600.

[43] Southampton Co. Marriage return, in *The Southside Virginian*, I, p. 69.

[44] Southampton Co. Land tax list 1783, taxed for 100 acres as Ann Mary.

[45] Southampton Co. Will Bk. 3, p. 230.

[46] Isle of Wight Co. Deed Bk. 8, 1747-52, p.256.

[47] Southampton Co. Deed Bk. 1, pp. 475-78.

[48] Charles Parish Register.

[49] Knorr, *Marriage Bonds ... Southampton County*, p. 82.

[50] Michael Pollock, *York County, Virginia, Marriages ... 1769-1853* (Athens, Ga., 1994), p. 64.

[51] York Co. Wills & Inventories 22, 1771-83, pp. 516-19.

[52] *W(1)* XI, pp. 264-66.

[53] York Co. Will Bk. 10, 1811-24, p. 83.

[54] Pollock, *op. cit.*, p. 65; *Virginia Gazette*, 12 Dec. 1777.

perhaps the Nancy Howard who was buried 15 Jan. 1832;[55] 63. Martha[6], born 4 Oct. 1761, married, (bond 13) Dec. 1784,[56] John Russell; 64. Francis[6], born about 1763, left will 18 April 1801-20 July 1801,[57] married (1) Elizabeth Robinson and (2) Ann Booker, who married (2) Richard Kerby and left will 8 Jukly 1812-19 Oct. 1812;[58] 65. Lucy[6], born 23 Jan. 1764, died after 1808, married, as his (2) wife, the Rev. Samuel Sheild, who was a student at the College of William and Mary, 1769, and its Botetourt medalist, 1773, minister of Drysdale Parish, King and Queen and Caroline counties, 1776, St. Asaph's Parish, 1785, York-Hampton Parish, 1786, and Charles Parish, 1790, was the minority choice for Bishop of Virginia, 1786 and 1790,[59] and died 1803;[60] 66. Henry[6], born about 1766.

33. SARAH[5] CALTHORPE (Charles[4], Elestrange[3], James[2], Christopher[1]), born March 1734/5. married, (bond 10) Aug. 1758,[61] Edmund Tyler.

Issue: [TYLER] 67. Jeremiah[6], left will 4 Feb. 1789-10 Dec. 1789,[62] married, (bond 7) Feb. 1783,[63] Elizabeth[7] Jarrell, daughter of Benjamin Jarrell and 88. Mary[6] Jones (see BENNETT, Edward), who married (2), (bond 10) Oct. 1792,[64] John Miles and died 1830 at Suffolk.[65]

34. FRANCES[5] CALTHORPE (Charles[4], Elestrange[3], James[2], Christopher[1]), born 6 Sept. 1737, died before 1811 in Person Co., N.C. She married Jesse Jones, son of William and Elizabeth (____) Jones,[66] of Sussex County, whom she joined in selling in three tracts, Nov. 1777, the land on Round Hill Swamp which he had patented 12 May 1759.[67] They moved to Caswell Co.,

---

[55] A. Bohmer Rudd, *Shockoe Hill Cemetery, Richmond, Virginia, Register of Interments*, I (Washington, 1960), p. 10, as aged 70.

[56] Pollock, *op. cit.*, p. 113.

[57] York Co. Wills & Inventories 23, pp. 579-80.

[58] York Co. Will Bk. 10, pp. 51-52.

[59] Edward Lewis Goodwin, *The Colonial Church in Virginia* (London, 1927), p. 306.

[60] *Norfolk Herald*, 22 Feb. 1803.

[61] Knorr, *op. cit.*, p. 106.

[62] Southampton Co. Will Bk. 4, p. 345.

[63] Knorr, *op. cit.*, p. 106.

[64] *Ibid.*, p. 75.

[65] Lyndon Hobbs Hart and Bromfield Bradford Nichol, *Ridley of Southampton* (n.p., 1992), p. 569.

[66] John Anderson Brayton, "The Descendants of Edward Jones, Sr. ..." (to be published in *Colonial Families of Surry and Isle of Wight Counties, Virginia*), p. 158.

[67] Southampton Co. Deed Bk. 5, pp. 240, 242, 243.

N.C., where he left will 28 Jan. 17880-Sept. 1780.[68]

Issue: [JONES][69] 68. Sally[6], died 1846,[70] married, (bond 19) Dec. 1786,[71] John Brown of Person Co., N.C., who died May 1837;[72] 69. Drury[6], died 1834, unmarried;[73] 70. Goodrich[6], died 25 Nov. 1828,[74] of Person Co., N.C., married Mary ___; 71. Willson[6], died about 1824 in Giles Co., Tenn.,[75] married, (bond 26) March 1803,[76] Rebecka McKissick.

35. JAMES[5] CALTHORPE (Charles[4], Elestrange[3], James[2], Christopher[1]), born 23 Jan. 1740/1, died by 25 April 1795 when his estate was appraised.[77] He married, (bond 2) Aug. 1775,[78] Lucy Bailey.

Issue:[79] 72. Mary Bailey[6], named in will of grandfather Barnaby Bailey, for whom Stephenson Blake gave bond as guardian, 20 Aug. 1798;[80] 73. Lucy[6].

38. JAMES BUTTS[5] CALTHORPE (Charles[4], Elestrange[3], James[2], Christopher[1]) chose Edward Calthorpe as his guardian, 12 Jan. 1769.[81] He married Lucy ____, who joined him, 22 Aug. 1777, in selling 375 acres he inherited from his father.[82]

Issue: 74. Mary[6], for whom John Hawkins Pond gave bond as guardian, 11 Dec. 1794.[83]

40. MARTHA[5] CALTHORPE (Charles[4], Elestrange[3], James[2], Christopher[1]) married Jonathan Bowen [Bowing], who moved to Franklin Co.,

---

[68] Caswell Co., N.C., Will Bk. A, p. 104.

[69] Brayton, *op. cit.*, pp. 162, 342-50.

[70] Person Co., N.C., Estate records, Sally Brown, 1846.

[71] Katharine Kerr Kendall, *Caswell County, North Carolina, Marriage Bonds, 1778-1868* (n.p., 1981), p. 15.

[72] Person Co., N.C., Estate records, John Brown, 1837.

[73] *Ibid.*, Drury Jones, 1834.

[74] *Ibid.*, Goodrich Jones, 1828.

[75] Giles Co., Tenn., Minute Bk. 1823-25, p. 296.

[76] Katharine Kerr Kendall, *Person County, North Carolina, Marriage Records, 1792-1868* (n.p., 1983), p. 48.

[77] Southampton Co. Will Bk. 4, p. 684.

[78] Knorr, *op. cit.*, p. 24.

[79] Southampton Co. Will Bk. 4, p. 42, will of Barnaby Bailey, 1 Sept. 1783-18 Nov. 1783.

[80] Southampton Co. Guardian's bond, in *The Virginia Genealogist*, XXV, pp. 133-34.

[81] Southampton Co. Order Bk. 1768-72, p. 118.

[82] Southampton Co. Deed Bk. 5, p. 320.

[83] Southampton Co. Guardian's bond, in *The Virginia Genealogist*, XXV, p. 133.

Ga., and died before Feb. 1796 when she gave bond as his administrator.[84]

Issue: [BOWEN][85] 75. Charles Butts[6], of Washington Co., Ga., when he purchased two tracts each of 202½ acres in Jones Co., Ga., 16 Dec. 1808 and 31 July 1809,[86] left will 15 June 1827-2 July 1827,[87] married (1) Eliza Williams and (2) Susan Pratt; 76. Edwin[6]; 77. Betsey[6]; 78. John[6].

41. ANNE[5] CALTHORPE (Charles[4], Elestrange[3], James[2], Christopher[1]) married, (bond 14) Nov. 1770,[88] James Summerell, who left will 24 Feb. 1800-21 July 1800.[89]

Issue: [SUMMERELL] 79. Silas[6]; 80. Lemuel Butts[6]; 81. Lucretia[6], married 103. Drewry [Drury][6] Branch; 82. Diana[6], married, (bond 30) Nov. 1803,[90] Benjamin Brister; 83. Sally[6]; 84. Eleanor[6].

42. ELENER CLIFTON[5] CALTHORPE (Charles[4], Elestrange[3], James[2], Christopher[1]), under 21 in 1764, married, (bond 29) April 1782,[91] John Hawkins Pond of Southampton County, who left will 23 July 1830-23 April 1832.[92]

Issue: [POND][93] 85. Calthorpe[6], died before 1825, of Southampton County, married (1), (bond 13 Sept. 1810,[94] Nancy Vick and (2), 20 Jan. 1814,[95] Harriet Whitehead, who married (2) James B. Wellons of Southampton County; 86. Patrick[6], died by 1822 when John H. Pond qualified as his administrator; 87. Peter[6], died by 1822 when John H. Pond qualified as his administrator, married, 23 April 1807,[96] Anna[7] Wellons, daughter of 90. William[6] Wellons; 88.

---

[84] Martha Walters Acker, *Franklin County, Georgia, Court of Ordinary Records, 1787-1849* (Birmingham, Ala., 1989), p. 4.

[85] Southampton Co. Deed Bk. 5, p. 249, deed, 2 Jan. 1777, of James Butts Calthorpe to sister Martha's children.

[86] Jones Co., Ga., Deed Bk. A, pp. 407-09, in *Georgia Genealogical Magazine*, no. 41, Summer 1971, p. 285.

[87] Jones Co., Ga., Will Bk. Will Bk. C, pp. 158-60.

[88] Knorr, *op. cit.*, p. 100.

[89] Southampton Co. Will Bk. 5, p. 197.

[90] *Ibid.*, p. 19.

[91] *Ibid.*, p. 86.

[92] Southampton Co. Will Bk. 11A, p. 12.

[93] Calthorpe, Patrick and Peter are indicated in Southall Papers, Earl Gregg Swem Library, College of William and Mary, folder 172, James City County.

[94] Southampton Co. Marriage Register, 1759-1853, p. 202.

[95] *Ibid.*, p. 666.

[96] *Ibid.*, p. 654.

Hawkins[6], married, 23 Nov. 1815,[97] Eliza C. Brittle; 89. Eleanor C.[6], married, 23 April 1823,[98] John Exum.

48. JOHN[5] WELLONS (Annamaria[4] Freeman, Barbara[3] Calthorpe, James[2], Christopher[1]), born 19 Oct. 1725, left will 16 July 1784-10 Dec. 1790.[99] He married Mary ___.

Issue: [WELLONS][100] 90. William[6], left will June 1810-18 Aug. 1810,[101] married (1), 25 Feb. 1783,[102] Anna Vasser and (2), (bond 20) Dec. 1784,[103] Mary Pond; 91. Benjamin[6], married, 26 Feb. 1783,[104] Lucretia Clarke, who left will 13 Oct. 1813-Nov. 1814;[105] 92. Rebecca[6], married Robert Exum, of Southampton County, who left will 7 Jan. 1804-20 Feb. 1810.[106]

49. HENRY[5] WELLONS (Annamaria[4] Freeman, Barbara[3] Calthorpe, James[2], Christopher[1]), born 30 July 1728, left will 10 June 1779-13 May 1784.[107] He married Eleanor ___.

Issue: [WELLONS] 93. Henry[6], as of Pulaski Co., Ky., and legatee of his father Henry Wellons, sold his one-fifth interest in 200 acres to his brother John;[108] 94. John[6]; 95. Robert[6]; 96. (perhaps) Charles[6], born 1762 in Southampton County, died 25 May 1840 in Johnston Co., N.C., served six short tours in Southampton County militia, 1778-81, moved to Johnston Co., N.C., 1783 or 1784, married there, 17 March 1782, Bethany ____, who died after 1850;[109] 97. (Child)[6].

50. CHARLES[5] WELLONS (Annamaria[4] Freeman, Barbara[3] Calthorpe, James[2], Christopher[1]) left will Jan. 1803-17 Dec. 1804.[110] He married ___.

Issue: [WELLONS] 98. Robert[6], deeded 100 acres by his father, Dec.

---

[97] *Ibid.*, p. 665.

[98] *Ibid.*, p. 690.

[99] Southampton Co. Will Bk. 4, p. 393.

[100] Southampton Co. Deed Bk. 7, p. 447.

[101] Southampton Co. Will Bk. 6, pp. 107-08.

[102] Knorr, *op. cit.*, p. 112.

[103] *Ibid.*

[104] *Ibid.*

[105] Johnston Co., N.C., Will Bk. 1, p. 399.

[106] Southampton Co. Will Bk. 5, pp. 469-70.

[107] Southampton Co. Will Bk. 4, p. 58.

[108] Southampton Co. Deed Bk. 13, pp. 323-25.

[109] Revolutionary War pension application, Charles Wellons, widow Bethany, W.3903, National Archives.

[110] Southampton Co. Will Bk. 6, pp. 4-5.

1800,[111] married, (bond 14) Jan. 1786,[112] Sally [Silvier] Wooton; 99. Westwood[6], left will 8 May 1806-21 July 1806,[113] married, 18 Nov. 1784,[114] Anna Gardiner; 100. Charles[6], married, 23 Dec. 1784,[115] Sarah Clarke; 101. Shadrack[6]; 102. Sally[6], married, 29 Dec. 1785,[116] Shadrack Worrell.

53. ELIZABETH[5] WELLONS (Annamaria[4] Freeman, Barbara[3] Calthorpe, James[2], Christopher[1]), born 25 Sept. 1740. She married Howell Branch, who left will 12 Oct. 1781-8 Nov. 1781.[117]

Issue: [BRANCH] 103. Drewry [Drury][6], married, (bond 1) March 1791,[118] 81. Lucretia[6] Summerell; 104. Peter[6], married, (bond 13) July 1796,[119] Patsy Britt; 105. Jesse[6], married (1), (bond 20) Sept. 1803,[120] Olive Holden and (2), (bond 9) March 1809,[121] Betsey Britt; 106. Martha[6].

---

[111] Southampton Co. Deed Bk. 9, pp. 314-15.

[112] Knorr, *op. cit.*, p. 112.

[113] Southampton Co. Will Bk. 6, p. 333.

[114] Knorr, *op. cit.*, as Western.

[115] *Ibid.*

[116] Knorr, *op. cit.*, p. 121.

[117] Southampton Co. Will Bk. 3, p. 346.

[118] Knorr, *op. cit.*, p. 17.

[119] *Ibid.*, p. 18.

[120] *Ibid.*

[121] *Ibid.*

CALVERT[1]

+1. GEORGE[1] CALVERT, born 1578 or 1579 at Kiplin, Yorkshire, was the son of Leonard Calvert and his wife Alice Crossland, daughter of John Crossland of Crossland, Yorkshire.[2] He matriculated at Trinity College, Oxford, 28 June 1594, aged 14, and received his B.A. 23 Feb. 1596/7.[3] He was a member of the Virginia Company and a subscriber to the Second Charter, 1609. He served as Under Secretary of State, Clerk of the Privy Council, 1605, was knighted 29 Sept. 1617, was member of Parliament for Bossiney, 1609-11, for York, 1620-22, and for Oxford University, 1624-25, and Secretary of State, Feb. 1618/9-1625. Admitted to the New England Company, 1622, he received a grant for the whole of Newfoundland, but the following year, by Royal Charter, was assigned the southeast peninsula of that land which he called the province of Avalon. Over this domain Calvert was given almost royal authority. He resigned all his preferments, Feb. 1624/5, having become a Roman Catholic, and was elevated to the Irish peerage, 16 Feb. 1624/5, as Baron Baltimore of Baltimore. In the summer of 1628 he took to Avalon his wife Lady Joane Baltimore, his family (except his eldest son Cecil[2]) and about forty colonists.[4]

The rigors of the climate proved too much a hardship for Lady Baltimore,[5] who sailed for Virginia, spending her time at Jamestown. Lord Baltimore followed her there, arriving Oct. 1629 "to view those parts," but met with a "cowlde" reception, the colonists fearing that the King might grant him a charter for the whole of Virginia. He was tendered the oath of supremacy, which he refused on account of his religion. The modified form of the oath agreeable to

---

[1] George Edward Cokayne, *The Complete Peerage*, I (2nd ed.; London, 1910), pp. 393-95.; Br. *Gen.*, pp. 841-42; John Bailey Calvert Nicklin, "Calvert Family," *MHM* XVI, pp. 50-59, 189-204, 313-18, 389-94; Ella Foy O'Gorman, *Descendants of Virginia Calverts* (n.p., 1947).

[2] Joseph Foster, ed., *The Visitation of Yorkshire ... 1612* (London, 1875), p. 500; Francis B. Culver, "Maternal Ancestry of Sir George Calvert," *MHM* XXIX, pp. 330-31; James W. Foster, "George Calvert: His Yorkshire Boyhood," *MHM* LV, pp. 261-74.

[3] Joseph Foster, *Alumni Oxonienses ... 1500-1714*, I (Oxford and London, 1891), p. 232.

[4] His son Leonard[2] Calvert and his son-in-law William Peaseley returned to England on the ship carrying a letter from Lord Baltimore. Leonard[2] petitioned the King that his father might have a share in certain prizes taken from the French by the ships *Benediction* and *Victory* (O'Gorman, *op. cit.*, pp. 56-57).

[5] Baltimore's letter to the King, dated "Ferryland," 19 Aug. 1629 (William Hand Browne, ed., *Proceedings of the Council of Maryland, 1636-1667* [*Archives of Maryland*, III; Baltimore, 1885], pp. 15-16).

him was not agreeable to the Virginia authorities. Consequently Lord Baltimore departed for England and upon his arrival there, 1630, sought a charter for land south of the James River. He was unsuccessful in securing this favor but the King finally agreed to assign him lands north and east of the Potomac.

Before the charter for this territory passed the seals, Lord Baltimore had died and was buried, 15 April 1632, at St. Dunstan's-in-the-West, London. He left a will, 14 April 1632-21April 1632, and his son and heir received the title to the Maryland[6] Charter, 20 June 1632.

George[1] Calvert married (1), 22 Nov. 1604, at St. Peter's Cornhill, London,[7] Anne Mynne, died 8 Aug. 1621, aged 42 years, 9 months, 18 days,[8] daughter of George Mynne of Hertingfordbury, Hertfordshire, and his wife Elizabeth Wroth, and (2), 1622-27, Joane ____, who sailed from Jamestown to England with several of Lord Baltimore's children in the *St. Claude*. The ship wrecked off the English coast before Oct. 1630, with the loss of all aboard.[9]

Issue:[10] (by 1) 2. CECELIUS[2]; 3. Ann[2], baptized 1 April 1607, died after 1672, married, before 1627, William Peaseley, who went to Avalon and returned; 4. Dorothy[2], baptized 18 Aug. 1608, buried 13 Jan. 1623/4; 5. Elizabeth[2], baptized 18 Nov. 1609, probably lost at sea with her step-mother; 6. LEONARD[2]; 7. GRACE[2]; 8. George[2], baptized 8 July 1613, drowned during a heavy storm in Virginia, left will 10 July 1634-19 Jan. 1634/5;[11] 9. Francis[2], living 20 March 1627/8 but not mentioned in his father's will, probably lost at sea with his step-mother; 10. HELLEN[2]; 11. Henry[2], baptized 8 March 1617/8, died at sea or abroad, unmarried, before 25 Nov. 1635 when administration on his estate was granted to his brother Cecil[2]; 12. John[2], baptized 31 Jan. 1618/9,

---

[6] Named in honor of the Queen of Charles I, Henrietta Maria.

[7] Granville W. G. Leveson Gower, ed., *A Register of all the Christninges, Burialls & Weddinges within the Parish of Saint Peeters Upon Cornhill* (Harleian Society, *Registers*, I; London, 1877), p. 244.

[8] Tombstone, St. Mary's Church, Hertingfordbury, Herts., in John Edwin Cussans, *History of Hertfordshire*, II, Hundred of Hertford (London and Hertford, 1876), p. 108, which names her ten children.

[9] According to an account of the death of Lady Baltimore by shipwreck, 1670 (Sloane Papers, British Museum, London, quoted in O'Gorman, *op. cit.*, p. 57), she with several of the Calvert children "was cast away" on the voyage from Virginia to England "in which ship his lordship lost a great deal of plate and goods of a great value."

[10] O'Gorman, *op. cit.*, pp. 53-54; *MHM* XXVII, pp. 334-35.

[11] P.C.C. 1 Sadler, in George Sherwood, *American Colonists in English Records*, I (London, 1932), p. 19; *MHM* I, pp. 363-64.

buried 1 Feb. 1618/9; (by 2) 13. PHILIP[2].

2. CECILIUS[2] CALVERT (George[1]), second Lord Baltimore, was born 8 Aug. 1605 and baptized 2 March 1605/6 at Boxley, Kent, and was originally called Cecil. He entered Trinity College, Oxford, 1621, and was admitted to Gray's Inn, 8 Aug. 1633.[12] As heir to the charter promised his father, he promoted, though in England, the settlement of Maryland. He married, (settlement 20) March 1627/8, Anne Arundell, "a most beautiful and accomplished woman," daughter of Thomas Arundell, first Lord Arundell of Wardour and his (2) wife Anne (Philipson) Thurgood. She died 23 July 1649 in her 34th year.[13] He died 30 Nov. 1675, leaving will 22 Nov. 1675-3 Feb. 1675/6,[14] and was buried at St. Giles-in-the-Fields, Middlesex.

Issue:[15] 14. Georgiana[3], born Aug. 1629, died in infancy; 15. Mary[3], born 18 July 1633, died aged 2 weeks; 16. George[3], born 15 Sept. 1634, died 6 June 1636; 17. Frances[3], born Nov. 1635, died 27 Dec. 1635; 18. Ann[3], born 9 Oct. 1636, died 6 May 1661; 19. CHARLES[3]; 20. Mary[3], born 30 Nov. 1638, died without issue 24 Sept. 1671, married, about 1650, Sir William Blakiston, of Gibside, Durham, who was admitted to ray's Inn, 10 Feb. 1640/1, succeeded his father as second Baronet, 1650, and was buried 26 Feb. 1691/2 at Whickham, Durham;[16] 21. Cecilius[3], born 23 Feb. 1639/40, died 4 Feb. 1640/1; 22. Elizabeth[3], buried 16 Jan. 1711/2, on whose estate administration was granted to her brother Charles[3] 25 Jan. 1711/2.[17]

6. LEONARD[2] CALVERT (George[1]), baptized 21 Nov. 1610, went to Avalon but returned to England, Aug. 1628. He was admitted to Gray's Inn, 8 Aug. 1633.[18] As agent for his elder brother, who fitted out the *Ark* and the *Dove* for the voyage across the Atlantic to settle Maryland, he and his brother George[2] sailed with the party from Gravesend, England, 18 Oct. 1633, reaching Maryland 3 March 1633/4. Upon landing the party founded the city of St. Mary's, 25

---

[12] Foster, *Alumni Oxonienses, loc. cit.*; Joseph Foster, *The Register of Admissions to Gray's Inn, 1521-1889* (London, 1889), p. 201.

[13] Monumental inscription, Tisbury, Wilts., in Arthur Collins, *The Peerage of England* (4th ed.; London, 1768), VI, pp. 598-99.

[14] P.C.C. 11 Bence, in *MHM* XXII, pp. 308-14.

[15] *MHM* XXII, p. 308.

[16] G. E. Cokayne, *Complete Baronetage*, II (Exeter, 1902), p. 188.

[17] *MHM* XXII, pp. 326-27.

[18] Foster, *The Register of Admissions ...*, *loc. cit.*

March 1634.[19] Leonard[2] was named by his brother Lieutenant-General of the Province and commissioned Governor, 1637.[20] Summoned by his brother to England, 1643, he is presumed to have married there. His wife, whose name is not known, was probably a member of the large Brent connection. He died at St. Mary's, having made an oral will on his death bed, to which Governor Thomas Greene testified, 19 June 1647,[21] naming Margaret Brent executrix and directing that she should "Take all, & pay all."

Issue: 23. WILLIAM[3]; 24. ANNE[3].

7. GRACE[2] CALVERT (George[1]), baptized 5 Feb. 1611/2, married, about 1630, Sir Robert Talbot, 2nd Baronet, of Cartown, County Kildare, Ireland. He succeeded to the baronetcy in March 1633 and served as a member of Parliament for County Wicklow, June-Oct. 1634. He was attainted in 1642 but was restored to his estates in 1665. Administration on his estate was granted 13 May 1671.[22] She was living 22 Nov. 1675 when bequeathed mourning by her brother Cecilius.[23]

Issue: [TALBOT] 25. Sir William[3], 3rd Baronet, came to Maryland and, 7 Aug. 1670, Cecilius, Lord Baltimore,"... reposing special trust and Confidence in the fidelity and Circumspection in our dear Nephew William Talbot, Esqr. ..." appointed him principal Secretary of the Province, Judge of Probate, public notary and member of the Council, but shortly after 7 June 1671, having succeeded on his father's death as 3rd Baronet, he returned to Ireland,[24] translated from the Latin *The Discoveries of John Lederer* (London, 1672), received a patent for 2000 acres in County Wicklow, 1677, was member for Meath of

---

[19] Harry Wright Newman, *The Flowering of the Maryland Palatinate* (Washington, 1961), pp. 180-84. St. Mary's City was named in honor of the Virgin Mary, it being the Feast of the Annunciation.

[20] Browne, *op. cit.*, III, pp. 49-55.

[21] William Hand Browne, ed., *Judicial and Testamentary Business of the Provincial Court, 1637-1650* (*Archives of Maryland*, IV; Baltimore, 1887), pp. 313-14.

[22] Cokayne,*Complete Baronetage*, I (Exeter, 1900), p. 248; John D'Alton, *Illustrations, Historical and Genealogical, of King James' Irish Army List 1689* (2nd ed.; London, 1861), p. 47.

[23] Will of Cecilius Calvert, note 13. O'Gorman, *op. cit.*, p. 54, states she died 15 Aug. 1672.

[24] William Hand Browne, ed., *Proceedings of the Council of Maryland, 1667-1687/8* (*Archives of Maryland*, V; Baltimore, 1887), pp. 70-75; Donnell MacClure Owings,*His Lordship's Patronage* (Baltimore, 1953), p. 126; *A Biographical Dictionary of the Maryland Legislature, 1635-1789*, II (Baltimore and London, 1985), pp. 797-98.

James II's Parliament at Dublin, 1689, and Master of the Rolls (vice-chancellor) of Ireland, 1689-91, but, as of Kilcarty, County Meath, was attainted in 1691 and his baronetcy forfeited, died without issue, 18 May 1691 in Galway, Ireland, married, (articles 10) Nov. 1683, Anne, daughter of Richard Nugent, Earl of Westmeath, and widow of Lucas, 6th Viscount Dillon of Costello-Gallen, who died 1711;[25] 26. Frances[3], died 1718, married Richard Talbot, of Malahide, County Dublin, Ireland, born 1638, died Aug. 1703, who was appointed Auditor General of Ireland by James II, 16 May 1689, and left descendants in Ireland.[26]

10. HELLEN[2] (ELLEN) CALVERT (George[1]), baptized 5 Dec. 1615, married James Talbot of Ballyconnell, County Cavan, Ireland, son of Walter Talbot, who was aged 10 when his father died in 1625.[27] He was a supporter of Charles I and was appointed high sheriff of County Cavan. He was dispossessed of his estates by the Cromwellian invasion of Ireland, retired for a short time to Dublin until all Papists were ordered to leave the city on pain of death, and then lived for a time in Connaught.[28] He petitioned in 1661 for restoration of his estates. In 1666 he was a signer of the Remonstrance of the Roman Catholic Nobility and Gentry of Ireland to the King.[29] He later made his home at Castle Rubey, County Roscommon.

Issue: [TALBOT] 27. GEORGE[3].

13. PHILIP[2] CALVERT (George[1]), born before 20 March 1627/8, came to Maryland, 1656, with commissions from his brother Cecelius[2] as councillor and Secretary. He served as President of the Council and justice of the Provincial Court until his death, was Secretary of the Province, 1656-60, Treasurer and Receiver General, 1659-60, Governor of Maryland, 1660-61, Deputy Governor, 1669, Chancellor, 1660-82, Commissary General, 1672-82, and mayor of St. Mary's City, 1668-71. He resided at "Pope's Freehold," St. Mary's Co., Md.,

---

[25] *A Biographical Dictionary ..., loc. cit.*; Cokayne, *The Complete Peerage*, IV (London, 1916), p. 359; D'Alton, *op. cit.*, pp. 49-50, 58, 71. He is omitted from the account in the *Complete Baronetage*, I, p. 248.

[26] *Genealogical Memoir of the Antient and Noble Family of Talbot of Malahide, in the County of Dublin* (Dublin, 1829), pp. 8, 10; Melville Henry Massue, Marquis de Ruvigny and Raineval, *The Jacobite Peerage ...* (London and Edinburgh, 1974), p. 246; *Burke's Genealogical and Heraldic History of the Peerage ...* (105th ed.; London, 1970), p. 2607.

[27] D'Alton, *op. cit.*, p. 47.

[28] *Calendar of State Papers Relating to Ireland ... 1663-1665* (London, 1907), pp. 483-84.

[29] *Ibid. ... September 1669-December 1670* (London, 1910), p. 563.

until 1679 and thereafter at "St. Peter's" in that county.[30]

He married (1), before 1656, Anne Wolseley, who accompanied him to Maryland, and (2), 1681, Jane Sewall, daughter of Henry and Jane (Lowe) Sewall and step-daughter of his nephew Charles[3] Calvert, third Lord Baltimore. He died late in Dec. 1682 leaving no issue and Jane Calvert was granted administration on his estate, 26 Feb. 1682/3.[31] As of St. Giles in the Fields, Middlesex, widow, she was buried 17 May 1692. She left will, 13 Jan. 1691/2-11 May 1693, which mentioned her mother, Lady Baltimore, and four god-children.[32]

19. CHARLES[3] CALVERT (Cecilius[2], George[1]), third Lord Baltimore, was born 27 Aug. 1637. He was Receiver General of Maryland, 1660, and was appointed Governor of Maryland by his father, 1661, serving until 1675, was Secretary of the Province, 1665-66, 1667-69, 1673-1673/4, and Collector of the Patuxent.[33] He remained in Maryland until the boundary dispute with William Penn of Pennsylvania required his presence in England, 1684. He died 20 Feb. 1714/5 leaving a will, 29 July 1714-20 May 1715,[34] and was buried at St. Pancras, Middlesex.

He married (1), about 1660, Mary Darnall, daughter of Ralph Darnall of Loughton, Herefordshire; (2), 1666, Jane (Lowe) Sewall, died 19 Jan. 1700/1, daughter of Vincent Lowe and widow of Henry Sewall who had served as Secretary of the Province of Maryland; (3), 6 Dec. 1701, Mary (Bankes) Thorpe, died 13 March 1710/11; and (4) Margaret Charlton, died 20 July 1731, daughter of Thomas Charlton of Hexham, Northumberland, who married (2), 9 Nov. 1718, Laurence Eliot of Yapton Place, Sussex, was buried at St. Pancras, and as Margaret, Lady Baltimore, left will 15 July 1731-21 July 1731.[35]

Issue:[36] (by 1) 28. Cecil[4], born 1661, buried 1 July 1681 at St. Giles-in-the-

---

[30] Browne, ed.,*Proceedings of the Council of Maryland, 1636-1667*, pp. 327-29, 392; *A Biographical Dictionary* ..., I (Baltimore and London, 1979), pp. 191-92.

[31] Maryland Testamentary Proceedings 13, p. 8.

[32] P.C.C. 77 Coker, in *MHM XXII*, pp. 324-26.

[33] Browne, ed., *Proceedings of the Council of Maryland, 1636-1667*, p. 439; *A Biographical Dictionary* ..., I, p. 187.

[34] P.C.C. 82 Fagg, in *MHM XXII*, pp. 327-30.

[35] P.C.C. 172 Isham, in *ibid.*, pp. 330-32.

[36] Cokayne, *The Complete Peerage*, I, p. 394. For discussion of the identity of Governor Charles Calvert (1680-1733), presumably son of the third Lord Baltimore but almost certainly illegitimate, see *MHM XIV*, pp. 317-18.

Fields; (by 2) 29. Clare[4], born 1670, died before 1694, married, about 1690, the Hon. Edward Maria Somersett; 30. Anne[4], born 1673, died 10 Feb. 1731/2, married (1), 26 May 1694, the Hon. Edward Maria Somersett, her sister's widower, and (2) William Paston of Horton, Gloucestershire; 31. BENEDICT LEONARD[4].

23. WILLIAM[3] CALVERT (Leonard[2], George[1]), born about 1643, was described in the petition of his guardian, 1661, to the Council of Maryland as "sonne and heire unto said Leonard Calvert" and heir of land patented by Leonard[2] in 1641.[37] He served as a member of the Lower House of the Maryland Assembly from St. Mary's County, 1663-64, 1666, and of the Upper House, 1669-82, was Attorney General, 1666-69, Secretary of the Province and judge of probate, 1669-70, 1673/4-1682, member of the Council and justice of the Provincial Court, 1669-82, alderman of St. Mary's City, 1668-71, and was colonel of militia by 1679 and commander of foot in St. Mary's County, 1681.[38] He died before 9 Jan. 1682/3 when administration on his estate was granted to his widow Elizabeth.[39]

He married, before 5 Nov. 1662, 25. *Elizabeth[3] Stone* (see GRAVES). She was living in Virginia with her son Richard about 1698.[40]

Issue: 32. CHARLES[4]; 33. ELIZABETH[4]; 34. (perhaps) George[4]; 35. (perhaps) William[4], of St. Mary's Co., Md., born 1670, died after 1696; 36. Richard[4], born 1672, died 11 Nov. 1718, unmarried; 37. (perhaps) Joshua[4], died 1733.

24. ANNE[3] CALVERT (Leonard[2], George[1]), born about 1645, came to Maryland, 1663. Her cousin Governor Charles[3] Calvert wrote his father, the second Lord Baltimore, Sept. 1663, that "att the same time my cozen Wms. sister arrived here & is now att my house, & has the care of my houshold affaires; as yett noe good Match does p'sent, but I hope in a short time she may find one to her owne content & yor Lo[rdshi]pps desire."[41] She married (1), about 1664, Baker Brooke, born at Battle, Sussex, England, 16 Nov. 1628, of De le Brooke

[37] Bernard Christian Steiner, ed., *Proceedings of the Provincial Court of Maryland, 1658-1662 (Archives of Maryland*, XLI; Baltimore, 1922), pp. 453-54.

[38] *A Biographical Dictionary* ..., I, p. 191.

[39] Maryland Testamentary Proceedings 12B, pp. 97-98. Nicklin, *loc. cit.*, states he was drowned while trying to ford the swollen Wicomoco River, but cites no source.

[40] Maryland Chancery Court Bk. 2, p. 706.

[41] *The Calvert Papers* (Maryland Historical Society, *Fund Publication*, XXVIII; Baltimore, 1889), I, p. 244.

Manor, Calvert Co., Md., member of the Maryland Council and justice of the Provincial Court, 1658-78, Surveyor General of the Province, 1671-78, and Deputy Governor, 1669-70,[42] who left will, 19 March 1678/9-26 March 1679, naming wife Anne and children.[43] She married (2) Henry Brent of Calvert Co., Md., who died before 6 Aug. 1694 when the inventory of his estate was made,[44] and (3) Col. Richard Marsham, justice of Prince George's Co., Md., who left will 14 April 1713-7 May 1713.[45]

Issue: (by 1) [BROOKE][46] 38. Charles[4], of St. Mary's Co., Md., died unmarried, left will 13 Feb. 1697/8-15 Aug. 1698;[47] 39. LEONARD[4]; 40. BAKER[4]; 41. MARY[4].

27. GEORGE[3] TALBOT (Hellen[2] Calvert, George[1]) came to Maryland and was granted by Lord Baltimore, 11 June 1680, the manor of Susquehanna, also known as New Connaught and Talbot manor, comprising 32,000 acres in Cecil Co., Md., with right of Court Leet and Court Baron.[48] He was a member of the Upper House of the Assembly, 1681-84, was commissioned as "our dear Cousen and Councellor Coll George Talbott, Esqr." to demand that William Penn relinquish land claimed by Charles, 3rd Lord Baltimore, 17 Sept. 1683, was sworn as Surveyor General of Maryland, 8 Nov. 1683, and was designated, as "our Dearly beloved Cozen George Talbott, Esqr.," as President of the Board of Deputy Governors established, 1 May 1684, to act during the minority of Benedict Leonard Calvert.

On 31 Oct. 1684 aboard his Majesty's ketch the *Quaker* in Patuxent River he stabbed Christopher Rousby, Collector of Customs for Patuxent District, "with a dagger newly prepared and sharpened, whereof he immediately dyed," and was put into irons but the captain of the ketch "conceiving the fact to have been committed as upon the seas carryed him into Virginia." He was imprisoned in Gloucester County but escaped and hid in the "mountains" north of his plantation in Cecil Co., Md., until he surrendered to the authorities. Tried by the General Court at James City in Virginia, 20 April 1687, he presented the King's

---

[42] *A Biographical Dictionary* ..., I, p. 168.
[43] Maryland Prerogative Court Wills 10, p. 1.
[44] Maryland Prerogative Court Inventories & Accounts 13A, p. 126.
[45] Maryland Prerogative Court Wills 13, p. 514.
[46] Christopher Johnston, "The Brooke Family," *MHM* I, pp. 69-70, 194-85.
[47] Maryland Prerogative Wills 6, p. 138.
[48] Harry Wright Newman, *Seigniory in Early Maryland* (n.p., 1949), pp. 25, 64.

pardon granted 9 Sept. 1686 and was released.[49]

In 1682 he was granted 3119 acres in County Roscommon, Ireland, for himself, his wife Sarah and their male issue.[50] He described himself as of Castleroory [Castle Rubey], County Roscommon, but now resident in Maryland, when he and his wife Sarah deeded a tract in Cecil County called "Bellaconell" and part of another tract called "Friendship," 7 June 1687, and as of Castlerowvy when he acknowledged the sale of a portion of Susquehanna Manor, 15 June 1687,[51] and later served in the army of James II, being outlawed in England for treason. His will, made in Spain, was never probated,[52]

George[3] Talbot married Sarah ___, who was with him in Maryland and is mentioned as going to Virginia while her husband was imprisoned there.

Issue: [TALBOT][53] 42. James[4], apparently died without issue; 43. Helen[4]; 44. Margaret[4].

31. BENEDICT LEONARD[4] CALVERT (Charles[3], Cecilius[2], George[1]), fourth Lord Baltimore, born 21 March 1678/9, died 16 April 1715, as an infant, upon his father's departure for England, was appointed by him Governor of Maryland under a Board of Deputies and after his conforming to the Established

---

[49] William Hand Browne, ed., *Proceedings and Acts of the General Assembly of Maryland, October 1678-November 1683* (*Archives of Maryland*, VII; Baltimore, 1889), p. 459; Browne, ed., *Proceedings of the Council of Maryland, 1667-1687/8* (*Archives of Maryland*, V; Baltimore, 1887), pp. 427-39; Browne, ed., *Proceedings of the County of Maryland, 1681-1685/6*, (*Archives of Maryland*, XVII; Baltimore, 1898), pp. 145, 249, 344, 477-83; Owings, *op. cit.*, p. 171; *A Biographical Dictionary ...*, II, p. 797.

[50] D'Alton, *op. cit.*, p. 50.

[51] Maryland Provincial Court Deed Bk. WRC 1, 1676-1700, pp. 462-65; Cecil Co., Md., Deed Bk. 1, pp. 196-202. The acknowledgment of the former deed stated they were bound on a voyage out of Maryland. He mortgaged Susquehannough or New Connaught Manor to Edward Pye to secure a debt of 50,000 pounds of tobacco due Isaac Allerton of Westmoreland County, 28 Dec. 1686, but Pye granted a discharge of the mortgage 27 June 1687 (Maryland Provincial Court Deed Bk. WRC 1, pp. 425-26, 439).

[52] William Hand Browne, ed., *Correspondence of Governor Horatio Sharp* (*Archives of Maryland*, XIV; Baltimore, 1895), pp. 403-04. Hugh Hammersley wrote to Governor Sharpe from London, 20 July 1767, that James Plunkett claimed Talbot Manor as heir at law of George Talbot and that William and John Crofton claimed under Talbot's will.

[53] D'Alton, *op. cit.*, p. 72. Following their father's death Helen and Margaret, by Patrick Talbot, their guardian, claimed the reversion of an estate tail in County Roscommon lands forfeited by George Talbot, such reversion being accruable if their brother James Talbot should die without issue. Their claim was allowed subject to such contingency, while James himself claimed and was allowed the estate tail and Sarah Talbot was allowed a jointure off said land.

Church, 1713, had the province of Maryland restored to him.[54] He left will 15 Aug. 1713-2 May 1716,[55] and was buried at Epsom, Surrey. He married, (license 2) Jan. 1698/9, Lady Charlotte Lee, born 13 March 1678/9, died 21 Jan. 1720/1, daughter of Edward Henry Lee, first Earl of Lichfield, and his wife Lady Charlotte Fitzroy, illegitimate daughter of Charles II by Barbara Villiers, created Duchess of Cleveland, from whom he separated, 1705, and who married (2), 6 Dec. 1719, Christopher Crowe (1681-1749) and was buried at Woodford, Essex.

Issue: 45. CHARLES[5]; 46. Benedict Leonard[5], born 20 Sept. 1700, died 1 June 1732 at sea, returning to England, member of Parliament for Harwich, 1726, and Governor of Maryland, 1727-32; 47. Edward Henry[5], born 31 Aug. 1701, died 1730, Commissary General of Maryland, 1728, married Margaret Lee, who married (2), 13 Oct. 1731, James Fitzgerald; 48. Cecilius[5], born 6 Nov. 1702, died 1765, Secretary of the Province of Maryland; 49. Charlotte[5], born 5 Nov. 1702, died 1744, married Thomas Brerewood; 50. Jane[5], born 19 Nov. 1703, married, 4 May 1720, John Hyde of Kingston Lisle, Berkshire; 51. Barbara[5], born 3 Oct. 1704, died in infancy; 52. Anne[5].

32. CHARLES[4] CALVERT (William[3], Leonard[2], George[1]) of Charles Co., Md., Stafford Co., Va., and later of St. Mary's Co., Md., deposed, 28 March 1721, he was aged 57 or thereabouts and, 14 Aug. 1722, he was aged 59 or thereabouts.[56] He left will 25 Oct. 1733-31 Dec.1733.[57] He married (1), 1690, Mary Howson, daughter of Robert Howson of Stafford County, and (2) Barbara Kirke, who married (2) Andrew Foy.

Issue:[58] 53. SARAH HOWSON[5]; 54. ANNE[5].

33. ELIZABETH[4] CALVERT (William[3], Leonard[2], George[1]), born 1666, died after 1684, married, shortly after 24 Dec. 1681,[59] James Neale of Wolleston Manor, Charles Co., Md., to whom Charles[4] Calvert conveyed, 27 Nov. 1707, 600 acres of the 3000 acre Piscataway tract in Charles County, "the which 3000 acres were granted to William Calvert, Esq., father of the said

---

[54] Browne, ed., *Proceedings of the Council of Maryland, 1667-1687/8*, p. 406.

[55] P.C.C. 91 Fox, in *MHM* XXII, pp. 334-37.

[56] Maryland Chancery Record Bk. PL, pp. 661, 750; John Bailey Calvert Nicklin, "Charles Calvert (1663-1733) and Some of His Descendants," *MHM* XXIV, pp. 126-32.

[57] Maryland Prerogative Court Wills 20, pp. 860-61.

[58] *MHM* xxiv, PP. 126-32.

[59] Maryland Provincial Court Deed Bk. WRC 1, 1676-1700, pp. 220-22.

Charles and the said 600 acres, part thereof aforesaid, was given or intended to be given in marriage with Elizabeth, daughter of the said William Calvert, to the said James Neale, by the said William."[60] He married (2), 1687, Elizabeth Lord and left will 1 April 1725-11 Oct. 1727.[61]

Issue: [NEALE][62] 55. MARY[5].

39. LEONARD[4] BROOKE (Anne[3] Calvert, Leonard[2], George[1]), of St. Mary's Co., Md., left will 1 Nov. 1716-2 April 1718.[63] He married Anne Boarman.

Issue: [BROOKE][64] 56. Charles[5], died unmarried before 1 July 1761 when his land was divided among his sisters; 57. ELEANOR[5]; 58. JANE[5]; 59. ANN[5].

40. BAKER[4] BROOKE (Anne[3] Calvert, Leonard[2], George[1]), of St. Mary's Co., Md., left will 5 Feb. 1697/8-27 May 1698.[65] He married Katherine Marsham who married (2) Samuel Queen.

Issue: [BROOKE][66] 60. Baker[5]; 61. RICHARD[5]; 62. LEONARD[5]; 63. ANNE[5].

41. MARY[4] BROOKE (Anne[3] Calvert, Leonard[2], George[1]) left will 29 Sept. 1760-24 May 1763.[67] She married Raphael Neale of Charles Co., Md., who left will 20 July 1743-10 Dec. 1743.[68]

Issue: [NEALE][69] 64. ELIZABETH[5]; 65. MARY[5]; 66. HENRIETTA[5]; 67. ANN[5]; 68. Monica[5], married 52. *Edward[5] Digges* (see DIGGES); 69. ELEANOR[5].

45. CHARLES[5] CALVERT (Benedict Leonard[4], Charles[3], Cecilius[2], George[1]), fifth Lord Baltimore, born 29 Sept. 1699, died 24 April 1751. He was Cofferer to Frederick, Prince of Wales, represented Surrey in Parliament, was a Fellow of the Royal Society and a Lord of the Admiralty but was widely known

---

[60] Westmoreland Co. Deeds & Wills 4, p. 96.

[61] Maryland Prerogative Court Wills 19, p. 246.

[62] *MHM* VII, p. 207.

[63] Maryland Prerogative Court Wills 14, p. 486.

[64] *MHM* I, p. 185.

[65] Maryland Prerogative Court Wills 6, p. 82.

[66] *MHM* I, p. 185.

[67] Maryland Prerogative Court Wills 31, pp. 993-94.

[68] Maryland Prerogative Court Wills 23, p. 294.

[69] *MHM* VII, p. 212; Harry Wright Newman, *The Maryland Semmes and Kindred Families* (Baltimore, 1956), p.301; Charles Co., Md., Deed Bk. A.1., pt. 2, p. 353-62, partition of Wollaston Manor, 26 June 1755.

for his "riotous living." He married, 20 July 1730, Mary Janssen, who died 25 March 1770 at Chaillot, near Paris, France.

Issue: 70. Frederick[6], sixth Lord Baltimore, born 6 Feb. 1731/2, died 4 Sept. 1771 at Naples, married, 9 March 1753, Diana, daughter of Scrope Egerton, Duke of Bridgewater, born 3 March 1731/2, died 13 Aug. 1758;[70] 71. Frances Dorothy[6], born 1734, died 5 March 1736; 72. Louisa[6], married John Browning; 73. Charles[6], born 21 Jan. 1737, died in infancy; 74. Caroline[6], married, 1765, Robert Eden, born 14 Sept. 1741 at Durham, England, died 2 Sept. 1784 at Annapolis, Md., who was commissioned lieutenant fireworker in the Royal Regiment of Artillery when about 16, served as captain in the Coldstream Guards in Germany during the Seven Years' War, was Governor of Maryland, 1769-76, where he was sympathetic with the point of view of the people but deprecated their militant methods, returned to England where he was created a baronet, 10 Sept. 1776, but later returned to Maryland to recover property and died there.[71]

53. SARAH HOWSON[5] CALVERT (Charles[4], William[3], Leonard[2], George[1]), born about 1694, married Nathaniel Jones of Westmoreland County, who left will 21 Jan. 1753-26 March 1754.[72]

Issue: [JONES][73] 75. John[6], died 1762, married, 16 Aug. 1744,[74] Eleanor Moss; 76. David[6], married, 18 Feb. 1763, Mary Boswell; 77. Nathaniel[6]; 78. Charles[6], left will, 25 Jan. 1771-2 March 1771;[75] 79. Calvert[6], left will 29 Aug. [1790]-7 April 1791;[76] 80. Mary[6], married ___ Peck; 81. Frances[6]; 82. Sarah[6], married ___ Franklin.

54. ANNE[5] CALVERT (Charles[4], William[3], Leonard[2], George[1]), born about 1696, married Thomas Porter of Stafford County, who died 26 Feb. 1739/40,[77] leaving undated will proved 8 April 1740.[78]

---

[70] Collins, *op. cit.*, II, p. 369.

[71] *Dictionary of American Biography*, VI (New York, 1931), pp. 16-17; *Biographical Dictionary of the Maryland Legislature*, I, pp. 299-300.

[72] Westmoreland Co. Deeds & Wills 12, pp. 75-78.

[73] O'Gorman, *op. cit.*, pp. 69, 73; *MHM* XXIV, p. 129.

[74] St Paul's Parish, King George Co., Register.

[75] King George Co. Will Bk. 1, pp. 317a-318.

[76] King George Co. Will Bk. 2, p. 128.

[77] Overwharton Parish, Stafford Co., Register.

[78] Stafford Co. Will Bk. M, p. 285.

Issue: [PORTER][79] 83. Anne[6], born 13 Oct. 1717, died 22 Sept. 1727;[80] 84. Calvert[6], born about 1718, married, 21 Sept. 1749,[81] Elizabeth Cash; 85. Thomas[6], born about 1720; 86. Benjamin[6], baptized 1 May 1725;[82] 87. Nicholas[6], born about 1725; 88. Joseph[6], born 7 Aug. 1726,[83] married, 26 Feb. 1756,[84] Jemima Smith; 89. Henry[6], baptized 1 May 1728;[85] 90. Charles[6], born about 1729; 91. Howson[6], born about 1730, died 11 April 1755,[86] married, 1 Jan. 1745/6,[87] John Stark, who married (2), 29 May 1756,[88] Hannah Eaves; 92. Anne[6], born 15 March 1731/2;[89] 93. John[6], born 4 Aug. 1734,[90] died 14 July 1754.[91]

55. MARY[5] NEALE (Elizabeth[4] Calvert, William[3], Leonard[2], George[1]) deposed 8 March 1721 she was aged about 39.[92] She married (1), by 10 April 1702,[93] Charles Egerton of "Piney Neck," St. Mary's Co., Md., on whose estate she was granted administration 5 March 1705,[94] (2), 1707, Jeremiah Adderton, who left will 11 April 1712-19 May 1713,[95] (3), by 9 April 1715,[96] Joseph Van Swearingen of St. Mary's Co., Md., who deposed, 28 Aug. 1717, he was aged about 35,[97] and died by 16 March 1721,[98] and (4), before 1 April 1725,[99] William Deacon.

---

[79] O'Gorman, *op. cit.*, pp. 69-70, 73; *MHM* XXIV, p. 130.
[80] St. Paul's Parish Register.
[81] Overwharton Parish Register.
[82] St. Paul's Parish Register.
[83] *Ibid.*
[84] Overwharton Parish Register.
[85] St, Paul's Parish Register.
[86] Overwharton Parish Register.
[87] *Ibid.*
[88] *Ibid.*
[89] St. Paul's Parish, Register.
[90] *Ibid.*
[91] Overwharton Parish Register.
[92] Maryland Chancery Bk. CL, p. 877.
[93] Prince George's Co., Md., Deed Bk. A, p. 449.
[94] Maryland Testamentary Proceedings 19C, p. 40.
[95] Maryland Prerogative Court Wills 15, pp. 90-93.
[96] Maryland Prerogative Court Inventories & Accounts 36B, p. 343.
[97] Maryland Chancery Bk. CL., p. 354.
[98] Maryland Prerogative Court Inventories 5, p. 105.
[99] Her father's will, *loc. cit.*

Issue: (by 1) [EGERTON]¹⁰⁰ 94. James⁶, of "Piney Neck," St. Mary's Co., Md., left will 16 Jan. 1765-26 July 1768,¹⁰¹ married ___; 95. Charles⁶, died before 13 Aug. 1739 when James Neale as administrator returned an accounting of his estate;¹⁰² (by 2) [ADDERTON] 96. James⁶; 97. (Child)⁶, unborn 1713.

57. ELEANOR⁵ BROOKE (Leonard⁴, Anne³ Calvert, Leonard², George¹) left will 28 Jan. 1760-16 Oct. 1760.¹⁰³ She married Clement Gardiner of St. Mary's Co., Md., who died before 18 June 1746.¹⁰⁴

Issue: [GARDINER] 98. Monica⁶, left will 24 Nov. 1772-1 Dec. 1772,¹⁰⁵ married (1) 110. Richard⁶ Brooke and (2) Henry Queen of St. Mary's Co., Md., who left will 21 Dec. 1767-2 Feb. 1768;¹⁰⁶ 99. Ann⁶, married 122. Richard Basil⁶ Boarman; 100. Mary⁶, married 123. George⁶ Boarman.

58. JANE⁵ BROOKE (Leonard⁴, Anne³ Calvert, Leonard², George¹) married John Smith of St. Mary's Co., Md., who left will 11 Aug. 1735-3 March 1735/6.¹⁰⁷

Issue: [SMITH] 101. Benjamin⁶, left land in Prince George's Co., Md., left will 21 March 1777-10 June 1777,¹⁰⁸ married 123. *Mary⁶ Neale* (see DIGGES); 102. Leonard⁶.

59. ANN⁵ BROOKE (Leonard⁴, Anne³ Calvert, Leonard², George¹) left will 4 Nov. 1785-7 Jan. 1786.¹⁰⁹ She married William Neale of St. Mary's Co., Md., who left will 3 Feb. 1763-8 Feb. 1763.¹¹⁰

Issue: [NEALE]¹¹¹ 103. William Chandler⁶, born 1743, died 1799 in England, Roman Catholic priest; 104. Leonard⁶, born 15 Oct. 1746 near Port Tobacco, Md., died 15 June 1817 at Georgetown, D.C., educated at St. Omer, Belgium, Jesuit priest professor at Bruges and a missionary at Demerara, British Guiana, 1779-83, before returning to Maryland, president of Georgetown

---

¹⁰⁰ *MHM* XXXV, pp. 296-97.
¹⁰¹ Maryland Prerogative Court Wills 36, p. 531.
¹⁰² Maryland Testamentary Proceedings 31, p. 38.
¹⁰³ Maryland Prerogative Court Wills 31, p. 7.
¹⁰⁴ Maryland Prerogative Court Inventories 33, p. 314.
¹⁰⁵ Maryland Prerogative Court Wills 39, p. 33.
¹⁰⁶ Maryland Prerogative Court Wills 36, p. 336.
¹⁰⁷ Maryland Prerogative Court Wills 21, p. 519.
¹⁰⁸ Charles Co., Md., Will Bk. AF7, p. 25.
¹⁰⁹ Charles Co., Md., Will Bk. AF9, pp. 174-75.
¹¹⁰ Maryland Prerogative Court Wills 31, p. 1027.
¹¹¹ *MHM* I, p. 216.

College, 1798-1806, nominated coadjutor Bishop of Baltimore, 1800, succeeded as Archbishop of Baltimore, 1815;[112] 105. Raphael[6], left will 5 March 1784-1 May 1784,[113] married, in England, Sarah Howard, who left will 1 [Jan.?] 1784-22 May 1784;[114] 106. Charles[6], born 10 Feb. 1751, died 1823 at Mount Carmel, near Port Tobacco, Md., aged 74,[115] Roman Catholic priest, superior of the Society of Jesus in the United States; 107. Francis Ignatius[6], born June 1756, died 1838; 108. Clare[6], married (1) Henry Brent of Charles Co., Md., who left will 23 Feb. 1769-22 May 1769,[116] and (2) George Slye of St. Mary's Co., Md., who left will 21 May 1773-20 June 1773;[117] 109. Mary[6], married William Matthews, of Charles Co., Md., who left will 30 Nov. 1776-23 Jan. 1777.[118]

61. RICHARD[5] BROOKE (Baker[4], Anne[3] Calvert , Leonard[2], George[1]) inherited part of "De le Brooke Manor," St. Mary's Co., Md., and left will 5 Dec. 1718-3 Aug. 1719.[119] He married Clare Boarman, who married (2) Richard Sherburne and left will 21 Feb. 1745-6 Aug. 1747.[120]

Issue: [BROOKE][121] 110. Richard[6], died 4 Dec. 1754,[122] married 98. Monica[6] Gardiner, who married (2) Henry Queen; 111. Baker[6], of St, Mary's Co., Md., left will 13 Feb. 1756-3 March 1756,[123] married Mary Simpson.

62. LEONARD[5] BROOKE (Baker[4], Anne[3] Calvert, Leonard[2], George[1]) of Prince George's Co., Md., left will June 1735-4 May 1736.[124] He married Ann ___, who left will 15 Dec. 1769-2 July 1770.[125]

Issue: [BROOKE][126] 112. Baker[6], left will 27 Oct. 1770-4 Jan. 1771,[127] of

---

[112] *The National Cyclopaedia of American Biography*, I (New York, 1898), p. 482.

[113] Charles Co., Md., Will Bk. B #1, p. 311.

[114] *Ibid.*, p. 319.

[115] *National Intelligencer*, 9 May 1823.

[116] Maryland Prerogative Court Wills 37, p. 117.

[117] Maryland Prerogative Court Wills 39, p. 350.

[118] Maryland Prerogative Court Wills 41, p. 279.

[119] Maryland Prerogative Court Wills 15, p. 178.

[120] Maryland Prerogative Court Wills 25, pp. 152-53.

[121] *MHM* I, pp. 284-85.

[122] Maryland Prerogative Court Inventories 58, p. 311.

[123] Maryland Prerogative Court Wills 30, p. 45.

[124] Maryland Prerogative Court Wills 21, p. 565.

[125] Maryland Prerogative Court Wills 38, pp. 178-79.

[126] *MHM* I, pp. 285, 376-77.

[127] Maryland Prerogative Court Wills 38, p. 194, which named uncle Henry Hill as an executor.

Charles Co., Md., married ____; 113. Oswald[6]; 114. Leonard[6], of Prince George's Co., Md., deposed 15 March 1757 he was aged 29,[128] left will 27 Oct. 1783-10 Feb. 1785,[129] captain of ship *Horatio*, married (1) 60. Anne[5] Darnall (see UTIE-BENNETT) and (2) Elizabeth ____; 115. Richard[6], of Charles Co., Md., left will 14 Jan. 1771-9 April 1771,[130] married ____; 116. Anna[6]; 117. Katherine[6]; 118. Jane[6]; 119. Mary[6]; 120. Henrietta[6].

63. ANNE[5] BROOKE (Baker[4], Anne[3] Calvert, Leonard[2], George[1]) married Benedict Leonard Boarman of Charles Co., Md., who deposed, 3 May 1745, he was aged 58,[131] left will 28 July 1754-11 March 1757.[132]

Issue: [BOARMAN][133] 121. Benedict Leonard[6], of Charles Co., Md., left will 14 Oct. 1791-3 Feb. 1794,[134] married Elizabeth ____; 122. Richard Basil[6], of St. Mary's Co., Md., left will 12 April 1777-8 Aug. 1782,[135] married 99. Ann[6] Gardiner; 123. George[6], of Charles Co., Md., left wil 7 April 1768-5 July 1768,[136] married 100. Mary[6] Gardiner; 124. Joseph[6], died before 1763; 125. Mary[6]; 126. Elinor[6], left will 22 July 1794-12 Oct. 1795,[137] unmarried; 127. Jane[6], left will 20 Sept. 1779-26 April 1783,[138] unmarried.

64. ELIZABETH[5] NEALE (Mary[4] Brooke, Anne[3] Calvert, Leonard[2], George[1]) died by 1743. She married John Lancaster of Charles Co., Md., who married (2) Mary ____ and left will 31 Jan. 1759-21 May 1760.[139]

Issue: [LANCASTER][140] 128. John[6], married ____; 129. Joseph[6], never married; 130. Raphael[6], born 1732, died before 26 May 1801 when a sale of his estate took place,[141] of "Spekes," Charles Co., Md., and, after 1783, of Nelson

---

[128] Prince George's Co., Md., Deed Bk. PP, pt. 2, p. 16.

[129] Prince George's Co., Md. Will Bk. T#1, p. 214.

[130] Maryland Prerogative Court Wills 38, p. 233.

[131] Charles. Co., Court Record Y#3, 1744-45, p. 342.

[132] Maryland Prerogative Court Wills 30, p. 277.

[133] Harry Wright Newman, *The Maryland Semmes and Kindred Families* (Baltimore, 1956), pp. 194-96, 201-06.

[134] Charles Co., Md., AK#11, pp. 203-05.

[135] St. Mary's Co., Md., Will Bk. JJ #1, pp. 200-01.

[136] Maryland Prerogative Court Wills 36, p. 491.

[137] Charles Co., Md., Will Bk. AK#11, pp. 287-90.

[138] Charles Co., Md., Will Bk, B#1, pp. 148-49.

[139] Maryland Prerogative Court Wills 31, p. 43.

[140] Samuel W. Lancaster, *The Lancaster Family of Maryland and Kentucky* (n.p., n.d.), pp. 14-15.

[141] Nelson Co., Ky., Will Bk. A, p. 624.

Co., Ky., married Eleanor Bradford, born 1835, died 1802; 131. Mary[6], married (1), 1746, Richard Holmes, mariner, who left will 6 May 1747 at Liverpool, Lancs.-6 Feb. 1749,[142] and (2) John Bradford, mariner of Prince George's Co., Md., who left will 29 Jan. 1770-14 Nov. 1770;[143] 132. Katherine[6], married Enoch Combs; 134. Elizabeth[6], never married.

65. MARY[5] NEALE (Mary[4] Brooke, Anne[3] Calvert, Leonard[2], George[1]) married Thomas Taney of St. Mary's Co., Md., who left will 1 Dec. 1762 [*sic?*]-1 June 1762.[144]

Issue: [TANEY] 134. John Francis[6]; 135. Raphael[6]; 136. Mary Eleanor[6], married ___ Combs; 137. Michael Thomas[6].

66. HENRIETTA[5] NEALE (Mary[4] Brooke, Anne[3] Calvert, Leonard[2], George[1]) left will 27 June 1773-16 June 1774.[145] She married Basil Brooke., son of Roger and Elizabeth (Hutchins) Brooke, born 16 Nov. 1717,[146] of St. Mary's Co., Md., who left will 14 May 1761-13 July 1767.[147]

Issue: [BROOKE][148] 138. Raphael[6], married Jane Thompson;[149] 139. Roger[6]; 140. James[6]; 141. Ann[6].

67. ANN[5] NEALE (Mary[4] Brooke, Anne[3] Calvert, Leonard[2], George[1]) married James Thompson, Jr., of St. Mary's Co., Md., who left will 10 Aug. 1749-codicil 14 Dec. 1749-18 Sept. 1750.[150]

Issue: [THOMPSON] 142. Raphael Francis[6]; 143. Mary Eleanor[6]; 144. James Charles[6].

69. ELEANOR[5] NEALE (Mary[4] Brooke, Anne[3] Calvert, Leonard[2], George[1]) married Bennett Hoskins, who left will 21 Feb. 1733/4-23 April 1734.[151]

Issue: [HOSKINS][152] 145. Mary Ann[6], left will 4 Jan. 1792-7 May 1792,[153]

---

[142] Maryland Prerogative Court Wills 27, p. 233, probated in Charles Co., Md.

[143] Maryland Prerogative Court Wills38, p. 112.

[144] Maryland Prerogative Court Wills 31, p. 666.

[145] Maryland Prerogative Court Wills 39, p. 697.

[146] *MHM* I, p. 288.

[147] Maryland Prerogative Court Wills 35, p. 407.

[148] *MHM* I, p. 288.

[149] Newman, *op. cit.*, p. 255; Maryland Prerogative Court Wills 38, p. 675, will of Henrietta Thompson, 20 March 1772-1 May 1772.

[150] Maryland Prerogative Court Wills 27, p. 397.

[151] Maryland Prerogative Court Wills 21, p. 52.

[152] Newman, *op. cit.*, pp. 206-08.

[153] Charles Co., Md., Will Bk. AK#11, pp. 87-90.

married Richard Bennett Boarman of Charles Co., Md., who left will 14 Sept. 1752-8 July 1758;[154] 146. Raphael[6], who, 1753, "is now and has been several years in Europe."[155]

---

[154] Maryland Prerogative Court Wills 30, p. 593.
[155] Charles Co., Md., Deed Bk. A1, p. 361.

CARSLEY

*1. HENRY[1] CARSLEY came to Virginia, 1623, in the *Providence* and at the age of 23 years when the muster was taken, Feb. 1624/5, was living at Newport News as one of Daniel Gookin's men.[1] The shipping and cattle breeding enterprise projected by Gookin did not prosper and Henry[1] Carsley migrated to the Eastern Shore where many settlers began to take up land after the 1622/3 massacre. On 19 Feb. 1633/4 Carsley petitioned the court held at Accawmack for a lease of 50 acres upon Old Plantation Creek on the south side of Fishing Creek.[2] Prior to that time he had married Elizabeth Berriman, step-daughter of Henry Wilson and daughter of the latter's wife Alice, whose will, recorded 1640, mentioned her granddaughter Frances[2] Carsley.[3] On 26 Nov. 1635 Elizabeth Caursley of Accawmack, "executrix of my right deere and well beloved husbound Henry Caursley," made a deed of gift to her two daughters, Agnis and Frances, and named "my ... father-in-law [step-father] Henry Wilson" overseer.[4]

Issue: 2. Agnes[2] [Ann], deceased by 27 Jan. 1647/8 when her sister Frances gave a power of attorney to "my uncle Thomas Johnson" to recover Ann's estate;[5] 3. FRANCES[2].

3. FRANCES[2] CARSLEY (Henry[1]), born in Virginia, called a minor in her grandmother Alice Wilson's will, 1640, married, (contract 18) May 1650,[6]

---

[1] Henry Casley was a headright named in Daniel Gookin's patent for 2500 acres in Upper Norfolk County, 29 Dec. 1637, pursuant to order of court, 25 Feb. 1634/5 (Patent Bk. 1, p. 511).

[2] Northampton Co. Orders, Deeds & Wills 1, 1632-40, p. 21.

[3] Northampton Co. Orders, Deeds & Wills 2, 1640-45, p. 7. Much of the will is missing; she made property bequests to daughter Jane Bessins (Bessons), so long as she remained a widow, named daughter Mary sole executrix, gave personal items to William Berriman, and identified a granddaughter Frances Carsley as a minor. By her (1) husband she also had children William Berriman (died 1644/5) and his sister Jane who married (1), by 1640, ___ Bessins (Bessons), (2) Jonas Jackson, and (3), by 1653, Richard Lemon. William Berriman had a patent for 800 acres in Northampton County which included acreage for the transportation of Jonah Jackson, Robert Jackson and Jane Jackson (Patent Bk. 1, p. 948).

[4] Northampton Co. Orders, Deeds & Wills 1, 1632-40, p. 83. On the same day William Berriman granted to Elizabeth Caursley his right and title to two male servants and gave her about thirty household items (*ibid.*, p. 84).

[5] Northampton Co. Orders, Deeds & Wills 3, 1645-51, p. 102.

[6] Northampton Co. Orders, Deeds & Wills 4, 1651-54, p. 48, drawn by her uncle Thomas Johnson, apparently her guardian. A judgment was acknowledged, 28 Oct. 1651, by Jeffrey Minshall to Thomas Johnson, Gent., "on the behalfe of Frances Carsley, Orphant, nowe the wife of the sd Jeffrey Minshall" (*ibid.*, p. 49).

Jeffrey Menshall, who deposed, 9 April 1655, that he was 34 years of age or thereabouts, but also deposed, 28 June 1655, that he was aged 30.[7] He came to Virginia before 1645[8] and by 17 Sept. 1666, with his wife and five children, had immigrated to the Province of Maryland where, on that date, he was assigned 400 acres called "Adventure," lying at the head of Marumsco in Somerset County.[9] He died 8 April 1675 and was buried at Marumsco.[10]

Issue: [MENSHALL][11] 4. MARY[3]; 5. JANE[3]; 6. JEFFREY[3]; 7. RANDOLPH[3]; 8. Elizabeth[3], buried 23 Nov. 1660;[12] 9. ANNE[3]; 10. ALICE[3]; 11. Elizabeth[3], born 28 Dec. 1668,[13] (twin of Alice?); 12. THOMAS[3].

4. MARY[3] MENSHALL (Frances[2] Carsley, Henry[1]), born in Virginia about 1651, was given 200 acres jointly with her sister Jane by Capt. Stephen Charlton, 29 Oct. 1654.[14] She married, Oct. 1666, Thomas Tull of Annemessex, Somerset Co., Md.,[15] who left will 14 Feb. 1717/8-28 June 1720, naming (2) wife Ann (___) Cox, her son William Cox, and his sons Thomas and John,[16] but before his death had married (3) Katherine ___.

---

[7] Northampton Co. Orders, Deeds & Wills 6, 1655-56, p. 3; Orders, Deeds & Wills 5, 1654-55, p. 124. His identification as the Jeffrey Menshall, son of Richard, baptized at Wistaston, County Chester, 26 March 1621, is incorrect; that Jeffrey died at the age of 4 (Bishop's Transcripts, Wistaston, Matthew M. Wise, *The Boston Family of Maryland* (2nd ed. rev.; Charlotte, N.C., 1986), p. 420.

[8] Northampton Co. Orders, Deeds & Wills 3, 1645-51, p. 24.

[9] Maryland Patent Bk. 10, pp. 133-34. "Jefry Mentiale of our Province of Maryl'd, planter, hath due unto him four hundred acres of land within our said province for transporting himself, Francis Mentiale, Mary Mentiale, Ann Mentiale, Jane Mentiale, his daughters, Jeffry and Randolph his sons and William Collet his serv[t] hither to inhabite as appears upon Record ... doe hereby grant ... Jeffry Mentiale a parcell of land called the Adventure, lying at the head of Marrumsco," 17 Sept. 1666. The survey was made 10 Feb. 1665/6 and he entered his rights 12 April 1666 (*ibid.*, p. 10).

[10] Somerset Co., Md., Deed Bk. IKL, p. 166.

[11] Clayton Torrence, *Old Somerset on the Eastern Shore of Maryland* (Richmond, 1935), p. 452; Wise, *loc. cit.*; Henry C. Peden and F. Edward Wright, *Colonial Families of the Eastern Shore of Maryland*, VIII (Westminster, Md., 2000), pp. 180-85, which differs in some identifications from the other accounts. The name appears also as Menchel, Minshal, Mentiale and frequently as Mitchell.

[12] Northampton Co. Deeds, Wills &c 1657-66, p. 110.

[13] Somerset Co., Md., Deed Bk. IKL, p. 162.

[14] Northampton Co. Orders, Deeds & Wills 6, 1655-56, p. 16.

[15] Somerset Co., Md., Deed Bk. IKL, p. 255.

[16] Maryland Prerogative Court Wills 16, p. 117.

Issue: [TULL][17] 13. THOMAS[4]; 14. RICHARD[4]; 15. JOHN[4]; 16. Mary[4], born 15 Jan. 1677/8, married [George?] Cullen.

5. JANE[3] MENSHALL (Frances[2] Carsley, Henry[1]), born in Virginia about 1653, married, 15 Feb. 1667/8, Samuel Long of Somerset Co., Md.,[18] and with him gave a deed, 20 April 1687, conveying her one-third interest in "Boston Adventure" to her brother Jeffrey[3] Menshall.[19] She died 5 Dec. 1692 and Samuel Long married (2), 22 Feb. 1693/4, Elizabeth King,[20] named with his children in his will, 26 Nov. 1695-10 Dec. 1695.[21]

Issue: [LONG][22] 17. Samuel[4], born 3 Oct. 1669 at Marumsco, buried 16 May 1673; 18 ELIZABETH[4]; 19. Daniel[4], born 8 Jan. 1673/4 at Marumsco, died as infant; 20. JOHN[5]; 21. DANIEL[5]; 22. JEFFREY[4]; 23. RANDOLPH [RANDALL][4]; 24. Jane[4]; 25. ANN[4]; 26. David[4], born 25 May 1687, left will 26 Nov. 1716-18 March 1716/7;[23] 27. William[4],born 16 Dec. 1689.

6. JEFFREY[3] MENSHALL [MITCHELL] (Frances[2] Carsley, Henry[1]), born in Virginia, left will dated 27 Jan. 1701/2,[24] married Hellena (Elinor) Connor, daughter of Philip Connor, Sr., who married (2) ___ Dikes before 21 Feb. 1720[/1?] when she and her son John sold land to Daniel Long.[25]

Issue: [MITCHELL][26] 28. Jeffrey[4], born 19 Dec. 1688, died young; 29. Sarah[4], born 11 Nov. 1691; 30. Ann[4]; 31. John[4], born 9 Dec. 1697, of Bath Co., N.C., 29 March 1739, when he sold land to Daniel Long;[27] 32. Thomas[4].

7. RANDOLPH[3] MENSHALL [MITCHELL] (Frances[2] Carsley, Henry[1]), born in Virginia, died after 7 March 1719 when he conveyed 150 acres of "Mitchell's Lot" to the vestry of Coventry Parish,[28] and probably about 1730

---

[17] Somerset Co., Md., Deed Bk. IKL, pp. 255, 257, 261; Wise, *op. cit.*, p. 433.

[18] Somerset Co., Md., Deed Bk. IKL, p. 261.

[19] Somerset Co., Md., Deed Bk. 7, p. 86.

[20] Somerset Co., Md., Deed Bk. IKL, p. 156.

[21] Somerset Co., Md., Original wills, Box 1, folder 34, Maryland State Archives.

[22] Somerset Co., Md., Deed Bk. IKL, pp. 32, 150-54, 257, 259; Wise,*op. cit.*, pp. 15-16, 411-12.

[23] Maryland Prerogative Court Wills 14, p. 358.

[24] Maryland Prerogative Court Wills 11, p. 354, without probate date. He died before 21 Feb. 1702/3, the date of his father-in-law's will (Maryland Prerogative Court Wills 3, p. 491).

[25] Somerset Co., Md., Deed Bk. IK, 1719-22, pp. 131-33.

[26] Somerset Co., Md., Deed Bk. IKL, pp. 172, 174.

[27] Somerset Co., Md., Deed Bk. MF #Y, pp. 64-66.

[28] Somerset Co., Md., Deed Bk. IK, p. 40.

when last taxed in Somerset Co., Md.[29] He married Alice, widow of Henry Potter and daughter of Ambrose Dixon.[30]

Issue: [MITCHELL] 33. Randolph[4], born 6 March 1690/1,[31] died young; 34. MARY[4].

9. ANNE[3] MENSHALL (Frances[2] Carsley, Henry[1]), born in Virginia, married, 23 Oct.1685,[32] John Moore of Coventry Parish, Somerset Co., Md., who left will 31 Dec. 1716-20 March 1717.[33]

Issue: [MOORE][34] 35. JOHN[4]; 36. William[4], born 30 Aug. 1689, died young; 37. Elizabeth[4], born 25 Jan. 1694/5, died young; 38. Thomas[4]; 39. Sarah[4].

10. ALICE[3] MENSHALL (Frances[2] Carsley, Henry[1]), born 27 Dec. 1668,[35] married John White. She was living 26 May 1729 when she signed the inventory of her brother Thomas[3] Mitchell as next of kin. He married (2) Jocina (Colehoune?) and died before 25 April 1737 when his estate was settled.[36]

Issue: [WHITE][37] 40. STEPHEN[4]; 41. Sarah[4], married Francis Carey and moved to "Princess Anne County of North Carolina" [*sic*];[38] 42. JOHN[4]; 43. William[4], left Somerset Co., Md., about 1734; 44. Thomas[4], of Somerset Co., Md., left will 1 Dec. 1766-21 Nov. 1770,[39] married Sarah ___; 45. Elizabeth[4], married John Matthews; 46. Isaac[4], left Somerset Co., Md., about 1731; 47. Rachel[4].

12. THOMAS[3] MENSHALL [MITCHELL] (Frances[2] Carsley, Henry[1]) was born 18 Aug. 1672[40] and died before 26 May 1729 when the inventory of his estate was made.[41] He married Ann Coulbourne, daughter of William

---

[29] J. Elliott Russo, *Tax Lists of Somerset County, Maryland, 1730-1740* (Westminster, Md., 1992), p. 2.

[30] Somerset Co., Md., Deed Bk. IKL, p. 171; Maryland Prerogative Court Wills 6, p. 22.

[31] Somerset Co., Md., Deed Bk. IKL, pp. 171.

[32] *Ibid.*, p. 170.

[33] Maryland Prerogative Court Wills 14, p. 572.

[34] Somerset Co., Md., Deed Bk. IKL, pp. 171, 174.

[35] *Ibid.*, p. 162.

[36] Maryland Prerogative Court Accounts 14, p. 331.

[37] *Ibid.*; Wise, *op. cit.*, p. 421.

[38] Somerset Co., Md., Deed Bk. X #1, pp 353-54, 20 May 1747.

[39] Maryland Prerogative Court Wills 38, p. 185.

[40] Somerset Co., Md., Deed Bk. IKL p. 164.

[41] Maryland Prerogative Court Inventories 14, pp. 134-37.

Coulbourne and his wife Ann Revell, born 9 April 1679.[42]

Issue:[43] 48. Thomas[4]; 49. Mary[4]; 50. ISAAC[4]; 51. Ann[4]; 52. RANDALL[4]; 53. Solomon[4], died before 20 July 1744 when his inventory was presented by Isaac Mitchell;[44] 54. STEPHEN[4].

13. THOMAS[4] TULL (Mary[3] Menshall, Frances[2] Carsley, Henry[1]), born 23 Oct. 1668 at Annamessix, died before 11 June 1720 when John and Esther Tull sold 37½ acres to his widow.[45] They resided in Somerset Co., Md. He married Sarah Handy, who left will 26 Nov. 1727-1 April 1728,[46] daughter of Samuel Handy, Sr.[47]

Issue: [TULL][48] 55. THOMAS[5]; 56. SAMUEL[5]; 57. Sarah[5], died 1796; 58. Rachel[5]; 59. Mary[5], married ___ Fountain; 60. William[5], under 18 in 1727; 61. ISAAC[5]; 62. Esther[5], under 18 in 1727, married William Miles, spinning wheel marker, who died 1786; 63. Grace[5], under 18 in 1727.

14. RICHARD[4] TULL (Mary[3] Menshall, Frances[2] Carsley, Henry[1]), of Somerset Co., Md., born 6 Dec. 1670 at Annamessix, left will 1 May 1710-2 Aug. 1710.[49] He married, 26 Jan. 1695/6, Elizabeth Turpin.

Issue: [TULL][50] 64. SOLOMON[5]; 65. Thomas[5]; 66. Richard[5]; 67. John[5].

15. JOHN[4] TULL (Mary[3] Menshall, Frances[2] Carsley, Henry[1]), born 8 June 1674 at Annamessix, resided in Somerset Co., Md., and left will 13 Dec. 1729-28 Jan. 1729/30.[51] He married Esther Costen, daughter of Stephen and Comfort (Furniss) Costen,[52] who was born 5 Oct. 1685 and left will 15 Feb. 1770- 21 March 1770.[53]

---

[42] Somerset Co., Md., Deed Bk. IKL, p. 40.

[43] Wise, *op. cit.*, p. 420. Son Randall was first taxed in the household of his motherr in 1738; Solomon and Stephen were first taxed in 1740 (Russo, *op. cit.*, pp. 150, 197).

[44] Maryland Inventories 31, p. 344.

[45] Somerset Co., Md., Deed Bk. IK, 1719-22, pp. 63-64.

[46] Maryland Prerogative Court Wills 19, p. 390.

[47] Maryland Prerogative Court Wills 17, p. 24, will of Samuel Handy, Sr., 15 May 1721-13 Sept. 1721.

[48] Wise, *op. cit.*, p. 433; Woodrow T. Wilson, *Thirty-Four Families of Old Somerset Co., Maryland* (Baltimore, 1977), pp. 272-76.

[49] Maryland Prerogative Court Wills 13, p. 134.

[50] *Ibid.*

[51] Maryland Prerogative Court Wills 20, p. 69.

[52] Wise, *op. cit.*, p. 391; Maryland Prerogative Court Wills 21, p. 735, will of Comfort Benton, 25 June 1735-17 Nov. 1736.

[53] Somerset Co., Md., Will Bk. ED #4, pp. 154-55.

Issue: [TULL][54] 68. JOHN[5]; 69. JOSHUA[5]; 70. MARY[5]; 71. Richard[5], planter of Somerset Co., Md., left will 25 March 1748/9-3 June 1749,[55] unmarried; 72. STEPHEN[5]; 73. ESTHER[5].

18. ELIZABETH[4] LONG (Jane[3] Menshall, Frances[2] Carsley, Henry[1]), born 19 Feb. 1671/2 at Marumsco, left will 12 March 1716/7-21 March 1716/7.[56] She married (1) Isaac Boston, son of Henry and Ann (___) Boston, who left will 3 Dec. 1700-9 April 1701,[57] and (2) Adrian Marshall, who predeceased her.

Issue: (by 1) [BOSTON][58] 74. ISAAC[5]; 75. Anne[5], placed under the care of her mother and "father-in-law" 6 June 1711, "being demented;"[59] 76. Elizabeth[3]; (by 2) [MARSHALL][60] 77. GEORGE[5]; 78. SAMUEL[5]; 79. THOMAS[5]; 80. Adrian[6], died young.

20. JOHN[4] LONG (Jane[3] Menshall, Frances[2] Carsley, Henry[1]), born 1 Jan. 1674/5 at Marumsco, left will 6 Nov. 1712-16 June 1718.[61] He married Ann Taylor, daughter of John and Anne (Coulbourn) Taylor, born 19 Feb. 1681/2 at Nassawaddox, Va.

Issue: [LONG][62] 81. ANN[5]; 82. Samuel[5], left will 18 June 1740-26 Dec. 1741,[63] unmarried; 83. JOHN[5]; 84. WILLIAM[5]; 85. DAVID[5]; 86. COULBOURNE[5].

21. DANIEL[4] LONG (Jane[3] Menshall, Frances[2] Carsley, Henry[1]), born 18 Oct. 1677, left will 10 Feb. 1737/8-4 Nov. 1741.[64] He married (1) Elizabeth Taylor, daughter of Hope and Margaret (Dennis) Taylor, who was born 11 Dec. 1684, and (2) Sarah Adams, daughter of Thomas Adams.

Issue: [LONG][65] (by 1) 87. DAVID[5]; 88. SOLOMON[5]; 89. Elizabeth[5], married Thomas Hall [Ball?]; 90. CHRISTIAN[5]; 91. DANIEL[5]; (by 2) 92. RACHEL[5]; 93. SARAH[5]; 94. Elisha[5], born 14 Oct. 1735,[66] married Mary ___,

---

[54] Wise, *op. cit.*, p. 433.

[55] Maryland Prerogative Court Wills 26, p. 125.

[56] Maryland Prerogative Court Wills 14, p. 281-82.

[57] Maryland Prerogative Court Wills 11, p.48.

[58] Wise, *op. cit.*, p. 16.

[59] Somerset Co., Md., Judicial Record 1711-12, pp. 101-02.

[60] Wise, *op. cit.*, pp. 452-53.

[61] Maryland Prerogative Court Wills 14, p. 625.

[62] Wise, *op. cit.*, pp. 411-12.

[63] Maryland Prerogative Court Wills 22, p. 446.

[64] Maryland Prerogative Court Wills 22, p. 414.

[65] Wise, *op. cit.*, p. 412.

[66] Coventry Parish, Somerset Co., Md., Register.

who joined him in a deed, 6 July 1757.[67]

22. JEFFREY[4] LONG (Jane[3] Menshall, Frances[2] Carsley, Henry[1]) left will 1 July 1731-17 June 1732.[68] He married Mary Seawell.

Issue: [LONG][69] 95. JANE[5]; 96. JEFFREY[5]; 97. SAMUEL[5]; 98. SEWELL[5]; 99. David[5], born 1717, died by 23 Sept. 1762 when his brother Sewell as administrator returned the inventory his estate,[70] shipwright of Anne Arundel Co., Md., married, 22 Oct. 1759,[71] Mary Boone; 100. Mary[5].

23. RANDALL[4] LONG (Jane[3] Menshall, Frances[2] Carsley, Henry[1]), born 4 Oct. 1682, left will 23 Dec. 1739-23 Feb. 1739/40.[72] He married Sarah (Cottingham) Hey, daughter of Thomas and Mary (Dixon) Cottingham and widow of George Hey, who was born 31 Aug. 1673 and died after 18 Nov. 1741 when she deeded "Mates Enjoyment" to her children Thomas and Ann Prior.[73]

Issue: [LONG] 101. ANN[5]; 102. MARY[5]; 103. Sarah[5], married 97. Samuel[5] Long.

25. ANN[4] LONG (Jane[3] Menshall, Frances[2] Carsley, Henry[1]), born 25 May 1685, married (1) [Thomas?] Wood and perhaps (2), as his (2) wife, Thomas Adams [Addams], who left will 29 March 1735-7 July 1735.[74]

Issue: (by 1) [WOOD] 104. WILLIAM[5]; 105. Mary[5]. deposed, 20 Oct. 1776, she was aged 60 and sister of William Wood,[75] married, 26 Sept. 1750,[76] as his (2) wife, Henry Potter of Somerset Co., Md., who left will 8 April 1769-2 May 1769.[77]

34. MARY[4] MITCHELL (Randolph[3], Frances[2] Carsley, Henry[1]), born 27 Sept. 1693,[78] married Thomas White.

---

[67] Somerset Co., Md., Deed Bk. B, pp. 184-85.

[68] Maryland Prerogative Court Wills 20, p. 402.

[69] Wise, *op. cit.*, p. 412.

[70] Maryland Prerogative Court Inventories 77, p. 179.

[71] St. Margaret's Parish Register.

[72] Maryland Prerogative Court Wills 22, p. 148.

[73] Somerset Co., Md., Deed Bk. MF #29, p. 254.

[74] Maryland Prerogative Court Wills 21, p. 442.

[75] Somerset Co. Judicial Record 1775-84, p. 112.

[76] Coventry Parish, Somerset Co., Md., Register.

[77] Maryland Prerogative Court Wills 37, p. 237.

[78] Somerset Co., Md., Deed Bk. IKL, p. 173.

Issue: [WHITE][79] 106. (Child)[5], died young.

35. JOHN[4] MOORE (Anne[3] Menshall, Frances[2] Carsley, Henry[1]), born 4 April 1686,[80] married ___.

Issue: [MOORE][81] 107. MARY[5]; 108. ANN[5]; 109. ELIZABETH[5]; 110. SARAH[5].

40. STEPHEN[4] WHITE (Alice[3] Menshall, Frances[2] Carsley, Henry[1]), born 10 Sept. 1693,[82] died by 1723.[83] He married ___.

Issue: [WHITE] 111. John[5], married Mary ___, who joined him in selling, 18 June 1740, land inherited from his grandfather;[84] 112. WILLIAM[5].

42. JOHN[4] WHITE (Alice[3] Menshall, Frances[2] Carsley, Henry[1]), born 3 Jan. 1697,[85] left will 10 April 1749-27 May 1748.[86] He married Mary (___) Prior[87].

Issue: [WHITE] 113. SARAH[5]; 114. BETTY[5]; 115. RACHEL[5]; 116. MARY[5]; 117. Alice[5], died after 15 Oct. 1765 when her husband sold the land slave and personalty devised to her by her father,[88] married John Juett, who died before 2 Aug. 1775 when the inventory of his estate was made.[89]

50. ISAAC[4] MITCHELL (Thomas[3], Frances[2] Carsley, Henry[1]) deposed, Jan. 1755, he was aged 45[90] and died by 1783 when his widow was charged with 68½ acres of "Amity." He owned 200 acres, "Amity," at Manokin, Somerset Co., Md. He married Bridget Waller, daughter of William and Bridget (Nelson) Waller.

---

[79] Somerset Co., Md., Deed Bk. A, 1748-53, pp. 155-56, sale, 25 Jan. 1750/1, by John Mitchell as heir at law of the eldest uncle of Mary (Mitchell) White by the father's side, of land in possession of Thomas White by curtesy of England.

[80] Somerset Co., Md., Deed Bk. IKL, p. 171.

[81] Somerset Co., Md., Deed Bk. X #1, pp. 135, 164, deeds, 20 March 1744/5 when the other heirs of John Moore sold to Beauchamp Davis, and, 18 July 1745, when he and wife Mary sold the land to Thomas Moore.

[82] Somerset Co., Md., Deed Bk. IKL, p. 287.

[83] Maryland Prerogative Court Accounts 14, p. 331.

[84] Somerset Co., Md., Deed Bk. MF #Y, 1738-42, p. 157.

[85] Wise, *op. cit.*, p. 421.

[86] Maryland Prerogative Court Wills 26, p. 123.

[87] Somerset Co., Md., Deed Bk. MF #Y, pp. 171-73, sale, 21 Aug. 1740, joined by Joshua Merrill and Sarah his wife, of land she bought, 18 Nov. 1719, while she was the widow Pryor.

[88] Somerset Co., Md., Deed Bk. D, p. 10.

[89] Somerset Co., Md., Will Bk. EB #1, p. 90., naming Mary Juett and Nathaniel Juett as nearest of kin.

[90] Somerset Co., Md., Judicial Record 1754-57, p. 61.

Issue: [MITCHELL][91] 118. WILLIAM[5]; 119. George[5], died before 1800; 120. Ann[5], deposed, 23 Sept. 1799, she was aged 56; 121. Thomas[5]; 122. Margaret[6]; 123. Isaac[6].

53. RANDALL[4] MITCHELL (Thomas[3], Frances[2] Carsley, Henry[1]) deposed, 22 Jan. 1755, he was aged 32[92] and died before 29 Dec. 1780 when Stephen Mitchell was granted administration on his estate.[93] He married Sarah ___, who joined him in selling land, 26 March 1752.[94]

Issue: [MITCHELL] 124. Stephen[5], who joined his father in selling land, 25 March 1772,[95] moved to Sussex Co., Del., left will dated 1 Dec. 1810,[96] married, by 6 May 1783, Elizabeth ___, widow of William Baggs Lacey.[97]

54. STEPHEN[4] MITCHELL (Thomas[3], Frances[2] Carsley, Henry[1]), born about 1724, left will 2 Dec. 1788-20 Jan. 1789.[98] He married Priscilla Ballard,[99] who left will 13 Sept. 1798-13 Nov. 1798.[100]

Issue: [MITCHELL] 125. Levin[5]; 126. Thomas[5]; 127. Henry[5]; 128. William[5]; 129. Mary[5], married ____ Johnson; 130. NANCY[5]; 131. Amelia[5], married ___ Morris.

55. THOMAS[5] TULL (Thomas[4], Mary[3] Menshall, Frances[2] Carsley, Henry[1]) left will 30 Oct. 1757-28 Oct. 1758.[101] He married, before 19 Nov. 1729 when they sold 100 acres of "Winter Range" which he inherited as heir at law of his grandfather,[102] Rachel ___, who married (2) 64. Solomon[4] Tull.

Issue: [TULL][103] 132. William[6], married (1), 10 Nov. 1756, Mary Newbold and (2) Taby ___, who relinquished dower then he sold land, 29 June 1765, to

---

[91] Wise, *op. cit.*, p. 421.

[92] Somerset Co., Md., Judicial Record 1754-57, p. 61.

[93] Sussex Co., Del., Estate Records A89, p.. 64.

[94] Somerset Co., Md., Deed Bk. B, p. 65.

[95] Somerset Co., Md., Deed Bk. E, p. 184.

[96] Sussex Co., Del., Probate 1810-13, Delaware State Archives, without probate entry.

[97] Sussex Co., Del. Estate Records A83, p. 29.

[98] Somerset Co., Md., Will Bk. EB #17, p. 41.

[99] Maryland Prerogative Court Wills 29, p. 509, will of Henry Ballard, 11 July 1755-24 July 1755.

[100] Somerset Co., Md., Will Bk. EB #17, pp. 689-90.

[101] Maryland Prerogative Court Wills 30, p. 634.

[102] Somerset Co., Md., Deed Bk. SH, p. 204.

[103] Woodrow T. Wilson, *Thirty-Four Families of Old Somerset Co., Maryland* (Baltimore, 1977), p. 275; Coventry Parish, Somerset Co., Md., Register.

his brother Thomas;[104] 133. Thomas[6], joiner of Somerset Co., Md., left will 31 Dec. 1816-24 Feb. 1818,[105] married, 11 May 1769, Elizabeth Merrill, born 15 June 1750; 134. Charles[6]; 135. Rhoda[6]; 136. Handy[6], died 1 Aug. 1796,[106] Revolutionary War soldier, married Eleanor ___, who married (2) ___ Mix; 137. Rachel[6], born 15 Feb. 1743/4, married, 1762, Elijah Coulbourn; 138. Samuel[6], born 13 Oct. 1746; 139. Levin[6] [Fearum], born 20 July 1749.

56. SAMUEL[5] TULL (Thomas[4], Mary[3] Menshall, Frances[2] Carsley, Henry[1]), born 6 April 1702,[107] died 1792. He married Sarah Maddux, who left will 30 Sept. 1796-8 Nov. 1796.[108]

Issue: [TULL][109] 140. Agnes[6], married ___ Stuett; 141. Levin[6], married Peggy ___, who joined him, 9 Oct. 1800. In selling to Littleton Dorsey the land of his father which he had taken at sale;[110] 142. Rebecca[6], died before 1810, married Richard Roe [Rowe]; 143. Eleanor[6], died before 1810, married Thomas Slocomb; 144. Sally[6], died before 1810, married John Wilson; 145. Leah[6], married Littleton Dorsey; 146. Henrietta[6], married Francis Murray; 147. Peggy[6]; 148. George[6], died before 1810, married ___; 149. Sarah[6], married Joshua Hall; 150. Samuel[6], died before his father, married ___; 151. Betsey[6], died before her father, married Thomas Hall; 152. Elijah[6], died before his father, married Bridget Fontaine.

61. ISAAC[5] TULL (Thomas[4], Mary[3] Menshall, Frances[2] Carsley, Henry[1]), born 16 Dec. 1718, died 1784. He moved to Lenoir Co., N.C., where he was a carpenter. He married, 24 Feb. 1743 in Baltimore Co., Md., Winifred (Watts) Caldwell, who was born 25 Oct. 1720 and died 18 May 1806, daughter of John and Ann (___) Watts.[111]

Issue: [TULL] 153. John[6], born 15 Oct.1744 at Baltimore, Md., died 21 Sept. 1820 in Lenoir Co., N.C., married, 23 Sept. 1779, Elizabeth Cannon, who died 30 Dec. 1820; 154. Charles[6], born 19 Oct. 1746 in Dobbs Co., N.C., died

---

[104] Somerset Co., Md., Deed Bk. C, p. 262.

[105] Somerset Co., Md., Will Bk. EB #23, p. 263.

[106] His estate was not settled until 13 Oct. 1838 in Woodford Co., Ky. (Wilson, *op. cit.*, p. 275).

[107] Somerset Co., Md., Judicial Record 1760-62, p. 215.

[108] Somerset Co., Md., Will Bk. EB #17, pp. 565-67.

[109] Somerset Co., Md., Judicial Record 1810, p. 394; Wilson, *op. cit.*, p 274.

[110] Somerset Co., Md., Deed Bk. T, pp. 572-73.

[111] Henry C. Peden, *Marylanders to Carolina* (Westminster, Md., 1994), pp. 159-60; Wilson, *op. cit.*, p. 275.

28 June 1747; 155. Elizabeth[6], born 6 Feb. 1748/9 at Baltimore, Md.; 156. Ann[6], born 23 May 1751; 157. Charles[6], born 22 Dec. 1753 at Baltimore, Md., died 8 Oct. 1836, served in the North Carolina militia during the Revolutionary War,[112] married, Jan. 1779, Sarah Handy, who was born 24 Oct. 1763 and died 12 Feb. 1843; 158. William[6], born 12 April 1756 in Johnston Co., N.C., died 8 Oct. 1818, private in North Carolina militia during the Revolutionary War, married Susannah ___; 159. Rev. Isaac[6], born 18 Nov. 1758, left will proved July 1813,[113] of Bourbon Co., Ky., first teacher at Bourbon Academy, 1800-02,[114] married (1) ___ and (2) Betsey ___; 160. Sarah[6], born 6 Dec. 1761.

64. SOLOMON[5] TULL (Richard[4], Mary[3] Menshall, Frances[2] Carsley, Henry[1]), of Somerset Co., Md., left will 20 July 1769-6 July 1773.[115] He married (1) Elizabeth ___, who joined him in the sale of land, 10 Aug. 1734,[116] and (2) Rachel (___) Tull, widow of 55. Thomas[5] Tull, who joined him in the sale of land 18 June 1766.[117]

Issue: [TULL] 161. Solomon[6].

68. JOHN[5] TULL (John[4], Mary[3] Menshall, Frances[2] Carsley, Henry[1]), of Somerset Co., Md., left will 27 April 1780-13 June 1780.[118] He married Alice ___.

Issue: [TULL] 162. Mary[6], married ___ Gray; 163. Rhoda[6], born 27 Oct. 1747,[119] married __ Hall; 164. Sarah[6]; 165. Martha[6], married William Warwick who left will 7 Jan. 1784-23 March 1784;[120] 166. Esther[6].

69. JOSHUA[5] TULL (John[4], Mary[3] Menshall, Frances[2] Carsley, Henry[1]), cordwainer of Somerset Co., Md., deposed 5 April 1762 he was aged 51[121] and left will 3 May 1795-16 Oct. 1798.[122] He married _____.

Issue: [TULL][123] 167. Thomas[6], of Somerset Co., Md., left will 9 Jan.

---

[112] Revolutionary War pension application, Charles Tull, S.7769, National Archives.

[113] Bourbon Co., Ky., Will Bk. D, p. 378.

[114] William Henry Perrin, ed., *History of Bourbon, Scott, Harrison and Nicholas Counties, Kentucky* (Chicago, 1882), p. 112.

[115] Maryland Prerogative Court Wills 39, p. 230.

[116] Somerset Co., Md., Deed Bk. AZ, p. 179.

[117] Somerset Co., Md., Deed Bk. D, pp. 30-31.

[118] Somerset Co., Md., Will Bk. EB #1, pp. 136-37.

[119] Coventry Parish, Somerset Co., Md., Register.

[120] Somerset Co., Md., Will Bk. EB #1, pp. 194-95.

[121] Somerset Co., Md., Judicial Record 1760-63, p. 215.

[122] Somerset Co., Md., Will Bk. EB #17, p. 682.

[123] Wise, *op. cit.*, p. 455.

1811-5 March 1811,[124] married Leah ___; 168. Esther[6], married Charles Hall; 169. Joshua[6], born 13 Nov. 1747, died 1812 at Baltimore, Md., Revolutionary War soldier, married, 22 Sept. 1780 in New York, Mary Thorp, born 30 April 1755,[125] died 7 Feb.1840.[126]

70. MARY[5] TULL (John[4], Mary[3] Menshall, Frances[2] Carsley, Henry[1]) is probably the daughter who married ___ Wharton.

Issue: [WHARTON] 170. Sophia[6].

72. STEPHEN[5] TULL (John[4], Mary[3] Menshall, Frances[2] Frances, Henry[1]) of Somerset Co., Md., left will 12 Nov. 1794-31 March 1795.[127] He married, 1747, 50. *Sarah[6] Hall* (see DAVIS), born 15 May 1725,[128] died before 12 Jan. 1812.[129]

Issue: [TULL][130] 171. Priscilla[6], born 4 Jan. 1750/1; 172. Richard[6], born 4 Feb. 1752/3; 173. James[6], born 19 April 1754; 174. Esther[6], born 12 Sept. 1757, married ___ Maddox; 175. Levi[6], born 14 Dec. 1760; 176. Betty[6], born 6 July 1765; 177. Sarah[6], born 25 March 1769, died 14 Dec. 1818, married, 21 Dec. 1786, as his (1) wife, Isaac[7] Harris, son of 197. Mary[6] (Marshall) Harris, who died 23 June 1824,[131] left will 21 March 1816-27 July 1824.[132]

73. ESTHER[5] TULL (John[4], Mary[3] Menshall, Frances[2] Carsley, Henry[1]) married ___ Beauchamp.

Issue: [BEAUCHAMP] 178. Edward[6].

74. ISAAC[5] BOSTON (Elizabeth[4] Long, Jane[3] Menshall, Frances[2] Carsley, Henry[1]), born about 1694, deposed 26 Aug. 1740 he was aged 45 and 31 Aug. 1744 he was aged 50[133] and left will 30 April 1751-28 Sept. 1751.[134] He married Rachel Tomlinson.

Issue: [BOSTON][135] 179. Isaac[6], planter and mariner of Somerset Co., Md.,

---

[124] Somerset Co., Md., Will Bk. EB #23, p. 168.

[125] Wilson, *op. cit.*, p. 272.

[126] *Sun*, Baltimore, Md., 11 Feb. 1840.

[127] Somerset Co., Md., Will Bk. EB #17, pp. 381-82.

[128] Coventry Parish, Somerset Co., Md., Register.

[129] Wise, *op. cit.*, p. 395.

[130] Coventry Parish, Somerset Co., Md., Register.

[131] Harris Bible, Maryland Historical Society; Wise, *op. cit.*, p. 398.

[132] Somerset Co., Md., Will Bk. JP #4, p. 85.

[133] Somerset Co., Md., Judicial Record 1740-42, pp. 43-45; Judicial Record 1742-44, p. 263.

[134] Maryland Prerogative Court Wills 28, p. 195.

[135] Wise, *op. cit.*, pp. 19, 21-23.

died after April 1765; 180. Abigail[6], born 24 Feb. 1724, married, 11 May 1746,[136] Henry White, who was born 20 July 1725 and died 16 Dec. 1756; 181. Samuel[6], died before 15 April 1765,[137] unmarried; 182. Sarah[6], died 1764-81, married ___ Evans; 183. David[6], died before 3 Sept. 1761,[138] unmarried; 184. Solomon[6], left will 1 Aug. 1806-26 Jan. 1807,[139] mariner and planter of Accomack County, married Elizabeth [Litchfield?]; 185. Naboth[6], died before 5 Aug. 1785 when his widow gave bond as his administratrix,[140] married Sarah (_____) Wharton; 186. Rebecca[6], left will 27 May 1784-9 Nov. 1784,[141] unmarried; 187. Martha[6], died after 1784 when named in Rebecca's will, unmarried; 188. Daniel[6], died before 16 Nov. 1832,[142] married (1) Sarah Collins and (2) Sally ___.

77. GEORGE[5] MARSHALL (Elizabeth[4] Long, Frances[3] Menshall, Frances[2] Carsley, Henry[1]) of Somerset Co., Md., deposed, 26 Aug. 1740, he was aged 36[143] and died before 2 Oct. 1760.[144] He married Mary Adams, daughter of Philip amd Ellis (___) Adams.[145]

Issue: [MARSHALL] 189. Ellis [Alice][6], married John Hall; 190. Sarah[6], married ___ Davis; 191. Samuel[6]; 192. Adrian[6], died before 23 Dec. 1777 when his widow petitioned for administration on his estate,[146] married Peggy ___; 193. Elizabeth[6], married John Swift; 194. Mary[6]; 195. George[6], born 1746, left will 9 Nov. 1802-18 Jan. 1803,[147] married (1) ___, (2) ___, and (3) Gertrude ___.

78. SAMUEL[5] MARSHALL (Elizabeth[4] Long, Frances[3] Menshall, Frances[2] Carsley, Henry[1]) deposed, 28 June 1753, he was aged 46 and, 1759, he

---

[136] Coventry Parish, Somerset Co., Md., Register.

[137] Somerset Co., Md., Deed Bk. 24, p. 251.

[138] Maryland Prerogative Court Accounts 76, p. 138.

[139] Accomack Co. Will Bk. 1806-09, pp. 36-37.

[140] Worcester Co., Md., Bonds JW #12, pp. 290-91.

[141] Somerset Co., Md., Will Bk. EB #1, p. 214.

[142] Somerset Co., Md., Bonds JP #8, pp. 235-36.

[143] Somerset Co., Md., Judicial Record 1740-42, p. 43. He also deposed 3 July 1742 as 39, 18 Nov. 1745 as 42, 31 May 1755 as 53, and 11 Aug. 1755 as 53 (*ibid.*, 1742-44, p. 152; 1744-47, p. 97; 1754-57, pp. 114,,136).

[144] Wise, *op. cit.*, p. 417.

[145] Maryland Prerogative Court Wills 38, p. 625, will of Philip Adams, 6 July 1769-30 Jan. 1772.

[146] Somerset Co., Md., Will Bk. EB #1, pp. 56-57.

[147] Somerset Co., Md., Will Bk. EB #23, p. 62.

was aged 56.[148] He married Grace Adams, daughter of Philip and Ellis (___) Adams, who married (2) his brother Thomas Marshall.

Issue: [MARSHALL][149] 196. (probably) Samuel[6], of Saxis Island, Accomack County.[150]

79. THOMAS[5] MARSHALL (Elizabeth[4] Long, Jane[3] Menshall, Frances[2] Carsley, Henry[1]) deposed 20 Oct. 1776 he was aged 69 but 20 May 1775 he was aged 60[151] and left will 24 April 1786-20 June 1786.[152] He married (1), by 18 May 1736, Jane (___) Haith, widow of Abraham Haith,[153] and (2) his sister-in-law Grace (Adams) Marshall.

Issue: [MARSHALL] (by 1) 197. Mary[6], married, 26 May 1757,[154] John Harris, who left will 13 Feb. 1788-13 Nov. 1793;[155] 198. Esther[6], born 6 Jan. 1742,[156] married, 25 March 1766, Thomas Marshall; 199. Martha[6], died 30 Sept. 1754; (by 2?) 200. Isaac[6], married, 17 Feb. 1768,[157] Sarah Tilghman; 201. Stephen[6], of Accomack County, married, 12 April 1770,[158] 322. Mary[6] Gunby, who was born 29 Dec. 1753[159] and died before 1800.[160]

81. ANN[5] LONG (John[4], Jane[3] Menshall, Frances[2] Carsley, Henry[1]) left nuncupative will 22 Oct. 1770-17 Dec. 1770.[161] She married James Trahern of Somerset Co., Md., who left will 28 Aug. 1769-23 March 1770.[162]

Issue: [TRAHERN][163] 202. Samuel[6], born about 1732, died 1804, married

---

[148] Somerset Co., Md., Judicial Record 1752-54, p. 127; 1760-63, p. 37.

[149] Vernon L. Skinner and F. Edward Wright, *Colonial Families of the Eastern Shore of Maryland*, X (Westminster, Md., 2000), p. 191.

[150] One Samuel Marshall of Saxis Island died before 28 April 1851 when administration was granted on his estate (Accomack Co. Order Bk. 1851-54, p. 2).

[151] Somerset Co., Md., Judicial Record 1775-84, pp. 112, 135.

[152] Somerset Co., Md., Will Bk. EB #1, p. 245.

[153] Maryland Prerogative Court Inventories 21, p. 371.

[154] Coverntry Parish, Somerset Co., Md., Register.

[155] Somerset Co., Md., Will Bk. EB #17, pp. 276-79.

[156] Coventry Parish, Somerset Co., Md., Register.

[157] *Ibid.*

[158] *Ibid.*

[159] *Ibid.*

[160] Wise, *op. cit.*, p. 395.

[161] Maryland Prerogative Court Wills 38, p. 186.

[162] Maryland Prerogative Court Wills 37, p. 508.

[163] Pauline Manning Batchelder, *A Somerset Sampler, Families of Old Somerset County, Maryland, 1700-1776* (n.p., 1994), p. 270.

Tabitha ___; 203. Cyrus[6], born 22 July 1746;[164] 204. Betty[6]; 205. Glepora[6], married ___ Silbet.

83. JOHN[5] LONG (John[4], Jane[3] Menshall, Frances[2] Carsley, Henry[1]) of Somerset Co., Md., left will 10 Feb. 1772-4 March 1775.[165] He married, 8 Nov. 1768,[166] Mary Adams.

Issue: [LONG] 206. Colbourne[6], born 28 Sept. 1769, left will 31 July 1801-17 Sept. 1801,[167] married, (license 30) Dec. 1800,[168] Sarah Price; 207. Elizabeth[6], born 7 March 1771, married ___ Lankford..

84. WILLIAM[5] LONG (John[4], Jane[3] Menshall, Frances[2] Carsley, Henry[1]) left will 27 May 1768-17 June 1768.[169] He resided in Worcester Co., Md., and married Naomi Griffin, daughter of William and Margaret (Tomlinson) Griffin.

Issue: [LONG] 208. John[6], joined his aunt and uncle, David and Abigail Long, 26 May 1770, in selling land,[170] died before 21 July 1770 when the inventory of his estate was made,[171].married Elizabeth ___; 209. Daniel[6]; 210. Abigail[6]; 211. Jesse[6]; 212. Isaac[6]; 213. Samuel[6]; 214. Molley[6].

85. DAVID[5] LONG (John[4], Jane[3] Menshall, Frances[2] Carsley, Henry[1]), of Worcester Co., Md., left will 24 Oct. 1782-21 July 1783.[172] He married Abigail Griffin, daughter of William and Margaret (Tomlinson) Griffin, who left will 2 Feb. 1784-26 March 1784.[173]

Issue: [LONG][174] 215. Samuel[5], of Worcester Co., Md.; 216. Elihu[6], of Worcester Co., Md., left will 2 Jan. 1791-1 Feb. 1791,[175] unmarried; 217. Hampton[6], died 22 Feb. 1840 in Pickaway Co., Ohio, aged 71,[176] married, (license 8) Oct. 1806,[177] Betsy Hargrove; 218. Solomon[6], died about 1800;

---

[164] Coventry Parish, Somerset Co., Md., Register.

[165] Maryland Prerogative Court Wills 40, p. 346.

[166] Coventry Parish, Somerset Co., Md., Register.

[167] Worcester Co., Md., Will Bk. JBR #1, p. 253.

[168] Worcester Co., Md., Marriage license.

[169] Maryland Prerogative Court Wills 36, p. 505.

[170] Worcester Co., Md., Deed Bk. H, p. 343.

[171] Maryland Prerogative Court Inventories 111, p. 7.

[172] Worcester Co., Md., Will Bk. JW #4, p. 527.

[173] Worcester Co., Md., Will Bk. JW #13, pp. 22-23.

[174] Wise, *op. cit.*, p. 412, 451-52.

[175] Worcester Co., Md., Will Bk. JW #18, p. 3.

[176] Gravestone, Greenland Cemetery, in Pickaway Plains Chapter DAR, "Index of Grave-Stones, Pickaway County, Ohio" (typewritten; n.p., 1936), p. 64.

[177] Worcester Co., Md., Marriage license.

married Comfort (___) White; 219. Margaret[6]; 220. David[6], died by 17 June 1778 when his administratrix gave bond,[178] married Elizabeth ___, who left will 21 July 1821-23 Sept. 1825;[179] 221. Charlotte[6]; 222. Ann[6], married Benjamin Gray, who died 1790; 223. Coulbourne[6], left will 9 Feb. 1809-14 Feb. 1809,[180] married, (license 22) Aug. 1799,[181] Mary (___) Davis, widow of Edward Davis; 224. Sally[6], married ___ Truitt.

86. COLBOURNE[5] LONG (John[4], Jane[3] Menshall, Frances[2] Carsley, Henry[1]) died about 1780.[182] He married (1) Easter ___, who died 3 May 1759, and (2), 29 Oct. 1759, Abigail Harris.

Issue: [LONG] (by 1)[183] 225. Martha[6], born 11 Aug. 1748; 226. Priscilla[6], born 22 Nov. 1751, married, 3 Nov. 1768, John Handy, born 27 Aug. 1749, of Nassawadux, Somerset Co., Md.;[184] 227. Leah[6], born 31 Aug. 1753, died 3 Sept. 1761; 228. Nancy[6], born 17 Nov. 1756.

87. DAVID[5] LONG (Daniel[4], Jane[3] Menshall, Frances[2] Carsley, Henry[1]) died 15 Sept. 1756.[185] He married Abigail Lidster, daughter of William and Jean (___) Lidster [Lister], who married (2) George Layfield and left will 20 Oct. 1773-21 Dec. 1773.[186]

Issue: [LONG][187] 229. Littleton[6], born 7 April 1738, left will 14 Aug. 1803-24 Oct. 1803,[188] married Sarah Merrill, born about 1748;[189] 230. Levi[6], born 24 June 1739; 231. David[6], born 2 Feb. 1742/3, died 29 April 1825, tailor of Worcester Co., Md., married (1) Eleanor White, born 17 May 1749, died 1 Feb. 1797, and (2), (license 17) Jan. 1801,[190] Sally Burnett; 232. Jesse Wing[6], born 18 Oct. 1745, left will 7 Dec. 1811-1 Jan. 1812,[191] of Worcester Co., Md.,

---

[178] Worcester Co., Md., Administration Bonds JW #12, pp. 50-51.

[179] Worcester Co., Md., Will Bk. MH #27, pp. 158-59.

[180] Worcester Co., Md., Will Bk. MH #4, p. 149, as Colevein.

[181] Worcester Co., Md., Marriage license.

[182] Wise, *op. cit.*, p. 412.

[183] Coventry Parish, Somerset Co., Md., Register.

[184] Isaac W. K. Handy, *Annals and Memorials of the Handys and their Kindred*, ed by Mildred Handy Ritchie and Sarah Rozelle Handy Mallon (Ann Arbor, Mich., 1992), pp. 78-79.

[185] Coventry Parish, Somerset Co., Md., Register.

[186] Maryland Prerogative Court Wills 39, p. 568.

[187] Coventry Parish, Somerset Co., Md., Register.

[188] Worcester Co., Md., Will Bk. JBR #6, p. 103.

[189] Wuse, *op. cit.*, p. 453.

[190] Worcester Co., Md., Marriage license.

[191] Worcester Co., Md., Will Bk. MH #4, p. 306.

married Rebecca ___, who left will 13 March 1815-1 Oct. 1816;[192] 233. Josiah[6], born 7 Oct. 1747, left will 28 March 1774-12 April 1774,[193] married Caty ___; 234. Levin[6], born 10 June 1752, died Oct. 1815 in Worcester Co., Md.,[194] married Margaret Chaille.

88. SOLOMON[5] LONG (Daniel[4], Jane[3] Menshall, Frances[2] Carsley, Henry[1]) deposed, 19 May 1740, he was aged 40[195] and left will 1 Oct. 1765-18 Feb. 1772.[196] He married (1) [Elizabeth?] Roach, daughter of Nathaniel and Elizabeth (Curtis) Roach, and (2), between 3 March 1735/6 and 11 July 1737,[197] Margaret Maddox, daughter of Thomas and Mary (___) Maddux.

Issue: [LONG][198] (by 1) 235. Elizabeth[6], married, 16 Jan. 1748/9,[199] Joseph Ward of Somerset Co., Md., who left will 2 Feb. 1772-25 July 1776;[200] 236. Daniel[6], died about 1750; 237. Mary[6], married William Morgan; (by 2)[201] 238. David, died before 23 Oct. 1804,[202] married (1) 272. Sarah[6] Long, born 18 Oct. 1745, and (2) Anne Gibbons, who married (2) Edward Beauchamp; 239. Jane[6], married John Howard; 240. Sarah[6], married, 14 Jan. 1762,[203] Brittain Powell, born 1737, of Coventry Parish, Somerset Co., Md., who left will 1 March 1796-15 March 1796;[204] 241. Matilda[6], married Henry Corker; 242. Solomon[6], captain of 2nd Maryland Regiment from Oct. 1776 to March 1778, farmer and merchant of "Trader's Branch," Somerset Co., Md., left will 17 Nov. 1797-2 Nov. 1798,[205] married Mary _____;[206] 243. Rebecca[6], married (1) 118. William[5]

---

[192] Worcester Co., Md., Will Bk. MH #10, p. 219.

[193] Maryland Prerogative Court Wills 39, p. 751.

[194] Wise, *op. cit.*, p. 414.

[195] Somerset Co., Md., Judicial Record 1742-44, p. 263.

[196] Maryland Prerogative Court Wills 38, p. 615.

[197] Somerset Co., Md., Will Bk. EB #9, p. 192; Maryland Prerogative Court Accounts 14, p. 334.

[198] Wise, *op. cit.*, pp. 412, 414.

[199] Coventry Parish, Somerset Co., Md., Register.

[200] Maryland Prerogative Court Wills 41, p. 112.

[201] Wise, *op. cit.*, pp. 412, 414; *Maryland Genealogical Society Bulletin*, XXX, pp. 253-56.

[202] Somerset Co., Md., Will Bk. EB #4, p. 110.

[203] Coventry Parish, Somerset Co., Md., Register.

[204] Somerset Co., Md., Will Bk. EB #17, pp. 496-500.

[205] Somerset Co., Md., Will Bk. EB #17, pp. 687-89.

[206] *Maryland Genealogical Society Bulletin*, XXX, p. 256, gives his wife as Sally Long Tingle.

Mitchell and (2) [James?] Hammond; 244. William[6], left will 4 May 1777-27 May 1777;[207] 245. Zadock[6], born 7 March 1756, died 3 Feb. 1838 at Princess Ann, Md., served in the Revolutionary War, left will 10 Dec. 1835-23 Feb. 1835,[208] married ___.

90. CHRISTIAN[5] LONG (Daniel[4], Jane[3] Menshall, Frances[2] Carsley, Henry[1]), living 19 Feb. 1772 when she signed the inventory of her brother Solomon as next of kin,[209] married (1) Edward Stogdell, who died before 12 April 1740 when the inventory of his estate was made, and (2), by 28 July 1740, John Howard.[210]

Issue: (by 1) [STOGDELL] 246. Jane[6]; 247. Sofia[6]; 248. Edward[6].

91. DANIEL[5] LONG (Daniel[4], Jane[3] Menshall, Frances[2] Carsley, Henry[1]) married Sarah Conner.

Issue: [LONG] 249. Solomon[6], born 6 May 1752.[211]

92. RACHEL[5] LONG (Daniel[4], Jane[3] Menshall, Frances[2] Carsley, Henry[1]) married Dennis Adams [Addams], son of William Addams, of Somerset Co., Md., who left will 8 March 1773-1 April 1777.[212]

Issue: [ADAMS] 250. Sebra[6]; 251. William[6].

93. SARAH[5] LONG (Daniel[4], Jane[3] Menshall, Frances[2] Carsley, Henry[1]) died about 1797.[213] She married (1) 96. Jeffrey[5] Long and (2), as his (2) wife, William Fleming, who deposed, 6 Jan. 1792, he was aged 78[214] and left will 14 Dec. 1798-codicil 9 Sept. 1800-8 Feb. 1803.[215]

Issue: (by 1) [LONG] q.v.; (by 2) [FLEMING][216] 252. William[6], died before 2 Sept. 1828, married (1) (license 3) April 1803,[217] Elizabeth[7] Tull, daughter of 167. Thomas[6] and Leah Tull, and (2), (license 7) Dec. 1813,[218] her sister Sarah[7] Tull.

---

[207] Somerset Co., Md., Will Bk. EB #1, p. 6.

[208] Somerset Co., Md., Will Bk. JP #5, pp. 17-19.

[209] Maryland Prerogative Court Inventories 113, p. 305.

[210] Maryland Prerogative Court Inventories 25, p. 149; Maryland Preorgative Court Accounts 18, p. 207.

[211] Coventry Parish, Somerset Co., Md., Register.

[212] Maryland Prerogative Court Wills 41, p. 337.

[213] Wise, *op. cit.*, p. 389.

[214] Somerset Co., Md., Judicial Record 1791-94, p. 92.

[215] Somerset Co., Md., Will Bk. EB #23, p. 63.

[216] Wise, *op. cit.*, p. 390.

[217] Somerset Co., Md., Marriage license.

[218] *Ibid.*

95. JANE[5] LONG (Jeffrey[4], Jane[3] Menshall, Frances[2] Carsley, Henry[1]) left will 24 Nov. 1781-9 Sept. 1783.[219] She married (1) Thomas Handy, son of Samuel Handy, who died before 3 Aug. 1737 when the inventory of his estate was made,[220] and (2), 28 Feb. 1737/8,[221] Thomas Seon, who left will 6 May 1780-codicil 15 Aug. 1780-17 Jan. 1781.[222]

Issue:[223] (by 1) [HANDY] 253. Sowell [Saywell][6], born about 1732, left will 27 March 1776-19 Nov. 1777,[224] merchant and planter of Somerset Co., Md., married 25 Feb. 1759, Mary Ann Sudler who left will 25 Jan. 1782-15 Oct. 1782;[225] 254. Samuel[6], born about 1734, died in infancy; 255. Thomas[6], born about 1736, died 10 June 1750; (by 2) [SEON][226] 256. Samuel[6], born 24 Dec. 1738, living Jan. 1766; 257. Martha[6], born 29 March 1740, died before 6 May 1780, married John Sudler who died about 9 April 1787.

96. JEFFREY[5] LONG (Jeffrey[4], Jane[3] Menshall, Frances[2] Carsley, Henry[1]), of Somerset Co., Md., died 19 May 1762,[227] leaving will 18 May 1762-17 July 1762.[228] He married 93. Sarah[5] Long, who married (2) William Fleming..

Issue: [LONG][229] 258. Orpha[6], married (1), 8 Nov. 1759, Levi Brittingham and (2), 14 July 1762, Hezekiah Turpin; 259. Mary[6]; 260. Saywell [Sewell][6], born 22 Dec. 1747. died 19 May 1762; 261. Rachel[6], born 29 July 1750, married, 27 Nov. 1772, John Perkins; 262. Permenes[6], born 13 July 1755, died young; 263. Sarah[6], born 3 March 1756, married John Fleming; 264. Asseneth[6], born 3 April 1757; 265. Mary[6], married (1) ___ Scott and (2) ___ Broughton; 266. Esther[6], born 16 March 1762.

97. SAMUEL[5] LONG (Jeffrey[4], Jane[3] Menshall, Frances[2] Carsley, Henry[1]) deposed 3 July 1742 that he was aged 35[230] and left will 13 June 1756-11 Sept.

---

[219] Somerset Co., Md., EB #1, p. 185.

[220] Maryland Prerogative Court Inventories 22, p. 530. A chart prepared by John D. Long, Baltimore, Md., 31 March 1960, says died about 3 June 1737.

[221] Coventry Parish, Somerset Co., Md., Register.

[222] Somerset Co., Md., Will Bk. EB #1, pp. 143-44.

[223] John D. Long chart, *loc. cit.*; Isaac W. K. Handy, *Annals and Memorials of the Handys and Their Kindred* (Ann Arbor, Mich., 1992), p. 21, 61-62; Coventry Parish Register.

[224] Somerset Co., Md., Will Bk. EB #1, pp. 49-50.

[225] *Ibid.*, pp. 168-69.

[226] Coventry Parish, Somerset Co., Md., Register.

[227] *Ibid.*

[228] Maryland Prerogative Court Wills 31, p. 723.

[229] Coventry Parish, Somerset Co., Md., Register.

[230] Somerset Co., Md., Judicial Record 1742-44, p. 152.

1756,[231] married 103. Sarah[5] Long.

Issue: [LONG] 267. Jean[6], married ___ Beauchamp; 268. William[6]; 269. Mary[6]; 270. Randolph [Randall][6], left will 27 Dec. 1767-3 Feb. 1768;[232] 271. Jeffrey[6]; 272. Sarah[6], born 18 Oct. 1745, married 238. David[6] Long.; 273. Samuel[6], born 22 April 1750, left will 17 Nov. 1801-25 Jan. 1803,[233] married Sarah ___.

98. SEWELL[5] LONG (Jeffrey[4], Jane[3] Menshall, Frances[2] Carsley, Henry[1]), a shipwright, deposed, 1 Aug. 1770, he was aged 53.[234] He died on Kent Island, Queen Anne's Co., Md., leaving will 25 Feb. 1774-31 March 1774.[235] He marrried (1), 28 May 1745,[236] Mary Brooksby, who was born 19 Sept. 1720 in Anne Arundel Co., Md., and died there 18 Sept. 1750,[237] and (2) Ann (Emory) Sudler, widow of Joseph Sudler, Jr.

Issue: [LONG][238] 274. Anne[6], born 23 July 1745, died about 27 May 1788 in Queen Anne's Co., Md., married, 28 Feb. 1758, Thomas Sudler, son of her step-mother, who died about 27 May 1788 in Queen Anne's Co., Md.; 275. Cornelius[6], born 25 June 1747, died young; 276. Mary[6], born 4 Nov. 1749, died 18 Sept. 1753; 277. David[6], born 11 Aug. 1751.

101. ANN[5] LONG (Randall[4], Jane[3] Menshall, Frances[2] Carsley, Henry[1]) left will 19 Dec. 1772-26 Jan. 1773.[239] She married Thomas Pryor of Somerset Co., Md., who left will 15 Dec. 1744-19 April 1745.[240]

Issue: [PRYOR][241] 278. Samuel[6]; 279. Thomas[6], left will 3 March 1772-Nov. 1772,[242] married Esther ____, who married (2) John Malcolm;[243] 280.

---

[231] Maryland Prerogative Court Wills 30, p. 143.

[232] Maryland Prerogative Court Wills 36, p. 289.

[233] Somerset Co., Md., Will Bk. EB #23, 1800-20, pp. 62-63.

[234] Queen Anne's Co., Md., Land Commission Bk. 1769-1801, p. 28.

[235] Maryland Prerogative Court Wills 39, p. 887. An inventory of his estate, 15 April 1774, Queen Anne's Co., Md., was signed by David Long, executor, and Jean Seon and Samuel Seon as next of kin (Maryland Prerogative Court Inventories 119, p. 270).

[236] St. Margaret's Parish, Anne Arundel Co., Md., Register.

[237] John D. Long chart, *loc. cit.*

[238] *Ibid.*

[239] Maryland Prerogative Court Wills 39, p. 137.

[240] Maryland Prerogative Court Wills 24, p. 101.

[241] Somerset Co. Md., Administration Accounts EB 11, p. 217; Maryland Prerogative Court Accounts 73, p. 268. Two daughters married William Taylor and Richard Tull.

[242] Maryland Prerogative Court Wills 39, p. 112.

[243] Somerset Co., Md., Will Bk. EB #16, p. 165.

Sarah[6]; 281. Randall [Randolph][6], married, 23 Jan. 1759,[244] Easter Cottingham; 282. Rhode[6], married [George?] Wilson; 283. Ann[6]; 284. Mary[6]; 285. David[6].

102. MARY[5] LONG (Randall[4], Jane[3] Menshall, Frances[2] Carsley, Henry[1]) deposed 18 April 1752 she was aged 30.[245] She married Thomas Cottingham, son of Charles and Anne (Broughton) Cottingham, who left will 9 June 1783-17 April 1791.[246]

Issue: [COTTINGHAM][247] 286. David[6], born 17 March 1742/3, left will 2 Sept. 1785-13 Aug. 1785,[248] married, 12 Nov. 1767, Mary Gunby, born 29 Dec. 1753; 287. Mary[6], born 6 July 1745; 288. Thomas[6], born 2 May 1747; 289. Hannah[6], born 18 Jan. 1749/50; 290. Randall[6], born 6 July 1755; 291. Ruth[6], born 25 May 1759; 292. Bridget[6], born 5 Nov. 1760.

104. WILLIAM[5] WOOD (Ann[4] Long, Jane[3] Menshall, Frances[2] Carsley, Henry[1]), of Somerset Co., Md., left will 26 Oct. 1760-25 July 1761.[249] He married Ann Adams, daughter of his step-father, who died 31 Jan. 1773,[250] leaving will 25 Jan. 1773-9 March 1773.[251]

Issue: [WOOD][252] 293. Rachel[6], born 30 May 1739; 294. William[6], born 24 Sept. 1741; 295. Leah[6], born 3 Oct. 1744; 296. Sarah[6], born 15 Nov. 1746, married, 14 Oct. 1767, William Hall; 297. Levi[6], born 30 Dec. 1749, died 23 Jan. 1773, left will 19 Jan. 1773-9 March 1773;[253] 298. Ebe[6], born 19 June 1752; 299. Elijah[6], married ___; 300. Martha[6], born 3 Feb. 1757, married 336. John[6] Tull.

107. MARY[5] MOORE (John[4], Anne[3] Menshall, Frances[2] Carsley, Henry[1]) married Beauchamp Davis of Somerset Co., Md.,, who left will 15 Dec. 1777-11 Feb. 1782.[254]

Issue: [DAVIS][255] 301. John[6]; 302. Joshua[6], born 17 May 1737; 303.

---

[244] Coventry Parish, Somerset Co., Md., Register.
[245] Somerset Co., Md., Judicial Record 1752-54, p. 22.
[246] Somerset Co., Md., Will Bk. EB #17, pp. 146-47.
[247] Coventry Parish, Somerset Co., Md., Register.
[248] Somerset Co., Md., Will Bk. EB #1, pp. 275-76.
[249] Maryland Prerogative Court Wills 31, p. 386.
[250] Coventry Parish, Somerset Co., Md., Register.
[251] Maryland Prerogative Court Wills 39, p. 128.
[252] Coventry Parish, Somerset Co., Md., Regiater.
[253] Maryland Prerogative Court Wills 39, p. 127.
[254] Somerset Co., Md., Will Bk. EB #1, p. 173.
[255] Coventry Parish, Somerset Co., Md., Register.

Beauchamp[6], born 30 Oct. 1738, married, 13 Feb. 1764, Naomi Beauchamp; 304. Mary[6], born 11 Feb. 1744, married, 17 Feb. 1765, Handy Beauchamp; 305. Tabitha[6], born 21 Aug. 1746, married, 1 May 1765, Levin Beauchamp.

108 ANN[5] MOORE (John[4], Anne[3] Menshall, Frances[2] Carsley, Henry[1]) married Josephus Potter of Worcester Co., Md., who left will 5 Dec. 1755-7 May 1756.[256]

Issue: [POTTER] 306. Anne[6]; 307. Sarah[6]; 308. Alice[6]; 309. Rachel[6]; 310. Leah[6].

109. ELIZABETH[5] MOORE (John[4], Anne[3] Menshall, Frances[2] Carsley, Henry[1]) married John Wilson of Somerset Co., Md.

Issue: [WILSON][257] 311. Ephraim[6], born 5 Aug. 1748; 312. John[6], born 28 Aug. 1750.

110. SARAH[5] MOORE (John[4], Anne[3] Menshall, Frances[2] Carsley, Henry[1]) married, 14 Dec. 1744, Thomas Langford.

Issue: [LANGFORD][258] 313. Leah[6], born 28 June 1745; 314. Ephraim[6], born 23 Sept. 1747; 315. Thomas[6], born 23 June 1749; 316. Elizabeth[6], born 24 Dec. 1750.

111. WILLIAM[5] WHITE (Stephen[4], Alice[3] Menshall, Frances[2] Carsley, Henry[1]) married ___.

Issue: 317. Stephen[6], left will 27 Mar 1760-6 May 1761,[259] married Elizabeth ___, who married (2) Thomas Bruff, silversmith of Somerset Co., Md., and died after 1800; 318. Elias[6], married, 28 Feb. 1756,[260] Sarah Dixon.

113. SARAH[5] WHITE (John[4], Alice[3] Menshall, Frances[2] Carsley, Henry[1]) married, 26 Nov. 1744,[261] James Gunby of Somerset Co., Md., who left will 24 May 1800-2 Dec. 1800.[262]

Issue: [GUNBY][263] 319. John[6], born 30 Sept. 1745, died 27 May 1807, left will 11 Feb. 1807-9 June 1807,[264] commissioned captain of the 2nd Independent Company of Somerset County, 2 Jan. 1776, lieutenant colonel of 7th Regiment,

---

[256] Maryland Prerogative Court Wills 30, p. 77.
[257] Coventry Parish, Somerset Co., Md., Register.
[258] *Ibid.*
[259] Maryland Prerogative Court Wills 31, p. 294.
[260] Coventry Parish, Somerset Co., Md., Register.
[261] *Ibid.*
[262] Somerset Co., Md., Will Bk. EB #23, p. 26.
[263] Wilson, *op. cit.*, pp. 310-12.
[264] Worcester Co., Md., Will Bk. MH #4, p. 75.

10 Dec. 1776, colonel, 17 April 1777, and breveted brigadier general 30 Sept. 1783, original member of the Society of the Cincinnati,[265] married (1) ____ (Stevenson) Hering, (2) Mrs. ___ Selby and (3) Amelia Charllier; 320. James[6], born 13 March 1747, of Somerset Co., Md., married ___; 321. Sarah[3], born 9 Feb. 1750, married William Adams; 322. Mary[6], married 201. Stephen[6] Marshall; 323. Isaac[6], born 1 [13?] Dec. 1756, died young; 324. Joseph[5], born 18 Jan. [May?] 1759, married 339. Esther[6] Coulbourn, born 13 Nov. 1762, died 16 Aug. 1838, who married (2), (license 28) Feb. 1797,[266] Joseph Schoolfield and with him gave bond, 16 Aug. 1797, as administrator of Joseph Gunby's estate;[267] 325. Benjamin[6], born 15 Feb. 1762, of Worcester Co., Md; 326. Elizabeth[6], born 18 [8?] May 1763, married ____ Schoolfield; 327. Stephen[6], born 31 Aug. 1766; 328. William[6], ship captain of Baltimore, Md.

114. BETTY[5] WHITE (John[5], Alice[3] Menshall, Frances[2] Carsley, Henry[1]) married. 3 Dec. 1747,[268] Abraham Outten.

Issue: [OUTTEN] 329. Sarah[6], born 13 Sept. 1748; 330. Mary[6], born 24 March 1751, married (1), as his (2) wife, David Lankford, who died 2 May 1774 leaving will 24 April 1774-14 July 1774,[269] and (2) Thomas Moore;[270] 331. John[6], born 28 Oct. 1753; 332. Easter[5], born 28 March 1756; 333. Abrom[6], born 13 June 1759; 334. Obed[6], born 22 Dec. 1760; 335. Bettey[6], born 10 May 1767.

115. RACHEL[5] WHITE (John[4], Alice[3] Menshall, Frances[2] Carsley, Henry[1]) married (1), 24 Dec. 1750,[271] James Tull, who died by 1761, and (2), 2 May 1762,[272] Elijah Coulbourn, who left will 27 Feb.1793-10 Feb. 1795.[273]

Issue:[274] (by 1) [TULL] 336. John[6], born 12 Dec. 1752, died 1810-20,[275] shipwright of Worcester Co., Md., corporal in 2nd Maryland Regiment in

---

[265] Rieman Steuart, *A History of the Maryland Line in the Revolutionary War, 1775-1783* (n.p., 1969), p. 89, which gives his birth as 10 March 1745.

[266] Worcester Co., Md., Marriage license.

[267] Worcester Co., Md., Administration Bonds 1793-98, pp. 346-48.

[268] Coventry Parish, Somerset Co., Md., Register.

[269] Maryland Prerogative Court Wills 39, p. 684.

[270] Wise, *op. cit.*, p. 451.

[271] Coventry Parish, Somerset Co., Md., Register.

[272] *Ibid.*

[273] Somerset Co., Md., Will Bk. EB #17, p. 361.

[274] Coventry Parish, Somerset Co., Md., Register; Wise, *op. cit.*, pp. 421-22.

[275] Willis Clayton Tull, "Corporal John Tull of the 2nd Maryland Regiment," *The Maryland and Delaware Genealogist*, XXX, pp. 136-40; *Maryland Genealogical Society Bulletin*, XXXIII, pp. 250-5; Wise, *op. cit.*, p. 395.

Revolutionary War, married 300. Martha⁶ Wood, born 3 Feb. 1757;²⁷⁶ 337. Sarah⁶, born 15 Feb. 1753; 338. James⁶, born 22 Sept. 1757; (by 2) [COULBOURN] 339. Esther⁶, married 324. Joseph⁶ Gunby; 340. Mary⁶, born 10 Feb. 1765, died before 1783; 341. Jane⁶, born 25 July 1767, married John Conner; 342. Betty⁶, born 30 Oct. 1771, married Benjamin Conner.

116. MARY⁵ WHITE (John⁴, Alice³ Menshall, Frances² Carsley, Henry¹) married, 13 March 1753,²⁷⁷ Killiam Lankford, who left will 28 Sept. 1783-18 Oct. 1796.²⁷⁸

Issue: [LANKFORD]²⁷⁹ 343. Elizabeth⁶, born 22 Feb. 1754, married Robert Hall, possibly son of 46. *John⁶ Hall* (see DAVIS), who left will 9 Dec. 1802-4 Jan. 1803;²⁸⁰ 344. Mary⁶, born 9 May 1756, married ____ Broughton; 345. Charity⁶, born 17 Feb. 1759, married (1), 23 Feb. 1775,²⁸¹ John Riggin and (2) William Betsworth, born 19 Jan. 1758, died 1796; 346. Sarah⁶, born 17 March 1762, married, 18 Dec. 1783, John Conner, born 23 July 1758; 347. Nukka⁶, born 4 Feb. 1764, died 22 Jan. 1765; 348. Zipporah⁶, born 1766, died 14 June 1770; 349. Noah⁶, born 13 April 1769, died 1821, of Somerset Co., Md., married (1) Elizabeth ____ and (2), (license) 28 Oct. 1800,²⁸² Mary Ann Bozman, born about 1780, died July 1849, left will 2 Aug. 1835-31 July 1849;²⁸³ 350. Benjamin⁶, born 13 Nov. 1772, died young.

118. WILLIAM⁵ MITCHELL (Isaac⁴, Thomas³, Frances² Carsley, Henry¹), born about 1735 at Manokin, Somerset Co., Md., left will 12 Feb. 1774-16 March 1774.²⁸⁴ He was described as a cordwinder when his father gave him 200 acres of "Amity," 19 June 1764.²⁸⁵ He married 243. Rebecca⁶ Long, who married (2) [James?] Hammond and left will 2 Feb. 1800-12 March 1800.²⁸⁶

Issue: [MITCHELL]²⁸⁷ 351. William⁶, deposed, 2 Sept. 1799, he was aged

---

²⁷⁶ Coventry Parish, Somerset Co., Md., Register.

²⁷⁷ *Ibid.*

²⁷⁸ Somerset Co., Md., Will Bk. EB #17, pp. 557-60.

²⁷⁹ Coventry Parish, Somerset Co., Md., Register; Wise, *op. cit.*, pp. 450-51.

²⁸⁰ Somerset Co., Md., Will Bk. EB #23, p. 60; Wise, *op. cit.*, p. 396.

²⁸¹ Somerset Parish, Somerset Co., Md., Register.

²⁸² Somerset Co., Md., Marriage license.

²⁸³ Somerset Co., Md., Will Bk. JP #9, p. 159.

²⁸⁴ Maryland Prerogative Court Wills 39, p. 747.

²⁸⁵ Somerset Co., Md., Deed Bk. C, p. 226.

²⁸⁶ Somerset Co., Md., EB #23, p. 4.

²⁸⁷ Wise, *op. cit.*, p. 421.

36,[288] died before 8 Oct. 1805, married Margaret ___; 352. Isaac[6]; 353. Nancy[6]; 354. Nelly[6]; 355. Zadock[6], deposed 2 Sept. 1799, he was aged 28;[289] 356. Margaret[6], born about 1773, Somerset Co., Md., probably married, (license 22) Jan. 1801,[290] Jesse Landon, who was born about 1770 and died 1815 at Pocamoke, Somerset Co., Md.[291]

130. NANCY[5] MITCHELL (Stephen[4], Thomas[3], Frances[2] Carsley, Henry[1]) married ___ Willis.

Issue: [WILLIS] 357. Priscilla[6].

---

[288] Somerset Co., Md., Judicial Record 1798-99, p. 406.

[289] *Ibid.*, p. 403.

[290] Somerset Co., Md., Marriage license.

[291] *Maryland Genealogical Society Bulletin*, XXXIII, p. 104.

CARTER[1]

1. WILLIAM[1] CARTER was in Virginia by 1 March 1623/4,[2] was listed in the muster, 1624/5, as residing on James Island, and was referred to, 14 Aug. 1626, as a "servant to Mr. Menefrey."[3] On 2 May 1654 he deposed that he was aged 54, and his wife Alice deposed she was aged 55.[4]

On 20 May 1636 he patented 700 acres about three miles from James River claiming as headrights his first wife Avis Turtley, second wife Ann Mathis and third wife Alice Croxon, and another 100 acres near the head of Lower Chippokes Creek, and on 15 Aug. 1637 an adjoining 200 acres.[5] In 1629 his wife, probably Avis Turtley, was ordered publicly to ask forgiveness for calling her "Cosen Grays wife" a "whoore."[6]

He died by Aug. 1655 when Edward Pettway patented 500 acres as being part of 1000 acres of William Carter, deceased.[7] On 18 Oct. 1655 his widow Alice entered into an agreement with Edward Pettaway who had married the widow of her step-son.[8] She married (2) Capt. Giles Parke, a justice of Surry County, who died by 5 Nov. 1657.[9] On 25 Jan. 1660/1 Alice Parke and her son George Carter gave a 99 year lease on land.[10] By 22 Aug. 1668[11] she had married (3), as his (1) wife, Edward Warren.

Issue: (by 1 or 2) 2. William[2], married Elizabeth ____, who married (2) Edward Pettway; (by 3) 3. GEORGE[7].

3. GEORGE[7] CARTER (William[1]), probably born about 1638, was given a power of attorney by his mother, 30 Jan. 1659/60[12] and was last mentioned 7

---

[1] B. C. Holtzclaw, "The Newsom Family and Related Families ... Appendix B: The Crawford and Carter Families," *V* XLVIII, pp. 74-77; John Anderson Brayton, *The Descendants of Robert Harris* (*Colonial Families of Surry and Isle of Wight Counties, Virginia*, II; Memphis, 1999), pp. 77-86, 138-47.

[2] *MCGC*, pp. 3-4.

[3] *Ibid.*, p. 107.

[4] Surry Co. Deeds, Wills &c 1, 1652-72, p. 42.

[5] Patent Bk. 1, pp. 359, 451. These tracts were repatented as 1000 acres, 21 May 1638 (*ibid.*, p. 572).

[6] *MCGC*, pp. 197-98.

[7] Patent Bk. 3, p. 361.

[8] Surry Co. Deeds,Wills &c 1, 1652-72, p. 75.

[9] *Ibid.*, p. 113.

[10] Surry Co. Deeds, Wills &c 2, 1674-84, p. 345.

[11] Surry Co. Deeds, Wills &c 1, 1652-72, p. 309.

[12] Surry Co. Deeds, Wills &c 1, 1652-72, p. 148.

May 1664 when he witnessed a deed.[13]   By 26 June 1665[14] his widow, Mary
__ married (2) William Hare, carpenter of Lawnes Creek Parish, who joined
Mary in leasing some of the Carter land, 6 Nov. 1674.[15]

Issue:[16] 4. ELIZABETH[3].

4 ELIZABETH[3] CARTER (George[2], William[1]) married Robert Crafford
with whom she, 1 and 3 Nov. 1684, deeded land which had been granted to
William Carter in 1638.[17] He held 1000 acres in 1704 and was described as a
miller when, 8 Sept. 1712, joined by his (2) wife Margaret ___, he deeded land
in Isle of Wight County.[18] Elizabeth died before 25 Jan. 1708/9 when her son
Carter deeded some of the Carter land.[19]   His will, 26 Oct. 1714-19 Jan.
1714/5,[20] named his children by both wives.

Issue: [CRAFFORD] 5. CARTER[4]; 6. Elizabeth[4], married 18. *Thomas[4]*
Newsom (see SPENCER); 7. Sarah[4], married (1) 16. *John[4] Newsom* (see
SPENCER) and (2), by 16 Feb. 1725/6,[21] William Ruffin; 8. Robert[4],
unmarried, left will 9 Oct. 1735-19 Nov. 1735.[22]

5. CARTER[4] CRAFFORD (Elizabeth[3] Carter, George[2], William[1]), born
1682-83, left will 5 Aug. 1743-15 Feb. 1743/4.[23] He married Sarah Swann,
daughter of Matthew and Mary (Harris) Spiltimber Swann, who survived him.

Issue: [CRAFFORD] 9. JOHN[5]; 10. CARTER[5]; 11. Faith[5], married 28.
Joseph[5] Hart (see SPENCER).; 12. Constant[5]; 13. MARY[5].

9. JOHN[5] CRAFFORD (Carter[4], Elizabeth[3] Carter, George[2], William[1]) of
Surry County, left will 31 July 1758-15 Aug. 1758,[24] married Mary ___, who
married (2), by 4 Dec. 1764,[25] John George Wills of Brunswick County, whom

---

[13] *Ibid.*, p. 246.

[14] *Ibid.*, p. 262.

[15] *Ibid.*, pp. 393-94.

[16] Mary Sue Mathys, "One Branch of a Colonial Carter Family," *The Virginia Genealogist*, XXX, pp. 117-26, states there were two sons, John and Joseph, but the cited sources
do not confirm this.

[17] Surry Co. Deeds, Wills &c 3, 1684-87, pp. 10-11.

[18] Isle of Wight Co. Deed Bk. 1, p. 225.

[19] Surry Co. Deeds, Wills &c 5, 1693-1709, p. 410.

[20] Surry Co. Deeds, Wills &c 6, 1709-15, p. 320.

[21] *Ibid.*, p. 623.

[22] Surry Co. Deeds, Wills &c 8, 1730-38, p. 537.

[23] Surry Co. Deeds, Wills &c 9, 1738-54, pp. 457-58.

[24] Surry Co. Will Bk. 10, p. 154.

[25] Surry Co. Deed Bk. 8, p. 243.

she survived.[26]

Issue: [CRAFFORD] 14. Ann[6]; 15. Carter[6], died about 1801,[27] deeded, aged 11, 15 March 1763, by his uncle Carter[5], Crafford's Mill,[28] married, (bond 19) May 1777,[29] 85. *Sarah[5] Marriott* (see GRAY); 16. John[6], deeded, aged 8, 18 Jan. 1762, by his mother, "Wickham" in Nansemond County;[30] 17. Mary[6], deeded, aged 4, 18 Jan. 1762, by her mother, slaves and personalty,[31] married, (bond 19) Sept. 1784,[32] Richard Crump of Williamsburg, who served as a captain in the Virginia State Line at the siege of Yorktown, 1781, and died 1798.[33]

10. CARTER[5] CRAFFORD (Carter[4], Elizabeth[3], George[2], William[1]) took the oath of a militia officer of Surry County, 15 March 1763,[34] and left will 14 Aug. 1781-22 Jan. 1782.[35] He married, by 20 Oct. 1747,[36] Elizabeth Kearney, daughter of Capt. Barnaby and Elizabeth (Godwin) Kearney of Nansemond County.

Issue: [CRAFFORD] 18. Henry[6], married, (bond 8) April 1780,[37] Jane White; 19. Leah[6], married 136. *Isaac[6] Hilliard* (see SPENCER); 20. Lucy[6], married __ Pitt; 21. Elizabeth[6], left will 22 Feb. 1815-24 April 1815,[38] married, (bond 19) Sept. 1786,[39] as his (2) wife, John Pettway of Surry County, widower of 130. *Lucy[6] (Holt) Barham* (see HOLT), who left will 29 Sept. 1791-29 Nov. 1799;[40] 22. Martha[6], married Joseph Arrington of Nash Co., N.C., who left will

---

[26] Surry Co. Will Bk. 11, p. 213, will of John George Wills, 22 Jan. 1781-23 Jan. 1782.

[27] Warwick Co. Land tax list, 1801, estate taxed.

[28] Surry Co. Deed Bk. 8, p. 161.

[29] Catherine Linsday Knorr, *Marriage Bonds and Ministers' Returns of Surry County, Virginia, 1768-1825* (Pine Bluff, Ark., 1960), p. 24.

[30] Surry Co. Deed Bk. 8, p. 95, with reversion if he died to Ann, Carter and Mary.

[31] *Ibid.*, p. 94.

[32] Knorr, *op. cit.*, p. 24.

[33] Margie G. Brown, *Genealogical Abstracts, Revolutionary War Veterans, Scrip Act 1852* (Oakton, Va., 1990), p. 255.

[34] Surry Co. Order Bk. 1757-63, p. 356.

[35] Surry Co. Will Bk. 11, p. 205.

[36] Surry Co. Deed Bk. 5, p. 139.

[37] Knorr, *loc. cit.*

[38] Surry Co. Will Bk. 3, p. 14.

[39] Knorr, *Marriage Bonds ... Surry County*, p. 65.

[40] Surry Co. Will Bk. 1, p. 354.

12 Nov. 1818-Feb. 1819.[41]

13. MARY[5] CRAFFORD (Carter[4], Elizabeth[3] Carter, George[2], William[1]) named in will of her uncle 8. Robert[4] Crafford, married Benjamin Newsom of Southampton County, who left will 14 Dec. 1799-17 Feb. 1800.[42]

Issue: [NEWSOM][43] 23. Crawford[6], baptized 3 Feb. 1760, died before 27 July 1799 when the sheriff of Southampton County as administrator sold his estate;[44] 24. Carter[6], baptized 26 April 1761; 25. Benjamin[6], born 15 Nov. 1762; 26. John[6], born 11 Oct. 1764; 27. Holliday[6], born 6 June 1766; 28. Elizabeth[6].

---

[41] Nash Co., N.C., Unrecorded wills.

[42] Southampton Co. Will Bk. 5, p. 181.

[43] Albemarle Parish Register.

[44] Southampton Co. Will Bk. 5, pp. 514-15.

CHAPLAINE

*1. Ensign ISAACK[1] CHAPLAINE came to Virginia, 1610, in the *Starr* and in the census, 1623/4, he, *Mrs. Chaplaine and *John Chaplaine are listed at "Chaplaine's Choice."[1] In the muster, 1624/5, Mrs. Chaplaine's name is given as Mary with the statement that she came in the *James*, 1622, and that John Chaplaine, aged 15, "kinsman" of Isaack[1], accompanied her along with four servants, including a maid servant. By the time they arrived, Isaack[1] Chaplaine appears to have been well established at one of the choice locations on the south side of James River.

In 1623 Mr. Greville Pooley, the minister, was authorized to "take the levy" at "Chaplaine's Choice."[2] The list of land titles sent to England, May 1626, credits Isaack[1] Chaplaine with 50 acres in Charles City and 200 acres in the "territory of Great Weyanoke."[3] Apparently other acreage was added, for a repatent of "Chaplaine's Choice" by Nicholas Wyatt, 30 Oct. 1686, lists 361 acres in the tract.[4]

Isaack[1] Chaplaine served as a member of the House of Burgesses from "Chaplaine's Choice" and "Jordan's Journey," 1624 and 1625, along with Nathaniel Cawsey.[5] He signed the "Laws and Orders by the Council and Assemblie" sent to England for approval.[6] He appeared as a witness, 1624, for Governor Yeardley in a suit brought against the Governor by Capt. John Martin and the following year before the suit was heard, Martin, one of the Council of State, sought to discredit him as a witness, stating "that Isack Chaplan is a perjured man ... a condemned man, and as yet never had his pardon for to acquit

---

[1] Hotten, p. 173. Alliterative names such as "Jordan's Journey," "Pace's Pains," "Beggar's Bush," and "Newport News" were not uncommon at this time. "Chaplaine's Choice" was on Bicker's (later Bicar's) Creek near "Jordan's Journey," on the south side of James River, opposite "Berkeley" and "Westover" (*Cra. Rep.*, p. 213).

[2] *R*, Va. Co. IV, p. 402.

[3] This included land on both sides of James River, as did Charles City. The territory on the south side of the river became Prince George County, 1702 (see "Chart of James River," *Cra. Rep.*, opposite p. 201).

[4] Patent Bk. 7, p. 531, which says the land had been many years in possession of Anthony Wyatt, father of Nicholas, and that a fire at the house of Anthony Wyatt had destroyed his patent and a fire in the Secretary's Office had destroyed the original.

[5] Leonard, pp. 5-6.

[6] *R*, Va. Co. IV, p. 558.

him, so that the said Ensign Chaplen is not capable in law to pursue him."[7]
Notwithstanding this charge, Ensign Chaplaine continued in the confidence of his
contemporaries and in 1626 was appointed a member of the commission to hold
court for the "Upper Parts" of the colony.[8] These commissioners were
authorized to hear and decide petty controversies not exceeding the value of 200
pounds of tobacco and also to consider petty offenses.

Apparently, Ensign Chaplaine was lost at sea some time before 8 Dec. 1628
when the General Court ordered "that John Chaplaine of 'Chaplaine's Choice'
shall have a commission granted unto him of the goods of Ensign Isack
Chaplaine, who is supposed to be cast away upon the sea."[9] This is the last
known reference to him.[10]

John Chaplaine, listed in the muster as "kinsman" to Isaack[1] Chaplaine,
continued to live in the area of "Chaplaine's Choice," for reference in patents is
frequently to Chaplaine's land and to John Chaplaine's land.[11] His degree of
kinship to Isaack[1] Chaplaine is undetermined; probably he was a nephew.

No issue of Isaack[1] and Mary Chaplaine has been established.[12]

---

[7] *MCGC*, pp. 37, 58.

[8] *Ibid.*, p. 106.

[9] *Ibid.*, p. 178. This shows how little reliance can be had in ages listed in the muster of
1624/5. If John Chaplaine had been but 15 years old then, he would have been but 19 in 1628,
but he was necessarily 21 to have been administrator of Isaack's estate.

[10] "List of Officers and Soldiers engaged in the American Expedition, who, during the year
1656, applied for arrears of pay, or on whose account such applications were made by widows
and representatives," Interregnum Entry Bk. CV, P.R.O., W. Noel Sainsbury, ed., *Calendar of
State Papers, Colonial Series, 1574-1660* (London, 1860), p. 455, includes the name of "Isaac
Chaplayn, Chaplain, deceased," but as this expedition was to Jamaica and Isaack Chaplaine of
"Chaplaine's Choice" was not a minister, this is a coincidence of names.

[11] Patent Bk. 1, pp. 579 (25 July 1638), 609 (12 Feb. 1638/9), 777 (10 Oct. 1641), 781 (10
March 1640/1); Patent Bk. 2, p. 168 (8 July 1647); Patent Bk. 5, p. 309 (287) (18 March
1662/3).

[12] Claimed children are: Mary Chaplaine as wife of Anthony Wyatt, primarily because
Wyatt was an early owner of "Chaplaine's Choice," but there is no evidence that Chaplaine had
a daughter or that Wyatt's wife was named Mary, and William Chaplaine of Calvert Co., Md.,
who left will, 9 Dec. 1669-5 Jan. 1669/70 (Maryland Prerogative Court Wills 1, p. 363), naming
wife Mary, daughters Elizabeth Chaplaine and Mary Chaplaine and son William, but to date no
documentary evidence in support of these claimed descents has been presented. Also unproved
is the claim that the wife of Isaack[1] Chaplaine was born Mary Calvert.

CHEW[1]

*1. JOHN[1] CHEW came to Virginia in the *Charitie*, which left England in April 1622, according to the muster of 1624/5, when he and his wife Sarah and three "servants" were living at Hog Island on the south side of James River. Sarah came in the *Seaflower* in 1621. As a merchant trading in commodities shipped from England in exchange for those obtained in the colony, he maintained a house and operated a store at Jamestown where he had been assigned 1 rod 9 poles "for the better conveniencie and more comaditye of his howse by him now erected and builded in the New Towne within the precincts of James Citty," adjoining north upon the back street, south upon Richard Stephens and east upon Capt. Hamor.[2]

Shortly after his arrival in Virginia, Chew was placed in charge of the business affairs of Robert Bennett, who died, 1623, soon after his arrival as manager of the Warascoyack plantation of his brother Edward Bennett, an English merchant.[3] John[1] Chew represented Wariscoyack in the General Assembly, 1624, and Hog Island in those of 1625, 1628 and 1629.[4] He was commissioned commander of Hog Island, 7 March 1628/9.[5]

---

[1] Francis B. Culver, "Chew Family," *MHM* XXX, pp. 157-75; Lawrence Buckley Thomas, *The Thomas Book* (New York, 1896), pp. 253-57; L. B. Thomas, *Genealogical Notes Containing: The Pedigree of the Thomas Family of Maryland* (Baltimore, 1877), pp. 55 *et seq.*; L. B. Thomas, *Pedigrees of Thomas, Chew, and Lawrence, A West River Register, and Genealogical Notes* (New York, 1883), pp. 1-35; "A Genealogical Table of the Family of [Chew of Vi]rginia, MS, written 1822 (?), photocopy, Archives Division, Library of Virginia; Rudolf Loeser, "Larkin Chew of Spotsylvania County and His Family," *The Virginia Genealogist*, XLVII, pp. 3-27, 107-34. Exact dates of birth, marriage and death for which no reference is cited appear, with some variations, in Culver and the three works by Thomas and presumably are derived from an ancient Chew Bible. J. Reany Kelly, *Quakers in the Founding of Anne Arundel County, Maryland* (Baltimore, 1963), pp. 44, 124, states that a part of the Bible had been found and was in his possession. Although his papers were given to the Maryland Historical Society, the Bible was not among them and its present whereabouts is unknown.

[2] Patent Bk. 1, p. 7; *MCGC*, pp. 37, 44, 51, 66. "Capt. Wm. Holmes Sworn and ex[amined] saith that Mr. Chew agreed with Mr. Calcar for a bed, a Covering, vallence Curtains, pewter &c to the vallew of 303[li] of tob: or there abouts for Mr. Willm. Ben[ets] use," 23 March 1623/4 (*ibid.*, p. 13).

[3] *R, Va. Co.* IV, p. 402. Chew was ordered to pay William Bennett, minister of Warascoyak, 1533 1/3 pounds of tobacco as salary for two years due William Bennett from Robert Bennett, deceased.

[4] Leonard, pp. 5-8.

[5] *MCGC*, p. 192.

Referred to by Governor Sir John Harvey and the Virginia Council in 1636 as one of the "ablest merchants in Virginia,"[6] Chew seized an opportunity in 1630 to acquire for himself a landed estate. At that time Governor John West and the Council opened a "tract of land called the forest bordering upon the chief residence of the Pamunkey King, the most dangerous head of the Indian enemy." By way of inducement for settlement, they offered 50 acres for persons "whoe the first yeare should adventure or bee inventured to seate and inhabite on the Southerne side of the Pamunkeye River now called Charles [York] River and then knowne by the Indian name of Chiscake" and 25 acres for those settling the second year.[7] John Chew's patent for 500 acres in the area, 6 July 1636, shows that he adventured himself and nine settlers the first year. Additional patents in the area were issued to him 7 July 1636, 9 Aug. 1637, 18 Feb. 1638/9, 22 Feb. 1638/9 and 10 Feb. 1641/2,[8] and, 16 Feb. 1642/3, he sold to Robert Kinsey and Henry Lowdy, churchwardens, 200 acres to be used as a glebe for York Parish, which embraced the area from the New Poquoson River to Morgan's Creek on the west side of the present site of Yorktown.[9] This was part of 750 acres on Chisman's Creek, patented 18 Feb. 1638/9. He sold 14 acres to Robert Parr, 3 May 1650.[10] In an Act of Assembly, 6 Jan. 1639/40, he was named a tobacco viewer between Back Creek and Wormeley's Creek.[11] Appointed justice of York County, 1634, he held that office until 1652. With his neighbors John Cheesman and Christopher Calthorpe, also early settlers in York, he represented that county in 1643 and 1644.[12]

His wife Sarah having died, on 3 April 1651 he signed a marriage contract, deeding "the Plantation and houses whereon I now live" to George Ludlowe and Richard Lee, Esqrs., in trust for "Mrs. Rachaell Counstable whome I intend (by God's grace) shortly to make my wife," as well as four Negro servants and a

---

[6] W. Noel Sainsbury, ed., *Calendar of State Papers, Colonial Series, 1574-1660* (London, 1860), pp. 291-92.

[7] Patent Bk. 1, p. 369.

[8] *Ibid.*, pp. 369, 445, 610, 616; Patent Bk. 2, p. 356.

[9] York Co. Deeds, Orders, Wills &c 2, 1645-49, p. 274; George Carrington Mason, *Colonial Churches of Tidewater Virginia* (Richmond, 1945), pp. 218-20.

[10] York Co. Deeds, Orders, Wills &c 4, 1664-72, p. 45, recorded 20 Dec. 1665.

[11] *W*(2) IV, p. 26.

[12] Leonard, pp. 21-22.

mare, but all to be void if Rachaell died before John and without issue by him.[13] The last reference to John[1] Chew is as a justice, 25 Sept. 1652, although "Mr. Chew" is mentioned in Dec. 1657, in retrospect.[14] Probably John[1] Chew died about 1652.

Issue:[15] (by 1) 2. SAMUEL[2]; 3. JOSEPH[2].

2. SAMUEL[2] CHEW (John[1]), born about 1626, settled in Maryland. On 3 Sept. 1658, without giving his residence, he gave power of attorney to "my brother Joseph Chew," who was still in York County,[16] and on 16 July 1659, he entered rights for 400 acres for transporting himself and three others to Maryland.[17] He acquired a substantial estate and extensive land holdings in Maryland where he was generally known as a well-to-do gentleman. At his plantation, "Herrington," located on Herring Creek in Anne Arundel County, he cultivated tobacco largely. He was a member of the Lower House of the Maryland Assembly, 1661, and of the Upper House, 1671-76, was sworn justice of the Provincial Court and Court of Chancery, 17 Dec. 1669, was a member of the Council from 1669 until his death, and was high sheriff, 1663-64, and justice, 1665-69, of Anne Arundel County and Keeper of the Seal of that county.[18]

On 24 Aug. 1668 Samuel[2] Chew, late of York Parish and County in Virginia, "now of Ann-Arundell County in the province of Maryland, sonne and heyre of John Chew late of Yorke County ... deceased," sold to Maj. James Goodwyn two tracts in York County, 500 acres patented to John Chew, 6 Aug. 1637 (should be 6 July 1636) and 700 acres adjoining (patented 7 July 1636), except a small piece sold by John Chew to Robert Parr. Anne, wife of Samuel[2] Chew, relinquished her dower rights.[19]

Samuel[2] Chew married, about 1658, Anne Ayres, died 13 April 1695, only daughter and heiress of William Ayres of Nansemond County. She was a prominent member of the Society of Friends [Quakers] and their monthly meetings were long held at her house at Herring Creek.

---

[13] York Co. Deeds, Orders, Wills &c 1, 1633-94, p. 132. The wife of Richard Lee was Ann Constable.

[14] *Ibid.*, p. 148; Deeds, Orders, Wills &c 3, 1657-62, p. 10.

[15] There were perhaps other children not now identified.

[16] York Co. Deeds, Orders, Wills &c 3, 1657-62, p. 58A.

[17] Maryland Land Office Bk. 4, p. 54.

[18] *A Biographical Dictionary of the Maryland Legislature, 1635-1789*, I (Baltimore and London, 1979), p. 218.

[19] York Co. Deeds, Orders, Wills &c 4, 1665-72, p. 201-02.

He died 15 March 1676/7. His will, 26 July 1676-12 June 1677,[20] and that of his widow Anne Chew, 20 Feb. 1694/5-5 May 1695,[21] both name their children.

Issue: 4. SAMUEL[3]; 5. JOSEPH[3]; 6. SARAH[3]; 7. Nathaniel[3], born about 1666, died after 20 Feb. 1695/6, who was bequeathed "Popping Jay" at Lyons Creek, Calvert Co., Md.; 8. WILLIAM[3]; 9. BENJAMIN[3]; 10. John[3], born about 1672, died 19 Feb. 1696/7, left will 13 Jan. 1696/7-15 March 1696/7;[22] 11. Caleb[3], born about 1674, died 8 May 1698, left will 5 May 1698-9 July 1698;[23] 12. Anne[3], born about 1676, died 28 Jan. 1699/1700.

3. JOSEPH[2] CHEW (John[1]) deposed, 29 July 1713, as a resident of Anne Arundel Co., Md., that he was then 76 years of age or thereabouts,[24] but he may well have been older as he was given responsible positions in York County in 1657 and 1658. On 18 Sept. 1658 he was acting guardian of Dennis English, whose guardian, Francis Holland, was then in England.[25] About 1659, he presented a petition to York County court stating that "he intended to leave the country and desired to deliver to the Court the estate of Dennis English, whose guardian he is."[26] Not until 4 Oct. 1668 did Dennis English, then of Baltimore Co., Md., quit-claim to Joseph[2] Chew.[27]

Joseph[2] Chew lived for a time in Cecil County in the extreme northeast corner of Maryland, adjacent to Delaware, where as attorney he is recorded in a number of legal transactions in New Castle County after 1672.[28] He is called "brother" in the will of Samuel[2] Chew, 1676. After his residence in Delaware, Joseph[2] Chew may have returned to Maryland[29] but it is also possible he was the Joseph Chew who lived in the Albemarle section of North Carolina from about 1680 to the early 1700s.[30] By 24-25 July 1710, when he witnessed a deed of

---

[20] Maryland Prerogative Court Wills 5, p. 241.

[21] Maryland Prerogative Court Wills 7, p. 59.

[22] *Ibid.*, p. 259.

[23] Maryland Prerogative Court Wills 6, p. 117.

[24] Maryland Chancery Record 3 [PL], 1712-24, p. 19.

[25] York Co. Deeds, Orders, Wills &c 3, 1657-62, p. 34.

[26] *Ibid.*, p. 175B.

[27] York Co. Deeds, Orders, Wills &c 4, 1665-72, p. 205.

[28] New Castle Co., Del., Minutes of the Court 1676-79, pp. 19, 72, 296.

[29] References to Joseph Chew in the records of Anne Arundel Co., Md., however, probably relate to his nephew.

[30] For a discussion of the North Carolina records concerning Joseph Chew, see Loeser, *op. cit.*, pp. 131-33.

Larkin[3] Chew,[31] he was living in Virginia. On 26 April 1712 he, Larkin Chew, Richard Buckner and John Sutton received two patents for 400 acres each on branches of the Mattapony River.[32]   By 1713 he was in Anne Arundel Co., Md.[33]

His nephew, Samuel[3] Chew, recorded among the deaths in his family Bible, "My onkel, Joseph Chew, 12th of twelfth month [February] 1715/6."[34]

Joseph[2] Chew married (1), 27 Dec. 1669,[35] Margaret (___) Mills, widow of Thomas Mills of Anne Arundel Co., Md., who died before 17 Dec. 1673,[36] and (2), possibly in Virginia, Ruth Larkin.[37] On 18 Jan. 1675/6 Joseph[2] Chew, "late of Cecil County in Maryland," and his wife Ruth made a deed to Nicholas Goodridge of London.[38] The will of Larkin[3] Chew, May 1728, refers to his mother as Ruth Green. It is possible that he and Ruth separated.   If he is the Joseph Chew of North Carolina, he married at least once again since records establish he married _____, widow of Nathaniel Batts,[39] and, by 15 March 1683/4,[40] was married to Elizabeth ___.

Issue: (by 2)[41] 13. LARKIN[3].

4. SAMUEL[3] CHEW (Samuel[2], John[1]), born about 1660, inherited at his mother's death half of his father's estate, including the plantation, "Herrington," and 300 acres called "Chew's Ridge" or "Poplar Ridge."   He married (1), 14 April 1682, Anne ___, who died 8 April 1702, and (2), 29 June

---

[31] Essex Co. Deeds & Wills 13, pp. 368-69.

[32] Patent Bk. 10, p. 58. The county was not entered but the land eventually fell into Spotsylvania County.

[33] Maryland Chancery Record. 3 [PL], 1712-24 , pp. 19-20.

[34] Quoted in Thomas, *The Thomas Book*, p. 254.

[35] This date, unconfirmed by any known record, is perhaps derived from the lost Chew Bible.

[36] Maryland Testamentary Proceedings 6, pp. 56-61.

[37] The surname is traditional. Ruth is said to be the daughter of John and Katherine Larkin of Anne Arundel Co., Md., but Ruth Larkin married William Goodman. For a discussion of the evidence see Leoser, *op. cit.*, pp. 124-26.

[38] Cecil Co., Md., Land Records 1, p. 50.

[39] J. R. B. Hathaway, ed., *North Carolina Historical and Genealogical Register*, I, p. 30. Batts married Mary, widow of 4. *Henry[2] Woodhouse* (see WOODHOUSE), but whether Joseph Chew married her or a later wife of Batts is unclear.

[40] Mattie Erma Edards Parker, ed., *North Carolina Higher-Court Records 1670-1696* (Raleigh, 1968), p. 452.

[41] If he was the Joseph Chew of North Carolina, he had at least one child by his marriage(s?) there, a daughter Sarah who died 26 Sept. 1697 (Hathaway, *op. cit.*, III, p. 403).

1704, Elizabeth (Thurston) Skipworth Coale, widow of William Coale, who died 27 Feb. 1709/10. He died 10 Oct. 1718, leaving will, as merchant of Anne Arundel County, 16 July 1718-31 Oct. 1718.[42]

Issue: 14. SAMUEL[4]; 15. Anne[4], born 2 July 1686,[43] died 28 Jan. 1694/5; 16. JOHN[4]; 17. Joseph[4], twin, born 1 April 1689; 18. Benjamin[4], twin, born 1 April 1689, died 18 April 1698; 19. NATHANIEL[4]; 20. Joseph[4], born 28 April 1696.

5. JOSEPH[3] CHEW (Samuel[2], John[1]), born about 1662, inherited from his father 450 acres called "Santetley." He married (1), 17 Nov. 1685,[44] Mary Smith, and (2), about 1689, Elizabeth (Hanslap) Battee, born about 1665, died May 1716, daughter of Henry and Elizabeth Hanslap who both mentioned her in their wills, 1698 and 1702, and widow of Seaborn Battee.[45] Joseph[3] Chew died 11 Feb. 1704/5, leaving undated will, proved 7 June 1705.[46] His widow left will, 23 April 1716-29 May 1716.[47]

Issue: (by 2) 21. JOSEPH[4]; 22. HENRY[4].

6. SARAH[3] CHEW (Samuel[2], John[1]), born about 1664, married Capt. Edward Burgess, born about 1655, son of William and Elizabeth (Robbins) Burgess.[48] He was a justice of Anne Arundel Co., Md., 1674-89. He was buried 4 March 1722/3 and left will 29 Aug. 1721-14 March 1722/3.[49] She left a will 26 Sept. 1738-12 May 1740.[50]

Issue [BURGESS][51] 23. William[4], born 19 Nov. 1684, buried 1 Dec. 1704, died without issue; 24. ANNE[4]; 25. Edward[4], born 1686, of Annapolis, Md., died

---

[42] Maryland Prerogative Court Wills 14, p. 669.

[43] West River Monthly Meeting records, *loc. cit.*

[44] West River Monthly Meeting records, in *Maryland Genealogical Society Bulletin*, XIV, no. 2, p. 4.

[45] Rudolf Loeser, "Ferdinando Battee of Anne Arundel County and His Two Families, *Maryland Genealogical Society Bulletin*, XXXVII, p. 477; Maryland Prerogative Court Wills 6, p. 163; Maryland Prerogative Court Wills 3, p. 8.

[46] Maryland Prerogative Court Wills 3, p. 447.

[47] Maryland Prerogative Court Wills 14, pp. 96-97.

[48] Donna Valley Russell, *First Families of Anne Arundel County, Maryland, 1649-1658*, I (New Market, Md., 1999), pp. 14-16.

[49] Maryland Prerogative Court Wills 18, pp. 144-46.

[50] Maryland Prerogative Court Wills 22, pp. 268-69.

[51] All Hallows Parish, Anne Arundel Co., Md., Register; Harry Wright Newman, *Ann Arundel Gentry* (Annapolis, 1970), I, pp. 14-21.

before 10 June 1715 when the inventory of his estate was made,[52] married, 12 Jan. 1713/4, Sarah ___, widow, who married (3), 27 Dec. 1716, James Crook; 26. ELIZABETH[4]; 27. SAMUEL[4]; 28. MARGARET[4]; 29. Sarah[4], with brother Samuel and sister Margaret baptized 13 Nov. 1698, married, 8 Sept. 1709, 6. *Benjamin[4] Gaither* (see GAITHER); 30. JOHN[4]; 31. SUSANNA[4].

8. WILLIAM[3] CHEW (Samuel[2], John[1]), born about 1668, married, 20 Dec. 1690,[53] Sidney Wynne, daughter of Dr. Thomas and Martha (Buttall) Wynne of Pennsylvania.[54] He died 28 Feb. 1709/10.

Issue: 32. BENJAMIN[4]; 33. William[4], of Baltimore Co., Md., died unmarried by 15 Nov. 1720 and his estate was divided among his sisters;[55] 34. ANNE[4]; 35. MARGARET[4]; 36. SIDNEY[4]; 37. Joanna[4]; 38. Elizabeth[4].

9. BENJAMIN[3] CHEW (Samuel[2], John[1]), born 13 Feb. 1670/1, married, 8 Dec. 1692,[56] Elizabeth Benson, daughter of John and Elizabeth (Smith) Benson and half-sister of the wives of his nephews 24. Samuel[4] and 16. John[4] Chew, to whom he devised by will, 26 Feb. 1699/1700-3 June 1700,[57] one-half of the 350 acre plantation, "Maidstone," including the dwelling. He died 3 March 1699/1700 and his widow married (2), 24 Sept. 1703,[58] Richard Bond, and died 1725.

Issue: 39. SAMUEL[4]; 40. ELIZABETH[4]; 41. Anne[4], born 14 Oct. 1696; 42. Mary[4], born Dec. 1698.

13. LARKIN[3] CHEW (Joseph[2], John[1]) "removed from Maryland to Virginia where he married into the respectable family of Roy."[59] He was first mentioned in Virginia, 24 July 1701, when the vestry of Petsworth Parish, Gloucester

---

[52] Maryland Prerogative Court Inventories & Accounts 36B, pp. 191-92.

[53] West River Monthly Meeting records, in *Maryland Genealogical Society Bulletin*, XIV, no. 2, p. 4.

[54] George E. McCracken, *The Welcome Claimants, Proved, Disproved and Doubtful* (Baltimore, 1970), pp. 575-76.

[55] Barnes, *op. cit.*, p. 108; Baltimore Co., Md., Original accounts, Box 4, folder 42, Maryland State Archives.

[56] West River Monthly Meeting records, in *Maryland Genealogical Society Bulletin*, XIV, no. 2, p. 4.

[57] Maryland Prerogative Court Wills 6, p. 379.

[58] West River Monthly Meeting records, in *Maryland Genealogical Society Bulletin*, XIV, no. 2, p. 4.

[59] Letter, 26 Sept. 1797, written by his grandson Joseph[5] Chew at Montreal, Canada, owned, 1952, by Mrs. Ronsone of Pittsburgh, Pa., photocopy, Archives Division, Library of Virginia.

County, instructed the churchwardens to bargain "with Larkin Chew for enlargement of Poplar Springs Church"[60] and on 11 April 1702 Larkin Chew of King and Queen County entered into an agreement with the justices of Essex County to erect a court house "according to the exact dementions and proprotions off King and Queen County Court house ... as the same was finished by the said Larkin Chew."[61] In 1704 he held 850 acres in Essex County and he eventually settled in Spotsylvania County which he represented in the General Assembly, 1723-26,[62] and was justice, 1722, and sheriff, 1727-28, captain of militia and vestryman of St. George's Parish.[63] By seventeen patents, 1712-23,[64] he acquired 34,939 acres on the Mattaponi River and 4,020 acres on the Rappahannock River. He resold the land in small holdings to new settlers.[65]

Larkin[3] Chew married, about 1700 in Virginia, Hannah Roy, probably sister of John Roy of Port Royal in what was then Essex but became Caroline County in 1728. His will, 11 May 1728-1 April 1729,[66] provided that "my mother Ruth Green" should have maintenance out of his estate. Thomas[4] Chew was granted administration on the estate of Hannah Chew, 3 Aug. 1743.[67]

Issue: 43. THOMAS[4]; 44. ANN[4]; 45. JOHN[4]; 46. LARKIN[4].

14. SAMUEL[4] CHEW (Samuel[3], Samuel[2], John[1]), born 28 May 1683,[68] died 31 Oct. 1736,[69] was a merchant who registered his own sailing vessels and left will 2 Oct. 1736-14 Dec. 1736.[70] He married, 26 Aug. 1703, Mary Harrison, born 10 Oct. 1684, died 4 Aug. 1725, daughter of Richard and Elizabeth (Smith) Benson Harrison.

---

[60] Churchill G. Chamberlayne, *Vestry Book of Petsworth Parish* (Richmond, 1933), pp. 68-69, 72. He was paid a total of 20,000 pounds of tobacco for the work.

[61] Essex Co. Wills & Deeds 10, p. 109.

[62] Leonard, p. 72.

[63] Vestry Book, St. George's Parish, Spotsylvania Co., 1726-45, pp. 7-8, in *The Virginia Genealogist*, XLI, p. 71.

[64] Patent Bks. 10 and 11, *passim*.

[65] William Armstrong Crozier, *Spotsylvania County, 1721-1800* (*Virginia County Records*, I; New York, 1905), pp. 88-107; T. J. Wertenbaker, *The Planters of Colonial Virginia* (Princeton, 1922), p. 154.

[66] Spotsylvania Co. Will Bk. A, p. 96.

[67] *Ibid.*, p. 367; Order Bk. 1738-49, p. 231.

[68] West River Monthly Meeting records, Anne Arundel Co., Md., in *Maryland Genealogical Society Bulletin*, XV, p. 101.

[69] Bible of Samuel Chew, in *Maryland Genealogical Society Bulletin*, XLII, p. 219.

[70] Maryland Prerogative Court Wills 21, p. 805.

Issue:[71] 47. Samuel[5], married 19. *Henrietta Maria[4] Lloyd* (see LLOYD); 48. ANN[5]; 49. Elizabeth[5], born 18 Oct. 1709, died 29 July 1719; 50. John[5], born 19 Sept. 1711, died 21 March 1726/7; 51. MARY[5]; 52. RICHARD[5]; 53. Francis[5], died 24 May 1720; 54. FRANCIS[5]; 55. Elizabeth[5], born 11 June 1725, died 25 June 1726.

16. JOHN[4] CHEW (Samuel[3], Samuel[2], John[1]), born 8 April 1687,[72] died 1718, was a merchant of Anne Arundel Co., Md. He married, 1708, Elizabeth Harrison, sister of the wife of his brother Samuel[4], who married (2), 1722, Elihu Hall.[73]

Issue:[74] 56. SAMUEL[5]; 57. ANNE[5]; 58. SARAH[5]; 59. MARY[5].

19. NATHANIEL[4] CHEW (Samuel[3], Samuel[2], John[1]), of Anne Arundel Co., Md., born 5 Aug. 1692, died 30 Jan. 1727/8, left will 12 Jan. 1727/8-21 Feb. 1727/8.[75] He married Mary __, who died 24 Aug. 1728, left will 23 Aug. 1728-26 Sept. 1728.[76]

Issue: 60. Nathaniel[5]; 61. JOSEPH[5]; 62. ANN[5].

21. JOSEPH[4] CHEW (Joseph[3], Samuel[2], John[1]), born about 1689, moved to Alexandria, Va., before 1752,[77] and was an inn-holder. He married (1), 23 Jan. 1710/11,[78] Mary Ford and (2) Mercy (__) Mauduit, died 5 Nov. 1775, aged 67,[79] who left will 1 Nov. 1775-19 Feb. 1776.[80]

Issue: (by 1) 63. Joseph[5], married __;[81] 64. John[5], born 1713, resided in Virginia; 65. Henry[5]; 66. SAMUEL[5]; 67. Elizabeth[5].

---

[71] *MHM* XXX, p. 162-63.

[72] *Ibid.*

[73] *MHM* VIII, pp. 295-96.

[74] *MHM* XXX, p. 163.

[75] Maryland Prerogative Court Wills 19, p. 521.

[76] *Ibid.*, p. 529.

[77] Fairfax Co. Will Bk. B, pp. 113-22, accounts of estate of Lawrence Washington.

[78] St. James' Parish, Anne Arundel Co., Md., Register.

[79] Tombstone, Evergreen Cemetery, Bladensburg, Md., cited in Jeann A. Sargent, ed., *Stones and Bones, Cemetery Records of Prince George's County, Maryland* (Bowie, 1984), p. 467.

[80] Fairfax Co. Will Bk. C, p. 243.

[81] Was his wife the Cassandra Chew, aged 47 in 1776 (census of Georgetown Hundred, Frederick Co., Md. [eventually part of District of Columbia], in Gaius Marcus Brumbaugh, *Maryland Records*, I [Baltimore, 1915], p. 196), left will 27 May 1807-5 Feb. 1811 (District of Columbia, Will Bk. 1, pp. 333-34 [186-87]), who before 1767 had two children by Robert Peter (*Maryland Genealogical Society Bulletin*, XXXVI, pp. 192-96)?

22. HENRY[4] CHEW (Joseph[3], Samuel[2], John[1]) deposed, 27 Aug. 1743, he was aged 50 years or upwards.[82] He was a vestryman and warden of All Saints Parish, Calvert Co., Md., then resident of Baltimore Co., Md., 1740-42, again of Calvert County to 1748, and briefly of Spotsylvania Co., Va., before moving to Carteret Co., N.C.,[83] where he left will May 1753-9 March 1758.[84] He married Elizabeth ___.

Issue:[85] 68 Henry[5], of Calvert Co., Md., and later of Carteret Co., N.C., unmarried; 69. JOSEPH[5]; 70. ELIZABETH[5]; 71. SARAH[5]; 72. JANE[5].

24. ANNE[4] BURGESS (Sarah[3] Chew, Samuel[2], John[1]), born 5 Dec. 1685, married, 22 Sept. 1709, Robert White of Prince George's Co., Md., who left will 9 Aug. 1758-14 April 1768.[86]

Issue: [WHITE] 73. James[5]; 74. Catherine[5]; 75. Burgess[5]; 76. SARAH[5]; 77. ANN[5].

26. ELIZABETH[4] BURGESS (Sarah[3] Chew, Samuel[2], John[1]), born 5 Aug. 16[_], was buried 13 March 1715/7. She married, 15 Aug. 1704, William Nicholson, merchant of Anne Arundel Co., Md., who was buried 6 Oct. 1719,[87] left will 25 Sept. 1719-19 Oct. 1719.[88]

Issue: [NICHOLSON] 78. William[5]; 79. Elizabeth[5], born Dec. 1705, buried 29 March 1711; 80. JOSEPH[5]; 81. Benjamin[5]; 82. Samuel[5]; 83. Edward[5].

27. SAMUEL[4] BURGESS (Sarah[3] Chew, Samuel[2], John[1]), died before 23 Jan. 1743/4 when the inventory of his estate was made.[89] He married, 19 April 1716, Elizabeth (Fowler) Durdain, daughter of Thomas and Susanna (Ijams) Fowler and widow of John Durdain, who was born 13 June 1697 and left will 12 Feb. 1757-9 May 1767.[90]

---

[82] Maryland Chancery Record 7 [IR #4], 1738-46, p. 469.

[83] Joseph Carroll Hopkins, "Colonel Henry Chew of Maryland and North Carolina," *Maryland Magazine of Genealogy*, V, pp. 51-65.

[84] Stephen E. Bradley, *Early Records of North Carolina*, VII, Wills 1750-1755 (From the Secretary of State Papers) (Keysville, Va., 1994), p. 21.

[85] *Maryland Magazine of Genealogy*, V, pp. 51-63.

[86] Maryland Prerogative Court Wills 36, p. 314, which also named grandchildren Zachariah White, Burgess White and Catherine Willson.

[87] All Hallows Parish, Anne Arundel Co., Md., Register.

[88] Maryland Prerogative Court Wills 15, p. 325.

[89] Maryland Prerogative Court Inventories 29, pp. 101-04.

[90] Maryland Prerogative Court Wills 35, p. 247.

Issue: [BURGESS][91] 84. Edward[5], baptized 14 April 1717; 85. Sarah[5], baptized 15 April 1719; 86. Richard[6], married Mary ___; 87. Ursula[5], baptized 11 Dec. 1726; 88. RACHEL[5]

28. MARGARET[4] BURGESS (Sarah[3] Chew, Samuel[2], John[1]), buried 28 July 1729,[92] married, 21 Dec. 1710, William Ware.

Issue: [WARE] 89. WILLIAM[5]; 90. Ann Balanda[5].

30. JOHN[4] BURGESS (Sarah[3] Chew, Samuel[2], John[1]), born 17 Aug. 1696, left will 4 Sept. 1773-10 Jan. 1774.[93] He married (1), 15 Dec. 1720, Jane Mackelfresh, born 1700, buried 11 March 1733/4, and (2), 27 Jan. 1733/4,[94] 73. *Matilda[4] Sparrow* (see WEST, Anthony).

Issue: [BURGESS][95] (by 1) 91. WILLIAM[5]; 92. Ann[5], born 4 March 1722/3, perhaps the daughter buried 19 Oct. 1732; 93. JOHN[5]; 94. JOSEPH[5]; 95. SARAH[5]; 96. Mary[5], born 27 Jan. 1730/1; 97. EDWARD[5]; (by 2) 98. SAMUEL[5]; 99. WEST[5]; 100. CALEB[5]; 101. MARY[5]; 102. Ann[5], born 30 March 1745; 103. Elizabeth[5], born 26 Nov. 1751; 104. Susanna[5], born 1 Feb. 1754/5, left will 28 Sept. 1792-12 Nov. 1792;[96] 105. Benjamin[5], married Priscilla ___.

31. SUSANNA[4] BURGESS (Sarah[3] Chew, Samuel[2], John[1]), born 14 March 1699/1700, married Thomas Richardson.of Prince George's Co., Md., who left will 5 March 1758-15 May 1758.[97]

Issue: [RICHARDSON] 106. Sophia[5], born 7 Dec. 1738;[98] 107. MARY[5]; 108. Thomas[5], born about 1744.

32. BENJAMIN[4] CHEW (William[3], Samuel[2], John[1]), born about 1700, left will 10 June 1761-4 Jan. 1763.[99] He moved to Cecil Co., Md., where he was a justice, 1743-60, disowned by Nottingham Friends Meeting, Oct. 1755. He

---

[91] Mother's will; All Hallows Parish, Anne Arundel Co., Md., Register. Newman, *op. cit.*, I, p. 20, also names children Benjamin and Elizabeth (without citation of any record naming them) and Jane (resulting from the apparent misidentification of 295. Husley [Ursula] Burgess who left will in 1792).

[92] Newman, *op. cit.*, I, p. 20.; All Hallows Parish Register.

[93] Maryland Prerogative Court Wills 39, pp. 833-34.

[94] All Hallows Parish, Anne Arundel Co., Md., Register.

[95] Newman, *op. cit.*, I, p. 18; All Hallows Parish, Anne Arundel Co., Md., Register.

[96] Anne Arundel Co., Md., Will Bk. JG #1, pp. 315-16.

[97] Maryland Prerogative Court Wills 30, p. 559.

[98] All Hallows Parish, Anne Arundel Co., Md., Register.

[99] Maryland Prerogative Court Wills 31, pp. 872-74.

married, Jan. 1726/7, Sarah Bond who left will 1 Nov. 1768-21 April 1769.[100]
Issue:[101] 109. BENJAMIN[5]; 110. Sarah[5], married _____ Johns; 111.
Phinehas[5], of Cecil Co., Md., died before 26 Feb. 1774 when the inventory of his
estate was proved by Cassandra Chew his administratrix;[102] 112. MARY[5]; 113.
ANN[5]; 114. HENRIETTA MARIA[5]; 115. ELIZABETH[5].

34. ANNE[4] CHEW (William[3], Samuel[2], John[1]) died after 1769 when she
was charged with 109 acres of "Stout," her dower in her (1) husband's land.[103]
She married (1) Christopher Randall, justice of Baltimore Co., Md., who died 2
Feb. 1734/5,[104] leaving will 23 Sept. 1734-28 March 1735,[105] and (2), by 7 May
1741, James Burke, who died by 1750.[106]

Issue: (by 1) [RANDALL][107] 116. ROGER[5]; 117. AQUILA[5]; 118.
Susanna[5], married 125. Benjamin[5] Brown; 119. John[5], born 3 July 1726, perhaps
the John whose estate was adminis-tered in 1770;[108] 120. Johanna[5], married 134.
Charles[5] Pierpoint; 121. Rachel[5], born 20 June 1732, married John Frost; 122.
Ruth[5], born 20 March 1734/5.

35. MARGARET[4] CHEW (William[3], Samuel[2], John[1]) married Capt. Joshua
Brown of Anne Arundel Co., Md., who left will 11 May 1774-9 June 1774.[109]

Issue: [BROWN][110] 123. JOHN[5]; 124. Joshua[5], of Anne Arundel Co., Md.,
left will 12 March 1753-22 March 1753,[111] unmarried; 125. BENJAMIN[5]; 126.
Susanna[5], married, 1753, _____; 127. Anne[5]; 128. Margaret[5], married 117.
Aquilla[5] Randall; 129. Jane[5]; 130. Hannah[5], married ___ Hiveley.

36. SIDNEY[4] CHEW (William[3], Samuel[2], John[1]), born about 1692, died
after 1755.[112] Her uncle Samuel[3] Chew gave 200 acres at Elk Ridge to her

---

[100] Maryland Prerogative Court Wills 37, pp. 65-66.

[101] *MHM* XXX, p. 165.

[102] Maryland Prerogative Court Inventories 117, p. 396.

[103] Debt Books, Baltimore Co., Md., 1754-69, Maryland State Archives.

[104] Dawn F. Thomas and Robert Barnes, *The Green Spring Valley* (Baltimore, 1978), I, pp.
45-46; II, pp. 82-83.

[105] Maryland Prerogative Court Wills 21, p. 314.

[106] Robert W. Barnes, *Baltimore County Families*, 1659-1759 (Baltimore, 1989), p. 528.

[107] *Ibid.*, pp. 85. 528.

[108] Maryland Administration Accounts 64, p. 187.

[109] Maryland Prerogative Court Wills 39, p. 819.

[110] Mackenzie, *op. cit.*, I, p. 47.

[111] Maryland Prerogative Court Wills 28, p. 444.

[112] Barnes, *op. cit.*, p. 507.

and her children John and Francis Pierpoint, 7 Oct 1712.[113] She married Charles Pierpoint who left will 1 July 1747-1 Aug. 1748.[114]

Issue:[115] [PIERPOINT] 131. JOHN[5]; 132. Henry[5], of Anne Arundel Co., Md., left will 17 Oct. 1786-1 April 1788;[116] 133. FRANCIS[5]; 134. CHARLES[5]; 135. Joseph[5], born 1726, died 8 April 1806 at Elk Ridge, Md., a preacher among the Friends for many years; 136. Miseal[5], dismissed by Gunpowder Monthly Meeting, 25 Jan. 1758, but admitted by West River Monthly Meeting, 17 July 1789; 137. Abraham[5], disowned by the Society of Friends for fighting, 1758; 138. Mary[5], married, 24 Jan. 1755 in Anne Arundel Co., Md., Benjamin Powell of Baltimore Co., Md.; 139. CHEW[5]; 140. CALIS[5]; 141. Bathsheba[5]; 142. MARGARET[5]; 143. ELIZABETH[5]; 144. Faithful[5], named as sister in will of 132. Henry[5].

39. SAMUEL[4] CHEW (Benjamin[3], Samuel[2], John[1]), born 30 Oct. 1693, inherited half of the "Maidsone" plantation. He was a physician, moved by 1740 to Dover, Del., and served as Chief Justice of the three lower counties, New Castle, Kent and Sussex, then belonging to Pennsylvania. He died 16 June 1743, administration on his estate being granted to Mary Chew, 30 July 1744.[117] He married (1), 7 Oct. 1715,[118] Mary Galloway, born 1697, died 26 May 1734, and (2), 29 Sept. 1736, Mary (Paca) Galloway, daughter of Aquila Paca and widow of Richard Galloway, on whose estate administration was granted to her step-son Benjamin Chew, 3 April 1747.[119]

Issue:[120] (by 1) 145. Sarah[5], born 23 July 1716, died Feb. 1717; 146. Ann[5], born 4 Jan. 1719, died 2 Oct. 1723; 147. Elizabeth[5], born 25 Nov. 1720, married 37. *Edward[4] Tilghman* (see LLOYD); 148. BENJAMIN[5]; 149. ANN[5]; 150. Mary[5], born 27 June 1727, died 28 May 1728; 151. Samuel[5], born 29 April 1728, died 29 June 1729; 152. Samuel[5], born 3 Aug. 1730, died 3 Nov. 1730; 153. Henrietta[5], born 17 March 1732, died June 1732; (by 2) 154. Samuel[5], born

---

[113] Baltimore Co., Md., Deed Bk. TR #A, pp. 207-08.

[114] Maryland Prerogative Court Wills 25, pp. 390-92.

[115] Barnes, *op. cit.*, p. 507; Hedman, *op. cit.*, pp. 53-56, 70-72, which omits Elizabeth and adds daughter Sidney.

[116] Anne Arundel Co., Md., Will Bk. JG #1, p. 6-7.

[117] Kent Co., Del., Will Bk. 1, p. 86.

[118] West River Monthly Meeting records, in *Maryland Genealogical Society Bulletin*, XIV, no. 2, p. 4.

[119] Kent Co., Del., Will Bk. 1, pp. 136-37.

[120] *MHM* XXX, p. 166.

24 Aug. 1737, died 25 May 1809, judge of the Supreme Court for the three lower counties of Delaware and judge of Oyer and Terminer, 1773, married Anna Maria Frisby, born 2 March 1740;[121] 155. Mary[5], born 6 Sept. 1739, died 1 May 1740; 156. John[5], born 21 March 1740, died 15 Dec. 1807 at Chestertown, Md., unmarried; 157. Phelopta[5], named in the will of her grandmother Martha Paca.[122]

40. ELIZABETH[4] CHEW (Benjamin[3], Samuel[2], John[1]), born 13 March 1694/5, died 9 Feb. 1726/7,[123] married, Nov. 1710, Kensey Johns, son of Richard and Elizabeth (Kensey) Johns,[124] born 12 June 1689,[125] died 2 April 1729,[126] left will 31 March 1729-16 July 1729.[127]

Issue: [JOHNS][128] 158. Richard[5], born 26 April 1712, died March 1730/31; 159. BENJAMIN[5]; 160. ELIZABETH[5]; 161. Samuel[5], born 3 March 1717/8; 162. Ann[5], born 27 Feb. 1719/20, died 30 July 1725; 163. KENSEY[5]; 164. Rachel[5], born 18 April 1724; 165. Mary[5], born 1724/5.

43. THOMAS[4] CHEW (Larkin[3], Joseph[2], John[1]), born about 1701, was sheriff of Spotsylvania County, 1724-25, and captain of militia, 1729, justice of Orange County on its formation, 1734, sheriff, 1745, major, 1735, and colonel of militia, 1741, vestryman and warden of St. Thomas' Parish, and left will written 24 March 1780-signed before witnesses 11 Nov. 1781-28 Feb. 1782.[129] He married Martha Taylor, daughter of Col. James Taylor.

Issue:[130] 166. JOSEPH[5]; 167. Larkin[5], deposed, 7 Feb. 1787, he was aged

---

[121] *MHM* XXXI, p. 346.

[122] Maryland Prerogative Court Wills 24, p. 496, will of Martha Paca, 27 Oct. 1746-17 Nov. 1746.

[123] Clifts Monthly Meeting records, Calvert Co., Md., in *Maryland Genealogical Society Bulletin*, XIV, no. 1, p. 10.

[124] James Bordley, *The Hollyday and Related Families* (Baltimore, 1962), p.236.

[125] Clifts Monthly Meeting records, in *Maryland Genealogical Society Bulletin*, XIII, no. 3, p. 23.

[126] Clifts Monthly Meeting records, in *Maryland Genealogical Society Bulletin*, XIV, no. 1, p.10.

[127] Maryland Prerogative Court Wills 19, p. 771.

[128] Clifts Monthly Meeting records, in *Maryland Genealogical Society Bulletin*, XIV, no. 1, pp. 9-11.

[129] Orange Co. Will Bk. 3, p. 39.

[130] "A Genealogical Table ..."; Letter of Joseph Chew, Montreal, Canada, 26 Sept. 1787, Virginia State Archives, Acc.23979; Horace E. Hayden, *Virginia Genealogies* (Wilkes Barre, Pa., 1891), p. 672; Jouett Taylor Cannon, Taylor Family Papers, The Filson Historical

about 62,[131] died 21 Sept. 1796,[132] lieutenant in 2nd Virginia Regiment in French and Indian War, arm shattered by a ball in action, May 1754, of Spotsylvania County;[133] 168. FRANCES[5]; 169. Hannah[5], unmarried; 170. Thomas[5], died as a young man; 171. Colby[5], in company with Dr. Thomas Walker on expedition through Cumberland Gap into Kentucky, 1750,[134] ensign in 1st Virginia Regiment, wounded by the Indians and drowned 1758 in Ohio River near Fort Duquesne;[135] 172. Betsy[5], unmarried; 173. Alice[5], married, 62. *Zachary[5] Taylor* (see WILLOUGHBY); 174. Mildred[5], died 10 Feb. 1788, married, 19 Dec. 1786,[136] James Coleman; 175. SAMUEL[5]; 176. JAMES[5].

44. ANN[4] CHEW (Larkin[3], Joseph[2], John[1]), born about 1703, died 1743, married (license 12) Oct. 1723,[137] as his (1) wife, Capt. William Johnston, born 1 Dec 1697,[138] left will, now lost, presented at court 13 July 1769,[139] of Gloucester, Spotsylvania and Caroline counties, merchant at Port Royal, justice of Spotsylvania, sheriff, 1731, captain of militia, 1729, member of the House of Burgesses from Spotsylvania, 1736-40.[140]

Issue: [JOHNSTON][141] 177. Joseph[5], unmarried; 178. LARKIN[5]; 179. JUDITH[5]; 180. Robert[5], died before 1789 when his executor advertised his estate for sale,[142] merchant and importer of Port Royal, married Ann Cook; 181.

Society, Louisville, Ky.

[131] *Virginia Revolutionary War State Pensions* (Virginia Genealogical Society, *Special Publications*, VII; Richmond, 1980), p. 22.

[132] *Virginia Herald*, Fredericksburg, 23 Sept. 1796.

[133] *The Virginia Genealogist*, XXX, p. 59.

[134] Journal of Dr. Thomas Walker, in Lewis Preston Summer, *Annals of Southwest Virginia, 1769-1800* (Abingdon, 1929), pp. 8, 16-19.

[135] Lloyd DeWitt Bockstruck, *Virginia's Colonial Soldiers* (Baltimore, 1988), pp. 127, 290.

[136] Francis Taylor Diary, Library of Virginia miscellaneous microfilm 114, entry for 22 Dec. 1786; Catherine Lindsay Knorr, *Marriages of Orange County, Virginia, 1747-1810* (Pine Bluff, Ark., 1959), p. 19, bond 18 Dec.

[137] Spotsylvania Co. orders, Will Bk. A, p. 3.

[138] Bible (London, 1605), quoted in Elbert Felton Johnston, *Johnston of Caroline County, Virginia* (Wolfe City, Tex., 1964), p. 52.

[139] Caroline Co. Order Bk. 1767-70, p. 397. Suit, Upshaw *vs.* Dickinson, Superior Court of Chancery for Richmond District, in *T* XX, pp. 167-69, gives will dates as 24 April 1769-12 Oct. 1769.

[140] Leonard, p. 77.

[141] "A Genealogical Table ..."

[142] *Virginia Herald*, Fredericksburg, 9 April 1789.

William[5], married (1) Ann Hunt and, perhaps, (2) Elizabeth Winn; 182. John[5], died young; 183. BENJAMIN[5]; 184. James[5], born 1736, married Mary Ware of Caroline County; 185. HANNAH[5]; 186. RICHARD[5]; 187. BETSY[5].

45. JOHN[4] CHEW (Larkin[3], Joseph[2], John[1]),born about 1706,was sheriff, 1737 and 1752, and justice of Spotsylvania County, and left will 11 May 1755-6 July 1756.[143]　He married, (license 26) June 1729,[144] Margaret Beverley, daughter of Capt. Harry and Elizabeth (Smith) Beverley, born 27 March 1704,[145] died between 1 July 1740 and 2 April 1751.[146]

Issue:[147] 188. ROBERT[5]; 189. MARY BEVERLEY[5]; 190. Margaret[5], died young; 191. JOHN[5]; 192. HANNAH[5].

46. LARKIN[4] CHEW (Larkin[3], Joseph[2], John[1]), deposed 27 July 1749 that he was aged 39.[148]　He was a justice of Spotsylvania County, sheriff, 1739 and 1754, and left will 27 March 1770-codicil 6 April 1770-21 Sept. 1770.[149]　He married, (license 30) Sept. 1733,[150] Mary Beverley, daughter of Capt. Harry and Elizabeth (Smith) Beverley, born 11 Nov. 1699.[151]

Issue:[152] 193. MARY[5]; 194. ELIZABETH BEVERLEY[5].

.　　48. ANN[5] CHEW (Samuel[4], Samuel[3], Samuel[2], John[1]) died 20 May 1777. She married, 11 Aug. 1724, as his (2) wife, Philip Thomas, born 1 March 1694, died 23 Nov. 1762 at "Lebanon," West River, Anne Arundel Co., Md., in his 70th year,[153] left will 29 Nov. 1760-codicil 23 Nov. 1762-31 Jan. 1763.[154]　He was a member of the Maryland Council, Judge and Register of the Land Office, and commissioner to settle the western boundary of Maryland, 1744.[155]

---

[143] Spotsylvania Co. Will Bk. B, p. 295.

[144] Spotsylvania Co. orders, Will Bk. A, p. 3.

[145] Christ Church Parish, Middlesex Co., Register.

[146] Spotsylvania Co. Deed Bk. C, pp. 383-85; Deed Bk. D, pp. 520-22.

[147] "A Genealogical Table ..."; John McGill, *The Beverley Family of Virginia* (Columbia, S.C., 1956), pp. 771-72, 775-76, 789-90, 743, 791, 811-12.

[148] Spotsylvania Co. Order Bk. 1749-55, p. 18, recorded 8 Nov. 1749.

[149] Spotsylvania Co. Will Bk. D, p. 431.

[150] Spotsylvania Co. orders, Will Bk. A, p. 121.

[151] Christ Church Parish, Middlesex Co., Register.

[152] McGill, *op. cit.*, pp. 686-87, 728-29, 737, 743.

[153] *Maryland Gazette*, 25 Nov. 1762.

[154] Maryland Prerogative Court Wills 31, p. 898.

[155] Mackenzie, *op. cit.*, I, p. 520.

Issue: [THOMAS][156] 195. Samuel[6], born 12 June 1725, died 17 July 1784, of "Perry Point," near Havre-de-Grace, Md., married Mary Thomas, born 3 Nov. 1731, died 4 March 1770; 196. Philip[6], born 23 July 1727, died 22 Feb. 1784, married, 30 April 1754,[157] Anne (Harris) Galloway; 197. Mary[6], born 1 Jan. 1731/2, married (1), 12 May 1748,[158] Henry Hill and (2), 7 Feb. 1760, 98. *Robert*[5] *Pleasants* (see JORDAN, Thomas); 198. Elizabeth[6], born 8 March 1732/3, died 30 Jan. 1790, married Samuel Snowden, born 2 Jan. 1728/9, died 27 June 1801, member of the Anne Arundel Co., Md., Committee, Nov. 1774;[159] 199. Richard[6], born 17 July 1736, married, 29 April 1760, Deborah Hughes; 200. John[6], born 26 Aug. 1743, died 3 Feb. 1805, married, 23 Aug. 1777, Sarah Murray.

51. MARY[5] CHEW (Samuel[4], Samuel[3], Samuel[2], John[1]) died 10 Aug. 1770 at Upper Marlboro, Md., in her 56th year.[160] She married John Hepburn, died 14 Aug. 1775 at Upper Marlboro in his 65th year,[161] left will 6 March 1775-20 Sept. 1775,[162] of Prince George's Co., Md., Judge of the Provincial Court.

Issue: [HEPBURN] 201. John[6], left will 30 March 1774-1 June 1774,[163] of Prince George's Co., Md., married 81. *Henrietta Maria*[6] *Waring* (see DIGGES), who married (2), (license 7) Dec. 1779,[164] Joseph Walker, Jr.; 202. Samuel Chew[6], died before 3 April 1807,[165] married ___, probably the Jane Hepburn who made many purchases at the sale of his estate; 203. Ann[6], married ___ Leeke.

52. RICHARD[5] CHEW (Samuel[4], Samuel[3], Samuel[2], John[1]), born 16 May 1716, died 24 June 1769 at Herring Bay, Anne Arundel Co., Md., left will 8 June

---

[156] West River Monthly Meeting records, Anne Arundel Co., Md., in *Maryland Genealogical Society Bulletin*, XV, p. 122.

[157] *Maryland Gazette*, 9 May 1754, "last week"; West River Monthly Meeting records, in *Maryland Genealogical Society Bulletin*. XV, p. 98.

[158] West River Monthly Meeting records, in *Maryland Genealogical Society Bulletin*, XIV, no. 3, p. 8.

[159] Mackenzie, *op. cit.*, I, pp. 488, 492.

[160] *Maryland Gazette*, 16 Aug. 1770; Bible of Francis Chew, in *Maryland Genealogical Society Bulletin*, XLII, pp. 217-18.

[161] *Maryland Gazette*, 24 Aug. 1775.

[162] Maryland Prerogative Court Wills 40, p. 447.

[163] Maryland Prerogative Court Wills 39, p. 874.

[164] Helen W. Brown, *Index of Marriage Licenses, Prince George's County, Maryland, 1777-1886* (Baltimore, 1973), p. 107.

[165] Prince George's Co., Md., Inventories TT #1, p. 221.

1769-22 Sept. 1769.[166]   He married, 5 Jan. 1749/50, Sarah (Lock) Chew, daughter of William Lock and widow of 56. Samuel[5] Chew, who died 1 Feb. 1791, aged 70,[167] leaving will 1 July 1790-10 March 1791.[168]

Issue: 204. Mary[6], born 27 Dec. 1750, died 23 Nov. 1793, married (1), 10 Feb. 1767, Alexander Hamilton Smith, died Nov. 1784, physician, merchant and justice of Calvert Co., Md., which he represented in the Lower House of the Maryland Assembly, 1779-80,[169] and (2), as his (2) wife, William Lyles, of "Red Hall," Calvert Co., Md., which he represented in the Lower House of the Assembly, 1773-74,[170] who left will 3 April 1790-3 Nov. 1790;[171] 205. Richard[6], born 10 April 1753, died 6 June 1801, captain and major of the Maryland Line in the Revolutionary War, married (1), 4 Feb. 1773, Margaret Mackall, born 1754, died 1779, and (2), 2 May 1780, Frances Holland, died 26 Sept. 1799; 206. Samuel[6], born 9 Dec. 1755, died 1 Feb. 1785, left will 28 Jan. 1785-23 June 1785;[172] 207. Lock[6], born 14 Nov. 1757, died 9 Dec. 1793, left will 22 Nov. 1793-6 Jan. 1794;[173] 208. Francis[6], born 10 July 1760; 209. Sarah Lock[6], born 20 Nov. 1761, married, 1788, Nathan Lane of Anne Arundel Co., Md., who left will 20 May 1791-7 Aug. 1791;[174] 210. Philemon Lloyd[6], born 23 July 1765, married, 28 Oct. 1790,[175] 439. *Ann[7] Bowie* (see GRAVES), born 1767, died 1827.

54. FRANCIS[5] CHEW (Samuel[4], Samuel[3], Samuel[2], John[1]), born 1721, died 11 Nov. 1775, married, 26 Feb. 1749/50, Mary Lingan, died 12 Feb. 1764.[176]

Issue: 211. Samuel[6], born 29 Jan. 1755; 212. Ann[6], born 15 May 1759; 213. Richard[6], born 19 Oct. 1761, died in Anne Arundel Co., Md., sergeant and ensign in the 4th Regiment, Maryland Continental Line.[177]

---

[166] Maryland Prerogative Court Wills 38, p. 336.

[167] Walter Worthington Bowie, *The Bowies and Their Kindred* (Washington, 1899), p. 383.

[168] Anne Arundel Co., Md., Will Bk. JG #1, pp. 220-22.

[169] *A Biographical Dictionary of the Maryland Legislature*, II, p.742.

[170] *Ibid.*, I, pp. 557-58.

[171] Maryland Chancery Record Bk. 48, p. 191.

[172] Anne Arundel Co., Md., Will Bk. TG #1, pp. 272-73.

[173] Anne Arundel Co., Md., Will Bk. JG #1, p. 370.

[174] Anne Arundel Co., Md., Will Nk. JG #1, pp. 243-45.

[175] Brown, *op. cit.*, p. 45, license 27 Oct.

[176] Bible of Francis Chew, *loc. cit.*

[177] Rieman Steuart, *A History of the Maryland Line in the Revolutionary War, 1775-1783* (n.p., 1969), p. 66.

56. SAMUEL[5] CHEW (John[4], Samuel[3], Samuel[2], John[1]) of Herring Bay, Anne Arundel Co., Md., died Feb. 1749 in London,[178] leaving will 23 Sept. 1748-21 July 1749.[179] He married Sarah Lock, born 1721, died 1791, who married (2), 5 Jan. 1749/50, 52. Richard[5] Chew.

Issue:[180] 214. Samuel[6], born 1737, died 20 Feb. 1790, of "Wells," Anne Arundel Co., Md., delegate of the Maryland Conventions of 1774-75 and of the Association of Freemen of Maryland, first lieutenant, 3rd Battalion, Flying Camp, June-Dec. 1776, captain, 3rd Regiment, Maryland Line, 10 Dec. 1776-Feb. 1777, married (1), 3 Feb. 1763,[181] Sarah Weems, died 30 Oct. 1763,[182] and (2) Priscilla Claggett; 215. John[6], left will 12 May 1785-codicil 26 May 1785-17 June/28 July 1785,[183] married ___; 216. William[6], born 1746, died 9 April 1801, aged 55,[184] married, 1768, Elizabeth Reynolds, died 12 April 1801;[185] 217. Elizabeth[6], married (1) ___ Smith and (2) ___ Sprigg; 218. (Daughter)[6].[186]

57. ANNE[5] CHEW (John[4], Samuel[3], Samuel[2], John[1]) married, 17 Aug. 1727,[187] Joseph Hopkins, born 2 Nov. 1706, left will 28 April 1783-30 Oct. 1784,[188] a Quaker, of Harford Co., Md.

Issue: [HOPKINS][189] 219. Joseph[6], born 1728, left will 27 Dec. 1784-24 Nov. 1795,[190] married, 9 Feb. 1769,[191] Elizabeth Gover; 220. Sarah[6], married, 25 Nov. 1759,[192] Skipwith Coale; 221. Margaret[6], married John Harris; 222.

---

[178] *Maryland Gazette*, 10 May 1749.

[179] Maryland Prerogative Court Wills 27, p. 1.

[180] Maryland Prerogative Court Wills 27, p. 272, will of William Lock, 22 April 750-15 May 1750.

[181] *Maryland Gazette*, 17 Feb. 1763.

[182] *Maryland Gazette*, 10 Nov. 1763.

[183] Anne Arundel Co., Md., Will Bk. TG #1, pp. 271-72, 275-76.

[184] Gravestone, All Saints Church, Sunderland Md., in Jerry and Mildred O'Brien and Merle L. Gibson, *Calvert Co. Maryland Old Graveyards* (Sunderland, Md., 1986), p. 3.

[185] *Ibid.* Bowie, *op. cit.*, p. 386, says 1 April.

[186] The will of Samuel, 1748, leaves to daughter Elizabeth a Negro girl "which was left to my Deceased Daughter."

[187] West River Monthly Meeting records, in *Maryland Genealogical Society Bulletin*, XIV, no. 3, p. 8.

[188] Harford Co., Md., Will Bk. AJ #2, pp. 298-99.

[189] Mackenzie, *op. cit.*, II, pp. 184, 362.

[190] Harford Co., Md., Will Bk. AJ #2, pp. 318-21.

[191] Deer Creek Monthly Meeting records, in Robert Barnes, *Maryland Marriages, 1634-1777* (Baltimore, 1975), p. 90.

[192] Nottingham Monthly meeting records, in Barnes, *op. cit.*, p. 35.

Mary[6], married 226. Charles[6] Worthington; 223. Elizabeth[6], married, 6 March 1760,[193] Samuel Hill.

58. SARAH[5] CHEW (John[4], Samuel[3], Samuel[2], John[1]), born 1 June 1705, died 1772, married, 5 Oct. 1732, as his (2) wife, Charles Worthington, of Harford Co., Md., born 20 Oct. 1701,[194] who married (1) 148. *Hamutel[5] Hammond* (see WILKINS) and left will 22 Nov. 1773-24 March 1774.[195]

Issue: [WORTHINGTON][196] 224. John[6], born 18 July 1733, left will 26 Feb. 1803-11/20 June 1803,[197] Harford Co., Md., married, 7 Nov. 1769,[198] Priscilla Wilson; 225. Elizabeth[6], born 22 July 1735, died 3 Aug. 1735; 226. Charles[6], born 6 July 1736, died about. 1799, married 222. Mary[6] Hopkins;[199] 227. Ann[6], born 10 June 1738, died unmarried before 1779; 228. Elizabeth[6], born 17 Jan. 1740, died 24 July 1747; 229. Sarah[6], born 17 Nov. 1743, died 7 March 1744/5; 230. Sarah Chew[6], born 15 Dec. 1746, married Josiah Lee.; 231. Mary[6], born 26 Jan. __, died unmarried; 232. Samuel Chew[6], born 8 Feb. 1755, died 1777, unmarried.

59. MARY[5] CHEW (John[4], Samuel[3], Samuel[2], John[1]), died 1779, married, 11 Oct. 1736,[200] Peregrine Ward, born 1709, who left will 4 July1759-1 Oct. 1759,[201] justice and sheriff, 1736, of Cecil Co., Md.

Issue: [WARD] 233. John[6], possibly the one of four John Wards of Cecil Co., Md., who served in the Lower House of the Maryland Assembly, 1776-78;[202] 234. Peregrine[6]; 235. Ann Chew[6], married Thomas Lloyd; 236. Mary[6].

61. JOSEPH[5] CHEW (Nathaniel[4], Samuel[3], Samuel[2], John[1]) died before 1762. He married ___.

Issue:[203] 237. Nathaniel[6], died 22 Dec. 1827 at West River, Anne Arundel

---

[193] *Ibid.*, in *ibid.*, p. 86.

[194] Sharon J. Doliante, *Maryland and Virginia Colonials* (Baltimore, 1991), p. 358.

[195] Maryland Prerogative Court Wills 39, p. 714.

[196] Worthington family record, in *Maryland Genealogical Society Bulletin*, XXIII, pp. 72-74.

[197] Harford Co., Md., Will Bk. AJ #C, pp. 153-60.

[198] Gunpowder Monthly Meeting records, in Barnes, *op. cit.*, p. 200.

[199] *Maryland Genealogical Society Bulletin*, XXXIII, p. 783.

[200] St. Stephen's Parish, Cecil Co., Md., in Barnes, *op. cit.*, p. 186.

[201] Maryland Proprietary Wills 30, p. 800.

[202] *A Biographical Dictionary of the Maryland Legislature*, II, pp. 859-60.

[203] Henrietta Maria (Chew) Dorsey made a bequest to the children , unnamed, of cousin Joseph Chew.

Co., Md., in 80th year,[204] married, (license 12) Dec. 1775,[205] Elizabeth Norris; 238. John[6], of Prince George's Co., Md., left will 9 May 1815-15 Nov. 1815,[206] married, (license 5) Jan. 1775,[207] Elizabeth Gott.

62. ANN[5] CHEW (Nathaniel[4], Samuel[3], Samuel[2], John[1]) left will 31 July 1783-10 Aug. 1784.[208] She married (1) ___ Tongue and (2), 29 Aug. 1747,[209] Nathaniel Dare of Anne Arundel Co., Md., who left will 13 Nov. 1763-17 Jan. 1764.[210]

Issue: (by 1) [TONGUE] 239. Thomas[6], married ___; (by 2) [DARE] 240. Nathaniel[6]; 241. Gideon[6]; 242. Ann[6], married, 28 Dec. 1775,[211] Richard Cowman; 243. Richard[6].

66. SAMUEL[5] CHEW (Joseph[4], Joseph[3], Samuel[2], John[1]) married, about 1746, Elizabeth Pratt.[212]

Issue:[213] 244. John[6], born 31 March 1749 at Alexandria, died 22 May 1838 in Loudoun County, married Margaret Reed;[214] 245. Roger[6], died 18 March 1792,[215] of Alexandria, married ____, possibly Anne, who married (2) ___ Moxley; 246. Elizabeth[6], died 1807,[216] married, 1785,[217] Richard Weightman, tailor and stays maker from London, who settled at Alexandria, 1785,[218] died 2

---

[204] *Maryland Gazette*, 3 Jan. 1828.

[205] Brown, *op. cit.*, p. 33.

[206] Prince George's Co., Md., Will Bk. TT #1, pp. 153-54.

[207] Brown, *op. cit.*, p. 33.

[208] Anne Arundel Co., Md., Will Bk. TG #1, pp. 191-94.

[209] St. James Parish, Anne Arundel Co., Md., Register.

[210] Maryland Prerogative Court Wills 31, p. 1054.

[211] St. James Parish, Anne Arundel Co., Md., Register.

[212] Affidavit of Eleanor Beall appended to power of attorney, 16 Feb. 1775, of Roger Chew to sell all Georgia lands he inherited from his father Samuel Chew (Georgia Colonial Conveyance Bk. CC, p. 563, in *Georgia Genealogical Magazine*, no. 8, April 1963, p. 425).

[213] Alexandria Co. Deed Bk. O, p. 224.

[214] *History of West Virginia, Old and New*, II (Chicago and New York, 1922), p. 321.

[215] Gravestone, Christ Episcopal Church graveyard, in Wesley E. Pippenger, *Tombstone Inscriptions of Alexandria, Virginia*, III (Alexandria, 1992), p. 136, which shows year as missing but supplies 1811; burial permit issued by Christ Church 19 March 1792 (*ibid.*, p. 146).

[216] *The Times & Alexandria Advertiser*, 6 Aug. 1807.

[217] *Virginia Journal and Alexandria Advertiser*, 14 April 1785.

[218] T. Michael Miller, *Artisans and Merchants of Alexandria, Virginia, 1780-1820* (Bowie, Md., 1992), II, p. 239.

March 1812, in his 52nd year,[219] left will 13 Dec. 1806-7 March 1812;[220] 247. Mary[6], married ___ McMasters.

69. JOSEPH[5] CHEW (Henry[4], Joseph[3], Samuel[2], John[1]), born 24 Aug. 1719, died 22 Jan. 1753, left will 15 1st month 1752-2 March 1753.[221] He lived in the portion of Baltimore Co., Md., which became Harford County. He married, 1745, Sarah Sheredine, born 18 Dec. 1726, died 7 Jan. 1784, who married (2) William Yates and as a widow continued to live in Baltimore Co., Md..[222] .

Issue:[223] 248. Elizabeth[6], born 16 July 1747, died 25 Sept. 1806, married, 24 Nov. 1768, John Hopkins, who was born 4 Jan. 1745/6 and died 25 Sept. 1806;[224] 249. Susan[6], born 25 Dec. 1749, died 15 Dec. 1784, married, (license 5) Sept. 1780,[225] Joseph Miller, born 1746, of Harford Co., Md.; 250. Thomas Sheredine[6], born 8 June 1752, died 15 Feb. 1821, married, 25 Feb. 1790,[226] Elizabeth Morgan, born 1 Nov. 1772.

70. ELIZABETH[5] CHEW (Henry[4], Joseph[3], Samuel[2], John[1]) died 29 Aug. 1806.[227] She married (1) Walter Smith of Calvert Co., Md., who left will 9 Oct. 1743-1 Feb. 1743/4,[228] (2) Job Hunt of Calvert Co., Md., born 16 Sept. 1718,[229] left will 1 Feb. 1753-11 Aug. 1753,[230] and (3), after 1770, John Bond.

Issue: (by 1) [SMITH] 251. Walter[6], born Jan. 1739, died 18 Feb. 1772,[231] left will dated 13 Aug. 1770,[232] of Baltimore Co., Md.; (by 2) [HUNT] 252.

---

[219] *Alexandria Herald*, 6 March 1812.

[220] Alexandria Co. Will Bk. 1, p. 157.

[221] Baltimore Co., Md., Original Wills, Box 8, folder 48, Maryland State Archives.

[222] Robert Barnes, *Baltimore County Families, 1659-1759* (Baltimore, 1989), pp. 108, 711; Census of Deer Creek Lower Hundred, Harford Co., Md., in Gaius Marcus Brumbaugh, *Maryland Records*, II (Lancaster, Pa., 1928), p. 160.

[223] *MHM* XXX, pp. 168, 173; Baltimore Co., Md., Administration Accounts 5, p. 335.

[224] Mackenzie, *op. cit.*, II, p. 351.

[225] Harford Co., Md., Marriage licenses.

[226] St. James Parish, Baltimore Co., Md., Register.

[227] Gravestone, Hunt Cemetery, Baltimore Co., Md.

[228] Maryland Prerogative Court Wills 23, p. 375.

[229] Clifts Monthly Meeting records, Calvert Co., Md., in *Maryland Genealogical Society Bulletin*, XIV, p. 9.

[230] Maryland Prerogative Court Wills 28, p. 527.

[231] *MHM* III, p. 385.

[232] Maryland Prerogative Court Wills 39, p. 95.

Henry[6]; 253. Job[6], died 18 Feb. 1809 in Baltimore Co., Md., in his 62nd year,[233] married ___; 254. Phineas[6], of Baltimore Co., Md.; 255. Samuel C.[6], of Baltimore Co., Md.

71. SARAH[5] CHEW (Henry[4], Joseph[3], Samuel[2], John[1]) married Richard Deale of Calvert Co., Md., who left will 15 Dec. 1767-17 Nov. 1770.[234]

Issue: [DEALE] 256. Richard[6], died before 1767, married ____; 257. William[6], died before 1767, married ____; 258. James[6]; 259. Joseph[6]; 260. Sheridine[6]; 261. Rachel[6], married ___ Hance; 262. Mary[6], married ___ Austin.

72. JANE[5] CHEW (Henry[4], Joseph[3], Samuel[2], John[1]) married (1) Reuben Parker, mariner of New Bern, N.C., and later merchant of Beaufort, Carteret Co., N.C., and justice 14 Dec. 1757, who left will 11 April 1760-May 1764,[235] and (2) Col. William Thompson of Carteret County, who died before Feb. 1803.[236]

Issue: (by 1) [PARKER] 263. Elizabeth[6], married ___ Dade; 264 Abigail[6], married ___ Jones; 265. Reuben[6]; 266. Joseph Henry Chew[6], on whose estate administration was granted, 21 Sept. 1786, to William Thompson.[237]

76. SARAH[5] WHITE (Anne[4] Burgess, Sarah[3] Chew, Samuel[2], John[1]), born 13 Feb. 1709,[238] married ___ Hawkes.

Issue: [HAWKES] 267. Robert[6].

77. ANN[5] WHITE (Anne[4] Burgess, Sarah[3] Chew, Samuel[2], John[1]) married John Fleming of Montgomery Co., Md., who left will Jan. 1795-16 Jan. 1797.[239]

Issue: [FLEMING] 268. Robert White[6]; 269. Ann[6], left will 1 June 1810-9 April 1814,[240] married Ninian Willett; 270. Catherine[6], born 22 Sept. 1747, died 26 Nov. 1821, married, 15 June 1778, as his (2) wife, Capt. Joseph Magruder, born 16 Oct. 1742, died 15 Aug. 1793, of Montgomery Co., Md.;[241] 271. John[6];

---

[233] *Federal Gazette*, Baltimore, 20 Feb. 1809.

[234] Maryland Prerogative Court Wills 38, p. 250.

[235] Secretary of State Records, Original wills, folder "Parker, Ruben, 1760." North Carolina State Archives; Carteret Co., N.C., Court Minutes 1747-64, p. 77, folio 1.

[236] Incomplete will, Carteret Co., N.C. Original wills, folder "Thomson, William, 1803," North Carolina State Archives.

[237] Carteret Co., N.C., Unbound original estate records, folder "Parker, Joseph Henry Chew, 1786," North Carolina State Archives.

[238] All Hallows Parish, Anne Arundel Co., Md., Register.

[239] Montgomery Co., Md., Will Bk. C, p. 315.

[240] Montgomery Co., Md., Will Bk. J, p. 22.

[241] Information provided to the American Clan Gregor Society by Richard Chowning Magruder, 1918.

272. James[6], left will 14 April 1792-12 June 1792;[242] 273. Margaret[6], married David Lowe.

80. Col. JOSEPH[5] NICHOLSON (Elizabeth[4] Burgess, Sarah[3] Chew, Samuel[2], John[1]), born 6 Aug. 1709,[243] died 1787. He resided at Chestertown, Md. He married (1) Hannah (Smith) Scott, daughter of James and Sarah (Hynson) Smith and widow of Edward Scott, and (2) Mary Hopper, daughter of William Hopper, who died about 1799.[244]

Issue: [NICHOLSON] (by 1) 274. Joseph[6], left will 14 Aug. 1781-11 Nov. 1786,[245] lawyer of Chestertown, Md., and later of "Chesterfield," Queen Anne's Co., Md., member of three of the Maryland conventions, 1774-76, and of the Senate, 1776-81, elected a delegate to the Continental Congress but did not attend,[246] married, 28 July 1757,[247] Elizabeth Hooper; 275. William[6]; 276. James[6], born about 1735, died 2 Sept. 1804 at New York, N.Y., in his 69th year,[248] went to sea and was present at the capture of Havana, 1762, thereafter resided in New York until 1771 when he returned to Maryland, was captain of the Maryland ship *Defence* and in 1776 of the *Virginia,* and in June 1776 was appointed commander-in-chief of the Continental Navy, later commanded the *Trumbull* which was taken by the British and he continued a prisoner of war to its conclusion,was an original member of the Society of the Cincinnati,[249] married ___; 277. Benjamin[6], died 1792, represented Baltimore Co., Md., in six of the Maryland conventions, 1774-76, lieutenant colonel of Baltimore County militia, judge of the Court of Admiralty, 1776-89, chief judge of the Baltimore city court, 1791-92,[250] married Mary Ridgely; 278. Samuel[6], born 1743, died 27 Dec. 1811 at Chestertown, Md., lieutenant on board the *Bon Homme Richard* in battle with

---

[242] Montgomery Co., Md., Will Bk. C, p. 1.

[243] All Hallows Parish, Anne Arundel Co., Md., Register.

[244] Robert W. Barnes and F. Edward Wright, *Colonial Families of the Eastern Shore of Maryland.* II (Westminster, Md., 1996), p. 239.

[245] Queen Anne's Co., Md., Will Bk. TW1, p. 42.

[246] *A Biographical Dictionary of the Maryland Legislature*, II, pp. 614-15; *MHM* XCVIII, pp. 134-35.

[247] *Maryland Gazette*, 4 Aug. 1757.

[248] *Baltimore American*, 6 Sept. 1804.

[249] Rieman Steuart, *A History of The Maryland Line in the Revolutionary War, 1775-1783* (n.p., 1969), p. 116; *The National Cyclopaedia of American Biography*, II (New York, 1900), p. 231.

[250] *A Biographical Dictionary of the Maryland Legislature*, II (Baltimore and London, 1985), pp. 612-13.

the *Serapis*, captain in the Continental Navy, 1779-83, first commandant of the Boston Navy Yard, original member of the Society of the Cincinnati,[251] married, 1780, Mary Dowse; 279. Thomas[6], died 1783, married, 1774, Rachel Ridgely; 280. Elizabeth[6], married Charles Gordon; 281. John[6], lieutenant and captain in the Continental Navy, original member of the Society of the Cincinnati;[252] (by 2) 282. Joseph Hopper[6]; 283. Mary[6]; 284. Henrietta[6], married (1) John Bracco, who died 1797, and (2) Robert Goldsborough.

88. RACHEL[5] BURGESS (Samuel[4], Sarah[3] Chew, Samuel[2], John[1]) left will 12 Sept. 1789-3 Dec. 1789.[253] She married James Disney, who left will 27 May 1778-25 July 1778.[254]

Issue: [DISNEY][255] 285. Ann[6], born 6 Nov. 1748; 286. James[6], born 11 April 1751; 287. Elizabeth[6], married ___ Nicholson; 288. Sarah[6], born 10 Aug. 1760, married, 1 Feb. 1782, Nicholas Watkins, born 1740; 289. Samuel Burgess[6], born23 Dec. 1762; 290. Rachel[6].

89. WILLIAM[5] WARE (Margaret[4] Burgess, Sarah[3] Chew, Samuel[2], John[1]), born March 1714,[256] married ___.

Issue: [WARE] 291. Richard[6], named in the will of his great-grandmother, 1740.

91. WILLIAM[5] BURGESS (John[4], Sarah[3] C hew, Samuel[2], John[1]), born 9 Oct. 1721,[257] of Anne Arundel Co., Md., left will 15 July 1757-codicil 3 April 1763-23 April 1763.[258] He married Sarah ___.

Issue: [BURGESS] 292. Ann[6], born 4 April 1743; 293. Samuel[6], born 19 Jan. 1744, died young; 294. Jane[6], born 14 Oct. 174[ ], married, as his (2) wife, Ephraim Duvall, born 12 July 1742, left will 25 March 1807-23 April 1807;[259] 295. Ursula [Husley][6], born 17 Nov. 1748, left will 26 Sept. 1787-10 April 1792;[260] 296. William[6], born 10 June 1751; 297. John[6], born 29 May 1753,

[251] Steuart, *op. cit.*, pp. 116-17.

[252] *Ibid.*, p. 116.

[253] Anne Arundel Co., Md., Will Bk. JG #1, pp. 109-10.

[254] Anne Arundel Co., Md., Will Bk. EV #1, pp. 70-71.

[255] All Hallows Parish, Anne Arundel Co., Md., Register.

[256] St. James Parish, Anne Arundel Co., Md., Register.

[257] All Hallows Parish, Anne Arundel Co. Md., Register.

[258] Maryland Prerogative Court Wills 31, p. 904.

[259] Anne Arundel Co., Md., Will Bk. JG #2, p. 388; Harry Wright Newman, *Mareen Duvall of Middle Plantation* (Washington, 1952), pp. 236-37.

[260] Anne Arundel Co., Md., Will Bk. 36, p. 275.

perhaps the John who left will 10 Jan. 1779-20 Dec. 1780,[261] married Rebecca ___; 298. Sarah[6], born 22 Dec. 1756; 299. Samuel[6], born after 1757.

93. JOHN[5] BURGESS (John[4], Sarah[3] Chew, Samuel[2], John[1]), born 8 June 1725,[262] died after 1793 when he was mentioned as an insolvent debtor. He was a justice of Anne Arundel Co., Md., 1777, judge of the Orphans Court, 1777-84, and sheriff, 1778. By 28 Feb. 1776 he had organized a company of militia and on 2 Nov. 1778 was appointed colonel of the Elk Ridge Battalion. He married Sarah Dorsey, daughter of Basil and Sarah (Worthington) Dorsey, who died before 12 March 1769.[263]

Issue: [BURGESS][264] 300. Achsah[6], married, (license 27) Nov. 1781,[265] John Green; 301. Sarah[6], married 310. Joshua[6] Burgess; 302. Basil[6], died 30 March 1824, ensign and lieutenant in the Maryland Line, 1780-83, original member of the Society of the Cincinnati,[266] moved to Mason Co., Ky., by 1800, married, (license 11) Jan. 1785,[267] Eleanor Dorsey; 303. John[6], born 24 Jan. 1766, died Oct. 1821,[268] left will 1 Oct. 1821-9 Oct. 1821,[269] of Montgomery and later of Frederick Co., Md., married, (license 27) July 1785,[270] Eleanor[7] Griffith, daughter of Henry and 393. *Ruth[6]* (*Hammond*) *Griffith* (see WILKINS), born March 1766.

94. JOSEPH[5] BURGESS (John[4], Sarah[3], Samuel[2], John[1]), born 5 March 1726/7,[271] of Anne Arundel Co., Md., left will 9 Sept. 1805-19 May 1806.[272] He entered service 10 Dec. 1776 as captain of a company of Elk Ridge militia in the 3rd Battalion, Maryland Flying Camp. He married, 13 June 1757, Elizabeth Dorsey, born 13 Dec. 1735, daughter of Michael and Ruth (Todd) Dorsey.

---

[261] Anne Arundel Co., Md., Will Bk. TG #1, pp. 13-14.

[262] All Hallows Parish, Anne Arundel Co., Md., Register.

[263] Maryland Prerogative Court Wills 39, p. 840, will of Sarah Dorsey, 12 March 1769-9 March 1774.

[264] Newman, *op. cit.*, I, pp. 23, 36-38.

[265] Anne Arundel Co., Md., Marriage license.

[266] Steuart, *op. cit.*, pp. 62-63.

[267] Anne Arundel Co., Md., Marriage license.

[268] *Frederick Herald*, 13 Oct. 1821.

[269] Frederick Co., Md., Will Bk. HS #2, p. 513.

[270] Anne Arundel Co., Md., Marriage license.

[271] All Hallows Parish, Anne Arundel Co., Md., Register.

[272] Anne Arundel Co., Md., Will Bk. JG #2, p. 357.

Issue: [BURGESS][273] 304. Lt. John[6], born 20 Nov. 1751, died before 19 March 1777 when the inventory of his estate was made,[274] married Sarah (___) Welch;[275] 305. Joseph[6], born 20 Jan. 1751, captain in 4th Regiment, Maryland Line, from 10 Dec. 1776 until 17 Nov. 1778,[276] died about 1780; 306. Michael[6], born 11 April 1754, died before 16 Dec. 1817 when the inventory of his estate was made,[277] ensign in the Maryland Flying Camp, 1776,[278] married, (license 22) Oct. 1783,[279] Sarah Warfield, who left will dated 23 Sept. 1823;[280] 307. Vachel[6], born 9 May 1752, died 30 March 1824,[281] ensign and lieutenant of 1st Maryland Regiment, 1777-79,[282] married, (license 1) Oct. 1782,[283] Rebecca Dorsey, daughter of Thomas Dorsey; 308. Richard[6], born 1 Sept. 1757, of Allegany Co., Md., married, (license 25) Feb. 1778,[284] Mary Gassaway; 309. Ruth[6], born and died 1759; 310. Joshua[6], born 3 July 1760, died 15 Oct. 1831, lieutenant in the Revolutionary War, 1776-83, original member of the Society of the Cincinnati, moved to Mason Co., Ky.,[285] married, (license 18) Dec. 1790,[286] 303. Sarah[6] Burgess; 311. Philemon[6], born 13 Dec. 1761, married, (license 18) Feb. 1800,[287] Mary Ridgely Dorsey, daughter of Thomas Dorsey; 312. Ruth[6], married 135. *Elisha[5] Warfield* (see GAITHER); 13. Elizabeth[6], born 25 May 1765, married, 11 Dec. 1792, Beall Israel; 314. Jane[6], born 6 Feb. 1769, married, (license 1)

[273] Newman, *op. cit.*, I, pp. 24-26, 39-42; Maxwell J. Dorsey, Jean Muir Dorsey and Nannie Ball Nimmo, *The Dorsey Family* (reprint, Baltimore, 2000), p. 84.

[274] Anne Arundel Co., Md., Administration Accounts EV #1, p. 122.

[275] Dorsey, *op. cit.*, p. 57, says she was Sarah Dorsey, died before 1769, daughter of Basil Dorsey.

[276] *Muster Rolls ... of Maryland Troops in the American Revolution* (*Archives of Maryland*, XVIII; Baltimore, 1900), p. 88.

[277] Anne Arundel Co., Md., Inventories JG #9, p. 519; Testamentary Papers, Box 149, folder 6, Maryland State Archives.

[278] Rieman Steuart, *A History of the Maryland Line in the Revolutionary War, 1775-1783* (n.p., 1969), p. 63.

[279] Anne Arundel Co., Md., Marriage license.

[280] Anne Arundel Co., Md., Will Bk. EVJG, p. 213, without probate date.

[281] *Alexandria Herald*, 5 May 1824, as aged 68.

[282] Steuart, *loc. cit.*

[283] Anne Arundel Co., Md., Marriage license.

[284] Baltimore Co., Md., Marriage license.

[285] Revolutionary War pension application, Joshua Burgess, BLWt.342-200, National Archives; Steuart, *loc. cit.*

[286] Baltimore Co., Md., Marriage license.

[287] *Ibid.*.

Feb. 1780,[288] Rezin Simpson; 315. Sarah[6], born 21 Jan. 1764; 316. William[6], born 9 Feb. 1771, died 1 Aug. 1804; 317. Honor[6], born and died 1772; 318. Honor[6], born 1 July 1773, married John Hobbs; 319. Nancy[6], born 15 Sept. 1775; 320. Lidey [Lydia][6], born 9 Dec. 1777, married (1) Isaac Barster and (2) William Maxwell; 321. Joseph[6], born 2 Sept. 1780.

95. SARAH[5] BURGESS (John[4], Sarah[3] Chew, Samuel[2], John[1]), born 2 Feb. 1717/8, married William Disney of Anne Arundel Co., Md., who left will 13 May 1762-21 June 1762.[289]

Issue: [DISNEY][290] 322. James[6], born 7 March 1745/6; 323. Ann[6], born 28 Sept. 1749; 324. William[6], born 23 Jan. 1750/1; 325. Jane[6], born 10 Jan. 1753; 326. Ezekiel[6], born 23 Dec. 1755.

97. EDWARD[5] BURGESS (John[4], Sarah[3] Chew, Samuel[2], John[1]), born about 1733, died 5 Dec. 1809. He was a captain of militia and served in the Flying Camp, 1776, was a planter of Montgomery Co., Md., justice, and member of the Lower House of the Maryland legislature, 1777-83, 1786-90, 1796.[291] He married 177. *Mary[5] Davis* (see GAITHER), born 22 Dec. 1733, died 1784.

Issue: [BURGESS][292] 327. John[6], died before 13 July 1813 when administration on his estate was granted to his widow,[293] married, (license 19) March 1800,[294] Helen Maccubbin; 328. Elizabeth[6], left will 25 Aug. 1824-12 Nov. 1824;[295] 329. Anne[6], left will 7 March 1826-3 April 1826;[296] 330. Edward[6], left will 27 Jan. 1824-11 May 1824;[297] 331. Margaret[6], married, (license 5) Sept. 1804,[298] Ninian Clagett; 332. Ephraim[6], of Montgomery Co., Md., unmarried, 1790, later of Allegany Co., Md., married Elizabeth ___; 333. Jane[6], left will 6 July 1825-8 Aug. 1825;[299] 334. Thomas[6]; 335. Mary[6], married John Shebell; 336. Sarah[6].

---

[288] Baltimore Co., Md., Marriage license.

[289] Maryland Prerogative Court Wills 31, p. 781.

[290] All Hallows Parish, Anne Arundel Co., Md., Register.

[291] *A Biographical Dictionary* ..., I, pp. 181-82.

[292] Newman, *op. cit.*, I, pp. 26, 44.

[293] Montgomery Co., Md., Will Bk. M, p. 84.

[294] Tressie Nash Bowman, *Montgomery County, Maryland, Marriages, 1796-1850* (n.p., 1966), p. 13.

[295] Montgomery Co., Md., Will Bk. O, p. 163.

[296] *Ibid.*, p. 373.

[297] *Ibid.*, p. 149.

[298] Bowman, *op. cit.*, p. 16.

[299] Montgomery Co., Md., Will Bk. P, p. 314.

98. SAMUEL⁵ BURGESS (John⁴, Sarah³ Chew, Samuel², John¹), born 28 Feb. 1735/6,³⁰⁰ died before 20 Jan, 1773 when the inventory of his estate was made.³⁰¹ He married Jane (Wyvill?), who left will 2 March 1776-10 May 1776.³⁰²

Issue: [BURGESS]³⁰³ 337. Matilda⁶; 338. Barbara⁶, married ___ Wood; 339. John West⁶, married (1), (license 3) Feb. 1787,³⁰⁴ Sarah Battie and (2), (license 29) Aug. 1790,³⁰⁵ Sarah Simmons; 340. Benjamin⁶, died before 6 Dec. 1793 when the inventory of his estate was made,³⁰⁶ married, 5 Nov. 1780,³⁰⁷ Agnes Battie, who married (2) Charles Cooke and lived in the District of Columbia.

99. WEST⁵ BURGESS (John⁴, Sarah³ Chew, Samuel², John¹), born 23 Nov. 1737, left will 2 March 1777-14 Sept. 1777.³⁰⁸ He married, 31 Oct. 1765,³⁰⁹ 143. *Elizabeth⁶ Warfield* (see GAITHER), who married (2), by 11 April 1780, John Dickerson.³¹⁰

Issue: [BURGESS]³¹¹ 341. Thomasine⁶, born 10 Sept. 1766; 342. Sander⁶; 343. Samuel West⁶, died before 2 May 1815 when West Burgess gave bond as his administrator,³¹² married ___ ; 344. John Brice⁶, left will 15 March 1815-18 April 1815;³¹³ 345. West⁶, born 1777, left will 28 March 1825-15 Aug. 1825,³¹⁴ of Frederick Co., Md., married, (license 3) Aug. 1803,³¹⁵ Rachel Warfield.

100. CALEB⁵ BURGESS (John⁴, Sarah³ Chew, Samuel², John¹), born 31

---

³⁰⁰ All Hallows Parish, Anne Arundel Co., Md., Register.
³⁰¹ Maryland Prerogative Court Inventories 116, p. 156.
³⁰² Maryland Prerogative Court Wills 40, p. 649.
³⁰³ Newman, *op. cit.*, I, pp. 29, 44-45.
³⁰⁴ Anne Arundel Co., Md., Marriage license.
³⁰⁵ *Ibid.*
³⁰⁶ Anne Arundel Co., Md., Inventories JG #3, pp. 339-42.
³⁰⁷ St. James Parish, Anne Arundel Co., Md., Register.
³⁰⁸ Anne Arundel Co., Md., Will Bk. EV #1, p p. 34-36.
³⁰⁹ Queen Caroline Parish, Howard Co., Md., Register.
³¹⁰ Anne Arundel Co., Md., Testamentary Papers, Box 2, folder 46, Maryland State Archives.
³¹¹ Newman, *op. cit.*, I, pp. 30, 45-47.
³¹² Anne Arundel Co., Md., Testamentary Proceedings, Box 117, folder 46, Maryland State Archives.
³¹³ Anne Arundel Co., Md., Will Bk. 38, p. 103.
³¹⁴ Frederick Co., Md., Will Bk. HS #3, p. 415.
³¹⁵ Margaret E. Myers, *Marriage Licenses of Frederick County, Maryland, 1778-1810* (2nd ed.; Westminster, Md., 1994), p. 19.

[*sic*] Sept. 1739,[316] died before 17 Feb. 1791 when his widow gave bond as his administratrix.[317] He married (1) 145. *Deborah⁵ Warfield* (see GAITHER), born 1752, and (2), (license 6) April 1787,[318] Susanna (___) Mercer, widow of John Mercer, who died before 11 June 1794 when the inventory of her estate was returned.[319]

Issue: [BURGESS] (by 1) 346. John⁶, married, (license 14) March 1798,[320] Rachel Thomas; 347. Caleb⁶, left will 2 Nov. 1817-1 Dec. 1817,[321] ensign of the Severn Battalion, Anne Arundel Co., Md., militia, 1778, later of Frederick Co., Md., married, (license 19) Aug. 1802,[322] Anne Warfield; 348. Samuel⁶, born 22 June 1782, died 28 Aug. 1822, married (1), (license 1) Dec. 1809,[323] Elizabeth Warfield and (2), 14 Dec. 1819,[324] Rachel Carmack, born 1785, died 10 Jan. 1857 at Johnsville, Md.; 349. Alexander⁶; 359. Phoebe [Dela] W., married, (license 2) Jan. 1790,[325] Rezin Spurrier; 351. Matilda⁶, married 255. *Joshua⁶ Simpson* (see GAITHER).

101. MARY⁵ BURGESS (John⁴, Sarah³ Chew, Samuel², John¹), born 25 Dec. 1743, married ___ Lusby.

Issue: [LUSBY] 352. Sarah⁶, married ___ Lumplough; 353. Robert⁶.

107. MARY⁵ RICHARDSON (Susannah⁴ Burgess, Sarah³ Chew, Samuel², John¹) married Henry Culver.

Issue: [CULVER] 354. Susannah⁶.

109. BENJAMIN⁵ CHEW (Benjamin⁴, William³, Samuel², John¹) died before 4 June 1779 when a final accounting of his estate was made.[326] He was captain of the privateer *Chase*, 20 men, six guns, 30 April 1777. He married, 1 May 1750, Cassandra Johns.

---

[316] All Hallows Parish, Anne Arundel Co., Md., Register.

[317] Anne Arundel Co., Md., Testamentary Papers, Box 22, folder 53, Maryland State Archives.

[318] Anne Arundel Co., Md., Marriage license.

[319] Anne Arundel Co., Md., Inventories JC #5, p. 361.

[320] Anne Arundel Co., Md., Marriage license.

[321] Frederick Co., Md., Will Bk. HS #2, pp. 125-26.

[322] Myers, *loc. cit.*.

[323] *Ibid.*.

[324] Margaret E. Myers, *Marriage Licenses of Frederick County, Maryland, 1811-1840* (Westminster, Md., 2000), p. 31, license 25 Nov.

[325] Anne Arundel Co., Md., Marriage license.

[326] Cecil Co., Md., Accounts Bk. 5, p. 80.

Issue:[327] 355. Samuel[6]; 356. Richard[5]; 357. Benjamin[6]; 358. Nathaniel[6], died 22 May 1827 in his 69th year, of Cecil Co., Md., midshipman, Continental Navy, in Revolutionary War, captured and confined in the Jersey prison ships,[328] and later a captain, married, 21 Nov. 1793, Margaret M. Rodgers, daughter of Commodore John Rodgers, U.S.N., who died 21 April 1848; 359. Ann[6]; 360. Sarah[6].

112. MARY[5] CHEW (Benjamin[4], William[3], Samuel[2], John[1]) married, 29 July 1765,[329] Thomas Elliott of Cecil Co., Md., and later of Baltimore Co., Md., who left will 21 Nov. 1805-26 Sept. 1807.[330]

Issue: [ELLIOTT] 361. Sarah Chew[6], married, 12 Oct. 1785,[331] John O'Donnell, colonel of militia and representative from Baltimore in the Maryland Legislature, who died 5 Oct. 1805 in Baltimore County, aged 56.[332]

113. ANN[5] CHEW (Benjamin[4], William[3], Samuel[2], John[1]) married, 27 Nov. 1768,[333] Capt. Isaac Van Bibber, born 25 Feb. 1736, died 21 April 1825,[334] of Cecil Co., Md.

Issue" [VAN BIBBER][335] 362. Washington[6], born 15 Feb. 1778, died 8 April 1848, married, 28 May 1807, Lucretia Emory; 363. Isaac[6], born 4 Jan. 1783, married ___; 364. Ann[6], born 25 Dec. 1786, died 17 Jan. 1834, married Hugh Neilson.

114. HENRIETTA MARIA[5] CHEW (Benjamin[4], William[3], Samuel[2], John[1]) left will 8 Aug. 1820-29 Aug. 1820.[336] She married (1), 1772, Samuel C. Davey and (2), 11 Oct. 1783,[337] John James.

Issue: (by 1) [DAVEY] 365. Capt. Hugh[6], married, 3 March 1808,[338] Elizabeth Weary; 366. Anna[6], never married; 367. Sarah[6], left will 4 April 1829-

---

[327] *Ibid.*, p. 85.

[328] Revolutionary War pension application, Nathaniel Chew, widow Margaret M., W.9383, National Archives.

[329] St. Mary Ann's (North Elk) Parish, Cecil Co., Md., Register.

[330] Baltimore Co., Md., Will Bk. 8, p. 245.

[331] Baltimore Co., Md., Marriage licenses, Scharf Papers, Maryland Historical Society.

[332] *Federal Gazette*, Baltimore, Md., 7 Oct. 1805.

[333] St. Mary Ann's (North Elk) Parish, Cecil Co., Md., Register.

[334] Mackenzie, op. cit., I, p. 538.

[335] *Ibid.*, p. 539.

[336] Baltimore Co., Md., Will Bk. 11, p. 171.

[337] Return of the Rev. William West, Baltimore Co., Md., Scharf Papers, Maryland Historical Society.

[338] *Baltimore American*, 4 March 1808.

28 June 1830,[339] married Samuel Harper Hadskiss, who left will 26 Dec. 1823-22 July 1825;[340] (by 2) [JAMES] 368. Deborah[6], married, 10 Feb. 1802,[341] Capt. William Robinson; 369. Molly Elliott[6], born 1788 at Baltimore, died 1862, married, 1803, William Jackson, born 1769, died 3 Feb. 1847,[342] major of cavalry at the battle of North Point, 1814, president of the Old Defenders Association of Baltimore.

115. ELIZABETH[5] CHEW (Benjamin[4], William[3], Samuel[1], John[1]) married, 30 June 1750,[343] Dr. Benjamin Crockett, who died before 24 Jan. 1760 when Gilbert Crockett gave bond as his administrator.[344]

Issue: [CROCKETT][345] 370. Benjamin[6], born 25 May 1751; 371. John[6], born 19 April 1754; 372. Gilbert[6], born 26 July 1756; 373. Sarah[6], named in will of her grandfather, 1761.

116. ROGER[5] RANDALL (Anne[4] Chew, William[3], Samuel[2], John[1]), born 3 Jan. 1720, died after Nov. 1754. He married, 26 Dec. 1742, Rachel Stevens.

Issue: [RANDALL] 374. Benjamin[6], born 2 Jan. 1744/5, died young; 375. Aquila[6], born 17 Nov. 1746; 376. Benjamin[6], born 11 Sept. 1749.

117. AQUILA[5] RANDALL (Anne[4] Chew, William[3], Samuel[2], John[1]), born 9 May 1723,[346] left will 20 June 1800-13 Oct. 1801.[347] He married 128. Margaret[5] Brown.

Issue: [RANDALL][348] 377. Christopher[6], married, (license 15) Nov. 1788,[349] Anne Crandall; 378. John[6]; 379. Aquila[6], married, 8 June 1779,[350] Rebecca Cord; 380. Delilah[6], married 86. Ichabod[6] Davis (see GAITHER); 381. Nathan[6], died 1806 in Anne Arundel Co., Md., married, 16 Oct. 1790, Ruth Davis; 382. Brice Chew[6], born 6 Aug. 1771, died 6 Aug. 1837,[351] moved to Fayette Co., Ky., married, Feb. 1795, Susanna Porter, born 11 Aug. 1780, died

---

[339] Baltimore Co., Md., Will Bk. 13, p. 428.
[340] Baltimore Co., Md., Will Bk. 12, p. 149.
[341] *Federal Gazette*, Baltimore, Md., 11 Feb. 1808.
[342] *Sun*, Baltimore, Md., 4 Feb. 1847.
[343] St. George's Parish, Baltimore Co., Md., Register.
[344] Baltimore Co., Md., Administration Bonds 1, p. 441.
[345] St. George's Parish, Baltimore Co., Md., Register; Barnes, *op. cit.*, p. 145.
[346] St. Paul's Parish, Baltimore Co., Md., Register.
[347] Anne Arundel Co., Md., Will Bk. JGH #37, p. 194.
[348] Thomas and Barnes, *op. cit.*, p. 83.
[349] Anne Arundel Co., Md., Marriage license.
[350] First Presbyterian Church, Baltimore, Md., Register.
[351] *Kentucky Gazette*, 10 Aug. 1837.

6 June 1857; 383. Ruth[6], married, 14 Oct. 1786, Michael Cramblett; 384. Anne [Nancy][6], married, 1 Sept. 1785,[352] Joseph Hobbs.

123. JOHN[5] BROWN (Margaret[4] Chew, William[3], Samuel[2], John[1]) was buried with wife and two children on part of "Ranters Ridge." He married __.

Issue: [BROWN] 385. (Child)[6]; 386. (Child)[6].

125. BENJAMIN[5] BROWN (Margaret[4] Chew, William[3], Samuel[2], John[1]) of Anne Arundel Co., Md., left will 9 June 1768-12 July 1768.[353] He married 118. Susannah[6] Randall, who died 5 Feb. 1804.[354]

Issue: [BROWN] 387. Samuel[6], born 9 Jan. 1747, died 6 Oct. 1833, of "Walnut Hill," Howard Co., Md., first lieutenant of Elk Ridge Battalion of militia, 1776, captain, 1778, married, 30 Nov. 1773, Achsah Riggs, born 27 Jan. 1745/6, died 9 Sept. 1817;[355] 388. Benjamin[6]; 389 Rachel[6], married __ Todd; 390. Ruth[6], married __ Todd; 391. Richard[6]; 392. Charles[6]; 393. Joshua[6]; 394. Vachel[6], married __ Hyatt; 395. Susanna[6]; 396. Ephraim[6].

131. JOHN[5] PIERPOINT (Sidney[4] Chew, William[3], Samuel[2], John[1]) left will 21 June 1753-8 Aug. 1753.[356] He resided in Anne Arundel Co., Md., and later settled in Frederick Co., Md. He married, 10 Aug. 1737,[357] Ann Gassaway, died before 18 Feb. 1757,[358] daughter of Nicholas and Elizabeth (_____) Gassaway.

Issue: [PIERPOINT][359] 397. Samuel[6]; 398. John[6]; 399. Henry[6]; 400. Ann[6], born 1744, died 17 July 1812; 401. Rachel[6], married ___, her cousin

133. FRANCIS[5] PIERPOINT (Sidney[4] Chew, William[3], Samuel[2], John[1]), born 1712, died 29 Aug. 1780. He moved to Fairfax County, Nov. 1750. He

---

[352] Baltimore Co., Md., Marriage returns, Scharf Papers, Maryland Historical Society.

[353] Maryland Prerogative Court Wills36, p. 476.

[354] *Maryland Genealogical Society Bulletin*, XXXI, p. 310, query, which, however, gives Benjamin's death as 4 Oct. 1768.

[355] John Beverley Riggs, *The Riggs Family of Maryland* (Baltimore, 1939), pp. 436-37; Brown Bible, in The Maryland Original Research Society of Baltimore, *Bulletin*, III (Baltimore, 1913), pp. 34-36.

[356] Maryland Prerogative Court Wills 29, p. 9.

[357] West River Monthly Meeting, Anne Arundel Co., Md., records, in *Maryland Genealogical Society Bulletin*, XIV, no. 4, p. 3.

[358] Maryland Prerogative Court Wills 30, p. 297, will of Nicholas Gassaway, 18 Feb. 1757-21 April 1757.

[359] Hedman, *op. cit.*, pp. 53-54.

married, 19 Jan. 1737/8,[360] Sarah Richardson, daughter of Joseph and Sarah Richardson, born 3 May 1719.[361]

Issue: [PIERPOINT][362] 402. Mary[6], born 12 Sept. 1738, married, 30 Sept. 1762, Richard Richardson, Jr., born 2 Dec. 1742,[363] died 1803, disowned by the Society of Friends, 1778, for his support of the American Revolution;[364] 403. Obed[6], born 3 Nov. 1740, died 3 April 1830, of Frederick Co., Md., married, 7 April 1773, Esther Myers, born 21 Aug. 1752, died 10 April 1839; 404. John[6], married Nancy Ann Morgan; 405. Charles[6], died unmarried; 406. Francis[6], married, July 1768, Sarah ___; 407. Eli[6]; 408. Elizabeth[6].

134. CHARLES[5] PIERPOINT (Sidney[4] Chew, William[3], Samuel[2], John[1]) deposed 20 Feb.1753/4 he was aged about 35,[365] left will 3 May 1785-23 May 1785.[366] He married, before 29 March 1745 when he was disowned by the Society of Friends for marrying his first cousin,[367] 120. Joanna[5] [Hannah] Randall, who died 19 Feb. 1815 at Baltimore, Md., aged 87 yrs. 21 days.[368]

Issue: [PIERPOINT][369] 409. Joseph[6], born 4 April 1747, died 1806; 410. Amos[6], of Frederick Co., Md.., disowned by the Society of Friends, 1787; 411. Benedick[6], disowned by the Society of Friends for neglecting meeting and fighting, 1785, married, 22 Oct. 1792, Milcah Griffith; 412. Samuel[6], disowned by the Society of Friends for neglecting meeting, 1787; 413. Walter[6], born 6 April 1770; 414. Thomas[6], born 12 July 1772; 415. Mary[6], died 17 Oct. 1857 at Baltimore, Md., aged 87,[370] married, 13 Oct. 1804 at Baltimore,[371] Felix McCurley, born 25 Dec. 1779, York Co., Pa., died 12 June 1845, Baltimore,

---

[360] West River Monthly Meeting, Anne Arundel Co., Md., records, in *Maryland Genealogical Society Bulletin*, XIV, no. 4, p. 3.

[361] West River Monthly Meeting, Anne Arundel Co., Md., records, in *Maryland Genealogical Society Bulletin*, XV, p. 120.

[362] Hedman, *op. cit.*, pp. 53-55; Hinshaw, VI, p. 547-48.

[363] Richardson Bible.

[364] Mackenzie, *op. cit.*, III, p. 47.

[365] Baltimore Co., Md., Deed Bk. HWS #14, p. 245.

[366] Baltimore Co., Md., Will Bk. 4, p. 33.

[367] Indian Springs Monthly Meeting (West River) Quarterly Minutes, 1698-1754, p. 208.

[368] *Baltimore American*, 28 Feb. 1815.

[369] Hedman, *op. cit.*, pp. 53, 55-56.

[370] Gravestone, Greenmount Cemetery, Baltimore, Md.; *Sun*, Baltimore, 19 Oct. 1857.

[371] War of 1812 Bounty land warrant 3342-120-55, Felix McCurley, widow Mary, National Archives.

Md.,[372] left will 8 June 1844-codicil 25 Jan. 1845-16 June 1845,[373] served as one of the defenders of Baltimore, Aug. 1814 for three months as private in Capt. Andrew Smith's company, Maryland militia; 416. John[6], died 12 Nov. 1802; 417. Ann[6], married, 6 Jan. 1773, Jacob Reed of Baltimore Co., Md.; 418. Deborah[6], died 3 Sept. 1802.

139. CHEW[5] PIERPOINT (Sidney[4] Chew, William[3], Samuel[2], John[1]) married, 25 Jan. 1748/9 at Gunpowder Meeting House, Md.,[374] Misael Deaver.

Issue: [DEAVER][375] 419. Abraham[6], born 13 Jan. 1749/50, died 1831, moved to Deavertown, Morgan Co., Ohio, married, (license 25) June 1778,[376] Ann Lakin, born 27 Sept. 1762, died 1842; 420. Miseal[6], born 6 Aug. 1751, died 1823, married (1) Rebecca ___ and (2), (license 26) Dec. 1799,[377] Sarah Frazier; 421. Mary[6], born 15 Sept. 1753; 422. Jonah[6], married, 4 Aug. 1786 at Baltimore, Md., Temperance Scott; 423. Margaret[6].

140. CALIS[5] PIERPOINT (Sidney[4] Chew, William[3], Samuel[2], John[1]) married, 28 Feb. 1750/1, [378] Thomas Taylor of Fairfax County and of Frederick Co., Md.

Issue: [TAYLOR][379] 424. Thomas[6], moved to Frederick Co., Md., 1793, married, May 1782 at Warrington Monthly Meeting, Pa., Sarah Musgrove; 425. Rachel[6], born 25 Sept. 1732, died 25 Jan. 1821, married, 30 Dec. 1788, as his (2) wife, Abraham Griffith, born 2 June 1746, died 26 May 1800;[380] 426. Joseph[6]; 427. Jesse[6]; 428. Sarah[6], married, 26 Dec. 1792, Benjamin Hough Canby and in 1817 moved to Boone Co., Ky.;[381] 429. Henry[6]; 430. Ann[6]; 431. Mary[6], married, 1 April 1775 at Monocacy Meeting House, Md., John West Plummer.

142. MARGARET[5] PIERPOINT (Sidney[4] Chew, William[3], Samuel[2], John[1]) married, 4 Nov. 1747 at Elk Ridge, Nicholas Gassaway, Jr., son of Thomas

---

[372] Gravestone, Greenmount Cemetery, *loc. cit.*; *Sun*, Baltimore, 14 June 1845.

[373] Baltimore, Md., Will Bk. 20, pp. 368-74.

[374] Hinshaw, VI, p. 486, as Basil.

[375] *Ibid.*; Hedman, *op. cit.*, pp. 57, 64, 70.

[376] Myers, *Marriage Licenses of Frederick County, Maryland, 1778-1810*, p. 36.

[377] *Ibid.*

[378] Elk Ridge Monthly Meeting, Harford Co., Md., records.

[379] Hinshaw, VI, p. 572; Hedman, *op. cit.*, pp. 71-72.

[380] Hinshaw, VI, p. 587.

[381] *Ibid.*, p. 480.

Gassaway, who settled in Baltimore Co., Md., by 1750.[382]

Issue: [GASSAWAY] 432. Rachel[6], born 15 Feb. 1750/1, married, 29 Oct. 1776,[383] John Wells.

143. ELIZABETH[5] PIERPOINT (Sidney[4] Chew, William[3], Samuel[2], John[1]) left will 28 June 1788-4 April 1791.[384] She married Valentine Brown, who died by 27 Nov. 1777 when his estate was administered.[385]

Issue: [BROWN] 433. Valentine[6]; 434. William[6]; 435. John[6]; 436. Sarah[6]; 437. Sidney[6]; 438. Elizabeth[6], married ___ Pierpoint; 439. Catherine[6], left will 4 1 mo. 1783-9 Dec. 1783;[386] 440. (Daughter)[6], married ____ Randall; 441. (Son)[6], married ___.

148. BENJAMIN[5] CHEW (Samuel[4], Benjamin[3], Samuel[2], John[1]), born 29 Nov. 1722 at "Maidstone," Anne Arundel Co., Md., died 20 Jan. 1810 at Philadelphia, Pa. He was a student at the Middle Temple, admitted to the bar, 1746, and began practice at Dover, Del., moved to Philadelphia and built "Cliveden" at Germantown, Pa., was Commissioner of Boundaries for the three lower counties of Delaware, 1751, Speaker of the House from the same district, 1753-58, Attorney General of Pennsylvania, 1754-69, Register General of Wills, 1765-76, with loyalist sympathies during the Revolutionary War, and Judge and President of the High Court of Errors and Appeals, 1791-1806.[387] He married (1), 13 June 1747,[388] Mary Galloway, died 1755, and (2), 12 Sept. 1757, Elizabeth Oswald, born 1732, died 1819.

Issue: (by 1) 442. Mary[6], born 10 March 1748, died 22 Aug. 1794, married, 18 May 1768, Alexander Wilcocks, born 1741, died 1801; 443. Anna Maria[6], born 27 Nov. 1749, died Nov. 1812, unmarried; 444. Elizabeth[6], born 10 Nov.

---

[382] Barnes, *op. cit.*, p. 246. Newman, *op. cit.*, I, pp. 156-57, however, names the parents of Nicholas Gassaway, Jr., as Nicholas and Elizabeth (___) Gassaway, states their marriage occurred 12 Sept. 1749 at West River, and names sons John, left will 20 Dec. 1767-30 Aug. 1768 (Maryland Prerogative Court Wills 36, p. 556) and. Nicholas, of Anne Arundel Co., Md., who left will 25 May 1810-8 Jan. 1815 (Anne Arundel Co., Md., Will Bk. JG #3, pp. 92-94), married, (license 9) Feb. 1785 (Baltimore Co., Md., Marriage license) Cassandra Randall, who left will 19 July 1820-31 Dec. 1829 (Anne Arundel Co., Md., Will Bk. TTS #1, p. 69).

[383] Gunpowder Monthly Meeting records, as Caleb Pierpoint.

[384] Anne Arundel Co., Md., Will Bk. JG #1, pp. 227-29.

[385] Anne Arundel Co., Md., Administration Accounts ED 1777-79, p. 28.

[386] Anne Arundel Co., Md., Will Bk. TG #1, pp. 144-45.

[387] *MHM* XXX, pp. 168-69; *Dictionary of American Biography*, IV (New York, 1930), p, 64.

[388] *Maryland Gazette*, 16 June 1747.

1751, married 131. *Edward⁵ Tilghman* (see LLOYD); 445. Sarah⁶, married 456. John⁶ Galloway; 446. Henrietta⁶, born Sept. 1755, died 1756; (by 2) 447. Benjamin⁶, born 30 Sept. 1758, died 30 April 1844, admitted to the bar at Philadelphia, Pa., 1786, married, 11 Dec. 1788, Katherine Banning, born 1770, died 1855; 448. Margaret Oswald⁶, born 16 Dec. 1760, died 29 May 1824, married, 18 May 1787, Col. John Eager Howard, born 4 June 1752 at "Belvedere," Baltimore Co., Md., died 12 Oct. 1827 at Baltimore, captain of the 2nd Battalion, Flying Camp (Baltimore Co., Md.), 16 July 1776, major of 4th Regiment, 10 Dec. 1776, lieutenant colonel of 2nd Regiment, 11 March 1779, and lieutenant colonal commandant of 5th Regiment, 3 June 1781, original member of the Society of the Cincinnati of Maryland and its president, 1804-27, Governor of Maryland, 1788-90, state senator, 1791-95, United States Senator 1797-1803, Federalist candidate for Vice President, 1816;[389] 449. Joseph⁶, born 9 March 1763, died Sept. 1764; 450. Juliana⁶, born 8 April 1765, married, 1 April 1793, as his (2) wife, Philip Nicklin, born in England, died 1806;[390] 451. Henrietta⁶, born 15 Sept. 1767, died 9 March 1848, unmarried; 452. Sophia⁶, born 13 Nov. 1769, married, 1796, Henry Philips, born 1767, died 1800, of Philadelphia, Pa.; 453. Maria⁶, born 22 Dec. 1771, died 27 March 1840, unmarried; 454. Harriet⁶, born 22 Oct. 1775, died 8 April 1861, married, 17 July 1800, Col. Charles Carroll, born 2 March 1775, died 3 April 1825, of "Homewood," Baltimore Co., Md.;[391] 455. Catherine⁶, born 3 May 1779, died 28 May 1831.

149. ANN⁵ CHEW (Samuel⁴, Benjamin³, Samuel², John¹), born 13 April 1725, married Samuel Galloway, of "Tulip Hill," Anne Arundel Co., Md., who left will 28 Oct. 1785-7 Nov. 1785.[392]

Issue: [GALLOWAY][393] 456. John⁶, of "Tulip Hill," Anne Arundel Co., Md., died 16 May 1810 at "Tulip Hill,"[394] married, 23 Oct. 1786, 445. Sarah⁶

---

[389] Steuart, *op. cit.*, p. 98; *Biographical Directory of the American Congress, 1774-1996* (Alexandria, Va., 1997), p. 1242.

[390] Mackenzie, *op. cit.*, IV, pp. 367-68, 395; *Evening Post*, Baltimore, Md., 6 Nov. 1806, died "last week."

[391] Mackenzie, *op. cit.*, IV, p. 73.

[392] Anne Arundel Co., Md., Will Bk. TG #1, pp. 291-92.

[393] George A. Hanson, *Old Kent: The Eastern Shore of Maryland* (Baltimore, 1876), pp. 66-67; *A Biographical Dictionary of the Maryland Legislature*, I, pp. 467-68.

[394] *Maryland Gazette*, 23 May 1810.

Chew, born 15 Nov. 1753, died 28 May 1826;[395] 457. Benjamin[6], student at Eton and Lincoln's Inn, settled and died at Hagerstown, Md.; 458. Mary[6], married 222. *Thomas[6] Ringgold* (see LLOYD); 459. Anne[6], married James Cheston.

159. BENJAMIN[5] JOHNS (Elizabeth[4] Chew, Benjamin[3], Samuel[2], John[1]) born 22 Jan. 1713/4, died 9 May 1750. He married Rachel __, who died 2 Jan. 1748.

Issue:[396] 460. Kensey[6], born Jan. 1744/5; 461. Benjamin[6], born Oct. 1746; 462. Richard[6], born 14 Nov. 1748.

160. ELIZABETH[5] JOHNS (Elizabeth[4] Chew, Benjamin[3], Samuel[2], John[1]), born 16 Jan. 1715/6, died 27 Aug. 1744. She married Benjamin Hance, Jr., of Calvert County, who left will 23 June 1748-10 Dec. 1748.[397]

Issue: [HANCE] 463. Benjamin[6]; 464. Kensey[6]; 465. Mary[6].

163. KENSEY[5] JOHNS (Elizabeth[4] Chew, Benjamin[3], Samuel[2], John[1]) born 11 May 1722, died 26 May 1763. He resided at West River, Anne Arundel Co., Md., and married, 15 Nov. 1750, Susanna Galloway.

Issue: [JOHNS] 466. Elizabeth[6], born 25 Aug. 1750, died 22 Jan. 1809, married, 19 Feb. 1778, 107. Judge *James[5] Tilghman* (see LLOYD); 467. Richard[6], born 1752, died 1816, married, 1774, Sarah Weems, died 1793;[398] 468. Kensey[6], born 14 June 1759 at West River, Md., died 1849 at New Castle, Del., served in Maryland militia during the Revolutionary War, studied law and settled at New Castle, member of the convention which framed the Delaware Constitution of 1792, appointed to United States Senate, 1794, but did not take his seat, appointed Chief Justice of Delaware, 1798, and Chancellor of the State of Delaware, 1830, married Ann Van Dyke.[399]

166. JOSEPH[5] CHEW (Thomas[4], Larkin[3], Joseph[2], John[1]) was

---

[395] *Maryland Gazette*, 1 June 1826.

[396] Clifts Monthly Meeting records, in *Maryland Genealogical Society Bulletin*, XIV, no. 1, p. 17.

[397] Maryland Prerogative Court Wills 25, p. 492.

[398] *Maryland Genealogical Society Bulletin*, XXIV, p. 129.

[399] *The National Cyclopaedia of American Biography*, V (New York, 1907), p. 196. They were the parents of John Johns, president of the College of William and Mary and Bishop of Virginia.

commissioner for Connecticut at the treaty of Fort Stanwix, 1768.[400] He married Grace Deshon of New London, Conn.

Issue:[401] 469. Joseph[6], died at Jamaica, unmarried; 470. William Johnston[6], officer in British army, killed at Niagara, 1812; 471. Frances[6], died 1820, married Gabriel Sistar [Swaine?] of New London, Conn.; 472. Grace[6], died at Montreal, Quebec, unmarried; 473. John[6], died at Montreal, Quebec, unmarried.

168. FRANCES[5] CHEW (Thomas[4], Larkin[3], Joseph[2], John[1]) died 8 Oct. 1784 in Mecklenburg Co., N.C. She married, by 6 Oct. 1758,[402] Henry Downs, who was captain of Augusta County militia, 1746, moved in 1762 from Orange and Augusta counties to the portion of Anson Co., N.C., which became Mecklenburg County, was captain of militia there and a signer of the Mecklenburg Declaration of Independence, and died 8 Oct. 1798 leaving will 2 April 1797-Oct. 1798.[403]

Issue: [DOWNS][404] 474. Jane[6], born 16 Jan. 1751, married, 17 July 1773, John Robinson of Mecklenburg Co., N.C.; 475. Henry Douglas[6], born 23 July 1754, died 2 Sept. 1774, married Elizabeth Davis; 476. Thomas[6], born 22 Aug. 1756 in Augusta County, died 27 Nov. 1839, served many short tours during the Revolutionary War and in 1781 was a lieutenant,[405] married Mary Courtney, born 1768, died 1828; 477. Samuel[6], born 7 May 1758, died at Atlanta, Ga., married _____ Crockett; 478. William[6], born 1759, colonel of the 2nd South Carolina Regiment, moved to Aberdeen, Miss., married Sarah Downs; 479. Mildred[6], born 27 July 1760, died after 1819 in Anderson Co., S.C., married, 1780, James Brewster, Revolutionary War soldier, born 1755, died before 10 April 1804 in Anderson Co., S.C.

175. SAMUEL[5] CHEW (Thomas[4], Larkin[3], Joseph[2], John[1]) commanded a vessel in the service of the Continental Congress and was killed in an engagement in 1779. He married, at New Haven, Conn., Lucy Miller, daughter of Capt. John Miller.

---

[400] Boyd Crumrine, ed., "Records of Deeds for the District of West Augusta, Virginia, for the Court held at Fort Dunmore (Pittsburgh, Pa.), 1775-1776," *Annals of the Carnegie Museum*, III (Pittsburgh, 1905), pp. 443, 449.

[401] Hayden, *loc. cit.*; Taylor Family Papers, *loc. cit.*

[402] Augusta Co. Deed Bk. 8, p. 63.

[403] Mecklenburg Co, N.C., Will Bk. C, p. 22.

[404] John Bennett Boddie, *Historical Southern Families*, VII (Kailua, Hawaii, 1963), pp. 213-16.

[405] Revolutionary War pension application, Thomas Downs, S.8337, National Archives.

Issue: 480. Coleby[6], died 1803 at sea, married Frances Larned of New London, Conn., died 1846; 481. Samuel[6], died 1834, married Mary Sabin of New London, Conn., died 1855; 482. Thomas John[6], born 1771, died 1846, married Aby Hortense Hallam of New London, Conn.

176. JAMES[5] CHEW (Thomas[4], Larkin[3], Joseph[2], John[1]) was a lieutenant stationed at Pittsburgh, Pa., 1764,[406] recommended as a justice at a court held at Fort Dunmore [Pittsburgh], 23 Feb. 1775 and 20 Aug. 1776,[407] was of Monongalia County, 1779,[408] and died by 1794.[409] He married Mary Caldwell.

Issue: 483. Colby[6], of Hampshire County when he purchased 177 acres there, 12 Feb. 1799,[410] of Berkeley County when he purchased 695½ acres, 17 May 1800, but of Hampshire County again when he sold that land, 9 Jan. 1805,[411] married Rebecca ___; 484. (perhaps) Joshua[6], born 27 April 1771, died 16 March 1859,[412] of Berkeley County, perhaps married (1), (bond 19) March 1804,[413] Polly Marquart and (2), (bond 12) May 1817,[414] Elizabeth McNelly [McNealy], born 14 June 1799, died 5 June 1873; 485. (perhaps) Henry[6], married, (bond 19) April 1813,[415] Amelia Gustine; 486. (perhaps) Mary[6], married, (bond 6) Oct. 1804,[416] James Daniel.

178. LARKIN[5] JOHNSTON (Ann[4] Chew, Larkin[3], Joseph[2], John[1]), born 1 May 1727 in Spotsylvania County, died 16 March 1816 in Jasper Co., Ga. He resided in Halifax County and in Person and Granville cos., N.C., before moving to Georgia. He married, 2 May 1745, Mary Rogers, born 22 Jan. 1727, died 25

---

[406] Bockstruck, *op. cit.*, p. 187.

[407] Boyd Crumrine, ed., "Minute Book of the Virginia Court Held at Fort Dunmore (Pittsburgh) for the District of West Augusta, 1775-1776," *Annals of the Carnegie Museum*, I (Pittsburgh, 1902), pp. 533, 565.

[408] Bockstruck, *op. cit.*, p. 277.

[409] Lyman Chalkley, *Chronicles of the Scotch-Irish Settlement of Virginia* (Roslyn, Va., 1912), II, p. 107; Berkeley Co., W.Va., Will Bk. 3, p. 488, accounting of estate of James Chew by George Hite, administrator.

[410] Clara McCormick Sage and Laura Sage Jones, *Early Records, Hampshire County, Virginia, now West Virginia* (Delavan, Wis., 1939), p. 14.

[411] Berkeley Co., W.Va., Deed Bk. 19, pp. 522-24.

[412] Chew family Bible owned by Mrs. Mary Stoltzfus, New York, N.Y.

[413] Guy L. Keesecker, *Marriage Records of Berkeley County, Virginia ... 1781-1854* (Baltimore, 1983), p. 37.

[414] *Ibid.*

[415] *Ibid.*

[416] *Ibid.*

Oct. 1800 at Hico, Person Co., N.C.[417]

Issue: [JOHNSTON][418] 487. William[6], born 25 Oct. 1746, died 29 Nov. 1759 in Granville Co., N.C.; 488. Ann[6], born 3 July 1749, married, 26 Aug. 1772, Samuel Cush [Cash]; 489. Larkin[6], born 11 July (O.S.) 1752, died 9 March 1757; 490. Lucy[6], born 15 May 1755 in Halifax County, died 9 Oct. 1832 in DeKalb Co., Ga., married, 30 Nov. 1783,[419] John Landers, who moved to DeKalb Co., Ga.; 491. Sarah[6], born 18 May 1758 in Granville Co., N.C., married (1), 25 Jan. 1778, Francis Howard and (2) Henry Fuller [Finlles?]; 492. Littleton[6], born 18 Feb. 1761 in Granville Co., N.C., died 7 July 1842 in Jasper Co., Ga., resided in Orange, Caswell, Granville and Person cos., N.C., and Elbert and Jasper cos., Ga., married (1), 4 Jan. 1781,[420] Lucy Chiles, born 30 Jan. 1756, died 9 June 1826, and (2), 12 Jan. 1828, Sarah (___) Durbin; 493. John[6], born 22 Dec. 1763, died 7 July 1842 in Jasper Co., Ga., aged 88 yrs. 4 mos. 2 days [*sic*], married (1) Leah [or Sarah?] Long and (2) Mary Warren [or Mary (___) Wansen?]; 494. Theodorick[6], born 20 Aug. 1768, married Elizabeth Stuard; 495. Sophia[6], born 15 Dec. 1769, married, 26 [or 20?] 1802, Larkin Herndon; 496. Richard[6], born 14 March 1778, died 17 Jan. 1837 in Walton Co., Ga., married, 4 March 1802, Elizabeth Hemphill.

181. JUDITH[5] JOHNSTON (Ann[4] Chew, Larkin[3], Joseph[2], John[1]) left will 23 Sept. 1793-3 Dec. 1793.[421] She married Robert Farish of King and Queen and Spotsylvania counties who left will 16 April 1768-2 Oct. 1769.[422]

Issue: [FARISH][423] 497. Robert[6], perhaps married Lucy Rogers and moved to Georgia; 498. John[6], moved to Kentucky, married ___; 499. Ann[6], born about 1749; 500. Sarah[6], married William Coleman; 501. Catey[6], married James

---

[417] Bible, in *Georgia Genealogical Magazine*, no. 4 (April 1962), p. 227, and in Memory Aldredge Lester, *Old Southern Bible Records* (Baltimore, 1974), p. 170, with variations.

[418] Hopewell L. Rogers, *Rogers, Some of the Descendants of Giles Rogers* (n.p., 1940), no pagination; Lorand V. Johnson, *Johnston of Caskieben, Crismond and Caiesmill* (Shaker Heights, Ohio, n.d.), p. 309.

[419] Elizabeth Hicks Hummel, *Hicks History of Granville County, North Carolina*, I (Oxford, N.C., 1965), p. 104, bond 29 Nov.

[420] *Ibid.*, p. 32, bond 3 June.

[421] Spotsylvania Co. Will Bk. E, pp. 1305-18.

[422] Spotsylvania Co. Will Bk. D, p. 526; Order Bk. 1768-74, p. 80.

[423] John Frederick Dorman, *The Farish Family of Virginia and its Forebears* (Richmond, 1967), pp. 20-21.

Stevens; 502. Dolley⁶; 503. Larkin⁶, born 10 April 1758,⁴²⁴ enlisted for three years as a marine, was taken prisoner aboard the ship *Musquito*, 4 June 1777, and sent to Barbados and never returned home;⁴²⁵ 504. Judith⁶, married, 13 April 1795,⁴²⁶ William Smith.

183. BENJAMIN⁵ JOHNSTON (Ann⁴ Chew, Larkin³, Joseph², John¹), born 1734, died before 5 April 1791 when administration on his estate was granted to William and Gabriel Johnston,⁴²⁷ was of Culpeper County by 17 March 1775 when he sold a lot in Fredericksburg,⁴²⁸ and of Washington Co., Pa., by Aug. 1782,⁴²⁹ before moving to Jefferson Co., Ky. He married Dorothy Jones, who left will 27 April 1792-5 June 1792.⁴³⁰

Issue: [JOHNSTON]⁴³¹ 505. William⁶, left will 18 Sept. 1794-6 March 1798,⁴³² of "Cave Hill," surveyor and later clerk of the court of Jefferson Co., Ky., married ___; 506. Gabriel Jones⁶, left will 26 April 1815-8 May 1815,⁴³³ attorney of Jefferson Co., Ky., married, (bond 25) Aug. 1788,⁴³⁴ 339. *Enfield⁶ Fowke* (see THOROWGOOD), born 28 May 1761,⁴³⁵ died 1818; 507. Mary Ann⁶, married John Harrison of Louisville, Ky.; 508. Benjamin⁶, lieutenant of Spotsylvania County militia, 1779, later of Jefferson Co., Ky., and St. Louis, Mo., married (1) Nancy ___⁴³⁶ and (2), (bond 24) Feb. 1790,⁴³⁷ Elizabeth ___, widow of Lawrence Muse; 509. Susannah⁶, married (1) George W. Lewis and (2), (bond 19) Feb. 1794,⁴³⁸ as his (2) wife, Davis Floyd, who moved to Harrison Co., Ind.; 510. General Washington⁶, born 10 Nov. 1776, died 26 Oct. 1833,⁴³⁹

---

⁴²⁴ Coleman *vs.* Rogers, Fredericksburg District Court.
⁴²⁵ Revolutionary War Rejected bounty land claims, Virginia State Archives.
⁴²⁶ Spotsylvania Co. Marriage Register 1795-1853, p. 1.
⁴²⁷ Jefferson Co., Ky., Minute Bk. 3, p. 32.
⁴²⁸ Spotsylvania Co. Deed Bk. J, pp. 129-31.
⁴²⁹ Spotsylvania Co. Deed Bk. K, pp. 62-64.
⁴³⁰ Jefferson Co., Ky., Will Bk. 1, p. 34.
⁴³¹ "A Genealogical Table ..."; Kentucky Court of Appeals Deed Bk. W, pp. 293, 383. 385.
⁴³² Jefferson Co., Ky., Will Bk. 1, p. 76.
⁴³³ Jefferson Co., Ky., Will Bk. 2, p. 25.
⁴³⁴ Jefferson Co., Ky., Marriage bond.
⁴³⁵ St. Paul's Parish, King George Co., Register, as Anphel.
⁴³⁶ Spotsylvania Co. Deed Bk. M, pp. 369-71.
⁴³⁷ Jefferson Co., Ky., Marriage bond.
⁴³⁸ *Ibid.*
⁴³⁹ Gravestone, Greenlawn Cemetery, Vincennes, Ind., in Alta Amsler and others, "Indiana, Knox County, City Cemeteries, VI-A (n.p., 1975), p. 117.

settled in Knox Co., Ind., 1793, admitted as an attorney at the first county court, Feb. 1799, member of the Indiana Territorial Legislature and its speaker two terms, captain of Knox County militia, 1813, and at battle of Tippecanoe, founder of the Masonic Grand Lodge of Indiana, 1817, presiding judge of Daviess Co., Ind., 1830-31,[440] married (1) Rosella Josetta Tromblay and (2) ____ Puryear;[441] 511. Ann [Nancy] Chew[6], died without issue, married John Thompson[7] Gray, son of George Gray and 292. *Mildred[6] Thompson* (see MARTIAU), born 1782, died 31 Jan. 1845, who married (2) Mary Ormsby; 512. Robert[6], died without issue before 26 Sept. 1794.

185. HANNAH[5] JOHNSTON (Ann[4] Chew, Larkin[3], Joseph[2], John[1]) died before 15 Feb. 1783 when her will was proved.[442] She married her step-brother 46. *Francis[6] Coleman* (see WYATT), of Caroline County, for whom Edmund Pendleton was appointed guardian, 11 Nov. 1749, and chose his guardian 14 March 1754,[443] was a member of the House of Burgesses, 1769,[444] and left will 20 July 1771-14 Nov. 1771.[445] He was licensed to keep an ordinary, 8 Feb. 1759,[446] and it was continued by his widow.

Issue: [COLEMAN][447] 513. William J.[6], left will 7 March 1806-23 June 1806,[448] of Fredericksburg, married Nancy Johnston; 514. Samuel[6], deposed 23 March 1790 he was aged 29, married (1), 18 Nov. 1778, Elizabeth Harris, who died 10 July 1784, and (2) Sarah McLean; 515. Francis[6]; 516. Ann[6], born 29 Oct. 1756, died 25 Aug. 1798, married, 24 Nov. 1774, as his (1) wife, David Dickinson, born 29 May 1756,[449] left will 3 April 1812-14 Sept. 1812,[450] of

---

[440] *Ibid.*; *History of Knox and Daviess Counties, Indiana* (Chicago, 1886), pp. 71, 174, 187, 208, 633.

[441] Alfred W. Harris, "Edward Harris, Jr., His Ancestors and Descendants, 1630-1900" (manuscript; Louisville, Ky., 1900).

[442] Caroline Co. Order Bk. 1781-85, p. 212.

[443] Caroline Co. Order Bk. 1746-54, pp. 182, 458.

[444] Leonard, p. 97.

[445] *T* XV, pp. 166-67.

[446] Caroline Co. Order Bk. 1759-63, p. 3.

[447] S. Bernard Coleman, Coleman family genealogical notes, Library of Virginia microfilm 428, pp. 124, 290-95; V LIV, pp. 259-61; suit, Dickinson *vs.* Muse, Caroline Co., in William Lindsay Hopkins, *Caroline County Court Records and Marriages, 1787-1810* (Richmond, 1987), p. 35.

[448] Fredericksburg Will Bk. A, p. 316.

[449] Bible, in *V* LVI, p. 261.

[450] Caroline Co. will, in suit Dickinson *vs.* Dickinson, Fredericksburg District Court.

"Chestnut Valley," Caroline County; 517. Elizabeth[6], married __ Triplett; 518. Frances[6], died Aug. 1795,[451] married, as his (1) wife, Capt. William Taylor of Fredericksburg who died there 29 Sept. 1809,[452] leaving will 15 July 1809-2 Oct. 1809;[453] 519. Lucy[6], married William Dickinson; 520. Jane Roy[6], died after 23 April 1823 when she made a deed to her children,[454] married (1), 19 Sept. 1789,[455] John Garland Duke, died 1811, of Louisa County, and (2) Samuel White, who moved to Green Co., Ky., and died before 9 Sept. 1816.[456]

186. RICHARD[5] JOHNSTON (Ann[4] Chew, Larkin[3], Joseph[2], John[1]) died 1789.[457] He was a lieutenant in Col. William Byrd's regiment on the Cherokee expedition, 1760. He married (1), about 1765, Dorothy Waller, daughter of Col. William and Ann (Stanard) Waller, born 1743, died 1770, and (2) Ann Smith, daughter of Maj. Charles Smith of Louisa County.

Issue: (by 1) [JOHNSTON] 521. Richard W.[6], for whom Joseph Brock gave bond as guardian, 5 Feb. 1788,[458] left will 2 March 1791-6 Sept. 1791,[459] unmarried; 522. William[6], born Oct. 1763, died after 1823, of Caroline County, given a power of attorney by his grandmother Ann Waller, 16 June 1786,[460] moved to Green Co., Ky., married, 2 Feb. 1785,[461] Ann Buckner, daughter of Capt. William and Mary (Madison) Buckner.[462]

187. BETSY[5] JOHNSTON (Ann[4] Chew, Larkin[3], Joseph[2], John[1]) died before 16 April 1772 when Benjamin Johnston was granted administration on her estate.[463] She married John Benger, son of Elliott and Dorothy (Brayne) Benger, of Spotsylvania County, who left will 14 Aug. 1766-3 Nov. 1766.[464]

Issue: [BENGER] 523. Ann Brayne[6], married, 21 Feb. 1780, Dr. George

---

[451] *Virginia Herald*, Fredericksburg, 21 Aug. 1795.

[452] *Ibid.*, 4 Oct. 1809.

[453] Spotsylvania Co. Will Bk. G, p. 465.

[454] Green Co., Ky., Deed Bk. 11, pt. 2, p. 13.

[455] Hopkins, *op. cit.*, p. 220.

[456] Walter Garland Duke, *Henry Duke, Councillor* (Richmond, 1949), pp. 205-06.

[457] *T* XX, p. 168.

[458] Spotsylvania Co. Will Bk. E, pp. 885-86 .

[459] Spotsylvania Co. Will Bk. E, p. 1086.

[460] Spotsylvania Co. Deed Bk. L, p. 12.

[461] Willock Bible (New York, 1824), in *The Kentucky Genealogist*, XI, p. 84.

[462] George H. S. King Papers, Virginia Historical Society. They were ancestors of Elizabeth Virginia (Bess) Wallace, wife of Harry S. Truman, President of the United States.

[463] Spotsylvania Co. Will Bk. D, pp. 508-09.

[464] Spotsylvania Co. Will Bk. D, p. 268.

French, born 1751, died 1 June 1824,[465] of Fredericksburg; 524. Dorothea Brayne[6], born 1 March 1765, died 26 Aug. 1839,[466] married (1), 6 April 1782, Col. William McWilliams, who died 17 April 1801,[467] left will 13 Nov. 1799-6 Oct. 1801,[468] captain and major in the Revolutionary War, mayor of Fredericksburg, and (2), as his (2) wife, 119. *George[6] Buckner* (see CROSHAW).

189. ROBERT[5] CHEW (John[4], Larkin[3], Joseph[2], John[1]), of Spotsylvania County, was a lieutenant in the French and Indian War, 1756, and left will 28 April 1778-17 Sept. 1778.[469] He married 105. *Mary[5] Perrott* (see CURTIS), who was born 18 Aug. 1733[470] and died 17 Sept. 1789, aged 57, in Spotsylvania County.[471]

Issue: 525. John[6], born 5 Aug. 1753 at Fredericksburg, died there 12 Feb. 1806, left will 19 May 1805-codicil 14 Oct. 1805-4 March 1806,[472] lieutenant in 6th Virginia Regiment, wounded 10 Oct. 1780 at Camden, S.C., in the arm which was amputated,[473] clerk of Spotsylvania County, 1782-1802, clerk of the Corporation Court of Fredericksburg, 1787-1806, married 557. Elizabeth Perrott[6] Smith; 526. Robert Beverley[6], died 30 Dec. 1791,[474] left will 28 Dec. 1791-7 Feb. 1792,[475] quartermaster sergeant, 6th Virginia Regiment, 1776, lieutenant, Virginia State Regiment, 1777-80, merchant of Fredericksburg; 527. Harry[6], born 23 Sept. 1758, served four tours as member of the Spotsylvania County militia in the Revolutionary war,[476] died after 1852; 528. Elizabeth Perrott[6], married 565. Larkin[6] Stanard; 529. Joseph[6], born 1769, died 1834, married Mary Winslow, died 22 Feb. 1793; 530. Mary[6].

---

[465] *Enquirer*, Richmond, 11 June 1824.

[466] *Political Arena*, Fredericksburg, 3 Sept. 1839; gravestone, "Braynefield," in Herbert Ridgeway Collins, *Cemeteries of Caroline County, Virginia*, II (Westminster, Md., 1995), p. 26.

[467] *The Courier*, Fredericksburg, 21 April 1801.

[468] Fredericksburg District Court Will Bk. A, p. 160.

[469] Spotsylvania Co. Will Bk. E, p. 281.

[470] Christ Church Parish, Middlesex Co., Register.

[471] *Virginia Herald*, Fredericksburg, 24 Sept. 1789.

[472] Spotsylvania Co. Will Bk. G, pp. 148-50.

[473] *Virginia Revolutionary War State Pensions*, p. 22.

[474] *Virginia Herald*, Fredericksburg, 5 Jan. 1792.

[475] Spotsylvania Co. Will Bk. E, p. 1143.

[476] Spotsylvania Co. Order Bk. 1829-32, pp. 443-45.

189. MARY BEVERLEY⁵ CHEW (John⁴, Larkin³, Joseph², John¹) married, 1749, Col. Joseph Brock, born 6 Nov. 1715, died before 2 March 1807.⁴⁷⁷ He was captain of Spotsylvania County militia, 1758, sheriff, 1766-68, and vestryman and warden of St. George's Parish, Spotsylvania County.

Issue: [BROCK] 531. John⁶, born 1751, murdered 8 Aug. 1792 in Spotsylvania County,⁴⁷⁸ administration on his estate granted to his father 4 Dec. 1792,⁴⁷⁹ married, 1774, Ann⁷ Curtis, daughter of 127. *Rice⁶ Curtis* (see CURTIS), born 1756; 532. Elizabeth⁶, married, (1), as his (2) wife, John Zachary Lewis of Spotsylvania County, who left will 7 March 1784-7 Sept. 1784,⁴⁸⁰ and (2), as his (1) wife, Col. Beverley Stubblefield of Spotsylvania County, who entered service as cadet in 6th Virginia Regiment, 10 Feb. 1776, was taken prisoner at Charleston, exchanged, and became captain 1781, member of the Society of the Cincinnati, moved to Todd Co., Ky., and died 25 Dec. 1828, aged 81;⁴⁸¹ 533. Mary⁶, married John Carter; 534. Catherine⁶, unmarried; 535. Joseph⁶, died 1806 in Spotsylvania County,⁴⁸² captain, United States Army, 1791-1800,⁴⁸³ married 541. Ann Fox⁶ Chew; 536. William⁶, merchant of Fredericksburg, married (1) ___ Barnes and (2), 14 Dec. 1795,⁴⁸⁴ Elizabeth⁷ Towles, daughter of Col. Thomas and 556. Mary Beverley⁶ (Smith) Towles, born 25 May 1774, died 21 Feb. 1835 at "Springfield," Culpeper County, who married (2) Capt. Philip Slaughter; 537. Susannah⁶, died 19 June 1794,⁴⁸⁵ married, Dec. 1787, Benjamin Robinson of Spotsylvania County who left will 11 Aug. 1785-1 Dec. 1795.⁴⁸⁶

191. JOHN⁵ CHEW (John⁴, Larkin³, Joseph², John¹) of Fredericksburg,

---

⁴⁷⁷ Spotsylvania Co. Will Bk. G, p. 227, bond of Joseph Brock as administrator of Joseph Brock (Clk).

⁴⁷⁸ *Virginia Gazette and General Advertiser*, Richmond, 22 Aug. 1792; *The Virginia Genealogist*,XXX, p. 58.

⁴⁷⁹ Spotsylvania Co. Will Bk. E, p. 1199.

⁴⁸⁰ Spotsylvania Co. Will Bk. E, pp. 610-13.

⁴⁸¹ McGill, *op. cit.*, p. 881.

⁴⁸² *Virginia Herald*, Fredericksburg, 4 April 1806, died "lately."

⁴⁸³ Francis B. Heitman, *Historical Register and Dictionary of the United States Army* (Washington, 1903), I, p. 246.

⁴⁸⁴ *Virginia Herald*, Fredericksburg, 18 Dec. 1795.

⁴⁸⁵ William W. Hening and William Munford, *Reports of Cases Argued and Determined in the Supreme Court of Appeals of Virginia* (2nd ed.; Flatbush, N.Y., 1806), I, p. 212.

⁴⁸⁶ Spotsylvania Co. Will Bk. Will Bk. E, p. 1484.

lieutenant and captain of Spotsylvania County militia, 1777-81, died 19 Sept. 1789, aged 49.[487] He married 144. *Ann*[6] *Fox* (see WEST), died 7 Oct. 1821 in her 67th year.[488]

Issue:[489] 538. John[6], born 1772, died 1827,[490] left will 11 Oct. 1837-2 July 1838,[491] of Urbanna and later of Fredericksburg; 539. Beverley[6], born 6 Feb. 1772, died 13 Jan. 1851 at New Orleans, La.,[492] merchant and later banker of New Orleans, sergeant in company of riflemen, Louisiana militia, during War of 1812, collector of the port of New Orleans, 1817-29, married, 14 June 1810 at New Orleans,[493] Maria Theodora Duer, born 9 July 1789,[494] died 21 July 1827 at New Orleans;[495] 540. Philadelphia Claiborne[6], born about 1795, died 1852,[496] married Capt. Bowker Waller, who died 23 July 1839 in Spotsylvania County in his 66th year,[497] leaving will Jan. 1838-7 Oct. 1839;[498] 541. Ann Fox[6], married 535. Joseph[6] Brock; 542. Robert[6], married Louise de Marcillon; 543 Thomas[6], died in Kentucky, unmarried; 544. Lucy[6], died 3 Oct. 1815, unmarried;[499] 545. Elizabeth[6], born 5 Oct. 1779,[500] died 12 Jan. 1838 at "Cold Hill," Spotsylvania County,[501] married, 6 Feb. 1800, as his (1) wife, Robert Cammack, born 17 April 1773,[502] died 18 Aug. 1853 at Warm Springs, Bath County,[503] left will 14

---

[487] *Virginia Herald*, Fredericksburg, 24 Sept. 1789.

[488] Gravestone, St. George's Churchyard, Fredericksburg.

[489] John Frederick Dorman and Claiborne T. Smith, *Claiborne of Virginia* (Baltimore, 1995), pp. 146, 152-58.

[490] Gravestone, Masonic Cemetery, Fredericksburg.

[491] Spotsylvania Co. Will Bk. P, pp. 469-70.

[492] Glenn R. Conrad, ed., *A Dictionary of Louisiana Biography*, I (New Orleans, 1988), p. 175,

[493] *Virginia Herald*, Fredericksburg, 1 Aug. 1810.

[494] Mrs. John King Van Rensselaer, *New York Families of the 19th Century* (New York, 1897), charts 16, 17.

[495] *The Bee*, New Orleans, 22 July 1837.

[496] Spotsylvania Co. Will Bk. U, pp. 32-33.

[497] *Political Arena*, Fredericksburg, 3 Aug. 1839.

[498] Spotsylvania Co. Will Bk. Q. pp. 1-2.

[499] Gravestone, St. George's Churchyard, Fredericksburg.

[500] Mansfield Papers, Virginia Historical Society, Mss.1 M3176a 795-825, Cammack.

[501] *Political Arena*, Fredericksburg, 16 Jan. 1838; gravestone, "Cold Hill," Spotsylvania Co.

[502] Mansfield Papers, *loc. cit.*

[503] *Weekly Advertiser*, Fredericksburg, 27 Aug. 1853.

April 1853-7 Nov. 1853,[504] of "Cold Hill," private in 16th Regiment, Virginia militia, 1814; 546. Claiborne[6], died 29 Jan. 1817 at Richmond,[505] merchant of Richmond.; 547. Caroline Matilda[6], died 12 April 1863,[506] married, 23 Aug. 1815,[507] John[7] Stanard, son of 565. Larkin[6] and 528. Elizabeth Perrott[6] (Chew) Stanard, died 23 Sept. 1833 at Washington, D.C., aged 47,[508] served as ensign to lieutenant colonel, United States Army, 1806-15, later marshal of the chancery court of Fredericksburg; 548. Mary[6], born about 1785, left will 15 April 1868-2 Aug. 1869.[509]

192. HANNAH[5] CHEW (John[4], Larkin[3], Joseph[2], John[1]) died 1821.[510] She married, as his (2) wife, John Carter, who left will 9 May 1778-codicil 13 Oct. 1783-18 Dec. 1783,[511] captain of Spotsylvania County militia in French and Indian War, 1758, and Revolutionary War, 1777-83, vestryman of St. George's Parish, sheriff, 1768, and justice, 1772.

Issue: [CARTER][512] 549. Mary Beverley[6], married Capt. Richard Stevens of Caroline or Spotsylvania County; 550. Margaret Chew[6], born 14 Jan. 1771, died 19 May 1822 at "Mt. Jolly," near Pendleton, S.C., married, 31 July 1802, Zachariah Taliaferro, born 28 April 1759 in Caroline County, died 14 April 1831 at "Mt. Jolly," Revolutionary soldier and lawyer near Pendleton, S.C.; 551. Judith[6], born 1773, died 1827, married Joseph Sutton, planter of Caroline County; 552. Lucy[6], born 1775, died 1831, married, as his (2) wife, Burton Taliaferro; 553. Robert[6], born 22 Feb. 1775, died 20 Feb. 1798;[513] 554. Elizabeth Matilda[6], born 1780, died 1799.

193. MARY[5] CHEW (Larkin[4], Larkin[3], Joseph[2], John[1]) was killed Nov.

---

[504] Spotsylvania Co. Will Bk. U, pp. 210-11.

[505] *Enquirer*, Richmond, 4 Feb. 1817.

[506] Gravestone, Masonic Cemetery, Fredericksburg.

[507] *Virginia Herald*, Fredericksburg, 25 Aug. 1815.

[508] Gravestone, Masonic Cemetery, Fredericksburg; *Virginia Herald*, Fredericksburg, 25 Sept. 1833.

[509] Spotsylvania Co. Will Bk. AA, pp. 453-54, probated in Orange Co., N.Y.

[510] W(1) XIX, p. 130.

[511] Spotsylvania Co. Will Bk. E, pp. 560-63. Hannah Carter was granted administration on the estate 7 Aug. 1810.

[512] W(1) XVIII, p. 102; XIV, pp. 133-37.

[513] Suit, Hannah Carter *vs.* Joseph Sutton, administrator of Robert Carter, in Hopkins, *op. cit.*, p. 23.

1803 by the oversetting of a carriage.[514]   She married (1) John Smith of "Rickahock," King and Queen County, who died before 6 April 1761 when Mary was granted administration on his estate,[515] and (2) Oliver Towles, born 1 Sept. 1736 in Middlesex County,[516] died 18 Nov. 1821, aged 80,[517] captain, major and lieutenant colonel in Revolutionary War, secretary of the Society of the Cincinnati in the State of Virginia, lawyer of Campbell County.

Issue: (by 1) [SMITH][518] 555. Larkin[6], died 28 Sept. 1813 at Fredericksburg,[519] left will 15 May 1813-22 Nov. 1813,[520] captain of cavalry in Revolutionary War, member of the House of Delegates, 1784-85, 1788-89, 1792-93, 1797-98, 1799-1802, and its Speaker 1799-1802,[521] justice of King and Queen County, 1784, and colonel of militia, 1796, collector of the port of Norfolk, married (1) Mary Eleanor Hill, who died 16 Jan. 1797,[522] and (2), 24 May 1804 at Norfolk,[523] Sophia Anne[7] (Tazewell) Taliaferro, daughter of 113. *Henry[6] Tazewell* (see GRAY) and widow of 473. *Benjamin[6] Taliaferro* (see BALEY-COCKE); 556. Mary Beverley[6], born 8 Sept. 1755, died 6 May 1813 at "Springfield," Culpeper County, married, 1773, Col. Thomas Towles, born 21 Feb. 1750, left will 29 April 1800-2 Sept. 1800,[524] of "Millbrook," Spotsylvania County, quartermaster of the Caroline County militia, 1776, later colonel of militia, member of the House of Delegates, 1782-85;[525] 557. Elizabeth Perrott[6], married 525. John[6] Chew; 558. Morris John[6]; (by 2) [TOWLES] 559. Ann[6], deeded 367 acres in Spotsylvania County by her father, 6 Feb. 1798;[526] 560. Molly[6], married, 27 Jan. 1785,[527] Archibald Dick, Jr., born 1764, died

---

[514] *Virginia Herald*, Fredericksburg, 29 Nov. 1803, "a few days since."

[515] Spotsylvania Co. Minute Bk. 1755-65, no pagination; Will Bk. B, pp. 520-21.

[516] Christ Church Parish, Middlesex Co., Register.

[517] *The Lynchburg Press*, 23 Nov. 1821.

[518] Spotsylvania Co. Minute Bk. 1755-65, no pagination; Will Bk. B, pp. 521-22, bond of Mary Smith as guardian, 6 April 1761.

[519] *Norfolk Gazette & Public Ledger*, 2 Oct. 1813; *Enquirer*, 8 Oct. 1813.

[520] Norfolk Borough Will Bk. 2, p. 98.

[521] Leonard, pp. 157, 169, 176, 188, 192, 208, 215-16, 219-20, 223-24, 228, xv.

[522] *Virginia Herald.*, Fredericksburg, 21 Feb. 1797.

[523] *Fredericksburg Gazette*, 5 June 1804.

[524] Spotsylvania Co. Will Bk. F, p. 133.

[525] Leonard, pp. 147, 151, 155.

[526] Spotsylvania Co. Deed Bk. P, p. 55.

[527] Information provided W. Festus Morgan, Jr., Cooperstown, N.Y., by Dr. Malcolm Hart Harris, West Point, source undetermined.

1849; 561. Oliver[6], born 1777, left will 28 Nov. 1819-codicil 20 Oct. 1820-14 Nov. 1823,[528] of Lynchburg, major and colonel in War of 1812, married, 1794, Agatha Lewis, born 1774, died 1843 at Cincinnati, Ohio; 562. Harry Beverley[6], lieutenant, United States Army, killed in battle of Maumee, 24 Aug. 1794; 563. Frances[6], married Robert Stevenson of Lewisburg, W.Va.

194. ELIZABETH BEVERLEY[5] CHEW (Larkin[4], Larkin[3], Joseph[2], John[1]) married (1), (license 19) April 1750,[529] Beverley Stanard, born 24 Feb. 1722, died 21 Feb. 1765[530] at "Roxbury," Spotsylvania County, left will 20 Feb. 1765- 1 July 1765.[531] He was a justice of Middlesex County, 1743, and later resided at "Roxbury," Spotsylvania County. She married (2) 36. Col. *Mordecai[6] Buckner* (see MATHEWS), who died between 7 June 1787 and 1 Jan, 1788.[532] He was quartermaster and captain in the French and Indian War and colonel of the 6th Virginia Regiment in Revolutionary War, but was cashiered 9 Feb. 1778 for shamefully misbehaving before the enemy.[533]

Issue: (by 1) [STANARD] 564. William[6], died Oct. 1807,[534] of "Roxbury" and "Stanardsville," Spotsylvania County, justice of Spotsylvania County, 1787, sheriff, 1802-04, married Elizabeth H. Carter, daughter of Edward Carter of Albemarle County, who died Feb. 1818 in Fredericksburg,[535] leaving will 7 Nov. 1817-2 March 1818;[536] 565. Larkin[6], born May 1760, died 1840, of "Stanfield," Spotsylvania County, served in Revolutionary War,[537] member of the House of Delegates, 1798-1804,[538] married 528. Elizabeth Perrott[6] Chew; 566. Beverley[6], born after Feb. 1765, whose guardian William Stanard gave bond 21 Dec. 1780,[539] probably the Beverley of Albemarle County who died 11 Nov. 1805 at

---

[528] Campbell Co. Will Bk. 4, p. 518.

[529] Spotsylvania Co. Will Bk. A, p. 512.

[530] Gravestone, "Roxbury," Spotsylvania Co.

[531] Spotsylvania Co. Will Bk. D, p. 207.

[532] Spotsylvania Co. Will Bk. E, pp. 881-82.

[533] John H. Gwathmey, *Historical Register of Virginians in the Revolution* (Richmond, 1937), p. 107; *Virginia Gazette* (Purdie), 7 March 1777.

[534] *Virginia Herald*, Fredericksburg, 20 Oct. 1807.

[535] *Ibid.*, 28 Feb. 1818.

[536] Spotsylvania Co. Will Bk. I-J, pp. 257-58.

[537] Spotsylvania Co. Order Bk. 1832-38, pp. 110-13; Revolutionary War pension application, Larkin Stanard, S.7607.

[538] Leonard, pp. 213, 217, 221, 225, 229, 233.

[539] Spotsylvania Co. Will Bk. E, p. 380-81.

the seat of William Stanard of Spotsylvania County;[540] 567. Elizabeth[6]; 568. Mary[6], married 214. Capt. *John[6] Montague* (see MONTAGUE); 569. Sarah[6]; (by 2) [BUCKNER][541] 570. John Chew[6], born 1770, died 1820;[542] 571. Baldwin Mathews[6], born 20 April 1772 at "Roxbury," died 27 Dec. 1827 at "Chestnut Hill," Orange County, married Fanny Burton, born 6 April 1780 at "Burtonsville," Orange County, died 5 Dec. 1872 at "Chestnut Hill."

---

[540] *Enquirer*, Richmond, 19 Nov. 1805.

[541] Spotsylvania Co. Will Bk. E, p. 882; William Armstrong Crozier, *The Buckners of Virginia* (New York, 1907), p.160.

[542] Margie G. Brown, *Genealogical Abstracts, Revolutionary War Veterans, Scrip Act 1852* (Oakton, Va., 1990), p. 347, gives death as 1830.

CHISMAN[1]

*1. THOMAS[1], *2. JOHN[1] and *3. EDWARD[1] CHEESMAN were listed 16 Feb. 1623/4 as living at Elizabeth City.[2] In the muster, 7 Feb. 1624/5, at the same place, Lieut. John[1] Chisman, aged 27, who came in the *Flying Hart*, 1621, and Edward[1] Chisman, aged 22, who came in the *Providence*, 1623, are enumerated.

1. THOMAS[1] CHEESMAN was in Virginia in Feb. 1623/4 but not in Feb. 1624/5. On 1 Oct. 1624 John Kent of Newport in the Isle of Wight and County of Southampton arranged for Elizabeth Baker, daughter of his sister-in-law Elizabeth Baker, to go to Virginia in the *Anne of London* in the charge of William Blackwell and Thomas Cheeseman of Newport Newes in Virginia, Gent., there to be married.[3] Thomas[1] is not mentioned again in Virginia. He married ___ and had

Issue: 4. Thomas[2], deceased by Dec. 1663 when John[1] Cheesman left tenements in Braban, Kent, to his heirs.

2. JOHN[1] CHEESMAN, Gent., of Kiccoughtan on 2 Sept. 1624 received a patent for 200 acres of land over against Kiccoughtan adjoining John Sipsey, due for the transportation of four servants, Thomas Fuller, Inocent Power, Peter Dickeson and Cuthbert Brookes, all of whom came in the *Southampton* in 1622.[4] When the area now York County became available for settlement in 1630, the Cheesmans located there. Lieut. John[1] Cheesman was a justice of Charles River (York) County by 8 April 1634.[5] His first patent in this region, 21 Nov. 1635, was for 600 acres on the New Poquoson River, due for the transportation of twelve persons.[6] He acquired much more land there, including, 8 March 1636/7, 300 acres due by deed of sale from Edward Chesman. On 19 Nov. 1638 Capt. John Cheesman of the New Poquoson in Virginia sold land "unto my brother

---

[1] *W*(1) I, pp. 89-93; Jean von Schilling, Computer files regarding the Chisman family, based in part on Thelma Ironmonger Hansford, "The Curtis Family of York County, Virginia," (ms, 1989). Also in early records CHEESMAN and CHEESEMAN.

[2] Hotten, p. 185.

[3] Virginia Colonial Records Project Survey Report 7076 (IW. 1), Town Clerk's Office, Newport, Isle of Wight.

[4] Patent Bk. 1, p. 47.

[5] York Co. Deeds, Orders, Wills &c 1, p. 9.

[6] Patent Bk. 1, p. 319.

Edmond Cheesman."[7] In an Act of Assembly, 6 Jan. 1639/40, he was named a tobacco viewer for the north side of New Poquoson River.[8]

John[1] Cheesman, successively lieutenant, captain and lieutenant colonel of militia, was a justice of Charles River (and its successor York) County from 1634 into the 1650s.[9] He was a member of the Assembly for York in 1643 and was a Councillor in 1652.[10] By 22 Aug. 1661 he had returned to England where, as of the parish of St. Mary Magdalene in Bermondsey in the County of Surrey, merchant, he made a power of attorney to Lawrence Smith. Under this, 1 April 1662, Smith leased for 21 years to Edmund[1] Cheesman, brother of John, all the latter's property in York County with the proviso that, if John[1] and Margaret his wife did not survive the lease, then as provided by the will of John[1], dated 6 Aug. 1658, the property should go to Edmund[1] and at his death to Edmund's sons, Edmund[2] and Thomas[2], and their heirs forever.[11]

John[1] Cheesman left will, Dec. 1663-2 May 1675,[12] which devised freeholds and copyholds in Hellen Norwood, Norcourt or Norcoke, Southall, Ealing alias Zeling, Old Brentford and New Brentford, Middlesex, to his wife Margaret to maintain his grandchild Anne Cheesman until her marriage or until 24 June 1670, and if they both died to his brother Edmund and then to his sons Edmund and Thomas, his tenements in Braban, Kent, to the heirs of his deceased nephew Thomas Cheesman, son of his eldest brother Thomas, and his estate in Gloucester Co., Va., to his grandchild Anne Cheesman. On 20 Sept. 1678 his widow Margaret gave a power of attorney to her "cozen Thomas Cheeseman of York River in Virginia."[13] She had been given a silk carpet in 1645/6 by the will of Humphrey Hanmore.[14] Judging by her will, 15 Jan. 1679/80-21 July 1680,[15]made as a resident of St. Mary Magdalen, Bermondsey, she was a close

---

[7] *Ibid.*, pp. 472, 718. The names Edward and Edmund were used interchangeably.

[8] *W*(2) IV, p. 27.

[9] York Co. Deeds, Orders, Wills &c 1, p. 152.

[10] Leonard, pp. xix, 21.

[11] York Co. Deeds, Orders, Wills &c 3, pp. 162-64.

[12] Public Record Office, London, B11/316/46. George Sherwood, *American Colonists in English Records* (London, 1932), p. 51, cited P.C.C. 46 Hyde and gives probate date as 2 May 1665.

[13] York Co. Deeds, Orders, Wills &c 3, p. 61.

[14] York Co. Deeds, Orders, Wills &c 2, p. 79.

[15] P.C.C. 92 Bath, in Waters, *Gleanings*, I, p. 691.

relation of the Francis[1] Mason family in Virginia.[16]

Issue: 5. (SON)[2].

3. EDMUND[1] (EDWARD) CHEESMAN owned 300 acres on the New Poquoson in Charles River County before 1637 when he deeded the land to his brother John[1], who in turn exchanged land with him the following year.[17] He also patented by 1650 land at Milford Haven in that part of Gloucester County which in 1791 became Mathews County.[18] He was a justice of York County 8 May 1652.[19] On 20 Sept. 1668 he patented 300 acres on the north side of Cheesman's Creek and Bay Tree Neck which had been patented 1654 by John[1] Cheesman and John Adleston but deserted.[20]

Edmund[1] Cheesman married before 20 Oct. 1646, probably as his (2) wife, Mary ___, widow of John Lilley who died after 1642. Edmund[1] is described as "father in law to John Lilley orphant of John Lilley."[21] Mary Cheesman was an ardent Quaker. On 10 Sept. 1659 the York Court ordered the sheriff and his deputies to prevent all private and other meetings of the "dangerous persons now in the County called Quakers." The order proved futile and, 1660, when the General Assembly issued a decree against the Quakers, the York Court ordered that the "sd. Chisman and his wife to have notice of the Governor's order and if shee [Mary Cheesman] shall hereafter offend in the like kind that the sd. order be put in effectual execution against hir and also that Mr. Chisman restreyn his said negroes & whole family from repairing to the said unlawfull assembly as at his perill."[22]

The will of Edmund Chisman Senior, liver of the New Poquoson parish inYork County, Virginia, 26 March 1673-23 Feb. 1673/4,[23] mentions land at Milford Haven.

Issue: 6. EDMUND[2]; 7. THOMAS[2]; 8. MARY[2]; 9. JANE[2].

5. (SON)[2] CHEESMAN (John[1]) apparently married ____, widow of 2.

---

[16] She may be the Margery Ganey named in Francis Mason's 1642 patent (Patent Bk. 1, p. 816) and a sister of Mason's wife Alice, whose granddaughter, Alice (Mason) Hodge Porten referred to her as aunt (Norfolk Co. Record Bk. 5, p. 197a).

[17] Patent Bk. 1, pp. 472, 718.

[18] Patent Bk. 2, p. 262.

[19] York Co. Deeds, Orders, Wills &c 1, p. 130.

[20] Patent Bk. 6, p. 273.

[21] York Co. Deeds, Orders, Wills &c 2, p. 180.

[22] York Co. Deeds, Orders, Wills &c 3, pp. 127, 125.

[23] York Co. Deeds, Orders, Wills &c 2, p. 180.

Samuel[2] *Mathews* (see MATHEWS), since the will of Margaret Cheesman mentioned John Matthews in Virginia, brother by the mother's side to her late granddaughter, Anne Cheeseman, deceased.

Issue: 10. ANNE[3], died unmarried.

6. EDMUND[2] CHEESMAN (Edmund[1]) qualified as justice of York County 25 July 1670.[24] He allied himself with Nathaniel Bacon and with the rank of major became one of the leaders of the Rebellion, 1676. After Bacon's death, he, with others, was taken captive in York by Robert Beverley and, held in prison, died "of feare, of griefe, or bad useage" before he could be brought to trial.[25] Nevertheless, he was named in an Act of Assembly, Feb. 1676/7, along with Bacon and William Hunt as having "escaped their due and just demerritts for their wicked and unheard of treasons and rebellions" and "adjudged, convicted and attainted of high treason to all intents and purposes."[26]

Edmond[2] married Lydia ___, perhaps Farlow, daughter of Mrs. Elizabeth Bushrod by her (1) husband and niece of Capt. George Farlow, also one of Bacon's supporters,[27] who deposed, April 1678, that she was aged about 29 years.[28] She was granted administration on the estate of Edmund[2] Chisman, April 1678,[29] married (2), 11 June 1678, Thomas Harwood and was "killed by thunder" 16 March 1694/5.[30]

Issue: 11. John[3], born 2 June 1669, died 13 June 1679.[31]

7. THOMAS[2] CHEESMAN (Edmund[1]) deposed 24 Jan. 1689/90 that he was aged 38 or thereabouts.[32] He was a justice of York, 24 Aug. 1680, captain of militia, vestryman of Charles Parish, and a member of the General Assembly of 1685-86 from York.[33] On 29 Sept. 1680 he patented 530 acres in Milford Haven, Gloucester County, 430 acres of which had been purchased by his

---

[24] York Co. Deeds, Orders, Wills &c 6, p. 296.

[25] *A Narrative of the Indian and Civil Wars in Virginia, In the Years 1675 and 1676* (Boston, 1814), p. 34.

[26] *H* II, p. 375.

[27] York Co. Deeds, Orders, Wills &c 5, p. 363; *A Narrative of the Indian and Civil Wars ..., loc. cit.*

[28] York Co. Deeds, Orders, Wills &c 6, p. 41.

[29] *Ibid.*, p. 35.

[30] Charles Parish Register; York Co. Orders, Wills &c 14, p. 125.

[31] Charles Parish Register.

[32] York Co. Deeds, Orders, Wills &c 8, p. 385.

[33] Leonard, p. 48.

father.[34] He held 1800 acres in York and 650 acres in Ware Parish, Gloucester, in 1704. He married 12. *Elizabeth³ Reade* (see MARTIAU), on whose estate Thomas³ Chisman was granted administration 16 Dec. 1717.[35] He left a will 25 Jan. 1710/1-18 July 1715.[36]

Issue:[37] 12. THOMAS³; 13. MILDRED³; 14. Elizabeth³, born 8 Nov. 1681, married ___ Lucas; 15. JOHN³; 16. Mary³, married ___ Athey, probably the Edward Athy, born 28 March 1675, son of Edward Athy, cooper, who was admitted to Christ's Hospital, London, from St. George Botolph Lane, April 1682, and on 28 Dec. 1689 sent to Col. Philip Ludwell of Virginia by consent of his brother John Athy, cooper,[38] and the Edward Athey of James City County who, 21 May 1710, sold to John Doswell, Jr., 23 acres in Charles Parish adjoining Capt. Chisman and, 21 Sept. 1713 with wife Mary sold an additional 73 acres to Doswell;[39] 17. Jane³, born 21 March 1686/7; 18. George³, born 5 Jan. 1688/9, died 6 Oct. 1710; 19. Sarah³, born 2 May 1690; 20. Anne, born 20 Dec. 1692.

8. MARY² CHEESMAN (Edmund¹) married, before March 1673, Robert Curtis and died 26 Jan. 1687/8.[40] On 21 Oct. 1687 Robert Curtis in right of his "now wyfe Mary" repatented 242 acres in New Poquoson Parish on the south side of Cheesman's Creek and the head of Ling's Creek which was part of the land conveyed by Col. John¹ Cheesman to his brother Edmund¹, who bequeathed to Mary.[41] Robert Curtis held 250 acres in York County, 1704, and was a vestryman of Charles Parish, 1708. His will, 11 Aug. 1713-21 May 1716,[42] named

Issue [CURTIS]: 21. EDMUND³; 22. THOMAS³; 23. Sarah³; 24. JANE³; 25. KATHERINE³; 26. Elizabeth³, married ___ Evans; 27. Robert³, buried 15 Jan. 1687/8.[43]

---

[34] Patent Bk. 7, p. 62.

[35] York Co. Orders & Wills 15, p. 171.

[36] York Co. Orders, Wills &c 14, 1709-16, pp. 434-36.

[37] Charles Parish Register.

[38] Peter Wilson Coldham, *Child Apprentices in America from Christ's Hospital London, 1617-1778* (Baltimore, 1990), pp. 18-19.

[39] York Co. Deeds & Bonds 3, 1713-29, pp. 5-6, 17-28.

[40] Charles Parish Register.

[41] Patent Bk. 7, p. 602.

[42] York Co. Orders, Wills &c 14, p. 515.

[43] Charles Parish Register.

9. JANE[2] CHEESMAN (Edmund[1]) married, as his (1) wife, 9. *Francis[3] Reade* (see MARTIAU).

Issue:[[READE][44] 28. Mary[3], married Edward Davis who held 100 acres in King and Queen County, 1704; 29. ELIZABETH[3].

12. THOMAS[3] CHISMAN (Thomas[2], Edmund[1]) was captain of militia, 1703, and held 600 acres in York County, 1704. He married Anne __ and died 11 Dec. 1722,[45] leaving will, 6 Nov. 1722-21 Jan. 1722/3,[46] which named

Issue: 30. EDMUND[4]; 31. JOHN[4]; 32. Anne[4]; 33. Mildred[4]; 34. GEORGE[4]; 35. Thomas[4], died 7 April 1727;[47] 36. Elizabeth[4].

13. MILDRED[3] CHISMAN (Thomas[2], Edmund[1]), born 19 Feb. 1675/6,[48] married, as his (1) wife, Col. Lawrence Smith, who married (2) 25. *Mildred[4] Reade* (see MARTIAU). He was captain of militia, 1703, justice and sheriff of York County, member of the House of Burgesses for York, 1718-34, and for Gloucester, 1736-38,[49] owned "Temple Farm," York County, and died 27 Feb. 1738/9[50] leaving will 11 March 1736/7-19 March 1738/9.[51]

Issue [SMITH]: 37. EDMUND[4].

15. JOHN[3] CHISMAN (Thomas[2], Edmund[1]), born 4 March 1682/3,[52] attained the rank of colonel in the militia, and died 19 Sept. 1728,[53] leaving will 18 Sept. 1728-17 Feb. 1728/9.[54] He married 22 Dec. 1708 Ellinor Hayward [Howard], born 25 July 1690, died 8 Feb. 1767,[55] daughter of Henry and Diana Hayward [Howard], who left will 20 Aug. 1753-16 Feb. 1767.[56]

---

[44] York Co. Deeds & Bonds 2, 1701-13, pp. 285-86, deed of 24 June 1708 for 170 acres known as Yorke Ridge from Edward Davis and Mary his wife and Paul Watlington and Elizabeth his wife, as coheiresses of their deceased mother Jane (Cheesman) Reade.

[45] *Ibid.*

[46] York Co. Deeds, Orders, Wills 16, p. 175.

[47] Charles Parish Register.

[48] *Ibid.*

[49] Leonard, pp. 69, 71, 73, 75-76.

[50] *Virginia Gazette*, 2 March 1738/9.

[51] York Co. Wills &c 18, pp. 487-88.

[52] Charles Parish Register; Chisman Bible, *W* (1) XIII, p. 70.

[53] *Ibid.*

[54] York Co. Deeds, Orders & Wills 16, p. 577.

[55] Chisman Bible, *loc. cit.*

[56] York Co. Wills & Inventories 21, p. 301.

Issue:[57] 38. Elizabeth[4], born 15 Dec. 1709, died 16 March 1717/8; 39. JOHN[4]; 40. DIANA[4]; 41. ELLINOR[4]; 42. HENRY[4]; 43. Mary[4], born 4 Nov. 1723, died 12 March 1781, married, 2 Oct. 1744, Harwood Jones, who was recommended as inspector of tobacco at Denbigh's, 2 Aug. 1750, took oaths as justice of Warwick County, 1 May 1755, as sheriff, 6 Aug. 1761, and as captain of militia, 2 July 1761,[58] and died 9 Feb. 1771.

21. EDMUND[3] CURTIS (Mary[2] Chisman, Edmund[1]) owned 200 acres in York County, 1704. He married Mary Wade, born 16 May 1683, daughter of Armiger and Elizabeth Wade.[59] He died 27 Oct. 1728,[60] leaving will 15 Oct. 1728-17 Feb. 1728/9.[61]

Issue [CURTIS]:[62] 44. Frances[4], born 26 Dec. 1706, left will 26 Oct. 1782-20 Aug. 1764,[63] married Edward Cross, who left will 4 May 1759-19 May 1760;[64] 45. Robert[4], born Dec. 1708, died 19 Jan. 1727/8; 46. Mary[4], born 14 March 1710/1, died 21 March 1710/1; 47. ELIZABETH[4]; 48. MARY[4]; 49. EDMUND[4].

22. THOMAS[3] CURTIS (Mary[2] Chisman, Edmund[1]) died 15 Dec. 1722,[65] leaving will 7 Dec. 1722-16 Sept. 1723.[66] He married Susannah (Dixon?), who married (2) Dunn Sheild and died 15 Nov. 1727.[67]

Issue [CURTIS]:[68] 50. ELIZABETH[4]; 51. Thomas[4], born 19 Jan. 1712/3, died 16 Jan. 1730/1; 52. SUSANNA[4]; 53. Mary[4], born 24 Dec. 1719; 54. Damazinah[4], born 26 Jan. 1721/2, died 6 Nov. 1722.

23. JANE[3] CURTIS (Mary[2] Chisman, Edmund[1]) married, as his (2) wife, John Trevilian, mentioned as in possession of Jackson's land near land of Capt.

---

[57] Chisman Bible, *loc. cit.*; Charles Parish Register.

[58] Warwick Co. Order Bk. 1748-62, pp. 66, 315, 652, 654.

[59] Charles Parish Register; York Co. Deeds, Orders, Wills &c 13, pp. 172-74, will of Armiger Wade, 12 Aug. 1708-24 Nov. 1708.

[60] Charles Parish Register.

[61] York Co. Deeds, Orders, Wills 16, p. 576.

[62] Charles Parish Register; York Co. Deeds, Orders, Wills &c 18, p. 19.

[63] York Co. Wills & Inventories 21, 1760-71, pp. 203-04.

[64] *Ibid.*, pp. 2-3.

[65] Charles Parish Register.

[66] York Co. Deeds, Orders, Wills 16, p. 230.

[67] Charles Parish Register; *W*(1) III, p. 269.

[68] Charles Parish Register.

Thomas Chisman in Charles Parish, York County, 1699,[69] and on the Warwick County quit rent roll, 1704, as holding 248 acres, "Patents out of the County."

Issue [TREVILIAN]:[70] 55. John[4], born 8 Aug. 1694; 56. Samuel[4], born 18 May 1696, died 25 May 1696; 57. Elizabeth[4], born 16 Dec. 1697.

24. KATHERINE[3] CURTIS (Mary[2] Chisman, Edmund[1]) married Edward Corley,[71] of York County, who patented 150 acres on the north side of Cheesman's Creek, 22 Sept. 1682,[72] which he continued to own, 1704. He left will 23 Dec. 1728-15 Dec. 1731.[73]

Issue [CORLEY]: 58. Christopher[4], left will 23 April 1772-10 May 1772,[74] naming as residuary legatees Edmund, Henry and Christopher Curtis, sons of Edmund Curtis, married Ann ___ who left will 16 Sept. 1780-17 June 1782;[75] 59. John[4]; 60. EDWARD[4]; 61. ELIZABETH[4]; 62. Sarah[4].

29. ELIZABETH[3] READE (Jane[2] Cheesman, Edmund[1]) married Paul Watlington, baptized 1678,[76] of Gloucester County.

Issue: [WATLINGTON][77] 63. PAUL[4]; 64. Francis[4], baptized March 1710/1; 65. JOHN[4]; 66. William[4], baptized 10 June 1716; 67. Isabella[4], baptized 29 Jan. 1720/1.

30. EDMUND[4] CHISMAN (Thomas[3], Thomas[2], Edmund[1]) left will 29 May 1735-18 Aug. 1735.[78] He married 11. *Elizabeth[3] Chapman* (see BENNETT-CHAPMAN), born 28 Dec. 1709,[79] left will 2 Aug. 1780-17 June 1782,[80] who married (2) James Goodwin.

Issue: [CHISMAN][81] 68. MARY[5]; 69. THOMAS[5]; 70. ANN[5]; 71. JOHN[5].

31. JOHN[4] CHISMAN (Thomas[3], Thomas[2], Edmund[1]), whose estate was

---

[69] Patent Bk. 9, p. 204.
[70] Charles Parish Register.
[71] Also as Calley, Corlee, Corlew, Colly.
[72] Patent Bk. 7, p. 184.
[73] York Co. Will Bk. 17, pp. 241-42.
[74] York Co. Will Bk. 22, p. 71.
[75] *Ibid.*, p. 519.
[76] Abingdon Parish Register.
[77] *Ibid.*
[78] York Co. Records, Wills & Inventories 18, p. 221.
[79] Charles Parish Register.
[80] York Co. Wills & Inventories 22, p. 511.
[81] *W*(1) I, pp. 97-98.

ordered appraised 18 Aug. 1755,[82] married Mary, daughter of Dr. Robert Phillipson.[83]

Issue:[84] 72. CATHERINE[5]; 73. ANNA[5]; 74. Elizabeth[5], born 26 July 1737, died 27 July 1737.

34. GEORGE[4] CHISMAN (Thomas[3], Thomas[2], Edmund[1]) left will 26 Oct. 1741-15 March 1741/2.[85] He married Mary ___.

Issue: 75. MILDRED[5].

37. EDMUND[4] SMITH (Mildred[3] Chisman, Thomas[2], Edmund[1]), surveyor and sheriff of York County, left will 13 Dec. 1750-18 March 1750/1.[86] He married Agnes Sclater, daughter of Richard and Mary (Nutting) Sclater, born 26 May 1707.[87]

Issue: [SMITH] 76. Mildred[5], died 10 Dec. 1778, aged 46,[88] married David Jameson of Yorktown, who died 10 July 1793[89] leaving will 14 Oct. 1792-codicil 21 May 1792-22 July 1793;[90] 77. LAWRENCE[5]; 78. THOMAS[5]; 79. Mary[5].

39. JOHN[4] CHISMAN (John[3], Thomas[2], Edmund[1]), born 25 June 1713, died 4 Sept. 1735, left will 4 Sept. 1735-17 Nov. 1735.[91] He married Frances ___.

Issue:[92] 80. JOHN[5].

40. DIANA[4] CHISMAN (John[3], Thomas[2], Edmund[1]), born 12 Oct. 1715, died 30 Nov. 1735, married James Goodwin, planter of York County who married (2) 11. *Elizabeth[4]* (*Chapman*) *Chisman* (see BENNETT-CHAPMAN) and died 8 Nov. 1757,[93] leaving will 9 Oct. 1757-19 Dec. 1757.[94]

Issue: [GOODWIN][95] 81. JOHN[5].

---

[82] York Co. Wills & Inventories 20, p. 384.

[83] *Ibid.*, p. 23, will of Dr. Robert Philipson.

[84] *W*(1) XIV, pp. 115-16; York Co. Deeds & Bonds 5, p. 143, deed of Robert Phillipson to his granddaughters Katharine and Ann Chisman, daughters of John Chisman, 26 July 1745.

[85] York Co. Wills & Inventories 19, p. 94.

[86] York Co. Wills & Inventories 20, p. 212.

[87] Charles Parish Register.

[88] Gravestone, "Temple Farm," York Co., in *W*(1) II, p. 12.

[89] *Virginia Gazette and Richmond and Manchester Advertiser*, 25 July 1793.

[90] Yorktown Hustings Court Records &c 1787-93, no pagination.

[91] York Co. Wills & Inventories 18, p. 241.

[92] *W*(1) I, p. 98.

[93] *W*(1) VI, Supplement, p. 15.

[94] York Co. Wills & Inventories 20, 1754-59, p. 454.

[95] *W*(1) VI, Supplement, pp. 14-16, 21, 23-24.

41. ELLINOR⁴ CHISMAN (John³, Thomas², Edmund¹), born 18 Nov. 1717, died 22 May 1765. She married John Sheild, born 24 Nov. 1719,⁹⁶ who left will 26 Dec. 1769-15 Jan. 1770.⁹⁷

Issue: [SHEILD]⁹⁸ 82. SARAH⁵; 83. MARY⁵; 84. ROBERT⁵; 85. ELEANOR⁵; 86. John⁵, born 29 Nov. 1757, died 16 Jan. 1783, left will 9 Sept. 1780-20 Jan. 1783, "being greviously wounded in an engagement to the Northward by which means am renduced to weak state of Health or Body ..."⁹⁹

42. HENRY⁴ CHISMAN (John³, Thomas², Edmund¹), born 3 Sept. 1720, died 17 April 1770.¹⁰⁰ He married Mary ___.

Issue:¹⁰¹ 87. Mary⁵, born 5 Feb. 1749; 88. John⁵, died 1781.

47. ELIZABETH⁴ CURTIS (Edmund³, Mary² Chisman, Edmund¹), born 21 Aug. 1712, married (1) 9. *Humphrey⁴ Harwood* (see HARWOOD) and (2), 1750, John Llewelling of Warwick County.

Issue: (by 1) [HARWOOD] see HARWOOD; (by 2) [LLEWELLING] 89. MARY⁵; 90. Elizabeth⁵.

48. MARY⁴ CURTIS (Edmund³, Mary² Chisman, Edmund¹) died 13 Feb. 1759. She married, 21 April 1737, James Dowsing, son of James and Elizabeth (Lucas) Dowsing, born Aug. ___, died 10 July 1800.¹⁰²

Issue: [DOWSING]¹⁰³ 91. Edmund Curtis⁵, born 8 May 1740, died 26 Dec. 1770, married, 17 Dec. 1763, Ann Wills; 92. James⁵, born 10 Jan. 1744, died 4 July 1748; 93. Everard⁵, born Sept. 1746, died 10 May 1747; 94. John⁵, born 27 Sept. 1746, died 7 Dec. [1775] in his 30th year, married (1), 10 Aug. 1771, Mary Read Godwin, daughter of Edmund and Susaner Godwin, born 11 Aug. 17_, died 7 Oct. 1774, and (2), 15 April 1775, Ann Minson, born 17 Sept. 1756; 95. Mildred⁵, born 4 Nov. 1748, died 17 April 1749; 96. EVERARD⁵; 97. Mary Stark⁵, born 20 Oct. 1754; 98. Thomas⁵, born 15 June 1756.

49. EDMUND⁴ CURTIS (Edmund³, Mary² Chisman, Edmund¹), born 16

---

⁹⁶ *W*(1) III, p. 269.
⁹⁷ York Co. Wills & Inventories 21, p. 483.
⁹⁸ *W*(1) III, pp. 269-70.
⁹⁹ York Co. Wills & Inventories 22, 1771-83, p. 574.
¹⁰⁰ Chisman Bible, in *W*(1) XIII, p. 70.
¹⁰¹ *W*(1) I, p. 98.
¹⁰² Dowsing Bible, in *The Daily Press*, Newport News, 16 July 1972.
¹⁰³ *Ibid.*

Sept. 1718, left will 7 March 1783-17 Jan. 1791.[104] He resided in York County. He married (1) Mary ___, (2) Elizabeth ___, who died 30 Dec. 1751, and (3) Ann Drewry.[105]

Issue: [CURTIS] (by 1) 99. Mary[5], born 14 Sept. 1742, probably the (2) wife of 71. John[5] Chisman; (by 2)[106] 100. Lucy[5], married 118. William[5] Patrick; 101. FRANCES[5]; 102. Elizabeth[5], born 9 Sept. 1748, married (1), (bond 15) Oct. 1772,[107] Robert Howard, born 1 Oct. 1745, died before 20 March 1791,[108] and (2) John Gayle; 103. Ann[5], born 21 March 1749/50, died 1786, married John Toomer; 104. Sarah[5], born 22 Oct. 1751, died young; (by 3)[109] 105. EDMUND[5]; 106. ROBERT[5]; 107. SARAH[5]; 108. HENRY[5]; 109. MARY[5]; 110. Christopher[5], born 26 Sept. 1769, died 1800, unmarried;[110] 111. THOMAS[5].

50. ELIZABETH[4] CURTIS (Thomas[3], Mary[2] Chisman, Edmund[1]), born 16 Nov. 1711, died 28 Dec. 1789. She married John Patrick of Charles Parish, son of John and Sarah (___) Patrick, born 26 July 1703, who left will.14 Jan. 1754-18 March 1754.[111]

Issue: [PATRICK] 112. JOHN[5]; 113. THOMAS[5]; 114. SARAH[6]; 115. CURTIS[5]; 116. William[5], born 23 April 1736, died 10 Oct. 1739; 117. MARY[5]; 118. WILLIAM[5]; 119. Susanna[5], born 26 July 1743, died 26 Aug. 1743; 120. Merrit[5], born 17 Nov. 1744, died young; 121. FRANCES[5]; 122 LUCY[5]; 123. EDMUND[5].

52. SUSANNA[4] CURTIS (Thomas[3], Mary[2] Chisman, Edmund[1]). born 9 Oct. 1717, died 1 Nov. 1744. She married John Hunt.

Issue: [HUNT] 124. Dinah[5], born 15 Nov. 1736, died 1 Nov. 1739; 125. John[5], born 8 Aug. 1738; 126. Susanna[5], born 29 May 1741; 127. THOMAS[5].

60. EDWARD[4] CORLEY (Katherine[3] Curtis, Mary[2] Chisman, Edmund[1])

---

[104] York Co. Wills & Inventories 23, pp. 225-26. He named son-in-law John Chisman whose relationship is unclear.

[105] Her surname is given as Drewry in notes made, 1915, by Virginia Cary (Curtis) Taylor and Maria Elizabeth (Whitaker) Curtis.

[106] Charles Parish Register.

[107] Pollock, *op. cit.*, p. 65.

[108] York Co. Wills & Inventories 23, pp. 577-78, earliest date in accounting of his estate returned 15 Jan. 1801 by Elizabeth Gales, late Elizabeth Howard.

[109] Charles Parish Register; York Co. Deed Bk. 12, p. 167.

[110] Southall Papers, *loc. cit.*, notation regarding his will, Warwick County.

[111] York Co. Wills & Inventories 20, pp. 318-20.

left will 14 ___ 1735-21 July 1735.[112] He married Anne ___.

Issue: [CORLEY] 128. William⁵, born 28 Feb. 1730, died 21 Sept. 1749;[113] 129. Francis⁶, apprenticed to William Moss by his mother, 19 June 1749.[114]

61. ELIZABETH⁴ CORLEY (Katherine³ Curtis, Mary² Chisman, Edmund¹) married Thomas Wooten.

Issue: [WOOTEN] 130. Ann⁵, born 9 March 1726/7.

63. PAUL⁴ WATLINGTON (Elizabeth³ Reade, Jane² Cheesman, Edmund¹), baptized 7 May 1706,[115] is presumably the Paul who married Elizabeth ___ and perhaps the Paul of Abingdon Parish, Gloucester County, who died 12 March 1777, aged 77 [*sic*].[116]

Issue: [WATLINGTON][117] 131. ARMISTEAD⁵; 132. Ann⁵, born 28 Dec. 1732, died 18 Sept. 1741; 133. Mildred⁵, baptized 25 July 1735; 134. FRANCIS⁵; 135. Elizabeth⁵, born 12 Nov. 1742; 136. (child)⁵, baptized and died 28 Aug. 1745; 137. Mary⁶, born 11 Aug. 1746; 138. Anne⁶, born 4 May 1750; 139. Fanny⁶, born 9 Nov. 1753.

65. JOHN⁴ WATLINGTON (Elizabeth³ Reade, Jame² Cheesman, Edmund¹), baptized 14 June 1713,[118] is perhaps the John who married Ann ___ and had

Issue: [WATLINGTON] 140. Mary⁶, born Dec. 1748.[119]

68. MARY⁵ CHISMAN (Edmund⁴, Thomas³, Thomas², Edmund¹) married (1), by 1757,[120] ___ Moss and (2) Isaac Hobday of Yorkhampton Parish.

Issue:[121] (by 1) [MOSS] 141. Elizabeth⁶, married (1), as his (2) wife, Thomas Pescud, born 7 March 1726/7, died 25 Sept. 1781, widower of 73. Anna⁵ Chisman, and (2), (bond 21) Dec. 1785,[122] Hawkins Reade; 142. Edward⁶, left will 24 Oct. 1784-15 Aug. 1785,[123] married Barbara ___; (by 2) [HOBDAY]

---

[112] York Co. Will Bk. 18, p. 212.
[113] Charles Parish Register.
[114] York Co. Judgments & Orders 1, 1746-52, p. 208, as Corlew.
[115] Abingdon Parish, Gloucester Co., Register.
[116] *Virginia Gazette*, 21 March 1777.
[117] Abingdon Parish Register.
[118] Abingdon Parish Register.
[119] *Ibid.*
[120] Will of step-father James Goodwin.
[121] *W*(1) XIV, pp. 115-17.
[122] Pollock, *op. cit.*, p. 108.
[123] York Co. Wills & Inventories 23, pp. 91-92.

143. Mary[6]; 144. Mildred[6]; 145. Nancy Buckner[6], born 30 March 1766.[124]

69. THOMAS[5] CHISMAN (Edmund[4], Thomas[3], Thomas[2], Edmund[1]) died 2 April 1770,[125] leaving will 29 March 1770-18 June 1770.[126] He married (1) Elizabeth ___, who died 23 April 1757,[127] and (2) Diana Moss, daughter of Edward and Elizabeth (Goodwin) Moss,[128] who was born 22 Dec. 1735. He was a justice, sheriff, and captain of York County militia, 1767.[129]

Issue: [CHISMAN][130] (by 1) 146. Edmund[6], born 20 May 1751, died 13 April 1784, left will 9 March 1784-20 Apil 1784,[131] vestryman of Charles Parish, 1774, took oath as lieutenant of York County militia, 21 April 1777,[132] married 206. *Mary[6] Robinson* (see MARTIAU), born 2 Dec. 1739, died 19 Nov. 1781; 147. Thomas[6], born 13 Nov. 1753, died 5 Dec. 1754; 148. Anne[6], married 62. *William[6] Howard* (see CALTHORPE); (by 2) 149. Thomas[6], born 3 July 1759, died 1798 or 1799 at Hampton, surgeon's mate on the *Dragon*, Virginia State Navy, 8 June 1777-20 Jan. 1779, was surgeon attending the guards when Dr. Thomas Walker surveyed the line between Virginia and North Carolina, and later was a physician of York County and schoolmaster at Hampton,[133] married __,[134] died about 1813, who married (2) Richard Garrett; 150. George[6], born 26 April 1761, apprenticed, 1777-82, to Hawkins Reade as a chairmaker and wheelwright,[135] recommended as first lieutenant of York County militia, 17 Feb. 1783,[136] died before 17 July 1786, when the inventory of his estate was ordered made;[137] 151. John[6], born 11 April 1763, died 14 Feb. 1782; 152. Diana[6], born

---

[124] Charles Parish Register.

[125] *Virginia Gazette*, 5 April 1770.

[126] York Co. Wills & Inventories 21, pp. 495-97.

[127] Charles Parish Register.

[128] *T* VI, p. 51.

[129] York Cp. Order Bk. 1765-68, pp. 330, 375.

[130] Charles Parish Register.

[131] York Co. Wills & Inventories 23, pp. 45-46.

[132] York Co. Order Bk. 4, 1774-84, p. 140.

[133] Revolutionary War pension application, Thomas Chisman, R. 27, Virginia Half Pay; Margie G. Brown, *Genealogical Abstracts, Revolutionary War Veterans, Scrip Act 1852* (Oakton, Va., 1990), p. 15.

[134] She was a near relation of Peter Goodwin (Brown, *loc. cit.*) and of Thomas Curtis (Revolutionary War pension application, Thomas Chisman, *loc. cit.*).

[135] York Co. Deed Bk. 7, pp. 550-51.

[136] York Co. Order Bk. 4, 1774-84, p. 315.

[137] York Co. Wills & Inventories 23, p. 124.

5 May 1765; 153. Mount Edward[6], died 30 July 1804,[138] of Elizabeth City County, collector of customs of the port of Norfolk, married ___, possibly the Mary Chesman resident in Hampton, 1810;[139] 154. James[6], born 24 April 1770.

70. ANN[5] CHISMAN (Edmund[4], Thomas[3], Thomas[2], Edmund[1]) married (1)___ Brown and (2) ___ Phillips.

Issue:[140] (by 1) [BROWN] 155. George[6]; 156. John[6]; (by 2) [PHILLIPS] 157. Elizabeth[6].

71. JOHN[5] CHISMAN (Edmund[4], Thomas[3], Thomas[2], Edmund[1]) left will 13 Sept. 1801-codicil 25 July 1802-20 June 1803.[141] He married (1) 34. *Mary[6] Buckner* (see MATHEWS), (2), probably, 99. Mary[5] Curtis, and (3) Elizabeth (Wills) Wills,[142] daughter of Thomas Wills and widow of William Wills, who left will 30 May 1807-16 Feb. 1808.[143] He was lieutenant of York County militia, 1763, and captain, 1764.

Issue: (by 1) 158. Mary[6], born 3 Nov. 1765, married Robert Tabb; 159. John Buckner[6], born 2 April 1768; (by 2) 160. Miles Cary[6], born 27 Jan. 1781; 161. George[6], born 8 June 1783; 162. Elias[6], left will 2 March 1812-18 April 1814,[144] married Mary R. ___; 163. Robert Todd[6]; 164. Martha[6].

72. CATHERINE[5] CHISMAN (John[4], Thomas[3], Thomas[2], Edmund[1]), born 3 July 1729,[145] married James Moss, who was.born 23 Aug. 1719[146] and left will proved 15 Nov. 1762.[147]

Issue: [MOSS][148] 165. John[6]; 166. Ann[6], married ___ Loyd; 167. Edward[6].

73. ANNA[5] CHISMAN (John[4], Thomas[3], Thomas[2], Edmund[1]), born 15 March 1730/1,[149] married, as his (1) wife, Thomas Pescud, born 7 March 1727,

---

[138] *Telegraph*, Baltimore, 14 Aug. 1804.

[139] Elizabeth City Co. 1810 census, Hampton, p. 283.

[140] The will of Elizabeth (Chapman) Chisman Goodwin appears to list her children and grandchildren in the order of birth. If so, the Brown and Phillips grandchildren, otherwise unidentified, are children of Ann Chisman.

[141] York Co. Wills & Inventories 23, pp. 622-23.

[142] W(1) I, p. 93, states she was Elizabeth Cary, daughter of Maj. Miles and Ann (___) Cary, but they are not identified in Fairfax Harrison, *The Virginia Carys* (New York, 1919).

[143] York Co. Wills & Inventories 23, pp. 723-24.

[144] York Co. Will Bk. 10, pp. 108-09.

[145] Charles Parish Register.

[146] *Ibid.*

[147] York Co. Wills & Inventories 21, pp. 116-17.

[148] *T* VI, p. 157.

[149] Charles Parish Register.

died 25 Sept. 1781, who married (2) 116. Elizabeth[6] Moss.

Issue: [PESCUD][150] 168. Mary[6], married 43. *Robert[5] Manson* (see BENNETT-CHAPMAN); 169. Robert[6], died in infancy.

74. MILDRED[5] CHISMAN (George[4], Thomas[3], Thomas[2], Edmund[1]), born 29 April 1739, died before 1775. She married, (bond 5) May 1762,[151] Michael Nicholson, born about 1740, of Surry County, who left will 6 March 1775-28 Jan. 1777.[152]

Issue: [NICHOLSON] 170. George[6]; 171. Robert[6]; 172. Michael[6]; 173. Chisman[6], of Sussex County; 174. Mary[6], married, (bond 16) Dec. 1784,[153] Marriott Davis, moved to Wilson Co., Tenn.,[154] left will 9 March 1830-29 June 1830.[155]

77. LAWRENCE[5] SMITH (Edmund[4], Mildred[3] Chisman, Thomas[3], Edmund[1]) of York County, paymaster, Virginia State Line,[156] left will 7 July 1787-15 Dec. 1788.[157] He married (1) ___[158] and (2) Elizabeth Tabb, who left will 28 Sept. 1811-19 Oct. 1812.[159].

Issue: [SMITH][160] (by 1) 175. John Tabb[6], of Yorktown and later of Norfolk, married (1) Janet Rule Cosby[161] and (2), 4 Sept. 1811 at Hampton,[162] Diana (Mallory) Wray; 176. Augustine[6], married ___; 177, Mildred[6]; (by 2)

---

[150] Elizabeth Hogg Ironmonger, *Three Courageous Women and Their Kin–A Pescud Family Genealogy* (Berryville, Va., 1965), pp. 9, 17.

[151] Catherine Lindsay Knorr, *Marriage Bonds and Ministers' Returns of Sussex County, Virginia, 1754-1810* (Pine Bluff, Ark., 1952), p. 58.

[152] Surry Co. Will Bk. 10A, p. 457.

[153] Knorr, *op. cit.*, p. 20.

[154] Richard N. Gookins, *A History and Genealogy of the Gookin Family* (rev. ed.; Salem, Ore., 1991), p. 116.

[155] Wilson Co., Tenn., Wills & Inventories 1830-33, pp. 36-37.

[156] *V* II, p. 362.

[157] York Co. Wills & Inventories 23, p. 167.

[158] The provisions of Lawrence Smith's will leaving his estate to his wife Elizabeth during widowhood towards the maintenance of his three youngest children, and then to all his children, and Elizabeth's will leaving a considerable estate only to sons Peyton and George, suggests he was married twice.

[159] York Co. Will Bk. 10, 1811-24, p. 52.

[160] *Ibid.*, naming only sons Peyton and George; Brown, *op. cit.*, p. 275, naming John Tabb, Peyton and Augustine; Garber, *op. cit.*, pp. 202-03, naming John Tabb and Mildred "among others."

[161] York Co. Deed Bk. 7, pp. 90-91.

[162] *Norfolk Herald*, 18 Sept. 1811

178. Peyton[6]; 179. George[6].

78. THOMAS[5] SMITH (Edmund[4], Mildred[3] Chisman, Thomas[2], Edmund[1]) of York County, married, 1766, Elizabeth Armistead, daughter of Westwood and Mary (Tabb) Armistead.

Issue: [SMITH][163] 180. Elizabeth[6], born 22 Aug. 1767, died 30 Jan. 1849, married, 8 Jan. 1789, Robert Armistead of Elizabeth City County, born 9 Aug. 1766, died 31 Aug. 1817; 181. Mary[6], married _____ Young and lived in Spotsylvania and Elizabeth City counties.

80. Col. JOHN[5] CHISMAN (John[4], John[3], Thomas[2], Edmund[1]) died before 18 June 1781.[164] He married.Mary Tabb, daughter of John and Diana (Moss) Tabb, who was born 9 Aug. 1755 and married (2) Lewis Charles.

Issue: 182. Edmund Tabb[6], left will 1 Aug. 1804-15 June 1807,[165] married Martha Moreland, who married (2) 211. Edmund[6] Curtis.

81. JOHN[5] GOODWIN (Diana[4] Chisman, John[3], Thomas[2], Edmund[1]), born 15 Nov. 1735, died 15 May 1783, was of Hanover County and lieutenant of militia, 21 March 1768. He married Elizabeth Doswell, died 16 Feb. 1814 in her 71st year.

Issue: [GOODWIN] 183. Diana Chisman[6], born 10 Feb. 1760, died 29 Sept. 1849,[166] married, 22 Dec. 1780, William Harris, born 13 Jan. 1753, died 26 Jan. 1802,[167] of "Cedar Hill," Hanover County, Revolutionary War soldier;[168] 184. Mary[6], born 3 July 1763, married John Harris, born 1756;[169] 185. Thomas[6], born 25 May 1765, Hanover County, died April 1838, Nelson County, private in Hanover County militia for two tours, 1781, of Louisa, Prince Edward, Prince William, King George, Amherst and Nelson counties,[170] married, 1789, Temperance Harris; 186. James[6], born 28 Nov. 1768, of Hanover County,

---

[163] Virginia Armistead Garber, *The Armistead Family* (Richmond, 1916), pp. 118-19.

[164] York Co. Order Bk. 4, p. 294. On 21 June 1785 Henry Charles was granted administration on the estate of 88. John Chisman, Sr., unadministered by 80. John Chisman, Jr. (Order Bk. 5, p. 170).

[165] York Co. Wills & Inventories 23, pp. 716-17.

[166] *The Virginia Genealogist*, XXII, p. 100; Alycon Trubey Pierce, *Selected Final Pension Payment* Vouchers, 1818-1864, Virginia: Richmond & Wheeling (Athens, Ga., 1996), I, p. 250.

[167] Harris Bible, in *Virginia Genealogical Society Quarterly*, VI, p. 42.

[168] Revolutionary War pension application, William Harris, widow Mary, W.4222.

[169] *The Virginia Genealogist*, XXII, p. 100.

[170] Revolutionary War pension application, Thomas Goodwin, S.13176.

married Fanny Harris;[171] 187. Frances[6], born 31 May 1772, married Robert Clough; 188. William Doswell[6], born 28 July 1774, died 12 Dec. 1827, farmer of Hanover County, soldier in War of 1812, married, 12 Nov. 1814, Mary Wingfield Cosby, born 17 March 1793,[172] died 28 Sept. 1872; 189. Edmund Chisman[6], born 30 Oct. 1776, farmer of Haywood Co., Tenn., married (1) ___ Anderson, (2), (bond 12) Sept. 1810,[173] Elizabeth Waddy, and (3) ____; 190. Elizabeth Doswell[6], born 28 July 1779, died 12 Jan. 1781; 191. Elizabeth Doswell[6], born 3 Sept. 1781, died 27 June 1849, married 78. *Littleton[6] Goodwin* (see BENNETT-CHAPMAN).

82. SARAH[5] SHEILD (Ellinor[4] Chisman, John[3], Thomas[2], Edmund[1]), born 21 Dec. 1745, died 18 Nov. 1811.[174] She married (1) William Dudley, lieutenant of York County militia, 1769, who died before 15 April 1771,[175] and (2) 86. *William[5] Cary* (see TAYLOR-CARY).

Issue: (by 1) [DUDLEY] 192. Maj. William[6], of York County, married 552. *Hannah[6] Cary* (see BALEY-COCKE), born 1770, died 1803; (by 2) see TAYLOR-CARY.

83. MARY[5] SHEILD, (Ellinor[4] Chisman, John[3], Thomas[2], Edmund[1]), born 16 Oct. 1747, married Simon Hollier.

Issue: [HOLLIER] 193. Mary[6], born April 1766.

84. ROBERT[5] SHEILD (Ellinor[4] Chisman, John[3], Thomas[2], Edmund[1]), born 12 March 1749/50, died 23 Oct. 1781, left will 13 Sept. 1781-20 May 1782.[176] He married Mary ___.

Issue: [SHEILD] 194. John Ferguson[6], born 1772, gave receipt, 21 Oct. 1793, to his guardian for his estate,[177] married Mitchell ___; 195. Robert[6], born 13 May 1774, died 1776; 196. Patrick[6], born 30 Sept. 1776; 197. Robert[6], born 4 April 1779; 198. Samuel[6], born 23 March 1781.

85. ELEANOR[5] SHEILD (Ellinor[4] Chisman., John[3], Thomas[2] Edmund[1]), born 23 March 1752, married Capt. William Mitchell of York County, who

---

[171] *The Virginia Genealogist*, XXII, p. 100.

[172] Walter Garland Duke, *Henry Duke, Councillor* (Richmond, 1949), pp.. 98, 324.

[173] Kathleen Booth Williams, *Marriages of Louisa County, Virginia, 1766-1815* (n.p., 1959), p. 42.

[174] *Enquirer*, Richmond, 3 Dec. 1811.

[175] York Co. Wills & Inventories 22, pp. 27-29.

[176] York Co. Wills & Inventories 22, pp. 507-08.

[177] York Co., Guardian Accounts p. 77.

married (2) Demaris (Gibbons) Smith, widow of 78. *Lawrence⁵ Smith* (see MARTIAU), and left will 12 Feb. 1786-17 April 1786.[178]

Issue: [MITCHELL] 199. William⁶, named in will of his uncle John Sheild.

89. MARY⁵ LLEWELLING (Elizabeth⁴ Curtis, Edmund³, Mary² Chisman, Edmund¹) died 1809. She married, 1773, Edmund Wynne, who was born 1744 in York County and died 1793 in Warwick County.

Issue: [WYNNE] 200. John⁶, born 1774, died 1776; 201. Edmund⁶, born 1776, died 1798; 202. Thomas⁶, born 1779, died 1815 in Warwick County, married, 11 Sept. 1813, Elizabeth Lee, born 19 Feb. 1793, died 29 Dec. 1836 in Warwick County; 203. Elizabeth Curtis⁶, married 34. *Humphrey Harwood⁶ Wynne* (see HARWOOD); 204. Lucy Hill⁶, born 1784, died 1813, married John Chisman, who died before 1810; 205. John⁶, born 1787, died 1816; 206. William⁶, born 1792, died 1810.

97. EVERARD⁵ DOWSING (Mary⁴ Curtis, Edmund³, Mary² Chisman, Edmund¹), born 21 July 1751, of Warwick County, married, 20 April 1783, Mildred Wills who died 23 May 1785.

Issue: [DOWSING] 207. Mary Curtis⁶, born 31 Jan. 1784, married, 2 Oct. 1800, William Augustine Moore.

101. FRANCES⁵ CURTIS (Edmund⁴, Edmund³, Mary² Chisman, Edmund¹), born 19 Nov. 1746, died about 1809. She married Matthew Wills, of Warwick County, who died about 1805.

Issue: [WILLS] 208. Matthew⁶, born 1780, died 1828, married, 1801, Lucy Moss Jones, who was born 1780 and died 1855 at "Briarfield," Elizabeth City County; 209. Sarah⁶.

105. EDMUND⁵ CURTIS (Edmund⁴, Edmund³, Mary² Chisman, Edmund¹), born 6 June 1754, left will 12 Nov. 1807-15 Jan. 1810.[179] He resided in Warwick County and later in York County. He married Ann⁷ Cary, daughter of 93. *Thomas⁶ Cary* (see TAYLOR-CARY), born 1769, died 1814.

Issue: [CURTIS][180] 210. Anne⁶, born 16 Feb. 1781;[181] 211. Edmund⁶, born 22 Aug. 1784, died 7 May 1857, soldier in War of 1812, married Martha (Moreland) Chisman, widow of 182. Edmund Tabb⁶ Chisman; 212. Thomas

---

[178] York Co. Wills & Inventories 23, p. 109.

[179] York Co. Wills & Inventories 23, pp. 757-58.

[180] Notes made, 1915, by Virginia Cary (Curtis) Taylor and Maria E. Curtis; York Co. Deed Bk. 12, p. 167.

[181] Charles Parish Register.

Cary[6], born 17 Feb. 1786, died 1851, farmer of Warwick County,[182] married, 15 Dec. 1816, Elizabeth Haynes of King and Queen County, born 22 Feb. 1792, died 27 May 1846 at "Rich Neck," Warwick County;[183] 213. Frances[6], died before 1807, married, 28 Jan. 1801, Josiah Thomas, who died before 1817; 214. Henry[6], died 1810; 215. Miles[6], born 9 Feb. 1791, died 26 May 1851, farmer of Lee's Mill, Warwick County,[184] married 25 Dec. 1816, Sarah Katherine Harwood, born 29 Nov. 1800, died 15 Oct. 1886;[185] 216. Sarah[6], married Samuel Presson, who was born 6 March 1775; 217. Christopher[6], born 2 Oct. 1795, died 1 Oct. 1830 in Warwick County, married, 16 Dec. 1819, Elizabeth Lee, born 19 Feb. 1793, died 29 Dec. 1836 in Warwick County; 218. Anne[6], born 1794, died about 1843, married, 17 March 1810, Willoughby Jordan of York County who died about 1829; 219. Mary[6], married 266. Clayton[6] Patrick; 220. Elizabeth[6], born 1797, married Lewis Charles of Williamsburg; 221. John[6], born 15 May 1801, died 29 Oct. 1844, married, 18 Dec. 1823, Virginia Goodwin of York County; 222. Mahala[6], died 1849, married (1) Bernard Elliott, born 1808, died 29 Dec. 1835 at Norfolk, and (2) Peter R. Goodwin, Jr., died 1844.

106. ROBERT[5] CURTIS (Edmund[4], Edmund[3], Mary[2] Chisman, Edmund[1]), born 11 Jan. 1757, died 1798. He married Hannah ___.

Issue: [CURTIS][186] 223. Elizabeth D.[6], died 1825, married Lewis Moreland, who died about 1849; 224. Hannah R.[6], born about 1794 in York County, married Hinde R. D. Brown, born about 1797 in Warwick County, where he was a farmer;[187] 225. Robert[6], died young.

107. SARAH[5] CURTIS (Edmund[4], Edmund[3], Mary[2] Chisman, Edmund[1]), born 15 May 1760, living 17 Oct. 1836, married (1), (bond 6) March 1786,[188] Thomas Minson, who died before 18 April 1796 when the inventory of his estate was returned,[189] and (2), (bond 31) March 1798,[190] Nicholas Presson, who left

---

[182] Warwick Co. 1850 census, p. 123 or 62, family 36-38.

[183] *Enquirer*, Richmond, 9 June 1846.

[184] Warwick Co. 1850 census, p. 123 or 62, family 37-39.

[185] Lyon G. Tyler, ed., *Encyclopedia of Virginia Biography* (New York, 1915), V, p. 941.

[186] Southall Papers, Earl Gregg Swem Library, College of William and Mary, folder 240; York Co. Deed Bk. 12, p. 167.

[187] Warwick Co. 1850 census, p. 122 or 61r, family 35-37.

[188] Pollock, *op. cit.*, p. 85.

[189] York Co. Wills & Inventories 23, pp. 461-62.

[190] Pollock, *op. cit.*, p. 105.

undated will proved 17 Jan. 1803.[191]

Issue: (by 1) [MINSON] 226. (Daughter)[6], died before 1815, married Lewis Burt; 227. Mary[6], died 1860, married (1), (bond 10) March 1800,[192] Joseph Monnett and (2) ___ Noel; 228. Thomas C.[6], born 1795, died 15 March 1858, married (1) Mary Thompkins Elliott, born 1806, died about 1841, and (2) Mary Archer; (by 2) [PRESSON] 229. James[6]; 230. Nancy Curtis[6], born 1802, married (1), (bond 25) Dec. 1826,[193] Thomas Stroud, died 1826, and (2) John Wright, Sr., died before 1850; 231. Samuel[6].

108. HENRY[5] CURTIS (Edmund[4], Edmund[3], Mary[2] Chisman, Edmund[1]), born 20 March 1763, died 4 Dec. 1804,[194] married Mary Prentis, who died 22 June 1810 in her 35th year.

Issue: [CURTIS] 232. Daniel Prentis[6], born 6 Jan. 1803 in Warwick County, died 23 March 1858, farmer of Warwick County,[195] married, 24 Dec. 1825, Elizabeth R.[7] Harwood, daughter of 42. *William*[6] *Harwood* (see HARWOOD), born 23 March 1810 in Warwick County;[196] 233. (Daughter)[6], married Simon Stubblefield.

109. MARY[5] CURTIS (Edmund[4], Edmund[3], Mary[2] Chisman, Edmund[1]), born 16 Oct. 1766, died by 17 Oct. 1836, married, (bond 27) Nov. 1786,[197] 280. Robert[6] Patrick, born 11 Feb. 1767.

Issue: [PATRICK][198] 234. William M.[6]; 235. John[6].

111 THOMAS[5] CURTIS (Edmund[4], Edmund[3], Mary[2] Chisman, Edmund[1]), born 25 July 1774, left will 14 Oct. 1840-12 Nov. 1840.[199] He married (1), 9 Jan. 1800, Ann Presson and (2), 16 June 1810, Nancy Gray, who died 1842.

Issue: [CURTIS] (by 1) 236. Christopher[6], born 19 Oct. 1800, died 8 Sept. 1873 in York County, married (1) Elizabeth Cary, born 1803, died 1835, (2), 21 May 1836,[200] Pamela (___) Smith, and (3) Sarah E. ___, died about 1889;

---

[191] York Co. Wills & Inventories 23, pp. 604-05.
[192] Pollock, *op. cit.*, p. 87.
[193] *Ibid.*, p. 120.
[194] Curtis family Bible (1868).
[195] Warwick Co. 1850 census, p. 119 or 60, family 8-8.
[196] Curtis family Bible (1868).
[197] Pollock, *op. cit.*, p. 97.
[198] York Co. Deed Bk. 12, p. 167.
[199] Southall papers, *loc. cit.*, folder 241, Warwick County.
[200] Pollock, *op. cit.*, p. 34.

237. Edmund[6], born about 1806 in Warwick County, where he resided,[201] married, 21 Feb. 1843,[202] Louisania Hay; 238. Thomas Crandol[6], died 1848, married, 14 Nov. 1844, Virginia Copeland, born 6 Dec. 1823, died 4 Jan. 1850;[203] (by 2) 239. Martha Jane[6], born 25 Nov. 1813, died 22 Jan. 1890, married (1) Thomas Haynes and (2) Edmund Chisman Charles, born 19 Oct. 1818 in York County, died 2 May 1880, farmer of Warwick County;[204] 240. Elizabeth Toplas[6], married Ro. T. Weymouth; 241. Ann [Nancy] Drewry[6], born 14 March 1818, died 27 July 1897, married John Toomer Garrow, born 15 Aug. 1820, died 19 March 1866. farmer of Warwick County;[205] 242. Matildy Crandol[6], born 1820, died 1823; 243. Samuel Gray[6], born 12 April 1823 in Warwick County, died 16 Nov. 1896, farmer of Warwick County,[206] married 14 Dec. 1844 Elizabeth Gibbs Wade, born 30 Nov. 1826, died 8 Nov. 1884; 244. William Henry[6], born 2 Feb. 1827, died Sept. 1903, farmer of Warwick County,[207] married Martha Harwood, born 3 April 1836, died 4 March 1911 at Denbigh; 245. Sarah Frances[6], born 1829, died in infancy; 246. Robert Gray[6], born 24 Feb. 1832, died 20 March 1899, married (1) Elmirah ___ and (2) Mattie Campbell; 247. Daniel Prentis[6], born 1833, died 1841.

112. JOHN[5] PATRICK (Elizabeth[4] Curtis, Thomas[3], Mary[2] Chisman, Edmund[1]), born 16 Oct. 1726, married 37. *Mary[5] Manson* (see BENNETT-CHAPMAN), born 3 Nov. 1726.[208]

Issue: [PATRICK][209] 248. Elizabeth[6], born 26 Oct. 1753, died 13 Feb. 1758; 249. Mary[6], born 11 Feb. 1755, died 29 July 1758; 250. Peter[6], born 11 Feb. 1757, died 3 Sept. 1766; 251. Nancy[6], born 12 April 1762, died 28 Oct. 1766; 252. Hannah[6], born 27 April 1765, died 14 June 1767.

113. THOMAS[5] PATRICK (Elizabeth[4] Curtis, Thomas[3], Mary[2] Chisman, Edmund[1]), born 6 Dec. 1728, died before 20 Aug. 1752 when the inventory of

---

[201] Warwick Co. 1850 census, p. 122 or 61r, family 31-33.

[202] Pollock, *op. cit.*, p. 34.

[203] Benjamin Copeland Bible, in Fillmore Norfleet, *Bible Records of Suffolk and Nansemond County, Virginia* ... (n.p., 1963), pp. 34, 36, which gives marriage as Oct. 1844.

[204] Warwick Co. 1850 census, p. 119 or 60, family 3-3.

[205] Warwick Co. 1850 census, p. 124 or 62r, family 47-51.

[206] Warwick Co. 1850 census, p. 122 or 61r, family 31-33.

[207] Warwick Co. 1850 census, p. 124 or 62r, family 46-50.

[208] Charles Parish Register.

[209] *Ibid.*; *W*(1) X, p. 113.

his estate was ordered made.[210] He married ___.

Issue: [PATRICK] 253. Mary[6].

113. SARAH[5] PATRICK (Elizabeth[4] Curtis, Thomas[3], Mary[2] Chisman, Edmund[1]), born 12 April 1731, married John Baptist of York County, who died 1781.[211]

Issue: [BAPTIST][212] 254. Mary[6], born 18 May 1755; 255. John[6], born 29 Aug. 1756, married, (bond 12) July.1774,[213] Betty Whitaker; 256. Sarah[6], born 18 June 1760; 257. Robert[6], born 10 May 1762; 258. Edward[6], born 21 Dec. 1765; 259. Frances[6], born 23 March 1768, married, (bond 20) Aug. 1787,[214] William Moore; 260. Nancy Gibbons[6], born 1776.

115. CURTIS[5] PATRICK (Elizabeth[4] Curtis, Thomas[3], Mary[2] Chisman, Edmund[1]), of Charles Parish, York County, born 13 Jan. 1733/4, died 1 Feb. 1784, left will 16 Sept. 1783-21 March 1785 [215] He married Martha Rogers, daughter of Clayton and Sarah (___) Rogers..

Issue: [PATRICK] 261. Susanna[6], born 29 Nov. 1755, married, (bond 29) Jan. 1774,[216] Thomas Presson, Jr.; 262. Sarah[6], born 16 Nov. 1758, married John Freeman; 263. Elizabeth[6], married (1) 127. Thomas[5] Hunt and (2) William Wright; 264. Patsy[6], married ___ Benjamin; 265. Thomas Curtis[6], born 5 May 1766, married Cressey ___; 266. Clayton[6], born 9 Feb. 1769, died before 15 July 1810,[217] married (1) Mary Powell Wright and (2) 219. Mary[6] Curtis; 267. Nancy[6], born 12 Nov. 1773.

117. MARY[5] PATRICK (Elizabeth[4] Curtis, Thomas[3], Mary[2] Chisman, Edmund[1]), born 26 July 1738, married John Giles of York County.

Issue: [GILES][218] 268. Mary[6], born 10 May 1765; 269. Mary[6], born 31 Dec. 1766; 270. Thomas[6], born 15 Oct.1768; 271. Betsey[6], born 14 Feb. 1771;

[210] York Co. Wills & Inventories 20, p. 303.

[211] York Co. Wills & Inventories 23, p. 428, accounting of estate returned 15 Dec. 1794 by William Patrick, administrator, earliest date 1781. The inventory of his estate was made pursuant to order 20 May 1782 (Wills & Inventories 22, p. 475).

[212] Charles Parish Register.

[213] Pollock, *op. cit.*, p. 8.

[214] *Ibid.*, p. 90.

[215] York Co. Wills & Inventories 23, p. 74.

[216] Pollock, *op. cit.*, p. 105.

[217] York Co. Will Bk. 10, p. 444, earliest date shown in estate account recorded 21 April 1823.

[218] Charles Parish Register.

272. John⁶, born 28 March 1773; 273. Frances Patrick⁶, born 15 Dec. 1774; 274. Hugh⁶, born 26 Nov. 1776; 275. Robert⁶, born 28 March 1779.

118. Capt. WILLIAM⁵ PATRICK (Elizabeth⁴ Curtis, Thomas³, Mary² Chisman, Edmund¹), born 30 March 1740/1, died before 4 Feb. 1794 when the inventory of his estate was made.[219] He married (1) 40. *Elizabeth⁵ Manson* (see BENNETT-CHAPMAN), born 18 May 1735,. and (2), (bond 6) Feb. 1772,[220] 100. Lucy⁶ Curtis, born 11 Jan. 1744/5, left will 4 Nov. 1796-16 Jan. 1797.[221]

Issue: [PATRICK] (by 1) 276. John⁶, born 23 April 1757; 277. Sarah⁶, born10 Oct. 1759; 278. Hannah⁶, born 30 June 1761, died young; 279. Mary⁶, born 25 Jan. 1765, married Thomas Powell; 280. Robert⁶, married 109. Mary⁵ Curtis; 281. Thomas⁶, born 14 Jan. 1768, married Mary Cooke; 282. Frances Manson⁶, born 9 Nov. 1768, died young; (by 2) 283. Elizabeth Topless⁶, born 23 Dec. 1772, married, (bond 17) April 1794,[222] Solomon Powell; 284. William⁶, born 17 June 1774, married (1) Ann ___, who died 1 Feb. 1815, and (2), 1817, Mary ___; 285. Edmund Curtis⁶, born 29 April 1777, died 9 Feb. 1826, left will 5 Nov. 1822-20 March 1826,[223] married 297. Lucy⁶ Wright, who died 14 Oct. 1836; 286. John C.⁶, died 16 Feb. 1826, married 301. Sally Clayton⁶ Patrick, born 12 March 1775, died 1839; 287. Nancy⁶, died 16 Nov. 1814; 288. Merritt Curtis⁶, died 23 Sept. 1818, married, 21) Feb. 1814,[224] Susan Cooke.

121. FRANCES⁵ PATRICK (Elizabeth⁴ Curtis, Thomas³, Mary² Chisman, Edmund¹), born 28 Oct. 1746, married Thomas Mallicott.

Issue: [MALLICOTT] 289. Thomas⁶.

122. LUCY⁵ PATRICK (Elizabeth⁴ Curtis, Thomas³, Mary² Chisman, Edmund¹), born 1749, married Benjamin Wright, who left undated will proved 21 Oct. 1792.[225]

Issue: [WRIGHT] 290. Elizabeth Curtis⁶, born 20 Nov. 1768, died 1839, married, (bond 22) Dec. 1787,[226] John Campbell and (2), (bond 4) Dec.

---

[219] York Co. Wills & Inventories 23, pp. 423-24.

[220] Pollock, *op. cit.*, p. 98.

[221] York Co. Wills & Inventories 23, p. 481.

[222] Pollock, *op. cit.*, p. 103.

[223] York Co. Will Bk. 11, pp. 99-100.

[224] Pollock, *op. cit.*, p. 97.

[225] York Co. Wills & Inventories 23, 1783-1811, p. 390.

[226] Pollock, *op. cit.*, p. 20.

1799,[227] Benjamin Stroud; 291. Benjamin[6], born 13 Aug. 1775, died 1803, married Willey ____; 292. Frances[6], born 12 Feb. 1778, died before 1808, married, (bond 4) Sept. 1799,[228] James Stroud; 293. Ann[6], born about 1780, married, (bond 15) Feb. 1801,[229] Lewis Hogg, born 1773, left will 16 Feb. 1852-20 Dec. 1852;[230] 294. John[6], born about 1785, died 1843, married, (bond 15) Aug. 1808,[231] Martha Belvin, born 1790, died 1850; 295. Edward E.[6], born about 1790, died 1821; 296. William[6], born 1793, died 1820; 297. Lucy[6], married (1) 285. Edmund Curtis[6] Patrick and (2) 300. Edmund Curtis[6] Patrick.

123. EDMUND[5] PATRICK (Elizabeth[4] Curtis, Thomas[3], Mary[2] Chisman, Edmund[1]), of Charles Pariish , York County, baptized 26 April 1752, left will 20 Sept. 1815-20 Nov. 1820.[232] He married Mildred ___.

Issue: [PATRICK] 298. John[6], born 22 Aug. 1772, married Elizabeth __; 299. Edmund[6], born 10 Feb. 1778, died young; 300. Edmund Curtis[6], born 22 Oct. 1780, married 297. Lucy[6] Wright, born about 1794, died 14 Oct. 1834; 301. Sally Clayton[6], married 286. John C.[6] Patrick; 302. Mildred[6], left will 12 Aug. 1839-21 Oct. 1839;[233] 303. Betsy[6], born 5 Oct. 1785.

127. THOMAS[5] HUNT (Susan[4] Curtis, Thomas[3], Mary[2] Chisman, Edmund[1]), born 30 Jan. 1741/2, left will 7 Dec. 1799-17 Feb. 1800.[234] He married (1) Mary ___, died 27 Dec. 1781, and (2) 263. Elizabeth[6] Patrick, born 12 Feb. 1761.

Issue: [HUNT][235] (by 1) 304. Martha[6], born 10 Feb. 1772, died before 4 Feb. 1800 when her estate account lists payment for her coffin;[236] 305. Frances[6], born 26 Feb. 1774, died before 23 Oct. 1802 when her sister Martha's estate account lists payment for her funeral expenses;[237] 306. Thomas[6], born 2 March 1776, left will 18 March 1804-16 April 1804;[238] 307. John[6], born 8 March 1778;

[227] *Ibid.*, p. 119.
[228] Pollock, *op. cit.*, p. 119.
[229] Pollock, *op. cit.*, p. 58.
[230] York Co. Will Bk. 15, pp. 199-200.
[231] Pollock, *op. cit.*, p. 136.
[232] York Co. Will Bk. 10, pp. 379-80.
[233] York Co. Will Bk. 12, pp. 197-98.
[234] York Co. Wills & Inventories 23, pp. 548-49.
[235] Charles Parish Register.
[236] York Co. Wills & Inventories 23, pp. 634-35.
[237] *Ibid.*
[238] York Co. Wills & Inventories 23, p. 648.

308. Diana[6], born 28 May 1781, twin; 309. Mary[6], born 28 May 1781, twin, died before Aug. 1803; (by 2) 310. William[6], born 29 Jan. 1784, died 7 Feb. 1784; 311. Curtis[6], born 28 Aug. 1785, sergeant in Capt. Samuel Sheild's Light Infantry 1813; 312. Susanna Curtis[6]; 313. Elizabeth[6].

131. Col. ARMISTEAD[5] WATLINGTON (Paul[4], Elizabeth[3] Reade, Jane[2] Cheesman, Edmund[1]), born 27 Dec. 1730, died 1807,[239] left will 2 Nov. 1803-codicil 18 April 1807-22 June 1807.[240] He resided in Halifax County where he was a justice, 1764, and also for a time in Pittsylvania County . He married Susannah Coleman, daughter of Thomas and Elizabeth (__) Coleman, who was born 16 Jan. 1735/6.[241].

Issue: [WATLINGTON] 314. Paul[6], captain of Halifax County militia during the Revolutionary War, married Mary Thompson; 315. John[6], died Jan. 1812, captain of artillery in the Virginia Line, married (1), (bond 23) Dec. 1781,[242] Elizabeth Allen and (2) Mary ___; 316. Thomas A.[6]; died before 23 May 1823;[243] 317. Elizabeth[6], married, 17 Jan. 1781,[244] Peter Barksdale, ensign of Halifax County militia, 1779, who married (2), (bond 16) Aug. 1818, Nancy (Sydnor) Logan and left will 5 May 1823-22 Jan. 1826;[245] 318. Fanny[6], married Joshua Boyd; 319. Polly[6], married (1), (bond 25) July 1787,[246] William Thompson, who died before 5 Dec. 1798,[247] and (2) William Terry.

134. FRANCIS[5] WATLINGTON (Paul[4], Elizabeth[3] Reade, Jane[2] Cheesman, Edmund[1]), baptized 2 Jan. 1737/8, married Rebecca ____, who married (2), (bond 6) Nov. 1780,[248] Benjamin Shelton..

Issue: [WATLINGTON][249] 320. Ann[6]; 321. Armistead[6]; 322. Edward[6]; 323. Francis[6].

---

[239] *Virginia Argus*, Richmond, 13 June 1807, which shows his age as 80.

[240] Halifax Co. Will Bk. 7, pp. 322-25.

[241] Abingdon Parish Register.

[242] Catherine Lindsay Knorr, *Marriage Bonds and Ministers' Returns of Halifax County, Virginia, 1753-1800* (Pine Bluff, Ark., 1957), p. 100.

[243] Halifax Co. Will Bk. 13, pp. 261-62, earliest date in estate account.

[244] Family Bible, in John A. Barksdale, *Barksdale Family History and Genealogy* (Richmond, 1940), p. 200; Knorr, *op. cit.*, p. 5, bond 11 July.

[245] Halifax Co. Will Bk. 14, pp. 9-11.

[246] Knorr, *op. cit.*, p. 91.

[247] Halifax Co. Will Bk. 6, pp. 59-60, estate inventoried.

[248] Knorr, *op. cit.*, p. 83.

[249] Halifax Co. Will Bk. 1, p. 174.